Psychology of Classroom Learning
An Encyclopedia

Psychology of Classroom Learning
An Encyclopedia

VOLUME 1
a–j

Eric M. Anderman
EDITOR IN CHIEF

Lynley H. Anderman
CO-EDITOR

MACMILLAN REFERENCE USA
A part of Gale, Cengage Learning

GALE
CENGAGE Learning™

Detroit • New York • San Francisco • New Haven, Conn • Waterville, Maine • London

GALE
CENGAGE Learning

Psychology of Classroom Learning: An Encyclopedia

Eric M. Anderman, Editor in Chief
Lynley H. Anderman, co-editor

Project Editor: Miranda H. Ferrara

Production Technology Support: Luann Brennan, Mark Springer, Mike Weaver

Manuscript Editors: Bryan Aubrey, Melodie Monahan

Proofreader: John K. Krol

Indexer: Do Mi Stauber Indexing Service

Product Design: Pamela A. E. Galbreath

Imaging: Lezlie Light

Graphic Art: GGS Information Services, Inc.

Rights Acquisition and Management: Margaret Abendroth, Beth Beaufore, Dean Dauphinais

Composition: Evi Abou-El-Seoud, Mary Beth Trimper

Manufacturing: Wendy Blurton

Product Manager: Leigh Ann Cusack

Publisher: Jay Flynn

For product information and technology assistance, contact us at
Gale Customer Support, 1-800-877-4253.
For permission to use material from this text or product,
submit all requests online at **www.cengage.com/permissions.**
Further permissions questions can be emailed to
permissionrequest@cengage.com

Since this page cannot legibly accommodate all copyright notices, the credits constitute an extension of the copyright notice.

Cover photographs reproduced by permission of Swerve/Alamy (Interior of American High School, Boston, Massachusetts); LWA-Dann Tardif/Zefa/Corbis (Students and Teacher Using Laptop in Classroom); JLP/Jose Luis Pelaez/Zefa/Corbis (Student Writing Languages on Blackboard); Pierre Tremblay/Masterfile www.masterfile.com (Students and Teacher in Classroom).

While every effort has been made to ensure the reliability of the information presented in this publication, Gale, a part of Cengage Learning, does not guarantee the accuracy of the data contained herein. Gale accepts no payment for listing; and inclusion in the publication of any organization, agency, institution, publication, service, or individual does not imply endorsement of the editors or publisher. Errors brought to the attention of the publisher and verified to the satisfaction of the publisher will be corrected in future editions.

EDITORIAL DATA PRIVACY POLICY: Does this product contain information about you as an individual? If so, for more information about our editorial data privacy policies, please see our Privacy Statement at www.gale.cengage.com.

Library of Congress Cataloging-in-Publication Data

Psychology of classroom learning : an encyclopedia / Eric M. Anderman, editor-in-chief; Lynley H. Anderman, co-editor.
   v. cm.
  Includes bibliographical references and index.
  ISBN 978-0-02-866167-4 (set : hardcover) -- ISBN 978-0-02-866168-1 (vol. 1) -- ISBN 978-0-02-866169-8 (v. 2)
   1. Learning, Psychology of--Encyclopedias. I. Anderman, Eric M. II. Anderman, Lynley Hicks.

LB1060.P89 2009
370.15'2303--dc22
                                       2008008737

Gale
27500 Drake Rd.
Farmington Hills, MI, 48331-3535

ISBN-13: 978-0-02-866167-4 (set)   ISBN-10: 0-02-866167-2 (set)
ISBN-13: 978-0-02-866168-1 (vol. 1)   ISBN-10: 0-02-866168-0 (vol. 1)
ISBN-13: 978-0-02-866169-8 (v. 2)   ISBN-10: 0-02-866169-9 (vol. 2)

This title is also available as an e-book.
ISBN-13: 978-0-02-866170-4 ISBN-10: 0-02-866170-2
Contact your Gale, a part of Cengage Learning sales representative for ordering information.

Printed in the United States of America
1 2 3 4 5 6 7 11 10 09 08

Editorial Board

Contents

Preface

NEED FOR *PSYCHOLOGY OF CLASSROOM LEARNING: AN ENCYCLOPEDIA (PCL)*

Children and adolescents spend much of their time in school environments. Indeed, the school social context has profound influences on children's and adolescents' psychological, academic, social, and physical development. When one considers that most students attend school for 180 days per year and spend at least six to seven hours per day at school for over a decade, the potential influence of the school environment on educational, developmental and personal outcomes becomes quite profound.

Teachers of course play an extremely important role in children's and adolescents' development. Students spend almost all of their in-school time in the presence of teachers. The daily practices that teachers use in their classrooms have important and enduring effects on students' self-perceptions, their understanding of their world, their identities, and their professional plans for the future.

In many teacher education programs, educators are required to take one course in Educational Psychology. That course typically covers theories of learning, theories of motivation, cognitive and social development, assessment, and behavior management. Consequently, a huge amount of material is covered in a brief period of time. In addition, these courses often are offered and required at the beginning stages of teacher education programs, or even prior to acceptance into a teacher education program. Thus for many teachers in training, the role of psychology in the classroom is taught early in the teacher preparation program, before students have a chance to spend time in classrooms and apply these important principles in actual schools. Oftentimes, students are taught all of the theory, but not the implications of that theory for practice.

The role of psychology in education has a long and important history. The role of psychology in education has been discussed by philosophers such as Artistotle and Plato, as well as by early psychologists such as William James, and later disciples such as B.F. Skinner. Woolfolk Hoy (2000) notes that the role of educational psychology in teacher preparation has changed during the past 100 years: in the early 1900s, the focus was on the application of laboratory-based studies of learning to classroom learning; however, in the later 1900s and more recently, focus shifted to how learning occurs in actual classrooms. In addition, whereas the early focus of educational psychology was on the characteristics of students as learners, the roles of the social context of the classroom (i.e., the teacher, curriculum, and the setting) have become better integrated into educational psychology in recent years.

In the beginning of the 21st century, it seemed important to us to produce an encyclopedia that summarizes much of the current research on the role of psychology in classroom learning. Both policy-makers and the general public realize that the interactions that students experience in school settings have important effects on many valued outcomes. Recent publicity regarding violence in schools, pregnancies during early adolescence, achievement gaps, and advances in neuroscience has kindled a renewed interest in the role of psychology in education. Our hope is that this encyclopedia will serve as an invaluable resource to practicing teachers, teacher education students, and to parents.

SCOPE AND CONTENTS OF *PSYCHOLOGY OF CLASSROOM LEARNING: AN ENCYCLOPEDIA*

Both psychology and education are extremely broad disciplines. One of the challenges in developing the scope and content for *Psychology of Classroom Learning: An Encyclopedia* involved providing thorough coverage of the content. As we describe below, the study of psychology and classroom learning is not confined to one field. Rather, research on the role of psychology in education emanates from extremely diverse fields within the social sciences.

Psychology and Classroom Learning: Studied by Diverse Scholars from Diverse Fields. The study of psychology is often broken down into sub-domains, such as developmental psychology, counseling psychology, clinical psychology, biological psychology, personality psychology, social psychology, organizational psychology, and of course educational psychology. Although these are considered distinct domains within the field of psychology, there is much overlap among these sub-groupings of psychology. Research related to classroom learning can be found in empirical journals in all of the sub-areas of psychology. In addition to educational psychology, research focused on the role of psychology in education appears quite often in journals in the domains of developmental psychology and social psychology.

In addition, the formal study of education is an extremely broad field. Whereas the study of the role of psychology in classroom learning is most commonly encountered in departments of educational psychology, there are individual scholars who study and publish about the role of psychology across a diverse array of fields within education. Indeed, when one examines the structures of schools and colleges of education, and the journals in the field of education, it is evident that there are extremely diverse divisions within the field. For example, colleges and universities often contain departments with varied names such as Foundations of Education, Urban Education, Higher Education, Teaching and Learning, Curriculum and Instruction, Educational Policy Studies, Educational Studies, Educational Administration, Educational Leadership, Special Education, Educational Research, and Educational Evaluation.

Within each of these organizational divisions there are individuals who conduct important research on the role of psychology in classroom learning. For example, in the field of Higher Education, many individuals study college student learning in the context of universities; in the field of Educational Administration, researchers examine the psychological effects of leadership on both teachers and students; in the field of Curriculum and Instruction, scholars study the roles of psychological variables across an array of subject domains (e.g., reading, mathematics, literacy, science, foreign language education, physical education, etc.).

In addition, when one examines peer-reviewed journals in the field of education, it is apparent that research related to the role of psychology in classroom learning is found in a large variety of journals. Whereas much of the research is published in predictable outlets (e.g., the *Journal of Educational Psychology, Contemporary Educational Psychology*, the *British Journal of Educational Psychology, Educational Psychologist, Learning and Individual Differences*, and *Educational Psychology Review*), much of the relevant research is also found in many other journals that span a variety of disciplines. For example, there are numerous studies about psychological aspects of science education in journals such as the *Journal of*

Research in Science Teaching; there are studies examining the role of psychology in literacy in journals such as *Reading Research Quarterly*; there are numerous studies that examine psychological issues in journals published by the American Educational Research Association (e.g., *American Educational Research Journal* and *Review of Educational Research*).

In addition, the role of psychology in education also is examined by scholars from other disciplines. In order to fully appreciate the many perspectives that are used to study this phenomenon, it also is important to consider research that emanates from other fields. For example, much important research about the interactions that occur in classroom settings is conducted by anthropologists. In addition, given the constantly changing research base on neurobiology, it is important to consider studies that emanate from the field of neurology. Numerous scholars from other academic domains also study the role of psychological variables in classroom learning.

Content Covered in *Psychology of Classroom Learning: An Encyclopedia.* The content that is covered in this encyclopedia is diverse. The editorial team spent much time discussing and examining many potentially relevant topics before we arrived at the specific entries that are included in this work. We wanted to make certain that the topics covered represented both (a) trends in current empirical research, and (b) the needs of practicing educators. We realize and acknowledge that sometimes there is not direct overlap in these areas. We also realize that practicing educators often do not feel that researchers study topics that are truly relevant to the daily lives of students and teachers; therefore, we worked diligently to provide coverage of topics that are both on the cutting-edge in the research world, and practical to the lives and concerns of educators.

Although *PCL* covers a large range of topics, there are some important themes that run through the entire work. First, many entries that examine the topic of learning in school contexts have been included. Obviously the study of learning is central, given that it is part of the title of this book. Nevertheless, we have tried to cover a broad range of perspectives on academic learning. These include entries examining various theories and perspectives on learning (e.g., operant conditioning; sociocultural theory), applications of learning theory (e.g., intelligence testing; concept learning), and learning in various subject areas (e.g., learning in mathematics, science, reading, writing, and foreign languages).

Second, *PCL* includes many entries that focus on academic motivation. Many educators comment that their students are not motivated, and many students who eventually drop out of school note that the material covered in school was "boring" or not relevant to their lives. We have included entries that focus on both the characteristics of motivated (and unmotivated) students, as well as on instructional practices that can be fostered by educators to enhance student motivation. Entries focus on theoretical frameworks for the study of motivation (e.g., goal orientation theory, attribution theory), applications of motivation to aspects of the instructional context (e.g., school transitions, school climate), and instructional practices that enhance or hinder motivation (e.g., rewards, praise).

Third, the user will find entries that examine developmental issues. It is extremely important to acknowledge the roles of psychological and social development in education. In addition, we particularly believe that it is extraordinarily important for educators to understand the role of cognitive development in education. Students may be of the same chronological age, but may be at very different levels of cognitive development. The instructional practices used to address these developmental differences can have profound effects on subsequent learning and motivation. For example, some 6-year-old children may be better able to learn simple mathematical concepts than are others; some educators may start using grouping practices during the first grade to better instruct students who are at different levels of development. However, such grouping practices may yield some beneficial effects (e.g., the teachers may be able to more easily provide appropriate instruction to slower learners), and some negative effects (e.g., the placement of some children into low-ability groups may lead to stigmatization, and such children may never be able to transition into average or high-ability groups). Thus it is extremely important for educators to have a comprehensive understanding of developmental issues. It also is important to realize that cognitive and social development do not stop at the end of childhood; rather, development continues to play an important role during the adolescent years, and even for adult learners. In *Psychology of Classroom Learning: An Encyclopedia*, we have included a broad range of entries examining developmental issues. Some of the entries examine theoretical frameworks in the study of development (e.g., information processing theories of development, Piaget's and Vygotsky's theories of development); other entries examine applications of developmental theory to instruction (e.g., development of core knowledge domains); and other entries focus on different albeit equally important areas of development (e.g., emotional development, epistemological development).

Fourth, there are many entries that focus on some of the empirical aspects of education. With the establishment of the Institute of Education Sciences in the early 21ˢᵗ century, well-controlled empirical experiments (i.e., clinical trails) in educational research have assumed an important role in the formation of educational policy. Although there is disagreement in the field about the importance of this recent trend, we believe that it is exceedingly important for educators and students of education to be able to critically read and understand current and forthcoming research. Therefore, we have included entries that focus on educational research methods (e.g., longitudinal research, design experiments, action research, experimental research, and quasi-experimental research).

In addition, the testing and assessment are extremely prevalent both in the United States and abroad. Tests are quite often used to determine high-stakes outcomes; indeed, many teachers' and principals' jobs are dependent on the outcomes of such assessments. Thus it is extremely important for educators to understand assessment. Therefore, we have included entries that examine important contemporary issues in the field of educational testing and assessment (e.g., reliability, item analysis, classical test theory, classroom assessment, item response theory, norm- and criterion-referenced testing, etc.).

Fifth are the entries that focus on the role of psychology in the learning of exceptional students. Children and adolescents in schools express diversity in many different ways, and it is extremely important for all educators to realize that some of their students will have unique needs. Therefore, we have included entries that examine some of the needs of exceptional learners. More specifically, we have included entries that examine specific categorizations of exceptionalities (e.g., gifted learners, bilingual learners, learning disabilities, orthopedic impairments, deafness/hard of hearing, mental retardation, autism spectrum disorders, and attention deficit hyperactivity disorder [ADHD]), as well as instructional practices that can be particularly useful with exceptional populations (e.g., goal-setting, behavioral objectives, token economies).

Sixth, *PCL* includes entries that describe instructional practices that are rooted in psychology. These various practices cut across issues of learning, motivation, development, assessment, and exceptionality. It is vital for educators to understand the theoretical rationale and development of various practices, so that they can apply and use these practices appropriately and effectively. Thus we have included entries that examine practices that focus on learning in groups (e.g., cooperative learning, reciprocal teaching), practices that involve parents (e.g., home schooling, homework, parent involvement), classroom instructional practices (e.g., gender bias in teaching, multicultural educational), and practices that involve entire schools (e.g., creation of positive school climates, promotion of feelings of school belonging, school size, etc).

Users of *PCL* will also find brief biographies of particularly noteworthy researchers. These individuals have spent their careers studying various aspects of the role of psychology in classroom learning and instruction. Many of these biographies have been written by researchers who have been acquainted with these eminent scholars either as their former students or colleagues. Biographies are included of scholars who contributed to the early development of important theories (e.g., Lev Vygotsky, Jean Piaget, William James), scholars who have contributed to better understanding the role of psychology in effective instruction (e.g., Wilbert McKeachie, Ann Brown, Jere Brophy), and individuals who have affected research and policy at a broad level (e.g., Albert Bandura, Urie Bronfenbrenner, David Berliner, Jerome Bruner).

Finally, we also have included some of the "classics." As in any field of study, there are certain theories and topics that have served as important bases for current research. Consequently, we have included entries that review some extremely important background topics that remain relevant in the 21st century. These include entries on topics such as behaviorism, classical conditioning, direct instruction, and parenting styles.

WHY NOW?

The timing of the release of the *Psychology of Classroom Learning* is important for several reasons. One of the main reasons that we developed this product was to provide a timely resource for teacher education students and practicing educators. The theories, research, and instructional practices that are reviewed in *PCL* provide a solid research base for examining contemporary educational problems, and potential solutions to those problems.

In the United States, we remain in the era of the *No Child Left Behind* legislation. The introduction of this legislation in the early 21st century led to many changes in educational policies and these changes, in turn, have had many implications for the relation between psychology and education. For example, the use of high-stakes assessments to determine whether or not schools are performing effectively has significant implications and ramifications. Many teachers and school administrators feel pressured to obtain high scores on these summative assessments; this has important implications for how teachers interact with students on a daily basis. If a school does not perform well on these assessments, the pressure to perform better in subsequent years may affect the types of instructional practices that teachers use in classrooms. This may impact student motivation and achievement in important ways.

Perhaps one of the most pervasive problems in education is the proliferation of the use of instructional practices that are not based in solid empirical research. As a parallel example, in the field of medicine, few patients would want their doctors to suggest the use of medical techniques that were not proven to be effective through extensive empirical research. Indeed, if you were told that you had high blood pressure, and your doctor informed you that she read an article on the internet suggesting that eating brown rice lowered blood pressure, you might be doubtful; you probably would feel more secure if the doctor learned of this new treatment via articles that were published in peer-reviewed medical journals. However, can we say that this same type of logic applies in education? Probably not; many educators try and use instructional techniques that are learned "on the fly" and which are not necessarily proven techniques. Of course we may not always want to apply the same standards that we use in the field of medicine to the field of education, but, as editors of this encyclopedia, we do strongly believe that practices should be based on empirical research.

There is evidence that educators do often adapt instructional practices that are not based on solid research. For example, many practicing educators base their instructional practices on Gardner's theory of multiple intelligences; however, as noted by Waterhouse (2006), there is little empirical support from either educational research or from research in cognitive neuroscience to support the direct application of this theory to educational practices.

In a recent chapter, Berliner (in press) describes several examples of the mismatch between contemporary educational practices and solid research evidence. First, he notes that although there is a 25 year history of the effectiveness of a reading comprehension technique known as *reciprocal teaching* (Palincsar & Brown, 1984), the technique is still seldom used in classrooms today. Second, Berliner notes that research clearly indicates that retaining students in their current grade for an extra year does not positively affect achievement, and often is predictive of subsequent educational problems, such as eventually dropping out of school. Nevertheless, Berliner describes recent national legislation that advocates against promotion of students who are failing into the next grade level; this legislation runs counter to research indicating that promoting students to the next grade, and providing them with appropriate educational support, would lead to better outcomes. Finally, Berliner reviews the extensive body of research on homework. Much of this research indicates that having students complete nightly homework has little positive effect on academic achievement for elementary school aged children; when homework is given, only small amounts are recommended for elementary school youth (e.g., Cooper, 2003). Nevertheless, the assignment of homework to young children remains prevalent.

Another currently relevant example involves the promotion of students' self-esteem. The self-esteem movement is very popular in American schools. Many schools offer self-esteem classes, and many teachers spend time on self-esteem programs. In addition, expensive curricula often are sold with the implicit guarantee that these curricula will raise children's and adolescents' self-esteem. Indeed, there is a pervasive belief among educators that self-esteem is related to positive social and educational outcomes, and that by increasing students' self-esteem, we may be able to both improve academic achievement and foster the avoidance of engagement in risky behaviors. Nevertheless, empirical research on self-esteem for the most part completely fails to support these contentions (e.g., Baumeister, Campbell, Krueger, & Vohs, 2003; Coley & Chase-Landsdale, 1998; Wylie, 1979). In fact, some research indicates that many criminals (e.g., murderers, rapists, etc.) have quite high self-esteem (Baumeister, Smart, & Bodeon, 1996). However, despite the compelling research, self-esteem continues to be an important entity in American education.

If These Practices are Not Based in Research, Why do They Remain So Popular in the Field of Education? One of the main reasons for the publication of *PCL* is to help both teacher educators and practicing teachers to be able to identify effective educational practices that are based on solid empirical research. All of the entries in this encyclopedia are written by scholars with expertise in each area and extensive lists of additional references are provided for further reading on each topic. We truly hope that some of the misconceptions about educational practices and some of the misuse of instructional practices that are currently prevalent will be altered with the publication of this encyclopedia.

Why do so many instructional practices that are not rooted in research remain popular in classrooms? There are several explanations for this. First, education is a field filled with traditions. Most practicing teachers remember how they were taught, and it is often difficult to break with well-learned habits. Thus, a teacher who was taught multiplication during his or her own childhood via rote memorization techniques may use the same practices 20 years later, simply out of force of habit. In addition, although a teacher who is new to the profession may have learned new research-based techniques in college or graduate school, it often is difficult for new teachers to introduce novel practices into a school environment that has operated in a particular way for many years (i.e., "we don't do it that way at this school").

Second, as noted by Berliner (in press), teaching is a highly private endeavor; what goes on in classrooms is seldom observed by outsiders. Therefore, it often may be difficult to communicate new, research-based instructional techniques to practicing educators. In addition, there often is little accountability for the use of new research-based techniques in education. Whereas a teacher may learn a new technique such as reciprocal teaching during a professional development seminar or in a graduate education course, there are few systems in place to verify that the teacher is using the technique during instruction. In addition, if the teacher is using the technique at all, consultations with experts to provide ongoing support in the use of the new technique are seldom provided.

Waterhouse (2006) uses the theory of multiple intelligences, the "Mozart" effect, and the theory of emotional intelligence as three examples of recent educational theories that have had strong effects on educational policy and practice, despite the fact that little sound empirical research supports these theories. Waterhouse suggests that these and other ideas remain popular and continue to influence policy and practice because they are appealing to teachers (i.e., they provide teachers with a sense of control over student learning), they provide quick fixes for enduring problems (i.e., they can help all students become better learners), and they provide simplified explanations for complex cognitive processes. In addition, the publication of materials and curricula on these topics is prevalent, and educational marketplaces are filled with materials that make extraordinary promises with little basis in well-conducted research. An examination of the reference list in many of these materials clearly proves this point—seldom are such materials referenced with extensive lists of peer-reviewed empirical studies that support the suggested practices.

PARAMETERS OF *PSYCHOLOGY OF CLASSROOM LEARNING: AN ENCYCLOPEDIA*

The relation of psychology to education is highly complex. Thus we acknowledged from the outset that we would be unable to include an exhaustive review of all of the relevant topics. As indicated above, we have tried to provide coverage of the important themes that are relevant in the field, and we also have tried to include entries that are related to current practical issues. Nevertheless, there are certainly limitations regarding coverage in the book.

First, the entries are focused on fairly recent research. Whereas there is a long history of the role of psychology in classroom learning, for the most part, we have included entries that examine research that has been conducted during the past 20 years. As mentioned earlier, there are some exceptions, including biographies of notable scholars and reviews of some of the classic theories and programs of research in the field. However, the majority of the entries focus on current research, as opposed to earlier research that was more focused on laboratory studies and decontextualized views of learning (see Woolfolk Hoy, 2000, for a review).

Second, the entries in *PCL* for the most part emanate from a western perspective on the role of psychology in education. We acknowledge that learning is deeply rooted in cultural beliefs and practices, and that many of the theoretical perspectives that are described in this encyclopedia may not seem directly relevant to educators in other parts of the world. Nevertheless, we truly hope that the vast array of entries in this encyclopedia can serve as important resources to teachers across a variety of cultures.

AUDIENCE AND ORGANIZATION

Psychology of Classroom Learning: An Encyclopedia is intended to serve a diverse audience. First and foremost, we have developed *PCL* to serve as a resource for teacher education students and for practicing teachers. There are over 300 topics covered in this encyclopedia, and we believe that there are entries that can be beneficial to educators at all grade levels, from preschool through postsecondary education. Issues of learning, motivation, development, and assessment are not unique to any one particular setting or age group; therefore, we believe that these entries will provide useful information for educators at all levels.

Second, we believe that *PCL* can serve as an excellent resource for graduate students in the fields of education and psychology. The research base for each entry is quite current and the bibliographies are extensive. This encyclopedia will be an excellent resource for graduate students who are preparing masters theses and doctoral dissertations in education.

Third, we also believe that *PCL* will be useful for parents. Parents need to be advocates for their children in schools. If a parent feels that a child or adolescent is not being served well by a particular school or teacher, then the parent who comes into the school with a reliable source of knowledge can more effectively argue for changes in policies and practices that will positively affect his or her children's learning. The entries in this encyclopedia have been written so that individuals without a strong background in psychology or education can understand the main points discussed in each entry.

The encyclopedia is organized alphabetically. As noted earlier, major themes such as learning, motivation, and assessment are evident in the book. Nevertheless, we organized the entire volume alphabetically so that both general readers and experts can easily locate information on topics using commonly used names for each entry. Each entry has been peer-reviewed for accuracy of content and contains an extensive bibliography of both print and electronic sources for further research.

PCL includes convenient cross-referencing of two types: "See" and "See Also" references. "See" references fall within the body of the work and refer the reader to articles discussing that topic. For example, if one wanted to find information about childhood and looked under "Childhood," there would not be an article, but rather the instruction to "SEE *Early Childhood Development*." "See Also" cross-references fall at the end of articles and direct the reader to one or more other articles that may shed more light on the topic. At the conclusion of the article on Aptitude Testing, for example, you will find "SEE ALSO *Accountability; High Stakes Testing; Intelligence: An Overview*." At the end of Volume 2, there is an extensive Index to terms and concept in the articles.

ACKNOWLEDGEMENTS

Psychology of Classroom Learning: An Encyclopedia would not have been possible without the contributions of many important individuals. First, we would like to acknowledge Miranda Ferrara at Macmillan Reference USA, our extraordinary product manager and task-master. Miranda managed the flow of manuscripts, invited all of the authors to contribute, and sent out those friendly "reminders" for late manuscripts. She monitored the review and revision process for over a year. Above all, she kept us organized, on task, and happy throughout this process.

We also want to acknowledge our extraordinary team of Associate Editors. We came up with three first-choices and we were delighted when all three said yes. Tamera Murdock of the University of Missouri–Kansas City handled many of the entries dealing with motivation and development; Lee Swanson, of the University of California–Riverside, reviewed the entries examining exceptional learners and cognition; and Clark Chinn worked with authors who wrote about issues related to learning and instructional practices. Given that there are over 300 entries in the encyclopedia, there was inevitably much overlap in the entries handled by each associate editor. All three were models of professionalism, and each brought his or her extraordinary expertise to the project. The comments that the associate editors provided to the contributors was always relevant, effective, and concise. In addition, the patience of each of the associate editors with the editors and the contributors was always and continues to be appreciated.

In addition, we are extremely grateful to the many scholars who contributed to this encyclopedia. When we look at the list of contributors, we are truly amazed at the extraordinary caliber of the contributors. We can truly state that the contributors to *PCL* represent a list of the most eminent scholars in the world on these topics. We are truly indebted to each author for contributing his or her knowledge, wisdom, and expertise to this volume.

Finally, we also must acknowledge our two children, Jacob and Sarah. They continue to remind us daily why we do the work that we do. The research that is presented in this encyclopedia can improve education for the next generation of learners. If the information contained in these entries helps even one teacher to improve the learning of one student, then the time will have been more than well spent.

Eric M. Anderman
Lynley H. Anderman
The Ohio State University

Baumeister, R. F., Campbell, J. D., Krueger, J. L., & Vohs, K. D. (2003). Does high self-esteem cause better performance, interpersonal success, happiness, or healthier lifestyles? *Psychological Science in the Public Interest, 4*, 1–44.

Baumeister, R. F., Smart, L., & Boden, J. M. (1996). Relation of threatened egotism to violence and aggression: The dark side of high self-esteem. *Psychological Bulletin, 103*, 5–33.

Coley, R.L., & Chase-Landsdale, P.L. (1998). Adolescent pregnancy and parenthood. *American Psychologist, 53*, 152–166.

Cooper, H. (2003). Homework for all – in moderation. *Educational Leadership, 60*, 34–38.

Waterhouse, L. (2006). Inadequate evidence for multiple intelligences, Mozart effect, and emotional intelligence theories. *Educational Psychologist*, 41, 247–255.

Woolfolk Hoy, A. (2000). Educational psychology in teacher education. *Educational Psychologist, 35*, 257–270.

Wylie, R.C. (1979). *The self-concept, volume 2*. Lincoln, NE: University of Nebraska Press.

List of Articles

Contributors

Margaret Alic
Eastsound, Washington
 LEARNING AND TEACHING
  MATHEMATICS *(sidebar)*
 LEARNING AND TEACHING SCIENCE
 SIMON, HERBERT (ALEXANDER)
 THEORY OF MIND

Eric M. Anderman
Ohio State University
 ATTRIBUTION THEORY
 GOAL ORIENTATION THEORY
 MAEHR, MARTIN L.
 NORMAL DISTRIBUTION
 RESEARCH METHODS: AN OVERVIEW
 SCHOOL TRANSITIONS: OVERVIEW
 SENSATION-SEEKING

Lynley H. Anderman
Ohio State University
 ATTRIBUTION THEORY
 SCHOOL BELONGING

Cynthia M. Anderson
University of Oregon
 APPLIED BEHAVIOR ANALYSIS

Lorin W. Anderson
University of South Carolina
 BLOOM'S TAXONOMY

Carey E. Andrzejewski
Ohio State University
 TEACHER BELIEFS

Doris B. Ash
University of California, Santa Cruz
 BROWN, ANN LESLIE
 COMMUNITIES OF LEARNERS

William Arthur Atkins
Pekin, Illinois
 CONCEPT MAPS

Chammie C. Austin
Saint Louis University
 IMPRESSION MANAGEMENT

Saul Axelrod
Temple University
 CLASSROOM MANAGEMENT:
  OVERVIEW

Doris Luft Baker
University of Oregon
 SECOND LANGUAGE ACQUISITION

Linda Baker
University of Maryland, Baltimore
County
 METACOGNITION

Sandra A. Baker
University of Maryland, College Park
 PEER RELATIONSHIPS: FRIENDSHIPS

Scott K. Baker
Pacific Institutes for Research
 SECOND LANGUAGE ACQUISITION

Robert L. Bangert-Drowns
University at Albany, State
University of New York
 FEEDBACK IN LEARNING

Carolyn Barber
University of Missouri–Kansas
City
 GENDER IDENTITY

Susan M. Barnett
Cornell University
 TRANSFER

Brigid Barron
Stanford University
 SHARED COGNITION

W. Robert Batsell
Kalamazoo College
 CLASSICAL CONDITIONING

Roy F. Baumeister
Florida State University
 SELF-ESTEEM

Anne S. Beauchamp
University of Kansas
 CHEATING
 KOHLBERG, LAWRENCE

Maria B. Benzon
University of Houston
 SOCIAL COGNITIVE THEORY

David A. Bergin
University of Missouri–Columbia
 OGBU, JOHN U(ZO)

Sheri Berkeley
University of Georgia
 PEER TUTORING

David C. Berliner
Arizona State University
CALFEE, ROBERT C.

Virginia W. Berninger
University of Washington
BRAIN AND LEARNING

David F. Bjorklund
Florida Atlantic University
CROSS-SECTIONAL RESEARCH
DESIGNS

Andrea Bjornestad
Sioux Falls, SD, School District;
University of South Dakota
FLOW THEORY

Peter Blatchford
University of London, United
Kingdom
CLASS SIZE

Patty Bode
Tufts University with The School of
the Museum of Fine Arts, Boston
MULTICULTURAL EDUCATION

Robert Bogdan
Syracuse University
QUALITATIVE RESEARCH

Ali Borjian
San Francisco State University
LEARNING AND TEACHING FOREIGN
LANGUAGES

Brian A. Bottge
University of Kentucky
ANCHORED INSTRUCTION

Marc A. Brackett
Yale University
EMOTIONAL INTELLIGENCE

Hilary Bradbury
University of Southern California
ACTION RESEARCH

Jeffery P. Braden
North Carolina State University
VALIDITY

Kelly D. Bradley
University of Kentucky
QUASIEXPERIMENTAL RESEARCH

Stephen Brand
University of Rhode Island
SCHOOL CLIMATE

Kelly Bridges
Florida Atlantic University
FIRST (PRIMARY) LANGUAGE
ACQUISITION

Stephen E. Brock
California State University,
Sacramento
TIME ON-TASK

Ray Brogan
Northern Virginia Community
College
COGNITIVE DEVELOPMENT:
INFORMATION PROCESSING
THEORIES OF DEVELOPMENT
GILLIGAN, CAROL
IDENTITY DEVELOPMENT
RELIABILITY
SOCIOECONOMIC STATUS

B. Bradford Brown
University of Wisconsin, Madison
PEER RELATIONSHIPS: PEER GROUPS

Paige Shalter Bruening
Ohio State University
PEER RELATIONSHIPS: SOCIOMETRIC
STATUS (sidebar)

Megan J. Bulloch
Ohio State University
CONCEPT DEVELOPMENT

Paul Burnett
Charles Sturt University
PRAISE

R. T. Busse
Chapman University
SOCIOMETRIC ASSESSMENT

James P. Byrnes
Temple University
AT-RISK STUDENTS
DECISION MAKING

Robert Calfee
Stanford University
BERLINER, DAVID CHARLES

Wayne J. Camara
The College Board
STANDARDS FOR EDUCATIONAL
AND PSYCHOLOGICAL TESTING

Gary L. Canivez
Eastern Illinois University
APTITUDE TESTS
STANFORD-BINET INTELLIGENCE
SCALES

Stephen J. Ceci
Cornell University
MISDIAGNOSES OF DISABILITIES
TRANSFER

Marilyn J. Chambliss
University of Maryland, College Park
PROVIDING EXPLANATIONS

Tabbye M. Chavous
University of Michigan
ETHNIC IDENTITY AND ACADEMIC
ACHIEVEMENT

Zhe Chen
University of California, Davis
ANALOGY

Clark A. Chinn
Rutgers University
ANDERSON, RICHARD C(HASE)
COGNITIVE STRATEGIES
COLLABORATIVE LEARNING
EPISTEMOLOGICAL BELIEFS

Lisa M. Chinn
Princeton University
COGNITIVE STRATEGIES
COLLABORATIVE LEARNING

Alexander W. Chizhik
San Diego State University
RESISTANCE THEORY

Estella W. Chizhik
San Diego State University
RESISTANCE THEORY

Douglas B. Clark
Arizona State University
CONSTRUCTIVISM: OVERVIEW

Andrea D. Clements
East Tennessee State University
HOME SCHOOLING

Marc Coenders
CPsquare
LAVE, JEAN

Allan Collins
Northwestern University (emeritus)
COGNITIVE APPRENTICESHIP
SITUATED COGNITION

Harris Cooper
Duke University
HOMEWORK
META-ANALYSIS

Lyn Corno
Columbia University
GAGE, NATHAN LEES
VOLITION

Brian D. Cox
Hofstra University
COGNITIVE DEVELOPMENT:
OVERVIEW

Anna Craft
University of Exeter and The Open
University, England
CREATIVITY

Donald Crawford
Baltimore Curriculum Project
DIRECT INSTRUCTION

Linda Crocker
University of Florida (emeritus)
SUBJECTIVE TEST ITEMS

Kathryn Cunningham
University of Kentucky
CLASSROOM ENVIRONMENT

Jerome V. D'Agostino
Ohio State University
CLASSROOM ASSESSMENT

Cynthia M. D'Angelo
Arizona State University
CONSTRUCTIVISM: OVERVIEW

Edward J. Daly, III
University of Nebraska, Lincoln
BEHAVIORISM

Fred Danner
University of Kentucky
BRONFENBRENNER, URIE

Helen Davidson
Rutgers University
ABILITY GROUPING
CONCEPT LEARNING
PEER RELATIONSHIPS: PEER PRESSURE

Heather A. Davis
Ohio State University
CARING TEACHERS
TEACHER BELIEFS
TEACHER EFFICACY

Tonya N. Davis
University of Texas at Austin
CLASSROOM MANAGEMENT: TOKEN
ECONOMIES

David Dean
University of Washington
CONSTRUCTIVISM: INQUIRY-BASED
LEARNING

Edward L. Deci
University of Rochester
SELF-DETERMINATION THEORY OF
MOTIVATION

Heidi H. Denler
Grosse Pointe, Michigan
MODELING *(sidebar)*

NEO-PIAGETIAN THEORIES OF
DEVELOPMENT *(sidebar)*
SOCIAL COGNITIVE THEORY
(sidebar)

Brent M. Drake
Purdue University
SCHOOL TRANSITIONS: MIDDLE
SCHOOL

Irit Dubrovsky
Hebrew University of Jerusalem
PROSOCIAL BEHAVIOR

Charles Dukes
Florida Atlantic University
CROSS-SECTIONAL RESEARCH
DESIGNS

George J. DuPaul
Lehigh University
ATTENTION-DEFICIT HYPERACTIVITY
DISORDER (ADHD)

Anthony Durr
Ohio State University
BULLIES AND VICTIMS *(sidebar)*

Carol S. Dweck
Stanford University
THEORIES OF INTELLIGENCE

Susan H. Eaves
Weems Division of Children and
Youth, Meridian, Mississippi
ITEM ANALYSIS

Jacquelynne S. Eccles
University of Michigan
EXPECTANCY VALUE MOTIVATIONAL
THEORY

Danielle Edelston
University of California, Riverside
LEARNING DISABILITIES

Nancy Eisenberg
Arizona State University
EMOTION REGULATION

Edmund T. Emmer
University of Texas at Austin
CLASSROOM MANAGEMENT:
WITHITNESS

Kurt E. Engelmann
National Institute for Direct
Instruction, Eugene, OR
DIRECT INSTRUCTION

Siegfried Engelmann
University of Oregon
DIRECT INSTRUCTION

Robert Epstein
University of California, San Diego
SKINNER, B(URRHUS) F(REDERIC)

Cynthia A. Erdley
University of Maine
DWECK, CAROL S(USAN)

Bradley T. Erford
Loyola College in Maryland
ITEM ANALYSIS

Dorothy L. Espelage
University of Illinois, Champaign
Urbana
BULLIES AND VICTIMS

Jose A. Espinoza
University of California, Riverside
OPPORTUNITY/ACHIEVEMENT GAP

Valerie A. Evans
Temple University
CLASSROOM MANAGEMENT:
OVERVIEW

David F. Feldon
University of South Carolina
EXPERTISE

Mark K. Felton
San José State University
ARGUMENTATION

Linda A. Fernsten
Dowling College
PORTFOLIO ASSESSMENT

Frank D. Fincham
Florida State University
LEARNED HELPLESSNESS

Dawn P. Flanagan
St. John's University
STANDARDIZED TESTING

Donna Y. Ford
Vanderbilt University
CULTURAL BIAS IN TESTING

Harriett H. Ford
Charlotte-Mecklenburg Schools;
Carolinas Medical Center
NORM-REFERENCED TESTING

Rachel L. Freeman
University of Kansas
BEHAVIORAL OBJECTIVES

Tierra M. Freeman
University of Missouri–Kansas City
DROPPING OUT OF SCHOOL
MACCOBY, ELEANOR E(MMONS)

Rebecca J. Frey
New Haven, Connecticut
ANXIETY

Tiffany L. Gallagher
Brock University
SELF-EXPLANATION

Brandon Gamble
California State University, Long
Beach
AUTHENTIC ASSESSMENT

Georgia Earnest García
University of Illinois-Champaign
Urbana
BILINGUAL EDUCATION

GNA Garcia
University of Connecticut
MORAL DEVELOPMENT

Howard Gardner
Harvard University
MULTIPLE INTELLIGENCES

Irene W. Gaskins
Benchmark School, Media, PA
(emeritus)
STRATEGIES INSTRUCTION

Mary Gauvain
University of California, Riverside
COGNITIVE DEVELOPMENT:
VYGOTSKY'S THEORY
ROGOFF, BARBARA

David C. Geary
University of Missouri–Columbia
COGNITIVE DEVELOPMENT:
BIOLOGICAL THEORIES

Sarah Gebhardt
Miami University of Ohio
CLASSROOM MANAGEMENT:
PUNISHMENT

Richard Gilman
Cincinnati Children's Hospital
Medical Center
INDIVIDUAL *VS.* GROUP
ADMINISTERED TESTS

Susan L. Golbeck
Rutgers University
GUIDED PARTICIPATION

Allen W. Gottfried
California State University, Fullerton
TEMPERAMENT

Sandra Graham
University of California, Los Angeles
WEINER, BERNARD

Steve Graham
Vanderbilt University
LEARNING AND TEACHING WRITING

Suzanne E. Graham
University of New Hampshire
LONGITUDINAL RESEARCH

DeLeon L. Gray
Ohio State University
TRANSFER *(sidebar)*

James G. Greeno
Stanford University (emeritus)
SITUATED COGNITION

Elena L. Grigorenko
Yale University
STERNBERG, ROBERT J(EFFREY)
TRIARCHIC THEORY OF
INTELLIGENCE

Jennifer Grisham-Brown
University of Kentucky
EARLY CHILDHOOD DEVELOPMENT

Robert W. Grossman
Kalamazoo College
CLASSICAL CONDITIONING

Diana Wright Guerin
California State University, Fullerton
TEMPERAMENT

Thomas R. Guskey
Georgetown College
MASTERY LEARNING

R. Trent Haines
Louisiana State University
VYGOTSKY, LEV SEMENOVICH

Leigh A. Hall
University of North Carolina,
Chapel Hill
LEARNING AND TEACHING READING

Nathan Hall
University of California, Irvine
ATTRIBUTIONAL RETRAINING

Daniel P. Hallahan
University of Virginia
SPECIAL EDUCATION

Diane F. Halpern
Claremont McKenna College
CRITICAL THINKING

Ronald K. Hambleton
University of Massachusetts,
Amherst
CRITERION-REFERENCED TESTS

Doug Hamman
Texas Tech University
ERIKSON, ERIK

Marcie W. Handler
The May Institute
CLASSROOM MANAGEMENT: RULES
AND PROCEDURES

Steven Hardy-Braz
U.S. Department of Defense; Fort
Bragg Schools
STANDARDIZED TESTING

Christopher J. Harris
University of Arizona
AUTHENTIC TASKS

Susan Harter
University of Denver
RELEVANCE OF SELF-EVALUATIONS
TO CLASSROOM LEARNING

Krista Healy
University of California, Riverside
NORM-REFERENCED SCORING

Daniel Hickey
Indiana University
SOCIOCULTURAL THEORIES OF
MOTIVATION

Nancy E. Hill
Duke University
PARENT INVOLVEMENT

Patrick L. Hill
University of Notre Dame
EGOCENTRISM

Cindy E. Hmelo-Silver
Rutgers University
CONSTRUCTIVISM: PROBLEM-BASED
LEARNING
CONSTRUCTIVISM: PROJECT-BASED
LEARNING

Barbara K. Hofer
Middlebury College
EPISTEMOLOGICAL DEVELOPMENT

Erika Hoff
Florida Atlantic University
FIRST (PRIMARY) LANGUAGE
ACQUISITION

Robin L. Hojnoski
Lehigh University
SCHOOL TRANSITIONS: ELEMENTARY
SCHOOL

Anthony C. Holter
University of Notre Dame
MORAL EDUCATION

Robert H. Horner
University of Oregon
APPLIED BEHAVIOR ANALYSIS
REWARDS

Cynthia Hudley
University of California, Santa
Barbara
AGGRESSION

Jason G. Irizarry
University of Connecticut
CULTURAL DEFICIT MODEL

Zeynep Zennur Isik-Ercan
Ohio State University
GUIDED PARTICIPATION (sidebar)

Nancy Ewald Jackson
University of Iowa
NEO-PIAGETIAN THEORIES OF
DEVELOPMENT

Patricia Jarvis
Illinois State University
SCHOOL TRANSITIONS: HIGH
SCHOOL

Joseph R. Jenkins
University of Washington
FORMATIVE AND SUMMATIVE
ASSESSMENT

Heisawn Jeong
Hallym University
TUTORING

Bonnie Johnson
Dowling College
HIGH STAKES TESTING

Dale D. Johnson
Dowling College
HIGH STAKES TESTING

David W. Johnson
University of Minnesota
CONFLICT RESOLUTION

Evelyn S. Johnson
Boise State University
FORMATIVE AND SUMMATIVE
ASSESSMENT

Roger T. Johnson
University of Minnesota
CONFLICT RESOLUTION

Lee Jussim
Rutgers University
TEACHER EXPECTATIONS

Constance Kamii
University of Alabama
PIAGET, JEAN

Tomoe Kanaya
Claremont McKenna College
MISDIAGNOSES OF DISABILITIES

Harrison Kane
Mississippi State University
SPEARMAN, CHARLES EDWARD

Avi Kaplan
Ben Gurion University of the Negev
ACHIEVEMENT MOTIVATION
INTRINSIC AND EXTRINSIC
MOTIVATION

Stuart A. Karabenick
University of Michigan
HELP-SEEKING

James M. Kauffman
University of Virginia
EMOTIONAL/BEHAVIORAL
DISORDERS

Alan E. Kazdin
Yale University
SINGLE-CASE DESIGNS

Timothy Z. Keith
University of Texas at Austin
WESCHLER INTELLIGENCE TEST

Ayesha Khurshid
Mississippi State University
SPEARMAN, CHARLES EDWARD

Makini L. King
University of Missouri–Kansas City
DROPPING OUT OF SCHOOL

Rachel B. Kirkpatrick
University of Missouri–Kansas City
DROPPING OUT OF SCHOOL

Femke Kirschner
Open University of the Netherlands
COGNITIVE LOAD THEORY

Paul A. Kirschner
Utrecht University; Open University
of the Netherlands
COGNITIVE LOAD THEORY

Ariel Knafo
Hebrew University of Jerusalem
PROSOCIAL BEHAVIOR

Timothy R. Konold
University of Virginia
APTITUDE TESTS

David R. Krathwohl
Syracuse University
BLOOM'S TAXONOMY

Deanna Kuhn
Columbia University
MICROGENETIC RESEARCH
STRATEGY DEVELOPMENT

Melanie R. Kuhn
Rutgers University
LEARNING STYLES

Revathy Kumar
University of Toledo
HOME-SCHOOL DISSONANCE

Haggai Kupermintz
University of Haifa
CRONBACH, LEE J(OSEPH)

Kathryn M. LaFontana
Sacred Heart University
PEER RELATIONSHIPS: SOCIOMETRIC
STATUS

Giulio Lancioni
University of Bari, Italy
CLASSROOM MANAGEMENT: TOKEN
ECONOMIES

Derek R. Lane
University of Kentucky
COMMUNICATION WITH STUDENTS
TO ENHANCE LEARNING

Daniel K. Lapsley
University of Notre Dame
EGOCENTRISM

Shawna J. Lee
Wayne State University; Merrill-
Palmer Institute for Child and
Family Development
POSSIBLE SELVES THEORY

Stephen Lehman
Denver Public Schools
INTEREST

Jian Li
Ohio State University
CORRELATIONAL RESEARCH

Jin Li
Brown University
BELIEFS ABOUT LEARNING

Richard G. Lomax
Ohio State University
CORRELATIONAL RESEARCH

Keisha Love
University of Kentucky
ATTACHMENT

Jens Möller
University of Kiel
SOCIAL COMPARISONS

Xin Ma
University of Kentucky
LEARNING AND TEACHING
    MATHEMATICS

Wendy Machalicek
University of Texas at Austin
CLASSROOM MANAGEMENT: TOKEN
    ECONOMIES

William E. MacLean
University of Wyoming
MENTAL RETARDATION

Ellie Martinez
California State University,
Sacramento
TIME ON-TASK

Ronald W. Marx
University of Arizona
AUTHENTIC TASKS

Jennifer T. Mascolo
St. John's University
STANDARDIZED TESTING

Emanuel J. Mason
Northeastern University
INTELLIGENCE: AN OVERVIEW

Margo A. Mastropieri
George Mason University
PEER TUTORING
TEST TAKING SKILLS

Richard E. Mayer
University of California, Santa
Barbara
CONSTRUCTIVISM: DISCOVERY
    LEARNING
EXPERIMENTAL RESEARCH
PROBLEM SOLVING

Megan M. McClelland
Oregon State University
SOCIAL SKILLS

Katherine M. McCormick
University of Kentucky
SERVICE-LEARNING

Matthew T. McCrudden
Victoria University of Wellington
INFORMATION PROCESSING THEORY

Karla K. McGregor
University of Iowa
SPEECH AND LANGUAGE
    IMPAIRMENTS

Wilbert J. McKeachie
University of Michigan
PINTRICH, PAUL ROBERT

James H. McMillan
Virginia Commonwealth University
GRADING

M. David Merrill
Utah State University
GAGNÉ, ROBERT MILLS

Michael Middleton
University of New Hampshire
ACADEMIC PRESS

Angela D. Miller
University of Kentucky
CLASSROOM ENVIRONMENT

Margery Miller
Gallaudet University
DEAF AND HARD OF HEARING

Kristen N. Missall
University of Kentucky
SCHOOL TRANSITIONS:
    ELEMENTARY SCHOOL

Donald Moores
University of North Florida
DEAF AND HARD OF HEARING

Christian E. Mueller
University of Memphis
MODELING

Kou Murayama
Tokyo Institute of Technology
OBJECTIVE TEST ITEMS

Tamera B. Murdock
University of Missouri–Kansas City
CHEATING

P. Karen Murphy
Pennsylvania State University
ALEXANDER, PATRICIA A.

Darcia Narvaez
University of Notre Dame
MORAL EDUCATION

Melissa M. Nelson
University of Pittsburgh
EXPERT-NOVICE STUDIES

Richard S. Newman
University of California, Riverside
HELP-SEEKING

Kim Nguyen-Jahiel
University of Illinois-Champaign
Urbana
ANDERSON, RICHARD C(HASE)

Sharon L. Nichols
University of Texas at San Antonio
ADOLESCENCE
BROPHY, JERE E(DWARD)
COMPETITION

Seth M. Noar
University of Kentucky
IMPULSIVE DECISION-MAKING

Angela M. O'Donnell
Rutgers University
CONSTRUCTIVISM: CASE-BASED
    LEARNING
MEMORY

Mark O'Reilly
University of Texas at Austin
CLASSROOM MANAGEMENT: TOKEN
    ECONOMIES

Teresa Odle
Albuquerque, New Mexico
EMOTIONAL DEVELOPMENT
EXPERIMENTAL RESEARCH *(sidebar)*
ORTHOPEDIC IMPAIRMENTS
VISUAL IMPAIRMENTS

Lori Olafson
University of Nevada, Las Vegas
KNOWLEDGE

Natalie G. Olinghouse
Michigan State University
LEARNING AND TEACHING WRITING

Pamella H. Oliver
California State University, Fullerton
TEMPERAMENT

John E. Opfer
Ohio State University
CONCEPT DEVELOPMENT

Gilda Oran
George Washington University
CULTURALLY RELEVANT PEDAGOGY

Jeanne Ellis Ormrod
University of Northern Colorado
(emerita); University of New
Hampshire
BRUNER, JEROME S(EYMOUR)

Jason W. Osborne
North Carolina State University
IDENTIFICATION WITH ACADEMICS

Steven J. Osterlind
University of Missouri–Columbia
CLASSICAL TEST THEORY
ITEM RESPONSE THEORY

Daphna Oyserman
University of Michigan
POSSIBLE SELVES THEORY

Fred Paas
Open University of the Netherlands;
Erasmus University, Rotterdam
COGNITIVE LOAD THEORY

Amado M. Padilla
Stanford University
LEARNING AND TEACHING FOREIGN
LANGUAGES

Frank Pajares
Emory University
BANDURA, ALBERT
JAMES, WILLIAM
SELF-EFFICACY THEORY

Aleksandra L. Palchuk
University of California, Davis
ANALOGY

Annemarie Sullivan Palincsar
University of Michigan
SOCIOCULTURAL THEORY

Erika A. Patall
Duke University
META-ANALYSIS

Helen Patrick
Purdue University
SCHOOL TRANSITIONS: MIDDLE
SCHOOL

Reinhard Pekrun
University of Munich
STUDENT EMOTIONS

Raymond P. Perry
University of Manitoba
ATTRIBUTIONAL RETRAINING

Larson Pierce
University of Kentucky
IMPULSIVE DECISION-MAKING

Sharon G. Portwood
University of North Carolina,
Charlotte
ABUSE AND NEGLECT

Kristin Powers
California State University, Long
Beach
AUTHENTIC ASSESSMENT

Richard S. Prawat
Michigan State University
DEWEY, JOHN

Sadhana Puntambekar
University of Wisconsin, Madison
SCAFFOLDING

Robert F. Putnam
The May Institute
CLASSROOM MANAGEMENT: RULES
AND PROCEDURES

Judi Randi
University of New Haven
VOLITION

Robert K. Ream
University of California, Riverside
OPPORTUNITY/ACHIEVEMENT GAP

Peter Reason
University of Southern California
ACTION RESEARCH

Johnmarshall Reeve
University of Iowa
AUTONOMY SUPPORT
REINFORCEMENT

Sally M. Reis
University of Connecticut
GIFTED EDUCATION

Joseph S. Renzulli
University of Connecticut
GIFTED EDUCATION

Cecil R. Reynolds
Texas A&M University
INTELLIGENCE TESTING

Todd L. Richards
University of Washington
BRAIN AND LEARNING

Susan E. Rivers
Yale University
EMOTIONAL INTELLIGENCE

Daniel H. Robinson
University of Texas at Austin
EVALUATION (TEST) ANXIETY

Samuel Rocha
Ohio State University
EPISTEMOLOGICAL BELIEFS
(sidebar)

Jeremy Roschelle
SRI International
SHARED COGNITION

Barak Rosenshine
University of Illinois (emeritus)
RECIPROCAL TEACHING

Sharon Scales Rostosky
University of Kentucky
SEXUAL ORIENTATION

Wolff-Michael Roth
University of Victoria, British
Columbia
DESIGN EXPERIMENT

Lisa. A. Ruble
University of Kentucky
AUTISM SPECTRUM DISORDERS

Shannon L. Russell
University of Maryland, College Park
PARENTING STYLES

Allison M. Ryan
University of Illinois-Champaign
Urbana
PEER RELATIONSHIPS: OVERVIEW
SOCIAL GOALS

Richard M. Ryan
University of Rochester
SELF-DETERMINATION THEORY OF
MOTIVATION

Sarah M. Ryan
University of California, Riverside
OPPORTUNITY/ACHIEVEMENT GAP

Mark C. Sadoski
Texas A&M University
DUAL CODING THEORY

Ala Samarapungavan
Purdue University
REASONING
THEORIES (AS A FORM OF
KNOWLEDGE)

Rosetta F. Sandidge
University of Kentucky
CLASSROOM MANAGEMENT:
ASSERTIVE DISCIPLINE

Kristin L. Sayeski
University of Nevada, Las Vegas
SPECIAL EDUCATION

Kathryn Scantlebury
University of Delaware
GENDER BIAS IN TEACHING
GENDER ROLE STEREOTYPING

Matthew Schlesinger
Southern Illinois University
CONNECTIONISM

Gregory Schraw
University of Nevada, Las Vegas
INFORMATION PROCESSING
THEORY
INTEREST
KNOWLEDGE
KNOWLEDGE REPRESENTATION

Dale Schunk
University of North Carolina,
Greensboro
GOAL SETTING
SELF-REGULATED LEARNING

Christian D. Schunn
University of Pittsburgh
ANDERSON, JOHN ROBERT
EXPERT-NOVICE STUDIES

Daniel L. Schwartz
Stanford University
BRANSFORD, JOHN D.

Amy Schweinle
University of South Dakota
FLOW THEORY

Sarah E. Scott
University of Michigan
SOCIOCULTURAL THEORY

Thomas E. Scruggs
George Mason University
PEER TUTORING
TEST TAKING SKILLS

Scott Seider
Harvard University
GARDNER, HOWARD
MULTIPLE INTELLIGENCES

Andrew Shtulman
Occidental College
DEVELOPMENT OF CORE
KNOWLEDGE DOMAINS

Thomas J. Shuell
University at Buffalo, State
University of New York (emeritus)
THEORIES OF LEARNING

Jeff Sigafoos
University of Tasmania, Australia
CLASSROOM MANAGEMENT: TOKEN
ECONOMIES

Sarah Kozel Silverman
Ohio State University
COGNITIVE DEVELOPMENT:
BIOLOGICAL THEORIES *(sidebar)*
TEACHER EFFICACY

Dorothy G. Singer
Yale University
COGNITIVE DEVELOPMENT:
PIAGET'S THEORY

Judith D. Singer
Harvard University
LONGITUDINAL RESEARCH

Robert E. Slavin
Johns Hopkins University and
University of York
COMPREHENSIVE SCHOOL
REFORM FOR HIGH-POVERTY
SCHOOLS

Carol L. Smith
University of Massachusetts, Boston
CONCEPTUAL CHANGE

Jeffrey K. Smith
University of Otago
LEARNING IN INFORMAL SETTINGS

John D. Smith
CPsquare
LAVE, JEAN

Elizabeth Soby
Grosse Pointe, Michigan
AT-RISK STUDENTS *(sidebar)*
CLASSROOM ENVIRONMENT
(sidebar)

Eun Hye Son
Ohio State University
QUESTIONING

Scott A. Spaulding
University of Oregon
REWARDS

Jason M. Stephens
University of Connecticut
MORAL DEVELOPMENT

Clayton L. Stephenson
Claremont Graduate University
CRITICAL THINKING

Ruby J. Stevens
University of Kentucky
CULTURAL BIAS IN TEACHING

*The Students of Dr. Carol
Midgley*
MIDGLEY, CAROL

Jeremy R. Sullivan
University of Texas at San Antonio
COMPETITION

H. Lee Swanson
University of California, Riverside
DYNAMIC ASSESSMENT
LEARNING DISABILITIES

April Z. Taylor
California State University,
Northridge
GRAHAM, SANDRA (HALEY)

Robert Thorndike
Western Washington University
THORNDIKE, E(DWARD) L(EE)

Martha L. Thurlow
University of Minnesota
ACCOUNTABILITY
INDIVIDUALIZED EDUCATION
PROGRAM (IEP)

Shauna Tominey
Oregon State University
SOCIAL SKILLS

Stephanie Touchman
Arizona State University
CONSTRUCTIVISM: OVERVIEW

Bruce W. Tuckman
Ohio State University
OPERANT CONDITIONING

Christina Tyler
University of Kentucky
STEREOTYPE THREAT

Kenneth M. Tyler
University of Kentucky
CLARK, KENNETH BANCROFT
CULTURAL BIAS IN TEACHING
STEREOTYPE THREAT

Aesha L. Uqdah
Chicago School of Professional
Psychology
CULTURAL BIAS IN TEACHING

Tim C. Urdan
Santa Clara University
SELF-HANDICAPPING

Carlos Valiente
Arizona State University
EMOTION REGULATION

Michelle Vander Veldt
California State University, Fullerton
KNOWLEDGE

Scott VanderStoep
Hope College
MCKEACHIE, WIBERT J(AMES)

Kim Walters-Parker
Georgetown College
COMMUNICATION WITH PARENTS
TO ENHANCE LEARNING

T. Steuart Watson
Miami University of Ohio
CLASSROOM MANAGEMENT:
PUNISHMENT

Tonya S. Watson
Miami University of Ohio
CLASSROOM MANAGEMENT:
PUNISHMENT

Michelle Weiner
Hebrew University of Jerusalem
PROSOCIAL BEHAVIOR

Etienne Wenger
CPsquare
LAVE, JEAN

Kathryn R. Wentzel
University of Maryland, College
Park
PARENTING STYLES
PEER RELATIONSHIPS: FRIENDSHIPS

Melissa Wheatley
University of Kentucky
AUTISM SPECTRUM DISORDERS

Gilman W. Whiting
Vanderbilt University
CULTURAL BIAS IN TESTING

Allan Wigfield
University of Maryland
ECCLES, JACQUELYNNE S.

Kaila Wilcox
Northeastern University
INTELLIGENCE: AN OVERVIEW

Nina C. Wilde
Temple University
CLASSROOM MANAGEMENT:
OVERVIEW

Ian A. G. Wilkinson
Ohio State University
DISCUSSION METHODS
QUESTIONING

John B. Willett
Harvard University
LONGITUDINAL RESEARCH

Patrick B. Williams
Claremont Graduate University
CRITICAL THINKING

Robert F. Williams
Lawrence University
DISTRIBUTED COGNITION

Merlin C. Wittrock
PROBLEM SOLVING

Vera E. Woloshyn
Brock University
PRESSLEY, G. MICHAEL
SELF-EXPLANATION

Christopher A. Wolters
University of Houston
SOCIAL COGNITIVE THEORY

Michael Yough
Ohio State University
GOAL ORIENTATION THEORY
(sidebar)

Thematic Index

The following classification of articles arranged thematically gives an overview of the variety of articles and the breadth of subjects treated in Psychology of Classroom Learning: An Encyclopedia. Along with the index and the alphabetical arrangement of PCL, this thematic outline should aid in the location of topics. It is our hope that it will do more, that it will direct the user to articles that may not have been the object of a search, and that it will facilitate the kind of browsing that invites the reader to discover new articles and new topics, related, perhaps tangentially, to those originally sought.

1. Assessment
2. Biography
3. Development
4. Exceptionalities
5. Group Differences
6. Grouping
7. Instruction
8. Intelligence
9. Learning
10. Literacy
11. Management
12. Methodology
13. Motivation
14. Philosophy
15. Policy
16. Psychological Characteristics
17. Social Context
18. Strategies

1. ASSESSMENT

Accountability
Aptitude Tests
Authentic Assessment
Classical Test Theory
Classroom Assessment
Criterion-Referenced Tests
Cronbach, Lee J(oseph)
Cultural Bias in Testing
Dynamic Assessment
Evaluation (Test) Anxiety
Formative and Summative Assessment
Grading
High Stakes Testing
Individual vs. Group Administered Tests
Intelligence Testing
Item Analysis
Item Response Theory
Misdiagnoses of Disabilities
Normal Distribution
Norm-Referenced Scoring
Norm-Referenced Testing
Objective Test Items
Portfolio Assessment
Reliability
Sociometric Assessment
Standardized Testing
Standards for Educational and
    Psychological Testing
Stanford-Binet Intelligence Scales
Subjective Test Items
Test Taking Skills
Validity
Weschler Intelligence Test

2. BIOGRAPHY

Alexander, Patricia A.
Anderson, John Robert
Anderson, Richard C(hase)
Bandura, Albert
Berliner, David Charles
Bransford, John D.
Bronfenbrenner, Urie
Brophy, Jere E(dward)
Brown, Ann Leslie
Bruner, Jerome S(eymour)
Calfee, Robert C.
Clark, Kenneth Bancroft
Cronbach, Lee J(oseph)
Dewey, John
Dweck, Carol S(usan)
Eccles, Jacquelynne S.
Erikson, Erik
Gage, Nathaniel Lees
Gagné, Robert Mills
Gardner, Howard
Gilligan, Carol
Graham, Sandra (Haley)
James, William
Kohlberg, Lawrence
Lave, Jean
Maccoby, Eleanor E(mmons)
Maehr, Martin L.
McKeachie, Wilbert J(ames)
Midgley, Carol
Ogbu, John U(zo)
Piaget, Jean
Pintrich, Paul Robert
Pressley, G. Michael
Rogoff, Barbara
Simon, Herbert (Alexander)
Skinner, B(urrhus) F(rederic)
Spearman, Charles Edward
Sternberg, Robert J(effrey)
Thorndike, E(dward) L(ee)
Vygotsky, Lev Semenovich
Weiner, Bernard

A

ABILITY GROUPING

Ability grouping is the practice of making student groupings based on ability and achievement in an attempt to provide instruction specifically relevant to each group's needs. Ability groups can differ in size and duration depending on the educational goals the groups are intended to meet. Groups can range from the small groups created for reading instruction in diverse elementary school classrooms to high school tracking methods that create just three broad ability groups within an entire high school population. Although ability grouping has become a standard educational practice in many schools, it continues to inspire heated debate and extensive research.

WITHIN-CLASS GROUPING

Within-class grouping is the practice of dividing a class of students with diverse abilities into groups based on ability and achievement level. This is commonly accomplished by assigning every member of the class to a particular group that they will be taught with during instruction in a particular subject. In some cases ability grouping is also accomplished by removing a few students from the class for the purpose of specialized instruction and allowing the rest of the class to be instructed together. This is sometimes done to provide specific instruction to a few students who are seen as very high achieving, and sometimes to provide more individualized assistance to students who are seen to be achieving significantly below their peers.

At the elementary school level, within-class grouping is a fairly established practice. A 2006 study by Chor-zempa and Graham found that 63% of primary grade teachers surveyed reported using ability groupings in reading instruction. In addition to reading instruction, mathematics instruction is also commonly taught in ability groups at the elementary school level. Ability grouping is less commonly used for other subjects such as science, social studies, and art.

Classrooms that practice within-class ability grouping for reading typically divide the children in the class into two or three reading groups. These groups are often assigned names, colors, or animals to differentiate them and to provide each group with a group identity. The way in which children are assigned to groups varies depending on the teacher making the assignments and any school or district-wide policies that provide grouping guidance. In many cases a variety of guidelines are in place with the classroom teachers having final authority for grouping decisions. Teachers may use testing, past performance, individualized evaluation of skills, or other factors to determine which reading group a child should be placed in. In most cases a combination of testing and observational methods may be used.

Ability-grouped reading instruction allows teachers to provide instruction that is attuned to the level of competency of the children in the group. For example, the lowest level reading group may benefit from extra work on sounding out words and using context clues to decipher meanings, whereas the most advanced group may be ready to tackle more complex sentences and concepts. Ability grouping also allows the teacher to focus on using instructional methods that are successful with different levels of learners. A lower-achieving reading group may benefit significantly from repetition, flash cards, and drills to help the students achieve basic mastery of recognizing phonemes. Repetition and drills may, however, frustrate a higher-achieving group of learners who are already able to read short sentences. Discussions of plot and character may motivate and engage the higher-level group, while it may frustrate another group of learners.

Ability groupings in math follow generally the same structure and purpose as ability groupings in reading. Because so many mathematical concepts build directly on previously learned material, it can be a frustrating and nonproductive experience for children who have not yet mastered one area to be rushed on to the next concept. Ability grouping in math allows children who have demonstrated mastery of a subject to move on, while allowing those who need more help or repetition the opportunity to achieve an understanding of the subject at their own pace.

Ability grouping in elementary education has many proponents who point to its success in providing more student-specific instruction in areas in which many students struggle. Opponents of ability grouping, while acknowledging that it does provide some small advantages over traditional whole-classroom education, argue that its potentially negative effects on students far outweigh any benefits derived from the student-specific curriculum.

Many of the arguments against ability grouping cite concern for the psychological and social well being of the children involved, especially children placed in the lower-achieving ability groups. Children become aware of differentiating characteristics very early on, and the emphasis placed on reading and math achievement by having some reading and math groups clearly labeled as the "slower" groups, while others are labeled as the "gifted" or "accelerated" groups, is not lost on children. This can lead to children being more aware of how other students perceive their achievement. One study found that students who were tracked in math had increased ego orientation, which led to students labeled high achieving being less willing to seek help, while not increasing the willingness of low achievers to seek help (Butler, 2008). Although teachers and other adults may try to treat all of the ability groups with equal respect, children show a very keen knowledge of their placement and the placement of others. This can lead to children placed in lower-ability groups to feel unsure of their educational potential, losing self-esteem, and developing low self-expectation.

It is not only the learners themselves that are affected by the assignment of children to ability-specific groups. Parents, and even teachers, have often demonstrated expectations of students that are ability-group specific. There is significant concern that low expectations can have negative results on academic achievement. Many educators and parents have also expressed concern about

designating children as remedial or advanced students at such an early age, fearing that such designations may continue with the children throughout their educational experience. Although many teachers and schools attempt to allow students to switch easily between ability groups if their achievement warrants it, such easy switching can be very difficult to implement. Additionally, if the lower-reading group spends a significant amount of time working on concepts the other groups have already mastered, it may be prohibitively difficult for a child to catch up without additional intervention.

Teaching time may also be negatively impacted by ability grouping. If teachers are focusing all their attention on the specific needs of one group of learners, the other learners will not be benefiting from the guided instruction of the teacher. This can often result in students participating in a large number of desk activities. Many classrooms utilize teacher aides, computer activities, learning groups, or even adult volunteers to help provide structured learning for students not currently engaged with the teacher. This however, may lead to a decreased quality of instruction during this time, and a loss of instruction time overall.

Although within-class grouping is an accepted practice in many elementary schools, it is not very common at the high school level. High schools rarely rely on students remaining in a single class throughout the day, with ability groups being formed for a few specific subjects. Instead, high schools are much more likely to rely on between-class grouping to provide ability-specific instruction.

BETWEEN-CLASS GROUPING

Between-class grouping is the system in which students are separated into different classes based on ability levels. It can also refer to the system in which students are placed into broad groups that all have the same classes, although not necessarily in a single classroom. This is often referred to as *tracking*. Tracking was once primarily used to refer to systems in which students destined for a specific educational outcome were grouped together and given classes specific to the perceived abilities of that group. In this way, many schools came to have a vocational track, a college prep track, and many other tracks. Over time the term *tracked* has come to refer generally to any system in which students are placed into groupings based on ability.

Forming whole classes of students based on ability is much more common in high school and junior high school than in elementary school. It has become the standard for many high schools, which often have Advanced Placement classes, college prep classes, remedial classes, and others designed to provide groups of students with instruction specific to their needs.

Between-class ability grouping was once more common, and more rigid, than it generally is in high schools in the early 21st century. In American high schools before the 1850s students were generally promoted each year based on ability and comprehension of the relevant material rather than age. In this way each grade of students was more a collection of individuals who had achieved a mastery of common material than it was a group of same-aged individuals. Although, strictly speaking, this was not between-class grouping it paved the way for between-class grouping. After the 1850s, age became a more relevant factor in promotion and determination of which grade a student was placed in. In the early 1900s, when more and more students stayed in school through high school, various educational tracks with specific emphases were proposed and adopted. Although many supporters of tracked education in its early days had noble ideals, tracking often served as a tool of discrimination against children who were economically disadvantaged or members of minority groups. Such children were often put into tracks in which vocational training was the main purpose, shutting them off from the opportunity for a more academically based education.

Although the specific emphasis of education changed over the years, many high schools still practiced a variety of tracking programs into the 1960s. Although many of these later programs were theoretically aimed at helping certain groups of students make progress by teaching to their specific needs, such as gifted students, remedial students, or students who needed English as a second language instruction, they still served to funnel students onto paths from which it was frequently very hard to deviate.

In the 1970s and 1980s a broad movement began against the use of tracking as a method for helping students achieve their educational goals. A number of studies and reports came out showing some of the dangers of rigid tracking systems and highlighting the children who were ill served by such systems. Many schools moved away from specifically tracked systems, eliminating the idea of labeling children as they entered the school.

Most high schools in the United States retain at least some form of between-class grouping for some or all classes. Schools with low levels of poverty, high numbers of students, racial diversity, and diverse student achievement levels are more likely to practice ability grouping (VanderHart, 2006). Math classes are especially likely to be grouped by ability. Classes are often designated as honors classes, and students of high achievement are grouped together to receive instruction that takes advantage of their strengths. These classes therefore cover more complex topics and include more in-depth discussions. Although some or all classes in a high school may be grouped, students themselves often do not receive special

designations. In this way students who excel at English may be in the honors English class, while also being in a remedial math class because that is a subject in which they experience difficulties. In this way students can receive instruction tailored to their ability in each subject and avoid many of the pitfalls of a whole-child designation.

Proponents of the between-classes grouping system cite its ability to provide targeted instruction. They also frequently suggest that lower-achieving students can ask questions in class without the risk of embarrassment in front of their higher-achieving peers. Higher achievers can benefit from more in-depth instruction that can focus on larger concepts and broader issues, whereas lower achievers can benefit from more extensive coverage of the core topics.

Although many people, especially parents, tend to be in favor of high schools structured along between-class grouping lines, many individuals believe that it can do significant harm, especially to the students placed into the lower-achieving classes. Several prominent groups, including the American Civil Liberties Union, the National Governors Association, the National Education Association, and the College Board, have all voiced their opposition to ability grouping. Many of the arguments against between-class ability grouping are similar to those against within-class ability grouping. Students who are grouped into one of the lower-achieving groups are at risk for lowered self-esteem and lowered self-expectations. They are also at risk for parents and teachers having low expectations of them, a circumstance which studies have shown can often be a self-fulfilling prophecy (Benner, 2007).

Another common concern with between-class ability grouping is that the lower-achieving groups may receive a lower quality of education overall than their higher-achieving peers. Lower-achieving classes tend to spend more classroom time on discipline than higher-achieving classes, with proportionately less time spent on subject matter instruction. Teachers of lower ability group classes are frequently found to be less qualified and less experienced than their peers who provide instruction to the highest achieving groups. This may be for a number of reasons, including the fact that teaching lower-achieving groups may be seen as less desirable, so such positions are assigned to less experienced educators. Additionally, teaching higher-level classes such as Calculus or Advanced Placement English often requires additional training or certification, resulting in teachers who have been more extensively trained.

Although thousands of studies have been conducted on ability grouping since the 1950s, the results are far from clear. Studies are often contradictory, and although one benefit may be shown repeatedly it still leaves room for spirited debate about whether the benefits are outweighed by possible side effects, and whose interests should take precedence in an educational setting that needs to serve everyone.

SEE ALSO *Bilingual Education; Gender Bias in Teaching; Special Education.*

BIBLIOGRAPHY

Benner, A.D., & Mistry, R.S. (2007). Congruence of mother and teacher educational expectations and low-income youth's academic competence. *Journal of Educational Psychology, 99*(1), 140–153.

Butler, R. (2008). Ego-involving and frame of reference effects of tracking on elementary school students' motivational orientations and help seeking in math class. *Social Psychology of Education, 11*(1), 5–34.

Chorzempa, B. F., & Graham, S. (2006). Primary-grade teachers' use of within-class ability grouping in reading. *Journal of Educational Psychology, 98*(3), 529–542.

Rees, D. I., Brewer, D. J., & Argys, L. M. (1997). *Ability grouping and student achievement in English, history, and science.* Denver, CO: Center for Research of Economic and Social Policy, University of Colorado.

Roberts, J. L., & Inman, T. F. (2007). *Strategies for differentiating instruction: Best practices for the classroom.* Waco, TX: Prufrock Press.

Tach, L. M., & Farkas, G. (2006). Learning-related behaviors, cognitive skills, and ability grouping when schooling begins. *Social Science Research, 35*(4), 1048–1080.

VanderHart, P. G. (2006). Why do some schools group by ability? Some evidence from the NAEP. *American Journal of Economics and Sociology, 65*(2), 435–463.

Helen Davidson

ABUSE AND NEGLECT

Although teachers' essential concern is with children's success in the school environment, it is clear that individual performance levels are affected by a host of factors outside of the classroom. Just as the home and neighborhood environments of children can enrich their school experiences, negative environments can have a detrimental impact on both students' academic performance and their classroom behavior. One of the most potentially damaging of these environmental factors is child maltreatment.

THE SCOPE OF CHILD ABUSE AND NEGLECT

Definitions of child maltreatment vary across states and jurisdictions, as well as across research studies. However, according to the 2003 Keeping Children and Families Safe Act, federal law defines child abuse and neglect as follows:

Any recent act or failure to act on the part of a parent or caretaker which results in death, serious physical or emotional harm, sexual abuse, or exploitation; or

An act or failure to act which presents an imminent risk of serious harm.

While child maltreatment may take many forms (e.g., sibling abuse, medical neglect, educational neglect), it is typically categorized into four domains: physical abuse, sexual abuse, psychological or emotional abuse, and neglect.

According to a compilation of reports from child protective services agencies across the United States, during the federal fiscal year 2005, approximately 3.3 million reports of suspected maltreatment, involving 6 million children, were received (U.S. Department of Health & Human Services, 2007). Of the 62.1% of reported cases screened for investigation, 28.5% included at least one child who was determined to be a victim of maltreatment. Overall, an estimated 899,000 children were substantiated as victims of abuse and/or neglect. In comparison, a 2005 national survey of children and caregivers reported that 14% of children were victims of child maltreatment (Finkelhor, Ormrod, Turner, & Hamby, 2005). Consistent with federal reports, the vast majority of children were identified as victims of neglect (60%), followed by physical abuse (18%), sexual abuse (10%), and emotional abuse (10%); although not reflected in this classification system, many children are victims of multiple forms of maltreatment (e.g., Sedlack & Broadhurst, 1996). Notably, more than half of children substantiated as victims of maltreatment by child protective service agencies were over the age of 7, that is, school-aged.

THE EFFECTS OF CHILD MALTREATMENT ON SCHOOL PERFORMANCE

Experiencing abuse and/or neglect may impact children's school performance in multiple ways, including lower grades, increased absences, increased disciplinary problems, and higher rates of school dropout (Putnam, 2006; Hurt, Malmud, Brodsky, & Giannetta, 2001). According to the National Clinical Evaluation Study, over 50% of abused children experienced some type of difficulty in school, including poor attendance and disciplinary problems; approximately 30% had some type of cognitive or language impairment; more than 22% showed evidence of a learning disorder; and approximately 25% required some type of special education services (Caldwell, 1992). At the extreme end of the continuum, severe physical injury—and head trauma in particular—may produce organic conditions that negatively impact learning,

---

Signs of child maltreatment for educators

Physical abuse:

Unexplained bruises, cuts, welts, bite marks, burns, or fractures
An explanation from the child that is inconsistent with the nature of the injury
A child's reporting an injury inflicted by his or her caretaker
A child's appearing extremely fearful or startling easily

Sexual abuse:

An abrupt change in behavior
Seductive behavior with other children and/or adults
Extreme behavior in regard to touching (e.g., inappropriate sexual touching, reluctance to be touched by an adult)
Age-inappropriate knowledge of sex
Consistent appearance of isolation, depression, or anger
Child complaints of itching, bleeding, or bruising in the genital area

Emotional abuse:

Impaired sense of self-worth
Failure to thrive
Intense fear, anger, and/or depression
Delayed physical, emotional, or intellectual development
Extreme behaviors (e.g., extreme compliance, passivity, or aggression)

Neglect:

Lack of supervision
Unaddressed medical problems
Evidence of caretaker drug or alcohol abuse
Inappropriate dress or hygiene
Hunger or fatigue

SOURCE: Lowenthal, 1996

Table 1 ILLUSTRATION BY GGS INFORMATION SERVICES. CENGAGE LEARNING, GALE.

---

motivation, and school performance. In addition, neuro-development can be impaired either by a lack of sensory experience (e.g., neglect) or through abnormally active neurons caused by traumatic experiences (e.g., abuse) (Lowenthal, 1999). In fact, there are data to suggest that maltreatment can lower children's IQs (Putnam, 2006). However, negative outcomes are not limited to the most extreme cases of child maltreatment.

In the past 10 to 15 years, improved methodologies (e.g., representative samples, increased sample size, use of adequate comparison groups, examinations of children's school performance longitudinally) have led to a growing consensus that maltreatment is significantly associated with deficits in school performance. Utilizing a community sample of 420 maltreated children in grades kindergarten through 12, matched with 420 nonmaltreated controls (on gender, school, grade level, residential neighborhood, and, when possible, classroom), Eckenrode, Laird, and Doris (1993) found that maltreated children performed at significantly lower levels on standardized tests and school grades. More specifically, among students in grades 2 through 8, maltreated children scored significantly below the comparison group in both reading and math. These negative effects exceeded those associated with living in poverty (i.e., having received public assistance). Further analysis revealed an interaction between maltreatment and grade level; reading deficiencies were more pronounced among maltreated children in the lower grades. Results also demonstrated that maltreated children were more likely to repeat a grade and had significantly more discipline referrals and suspensions than comparison students. However, there were few differences between groups of older students (grades 9 through 12) in grades and grade repetition, suggesting that there may be a selective process of dropping out of school among maltreated children.

Leiter and Johnsen (1994) identified school outcomes in three domains: cognitive learning, participation, and integration (i.e., socialization). Comparing these outcomes between a sample of maltreated children drawn from the North Carolina Central Registry of Child Abuse and Neglect and a general school sample, the researchers found that abused children performed significantly worse on all school measures, including grades, standardized test scores, grade retention, and absences. Moreover, the dropout rate for abused children was more than three times higher than that of their nonabused counterparts. These deficits appeared to exceed those of children suffering other forms of social disadvantage.

In a comparison of abused, neglected, and nonmaltreated children's school performance, socioemotional development, and adaptive behavior, Wodarski, Kurtz, Gaudin, and Howing (1990) found that, controlling for socioeconomic status (SES), both abused and neglected children scored lower on a composite index of overall school performance. In regard to behavior, teachers rated both abused and neglected children more negatively on the Child Behavior Checklist—Teacher form. Overall, children who had experienced physical abuse were viewed as more problematic in school, "displaying academic deficits, problem behaviors, lowered self-esteem, delinquency, and elevated feeling of aggression, and pervasive adjustment difficulties in a variety of contexts" (p. 510). On a more hopeful note, older children in both maltreatment groups demonstrated areas of strength in adaptive behaviors.

DIFFERENT IMPACTS OF VARIOUS MALTREATMENT TYPES

As data have accumulated to evidence the detrimental effects of maltreatment on school performance, researchers have begun to explore the differential impact of specific types of maltreatment, as well as the processes through which maltreatment influences academic achievement (Leiter, 2007). For example, in their 1993 study, Eckenrode and colleagues found that for both grades and test scores, children who had experienced neglect, either alone or in combination with abuse, performed most poorly, while children who had experienced physical abuse had the most discipline problems. In a secondary analysis of the Eckenrode et al. (1993) data, Kendall-Tackett and Eckenrode (1996) examined the developmental course of children who had experienced neglect alone or in combination with other abuse. When effects for gender and SES were controlled, results showed that neglected children performed more poorly than their peers, with a marked drop during the transition from elementary to junior high school. Neglect alone had a negative impact on grades and number of suspensions regardless of whether it occurred alone or in combination with physical or sexual abuse. However, the combination of abuse and neglect had a particularly strong negative effect on number of disciplinary referrals and grade repetitions. In contrast to the growing body of evidence that particularly severe deficits may follow from neglect, the results of studies investigating the impact of sexual abuse on academic development have been mixed (Trickett & McBride-Chang, 1995).

Child maltreatment may further impair children's school performance when combined with other challenges. For example, Kerr, Black, and Krishnakumar (2000) found that children with both failure-to-thrive and maltreatment demonstrated more behavior problems and worse cognitive performance and school functioning than did those with only one of these risk factors. Because of its association with poor school performance, poverty has been a subject of particular interest to researchers examining the academic effects of child maltreatment. Using the Hahnemann Elementary School Behavior Rating Scale, Reyome (1994) compared teachers' ratings of achievement-related classroom behaviors for (1) a group of sexually abused or neglected children in grades K to 6, (2) nonmaltreated children receiving public assistance, and (3) nonmaltreated lower middle class children. For 13 of the 14 factors measured, there was a statistically significant difference between the three groups. Compared to nonmaltreated lower middle class children, the abused or neglected students exhibited fewer classroom behaviors positively associated with academic achievement (for example, originality, classroom involvement) and more classroom behaviors negatively associated with

academic achievement (e.g., disruptive social involvement). However, when compared to students from similarly disadvantaged socioeconomic backgrounds, the maltreated students showed few differences in negative classroom behaviors (with the exception of withdrawn behavior). Maltreated children were nonetheless less original, independent, and involved in classroom work than were the comparison children.

In an effort to develop better responses to maltreated children in the schools, researchers have sought to elucidate the processes through which abuse and neglect affect academic performance. Some of the first longitudinal studies of the development of maltreated children, which focused on infants and preschool children, indicated that at these early ages, children display more insecure attachments; lower intelligence scores; impaired cognitive development, including language; lower levels of effectance motivation; more negative and less positive affect; and fewer prosocial behaviors, along with more aggressive and noncompliant behavior. As noted by Eckenrode et al. (1993), taken together, these findings suggest "a continuity of disadvantage for maltreated children with regard to the negotiation of age-appropriate developmental tasks" (p. 59).

Subsequent studies suggest that this pattern of compounding deficits continues through the school years. For example, Rowe and Eckenrode (1999) demonstrated that there was a time element associated with risk; abused children were at substantially higher risk of repeating kindergarten and first grade than were their nonabused counterparts. This differential was not detected in grades 2 through 6, suggesting that academic difficulties appear early in a child's school career. Such early academic difficulties have been associated with increased risk of school drop out.

Leiter (2007) examined the temporal pattern of declines in school performance, exploring the trajectory of school performance after an initial report of maltreatment. An analysis of data from a large urban school district and state child protective service records for 715 children demonstrated that for study outcomes, absenteeism, and grades, adverse influences accumulated with time; however, the rate at which these adverse influences accumulated was more rapid for older maltreated children. Maltreatment beginning early in a child's life impacted absenteeism more negatively than did maltreatment with a later onset. The negative impact of maltreatment on attendance was almost immediate—and exceeded the impact on grades, especially immediately after an initial report. The negative effects on grades appeared over longer periods of time. In addition, maltreatment heightened the negative impact of aging on school performance. Letier noted that as children age, school grades may decline for reasons unassociated with learning ability (e.g., higher standard imposed by high school teachers); however, increased absenteeism may, in fact, reflect an increased level of disengagement from school that proves equally detrimental to academic achievement. Intervention by child protective services did evidence some ability to offset the impact of maltreatment—more for grade point average (e.g., school performance) than for absenteeism (e.g., school participation).

In one study designed to explore the motivational patterns of maltreated children, younger (6- and 7-year-old) children tended to present themselves in a positive manner that was inconsistent with their descriptions by teachers and nonabused peers (Barnett, Vondra, & Shonk, 1996). Although their perceptions of peer acceptance dropped, older (8- to 11-year-old) maltreated children, like their younger counterparts, held views of their competence and acceptance that were inconsistent with those of their teachers. While there were few differences in regard to scholastic functioning and motivational orientations, existing differences did favor nonmaltreated children. Abused children tended to score lower on verbal intelligence and higher for special education status than did their nonabused peers. As noted by the researchers, these findings suggest that negative views about oneself may actually predict working harder and engaging more with schoolwork among maltreated children, a pattern of motivational orientation that is virtually the opposite of the pattern observed among nonabused children.

SUGGESTIONS FOR EDUCATORS

As of 2007, there are laws in all 50 states that require reporting of suspected cases of child maltreatment. While these laws vary in the scope of professionals and other adults included as mandatory reporters, teachers and other school personnel are clearly bound by these requirements; in fact, teachers may be personally liable for reporting abuse (Lowenthal, 1996). Although data suggest that teachers are generally reluctant to report (Tite, 1993), in order to satisfy their legal obligations, educators should make a report of any suspected abuse or neglect within 24 hours and place a detailed record of the observed indicators of abuse in the student's file.

Summarizing previous work, Lowenthal (1996) identified the potential signs of child maltreatment for educators. The specific indicators for physical abuse, sexual abuse, emotional abuse, and neglect are listed in Table 1.

Although frequently concerned that they have received limited to no training on how to identify child abuse, teachers do appear to have accurate perceptions of the effects of maltreatment on classroom behavior, indicating that they should have confidence in their ability to serve effectively as reporters (Yanowitz, Monte, & Tribble, 2003).

Ultimately, the decision of whether maltreatment is substantiated lies with children's protective services; however, teachers can employ various strategies to assist possible victims, including adopting an accepting, caring attitude; honoring confidentiality in the case of disclosure (excluding the legal duty to report); being sensitive to students' cues; developing active listening skills; setting reasonable goals to enhance students' confidence and success; establishing a structured classroom environment; engaging the student in class activities; emphasizing the student's strengths and abilities; and working with other professionals to identify and to implement appropriate interventions (Lowenthal, 1996).

SEE ALSO *At-risk Students; Emotional Development.*

BIBLIOGRAPHY

Barnett, D., Vondra, J.I., & Shonk, S.M. (1996). Self-perceptions, motivation, and school functioning of low-income maltreated and comparison children. *Child Abuse & Neglect, 20,* 397–410.

Belsky, J. (1993). Etiology of child maltreatment: A developmental-ecological analysis. *Psychological Bulletin, 114,* 413–434.

Caldwell, R. (1992). *The costs of child abuse vs. child abuse prevention: Michigan's experience.* Lansing: Michigan's Children's Trust Fund.

Eckenrode, J., Laird, M., & Doris, J. (1993). School performance and disciplinary problems among abused and neglected children. *Developmental Psychology, 29,* 53–62.

Finkelhor, D., Ormrod, H., Turner, H., & Hamby, S. (2005). The Victimization of children and youth: A comprehensive national survey, *Child Maltreatment, 10,* 5–25.

Hurt, H., Malmud, E., Brodsky, N.L., & Giannetta, J. (2001). Exposure to violence: Psychological and academic correlates in child witnesses. *Archives of Pediatrics and Adolescent Medicine, 155,* 1351–1356.

Kendall-Tackett, K.A., & Eckenrode, J. (1996). The effects of neglect on academic achievement and disciplinary problems: A developmental perspective. *Child Abuse & Neglect, 20,* 161–169.

Kerr, M. A., Black, M. M., & Krishnakumar, A. (2000). Failure-to-thrive, maltreatment and the behavior and development of 6-year-old children from low-income, urban families: A cumulative risk model. *Child Abuse & Neglect, 24,* 587–598.

Leiter, J. (2007). School performance trajectories after the advent of reported maltreatment. *Children & Youth Services Review, 29,* 363–382.

Leiter, J., & Johnsen, M.C. (1994). Child maltreatment and school performance. *American Journal of Education, 102,* 154–189.

Lowenthal, B. (1996). Educational implications of child abuse. *Intervention in School & Clinic, 32,* 21–26.

Lowenthal, B. (1999). Effects of maltreatment and ways to promote children's resiliency. *Childhood Education,* Summer 1999, 204–209.

Putnam, F. W. (2006). The impact of trauma on child development. *Juvenile and Family Court Journal, 57,* 1–11.

Reyone, N.D. (1994). Teacher ratings of the achievement-related classroom behaviors of maltreated and non-maltreated children. *Psychology of the Schools, 31,* 253–260.

Rowe, E., & Eckenrode, J. (1999). The timing of academic difficulties among maltreated and nonmaltreated children. *Child Abuse & Neglect, 8,* 813–832.

Sedlack, A., & Broadhurst, D. (1996). Executive summary of the third national incidence study of child abuse and neglect (NIS–3). National Clearinghouse on Child Abuse and Neglect Information. Washington, DC: U.S. Department of Health and Human Services. U.S.

Tite, R. (1993). How teachers define and respond to child abuse: The distinction between theoretical and reportable cases. *Child Abuse & Neglect, 17,* 591–603.

Trickett, P. K., & McBride-Chang, C. (1995). The developmental impact of different forms of child abuse and neglect. *Developmental Review, 15,* 311–337.

U.S. Department of Health & Human Services, Administration on Children, Youth and Families (2007). Child maltreatment 2005. Washington, DC: U.S. Government Printing Office.

Wodarski, J.S., Kurtz, P.D., Gaudin, J.M., & Howing, Ph.T. (1990). Maltreatment and the school-age child: Major academic, socioemotional, and adaptive outcomes. *Social Work, 35,* 506-513.

Yanowitz, K.L., Monte, E., & Tribble, J.R. (2003). Teachers' beliefs about the effects of child abuse. *Child Abuse & Neglect, 27,* 483-488.

Sharon G. Portwood

ACADEMIC PRESS

Educational demands are sometimes characterized as academic press. With increased calls for teachers to make classrooms demanding, researchers and practitioners need clarification on how academic press is defined and measured and how press relates to educationally relevant outcomes.

ACADEMIC PRESS DEFINED

Human behavior has been conceptualized in terms of both personal needs and environmental press. Henry A. Murray labeled demands from the environment that prompt behavior as *press* and urged psychologists to develop models of behavior that include both personal needs and demands from the environment. Such a press can be characterized from an individual's perception of demand or from an objective view of environmental demands. Moreover, press does not operate independent of its context but acts within a "patterned meaningful whole" (Murray, 1938, p. 40) in the total environment. An academic press, therefore, describes the pattern of demands for engagement with academic work placed on a learner within the classroom and school environment.

TYPES OF PRESS

Three broad categories of academic press emerge from the research literature—press for completion, for performance, and for understanding.

Press for completion. The demand to achieve a list of objectives or meet academic standards within a set period of time can be called a press for completion or coverage of material and is often independent of the quality of the work being completed. This press has been described as the number of students who complete certain courses or grade levels, such as the percentage of students completing high school or taking algebra in the eighth grade, and number of semesters of a particular subject area completed. Press for completion in classrooms is reflected in an emphasis on completing a curriculum and assignments, on the number of hours of homework, or on doing work exactly as students are directed rather than having them think about the task at hand.

Press for performance. A press for performance emphasizes a demand for a level of achievement such as a specific passing grade or test scores or scoring better in comparison to others. Academic press may be thought of as "the degree of normative emphasis placed on academic excellence by members of the organization" (Shouse, 1996, p. 175). Such a press may encompass a variety of school policies meant to improve the "academic climate" or emphasis on academic success, such as the degree to which a school honors student achievement, whether competition for grades is encouraged, and the use of *absolute achievement* grading practices.

Press for understanding. Finally, academic press can be thought of as a press for understanding or the degree to which students are required to engage in higher-order thinking skills, such as linking understanding to previous knowledge, checking answers against what they already know, and demonstrating conceptual understanding. Press for understanding has been described by instructional practices, such as attention on the main point, checking for understanding, asking high level questions, demanding justification or clarification, encouraging connection making, and sustaining an expectation for explanation.

LEVEL OF PRESS

The environmental level at which press operates adds another dimension to understanding academic press.

School Level. In an attempt to create better schools and improve student achievement, several studies have examined the influence of academic press at the school level as it contributes to school climate. Schools that implement certain policies to emphasize academic excellence are considered to have a stronger climate of academic press than those that implemented fewer of the policies.

Classroom Level. Academic press may have greater impact on student outcomes in the immediate environment of the classroom rather than at the more distant school level. Studies of classroom academic press often emphasize instructional practices. Press for understanding is typically demonstrated by teachers pressing students to explain, justify, and relate ideas as opposed to relying on students' perceptions of the school as affecting what they might do in the classroom.

COMMON WAYS TO MEASURE ACADEMIC PRESS

Early research on press differentiated forms of press. The lack as of 2008 of conceptual consistency regarding types and levels of academic press has led to the development of several divergent measures. One approach has been to form a comprehensive index that includes several types of press; however, this approach does not provide an understanding of the relative importance of different forms of press or their relation to outcomes. Academic press has also been measured by the presence or absence of school policies such as ability grouping, incrementally based grading, remediation, promotion based on mastery, or discipline codes. Student self-report measures are also a common way to measure perceptions of academic press. These measures report student perceptions formed over an extended period of time and are closely linked to reported educational beliefs and behaviors. One advantage of this method is that aggregate perceptions of all students in the class can provide a classroom measure of academic press. Observation measures of academic press have focuses on instructional practices and teacher-student discourse. This approach to measurement, which provides rich classroom description of related classroom features, however, may introduce observer bias and contradicts the assertion that perceptions of press are most closely linked to an individual's behavior.

EDUCATIONAL OUTCOMES ASSOCIATED WITH PRESS

Most descriptions of academic press start with the premise that the teacher is central in creating classroom demands. As Meece (1991) states, "We assumed that teachers who frequently probed students' levels of understanding and asked for explanations, rather than simply affirming or negating answers, create a 'press' for mastery in their classroom" (p. 271). However classroom character is not determined by one factor, such as the teacher, but is related to a constellation of characteristics. The learner experiences many elements of the classroom that can serve as agents of academic press, such as the teacher, the task, and peers; similarly, the learner may experience external sources such as parents.

Outcomes. Academic press has been related to short-term achievement outcomes such as grades even for low achieving students when accompanied by increased effort. Press also may moderate the relationship between other aspects of the environment, such as social support, and learning. Moreover, academic press works in combination with instructional pacing, support, and scaffolding to support learning. Academic press also has been associated positively with self-efficacy, self-regulation, and school belongingness and negatively with avoiding help-seeking and bullying.

Group Differences. Variation in student experience of press may be a result of different treatment or different perceptions. Press has been found to have different effects on different groups such as diminishing the avoidance of help-seeking in girls in math classrooms or enhancing academic interest in African-American middle school students. Even in the same classrooms lower achieving students have reported experiencing lower press than high achieving students. Gender, race, and prior achievement may play a key role in the how press operates in classrooms.

Academic press has been used to describe the emphasis, value, and opportunity for learning presented by the environment. However, the theoretical conception and empirical measurement of academic press varies in educational research by type of press, source of press, and reported outcomes. Research on the processes by which press serves to enhance learning or achievement and how it interacts with other features of the learning environment would enhance understanding of this factor in education.

SEE ALSO *Achievement Motivation.*

BIBLIOGRAPHY

Ames, C. (1992). Classrooms: Goals, structures, and student motivation. *Journal of Educational Psychology, 84,* 261–271.

Blumenfeld, P. C. (1992). The task and the teacher: Enhancing student thoughtfulness in science. In J. Brophy (Ed.), *Advances in Research in Teaching:* Volume 3 (pp. 81–114). JAI Press.

Doyle, W. (1983). Academic work. *Review of Educational Research, 53,* 159–199.

Epstein, J. L. (1989). Family structures and student motivation: A developmental perspective. In C. Ames & R. Ames (Eds.), *Research on motivation in education,* Vol. 3 (pp. 259–295). New York: Academic Press.

Henningsen, M., & Stein, M. K. (1997). Mathematical tasks and student cognition: Classroom-based factors that support and inhibit high-level mathematical thinking and reasoning. *Journal for Research in Mathematics Education, 28,* 524–549.

Hoy, W. K., Sweetland, S. R., & Smith, P. A. (2002). Toward and organizational model of achievement in high schools: The significance of collective efficacy. *Educational Administration Quarterly, 38,* 77–93.

Kempler, T.M. (2007). Optimizing students' motivation in inquiry-based learning environments: The role of instructional practices. *Dissertation Abstracts International Section A: Humanities and Social Science.*

Lee, V. E., & Smith, J. B. (1999). Social support and achievement for young adolescents in Chicago: The role of school academic press. *American Educational Research Journal, 36,* 907–945.

Ma, X. (2002). Bullying in middle school: Individual and school characteristics of victims and offenders. *School Effectiveness and School Improvement, 13,* 63–89.

Ma, X. (2003). Sense of belonging to school: Can schools make a difference? *Journal of Educational Research, 96,* 340–349.

Marshall, H. H., & Weinstein, R. S. (1984). Classroom factors affecting students' self-evaluations: An interactional model. *Review of Educational Research, 54,* 301–325.

Meece, J. L. (1991). The classroom context and students' motivational goals. In P. Pintrich & M. L. Maehr (Eds.), *Advances in motivation and achievement:* Vol. 7. *Goals and self-regulatory processes.* Greenwich, CT: JAI Press.

Middleton, M. J. (2004). Motivating through challenging: promoting a positive press for learning. In P. R. Pintrich & M. L. Maehr (Eds.), *Advances in Motivation and Achievement,* Vol. 13. Greenwich, CT: JAI Press.

Middleton, M. J., & Midgley, C. (2002). Beyond motivation: Middle school students' perceptions of press for understanding in math. *Contemporary Educational Psychology, 27,* 373–391.

Murphy, J. F., Weil, M., Hallinger, P., & Mitman, A. (1984). Academic press: Translating high expectations into school policies and classroom practices. *Educational Leadership, 40,* 22–26.

Murray, H. A. (1938). *Explorations in personality.* New York: Oxford University Press.

Pace, C. R., & Stern, G. C. (1958). An approach to the measurement of psychological characteristics of college environments. *Journal of Educational Psychology, 49,* 269–274.

Phillips, M. (1997). What makes schools effective? A comparison of the relationships of communitarian climate and academic climate to mathematics achievement and attendance during middle school. *American Educational Research Journal, 34,* 633–662.

Roderick, M., & Engel, M. (2001). The grasshopper and the ant: Motivational responses of low-achieving students to high-stakes testing. *Educational Evaluation and Policy Analysis, 23,* 197–227.

Shouse, R. C. (1996). Academic press and sense of community: Conflict and congruence in American high schools. *Research in Sociology of Education and Socialization, 11,* 173–202.

Stevenson, J. (1998). Performance of the cognitive holding power questionnaire in schools. *Learning and Instruction, 8,* 393–410.

Stone, S. I., Engel, M., Nagaoka, J., & Roderick, M. (2005). Getting it the second time around: Student classroom experience in Chicago's Summer Bridge program. *Teachers College Record, 107,* 935–957.

Walker, W. J., & Richman, J. (1984). Dimensions of classroom environmental press. *Psychological Reports, 55,* 555–562.

Michael Middleton

ACCOUNTABILITY

Accountability permeates education in the United States. It focuses on both the processes and products of education. Responsibility is assigned to individuals or groups, including educational leaders, administrators, teachers, other school staff, and students themselves. Measures are used to determine whether the process or products meet the desired goals, and criteria are set for whether the targets are met. The consequences attached to the accountability systems may be simply labels assigned to the individual or group to which responsibility has been assigned, or they can involve withdrawal of funding or removal of the individual or group from continuing in the same role.

DEFINITION

Accountability is the assignment of responsibility for conducting activities in a certain way or producing specific results. A primary motivation for increased accountability is to improve the system or aspects of it. To have a workable accountability system, there must be a desired goal (e.g., compliance with legal requirements, improved performance), ways to measure progress toward the goal (e.g., indicators of meeting legal requirements; indicators of performance), criteria for determining when the measures show that the goal has or has not been met, and consequences for meeting or not meeting the goal. Each of these aspects of an accountability system can vary in a number of ways.

EDUCATIONAL ACCOUNTABILITY

Educational accountability targets either the processes or results of education. A desired goal is identified (e.g., compliance with the legal mandates of providing special education, highly qualified teachers, improved student performance), and measures are identified for determining whether the goal is met (e.g., a checklist of indicators that the legal mandates have been met, a target of 90% correct for teachers taking a test of current knowledge and skills, a target of 60% of students performing at grade level by the end of each school year). Criteria for determining whether the goal has been met can involve specific determinations of ways that the goal may and may not be met (e.g., deciding how many indicators in the checklist must be marked to be considered meeting the legal mandates, determining the specific content that does or does not count for specific types of teachers, determining how to calculate the percentage of students performing at a proficient level, and how to define grade-level performance).

Accountability occurs in many ways in educational systems. One type of educational accountability system is that in which the school is held responsible for the performance of its students. Another type of educational accountability is a system in which teachers or administrators are individually held responsible for the performance of their students. Accountability systems in which schools or individual school personnel are held responsible for aspects of the educational process are most often used as ways to adjust the processes of education. Whether the school or individual teachers or administrators are held responsible, the educational accountability approach is termed *system accountability*.

Educational accountability may also hold individuals responsible for their own performance. For example, students may be held responsible for their performance in school (such as through promotion tests or graduation exams). Teachers may be held responsible for their performance on content and pedagogy through entry examinations or periodic tests of knowledge and skills.

System Accountability. Educational accountability in which the system is held responsible for the results of its students gained popularity in the early 1990s. Although some school districts and some states had their own accountability systems, the first use of this type of accountability across the United States was the 1994 reauthorization of the Elementary and Secondary Education Act (ESEA) known as Improving America's Schools. Accountability consequences were increased significantly in the 2001 reauthorization of Elementary and Secondary Education Act known as the No Child Left Behind Act (NCLB). NCLB required that schools, local education agencies, and states be held accountable for the performance of all students in the public education system.

The accountability system focused on school responsibility for student achievement, as in No Child Left Behind, demonstrates the components of educational accountability systems. The desired goal is improved student achievement. It is measured in terms of increases in the reading and math performance of groups of students. Measurement occurs through the administration of state assessments of reading and mathematics (such as compliance with legal requirements, improved performance), and ways to measure progress toward the goal (such as indicators of meeting legal requirements; indicators of performance). The criteria for determining when the measures show that the goal has or has not been met are defined in terms of benchmarks toward an ultimate target for performance,

with specific rules for how the performance is aggregated and counted. The consequences for not meeting the goal include requiring schools that do not meet benchmarks to offer students the opportunity to attend a school that did meet benchmarks, requiring schools that did not meet benchmarks to provide additional educational services to students, and eventually closing schools that do not meet benchmarks for a certain number of years in a row.

Accountability for the process of education is a common form of educational accountability. Schools are required to meet accreditation criteria. Special education programs must demonstrate that they have provided services and maintained Individualized Education Programs (IEPs) in a manner consistent with the law. The desired goal of educational accountability focused on process is to improve the process that is targeted. Special education IEPs are an example of a process targeted for accountability. Meeting the process requirements means demonstrating compliance with a number of requirements in the law and in regulations for IEPs. Measurement occurs through the completion of a checklist, for example, that identifies the requirements (such as providing notice within a certain period of time, having specific signatures on the IEP document, and so on). The criteria for determining when the measures show that the goal has or has not been met are defined in terms of numbers of elements that must be checked. The consequences for not meeting the goal generally include a letter identifying the problems in the process. In some cases, repeated failure to meet the criteria results in penalties, such as reduction of funding, to the educational system.

Individual Accountability. Student accountability implemented via promotion or exit exams is a common type of individual accountability in schools. Students are required to pass a test to demonstrate that they are ready to move either from one grade to the next (promotion) or leave the educational system with a credential certifying successful completion (exit). The tests that are administered to students generally cover those topics that the school system or its public have deemed important for individual students to demonstrate at a certain point in time. The criteria for determining when the measures show that the goal has been met (for instance, that the student is ready to move from one grade to the next) are defined in terms of passing scores on the test. In some cases alternative criteria are available to certain students who either are not able to pass the tests or who need to demonstrate that they have met criteria through other means.

Individual accountability for the adults in the education system include such variations as teachers being held responsible for passing tests to obtain or keep jobs, or principals and educators receiving salary bonuses on the basis of student achievement. This type of accountability includes the same components as other educational accountability systems, with goals, measures, and other criteria for determining when the goal has been met, and rewards and sanctions for meeting or not meeting the criteria.

ACCOUNTABILITY MEASURES

The most common forms of educational accountability use measures such as checklists of the process or assessments of student performance. The content of measures of educational accountability for process typically focus on resources (such as number of teachers or teacher-student ratio) or elements of a process (such as the elements of an Individualized Education Program). The content of measures of student performance focus on various student outcomes (such as what students should know and do at various grade levels, or percentage of students graduating with a standard diploma). States have defined content standards that identify what students at various grade levels should know and be able to do. Reading/English language arts and mathematics are common content areas in which standards have been set and assessments developed to measure student performance.

The measures of student achievement are nearly always large-scale assessments. These assessments are data collection instruments that usually have multiple-choice items in which students select from a list of answer choices, and also may have extended response items in which students write a response to a question. To lessen the unintended exclusion of some students from the accountability system because of their inability to be assessed on typical large-scale assessments, the assessments are designed to be widely inclusive of students of all characteristics. When the regular large-scale assessment cannot include all students, even with accommodations provided for students with disabilities and English language learners, alternative forms of measurement usually are provided (such as requiring students to demonstrate that they have the required knowledge and skills). Results of the large-scale assessments and alternatives, if available, are aggregated (added together) to produce a school score.

COMPARISON OF ACCOUNTABILITY APPROACHES

School accountability systems based on student performance provide explicit scores for schools and also attach labels that determine rewards and sanctions. The way in which the accountability systems incorporate student performance to obtain a score may vary from one place to another. Approaches to school accountability may be either cross-sectional, which are based on groups of students who may not be the same students from one year to the next, or longitudinal, which are based on individual students who

are tracked across time. Specific models of accountability within these approaches include four models: status, status change, cohort gain, and individual gain score.

The *status model* is a cross-sectional approach that uses an average score to determine a school's level of performance. This model has also been called a school-mean performance approach because it adds together students' performance scores and then determines the average to represent school performance. Status models of accountability rely on student performance scores in a single year. Schools are rated and consequences assigned based on the single year scores. In some cases, additional information such as absenteeism rate or graduation rate may be added to student performance to determine an average school score. The major drawback of this approach is that it does not recognize many of the factors that might have a significant impact on performance, such as differences in student body composition and instructional or programming factors, and does not allow for error in the measurement of performance. Measurement error is greater when the group of interest is smaller, thus complicating inferences from adding together information from small groups to reach conclusions about school performance.

A *status change model* is similar to the status model, but adds the dimension of time. It is sometimes called an improvement model. Average student performance, or a combination of student performance and absenteeism, for example, is examined over time. Typically school scores are compared year to year to see whether there are improvements in the performance of the school. For example, the percentage of students scoring proficient and above is compared from one year to the next. The major drawback of the status change model is that it is cross-sectional with different students included in the school averages from year to year, meaning that the performance of students who may be different on a variety of factors is compared. As mobility rates increase, as in the United States in the early 21st century, so do the drawbacks of the status change model. Another drawback of the status change approaches that focus on the percentage of students reaching a certain performance level is that the model does not recognize movement of students within levels, such as a student who moves from the bottom scores in a level of performance to high scores in that level, or across lower levels, such as a student who moves from the bottom level to the next higher level but is still below the targeted performance level for counting.

Another accountability model is known as the *cohort gain model*. This model uses a longitudinal approach to focus on changes in performance of individual groups of students over time. For example, those students in grade 7 in one year are compared to the performance of those students in grade 6 the previous year, with the assumption that the students in grade 6 moved to grade 7 and therefore the large majority of students are included in the comparison. The U.S. Department of Education has required each state to use this accountability model to receive NCLB Title I funds. To the extent that the assumption of minimal mobility of students from one grade to the next is upheld, the model has the advantage of not comparing different groups of students. To the extent that the assumption of a stable student population is not upheld, the model has some of the drawbacks of the cross-sectional models of accountability.

The *individual gain score model* of accountability is a longitudinal approach that focuses on the changes in performance of individual students over time. Growth models designed to evaluate the extent to which there has been growth in the achievement of individual students and value-added statistical models that factor in teacher or school variables and define growth expectations are versions of the individual gain score model. The advantage of the individual gain score approach is that comparisons evaluate changes for exactly the same group of students, thereby eliminating any error that is introduced due to the changing students in the groups over time. A disadvantage of this approach is that it only includes those students who have data at every point in time being compared. It is often the case that a number of students are left out, and this number increases with greater student mobility or with more years in the comparisons.

In practice, the accountability models can be altered in a number of ways, and the status and longitudinal approaches can be combined. Under NCLB, numerous adjustments have been made to accountability models to meet the needs and characteristics of individual states. Some researchers have argued that regardless of the approach, the results should not be interpreted as identifying the causes of good or poor performance, or a source for explaining why one school is better than another, but rather as a source of descriptive information that requires further investigation.

SEE ALSO *High Stakes Testing; Standardized Testing.*

BIBLIOGRAPHY

Erpenbach, W. J., & Forte, E. (2007). *Statewide educational accountability systems under the NCLB Act: A report on 2007 amendments to state plans.* Washington, DC: Council of Chief State School Officers.

Goldschmidt, P., Roschewski, P., Choi, K., Auty, W., Hebbler, S., Blank, R., and Williams, A. (2005). *Policymakers' guide to growth models for school accountability: How do accountability models differ?* Washington, DC: Council of Chief State School Officers.

Hanushek, E. A., Kain, J. F., & Rivkin, S. G. (2004). Disruption versus tiebout improvement: The costs and benefits of switching schools. *Journal of Public Economics, 88*(9), 1721–1746.

Heubert, J., & Hauser, R. (1999). *High stakes: Testing for tracking, promotion, and graduation.* Washington, DC: National Academy Press.

Linn, R. L. (2004). Accountability models. In S. H. Fuhrman & R. F. Elmore (Eds.), *Redesigning accountability systems for education* (pp. 73–95). New York: Teachers College Press.

Linn, R. L., Baker, E. L., & Betebenner, D. W. (2002). Accountability systems: Implications of requirements of the No Child Left Behind Act of 2001. *Educational Researcher, 31*(6), 3–16.

Linn, R. L., & Haug, C. (2002). The stability of school building scores and gains. *Educational Evaluation and Policy Analysis, 24*(1), 27–36.

McCaffrey, D. F., Lockwood, J. R., Koretz, D. M., & Hamilton, L.S. (2003). *Evaluating value-added models for teacher accountability.* Santa Monica, CA: RAND.

Raudenbush, S.W. (2004). *Schooling, statistics, and poverty: Can we measure school improvement? The ninth annual William H. Angoff Memorial Lecture.* Princeton, NJ: Educational Testing Service.

Singer, J., & Willet, J. (2003). *Applied longitudinal data analysis: Modeling change and event occurrence.* New York: Oxford University Press.

Martha L. Thurlow

ACHIEVEMENT GAP

SEE *Opportunity/Achievement Gap.*

ACHIEVEMENT MOTIVATION

A quick survey of scientific literature and popular language would reveal that, while the word "motivation" has many meanings, fundamentally they refer to processes that impel an organism to act. Indeed, "motivation" comes from the Latin verb *movere*, which means "to move." Hence, motivation refers to the processes that lead to the instigation, continuation, intensity, and quality of behavior. Accordingly, the term *"achievement* motivation" denotes processes leading to behavior that aims to achieve a certain criterion or standard. The criterion can be any goal or objective, formal or informal, set by an individual or by others, in any professional or leisure domain (e.g., school, sports, work, music, gardening, even social relationships and moral conduct), which provides a guide for evaluating success and failure.

Because achievement of standards is a fundamental human endeavor, achievement motivation has been an important domain in psychological inquiry. During the century that has passed since psychology became a scientific discipline in the late 1800s, numerous theories have been developed to explain the processes underlying achievement-oriented behavior. To a large degree, these various theories reflect the scientific zeitgeist of the time of their development, as well as the ideological beliefs of the researchers who developed them.

EARLY MOTIVATION THEORIES

Early twentieth-century theories of motivation were strongly influenced by the general scientific developments of the late 19th century—especially Darwin's theory of evolution in biology and Helmholz's law of the conservation of energy in physics. These scientific ideas led to the conception of living organisms as types of machines, with motivation as the energy that fuels the machine (Weiner, 1990). The organism was thought to strive toward homeostasis, or an optimal state of no motion. Motivation for action was thought to derive from a deprivation that created a disruption to, or disequilibrium of, this homeostatic state. For example, deprivation of nourishment leads to motivation to seek food, and deprivation of interesting surroundings leads to motivation to seek stimulation. In these theories, the main explanatory concept—or motivational mechanism—was termed "Drive," and it was thought to represent responses to such physiological deficits that aimed to restore homeostasis to the organism.

"Instincts," "Needs," and other related motivational concepts of the early twentieth century were similar in their emphasis on the general organismic and "energetic" character of behavior. Motivational theories of the period explained how the energy provided by the drive, instinct, or need combined with the organism's skill in a certain behavior (i.e., how much practice it had) and the relative value of the behavior's reward (e.g., going for a tasty rather than a bland food) to elicit and guide action (see, for example, Hull, 1952). Theorists of the time were faced with formidable challenges as they attempted to decide how many drives, instincts, and needs existed, how to measure them, and which were primary or secondary (for example, Murrey, 1938). As motivational systems were thought to operate according to similar principles in all organisms, much of the research during this era was conducted with animals. It was much easier to create deprivation and test instigation of behaviors aiming at different rewards among animals than among people: e.g., among rats in a maze.

It was ideological beliefs as much as empirical investigations and clinical understandings that led to developments in motivational theories during the first half of the 20th century. For example, the fundamental belief that scientific psychology should focus on observable behavior and avoid any reference to "mentalism" was the impetus for B. F. Skinner's (1938) version of behaviorism, which focused exclusively on observable reinforcements and punishments for explaining the likelihood of behavior. Another important ideological perspective—"Humanism"—led Abraham Maslow (1955) to distinguish the human motivation system from that of animals, and to arrange human needs according to a hierarchy in which general physiological needs were at the bottom and the unique human self-actualizing needs were at the top. And it was as much an ideological battle as a scientific one that framed the fierce debate about the role of cognition in motivation. "Drive" theorists, led by Hull (1952), held fast to the automatic machine metaphor, whereas the "Cognitivists," led by Tolman (1932), argued that cognitive processes, such as *expectations* for a reward, must be included to explain variation in motivation.

THEORIES OF THE MID-1900S

The Hull-Tolman debate was decidedly won by the proponents of cognition and led to the inclusion of cognitive processes, such as expectancies for success and perceptions of its value, alongside drives and needs in the major theories of achievement motivation of the middle of the 20th century. Arguably, the most notable among these theories was that of David McClelland, John Atkinson, and their colleagues (McClelland, Atkinson, Clark & Lowell, 1953). For these researchers, achievement motivation was based in a personality characteristic that manifested as a dispositional need to improve and perform well according to a certain standard of excellence. This achievement motive, which the researchers labeled *n Achievement*, or *nAch*, was believed to form during the first years of life through parents' child-rearing practices: primarily, how early parents expected and rewarded—either tangibly or affectively with warmth and affection—independence in their children. McClelland and his colleagues hypothesized that these early experiences led to the propensity to experience a strong emotional arousal when cues in the environment were interpreted as an opportunity to achieve. Individuals were thought to differ from each other in the strength of this arousal and in the breadth of cues that elicited it.

As need for achievement was thought to be based in affective associations established in the first years of life, McClelland, Atkinson, and their colleagues believed that people were not conscious of this characteristic of their personality. Therefore, these researchers considered it inappropriate to assess people's need for achievement by asking them directly to talk about their motivation. Instead, they chose to assess this need indirectly through a projective instrument called the Thematic Apperception Test (TAT) that purportedly elicits unconscious processes. In this instrument, people are asked to write a story describing the thoughts, emotions and behaviors of a person in an ambiguous picture or drawing (for example, a child sitting in front of a violin). The stories are then coded for achievement-related content including indicators of competition, accomplishments, and commitment to achieve. This technique, labeled the Picture Story Exercise (PSE), was used in numerous studies that tested the relations of *nAch* with various indicators of performance. The PSE was also used to investigate the way different environmental cues (e.g., success and failure feedback) were related to elicitation of the achievement need, and to investigate differences in level of *nAch* among people from different social groups (e.g., McClelland, 1961). This latter work was rather controversial due to its stereotype-promoting implication that people from certain groups were inherently low in need for achievement. About a decade later, Maehr (1974) challenged this deterministic implication by highlighting the role of contexts and situations over that of personality in motivation and achievement.

It was not long before research, observations, and earlier notions of human motivation suggested that *nAch* was not the only achievement motive. Analyses of the PSE indicated that while some people had ample positive imagery related to achievement (and were identified as high on *nAch)* and others had very little (and were identified as low on *nAch)*, many people actually had strong *negative* imagery associated with achievement. Researchers realized that a more complete description of the achievement motive would require supplementing the positive affective arousal triggered by the potential for achievement, or *Hope of Success* (HS), with the negative affective arousal triggered by the potential for failure, labeled *Fear of Failure* (FF). Similar to HS, FF was believed to be shaped during the early years of life through child-rearing practices that included punishment—again, either tangible or affective, such as love withdrawal—for failing to meet parents' expectations. Thus, in addition to outcomes associated with high HS, research during the middle of the 20th century paid much attention to the processes and outcomes associated with FF and its related construct of "Anxiety about Failure." These two motives later came to represent an important distinction in the achievement motivation literature between *approach* and *avoidance* motivations (Elliot & Covington, 2001).

Much of the research during the 1950s and 1960s in the need for achievement framework relied on the PSE. However, while the PSE proved to be a successful measure of *nAch*, it had critics who questioned its reliability and validity. These criticisms led researchers to construct alternative measures to assess achievement needs: summated scales. This method involves giving a questionnaire to participants and asking them to rate their agreement with a number of statements describing characteristics or emotional reactions that define *nAch* and FF (e.g., "I will not be satisfied until I am best in my field of work," Jackson, 1984). The ratings on the different items are then summed to provide a score indicative of the person's level of achievement motivation.

The construction of these easily used scales increased the number of studies relating self-reported *nAch* and FF to a wide range of outcomes. However, unlike the PSE, summated scales ask people directly about their motivation. Interestingly, research found that responses on the scales do not correlate with scores of *nAch* derived from the PSE. Moreover, scores from these two types of measures seem to be associated with different outcomes. Years later, these findings led McClelland and his colleagues (McClelland, Koestner & Weinberger, 1989) to argue that the two measures tap into two different motivational systems. They argued that the PSE indeed assesses *nAch*, which is the unconscious, or "implicit," emotional arousal that is experienced in response to achievement cues. In contrast, the scales assess conscious cognitive perceptions and evaluations, which are self-attributed, or "explicit." These explicit motives were thought to be influenced by social norms and expectations and were closer in meaning and psychological function to the other cognitive concepts that became dominant in motivational theories during the second half of the 20th century: expectancies for success, perceived value, perceptions of control, and goals.

COGNITIVE PROCESSES IN MOTIVATION

In its theoretical formulation, Atkinson's (1957) and McClelland's (1985) theory of achievement motivation combined *nAch* with cognitive expectations of success and with the value of such success to a person. In fact, this theory was often referred to as the Expectancy-Value model of achievement motivation. The inclusion of cognitive processes as central concepts in the explanation of human behavior indicated a shift in the metaphor that guided motivation theory: from that of a machine to that of a rational decision-maker (Weiner, 1991). Atkinson held, for example, that people would rationally construct the value of success to be higher on difficult than on easy tasks. Similarly, he expected people to have lower expectancies for success on difficult than on easy tasks. Atkinson contended that these two perceptions interacted to result in a person's behavioral tendency to engage in a task, which was highest at moderate levels of task difficulty, and zero at both very low and very high levels. However, in Atkinson's theory, this relationship was still thought to be affected by people's unconscious need for achievement, and to be strong only for individuals with high need for achievement. For individuals with low need for achievement, the behavioral tendency to engage was expected to be low regardless of task difficulty.

The cognitive processes of expectancies for success and perceived value continued to be important motivational concepts throughout the second half of the 20th century and the beginning of the 21st century. Indeed, the "cognitive revolution" in psychology in the middle of the 20th century, combined with criticisms of the *nAch* perspective, resulted both in increased attention to cognitive processes in motivation and in waning interest in the concepts of the past. Rather than striving toward homeostasis, humans were now considered to be continuously active, and motivation was thought of as the process underlying the behavioral choices that they made. But it was also becoming clear that people were not rational decision-makers (Weiner, 1991). People constructed different meanings for the same task that guided their perceptions, expectations, and valuing. These meanings were considered to be as much a result of social interactions as of personal dispositions. Thus, the focus during the last three decades of the 20th century was on people's subjective experiences of success and failure (created in the laboratory or in natural social settings such as schools), the attributions they made to these events, their evaluations of their competence, their expectations of success or failure in the future, and the goals they adopted for engagement.

MOTIVATION THEORY AT THE LATE-TWENTIETH CENTURY

Unlike the grand theories of the early decades of the 20th century, no single theory dominated the field of achievement motivation in its late decades. Instead, several theoretical frameworks developed side by side, employing various social-cognitive concepts and mechanisms. These different frameworks highlighted processes as applied to different units of analysis (e.g., the academic task at hand, the subject matter, academic learning, achievement generally, life goals); they emphasized the role of the individual, the environment, or their interaction; and they focused on somewhat different indicators of motivation (e.g., choice, persistence, quality of engagement, affective experience). Arguably, the dominant concepts of the last decades of the 20th century could be said to be *Self* and *Goals*. Self processes, including perceived competence, sense of control, and sense of autonomy, as well as the values and goals that defined the criteria of success and failure, appeared in one form or another in almost all the theoretical frameworks. These cognitive structures, which emphasize the agentic nature of behavior, seem to characterize the zeitgeist of motivational theorizing of this period. Along with the reliance on cognitive processes, the most common method of assessing motivational processes within these frameworks is summated scales, although other methods including interviews, observations, and experiments are employed as well.

Today, in the first decade of the 21st century, one can identify several directions in motivational theorizing.

The cognitive concepts of *Self* and *Goals* continue to play a prominent role. However, current theorizing places greater weight on the social-cultural foundation of these cognitive processes (Volet & Järvelä, 2001). Thus, the importance of culture, the social context, and social relations and interactions to achievement motivation is receiving more and more attention. Another apparent trend is the integration of earlier motivational concepts, primarily achievement needs, with the later cognitive processes (Elliot & Thrash, 2001; for an integration of cognitive processes with humanistic needs see Deci & Ryan, 2000). Conceiving of implicit and explicit motives as complementary systems, and identifying corresponding neurological systems in the brain, is likely to instigate further research and theoretical developments (Schultheiss & Brunstein, 2005). Finally, emotional processes, which were rather neglected during the heavy emphasis on cognitive concepts, are receiving recognition as important energizing concepts in their own right, and research on the emotional nature of achievement motivation is beginning to bear interesting fruit (Linnenbrink, 2006).

FACILITATING ACHIEVEMENT MOTIVATION IN SCHOOL

In conclusion, motivational theories reflect the zeitgeist as well as the ideology of their authors. Different theories represent different metaphors of human action, emphasize different underlying processes, and focus on different outcomes. When attempting to understand student motivation, for example, educators and researchers should be critical consumers and consider the fit of a theory with their own values and needs. Such consideration should include the methods for assessing motivation, as these methods are inextricably embedded in theoretical assumptions. Finally, theoretical assumptions are tied with implications for motivational interventions. Motivational theories that emphasize stable personality characteristics are, by nature, more pessimistic with regard to interventions (although see McClelland, 1965, 1978). Arguably, educators might find most useful those theoretical perspectives that emphasize the role of the social environment in students' motivation. Among these, it seems, there is relative agreement: quality achievement motivation among all students is facilitated by caring and safe environments that promote meaningful relationships between and among adults and children, in which the emphasis is on personal development and collaboration rather than on competition and social comparison, in which students are encouraged to pursue their interests and to learn from mistakes, and in which feedback is geared towards learning and not merely evaluation (Pintrich & Schunk, 2002).

SEE ALSO *Attribution Theory; Expectancy Value Motivational Theory; Goal Orientation Theory; Self-Efficacy Theory.*

BIBLIOGRAPHY

Atkinson, J.W. (1957). Motivational determinants of risk-taking behavior. *Psychological Review, 64*, 359–372.

Elliot, A. J., & Covington, M. V. (2001). Approach and avoidance motivation. *Educational Psychology Review, 13*, 73–92.

Elliot, A. J., & Thrash, T. M. (2001). Achievement goals and the hierarchical model of achievement motivation. *Educational Psychology Review, 13*, 139–156.

Hull, C. L. (1952). *A behavior system.* New Haven, CT: Yale University Press.

Jackson, D. N. (1984). *Personality research form* (3rd ed.). Port Huron, MI: Sigma Assessment Systems.

Linnenbrink, L. E. (Guest Ed.), (2006). Special issue on: Emotion research in education: Theoretical and methodological perspectives on the integration of affect, motivation, and cognition. *Educational Psychology Review, 18*.

Maslow, A. (1955). Deficiency motivation and growth motivation. In M. Jones (Ed.), *Nebraska symposium on motivation.* Lincoln, NB: University of Nebraska Press.

McClelland, D. C. (1961). *The achieving society.* New York: Free Press.

McClelland, D. C. (1965). Toward a theory of motive acquisition. *American Psychologist, 20*, 321–333.

McClelland, D. C. (1978). Managing motivation to expand human freedom. *American Psychologist, 33*, 201–210.

McClelland, D. C. (1985). How motives, skills, and values determine what people do. *American Psychologist, 40*, 812–825.

McClelland, D. C., Atkinson, J. W., Clark, R. A., & Lowell, E. L. (1953). *The achievement motive.* New York: Appleton-Century-Crofts.

McClelland, D. C., Koestner, R., & Weinberger, J. (1989). How do self-attributed and implicit motives differ? *Psychological Review, 96*, 690–702.

Pintrich, P. R., & Schunk, D. (2002). *Motivation in education: Theory, research and applications* (2nd ed.). Upper Saddle River, NJ: Prentice-Hall.

Ryan, R. M., & Deci, E. L. (2000). Self-determination theory and the facilitation of intrinsic motivation, social development, and well-being. *American Psychologist, 55*, 68–78.

Schultheiss, O. C., & Brunstein, J. C. (2005). An implicit motive perspective on competence. In A. J. Elliot & C. S. Dweck (Eds.), *Handbook of competence and motivation* (pp. 31–51). New York: Guilford.

Skinner, B. F. (1938). *The behavior of organisms: An experimental analysis.* Englewood Cliffs, NJ: Prentice-Hall.

Tolman, E. C. (1932). *Purposive behavior in animals and man.* New York: Appleton Century-Crofts.

Volet, S., & Järvelä, S. (Eds.), (2001). *Motivation in learning contexts: Theoretical advances and methodological implications* (pp. 33–55). Oxford, UK: Pergamon.

Weiner, B. (1990). History of motivational research in education. *Journal of Educational Psychology, 82*, 616–622.

Weiner, B. (1991). Metaphors in motivation and attribution. *American Psychologist, 46*, 921–930.

Avi Kaplan

ACTION RESEARCH

Action researchers develop actionable knowledge. They do not merely study problems from a distance. Participants become empowered and aligned around the truths created/discovered in the action research so that desirable change results.

WHERE TRUTH MEETS POWER

The work of action researchers challenges much received wisdom in both academia and among social change and development practitioners, not least because it is a practice of participation, engaging those who might otherwise be subjects of research or recipients of interventions as inquiring co-researchers. Action researchers do not start from a desire of changing others out there, although their work may eventually have that result, rather it starts from an orientation of change with others. Action research is therefore not a methodology but an orientation to inquiry that comprises a great variety of practices.

In the often-cited definition given by Peter Reason and Hilary Bradbury in their *Handbook of Action Research* (2001, 2006, 2008), action research is described as

"a participatory process concerned with developing practical knowing in the pursuit of worthwhile human purposes ... It seeks to bring together action and reflection, theory and practice, in participation with others, in the pursuit of practical solutions to issues of pressing concern to people."

OVERVIEW OF STEPS AND PROCEDURES

Common among the varieties of action research is a holistic approach that integrates reflection and action. Thinking together in dialogue is especially valued because innovation and coordinated action is thereby generated. A review of a large variety of action research projects over the years shows that action research has the following characteristics:

- grounded in real life experience,

- developed in partnership,

- addresses significant needs,

- develops new ways of seeing/interpreting the world (i.e., theory),

- works with (rather than simply studying) people,

- uses methods that are appropriate to the audience and participants at hand,

- develops needed structures to allow for follow up or institutionalization of new practices so that the work may have a lasting, positive impact.

While there are many ways of doing action research, the following steps suggest how a generic action research project evolves over time:

- Co-scoping the work in an insider/outsider team (e.g., scholar/practitioner),

- Mapping the entire system in which the need for change is perceived,

- Identifying key stakeholders and possible leverage for desired change,

- Collecting targeted data, often including interviews and focus groups,

- Meeting with stakeholder on preliminary findings and design of participatory implementation,

- Ensuring infrastructure that will sustain the work,

- Presenting findings for wider audiences with use of metrics to support the effort.

ASSESSING VARIETIES OF ACTION RESEARCH

The best way of understanding action research is to be immersed in a project. Perhaps second best is to read rich descriptions. The following constructs, selected from *The Handbook of Action Research* and the Sage journal *Action Research,* offer a way of appreciating what can otherwise seem like a bewildering array of projects.

The construct of context refers to the manifold types of places and organizations in which action research takes place. Action research happens in private spaces; in urban communities; in business, healthcare, and development contexts; and in the ministerial offices of nation states.

The term *leadership* refers to the core group of movers in the action research projects. In most cases the movers design a project that envelops larger numbers of people at different levels of engagement over time—from supporters to active co-researchers. However, sometimes those who generate the original design for the action research also experience it, as for example with collaborative inquiry aimed at professional improvement for all participants.

First-, second-, and third-person modes of inquiry often coexist in one project. But for the sake of overview it is helpful to differentiate which predominates as the cause of a project's impact. First-person mode refers to the work that each individual does with regard to cultivating an orientation of learning. Second-person mode refers to the work of group learning that usually underpins the participative approach in action research projects, within which people engage with one another. Third-person mode refers to efforts to involve or share information with those not originally involved in the work, which typically happens through publication or invitation for others to join an on-going effort.

The level of impact refers to the place in a system where impact is felt, for example, at the level of the individual; the small group organization or unit of community; or at the level of the whole society.

Finally, people who study action research ought to look at the order of change. First order change or single loop change refers to the degree to which concrete results are experienced by project participants. Second order or double loop change refers to the change occurring at the level of operating theories and values.

METHODOLOGICAL STRENGTHS AND WEAKNESSES

Action research typically involves two sets of actors whose roles may blur. One set is directly responsible for effecting change in a system while the other helps frame and theorize the work. Strengths and weaknesses are therefore viewed through different lenses—the need to act and the need to understand.

For practitioners it is often that a good balance between first and second order outcomes (immediate results and value added learning) helps to better commend the action research approach as it allows for momentum to build around small wins.

For those situated in a scholarly context, methodology must include the question of how to relate to conventional social science and especially how to work with the issue of partial objectivity. In the West, most action researchers have been brought up in a broadly Cartesian worldview, which channels their thinking in significant ways. It views the world as made of separate things. These objects of nature are composed of inert matter, operating according to causal laws. They have no subjectivity or intelligence, no intrinsic purpose or meaning. The philosophy of Descartes states that mind and physical reality are separate. Humans alone have the capacity for rational thought and action and for understanding and giving meaning to the world. This split between humanity and nature, and the abrogation of all mind to humans, is what Max Weber meant by the disenchantment of the world. Participation therefore becomes an epistemological principle with methodological implications. An attitude of inquiry includes developing an understanding that people are embodied beings that are part of a social and ecological order, that they are radically interconnected with all other beings, not bounded individuals experiencing the world in isolation. This all leads to individual researchers suggesting that there can never be one right way of doing action research.

In addressing the important question of how one knows if action research can be deemed good (Bradbury & Reason, 2003; Bradbury, 2007), Bradbury and Reason argue that a key dimension of quality is for action researchers to be aware of their choices for quality and to make those choices clear, transparent, articulate, to themselves, to their inquiry partners, and, when they start writing and presenting, to the wider world. This is akin to the crafting of research that Kvale (1995) advocates, or following Lather (2001), away from validity as policing toward incitement to dialogue. The degree of actionability in the work of Bradbury and Reason is a function of how rigorously they can address issues of quality in their knowledge generation efforts.

Generally then Bradbury and Reason suggest that action researchers keep an eye on a handful of issues and address them early and often in the life of a project. Those are considerations of quality with regard to the following:

1. Quality of partnership,

2. Quality of practical outcome,

3. Quality of methodological and theoretical rigor (being careful to include the multiple ways of knowing best suited to participants),

4. Quality of infrastructure.

ACTION RESEARCH, INSTRUCTION, AND EDUCATION

Action research can be undertaken by people in all walks of life as they study and attempt to change their world. It does not have to be part of a formal academic project. It can be facilitated by scholars and those in graduate training at universities, by those in think tanks and nongovernmental organizations around the world. Scholarly action researchers are called upon to unify oppositional approaches that include the integration of theory and practice, action and reflection, empirical analysis and normative vision, critique and appreciation, explanation and action, vision and current reality. In academic cultures that more readily replace *and* with *or*, this will always be a challenge. Thankfully this challenge also offers opportunity for experiencing that the action research approach makes a positive difference, especially as researchers contribute to a more sustainable world.

SEE ALSO *Research Methods: An Overview.*

BIBLIOGRAPHY

Bradbury, H. (2007). Quality and actionability: What action researchers offer from the tradition of pragmatism. In A. B. (Rami) Shani, S.A. Mohrman, W. Pasmore, B. Stymne, & N. Adler (Eds.), *Handbook of Collaborative Management Research*, pp. 583–600. Thousand Oaks, CA: Sage.

Bradbury, H., & Reason, P. (2003). Action research: An opportunity for revitalizing research purpose and practices. *Qualitative Social Work, 2* (2) 173–183.

Kvale, S. (1995). The social construction of validity. *Qualitative Inquiry, 1*(1), 19–40.

Lather, P. (2001). Validity as an incitement to discourse: qualitative research and the crisis of legitimation. In V. Richardson (Ed.), *Handbook of Research on Teaching*, 4th ed., pp. 241–250. Washington DC: American Education Research Association.

Reason, P., & Bradbury, H. (Eds.). (2001). *The handbook of action research: participative inquiry and practice.* Thousand Oaks, CA: Sage.

Reason, P., & Bradbury, H. (Eds.). (2006). *The handbook of action research: Concise paperback edition.* London: Sage.

Reason, P., & Bradbury, H. (Eds.). (2008). *The handbook of action research: participative inquiry and practice.* 2nd ed. Thousand Oaks, CA: Sage.

Hilary Bradbury
Peter Reason

ADHD

SEE *Attention Deficit Hyperactivity Disorder (ADHD).*

ADOLESCENCE

Research on adolescence is over 100 years old and can be characterized by two main trends (Lerner & Steinberg, 2004). In the first 70 years or so, research was mainly confined to separate disciplines. Biologists described physical development and the changes that accompany puberty; psychologists studied cognitive development; sociologists examined how various social arenas influenced adolescents; and educational psychologists studied how adolescents' motivation differed across school and classroom settings. This research produced a detailed account of how adolescents develop. More recently, however, researchers have generated more complex understandings of youth. Instead of, for example, studying biological or social development separately, researchers are increasingly examining how different areas of life interact and affect one another.

Another trend consists of changing assumptions about adolescence. Throughout the first 70 years of research, there was a common assumption that adolescence was a time of "storm and stress" (Hall, 1904). Indeed, many believed that puberty brought an inevitable upheaval that led to antisocial attitudes and recklessness. However, since that time, these generalized assumptions have been challenged. Data suggest that for most, the transition from childhood to adulthood is relatively smooth (Arnett, 1999).

The long history of research into adolescent development has resulted in a wealth of practical implications for educators who work with adolescents and strive to provide proactive, healthy opportunities that will facilitate youth's optimal development.

DEFINITIONS OF ADOLESCENCE

Notions of adolescence are defined by biology and culture and are best understood in a social-historical context. The most longstanding definition of the onset of adolescence links it to puberty, when hormone activity produces the development of secondary sex characteristics (pubic hair and voice change in males; breast development and menarche in females). However, while these biological changes are evidence of the transition from childhood to adolescence, the transition out of adolescence is less well defined. The adage that "adolescence begins in biology and ends in culture" reflects the variable understanding of when adolescence ends. However, theories and models have emerged to explain the transition out of adolescence into early adulthood (Arnett, 2000).

Culturally, definitions of the timing and meaning of adolescence have changed over the years as expectations of youth shifted. A hundred years ago, notions of adolescence were scarcely understood, since teens did not attend high school and most assumed adult roles of providing for their family and getting married at average ages of 14 and 15. Expectations that teens assume adult roles at young ages precipitated the transition into adulthood at much earlier ages than is the case in the 21st century.

However, during the twentieth century expectations of youth began to shift in response to the demands of a changing economy. The need for a better-educated workforce, along with the child welfare movement, propelled youth out of the workforce and into high schools, thus delaying their entry into adult roles. This trend has continued into the present. Now, young people are expected to stay in school much longer, which means they spend more time with same-age peers and enter adulthood later than ever before. These shifts have influenced views of what it means to be an adolescent (e.g., Nichols & Good, 2004).

As a result of these economic and cultural shifts, the time period of adolescence has been extended to include the ages of 10 through the mid twenties, with most researchers dividing the age span into early (10–13), middle (14–17) and late (18–mid twenties) adolescent (Smetana, Campione-Barr, & Metzger, 2006). This division corresponds to American school structures, allowing analyses of development and context according to middle school, high school, and college.

ADOLESCENT DEVELOPMENT

Adolescence represents a period of significant growth. Individually, adolescents experience rapid physical growth and changes, accompanied by shifts in cognitive and emotional capacities. At the same time, the development from childhood into young adulthood brings new cultural and societal opportunities and expectations. At no other time in life do so many shifts in development and social contexts occur simultaneously.

Physical Growth and Change. Most physical growth occurs during the early and middle phases, with the onset of puberty the most characteristic feature of adolescence. The biological changes of adolescence include hormonal changes leading to growth of secondary sex characteristics, growth in height and weight, and changes in body composition (changes in bone, muscle, and fat). The onset of puberty, as marked by hormone changes, starts as early as age 8 in girls and age 9 in boys, with the development of external characteristics typically appearing a few years later. Over time, females are maturing and developing at younger and younger ages, although this is not the case for males.

Puberty-related changes in the body at earlier ages have implications for how youth cope with these changes—especially for girls. Researchers have investigated how biological and social factors affect one another by looking at puberty status, which refers to the degree of physical maturation (hormone changes, breast development, voice change), and puberty timing, which refers to puberty status relative to same-age peers (Susman & Rogol, 2004). One theory that has been advanced to explain the effects of puberty timing is referred to as the Maturational Deviance Hypothesis. It suggests that adolescents who are "off time (earlier or later) in their pubertal development experience more stress than do on-time adolescents" (Susman & Rogol, 2004, p. 30). Studies reveal that youth who mature earlier or later than their same-age peers are vulnerable to at-risk outcomes such as problems with coping, antisocial behavior, and emotional distress (Brooks-Gunn, Peterson & Eichorn, 1985). Early-developing girls are especially at risk for poor body image, higher levels of depression, and substance abuse. By contrast, late-developing boys seem to be at greater risk for depressed mood, lower self-esteem or confidence, and lower achievement.

While late-maturing boys may be vulnerable to some negative outcomes, this finding is not consistent across studies. By contrast, the finding that early development is disadvantageous for girls is more consistent. Often referred to as the early-maturational or early-timing hypothesis, research studies more or less consistently show how early maturation among girls is associated with negative outcomes. There is also data to suggest that boys too may be disadvantaged if they mature before their peers. In general, research seems to suggest that for both boys and girls, off-timing puberty may have negative effects.

Cognitive Growth and Change. Jean Piaget's theories have provided a starting point in the study of the changing nature of cognitive processing in the development from childhood to adolescence. Piaget described how adolescence brings forth the capacity to think logically and abstractly (Piaget, 1955). Since Piaget's time, researchers have sought to understand more complex questions of how processes such as memory, reasoning or problem-solving skills, and expert knowledge develop through adolescence. In short, these interrelated processes seem to develop together, which means researchers cannot determine their individual developmental paths. Instead, a review of literature on cognitive processing as a whole suggests that adolescence brings the "attainment of a more fully conscious, self-directed, and self-regulating mind" (Keating, 2004, p. 48). Thus, in contrast to children, adolescents become more aware of their surroundings and able to direct their own thinking, learning, and problem solving.

Two areas of cognitive development have received much attention: moral reasoning and changes in interpersonal perspective taking. Lawrence Kohlberg (1984) has significantly contributed to understanding of how adolescents reason in their moral decision making. Drawing from Piaget's work, Kohlberg theorizes that the capacity to morally reason grows more complex and differentiated over time. Kohlberg argues that in general, data suggest that early adolescents typically reason according to his stage two—individualism, instrumental purpose, and exchange, but by about age 13, reasoning progresses to include mutual understandings. Thus, for a 12-year-old, being "good" is about following the rules for one's own good, whereas in stage three, the capacity to understand another person's experiences broadens notions of morality to include a concern for others and the nature of varying circumstances. In short, one's frame of reference moves from childhood moral reasoning that is based on personal perspectives or "what is right is what is good for me" to adolescent moral reasoning that is based in greater appreciation for others' perspectives and experiences or "what is right is for one may not be right for another."

Robert Selman's 2003 work on the development of perspective-taking has built on the work of Kohlberg and others to shape understanding of adolescent social and moral cognition. Selman studied the progression of perspective-taking skills, referred to as interpersonal understanding, throughout development to understand how cognitive changes in the capacity to understand someone else's perspective influences relationships. At the earlier stages in childhood, perspectives are limited to a single view of the world with very little back and forth understanding. By level two (around early adolescence), adolescents are better able to understand that people have different perspectives. This stage is marked by reciprocity, in which what they give to others is linked to expectations of what they will receive in return. Level three is also marked by mutual understanding that is characterized by genuine giving and caring for another person without expectation for a return. Early adolescents operate consistently at level two, but as they grow older, they operate more frequently at level three.

Selman's work, along with that of Kohlberg and others (e.g., Gilligan, 1982) suggests that adolescents are cognitively different from their childhood counterparts in that adolescents have the capacity to see and understand the world as others see it. Morally and cognitively, this means that adolescents (both early and middle) are more generally prosocial in thought and action than their childhood counterparts (Eisenberg & Morris, 2004). Further, it suggests that for adolescents, fostering and maintaining relationships become more complex as the ability to imagine multiple roles for themselves and multiple perspectives of others deepens.

Social and Emotional Changes. Erik Erikson's 1950 theory of identity development has had a significant impact on the understanding of adolescent social and emotional development. According to Erikson, people's sense of who they are unfolds throughout their lives and is driven by the struggle between their "internally defined selves and those selves that are defined, confirmed, or denied by others" (Nakkula & Toshalis, 2006, p. 19). The constant negotiation between these two selves shapes who a person is and who he or she will become. There are eight stages in life during which certain struggles are primary. During adolescence, the primary struggle is over the central question of "Who am I?" Adolescents yearn to be themselves both in relation and reaction to others, and they need relationships in which experiments with identity will be embraced. The struggle to find a balance between individuation and connection drives identity experimentation and the fleeting passions that often accompany it (Nakkula & Toshalis, 2006, p. 22).

Theory on identity development was advanced by James Marcia, who proposed four identity states: foreclosure, moratorium, diffusion, and identity achieved. Each state is characterized by varying levels of exploration and commitments (Marcia, 1966). In Marcia's concept of identity achieved, a person has undergone explorations of possible selves and come to some level of commitment as a result of those explorations. Identity diffusion is the opposite. It applies to someone who has made no commitments and has not gone through any period of exploration. Identity moratorium applies to someone who is actively experimenting or exploring but who has not yet made any commitments, whereas in foreclosure, a person has made commitments without having explored possible options.

The value of these identity status constructs is that they provide a theoretically based framework for understanding the path to healthy identity formation. At the core of these theories is the implication that struggle, experimentation, or exploration is fundamental to the acquisition of healthy identity. Further, these theories imply that the path to an achieved identity involves negotiation between the inner self and social, cultural definitions of the self. Research suggests that identity exploration is often triggered by cognitive and social shifts in which emerging understandings of how others see the world challenge previous definitions. These challenges often unfold in complex social contexts such as schools, peer groups, media environment, and families. In general, at some point, adolescents' views of who they are meet competing definitions that raise the possibility that their own beliefs may be wrong. The resulting challenges often propel teens into exploration, including the taking of risks and pushing of boundaries, in order to better understand their own and others' views of themselves.

Identity struggles emerge because of competing expectations from peers and cultural institutions of which youth are a part. This is true for a wide range of identity constructs, including gender, ethnicity, race, class, and sexual orientation. For example, researchers have long sought to understand the achievement gap between privileged, White cultures and disadvantaged, largely minority cultures. Theorists argue that the achievement gap in the United States is partly explained by a minority culture's distrust of an educational system that is largely based on European values that are perceived as perpetuating segregation and discrimination (Ladson-Billings, 1995). For teens trying to discover their true academic, ethnic, and gendered identity commitments and values, competing expectations cause a dilemma. For minority teens, school may be valued at home, but among peers, doing well in school may be viewed as "acting White" or as abiding by the rules established by another culture. The implicit accusation, that a person has "abandoned" his or her own culture in favor of someone else's, forces minority youth to examine the meaning of school and culture in their lives.

SOCIAL CONTEXTS OF DEVELOPMENT

Adolescent physical, cognitive, and emotional development occurs within social institutions, including families, friends, and schools. Therefore, understanding the nature of development necessitates understanding the social contexts in which it occurs. For adolescents, families, peers, and schools constitute the most important cultural contexts in which development unfolds.

Parents and Families. Notions of adolescence as a time of "storm and stress" suggest that this time period will be marked by rebellion, antisocial attitudes, and conflict with parents. However, research suggests that this is the exception rather than the norm. Data reveal that between 5% and 15% of teens are antisocial and excessively rebellious of adult authority (e.g., Collins & Laursen, 2004). Therefore, in family interactions, a majority of youths proceed through adolescence in a relatively stable, healthy, prosocial fashion.

Still, parent-adolescent relationships change in certain ways during the transition from childhood to adulthood. For example, disagreements grow in number and severity throughout adolescence as teens seek out autonomy and independence from parental rules. Thus, conflicts, when they do arise, are typically about rule negotiation, with teens seeking more independence and parents struggling to know when and how to accommodate them. One meta-analysis of studies examining longitudinal patterns in parent-child conflict suggests that frequency of conflicts grows from early to mid adolescence and then tapers off in later adolescence, whereas the intensity of conflicts grows through mid adolescence and stays about the same through later adolescence (Laursen, Coy, & Collins, 1998). Data suggest that this pattern holds relatively the same for parent-child relationships in different cultures.

Peers. Research suggests that adolescent peer groups are dynamic systems that grow bigger and more important with the transition from elementary through middle and high school. Although it has been known since 1900 that a teen's peer group is important, recent research has provided a more complex picture of the role and influence of such groups. Brown (2004) comments on a few basic themes uncovered by this rich literature, pointing out that teen friendships are relatively unstable over time. It has been suggested that fewer than half of "reciprocrated" best friends last more than one full year, and between one third and one half of peer groups dissolve with time (Brown, 2004). One way of studying this is through nomination procedures in which teens identify popular and well-liked kids and those who are not. These status ascriptions are relatively stable in the short term, but they often vary over the long term. Peer groups are therefore fluid systems that change over time.

Another research topic has been how adolescents manage their friendships. As a way of understanding peer-peer relationships, researchers have studied how adolescents manage conflict. In one set of studies, it was found that youth vary with respect to how they respond to aggressive acts. For example, prosocial youth are less likely to attribute aggression to intentional hostility and are more likely to seek out reconciliation than youth who are characterized as withdrawn or rejected.

Bullying has also received increased attention over the years in the wake of incidents such as the shootings at Columbine High School, Colorado, in 1999. A national survey of youth in grades 6–10 reveals that approximately 29% of students report being involved in bullying (as the bully, victim, or both), and that 13% report engaging in moderate or frequent bullying of others (Nansel et al., 2001). Further, bullying more often occurs in grades 6 through 8, with males as the bully and/or victim more often than females. Males are typically more involved in physical bullying whereas females are often more involved in indirect, relational bullying, such as gossip, rumors, and exclusion. The consequences of bullying can be significant because victims often are lonely, depressed, and have low self-esteem. By contrast, students who are infrequently bullied tend to be more strongly bonded to the school and invested in prosocial behaviors and beliefs (Cunningham, 2007).

SCHOOL CONTEXTS: IMPLICATIONS FOR TEACHERS

One consistent theme throughout the literature on adolescence is the notion of "struggle" or "exploration." The concomitant emergence of cognitive changes, identity conflicts, and changing role expectations as adolescents progress through school requires that they have open, safe places in which to test, explore, and discover for themselves their identities. For cognitive development, this requires having opportunities to form understandings about right and wrong. For emotional development, it means having safe environments for testing identities in multiple contexts (e.g., in peer groups, through school-based and after-school activities). For social development, it means exploring role definitions through interactions with friends, peer groups, and adult role models and mentors. Teachers can help youth manage these learning experiences through active listening, authoritative management styles, and by helping youth feel like they belong and have safe places in which to explore. This is especially important for middle school contexts in which young adolescents are especially vulnerable to disengagement from school (Eccles, 2004).

The Search Institute has summarized developmental assets for positive youth development that offer ideas for helping youth achieve their potential. These include four external and four internal assets. External assets include (a) having supportive, positive fulfilling relationships with members of one's communities (schools, families, friends); (b) empowerment (being perceived positively by members of the community); (c) knowing clearly what

family and school expects, (d) a community that provides a safe place with rich opportunities for exploration. Internal assets include (a) being committed to learning, (b) positive values for making good choices, (c) social competencies to engage in familiar and new situations, and (d) positive self concept (Scales & Leffert, 2004). Using these developmental assets as a guide, teachers can assist youth by arranging environments that foster external assets and engaging in relationships that facilitate internal assets.

Teachers play a significant role in the lives of adolescents, and knowledge of adolescence equips them to be sensitive to the diversity in youth's experiences and the competing forces in their lives. Armed with this knowledge, teachers can offer safe spaces for youth to explore and test their emerging ideas of who they are and who they want to become.

BIBLIOGRAPHY
Arnett, J. J. (1999). Adolescent storm and stress, reconsidered. *American Psychologist, 54*(5), 317–326.

Arnett, J. J. (2000). Emerging adulthood: A theory of development from the late teens through the twenties. *American Psychologist, 55*(5), 469–480.

Brooks-Gunn, J., Petersen, A. C., & Eichorn, D. (1985). The study of maturational timing effects in adolescence. *Journal of Youth and Adolescence, 14*(3), 149–161.

Brown, B. B. (2004). Adolescents' relationships with peers. In R. M. Lerner & L. Steinberg (Eds.), *Handbook of adolescent psychology* (2nd ed., pp. 363–394). Hoboken, NJ: John Wiley & Sons.

Collins W. A., & Laursen, B. (2004). Parent-adolescent relationships and influences. In R. M. Lerner & L. Steinberg (Eds.), *Handbook of adolescent psychology* (2nd ed., pp. 331–361). Hoboken, NJ: Wiley.

Cunningham, N. J. (2007). Level of bonding to school and perception of the school environment by bullies, victims, and bully victims. *Journal of Early Adolescence, 27*(4), 157–178.

Eccles, J. S. (2004). Schools, academic motivation, and stage-environment fit. In R. M. Lerner & L. Steinberg (Eds.), *Handbook of adolescent psychology* (2nd ed., pp. 125–153). Hoboken, NJ: Wiley.

Eisenberg, N., & Morris, A. S. (2004). Moral cognitions and prosocial responding in adolescence. In R. M. Lerner & L. Steinberg (Eds.), *Handbook of adolescent psychology* (2nd ed., pp. 155–188). Hoboken, NJ: Wiley.

Erikson, E. (1950). *Childhood and society.* New York: Norton.

Gilligan, C. (1982). *In a different voice: Psychological theory and women's development.* Cambridge, MA: Harvard University Press.

Hall, G. S. (1904). *Adolescence: Its psychology and its relation to physiology, anthropology, sociology, sex, crime, religion, and education* (Vols. I & II). Englewood Cliffs, NJ: Prentice-Hall.

Keating, D. P. (2004). Cognitive and brain development. In R. M. Lerner & L. Steinberg (Eds.), *Handbook of adolescent psychology* (2nd ed., pp. 45–84). Hoboken, NJ: John Wiley & Sons.

Kohlberg, L. (1984). *The psychology of moral development: The validity of moral stages.* San Francisco: Harper & Row.

Ladson-Billings, G. (1995). Toward a theory of culturally relevant pedagogy. *American Educational Research Journal, 32*(3), 465–491.

Laursen, B., Coy, K. C., & Collins, W. A. (1998). Reconsidering changes in parent-child conflict across adolescence: A meta-analysis. *Child Development, 69*(3), 817–832.

Lerner, R. M., & Steinberg, L. (Eds.). (2004). *Handbook of adolescent psychology* (2nd ed.). Hoboken, NJ: Wiley.

Marcia, J. E. (1966). Development and validation of ego-identity status. *Journal of Personality and Social Psychology, 3,* 551–558.

Nansel, T. R., Overpeck, M., Pilla, R. S., Ruan, W. J., Simons-Morton, B., & Scheidt, P. (2001). Bullying behaviors among US Youth: Prevalence and association with psychosocial adjustment. *Journal of American Medical Association, 285*(16), 2094–2100.

Nakkula, M. J., & Toshalis, E. (2006). *Understanding youth: Adolescent development for educators.* Cambridge, MA: Harvard Education Press.

Nichols, S. L., & Good, T. L. (2004). *America's teenagers—Myths and realities: Media images, schooling, and the social costs of careless indifference.* Mahwah, NJ: Erlbaum.

Piaget, J. (1955). *The language and thought of the child.* New York: Meridian Books.

Scales, P. C., & Leffert, N. (2004). *Developmental assets: A synthesis of the scientific research on adolescent development* (2nd ed.). Minneapolis, MN: Search Institute.

Selman, R. (2003). *The promotion of social awareness: Powerful lessons from the partnership of developmental theory and classroom practice.* New York: Russell Sage Foundation.

Smetana, J. G., Campione-Barr, N., & Metzger, A. (2006). Adolescent development in interpersonal and societal contexts. *Annual Review of Psychology, 57,* 255–284.

Susman, E. J., & Rogol, A. (2004). Puberty and psychological development. In R. M. Lerner & L. Steinberg (Eds.). (2004), *Handbook of adolescent psychology* (2nd ed., pp. 15–44). Hoboken, NJ: Wiley.

Sharon L. Nichols

AGGRESSION

The psychological literature generally concurs that human aggression is any behavior intended to harm another living being who is motivated to avoid such behavior. Aggressive behavior can be physical, verbal, or relational; implies action or the threat of action; and can be characterized as either direct or indirect. Physical and verbal aggression, as their names suggest, describe physical harm or insults or threat of such actions. Relational aggression, by contrast, refers to behaviors that cause emotional harm by manipulating or damaging a victim's relationships with his or her peers or by injuring one's feelings of group acceptance (Dodge, Coie, & Lynam, 2006). Both physical and verbal aggression can be direct (e.g., a physical assault or a derogatory remark) or indirect (e.g., destroying another's prized possession or insulting a victim behind his or her

back). Some, but not all research (see Bushman & Anderson, 2004) further distinguishes two types of aggression by the motives underlying the behavior. Proactive or instrumental aggression is a means to another end; the harm is directed toward attaining objects, privileges, or similar self-serving ends. Reactive, retaliatory, or hostile aggression is behavior motivated to harm another that is displayed in anger as a response to a perceived threat or provocation (Dodge, Coie, & Lynam, 2006).

THEORIES OF AGGRESSION

Aggression in childhood and adolescence has typically been framed in one of a few prominent theories. Social learning theory (Bandura, 1973) is one of the earliest and most enduring theories of aggression that influenced thinking on children's aggressive behavior. Bandura theorized that children learned aggression by observing the behavior and the consequences of that behavior for others, a proposition made famous through the various "Bobo" studies that demonstrated the power of both live and filmed models to influence children to enthusiastically hit a Bobo doll. Closely related to modeling, this theory asserts that children who are positively reinforced or who observe others being positively reinforced for aggression are much more likely to persist in this behavior. Models provided through the mass media extend the power of observational learning far beyond the child's immediate environment. Importantly, media models are typically reinforced for aggression (Wilson et al., 2002), making them extremely powerful according to social learning theory.

Other recent theories have implicated family process in the development of aggression in childhood. Chief among them is coercion theory (Patterson, 2002), which postulates that the development of aggression is largely explained by coercive family processes in which parents and children mutually train one another's behavior. Children aggress, parents demand compliance, children escalate their aversive behavior, and parents escalate their demands but ultimately yield to the child's behavior, tacitly reinforcing children's aggressive behavior and perhaps modeling aggression in the process.

Social information processing theory (Dodge, Coie, & Lynam, 2006)) has been another generative model for the study of childhood aggression. Dodge (1986) originally developed a model of information processing that identified a hostile attributional bias as a foundation for the display of children's angry or reactive aggression in social situations His five-step model posited that children first encode and then interpret cues; highly aggressive youth may presume hostility from peers and selectively attend to cues that support that hostile attributional bias. The next steps include access or construction of a response, selecting a response, and enacting that response; for aggressive children with a hostile attributional bias, that response is most often aggressive. A further elaboration included an additional intermediate step of selecting a goal or preferred outcome of a response. As well, reciprocal effects between the child and the child's social environment (e.g., peer influences and reactions) and existing cognitive structures (e.g., memory stores, social schemas) that the child brings to the situation, were incorporated into the model.

The addition of constructs from social psychology (e.g., schemas) foregrounded linkages between this and another social information processing model of childhood aggression (Huesmann, 1988) that has influenced the study of media effects and aggression. Huesmann and colleagues argued that a child acquires aggressive scripts through observational learning (in both the proximal environment and the media) and perceived reinforcement of aggressive behavior. The accumulation and subsequent networking of multiple aggressive scripts into cognitive schemas results in social behavior that emphasizes aggression. Normative beliefs, or cognitions about what is right for the self, are also key cognitive structures in the Huesmann model. Aggressive children are presumed to have a greater store of aggressive scripts as well as normative beliefs that condone more aggression.

These information processing theories have been blended into a unified model (Huesmann, 1988) that highlights four decision points. A youth first perceives danger from the environment and next searches for and retrieves scripts from memory that are relevant to the situation. The youth then evaluates scripts stored in memory to decide what actions are acceptable, what actions lead to the most desired goal, and which actions are actually feasible. Finally, the youth evaluates the expected responses to any action. An aggressive child will selectively perceive cues and inappropriately attribute hostility when none exists. That child will also have a larger store of aggressive scripts from which to select and a greater propensity to positively evaluate aggressive scripts. This combination typically leads to a display of aggression.

The most comprehensive of the developmental theories of aggression, the biopsychosocial model (Dodge, Coie, & Lynam, 2006) is a transactional developmental model that incorporates biological dispositions; sociocultural contexts; and experiences with parents, peers, and social institutions. This model proposes that genetic bases and prenatal insults; life experiences that involve harsh treatment, rejection, and failure; family experiences that include poverty, neighborhood and family instability, harsh discipline, and limited parental education; and excessive early exposure to media violence all unfold in a transactional relationship during the child's develop-

ment. Many of these factors also represent negative social experiences that can lead to dysfunctional patterns of social information processing, and these information processing patterns link the broad life experiences to the individual display of aggression. This comprehensive model most effectively demonstrates the multiple points of convergence (e.g., observational learning, social information processing, reinforcement) in all of the major theories of aggression in childhood and adolescence.

MEASURES OF AGGRESSION

One common measurement strategy is checklists or rating scales that are completed by any combination of teachers, parents, and the child. A typical instrument widely used in research, schools, and clinical practice is the Achenbach Child Behavior Checklist, a scale with separate forms for parents (CBCL), teachers (TRF), and students (YSR). Scores on the multiple forms can be compiled to examine distinct problem areas across informants, including aggression and delinquent behavior. Other multiple informant rating scales for aggression in childhood and adolescence include the Social Skills Rating System, the Eyberg Child Behavior Inventory and Sutter-Eyberg Student Behavior Inventory, and the Behavioral Assessment Scale for Children (Buros Institute, 2007).

Direct behavioral observation, often described as naturalistic observation, is considered by some (Hudley, 2006) to be the most effective strategy for assessing aggression in childhood and adolescence. Behavior does not occur in a vacuum, and direct observations are able to capture the interactive environment in which the behavior exists, including the antecedent conditions and the consequences that elicit and maintain aggressive behavior. Naturalistic observations include recording behaviors in their natural setting and a descriptive coding system that requires a minimum of inference from observers and coders. Observational codes can measure behavior in several ways. Event recording simply tallies the frequency of a given behavior during the observation period. Interval recording similarly captures frequency, but divides the observation period into segments and counts the number of segments in which the target behavior is displayed, either throughout the interval or at a particular time point in the interval. Duration recording measures the length time a behavior lasts. Functional behavior assessment, an observational strategy, assesses antecedents, frequency, duration, and consequences of the aggressive behavior for the target child and others in the environment to determine the functions that the aggressive behavior serves for the child. In spite of obvious benefits of direct observation, the strategy can be limited by several problems (Hudley, 2006). Behaviors must be clearly defined, and observers must be trained to fully understand the exact behaviors that are to be captured. Observer bias or the tendency to see what one expects to see is especially troublesome in direct observation of aggression. In addition, particularly with adolescents, participant reactivity to the presence of observers can change or eliminate the exact behaviors that are the target of the observation. Finally, in school settings direct observations can be labor intensive and exceed the resources that are available on site.

Sociometric assessments continue to be used widely in research on childhood aggression, although their use in educational and clinical practice has declined dramatically (Hutton, Dubes, & Muir, 1992). The most common sociometric strategies involve children providing assessments of peers in school. These strategies have demonstrated substantial predictive validity for future negative outcomes. Peer nomination assessments typically ask students to nominate classmates or students in their grade who fit certain characteristics (e.g., starts fights), students they prefer (like most), or reject (like least) (see Hudley & Graham, 1993). The Class Play (Masten, Morrison, & Pelligrini, 1985), a variant of peer nomination techniques, directs children to cast their classmates in a variety of roles, either positive or negative, in a hypothetical play that the class will perform. In contrast, peer-rating procedures allow each child to rate every other student in the class on specified characteristics, preferences, or rejection. For young children, responses can be recorded with a series of faces rather than a numerical rating scale. Ethical concerns surrounding children expressing negative opinions about their peers have been raised, but no harmful reactions from participation in sociometric procedures have been documented (Iverson & Iverson, 1996).

DEVELOPMENTAL CHANGE IN AGGRESSION ACROSS CHILDHOOD AND ADOLESCENCE

Physical aggression in childhood is a relatively stable phenomenon. Highly aggressive boys and girls in middle childhood often continue to be aggressive in adolescence and adulthood, although the links between early and later behavior may not be as strong for girls as they are for boys (Dodge, Coie, & Lynam, 2006). Certainly not all highly aggressive children are aggressive and violent as they grow older, but such children are overrepresented in the population of aggressive and violent adolescents and adults. For example, longitudinal research has found that children at age 8 who were rated by their peers as highly aggressive self-reported high rates of aggression at age 18 and physical aggression toward spouses and children at age 30. Most troubling, those who were parents by age 30 reported high aggression for their children (Huesmann, Eron, Lefkowitz, & Walder, 1984).

From early infancy to the early school years, children's aggression is typically expressed through temper tantrums and direct physical means (hitting, pulling, pushing, etc.). In the general population, simple displays of direct aggression peak between 2 and 3 years of age and then decline, largely due to children's developing social and cognitive abilities. However, some children remain aggressive through adolescence and beyond, and the form of their aggressive behavior changes across development. These children may show any combination of increasingly dysfunctional social cognitions, increasing aggression in interpersonal situations, and steady declines in prosocial behavior (Dodge, Coie, & Lynam, 2006). As well, children shift the site of their behaviors from early childhood through adolescence, as increasing age allows them to spend more time in the community and less time under direct adult supervision. As the setting for behavior changes, new forms of behavior may emerge; the 8 year old who fights at school may engage in physical mugging at 17. Finally, the intensity or force of aggression also changes over time for some aggressive children, in a trajectory that moves from simple hitting and pushing in early childhood to physical assaults with deadly objects in late adolescence and early adulthood.

OUTCOMES FOR HIGHLY PHYSICALLY AGGRESSIVE CHILDREN

Childhood aggression carries a host of negative developmental consequences that persist and accumulate over time, including delinquency and criminality, peer rejection, poor school adjustment, and mental health concerns. Although highly, overtly aggressive elementary age children are often rejected by their peers, not all aggressive children are rejected; those most likely to be rejected are socially incompetent and retaliate aggressively at times when peers find the behavior unwarranted and in violation of peer norms. Children and adolescents who are both rejected and aggressive in elementary school experience significantly higher rates of self reported depression and lower rates of peer rated friendship than their average peers. Aggressive children therefore may find themselves part of a deviant peer group composed of other, similar children who reinforce aggression, delinquency, and other behaviors (Dodge, Coie, & Lynam, 2006).

Another robust consequence of early aggressive behavior is adolescent delinquency and adult criminality, particularly among men. Longitudinal data find that men convicted of a violent crime by age 30 were more than three times as likely to have been rated by teachers and parents as highly aggressive in childhood or early adolescence than a comparison group of men who were not convicted of such crimes (Loeber et al., 2005). Highly aggressive students are also perceived as generally less academically successful, more behaviorally disruptive, and less motivated in class (e.g., off task, not doing homework) in comparison to their nonaggressive peers (Cairns, Cairns, & Neckerman, 1989). Finally, high levels of aggression have been cited as among the primary reasons that children and adolescents are referred to mental health services (Dodge, Coie, & Lynam, 2006).

SCHOOL- AND FAMILY-BASED INTERVENTION

Because cognitive mediators have been firmly linked to children's aggressive behavior, school based programs have often focused on cognitive-behavioral interventions. Cognitive-behavioral strategies address specific cognitive distortions that cause the display of aggression. One such program, the BrainPower Program (Hudley, 2003; Hudley et al., 1998), modifies attributional bias that supports childhood aggression, as described earlier. This program teaches aggressive children to recognize that negative social outcomes with peers may sometimes be caused by accidental rather than intentionally hostile causes. Students are taught to effectively search for social cues, initially attribute ambiguous negative outcomes to accidental causes, and develop less verbally and physically aggressive behavioral responses.

However, given the overwhelming evidence that multiple interpersonal processes regulate childhood aggression (Dodge, Coie, & Lynam, 2006), aggression reduction programs are most effective as one part of a comprehensive intervention to support the healthy development of children, families, and communities. One example of many such programs, Families and Schools Together (FAST) (McDonald & Sayger, 1998), incorporates the full range of relationships and settings impacted by youths' antisocial behavior. FAST builds, sustains, and enhances relationships between youth and their families, peers, teachers, and other community members. FAST brings a group of families from the same community together for weekly activities and two years of monthly school-community meetings to facilitate the development of mutual support networks in the community and the school.

Classrooms with lax and inconsistent discipline and schools that do not address problems of aggression and bullying see more physical aggression among students (Osher et al., 2004). Witnessing aggression (e.g., fighting, bullying, weapons) in school increases physically aggressive behavior, more so for girls than for boys (O'Keefe, 1997). However, zero tolerance discipline policies for physically aggressive behavior reduce attendance, motivation, and engagement in school among those students who do not run afoul of the policy. These negative policies typically do not reduce physical fighting in schools and actually promote aggression and youth violence in the community by expelling children who need the structure and education provided by school. The overall goal for schools must be the two-sided process of reducing aggressive behavior and promoting a peaceful, positive climate, and that responsibility can be shared by students and adults alike. School groups organized specifically to promote non-violence often benefit from improved school climate and reduced levels of aggressive, antisocial behavior, including bullying, fighting, and teasing (Office of Elementary and Secondary Education, 2002).

BIBLIOGRAPHY

Bandura, A. (1973). *Aggression: A social learning analysis.* Englewood Cliffs, NJ: Prentice-Hall.

Barnow, S., Lucht, M., & Freyberger, H. (2005). Correlates of aggressive and delinquent conduct problems in adolescence. *Aggressive Behavior, 31,* 24–39.

Buros Institute (2007). Test Reviews Online. Retrieved April 4, 2008 from http://buros.unl.edu/buros/jsp/clists.jsp?cateid=19&catename=Behavor+Assessment.

Cairns, R., Cairns, B, & Neckerman, H. (1989). Early school dropout: Configurations and determinants. *Child Development, 60,* 1437–1452.

Dodge, K. (1986). A social information processing model of social competence in children. In M. Perlmutter (Ed.), *The Minnesota Symposium on Child Psychology* (Vol. 18, pp. 77–125). Hillsdale, NJ: Erlbaum.

Dodge, K., Coie, J., & Lynam, D. (2006). Aggression and antisocial behavior in youth. In W. Damon & R. Lerner (Series Eds.) & N. Eisenberg (Vol. Ed.), *Handbook of child psychology:* Vol. 3. *Social, emotional, and personality development* (6th ed., pp.719–788). New York: Wiley.

Hudley, C. (2003). Cognitive-behavioral intervention with aggressive children. In M. Matson (Ed.), *Neurobiology of aggression: Understanding and preventing violence* (pp. 275–288). Totowa, NJ: Humana Press.

Hudley, C. (2006). Who's watching the watchers? The challenge of observing peer interactions on elementary school playgrounds. *New Directions for Evaluation, 110,* 73–85.

Hudley, C., Britsch, B., Wakefield, W., Smith, T., DeMorat, M., & Cho, S. (1998). An attribution retraining program to reduce aggression in elementary school students. *Psychology in the Schools, 35,* 271–282.

Huesmann, L. R. (1988). An information processing model for the development of aggression. *Aggressive Behavior, 14,* 13–24.

Huesmann, L. R., Eron, L., Lefkowitz, M., & Walder, L. (1984). Stability of aggression over time and generations. *Developmental Psychology, 20,* 1120–1134.

Hutton, J., Dubes, R., & Muir, S. (1992). Assessment practices of school psychologists: Ten years later. *School Psychology Review, 21,* 271–284.

Iverson, A., & Iverson, G. (1996). Children's long-term reactions to participating in sociometric assessment. *Psychology in the Schools, 33,* 103–112.

Loeber, R., Pardini, D., Homish, D., Wei, E., Crawford, A., Farrington, D., et al. (2005). The prediction of violence and homicide in young men. *Journal of Consulting and Clinical Psychology, 73,* 1074–1088.

Masten, A., Morrison, P., & Pelligrini, D. (1985). A revised class play method of peer assessment. *Developmental Psychology, 21,* 523–533.

McDonald, L., & Sayger, T. (1998). Impact of a family and school based prevention program on protective factors for high risk youth. *Drugs and Society, 12,* 61–86.

Office of Elementary and Secondary Education. (2002). *Student-led crime prevention: A real resource with powerful promise.* Washington DC: U.S. Department of Education, Safe and Drug-Free Schools Program.

O'Keefe, M. (1997). Adolescents' exposure to community and school violence: Prevalence and behavioral correlates. *Journal of Adolescent Health, 20,* 368–376.

Osher, D., VanAcker, R., Morrison, G., Gable, R., Dwyer, K., & Quinn, M. (2004). Warning signs of problems in schools: Ecological perspectives and effective practices for combating school aggression and violence. *Journal of School Violence, 3,* 13–37.

Patterson, G. (2002). The early developmental of coercive family process. In J. Reid, G. Patterson, & J. Snyder (Eds.), *Antisocial behavior in children and adolescents: Developmental theories and models for intervention* (pp. 25–44). Washington, DC: American Psychological Association.

Wilson, B., Smith, S., Potter, W. J., Kunkel, D., Linz, D., Colvin, C., et al. (2002). Violence in children's television programming: Assessing the risks. *Journal of Communication, 52,* 5–35.

Cynthia Hudley

Patricia A. Alexander PHOTO COURTESY OF PATRICIA ALEXANDER.

ALEXANDER, PATRICIA A.
1947–

Patricia A. Alexander was born in Washington, DC, on October 28, 1947, to a first-generation Italian immigrant mother and a father who came to the city from the Virginia Mountains as a result of the World War II draft. Alexander's life is one of classic blue-collar America. She attended a Catholic primary school where she struggled in basic subjects like reading and writing. Upon occasion Alexander has recounted a story of the day that she realized that all of her second-grade peers could read words that she had no idea how to understand. That day she decided that learning to read and write was going to require a great deal of hard work. Despite these early struggles, Alexander went on to graduate from Hammond High School, Alexandria, Virginia, in 1966, and was the first member of her family to attend college.

In 1970, she graduated from Bethel College, McKenzie, Tennessee, with a degree in elementary education. Following her degree, Alexander worked for nine years as a middle school language arts and science teacher primarily in rural Virginia in the Shenandoah County Public Schools (SCPS). In her final three years with the SCPS, she was given the opportunity to teach students with exceptionalities reading and mathematics in a laboratory setting. This experience was fundamental in Alexander's career as it turned her attention to the issue of individual differences in children and ways that educators could foster positive academic growth for all learners. Following this experience, she enrolled in James Madison University, Harrisonburg, Virginia, where in 1979 she obtained a Masters of Education degree in reading/elementary and early childhood education. In 1981 she received her Doctorate in Philosophy in reading from the University of Maryland, College Park, Maryland. Alexander accepted her first faculty position as an assistant professor of educational curriculum and instruction at Texas A&M University in 1981. Less than a decade later she was a full professor with a joint appointment in educational psychology and educational curriculum and instruction at Texas A&M University, and in 1995 she returned to the University of Maryland at College Park as professor of human development and convener of the educational psychology specialization. In 2000 she was named Distinguished Scholar-Teacher in Human Development at the University of Maryland in recognition of her outstanding research and teaching.

MAJOR CONTRIBUTIONS TO EDUCATIONAL PSYCHOLOGY

Alexander has made seminal contributions to many areas of learning and instruction. Among her notable contributions are her research on the role of strategic processing and analogical reasoning in reading comprehension and problem solving (e.g., Alexander, Willson, White, & Fuqua, 1987), explorations on interest in student learning (e.g., Alexander, Kulikowich, & Schulze, 1994), and investigations regarding the powerful influence of knowledge and beliefs in the acquisition of domain-specific expertise (e.g., Alexander, Murphy, & Kulikowich, 1998; Alexander, Schallert, & Hare, 1991; Garner & Alexander, 1994). Perhaps her most noteworthy contribution, however, is the *model of domain learning* (MDL) (Alexander, 1997). The MDL depicts the journey toward expertise in a domain in terms of select cognitive and affective components (i.e., subject-matter knowledge, learner interest, and general strategic processing) in a way that was groundbreaking in the field of educational psychology.

These components are positioned within a framework that addresses both stages (i.e., long-term characterizations) and phases (i.e., recurrent, iterative aspects) of domain learning. The stages predicted in the MDL are essentially non-regressive and non-recursive and aligned with the experiences, schooling, and work that tend to be age-associated. While the stages are meant to depict step-like changes in domain learning trajectories, the phases are intended to capture the fluidity within the learning process. It is the recurring patterns emerging from the phases that give rise to the profiles indicative of a particular stage of domain learning. The MDL entails three stages: *acclimation, competence,* and *proficiency/expertise.* Woven through these three stages are the critical forces of subject-matter knowledge, interest, and strategic processing that serve as catalysts for structuring and restructuring within and across each stage. Thus, it is the configuration of these components that bridges the stages and gives them identifiable characteristics.

Acclimation, the initial stage of development toward expertise, represents that point when individuals are confronted with a domain for which they possess little relevant knowledge, interest, or strategies. Overall, individuals in the acclimation stage demonstrate limited and fragmented knowledge of the subject, rely heavily on surface-level strategies, and report relatively higher levels of situational interest than individual interest.

A number of changes take place during the phases of acclimation on the road to competence. Specifically, the indicators of competence within a domain include a distinct increase in the breadth and depth of subject-matter knowledge, a deeper personal investment in the domain combined with decreased reliance on situationally interest-

ing conditions, and finally a willingness to exert the effort necessary to employ deep-level processing strategies.

The change from competence to proficiency requires a synergy among subject-matter knowledge, interest, and strategic processing. Those individuals fortunate enough to achieve proficiency in a domain are distinguishable from competent learners in several ways. First, the subject-matter knowledge of an expert becomes increasingly dense and cohesive, and proficient learners actually generate knowledge. In addition, individual interest and knowledge combine as a unified force. Finally, they may experience a slight rise in deeper strategic processing due to the knowledge generation and solving of novel domain problems, and a concomitant decrease in surface-level strategies.

Through her pioneering work, Alexander has given researchers and educators new ways to envision individual differences in student learning within a domain. Essentially, the MDL lays out a developmental trajectory of expertise; that is, a road map to proficiency. In addition, the domain-specific nature of the model lends versatility to its application in diverse settings such as those commonly found in schools and the workplace. This is so much the case that the MDL has become foundational in programs designed to train the teacher leaders of tomorrow such as the KEYS initiative (Hawley & Rollie, 2002). In the end, Alexander's MDL exemplifies the 1930 admonition of John Dewey (1859–1952) "No act can be understood apart from the series to which it belongs" (p. 412). The MDL calls on researchers and educators alike to think more deeply about learning and individual differences in developmental and multidimensional ways.

BIBLIOGRAPHY

WORKS BY

Alexander, P. A. (1997). Mapping the multidimensional nature of domain learning: The interplay of cognitive, motivational, and strategic forces. In M. L. Maehr & P. R. Pintrich (Eds.), *Advances in motivation and achievement* (Vol. 10, pp. 213–250). Greenwich, CT: JAI Press.

Alexander, P. A., Kulikowich, J. M., & Schulze, S. K. (1994). How subject-matter knowledge affects recall and interest. *American Educational Research Journal, 31,* 313–337.

Alexander, P. A., Murphy, P. K., & Kulikowich, J. M. (1998). What responses to domain-specific analogy problems reveal about emerging competence: A new perspective on an old acquaintance. *Journal of Educational Psychology, 90,* 397–406.

Alexander, P. A., Schallert, D. L., & Hare, V. C. (1991). Coming to terms: How researchers in learning and literacy talk about knowledge. *Review of Educational Research, 61,* 315–343.

Alexander, P. A., Willson, V. L., White, C. S., & Fuqua, J. D. (1987). Analogical reasoning in young children. *Journal of Educational Psychology, 79,* 401–408.

Garner, R., & Alexander, P. A. (Eds.). (1994). *Beliefs about text and about instruction with text.* Hillsdale, NJ: Erlbaum.

P. Karen Murphy

ANALOGY

Analogical thinking lies at the core of human cognition and is a key component for a multitude of functions such as problem solving, reasoning, and discovery and learning. It has been argued that the very act of forming an analogy requires a kind of "mental leap," inasmuch as it necessitates seeing one thing as if it were another (Holyoak & Thagard, 1995). Many scientific discoveries frequently rely on these mental leaps, and analogy forms the basis for our everyday problem solving, from the simplest instance to the most sophisticated reasoning strategy. Analogical reasoning has been classified into two common types: classic analogy and analogical problem solving. Both types of analogical reasoning involve analogical mapping, a central process of discovering which elements in the target correspond to specific elements in the source and aligning them together.

CLASSIC ANALOGY AND ANALOGICAL PROBLEM SOLVING

Classic analogy usually applies knowledge from a set of familiar elements (the relation of A to B) to relations about yet unknown elements (the relation of C to D) (Sternberg, 1977). Classic analogical problems are states A:B::C:? For example, *dog* is to *puppy* as *cat* is to ___? The answer is *kitten.* By knowing the relation between the first two elements (a *puppy* is a baby *dog*), one can use that knowledge to complete the analogy for a new item (*cat*). Because analogies are based on similarities, one must understand the relational similarity between dogs and cats and puppies and kittens in order to solve the analogical problem above.

Analogical problem solving, the second type of analogical reasoning, consists of a source case (which is generally already understood to some extent) and a target case (about which new knowledge is desired), and a relation that maps these elements from one case to the other. The analogical problem is considered solved when individuals can successfully transfer their knowledge from the source set and apply it correctly to the target set. A classic study by Gick and Holyoak had the participants attempting to solve the "tumor" problem. They were presented with a situation in which a doctor was trying to save his patient's life by eradicating a stomach tumor. The participants needed to advise the doctor on the kind of ray that at sufficiently high intensity can destroy the tumor but not harm the surrounding healthy tissue. The solution was to aim multiple low-intensity rays at the tumor from many angles; the rays would "meet" at the site of the tumor and their "sum" would equal the full strength of the ray. Gick and Holyoak found that the problem was quite difficult to solve. To determine whether participants could transfer a solution from an analogous problem to the tumor problem, they had participants first read an analogous story about the "general and a fortress" in which the general had to divide his troops into many small groups and attack the fortress from different directions. Having an analogous story in structure (source set) prior to reading the target problem allowed the participants to transfer their previous knowledge and correctly solve the analogy. However, most participants required a hint before they noticed that the solution "general and a fortress" problem could be applied to the "tumor" problem.

The analogy helps learners make connections between the pre-existing source knowledge and the new target. It has also been suggested that analogies facilitate abstraction from individual cases to general schemata (Gick & Holyoak, 1983) or help the learner generate new inferences about the target. Studies have shown that analogies can support productive conceptual change when neither the target nor the source are well understood; knowledge of each can be enriched through a process of "bootstrapping" (Kurtz, Miao, & Gentner, 2001). Investigations have demonstrated how analogies are used in non-experimental settings such as political debates (Blanchette & Dunbar, 2001), as well as in more naturalistic settings, such as scientific laboratory meetings. Although analogical transfer is an important component in human thinking and reasoning, lab studies do not always demonstrate effective use of analogies in solving problems. Some studies indicate that in lab scenarios in which participants typically use source information to solve problems superficially similar to the source, scientists often use structural features and higher-order relations in making the analogy during the discovery process.

COMPONENTS AND PROCESSES INVOLVED IN ANALOGICAL REASONING

Analogical problem solving can be functionally divided into multiple processes. The first component involves representing the source information. Studies have demonstrated that individuals' ways of encoding source analogues and the characteristics and quality of the representations influence subsequent transfer. For example, children who formed a goal structure of a source problem (e.g., goal of the main character; obstacle; and action to overcome obstacle and achieve goal) transferred more readily than those who encoded only specific details (e.g., Brown, 1989). Differences in breadth of learning are related to differences in the depth of initial learning, and this more

30

"robust learning" partially explains the better retention and wider generalization evident in subsequent transfer.

The second component is perceiving the analogical relationship, and a major obstacle to transfer is the failure to access spontaneously a source analogue. Informing problem solvers about the potential usefulness of source analogues, increasing the superficial similarities between tasks, and encouraging solvers to extract a more abstract principle from the source analogues have proved useful in improving the accessing process (Gentner & Rattermann, 1991).

Once a source analogue has been retrieved, the correspondences between the problems' key elements need to be mapped. The mapping process is guided by the common relational structures between analogous tasks, and perceiving these underlying structures presents a great challenge to successful transfer, often not only for young children but also for some adults. It is important to note that the difficulty in analogical transfer is not simply a developmental problem, but in various contexts may pose difficulty for all learners. Accessing an analogue and mapping relations do not ensure successful implementation of a solution. The last component involves executing an acquired strategy or principle. When the source and target problems share only a solution principle but differ in specific procedures, children might experience an obstacle in executing a source solution, despite the availability of the strategy (e.g., Ross, 1989). Experiencing diverse procedures illustrating a solution principle facilitates the extraction of a strategy, which is not embedded in a specific procedure, and its flexible and effective generalization to relevant problems.

The conceptual model concerning transfer processes and the age differences associated with each component addresses the observation that children in particular often experience difficulty with analogical transfer. This model also addresses questions of why some analogues are more difficult to use in problem solving than others and helps pinpoint how people at different age levels differ in solving analogous tasks, and how various factors influence transfer performance.

THEORIES OF ANALOGICAL REASONING

While it is well documented that analogical reasoning is a sophisticated conceptual process that is central to everyday thinking and learning, many underlying mechanisms that support the development of analogical reasoning are not yet well understood. Previously established theoretical accounts of analogy have two important processes: *relational processes*, which establish correspondences based on similar relations among the objects in the two problems, and *object-matching processes*, which create correspondences based on the similarity of an object in the

target problem to one in the source problem. However, research has shown existing evidence of consistent developmental differences in drawing analogies, and efficiency in analogical problem solving has been offered as a sensitive index of age-related differences. Younger children are more prejudiced by surface features than by structural or deeper causal properties and they are more dependent on hints pointing to the relations between problems. With age and experience, an expanding knowledge base, and increasing mental resources, children become more effective in perceiving deep relations or causal structures. Theorists have put forth three major hypotheses to account for age-related differences in analogical reasoning.

The first hypothesis is *increased domain knowledge*. In the late 1970s Piagetian studies suggested that young children are unable to reason analogically prior to achieving formal operations at approximately 13 or 14 years of age. Goswami and Brown have greatly disagreed with that claim and proposed in their 1989 study a "relational primacy hypothesis," arguing that analogical reasoning is fundamentally available as a capacity from early infancy but that children's analogical performance increases with age due to the accumulation of knowledge about relevant relations. While Piaget's tasks frequently involved uncommon tasks (e.g., a "steering mechanism") which were likely unfamiliar to youngsters, Goswami presented analogical reasoning tasks that were more relevant to children as young as 3 years old, who in turn, demonstrated knowledge about those relations. That said, having knowledge about relevant relations still cannot fully account for age-related effects in young children's performance on analogical reasoning tasks since children still seem to fail on analogies in systematic ways even when they possess relational knowledge relevant to the task.

The second hypothesis, an alternative explanation of young children's observed age-related increase in analogical reasoning performance, is *relational shift*. In a 1991 study, Gentner and Rattermann suggested that children primarily begin to attend to feature similarity between objects and will reason on the basis of perceptual features rather than on the basis of relational similarity. Following a relational shift, or a fundamental maturational change in their thinking, children can and will reason on the basis of relational features. Developmental literature has shown support for this hypothesis, demonstrating the interrelations between young children's processing of object similarity and their processing of relational similarity.

A third explanation for developmental changes in analogical reasoning shows the limits on children's working memory capacity that affect their ability to process multiple relations simultaneously. In a 2002 study Andrews and Halford defined *relational complexity* in terms of the number of sources of variation that are related and must be processed in parallel. In a binary relation in which "a dog chases a cat," the chase itself is a single relation, while the interaction between the dog and the cat become the arguments or the second relation. A child would need to hold both arguments, dog and cat, as well as the relevant relation in mind to reason on the basis of this relation. Andrews and Halford argued that for a developmental continuum in children's working memory capacity, children can process binary relations (a relation between two objects) after 2 years of age and can go on to process ternary relations (a relation between three objects) after 5 years of age. Age deepens children's development of executive functions, particularly the ability to reflect on the relation between two rules. Cognitive maturation also allows children to efficiently solve analogical problems with higher levels of complexity once they have an increased control over their thoughts and actions.

THE ROLE OF ANALOGY IN COMPREHENSION, TRANSFER, AND DEVELOPMENT

Whether and how children retrieve relevant information and use examples acquired in the past to solve analogous problems is a fundamental issue in the study of cognitive development. Experimental investigations of analogical transfer can be traced back to the beginning of the 20th century (e.g., Thorndike & Woodworth, 1901); however, the centrality of transfer to children's thinking and learning still remains a rather peripheral aspect in developmental psychology.

In broad terms, analogical thinking involves metaphor comprehension (e.g., Gentner & Markman, 1997), similarity and relational mapping (Markman & Gentner, 2002), classical analogy (Goswami & Brown, 1989), and problem solving by analogy (Brown, 1989). The transfer of strategies from familiar situations to novel problems reflects how deeply children acquire strategies, how broadly they generalize them to different situations, and how flexibly they think and reason. Strategy generalization is one of five critical dimensions of strategic change in children's thinking (Siegler, 2000) and is an ultimate measure of children's learning.

While traditional Piagetian accounts of analogical reasoning suggested that it is an ability that develops later in life, early competencies in solving analogical problems were demonstrated with infants as young as 10 to 12 months. The infants first observed their parent solving a problem and then were able to transfer the strategy themselves to a new problem, which shared the same underlying structure but differed in superficial features.

Substantial evidence further demonstrates that preschool children who observed an experimenter demonstrating with an appropriate tool (a rake that was both

long enough to reach the toy and had a functional head with which to pull the toy closer) transferred more effectively than did those who received only a hint about using the tool. Specifically, these children were increasingly likely to choose a tool that was similar in causal function to the source tool (e.g., a long cane) instead of tools sharing only perceptual similarities (e.g., a rake head without a handle or a handle without an effective head). Receiving a hint still proved somewhat helpful; children offered a hint outperformed those who received neither demonstration nor hint. These findings reveal that from a very early age children not only have a rudimentary ability to analogize in problem solving but that help provided by the adult allows the children to move beyond simply understanding analogies based on perceptual similarity and conceptualize them based on their causal function.

With the emergence of evidence that outlines the consistent developmental differences, it is well known that younger children are more prejudiced by surface features than by structural or deeper causal properties, and they are more dependent on hints pointing to the relations between problems. By providing direct instruction in the original learning situation teachers facilitate an effective way of subsequent transfer of strategies. Children's strategy transfer also benefits from specific probing questions that encourage self-explanations that give the children the opportunity to explain both the reasoning behind their strategy choices as well as the conclusions they drew from their design (Siegler, 2000). Children's superior performance in learning and transferring in such a probe condition suggests that direct instruction and asking children to generate self-explanations enhances learning and transfer.

INSTRUCTIONAL USES OF ANALOGIES

There are numerous research findings in support of analogy-enhanced teaching and learning. The widespread use of analogies as explanatory tools in introducing new concepts occurs across various disciplines in middle schools, high schools, and colleges. This has proved a reliable method of teaching in many countries worldwide.

Analogies, models, and modelling have been recognized as key tools for scientists, science teachers, and science learners. The familiar situation base or source analogue provides a kind of model for making inferences about the unfamiliar situation or the target analogue. By finding a structural alignment between a novel situation and the familiar situation learners are able to bring new ideas or concepts closer to their understanding and achieve eventual mastery.

Classroom-based research demonstrates that the use of models and analogies within the pedagogy of science education may provide an effective understanding of the nature of science. Studies show that in order successfully to develop conceptual understanding in science, learners need to be able to reflect on and discuss their understanding of scientific concepts as they are developing them. Furthermore, it has been found that pedagogies that involve various types of modelling are most effective when students are able to construct and critique their own and scientists' models. Research also suggests that group work and peer discussion are important ways of enhancing students' cognitive and metacognitive thinking skills. Lastly, understanding of science models, analogies, and the modelling process enables students to develop an awareness of scientific knowledge, as well as providing the tools to reflect on their own scientific understanding.

A vast body of research shows the importance of analogy use in math learning. Novice learners have great difficulty spontaneously noticing the similarity between two problems or instances that embody the same principle but have a different form (e.g., Gick & Holyoak, 1983). For example, a novice learner who correctly solves one math problem will have difficulty noticing that a second problem has the same conceptual structure if its form is changed into a word problem, if it is written in an alternate way, or if semantic cues in the problem invoke different background knowledge. Since analogical reasoning follows a series of specific steps that can lead to deep processing of novel information, yielding the capacity to learn and transfer knowledge to unfamiliar targets, the application to learning mathematics is especially relevant.

Mathematics is characterized by abstract structure in which underlying relationships remain the same but the object slots can be filled in various ways. Noticing higher-order similarity relationships between such instances of structural similarity is at the core of complex mathematical thinking. For instance, students may not at first notice the similarity between addition of numbers and addition of variables because variables are different at the surface level. However, with assistance or an increase of expertise, they could generate an analogy between these objects and use what they know about addition of numbers to inform their reasoning about addition involving variables. This simple case illustrates the power of analogy in enabling reasoners to apply information from one mathematical topic to other topics that are structurally similar.

In a 2004 study conducted in eighth-grade mathematics classrooms, Richland, Holyoak, and Stigler discovered that teachers used verbal analogies on a regular basis. When explaining a problem, non-math sources were used almost exclusively when instructors were developing analogies to teach mathematical concepts and when using analogies for socialization purposes. Conversely, when explaining mathematical procedures, teachers were most likely to use non-contextualized math

problems. These findings suggest that teachers were explicitly or implicitly tailoring their analogy production to the cognitive needs of students. When students were showing difficulty, teachers generated sources and targets with higher surface similarity, thus making analogy more transparent for learners.

In summary, the use of analogies for instruction, whether initiated by text, by the teacher, or by the students themselves, has been shown to improve conceptual learning. Studies show that analogies presented to students in a school setting, usually via instructional materials or teachers' spontaneous use, promote flexible conceptual learning and problem solving. Analogy allows students to use commonalities of one subject to help understand novel problems or concepts either within a single domain (e.g., physics concept of water pressure confined to a tower) or apply it to a vastly different area of knowledge across domains (e.g. using the water-tower analogy for understanding the cardiovascular system), thereby contributing to integral components of overall cognitive proficiency. Scientific research has increasingly placed analogical reasoning in the foreground, giving further support to notion that reasoning by analogy may indeed be the main engine of inventive thinking.

SEE ALSO *Providing Explanations.*

BIBLIOGRAPHY

Andrews, G., & Halford, G. S. (2002). A cognitive complexity metric applied to cognitive development. *Cognitive Psychology, 45,* 153–219.

Blanchette, I., & Dunbar, K. (2001). Analogy use in naturalistic settings: The influence of audience, emotion, and goals. *Memory & Cognition, 29,* 730–735.

Brown, A. L. (1989). Analogical learning and transfer: What develops? In S. Vosniadou & A. Ortony (Eds.), *Similarity and analogical reasoning* (pp. 369–412). London: Cambridge University Press.

Chen, Z., Sanchez, R. P., & Campbell, T. (1997). From beyond to within their grasp: The rudiments of analogical problem solving in 10- and 13-month-olds. *Developmental Psychology, 33,* 790–801.

Gentner, D., & Markman, A. B. (1997). Structure mapping in analogy and similarity. *American Psychologist, 52,* 45–56.

Gentner, D., & Rattermann, M. J. (1991). Language and the career of similarity. In S. A. Gelamn & J. P. Byrnes (Eds.), *Perspectives on thought and language: Interrelations in development* (pp. 225–277). London: Cambridge University Press.

Gick, M. L., & Holyoak, K. J. (1983). Schema induction and analogical transfer. *Cognitive Science, 15,* 1–38.

Goswami, U., & Brown, A. L. (1989). Melting chocolate and melting snowmen: Analogical reasoning and causal relations. *Cognition, 35,* 69–95.

Holyoak, K. L., & Thagard, P. (1995). *Mental leaps: Analogy in creative thought.* Cambridge, MA: MIT Press.

Kurtz, K., Miao, C. H., & Gentner, D. (2001). Learning by analogical bootstrapping. *Journal of the Learning Sciences, 10,* 417–446.

Richland, L. E., Holyoak, K. J., & Stigler, J. W. (2004). Analogy use in eighth-grade mathematics classrooms. *Cognition and Instruction, 22*(1), 37–60.

Ross, B. H. (1989). Distinguishing types of superficial similarities: Different effects on access and use of earlier problems. *Journal of Experimental Psychology: Learning, Memory, & Cognition, 15,* 456–468.

Siegler, R. S. (2000). The rebirth of children's learning. *Child Development, 71,* 26–35.

Sternberg, R. J. (1977). A component process in analogical reasoning. *Psychological Review, 84*(4), 353–378.

Thorndike, E. L., & Woodworth, R. S. (1901). The influence of improvement in one mental function upon the efficiency of other functions. II. The estimation of magnitudes. *Psychological Review, 8,* 384–395.

Aleksandra L. Palchuk
Zhe Chen

ANCHORED INSTRUCTION

Anchored instruction is a teaching approach that situates, or anchors, problems in authentic-like contexts that people can explore to find plausible solutions. Anchored instruction in education is closely related to problem-based and case-based learning in other fields (e.g., business, medicine), but it differs somewhat because all the information for solving anchored problems is available whereas it may not be in actual problem solving situations. Anchors are typically shown in a short video (8-to-12 minutes), which students search to find information they need for solving the embedded problems. In a typical classroom using anchored instruction, students work together to formulate strategies for solving the subproblems embedded in the anchor. The problems are of high interest, and most students work for several days to help the main characters in the video solve the problems.

Presenting anchored problems in video format has several advantages. One important quality of an anchored problem is its ability to directly immerse students in a rich array of problem contexts, which helps to eliminate the barriers many students with low achievement in both math and reading confront when attempting typical text-based problems. Second, the dynamic nature of video enables students to notice subtleties in the mix of auditory and visual cues, which are missing in text-based problems. Finally, multimedia scaffolds enable students to access help stations as they work on generating solutions they think are plausible.

Theoretical underpinnings of anchored instruction are derived from well-known theorists such as John Dewey (1933) who stressed the importance of viewing knowledge as tools. When people (students) acquire new knowledge that they understand can help them solve problems in particular contexts, they view knowledge more as a tool than as disconnected facts and procedures. The role that context plays in helping students recognize how and when to use these tools (i.e., transfer) is one of the key components of anchored instruction. The importance of context on cognition has been termed "situated cognition" (e.g., Brown, Collins, & Duguid, 1989) and "cognitive apprenticeship" (e.g., Collins, Brown, & Newman, 1989). Contextual factors in everyday problem solving have been shown to affect learning situation-specific practices and their transfer among people across cultures (e.g., Lave, Smith, & Butler, 1988).

A primary goal of anchored instruction is to engage students in problem-solving activities that can help reduce the "inert knowledge" problem that Alfred North Whitehead (1929) identified decades ago. Knowledge presented as isolated disconnected facts remains inert and thus fails to transfer. In contrast, when knowledge and skills are contextualized as they are in anchored instruction, students are more apt to recognize when to appropriately apply them and use their prior knowledge to solve similar problems they encounter in the future. Research in educational settings suggests expertise is developed through problem-solving activities that involve active construction of knowledge results (Bransford, Brown, & Cocking, 2000). Thus, anchored learning environments are generative because they motivate students to actively search for relevant information, use the information to plan strategies for solving the problem, and test their solutions.

ANCHORED INSTRUCTION IN MATHEMATICS

A well-known series of anchors for improving students' problem-solving skills in mathematics is called *The Adventures of Jasper Woodbury* (CTGV, 1997). The entire set of Jasper Adventures consists of twelve episodes, each one including a video-based problem and related extension problems. Three episodes were developed for each of four mathematical areas of study: Distance/Rate/Time, Statistics, Geometry, and Algebra. The early versions of Jasper were presented on random access videodisc technology, which enabled students to keep track of the frame numbers and to access information almost instantly with the videodisc controller or barcode reader. This feature was far superior to access methods in linear-based videotape and VCR technology.

Kim's Komet is one of the Jasper Adventures that helps students develop their informal understanding of pre-algebraic concepts, such as variable, linear function, rate of change (slope), line of best fit, and reliability and measurement error. The video-based anchor involves two girls who compete in a car competition called the Grand Pentathalon in which competitors have to predict where on a ramp they should release their cars to navigate five tricks attached to the end of ramp straightaway. *Kim's Komet* first helps show students how to calculate speeds when times and distances are known. They do this watching the time trials in the video held the day before the Grand Pentathalon. The challenge is to identify the three fastest qualifiers in three regional races, where times and distances are known but the distances vary. For example, students explain whether a car that travels 15 feet in 0.9 seconds is faster or slower than a car that travels 20 feet in 1.3 seconds.

The next challenge is more difficult: It asks students to use their own stopwatches to time Kim's car in time trials prior to the Grand Pentathalon. The software allows students to pick various release points (i.e., heights) on the ramp so they can compute the speeds of Kim's car along the length of straightaway. Eventually the students realize that they should time Kim's car from the beginning to the end of the straightaway, where the car's speed is relatively constant, rather than on the ramp, where the car is accelerating. After computing these speeds, students plot on their graph the speed of Kim's car for each of the release points and then draw a line of best fit. Students use this line to predict speeds for all possible release points.

On the day of the Grand Pentathalon, the teachers reveal to students the critical speed range of Kim's car for each of five tricks, which are attached to the end of the straightaway. Students earn points for helping Kim successfully accomplishing each trick. The software enables students to enter the height of the release point for each event and to watch Kim as she releases her car from that height. If students provide Kim with the correct release point, they can watch as Kim's car successfully navigates the trick. However, when speeds and release points have been incorrectly computed, they watch as Kim's flies off the trick and crashes. Foundation skills needed to solve this problem include computation with whole numbers and decimals.

ENHANCED ANCHORED INSTRUCTION

An instructional method based on the concept of anchored instruction is called Enhanced Anchored Instruction (EAI; Bottge, 2001). EAI has two main components. Like the Jasper series, problems are presented in video format that students navigate to find solutions to an overarching problem. Multimedia-based learning opportunities built into newer technology enable students to access technology-mediated scaffolds, which are of particular benefit to many low-achieving students. In addition, EAI extends AI by affording students additional opportunities to practice their skills as they solve new but analogous problems in applied, motivating, and challenging hands-on contexts.

One example of EAI is a multimedia-based problem called *Fraction of the Cost* and its hands-on related problem called the *Hovercraft Challenge*. *Fraction of the Cost* stars three middle school students who wonder if they can afford materials to build a skateboard ramp. The main instructional purpose of the problem is to help students improve their math skills in the areas of rational numbers and measurement. After students solve the problems posed in *Fraction of the Cost*, they work on solving a related problem, the *Hovercraft Challenge*, in which students have to plan and construct a rollover cage for a hovercraft out of PVC pipe. The teacher divides the class into groups of three students, and each group plans how they can make the cage in the most economical way. When students have constructed their cages, they lift them onto a 4-by-4-foot plywood platform (i.e., hovercraft). A leaf blower inserted into a hole in the plywood powers the hovercraft, which inflates the plastic attached to its underside and elevates it slightly above the floor. The last day of the project students ride on their hovercrafts in relay races up and down the halls of the school.

RESEARCH FINDINGS OF AI AND EAI

Results of formative evaluations with Jasper materials were reported in CTGV (1997). In these studies, teachers were provided extensive training on the content and use of the anchored materials. Findings suggested students in the anchored instruction groups developed more sophisticated math skills and positive attitudes compared to students in comparison groups. In a later study conducted in fifth grade classrooms (Hickey, Moore, & Pellegrino, 2001), two pairs of closely matched schools were randomly assigned to assess the effects of several Jasper series adventures on students' math achievement and motivational responses. Results showed that the anchored instruction materials had positive effects on math achievement and motivation of students in both high-SES and low-SES schools. This latter finding was especially important because it suggests that low-achieving students can profit from complex problem-solving activities without negative or motivational consequences if they are designed appropriately.

A series of quasi-experimental studies comparing EAI to traditional modes of instruction with students at several achievement levels (i.e., low, average, high) have confirmed and expanded the earlier findings with AI. These studies have yielded medium-to-large effect sizes (η^2) on curriculum-aligned problem solving tests (.31 to .79) and transfer tasks among students without disabilities (.14 to .38) (e.g., Bottge, 1999; Bottge, Heinrichs, Mehta, & Hung, 2002).

Similar results have been found in studies involving students with learning disabilities (Bottge et al., 2007) and emotional/behavioral disabilities (Bottge et al., 2006). An important finding generated from these studies suggests that teachers need substantial amounts of training to teach EAI effectively. This training should include both pedagogical methods for teaching EAI and deep understanding of the math principles embedded in the EAI problems.

Although studies suggest that AI and EAI can have positive effects on students' problem-solving skills, they have also identified some points for consideration. First, teachers need considerable training in methods and math content to teach with anchored instruction. Second, low-achieving students require explicit just-in-time instruction to help them perform difficult mathematics computation procedures (e.g., adding fractions) and understand mathematical concepts (e.g., variables). Third, EAI uses instructional technology (i.e., computer and hands-on applications), which some schools may not have or cannot afford to buy. Finally, anchored instruction may not fit neatly within traditional curricula.

Anchored instruction has the potential for helping students across a range of abilities improve their problem-solving skills. Results of several studies suggest that the contextualized nature of the anchors interest students and engage them for extended periods in problem solving activities. With low-achieving students, the related hands-on problems and learning scaffolds are especially important for solidifying the concepts embedded in the video-based anchors. One of the most important implications of these findings is that success or failure on academic tasks should not be predicted on students' prior achievement but rather on the design quality of the instructional material.

SEE ALSO *Constructivism.*

BIBLIOGRAPHY

Bottge, B. A. (1999). Effects of contextualized math instruction on problem solving of average and below-average achieving students. *Journal of Special Education, 33,* 81–92.

Bottge, B. A., Heinrichs, M., Chan, S., & Serlin, R. (2001). Anchoring adolescents' understanding of math concepts in rich problem solving environments. *Remedial and Special Education, 22,* 299–314.

Bottge, B. A., Heinrichs, M., Mehta, Z., & Hung, Y. (2002). Weighing the benefits of anchored math instruction for students with disabilities in general education classes. *Journal of Special Education, 35,* 186–200.

Bottge, B. A., Rueda, E., LaRoque, P. T., Serlin, R. C., & Kwon, J. (2007). Integrating reform-oriented math instruction in special education settings. *Learning Disabilities Research and Practice, 22,* 96–109.

Bottge, B., Rueda, E., & Skivington, M. (2006). Situating math instruction in rich problem-solving contexts: Effects on adolescents with challenging behaviors. *Behavioral Disorders, 31,* 394–407.

Bransford, J. D., Brown, A. L., Cocking, R. R., Donovan, M. S., & Pellegrino, J. W. (Eds.). (2000). *How people learn: Brain, mind, experience, and school.* Washington, DC: National Academy Press.

Brown, J. S., Collins, A., & Duguid, P. (1989). Situated cognition and the culture of learning. *Educational Researcher, 17*(1), 32–41.

Cognition and Technology Group at Vanderbilt University. (1990). Anchored instruction and its relationship to situated cognition. *Educational Researcher, 19*(3), 2–10.

Cognition and Technology Group at Vanderbilt University. (1991). Technology and the design of generative learning environments. *Educational Technology, 31*(5) 34–40.

Cognition and Technology Group at Vanderbilt University. (1997). *The Jasper Project: Lessons in curriculum, instruction, assessment, and professional development.* Mahwah, NJ: Erlbaum.

Collins, A., Brown, J. S., & Newman, S. E. (1989). Cognitive apprenticeship: Teaching the crafts of reading, writing, and mathematics. In L. B. Resnick (Ed.), *Knowing, learning, and instruction: Essays in honor of Robert Glaser* (pp. 453–494). Hillsdale, NJ: Erlbaum.

Dewey, J. (1933). *How we think* (Rev. ed.). Boston: Heath.

Hickey, D. T., Moore, A. L., & Pellegrino, J. W. (2001). The motivational and academic consequences of elementary mathematics environments: Do constructivist innovations and reforms make a difference? *American Educational Research Journal, 38,* 611–652.

Lave, J., Smith, S., & Butler, M. (1988). Problem solving as an everyday practice. In R. I. Charles & E. A. Silver (Eds.), *The teaching and assessing of mathematical problem solving* (pp. 61–81). Reston, VA: National Council of Teachers of Mathematics.

Whitehead, A. N. (1929). *The aims of education.* New York: Macmillan.

Brian A. Bottge

ANDERSON, JOHN ROBERT
1947–

John Robert Anderson was born August 27, 1947, in Vancouver, British Columbia. He obtained his undergraduate training in psychology at University British Columbia, and he completed his PhD at Stanford University working with Gordon Bower. After a brief faculty appointment at Yale, he moved to Carnegie Mellon University in 1978 and has remained there into the early 2000s, with faculty appointments in psychology and computer science. He is married to cognitive psychologist Lynne Reder and has collaborated with her on a number of projects throughout his career. He has received a number of important recognitions of his excellence in basic psychological and cognitive science research: the American Psychological Association's Early Career Award in 1978; APA's Distinguished Scientific Contribution Award in 1994; election to the National Academy of Sciences and the American Academy of Arts and Science in 1999; the David Rumelhart Prize for Contributions to the Formal Analysis of Human Cognition in 2004; and the Dr. A. H. Heineken Prize for Cognitive Science in 2006. He has also served as president of the Cognitive Science Society.

John Anderson's most famous contribution is the ACT theory in its various incarnations: ACT, ACT*, and ACT-R (as of 2007 on version 6.0). Interestingly, the ACT acronym matches the titles of some of Anderson's highly influential books such as *Atomic Components of Thought*, but in fact, the acronym does not stand for anything in particular. The ACT theories formally describe cognition in computational terms (i.e., with great depth), but in a way that unifies a broad range of cognitive activities (i.e., with great breadth). The framework is unifying in that it carefully describes many components of cognition (e.g., perception, categorization, memory, analogy, decision making, and problem solving) and has been used to understand many behaviors (e.g., a vast array of memory experiments, language learning, mathematical problem solving, scientific reasoning, and car driving, to name just a few examples). The theoretical framework has also been unifying in that it shows how cognition can have symbolic elements (i.e., knowledge and skills with complex, hierarchical structure) and subsymbolic elements (i.e., knowledge and skills acquired and applied gradually), an issue that has been somewhat divisive among other computational theories of cognition. Finally, the theoretical framework is unifying in that as of 2007 over 100 researchers worldwide directly use, build upon, and adapt the ACT-R theory in their own research.

To educational psychology, the ACT theories provide a theoretical framework for dividing any complex task into core elements whose acquisition can be carefully tracked and predicted. In all the ACT theories, there is a large division between procedural knowledge (knowing how) and declarative knowledge (knowing that), with different learning mechanisms for each. Performance in any task requires a combination of both kinds of knowledge (e.g., even a simple memory task requires knowing the rules of the memory task). The ACT theories describe how individual procedural and declarative knowledge elements are acquired through practice and gradually lost with time and how performance at any point in time can be precisely predicted through careful analysis of the learning history.

The ACT* theory formed the basis of a series of intelligent tutoring systems called Cognitive Tutors, the most influential of which is a high school Algebra tutor widely deployed in many high schools throughout the United States. The core insight behind the Cognitive Tutors is that feedback and practice can be optimized on a per student basis if student progress on individual knowledge elements is tracked. Experimental evaluations on the Cognitive Tutors have regularly found a one standard deviation improvement in student learning over traditional classroom learning. The Cognitive Tutors have also served as an important validation of the ACT approach because the highly irregular learning and performance curves associated with students learning a complex task become smooth learning curves when analyzed according to ACT predictions. These Cognitive Tutors have also provided a powerful research tool for testing various theoretical questions about learning with strong experimental precision but doing so in real classroom settings.

The move from ACT* to ACT-R reflected Anderson's highly influential rational analysis of cognitive behavior. Prior to this rational analysis, cognition was widely thought of as basically defective, and the job of psychology was to document those defects. Anderson's rational analysis showed how the general structure of the human cognitive architecture was essentially a highly rational system that tries to optimize problem-solving performance with limited resources in a complex but somewhat regular environment. For example, he showed how memory-forgetting functions closely approximated the way the world gradually changes with time and context. To educational psychology, this work shows how important it is to attend not only to the general presence or absence of information in the learner's environment, but also how critical the statistical regularities of that input (e.g., when tests are given) are to shaping student learning.

BIBLIOGRAPHY

WORKS BY

Anderson, J. R. (1976). *Language, memory, and thought.* Hillsdale, NJ: Erlbaum.

Anderson, J. R. (1990). *The adaptive character of thought.* Hillsdale, NJ: Erlbaum.

Anderson, J. R. (2000). *Cognitive psychology and its implications* (5th ed.). New York: Worth.

Anderson, J. R., Corbett, A. T., Koedinger, K., & Pelletier, R. (1995). Cognitive tutors: Lessons learned. *Journal of Learning Sciences, 4,* 167–207.

Anderson, J. R., & Lebiere, C. (1998). *The atomic components of thought.* Mahwah, NJ: Erlbaum.

Christian D. Schunn

ANDERSON, RICHARD C(HASE)
1934–

Richard Chase Anderson is an American educational psychologist and reading educator. He has strongly influenced educational theory and practice through his own research as well as through a teaching career in which he has mentored many leading researchers in educational psychology and reading education. To date, he has written two books, edited or co-edited another six books, and written about 200 articles and book chapters.

Born in 1934, Anderson grew up in River Falls, Wisconsin. He received a bachelor's degree, cum laude, in American history in 1956 and a master's degree in social science education in 1957 from Harvard University. He earned a doctorate of education at Harvard University in 1960, working with John Carroll, a pioneer in psycholinguistics. He worked as an assistant superintendent in East Brunswick, New Jersey, for three years, and then accepted a faculty position at the University of Illinois at Urbana-Champaign, where he has remained throughout his career.

Anderson has received numerous awards, including several of the most prestigious awards in education. In 1997 Anderson won the American Psychological Association Edward Thorndike Award for distinguished career-long contributions to the psychological study of education. In 2006 he was honored by the American Educational Research Association with the Sylvia Scriber Award for his research on learning and instruction.

Anderson was at various times director or co-director of one of the most prolific and influential research centers in U.S. educational history, the Center for the Study of Reading at the University of Illinois at Urbana-Champaign. Many eminent researchers participated in the work of the Center during its 15 years of federal funding. These included senior scientists as well as visiting scholars and graduate students who trained at the center before moving on to positions of scholarship and leadership throughout the world.

Anderson's research has encompassed many topics of great relevance to educators. Among these are schema theory, vocabulary development, learning to read, cross-cultural analyses of learning to read, and collaborative reasoning. Several of his key contributions are summarized below.

Anderson was among the leaders in developing schema theory and applying it to reading education. According to schema theory, when readers read texts, they use their prior knowledge to help them make sense of these texts. Hence, reading comprehension is facilitated when readers have relevant organized knowledge packets, called *schemas*, that they can use to interpret the information. When reading a narrative of a wedding, for example, readers apply their schema of typical wedding events (prior knowledge of the processional, the vows, the reception, and so on) and fill the slots in the schema with the details of the particular wedding described in the narrative (e.g., the details of this particular processional, vow, reception, and so on). When readers lack relevant schemas, or when they fail to activate their schemas, they understand and recall less of the new material. Schema theory can help teachers understand some of the difficulties that students have while reading, and it suggests that building relevant schemas and activating them can enhance reading comprehension.

Anderson and his colleagues also conducted a variety of studies of vocabulary acquisition. One finding emphasized that most words are learned not from explicit study but by incidental learning of word meanings from reading texts. An instructional implication of this finding is that encouraging students to read widely is important in vocabulary development.

Another line of Anderson's work focused on processes of learning to read in elementary school. A particularly important achievement was the 1985 book *Becoming a Nation of Readers*. Anderson was the lead author of this book, which arose from the work of the Commission on Reading, sponsored by the National Academy of Education. The book synthesized a broad array of research on learning to read. The authors presented this research in a way that was at once a scholarly review of the literature and a report that was highly accessible to teachers.

Anderson's later work had two tracks. In one track, he teamed with Chinese scholars to investigate learning to read Chinese. The research not only laid the foundation for building the essential literacy skills of Chinese children but also impacted the way Chinese children learn to read—with an emphasis on reading more and reading for pleasure.

In the other track, beginning in the early 1990s, he and his research team developed an approach to classroom discussions called *Collaborative Reasoning*. In Collaborative Reasoning, students engage in constructive argumentation in which they give reasons and evidence for positions they take. The argumentation centers around a central question relating to material students have read. For example, after reading material relating to wolves and wolf re-introduction and management policies, students discuss whether a town should be allowed to hire professional hunters to kill the wolves that wander near the town. Anderson and his collaborators found that Collaborative Reasoning has very positive effects on classroom discourse and also improves students' reasoning and argumentation.

In his career, Anderson forged new ways of thinking about reading, learning, and classroom discussions. He conducted rigorous studies in both the laboratory and in the complexities of the classroom, and he trained new generations of educational researchers, to whom he was a great mentor and friend.

BIBLIOGRAPHY

WORKS BY

Anderson, R. C. (1959). Learning in discussions: A resume of the authoritarian-democratic studies. *Harvard Educational Review, 29*, 201–215.

Anderson, R. C. (1977). The notion of schemata and the educational enterprise. In R. C. Anderson, R. J. Spiro, and W. E. Montague (Eds.), *Schooling and the acquisition of knowledge.* Hillsdale, NJ: Erlbaum, 415–431.

Anderson, R. C. (1994). Role of reader's schema in comprehension, learning, and memory. In R. Ruddell and M. Ruddell (Eds.), *Theoretical Models and Processes of Reading* (pp. 469–482). Newark, DE: International Reading Association.

Anderson, R. C., Chinn, C., Chang, J., Waggoner, M., & Yi, H. (1997) On the logical integrity of children's arguments. *Cognition and Instruction, 15(2),* 135–167.

Anderson, R. C., Hiebert, E. H., Scott, J. A., Wilkinson, I. G. (1985). *Becoming a Nation of Readers.* Champaign, IL: Center for the Study of Reading.

Anderson, R. C., & Li, W. (2005). A cross-language perspective on learning to read. In A. McKeough, J. L. Lupart, L. Phillips, and V. Timmons (Eds.), *Understanding Literacy Development: A Global View* (pp. 65–91). Hillsdale, NJ: Erlbaum.

Anderson, R. C., Nguyen-Jahiel, K., McNurlen, B., Archodidou, A., Kim, S.-Y., Reznitskaya, A., et al. (2001). The snowball phenomenon: Spread of ways of talking and ways of thinking across groups of children. *Cognition and Instruction,* 19, 1–46.

Chinn, C., Anderson, R. C., Waggoner, M. (2001). Patterns of discourse during two kinds of literature discussion. *Reading Research Quarterly,* 36, 378–411.

Kim, I., Anderson R. C., Nguyen-Jahiel, K., & Archodidiou, A. (2007). Discourse patterns in children's collaborative online discussions. *The Journal of the Learning Sciences,16,* 333–370.

Kuo, L.-J., & Anderson, R. C. (2006). Morphological awareness and learning to read: A cross-language perspective. *Educational Psychologist,* 41, 161–180.

Reznitskaya, A., Anderson, R. C., & Kuo, L.-J. (2007). Teaching and learning argumentation. *Elementary School Journal,* 107, 449–472.

Clark A. Chinn
Kim Nguyen-Jahiel

ANXIETY

Anxiety is an important subject in educational psychology because it is known to interfere with children's ability to learn, the level of their classroom performance, and their relationships with classmates. Anxiety can be understood as a multisystem response to an object or event that arouses apprehension. It involves biochemical and neuromuscular changes in the body, memories of past events (including personal history), anticipation of future outcomes, and appraisal of the present situation. While animals clearly experience fear, as far as is known only humans experience anxiety. Children who feel anxious in school interpret some aspect of the classroom situation through the lens of their past experiences and anticipate negative outcomes. According to Lagattuta, children begin to worry about the future because of a negative past event at some point between the ages of three and five. The specific trigger of classroom anxiety is commonly a test or task of some kind, but it may also be a feature of the social environment, such as a recent move to a new school, general feelings of isolation or rejection, verbal criticism from the teacher, or bullying by schoolmates. In general, schoolchildren are most likely to experience anxiety when they are worried about something bad happening in the future but feel powerless to avoid it, prevent it, or otherwise influence the outcome.

DEFINITIONS

In 1972 Spielberger introduced the distinction between state and trait anxiety that is commonly used by school psychologists in the early 21st century. State anxiety refers to the unpleasant sensation of fear experienced in the face of a threat, whether physical or psychological. State anxiety presupposes a cognitive perception or appraisal of a threat; that is, individuals must know or believe on some level that a specific situation is in fact dangerous or threatening. Test anxiety is a commonly encountered form of state anxiety, as is anxiety related to a public athletic competition or musical performance. Typically, children or adolescents feel less anxious after the stressful event is over. Trait anxiety, by contrast, is an aspect of personality—namely, a tendency to experience state anxiety when confronted with a threat—that remains stable in a specific individual over time but varies from one individual to another. High levels of trait anxiety are closely linked to neuroticism as defined by Eysenck and Eysenck (1991).

In 1980 Spielberger distinguished between two features of both state and trait anxiety, namely worry and emotionality. Worry is related to the cognitive dimension of anxiety; that is, how individuals assess the danger and their competence or incompetence for handling it. Emotionality refers to the feelings and physical sensations associated with anxiety, such as sweating, breathing heavily, feeling nauseated, or having a dry mouth. Worry and emotionality are usually present at the same time; however, they are not necessarily closely related to each other.

Thus it is possible for children to be intensely worried but to experience only a moderate level of physical arousal or vice versa.

The physical symptoms that children may experience when they are feeling anxious are related to the so-called fight-or-flight reaction to stress. Some essential body functions, such as breathing, heart rate, and sweating, speed up or intensify, while other functions such as digestion, secretion of saliva, and blood flow within the skin slow down. Children may experience a wide range of bodily sensations, including dry mouth, nausea, vomiting, diarrhea, or abdominal cramps; dizziness, choking sensations, or shortness of breath; rapid pulse or heartbeat, irregular heart rhythms, headache, or heavy sweating; muscle tension or cramps, chest pain, shakiness and impaired physical coordination, general fatigue, or stiff or sore joints. Parents or teachers may notice other signs such as insomnia, general restlessness, or pacing the floor.

Behavioral changes associated with anxiety in children include general irritability and moodiness; regression to earlier stages of development, often around eating habits or toilet training issues; crying, angry outbursts, or temper tantrums; clinging to parents or caregivers; or avoidance behaviors, which may include school refusal, avoidance of after-school activities, or selective mutism (being unable to speak during anxious periods but able to do so normally at other times).

EVALUATION AND ASSESSMENT

Evaluation and assessment of school-related anxiety in children is a difficult and complex process. First, anxiety is a universal human experience that most children are able to manage. According to Huberty (2004), most schoolchildren cope satisfactorily with anxiety or can be taught to cope more effectively without the need for formal therapy. Between 15 and 20 percent of children in the United States, however, may eventually require treatment for a childhood anxiety disorder.

Second, some childhood fears are age-related; for example, separation anxiety is normal in children between the ages of 18 months and 3 years but usually resolves by the time the child is 4 years or older. At some point around age 8, children's anxieties become less specific; they are replaced by more abstract worries. In other words, children worry less about a mean dog next door or a monster under the bed and more about fitting in with new classmates or making friends at school. Older children and adolescents commonly experience anxiety related to schoolwork, social popularity, and other areas of competition, as they become aware that academic and social competencies are important for success in the workplace as well as in marriage and in procreation. But because children vary in their developmental timetables, it can be difficult to assess whether an anxious child is simply going through a phase or requires closer evaluation.

Third, recent changes in a child's life, such as geographical relocation, starting a new grade, changes in the family structure (such as divorce, death, or remarriage), chronic illness, or parental job loss can affect the child's normal reactions to tests and other anxiety-provoking experiences in school. It may take time to discern whether the child is adjusting to a new situation or whether the child needs additional help. Huberty recommends looking at the child's daily functioning to determine whether professional help is needed. If children are having difficulty with everyday classroom activities, then the anxiety must be addressed regardless of its cause. Evaluating the degree to which the anxiety is interfering with daily life will guide answers to such questions as whether the anxiety is typical for the child's age, whether it is limited to specific learning situations (such as mathematics or foreign-language classes), or whether it appears across a range of activities in the child's life.

Fourth, the physical symptoms associated with anxiety may be caused by a range of other diseases and disorders; thus it is important to rule out such disorders before giving the child a psychological evaluation. In addition, side effects to some medicine should be considered. For example, some cold or asthma medications may cause anxiety symptoms in some children.

If the physical examination gives normal results, and if children still have difficulty with homework or other school-related activities, they may need further evaluation by one or more professionals qualified to diagnose and treat anxiety-related problems in children or adolescents. They may give children one or more brief self-report instruments to screen for excessive anxiety as well as clinician-administered tests.

The State-Trait Anxiety Inventory for Children (STAIC), first used in 1973, is a widely used clinician-administered instrument for measuring state and trait anxiety in children. As of 2008, it was considered the standard in the field and had been translated into more foreign languages than any other measure of anxiety in children. The STAIC is designed for use in children from 9 to 12 years of age and requires about 10 to 20 minutes to complete. It has two 20-item scales: an S-anxiety scale that measures how the child feels at the specific point in time when completing the inventory, and a T-anxiety scale that elicits the child's general feelings of anxiety over time. The STAIC has been used to measure differences in trait anxiety between boys and girls as well as differences between children from different social classes. It has also been used to evaluate the effect of state anxiety on children's ability to recall information accurately.

Another clinician-administered instrument, the Beck Anxiety Inventory (BAI), is used to distinguish between anxiety and depression in children over the age of 7. The STAIC and the BAI are used in psychological research as well as in clinical diagnosis.

Common screening measures include the Screen for Child Anxiety Related Disorders (SCARED), which consists of 41 items; or the Multi-dimensional Anxiety Scale for Children (MASC), which consists of 39 items. These two instruments are designed for children between the ages of 8 and 19 and can be completed in five to 15 minutes. The Spence Children's Anxiety Scale (SCAS), intended for children between 8 and 12 years of age, consists of 45 items and can be completed in five to 10 minutes. A 34-item version of the SCAS for children from 2.5 to 6.5 years of age is designed to be completed by parents. Muris and colleagues (2002) reported that these screeners are reliable and internally consistent instruments that yield results strongly correlated with scores on the STAIC.

ASSOCIATED FACTORS

One question that has surfaced repeatedly is whether children in the early 2000s are more anxious than their counterparts in previous generations. This question has been asked in connection with state as well as trait anxiety. Twenge reviewed three major explanations for the reported increase in trait anxiety in children between the 1950s and 1990s, namely an increase in overall threats to life and health; increased economic hardship; and loss of social connectedness. After analyzing a number of studies, she came to the conclusion that self-reported levels of anxiety have risen "about a standard deviation between the 1950s and 1990s, a result consistent across samples of college students and children and across different measures" (Twenge, 2000, p. 1018). She attributes the rise in children's anxiety to a combination of worry about personal safety and loss of social connectedness, with economic conditions having a smaller impact.

On the individual level, some children appear to be genetically predisposed to high levels of trait anxiety, as Eley and others have reported in twin studies. Children with a temperament marked by behavioral inhibition (avoidance of new stimuli) are also more likely to develop high levels of trait anxiety. By contrast, Degnon and Fox reported in 2007 that behavioral inhibition is itself a trait that changes over time in many children, with some who were extremely inhibited as toddlers becoming more resilient in later childhood. The researchers attribute these changes in temperament to the development of adaptive attention skills, the influence of parenting, and the child's gender. With regard to gender in particular, Huberty cites findings that girls have higher levels of general anxiety than boys, as well as higher levels of anxiety related specifically to social acceptance. He attributes these findings to the social roles that girls are expected to maintain in contemporary society.

An external factor that increases children's risk of high levels of trait anxiety is low socioeconomic status (SES). According to Papay and Hedl, there is a clear correlation between higher levels of trait anxiety in schoolchildren and lower socioeconomic status.

Some parenting styles have been associated with an increased risk of high levels of trait and state anxiety in children. Parental verbal abuse has been associated with anxiety in children, as have overly controlling parental behavior and negative or rejecting attitudes toward the child. The combination of excessive control and emotional rejection by parents has been shown to have a particularly strong correlation with high levels of anxiety in school-age children.

ANXIETY AND CLASSROOM OUTCOMES

Anxiety in children is a major concern to educators because of its long-term toll on future academic success and social adjustment. High levels of anxiety increase the likelihood that a child will make mistakes in schoolwork, thus drawing criticisms from teachers and parents that typically reinforce the anxiety. Test taking, bullying, and other anxiety-provoking situations in school may lead to school refusal, which in turn has both short-term and long-term consequences. The short-term consequences include falling behind academically, weakened relationships with peers, and increased stress and conflict within the family. Over the long term, a child with a high level of school-related anxiety is at risk for lifelong academic underachievement, substance abuse, mental disorders in late adolescence or adulthood, recurrent difficulties in social relationships, and employment problems. Other possible outcomes include low self-esteem, underestimation of competencies, and poor problem-solving skills.

Anxiety related to specific intellectual tasks—mathematical problem solving and recitation in foreign-language classes are the two most frequently mentioned—is known to affect eventual career planning. Some students decide against careers that require skill in these fields because they are made anxious by past experiences of difficulty or failure with math or foreign languages.

Bullying in the school environment is another factor in anxiety shown to affect classroom outcomes. According to Grills and Ollendick (2007), girls are more severely affected in their academic performance by anxiety related to bullying than are boys, even though boys are bullied more frequently.

MANAGEMENT OF ANXIETY

A multimodal approach is the most common recommendation for the treatment of anxiety in school-age children, in that anxious children vary widely in the nature and severity of their symptoms as well as the causes of their anxiety and the degree of their functional impairment. Teachers and other school personnel are usually consulted when a child's treatment is being planned.

Huberty recommends beginning the treatment of anxiety in children with psychotherapy rather than medications. Although the use of medications in treating anxiety in children is no longer controversial, these drugs should not be used as the only form of treatment. They are usually prescribed for children whose anxiety symptoms need to be reduced as quickly as possible, who suffer from concurrent diseases or disorders, or who have not responded to psychotherapy within a reasonable amount of time.

Several forms of psychotherapy have been shown to be effective in managing anxiety in children. Cognitive-behavioral therapy (CBT) is the approach most frequently recommended for children over the age of 6 or 7; between 70 and 80 percent of children respond favorably to it, with 50 percent maintaining their improvement over seven years. CBT helps children improve their sense of mastery and self-esteem as it reduces anxiety symptoms. It is also useful in correcting the cognitive distortions that contribute to anxiety in children; many studies indicate that anxious children tend to focus their attention selectively on threatening rather than positive or neutral features of their classroom. A CBT therapist teaches the child to identify anxious self-talk, to challenge it (with such statements as "That's just my fear talking"), and to substitute positive statements ("I can get through this!"). Key factors in the success of CBT include the child's willingness to practice the new behaviors when the child is not anxious and the parents' willingness to practice the new skills with the child.

A version of CBT introduced by Kendall in the 1990s is the Coping Cat program. The program teaches children to (1) recognize worry and physical reactions to anxiety; (2) clarify their feelings in anxiety-provoking situations; (3) develop a plan to cope effectively with a specific situation; and (4) evaluate their performance and administer self-reinforcement afterward.

Christophersen and Mortweet discuss the ways in which CBT can be used effectively in treating groups of anxious children as well as individuals. According to these authors, forms of psychotherapy that have been shown to be effective in anxious children include child psychoanalysis and psychodynamic psychotherapy. Parent-child interventions include family therapy for parents with problematic parenting styles and inclusion of the parents in the child's CBT therapy.

The American Academy of Child and Adolescent Psychiatry recommended in 2007 that teachers should be involved in the treatment of anxious children when the child's anxiety is interfering with classroom work. Specific suggestions include tailoring the length of homework assignments to the student's capacity to complete them without increased anxiety; identifying an adult outside the classroom who can assist the child with problem-solving and coping strategies; administering tests in quiet or private environments; and writing such accommodations into the child's Individualized Education Plan.

SEE ALSO *Evaluation (Test) Anxiety.*

BIBLIOGRAPHY

Almerigogna, J., Ost, J., Bull, R., & Akehurst, L. (2006). A state of high anxiety: How non-supportive interviewers can increase the suggestibility of child witnesses. *Applied Cognitive Psychology.* Retrieved April 7, 2008, from http://www.port.ac.uk/departments/academic/psychology/staff/downloads/filetodownload,62622,en.pdf.

Christophersen, E. R., & Mortweet, S. L. (2001). *Treatments that work with children: Empirically supported strategies for managing childhood problems.* Washington, DC: American Psychological Association.

Degman, K. A., & Fox, N. A. (2007). Behavioral inhibition and anxiety disorders: Multiple levels of a resilience process. *Development and Pathology, 19,* 729–746.

Eley, T. C. (2001). Contributions of behavioral genetics research: Quantifying genetic, shared environmental, and nonshared environmental influences. In M. W. Vasey & M. R. Dadds (Eds.), *The Developmental psychopathology of anxiety.* New York: Oxford University Press.

Eysenck, H. J., & Eysenck, S. B. G. (1991). *The Eysenck Personality Questionnaire* (Rev.). Sevenoaks, Kent, UK: Hodder & Stoughton.

Fremont, W. P. (2003). School refusal in children and adolescents. *American Family Physician, 68,* 1555–1564.

Grills, A. E., & Ollendick, T. H. (2002). Peer victimization, global self-worth, and anxiety in middle school children. *Journal of Clinical Child and Adolescent Psychology, 31,* 59–68.

Huberty, T. J. (2004). *Anxiety and anxiety disorders in children: Information for parents.* Bethesda, MD: National Association of School Psychologists.

Hudson, J. L., & Rapee, R. M. (2001). Parent-child interactions and anxiety disorders: An observational study. *Behaviour Research and Therapy, 39,* 1411–1427.

Kendall, P. C., & Hedtke, K. A. (2006). *Coping cat workbook* (2nd ed.). Ardmore, PA: Workbook.

Lagattuta, K. H. (2007). Thinking about the future because of the past: Young children's knowledge about the causes of worry and preventative decisions. *Child Development, 78,* 1492–1509.

Muris, P., et al. (2002). Three traditional and three new childhood anxiety questionnaires: their reliability and validity in a normal adolescent sample. *Behaviour Research and Therapy, 40,* 753–772.

Onwuegbuzie, A. J., Bailey, P., & Daley, C. (1999). Factors associated with foreign language anxiety. *Applied Psycholinguistics, 20,* 217–239.

Papay, J. P., & Hedl Jr., J. J. (1978). Psychometric characteristics and norms for disadvantaged third and fourth grade children on the state-trait anxiety inventory for children. *Journal of Abnormal Child Psychology, 6,* 115–120.

Puliafico, A. C., & Kendall, P. C. (2006). Threat-related attentional bias in anxious youth: A review. *Clinical Child and Family Psychology Review, 9,* 162–180.

Spence, S. H. (1998). A measure of anxiety symptoms among children. *Behavior Research and Therapy, 36,* 545–566.

Spielberger, C. D. (1972). *Anxiety: Current trends in theory and research* (Vol. 1). New York: Academic Press.

Spielberger, C. D. (1980). *Test Anxiety Inventory. Preliminary professional manual.* Palo Alto, CA: Consulting Psychologists Press.

Twenge, J. M. (2000). The age of anxiety? Birth cohort change in anxiety and neuroticism, 1952–1993. *Journal of Personality and Social Psychology, 79,* 1007–1021.

Rebecca J. Frey

APPLIED BEHAVIOR ANALYSIS

Applied behavior analysis is the application of behavioral science to address socially important problems. It is one element of the larger discipline of behavior analysis, which consists of the experimental analysis of behavior, radical behaviorism, and applied behavior analysis. The field of applied behavior analysis emerged in the 1950s and 1960s from early theory (Skinner, 1938, 1953; Terrace, 1966) and animal research identifying basic principles of behavior (Honig, 1966). Behavioral principles, such as positive reinforcement, generalization, and extinction, began to be applied to socially important human behavior with startling and encouraging results. Sidney Bijou and Donald Baer (1961), for example, demonstrated that children with intellectual disabilities and very limited communication skills could learn to interact effectively when provided with instruction based on behavioral principles. Children with self-injury and severe aggression learned alternative skills and reduced their dangerous behavior. These early examples of behavior change emphasized that behavior analysis was both a scientific approach for studying behavior and a technology that could be harnessed for positive social change. This distinction between applied behavior analysis as a field of science, and applied behavior analysis as a technology for intervention, is important. The core features of applied behavior analysis exist in both, but are emphasized differently when the goal is to advance the science of human behavior rather than address a personal intervention need.

Applied behavior analysis became a distinct field of study in 1968 with the launching of the *Journal of Applied Behavior Analysis* and the classic, inaugural article by Donald Baer, Montrose Wolf, and Todd Risley (1968). These authors used this article to describe eight defining dimensions of applied behavior analysis: (a) applied (b) behavioral, (c) analytic, (d) technological, (e) conceptually systematic, (f) effective, (g) generalizable, and (h) durable. These dimensions warrant review for anyone interested in understanding and contributing to the field.

MEANING OF APPLIED

Applied behavior analysis is a science guided by values. While behavior analysis as a field focuses on variables affecting behavior (and that can be any behavior by any organism) applied behavior analysis is the study of variables that affect socially valued human behavior. The very first feature of an applied behavior analysis research study is description of the social issue or concern under study. What is the behavior of study, and what criterion would make that behavior appropriate and acceptable for that individual in his context? Applied behavior analysis is a science/technology with an overt goal of improving society, of assisting people to achieve identified goals, and of applying the science of human behavior toward those ends.

It is worth noting that the initial dimension selected by Baer, Wolf, and Risley to define applied behavior analysis was that the analysis must focus on problems in which society shows a clear interest and concern. The applied element of applied behavior analysis is defined not in technology, procedure, or science, but in the social value of the issues under study. As such, research and practice in applied behavior analysis typically will not only focus on highly valued behavior (e.g., reading, speaking, social interaction, play) but will examine that behavior in the actual context where it typically occurs. One of the underlying messages from behavior analysis is the central role that contextual variables (prompts, social opportunities, consequences) have on behavior. Thus an applied understanding of human behavior requires study of that behavior in natural contexts. For example, an applied study of reinforcement would be more likely to occur with a valued behavior, such as reading, in a natural context, such as a school or home, rather than with a behavior such as lever pressing studied in a laboratory setting. Some applied behavior analysis research may occur in atypical contexts such as clinics when the goal is to isolate variables that are causing the behavior, but even then the ultimate goal is to apply what is learned to more natural settings. For example, a child who exhibits self-injury may receive assessment in a clinic in which conditions can be managed with precision and safety to determine what triggers and maintains the behavior. The goal of the resulting intervention, however, would be to achieve behavior change in the child's typical home and school. The applied dimension of applied behavior analysis emphasizes valued behavior in typical contexts.

FOCUS ON BEHAVIOR

Applied behavior analysis focuses on observable human behavior. There are increasingly sophisticated definitions of behavior (Johnston & Pennypacker, 1980), but the basic message is that the focus of an applied behavior analysis is human behavior that can be observed and counted. The emphasis on observable behavior is part of the precision that makes applied behavior analysis a science. Importantly, observed does not necessarily imply a focus only on behavior that is observable by others—simply that the behavior be observable at least by the person exhibiting that behavior (Skinner, 1953). Thus, thinking is considered a behavior but inferred, internal states such as anger would not be a focus for applied behavior analysis, but hitting, kicking, screaming, throwing would be observable and countable behaviors suitable for study. Because applied behavior analysis focuses on changing behavior via altering events around the behavior, the focus most often is on behaviors that are observable to others as well as to the person exhibiting the behavior.

The goal in applied behavior analysis is the direct study of behavioral phenomena. If eating were the focus of the analysis, then the study would likely involve observing and counting bites or calories ingested. The study would not, for example, focus on verbal descriptions of what was eaten. Verbal descriptions would be an indirect measure of what was eaten (though a direct measure of talking about eating). Similarly, if a study were examining a child's screaming, the analysis would not focus on fear or anxiety (which are not observable or countable) but on the behavior of screaming, and the conditions when screaming was most and least likely.

The emphasis on direct study of observable behavior reflects concern about the potential for confusion and miss-calculation that can occur when inferred emotions, intentions, and motivations are used as the heart of an analysis. A hallmark of applied behavior analysis is excruciating precision in the definition of, and direct observation of, the behavior under study.

ANALYTIC METHOD

Both as an approach to studying behavior and as a technology for behavior change, applied behavior analysis is analytic. As a science, applied behavior analysis incorporates a systematic process characterized by (a) valid, reliable measurement of behavior, (b) operational description of intervention procedures, (c) utilization of research designs that allow demonstration of experimental control, and (d) replication of findings. In most cases, research examples of applied behavior analysis involve a process in which individuals are observed over time and the researcher manipulates a specific feature of the context or setting to determine if this feature (e.g. the consequence following a behavior) will affect the frequency, duration or form of the behavior under study. The presentation of a consequence, such as praise, for example, would be manipulated within a formal experimental design that allowed the researchers to determine (a) if the behavior changed when praise was provided as a consequence and (b) if change in the behavior was functional related (causally related) to manipulation of the consequence (presentation of contingent praise).

As a technology of behavior change, applied behavior analysis is analytic in that repeated and precise measurement of behavior continues to be essential. When the technology of applied behavior analysis is used in home, school, work, and community settings it is not always expected that a formal research study will be performed. Rather, the expectation is that the procedures used in the behavior change effort will be drawn from previous studies, that the behavior of the focus individual will still be measured directly to determine if desired behavior change is achieved, and implementation of the intervention or practice will be done with precision (and most often with measurement of fidelity).

TECHNOLOGICAL FACTORS

Applied behavior analysis is a technology as well as a science. As with any technology it is essential that the specific elements of an intervention or practice are described with sufficient clarity and precision that someone reading the description can replicate what was done. This is often easier to say than to do. It would be one thing for an individual to describe her morning routine for getting out of bed and preparing for the day. It would be another thing entirely to describe her routine with sufficient precision that it could be replicated by someone reading her account. The same is true for describing how to teach reading or how to respond to a behavioral tantrum. Both as a science and as an approach to behavior change, applied behavior analysis is characterized by careful, complete, and specific description of procedures.

CONCEPTUALLY SYSTEMATIC

Applied behavior analysis is the application of behavioral principles. Behavioral principles have been defined from research in the experimental analysis of behavior and have been shown to be useful for explaining the conditions under which a behavior will or will not occur. Principles commonly applied in applied behavior analysis include reinforcement, punishment, extinction, stimulus control, generalization, and maintenance. There are countless ways these principles can be applied, and many examples of applied behavior analysis offer innovative applications. The use of positive reinforcement, for example, may include the delivery of praise and/or toys to develop toilet training skills with young children. But from a conceptual perspective it is not the praise or toys per se that are important, but the systematic application of positive reinforcement as a conceptual principle of behavior. Thus, applied behavior analysis should not be perceived as a particular procedure or set of intervention tricks (e.g., prompts to perform desired behavior; praise following correct behavior; correction, reprimand, or redirection following incorrect behavior), but the application of behavioral principles. It is this conceptual foundation that links the science and technology of applied behavior analysis.

EFFECTIVENESS

Applied behavior analysis is a pragmatic enterprise. The focus is on using principles of behavior to achieve not just improved behavior, but behavior that is improved to a level that it is socially important. It is useful, but unimpressive, to reduce bouts of screaming from 20 events in a day to 15 events in a day. This is clearly an improvement, but 15 bouts of screaming in a day will likely remain socially unacceptable. When screaming has reduced to once per week, the family may define the intervention as successful. Both the science and technology of applied behavior analysis are held to a standard of change defined by the values of the people in the applied setting. The goal is to change behavior to a socially important level. For example, in determining how many screams are acceptable those concerned with the child's screaming (e.g., parents, teachers, the child) need to say what is and is not acceptable. The task of someone using applied behavior analysis is to apply behavioral principles to create a context that produces acceptable and valued levels of behavior.

Generalized Effects. In their seminal article Baer, Wolf, and Risley (1968) established the expectation that applied behavior analysis should focus not just on isolated behavior change, but generalized behavior change. Socially important change seldom is contained in a single context. Working successfully with one teacher in one room is an excellent accomplishment for a young child who has autism and a history of severe self-injury. But for this accomplishment to meet the standards of applied behavior analysis one would look for an approach that produces student success across locations, across instructional contents, and across instructors. Most important behaviors must be performed across many contexts or settings to be practical, useful, and functional for the individual. The

focus on applied outcomes led the founders of applied behavior analysis to see generalization of behavior as a particularly valued achievement.

Maintenance of Effects. The strategies for producing a socially important change in behavior are not always the same ones used to maintain the effect across time. Although often discussed together, maintenance is different from generalization. Maintenance is based on a different outcome measure (durable responding across time) and also is affected by different variables (typically the type, level, and consistency of consequences). But like generalization, maintenance is important for applied behavior analysis due to its applied relevance: behavior change typically becomes socially important only if it endures for socially significant periods of time. It is wonderful to demonstrate that a child who previously refused to eat has learned to eat new foods and has been eating a healthy diet for a week. But the social importance of that demonstration lies in maintenance of the effect for months and years. Applied behavior analysis is a science and technology focused on practical, socially important behavior change. As such applied behavior analysis includes careful attention to the variables that affect maintenance.

CONTRIBUTIONS OF APPLIED BEHAVIOR ANALYSIS

Between the 1950s and the early 2000s applied behavior analysis demonstrated increasing value both as a science for understanding human behavior and as a technology for helping people achieve desired behavior change. Early applications of applied behavior analysis were most common with children and adults with severe disabilities, for whom other intervention approaches had proven less effective. As successful demonstrations of behavioral and lifestyle change became more common, the application of applied behavior analysis to typical work, school, and community contexts has increased. Descriptions of applied behavior analysis addressing extreme aggression by individuals with severe intellectual disabilities are now matched by examples of applied behavior analysis being used to teach social play skills, to decrease classroom talking out by children without disabilities, and to affect the quality and quantity of organizational outcomes.

An overarching message from this work is that the setting or context matters. Human behavior is more than personal willfulness. The physical conditions, social interactions, activities, and consequences within a setting do, over time, affect how people behave. Understanding why, when, and how these effects occur is at the heart of applied behavior analysis, and this is the promise that applied behavior analysis brings to help people understand both their current patterns of behavior and how to change dangerous and undesirable patterns of behavior.

TWO-PART LEGACY

Amidst the scientific legacy of applied behavior analysis two messages warrant emphasis. The first is that the consequences that follow a behavior will, over time, affect the likelihood of that behavior in the future. If a behavior (e.g., crying) is followed by a positive consequence (e.g., attention), then it is likely that under similar conditions in the future crying will become more likely. If a behavior (e.g., hitting) is followed by negative consequences (e.g., reprimand), then it is likely that under similar conditions in the future hitting will become less likely. Importantly, positive or negative cannot be determined a priori; what is negative for some people may actually be very reinforcing for others. This "law of effect" (Herrnstein, 1970) has an extensive research foundation and has been characterized in applied behavior analysis as the "function of the behavior." Research indicates that an individual need not overtly define that he is engaging a behavior to achieve a particular function (i.e., to get or avoid something) for that function to occur. A person's behavior is being changed continually by the consequences in his world, whether he is aware or not of that process.

The importance of understanding the function of a behavior has become especially important for those using applied behavior analysis as a behavior change technology. Building on the basic research and philosophical foundations of B. F. Skinner and others, Sidney Bijou is recognized as among the first to encourage the careful recording and manipulation of antecedents and consequences in his early research on child communication (Bijou, Peterson & Ault, 1968). Then in 1977 Edward Carr wrote a compelling analysis of how access to positive and negative consequences affects the self-injurious behavior of children with severe disabilities. The model proposed by Carr created a taxonomy of behavioral functions that has direct relevance for both assessment of behavior problems and development of behavioral interventions. Carr's paper was followed in 1982 by a research analysis conducted by Brian Iwata and his colleagues (Iwata, Dorsey, Slifer, Bauman & Richman, 1982) that has become foundational reading for all students of applied behavior analysis. Iwata et al. (1982) documented effects of different behavioral consequences on the self-injury of adolescents and adults with severe intellectual disabilities. Their results were consistent with Carr's model and provided the foundation for both future research and clinical intervention. Iwata et al. found that when designing interventions for an individual with problem behavior, it is as (if not more) important to understand the behavioral function of the problem behavior (the specific consequence maintaining the behavior) as

it is to define the type of disability or clinical diagnosis. An intervention that may be effective for a person who engaged in kicking maintained by attention may be completely ineffective for a different person who also engages in kicking but does so to avoid unpleasant tasks.

The impact of the vision, theory, and research that Bijou, Carr, and Iwata provided resulted in a major transformation in applied behavior analysis. Any current research or clinical intervention employing applied behavior analysis is in the early 2000s likely to include a functional analysis (the systematic analysis of behavioral function) or a functional behavioral assessment (the use of interviews, direction observation, and/or systematic analysis to define behavioral function). Because the consequences following a behavior are so important, it has become a professional expectation (and in many states a legal requirement) that care will be taken to assess the behavioral function of a behavior prior to designing behavioral interventions and supports.

The second major message in applied behavior analysis research in the early 2000s has been emphasis on investing in prevention of problem behavior. This means understanding and changing the events and conditions that occur before problem behaviors are performed. Since H. S. Terrace (1966) first summarized the scientific understanding of how stimuli (events, actions, and objects perceptible to the senses) can control behavior, there has been on-going study of how stimuli come to influence when and how behavior patterns develop. This research is important for understanding practical issues such as how the stimulus *b* comes to control the sound /*b*/ for a child learning to read, and how the stimulus "please help wash the dishes" from a parent comes to control the response "whine and cry" from a child who does not find dish washing reinforcing.

Applied behavior analysis emphasizes the important role of consequences, but research results also demonstrate the key role of events that precede target behaviors. Events that reliably precede behavior are important if specific consequences differentially occur in their presence or absence. For example, if a student's talking out is ignored by substitute teachers but reprimanded by the regular teacher, then the presence of who is teaching comes to control the behavior: The student is more likely to talk out when the substitute is there. Clinical applications of applied behavior analysis now regularly involve (a) manipulating the antecedent stimuli in a setting, and (b) investing in teaching new skills that produce functional outcomes for an individual, as ways to prevent problem behaviors. If a child with autism, for example, finds the background hum of florescent lights highly aversive, she may engage in screaming, throwing, and hitting as behaviors that result in her removal from the room with the aversive noise.

Attention to prevention would suggest (a) remove the aversive noise by using lights that do not produce the negative hum, and (b) teach the child a communication skill that she can use to tell adults when she is in distress (without engaging in aversive histrionics). Changing the lights removes the aversiveness of the room and hence the function of screaming, throwing, and hitting—removal from the situation—no longer is relevant. Teaching her an alternative communication skill that produces the same effect (removal from aversive noise) gives her a socially appropriate (and more efficient) strategy for achieving the maintaining function.

The message from this example is that applied behavior analysis has matured beyond just the manipulation of positive and negative consequences. Both the research being done in the early 2000s, and the clinical applications of the technology, focus extensively on (a) the events that set the occasion (or prompt) problem behavior, and (b) alternative skills that can be taught to make problem behaviors unnecessary. In essence applied behavior analysis is being used to apply the principles of human behavior to the design of effective school, work, play, and home environments. This is an exciting development in that applied behavior analysis is being used as a technology to create situations that prevent problems as well as a technology to address problems when they develop.

The field of applied behavior analysis remains promising, but under-utilized in U.S. society. The contributions that basic principles of behavior can make to improve living and learning opportunities far outstrip current applications. The early decades of the twenty-first century are anticipated to show elaboration and scaling of these contributions. For the first years of the 2000s, however, (a) research in applied behavior analysis can be expected to improve the on-going understanding of how the environment affects human behavior, and (b) any clinical application of applied behavior analysis can be expected to (1) be based in application of basic behavioral principles, (2) include an initial functional behavioral assessment or functional analysis to identify the consequences maintaining the target behavior(s), (3) employ behavioral interventions that combine manipulation of prevention variables (e.g. antecedent stimuli and instruction on new skills) in addition to consequences, and (4) include measurement of behavior over time to assess effects.

SEE ALSO *Classroom Management.*

BIBLIOGRAPHY

Baer, D., Wolf, M., & Risley, T. (1968). Some current dimensions of applied behavior analysis. *Journal of Applied Behavior Analysis. 1,* 91–97.

Bijou, S., & Baer, D. (1961). *Child development I: A systematic and empirical theory.* Upper Saddle River, NJ: Prentice Hall.

Bijou, S., Peterson, R., & Ault, M. (1968). A method to integrate descriptive and experimental field studies at the level of data and empirical concepts. *Journal of Applied Behavior Analysis, 1,* 175–191.

Carr, E. G. (1977). The motivation of self-injurious behavior: A review of some hypotheses. *Psychological Bulletin, 84,* 800–816.

Herrnstein, R. J. (1970). On the law of effect. *Journal of the Experimental Analysis of Behavior, 13,* 243–266.

Honig, W. (1966). *Operant behavior: areas of research and application.* Upper Saddle River, NJ: Prentice-Hall.

Iwata, B., Dorsey, M., Slifer, K., Bauman, K., & Richman, G. (1982). Toward a functional analysis of self-injury. *Analysis and Intervention in Developmental Disabilities, 2,* 3–20.

Johnston, J., & Pennypacker, H. (1980). *Strategies and tactics of human behavioral research.* Mahwah, NJ: Lawrence Erlbaum.

Sidman, M. (1960). *Tactics of scientific research: evaluating experimental data in psychology.* Boston: Authors Cooperative.

Skinner, B. F. (1938). *The behavior of organisms.* New York: Appleton-Century Crofts.

Skinner, B. F. (1953). *Science and human behavior.* New York: Macmillan.

Terrace, H. S. (1966). Stimulus control. In W. Honig (Ed.), *Operant Behavior: Areas of Research and Application* (pp.271–344). Upper Saddle River, NJ: Prentice Hall.

Robert H. Horner
Cynthia M. Anderson

APTITUDE TESTS

Perhaps no other construct in psychology or education has elicited as much debate as the question of what constitutes mental ability, how one might go about measuring it, and even how the resulting tests should be labeled. Most tests of mental ability include in their title some reference to intelligence (i.e., IQ) or aptitude. At the same time, some authors are moving away from the use of either of these terms for fear of the negative connotations they often elicit regarding their historically incorrect associations with invariant hereditability. An example would be the change in how the SAT is known. That "the *Scholastic Aptitude Test* became the *Scholastic Assessment Test,* and later simply the *SAT*" (Hogan, 2003, p. 279) is an example of an organization's move away from these highly charged terms.

Beyond labels, different theories of mental abilities focus on different aspects of and emphases on mechanisms and processes. There is no universal agreement or clear consensus as to which human processes are responsible for giving rise to intelligent behavior. It is, however, fair to say that most definitions and theories of mental ability include the use of the term *capacity* in one or more ways. For example, the capacity to learn, process information, learn from experience, adapt to one's environment, and think abstractly. Tests of mental ability are designed to quantify a variety of cognitive processes that underlie individual capacity.

INTELLIGENCE AND APTITUDE

Differentiation of mental ability in terms of intelligence and aptitude is often very subtle and difficult to disentangle. The problem is further complicated by the fact that scientists and test authors often use the terms synonymously, frequently making a separation between the two concepts a matter of semantics. However, examination of the content and purported uses of tests that include either intelligence or aptitude in their title allows for some differentiation between the two terms. Examples of intelligence and aptitude tests are presented in many major psychological measurement and testing texts such as Anastasi and Urbina (1997) and Kaplan and Saccuzzo (2005). Perhaps the most obvious difference relates to the purposes of their intended use. Both are primarily useful for predicting future outcomes or gauging potential for success. Whereas intelligence tests are typically used for predicting classroom or scholastic achievements, aptitude tests tend to be used more for gauging occupational success (e.g., informing job selections and military placements). Another distinguishing feature is that tests that in title purport to measure aptitude tend to be group administered, whereas those tests that advertise themselves as measuring intelligence are more often individually administered.

Beyond these differences related to use and administration, there are often only slight differences in the content of the measures. Most aptitude tests are comprised of large doses of content devoted to the measurement of cognitive ability constructs that would typically be found on an intelligence test (e.g., verbal ability, perceptual ability). Historically, aptitude tests were differentiated from intelligence tests by providing a broader assessment of abilities than the single IQ score afforded by intelligence tests. However, later developments resulted in an explosion of cognitive theories and accompanying IQ batteries that provide a much broader assessment of individual strengths and weaknesses, causing this line of distinction to become increasingly blurred. These same theories also provide the foundation underlying tests of aptitude. In addition, although aptitude tests may contain portions that are more obviously (i.e., as indicated by subtest labels) achievement related, many intelligence tests require acquired knowledge on the part of the examinee. These issues are addressed in greater detail below.

HISTORY OF MEASURING MENTAL ABILITY

The first attempt at measuring mental ability can be traced back to the early 1800s and the work of Sir Francis Galton (1822–1911). Galton's first attempts at measuring mental

Popular Aptitude Battery Subtests (and their Linkages to CHC Constructs)

Differential Aptitude Tests - Fifth Edition (DAT) and the Differential Aptitude Tests - Computerized Adaptive Edition (DAT Adaptive)

Verbal Reasoning (Gc), Numerical Reasoning (Gq), Abstract Reasoning (Gf), Perceptual Speed and Accuracy (Gt), Mechanical Reasoning (Gv), Space Relations (Gv), Spelling (Grw), Language Usage (Grw)

General Aptitude Test Battery (GATB)

General Learning Ability (Gf), Verbal Aptitude (Gc), Numerical Aptitude (Gq), Spatial Aptitude (Gv), Form Perception (Gv), Clerical Perception (Gv), Motor Coordination (Gp), Finger Dexterity (Gp), Manual Dexterity (Gp)

Multidimensional Aptitude Battery (MAB)

Information (Gc), Comprehension (Gc), Arithmetic (Gf), Similarities (Gc), Vocabulary (Gc), Digit Symbol (Gs), Picture Completion (Gv), Spatial (Gv), Picture Arrangement (Gv), Object Assembly (Gv)

Occupational Aptitude Survey and InterestSchedule - Third Edition (OASIS - 3)

General Ability (Gf), Verbal Aptitude (Gc), Numerical Aptitude (Gq), Spatial Aptitude (Gv), Perceptual Aptitude (Gv), Manual Dexterity (Gp)

Note: Gf = Fluid Intelligence, Gq = Quantitative Knowledge, Gc = Crystallized Intelligence, Grw = Reading and Writing, Gv = Visual Processing, Gs = Processing Speed, Gt = Reaction Time, and Gp = Psychomotor Abilities.

Table 1 ILLUSTRATION BY GGS INFORMATION SERVICES. CENGAGE LEARNING, GALE.

ability were met with criticism and largely failed to stand the test of time. This was most likely the result of his failure formally to understand and define the construct he was attempting to measure. Further, Galton's measures were primarily physical and sensory rather than mental or cognitive in nature. Modern theories of mental ability can be traced back to the mid to late 1800s and the theoretical work of Alfred Binet (1857–1911), Victor Henri (1872–1940), and Theodore Simon (1872–1961). Binet's early theories were operationalized in the Binet-Simon Intelligence Scale (1905), an instrument that was largely successful in identifying children with mental retardation. Success of the Binet-Simon Scales of Intelligence led to their translation and adaptation for use in the United States, and ultimately led to the first Stanford-Binet Intelligence Scale (Terman, 1916). Soon to follow were the group administered Army Alpha and Army Beta tests of mental ability. The former consisted of 10 scales designed for use with examinees proficient and literate in English, and the latter seven scales designed for use with those unfamiliar with or lacking proficiency in English literacy.

The eventual declassification of the Army Alpha-Beta scales led to a proliferation of commercially available tests through the mid 1900s, including the first Scholastic Aptitude Test (SAT; 1926). Wasserman and Tulsky

(2005) give a more detailed historical account of the origins of cognitive assessment.

Many of the historical attempts at measuring cognitive ability were often criticized for lacking a strong underlying theoretical basis. In addition, the primary benefit of these measures was largely in the prediction of academic outcomes and in the identification of children in need of special services. Despite the importance of these objectives, educators often sought ways in which the results of cognitive assessments could inform instructional practices. These attempts, however, largely failed to obtain empirical support. Several contemporary theories of human abilities have been proposed that hold greater promise for informing instructional interventions. The advantage of mapping test designs onto models of cognitive development that are both theoretically meaningful and empirically supported is that the assessment results hold greater promise for academic interventions that can be more directly applied to optimize student success in the classroom.

THEORIES AND MODELS OF COGNITIVE ABILITY

New and revised theories of cognitive ability, which are strongly rooted in the more empirically researched paradigm of information processing, have paved the way for new instruments and revisions of past traditions. Broadly, information processing theories are concerned with the cognitive processes involved in performing various tasks. Most contemporary theories operate within this paradigm, differing largely in terms of the number of processes believed to be involved, how the processes are related to one another, and the level of detail required for a proper assessment of children's strengths and weaknesses that are useful for informing interventions and predicting future success. Examples of operational models of mental ability that derive roots within the information processing paradigm include the Planning, Attention, Simultaneous, and Successive (PASS) theory (Naglieri & Das, 1990); the Gf-Gc theory (Horn & Cattell, 1966); Carroll's 1993 three-stratum theory; and the Cattell-Horn-Carroll (CHC) theory of cognitive abilities.

Although no single representation of the structure of cognitive ability is universally accepted among researchers, the CHC model appears to be drawing the most attention in terms of academic research and its influence on the development and revision of cognitive tests. (Interested readers may consult McGrew's 2005 study for a fascinating discussion of the birth of the CHC model.) The CHC model integrates the Gf-Gc (Cattell & Horn) and three-stratum (Carroll) models. Gf-Gc originates from the earliest model of the theory that consisted of only two abilities: fluid (inductive and deductive) reasoning (Gf) and

crystallized intelligence (Gc) largely characterized by knowledge acquired through acculturation. Evolutions of both the original Gf-Gc model and Carroll's three-stratum theory have occurred over time.

The CHC model is characterized by several broad-band abilities, including fluid intelligence (Gf), quantitative knowledge (Gq), crystallized intelligence (Gc), reading and writing (Grw), short-term memory (Gsm), visual processing (Gv), long-term storage and retrieval (Glr), processing speed (Gs), reaction time (Gt), and psychomotor abilities (Gp). Underlying each of these broad-band abilities are numerous narrow abilities that are useful for operationalizing the multidimensional aspects of the broad-band ability constructs. For example, fluid intelligence (broad-band ability) is influenced by several narrow abilities including general sequential reasoning, induction, quantitative reasoning, Piagetian reasoning, and speed of reasoning. Interested readers may consult Alfonso, Flanagan, and Radwan (2005); and McGrew and Flanagan (1998) for a more detailed description of the CHC model.

MEASUREMENT INSTRUMENTS

Recent decades have witnessed a swelling of cognitive tests on the market. The majority of these new or recently revised instruments are rooted within the CHC model of cognitive ability and measure, to varying degrees, at least some of the broad-band and narrow-band abilities represented in the CHC model. Examples of such instruments that are appropriate for use with children and adolescents in school settings include Kaufman Adolescent and Adult Intelligence Test (KAIT; Kaufman & Kaufman, 1993), Kaufman Assessment Battery for Children, second edition (KABC-II; Kaufman & Kaufman, 2004), Reynolds Intellectual Assessment Scales (RIAS; Reynolds & Kamphaus, 2003), Stanford-Binet Intelligence Scales, fifth edition (SB-5; Roid, 2003), Wechsler Intelligence Scale for Children, fourth edition (WISC-IV; Wechsler, 2003), Wechsler Preschool and Primary Scale of Intelligence, third edition (WPPSI-III; Wechsler, 2002), Wechsler Adult Intelligence Scale, third edition (WAIS-III; Wechsler, 1997), Wide Range Intelligence Test (WRIT; Glutting, Adams, & Sheslow, 2002), and Woodcock-Johnson III Tests of Cognitive Abilities (WJ-III; Woodcock, McGrew, & Mather, 2001). The 2005 study by Alfonso and colleagues contains descriptions of the specific CHC model components and influences embedded within these psychodiagnostic measures.

It is notable that the same CHC ability constructs that serve as templates for the development of tests that feature "intelligence" in their titles also factor prominently into measures of "aptitude." Table 1 lists several popular aptitude batteries along with the subtests that comprise them. It is also shown that each of the components of these batteries aligns with one of the broad or narrow constructs of the CHC model. As described in an earlier section of this entry, this illustrates the substantial overlap in the constructs typically assessed by labeled tests of intelligence and aptitude. Similarly, although aptitude tests may contain portions that are more obviously (i.e., as indicated by subtest labels) achievement related, many intelligence tests also require acquired knowledge on the part of the examinee. The popular Wechsler Intelligence Scale for Children, for example, contains several subtests that assess previously learned material (e.g., vocabulary, information).

IMPLICATIONS FOR LEARNING

The prediction of academic achievement and future occupational success remains a common practice in education as a means for guiding decisions related to student selection, diagnosis, and placement. Historically, interest in the prediction of academic achievement emerged from a variety of sources. One of these sources was the need for institutions of higher education to select students who demonstrated academic potential (Laven, 1965). A second source was from interest in the early diagnosis of students likely to suffer from academic failure, so that remedial interventions could be provided in a timely fashion (Keogh & Becker, 1973).

A variety of variables have been linked to school achievement, including cognitive ability, academic skills/readiness, language abilities, motor skills, behavioral-emotional functioning, achievement motivation, peer relationships, and student-teacher relationships (Tramontana, Hooper, & Selzer, 1988). As a result, it is important to note that any assessment of children's potential strengths and/or weaknesses should consider multiple inputs and sources. Nonetheless, evaluations of children's capacity to learn as measured by many tests of cognitive ability remain at the forefront of developing hypotheses about potential learning problems.

Psychodiagnostic tests have a rich history of accounting for meaningful levels of achievement variance (Bracken & Walker, 1997; Brody, 2002; Flanagan, Andrews & Genshaft, 1997; Grigorenko & Sternberg, 1997; Jensen, 1988; McDermott, 1984). In fact, it is often said that one of the most important applications of such tests is their ability to predict student achievement and future outcomes (Brown, Reynolds, & Whitaker, 1999; Weiss & Prifitera, 1995). From this perspective, cognitive tests can be considered useful for identifying children who are at risk for academic failure.

At the same time, there has been movement in the field to inform users of alternative ways in which aptitude

tests can be more directly tied to individual educational treatment plans. A few examples of the many ways in which aptitude test results can be used to guide individual instruction, enhance academic success, and suggest useful accommodations are provided below, and interested readers may consult Mather and Wendling's 2005 study for more details. Drawing from this source, the following examples illustrate how cognitive assessment results can be useful for guiding instruction and enhancing the learning of children. The examples are not contained within any one of the many available aptitude tests listed above, rather, they are general processes involved in different ways to student learning. As noted above, most of these contemporary tests have been constructed to tap into some aspect of the information processing system responsible for learning. As a result, these processes are largely measured in one way or another by most contemporary tests of intellectual processing.

Early language development is dependent upon children's phonological processing capacity. Children with identified deficits in phonological processing often benefit from direct instruction emphasizing linkages between phonemes and graphemes. The ability to retain and recall information over long periods of time is an important component of cognitive functioning. Children with identified long-term retrieval problems are likely to benefit from additional practice when learning new material. Including dynamic visual instruction diagrams or organizers will benefit children struggling with visual-spatial thinking, and children with processing speed deficits will often require more concise definitions of required tasks and longer periods of time to complete them.

It is important to note, however, that children at risk may have more than one type of aptitude deficit, and may also possess one or more strengths. As a result, it is important that educators take into consideration how these processes may be operating in concert. In addition, it is important to emphasize that while aptitude tests hold much promise for helping to understand the needs of children, no single test score should be used as the sole basis for decisions. A complete understanding of the potential influences of learning problems involves multiple inputs from multiple sources. It is equally important to remember that while aptitude tests explain a good portion of the variance in student achievements, they are in no way self-determining of academic success. Children's motivation, personality, classroom environment, self-image, peer relationships, student-teacher relationships, teacher instructional effectiveness, and so on also contribute to student success.

SEE ALSO *Accountability; High Stakes Testing; Intelligence: An Overview.*

BIBLIOGRAPHY

Alfonson, V. C., Flanagan, D. P., & Radwan, S. (2005). The impact of the Cattell-Horn-Carroll theory on test development and interpretation of cognitive abilities and academic abilities. In D. P. Flanagan & P. L. Harrison (Eds.), *Contemporary intellectual assessment: Theories, tests, and issues* (2nd ed., pp. 185–202). New York: Guilford.

Anastasi, A., & Urbina, S. (1997). *Psychological testing* (7th ed.). New York: Prentice Hall.

Bracken, B. A., & Walker, K. C. (1997). The utility of intelligence tests for preschool children. In D. P. Flanagan, J. L. Genshaft & P. L. Harrison (Eds.), *Contemporary intellectual assessment: Theories, tests, and issues* (pp. 484–502). New York: Guilford.

Brody, N. (2002). g and the one-many problem: Is one enough? In *The nature of intelligence. Novartis Foundation Symposium 233* (pp. 122–135). New York: Wiley.

Brown, R. T., Reynolds, C. R., & Whitaker, J. S. (1999). Bias in mental testing since bias in mental testing. *School Psychology Quarterly, 14,* 208–238.

Flanagan, D. P., Andrews, T. J., & Genshaft, J. L. (1997). The functional utility of intelligence tests with special education populations. In D. P. Flanagan, J. L. Genshaft & P. L. Harrison (Eds.), *Contemporary intellectual assessment: Theories, tests, and issues* (pp. 457–483). New York: Guilford.

Glutting, J. J., Adams, W., & Sheslow, D. (2002). *Wide range intelligence test.* Wilmington, DE: Wide Range.

Grigorenko, E. L., & Sternberg, R. J. (1997). Styles of learning, abilities, and academic performance. *Exceptional Children, 63*(3), 295–312.

Hogan, T. P. (2003). *Psychological testing: A practical introduction.* Hoboken, NJ: Wiley.

Horn, J. L., & Cattell, R. B. (1966). Refinement and test of the theory of fluid and crystallized general intelligences. *Journal of Educational Psychology, 57,* 253–170.

Individuals with Disabilities Education Act Amendments of 1997, Pub. L. No. 105–17, 20 U.S.C. 33. (1997).

Jensen, A. R. (1981). *Straight talk about mental tests.* New York: The Free Press.

Kaplan, R. M., & Saccuzzo, D. P. (2005). *Psychological testing: Principles, applications, and issues* (6th ed.). Belmont, CA: Wadsworth/Thomson.

Kaufman, A. S., & Kaufman, N. L. (1993). *Kaufman adolescent and adult intelligence test.* Circle Pines, MN: American Guidance Service.

Kaufman, A.S., & Kaufman, N.L. (2004). *Kaufman assessment battery for children* (2nd ed.). Circle Pines, MN: American Guidance Service.

Keogh, B. K., & Becker, L. D. (1973). Early detection of learning problems: Questions, cautions, and guidelines, *Exceptional Children, 39,* 5–11.

Laven, D. E. (1965). *The prediction of academic performance.* Hartford, CT: Connecticut Printer.

Mather, N., & Wendling, B.J. (2005). Linking cognitive assessment results to academic interventions for students with learning disabilities. In D. P. Flanagan & P. L. Harrison (Eds.), *Contemporary intellectual assessment: Theories, tests, and issues* (2nd ed., pp. 269–294). New York: Guilford.

McDermott, P. A. (1984). Comparative functions of preschool learning style and IQ in predict future academic performance. *Contemporary Educational Psychology, 9,* 38–47.

McGrew, K.S. (2005). The Cattell-Horn-Carroll theory of cognitive abilities: Past, present, and future. In D. P. Flanagan & P. L. Harrison (Eds.), *Contemporary intellectual assessment: Theories, tests, and issues* (2nd ed., pp. 136–181). New York: Guilford.

McGrew, K. S., & Flanagan, D. P. (1998). *The intelligence test desk reference (ITDR): Gf-Gc cross battery assessment.* Boston: Allyn & Bacon.

Naglieri, J. A. & Das, J. P. (1990). Planning, attention, simultaneous, and successive (PASS) cognitive processes as a model for intelligence. *Journal of Psychoeducational Assessment, 8,* 303–337.

Reynolds, C. R., & Kamphaus, R.W. (2003). *Reynolds intellectual assessment scales.* Lutz, FL: Psychological Assessment Resources.

Roid, G. H. (2003). *Standford-Binet intelligence scale* (5th ed.). Itasca, IL: Riverside.

Terman, L. M. (1916). *The measurement of intelligence.* Boston: Houghton Mifflin.

Tramontana, M. G., Hooper, S. R., & Selzer, S. C. (1988). Research on the preschool prediction of later academic achievement: A review. *Developmental Review, 8,* 89–146.

Wasserman, J. D., & Tulsky, D. S. (2005). The origins of intellectual processing. In D. P. Flanagan & P. L. Harrison (Eds.), *Contemporary intellectual assessment: Theories, tests, and issues* (2nd ed., pp. 3–38). New York: Guilford.

Wechsler, D. (1997). *Wechsler adult intelligence scale* (3rd ed.). San Antonio, TX: Psychological Corporation.

Wechsler, D. (2002). *Wechsler preschool and primary scale of intelligence* (3rd ed.). San Antonio, TX: Psychological Corporation.

Wechsler, D. (2003). *Wechsler intelligence scale for children* (4th ed.). San Antonio, TX: Psychological Corporation.

Weiss, L. G., & Prifitera, A. (1995). An evaluation of differential prediction of WIAT achievement scores from WISC-III FSIQ across ethnic and gender groups. *Journal of School Psychology, 33,* 297–304.

Woodcock, R. W., McGrew, K. S., & Mather, N. (2001). *Woodcock-Johnson III tests of cognitive abilities.* Itasca, IL: Riverside.

Timothy R. Konold
Gary L. Canivez

AR

SEE *Attributional Retraining.*

ARGUMENTATION

Argumentation is a form of discourse in which individuals take a position, justify that position with claims and evidence, and address possible counterarguments. In school settings, argumentation may involve contrasting alternative hypotheses in a lab, questioning the sources used to construct an historical account, or revising a literary analysis to include more textual support. In each of these activities, students engage in dialogue with a peer, an author, or themselves to evaluate claims and evidence. Whether it occurs socially, as it would in conversation or debate, or privately, as in writing or thought, argumentation involves building knowledge by considering claims in a framework of alternatives. Seen in this light, argumentation holds at least two important benefits for classroom learning: First, it can be used as an instructional tool to enhance learning. The process of argumentation can be used to prompt students to build and test the explanatory foundations of their knowledge. Second, argumentation can serve as a context for developing students' disciplinary thinking skills. Argumentation lies at the heart of all academic discourse, and when students learn to argue in the classroom, they learn to adopt the language, standards, and procedures for building knowledge in that discourse community.

ARGUING TO LEARN

Argumentation can help students develop a strong base of content knowledge in a number of ways. First, it provides a context within which students can elaborate their knowledge. When students engage in elaborative processing, they seek to understand the reasons why something is the case, rather than simply accepting that it is the case. They go beyond what is explicitly stated in a text or conversation to produce knowledge that is more complex, integrated, and, ultimately, more meaningful to them. This deeper processing of information, in turn, promotes memory and comprehension of the material to be learned. When students argue, they engage in a form of elaborative questioning in which they ask partners to clarify statements, justify claims, and respond to counterarguments (Kuhn, 2005). In these argumentative exchanges, students must move beyond accepting or advancing a simple assertion to questioning, critiquing, or establishing the grounds on which the assertion rests (Chinn, Anderson, & Waggoner, 2000). This process of argumentation, in turn, allows students to fill in gaps in their understanding, examine claims and evidence, and consider alternative perspectives. Students can gain similar benefits from the elaborative effects of writing arguments. For example, when students write arguments to link information in the texts they read, they are more likely to grasp the underlying causal relationships between events described in the text than when they write narratives, summaries, or explanations (Wiley & Voss, 1999). Thus, engaging in argumentation, whether collaboratively or on one's own, prompts students to make sense of content knowledge in a way that other more processes do not.

Argumentation can also be used to address student misconceptions in content knowledge. Science educators,

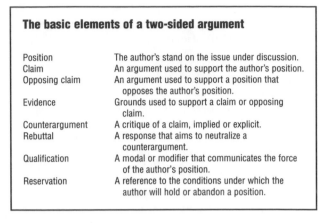

The basic elements of a two-sided argument

Position	The author's stand on the issue under discussion.
Claim	An argument used to support the author's position.
Opposing claim	An argument used to support a position that opposes the author's position.
Evidence	Grounds used to support a claim or opposing claim.
Counterargument	A critique of a claim, implied or explicit.
Rebuttal	A response that aims to neutralize a counterargument.
Qualification	A modal or modifier that communicates the force of the author's position.
Reservation	A reference to the conditions under which the author will hold or abandon a position.

Table 1 ILLUSTRATION BY GGS INFORMATION SERVICES. CENGAGE LEARNING, GALE.

for example, have long struggled with the problem of how to promote conceptual change when students hold misconceptions that interfere with learning. Challenging students to confront misconceptions can be exceedingly difficult because students may ignore conflicting information, misinterpret it, or, in some cases, even accept incompatible beliefs as true without realizing. Early research in promoting conceptual change yielded mixed results in part because confronting students with an experience that contradicts their beliefs does not prove to be enough to advance their understanding (Limón, 2001). Several studies have explored the effects of argumentation as an intervention for helping students to address prior misconceptions. When students argue with peers about the meaning and implication of conflicting data, they can prompt one another to re-examine their beliefs and assumptions (Bell & Linn, 2000), reconcile discrepancies in their collective understanding (Nussbaum & Sinatra, 2003), and fortify their conceptual knowledge (Zohar & Nemet, 2002). Studies such as these suggest that argumentation encourages conceptual change by making students' beliefs explicit and open to evaluation (Kuhn, 2005).

Of course, not all argumentation is conducive to learning. Social psychologists have long been aware of the potential in argumentation for polarizing people, making individuals resistant to examining or revising their beliefs (Lord, Ross & Lepper, 1979). These negative effects are heightened by a phenomenon called *confirmation bias*, or the tendency for individuals to seek out evidence that supports their beliefs, while overlooking, ignoring, or undervaluing evidence that contradicts their beliefs (Wason, 1960).

Here it is useful to distinguish two overlapping activities: dispute and deliberation. These kinds of discourse involve contrasting alternative claims, but they can be distinguished by their goals. In dispute the goal is to win the argument, whereas in deliberation the goal is to choose a best explanation or course of action. These divergent goals affect how individuals respond to alternative claims and evidence. In dispute, alternatives must be effectively eliminated, neutralized, or ignored. In deliberation, alternatives may be rebutted, but they may also be adopted, integrated, or change through compromise. However individuals choose to respond to them, alternatives are addressed in such a way that avoids bias and seeks coalescence of the arguments and evidence (Gilbert, 1997).

In the classroom context, students may have difficulty grasping the deliberative goals of argumentation. Many students have little experience with deliberation before they enter school, and by habit they follow the goals and structure of dispute. But in many ways, the classroom is the ideal context in which to introduce older children and adolescents to deliberation. Because it is so rare in everyday argument and because it goes against certain mental habits, students need to have deliberation taught in school where teachers can assist them in the process.

LEARNING TO ARGUE

Learning how to argue begins in the home and on the playground long before children come to school (Eisenberg & Garvey, 1981). Typically, by age five, when most children enter formal schooling, they have had extensive experience with argumentation in their everyday dialogue with adults, siblings, and peers. Whether fighting with a playmate over a toy or pleading with parents to stay up a little later, children come to understand that people can hold conflicting goals and desires. At some time during preschool, they realize that they must be able to produce reasons and evidence to substantiate their requests in response to the questions and claims of others. In these early conflicts, children often invoke personal preferences and motives to justify their assertions (e.g., "I want to play with the truck now because it's fun for me"). But as they develop, they come to recognize that arguments must be won not only by asserting a position, but also by addressing the legitimacy of that position in light of alternatives. They realize that they must appeal to mutually acceptable justifications to prevail and they must demonstrate that one position is better substantiated than others (e.g., "I want to play with the truck now, because you've had a turn with it and we all have to share.") This advance marks a critical turning point in two-sided thinking and lays the foundation for academic forms of argumentation in two ways: children begin to recognize the need for evidence to support their claims, and they recognize the need to address alternatives.

By middle school, most adolescents have learned to advance, contrast, and reconcile perspectives, pushing themselves and their peers to strengthen arguments by asking questions, requesting evidence, or proposing counterclaims in conversational contexts (Felton & Kuhn, 2001). In dialogue, young adolescents demonstrate a clear competence in producing the basic elements of argument as they respond to their peers' claims, questions, and challenges. But these sophisticated skills of argument are often limited to the highly supportive context of dialogue on familiar and generally non-academic topics (Stein & Miller, 1991). Despite the growing consensus that students come to school with the basic skills in argumentation intact, in academic contexts, they nonetheless produce simple, unsubstantiated claims that fail to address alternative claims and evidence. This gap seems to result from the unique demands that academic argumentation places on learners. Ultimately, students must learn how to adapt their basic skills of argument to meet the academic demands of classroom argumentation.

ADDRESSING DIFFERENCES IN CONTENT KNOWLEDGE

Due to differences in content knowledge, some students are better prepared than others to argue in academic contexts. When two children argue about who is the best pitcher in a baseball league, the quality of their discourse will depend on their knowledge of performance statistics and the qualities of good pitching. Similarly, to argue well in school, students need ready access to disciplinary knowledge in order to construct valid and effective arguments (Stein & Miller, 1991). For this reason, teachers should embed argumentation in units that offer students direct access to information and evidence in classroom discussions.

Limited content knowledge can also have a negative effect on students' ability to process and recall arguments that contradict their own views. More knowledgeable students have extensive resources to support the processes of encoding, retrieving, and reconstructing opposing side arguments, while less knowledgeable students are left to rely only on their position. As a result, less knowledgeable students are less likely to represent two-sided arguments in memory. However, presenting students with alternative arguments, especially when they are juxtaposed on point-counterpoint fashion, can reverse the biasing effects of limited content knowledge on memory (Wiley, 2005). Therefore, teachers should take care that students have direct access not only to information and evidence when they argue, but also to claims and counter-claims. Over time, with access to claims and evidence, students will be equipped to engage in effective argumentation and gain access to its beneficial effects on knowledge building.

DEVELOPING STANDARDS FOR EVIDENCE USE

Successful students produce better arguments because they are more familiar with content knowledge and because they understand how to use evidence to advance and evaluate claims in a discipline. In history class, for example, students must learn to cite primary and secondary sources while taking the biases of these sources into account. They also learn to draw legitimate cause-and-effect relationships and to argue effectively from historical precedent. Argumentative dialogue in the classroom creates a context for students to develop these skills. In the process of arguing with peers, students discover what questions need to be asked, what claims need to be proven, and what evidence might be used to prove it (King, 1990). They have evidence-use modeled for them by peers, and they also have the opportunity to make judgments about the legitimate use of evidence to support a claim. A history student, for example, might cite a textual source to prove a point, only to have a partner question the reliability of that source. A science student might cite data to support a hypothesis, only to have a peer use the same data to support an alternative hypothesis. Such exchanges provide more than a forum for testing understanding: They offer an opportunity for students to explore questions about why, when, and how evidence can be used to advance claims in a discipline.

But argumentative dialogue in this case is only the impetus for learning about evidence use. Teachers must follow up peer dialogues with discussions about disciplinary sources of evidence and standards of evaluation as students discover a need for them. In the history example above, teachers might follow up an argument about source bias with samples of two conflicting accounts and a discussion about detecting bias. The science teacher in the example above might prompt students to argue alternative hypotheses and then discuss the experimental control of variables. In short, argumentation can enhance the existing curriculum by providing anchor experiences that illustrate the essential role that evidence and its analysis play in knowledge construction. It gives students a concrete and immediate context in which to learn about evidence. Coordination of peer-dialogue and teacher-led discussion is essential for advances in the use of evidence. Without the addition of teacher-guided reflection, argumentative dialogue among peers runs the risk of perpetuating low standards and misconceptions about the appropriate use of evidence (Anderson, Howe, Soden, Halliday, & Low, 2001).

INTERNALIZING ARGUMENT STRUCTURE

To be successful in academic tasks, students must also learn to transfer the skills of argument from collaborative to independent settings. Whether they are writing an essay, taking a test, or preparing a report, students must be able to produce claims, evidence, counterarguments, and rebuttals without relying on their peers to prompt them. They must internalize the dialectical process, so that they can independently advance and critique opposing perspectives. Argumentative dialogue offers an excellent opportunity for students to discover that they already produce the elements of argument spontaneously. This discovery, in turn, can serve as a point of entry for developing a model of what complete arguments must include. To harness these skills of argument, teachers must introduce students to the vocabulary and structure of argument, helping them to see beyond the content of dialogue to its underlying structure.

In his seminal work "The Uses of Argument" (1958) Stephen Toulmin offers a useful framework for describing the elements of argument that has been adapted for use in a variety of instructional contexts and disciplines. Simplified versions like the one in Table 1 have been effective in introducing students to the basic elements of argument. But it is essential to introduce these elements in the context of real argumentation—either in dialogue or in written materials. Without reference to concrete argumentation, terms such as these are vague and offer few benefits to students. In a single introductory lesson, teachers can introduce students to these elements by helping them apply them to a brief conversation. With practice applying these terms to their dialogues (Felton, 2004; Osborne, Erduran & Simon, 2004), as well as prompts from teachers to include these elements during whole-group discussions (Reznitskaya et al., 2001) students can learn to produce the elements of argument more consistently on their own. The combination of firsthand experience in argumentation, and critical reflection on the strengths and weaknesses of the arguments they produce, sets the stage for internalizing dialectal reasoning.

Once teachers have introduced students to a vocabulary for describing argument and modeled its application to dialogue, they can then scaffold the transfer to writing. There are a number of reasons why argumentative writing is particularly challenging for students. First, novice writers often have difficulty discerning the underlying goals and purposes of writing tasks. Without direct instruction embedded in content, they misrepresent the purpose of writing, or more often, they write without elaborated goals to guide the planning and composing process. However, with explicit directives in goal setting, students can write more complete arguments (Graham, MacArthur, & Schwatz, 1995). In addition, students often have difficulty with the structure of genre-specific writing. Argumentative writing calls for new text structures that require greater organizational and linguistic processing than is required from genres emphasized earlier in the school curriculum (Coirier, Andreissen, & Chanquoy, 1999). Therefore, most students need support in developing the text structures that allow them to organize and examine their writing. This can be accomplished with the use of question stems, graphic organizers, or mnemonic cues (King, 1990; Osborne, Erduran, & Simon, 2004). Whatever the method, teachers should provide support to help students structure their essays. With consistent exposure to scaffolds like these, students learn to produce written arguments that acknowledge alternative viewpoints, cite and rebut counterarguments, and provide evidence to support their claims.

CLASSROOM IMPLICATIONS

To optimize its effects on student learning, teachers must make argumentation an integral part of the classroom experience. The questions teachers pose and the conversations that ensue have a direct impact on what students see as the purpose and form of academic work in general and argumentation in particular (Halldén, 1994). Through classroom discourse, teachers communicate their assumptions about the degree to which students must draw on evidence and justification to undergird their knowledge of the content. They also set implicit expectations on what it means to know or understand the content. Studies suggest that when readings, writing, and classroom discourse align regarding the goals of argumentation, students show measurable improvements in their ability to produce elaborated arguments (Nystrand, 1997). Conversely, when there is a lack of alignment in the curriculum, students do not show comparable improvements. Direct instruction in argumentative text structures and the goals of argumentative writing are insufficient in promoting change when classroom discourse lacks opportunities for authentic argumentative discourse.

Unfortunately, all too often, classroom discourse is dominated by direct instruction or recitation with few opportunities for students to engage in the meaningful examination of knowledge (Nystrand, 1997). Driven by the demands of a dense curriculum and high-stakes testing many teachers may feel that they cannot afford the time to teach thinking skills. Nonetheless, when compared to traditional recitation-based lessons, student-centered argumentative discourse is more effective in promoting student engagement and deeper cognitive processing of the content (Chinn, Anderson, & Waggoner, 2001). When students have the opportunity to collaborate in constructing arguments and examining evidence, they are more likely to find meaning in the content. A growing body of research suggests that while argumentation may take time away from coverage in the curriculum, it may also promote lasting effects in both content knowledge and disciplinary thinking.

SEE ALSO *Constructivism: Inquiry-Based Learning; Critical Thinking; Reasoning.*

BIBLIOGRAPHY

Anderson, T., Howe, C., Soden, R., Halliday, J., & Low, J. (2001). Peer interaction and the learning of critical thinking skills in further education students. *Instructional Science, 29*(1), 1–32.

Bell, P., & Linn, M. C. (2000). Scientific arguments as learning artifacts: Designing for learning from the Web with KIE. *International Journal of Science Education, 22*(8), 797–817.

Chinn, C. A., Anderson, R. C., & Waggoner, M. A. (2001). Pattern of discourse in two kinds of literature discussion. *Reading Research Quarterly, 36,* 378–411.

Coirier, P., Andriessen, J., & Chanquoy, L. (2000) Form planning to translating: The specificity of argumentative writing. In P. Coirier, C. Pierre, & J. Andriessen (Eds.), *Foundations of argumentative text processing.* Amsterdam: Amsterdam University Press.

Driver, R., Newton, P., & Osborne, J. (2000). Establishing the norms of scientific argumentation in classrooms. *Science Education, 84*(3), 287–312.

Eisenberg, A. R., & Garvey, C. (1981). Children's use of verbal strategies in resolving conflicts. *Discourse Processes, 4,* 149–170.

Felton, M. (2004). The development of discourse strategy in adolescent argumentation. *Cognitive Development, 19*(1), 39–58.

Felton, M., & Kuhn, D. (2001). The development of argumentive discourse skills. *Discourse Processes, 29*(2–3), 135–153.

Gilbert, M. A. (1997). *Coalescent Argument.* Mahwah, NJ: Erlbaum.

Graham, S., MacArthur, C. A., & Schwartz, S. S. (1995). The effects of goal setting and procedural facilitation on the revising behavior and writing performance of students with writing and learning problems. *Journal of Educational Psychology, 87,* 230–240.

Halldén, O. (1994). On the paradox of understanding history in an educational setting. In G. Leinhardt, I. L. Beck, & C. Stainton (Eds.), *Teaching and learning in history* (pp. 27–46). Hillsdale, NJ: Erlbaum.

King, A. (1990). Enhancing peer interaction and learning in the classroom through reciprocal questioning. *American Research Association Journal, 27*(4), 664–687.

Kuhn, D. (2005). *Education for thinking.* Cambridge, MA: Harvard University Press.

Limón, M. (2001) On the cognitive conflict as an instructional strategy for conceptual change: a critical appraisal. *Learning and Instruction, 11,* 357–380.

Lord, C. G., Ross, L., & Lepper, M. R. (1979). Biased assimilation and attitude polarization: The effects of prior theories on subsequently considered evidence. *Journal of Personality and Social Psychology, 37*(11), 2098–2109.

Newton, P., Driver, R., & Osborne, J. (1999). The place of argumentation in the pedagogy of school science. *International Journal of Science Education, 21*(5), 553–576.

Nussbaum, E. M., & Sinatra, D. (2003). Argument and conceptual engagement. *Contemporary Educational Psychology, 28,* 384–395.

Nystrand, M. (1997). *Opening dialogue: Understanding the dynamics of language and learning in the English classroom.* New York: Teachers College Press.

Osborne, J., Erduran, S., & Simon, S. (2004). Enhancing the quality of argumentation in school science. *Journal of Research in Science Teaching, 41*(10), 994–1020.

Reznitskaya, A., Anderson, R., McNurlen, B., Nguyen-Jahiel, K., Archidou, A., & Kim, S. (2001). Influence of oral discussion on written argument. *Discourse Processes, 32*(2–3), 155–176.

Stein, N. L., & Miller, C. A. (1991). I win—you lose: The development of argumentative thinking. In J. F. Voss, D. N. Perkins, & J. W. Segal (Eds.), *Informal Reasoning and Education.* Hillsdale, NJ: Erlbaum.

Wason, P.C. (1960). On the failure to eliminate hypotheses in a conceptual task. *Quarterly Journal of Experimental Psychology, 12*, 129-140.

Wiley, J. (2005). A fair and balanced look at the news: What affects memory for controversial arguments? *Journal of Memory and Language, 53*(1), 95–109.

Wiley, J., & Voss, J. (1999). Constructing arguments from multiple sources: Tasks that promote understanding and not just memory for text. *Journal of Educational Psychology, 91*(2), 1–11.

Wood, T. (1999). Creating a context for argument in mathematics class. *Journal for Research in Mathematics Education, 30*(2), 171–191.

Mark K. Felton

ASSERTIVE DISCIPLINE

SEE *Classroom Management: Assertive Discipline.*

AT-RISK STUDENTS

The construct of being at-risk originated in the field of epidemiology. When epidemiologists conduct studies, they try to identify so-called risk factors (e.g., obesity), which are characteristics of people or environments that are predictive of health problems (e.g., heart disease). After risk factors have been identified in the first wave of studies, epidemiologists then create interventions to reduce the incidence of health problems by targeting the risk factors that are both highly predictive and modifiable.

When the term at-risk is applied to the field of education, it pertains to children who are identified as being more likely than other students to experience undesirable educational outcomes such as low achievement, suspensions, or dropping out of high school. After identifying the children who are particularly at risk for such outcomes, the goal then becomes one of creating interventions to help these children be more successful.

EVOLUTION OF THE CONSTRUCT

In the 1970s and 1980s, the phrase *at-risk students* slowly replaced the phrase *disadvantaged students* in the educational, psychological, and sociological literatures (though the latter continued in use into the early 2000s). Since the early 1990s, however, an increasing number of scholars have advocated using the phrase *students placed at risk* instead of *at-risk students.* The reasons for these multiple shifts in reference pertain to arguments that have been made regarding the implications of these expressions for the causes of educational failures, optimal research methodologies, and intervention strategies. For example, it could be argued that the term *disadvantaged* conveys the idea that group differences in achievement are primarily due to differences in family income and educational opportunity. This term does not seem to commit the speaker to a particular research strategy for revealing the nature of achievement differences, but authors who use the term would presumably agree that achievement differences could be ameliorated by providing increased opportunity to the disadvantaged group.

In contrast, the descriptor *at-risk for educational failure* focuses the reader's attention on the outcome rather than on the cause of learning problems and does not necessarily imply that income and opportunity are the primary or sole factors that are predictive of educational failure. In addition, authors who use the *at-risk* phrase seem (intentionally or unintentionally) to commit themselves to endorsing the idea that the epidemiological model is a useful approach for understanding ways to promote educational achievement and prevent educational failure. Endorsement of the epidemiological model, in turn, commits one to acknowledging the benefits of a research strategy in which researchers (a) take a longitudinal, developmental perspective in which they follow children from the time they enter school until they experience educational problems, and (b) gather data on various characteristics of students and their environments to see which factors are most predictive of subsequent educational problems (i.e., risk factors). Moreover, the epidemiological model specifies that interventions should target the most predictive risk factors that are modifiable (as noted earlier).

Although the standard epidemiological approach has remained prevalent in the literature, some scholars have rejected it for several reasons. First, they argue that it seems to place the blame on students themselves by focusing on their personal characteristics (e.g., their poverty or lack of readiness) instead of focusing on the characteristics of schools and other societal institutions (e.g., communities; school systems; legislators and policy makers); in so doing, schools and other societal entities are apparently freed from having any responsibility for children not succeeding. Hence, the perspective suggests that students should be the targets of intervention, and schools do not have to change how they treat at-risk students. Advocates of the *placed at risk* phrase argue further that many of the predictors of failure that have been identified in epidemiological studies (e.g., poverty) pertain to what is lacking in children and their families. As a result, the focus becomes one of remediating deficiencies in children and using the deficiencies as a reason for restricting access to quality educational experiences.

Critics of the *at risk* phrase argue for using the substitute phrase *students placed at risk* because it carries the connotation that others (e.g., teachers, school systems) have placed students at risk by treating them in certain ways. Instead of merely remediating deficiencies, they argue, school systems should focus on building on the strengths that students bring to school (e.g., their knowledge, talents, and interests). Moreover, advocates of the *placed at risk* phrase argue that educational failure is really the result of a poor fit between student characteristics and the classroom environment. To improve the fit and help students be more successful, interventions should focus on creating changes in both students and the classrooms in which they find themselves.

Other scholars have pointed out two further aspects of the epidemiological model that they believe to be problematic. The first is that the model seems to assume that risk factors work in an additive fashion rather than in an interactive fashion. For example, in an additive model, factors such as poverty and inadequate instruction each increase the risk of failure by a certain amount and the total amount of risk is determined by adding together the amount supplied by each of the two factors. However, if risk is defined by the lack of fit between student characteristics and characteristics of schools, such an additive account fails to capture what is really going on. A more apt account, they argue, would be one that describes the interacting effects of multiple factors. If a school uses ability grouping, for example, and a student comes to school with a high degree of aptitude for learning the material presented to the top ability group (i.e., the student has the prerequisite knowledge and motivation needed to take advantage of this enriched environment), such a combination would lead to highly favorable outcomes. Other combinations, in contrast, would lead to much less favorable outcomes because there would be a poorer fit between students and classrooms.

One additional problematic aspect is that the epidemiological model tends to ignore the fact that risk categories are not perfectly predictive, that individual cases fail to conform to expectations. Although it may be true that many or most children from low-income families fail to attain adequate levels of competencies in reading and mathematics, for example, some do achieve in spite of their circumstances. Conversely, although it is true that

many or most children from affluent families attain adequate levels of competence in reading and mathematics, some do not in spite of their access to high quality environments. The focus on the degree of fit between individual children and their potentially unique circumstances at home or school allows one to explain both the cases that conform to expectations and cases that do not conform.

FURTHER ELABORATIONS

The phenomenon in which children attain favorable developmental or educational outcomes in spite of the adversity they face is called resilience. As noted earlier, variables that increase the probability of negative outcomes (e.g., low achievement) are called risk factors. Studies suggest that the likelihood of academic failure increases dramatically each time additional risk factors accumulate in a child's life. In contrast, variables that counteract or buffer the effects of risk factors are called protective factors. As the level or number of protective factors in students' lives increases, students are increasingly likely to demonstrate resilience. A third class of factors called promotive factors also increase the likelihood of favorable educational outcomes but do not operate to buffer the effects of risk factors per se. Instead, they promote academic achievement in both disadvantaged children (who are exposed to multiple risk factors) and advantaged children (who are not exposed to the same risk factors). The fact that variables in the third category promote achievement in advantaged children means that they are not working to buffer the negative effects of risk factors.

The risk factors that have been found to be predictive of academic failure include poverty, race, gender, presence of a learning disability or attentional disorder, mental health problems, inadequate levels of prerequisite skills upon school entry, exposure to multiple stressful events, living in a single-parent family, alliance with non-academically oriented peers, and repeatedly transferring to new schools. More specifically, children are more likely to experience educational failure if they (a) come from a low-income home, (b) are African American, Hispanic, or Native American, (c) are male, (d) have a learning disability, attentional disorder, or emotional disorder, (e) enter first grade without foundational abilities in language (i.e., a large spoken vocabulary and knowledge of syntax), literacy (i.e., the ability to identify sounds in words and recognize letters), and mathematics (i.e., counting skills), (f) have to repeatedly deal with stressful events such as marital discord, parental job losses, and violent acts, (g) live with just one parent, (h) have friends who are not good role models for academic achievement and engagement, and (i) move to new schools multiple times throughout their elementary school years.

COMPARISON OF SCHOOL ENVIRONMENTS FOR STUDENTS OF DIFFERING ECONOMIC STATUS

Low Income: Administrators encourage teachers to emphasize basic skills and mastery of those skills before higher level thinking is introduced. **Middle/Upper Class Income:** Classroom teachers are encouraged to emphasize both basic skills and high level thinking skills.

Low Income: The goals or expectations seem to be lower than the state benchmarks. **Middle/Upper Class Income:** State mandated benchmarks are the goals for at-risk students in this group.

Low Income: Skills are subject areas are taught as distinct and usually in isolation from each other. **Middle/Upper Class Income:** Skills and subjects are integrated and students have the opportunity to experience a more balanced curriculum.

Low Income: An ideal classroom is one where the students are sitting at their desks, quietly working. The teacher is in charge of all information and the dispenser of information. **Middle/Upper Class Income:** The teacher often sets up situations where there is collaborative learning is encouraged. There is a great deal of conversation and guided practice. Independent learning is the goal in this situation. Peer coaching, group discussions, hands-on activities, differentiated instruction are just a few of the ways that teachers secure success for at-risk students.

Low Income: Programs for at-risk students in Title One or low-income schools often involves the implementation of pull-out programs taught by Special Education Teachers where special skills are addressed away from the context of the regular education classroom. **Middle/Upper Class Income:** Programs in these schools tend to use the Special Education Teacher as a resource in the regular education classroom. Often the Special Education Teacher acts as a Collaborative Teacher in the regular education classroom. In addition, Special Education Teachers are used as pedagogical consultants.

Low Income: Although individual educational assessment meetings occur, it is difficult to evaluate the effectiveness of the plan by the regular classroom teacher. Often the classroom teacher does not know the accommodations. **Middle/Upper Class Income:** Because students are usually in a regular education classroom, the teacher is able to monitor the plan developed in the individual educational assessment.

Low Income: For various reasons, lack of parent in the home, transience, and unsettled living situations, there is very little family participation in learning. It is difficult to communicate with parents because they may not have a phone or are unavailable during the school day. **Middle/Upper Class Income:** Family participation in learning seems to be a key factor in success of students in this group. There are frequent phone calls and parent conferences. In addition, parents are encouraged to volunteer in the school.

Low Income: The Core Curriculum is static and doesn't reflect current thinking in pedagogy. Although encouraged to do so, the opportunity to attend workshops and seminars is not often presented to the teacher. **Middle/Upper Class Income:** The Core Curriculum is dynamic and reflects the needs of the school community and the community at large. Teachers are encouraged to investigate new and different ways to make learning happen. Workshops, seminars are made available to classroom teachers.

Low Income: The teacher is the holder to the key to the information or a dispenser of knowledge. **Middle/Upper Class Income:** As a partner in learning, the teacher is respected as the "go to" person for information on how to help the child be more successful.

Low Income: There is higher level of violence and non-standard social behavior in the classroom and the school community. **Middle/Upper Class Income:** In higher income level school communities, programs like Alternative Education or Alternative Schools are possible because of the additional funds available for such programs.

Low Income: For a variety of reasons, students in this population spend more time at home. Some researchers believe that this isolation causes poor academic success. **Middle/Upper Class Income:** Students who have neighborhood and community support can also find success in school.

Low Income: Students living in areas of extreme poverty often distrust adults, avoid making friendships, seem hopeless or disinterested, and respond only to orders. **Middle/Upper Class Income:** Students in this population are more open, seem to have a number of friends inside and outside the classroom.

Low Income: Teachers incorporate multicultural elements into the lesson plans. **Middle/Upper Class Income:** Teachers accept and encourage students' racial, ethnic and cultural differences.

Elizabeth Soby

In contrast, the factors that have been found to play either a promotive or protective role include average or above average levels of general intelligence, average or above average levels of specific academic skills (e.g., math skills), high levels of self-efficacy, positive relationships with teachers and other adults (e.g., clergy, counselors, coaches), engagement in and attachment to, school, alliance with academically oriented peers, parental monitoring and parental engagement in offspring learning process, adaptive coping skills for dealing with stressful life events, and ethnic identity.

These variables, described more fully in the next section, operate at different ecological levels. Whereas some are characteristics of neighborhoods, others pertain to family, peers, classrooms and schools. Moreover, some are modifiable and others are not. Of particular importance are those factors that have been found to mediate between risk factors and undesirable educational outcomes. Studies suggest, for example, that some children manage to fare well in school even though they live in low-income, high crime neighborhoods and attend schools that are plagued with staffing problems and lack resources. Those children who achieve in spite of such circumstances come from homes in which their parents demonstrate optimal parenting practices and utilize community resources (e.g., sport teams, church groups, libraries). School improvement programs can also be effective for mediating between risk and outcomes.

However, researchers are still in the process of determining the complete and definitive list of such factors and their relative importance (i.e., which ones are more strongly predictive than others). The provisional state of knowledge in this regard derives from the fact that researchers have generally not taken a comprehensive approach in which they assessed the role of all of the above factors in the same study. It has often been found that certain factors (e.g., parent involvement in their child's school) are predictive of academic outcomes when examined alone or in combination with a few other factors that do not predict strongly, but are no longer predictive when a larger list of factors is examined or when particularly powerful predictors are included in addition to the focal factor (e.g., prior achievement). Moreover, many of the risk factors listed above co-occur in the same individual. For example, African American students (risk factor 1) are more likely than European American students to enter school without the foundational skills they need to be successful (risk factor 2) and are also more likely to live in a low-income (risk-factor 3), single parent home (risk factor 4) and attend a school with a higher percentage of uncertified teachers (risk-factor 5) and peers who eventually drop out of school (risk-factor 6). When only one of the risk factors is studied in isolation and is found to be predictive (e.g.,

race), its predictive role may actually reflect its association with other predictors that are more authentically connected to, or causally responsible for, academic failure (e.g., poverty or lack of foundational skills).

THE IMPORTANCE OF A COMPREHENSIVE THEORY

Identification of the complete set of authentic and modifiable factors in the risk, promotive, and protective categories is the first step in creating more effective forms of intervention. The second step is to identify the most powerful of these predictors so that interventionists can know which factors should be specifically targeted as a means of producing more immediate or larger effects. The third step is to combine the set of identified factors into a coherent causal story using an integrative theoretical model. In other words, it is useful to know that particular factors are predictive, but it is even more useful to understand why these factors are predictive and how they conspire over time to produce educational outcomes. When the association between a predictor and an outcome is somewhat mysterious, it is not clear how one should intervene and some inferences could lead to the implementation of ineffective strategies. For example, in the association between poverty and low achievement, it does not follow that higher achievement would immediately ensue if additional funds were to be supplied to low-income families. The association may be due to the fact that high income parents provide opportunities at home that instill prerequisite skills in their preschoolers before they start first grade. If so, a more effective form of intervention than simply providing funds would be one in which parents of low-income preschoolers are taught how to instill reading and math readiness skills in their children.

A number of scholars have suggested that Urie Bronfenbrenner's Ecological Model can be used to integrate various factors into a coherent explanatory account of educational success or failure. In this model, factors are categorized in terms of the sociocultural level at which they influence developmental outcomes. The most proximal factors that operate within a student's immediate environment are said to be part of the microsystem of influences. This level includes factors such as a student's personal characteristics and behaviors (e.g., current knowledge and beliefs) and relationships with others such as parents. Operating at a more distal level are factors that influence other students in the same community and subculture such as local cultural norms, local educational policies, and belief systems shared by the local community. Collectively, such variables comprise the mesosystem of influences. At the most distal level are influences that comprise the macrosystem of the model such as national school policies and the belief systems shared by the larger culture of an embedded local subculture. Advocates of the Ecological Model argue that interventions must target factors from each of these levels in order to be effective and that certain factors at specific levels can mediate between risks and outcomes.

Alternatively, factors can also be integrated within an Opportunity-Propensity framework. Opportunity factors are those variables pertaining to the provision of high quality educational experiences. Students have been given excellent opportunities to learn when they are presented with the content required on achievement tests in an accurate and effective manner by a skilled teacher. Propensity factors are characteristics of students that pertain to their ability and willingness to take advantage of opportunities to learn (e.g., intelligence, prerequisite skills, motivation, and self-regulation). Factors in a third category explain the emergence of opportunities and propensities (i.e., why some students are given more opportunities and are more likely to take advantage of these opportunities): family socio-economic status, parental expectations, gender, race, and school policies regarding ability grouping. Because the latter factors operate earlier in time than opportunity factors and propensity factors, they are called distal factors. The Opportunity-Propensity framework suggests that interventions are more effective when they target opportunity factors, propensity factors, and distal factors.

EFFECTIVE PROGRAMS FOR AT-RISK STUDENTS

Arthur J. Reynolds of the University of Minnesota examined the extensive literature on early interventions and developed the following eight principles of effective early childhood programs: (1) target the children who are at highest risk of school difficulties, (2) begin participation early and continue until second or third grade, (3) provide comprehensive child development services, (4) encourage active and multi-faceted parent involvement, (5) use a child-centered, structured curriculum approach, (6) limit class size and teacher/child ratios, (7) include regular staff development and in-service training for certified teachers, and (8) engage in systematic evaluation and monitoring. Programs that conform to these principles and produce significant effects (according to meta-analytic reviews) include the High Scope/Perry Preschool program, the Abecedarian Project, and the Chicago Child-Parent Center program. All of these programs target a number of factors identified earlier as being promotive, protective, or relevant to educational opportunities and propensities.

In terms of programs for elementary and middle school students, Olatokunbo Fashola and Robert Slavin in 1997 published a best evidence synthesis of the effectiveness literature in which they included any program in which (a) the performance of students in the intervention schools was compared to the performance of students in appropriate comparison schools, (b) the program was implemented in more than one school and success did not appear to depend on unique or specifically favorable conditions at one school, and (c) the program was found to be effective for low-income and minority students. Thirty programs were found to meet these three criteria for inclusion. Fashola and Slavin concluded that programs tend to be more successful when they (a) have clear goals and monitor student progress toward these goals, (b) have well specified programs, materials, and professional development procedures, and (c) are disseminated by organizations that monitor fidelity of implementation.

In terms of interventions for older students, Fashola and Slavin published a follow-up best evidence synthesis of the literature on dropout prevention programs and college attendance programs for at-risk high school students. Two dropout prevention programs met the inclusion criteria for having credible comparison groups, being effective, and being replicable across settings: the Coca Cola Valued Youth Program and the Achievement for Latinos for Academic Success program. Four college attendance programs met these criteria as well: Upward Bound, SCORE, Project Advancement via Individual Determination, and Graduation Really Achieves Dreams. These programs were apparently successful because they focused on multiple causes of these educational outcomes such as self-efficacy, relationships with others, school-parent connections, and enhancement of prerequisite skills.

SEE ALSO *Bronfenbrenner, Urie.*

BIBLIOGRAPHY

Becker, B. E., & Luthar, S. S. (2002). Social-emotional factors affecting achievement outcomes among disadvantaged students: Closing the achievement gap. *Educational Psychologist, 37,* 197–214.

Boyki, A. W. (2000). Foreword. In M. G. Sanders (Ed.), *Schooling students placed at risk: Research, policy, and practice in the education of poor and minority adolescents* (pp. xi–xiii). Mahwah, NJ: Erlbaum.

Fashola, O., & Slavin, R. E. (1997). Promising programs for elementary and middle schools: Evidence of effectiveness and replicability. *Journal of Education for Students Placed at Risk, 2,* 251–307.

Fashola, O., & Slavin, R. E. (1998). Effective dropout prevention and college attendance programs for students placed at risk. *Journal of Education for Students Placed at Risk, 3,* 159–183.

Furstenberg, F. F., Cook, T. D., Eccles, J., Elder, G. H., & Sameroff, A. (1999). *Managing to make it: Urban families and adolescent success.* Chicago: University of Chicago Press.

Gutman, L. M., Sameroff, A. J., & Eccles, J. S. The academic achievement of African American students during early adolescence: An examination of multiple risk, promotive, and protective factors. *American Journal of Community Psychology, 30,* 367–399.

Johnson, G. M. (1994). An ecological framework for conceptualizing educational risk. *Urban education, 29,* 34–49.

Reynolds, A. J. (1998). Developing early childhood programs for children and families at risk: Research-based principles to promote long-term effectiveness. *Children and Youth Services Review, 20,* 503–523.

James P. Byrnes

ATTACHMENT

Emerging in the 1940s, attachment theory is the joint work of John Bowlby (1907–1990) and Mary Ainsworth (1913–1999). Attachment theory relates to strong, affectionate bonds that human beings share with each other. Bowlby specifically defined parental attachments as inherent, affectionate bonds between infants and their primary caregivers. Attachment relationships tend to be relatively enduring throughout the lifespan and serve two primary purposes. First, they provide infants with the comfort, care, and security that they need for survival. Second, they serve as templates for relationships that infants develop later in life with others such as friends, teachers, colleagues, and romantic partners. Since its inception, attachment theory has been examined by a number of scholars and continues to be researched in new areas. For instance, research regarding attachment relations among persons of color has begun to emerge. In addition, beginning back in the 1980s, several contemporary, key scholars began examining of the influence of attachment relationships on numerous outcomes such as motivation, student-teacher relationships, transitions to college, psychological health, and social adjustment, to name a few.

Several key figures in the attachment literature beyond Bowlby and Ainsworth have emerged throughout the decades (from the 1940s to the early 21st century), and new scholars continue to supply meaningful contributions. Ellen Moss, who examines attachment relationships and behavioral problems among school age students, has published numerous academic articles on the subject. Diane St. Laurent studies the influence of parental attachment relationships on peer relationships, academic outcomes, and behavioral outcomes among primary and elementary school children. Kathryn Wentzel examines the influence of parent and peer attachments, and teacher pedagogical caring (perceptions that students have of their teacher providing care and support) on motivation, student adjustment, and academic adjustment among students from a variety of ages. Other key figures include Maureen Kenny, who researches the influence of parental attachment relationships on mental

health outcomes among adolescents and young adults. Lastly, Kenneth Rice examines the influence of parental attachment relationships on outcomes such as psychological, social, and emotional well-being to predict students' adjustment to college. A review of the work of any of these scholars will provide an insightful, informative look into the theoretical and practical aspects of attachment theory. However, the following entry provides a basic understanding of attachment relationships and their relation to various outcomes.

FORMATION OF ATTACHMENT BONDS

Parenting behaviors are said to give rise to the formation of the relationships. Attachments are based upon two primary behaviors that caregivers display towards their children: (1) the caregiver's accessibility and responsiveness, and (2) the caregiver's ability to provide protection and security. Attachment relationships are represented in the form of cognitive working models (i.e. thoughts) that infants hold of themselves and others based upon the two primary caregiver behaviors. Infants whose caregivers are affectionate, warm, and responsive to their basic needs for care develop a positive self-view, for they know that they are worthy and deserving of love. Conversely, infants whose caregivers are cold, aloof, neglectful, or inconsistent develop a negative view of themselves because they think that they are not worthy or deserving of love. The extent to which the caregivers provide security and protection shapes infants' view of others and the world. On the one hand, caregivers who protect their infants from harm and provide security prime their infants to develop positive views of others and the world for they see others as reliable and trustworthy and view the world as safe for exploration. On the other hand, caregivers who do not provide security prime their children to view others as unreliable and untrustworthy and to view the world as unsafe.

INDIRECT INFLUENCES OF ATTACHMENT RELATIONSHIPS

While parenting behaviors are the primary catalysts that shape attachment relationships, other contextual (i.e. environmental) factors have also been found to indirectly contribute to the formation of attachment relationships, making attachment bonds complex. For instance, parents with better psychological health provide their infants with higher quality care. Hence, infants of these caregivers tend to be attached more securely (or positively) than infants whose caregivers are psychologically maladjusted or distressed. For instance, clinically depressed mothers or caregivers who engage in intrusive, hostile, and/or unresponsive care giving due to their depression are likely to have children who are insecurely attached (negatively attached).

Greater marital or relationship satisfaction is also associated with attachment security, as these caregivers tend to display more sensitive parenting skills that contribute to the formation of secure attachments.

Both Bowlby and Ainsworth argue for the universality of attachment relationships, stating that attachment relationships occur cross-culturally due to their biological basis. However, demographic factors, including race/ethnicity and socioeconomic status (SES), have also been shown to contribute to the formation of attachment relationships, and even influence views of the ideal attachment relationship. As Robert Hinde (1991) states: "what is biologically best in one situation may not be so in another. Natural selection tends to produce not rigid types of behavior, but alternative strategies … so while a secure mother-child relationship may be best in some instances, other types of relationships may be better in others" (pp. 160-161). The presence of attachment relationships has not been challenged, but the criteria utilized to classify individuals as secure or insecure has been challenged. For instance, caregivers in Japan would fault caregivers in the United States who encourage their infants to be explorative and autonomous because Japanese caregivers value continuous, close proximity and contact with their infants. Therefore, cultural contexts must be considered when evaluating attachment relationships.

Caregivers from lower incomes often have to contend with added stressors such as financial worries and being able to provide adequate clothing and shelter for their children. Continuous exposure to these stressors has been known to create psychological maladjustment (e.g. depression and/or anxiety) that negatively affects the quality of the attachment relationship. Despite the negative influence that a lack of resources may have on attachment security, additional support from extended family and friends may minimize these negative influences. Social support networks can provide children with the opportunity to form secure bonds with other adult caregivers or may afford parents the opportunity to provide better quality care for their children by lessening the burden of fulfilling other obligations that may detract from providing quality care.

A majority of research related to attachment theory focuses on parents' influences on their children. However, attachment relationships are bi-directional in that parental and infant characteristics influence the attachment bond. For instance, oftentimes overlooked, infants' temperament is one such factor that is said to influence attachment bonds. While numerous definitions of temperament exist, temperament generally refers to basic, inherent dispositions that guide human behaviors, such as expression, reactivity, emotionality, and sociability.

Thomas and Chess identify three temperament styles: Easy, Difficult, and Slow-to-Warm. Children with Easy temperaments develop regular sleeping and feeding schedules, smile at strangers, are interpersonally pleasant and joyful, adapt easily to new situations, accept most frustration with little fuss, and are typically easy to parent. By contrast, Difficult children are irregular in their biological functions, irritable, fussy, non-adaptive, withdraw from new stimuli, and are generally difficult to parent. Slow-to-Warm children have mild intensity in expression, are somewhat regular in their biological functions, and tend to approach new situations, but they also tend to take longer to adapt to new situations and are slower to warm interpersonally than Easy children are. Thomas and Chess estimate that 40-50% of infants are Easy, 10-20% are Difficult, and 15-25% are Slow-to-Warm.

How does temperament relate to attachment relationships? Caregivers often report that it is more challenging to interact meaningfully with Difficult children because they are fussy, irritable, and non-adaptive. Therefore, it is difficult to form an affective bond with these children. However, children with Easy or Slow-to-Warm temperaments are interpersonally pleasant, adaptive, and not fussy, which makes bonding easier, so children with these type of temperaments help facilitate bonding.

CLASSIFICATION AND MEASUREMENT OF ATTACHMENT STYLES

Ainsworth identified three types of attachment styles based upon observations of caregivers interacting with their infants (roughly 1 year of age) during a research experiment called The Strange Situation. The attachment styles include the insecure-avoidant (pattern A) style, the secure (pattern B) style, and the insecure-ambivalent (pattern C) style. The Strange Situation is a 20-minute experimental drama designed to reveal infants' attachment style (Ainsworth, 1978). During the experiment, the mother and infant are introduced to a laboratory playroom in which the infant is allowed to explore the room and play with toys while the mother watches. After a brief period, an unfamiliar woman enters the playroom, initially speaks with the mother, and then proceeds to interact with the infant. While the stranger plays with the infant, the mother leaves the room briefly but returns. A second separation occurs in which the infant is left completely alone for a brief period. The stranger returns first, and then the mother returns. The infant's responses to the separations from his/her mother and the reactions upon the mothers' return were documented and used to classify infants as securely or insecurely attached. Infants who were comfortable exploring the room in their mother's presence, cried in their mother's absence, and were comforted by their mother's return to the room were labeled "secure." Infants who refused to leave their mothers to play with the toys, cried in their mother's absence, and failed to be consoled by their mother's comfort upon returning were labeled "insecure-ambivalent (anxious)." Infants who seemed unaffected by their mother's presence or absence in the room were labeled as "insecure-avoidant."

Methodologies similar to The Strange Situation are commonly used to measure attachment styles from infancy to kindergarten. Among older elementary school children, self-report questionnaires are commonly used to measure attachment styles. Self-report questionnaires, which solicit information directly from children, or their parent(s), hence the name self-report, require children to read or listen to a set of statements or questions and choose the response that most closely applies to them. For instance, the Parental Attachment Questionnaire, a self-report questionnaire, has been widely used among children to measure attachment styles. Among adolescents and adults, several self-report questionnaires such as the Parental Attachment Questionnaire, the Parental Bonding Instrument, the Inventory of Parent and Peer Attachment, and West and Sheldon's (1988) Measure of Insecure Attachment are commonly used to measure attachment relationships.

OVERVIEW

According to Ainsworth, secure infants experience warm, responsive relationships with their primary caregivers that are encouraging of autonomy. Infants with secure attachments cognitively have positive views of themselves and others because they know that they are worthy of love and equate security and protection with their caregivers. As adults, these infants are comfortable with closeness and separateness in their relationships with others, are self-reliant and self-confident, cooperative, helpful toward others, have high self-esteem, tend to be successful, and view the world as a place to be explored. Data have consistently demonstrated that a majority of children worldwide, roughly 65–70%, have secure attachment relationships. For instance, approximately 67% of children raised in the United States and Britain have secure relationships. Likewise, among Gusii women of Kenya, Kermoian and Leiderman classified 61% of infants as secure, 20% as anxious, and 19% as ambivalent.

Insecure-ambivalent (anxious) infants tend to experience warmth from their primary caregivers, but their caregivers do not respond to their needs for basic care promptly and consistently or provide security and protection (Ainsworth, 1989). These infants learn that they are worthy of love, but view their caregivers as unreliable and untrustworthy, which tends to paint their view of the world as unsafe. As a result, these infants tend to develop "clingy" behavior toward their caregivers and fear abandonment because they never know if the caregiver will be available to respond to their needs. As adults, they tend to fear being separated from or abandoned by their romantic partners or friends; they may become overly dependent on others and tend to act immature. Furthermore, under times of stress, these individuals are apt to develop symptoms such as depression or phobias. Roughly 15% of infants have an avoidant attachment style. Among a sample of Chinese infants in China, Hu and Meng found that 68% of infants had secure attachments with their maternal figures, 16% were considered ambivalent, and 16% were considered avoidant.

Insecure-avoidant infants tend to experience neglectful relationships with their primary caregivers. These infants' caregivers are unresponsive and do not provide warmth or a sense of protection and security. These infants learn that they are not worthy of love and view others as unresponsive, unreliable, and unsafe. As adults, these individuals have difficulty trusting others, do not believe that they are worthy of love, and do not expect others to be responsive to their needs (Ainsworth, 1989). These infants are prone to having later interpersonal difficulties with others due to difficulty bonding, tend to suffer from low self-esteem, lack confidence, and have difficulty adapting. Roughly 15% of children have an avoidant attachment style.

Based upon interviews that they conducted with individuals, in the early 1990s, Bartholomew and Horowitz created more contemporary classifications of attachment styles. Four different categories of attachment styles emerged from Bartholomew and Horowitz's research and they labeled them: secure, preoccupied, dismissing, and fearful. According to Bartholomew and Horowitz, individuals with a "secure" attachment style cognitively have a sense of worthiness and lovability (a positive view of the self) and believe other people are accepting and responsive (a positive view of others). Individuals with a "fearful" attachment style have a sense of worthlessness and feelings of being unloved (a negative view of the self) and believe others will be untrustworthy and rejecting (a negative view of others). Individuals with a "dismissing" attachment style tend to have a sense of worthiness and lovability (a positive view of the self) but have a negative disposition towards others (a negative view of others). Individuals with a "preoccupied" attachment style have a sense of worthlessness and feelings of being unloved (a negative view of the self) but have a positive disposition of others (a positive view of others).

THE INFLUENCE OF ATTACHMENT STYLES ON EDUCATIONAL OUTCOMES

In addition to influencing psychological, social, and emotional outcomes, parental attachment relationships influence students' academic success through several mediums.

For instance, children's attachments to their parents serve as templates for relationships in which they engage with others such as teachers. Given this affiliation, teacher-child attachments, or bonds that children form with their teachers, are likely to mirror the attachments that children have with their parents. In essence, children with secure parental attachments are likely to have secure teacher-child attachments, while those with avoidant or ambivalent attachments are likely to have the same type of relationship with their teachers.

O'Conner and McCartney found support for this claim by demonstrating that students with insecure parental attachments also had insecure teacher attachments in three independent samples of preschool, kindergarten, and first-grade students. Teachers are likely to have a more difficult time bonding with students with insecure attachments because these children tend to harbor negative views of the teacher that will impede the bonding process. Subsequently, it may be difficult for teachers to learn about these children's needs to respond to them in a manner that facilitates learning and adjustment. As a result, insecure children are more likely to struggle academically than secure children are because secure children are able to successfully establish secure attachments with their teacher, view their teacher favorably, have the confidence necessary to succeed, and utilize the teacher as a secure base from which to explore and engage in academic tasks and challenges.

Furthermore, studies have demonstrated that parental attachments strongly influence attachments that students develop with their peers. Similar to teacher attachments, peer attachments often mirror those of parental attachments. Peer attachments have been linked to a number of educational outcomes through various studies, thereby indirectly connecting parental attachments to educational outcomes in yet another facet. For instance, students with secure peer attachments typically demonstrate greater motivation, academic achievement, and prosocial behaviors. In contrast, students with insecure attachments are more prone to exhibiting problematic behaviors and typically achieve less academic success.

Attachment also influences self-efficacy (individuals' belief in their ability to successfully complete tasks), self-confidence (individuals' positive perceptions of their general abilities), and self-esteem (individuals' feeling of self-worth and satisfaction with oneself), all of which are vital to academic success. Secure children have the confidence, esteem, and security that they need to complete academic tasks successfully, are more likely to be engaged in classroom activities, and tend to be more motivated than their insecure peers are. Soares, Lemos, and Almeida found that secure adolescents are more likely to engage in goal-oriented behavior, engage in active problem solving, and

be motivated to attempt challenging academic tasks than insecure children. As a result, secure children often attain greater academic achievement than their insecure counterparts do.

Among a sample of sixth grade and ninth grade students, Wong, Wiest, and Cusick found that children who had high self-esteem, high scholastic self-efficacy (confidence in their ability to academically excel), and secure parental attachments preferred to be academically challenged and were motivated to learn for the sake of mastering the course content. By contrast, their insecure counterparts who lacked self-esteem and scholastic self-efficacy did not achieve at as high a level. Additionally, among the ninth grade students, teacher support was associated with greater academic achievement, which is consistent with findings from others who have demonstrated positive associations between teacher attachment security and higher grade point averages.

Lastly, attachment styles are associated with various behavioral outcomes that influence educational outcomes. For instance, secure children tend to be resilient, confident, and independent, which facilitates learning and academic success. However, avoidant children are likely to be clingy and unsure, while ambivalent children are likely to exhibit problem behaviors (e.g. hostility and aggression) and have interpersonal difficulties with their peers. All of these behavioral difficulties may hinder educational success. Furthermore, attachment insecurity has also been associated with attention problems such as Attention Deficit Disorder and/or Attention Deficit-Hyper Activity Disorder. Jacobson and Hofmann found insecurely attached children at ages 9, 11, and 15 had decreased attention spans, resulting in these children having difficulty attuning to instructions and engaging in classroom activities for extended amounts of time, both of which have been shown to impede learning.

In conclusion, attachment relationships influence numerous aspects of our lives from learning and achievement to psychological and social outcomes. Attachments are not just limited to parental attachments, as peer attachments and teacher attachments have also been shown to predict numerous outcomes. Therefore, fostering attachment styles that promote healthy, adaptive functioning throughout the lifespan is critical to well being.

SEE ALSO *Parenting Styles; Temperament.*

BIBLIOGRAPHY
Ainsworth, M. (1978). *Patterns of attachment: A psychological study of the strange situation.* Hillsdale, NJ: Eribaum.
Ainsworth, M. (1989). Attachments beyond infancy. *American Psychologist, 44 (4)*, 709–716.
Armsden, G., & Greenberg, M. (1987). The inventory of parent and peer attachment: individual differences and their

relationship to psychological well-being in adolescence. *Journal of Youth and Adolescence, 16 (5)*, 427–454.

Bartholomew, K., & Horowitz, L. (1991). Attachment styles among young adults: a test of a four-category model. *Journal of Personality and Social Psychology, 61(2)*, 226–244.

Bowlby, J. (1977). The making and breaking of affectional bonds: Aetiology and psychopathology in the light of attachment theory. *British Journal of Psychiatry, 130*, 201–210.

Bretherton, I. (1992). The origins of attachment theory: John Bowlby and Mary Ainsworth. *Developmental Psychology, 28(5)*, 759–775.

Cassidy, J., & Shaver, P. (1999). *Handbook of attachment: Theory, research, and clinical applications.* New York: Guilford.

Harwood, R., Miller, J., & Irizarry, N. (1995). *Culture and Attachment.* New York: Guilford.

Hinde, R. (1991). Relationships, attachment, and culture: A tribute to John Bowlby. *Infant Mental Health Journal, 12 (3)*, 154–163.

Holmes, J. (1993). *John Bowlby and Attachment Theory.* New York: Routledge.

Hu, P., & Meng, Z. (1996). An examination of mother-infant attachment in China. Poster presented at the meeting of the International Society for the study of Behavioral Development, Quebec City, Quebec, Canada.

Goldsmith, H., Buss, A., Plomin, R., Rothbart, M., Chess, S., Hinde, R., et al. (1987). Roundtable: What is temperament? Four approaches. *Child Development, 58*, 505–529.

Jacobsen, T., & Hofmann, V. (1997). Children's attachment representations: Longitudinal relations to school behavior and academic competency in middle childhood and adolescence. *Developmental Psychology, 33 (4)*, 703–710.

Kenny, M. (1987). The extent and function and parental attachment among first-year college students. *Journal of Youth and Adolescence, 16* (1), 17–29.

Kenny, M.E., & Perez, V. (1996). Attachment and psychological well-being among racially and ethnically diverse first year college students. *Journal of College Student Development, 37* (5), 527–535.

Kermoian, R., & Leiderman, P. (1986). Infant attachment to mother and child caretaker in an East African community. *International Journal of Behavioral Development, 9*, 455–469.

Main, M. (1983). Exploration, play, and cognitive functioning related to infant-mother attachment. *Infant Behavior and Development, 6 (2)*, 167–174.

Main, M., & Solomon, J. (1990). Procedures for identifying infants as disorganized/disoriented during the Ainsworth strange situation. In M. Greenberg, D. Cicchetti, & E. Cummings (Eds.), *Attachment in the preschool years* (pp. 121–160). Chicago: University of Chicago Press.

Moss, E., & St. Laurent, D. (2001). Attachment at school age and academic performance. *Developmental Psychology, 37 (6)*, 863–874.

O'Conner, E., & McCartney, K. (2006). Testing associations between young children's relationships with mothers and teachers. *Journal of Educational Psychology, 98 (1)*, 87–98.

Parker, G., Tupling, H., & Brown, L. (1979). A parental bonding instrument. *British Journal of Medical Psychology, 52*, 1–10.

Rice, K.G., Cunningham, T., & Young, M. (1997). Attachment to parents, social competence, and emotional well-being: A comparison of black and white late adolescents. *Journal of Counseling Psychology, 44* (1), 89–101.

Rothbaum, F., Weisz, J., Pott, M., Miyake, K., & Morelli, G. (2000). Attachment and culture: security in the United States and Japan. *American Psychologist, 55 (10)*, 1093–1104.

Sagi, A., Lamb, M., Lewkowicz, K., Shoham, R., Dvir, R., & Estes, D. (1985). Security of infant-mother, -father and metapelet attachments among kibbutz-reared Israeli children. In I. Bretherton & E. Waters (Eds.), *Growing points of attachment theory and research. Monographs of the Society for Research in Child Development, 50 (1–2)*, 257–275.

Soares, I., Lemos, M., & Almeida, C. (2005). Attachment and motivational strategies in adolescence: Exploring links. *Adolescence, 40 (157)*, 129–154.

Thomas, A., & Chess, S. (1977). *Temperament and Development.* New York: Brunner/Mazel.

West, M., & Sheldon, A. (1988). Classification of pathological attachment patterns in adults. *Journal of Personality Disorder, 2*, 153–159.

Wentzel, K. (2002). Are effective teachers like good parents? Teaching styles and student adjustment in early adolescence. *Child Development, 73* (1), 287–301.

Wentzel, K. (1998). Social relationships and motivation in middle school: The role of parents, teachers, and peers. *Journal of Educational Psychology, 90* (2), 202–209.

Wong, E., Wiest, D., Cusick, L. (2002). Perceptions of autonomy support, parent attachment, competence and self-worth as predictors of motivational orientation and academic achievement: An examination of sixth and ninth grade regular education students. *Adolescence, 37 (146)*, 255–266.

Keisha Love

ATTENTION-DEFICIT/ HYPERACTIVITY DISORDER (ADHD)

Problems with attention, impulse control, and activity level are among the most common behavior difficulties exhibited by children and adolescents in the United States (Barkley, 2006). In fact, approximately 3 to 5 percent of school-aged children could be diagnosed with Attention-Deficit/Hyperactivity Disorder (ADHD), a psychiatric condition applied to individuals who exhibit developmentally inappropriate levels of inattention and/or impulsivity/overactivity (American Psychiatric Association, 2000).

DEFINITION OF ADHD

To meet DSM-IV-TR (American Psychiatric Association, 2000) criteria for ADHD, individuals must exhibit at least six inattention or at least six hyperactive-impulsive symptoms prior to the age of 7, for at least 6 months, and with concomitant academic and/or social impairment. Boys with ADHD outnumber girls with this disorder at about a 2:1 to 5:1 ratio (Barkley, 2006). Given that most public school classrooms in the United States include 20 to 30 students, approximately one to two students in every classroom will have ADHD. Further, ADHD symptoms typically persist from early childhood through at least adolescence for a majority of individuals (Barkley, Murphy, & Fischer, 2007). Thus, ADHD typically is viewed as a lifelong disorder that must be addressed through ongoing intervention that is developmentally appropriate and addresses the unique needs and specific impairment of individual children (DuPaul & Stoner, 2003).

CHARACTERISTICS AND ASSOCIATED DIFFICULTIES

Children and adolescents with ADHD typically exhibit a variety of difficulties with school functioning. First, students with this disorder frequently are inattentive and exhibit significantly higher rates of off-task behavior relative to their non-ADHD classmates (e.g., Vile Junod, DuPaul, Jitendra, Volpe, & Cleary, 2006). Second, hyperactive-impulsive behaviors that characterize ADHD typically lead to disruptive behaviors (e.g., talking without permission, bothering other students, and leaving assigned area) in the classroom and other school settings. Third, ADHD frequently is associated with deficits in academic skills and/or performance. On average, children with ADHD score between 10 to 30 points lower than non-ADHD control children on norm-referenced, standardized achievement tests (e.g., Barkley, 2006). In fact, approximately 20 to 30 percent of children with ADHD are classified as having learning disabilities because of deficits in the acquisition of specific academic skills (DuPaul & Stoner, 2003). Further, the results of prospective longitudinal investigations of children with ADHD into adolescence and adulthood indicate significantly higher rates of grade retention, placement in special education classrooms, and school drop-out relative to their non-ADHD classmates as well as significantly lower high school grade point average, enrollment in college degree programs, and socioeconomic status (for review, see Barkley et al., 2007).

Children and adolescents with ADHD are at higher than average risk for a variety of behavioral difficulties including defiance toward authority figures, physical and verbal aggression toward peers, and antisocial acts such as lying, stealing, and vandalism (American Psychiatric Association, 2000; Barkley, 2006). As a result of defiant and aggressive behavior, individuals with ADHD often have significant difficulty developing and maintaining positive relationships with peers, teachers, and other school personnel. Not surprisingly, several investigations have found children with ADHD to be less well-liked, more often rejected, and have fewer friends than their non-ADHD peers (e.g., Hoza, Gerdes, Mrug, Hinshaw, Bukowski, Gold et al., 2005).

SUBTYPES OF ADHD

The DSM-IV identifies three subtypes of ADHD: combined type, predominantly inattentive type, and predominantly hyperactive-impulsive type (American Psychiatric Association, 2000). Individuals with ADHD combined type exhibit significant symptoms of both inattention and hyperactivity-impulsivity, while those with predominantly inattentive and hyperactive-impulsive types display significant symptoms of only one of the two dimensions. Prevalence figures in the child population are approximately equal for ADHD combined and predominantly inattentive types, with these two subtypes outnumbering hyperactive-impulsive type by a 2:1 margin (Hudziak, Heath, Madden, Reich, Bucholz, Slutske et al., 1998).

Most of the research on ADHD conducted as of the early 2000s has focused on children and adolescents with ADHD combined type. Between 1985 and 2005, studies examining individuals with predominantly inattentive type have found that the latter are more likely to exhibit learning problems and possibly internalizing disorder symptoms, and less likely to have comorbid disruptive behavior disorders relative to children with ADHD combined type (Barkley, 2006), although these findings are not consistent across studies. Given that the predominantly hyperactive-impulsive type was not included in the DSM nomenclature until 1994, very little research has focused on this subtype. What little data are available suggest that the hyperactive-impulsive subtype may be more prominent in younger children and could be an early childhood manifestation of what eventually will be ADHD combined type (e.g., Riley, DuPaul, Pipan, Kern, Van Brakle, & Blum, in press). Importantly, very little research has examined differential treatment response across subtypes; thus, as of 2007, treatment components are not modified based on ADHD subtype.

ASSESSMENT OF ADHD

The assessment of children and adolescents suspected of having ADHD involves the use of multiple assessment tools (e.g., rating scales and diagnostic interviews) to obtain information on symptomatic behavior and associated functioning from the perspectives of multiple individuals (i.e., parent, teacher, and child) (Barkley, 2006). No single assessment method or source alone is adequate for making the diagnosis; clinicians must examine child functioning as comprehensively as possible (American Academy of Child and Adolescent Psychiatry, 2007).

The assessment process can be viewed as a five-stage process, including screening, multimethod assessment, interpretation of data, treatment design, and treatment evaluation (DuPaul & Stoner, 2003). The goal of this assessment process is not only to determine if an individual has ADHD, but also to identify possible comorbid conditions, delineate potentially effective treatment strategies, and evaluate whether intervention is successful.

The first stage of the assessment process is screening for ADHD symptoms in all cases where an individual is reported to have problems with attention, impulsivity, or activity level. Typically, screening entails obtaining parent and/or teacher report on the extent to which ADHD symptoms are evident in home or school settings. For example, the parent or teacher could complete an 18-item rating scale that contains the DSM-IV ADHD symptoms. If a significant number of inattentive and/or hyperactive-impulsive symptoms are reported, then more assessment data will be gathered at the next stage of the process.

The multimethod assessment stage involves gathering extensive information about symptoms of ADHD and other psychopathological disorders; the child's developmental, medical, and family histories; and the extent to which academic and social functioning are impaired by symptoms (Barkley, 2006; DuPaul & Stoner, 2003). A major component of the assessment is a diagnostic interview with the child's parent (and teacher, if possible). There are various interview formats available, but the key information to obtain is parental perception of the frequency and chronicity of ADHD symptoms, presence of symptoms of other disorders (e.g., oppositional defiant disorder), prior attempts to treat these difficulties, developmental history, and family history (Barkley, 2006). Behavior ratings also must be obtained from parents and teachers. Ideally, rating scales that assess a broad band of psychopathological behaviors (e.g., Child Behavior Checklist; Achenbach, 1991) and a narrow band of behaviors related to ADHD (e.g., ADHD Rating Scale-IV; DuPaul, Power, Anastopoulos, & Reid, 1998) should be used. If possible, direct observations of classroom behavior should be used to assess the degree to which ADHD-related behaviors are evident as compared to classroom peers as well as to identify possible environmental factors that could be eliciting and/or maintaining challenging behaviors. Finally, data regarding social (e.g., Social Skills Rating Scale; Gresham & Elliott, 1990) and academic (e.g., curriculum-based measurement probes) functioning should be gathered to determine the degree of impairment associated with ADHD symptoms.

It should be noted that traditional psychological and neuropsychological tests (e.g., Wechsler scales) have limited value in the assessment of ADHD symptoms. Although individuals with ADHD may perform below their non-ADHD peers on some of these instruments, score profiles specific to ADHD have not been identified and these data have limited ecological validity (Barkley, 2006). In similar fashion, medical assessment procedures

(e.g., MRI, EEG) do not provide specific data to inform diagnostic decisions at the individual level.

The next stage in the assessment process is to interpret the data obtained through multiple measures. Specifically, one must determine the degree to which clinically significant ADHD symptoms are evident across settings and the degree to which these symptoms are associated with academic, social, and/or occupational impairment. Further, alternative hypotheses for the display of apparent ADHD symptoms should be considered. For example, attention difficulties may be due to an anxiety or depressive disorder. Finally, possible comorbid diagnoses should be considered given that most individuals with ADHD will have one or more additional disorders (Barkley, 2006). The disorders most commonly associated with ADHD include oppositional defiant disorder, conduct disorder, and learning disabilities.

The final two stages of the assessment process are designed to move beyond diagnosis and are focused on treatment development and evaluation. Assessment data are used to determine the most appropriate course of action for intervention. For example, the more severe the ADHD symptoms and the more these symptoms are associated with multiple comorbid disorders, the more likely that a combination of psychotropic medication and behavior modification will be necessary (Jensen, Hinshaw, Kraemer, Lenora, Newcorn, Abikoff et al., 2001). Also, data regarding the antecedent and consequent events that serve as a context for classroom disruptive behavior can aid in determining the function of target behaviors and, ultimately, can lead to the development of an intervention that directly addresses this behavioral function (DuPaul & Stoner, 2003). Finally, once a treatment plan is developed and put into action, assessment data are collected periodically to determine whether the plan is successful and to delineate potential treatment modification.

INTERVENTIONS AND INSTRUCTIONAL STRATEGIES

The two primary interventions for ADHD are psychostimulant medication (e.g., methylphenidate) and behavior modification strategies implemented in home and school settings (Barkley, 2006). These intervention strategies have been found to reduce ADHD symptoms and associated behavior difficulties (e.g., noncompliance and aggression) as well as enhance peer interactions and academic performance for most study participants (for review see Barkley, 2006).

Psychotropic Medication. Central nervous system (CNS) stimulants are the most common and widely studied class of psychotropic medication used in the treatment of

ADHD (Connor, 2006). In fact, methylphenidate and other CNS stimulants are the single most effective treatment for reducing ADHD symptoms in children (MTA Cooperative Group, 1999, 2004). Further, numerous studies have shown methylphenidate and amphetamine compounds to improve classroom attention, behavior control, and interactions with peers and authority figures as well as enhance productivity and accuracy on academic tasks and curriculum-based measurement probes (for review, see Brown, Antonuccio, DuPaul, Fristad, King, Leslie et al., 2007; Connor, 2006). Alternatively, long-term effects on academic achievement (as measured by standardized achievement tests) have been either very small or non-existent (e.g., Jensen, Arnold, Swanson, Vitiello, Abikoff, Greenhill et al., 2007; MTA Cooperative Group, 1999, 2004). Because some individuals may experience limited success and/or adverse side-effects with CNS stimulants, several non-stimulant medications have been studied. For example, atomoxetine (Spencer et al., 2002) and clonidine (Connor, Fletcher, & Swanson, 1999) have been successful in reducing ADHD symptoms. The effects of non-stimulants on academic performance and social interactions with peers have not been studied extensively and are as of 2007 essentially unknown.

Interventions Based on Behavioral Principles. Contingency management interventions that manipulate consequences to change specific target behaviors are widely used to treat ADHD symptoms and comorbid behavioral difficulties. The two consequence-based interventions that have the strongest empirical support are token reinforcement and response cost (Pelham, Wheeler, & Chronis, 1998). Token reinforcement programs involve providing individuals with immediate reinforcement in the form of tokens contingent on the display of appropriate behavior (e.g., Pfiffner, Rosen, & O'Leary, 1985). Alternatively, response cost involves the removal of token reinforcers following the display of inappropriate behavior (Rapport, Murphy, & Bailey, 1982). Both of these strategies have been found to reduce inattentive, disruptive behaviors to a significant degree relative to baseline conditions. When possible, behavioral interventions should be designed using functional assessment data (O'Neill, Horner, Albin, Sprague, Storey, & Newton, 1997). In fact, several single subject design studies that included students exhibiting ADHD symptoms (e.g., Eckert, Martens, & DiGennaro, 2005) have indicated the value of an assessment-based approach to the design of behavioral interventions.

Combined Medication and Behavioral Intervention. Investigations systematically comparing the combination of CNS stimulants, behavioral interventions and their combination (i.e., multimodal treatment) have found stimulants to be superior to behavioral treatments in reducing ADHD symptoms (MTA Cooperative Group, 1999, 2004). Alternatively, the greatest effects on problems associated with ADHD (e.g., oppositional behavior and social performance difficulties) typically are obtained with the combination of stimulants and behavior modification (Conners, Epstein, March, Angold, Wells, Klaric et al., 2001). Further, children with multiple comorbid disorders (Jensen et al., 2001) and individuals from ethnically or socioeconomically diverse backgrounds (Arnold, Elliott, Sachs, Bird, Kraemer, Wells et al., 2003) are most successful when these treatment modalities are combined.

Academic Interventions. Stimulants and behavioral interventions are associated with small effects, at best, on academic achievement. Although academic interventions for students with ADHD have not been as widely studied as behavioral treatments, studies in the late 1990s and early 2000s have provided preliminary support for instructional and remediation strategies. Specifically, computer-assisted instruction (Mautone, DuPaul, & Jitendra, 2005), classwide peer tutoring (DuPaul, Ervin, Hook, & McGoey, 1998), home-based parent tutoring (Hook & DuPaul, 1999) or homework support (Power, Karustis, & Habboushe, 2001), self-regulated strategy for written expression (Reid & Lienemann, 2006), and directed note-taking (Evans, Pelham, & Grudberg, 1995) are associated with improvements in specific academic skills and outcomes. Further, a large scale examination of consultation-based academic strategies found significant growth in reading and math skills for elementary students with ADHD (DuPaul, Jitendra, Volpe, Tresco, Lutz, Vile Junod et al., 2006).

Children and adolescents with ADHD experience significant academic, social, and behavioral difficulties in home and school settings. The assessment of ADHD involves collection of data across settings and sources to identify whether significant symptoms are present, whether these are better accounted for by other disorders, and what environmental variables can be altered as part of the treatment protocol. Empirical studies support the use of psychotropic medication (most notably stimulants and atomoxetine), behavioral strategies in home and school settings, and modifications to academic instruction in reducing ADHD symptoms and enhancing academic and social functioning. Nevertheless, there are many important gaps in the extant treatment literature, including the need (a) to evaluate effects on academic and social functioning, (b) to assess treatment integrity and acceptability, and (c) to document how the combination of stimulant medication and behavioral interventions can be optimized.

SEE ALSO *Emotional Development; Learning Disabilities.*

BIBLIOGRAPHY

Achenbach, T. M. (1991). *Manual for the child behavior checklist and revised child behavior profile.* Burlington, VT: University of Vermont, Department of Psychiatry.

American Academy of Child and Adolescent Psychiatry. (2007). Practice parameter for the assessment and treatment of children and adolescents with attention-deficit/hyperactivity disorder. *Journal of the American Academy of Child and Adolescent Psychiatry, 46,* 894–921.

American Psychiatric Association (2000). *Diagnostic and statistical manual of mental disorders* (4th ed.). Washington, DC: Author.

Arnold, L. E., Elliott, M., Sachs, L., Bird, H., Kraemer, H. C., Wells, K. C., et al. (2003). Effects of ethnicity on treatment attendance, stimulant response/dose, and 14-month outcome in ADHD. *Journal of Consulting and Clinical Psychology, 71,* 713–727.

Barkley, R. A. (Ed.). (2006). *Attention-deficit hyperactivity disorder: A handbook for diagnosis and treatment* (3rd ed.). New York: Guilford.

Barkley, R. A., Murphy, K., & Fischer, M. (2007). *ADHD in adults: What the science says.* New York: Guilford.

Brown, R. T., Antonuccio, D., DuPaul, G. J., Fristad, M., King, C. A., Leslie, et al. (2007). *Childhood mental health disorders: Evidence base and contextual factors for psychosocial, psychopharmacological, and combined interventions.* Washington, DC: American Psychological Association.

Conners, C. K., Epstein, J. N., March, J. S., Angold, A., Wells, K. C., Klaric, J., et al. (2001). Multimodal treatment of ADHD in the MTA: An alternative outcome analysis. *Journal of the American Academy of Child and Adolescent Psychiatry, 40,* 159–167.

Connor, D. F. (2006). Stimulants. In R. A. Barkley (Ed.), *Attention deficit hyperactivity disorder: A handbook for diagnosis and treatment* (3rd ed., pp. 608–647). New York: Guilford.

Connor, D. F., Fletcher, K. E., & Swanson, J. M. (1999). A meta-analysis of clonidine for symptoms of attention-deficit hyperactivity disorder. *Journal of the American Academy of Child and Adolescent Psychiatry, 38,* 1551–1559.

DuPaul, G. J., Ervin, R. A., Hook, C. L., & McGoey, K. E. (1998). Peer tutoring for children with Attention Deficit Hyperactivity Disorder: Effects on classroom behavior and academic performance. *Journal of Applied Behavior Analysis, 31,* 579–592.

DuPaul, G. J., Jitendra, A. K., Volpe, R. J., Tresco, K. E., Lutz, J. G., Vile Junod, R. E., et al. (2006). Consultation-based academic interventions for children with ADHD: Effects on reading and mathematics achievement. *Journal of Abnormal Child Psychology, 34,* 633–646.

DuPaul, G. J., Power, T. J., Anastopoulos, A. D., & Reid, R. (1998). *AD/HD Rating Scale-IV: Checklist, norms, and clinical interpretation.* New York: Guilford.

DuPaul, G. J., & Stoner, G. (2003). *ADHD in the schools: Assessment and intervention strategies* (2nd ed.). New York: Guilford.

Eckert, T. L., Martens, B. K., & DiGennaro, F. D. (2005). Describing antecedent-behavior-consequence relations using conditional probabilities and the general operant contingency space. A preliminary investigation. *School Psychology Review, 34,* 529–536.

Evans, S. W., Pelham, W., & Grudberg, M. V. (1995). The efficacy of notetaking to improve behavior and comprehension of adolescents with Attention Deficit Hyperactivity Disorder. *Exceptionality, 5,* 1–17.

Gresham, F. M., & Elliott, S. N. (1990). *Social skills rating system.* Circle Pines, MN: American Guidance Service.

Hook, C. L., & DuPaul, G. J. (1999). Parent tutoring for students with attention deficit hyperactivity disorder: Effects on reading at home and school. *School Psychology Review, 28,* 60–75.

Hoza, B., Gerdes, A. C., Mrug, S., Hinshaw, S. P., Bukowski, W. M., Gold, J. A., et al. (2005). Peer-assessed outcomes in the Multimodal Treatment Study of children with Attention Deficit Hyperactivity Disorder. *Journal of Clinical Child and Adolescent Psychology, 34,* 74–86.

Hudziak, J. J., Heath, A. C., Madden, P. F., Reich, W., Bucholz, K. K., Slutske, W., et al. (1998). Latent class and factor analysis of DSM-IV ADHD: A twin study of female adolescents. *Journal of the American Academy of Child and Adolescent Psychiatry, 37,* 848–857.

Jensen, P. S., Arnold, L. E., Swanson, J. M., Vitiello, B., Abikoff, H. B., Greenhill, L. L., et al. (2007). Three-year follow-up of the NIMH MTA study. *Journal of the American Academy of Child and Adolescent Psychiatry, 46,* 989–1002.

Jensen, P. S., Hinshaw, S. P., Kraemer, H. C., Lenora, N., Newcorn, J. H., Abikoff, H. B., et al. (2001). ADHD comorbidity findings from the MTA study: Comparing comorbid subgroups. *Journal of the American Academy of Child and Adolescent Psychiatry, 40,* 147–158.

Mautone, J. A., DuPaul, G. J., & Jitendra, A. K. (2005). The effects of computer-assisted instruction on the mathematics performance and classroom behavior of children with attention-deficit/hyperactivity disorder. *Journal of Attention Disorders, 8,* 301–312.

MTA Cooperative Group. (1999). A 14-month randomized clinical trial of treatment strategies for Attention-Deficit/Hyperactivity Disorder. *Archives of General Psychiatry, 56,* 1073–1086.

MTA Cooperative Group (2004). National Institute of Mental Health multimodal treatment study of ADHD Follow-up: 24-month outcomes of treatment strategies for attention-deficit/hyperactivity disorder. *Pediatrics, 113,* 754–761.

O'Neill, R. E., Horner, R. H., Albin, R. W., Sprague, J., Storey, K., & Newton, J. S. (1997). *Functional analysis and program development for problem behavior: A practical handbook.* Pacific Grove, CA: Brooks/Cole.

Pelham, W. E., Wheeler, T., & Chronis, A. (1998). Empirically-supported psycho-social treatments for ADHD. *Journal of Clinical Child Psychology, 27,* 190–205.

Pfiffner, L. J., Rosen, L. A., & O'Leary, S. G. (1985). The efficacy of an all-positive approach to classroom management. *Journal of Applied Behavior Analysis, 18,* 257–261.

Power, T. J., Karustis, J. L., & Habboushe, D. F. (2001). *Homework success for children with ADHD: A family-school intervention program.* New York: Guilford.

Rapport, M. D., Murphy, A., & Bailey, J. S. (1982). Ritalin vs. response cost in the control of hyperactive children: A within subject comparison. *Journal of Applied Behavior Analysis, 15,* 205–216.

Reid, R., & Lienemann, T. O. (2006). *Strategy instruction for students with learning disabilities: What works for special needs learners.* New York: Guilford.

Riley, C., DuPaul, G. J., Pipan, M., Kern, L., Van Brakle, J., & Blum, N. J. (in press). ADHD-combined subtype vs. ADHD-hyperactive/impulsive subtype: Is there a difference in functional impairment? *Journal of Developmental and Behavioral Pediatrics.*

Spencer, T. J., Heiligenstein, J., Biederman, J., Faries, D., Kratochvil, C., Conners, C. K., et al. (2002). Atomoxetine in children with ADHD: Results from two randomized, placebo-controlled studies. *Journal of Clinical Psychiatry, 63,* 1140–1147.

Vile Junod, R. E., DuPaul, G. J., Jitendra, A. K., Volpe, R. J., & Cleary, K. S. (2006). Classroom observations of students with and without ADHD: Differences across types of engagement. *Journal of School Psychology, 44,* 87–104.

George J. DuPaul

ATTRIBUTION THEORY

Attribution theory provides an important method for examining and understanding motivation in academic settings. It examines individuals' beliefs about why certain events occur and correlates those beliefs to subsequent motivation. The basic premise of this theory is that people want to understand their environments and, therefore, strive to understand why certain events happen. In the classroom, the understanding students have about the causes of past events influences their ability to control what happens to them in the future. For example, if students fail a test, they will probably attribute that failure to a specific cause, such as (1) lack of ability, (2) lack of effort, or (3) poor instruction. The selected attribution will affect their subsequent motivation to engage in similar learning activities.

WEINER'S MODEL OF ATTRIBUTIONS

The study of attribution was initially associated with Fritz Heider (1896–1988) (1958). Later Bernard Weiner (1935–) of the University of California at Los Angeles developed a more comprehensive and extensive model of human attributions. Weiner's model is particularly informative in research on student learning in school settings. In his model, Weiner outlined the processes through which learners form causal beliefs (Weiner 1985, 2005). A basic assumption of Weiner's model of attributions is that learners are affected by both environmental factors (e.g., characteristics of the students' home or school) and by personal factors (e.g., prior experiences and prior knowledge). These background variables affect the types of attributions that individuals are likely to make.

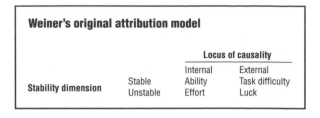

Attribution diagram based on the work of Bernard Weiner.

When an achievement-related event occurs (e.g., a student fails an examination), especially if the outcome was unexpected, Weiner proposes that learners undertake an attributional search, trying to understand what happened. The perceived cause of the event is important regardless of any objective explanation because whatever learners perceive as being the cause of the event will affect their future motivation toward engagement with similar tasks. For example, suppose a group of students performs poorly on an examination because of poor instruction. Those individuals who attribute their failure to poor teaching will have a different level of motivation in subsequent examinations than those who attribute their failure to their own lack of innate ability.

One important feature of Weiner's theory is that the specific attribution being made (luck, effort, etc.) is less important than the characteristics of the attribution, which are classified along three causal dimensions: locus, stability, and controllability. These important dimensions affect learners' subsequent motivation toward the task or activity. The locus dimension refers to whether the cause of the event is perceived as internal to the individual or external. If a learner believes that she failed an exam because she lacks ability, she is choosing an internal cause because ability is internal to the learner. In contrast, if a learner believes that he failed an exam because the teacher is incompetent, he is choosing an external cause because teacher incompetence is external to the student. The stability dimension refers to whether the cause is stable or unstable across time and situations. If a learner believes that he failed a science exam because he lacks ability in science, then his cause is stable, particularly if he believes that his lack of ability in science is a permanent quality. In contrast, if a learner believes that he failed the exam because he was ill at the time of the exam, then the cause is unstable in cases in which the illness is a temporary factor. When a student experiences success, attributions to stable causes lead to positive expectations for success in the future. In the face of failure, however, attributions to stable causes can result in low expectations for the future. The controllability dimension refers to whether the cause of the event is perceived as being under the control of the individual.

If a runner believes that he lost a race because he did not get enough practice before the event, the cause is controllable because he could have decided to spend more time practicing; in contrast, if he feels that he lost the race because he simply lacks ability as a runner, then the cause is uncontrollable. By definition, only internal attributions can be considered controllable.

In addition to the effect of individuals' motivation and expectations on future success, Weiner's model also indicates that certain emotional responses are associated with various causal dimensions (Weiner 1985, 2006). Consideration of emotional outcomes is rare in the study of academic motivation, given that most current motivation theories do not examine emotions. Weiner and others have demonstrated that the locus dimension is related to feelings of pride and self-esteem: People are more likely to experience a sense of pride in accomplishment if they believe that the cause is due to an internal characteristic or behavior. The stability dimension is related to feelings of hopefulness or hopelessness; attributions to unstable causes, by contrast to stable causes, suggest the possibility of a different outcome in the future. Finally, the controllability dimension is related to such feelings as shame, guilt, anger, gratitude, and pity. For example, students who believe their poor performance in a class is due to a controllable attribution (such as lack of effort) may experience guilt, whereas classmates who believe their failure is due to an uncontrollable cause (such as lack of ability) are more likely to experience feelings of shame (Weiner 1985). Emotional consequences of attributions ultimately affect individuals' subsequent motivation to engage in a particular behavior.

Finally, Weiner's model posits that the aforementioned psychological processes lead to behavioral consequences. For example, students' decision regarding whether to enroll in a mathematics course in the future may be partially determined by their attributions for successes or failures on previous mathematics examinations; athletes' subsequent effort in a competitive sports event may be determined by their attributions for successes or failures in previous events.

HOW ATTRIBUTIONS INFLUENCE BEHAVIOR

Many studies indicate that the types of attributions that individuals make influence their subsequent behaviors in predictable ways. Both the expectancy beliefs and the emotions that individuals experience as a result of the attributional process tend to determine future behaviors. Research generally indicates that academic achievement is improved and enhanced when learners attribute academic outcomes to factors such as effort and the use of appropriate study strategies; in contrast, academic achievement is hindered when learners attribute their failure to factors such as lack of ability or chronic health problems and attribute their success to luck. Consequently, a student who attributes failure on an examination to a lack of effort (e.g., she did not study enough the week before the exam) may be motivated to put forth additional effort when preparing for a subsequent exam. In contrast, a student who attributes failure on an examination to a lack of ability (i.e., she believes that she does not have adequate ability in the examination area) will be unlikely to exert effort for a subsequent examination.

HOW ATTRIBUTIONS ARE COMMUNICATED TO LEARNERS

Attributional information is communicated to learners in a variety of ways. Teachers communicate important information to their students through their feedback on assignments, on graded exams, and during classroom instruction. When teachers communicate to students that failures are due to the use of inappropriate strategies or due to inappropriate effort, students are likely to be motivated to try harder or to use more appropriate strategies in the future. Teachers provide this feedback to students in a variety of ways. One common way is through comments on written work. Some teachers provide general feedback, using phrases such as "Good work" or "Needs work." Research indicates that specific feedback is more useful to students because it can assist students in developing adaptive attributional beliefs. Therefore, it is may be effective to write a more specific comment (e.g., "I know you can do better; you need to spend more time studying the night before a test") when a teacher knows that a student has not been putting forth enough effort. It is important, however, to be sure that lack of effort truly is the problem. Researchers such as Martin Covington caution that when teachers encourage students to make attributions to effort (i.e., "You didn't try hard enough"), some students may interpret such comments as an indication of the teachers' lack of belief in the students' true abilities. In many instances, helping students to attribute their failure to not using appropriate strategies or to their lack of specific content knowledge may be more appropriate than assuming students are not trying.

Teachers also need to provide differential feedback to students. Educators must acknowledge that progress and achievement will be different for individual students. If students raise their grades from a "D" to a "C," teachers might choose to offer praise, if this change represents an important, meaningful new accomplishment for the students. In terms of attributions, scholars who study the effects of feedback and learning, such as Jere Brophy, would argue that teachers should provide feedback that will promote attributions to effort or appropriate strategy use (e.g., "You did great! I am proud of you. The fact that you used the correct formulas this time to solve the math problems shows me that you have really worked on learning when and why to use the appropriate formulas, good job!").

Parents also communicate information to children and adolescents that affect their attributions. If a participant loses a gymnastics competition, one parent might comment, "It is okay; gymnastics is very difficult," whereas another parent might state, "You didn't use the techniques that your coach showed you last week." The first statement might produce ability attributions (e.g., "This is difficult; I don't expect you to be able to do well"), whereas the latter statement might encourage the gymnast to attribute the failure to a controllable cause, to something that can be altered for a better outcome next time.

The information that parents communicate to children and adolescents may be based at least in part on parents' own attributions for their children's successes and failures. When children succeed or fail at tasks in school, parents form their own beliefs about the causes of their children's experiences. Some research suggests that there may be predictable patterns to these parental beliefs. For example, as indicated by Yee and Eccles, some research indicates that in the domain of mathematics, parents are more likely to attribute their daughter's success to effort, but to assume the same success in their son is due to mathematical ability.

INDIVIDUAL DIFFERENCES IN ATTRIBUTIONS

Attributional patterns differ among individuals. Development also plays a role in attribution. For instance, according to Nicholls, young children and older adolescents have different understandings of concepts, such as ability, that are central to attribution theory. Younger children do not easily differentiate between concepts, such as ability and effort, whereas older adolescents are better able to understand such distinctions. Consequently, attributions may take on different meanings for students at different stages of cognitive development.

Although there has not been much research on ethnic differences in attributions, Sandra Graham has summarized the findings to date of research in this area. Graham notes African-American students tend to make external attributions more often than white students. Although internal attributions are generally considered more adaptive for white students, Graham suggests that greater belief in external causes may be adaptive for African American students (1994). Graham also notes that in order to truly understand the role of attributions in the study of motivation in minority students, it is important to consider the complex relations between gender and ethnicity (1997).

Studies of gender differences in attributions have yielded somewhat mixed results. Some studies indicate that female students are more likely to attribute negative outcomes to internal and stable causes and to attribute successful outcomes to unstable, external causes (e.g., "My successes are due to good teaching and good luck; my failures are because I'm not good enough"); however, other research suggests that there are no gender differences in attributional patterns. Clearly, additional research on this topic is needed.

IMPLICATIONS OF ATTRIBUTION THEORY FOR EDUCATORS

There are many practical implications of attribution theory for educators. First, teachers need to realize that they can affect the types of attributions that students make. Teachers affect students' attributions on a daily basis, through their comments to students, feedback on assignments and examinations, and the types of praise that they offer during instruction. These comments can have important long-term effects on student learning and motivation. A student who consistently learns to attribute failures to a lack of ability in a particular subject area is unlikely to continue to be motivated to achieve in that subject area in the future. Educators need to remember the power they have in shaping students' attributions.

Second, teachers can educate parents about attributions. Since parents provide feedback and make comments to their children about performance on academic work, teachers can encourage parents to provide effective feedback. For example, teachers can send home a weekly newsletter to parents explaining what is being learned in class and offering specific suggestions to parents about providing appropriate feedback to children.

Finally, educators should be aware that students do think about the causes of their own successes and failures. Teachers can engage students in conversation to learn about their students' attributions and to monitor potentially inaccurate and harmful beliefs. Teachers may be surprised by some of their students' attributional beliefs; one-on-one conversations may provide insight to teachers and provide opportunities for shaping students' beliefs about their performance.

SEE ALSO *Attributional Retraining; Student Emotions; Weiner, Bernard.*

BIBLIOGRAPHY
Brophy, J. (1981) Teacher praise: A functional analysis. *Review of Educational Research, 51*(1), 5–32.

Covington, M. V. (1992). *Making the grade: A self-worth perspective on motivation and school reform.* New York: Cambridge University Press.

Graham, S. (1994). Motivation in African Americans. *Review of Educational Research, 64,* 55–117.

Graham, S. (1997). Using attribution theory to understand social and academic motivation in African-American youth. *Educational Psychologist, 32*(1), 21–34.

Heider, F. (1958). *The psychology of interpersonal relations.* New York: Wiley.

Nicholls, J. G. (1990). What is ability and why are we mindful of it? A developmental perspective. In R. Sternberg & J. Kolligian (Eds.), *Competence considered* (pp.11–40) New Haven, CT: Yale University Press.

Weiner, B. (1985). An attribution theory of achievement motivation and emotion. *Psychological Review, 92,* 548–73.

Weiner, B. (2005). Motivation from an attributional perspective and the social psychology of perceived competence. In A. J. Elliot and C. S. Dweck (Eds.), *Handbook of Competence and Motivation* (pp.73–84). New York: Guilford.

Weiner, B. (2006). *Social motivation, justice, and the moral emotions: an attributional approach.* Mahwah, NJ: Lawrence Erlbaum Associates.

Yee, D. K., & Eccles, J. S. (1988). Parent Perceptions and Attributions for Children's Math Achievement. *Sex roles, 19,* 317–333.

Eric Anderman
Lynley Anderman

ATTRIBUTIONAL RETRAINING

Attributional retraining (AR) is a motivational treatment developed in the latter half of the 20th century in concert with social cognition theories that focused on how individuals explain life experiences (Heider, 1958; Weiner et al., 1972). AR is closely linked with Weiner's attribution theory (1974, 1985, 2006) which posits that negative, unexpected, and important outcomes trigger explanatory thinking in achievement settings. The ensuing explanations or causal attributions have three properties in common: locus of causality (within/outside the individual), stability (transient/enduring), and controllability (not modifiable/modifiable). Students' attributions for success and failure influence learning-related emotions, cognitions, and motivation because each dimension has unique cognitive and affective consequences.

The locus dimension fosters feelings of pride following an internal attribution for success. The stability dimension influences expectations about the reoccurrence of the event and feelings of hope for future success (hopefulness/hopelessness). The controllability dimension determines responsibility judgments concerning the event and guilt and shame emotions related to negative events. Following failure, a low ability attribution is motivationally dysfunctional because it affirms the expectation that failure can reoccur (stable/uncontrollable failure), while increasing feelings of shame. Lack of effort enhances motivation because it promotes expectations that change is possible (unstable/controllable failure) and engenders feelings of guilt. Because of these attribution-affect-cognition linkages, unstable and controllable causes intensify motivation and persistence when failure occurs; uncontrollable and stable causes do the opposite.

In achievement settings, a variety of AR treatments have been used that differ in terms of attributional content, delivery formats, and audience targets (Försterling, 1985; Perry et al., 1993; Weiner, 1988; Wilson et al., 2002). AR content ranges from modifying individual attributions to changing the dimensional properties of attributions based on Weiner's theory (1985; 2006). Some treatments specifically encourage effort instead of ability attributions as explanations of failure; others seek to change ability from a stable to an unstable attribution that changes with time. Still others primarily seek to increase controllable attributions for negative experiences (effort, strategy), or to decrease uncontrollable attributions (test difficulty, luck). For example, an AR treatment focusing on controllable attributions may highlight lack of effort or poor note-taking as causes of failure because they can be increased by studying harder, taking clearer notes, or attending more classes.

AR treatments also differ in terms of the delivery format used to present the attributional content. Past studies have delivered the content via written material, videotape simulations, and structured lectures separately or in combination. These formats vary in length and in whether they are delivered to recipients individually or in groups. Individual presentations are often face-to-face and group presentations are some combination of written material, videotape, and lecture. In a typical experiment, recipients are encouraged to think about past performance outcomes (e.g., class tests, course grades) or receive feedback on a task designed to activate attributional thinking. The AR treatment is administered immediately thereafter via some combination of delivery formats. Prior to the activation task and following the AR treatment, attributional measures are administered to assess pre/post treatment effects.

The recipients of AR treatments can be differentiated largely in terms of age (children versus adults), and these can be further segregated into sub-groupings based on demographic and psycho-social variables. Depending on the target audience, the objectives and the format of the treatment will vary in accordance with audience characteristics. An AR treatment administered to college students, for example, can use more complex attributional content than would be possible with children that may include a broader range of specific attributions and formats. It may also be more readily presented in a group context rather than in an individualized, face-to-face context as may be necessary with children.

With younger students, AR information is typically administered through repeated face-to-face or computer-based attributional feedback in response to performance. Attributional feedback often involves highlighting the importance of investing effort ("You've been working very hard"; Schunk, 1983) or noting insufficient effort following failure ("You should have tried harder"; Dweck, 1975). Examples of other AR techniques include the modeling of adaptive attributions during mock performance trials with learning-disabled children (Borkowski et al., 1988) and reinforcing student-generated statements involving effort (Fowler & Peterson, 1981).

With university students, AR typically comprises one-time, mass informational seminars presenting controllable attributions verbally, in written format, or via videotaped interviews (Perry et al., 1993). Following the presentation, an activity that encourages students to reflect concretely (e.g., by completing a difficult test) or abstractly (e.g., group discussion, writing exercise) on the information is administered, with both the presentation and consolidation typically required for AR to be successful (Perry et al., 2005).

AR IN SCHOOLS

In elementary classrooms, AR is effective in improving academic motivation and performance in struggling students, demonstrated originally by Dweck (1975) and Miller et al. (1975). An AR intervention encouraging effort attributions for failure improved performance on a mathematics problem-solving task, particularly for students who have learned helplessness. These findings have been replicated primarily with underachieving students, showing AR techniques not only to improve performance, but also to increase motivation, self-efficacy, success expectations, and controllable attributions, as well as to lower uncontrollable attributions (e.g., Andrews & Debus, 1978, Fowler & Peterson, 1981; Schunk, 1983). AR methods can also reduce aggressive behavior in school classrooms (Hudley et al., 1998) and can be beneficial for children with learning disabilities (Robertson, 2000).

These studies suggest AR procedures that promote self-talk concerning adaptive attributions may be better than direct persuasion by the instructor (e.g., "You should work harder"; Fowler & Peterson, 1981; Miller et al., 1975). Instructor-initiated AR in intact classrooms may be less effective than smaller experimenter-led sessions (Craven et al., 1991; Robertson, 2000). Many AR interventions for children are administered as part of

larger training programs focusing on learning or social skills, particularly for students with learning disabilities (e.g., Borkowski et al., 1988; Schunk, 1983). Although some results suggest that ability-related feedback following success may improve self-efficacy and performance (Schunk, 1983), other findings indicate the simultaneous combination of ability feedback (e.g., "You're good at this") and effort feedback does not improve AR effectiveness (e.g., Ho & McMurtie, 1991; Schunk, 1983).

AR research on middle- and high-school students shows that intensive, in-person AR programs can increase perceptions of control, persistence, and achievement (e.g., Dresel, 2000; Ziegler & Heller, 1998), particularly for failing or depressed students (Dieser & Ruddell, 2002). Computer-based AR can also improve mathematics performance by providing attributional feedback contingent upon students' performance (failure equals effort; success equals ability; Okolo, 1992) and on their progress (success first attributed to effort, then ability; Dresel & Ziegler, 2006). Research by Heller, Ziegler, and colleagues further illustrates the effectiveness of brief AR techniques (e.g., videotape presentation) for gifted students, particularly for females in the natural sciences (Heller, 1999, 2003; Heller & Ziegler, 1996; Ziegler & Heller, 2000; Ziegler & Stoeger, 2004). AR also plays a critical role in resolving group discipline problems (Lapointe & Legault, 2004) and assisting with career-related decision-making (Szabo, 2006).

AR IN POSTSECONDARY EDUCATION

In college classrooms, AR researchers have focused extensively on students' scholastic development, particularly the transition from high school to college. Since classic studies by Wilson and Linville (1982, 1985), AR programs that encourage the changeable nature of academic performance have improved motivation, emotions, and course performance (Perry et al., 1993, 2005; Wilson et al., 2002). Successful AR techniques for college students are typically brief and consist of two phases. The initial presentation phase often includes a videotaped dialogue between senior students (Noel et al., 1987; Perry & Penner, 1990; Van Overwalle et al., 1989; Wilson & Linville, 1982, 1985) or an informational handout (Haynes et al., 2006; Jesse & Gregory, 1986–1987; Ruthig et al., 2004) outlining the benefits of attributing poor performance to, for example, insufficient effort and poor study strategies.

Following the AR presentation, a consolidation phase is administered that encourages students to elaborate on the information through exercises such as group discussions (e.g., Ruthig et al., 2004; Struthers & Perry, 1996), aptitude or achievement tests (e.g., Hall et al., 2007; Menec et al., 1994), or writing assignments (e.g.,

Hall et al., 2007). Similar to findings for younger students, AR conducted in intact classrooms by course instructors appears to be less effective than smaller-scale, experimenter-led sessions (Hladkyj et al., 1998), and computer-based AR involving the Internet can contribute to better course grades (Hall et al., 2005). AR can also facilitate career-related decision-making (Luzzo et al., 1996) and success in employment interviews for upper-level undergraduates (Jackson et al., in press).

AR research with college students has focused not only on the development of intervention techniques, but also on targeting students with specific risk characteristics. For example, AR is especially beneficial for students at risk of failure due to previous poor performance (Wilson & Linville, 1982, 1985; Van Overwalle et al., 1989), uncontrollable attributions (Struthers & Perry, 1996), an external locus of control (Menec et al., 1994; Perry & Penner, 1990), and insufficient use of elaborative learning strategies (Hall et al., 2007). Students with overly optimistic beliefs are particularly at risk and respond especially well to AR interventions (Hall et al., 2006; Haynes et al., 2006; Ruthig et al., 2004).

APPLICATIONS TO CLASSROOMS

As most educators know, attributional exchanges commonly occur in the daily functioning of classrooms. However, these informal, spontaneous, and anecdotal attributional exchanges are rarely informed by scientific theory and evidence and too often involve the communication of maladaptive (uncontrollable/stable) attributions for failure (e.g., low ability: "If you did poorly on the exam, this class isn't for you."). Such maladaptive attributional exchanges raise serious questions about the ethics of their use in teaching practices intended to foster motivation. In contrast, research-informed AR has several strengths as a motivation-enhancing treatment: It is derived from a well-established attribution theory (Weiner, 1985, 2006); it is supported by a solid body of empirical evidence (Perry et al., 1993, 2005), and it can be readily adapted to achievement settings (Perry, 1991, 2003; Wilson et al., 2002).

Assuming that AR is to be implemented in a classroom, four guiding principles are recommended. First, the attributional content should be strongly informed by the scientific evidence on effective AR procedures and reviewed by responsible professionals. Second, screening procedures should be used to identify students most likely to benefit from the program. Such diagnostic procedures may include course tests, informal teacher/student exchanges, formal questionnaires, etc. Third, the intervention format should be selected based on empirical evidence regarding effective procedures for specific student populations (e.g., one-time seminars for gifted or older students; repeated performance feedback for younger or learning-disabled students).

Finally, follow-up assessments of subjective (e.g., attributions, motivation) and objective outcomes (e.g., attendance, performance) are required to accurately determine the effectiveness of AR on classroom adjustment and performance.

SEE ALSO *Attribution Theory; Learned Helplessness.*

BIBLIOGRAPHY

Andrews, G. R., & Debus, R. L. (1978). Persistence and the causal perception of failure: Modifying cognitive attributions. *Journal of Educational Psychology, 70,* 154–166.

Borkowski, J. G., Weyhing, R. S., & Carr, M. (1988). Effects of attributional retraining on strategy-based reading comprehension in learning-disabled students. *Journal of Educational Psychology, 80,* 46–53.

Craske, M. L. (1988). Learned helplessness, self-worth motivation and attribution retraining for primary school children. *British Journal of Educational Psychology, 58,* 152–164.

Craven, R. G., Marsh, H. W., & Debus, R. L. (1991). Effects of internally focused feedback and attributional feedback on enhancement of academic self-concept. *Journal of Educational Psychology, 83,* 17–27.

Dresel, M., & Ziegler, A. (2006). Langfristige förderung von Fähigkeitsselbstkonzept und impliziter Fähigkeitstheorie durch computerbasiertes attributionales Feedback [Long-term enhancement of academic self concept and implicit ability theory through computer-based attribution feedback]. *Zeitschrift für Pädagogische Psychologie, 20,* 49–63.

Dweck, C. S. (1975). The role of expectations and attributions in the alleviation of learned helplessness. *Journal of Personality and Social Psychology, 31,* 674–685.

Försterling, F. (1985). Attributional retraining: A review. *Psychological Bulletin, 98,* 495–512.

Fowler, J. W., & Peterson, P. L. (1981). Increasing reading persistence and altering attributional style of learned helpless children. *Journal of Educational Psychology, 73,* 251–261.

Hall, N. C., Perry, R. P., Chipperfield, J. G., Clifton, R. A., & Haynes, T. L. (2006). Enhancing primary and secondary control in achievement settings through writing-based attributional retraining. *Journal of Social and Clinical Psychology, 25,* 361–391.

Hall, N. C., Perry, R. P., Goetz, T., Ruthig, J. C., Stupnisky, R. H., & Newall, N. E. (2007). Attributional retraining and elaborative learning: Improving academic development through writing-based interventions. *Learning and Individual Differences, 17,* 280–290.

Hall, N. C., Perry, R. P., Ruthig, J. C., Haynes, T. L., & Stupnisky, R. H. (2005, April). *Internet-based attributional retraining: Longitudinal effects on academic achievement in college students.* Montreal, QC, Canada: American Educational Research Association.

Haynes, T. L., Ruthig, J. C., Perry, R. P., Stupnisky, R. H., & Hall, N. C. (2006). Reducing the academic risks of overoptimism: The longitudinal effects of attributional retraining on cognition and achievement. *Research in Higher Education, 47,* 755–779.

Heider, F. (1958). *The psychology of interpersonal relations.* New York, NY: Wiley.

Heller, K. A. (2003). Attributional retraining as an attempt to reduce gender-specific problems in mathematics and the sciences. *Gifted and Talented, 7,* 15–21.

Heller, K. A., & Ziegler, A. (1996). Gender differences in mathematics and the natural sciences: Can attributional retraining improve the performance of gifted females? *Gifted Child Quarterly, 40,* 200–210.

Hladkyj, S., Hunter, A. J., Maw, J., & Perry, R. P. (1998, April). Attributional Retraining and Elaborative Learning in the College Classroom. Paper presented at the American Educational Research Association annual meeting, San Diego, CA.

Jackson, S. E., Hall, N. C., Rowe, P., & Daniels, L. M. (in press). Getting the Job: Attributional Retraining and the Employment Interview. *Journal of Applied Social Psychology, .*

Jesse, D. M., & Gregory, W. L. (1986–1987). A comparison of three attributional approaches to maintaining first year college GPA. *Educational Research Quarterly, 11,* 12–25.

Lapointe, J. M., & Legault, F. (2004). Solving group discipline problems without coercion: An approach based on attribution retraining. *Journal of Classroom Interaction, 39,* 1–10.

Luzzo, D. A., James, T., & Luna, M. (1996). Effects of attributional retraining on the career beliefs and career exploration behavior of college students. *Journal of Counselling Psychology, 43,* 415–422.

Menec, V. H., Perry, R. P., Struthers, C. W., Schonwetter, D. J., Hechter, F. J., & Eichholz, B. L. (1994). Assisting at-risk college students with attributional retraining and effective teaching. *Journal of Applied Social Psychology, 24,* 675–701.

Miller, R. L., Brickman P., & Bolen, D. (1975). Attribution versus persuasion as a means for modifying behavior. *Journal of Personality and Social Psychology, 31,* 430–441.

Noel, J. G., Forsyth, D. R., & Kelley, K. N. (1987). Improving performance of failing students by overcoming their self-serving attributional biases. *Basic and Applied Psychology, 8,* 151–162.

Perry, R. P., Hall, N. C., & Ruthig, J. C. (2005). Perceived (academic) control and scholastic attainment in higher education. In J. Smart (Ed.), *Higher education: Handbook of theory and research* (vol. 20, 363–436). The Netherlands: Springer.

Perry, R. P., Hechter, F. J., Menec, V. H., & Weinberg, L. E. (1993). Enhancing achievement motivation and performance in college students: An attributional retraining perspective. *Research in Higher Education, 34,* 687–723.

Perry, R. P., & Penner, K. S. (1990). Enhancing academic achievement in college students through attributional retraining and instruction. *Journal of Educational Psychology, 82,* 262–271.

Robertson, J. S. (2000). Is attribution training a worthwhile classroom intervention for K–12 students with learning difficulties? *Educational Psychology Review, 12,* 111–13.

Ruthig, J. C., Perry, R. P., Hall, N. C., & Hladkyj, S. (2004). Optimism and attributional retraining: Longitudinal effects on academic achievement, test anxiety, and voluntary course withdrawal in college students. *Journal of Applied Social Psychology, 34,* 709–730.

Schunk, D. H. (1983). Ability versus effort attributional feedback: Differential effects on self-efficacy and achievement. *Journal of Educational Psychology, 75,* 848–856.

Struthers, C. W., & Perry, R. P. (1996). Attributional style, attributional retraining, and inoculation against motivational deficits. *Social Psychology of Education, 1,* 171–187.

Szabo, Z. (2006). The influence of attributional retraining on career choices. *Journal of Cognitive and Behavioral Psychotherapies, 6,* 89–103.

Van Overwalle, F., Segebarth, K., & Goldchstein, M. (1989). Improving performance of freshman through attributional testimonies from fellow students. *British Journal of Educational Psychology, 59,* 75–85.

Weiner, B. (1974). Motivational psychology and educational research. *Educational Psychologist, 11*(2), 96–101.

Weiner, B. (1985). An attributional theory of achievement motivation and emotion. *Psychological Review, 92,* 548–573.

Weiner, B. (1988). Attribution theory and attributional therapy: Some theoretical observations and suggestions. *British Journal of Clinical Psychology, 27,* 93–104.

Weiner, B. (1995). *Judgments of responsibility: A Foundation for a theory of social conduct.* New York: Guilford Press.

Weiner, B. (2006). *Social motivation, justice, and the moral emotions: An attributional approach.* Mahwah, NJ: Lawrence Erlbaum Associates.

Weiner, B., Frieze, I., Kukla, A., Reed, L., Rest, S., Rosenbaum, R. (1972). Perceiving the causes of success and failure. In E. E. Jones, D. Kanouse, H. H. Kelley, R. E. Nisbett, S. Valins, and B. Weiner. *Attribution: Perceiving the Causes of Behavior.* Morristown, NJ.: General Learning Press.

Wilson, T. D., Damiani, M., & Shelton, N. (2002). Improving the academic performance of college students with brief attributional interventions. In J. Aronson (Ed.), *Improving academic achievement: Impact of psychological factors on education* (pp. 88–108). San Diego, CA: Academic Press.

Wilson, T. D., & Linville, P. W. (1982). Improving the academic performance of college freshmen: Attributional therapy revisited. *Journal of Personality and Social Psychology, 42,* 367–376.

Wilson, T. D., & Linville, P. W. (1985). Improving the performance of college freshmen with attributional techniques. *Journal of Personality and Social Psychology, 49,* 287–293.

Ziegler, A., & Stoeger, H. (2004). Evaluation of an attributional retraining (modeling technique) to reduce gender differences in chemistry instruction. *High Ability Studies, 15,* 63–83.

Raymond P. Perry
Nathan Hall

AUTHENTIC ASSESSMENT

Authentic assessment comprises a variety of assessment techniques that share the following characteristics: (1) direct measurement of skills that relate to long-term educational outcomes such as success in the workplace; (2) tasks that require extensive engagement and complex performance; and (3) an analysis of the processes used to produce the response. Authentic assessment is often defined by what it is not: Its antonyms include: norm-referenced standardized tests; fixed-choice multiple-choice or true/false tests; fill-in-the-blank tests. Synonyms include: performance assessment, portfolios, and projects. Dynamic (Lidz, 1991) or responsive assessment (Henning-Stout, 1991) are other terms associated with authentic assessment. Authentic assessment has been a popular method for assessing student learning among specific populations of students such as those with severe disabilities (Coutinho & Malouf, 1993), very young children (Grisham-Brown, Hallam, & Brookshire, 2006), and gifted students (Moore, 2005). In addition, specific disciplines such as the arts (Popovich, 2006), science (Oh, Kim, Garcia, & Krilowicz, 2005) and teacher education (Gatlin & Jacob, 2002) have embraced authentic assessment for its emphasis on process over product. Grant Wiggins described authentic assessments as "faithful representations of the contexts encountered in a field of study or in the real-life 'tests' of adult life" (1993, p. 206).

THE HISTORY OF AUTHENTIC ASSESSMENT

Authentic assessment was a significant component of the 1990s education reform zeitgeist, and Wiggins was one its most prolific and convincing proponents (Terwilliger, 1997). Wiggins (1993) asserted that traditional methods of student assessment (i.e., forced choice tests such as multiple-choice, true/false test, etc.) fail to elicit complex intellectual performance valued in real life experiences and result in a narrowing of the curriculum to basic skills, including test taking skills. At a time when standardized minimum competency tests had been largely rejected for reducing or diminishing the curriculum, and content standards emphasizing higher-ordered thinking skills were articulated within many disciplines and states, authentic assessment gained considerable traction.

Subsequently, educators may have engaged in authentic assessment to rebel against the top-down accountability of high-stakes standardized testing (Salvia

& Ysseldyke, 2004). Since the 2002 No Child Left Behind (NCLB) Act, there has been a greater focus on large-scale standardized testing. There is a lack of connection between the federal and state policy makers and public school educators. In an ideal educational setting, professional educators in all arenas would guide the learners' movement toward the standards. This would be developed in an organic process with student, site, and community input. However, the current practice is that standards are developed by remote government bureaucrats in state or federal buildings far removed from the students and those who are in contact with the students on a daily basis (Henning-Stout, 1996). There is a feeling of imposition on school site educators by state and federal officials, which compounds the challenges towards the ideal development of authentic assessment.

Educators' desire for authenticity in assessment and learning is not free from the polemics of political climates that define that nature of modern education.

AUTHENTIC ASSESSMENT DATA ANALYSIS

Assessment data are used for multiple purposes, including making accountability, eligibility, and instructional decisions. The purpose of the assessment directs the analyses. For example, authentic assessment data collected for determining whether a school, district, or state is sufficiently educating students will require data to be aggregated at the systems level, as well as disaggregated by various sub-populations of students, in order to make such accountability decisions. Authentic assessment to determine whether a student meets specific state or national special education criteria must be corroborated by other types of data given the significant ramifications for the student (Lidz, 1991). Data collected to inform instruction must be analyzed relative to the curriculum and instruction provided to the students in a particular class. Authentic assessment data can be analyzed by qualitative or quantitative methods.

Examples of authentic assessments

Assessment	Standard
Students writing to their councilperson about an improvement they could make in their neighborhood	Second grade social studies standards
Students work in teams to build small-scale models of California missions or Indian villages	Fourth grade history standard
Classroom presentation in the form of a play on civil rights struggle. The play is shared with the student body, civic organizations, and other schools (Hilliard, 2003)	Sixth grade history standard
Summative science fair presentation that integrates applying scientific method, mathematical problem solving, history of the area of study, writing, visual presentation, and public speaking skills (Meyer, 1992)	High school science standards
Reflective meta-cognitive journal entries about how artifacts in the school psychology formative program portfolio relate to the eight domains for training (Hass & Osborne, 2002)	National Association of School Psychologists training standards

Table 1 ILLUSTRATION BY GGS INFORMATION SERVICES. CENGAGE LEARNING, GALE.

A qualitative analysis of a student's performance typically describes skills that were demonstrated and errors that were made thereby providing a narrative of what the student knows and is able to do, and what the student needs to learn or improve upon. Narratives also allow the student's performance to be considered within the context of the assessment. For example, Alverno College is nationally recognized for its narrative assessments of eight core abilities in a manner that is contextually relevant for each discipline (Alverno College Faculty, 1994).

A quantitative analysis of authentic assessment data applies a scoring rubric or checklist to judge student responses relative to criteria within a restricted range of four or more proficiency levels (e.g., advanced proficient, proficient, partially proficient, and failure). Scoring rubrics can be either analytic or holistic. Analytic analyses require defining and assessing different dimensions of a task. For example, the spelling, sentence structure, vocabulary, accuracy, level of detail, and coherence of an essay may be judged independently. Holistic analysis assigns an overall score to a student's performance, like judging an Olympic gymnastic competition.

VARIATIONS OF AUTHENTIC ASSESSMENTS

Three variations of authentic assessments most frequently discussed are dynamic (Hilliard, 1995; Lidz, 1991), performance, and portfolio assessment (Salvia & Ysseldyke, 2004). Proponents of authentic assessment (Hilliard, 1995; Lidz, 1991; Meyer, 1992) have observed that many people think they are conducting it when in fact they are not. The multiple purposes for assessments and the general nature of many of the terms associated with authentic assessment has resulted in variation among researchers and practitioners in what is considered authentic or dynamic assessment (Cumming & Maxwell, 1999; Newton, 2007).

Dynamic assessment is conducted within a test-intervene-retest format or process. For example, an educator first administers a test to a student; then the adult intervenes by asking questions about the child's incorrect or unexpected answers to improve the student's cognitive processes. Finally, the adult administers the same or a similar test to the child to see if the child has developed a new strategy for solving the problem. Thus, dynamic assessment attempts to measure the student's level of modifiability.

Compared to dynamic assessment, performance and portfolio assessment are more commonly used in classroom settings (Salvia & Ysseldyke, 2004). Performance assessments require students to complete or demonstrate the behavior that educators want to measure (Meyer, 1992). For a performance task to be authentic, it must be completed within a real-world context, which includes shifting the locus of control to the student in that the student chooses the topic, the time needed for completion, and the general conditions under which the writing sample is generated (Meyer, 1992). Portfolio assessments are an accumulation of artifacts that demonstrate progress toward valued real-world outcomes, are often produced in collaboration, require student reflection, and are evaluated on multiple dimensions (Salvia & Ysseldyke, 2004).

METHODOLOGICAL STRENGTHS AND LIMITATIONS OF AUTHENTIC ASSESSMENT

A major strength of authentic assessment is its connection to real-life skills (Meyer, 1992). Proponents of authentic assessment are quick to point out that life is not a series of isolated multiple-choice questions but full of complex, embedded problems to be solved (Wiggins, 1993). Accordingly, authentic assessments require students to solve complex problems or produce multi-step projects, often in collaboration with others. In this way, higher-ordered learning skills such as synthesis, analysis, collaboration, and problem solving are assessed. In fact, the purpose of authentic assessment is to measure students' ability to apply their knowledge and thinking skills to solving tasks that simulate real-world events or activities (see Table 1, for examples; Wiggins, 1993).

Authentic assessments attempt to seamlessly combine teaching, learning, and assessment to promote student motivation, engagement, and higher-ordered learning skills (Eder, 2004). Because assessment is part of instruction, teacher and students share an understanding of the criteria for performance; in some cases, students even contribute to defining the expectations for the task. The assumption is that students perform better when they know how they will be judged. Often students are asked to reflect and evaluate their own performance in order to promote deeper understanding of the learning objectives as well as foster higher order learning skills (i.e., self-reflection and evaluation).

Authentic assessments are often described as developmental because of the focus on students' burgeoning abilities to learn how to learn in the subject (Wiggins, 1993). For example, students' shortcomings in knowledge and how they apply their knowledge can be examined through carefully analyzing of their log books or by asking probing questions, in order to identify what needs to be taught or re-taught. Thus, the process by which students arrived at their final response or product is assessed (Mehrens, 1992).

Authentic assessments also have limitations. These include subjectivity in scoring, the costliness of administering and scoring, and the narrow range of skills that are typically assessed (Mehrens, 1992). By emphasizing complexity and relevance rather than structure and standardization, inter-rater reliability can be difficult to achieve with authentic assessment. Inter-rater agreement is increased with clearly defined criteria, including exemplars and non-exemplars and initial and on-going training of the evaluators. Unfortunately educators rarely have adequate guidelines to help analyze and score student products (Ysseldyke & Salvia, 2004). The logistics and training demands of authentic assessment have made its wide-spread adoption among general education prohibitive. Selecting artifacts to include in a portfolio can also be a challenge. In order to avoid the portfolio's becoming a meaningless accumulation of student work, there needs to be some selection process that distinguishes critical works from mementos (Hass & Osborne, 2002). Lastly, the emphasis on assessing knowledge in-depth or in application, often limits the amount of content knowledge that is assessed. For example, an authentic assessment that requires students in a biology class to design the ideal zoo would not test what students know about photosynthesis. Terwilliger proposed that the specificity of authentic assessment evaluation criteria to a particular task may limit its value as a measure of general learning outcomes.

HOW AUTHENTIC ASSESSMENT INFORMS INSTRUCTION AND INTERVENTIONS

Henning-Stout (1996) stated, "Academic assessment is authentic when it reflects performance on tasks that are meaningful to the learner" (p. 234). One strength of authentic assessment is the strong connection to the development of lessons and interventions that have real-life applications. If the learners being assessed are aware of their ability to self-regulate (Dembo, 2004) and make the appropriate changes during the learning process, they will achieve the transfer of knowledge that is necessary for learning to occur (Lidz, 1991). More importantly, they should be able to solve real-world tasks and be able to process new information within the construct of that task.

When given clear standards (Henning-Stout, 1996) and reliable and valid methods (Salvia & Ysseldke, 2004) for conducting authentic assessment, teachers can inform students of the level of expected performance and provide direct feedback about students' process towards meeting those standards. With dynamic assessment students receive immediate feedback about their process and their own problem-solving skills. The portfolio assessment provides individual students with an opportunity to physically and cognitively organize and monitor their learning process.

For educators concerned with social justice in the development of curriculum, pedagogy and assessment, authentic assessment provides ways for students outside the norm of the standard assessment to express their understanding of material (Henning-Stout, 1996; Hilliard, 1995; Louise, 2007; Newfield, Andrew, Stein, & Maungedzo, 2003). For example, the government of South Africa has moved away from high stakes standardized assessments for categorizing, labeling, and tracking students towards portfolio assessments that are developed in conjunction with local communities (Newfield et al., 2003).

Authentic assessment has also been used to train professionals. School administrators and teachers have been evaluated using portfolio assessments (Gatlin & Jacobs, 2002; Meadows & Dyal, 1999) as well as school psychology graduate students (Hass & Osborn, 2002; Prus, Matton, Thomas, & Robinson-Zañartu, 1996).

SEE ALSO *Classroom Assessment.*

BIBLIOGRAPHY

Alverno College Faculty. (1994). *Student assessment-as-learning at Alverno College.* Milwaukee, WI: Alverno Productions.

Coutinho, M., & Malouf, D. (1993). Performance assessment and children with disabilities: Issues and possibilities. *Teaching Exceptional Children, 25*(4), 63–67.

Cumming, J. J., & Maxwell, G. S. (1999). Contextualizing Authentic Assessment. *Assessment in Education, 6*(2), 177–194.

Dembo, M. H. (2004,). Don't lose sight of the students. *Principal Leadership,* April, 37–42.

Edger, D. J., (2004). General education assessment within the disciplines. *Journal of General Education, 53*(2), 135–157.

Gatlin, L., & Jacob, S. (2002). Standards-based digital portfolios: A component of authentic assessment for preservice teachers. *Action in Teacher Education, 23*(4), 28–34.

Grisham-Brown, J., Hallam, R., & Brookshire, R. (2006). Using authentic assessment to evidence children's progress toward early learning standards. *Early Childhood Education Journal, 34*(1), 45–51.

Hass, M., & Osborn, J. (2002). Using formative portfolios to enhance graduate school psychology programs. *California School Psychologist, 7,* 75–84.

Hilliard, A. G. (1995). *Testing African American Students* (2nd ed.). Chicago: Third World Press.

Lidz, C. (1991). *Practitioner's Guide to Dynamic Assessment.* New York: Guilford Press.

Meadows, R. B., & Dyal, A.B. (1999). Implementing portfolio assessment in the development of school administrators: improving preparation for educational leadership. *Education, 120*(2), 304–314.

Mehrens, W. A., (1992, Spring). Using performance assessment for accountability purposes. *Educational Measurement: Issues and Practice, 11*(1), 3–20.

Meyer, C. (1992). What's the difference between authentic and performance assessment? *Education Leadership, 49*(8), 39–40.

Moore, M. (2005). Meeting the educational needs of young gifted readers in the regular classroom. *Gifted Child Today, 28*(4), 40–47, 65.

Newfield, D., Andrew, D., Stein, P., & Maungedzo, R. (2003). 'No number can describe how good it was': assessment issues in the multimodal classroom. *Assessment in Education, 10* (1), 61–81.

Oh, D. M., Kim, J. M., Garcia, R. E., & Krilowicz, B. L. (2005). Valid and reliable authentic assessment of culminating student performance in the biomedical sciences. *Advances in Physiology Education, 29*(2), 83–93.

Popovich, K. (2006). Designing and implementing 'exemplary content, curriculum, and assessment in art education.' *Art Education, 59*(6), 33–39.

Prus, J., Matton, L., Thomas, A., & Robinson-Zañartu, C. (1996). Using portfolios to assess the performance of school psychology graduate students. Paper presented at the meeting of the National Association of School Psychologists, Atlanta, Georgia.

Salvia, J., & Ysseldyke, J. E. (2004). *Assessment in special and inclusive education* (9th ed.). New York: Houghton Mifflin.

Terwilliger, J. (1997). Semantics, psychometrics and assessment reform: A close look at 'authentic' assessments. *Educational Researcher, 26*(8), 24–27.

Wiggins, G. (1993). Assessment: Authenticity, context and validity. *Phi Delta Kappan, 75*(3), 200–214.

Kristin Powers
Brandon Gamble

AUTHENTIC TASKS

The instructional activities teachers provide for their students play an integral role in shaping what is learned in classrooms. These activities, often referred to as tasks, are what students do to learn academic content and skills. Tasks provide a structure and goal for learning in classrooms and require time to accomplish. They are meant to engage students in an action, or sequence of actions, that require the application and production of knowledge. Some types of tasks are authentic, which means they are situated in meaningful contexts that reflect the way tasks might be found and approached in real life. Authentic tasks can encompass everyday situations, such as organizing to make and sell t-shirts for a community fundraiser, or real-world activities undertaken in disciplines, such as conducting an historical inquiry into the Lewis and Clark expedition. Authentic tasks are not the norm in schools and classrooms, but research and contemporary perspectives on how students learn suggest that these types of tasks are powerfully effective for learning.

A distinguishing feature of authentic tasks is that they have value and meaning beyond the classroom. When students engage in authentic tasks, they do and experience what they, or other people, might do or experience in a real-life setting. In a classroom, this might mean participating in real-world tasks that are similar to the kind of tasks that experts engage in. For example, authentic tasks in a science classroom might require students to conduct scientific investigations in a manner similar to how scientists conduct their work, but in ways that are appropriate and meaningful for students. In this kind of science classroom, students might investigate the air and water quality of their neighborhoods, examine how invasive species impact local habitats, or design and construct a model erosion management system for a city park. As students engage in these tasks, they learn important science content, develop skills that mirror the practices of expert scientists, and learn first-hand how to apply their skills and knowledge in real-life, problem-solving contexts.

Authentic tasks are important because they provide meaning and motivation for learning. They provide students with opportunities to relate to real-world situations, make connections to their own interests, and engage deeply with subject matter. One of the key benefits of authentic tasks is that they introduce students to ways of reasoning and problem solving that represent the work of professionals in practice, which has the advantage of helping students build real-world expertise. As students engage in authentic tasks, they create products or artifacts that showcase the skills and knowledge they have acquired. Often, these artifacts can be used for assessment purposes in a manner that reflects the complexity of how performance is evaluated in the real world.

THEORETICAL PERSPECTIVES

In the early 20th century, the educator and philosopher John Dewey (1933) advocated the use of authentic tasks to help students acquire and deepen subject matter knowledge and enhance their logical reasoning and self-regulation skills. Central to Dewey's view was that children learn best through purposeful activity and that real-world tasks are ideal for developing useful skills and knowledge. In subsequent decades, education researchers and learning theorists elaborated further on the notion of authenticity. Their work sought to explain how authentic tasks support thinking and to gain insight into the classroom conditions under which authentic tasks are most effective.

An important idea that emerged from learning theory and research is that students construct more useful, robust, and integrated knowledge when they are engaged in their learning and helped to develop sophisticated understanding. Requiring students to merely carry out a task will not ensure learning. All too often, classroom tasks result in the acquisition of discrete information that is not very meaningful, memorable, or usable. Psychologist David Perkins (1993) calls such information, which often results from rote memorizing and is not easily transferred to other situations, inert knowledge. For meaningful learning to occur, students need to be cognitively engaged, or intellectually invested, and active in applying ideas. Cognitive engagement depends not only on the task itself, but also on the context in which the task is situated. This idea is referred to as situated cognition (Brown, Collins, & Duguid, 1989). Situated cognition emphasizes that the activity and the context in which the activity unfolds are integral to what is learned.

According to the situated cognition perspective, when students learn new information in the context of authentic tasks, they are able to make sense of the new information and relate it to what they already know or have experienced. In such cases new ideas are more likely to become intelligible because they are put in context. Context provides students with a mental frame for making sense of the learning experience. Without some framework in which to connect new ideas, students face difficulty in bringing together new information and organizing it in a way that can be easily recalled and put to use.

Situated cognition also suggests that when students participate in authentic tasks, they acquire information about the conditions and situations in which it is useful to know and apply what they have learned. As a result, they are more likely to be able to take what they have learned in one situation and transfer it to another. Additionally, students are more likely to make relevant connections between their academics and their personal lives. As viewed through the situated cognition lens, authentic tasks engage students cognitively by providing opportunities to actively think about, integrate, and apply ideas in situations that are relevant beyond the classroom. This experience often results in learning that is personally meaningful and motivating for students.

AUTHENTIC TASKS IN CLASSROOMS

Authentic tasks are used in a wide range of classroom settings, including mathematics, science, and history classrooms. Furthermore, an increasing number of instructional programs feature authentic tasks as a means to situate learning in real-world contexts (Blumenfeld, Marx, & Harris, 2006). One example is Project-Based Science (PBS), a program for middle-school science classrooms developed by Joseph Krajcik and colleagues at the University of Michigan (Krajcik, et al., 2000) in which students engage in authentic tasks in ways that are similar to how scientists conduct their work. In PBS classrooms, students take part in scientific inquiry projects that are framed by driving questions that guide instruction and serve to organize students' investigations. For instance, in a project focusing on the physics of collisions, students learn about force and motion by engaging in tasks pertaining to the question, "Why do I need to wear a helmet when I ride my bike?" This question situates the science topic in a context that is likely to be of interest to young students. As they pursue answers to the driving question, they conduct investigations, collect data, weigh evidence,

write explanations, and discuss and present findings. The authentic tasks help students learn scientific content and practices relevant and necessary to construct an evidence-based response.

Another instructional program that features authentic tasks is a video-based mathematics series called *The Adventures of Jasper Woodbury*, developed by John Bransford and his research group (Cognition and Technology Group at Vanderbilt, 1997). The program materials consist of video-based narrative adventures that present students in grades five and up with real-world mathematical challenges. For example, in a statistics and probability adventure called *The Big Splash*, students help a character develop and evaluate a business plan for raising funds for a student-run project. In another adventure called *Blueprint for Success*, students learn geometry as they help characters design a playground. A central purpose of the narrative adventures is to create experiences that are similar to the type of learning that takes place in real life. Additionally, the challenges provide students with opportunities to apply mathematics concepts and skills in realistic situations.

IMPACT ON LEARNING AND MOTIVATION

When tasks are authentic and situated in real-world contexts, students are more likely to be motivated. Motivation is important because it can lead to increased cognitive engagement and thereby enhance learning (Blumenfeld, Kempler, & Krajcik, 2006). For instance, authentic tasks often create compelling and relevant need-to-know situations for learning that heightens interest and motivates students to invest in their learning. More interest and investment in learning can lead to higher levels of engagement. In turn, sustained cognitive engagement helps students to acquire knowledge and skills as they go about working on tasks. A key benefit of authentic tasks, then, is that they provide a meaningful and motivating backdrop for learning that affords opportunities to actively think about and apply important ideas.

Research on authentic tasks indicates that when they are implemented they are associated with increased achievement and motivation for learning (e.g., Hickey, Moore, & Pelligrino, 2001). Authenticity may be particularly important for students from diverse backgrounds, especially those whose language and cultural backgrounds differ from the mainstream, and who may not perceive relevant connections between school and their everyday interests and lives. Luis Moll and colleagues (1992), for example, describe how teachers designed integrated science and mathematics projects that involved parents sharing their knowledge and expertise regarding topics connected to the surrounding community. Moll and his colleagues found that when teachers draw from students' funds of knowledge—the cognitive, linguistic, and cultural resources that they bring to school—to create tasks that help students make connections, students find meaning in what they are learning and a reason to understand. Overall, the research evidence on authentic tasks with learners in diverse school settings is encouraging: Students benefit academically and show increased interest, motivation, and engagement. Tasks that help students make connections also appear to help them to develop a more comprehensive and nuanced grasp of new material as well as an appreciation for why it is important.

DEVELOPING AND USING AUTHENTIC TASKS

To develop authentic tasks, teachers need to know their students' backgrounds and interests, school and community resources, as well as disciplinary content and practices. A high quality authentic task has several features, including real-world relevance, accessibility, feasibility, sustainability, and alignment to learning goals. Real-world relevance refers to the extent to which the task connects to issues or experiences beyond the classroom. Authentic tasks are most effective when they have personal value and meaning that extends to the surrounding world, thus providing students with a sense of purpose for engaging in the tasks. Accessibility highlights the appropriateness of the task given the prior knowledge and skills of students and its potential for helping students advance in their understanding. An authentic task that is accessible will help students learn important content and develop skills and enhance understanding about the situations in which the newly acquired knowledge and skills can be applied. Feasibility addresses the available school and community resources and whether students can carry out the task given the resources and materials at hand. Sustainability is the ability of a task to sustain cognitive engagement over time. This feature is critical for ensuring that students learn while participating in authentic tasks. A final key feature is alignment to learning goals. Authentic tasks that do not match important learning goals found in district or state standards are unlikely to be usable in school settings.

Teachers can develop high-quality authentic tasks in various ways. One approach is to use learning goals as a starting point. With learning goals in mind, teachers can then brainstorm tasks that will interest students and encompass important ideas and skills. Another way is to use existing curriculum materials and identify opportunities within the materials to create authentic tasks that connect to students' everyday lives and curiosities. Teachers can also develop authentic tasks by listening to students and drawing directly from their ideas, interests, and experiences, as well as issues in their communities.

Another approach involves teachers collaborating with students to identify and structure possible tasks. Finally, teachers can work with community experts, such as writers, architects, scientists, engineers, and historians, to develop meaningful and engaging tasks that help students learn about professional practices.

Using authentic tasks effectively with students requires that teachers attend to several features of the classroom environment. Foremost, teachers need to create classroom conditions that support students in learning from authentic tasks (Newmann & Wehlage, 1993). It is necessary to provide guidance to students in how to engage in tasks and how to learn from them. Without specialized support, or scaffolding, from a teacher, students will not develop the skills and knowledge to successfully engage in authentic tasks. Teachers must also create a social climate that supports students in working together productively and encourages students to take risks and try hard on tasks. Another important feature is assessment. Teachers need to provide for authentic assessment of learning that is integrated within the tasks and reflective of the purposes and complexity of the tasks.

LIMITATIONS IN USING AUTHENTIC TASKS

Using authentic tasks in classrooms is complex and difficult. Teachers can be challenged because they may have never participated in authentic tasks and may not know how to enact them. In contrast to typical classroom tasks, authentic tasks are carried out over days or weeks rather than minutes or hours. Teachers need to carefully sequence activities so that students acquire the appropriate skills and knowledge as they work over time. They also need to orient their students to new ways of learning. Students are expected to take on more responsibility and be more self-directed in their learning. Participation alone is not sufficient: Students need to be interested in the task and find personal relevance in it. Yet not all students will find tasks personally meaningful. In such instances, teachers need to use instructional strategies to support students' motivation and cognitive engagement. Another challenge for students is that effective participation in authentic tasks often involves solving problems in which there are no quick and easy solutions. Students can become discouraged with the difficulty of completing tasks. If teachers are to use authentic tasks effectively, they must address the challenges of organizing instruction and supporting students.

A major limitation in using authentic tasks is that they do not fit well within existing school organization and culture (Resnick, 1987). The organizational features of schools, including teacher workload, class scheduling, material resources, and assessments that measure knowledge of simple facts, are structured for traditional instruction and narrow assessment. Furthermore, school norms typically involve students in learning directly from either the teacher or textbook. Teachers, students, and parents expect tasks to fit this model of instruction. Authentic tasks involve a different way of thinking about tasks in classrooms. They require more instructional time and resources, a different instructional stance on the part of teachers, and more effort on the part of students.

Although the benefits in using authentic tasks are clear, the widespread use of these tasks will require changes in the roles of teachers and students, as well as changes in the structure of schools. Though formidable, such changes promise to transform classrooms into places where students engage in complex tasks that are meaningful to them, relate to real-world situations, and help them develop usable knowledge and robust understandings. This kind of learning environment may prove advantageous for all learners.

SEE ALSO *Goal Orientation Theory.*

BIBLIOGRAPHY

Blumenfeld, P. C., Kempler, T., & Krajcik, J. S. (2006). Motivation and cognitive engagement in learning environments. In R. K. Sawyer (Ed.), *Cambridge Handbook of the Learning Sciences.* New York: Cambridge University Press.

Blumenfeld, P. C., Marx, R. W. & Harris, C. J. (2006). Learning environments. In W. Damon, R. M. Lerner, K. A. Renninger, and I. E. Sigel (Eds.), *Handbook of Child Psychology* 6th ed., Vol. 4: *Child Psychology in Practice.* Hoboken, NJ: Wiley.

Brown, J. S., Collins, A. & Duguid, P. (1989). Situated cognition and the culture of learning. *Educational Researcher, 18*(1), 32–42.

Cognition and Technology Group at Vanderbilt. (1997). *The Jasper project: Lessons in curriculum, instruction, assessment, and professional development.* Mahwah, NJ: Erlbaum.

Dewey, J. (1933). *How we think* (2nd ed.). Boston: D. C. Heath.

Hickey, D. T., Moore, A. M., & Pellegrino, J. W. (2001). The Motivational and Academic Consequences of Elementary Mathematics Environments: Do Constructivist Innovations and Reforms Make a Difference? *American Educational Research Journal, 38*(3), 611–652.

Krajcik, J. S., Blumenfeld, P. C., Marx, R. W., & Soloway, E. (2000). Instructional, curricular, and technological supports for inquiry in science classrooms. In J. Minstrell & E. H. van Zee (Eds.), *Inquiring into inquiry learning and teaching in science.* Washington, DC: American Association for the Advancement of Science.

Moll, L. C., Amanti, C., Neff, D., & Gonzalez, N. (1992). Funds of knowledge for teaching: Using a qualitative approach to connect homes and classrooms. *Theory into Practice, 31*(2), 132–141.

Newmann, F. M., & Wehlage, G. G. (1993). Five standards of authentic instruction. *Educational Leadership, 50*, 8–12.

Perkins, D. N. (1993). Teaching for understanding. *American Educator, 17*(3), 8, 28–35.

Resnick, L. B. (1987). Learning in school and out. *Educational Researcher, 16*(9), 13–20.

Christopher J. Harris
Ronald W. Marx

AUTISM SPECTRUM DISORDERS

Autism was first described in 1943 by child psychiatrist Leo Kanner. About fifty years later, in 1991, autism became its own eligibility category for special education services. Until the end of the twentieth century, autism was considered a low incidence disability. Over the years, research resulted in a broader definition of autism as well as better trained professionals who had increased knowledge and reliable tools to identify children with autism in the preschool years. Autism is recognized as a relatively common developmental disorder, more prevalent than childhood cancer, diabetes, and Down syndrome. Classroom teachers as well as school psychologists can expect to work with children with autism and related disorders.

AUTISM DEFINED

Autism is a neurodevelopmental disorder defined by behaviors rather than by medical tests. That is, there are no blood tests, brain scans, or medical procedures available to identify autism. Instead, a diagnosis is based on observation of social and communication behaviors that take into account a spectrum of symptom expression which ranges from severe to mild and also varies with age and developmental level. Autism is a retrospective diagnosis, and in order to make a differential diagnosis, careful assessment of developmental history is essential. Finally, the complexity of diagnostic assessment of autism is increased because it frequently occurs in association with other syndromes and developmental disabilities, such as Down syndrome, fragile X, and intellectual disability. Research suggests that the prevalence of autism may be about 1 in 600 children and when combined with related disorders, the incidence increases to about 1 in about 160 (Chakrabarti & Fombonne, 2001).

CHARACTERISTICS

The *Diagnostic and Statistical Manual of Mental Disorders, Text Revision* (4th ed., DSM-IV-TR; American Psychiatric Association, 2000) describes the diagnostic criteria for pervasive developmental disorders (PDDs) used by medical personnel. PDD is an umbrella term that includes the diagnosis of autism as well as four other

Autistic children and their teachers working on an art project **AP IMAGES.**

PDDs. The DSM is independent from the classification system established by State Departments of Education. Although autism has been defined in the Individuals with Disabilities Education Act (IDEA; 1997), classification criteria may vary considerably from state to state as states execute their own discretion in developing special education eligibility criteria using IDEA criteria as the minimal standard (see Table 1). Some states use DSM-IV criteria, and other states use their own criteria.

VARIATIONS AND SUBGROUPS

The PDDs have some features in common. But of the five PDDs, three have the most overlap with one another—autistic disorder, Asperger disorder (AD), and pervasive developmental disorder not otherwise specified (PDD-NOS). The shared social impairments are the hallmark features of the PDDs that distinguish them from other childhood disorders. Also, instead of the term PDD, some researchers advocate for the term Autism spectrum disorder (ASD) to emphasize both the shared overlap and lack of clear distinctions between these PDDs and the fact that these children often benefit from the same services (Lord & Risi, 2001) even though AD and PDD-NOS are not recognized as independent special education eligibility cat-

egories. If a student is performing well academically, problems with social interaction with peers and pragmatic language use should be addressed in educational programs. These skills are critical for success on the job after high school. Therefore, it is suggested that these students be classified under autism for educational purposes (Schopler, 1998). The DSM-IV-TR criteria are presented below.

DIAGNOSTIC CRITERIA OF AUTISTIC DISORDER

Although autism becomes evident within the first three years of life, it often remains undiagnosed until 4 years of age. This delay is unfortunate because research indicates that children can be identified reliably before 3 years of age (Lord, 1995; Stone, 1999), and an early diagnosis is critical because it allows the child the opportunity to obtain specialized early intervention services that have been shown to result in significant developmental gains (NRC, 2001).

The first component of the definition of autism, social impairment, is characterized by significant impairment in at least two of the following four areas: (a) coordinated use of nonverbal behaviors to regulate social and communicative interactions (e.g., eye-to-eye gaze, gestures, facial

---

U.S. Department of Education criteria for autism

"Autism" means a developmental disability significantly affecting verbal and nonverbal communication and social interaction, generally evident before age 3, that adversely affects a child's educational performance. Other characteristics often associated with autism are engagement in repetitive activities and stereotyped movements, resistance to environmental change or change in daily routines, and unusual responses to sensory experiences.

Table 1 ILLUSTRATION BY GGS INFORMATION SERVICES. CENGAGE LEARNING, GALE.

Comparison of autism spectrum disorders using DSM-IV-TR

	Autistic disorder	Aspergers disorder	Pervasive developmental disorder—not otherwise specified
Disordered social interaction	Present	Present	Present
Disordered communication	Present		Present[a]
Restricted and repetitive behaviors	Present	Present	Present[a]
Age of onset	Prior to 36 months		
Average intelligence		Present	
Incidence[b]	16.8/10,000	8.4/10,000	36.1/10,000
Male/female ratio	3 to 4:1	More common in males	More common in males

[a]Either disordered communication or restricted behaviors must be present
[b]Chakrabarti & Fombonne, (2001)

Table 2 ILLUSTRATION BY GGS INFORMATION SERVICES. CENGAGE LEARNING, GALE.

---

expressions); (b) development of peer relationships appropriate to the child's developmental level; (c) active pursuit of shared enjoyment, interests, and achievements with others; and (d) establishment of social and emotional reciprocity (e.g., the ability to engage in social play for older children or peek-a-boo for younger children).

The second feature of autism, impaired communication, is characterized by significant impairment in at least one of the four areas: (a) problems in development of spoken language (also accompanied by a lack of compensation through other modes of communication such as gestures); (b) inability to initiate or sustain a conversation with others in individuals with spoken language; (c) the presence of stereotyped and repetitive use of language or idiosyncratic use of language (e.g., repetition of words or phrases without regard to meaning); and (d) a lack of varied, spontaneous make-believe play or social imitative play consistent to the child's developmental level.

The third and final area of impairment is restricted, repetitive, and stereotyped patterns of behavior interests, and activities in at least one of the following four areas: (a) preoccupation with one or more stereotyped and restricted patterns of interest that is abnormal in intensity or focus; (b) inflexible adherence to specific nonfunctional routines or rituals; (c) stereotyped and repetitive motor mannerisms; and (d) a persistent preoccupation with parts of objects.

In addition to meeting the criteria described above, the child must also demonstrate abnormal functioning in at least one of the following areas prior to 3 years of age: (a) social interaction; (b) language as used in social communication; and (c) symbolic or imaginative play.

DIAGNOSTIC CRITERIA OF ASPERGER DISORDER

In the early 2000s debate continued whether Asperger disorder (AD) can be distinguished from high functioning autism (children with autism who do not have cognitive impairment) (Klin & Volkmar, 1997; Schopler, 1998). In order to meet criteria for AD, the child must

demonstrate impairments in two of the areas previously described for autistic disorder: (a) social interaction and (b) restricted, repetitive patterns of behavior, interests, and activities. The child must not demonstrate any clinically significant general delay in language and should use single words by age 2 and communicative phrases by age three. In addition, the child also must not exhibit any significant delay in cognitive development or adaptive behavior (except for social interaction), and show curiosity about the environment in childhood.

DIAGNOSTIC CRITERIA OF PDD-NOS

Pervasive developmental disorder not otherwise specified (PDD-NOS) is diagnosed when a child does not meet criteria for autism because of late age at onset, atypical symptomatology, or subthreshold symptomatology. Children with PDD-NOS do demonstrate the (a) social impairments and either (b) communication impairments or (c) restricted, repetitive patterns of behavior, interests, and activities.

The other two PDDs, childhood disintegrative disorder (CDD) and Rett disorder, are degenerative disorders, a feature not present in the other PDDs. Table 2 provides a brief comparison between the most related of the ASDs.

National Research Council recommendations (2001)
• Immediate entry into intervention programs after the diagnosis • Active engagement in intensive programming for a minimum of 25 hours a week, equivalent to a full school day for 5 days a week, with full year programming based on a child's age and developmental level • Planned and repeated teaching opportunities appropriate to the developmental level and with sufficient attention from adults in varied settings to meet needs • Low ratio of students to teacher (at least 1 adult for 2 young children with autism) • Inclusion of family component and parent training • Ongoing assessment and evaluation to measure progress and make adjustments

Table 3 ILLUSTRATION BY GGS INFORMATION SERVICES. CENGAGE LEARNING, GALE.

Quality and content indicators analyzed
• Social skills to improve involvement in school and family activities • Expressive, receptive and non-verbal communication skills (as appropriate) • Symbolic functional communication system • Engagement in tasks or play that are developmentally appropriate, including an appropriate motivational system • Fine and gross motor skills to be utilized when engaging in age appropriate activities • Basic cognitive and academic thinking skills • Replacement of problem behaviors with appropriate behaviors • Organizational skills and other behaviors that underlie success in a general education classroom • Goals are individualized and adapted from the academic content standards

Table 4 ILLUSTRATION BY GGS INFORMATION SERVICES. CENGAGE LEARNING, GALE.

ASSESSMENT OF CHARACTERISTICS

The development of appropriate and specialized intervention programs begins with a diagnostic assessment. One issue that may pose a barrier for children obtaining a diagnosis is the presumed stigma of labeling. Ideally, a label facilitates communication among professionals and families, allows access to intervention services, provides a basis for research and prevention, leads to appropriate treatment planning and intervention, and provides a framework for gathering information on outcome, etiology, and associated problems. Most importantly, a label allows teachers as well as parents to become informed. It gives professionals and families the basis to gather information, read, join support groups, advocate, and become organized in their efforts to obtain resources and improve outcomes. From the point of view of many helping professionals, the benefits of a diagnosis/identification far outweigh the liabilities.

Assessment of the characteristic features of autism—social and communication impairments and restricted patterns of behaviors and interests—require varied assessment approaches. Two gold standard tools are the Autism Diagnostic Observation Schedule (ADOS-G; Lord, Rutter, DiLavore, & Risi, 1999) and the Autism Diagnostic Interview (ADI-R: Lord, Rutter, & Le Couteur, 1994). The ADOS-G is a child interaction assessment and the ADI-R is a parent interview.

Social assessment consists of two main strategies: structured and unstructured observation and parent interview. In the very young child, the social impairments may be expressed by reduced play in baby games such as peek-a-boo; reduced attempts to draw attention to themselves for the purpose of showing off to adults; reduced ability to imitate vocal sounds, body movements, and actions with objects; and reduced ability to point to objects, show objects, and follow an adult's point to objects for purely social reasons.

Communication assessment consists of informal and formal testing, observational assessment, and parent interview. Assessment should also include information on the child's functional communication abilities, that is on the forms (how child communicates), the functions or purposes (what child communicates), and the contexts (where and with whom child communicates) of communication. Young children with autism demonstrate difficulty understanding and using nonverbal means, such as gestures, to communicate. Children with autism who have verbal speech may exhibit both the difficulty understanding the meaning of words and phrases (semantics) and using communication in a functional manner with others (pragmatics).

Assessment of repetitive behaviors and restricted range of activities and interests is best conducted by parent interview and observations. Resistance to change in environment and new routines and an insistence on following familiar routines characterize these behaviors. Parents can provide information on the child's narrow interests and unusual attachment to objects. Often sensory input that incorporates a visual, auditory, tactile, olfactory, or motor component is either excessively sought or strongly avoided. An example of a visual interest is a child who enjoys spinning objects, twirling, and watching fans or objects that rotate. The stereotypic behaviors of these children include jumping up and down and hand flapping when excited, flipping fingers in front of their eyes, and rocking their body.

INTERVENTION AND INSTRUCTIONAL PROCEDURES

Education is considered one of the primary methods of intervention for ASD (NRC, 2001). Recognizing its critical role in the education and treatment of children with autism, the U.S. Department of Education's Office of Special Education Programs requested the National Research Council to report on the scientific evidence regarding educational interventions for young children with autism (from three to eight years) (see Table 3). The NRC also provided guidelines on content areas critical in the educational plans of students with autism (see Table 4).

Several types of teaching strategies have been evaluated for children with autism. These methods include structured teaching (Schopler, Mesibov, and Hearscy, 1995), incidental teaching (McGee, Morrier, & Daly, 1999), discrete trial training (Smith, Eikeseth, Klevstrand, & Lovaas, 1997), pivotal response training (Koegel, Koegel, Shoshan, & McNerney, 1999), and functional communication training (Carr, 1993). All of these approaches are research supported and represent systematic and planful teaching techniques designed to increase desired behaviors, decrease undesirable behaviors, and teach new skills. Applied behavior analysis (ABA) is a framework that takes these techniques into account. No single teaching method, however, has been reported as of the early 2000s as being more effective than any other approach; in fact, all have demonstrated effectiveness, and it is likely that a multi-component approach is most effective. Regardless of which approach is selected, it is essential to first generate treatment goals based on the results of individualized assessments of the child's various areas of development and make adjustments of the treatment goals and methods based on the child's progress.

ISSUES OF ASSESSMENT AND INSTRUCTION

Not all children respond the same way to the same intervention. Children have individual learning styles and preferences and respond differently to various research supported approaches. The selection of an intervention must be based on individualized assessment of needs and ongoing monitoring of progress. It is not uncommon for a teacher to use many different methods to meet the needs of the children in the room (i.e., discrete trial, incidental teaching, and structured teaching).

The unique issues of autism require specialized planning on the IEP. The social and communication deficits in autism are often accompanied by intellectual impairment or issues with thinking and learning that often require the explicit teaching of skills that other children typically pick up naturally. These issues require that close attention be paid to the sequence of skills being taught and ensure that one skill builds upon another (Smith & Slattery, 1993).

Some teachers experience frustration understanding and managing the behavior of students with autism. They find that discipline strategies that work for other students do not work for these students. When confronted with challenging behaviors, it is necessary to consult a specialist in autism and behavior. The specialist can provide a functional behavioral analysis (FBA) to develop positive behavior supports. If problem behaviors are interfering with educational participation, it is necessary to have an FBA and a positive behavior support plan as part of the IEP.

School personnel have tools available to identify students with autism and select and implement effective teaching plans. The success of a teaching plan, however, depends on the quality of the teacher-student interaction as well was a teacher's ability to engage the student. Engagement is a key factor in an effective program (NRC, 2001), and research shows that both child and environmental factors influence engagement (Ruble & Robson, 2007). Establishing a collaborative relationship with former teachers of these children, their parents, and autism specialists is essential for optimal educational experiences and outcomes.

SEE ALSO *Mental Retardation; Special Education.*

BIBLIOGRAPHY

American Psychiatric Association. (2000). *Diagnostic and statistical manual of mental disorders* (4th ed., Test Revision ed.). Washington, DC: American Psychiatric Association.

Carr, E. (1993). Reduction of severe behavior problems in the community using a multicomponent treatment approach. *Journal of Applied Behavior Analysis, 26*(2), 157–172.

Chakrabarti, S., & Fombonne, E. (2001). Pervasive developmental disorders in preschool children. *Journal of the American Medical Association, 285*(24), 3093–3099.

Klin, A., & Volkmar, F. (1997). *Asperger's syndrome* (2nd ed.). New York: Wiley.

Koegel, L., Koegel, R., Shoshan, Y., & McNerney, E. (1999). Pivotal response intervention II: Preliminary long-term outcome data. *Journal of the Association of Persons with Severe Handicaps, 24*(3), 186–198.

Lord, C. (1995). Follow-up of two-year-olds referred for possible autism. *Journal of Child Psychology and Psychiatry, 36*(8), 1365–1382.

Lord, C., & Risi, S. (1998). Frameworks and methods in diagnosing autism spectrum disorders. *Mental Retardation and Developmental Disabilities Research Review, 4*(2), 90–96.

Lord, C., & Risi, S. (2001). Diagnosis of autism spectrum disorders in young children. In A. W. B. Prizant (Ed.), *Autism Spectrum Disorders* (Vol. 9, pp. 11–30). Baltimore: Brookes.

Lord, C., Rutter, M., & Le Couteur, A. (1994). Autism diagnostic interview-revised: A revised version of a diagnostic interview for caregivers of individuals with possible pervasive developmental disorders. *Journal of Autism and Developmental Disorders, 24*(5), 659–685.

McGee, G. G., Morrier, M. J., & Daly, T. (1999). An incidental teaching approach to early intervention for toddlers with autism. *Journal of the Association for Persons with Severe Handicaps, 24*(3), 133–146.

National Research Council. (2001). *Educating children with autism.* Washington, DC: National Academy Press.

Ruble, L., & Robson, D. (2007). Individual and environmental influences on engagement. *Journal of Autism and Developmental Disorders, 37,* 1457–1468.

Schopler, E. (1998). Premature popularization of Asperger syndrome. In G. M. E. Schopler (Ed.), *Asperger syndrome or high-functioning autism?* (pp. 385–400). New York: Plenum.

Schopler, E., Mesibov, G., & Hearsey, K. (1995). Structured teaching in the TEACCH system. In E. Schopler, & Mesibov, G. (Ed.), *Learning and cognition in autism* (pp. 243–268). New York: Plenum.

Smith, T., Eikeseth, S., Klevstrand, M., & Lovaas, O. (1997). Intensive behavioral treatment for preschoolers with severe mental retardation and pervasive developmental disorder. *American Journal Mental Retardation, 102*(3), 238–249.

Smith, S. W., & Slattery, W. J. (1993). Developing individualized education programs that work for students with autism. *Added Focus on Autistic Behavior, 8,* 1–15.

Stone, W., Lee, E., Ashford, L., Brissie, J., Hepburn, S., Coonrod, E., et al. (1999). Can autism be diagnoses accurately in children under three years? *Journal of Child Psychology and Psychiatry, 40,* 219–226.

U. S. Department of Education. (1997). *Individuals with Disabilities Education Act Amendment of 1997,* P.L. 105–117. Washington, DC: Author.

Lisa. A. Ruble
Melissa Wheatley

AUTONOMY SUPPORT

Autonomy is the experience of being the author and origin of one's behavior—the subjective sense that one's moment-to-moment activity authentically expresses the self and its inner motivation. Behavior is autonomous when students freely endorse what they are doing in the classroom, and this inner endorsement of one's actions is most likely to happen when students' inner motivational resources (e.g., needs, interests, preferences) guide their on-going classroom engagement. Given this understanding of the nature of student autonomy, a definition of teacher-provided autonomy support can be offered. Autonomy support is the interpersonal behavior teachers provide during instruction to identify, nurture, and build students' inner motivational resources (Deci & Ryan, 1985; Reeve, Deci, & Ryan, 2004).

The opposite of autonomy support is controllingness. Controllingness is the interpersonal behavior teachers enact during instruction to gain students' compliance with a teacher-prescribed way of thinking, feeling, or behaving. As opposites, autonomy support and controllingness represent a single bipolar continuum of a teacher's motivating style toward students (Deci, Schwartz, Sheinman, & Ryan, 1981). When controlling, teachers have students put aside their inner motivational resources and instead adhere to the teacher's prescribed way of thinking, feeling, or behaving. Controlling teachers motivate students by using extrinsic incentives and pressuring language to the point that students' classroom participation is regulated by external contingencies and pressuring language, not by their inner motivational resources.

BENEFITS OF AN AUTONOMY-SUPPORTIVE MOTIVATING STYLE

Compared to students in classrooms managed by controlling teachers, students with autonomy-supportive teachers experience a wide range of educationally and developmentally important benefits. These benefits include not only greater perceived autonomy and greater psychological need satisfaction during learning activities but also greater classroom engagement, more positive emotionality, higher mastery motivation, greater intrinsic motivation, a preference for optimal challenge over easy success, higher creativity, enhanced psychological well-being, active and deeper information processing, greater conceptual understanding, higher academic achievement, and greater persistence in school versus dropping out (Black & Deci, 2000; Koestner, Ryan, Bernieri, & Holt, 1984; Reeve, Jang, Carrell, Barch, & Jeon, 2004; Vallerand, Fortier, & Guay, 1997).

WHAT AUTONOMY-SUPPORTIVE TEACHERS SAY AND DO DURING INSTRUCTION

Because autonomy support promotes students' positive functioning in so many ways, researchers have worked to identify what specific instructional behaviors teachers with an autonomy-supportive style enact that differentiates their style from teachers with a relatively controlling style (Assor, Kaplan, & Roth, 2002; Assor, Kaplan, Kanat-Maymon, & Roth, 2005; Deci, Spiegel, Ryan, Koestner, & Kauffman, 1982; Reeve, Bolt, & Cai, 1999; Reeve & Jang, 2006). Table 1 defines the central feature of both an autonomy-supportive and a controlling motivating style, and it lists the four essential features associated with both styles.

The essential core of an autonomy-supportive motivating style is the teacher's willingness to take the student's perspective during instruction and to deeply value, understand, and appreciate that perspective. When doing so, teachers work hard to identify, nurture, and build students' inner motivational resources. More concretely, the moment-to-moment expression of an autonomy-

Defining features of an autonomy-supportive (and controlling) motivating style

Autonomy-supportive motivating style	Controlling motivating style
Core feature of autonomy support	*Core feature of controllingness*
Understands and highly values the student's perspective during instruction	A teacher-targeted agenda paired with some type of pressure to comply with that agenda
Four aspects of autonomy support	*Four aspects of controllingness*
• Nurtures inner motivational resources	• Relies on extrinsic sources of motivation
• Relies on noncontrolling, informational language	• Relies on controlling, pressuring language
• Promotes valuing	• Neglects valuing
• Acknowledges and accepts expressions of negative affect	• Power assertion

Table 1 ILLUSTRATION BY GGS INFORMATION SERVICES. CENGAGE LEARNING, GALE.

supportive style can be seen in the instructional behaviors of nurturing students' inner motivational resources, relying on noncontrolling and informational language, promoting valuing, and acknowledging and accepting students' expressions of negative affect. Nurturing inner motivational resources means identifying and supporting students' needs, interests, and preferences during instruction. Relying on noncontrolling and informational language means uttering information-rich, competence-affirming messages that diagnose and explain why students are doing well and making progress. Promoting value means providing rationales to explain the underlying importance or usefulness of a requested activity, behavior, or procedure. Acknowledging and accepting students' expressions of negative affect means treating students' complaints and points of resistance as a valid reaction to imposed classroom structures and demands. These behaviors are all positively intercorrelated and, collectively, they set the stage for students to experience personal autonomy, psychological need satisfaction, and positive functioning in general (Ryan & Deci, 2000).

The essential core of a controlling motivating style is the teacher's insistence on a prescribed right or best way of thinking, feeling, or behaving. That insistence is routinely paired with the use of pressuring language and extrinsic incentives to gain students' compliance with that prescription. In practice, the moment-to-moment expression of a controlling style during instruction can be seen in teachers' reliance on extrinsic sources of motivation (incentives, consequences, directives, compliance requests), relying on controlling and pressuring language (uttering a steady stream of "shoulds," "have to's," "got to's," and "musts"), neglecting valuing (making little or no effort to explain why they are asking students to do unappealing or uninteresting activities), and power assertion (countering students' negative affect with authoritarian power assertions such as "Shape up" and "Just get the work done and quit your complaining").

AUTONOMY-SUPPORTIVE PARENTING

As is the case with autonomy-supportive teaching, autonomy-supportive parenting revolves around involving and nurturing (rather than neglecting and frustrating) students' psychological needs, personal interests, and integrated values (i.e., their inner motivational resources; Grolnick, 2003). An additional aspect of an autonomy-supportive style that is especially important during parenting is sensitivity to children's and adolescents' temperament-related dispositions (e.g., shyness, sociability). Sensitivity to students' temperament is autonomy-supportive because it allows students to act in ways that fit their internal dispositions, including their preferred activities, preferred pace of instruction, and preferred way of doing things.

MEASURING MOTIVATING STYLE

Researchers assess motivating style with both self-report questionnaire measures and observational ratings from trained raters. Self-report measures include both teacher (and parent) reports of their own style as well as students' reports of the teacher's (and parent's) style. For the former, teachers rate their style using the Problems in Schools questionnaire. For the later, students rate their teachers' style using questionnaires such as the Learning Climate questionnaire (Williams & Deci, 1996) and the Perceptions of Parents Scale (Grolnick, Ryan, & Deci, 1991). Most self-report measures of motivating style are available on-line. In addition, several studies rely on trained raters to objectively score teachers' motivating style during instruction. Raters score aspects of teachers' motivating style using the four bipolar scales summarized in Table 1.

IMPLICATIONS FOR TEACHERS

During class, students can be curious, proactive, and highly engaged, or they can be alienated, reactive, and passive. Just how engaged students are during instruction and how much they develop themselves as autonomous learners depends, in part, on the autonomy supportive quality of the teacher's motivating style. From this point of view, students' motivation, engagement, and positive functioning during instruction are an interpersonally coordinated process between teacher and students. When teacher-student interactions go well—that is, when teachers support students' autonomy rather than control their behavior—teachers function both as a guide to structure students' learning opportunities and as a support system to nurture their existing inner resources and to help them develop new and constructive sources of autonomous motivation, such as internalized values.

The implication for teachers (and parents) is that supporting students' autonomy, rather than neglecting or even interfering with their autonomy, creates the conditions during learning activities in which students can experience an engagement-fostering congruence between what they want to do (their inner guides) and what they actually do during class. The positive implications of autonomy support, and the negative implications of teacher control, are many and wide-reaching. This is an exciting conclusion because classroom-based intervention research shows that teachers can learn how to be more autonomy supportive during instruction and also that the more teachers learn how to expand their style to incorporate a greater use of autonomy-supportive acts of instruction, the more their students benefit in terms of classroom engagement and academic achievement (deCharms, 1976).

TEACHERS' CONCERNS ABOUT AUTONOMY SUPPORT

Even when they acknowledge the strong relationship between supporting students' autonomy and students' positive classroom functioning, teachers often express two concerns over the practice of autonomy support. The first is the fear that if teachers' support students' autonomy, then student engagement would be uneven, off-task, or even irresponsible. But supporting autonomy does not mean removing structure. Instead, providing structure is a crucial aspect of effective instruction, so the crucial issue is not whether teachers provide structure but, rather, whether they provide that structure in an autonomy-supportive or in a controlling way (Reeve, 2006). The second concern is that autonomy-supportive instruction may not apply to all students in all educational contexts. This concern has been allayed by researchers showing the benefits of autonomy support for a diverse range of students, including students with special needs (Algozzine, Browder, Karovnen, Test, & Wood, 2001), international students in collectivistic cultures (Chirkov & Ryan, 2001), religiously motivated home school students (Cai, Reeve, & Robinson,

2002), and at-risk high school students in alternative school settings (Forstadt, 2006). The conclusion is that all students want and need autonomy and autonomy support and also that they benefit when teachers support their autonomy rather than control their behavior.

SEE ALSO *Classroom Environment; Intrinsic and Extrinsic Motivation; Self-Determination Theory of Motivation.*

BIBLIOGRAPHY

Algozzine, B., Browder, D., Karovnen, M., Test, D. W., & Wood, W. M. (2001). Effects of interventions to promote self-determination for individuals with disabilities. *Review of Educational Research, 71*, 219–277.

Assor, A., Kaplan, H., Kanat-Maymon, Y., & Roth, G. (2005). Directly controlling teacher behaviors as predictors of poor motivation and engagement in girls and boys: The role of anger and anxiety. *Learning and Instruction, 15*, 397–413.

Assor, A., Kaplan, H., & Roth, G. (2002). Choice is good, but relevance is excellent: Autonomy-enhancing and suppressing teaching behaviors predicting students' engagement in schoolwork. *British Journal of Educational Psychology, 27*, 261–278.

Black, A. E., & Deci, E. L. (2000). The effects of instructors' autonomy support and students' autonomous motivation on learning organic chemistry: A self-determination theory perspective. *Science Education, 84*, 740–756.

Cai, Y., Reeve, J., & Robinson, D. T. (2002). Home schooling and teaching style: Comparing the motivating styles of home school and public school teachers. *Journal of Educational Psychology, 94*, 372–380.

Chirkov, V. & Ryan, R. M. (2001). Parent and teacher autonomy-support in Russian and U.S. adolescents: Common effects on well-being and academic motivation. *Journal of Cross Cultural Psychology, 32*, 618–635.

deCharms, R. (1976). *Enhancing motivation: Change in the classroom.* New York: Irvington.

Deci, E. L., & Ryan, R. M. (1985). *Intrinsic motivation and self-determination in human behavior.* New York: Plenum.

Deci, E. L., Schwartz, A., Sheinman, L., & Ryan, R. M. (1981). An instrument to assess adult's orientations toward control versus autonomy in children: Reflections on intrinsic motivation and perceived competence. *Journal of Educational Psychology, 73*, 642–650.

Deci, E. L., Spiegel, N. H., Ryan, R. M., Koestner, R., & Kauffman, M. (1982). Effects of performance standards on teaching styles: Behavior of controlling teachers. *Journal of Educational Psychology, 74*, 852–859.

Grolnick, W. S. (2003). *The psychology of parental control: How well-meant parenting backfires.* Mahwah, NJ: Lawrence Erlbaum.

Grolnick, W. S., Ryan, R. M., & Deci, E. L. (1991). Inner resources for school achievement: Motivational mediators of children's perceptions of their parents. *Journal of Educational Psychology, 83*, 508–517.

Koestner, R., Ryan, R. M., Bernieri, F., & Holt, K. (1984). Setting limits on children's behavior: The differential effects of controlling versus informational styles on intrinsic motivation and creativity. *Journal of Personality, 52*, 233–248.

Reeve, J. (2006). Extrinsic rewards and inner motivation. In C. M. Evertson & C. S. Weinstein (Eds.), *Handbook of classroom management: Research, practice, and contemporary issues* (pp. 645–664). Mahwah, NJ: Lawrence Erlbaum.

Reeve, J., Bolt, E., & Cai, Y. (1999). Autonomy-supportive teachers: How they teach and motivate students. *Journal of Educational Psychology, 91,* 537–548.

Reeve, J., Deci, E. L., & Ryan, R. M. (2004). Self-determination theory: A dialectical framework for understanding the sociocultural influences on student motivation. In D. McInerney & S. Van Etten (Eds.), *Research on sociocultural influences on motivation and learning: Big theories revisited* (Vol. 4, pp. 31–59). Greenwich, CT: Information Age Press.

Reeve, J., & Jang, H. (2006). What teachers say and do to support students' autonomy during a learning activity. *Journal of Educational Psychology, 98,* 209–218.

Reeve, J., Jang, H., Carrell, D., Barch, J., & Jeon, S. (2004). Enhancing high school students' engagement by increasing their teachers' autonomy support. *Motivation and Emotion, 28,* 147–169.

Ryan, R. M., & Deci, E. L. (2000). Self-determination theory and the facilitation of intrinsic motivation, social development, and well-being. *American Psychologist, 55,* 68–78.

Vallerand, R. J., Fortier, M. S., & Guay, F. (1997). Self-determination and persistence in a real-life setting: Toward a motivational model of high school dropout. *Journal of Personality and Social Psychology, 72,* 1161–1176.

Williams, G. C., & Deci, E. L. (1996). Internalization of biopsychosocial values by medical students: A test of self-determination theory. *Journal of Personality and Social Psychology, 70,* 115–126.

Johnmarshall Reeve

B

BANDURA, ALBERT
1925–

Albert Bandura was born on December 4, 1925, in a hamlet in northern Alberta, Canada, the only son in a family of five older sisters. In 1949 he graduated from the University of British Columbia. He attended graduate school at the University of Iowa and, while there, married Virginia Varns. Bandura received his M.A. degree in 1951 and his Ph.D. in 1952 under the direction of Arthur Benton. Al and "Ginny" became parents to two daughters, Carol and Mary.

Bandura joined the faculty at Stanford University in 1953, where he has remained throughout his career. In collaboration with Richard Walters, his first doctoral student, Bandura conducted studies of social learning and aggression. Their joint efforts illustrated the critical role of modeling in human behavior and led to a program of research into observational learning (part of which is known in the history of psychology as the "Bobo Doll studies"). The program also led to Bandura's first book, *Adolescent Aggression*, written in collaboration with Walters and published in 1959. In 1974, Bandura became David Starr Jordan Professor of Social Science in Psychology. In 1977, he published the ambitious *Social Learning Theory*, which sparked the interest in social learning and psychological modeling that took place during the last two decades of the 20th century.

Bandura has collaborated in projects with internationally renowned scholars such as Jack Barchas and Barr Taylor in psychiatry, Robert DeBusk in cardiology, Halsted Holman in internal medicine, and Philip Zimbardo in psychology. One of these projects studied how people's perceptions of their own ability to control what they viewed as threats to themselves influence the release of neurotransmitters and stress-related hormones into the bloodstream. A major finding that resulted from these studies was that people can regulate their level of physiological activation through their belief in their own capabilities to do so, or their self-efficacy beliefs. In the course of investigating the processes by which modeling alleviates phobic disorders, Bandura again found that changes in behavior and fear arousal were mediated through the beliefs that individuals had in their own capabilities to alleviate their phobia. From the late 1970s, a major share of his research attention was devoted to exploring the role that these self-efficacy beliefs play in human functioning.

With the publication of *Social Foundations of Thought and Action: A Social Cognitive Theory* in 1986, Bandura put forth a view of human functioning in which individuals are agents proactively engaged in their own development and can make things happen by their actions. From this perspective, the beliefs that people have about themselves are critical elements in their exercise of control and personal agency. In his 1997 book, *Self-Efficacy: The Exercise of Control*, Bandura set forth the tenets of his theory of self-efficacy beliefs and its applications to diverse fields of human accomplishment.

Self-efficacy has generated research in areas as diverse as medicine, business, sports, and, of course, psychology. Research has been especially prominent in education, where researchers have established that self-efficacy beliefs and educational attainments are highly correlated and that self-efficacy is an excellent predictor of academic success. In fact, self-efficacy has proven to be a more consistent predictor of educational outcomes than has any other motivation construct.

Albert Bandura **ARCHIVES OF THE HISTORY OF AMERICAN PSYCHOLOGY. THE UNIVERSITY OF AKRON.**

from the International Society for Research in Aggression, and the Distinguished Scientist Award of the Society of Behavioral Medicine. He was elected to the American Academy of Arts and Sciences and to the Institute of Medicine of the National Academy of Sciences.

SEE ALSO *Self-Determination Theory of Motivation; Self-Efficacy Theory; Social Cognitive Theory; Teacher Efficacy.*

BIBLIOGRAPHY

WORKS BY

Bandura, A. (1973). *Aggression: A social learning analysis.* Englewood Cliffs, NJ: Prentice-Hall.

Bandura, A. (1977). *Social learning theory.* Englewood Cliffs, NJ: Prentice-Hall.

Bandura, A. (1986). *Social foundations of thought and action: A social cognitive theory.* Englewood Cliffs, NJ: Prentice-Hall.

Bandura, A. (1997). *Self-efficacy: The exercise of control.* New York: W. H. Freeman.

WORKS ABOUT

Richard I. Evans, R. I. (1989). *Albert Bandura, the man and his ideas—a dialogue.* New York: Praeger.

Frank Pajares

As the new century dawned, Bandura broadened the scope of his thinking to expound a social cognitive theory capable of encompassing the critical issues of the new millennium. He has written on escaping homelessness, environmental sustainability, and population growth. He has proposed a social cognitive view of mass communication, explained the self-regulatory mechanisms governing transgressive behavior, and shown how perceived social inefficacy can lead to depression and substance abuse. Exploring the moral disengagement in the perpetration of inhumanities, Bandura outlined the psychosocial tactics by which individuals and societies selectively disengage moral self-sanctions from inhumane conduct and called for "a civilized life" in which humane standards are buttressed "by safeguards built into social systems that uphold compassionate behavior and renounce cruelty."

As of 2007, Bandura has authored seven books and edited two others, and he has written over 250 articles and book chapters. In 1974 he was elected president of the American Psychological Association (APA). His contributions to psychology have been recognized in the many honors and awards he has received. He has received the Distinguished Scientific Contributions Award of the APA, the William James Award from the Association for Psychological Science, the Distinguished Contribution Award

BEHAVIORAL OBJECTIVES

Everyone has had some experience setting personal goals. Perhaps the most common goal people set is the New Year's resolution when an individual identifies a broad goal to lose weight, stop smoking, or exercise more frequently as part of a personally valued way to begin the new year. The first consideration in setting such a goal is determining that it is truly a valued accomplishment for the person who resolves to achieve it.

The next important consideration in setting a broad goal is making sure that it is stated clearly in specific behavioral terms. Using these behavioral terms is one way to operationally define the goal, that is, by statements about the observable behaviors that are essential parts of attaining it. Making clear statements about these component behaviors requires careful analysis of the sequence of smaller units of behaviors that, when put together, lead to attainment of the broader behavioral goal. These statements define the goal for purposes of knowing when it is achieved. They also help ensure that the person working toward the goal knows which behaviors to perform to increase the likeliness of success in achieving the broader behavioral goal.

STEPS FOR REACHING EFFECTIVE GOALS

Many people who set a New Year's resolution fail at some point to keep working toward their goal. This outcome is often related to their earlier failure to break their broader goal down into a logical sequence of smaller achievable objectives, which can help them to keep working toward their broader goal because they experience success along the way. This approach to setting goals requires that individuals determine ways to evaluate both the achievement of their smaller successes and, ultimately, the accomplishment of their broader goal. Thus, a reason many people do not stick to New Year's resolutions is that they do not develop ways to evaluate their progress over time. Reaching an effective goal is particularly important in education. Teachers use goal-setting strategies to ensure students are learning and experiencing academic success.

Teachers and students are more successful when the goals they set a) are realistic (achievable), b) are publicly stated rather than private internal commitments, c) include deadlines, and d) include feedback on progress over time (Martin & Pear, 1996). In fact, research on goal setting has shown that the most effective goals are those that are broken down into smaller, clearly defined and achievable steps or components that facilitate reinforcement of success on a regular basis and evaluation of progress (Bandura, 1969).

BEHAVIOR GOALS AND OBJECTIVES IN EDUCATION

An effective way to break larger goals down into smaller units is to define and set behavioral objectives. Behavioral objectives are the smaller, observable, and measurable intermediate goals that build in a stepwise fashion toward the completion of the broader long-term goal that is often more complicated and comprehensive. Behavioral objectives that are stated in observable and measurable terms help goal setters understand whether the strategies they are using to achieve their goal are resulting in change or whether they need to modify their efforts to improve the likelihood of accomplishing the desired outcome.

Behavior change is not a new concern. Information about creating effective behavioral goals and objectives to facilitate behavior change has a very long history in areas such as industry, sports, human service organizations, and education (Mager, 1961; Sulzer-Azaroff & Mayer, 1977; Locke & Latham, 1985, 1990). Teachers use behavioral objectives to guide and improve classroom instruction for groups of students, manage classroom social behaviors, and support individual students in need of more intensive social and academic instruction and support (Alberto & Troutman, 1999; Maag, 2004). Behavioral goals and objectives are included in Individual Education Plans (IEPs) for students in need of special education services. The development of educational goals and behavioral objectives was included as one of the mandates of the Education for all Handicapped Children Act of 1975 (PL 94-142) and continued thereafter to be considered an important element for facilitating behavior change resulting from the instructional process.

CHARACTERISTICS OF BEHAVIORAL OBJECTIVES

According to Alberto and Troutman (1999), each behavioral objective should identify the following elements:

1. person(s) for whom the objective is written (the learner),
2. behavior targeted for change,
3. conditions under which a behavior will be performed
4. criteria for determining when the acceptable performance of the behavior occurs.

The learner(s) can be an individual person or a group of individuals. For instance, a learner identified within a behavioral goal could be a student, a classroom, a group of individuals participating in specific track and field activities, or an entire basketball team. Once the learner is defined, the behavior targeted for change must be likely to be repeated over time and must be clearly defined operationally in behavioral terms so that whenever it is performed, it can be observed and measured across repeated occasions. An effective definition of the desired behavior ensures that an outside observer will be able to confirm that the target behavior has occurred.

Thus, it is important when defining the target behavior to avoid words and phrases such as "being disruptive," "staying on task," or "enjoying a story" that have not been operationally defined in behavioral terms. These words and phrases can mean different behaviors to different people. For instance, a substitute teacher may define "being disruptive" as a student tapping a pencil on the desk loudly enough that it can be heard throughout the room. The student's teacher, however, may only be recording "being disruptive" when the child begins yelling so loudly that it can be heard out in the hallway. Behavior definitions that are not stated clearly enough (operationally in specific behavioral terms), for everyone to interpret in the same way, can confuse both the learner and the individuals monitoring the learner's performance. This confusion is likely to lead to further decrease in the likelihood that a goal will be achieved by the learner.

The definition of the behavior should also identify elements of the teaching/learning context that are important for determining the conditions in which a behavior is to occur. The circumstances, requests, materials, and instructions that are identified in the behavioral objective as important elements in the context in which a behavior should be performed must be sufficiently detailed to allow a teaching/learning context to be provided repeatedly. The specific environmental cues that are present when a behavior is expected to occur must be described in enough detail to ensure there will be clear and consensual understanding of exactly what such cues include. Frequently the statement of an objective begins with condition statements, such as the following:

Given a map of the United States ...

Given independent study time ...

After reading this a paragraph about ...

The final information necessary in an effective behavioral objective must be statements of the criteria for acceptable performance of the targeted behavior. This statement must define the minimal performance necessary to consider a behavioral response correct and sets a standard for evaluation purposes. There are a number of ways in which to evaluate a response: accuracy (number of items correct), frequency of occurrence (number of behaviors performed), duration (behavior occurring within a time period), or latency (time taken until a response occurs). Another consideration in determining criteria for successful accomplishment of behavioral objectives involves how many times a learner must meet a criterion before the behavior is considered learned. Information about the criteria for evaluating a correct response will guide the ways in which learner performance of the behavioral objective will be measured.

Alberto and Troutman (1999) suggest writing each element of a behavioral objective as a guideline or format, as the following example illustrates:

Goal: Cindy writes effective behavioral goals and objectives for all students needing additional academic support in her math class.

Learner: Cindy

Condition: Cindy identifies a student who is not succeeding on a math assignment in her class.

Behavior: Cindy will write a behavioral goal for that student, breaking the goal down into behavioral objectives that facilitate or assist the student in being successful.

Criteria: Cindy will write a behavioral goal that includes two or more behavioral objectives for two general education students who receive a D or lower on three consecutive assignments in her class with 100% accuracy for three months.

Over time, the criteria for successful accomplishment of each behavioral objective are raised until the learner is able to accomplish the long-term goal that has been identified. Cindy may begin by writing behavioral goals and objectives for only two students in her class who are receiving a D on three assignments. Each subsequent behavioral objective will include criteria that increase in complexity until Cindy is providing support to all of her students who need individualized behavioral goals and objectives and Cindy can show that student performance is increasing using evaluation data for each student.

IMPORTANT CONSIDERATIONS FOR DESIGNING BEHAVIOR OBJECTIVES

Behavioral objectives must be written in such a way that the aim is for the individual learner to remain positively motivated to continue working on the long-term goal by experiencing success on the smaller-scope behavioral objectives. If a behavioral objective is too broad, complex, and difficult, a learner may stop trying to perform the behavior. Behavioral objectives are intended to provide feedback for successful performance over time, and this progress can reinforce the learner with positive feedback. The learner's motivation also may decrease if behavioral objectives are too easy. The person working on a behavioral objective that is easily accomplished can become bored with the learning opportunity. Or it may take a long time to achieve the stated goal because there are too many objectives that must be met, which makes the goal seem unobtainable to the learner.

Individuals designing behavioral objectives must balance the number of objectives within each long-term goal as well as the level of difficulty involved in each behavioral objective to help ensure the learner will continue working on a long-term goal. Developing effective behavioral objectives can be challenging. Individuals who write behavioral objectives must monitor progress closely and make modifications as needed over time to help ensure that motivation on the part of the learner remains high, the criteria identified for judging success are effective for evaluating progress, and progress toward the overall goal is being made in a timely manner.

SEE ALSO *Direct Instruction; Mastery Learning.*

BIBLIOGRAPHY

Alberto, P. A., & Troutman, A. C. (1999). *Applied behavior analysis for teachers.* New Jersey: Merrill.

Bandura, A. (1969). *Principles of behavior modification.* New York: Holt, Rinehart, & Winston.

Locke E. A., & Latham, G. P. (1985). The application of goal setting to sports. *Journal of Sport Psychology, 49,* 205–222.

Locke, E. A., & Latham, G. P. (1990). *A theory of goal setting and task performance.* Englewood Cliffs, NJ: Prentice-Hall.

Maag, J. W. (2004). *Behavior management: From theoretical implications to practical applications.* Belmont, CA: Thomson Learning.

Mager, R. F. (1961). *Preparing objectives for programmed instruction.* San Francisco, CA: Fearon.

Martin, G., & Pear, J. (1996). *Behavior modification: What it is and how to do it.* Upper Saddle River, NJ: Prentice Hall.

Sulzer-Azaroff, B., & Mayer, G. R. (1977). *Applying behavior-analysis procedures with children and youth.* New York: Holt, Rinehart, & Winston.

Rachel L. Freeman

BEHAVIORISM

Behaviorism is the scientific study of observable behavior of living organisms in relation to environmental events. Behaviorists view observable behavior as an important subject matter in its own right and avoid interpreting behavior as a sign of some other psychological phenomenon as other psychological systems do (e.g., interpreting behavior as an indication of repressed psychological content in a Freudian model). Instead, behaviorists seek to identify predictable relationships between environmental events and behavior (Alberto & Troutman, 2003; Cooper, Heron, & Heward, 2007; Miltenberger, 2008). Although the totality of all possible environmental events is theoretically limited only by natural physical laws, behaviorism categorizes all environmental events into three types: neutral events, antecedents, and consequences. Only antecedents and consequences are of interest to behaviorists, who refer to them as stimulus events. Behaviorists study stimulus events that cause behavior to occur, stop occurring, or change in some way as a function of antecedents or consequences to behavior. Behavioral scientists recognize, however, that environmental events that affect behavior as antecedents or consequences often vary from person to person and have developed an experimental methodology that allows them to study these phenomena at the level of the individual organism (single-case experimental designs).

RESPONDENT AND OPERANT CONDITIONING

The two main traditions of behaviorism are respondent conditioning and operant conditioning (Alberto & Troutman, 2003; Cooper et al., 2007; Miltenberger, 2008). Respondent conditioning studies antecedent events that cause reflexive behavior to occur. For example, if an otherwise neutral stimulus (e.g., a pungent spice) is paired with a noxious stimulus (e.g., spoiled meat) that causes a reflexive action (e.g., upset stomach), the previously neutral stimulus may cause that response in the future (becoming a conditioned stimulus). A relationship between a stimulus and a response that did not exist prior to the pairing has been created: the pungent spice now causes upset stomach.

Operant conditioning studies a different class of behaviors, behaviors that are caused by consequences. Behavior changes the environment in some way, and those changes can become consequences that affect future behavior. For example, if a child's inappropriate comments in the classroom result consistently in laughter such that a contingent relationship is formed and there is an increase over time in the frequency of those comments, then the laughter (social attention) is the consequence that causes the behavior to occur. There are four types of consequences that affect the future probability of behavior, two of which are reinforcers and two of which are punishers. A consequence that increases the future probability is a reinforcer. If an environmental stimulus is *added* following the occurrence of behavior and the behavior is more likely to occur in the future, the consequence is a positive reinforcer (Miltenberger, 2008). For example, laughter is the positive reinforcer that increases the future probability of inappropriate comments in the previous example. If an environmental event is *removed* following the occurrence of behavior and the behavior is more likely to occur in the future, the consequence is a negative reinforcer (Miltenberger, 2008). For example, if a child is sent to time-out for crying and screaming when asked to pick up toys and clean up the room, the child may be reinforced by the removal of the demand (picking up toys and cleaning the room) that occurs when the child is sent to time-out. As a result, crying and screaming are more likely in the future when the child is asked to pick up toys.

Punishment is the other consequence that affects the future probability of behavior. However, its effect is opposite that of reinforcement; it decreases behavior. If an environmental stimulus is *added* following the occurrence of behavior and the behavior is less likely to occur in the future, the consequences is a positive punisher (Miltenberger, 2008). For example, if a mother gives a stern look at her child when he is making noise in church and the child is less likely to make noise in church in the future, the stern look is a positive punisher. If an environmental stimulus is *taken away* following the occurrence of behavior and the behavior is less likely to occur in the future, the consequence is a negative punisher (Miltenberger, 2008). For example, when parents take driving privileges away from their adolescent daughter because she was late in returning home and the daughter is less likely to be late in the future, taking away privileges serves as a negative punisher.

Although the primary focus of operant research is on consequences that cause behavior to occur, behavioral scientists are also interested in antecedent influences on operant behavior (Alberto & Troutman, 2003; Cooper et al., 2007; Miltenberger, 2008). An antecedent is any stimulus present when a behavior is reinforced that has a predictable relationship with the occurrence of reinforcement. For example, if laughter following a child's comment occurs only when a particular person (e.g., a friend) is present and does not occur when that person is not present, the antecedent stimulus (presence of friend) is said to exert stimulus control over the behavior (student comment). It is the laughter (social attention) that causes the behavior to occur; however, the antecedent stimulus sets the occasion for the occurrence of the behavior by virtue of its pairing with the consequence.

STUDYING ENVIRONMENTAL FACTORS AND THEIR EFFECT ON BEHAVIOR

Behaviorism assumes that behavior is governed by natural laws that can be meaningfully studied and identified (Bijou, 1970). Behaviorists seek scientific explanations that predict the occurrence of behavior as it relates to environmental events so that the environment can be arranged to foster the organism's (human or animal) ability to adapt to its environment. When a class of environmental events is shown experimentally to have a predictable effect on behavior, behaviorists say that a functional relationship has been established (Alberto & Troutman, 2003; Cooper et al., 2007; Miltenberger, 2008). For example, aberrant human behavior has been shown to increase in frequency as a function of different classes of stimulus events (consequences) such as contingent access to preferred stimuli (e.g., social attention, toys, food) and contingent removal of aversive stimuli (e.g., instructional demands) (Iwata et al., 1994). Behaviorism also assumes that deviant behavior can be treated through its learning paradigm by rearranging stimulus events.

For behaviorists, all types of problem behavior fall into one of two categories; behavioral excesses (i.e., too much behavior) or behavioral deficits (i.e., too little behavior). Identifying existing functional relationships, therefore, allows behaviorists to rearrange the environment to establish more adaptive functional relationships. In the earlier example of a functional relationship between a child's inappropriate comments in the classroom caused by laughter of a friend, the inappropriate comments constitute the behavioral excess and the presence and laughter of the friend are the controlling events. Rearranging the contingencies to reduce the problem through a behavioral treatment could occur in a variety of ways. For example, removing the friend removes the antecedent to problem behavior; rewarding the friend for not laughing eliminates the consequence for problem behavior; rewarding the child who makes inappropriate comments for reducing or eliminating inappropriate comments by allowing him or her to have time with the peer is a means of offering a consequence that may compete effectively with the natural consequence supporting the occurrence of the behavior (peer laughter).

TWENTIETH-CENTURY BEHAVIORAL RESEARCH

The assumptions, methods, and practices of behaviorism make it an ecological model of learning. Behaviorists spend as much time examining the context for the occurrence of behavior as they do behavior itself. This dimension of behaviorism has developed over time. Early behavioral research in the twentieth century gave rise to the tradition of the Experimental Analysis of Behavior, which used single-case experimental methodology to study a wide variety of types of behavior-environment relationships largely in animals. During this phase of the field's development, the research was largely conducted in carefully designed and controlled experimental contexts. Toward the middle of the twentieth century, behaviorists began to see potential application of the principles and methods to human environments, which resulted in the emergence of the tradition of Applied Behavior Analysis (Baer, Wolf, & Risley, 1968). The field of Applied Behavior Analysis was particularly concerned with addressing human problems (e.g., psychopathology, educational learning, work related difficulties) in their natural context.

Early behavioral treatments often imposed novel and complex generated reinforcement contingencies (e.g., token economies) on existing, natural conditions (Martens, Witt, Daly, & Vollmer, 1999). As the field matured, researchers and clinicians began examining contingencies (antecedents, reinforcers, and punishers) that were already in existence in the natural environment prior to prescribing behavioral treatments. As a result, behavioral treatments became less cumbersome and were better adapted to the environments in which they were being applied. The earlier example of how to respond to inappropriate classroom comments demonstrates how an analysis of classroom contingencies can lead to a treatment that is uniquely adapted to the context in which the problem occurs. An important and unique aspect of the tradition of Applied Behavior Analysis is that both the principles of behavior (e.g., positive and negative reinforcement, punishment, stimulus control) and the actual methodology for studying behavior (use of single-case experimental design elements) can be applied in educational and clinical situations.

BENEFITS OF APPLIED BEHAVIOR ANALYSIS IN EDUCATION

Applied Behavior Analysis is the version of behaviorism that is best suited to educational settings because it has produced the most useful technologies for addressing student learning and problems students typically encounter in schools. Applied Behavior Analysis is the standard of practice in the field of developmental disabilities, both in terms of teaching adaptive behavioral repertoires (e.g., self-help skills, safety behaviors, vocational training) and addressing maladaptive problem behaviors (e.g., self-injury) that are all too frequent in this population (Miltenberger, 2008). Functional analysis of behavior is a well-developed protocol (based on hundreds of studies) for identifying stimulus events that control problem behavior as a basis for developing behavioral treatments and has been studied extensively regarding individuals with developmental disabilities, behavioral disorders, educational disabilities, and those at-risk for learning and behavior problems (O'Neill et al., 1997). In schools, functional behavioral assessment (which involves intensive and systematic study of functional relationships in natural classroom settings using methods of Applied Behavior Analysis) is a requirement of federal special educational law under some circumstances. Positive Behavior Support is an outgrowth of functional behavioral assessment that applies methods of Applied Behavior Analysis at the school building or district level for reducing the overall level of problem behaviors.

There are also teaching models that have been developed based on the science of Applied Behavior Analysis. Direct Instruction, an instructional package that has been shown to produce strong academic learning effects over thirty years of implementation and evaluation (Adams & Carnine, 2003), was originally developed based on a stimulus control paradigm: Instructional materials and lessons are designed to assure the clearest possible presentation of instructional tasks and occasion high rates of student responding to foster strong functional relationships between academic tasks and student responding.

A related development in instructional technology is Precision Teaching (Johnson & Layng, 1992), which uses behavioral fluency training and frequent student monitoring to produce generalizable skill repertoires that make harder tasks easier to learn as students progress through the curriculum. In the field of autism, discrete trial training has achieved enormous popularity. The Comprehensive Application of Behavior Analysis to Schooling (CABAS) is another model used for children with autism and other disabilities (Greer, 1994). CABAS applies frequent and systematic prompting and consequences (learn units) to student academic responding. Behaviorism in its early 21st century form has developed into a number of applications that share a common view of the importance of measuring observable relationships between behavior and the natural contexts in which it occurs.

SEE ALSO *Applied Behavior Analysis.*

BIBLIOGRAPHY

Adams, G., & Carnine, D. (2003). Direct instruction. In H. Lee Swanson, K. R. Harris, & S. Graham (Eds.), *Handbook of learning disabilities* (pp. 403–416). New York: The Guilford Press.

Alberto, P. A., & Troutman, A. C. (2003). *Applied behavior analysis for teachers* (6th ed.). Upper Saddle River, NJ: Merrill Prentice Hall.

Baer, D. B., Wolf, M. M., & Risley, T. R. (1968). Some current dimensions of applied behavior analysis. *Journal of Applied Behavior Analysis, 1,* 91–97.

Bijou, S. W. (1970). What psychology has to offer education—now. *Journal of Applied Behavior Analysis, 3,* 65–71.

Cooper, J. O., Heron, T. E., & Heward, W. L. (2007). *Applied behavior analysis* (2nd ed.). New York, NY: Macmillan.

Greer, R. D. (1994). The measure of a teacher. In R. Gardner III, D. M. Sainato, J. O., Cooper, T. E. Heron, W. L. Heward, J. W. Eshleman, & T. A. Grossi. (Eds.), *Behavior analysis in education: Focus on measurably superior instruction* (pp. 161–172). Pacific Grove, CA: Brooks/Cole Publishing Co.

Iwata, B. A., Dorsey, M. F., Slifer, K. J., Bauman, K. E., & Richman, G. S. (1994). Toward a functional analysis of self-injury. *Journal of Applied Behavior Analysis, 27,* 215–240. (Reprinted from *Analysis and Intervention in Developmental Disabilities, 2,* 1–20, 1982).

Johnson, K. R., & Layng, T. V. J. (1992). Breaking the structuralist barrier: Literacy and numeracy with fluency. *American Psychologist, 47,* 1475–1490.

Martens, B. K., Witt, J. C., Daly, E. J., III, & Vollmer, T. R. (1999). Behavior analysis: Theory and practice in educational settings. In C. R. Reynolds & T. B. Gutkin (Eds.), *The handbook of school psychology* (3rd ed., pp. 638-663). New York, NY: John Wiley & Sons.

Miltenberger, R. G. (2008). *Behavior modification: Principles and procedures* (4th ed.). Belmont, CA: Wadsworth/Thomson Learning.

O'Neill, R. E., Horner, R. H., Albin, R. W., Sprague, J. R., Storey, K., & Newton, J. S. (1997). *Functional assessment of problem behavior: A practical assessment guide* (2nd ed.). Pacific Grove, CA: Brooks/Cole.

Edward J. Daly, III

BELIEFS ABOUT LEARNING

Beliefs about learning (BLs) make up the belief system that learners have about learning anything. BLs are central to children's formal education. BLs are not domain or task specific, but general about oneself as a learner. Although researchers may have referred to BLs previously,

Jin Li used the term to study European American (EA) and Chinese students' BLs systematically in the early 2000s. BLs include four broad areas: (1) one's own purposes of learning, (2) understanding of one's learning process, (3) affect associated with one's learning, and (4) social perceptions surrounding one's learning. These four areas jointly influence learners' motivation, self-regulation, and ultimately their achievement.

DEFINING THE CONCEPTS OF BELIEFS ABOUT LEARNING

One's purposes pertain to the central question "why do I need to learn?" to which all learners can respond. Some learners may believe that learning is for a better job in the future; others may believe that learning enables them to understand the world. Some learners may have few purposes whereas others may have multiple purposes. Understanding of one's learning process addresses what learners believe it takes for them to learn something. This set of beliefs includes those about how one's mind works, about the steps one takes to tackle a learning task, and about more abstract approaches of planning, self-monitoring, and overcoming challenges. Affect associated with one's learning is the range of emotions and other feelings learners have about their own learning. These responses can be positive and negative. Joy, excitement, passion, interest, flow, confidence, and pride are examples of positive affects. Dread, anxiety, low self-esteem, embarrassment, shame, guilt, and jealousy are examples of negative affects. Affect is part of the belief system because learners' beliefs are linked to these affective experiences in learning situations. Finally, social perceptions surrounding one's learning concern how learners perceive social aspects in their own learning. All students have such perceptions, for example, regarding what teachers are supposed to do, how learners are supposed to relate to teachers, what good versus poor teaching is, what high versus low-achieving peers are like, how oneself relates to them, how learners view parental and school pressure for learning, and how learners understand the social resources available to themselves.

INDIVIDUAL DIFFERENCES AMONG STUDENTS

Large individual differences exist in all four areas of BLs. Few BLs are attributable only to the individual him- or herself, but are subject to developmental, social, and cultural/ethnic influences. With regard to purposes, EA preschoolers, for instance, believe that learning makes them smart because they learn concrete pieces of knowledge such as names of animals. Older children believe that learning makes them understand things, but not necessarily that it makes them smart. Middle-class students may focus on developing their personal talents; low-income students may be more concerned about

changing their economic status. A given student may have one clear purpose; another may have a combination of purposes (Li, 2006; Li & Fischer, 2004). For example, a Chinese American student may have the individual purpose of studying medicine but at the same time may purposefully intend to fulfill her family's expectations.

Individual learners also vary greatly in what they think it takes for them to learn something. Young children believe that if a person wants to learn something, that person will learn it. Older children realize that desire alone may not guarantee successful learning; one needs to be exposed to the knowledge and to have the intention to learn it. Some students may not see any utility in learning things by heart; others may believe that memorization is a helpful step. Whereas older EA students may focus on thinking, active involvement, and verbal communication, Asian students may stress the so-called personal virtues of diligence, endurance of hardship, concentration, quiet contemplation, persistence, and humility (Li, 2003; Sobel, Li, & Corriveau, 2007).

How learners feel about learning in school is essential to their actual engagement in learning. Individuals' affective experiences with learning vary widely, and they are strongly shaped by their social and cultural context, particularly their home. For example, if a child's personal curiosity is allowed to flourish, that child is likely to grow up feeling that it is natural to ask questions. If a child is socialized to take pride in overcoming challenges, that child may be more inclined to persist through challenges. However, if a child is shielded from making mistakes and failing, that child may develop an aversion toward failure and be less ready to face setbacks. Or if a child is made to feel that not making great effort to learn brings shame to his or her family, that child may be willing to work harder (Li, 2002).

Individuals' perceptions of social aspects of learning can also differ largely. For example, while younger children view teachers as authority figures who must be obeyed, regardless of the teachers' quality, older children may not have such a generalized view of teachers. Instead, they judge teachers individually according to the standards teachers should display and personal qualities such as professional responsibility, integrity, and the care they give to students. Different students may also have different attitudes toward parental pressure for learning. Whereas African American students may regard parental demand as a form of caring, EA students may regard the same parental behavior as interference with their autonomy (Delpit, 1995).

Of particular significance are learners' perceptions of their high- versus low-achieving peers. Social comparison for learning is common among children of all ages. Yet, EA preschoolers are not concerned about how their self-celebratory announcement of their achievement can

100

negatively impact their lesser achieving peers. However, older children, while seeking information about others' achievement, will try to conceal their own higher achievement to avoid negative social consequences for themselves (e.g., peer rejection). Lower achievers also conceal their achievement in order to avoid negative opinions of their lack of ability. Instead, students with similar achievement reveal their information to each other because the perceived negativity for the self is minimal. In contrast, Chinese higher achievers do not feel a need to conceal their level, and their disclosure is taken as an offer of help extended to the lower achievers. Similarly, lower achievers disclose their information to higher achievers to solicit help from them. These differences reflect diverging cultural values and norms, with EA culture emphasizing the self as unique and stable, while the Chinese culture stresses the self as in constant need of improvement (Li & Wang, 2004).

HOW BELIEFS ABOUT LEARNING GUIDE STUDENT PERFORMANCE

Conscious human behavior is guided by human beliefs. However, how specifically BLs guide student learning has not been well studied. Because BLs are conceptualized as the core of the student's self-view as a learner, not necessarily to a particular learning task or achievement situation, BLs are assumed to guide student learning more broadly. Available evidence suggests that the more numerous and the longer-term purposes students have, the more readily they are engaged to pursue those purposes. For example, if students believe that learning makes them understand the world, gives them good grades for college, and prepares them for a desirable career, allows them to serve their community better, and to earn respect from people, then those students are likely to be more ready to learn. If, however, students believe that school is only about getting a diploma, they may be less motivated to learn.

Similarly, if students believe that keeping an open-mind, always questioning, collecting and using a variety of study skills, paying attention to what is taught, resisting distractions, persisting through the task without giving up, and seeking help when they need it, they are more likely to learn well than students who want to get through each task as quickly and effortlessly as possible. The former students have a set of beliefs that will allow them to meet most academic challenges; the latter hold BLs that foster resignation and avoidance.

Learning without affect is boring. Unfortunately, many students pass through school with such indifference. Students learn much better when they are affectively attuned. Research shows that both positive and negative affects promote learning, depending on how these affects are organized. Self-defeating affects such as low self-esteem and learned helplessness are detrimental to learning. However, having a sense of shame or guilt for not working hard or for not taking responsibility can motivate a student to seek ways to improve. This tendency is especially true for students from cultural/ethnic backgrounds such as Asians who emphasize social accountability and self-improvement. Regardless of their cultural background, it is better for students to have both positive and negative emotions that are activated appropriately. If students have passion for learning, they will learn better. If students learn well, they should feel proud. If they behave irresponsibly, they should feel a sense of remorse and strive to improve (Li & Fischer, 2004).

Students' perceptions of teachers, peers, and parental and school demands can influence their learning emphatically. In fact, the social world has the most impact on children's BLs. If children view their high achieving peers as models to emulate, they will not reject such peers. If low-achieving students can be encouraged to seek help from their peers without the risk of being viewed as unintelligent, those students will learn much more (Li & Wang, 2004). If teachers teach with deep understanding, appropriate pedagogy, and moral embodiment, students are likely to view them as serious, responsible, and caring adult exemplars. Parental attitude toward school learning is also essential in influencing children's attitudes. If parents emphasize open-mindedness, inquiry, thinking, hard work, perseverance, concentration, and perhaps even a degree of humility, and if they act consistently, their children are likely to follow their examples and act accordingly in school.

SEE ALSO *Epistemological Beliefs.*

BIBLIOGRAPHY

Delpit, L. D. (1995). *Other people's children: Cultural conflict in the classroom.* New York: New Press.

Li, J. (2002). Models of learning in different cultures. In J. Bempechat & J. G. Elliott (Eds.), *New directions in child and adolescent development, no. 96: Achievement motivation in culture and context: Understanding children's learning experiences.* San Francisco: Jossey-Bass.

Li, J. (2003). U.S. and Chinese cultural beliefs about learning. *Journal of Educational Psychology, 95,* 258–267.

Li, J. (2006). Self in learning: Chinese adolescents' goals and sense of agency. *Child Development, 77,* 482–501.

Li, J. & Fischer, K. W. (2004). Thoughts and emotions in American and Chinese cultural beliefs about learning. In D. Y. Dai & R. Sternberg (Eds.), *Motivation, emotion, and cognition: integrative perspectives on intellectual functioning and development.* Mahwah, NJ: Erlbaum.

Li, J. & Wang, Q. (2004). Perceptions of achievement and achieving peers in U.S. and Chinese kindergartners. *Social Development, 13,* 413–436.

Sobel, D., Li, J., & Corriveau, K. (2007). "It danced around in my head and I learned it": What children know about learning. *Journal of Cognition and Development, 8*, 1–25.

Jin Li

BERLINER, DAVID CHARLES
1938–

Experimental psychologist, educational researcher, psychometrician, teacher educator, policy wonk, activist, administrator—David Berliner realized a full life during seven decades during the 20th century and into the 21st, and as of 2008 showed little sign of slowing his pursuit of enhancing the quality of U.S. public schools and of searching out, understanding, and remedying inequities in the system. Seen by some as a troublemaker, he is viewed by many as a mover and shaker.

Born in 1938 in New York, Berliner moved west for academic work at University of California, Los Angeles, Los Angeles City College, and a 1968 doctorate at Stanford University. In 1977 he moved to Arizona, first to Tucson, and in 1997 to Arizona State University for several years as dean and subsequently as regents professor. In 1985 he was elected president of the American Educational Association; his awards and honors are numerous and come from various places around the world. This entry organizes Berliner's accomplishments by the four seminal topics that emerged over the decades: (1) academic learning time; (2) looking at classrooms; (3) classroom expertise; and (4) the public image of teachers and teaching.

Schools have a plentitude of learning time; in the United States, most students spend almost 12,000 hours in classrooms, surely enough time to learn. In the 1980 Beginning Teacher Evaluation Study (BTES), Berliner and his colleagues used ethnographic methods to document the details of classroom life (Fisher & Berliner, 1985). The result was a rich and textured account of how individual teachers moved the minds and motives of students toward mandated academic and social outcomes. They discovered that time was a critical but complex metric. In a mindless application of the *time-on-task* principle, administrators in the early 2000s mandated prescribed time to specified tasks. For example, they might specify that the teacher spend two hours daily on reading. Berliner showed time to be an essential ingredient, often lost through poor management practices. But he also found that how time was spent was an equally if not more important consideration.

BTES was unique as a large-scale ethnographic study, relying on qualitative methods to collect generalizable data. It was also an example of a *mixed-methods* strategy, where many claims relied on qualitative (statistical) techniques. The data included classroom observations, along with psychometrically designed student outcomes, teacher interviews, and focus-group techniques. At about this time, an acrimonious debate emerged between quantitative and qualitative camps. Berliner finessed this debate. Focused on understanding the contextual influences on classrooms, he relied on the mix of methods best suited to a particular problem.

Berliner's interest in expertise emerged from observations and interviews during the BTES study (Berliner, 1994). The new approaches of cognitive psychology revealed that expertise could illuminate the exploration of well-organized minds. His decade of work in this field brought out that pedagogical expertise was wonderful to behold, could be studied experimentally, and appeared across a broad spectrum of contexts.

Findings from the annual Gallup poll on the state of U.S. schools (Phi Delta Kappan) are remarkably consistent. In general, respondents say that U.S. schools are in a sorry state. Parents view their local schools as good, but schools in general as quite bad. The poll, a crude index, raises puzzling questions. For instance, how does a non-parent form opinions of schools? In a seminal work with Bruce Biddle (*Manufactured Crisis*, 1995) and with Sharon Nichols (*Collateral Damage* [2007]) Berliner analyzed media portrayals of public school. Reporters spend little time in classrooms and rely on the opinions of opinion-makers. Bad news sells. Driven by anecdotes more than evidence, the policy environment of the early 2000s portrays schools as poorly managed, teachers as incompetent, and graduates as lacking basic skills. To ensure that "no child is left behind," the corrective is the use of multiple-choice tests to pressure public schools to raise test scores by whatever means possible, threatening dire consequences for those who fail to attain ever-increasing levels. Berliner's work raises questions about every aspect of this policy environment—but most significantly, Berliner takes to task the media—especially those who persist in reporting so-called facts that are demonstrably false.

Berliner's influence comes about in several ways. He is a prolific writer. For example, he wrote the bestselling textbook, *Educational Psychology*, with mentor and colleague Nate Gage (Gage & Berliner, 1998) and co-edited the larger volume, *The Handbook of Educational Psychology* with Robert Calfee (1996). His numerous journal articles and readings, many with Ursula Casanova, have reached large audiences. He is at his best with a live audience, combining an avuncular style with passion and sensitivity. He has a remarkable ability to match style with audience—general public, researchers, practitioners, legislators. He does not lack for detractors, quite the contrary, but he persistently presses for equal and quality public education, through policies more than politics, through cumulative evidence more than quick fixes, through reasoned analysis more than one best answer.

A final anecdote illustrates Berliner employing evidence to cut to the core of a problem, simultaneously confounding all parties. Shortly after he became dean at Arizona State, the Arizona legislature asked him how to reduce the costs of public schooling. Berliner told the committee that they could reduce costs substantially by one simple act—eliminate retention in grade. The evidence is clear: Keeping a student behind has no positive effect on learning, but rather a variety of negative motivational and social consequences. The economic consequences are obvious: Retention adds another year of costs to the education. The legislators were confounded. The evidence was unassailable, but the recommendation was unacceptable. Berliner's delivery was calm but persistent: If the legislators really wanted to save money, then they would do away with retention and find more cost-effective ways to help students who were not doing well. The legislative committee thanked him for his words and moved on to other issues. But Berliner was not discouraged, for there was much for him to do.

BIBLIOGRAPHY

WORKS BY

Berliner, D. C. (1994). Expertise: The wonders of exemplary performance. In J. N. Mangieri and C. Collins Block (Eds.), *Creating powerful thinking in teachers and students* (pp. 141–186). Ft. Worth, TX: Holt, Rinehart and Winston.

Berliner, D. C., & Biddle, B. J. (1995). *The manufactured crisis: Myths, fraud, and the attack on America's public schools.* New York: Addison-Wesley.

Berliner, D. C., & Calfee, R. C. (Eds.). (1996). *The handbook of educational psychology.* New York: Macmillan.

Fisher, C. W., & Berliner, D. C. (1985). (Eds.). *Perspectives on instructional time.* New York: Longman.

Gage, N. L., & Berliner, D. C. (1998). *Educational psychology* (6th ed.). Boston: Houghton Mifflin.

Nichols, S. N. & Berliner, D. C. (2007). *Collateral Damage: How high-stakes testing corrupts America's schools.* Cambridge, MA: Harvard Education Press.

Robert Calfee

BILINGUAL EDUCATION

Bilingual education refers to instruction in two languages. Typically, bilingual education is offered in the societal language and in another language. In the United States, bilingual education usually refers to the type of instruction provided to students who are limited-English-proficient, also known as English language learners. These students receive instruction in their native or home language and in English. Most programs focus on Spanish and English because the majority of English language learners are Spanish speakers. In international contexts, bilingual education is offered to students who do not know the societal language and to students who are native speakers of the societal language. When the latter students are given the opportunity to learn a second language, bilingual education becomes prestigious and is viewed as an educational advantage.

HISTORY OF BILINGUAL EDUCATION IN THE UNITED STATES

Although James Crawford reports that bilingual education existed during the early history of the United States, it was not until 1968, when the United States Congress authorized bilingual education through the Bilingual Education Act, or Title VII of the Hawkins-Stafford Elementary and Secondary Education Act, that it became an approved means of education for students who were limited-English-proficient. A Supreme Court ruling, *Lau v. Nichols* (1974), contributed to the spread of bilingual education when the Court declared that placing Chinese students who were limited-English-proficient in regular classrooms, without special efforts to address their second-language status, was a violation of their civil rights. The Office of Civil Rights in the United States Department of Education then decided that the preferred method to address students' second-language status was bilingual education.

Crawford explains that after 1987, the types of programs funded under the heading of bilingual education expanded to include English instruction without a native-language component. For example, in 1987–1988, Congress allowed up to 25 percent of federal funding to be used for all-English programs. In the late 1990s and early 2000s, a few states restricted or outlawed bilingual education programs with native-language instruction, providing English-language learners only with some form of English instruction. In 2002, with the passage of the No Child Left Behind Act, the English Language Acquisition Act (Title III), replaced the Bilingual Education Act. States now could choose how to address the second-language needs of English-language learners, as long as they established English proficiency standards, quality academic instruction in reading and mathematics, and quality language instruction based on scientific research for English acquisition. They also had to provide English language learners with highly qualified teachers and annually assess the English proficiency and reading and mathematics performance of English-language learners. In 2005, forty states still had bilingual education programs that used the native language and English, with the rest offering some type of English-as-a-second-language (ESL) instructional program.

BILINGUAL EDUCATION VERSUS INSTRUCTION IN THE SOCIETAL LANGUAGE

Opponents of bilingual education often claim that their grandparents were immigrants who learned the societal language and acquired jobs without bilingual education. They warn that students will not learn the societal language if they are not immersed in it at an early age. They voice concerns about students not acquiring the societal language as fast as possible and argue that time on task is important for language acquisition.

Katharine Davies Samway and Denise McKeon explain that past immigrants had less need for a high school education and could survive with lower levels of English proficiency than current immigrants due to the types of employment available. Diane August and Kenji Hakuta counter the early immersion and time-on-task warning by explaining that older students, who already have acquired their native language, are more effective second-language learners than younger students. The older students can use what they have learned about their native language to approach learning about a second language. Additionally, Stephen Krashen explains that mere exposure to a second language is not enough for second-language acquisition because students need to receive structured course content that is comprehensible to them.

Jim Cummins (1979, 1981) points out that it takes time for English language learners to acquire the type of language needed to perform at grade level in English. He distinguishes between the skills needed to communicate orally in English and academic language proficiency—the skills needed to read and write in English and learn new material at grade level in English, Cummins observes that English-language learners can acquire English oral proficiency in two to three years of instruction but may need four to seven years of instruction to acquire academic language proficiency.

Cummins (1979) also argues that students who have developed academic language proficiency in one language can make use of this proficiency for learning in a second language. Virginia Collier's synthesis of research with immigrant children from advantaged backgrounds provides some evidence that supports Cummins's theory. Collier found that English-language learners who had no formal instruction in their home countries, needed seven to ten years of instruction in English to reach grade-level in English, whereas English-language learners

who had two to three years of formal schooling in their home countries and who entered schools in the United States between ages 8 and 12 needed five to seven years of instruction in English to reach grade level. In a review of empirical data, Diane August and her colleagues (2008) also support Cummins's claim. They concluded, "Language minority children who are literate in their first language are likely to be advantaged in the acquisition of English literacy. Studies demonstrate that language minority students instructed in the native language (usually Spanish) and English perform, on average, better on English reading measures than language-minority students instructed only in English" (p. 171).

TYPES OF PROGRAMS

There are different types of bilingual education programs. The most common program is Transitional Bilingual Education, which typically is offered to English-language learners in the elementary grades for up to three years, most often from grades 1 to 3. Students usually receive some amount of native language instruction so that they do not fall behind in their literacy or content learning as they are acquiring English. The percent of time that they are taught literacy and content in the native language changes so that by the end of third grade, most, if not all of their literacy and content instruction is in English. Teachers in these programs are supposed to be proficient in both English and the native language and state certified for teaching at the particular grade level and in bilingual education. Although funding for this type of program is available for three years, individual students are exited from the program as soon as they are classified as English proficient. Once exited, they are placed in all-English classrooms without additional second-language services.

Another type of program is called maintenance, developmental, or late-exit bilingual education. English-language learners typically stay in these programs throughout elementary school, or from grades K–5 or 6. Similar to those teaching in transitional bilingual education, teachers in this program should be proficient in English and the native language and state certified at the respective grade level and in bilingual education. Students learn literacy and content areas in their native language as they are taught ESL. However, their transition to instruction in English is more gradual than in transitional bilingual education, and they continue to receive instruction in their native language throughout elementary school. For example, beginning in fourth grade, students usually receive 40 percent of their instruction in the native language and 60 percent in English. When students graduate from elementary school to middle school, they usually are placed in all-English classrooms and no longer receive bilingual education services.

Dual language or two-way immersion is a third type of bilingual education program. In these programs, two types of students are enrolled in the same classroom or program: native English-speaking students and English-language learners. Instruction is presented in two languages: English and the native language of the English-language learners. The goal of the instruction is for both groups of students to become fluently bilingual. A certified bilingual education teacher or a pair of teachers—one fluent in English and with grade-level and ESL certification, and the other fluent in the native language and English with grade-level and bilingual education certification—teach the students, making sure to use second-language techniques to introduce content and literacy to the students not fluent in the specific language of instruction. Typically, students in first grade receive 80–90 percent of their instruction in the native language, and 10–20 percent of their instruction in the other language. By fourth grade, students receive instruction for half the school day in each language. In a few programs, starting with first grade, students receive instruction in both languages 50 percent of the time. Students stay in this type of program throughout elementary school.

A fourth type of program is structured English immersion. This program is only for English-language learners and does not involve any formal instruction in the native language. All of the students' instruction is in English. To help students understand the instruction, the teacher adapts her instruction by using ESL techniques. However, in some classrooms the teacher may speak the native language and allow the students to interact with each other in the native language. Students typically are in this program for one to three years. Once exited from the program, students no longer receive any second-language services.

When students are not in one of the above bilingual education programs, they may participate in an ESL pullout program for part of the school day, or be placed in an all-English classroom without any second-language services. The latter is called submersion, or sink-and-swim, because students either do not do well (sink) in school or do well in school (swim).

In Canada, majority native-English speaking students may enroll in French immersion programs. These programs are similar to structured English immersion in terms of the teacher's qualifications and the use of second-language techniques to present instruction in a second language, in this case, French. However, beginning in first grade, a native-language or English component often is included, making them more similar to transitional bilingual education or late exit/maintenance bilingual education. Also, these programs tend to serve middle or upper class students rather than students of immigrant families.

EVALUATIONS OF PROGRAM EFFECTIVENESS

One reason that bilingual education has continued to be controversial in the United States is that large-scale evaluations are difficult to conduct due to the lack of random assignment of students to instructional programs and the range of variables that need to be controlled, such as variation in program design, amount of native language and English used for instruction, previous student experience in bilingual education, and differences in teacher qualifications and students' levels of English proficiency and socio-economic status. The conclusions of national evaluations that have reported non-significant or negative findings for bilingual education have been questioned due to serious flaws in their evaluation designs. Meta-analyses of bilingual education programs, which statistically control for many design problems noted above, have favored bilingual education programs.

Critics of bilingual education usually cite two early evaluations of bilingual education programs. In 1977–1978 the American Institutes for Research (AIR) conducted a national evaluation of 38 bilingual programs. Crawford explains that the AIR evaluation compared the performance of Spanish-background students enrolled in bilingual education to that of Spanish-background students enrolled in all-English classrooms on pre- and post-measures in English in reading, oral comprehension, and mathematics, and in Spanish on reading and oral comprehension. AIR concluded that bilingual education had not had a positive impact because there were no differences in performance between the two groups in oral English comprehension and mathematics, and children in the all-English classrooms outperformed those in bilingual education on standardized measures of English reading. However, one of the major flaws with the AIR evaluation was that two-thirds of the Spanish-background students included in the all-English sample had previously been enrolled in bilingual education.

In 1983 Keith Baker and Adriana de Kanter published their evaluation of bilingual education. They used 28 of 300 program evaluations, excluding most of the program evaluations because they deemed them methodologically unsound. They included the AIR evaluation and evaluations of Canadian French immersion programs. To determine effectiveness, Baker and de Kanter counted the number of program evaluations that reported higher test scores for students in transitional bilingual education classrooms compared to students in other types of classrooms (all-English, structured English immersion, Canadian French immersion, pull-out ESL). Baker and de Kanter concluded that the results were ambiguous because students in bilingual education did not outperform students who were not in bilingual education. Crawford reports that Baker later stated that one in three studies favored bilingual education, while one in four favored all-English. This evaluation was criticized because Baker and de Kanter did not control for a number of teaching and student variables; considered the Canadian French Immersion studies to be similar to structured English immersion; and in their narrative tally did not take into account the different numbers of students who participated in the individual program evaluations (e.g., an evaluation with 50 students was considered equal to an evaluation with 200 students).

In 1996, Chrisine Rossell and Keith Baker published another narrative comparison of bilingual education programs and non-bilingual education programs, which again included the Canadian French Immersion programs along with other types of Canadian programs. This time they included 72 out of 300 evaluation studies. On English reading measures, they reported that 45 percent of the findings were inconclusive, while 22 percent of the transitional bilingual education programs outperformed structured immersion, and 33 percent of the structured immersion programs (primarily the Canadian French Immersion programs) outperformed transitional bilingual education programs. According to Crawford, Canadian researchers warned that many of the Canadian programs were not equivalent to the program types in the United States. In some program evaluations, students received native language instruction in both the control and experimental groups, invalidating the comparison. Other researchers complained that they could not find all the studies in the Rossell and Baker evaluation.

Three meta-analyses of bilingual education programs conducted between 1985 and 2008 have reported favorable findings for bilingual education. In 1985, Ann Willig used meta-analysis to reanalyze 23 of the 28 studies originally included in the Baker and de Kanter evaluation, excluding the Canadian French Immersion studies and secondary studies. On English measures of language, mathematics, overall achievement, and reading (and on similar measures in Spanish, plus listening comprehension, writing, social studies, attitudes about school and self), she found small-to-moderate differences in favor of bilingual education. When random assignment had been used in the evaluations, the effect size was even greater for bilingual education. Crawford explains that in 1999, Jay Greene also used meta-analysis to re-analyze the methodologically sound studies that could be located from the Rossell and Baker evaluation, purposefully excluding the Canadian studies. He found 11 studies. To avoid the confounding of program type, he ignored the program labels and based his comparison on the use or non-use of the native-language for the instruction of English language learners. His results were similar to Willig's meta-analysis:

He found small to moderate differences favoring bilingual education on the same types of measures.

Diane August and her colleagues (2008) chose to conduct a meta-analysis that only focused on studies with experimental designs and in which students had been taught for at least six months. They limited their comparison to the English reading test performance of students in bilingual programs and students in programs that only used English. Sixteen programs from the United States and four from Canada were included in the meta-analysis. August and her colleagues concluded that "bilingual education has a positive effect on English reading outcomes that is small to moderate in size" (p. 139). Further, they reported: "children in the bilingual programs ... also developed literacy skills in their native language. Thus, they achieved the advantage of being bilingual and biliterate" (p. 140).

RELATIONS AMONG LANGUAGE STATUS, AFFECTIVE FACTORS, AND LEARNING

According to Walter Lambert, subtractive bilingualism occurs when students lose proficiency in one language as they develop proficiency in the other language. Several experts have warned that participation in all-English classrooms, structured English immersion, or transitional bilingual education may contribute to subtractive bilingualism. When language-minority students are not fully accepted by native speakers of the societal language because of their accented speech or racial/ethnic appearance the loss of proficiency or lack of further development in their native language can result in low self-esteem and negative self-image. Lilly Wong Fillmore described the psychological problems that occurred when young English-language learners, enrolled in all-English classrooms, lost their ability to communicate with family members in their native language.

Additive bilingualism is viewed as contributing to students' self-esteem. According to Lambert, additive bilingualism occurs when students add proficiency and competency in a second language to the native language without loss or retardation of the native language. The latter is likely to occur for language majority students who are acquiring a minority language, such as in Canada. Participation in maintenance, developmental, or late-exit bilingual education and dual language or two-way immersion programs also can promote additive bilingualism. The length and design of these programs usually provide English-language learners with the opportunity to acquire academic language proficiency in English as students continue to use and further their native-language development. Participation in these programs also may aid students in making effective use of cross-linguistic transfer when instruction across the two languages is coordinated, so that students learn new and difficult concepts in the language they know best, while being taught the vocabulary and discourse to access this knowledge in English. In a comparison of the performance of Spanish-speakers in transitional bilingual education, structured English immersion, and late-exit bilingual education, David Ramirez found that students in the latter programs had the highest growth curve in English learning as measured on standardized tests, indicating that with additional time in school they would be at a grade level.

SEE ALSO *Learning and Teaching Foreign Languages; Multicultural Education.*

BIBLIOGRAPHY

August, D., Beck, I. L., Calderón, M., Francis, D. J., Lesaux, N. K., Shanahan, T., et al. (2008). Instruction and professional development. In D. August and T. Shanahan (Eds.), *Developing reading and writing in second-language learners: Lessons from the report of the National Literacy Panel on Language-Minority Children and Youth* (pp. 131–250). New York: Routledge, International Reading Association, and Center for Applied Linguistics.

August, D., & Hakuta, K., (Eds.). (1997). *Improving schooling for language-minority children: A research agenda.* Washington, DC: National Academy Press.

Baker, K. A., & de Kanter, A. A. (1983). *Bilingual education: A reappraisal of federal policy.* Lexington, MA: Lexington Books.

Collier, V. P. (1989). How long? A synthesis of research on academic achievement in a second language. *TESOL Quarterly, 23(3),* 509–31.

Crawford, J. (2004). *Educating English learners: Language diversity in the classroom* (5th ed.). Los Angeles: Bilingual Education Services.

Cummins, J. (1979). Linguistic interdependence and the educational development of bilingual children. *Review of Educational Research, 49(2),* 221–51.

Cummins, J. (1981). The role of primary language development in promoting educational success for language minority students. In Leyba, C. F. (Ed.), *Schooling and language minority students: A theoretical framework.* Los Angeles: Evaluation, Dissemination, and Assessment Center.

Krashen, S. (1985). *The input hypothesis: Issues and implications.* New York: Longman.

Lambert, W. E. (1975). Culture and language as factors in learning and education. In A. Wolfgang (Ed.), *Education of immigrant students* (pp. 55–83). Toronto: Ontario Institute for Studies in Education.

Ramirez, J. D. (1991). Executive summary. *Bilingual Research Journal, 16(1–2),* 1–62.

Rossell, C. H., & Baker, K. (1996). The educational effectiveness of bilingual education. *Research in the Teaching of English, 30(1),* 7–74.

Samway, K. D., & McKeon, D. (2007). *Myths and realities: Best practices for English language learners* (2nd ed.). Portsmouth, NH: Heinemann.

Willig, A. C. (1985). A meta-analysis of selected studies on the effectiveness of bilingual education. *Review of Educational Research, 55(3),* 269–317.

Wong Fillmore, L. (1991). When learning a second language means losing the first. *Early Childhood Research Quarterly, 6,* 323–346.

Georgia Earnest García

BIOLOGICAL THEORIES OF COGNITIVE DEVELOPMENT

SEE *Cognitive Development: Biological Theories.*

BLOOM'S TAXONOMY

The Taxonomy of Educational Objectives: Handbook I, The Cognitive Domain (Bloom, 1956) is a framework intended to classify any curriculum objective in terms of its explicit or implicit intellectual skills and abilities. Curriculum objectives describe the intended outcomes of instruction—its goals. Despite their age, the taxonomies have provided a basis for test and curriculum development in the United States as well as throughout the world (Chung, 1994, Lewy and Bathory, 1994, Postlethwaite, 1994). *The Taxonomy* was cited as one of the significant writings influencing curriculum in the twentieth century (Shane, 1981, Kridel, 2000). A Yahoo search showed "Bloom's Taxonomy" appeared in more than 455,000 entries.

Its six categories—Knowledge, Comprehension, Application, Analysis, Synthesis, and Evaluation—were tested with sets of actual objectives to assure inclusiveness. The distinctions between categories were intended to reflect those that teachers make in curriculum development and teaching. Although each category was also broken into subcategories, most applications of the framework involved mainly the major categories.

Intended to be logically internally consistent, the underlying ordering dimensions were those of simple to complex and concrete to abstract. Because each category assumed mastery of the previous ones, the framework formed a cumulative hierarchy. For example, comprehension of a rule is assumed necessary to the rule's proper application to a problem. Therefore, one must assume certain background knowledge and skills in order to properly classify objectives for particular students.

Developed by faculty involved in building achievement tests for university courses, *The Taxonomy* was intended to ease communication among test makers so they could trade items designed to test the same objectives. Thus, the handbook included a large number of sample items for each major category as models. But the framework has found considerable use beyond this. By providing a panorama of the breadth of objectives, it became a standard against which sets of objectives could be compared. Therefore, a major application was the analysis of course objectives to determine the balance of goals across the categories. Repeatedly finding an overbalance of knowledge objectives compared to few, if any, skills and abilities objectives (comprehension through evaluation) led to increased emphasis on higher—level behaviors.

The cognitive domain was the first of three taxonomies developed to cover the objectives spectrum. The second, the affective domain (Krathwohl, Bloom, and Masia, 1964), covered interest, attitude, appreciation, value and adjustment objectives. Objectives dealing with motor coordination and physical movement were the subject of the psychomotor taxonomies of Simpson (1966) and Harrow (1972).

All these authors assumed that each field would create subdivisions to make the framework fit its own emphases, language, and characteristics. Indeed, Bloom, Hastings and Madaus (1971) provided examples of how it could be adapted. *The Taxonomy's* wide adoption (including translation into more than twenty languages) showed the usefulness of such frameworks and stirred development of alternatives. Bloom's introduction of taxonomy to the field of education with all the term implied was important. A chapter in *The Taxonomy Revision* describes 19 of numerous competing frameworks, many claiming to be taxonomies.

THE REVISION OF *THE TAXONOMY*

Advances in cognitive psychology suggested a need for revision. In 1995 Krathwohl and Anderson formed a committee composed of P. W. Airasian, K. A. Cruikshank, R. E. Mayer, P. R. Pintrich, J. Raths, and M. C. Wittrock. Their revision was Anderson and Krathwohl (Eds.) (2001). The revision made 12 major changes that fall in three categories, changes in emphasis, terminology, and structure.

Changes in Emphasis. First, the primary audience is elementary and secondary teachers. Second, instead of providing many sample test items, the revision emphasizes the alignment of curriculum, instruction, and assessment. Third, rather than providing models, the sample assessment tasks illustrate and clarify the category's meaning. Finally, subcategories are used to define the major categories.

Changes in Terminology. First, the nouns forming the categories on the cognitive process dimension were rewritten as verbs. Second, the term *Knowledge* became *Remember*, but remained the least complex cognitive process. Third, *Comprehension* and *Synthesis* were renamed *Understand* and *Create*. Finally, the subcategories were completely renamed, reorganized, and were written as verbs.

Changes in Structure. The grammatical structure of educational objectives is subject-verb-object. In numerous elementary classrooms one sees the letters TLW, standing for "The Learner Will," written as a lead-in to objectives written on chalkboards or whiteboards. The subject of educational objectives is the student or the learner. The first structural change was to classify each objective in two dimensions according to the verb and object. Second, the verb—what is to be done with or to knowledge—became the cognitive process dimension with Remember, Understand, Apply, Analyze, Evaluate and Create categories. The object—what content is dealt with—became the Knowledge Dimension with Factual, Conceptual, Procedural, and Metacognitive categories. Third, the two dimensions became the basis for the Taxonomy Table described below. Fourth, the claim that the cognitive process dimension was a cumulative hierarchy was eliminated.

THE TAXONOMY TABLE

The taxonomy table provides a useful way of analyzing the objectives and instructional activities of a curriculum in terms of *The Taxonomy Revision* framework to show how well objectives and objectives are aligned and how they contribute to the larger course of study of which it is a part.

The Taxonomy Table's Cognitive Process Dimension. Verbs in this dimension usually name the columns of the Taxonomy Table (see Table 1). The learner will remember. The learner will classify. The learner will apply. The learner will organize.

Its Knowledge Dimension. The objects of objectives are derived most frequently from the curriculum content: The learner will remember the major exports of countries; be able to classify poems as ballads, sonnets, etc.; apply algorithms to mathematical operations; organize tree leaves based on botanical principles. Knowledge's four classifications of this content transcend subject matter and grade level and form the rows of the Table (see Table 1). 1) Factual knowledge includes knowledge of terms and facts. "Major exports of countries" is an example of factual knowledge. 2) Conceptual knowledge includes knowledge of categories, principles, theories, and models. "Ballads, sonnets, odes, and epics" are all categories of poems. 3) Procedural knowledge includes knowledge of techniques and methods. Addition, subtraction, multiplication, and division algorithms are

---

A taxonomy table example

The columns of the table are the Cognitive Process categories and the rows are the Knowledge categories. The sample objective is classified at the intersection of Understand and Conceptual Knowledge.

	Remember	Understand	Apply	Analyze	Evaluate	Create
Factual						
Conceptual		The learner will compare democracies and autocracies				
Procedural						
Metacognitive						

Table 1 ILLUSTRATION BY GGS INFORMATION SERVICES. CENGAGE LEARNING, GALE.

---

mathematical procedures. 4) Metacognitive knowledge includes knowledge of general strategies, school tasks, and oneself. Knowing how to write an essay that meets the approval of the teacher is an aspect of metacognitive knowledge.

APPLICATIONS OF *THE REVISED TAXONOMY*

Because the format of the Taxonomy Table mirrors the grammatical structure of objectives, it can be used (1) to increase understanding of educational objectives, (2) to design assessments that are aligned with specified educational objectives, and (3) to develop instruction that is aligned with both the objectives and the assessments. Each of these applications is described briefly in the sections that follow.

Increased Understanding of Objectives. The Taxonomy Table provides a framework for showing the underlying similarities across subjects and grades. Consider the following objective: "The learner will compare democracies and autocracies." In this objective, "compare" means the student will understand the similarities and differences of two forms of government. Because "compare" is a cognitive process associated with "Understand" in the Taxonomy Table and because "democracies" and "autocracies" are forms (classifications) of government, this objective would be classified as "Understand Conceptual Knowledge" (see Table 1).

Now, consider an objective dealing with important science concepts: "The learner will compare weather and climate." This objective, like the first, would be classified as "Understand Conceptual Knowledge." The Taxonomy Table, thus, allows educators to move beyond rather superficial subject matter differences (social studies versus science) to a deeper understanding of the objectives in terms of intended student learning.

Designing Valid Assessments. Far too often, educators focus on the objects of the objectives with only a secondary concern for the verbs included in them. Numerous test items can be written about democracies and autocracies or weather and climate. To conform to the objective's real meaning, however, the items cannot ask students to provide or identify memorized concept definitions (which would be less complex, cognitively speaking), nor can the items ask students to evaluate the relative merits of each concept (which would be much more complex, cognitively speaking). If they are to be valid, the items need to determine whether students can compare two forms of government or two meteorological categories in terms of their similarities and differences. One method of improving the alignment between objectives and test items, which is consistent with the Taxonomy Table, is to build items using item formats designed to test these complex objectives (Haladyna, 1999; Roid and Haladyna, 1982).

Planning Effective Instruction. One of the insights many educators gain from using the Taxonomy Table to plan instruction is that objectives that are classified into the same cells of the Table are taught in much the same way. For example, both of the objectives used as examples in the previous sections would be classified as "Understand Conceptual Knowledge." Based on a great deal of research, much is known about teaching students to understand conceptual knowledge (Klausmeier, 1980; Tennyson and Cocchiarella, 1986). Teaching concepts in context, teaching defining features, and using examples and non-examples are all empirically verified ways of teaching concepts.

CRITICISM OF THE TAXONOMIES

Much of the written criticism has been directed toward *The Taxonomy*. Furst (1994) questioned the assumption that *The Taxonomy* was a "purely descriptive scheme in which every kind of goal could be represented in a relatively neutral way." (p. 28). He also questioned whether *The Taxonomy* was sufficiently comprehensive, suggesting that omitting the term understanding was an error. Bereiter and Scardamalia (1998) criticized the placement of knowledge on the same continuum as intellectual skills and abilities, particularly its placement at the lowest end of the continuum. Still others resist the objectives-based-movement as overly simplistic or as slicing and dicing the curriculum so as to destroy holistic processes (Marsh, 1992). The taxonomy revision attended to many of these criticisms, including a separate knowledge dimension as well as understanding as a primary cognitive process category. The focus on curriculum standards by both state and federal governments has reminded educators of the importance of objectives.

Shulman (2002) had the right idea when he wrote: "what is important about these taxonomies is that they are ... heuristics. They help us think more clearly about what we're doing, and they afford us a language through which we can exchange ideas and dilemmas" (p. 42).

SEE ALSO *Questioning.*

BIBLIOGRAPHY

Anderson, L. W., & Krathwohl, D. R. (Eds.). Airasian, P. W., Cruikshank, K. A., Mayer, R. E., Pintrich, P. R., Raths, J. and Wittrock, M. C. (2001). *A taxonomy for learning, teaching and assessing: A revision of Bloom's Taxonomy of Educational Objectives.* New York: Allyn Bacon Longman.

Anderson, L. W., & Sosniak, L. A. (Eds.). (1994). *Bloom's taxonomy: A forty- year perspective. Ninety-third Yearbook of the National Society for the Study of Education.* Chicago: University of Chicago Press.

Bereiter, C. & Scardamalia, M. (1999). Beyond Bloom's Taxonomy: Rethinking Knowledge for the Knowledge Age. In Hargreaves, A., Libermann, A., Fullan, M., & Hopkins, D. (Eds.), *The International Handbook of Educational Change* (pp. 675–692). Dordrecht, The Netherlands: Kluwer Academic Publishers.

Bloom, B. S. (Ed.). Engelhart, M. D., Furst, E. J., Hill, W. H., Krathwohl, D. R. (1956). *Taxonomy of educational objectives: Handbook I: The cognitive domain.* New York: David McKay.

Bloom, B. S., Hastings, J. T., & Madaus, B. B. (1971). *Handbook of formative and summative evaluation of student learning.* New York: McGraw-Hill.

Chung, B. M. (1994). The Taxonomy In The Republic of Korea. In L. W. Anderson & L. A. Sosniak (Eds.), *Bloom's Taxonomy: A Forty-Year Retrospective.* Ninety-Third Yearbook of the National Society for the Study of Education (pp. 129–186). Chicago: University of Chicago Press.

Haladyna, T. H. (1999). *Developing and validating multiple-choice test items.* Mahwah, NJ: Erlbaum.

Harrow, A. (1972). *A taxonomy of the psychomotor domain: A guide for developing behavioral objectives.* New York: David McKay.

Klausmeier, H. J. (1980). *Learning and teaching concepts.* New York: Academic Press.

Krathwohl, D. R., Bloom, B. S., & Masia, B. B. (1964). *Taxonomy of Educational objectives: Handbook II: The affective domain.* New York: David McKay.

Kridel, C. (1999). Some books of the century. *Education Week. 19* (16), 40–41, 60.

Lewy, A. & Bathory, Z (1994). The Taxonomy of Educational Objectives in Continental Europe, the Mediterranean, and the Middle East. In L. W. Anderson & L. A. Sosniak (Eds.), *Bloom's Taxonomy: A Forty-Year Retrospective.* Ninety-Third Yearbook of the National Society for the Study of Education (pp. 129–186). Chicago: University of Chicago Press.

Postlethwaite, T. N. (1994). Validity vs. Utility: Personal Experiences with the Taxonomy. In L. W. Anderson & L. A. Sosniak (Eds.), *Bloom's Taxonomy: A Forty-Year Retrospective.* Ninety-Third Yearbook of the National Society for the Study of Education (pp. 129–186). Chicago: University of Chicago Press.

Roid, G. H., & Haladyna, T. H. (1982). *A technology for test-item writing.* New York: Academic Press.

Shane, H. G. (1981). Significant Writings That Have Influenced The Curriculum. *Phi Delta Kappan, 63,* 311–314.

Shulman, L. (2002). Making Differences: A Table of Learning, *Change, 34*(6), 36–44.

Simpson, B. J. (1966). The classification of educational objectives: Psychomotor domain. *Illinois Journal of Home Economics, 10*(4), 110–144.

Tennyson, R. D., & Cocchiarella, M. J. (1986). Empirically based instructional design theory for teaching concepts. *Review of Educational Research, 56,* 40–71.

David R. Krathwohl
Lorin W. Anderson

BRAIN AND LEARNING

This entry discusses "Reading, Writing, and Math Brains" and the relevance of brain research to teaching and learning.

Knowledge of the structure and function of the normal brain in living human beings expanded exponentially during the last decade of the 20th century. Fueled by financial support from the United States government and advancements in brain imaging technology, neuroscientists scanned brains of mostly adults and sometimes children while they performed tasks. Likewise, neuroscientists in other countries contributed to the rapidly growing knowledge of brain-behavior relationships. Prior to this period in neuroscience history, most knowledge of brain-behavior relationships was based on autopsies of individuals who died of brain-related disease or injury.

Educational professionals expressed various reactions to this knowledge explosion, ranging from fascination and enthusiasm to skepticism. Is it really possible to go from brain scan to lesson plan? Many did not see the relevance of this basic research knowledge to their day-to-day practices as teachers in real-world classrooms. In part, the reluctance to embrace this new knowledge may be related to feeling intimidated by the complexity and terminology of neuroscience, which was not easily accessible by non-neuroscientists.

Typically, few pre-service or graduate students in teacher education are required to take courses on the brain as are students in medical, speech, hearing, and language sciences, occupational therapy, and physical therapy. Considering that the brain is the organ of learning, this oversight seemed shortsighted to some professionals. Virginia Berninger and Todd Richards, the authors of this entry, wrote *Brain Literacy for Educators and Psychologists* to introduce to educators the terminology and concepts needed to read the emerging research literature relevant to the brain and instruction and learning. Other books written for an educational audience for the same purpose are listed below under Suggestions for Further Reading. A Web site included under Electronic Resources by Eric H. Chudler is specifically directed to teachers and includes lesson plans for teaching students about their brains.

This entry provides an overview of some of what is known about reading, writing, and math brains. It also seeks to make the case that the brain and knowledge of it are relevant to teaching. Included is a brief overview of important general principals regarding the brain's role in learning and discussion of how brain research increased understanding of how reading brains, writing brains, and math brains develop as the brain interacts with the educational environment.

BRAIN'S BIDIRECTIONAL, MEDIATING RELATIONSHIPS WITH ENVIRONMENTAL INTERACTIONS

All learning is mediated by the brain's response to either instruction or other educational experience. Whether that instruction or experience is teacher-directed, teacher-guided (through scaffolding or questioning rather than knowledge dissemination), or self-generated and self-directed, the brain receives input from the environment. However, neither teaching nor other environmental input directly programs the brain as the software engineer directly creates programs or the computer-user enters data into the system. Rather, the environmental input indirectly exerts its effects on subsequent learning processes via the brain's attentional system, which selects a subset of the incoming stimuli for focus of attention, and the memory system, which codes the incoming information for temporary or permanent storage. Selection of stimuli for attentional focus may occur at the unconscious level in implicit memory or the conscious level in explicit memory.

The human brain codes incoming information in multiple formats depending on the physical properties of the incoming signal (e.g. visual or auditory) and existing coding formats higher in the system that are uniquely designed for

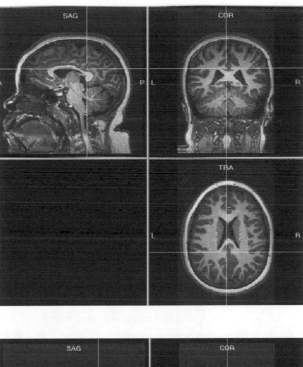

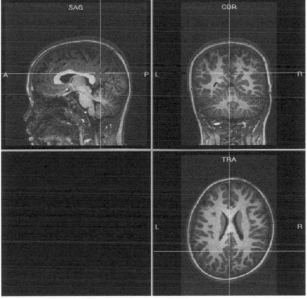

Figure 1—*View from 3 Imaging Perspectives of Two Typically Developing Brains. SAG = sagittal side view of the brain section; COR = coronal frontal view of the brain section; TRA = transverse which means a top view of the brain section.* COURTESY OF DR. TODD RICHARDS AND THE UNIVERSITY OF WASHINGTON LEARNING DISABILITY CENTER.

special kinds of sensory input (e.g. orthographic for visual or phonological for auditory). Working memory is a specialized brain system in explicit memory for consciously selecting, storing, maintaining, and processing incoming information and existing information in the brain for goal-directed purposes or tasks. Some of these processes may be automatic and executed in implicit memory thus freeing up limited conscious awareness in explicit working memory.

Once it is coded into working memory, further processing of the new input is influenced more by the learner's existing knowledge than the teacher's instructional input, guidance, or learning activities to foster self-guided learning. Whether the student has learned to learn, that is, created mental sets or strategies for regulating the learning process, is invisible to an observer but will determine what happens next in the learning process. However, some kinds of instruction or learning activities require that the student act on the environment, that is, produce observable behavior. The brain's motor systems are involved in such behavior generation: gross motor systems for arms, legs, body trunk or fine motor system for mouth and articulation and hand for finger movements.

How the brain mediates the teacher's instructional input or other relevant input is not directly observable, but the brain's behavioral response to that instruction is. Brain differences between students with and without developmental and behavioral problems show pretreatment differences and individual differences in response to the same instruction (e.g., Berninger & Richards, 2002). Likewise, typically developing readers in first grade instructional groups showed normal variation in response to the same reading instruction (Berninger & Abbott, 1992), as did individual at-risk readers and writers (Abbott, Reed, Abbott, & Berninger, 1997).

Children probably exhibit such normal variation in response to instruction because of normal variation in the neuroanatomical structures and functions of individual brains. No two brains are exactly alike. See Figures 1 and 2. Each of these brains shown in a magnetic resonance imaging scan (MRI) has the same parts—but they vary markedly in the way the gray and white matter are organized in the convolutions (folds) of cortex on top of the brain, corpus callosum (band of white fibers connecting right and left cortex), and four ventricles filled with cerebrospinal fluid. These MRI scans are not photographs of the exquisite detail of a child's neuroanatomy but rather images that are reconstructed by computer program based on water molecules in the human brain to provide spatial information about brain structures. These scans are not invasive; that is, no radiation is used and that makes them ideal for research purposes with children and youth.

Furthermore, the brain is not only an independent variable that influences response to instruction but also a dependent variable that may change as a result of learning. In some cases the changes involve what is represented—factual or procedural knowledge. In other cases changes involve how the brain functions—amount of activation in specific brain regions that vary in the physical properties of their neurons and presumable their computational capabilities.

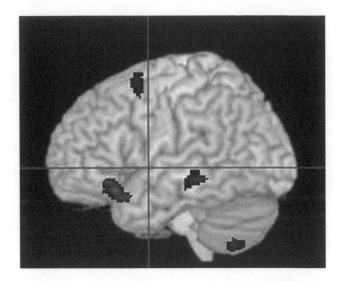

Figure 2—fMRI Functional imaging of brain of a fifth grader deciding if words are correctly spelled real words. Significant Blood-Oxygen-Level-Dependent (BOLD) activation occurred in left cerebellum, left temporal pole, left inferior frontal gyrus, and bilateral supplementary motor area. COURTESY OF DR. TODD RICHARDS AND THE UNIVERSITY OF WASHINGTON LEARNING DISABILITY CENTER.

To summarize, the brain may influence the learner's response to instruction or learning activities, and the learner's behavior in response to instruction may in turn influence the brain's representations or functions. Teaching and learning are not synonymous—the learner may not attend to and encode into memory some or all of the environmental input from teaching or learning activities. Learning depends as much on what the brain imposes on input from the environment and operating on the environment as on the input itself. At some point in time the learner's internal learning mechanism may override the external input from teaching. As shown in the MRI images in Figure 1, the mediating brain is not a black box but rather a gray and white complex structure housed within three thin membranes inside a bony skull. General principles of organizing structure and function of this remarkable, dynamic organ are considered below.

GENERAL PRINCIPLES OF BRAIN AND LEARNING

Two general principles underlie the role of brain in learning. The first is that many different levels of analysis can be applied to the brain's structures and functions. The second is that a system approach is needed to understand how the various component functions might be organized when a brain performs a reading, writing, or math task.

Levels of Structure and Function. Brain structures and functions contribute to learning at the macro-level and micro-level. Examples of structures at the macro-level are shown in Figure 1 and are visible to the human eye. What is not visible is the labeling schemes that evolved over the 20th century to describe specific regions of interest within these structures. Some schemes use names for regions such as inferior frontal gyrus or intraparietal sulcus to indicate location of region in the four lobes of cerebral cortex: occipital, temporal, parietal, or frontal. The adjective indicates where the gyrus (ascending up like a mountain) or sulcus (ascending below like a valley) is in reference to convolutions (grey folds in cortex) surrounding the cerebrum, which contains many visible white fiber tracts (see Figure 1). Other schemes use the numbers a neurosurgeon named Brodmann assigned to specific regions, for example, Brodmann's Area (BA) 8, which is Exner's Area, one of the writing centers in the brain (for more information on the names of brain regions and structures, see Bear, Connors, & Paradiso, 2007; Berninger & Richards, 2002; Chudler Web site; and the *Digital Anatomist Collection Manager* Web site).

Under the microscope the micro-level of brain structure becomes visible. The basic building block of the central nervous system (brain and spinal cord) is the neuron, which consists of a cell body, dendrites that receive electrochemical signals from other neurons, and axons that send electrochemical signals to the dendrites of other neurons. The space that separates the axon of one neuron from the dendrites of the other neuron is a synapse. The individual, microscopic neurons communicate only when an electrical impulse travels over the synapse causing the spatially separate neurons to become functionally connected for the moment until the electrical impulse subsides. Complex neurochemical events are involved in this electrical transmission (see Bear, Connors, & Paradiso, 2007, for research regarding the protein chemistry that regulates electrical transmission across synapses). The gray matter of cerebral cortex is collections of millions of neuronal cell bodies where computation occurs and the white matter of the cerebrum below is a collection of millions of axons bundled together for electrochemical transmission.

The unique computational properties of the human brain are related to this two-layer micro-level and macro-level organization. At the micro-level, spatially separated neurons communicate individually in linear time via dendrites, which look like tree branches and receive analogue signals graded in degree that are summated according to different computational mechanisms in the cell body until reaching a threshold that causes the axon to fire in a digital all-or-none manner. At the macro-level neurons containing the same parts but with somewhat different physical and functional capabilities are arranged in spatially separated cortical or subcortical regions. Large numbers of individual neurons in regional groupings with specialized computa-

tion properties communicate collectively across spatially distributed networks in the brain in multi-dimensional, non-linear, momentary time—at any moment in time the constellation of which regional groups of neurons are communicating with other regional groups of neurons varies, but their momentary spatial-temporal communication gets synthesized in real time (linear). (See Minsky, 1986, for discussion of the distinction between momentary and real time.) Thus, the human brain is an electrochemical, cross-talking network of multiple computers that communicate sequentially in time at the micro-level and in parallel at the macro-level in multidimensional space-time constellations.

The lower branches of the dendrites are under genetic control and thus influenced by inheritance and maturation, whereas the upper branches are under environmental control and influenced by education and experience (Diamond & Hobson, 1998; Jacobs et al., 1993). Consequently, the human brain develops through nature-nurture interactions to construct inner mental worlds (the mind) and overt interactions with the external world (behavior). This construction process is thought to occur through hierarchically ordered sensation (perception)-action (production) cycles with feedback and feedforward mechanisms. Without teaching and other kinds of environmental input, brains would not learn and develop, but without their internal computational mechanisms at the micro-level and macro-level, they would not learn.

System Approach to Brain Functions. Like brain structure, brain function is also complex. Alexander Luria (1902–1977), the pioneering Russian neuropsychologist, based on astute clinical observations, proposed four basic principles of organization of the working human brain for managing this complexity and creating multiple functional systems (1962, 1973):

Many different component processing units are involved in each functional system.

Regions distributed throughout the brain participate in any one functional system.

Different functional systems draw on common and unique processing units (i.e. brain regions).

Any one brain region may participate in multiple functional systems.

Having the same brain region participate in multiple functional systems and using the same common component brain regions across functional systems organized to achieve different goals lends efficiency to the fuel and energy requirements for supporting brain functions.

Brain imaging research results mesh with Luria's observations in a pre-imaging era. A consensus has developed that although certain kinds of functions tend to be associated with certain local brain regions the brain's operating system is more complex than one brain region having one corresponding function (e.g., Just & Varma, 2007). A particular brain region may be involved in more than one function and usually within the context of a neural network distributed spatially across more than one brain region. The sensory and motor processes have direct contact with the external world and code incoming information in local, primary regions, but subsequent processes draw on multiple codes, integrate them, and create more abstract representations, involving distributed space-time networks in association areas throughout the brain. Multiple, but not all, brain regions co-activate at the same time in a spatially distributed network of brain regions that are not communicating with each other constantly but rather at certain moments in time to achieve specific task-related goals. Brain functions may depend on sequences of these momentary spatial-temporal constellations being coordinated in real time, much as an orchestra conductor creates music by keeping the individual musical instruments, which do not all play at the same time, playing in temporal synchrony across time (Posner, Petersen, Fox, & Raichle, 1988).

Temporal Coordination of Components in Functional Systems. Fuster (1997) devoted his career to studying the frontal lobe, which is larger in humans than other species, especially in dorsal lateral prefrontal cortex (DLPFC), and houses executive functions, including but not restricted to temporal coordination. Based on a life-time of empirical studies, many with white rats, he proposed a model of cross-temporal contingencies for orchestrating the component processes of functional systems in time. The model has three networks:

1. A bottom-up pathway that originates in the sensory areas in the back of the brain that have direct contact with the external world and project incoming information to the association areas that do not have direct contact with the external world;

2. A top-down pathway that originates in the abstract association areas of DLPFC in frontal lobe and projects to midlevel premotor and supplementary motor cortex and then on to primary motor cortex (all in frontal lobe) and finally to spinal cord that generates the elements of movement that act on the world;

3. A cortical-subcortical pathway (including the cerebellum below the cortex and behind the cerebrum that has about half the neurons in the brain) for temporal coordination of the sequential and simultaneous communication of the other pathways.

Working Memory Component in Functional Systems for Reading, Writing, and Math. A common subsystem in the functional systems for reading, writing, and math functions is the working memory system that supports conscious, goal-directed behavior. Working memory is thought to consist of storage and processing units coordinated through a central executive (e.g., Baddeley, Gathercole, & Papagno, 1998; Swanson, in press). Although the phonological loop was first proposed as a mechanism for maintaining information over time in working memory, it has also been investigated for its role in regulating language learning involving overt or covert naming (e.g., vocabulary words that involve cross-code mapping of visual codes, name codes, and concept codes) (Baddeley et al., 1998). In addition, recent evidence for an orthographic loop for integrating orthographic codes and grapho-motor codes for output by hand was mounting (e.g., Beringer, Raskind et al., in press).

Fuster (1997) proposed implications of his model for working memory. The bottom-up sensory pathways may play an important role in coding and storing incoming information in working memory. The top-down pathway emanating in the dorsolateral prefrontal cortex (DLPFC) may play an important role in the central executive processes of working memory, including supervisory attention and self-regulation of acts upon the world during task completion. The cortical-subcortical pathway may contribute the temporal coordination of the executive functions coordinating codes and/or processes. The cortical path involves DLPFC, including middle frontal gyrus, and the subcortical path includes the cerebellum.

Because working memory is a critical component of all reading, writing, and math brains, this entry focuses on its possible brain basis in creating reading, writing, and math brains through nurture-nature interactions as the learning brain interacts with the external, learning environment. A word of caution is in order. In the initial studies of academic learning during the Decade of the Brain, the focus was on identifying regions of interest that were associated with particular cognitive functions (and presumably computations). Although much progress was made on this front, it is increasingly clear in the early 2000s that academic skills such as reading, writing, and math draw on neural networks distributed in space-time constellations throughout the brain and increasingly brain imaging researchers are studying the temporal connectivity of distributed networks or the temporal unfolding of neural events in complex functional systems rather than focusing on a single region of interest (e.g., Richards & Berninger, 2007; Shaywitz et al., 2003; Stanberry et al., 2006). Moreover, localizing a function to one brain region does not explain a learning process; it merely pinpoints where some of the action is.

How the brain works is not yet fully understood. For one thing, language processing, which is needed for learning to read, write, and do math, activates both right and left cortical regions. Is the side of the brain activated related to the nature of code for the stimulus storage or processing or to one hemisphere (side of cortex and cerebrum) taking the lead and the other inhibiting networks in the same structure on the other side? When some neurons fire, the electrical signal travels across the synapse causing the receiving neuron to fire in turn or not to fire. The first kind of neuron is excitatory, and the second kind of neuron is inhibitory. Up to two-thirds of the neurons in the human brain may be inhibitory. Children who fail to learn or behave appropriately may not choose not to learn or behave appropriately; rather, they may have neurons that have not yet myelinated, that is, formed a white sheath of myelin that improves the speed and efficiency of neural conduction in networks supporting inhibition and/or excitation.

Thus, the next section of this entry will not, for the most part, identify a single brain region of interest for each function, but rather will offer a conceptual model for a system of component processes that involve local brain regions in distributed spacetime networks, which when coordinated in working memory achieve reading, writing, or math goals. Teachers may find this conceptual model useful in thinking about individual differences in learners who vary in where they have their strengths and weaknesses in working memory components and the related instructional implications. For each content domain, codes represent and store incoming domain-specific information, loops integrate codes with end organs for input and output, and executive functions manage working memory components supporting conscious, task-oriented functions; these working memory components are in boldface in Tables 1, 2, and 3. This working memory architecture is necessary but not sufficient. Issues also considered are (a) other processes supported by working memory to reach goals, (b) the previously discussed three cross-temporal contingencies, and (c) the distinction between internal cognition in invisible/inaudible working memory and external cognition, a kind of extramemory in the visible/audible external world. Coupling internal working memory and external cognition may facilitate learning (Winn, Li, & Schill, 1991).

THE DEVELOPING READING BRAIN

This section illustrates how each of the working memory components contributes to development of a functional system for a reading brain.

Codes and Storage. To learn to read, children must code written words and letters into working memory; this code is called orthographic word-form. The goal is to translate that orthographic word-from into a spoken word (phonological word-form). Once children hear what is pronounced, that spoken word is then coded as an audible

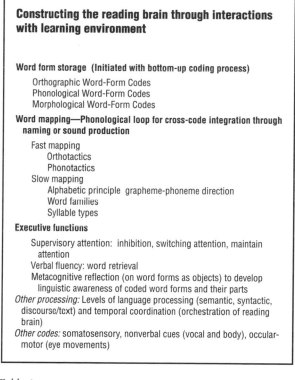

Constructing the reading brain through interactions with learning environment

Word form storage (Initiated with bottom-up coding process)
> Orthographic Word-Form Codes
> Phonological Word-Form Codes
> Morphological Word-Form Codes

Word mapping—Phonological loop for cross-code integration through naming or sound production
> Fast mapping
>> Orthotactics
>> Phonotactics
> Slow mapping
>> Alphabetic principle grapheme-phoneme direction
>> Word families
>> Syllable types

Executive functions
> Supervisory attention: inhibition, switching attention, maintain attention
> Verbal fluency: word retrieval
> Metacognitive reflection (on word forms as objects) to develop linguistic awareness of coded word forms and their parts
> *Other processing:* Levels of language processing (semantic, syntactic, discourse/text) and temporal coordination (orchestration of reading brain)
> *Other codes:* somatosensory, nonverbal cues (vocal and body), occular-motor (eye movements)

Table 1 ILLUSTRATION BY GGS INFORMATION SERVICES. CENGAGE LEARNING, GALE.

phonological word-form that provides sensory feedback about the sounds in the word. When children master the decoding process of translating written to spoken words, they no longer need to read aloud for this phonological feedback which is now accessible through inner speech (covert sound code that is not audible but codes the phonemes that correspond to alphabet letters, that is, alphabetic principle). Both the orthographic and phonological word-form may also have morphological structure (base word plus prefix and/or suffix/es), which the reader may also code. See Table 1.

Processing. Written words are accessible for processing once they are coded as orthographic word forms. Two kinds of cross-word form processing—fast and slow—may convert orthographic word-forms into phonological word-form (and morphological word-forms). Both are regulated by the phonological loop for cross-word form integration via the act of naming the whole written word or part of it, thereby, making a close-connection in time between an orthographic and phonological code. The codes are probably stored and processed in word-form regions in the back of the brain (e.g., fusiform gyrus, lingual gyrus, inferior temporal gyrus) and may be integrated in Brodmann's Area (BA) 37. Wernicke's Wortshatz (treasure house for words) (see Berninger &

Creating a writing brain through interactions with learning environment

Executive function: idea generation and goal setting (Initiated by top-down process)

Executive function: translating ideas into different *levels of written language*:

Letters (handwriting) Orthographic letter code

Words (spelling, vocabulary)

    Word form coding

        Phonological Word Form
        Orthographic Word Form
        Morphological Word Form (bases and affixes)

    Word-form mapping—Orthographic loop for cross-code integration through letter or word writing

        Fast mapping for whole words
            Phonotactics
            Orthotactics
        Slow mapping of subword units
            Alphabetic principle grapheme-phoneme direction
            Onset rimes (Onset phonemes 1 rime word families)
            Syllable types

    Discourse/text production

        Semantics construction
        Syntax construction
        Discourse schema construction

Executive function: reviewing/revising

Other processing: Temporal coordination of all processes (orchestration of writing brain)

Other codes: Grapho-motor: (fine motor planning of sequential and non-sequential finger movements, find motor execution of these movements)

Othographic-motor integration: (integrating internally represented letter forms with the fine motor codes for producing letter forms)

Visual-motor integration: (integrating non-letter visual drawings with the motor codes)

Spatial: (placement of letter forms on lines, relative size of strokes, absolute size of letter form)

Table 2 ILLUSTRATION BY GGS INFORMATION SERVICES. CENGAGE LEARNING, GALE.

Richards, 2002) outside the primary visual areas; but larger temporal-parietal (and visual association areas of occipital) regions are likely to be involved too (Pugh et al., 1996). The phonological loop may involve a right cerebellar-left inferior frontal gyrus network (Eckert et al., 2003; Richards et al. 2006b). Developing reading brains need instructional activities for both fast mapping and slow mapping (see Table 1).

Fast mapping occurs from one or a few exposures (McGregor, 2004), in this case to a seen written word and a heard spoken word close in time, forming a connection between them through association. Once the cross-word-form map is completed, the child automatically recognizes the word, that is, can pronounce it or recognize it through inner speech. Teachers often refer to words learned through fast mapping as sight word vocabulary, but orthographic and phonological codes are involved not just primary visual

regions of brain. Orthotactics (permissible letter sequences and letter positions in words) and phonotactics (permissible sound sequences and sound positions in words) may underlie ease of learning to read as well as spell (see Apel, Oster, & Masterson, 2006) through fast mapping. Some children may struggle with automatic word recognition because of undiagnosed and untreated phonotactic and/or orthotactic problems.

Slow mapping requires a longer learning period and involves more refined units of correspondence between two codes (McGregor, 2004). This slow mapping, which typically requires explicit instruction to bring the corresponding codes to the child's conscious attention, benefits from teaching multiple connections between graphemes (one- or two-letter units) and phonemes (the sounds in spoken words that correspond to alphabet letters); written rimes (part of the syllable remaining when onset phoneme or blend is deleted) and spoken rimes; syllable types (closed, open, silent *e*, vowel teams, *r*-controlled, and the *-le* syllable; and morphological structures for transforming base words by adding prefixes or suffixes. The first kind of slow mapping is the alphabetic principle that is fundamental to phonological decoding of written words. The second kind of slow mapping is word families, which also benefit phonological decoding, especially when the orthographic-phonological correspondence is more predictable for multi-letter units that may exceed two letters (e.g., -ight in right or light). Mapping syllables by classifying them has been found to be more helpful than teaching children to merely mark where one syllable ends and another begins because in English syllable boundaries can be altered by the speed at which a word is said. The morphological mapping is critical for developing vocabulary meaning and a bridge from cross-code word maps to the text-level comprehension processes (e.g., Nagy, Berninger, & Abbott, 2006; Nagy, Berninger, Abbott, Vaughan, & Vermeulen, 2003). Although many children acquire these maps during the first three grades, others require a longer period of explicit instruction in slow mapping well into middle school and even high school years, possibly because of individual differences in the rate of myelination already defined.

Executive Functions. Frontal and subcortical cerebellar regions and the many neural pathways among them and the anterior cingulate (a region involved in conflict management) play important roles in regulating the process of learning to read and then reading to learn: Lower-level executive functions, especially inhibition and switching attention (Altemeier, Abbott, & Berninger, 2007) but also maintaining attention over time (Amtmann, Abbott, & Berninger, 2006). Inhibition is the ability to focus on what is relevant and suppress or ignore what is irrelevant. Switching attention is the ability to release from focus of attention what was relevant and switch to what is now relevant.

Maintaining attention is the ability to stay focused over time for goal-directed activity, especially when orthographic-phonological code integration is involved. Children who struggle with reading may have difficulty with any of these (Altemeier et al., 2007; Amtmann et al., 2006). Executive functions involving supervisory attention influence orthographic word-form processing (Thomson et al., 2005). Teachers can incorporate in lesson plans, for those children who struggle with attention regulation for written words, strategies for focusing on the relevant, switching attention focus, and maintaining attention over time.

Higher-order executive functions are also involved in reading such as verbal fluency (word finding) and linguistic awareness (see Table 1). Readers need to find in long-term memory associated names (phonological word-form) and meanings for written words. Long-term memory stores complex cognitive representations in associational networks or webs, hierarchical, categorical classification systems, and nonverbal visual images (see Stahl & Nagy, 2005). They also need to reflect upon the word-forms and their parts to develop orthographic awareness, phonological awareness, and morphological awareness (see Berninger & Richards, 2002, Chapter 8).

Other Processing Jobs. If the task is to comprehend the written text, accurate identification of single written words is necessary but not sufficient. Syntax emerges during the preschool years for storing accumulating words in working memory for the purpose of comprehending the incoming oral language message; the sum is greater than the parts in the syntactic constructions based on single words. Children who have problems with ordering accumulating words in working memory according to the syntax structures of the language may have problems in comprehending both oral and written language and persistent reading comprehension problems during the school years (Berninger, in press). However, reading comprehension depends on many levels of language, ranging from vocabulary meaning for single words or idioms of the language to sentence syntax structures to discourse schema (see Table 1). Many parts of the brain are involved in reading comprehension both in the back of the brain (e.g. Wernicke's Area) and front of the brain (e.g. DLFFC and superior frontal gyrus) (see Berninger & Richards, 2002, Chapter 5).

Top-down, Bottom-up, and Cortical-Subcortical Temporal Coordination. Both learning to read and reading to learn require engagement of the bottom-up system (incoming visual information from the written text that proceeds upwards in the system to be coded for orthographic, phonological, and morphological word-forms, syntax, and semantics—the links between language and cognition), the top-down system (existing factual and conceptual knowledge in long-term memory from life experience and

prior reading as well as cognitive procedures for abstracting the gist and details from incoming text and summarizing what is read), and cortical-subcortical temporal coordination (the grand orchestra conductor of mind for coordinating all the processes in momentary and real time).

Even if purpose-setting questions and discussion of background knowledge (top-down processing) precede the actual act of reading written text, the initial process in the actual reading begins with bottom-up brain processing initially in visual cortex but subsequently in temporal-parietal-frontal networks. At some point in this process, top-down and cortical-subcortical temporal coordination processes activate and can influence reading outcomes.

Internal and External Cognition. Input codes that are not exclusively visual and several output codes may externalize cognition in ways that support internal working memory during reading. The first are ocular motor codes that regulate eye movements as the eyes move forward, then backward, and then pause to fixate on external word information while it is being processed; see Berninger and Richards, 2002 for the multiple central (brain and spinal cord) and peripheral (outside brain and spinal cord) regions of the nervous system involved in eye movements. The second is the mouth's oral-motor system that turns written language, which is originally only visible, into audible language, that is, one's first language. That is why oral reading provides important external feedback in learning to read written language. The third is nonverbal cues, including vocal cues (the intonation or musical melodies of spoken language) and bodily expression that may facilitate the translation of written into oral language. For example, some students who struggle to read textbook text orally become fluent when reading play scripts allowing them to act out concepts underlying language and drawing on the intonation of oral language. The fourth is grapho-motor codes that support writing words by hand. Spelling words in writing transferred to improved word reading; and written composition instruction may benefit reading comprehension (e.g., Berninger, 2008). The postcentral gyrus (primary somatosensory area in parietal lobe) receives information from the environment through touch and kinesthetic movement via hands engaged in writing-related reading activities. This somatosensory stimulation may be transmitted to nearby supramarginal gyrus (a phonological processing center) through explicit phonological activities involving hands (e.g. counting syllables or phonemes and writing letters that go with phonemes or hands-on, science problem-solving activities with virtual reality) (Richards et al., 2007).

THE DEVELOPING WRITING BRAIN

Writing has many component processes (see Table 2), but most brain imaging has been done on transcription skills (handwriting and spelling). Acquired writing disorders in adults are associated with three brain regions: (a) left posterior middle frontal gyrus (Exner's Area BA8) (Exner,1881) thought to support coactivation of movement sequences during letter generation (Anderson, Damaisio, & Damaisio, 1990); (b) left superior parietal lobule where internal letter codes are thought to form for production (Basso, Taborelli, & Vignolo, 1978); and (c) left premotor (BA6) thought to store the grapho-motor codes for writing letters (Brain, 1967). A close relationship exists between letter production and letter perception—both motor and visual regions are involved in handwriting (James & Gauthier, 2006; Longcamp et al., 2003).

At the end of fifth grade good and poor writers, who differed significantly on behavioral measures of handwriting and spelling, also differed significantly in blood-oxygen-level-dependent (BOLD) activation in each of these regions identified for acquired writing disorders during a functional magnetic brain imaging (fRMI) Finger Succession task controlled for non-successive finger tapping (Richards et al., submitted 2008). In that same study, the good and poor writers differed significantly in left fusiform gyrus in lower non-motor temporal regions on a Handwriting Contrast between a novel configuration and a familiar letter equated for motor movements in formation; fusiform codes letter forms, showing that handwriting is not just a motor skill. Prior findings from two studies with adult writers (Matsuo, Kato, Ozawa et al., 2001; Matsuo, Kato, Tanaka et al., 2001b) replicated for children. Both the good and poor writers activated fewer brain regions when a letter form could be phonologically coded (associated with a phoneme) than when it could not. Alphabetic principle for mapping graphemes onto phonemes may have a brain advantage for more efficient letter writing.

Brain imaging of normal adults during spelling tasks showed that orthographic word-form activated inferior temporal (e.g., fusiform) more robustly than primary visual (occipital) regions in response to linear arrays of visual elements that can be linguistically coded (e.g., Cohen et al., 2002; Dehaene et al., 2002). Phonological-orthographic mapping activated left fusiform gyrus (Booth et al., 2002), posterior parietal cortex (Bitan et al. 2007), and left inferior frontal gyrus (Booth et al., 2007). The time course proceeded from occipital visual association areas to Wernicke's Area (cross-code integration), to left inferior frontal gyrus (Dhond et al., 2001). For the good spellers in grades 4 to 6, significant BOLD activation during an fMRI spelling task occurred in medial superior frontal gyrus, bilateral middle frontal and inferior frontal gyri, middle temporal, fusiform and lingual gyri, right orbital and posterior parietal regions, left superior temporal and inferior temporal gyri, and anterior cingulate and anterior insula, (Richards et al., 2006a). Two conclusions can be drawn—spelling like reading is not a purely visual

process and the temporal and parietal regions involved in orthographic and phonological word-forms and their integration appear to activate word-form regions during spelling as well as reading in children. Also, the inferior frontal gyrus involved in the highest level of executive function for coordinating the language systems is activated in brain during spelling as well as reading in children.

Prior to treatment, good and impaired spellers differed significantly in BOLD activation in right inferior frontal gyrus and right posterior parietal BOLD activation, but after orthographic (not morphological control) treatment, the poor spellers normalized in both regions compared to good spellers (Richards et al., 2006a). Based on common core and unique BOLD activation across phonological, orthographic, and morphological word-form tasks (e.g., Richards et al., 2006b), Richards et al. (2005) compared two of these at a time to identify common core and unique brain activation underlying phonological-orthographic, orthographic-morphological, and phonological-morphological mapping in children aged 9 to 13. Results showed a common core of many brain regions and a sizable number of uniquely activated brain regions more associated with one word-form than the other. Clearly, large distributed networks involving many language areas are involved in cross-word form mapping of phonological, orthographic, and morphological word-forms in spelling in children. This cross-word mapping may begin in the posterior word-form centers in temporal-parietal regions and culminate in the left inferior frontal gyrus for phonological mapping and the right inferior frontal gyrus for orthographic mapping (Richards et al., 2005).

Figure 2 shows an individual fifth grader's brain while deciding whether each of two words (always pronounced the same) were real, correctly spelled words. All components of a working memory architecture showed significant BOLD activation: a left temporal region for orthographic word-form and phonological word-form storage and processing, left cerebellum that may be involved in orthographic for cross-code integration in spelling, and two frontal regions (one on left associated with executive functions for language and the supplementary motor area involved in motor planning on both sides).

Top-down, Bottom-up, and Cortical-Subcortical Temporal Coordination. Writing is not the inverse or mirror image of reading (Read, 1981). Note that different component processes are at the top of Table 1 and top of Table 2 for reading and writing, respectively. Also see Chapters 8 and 9 of Berninger and Richards (2002) for further discussion of the differences between the developing reading brain and the developing writing brain. Instead of beginning like reading with a bottom-up pathway, writing begins with a top-down pathway during idea generation and goal-setting of the planning/proposing processes (Hayes &

Creating the math brain through interactions with the learning environment

Concepts initiated by quantitative, visual-spatial, or scientific (mathematics, physics, psychological, behavioral) concept or problem solving
Examples of cardinal concepts in early math development
    Counting
        One-to-one correspondence
        Internal mental line
    Place value
    Part-whole relationships
Codes for storage and/or production of math concepts and symbols
    Visual numeric symbols for single digits
    Visual numeric representation of multiplace numbers
    Auditory number names
    Auditory numeric representations of multiplace number names
    Quantitative concept
    Grapho-motor codes for producing written numeric symbols
Quantitative processing
    Number fact acquisition and retrieval
    Arithmetic algorithms
    Written calculations
    Mental calculation
    Math problem solving (exact and/or estimated)
Executive functions for self-monitoring and repairing errors

Table 3 ILLUSTRATION BY GGS INFORMATION SERVICES. CENGAGE LEARNING, GALE.

Flower, 1980; Hayes, in press); Good writers and poor writers at the end of fifth grade differed in BOLD activation in the superior and middle frontal gyri (including DLPFC) while their brain was scanned during fMRI Idea Generation; when they left the scanner, they wrote compositions on what they learned during the summer that they had not learned in school (Berninger et al., 2008). Where they differed suggested that good writers engaged working memory more than poor writers as early as idea generation that initiates the writing process.

Processing. Cognitive processes such as planning, translating (ideas into language), transcribing, and reviewing and revising are important throughout the writing process of skilled adults (e.g., Chenoweth & Hayes, 2001, 2003; Hayes, 2004, in press; Hayes & Flower, 1980), and some progress has been made in how to teach these cognitive processes effectively to young children and middle school students (for review, see Berninger, 1998). Translating occurs at many different levels of language ranging from letters to words to sentences and discourse structures (see Table 1). Additional research is needed to determine whether all these translation processes occur simultaneously or sequentially or both or depend on expertise level and writing purpose.

Codes for Storage and Mapping. In contrast to reading that maps orthographic word-forms onto phonological word-forms, writing maps phonological word-forms (spoken or analyzed with inside voice) onto orthographic word-forms. Like reading, the mapping may be fast or slow and fast mapping may be influenced by phonotactic and orthotactic knowledge, as defined in reading section. English spelling is hard because slow mapping has more alternations or possible spellings for a given phoneme than possible sounds for a given one- or two-letter grapheme (Venezky, 1970, 1999). Both the phonological and orthographic word forms may also have morphological structure. In the case of writing, these morphological structures for transforming base words by adding affixes (Carlisle, 2000) may facilitate word choice during the text generation process, which like reading, occurs at multiple levels of analysis ranging from word to sentence to discourse schema (see Table 2).

Executive Functions. Writing is more complex than reading because it places more demands on executive functions (e.g., Hooper et al., 2002). In addition to low-level executive functions in frontal and cingulate regions, high-level executive functions are required such as (a) planning that involves both idea generation and goal setting for tasks requiring space-, time-, and resource-limited conscious working memory, (b) translating cognitive representations into linguistic representations at multiple levels of written language and translating those levels of language via transcription into written symbols, and (c) reviewing (self-monitoring) text produced and revising it as needed (not only surface feature edits but also repairing deep structures through substantial rewriting).

Internal and External Cognition. The executive juggling act of writing may place greater demands on internal working memory than reading does, but writing has the advantage that it externalizes cognition making it visible via written language to become an object for reflection and repair. Moreover, learners often do not have access to what they are thinking in implicit memory until it becomes consciously available through writing in explicit memory and externalized cognition (see Hayes & Flower, 1980).

THE DEVELOPING MATH BRAIN

Brain imaging studies with adults produced mixed results when localized regions for coding operations during math were investigated, but they clearly support a major role for the parietal cortex and the representation of an internal number line that codes quantity; exact and estimated math appear to be represented in different neural networks. The math brain draws on many of the regions that reading and writing do because math involves verbal as well as quantitative and visual spatial representations and procedures. However, one brain region uniquely involved in the math brain but not the reading or writing brains is the lenticular nucleus (for review of imaging studies in math and instructional implications, see Berninger and Richards [2002, Chapters 7 and 10]). Math, which has many branches and subspecializaitons, begins with the concepts underlying this knowledge domain.

Concepts. Counting is the fundamental cornerstone of math in early math development and the work of mathematicians engaged in discovery of mathematical truth (see Hoffman, 1998, for account of Erdös the mathematician who loved only numbers). Numbers can extend in either direction infinitely and be real or imaginary. Some mathematicians devote their careers to detecting complex patterns in the number line that are then used to solve important problems about the physical universe. Multiple number lines (one for each continuous dimension) can be used to describe quantitatively how changes in one distribution affect changes in another distribution and to solve problems involving multiple number lines, each on different scales (e.g., seconds, minutes, hours, half days for telling time). Another key concept is place value, which is the syntax for numbers and allows the math brain to represent an infinite number of numbers with just ten symbols if one of them is zero to indicate nothingness. The part-whole concept is another cornerstone of math underlying fractions, mixed numbers, telling time, measurement, and algebraic reasoning. Children first learn that objects have permanence in the mind even if not in the external world and then they must learn that quantity for objects is not absolute—the magnitude depends on how many parts the object has. One-fourth is less than one-half no matter what the absolute size of an object even though four is a larger quantity than two (see Table 3).

Codes and storage. A number is an internal representation of quantity, that is, a quantitative code, abstracted from counting many objects, but a numeral or digit is an external symbol written by hand for that number by the graphomotor system and is visible to primary visual area of brain. Numbers also have names that stimulate the primary auditory area and are audible to the brain. Letters and numerals may be represented in different locations in brain (Anderson et al., 1990) even though grapho-motor codes for writing them may be the same (see Table 3).

Processing. Arithmetic is often confused with mathematics, which is higher-order problem solving, including proving theorems and applying science to the physical universe and human behavior. Arithmetic involves number facts (learning them and retrieving them are separable processes), and arithmetic algorithms for calculation (steps of basic addition, subtraction, multiplication, and division operations). Math fact learning and retrieval and calculation operations may be executed in internal working memory (mental math) or coupled with the external environment through written calculation (see Table 3).

Executive Functions. All low-level supervisory attention functions influencing reading and writing brains may also influence the math brain. In addition, math calculation and problem solving require planning, thinking, translating metaknowledge about math, and self-monitoring and correction.

Top-down, Bottom-up, and Cortical-Subcortical Temporal Coordination. Math problem-solving typically initiates with top-down pathways, but math fact retrieval and calculation may begin with bottom-up pathways. As with the reading and writing brain, the math brain requires orchestration in time of all the relevant processes to the task at hand (see Table 3).

Internal and External Cognition. Hand-held calculators and other technology tools provide external cognition support for overcoming weaknesses in internal working memory that support math problem solving. However, unless math is taught in a way that includes mental math as part of the coupling of working memory and external cognition supports, learners will never become skilled in math. Ultimately mathematical thinking and applications occur in the math mind—the math brain at work.

FROM BRAIN SCAN TO COMPASSION AND INDIVIDUALLY TAILORED LEARNING ENVIRONMENTS

Knowledge of the developing brain and its influences on learning to read, write, and do math is not absolutely necessary for individuals to be effective teachers for many students. Such knowledge may matter for designing and implementing specialized instruction for students with biologically based developmental and learning disorders and for optimizing academic achievement of all students. Working memory components and other processes in Tables 1, 2, and 3, may break down or be a talent in individual students. Whether such knowledge translates directly to daily lesson plans may depend on teachers' grasp of the whole system of processes involved in learning and not just teaching reading, writing, and math and individual differences among learners that affect response to instruction. At a time in the history of education when educators are becoming aware of diversity due to multicultural backgrounds of learners, it is equally important to understand that biodiversity is also relevant to academic achievement.

Students may differ in meaningful ways in the kinds of learning environments in which they learn most appropriately. Educators and students need a no-fault approach to education. Academic underachievement cannot be attributed only to teachers or only to students. Not all students learn the same way and learning is harder for some than it is for others because of brain differences. Improving teachers' knowledge of the brain may lead to greater compassion for learners who do not learn easily and may stimulate teachers to discover creative alternative instructional approaches for improving the match between how individual students learn and the environmental conditions under which they may realize their biologically influenced talents and overcome their weaknesses.. Increasing pre-service teachers' knowledge of brain and biodiversity along with multicultural diversity may contribute to this next step in educational evolution that leaves no teacher or student behind (see Berninger & Richards, 2002, Chapter 12).

BIBLIOGRAPHY

SUGGESTIONS FOR FURTHER READING

Bear, M. F., Connors, B., & Paradiso, M. (2007). *Neuroscience: Exploring the brain.* 3rd ed. Philadelphia: Lippincott Williams & Wilkins.

Blakemore, S. & Frith, U. (2005). *The learning brain. Lessons for education.* Malden, MA: Blackwell Press.

Diamond, M., & Hopson, J. (1998). *Magic trees of mind. How to nurture your child's intelligence, creativity, and healthy emotions from birth to adolescence.* New York: Penguin Books.

Eliott, L. (1999). *What's going on in there? How the brain and mind develop in the first five years of life.* New York: Bantam Books.

Fuster, J. (1997). *The prefrontal cortex. Anatomy, physiology, and neuropsychology of the frontal lobe* (3rd ed., pp. 209–252). New York: Raven Press.

Papanicolaou, A. C. (1998). *Foundations of functional imaging. A guide to the methods and their and their applications to psychology and behavioral neuroscience.* New York: Psychology Press.

Posner, P., & Rothbart, M. (2007). *Educating the human brain.* Washington, DC: American Psychological Association.

ELECTRONIC RESOURCES

Chudler, Eric. Neuroscience for Kids. Retrieved April 10, 2008, from http://faculty.washington.edu/chudler/baw.html.

Digital Anatomist Image Collection Manager. Retrieved April 10, 2008, from http://vertex.biostr.washington.edu/repos/image_repo/.

REFERENCES CITED

Abbott, S., Reed, L., Abbott, R., & Berninger, V. (1997). Year-long balanced reading/writing tutorial: A design experiment used for dynamic assessment. Learning *Disability Quarterly, 20,* 249–263.

Altemeier, L., Abbott, R., & Berninger, V. (2007). Executive functions for reading and writing in typical literacy development and dyslexia. *Journal of Clinical and Experimental Neuropsychology, 30,* 588–606.

Amtmann, D., Abbott, R., & Berninger, V. (2006). Mixture growth models for RAN and RAS row by row: Insight into the reading system at work over time. *Reading and Writing. An Interdisciplinary Journal, 20,* 785–813.

Anderson, S., Damasio, A., & Damasio, H. (1990). Troubled letters but not numbers: Domain specific cognitive impairments following focal damage in frontal cortex. *Brain, 113,* 749–760.

Apel, K., Oster, J., & Masterson, J. (2006). Effects of phonotactic and orthotactic probabilities during fast-mapping on five year-olds' learning to spell. *Developmental Neuropsychology, 29,* 21–42.

Baddeley, A., Gathercole, S., & Papagno, C. (1998). The phonological loop as a language learning device. *Psychological Review, 105,* 158–173.

Basso, A., Taborelli, A., & Vignolo, L. (1978). Dissociated disorders of speaking and writing in aphasia. *Journal of Neurology, Neurosurgery, and Psychiatry, 41,* 556–563.

Berninger, V. (2004). The reading brain in children and youth: A systems approach. In B. Wong (Ed.), *Learning about learning disabilities* (3rd ed., pp. 197–248). San Diego: Academic Press (Elsevier Imprint).

Berninger, V. (2008). Evidence-based written language instruction during early and middle childhood. In R. Morris & N. Mather (Eds.), *Evidence-based interventions for students with learning and behavioral challenges* (pp. 215–235). Mahwah, NJ: Erlbaum.

Berninger, V. (in press). Defining and differentiating dyslexia, dysgraphia, and language learning disability within a working memory model. In E. Silliman & M. Mody (Eds.), *Language impairment and reading disability-interactions among brain, behavior, and experience.* New York: Guilford.

Berninger, V., & Abbott, R. (1992). Unit of analysis and constructive processes of the learner: Key concepts for educational neuropsychology. *Educational Psychologist, 27,* 223–242.

Berninger, V., Raskind, W., Richards, T., Abbott, R., & Stock, P. (in press). A multidisciplinary approach to understanding developmental dyslexia within working-memory architecture: Genotypes, phenotypes, brain, and instruction. *Developmental Neuropsychology.*

Berninger, V., & Richards, T. (2002). *Brain literacy for educators and psychologists.* New York: Academic Press.

Berninger, V., Richards, T., Stock, P., Abbott, R., Trivedi, P., Altemeier, L., et al. (2008). From idea generation to idea expression in language by hand. *British Journal of Educational Psychology Monograph.*

Bitan, T., Cheon, J., Lu, D., Burman, D. Gitelman, D. Mesulam, M., et al. (2007). Developmental changes in activation and effective connectivity in phonological processing. *NeuroImage, 38,* 564–575.

Booth, J., Cho, S., Burman, D., & Bitan, T. (2007). Neural correlates of mapping from phonology to orthography in children performing an auditory spelling task. *Developmental Science, 10,* 441–451.

Booth, J. R., Burman, D. D., Meyer, J. R., Gitelman, D. R., Parrish, T. B., & Mesulam, M. M. (2002). Functional anatomy of intra- and cross-modal lexical tasks. *Neuroimage, 16*(1), 7–22.

Brain, L. (1967). *Speech disorders: Aphasia, apraxia, and agnosia.* London: Butterworth.

Chenoweth, N., & Hayes, J. R. (2001). Fluency in writing. Generating text in L1 and L2. *Written Communication, 18,* 80–98.

Chenoweth, N., & Hayes, J. R. (2003). The inner voice in writing. *Written Communication, 20,* 99–118.

Cohen, L., Lehéricy, S., Chhochon, F., Lemer, C., Rivaud, S., & Dehaene, S. (2002). Language-specific tuning of visual cortex? Functional properties of the Visual Word Form Area. *Brain, 125,* 1054–1069.

Connelly, V., Campbell, S., MacLean, M., & Barnes, J. (2006). Contribution of lower-order skills to the written composition of college students with and without dyslexia. *Developmental Neuropsychology, 29,* 175–196.

Dehane, S., Le Clec, H. G., Poline, J-B., Bihan, D., & Cohen, L. (2002). The visual word form area: A prelexical representation of visual words in the fusiform gyrus. *Brain Imaging, 13,* 321–325.

Dhond, R., Buckner, R., Dale, A., Marinkovic, K., & Halgren, E. (2001). Spatiotemporal maps of brain activity underlying word generation and their modification during repetition priming. *Journal of Neuroscience, 21,* 3564–3571.

Eckert, M., Leonard, C., Richards, T., Aylward, E., Thomson, J., & Berninger, V. (2003). Anatomical correlates of dyslexia: Frontal and cerebellar findings. *Brain, 126* (2), 482–494.

Exner, S. (1881). *Untersuchungen über die Lokalisation der Funktionen in der Grosshirnrinde des Menschen.* Vienna: Wilhelm Braumuller.

Fuster, J. (1997). The prefrontal cortex. *Anatomy, physiology, and neuropsychology of the frontal lobe* (3rd ed., pp. 205–252). New York: Raven Press.

Garcia, N. (2007). *Phonological, orthographic, and morphological contributions to the spelling development of good, average, and poor spellers.* Unpublished doctoral dissertation. University of Washington.

Hayes, J. R. (in press). From idea to text. In R. Beard, D. Myhill, M. Nystrand, & J. Riley (Eds.), *SAGE Handbook of Writing Development.* Thousand Oaks, CA: Sage.

Hayes, J. R., & Chenoweth, N. (2006). Is working memory involved in the transcribing and editing of texts? *Written Communication, 23,* 135–149.

Hayes, J. R., & Flower, L. S. (1980). Identifying the organization of writing processes. In L.W. Gregg & E.R. Steinbert (Eds.), *Cognitive processes in writing* (pp. 3–30). Hillsdale, NJ: Erlbaum.

Hoffman, P. (1998). *The man who loved only numbers: The story of Paul Erdös and the search for mathematical truth.* New York: Hyperion.

Hooper, S. R., Swartz, C. W., Wakely, M. B., de Kruif, R.E.L., & Montgomery, J. W. (2002). Executive functions in elementary school children with and without problems in written expression. *Journal of Learning Disabilities, 35,* 37–68.

Jacobs, B. Schall, M., & Scheibel, A. (1993). A qualitative dendritic analysis of Wernicke's area in humans. II. Gender, hemispheric, and environmental factors. The *Journal of Comparative Neurology, 327,* 97–111.

James, K. H., & Gauthier, I. (2006). Letter processing automatically recruits a sensory–motor brain network. *Neuropsychologia 44,* 2937–2949.

Jenkins, J., Johnson, E., & Hileman, J. (2004). When is reading also writing: Sources of individual differences on the new reading performance assessments. *Scientific Studies in Reading, 8,* 125–151.

Jones, D. (2004). *Automaticity of the Transcription Process in the Production of Written Text.* Unpublished doctoral dissertation. Graduate School of Education, University of Queensland, Australia, Brisbane.

Jones, D., & Cristensen, C. (1999). The relationship between automaticity in handwriting and students' ability to generate written text. *Journal of Educational Psychology, 91,* 44–49.

Just, M., & Varma, S. (2007). The organization of thinking; What functional imaging reveals about the neuroarchitecture of complex cognition. *Cognitive, Affective, & Behavioral Neuroscience, 7,* 153–191.

Longcamp, M., Anton, J. L, Roth, M., & Velay, J. L. (2003). Visual presentation of single letters activates a premotor area involved in writing. *Neuroimage 19,* 1492–1500.

Luria, A. R. (1973). *The working brain.* New York: Basic Books.

Matsuo, K., Kato, C., Ozawa, F., Takehara, Y., Isoda, H., Isogai, S. et al. (2001). Ideographic characters call for extra processing to correspond with phonemes. *NeuroReport, 12,* 2227–2230.

Matsuo, K., Kato, C., Tanaka, S., Sugio, T., Matsuzawa, M., Inui, T. et al. (2001b). Visual language and handwriting movement: Functional magnetic resonance imaging at 3 tesla during generation of ideographic characters. *Brain Research Bulletin, 55,* 549–554.

McGregor, K. (2004). Developmental dependencies between lexical semantics and reading. In C. A. Stone, E. Silliman, B. Ehren, & K. Apel (Eds), *Handbook of language and literacy* (pp. 302–317). New York: Guilford.

Minsky, M. (1986). *Society of mind.* New York: Simon and Schuster.

Nagy, W., Berninger, V., & Abbott, R. (2006). Contributions of morphology beyond phonology to literacy outcomes of upper elementary and middle school students. *Journal of Educational Psychology, 98,* 134–147.

Nagy, W., Berninger, V., Abbott, R., Vaughan, K., & Vermeulen, K. (2003). Relationship of morphology and other language skills to literacy skills in at-risk second graders and at-risk fourth grade writers. *Journal of Educational Psychology, 95,* 730–742.

Posner, M., Petersen, S., Fox, P., & Raichle, M. (1988). Localization of cognitive operations in the human brain. *Science, 240,* 1627–1631.

Pugh, K., Shaywitz, B.,Shaywitz, S., Constable, T.,Skudlarski, P., Fullbright, R. et al. (1996). Cerebral organization of component processes in reading. *Brain, 119,* 1221–1238.

Read, C. (1981). Writing is not the inverse of reading for young children. In C. Frederickson & J. Domminick (Eds.), *Writing: The nature, development, and teaching of written communication* (Vol. 2, pp. 105–117. Hillsdale, NJ: Erlbaum.

Richards, T., Aylward, E., Berninger, V., Field, K., Parsons, A., Richards, A., et al. (2006a). Individual fMRI activation in orthographic mapping and morpheme mapping after orthographic or morphological spelling treatment in child dyslexics. *Journal of Neurolinguistics, 19,* 56–86.

Richards, T., Aylward, E., Raskind, W., Abbott, R., Field,. K., Parsons, A., et al. (2006b). Converging evidence for triple word form theory in children with dyslexia. *Developmental Neuropsychology, 30,* 547–589.

Richards, T., & Berninger, V. (2007). Abnormal fMRI connectivity in children with dyslexia during a phoneme task: Before but not after treatment. *Journal of Neurolinguistics.* Published on line by ScienceDirect for Elsevier.

Richards, T., Berninger, V., Aylward, E., Richards, A., Thomson, J., Nagy, W., et al. (2002). Reproducibility of proton MR spectroscopic imaging (PEPSI): Comparison of dyslexic and normal reading children and effects of treatment on brain lactate levels during language tasks. *American Journal of Neuroradiology. 23,* 1678–1685.

Richards, T., Berninger, V., Nagy, W., Parsons, A., Field, K., Richards, A. (2005). Brain activation during language task contrasts in children with and without dyslexia: Inferring mapping processes and assessing response to spelling instruction. *Educational and Child Psychology, 22*(2), 62–80.

Richards, T., Berninger, V., Winn W., Stock, P., Wagner, R., Muse, A., et al. (2007). fMRI activation in children with dyslexia during pseudoword aural repeat and visual decode: Before and after instruction. *Neuropsychology. 21,* 732–747.

Shaywitz, S., Shaywitz, B., Fulbright, R., Skudlarski, P., Mencl, W., Constable, R., et al. (2003). Neural systems for compensation and persistence: Young adult outcome of childhood reading disability. *Biological Psychiatry, 54,* 25–33.

Stahl, S., & Nagy, W. (2005). *Teaching word meaning.* Mahwah, NJ: Erlbaum.

Shaywitz, S., Shaywitz, B., Fulbright, R., Skudlarski, P., Mencl, W., Constable, R., et al. (2003). Neural systems for compensation and persistence: Young adult outcome of childhood reading disability. *Biological Psychiatry, 54,* 25–33.

Stanberry, L., Richards, T., Berninger, V., Nandy, R., Aylward, E., Maravilla, K., et al. (2006). Low frequency signal changes reflect differences in functional connectivity between good readers and dyslexics during continuous phoneme mapping. *Magnetic Resonance Imaging,* 24, 217–229.

Swanson, H.L., & Berninger, V. (1996). Individual differences in children's working memory and writing skills. *Journal of Experimental Child Psychology,* 63, 358–385.

Swanson, H. L. (2006). Working memory and reading disabilities: Both phonological and executive processing deficits are important. In T. Alloway, & S. Gathercole (Eds.), *Working memory and neurodevelopmental conditions* (pp. 59–88). London: Psychology Press.

Thomson, J., Chennault, B., Abbott, R., Raskind, W., Richards, T., Aylward, E., et al. (2005). Converging evidence for attentional influences on the orthographic word form in child dyslexics. *Journal of Neurolinguistics. 18,* 93–126.

Venezky, R. (1970). *The structure of English orthography.* The Hague. Mouton.

Venezky, R. (1999). *The American way of spelling.* New York: Guilford.

Wagner, R. K., Torgesen, J. K., & Rashotte, C. A. (1999). *The comprehensive test of phonological processing.* Austin, TX: Pro-Ed.

Winn, W. D., Li, T-Z., & Schill, D. E. (1991). Diagrams as aids to problem solving: Their role in facilitating search and computation. *Educational Technology Research and Development, 39,* 17–29.

Virginia W. Berninger
Todd L. Richards

BRANSFORD, JOHN D.

John D. Bransford helped start the cognitive revolution and used cognitive theory to create ground-breaking instructional designs. Bransford received his PhD in cognitive psychology at the University of Minnesota in 1970. His early experimental research demonstrated the constructive nature of understanding and learning. In a classic study, Bransford, Barclay, and Franks (1972) asked people to read sentence pairs such as "The turtle was sitting on the log," and "The fish swam under the log." Afterwards, participants completed a verification task in which they decided whether they had seen a given sentence verbatim. People demonstrated systematic errors that indicated they had constructed a mental model of the situation. For instance, they incorrectly verified that they had read, "The turtle swam under the frog," when, in fact, the sentences never stated that explicitly. Prevailing theories of behaviorism could not explain why people made this mistake because behaviorism could only refer to the stimulus and not what might or might not be going on in the mind.

A central tenet of Bransford's constructivism is that learning builds on prior knowledge. Prior knowledge was not in the lexicon of the prevailing theory of behaviorism, which explained human behavior through reinforcement not knowledge. Bransford and Johnson (1972) demonstrated the significance of prior knowledge by showing participants passages that were largely unintelligible. For example, "The procedure is actually quite simple. First you arrange things into groups. Of course, one pile may be sufficient depending on how much there is to do. If you have to go somewhere else due to lack of facilities, that is the next step." Bransford showed that a simple phrase that elicits the correct prior knowledge can make the unintelligible become meaningful. In this example, the phrase would be "washing clothes."

These early demonstrations presaged a career of high creativity and theoretical edge. Initially, journal editors were incredulous of his findings and he had difficulty publishing. However, he demonstrated the effects on the editors themselves, and they realized that they had been blinded by their theories.

As of 2007, Bransford had published roughly 90 journal articles, 90 book chapters, 6 authored books, and 4 edited volumes. His work has been translated into various languages, including French and Japanese. One explanation for Bransford's high level of productivity and reach is his combination of curiosity and collaborative abilities. Only four of his publications are sole-authored. His collaborative efforts enabled him to expand his scholarship into publications that appear in psychology, reading, medicine, engineering, technology, business, science, math, and special education outlets; the work is further cited in fields as diverse as animal neuroscience and economics.

One of his most broadly collaborative periods involved the development of the Cognition and Technology Group at Vanderbilt (CTGV). Bransford gathered a diverse collection of scholars who dedicated themselves to designing effective, technology-driven educational lessons and assessments in multiple content areas. Much of the work stemmed from his theory of transfer appropriate processing, which attempted to explain why people sometimes fail to apply their prior knowledge. Of the many original creations of the CTGV (1997), one of the most notable is the "Adventures of Jasper Woodbury." The Jasper series helped students engage in sustained mathematical problem solving, so they could learn to solve problems that might arise in everyday life and not just word problems. Bransford recognized that students could not learn complex problem solving at school unless they had a strong body of prior knowledge to help anchor their reasoning. To solve this problem, Bransford created anchored instruction: Each Jasper adventure was presented as a twenty-minute video narrative. In one adventure, for example, students had to create a plan to rescue an eagle that had been injured. The video developed the context, constraints, quantities, and the goal of the problem. The anchor created the prior knowledge that enabled students to experience complex problem solving with mathematics, and students developed the type of knowledge that was likely to transfer to everyday settings.

In the late 1990s, Bransford led a team of federally commissioned scholars to author the volume, *How People Learn* (2000). This book brought learning back into the spotlight and has had a tremendous impact on the research agenda in the United States and internationally.

SEE ALSO *Anchored Instruction; Metacognition.*

BIBLIOGRAPHY

WORKS BY

Bransford, J. D., Barlay, J. R., & Franks, J. J. (1972). Sentence memory: A constructive vs. interpretive approach. *Cognitive Psychology, 3,* 193–209.

Bransford, J. D., & Johnson, M. K. (1972). Contextual prerequisites for understanding: Some investigations of comprehension and recall. *Journal of Verbal Learning and Verbal Behavior, 11,* 717–726.

Cognition and Technology Group at Vanderbilt. (1997). *The Jasper Project: Lessons in curriculum, instruction, assessment, and professional development.* Mahwah, NJ: Erlbaum.

Bransford, J. D., Brown, A. L., & Cocking, R. R. (2000). *How people learn: Brain, mind, experience, and school.* Washington, DC: National Academy Press.

Daniel L. Schwartz

BRONFENBRENNER, URIE
1917–2005

Urie Bronfenbrenner was born in Russia in 1917 and came to the United States at the age of 6. He went to high school in Haverstraw, New York, and completed a double major in psychology and music at Cornell University in 1938. He received a master's degree in education from Harvard University in 1940 and a doctorate in developmental psychology from the University of Michigan in 1942. After completing his doctoral work he was inducted into the U.S. Army, where he served as a psychologist in the Army Air Corps and the Office of Strategic Services. After his military service he worked briefly as a research psychologist for the VA Clinical Psychology Training Program, before returning to the University of Michigan as an assistant professor of psychology. Two years later, in 1948, he accepted a faculty position in Human Development, Family

Urie Bronfenbrenner COURTESY OF LIESA BRONFENBRENNER.

Studies, and Psychology at Cornell University, where he remained for the rest of his professional life. He continued his research and writing as a professor emeritus of Human Development and Psychology in Cornell's College of Human Ecology until he died on September 25, 2005.

It is fitting that Bronfenbrenner spent most of his professional career in a department with a name that encompasses three separate fields and ended it in a college named Human Ecology–a field that he did much to inspire. He was dissatisfied with what he saw as fragmented approaches to the study of human development, each with its own level of analysis (child, family, society, economics, culture, etc.), and was fond of saying that "Much of contemporary developmental psychology is the science of the strange behavior of children in strange situations with strange adults for the briefest possible periods of time" (Bronfenbrenner, 1977, p. 513).

In response Bronfenbrenner developed an ecological systems theory, detailed in his 1979 book *The Ecology of Human Development.* In this theory the child is at the center of many levels of contexts (or systems) that interact to influence development over time. He described five systems, each of which is progressively distant from the child but which nevertheless impact development. The microsystem includes those relationships and interactions that are closest to the child, such as family, peers, and school. The mesosystem comprises the connections between the influences closest to the child, such as the relationships between parents or between parents and schools. The exosystem includes the larger social context, such as the surrounding community, that impacts children indirectly through their parents. The fourth level, the macrosystem, is the most distant from the child and includes cultural values, economic conditions, political systems, and laws, all of which flow back through the inner levels to influence the child. Finally the chronosystem incorporates the unique influence of a child's personal history. Later formulations of his theory included the child's biological system as an important but not decisive factor in development (Bronfenbrenner & Ceci, 1994; Bronfenbrenner, 2001).

Bronfenbrenner's theory, with its emphasis on the powerful influence of multiple contexts on the child, both directly and indirectly through his/her parents, has had a profound effect on how others view a child who has difficulties in school. It is no longer sufficient to simply blame the parents or conclude that the child has a low aptitude for learning. In fact, Bronfenbrenner explicitly argued that it is the cumulative effect of the specific, enduring, supportive interactions children have with all of the individuals in their lives that allows them to live up to their biological potential. He called these interactions "proximal processes" and asserted that others share responsibility for both directly providing such interactions to children and creating social conditions that allow their parents to do so.

Bronfenbrenner, a tireless advocate for more humane and supportive contexts for children and their families, helped to establish the Head Start program and taught an entire generation of social science researchers to take a broader more inclusive look at the forces acting on children. Perhaps his most enduring legacy will be his insistence that people must not only strive for a more accurate picture of human development, but also act on this knowledge to improve the lives of children.

In the forward to one of Bronfenbrenner's last books, Richard Lerner wrote: "For more than 60 years, Urie Bronfenbrenner has been both the standard of excellence and the professional conscience of the field of human development, a field that–because of the scope and synthetic power of his vision–has become productively multidisciplinary and multiprofessional" (2005, p. ix).

BIBLIOGRAPHY

WORKS BY

Bronfenbrenner, U. (1977). *Toward an experimental ecology of human development. American Psychologist, 32,* 513–531.

Bronfenbrenner, U. (1979). *The ecology of human development: Experiments by nature and design.* Cambridge, MA: Harvard University Press. (Republished in 2006).

Bronfenbrenner, U., & Ceci, S. (1994). Nature-nurture reconceptualized in developmental perspective: A bioecological model. *Psychological Review, 101,* 568–586.

Bronfenbrenner, U. (2001). The bioecological theory of human development. In N. Smelser & P. Baltes (Eds.), *International encyclopedia of the social and behavioral sciences* (Vol. 10, pp. 6963–6970). New York: Elsevier.

Bronfenbrenner, U. (2005). *Making human beings human: Bioecological perspectives on human development.* Thousand Oaks, CA: Sage.

Fred Danner

BROPHY, JERE E(DWARD)
1940–

Jere Edward Brophy was born in Chicago in 1940. He received his BA from Loyola in 1962 and his PhD from the University of Chicago in 1967 in Human Development and Clinical Psychology. He took his first position at the University of Texas at Austin in 1968 in the Department of Educational Psychology. From there he moved in 1976 to Michigan State University where in 1990 he was named University Distinguished Professor of Teacher Education and Educational Psychology. His earlier training in clinical psychology and human development helped him to become a pioneer in understanding how teachers think about their students and the ways in which their beliefs affect their behavior. Steadily, and throughout his career, in his capacity to translate theory and research into concrete applications for the practitioner, Jere Brophy contributed to the way in which teachers are educated. His two main contributions are teacher expectation effects and student motivation in learning.

TEACHER EXPECTATION EFFECTS

In the field of educational psychology, Brophy collaborated with Tom Good on teacher expectation effects and self-fulfilling prophecies (e.g., Brophy, 1983; Brophy & Good, 1970). At that time, data suggested that teachers' beliefs about students' academic potential could impact students' achievement in positive or negative ways. Brophy and Good provided some of the first studies to examine how these beliefs transformed teacher practice and ultimately student outcomes. From this body of research, Brophy and Good developed models to explain teacher expectation effects as well as specific strategies to help teachers become more aware of their achievement expectations and how they are communicated to students (Brophy & Good, 1986). These initial sets of studies spawned a generation of researchers interested in understanding how teacher expectations are formed, communicated, and received by students (see Brophy, 1998).

Brophy's classroom research on teacher expectation effects led to questions about what made teachers effective. In collaborations with Evertson and McCaslin and others, Brophy studied experienced teachers to understand the nature and impact of their instructional and classroom management practices (Brophy, 1996; Brophy & McCaslin, 1992; Brophy & Evertson, 1981). Studies looking at how expert teachers think about student behavioral and achievement problems and subsequently address them generated numerous publications offering teachers practical strategies for how to think about classroom management in general and problem behaviors specifically (e.g., Brophy, 1992, 2004).

MOTIVATION TO LEARN

The impact of Brophy's work on the field of educational psychology rests with his enduring concern for helping teachers with their daily practice. Nowhere is this more evident than in his work on student motivation. In his 2004 book *Motivating Students to Learn*, Brophy synthesizes the motivational literature while drawing upon his research and clinical background to provide one of the most practical resources for teachers in helping them think about how to motivate their students. Brophy's opus provides a fresh and practical perspective on learning and motivation that is critical of theorists who argue that learning should be made enjoyable. Instead, he

argues that the field should reconstruct motivation to focus on what Brophy calls "motivation to learn" which he defines as, "a student tendency to find academic activities meaningful and worthwhile and to seek to get the intended learning benefits from them, whether or not they find the content interesting or the processes enjoyable" (Gaedke & Shaughnessy, 2003, p. 207).

Brophy's view of motivation stems from criticisms that traditional motivational researchers do not adequately account for the learning context (the real constraints and affordances in day-to-day classroom life) or the student perspective (e.g., Brophy, 2005). Brophy filled this void by providing an unparalleled body of work that is organized by the common goal of understanding where theory and research intersects with daily practice. The result was over 300 articles, chapters, and technical reports, and numerous authored, co-authored, and edited books that provide teachers with valuable resources for helping them to improve their instructional practice.

Brophy's work in the early 2000s focused on issues related to social studies curricula and assessment. In this vein, Brophy brought his concern for students and teachers in practical settings to analyses of curricular content and instructional method issues involved in teaching social studies for understanding, appreciation, and life application (e.g., Brophy & Alleman, 2007).

IMPACT AND LEGACY

Brophy's impact on the field is extensive. His editorial efforts brought scholars together to comment on enduring issues related to teachers, teaching, and classroom life (e.g., Brophy 1992, 1998). His empirical work generated a rich literature for understanding the underlying processes of teaching and teacher-student relationships. And his texts have provided valuable tools for helping teachers to think about how to manage classrooms and cope with students presenting all sorts of motivational and achievement-related dispositions. One of his most enduring legacies is the single text that was used for 30 years in the field and as of 2008 was in its tenth edition. Co-authored with Tom Good of the University of Arizona, *Looking in Classrooms* is widely regarded as one of the most authoritative texts to synthesize research on classroom life.

Jere Brophy was the 2007 recipient of the Thorndike Award for career achievement in educational psychology, by Division 15 of the American Psychological Association. This honor underscores Jere Brophy's legacy as having made an indelible impact on the field of teaching and teacher education.

SEE ALSO *Praise.*

BIBLIOGRAPHY

WORKS BY

Brophy, J. E. (1983). Research on the self-fulfilling prophecy and teacher expectations. *Journal of Educational Psychology, 75*(5), 631–661.

Brophy, J. (1992) (Ed.). *Planning and managing learning tasks and activities: Advances in Research on Teaching* (Vol. 3). Greenwich, CT: JAI Press.

Brophy, J. (1996). *Teaching problem students.* New York: Guilford.

Brophy, J. (1998) (Ed.). *Advances in research on teaching: Expectations in the classroom.* Greenwich, CT: JAI Press.

Brophy, J. (2004). *Motivating students to learn* (2nd ed.). Mahwah, NJ: Erlbaum.

Brophy, J. (2005). Goal theorists should move on from performance goals. *Educational Psychologist, 40*(3), 167–176.

Brophy, J., & Alleman, J. (2007). *Powerful social studies for elementary students* (2nd ed.). Belmont, CA: Wadsworth.

Brophy, J., & Evertson, C. (1981). *Student characteristics and teaching.* New York: Longman.

Brophy, J., & Good, T. (1970). Teachers' communication of differential expectations for children's classroom performance: Some behavioral data. *Journal of Educational Psychology, 61,* 365–374.

Brophy, J., & Good, T. (1974). *Teacher-student relationships: Causes and consequences.* New York: Holt, Rinehart & Winston.

Brophy, J., & Good, T. (1986). Teacher behavior and student achievement. In M. Wittrock (Ed.), *Handbook of research on teaching* (3rd ed., pp. 328–375). New York: Macmillan.

Brophy, J., & McCaslin, M. (1992). Teachers' reports of how they perceive and cope with problem students. *Elementary School Journal, 93*(1), 3–68.

Good, T. L., & Brophy, J. E. (2008). *Looking in Classrooms* (10th ed.). New York: Pearson.

WORKS ABOUT

Gaedke, B., & Shaughnessy, M. F. (2003). An interview with Jere Brophy. *Educational Psychology Review, 15*(2), 199–211.

Sharon L. Nichols

BROWN, ANN LESLIE
1943–1999

Ann Leslie Brown, a leading educational psychologist, was the first in her family to go to college. In spite of having difficulty learning to read as a child, only becoming fluent at 13, she was to become one of the leading scholars on memory, metacognition, how people learn, and classroom-based learning research. Brown pioneered the term *metacognition*, which referred to individuals' understanding and control of their own mental processes. Using this approach, she and Annemarie Palincsar designed an interventional reading program, reciprocal teaching, which was designed to help students improve their ability to understand what they were reading by using metacognitive strategies such as clarifying, questioning, predicting, and summarizing during collaborative reading of content-rich text.

Brown emphasized "design experiments" (1992) in which "first principles guide the engineering and investigation of educational innovation" (Palincsar, 1999, p. 33). Using "first principles" Brown and her chief collaborator and husband, Joe Campione, built the Fostering a Community of Learners (FCL) project in West Oakland, California. The FCL research project demonstrated that underperforming schools could effectively create learning communities characterized by an ethos of trust and respect, in which students learned a great deal of complex science while developing literacy and technology skills (Brown & Campione, 1994, 1996).

Brown was known for her ability to comfortably travel between theory and practice. Her theories about how children learn and classroom design have spread across the world of teaching as well as to numerous branches of educational research. Brown took laboratory-informed theories and tested them, using rigorous research methods, in real classrooms. Her research trajectory from laboratory to classroom and back has set a high standard for those involved in classroom research.

Brown's PhD degree in psychology was completed at the University of London in 1967; her dissertation was titled "Anxiety and Complex Learning Performance in Children." She held faculty positions at the University of Sussex, England; University of Illinois, Champagne Urbana; Harvard University; and the University of California, Berkeley. Brown co-edited *How People Learn: Brain, Mind, Experience and School* (1999), served as president of The American Educational Research Association and the National Academy of Education and won major career awards from national associations in psychology and education.

Brown was described by her collaborator and friend Annemarie Palincsar in this way:

> Ann's work can be characterized as a journey—a journey toward a theoretical model of learning and instruction—a journey in which she integrated and applied her vast knowledge of teaching, learning, curriculum, assessment, and the social contexts of classrooms and schools—a journey always focused on the goal of expanding learners' capabilities. (Palincsar, 1999, p. 33)

At her American Educational Research Association president's talk in 1993 Brown explained that "her talk would be a 'kind of odyssey of her life,'" examining how her own professional journey paralleled changes and developments in education and research on education. Brown argued that educational researchers "throw the baby out with the bath water" when they should strive to build cumulatively (Brown,

1994; Rutherford & Ash, in press). Brown argued for a synthetic approach, which included designing strong learning communities through a process she described as "design experiments" (Brown, 1992). Brown explained:

> A major part of my personal effort in the design experiment of creating community is to contribute to a theory of learning that can capture and convey the core essential features. The development of theory has always been necessary as a guide to research, a lens through which one interprets, that sets things apart and pulls things together. But theory development is essential for practical implementation as well. (Brown, 1994)

The practical outcome of this goal, the Fostering Communities of Learners project, occupied much of Brown's time at the University of California, Berkeley. Working with teachers, principles, and other educators in urban schools, Brown viewed "classrooms as contexts in which diversity was not only tolerated but was, in fact, integral to success" (Palincsar, 1999, p. 34). Such learning environments, based on "first principles" carefully conceived and grounded in the particulars of the context, guided the development of communities that foster intellectual curiosity and engagement so that all students may learn how to learn (Rutherford & Ash, in press).

Brown loved being in the classroom, often talking comfortably with her students as they were actively involved in learning how to learn. The students also loved Brown. One FCL student, Florencia Tuaumu, remarked in 2004 about her 1992–1993 FCL classroom, "It was almost like a homecoming of sorts … it was something we had always been able to do but never actually had the chance … and now, the possibilities were seemingly endless" (Rutherford & Ash, in press, p. 2). Florencia's remarks convey "the essence of a silver thread that ran through all of Ann Brown's work—a deep passion and commitment to create the ways and means for young people to learn to use their minds well" (Rutherford & Ash, p. 2).

SEE ALSO *Analogy; Communities of Learners; Metacognition; Reciprocal Teaching.*

BIBLIOGRAPHY

WORKS BY

Bransford, J., Brown, A., & Cocking, R. (Eds.). (1999). *How people learn: Brain, mind, experience, and school.* Washington, DC: National Academy Press.

Brown, A. L. (1975). The development of memory: Knowing, knowing about knowing, and knowing how to know. In H. W. Reese (Ed.), *Advances in child development and behavior* (Vol. 10, pp. 103–152). San Diego, CA: Academic Press.

Brown, A. L. (1980). Metacognitive development and reading. In R. J. Spiro, B. C. Bruce, & W. F. Brewer (Eds.), *Theoretical issues in reading comprehension* (pp. 453–481). Hillsdale, NJ: Erlbaum.

Brown, A. L. (1990). Domain-specific principles affect learning and transfer in children. *Cognitive Science, 14,* 107–133.

Brown, A.L. (1992). Design experiments: Theoretical and methodological challenges in creating complex interventions in classroom settings. *The Journal of the Learning Sciences, 2*(2), 141–178.

Brown, A. L., & Campione, J. C. (1994). Guided discovery in a community of learners. In K. McGilly (Ed.), *Classroom lessons: Integrating cognitive theory and classroom practice* (pp. 229–270). Cambridge, MA: MIT Press/Bradford Books.

Brown, A. L., & Campione, J. C. (1996). Psychological theory and the design of innovative learning environments: On procedures, principles, and systems. In L. Schauble & R. Glaser (Eds.), *Innovations in learning: New environments for education* (pp. 289–325). Mahwah, NJ: Erlbaum.

Brown, A. L., Bransford, J. D., Ferrara, R. A., & Campione, J. C. (1983). Learning, remembering, and understanding. In P. H. Mussen (Series Ed.) & J. M. Flavell & E. M. Markman (Vol. Eds.), *Handbook of child psychology* (Vol. 3, 4th ed., pp. 77–166). New York: Wiley.

Palincsar, A. S., & Brown, A. L. (1984). Reciprocal teaching of comprehension-fostering and comprehension-monitoring activities. *Cognition and Instruction, 1*(2), 117–175.

WORKS ABOUT

Palincsar, A. S. (1999). In Memoriam: Ann L. Brown (1943–1999) *Educational Researcher, 28*(7), 33–34.

Rutherford, M., & Ash, D. (in press). The Ann Brown Legacy: Still Learning After All These Years. In *Children's learning in and out of school: Essays in honor of Ann Brown.*

Doris Ash

BRUNER, JEROME S(EYMOUR)
1915–

Jerome Seymour Bruner is a psychologist whose contributions to cognitivist and constructivist views of human learning and child development spanned several decades.

Bruner first encountered the field of psychology in the 1930s as an undergraduate and (for a short time) graduate student at Duke University, where his early research in collaboration with behaviorists convinced him that even laboratory rats were thinking creatures whose behavior could not be reduced to simple stimulus-response connections. He followed up with graduate study at Harvard University, earning his Ph.D. in 1941.

After a four-year stint working for the federal government during World War II, Bruner returned to Harvard as a faculty member. There he soon felt at odds with current mainstream views in American psychology, and especially with the behaviorist idea that thought processes

Jerome Seymour Bruner ARCHIVES OF THE HISTORY OF AMERICAN PSYCHOLOGY. THE UNIVERSITY OF AKRON.

center was a fertile cross-breeding ground for new ideas (including those of developmentalists Jean Piaget [1896–1980] and Lev Vygotsky [1896–1934]) and was a key player in turning the tide in American psychology from behaviorism to a more cognitively oriented perspective.

By 1972 cognitive theories, especially information processing theory, had become the mainstream point of view in American psychology. That year Bruner moved to England to join the faculty at Oxford University, where much of his research addressed cognition and cognitive development in infants. Upon his return to the United States in 1980, he spent another year at Harvard and then in 1981 joined the faculty at New York University. At NYU he continued his work in cognition into the early years of the twenty-first century, with a particular focus on the ways in which human beings impose meanings on the world around them.

Despite his many contributions to psychology, Bruner is probably best known for his work in education. In his 1960 book *The Process of Education*, Bruner argued against the prevailing notion that lack of readiness prevents young children from understanding difficult subject matter. He advocated a spiral curriculum in which children tackle challenging topics in age-appropriate ways even in the primary grades, revisiting these topics year after year and each time building and expanding on previous acquisitions. In a later book, *Toward a Theory of Instruction* (1966), Bruner suggested that children mentally represent events in three ways—first as physical actions (enactively), then as mental images (iconically), and eventually as language (symbolically). Through concrete manipulatives and carefully designed activities, children can discover important ideas and principles on their own, first representing them enactively, then iconically, and finally symbolically. Thus, Bruner was an early advocate of discovery learning. Furthermore, he contended, children are intrinsically motivated to master new skills, particularly when those skills are sequenced to enable frequent success.

In the 1990s and early 2000s, Bruner increasingly emphasized the many ways that culture shapes the mind, both in school and in the world beyond it. In his *The Culture of Education* (1996), Bruner emphasized a point that many contemporary sociocultural psychologists share: Culture provides general frames of reference that permeate the meanings people impose on daily events and classroom lessons. Rather than assume that students will absorb classroom subject matter exactly as it is presented, educators must engage students in ongoing dialogues, assessing existing beliefs and understandings and modifying instruction in light of them. Education, then, must always involve two-way communication, continually informing both student and teacher alike.

could not be observed and so could not be studied scientifically. Furthermore, Bruner's research on perception in the late 1940s and early 1950s (much of it conducted with collaborator Leo Postman) consistently pointed to the same conclusion: People's perceived realities were often quite different—and different in predictable ways—from the information their various senses actually detected in the environment. In the 1950s, Bruner also ventured into new territory by looking at how people form categories. In 1956 he published *A Study of Thinking* with coauthors Jacqueline Goodnow and George Austin. Although the book was justifiably criticized for its study of people's behaviors in an artificial concept-learning exercise, central to its discussion was an important insight: Rather than being merely the unwitting victims of environmental circumstances, human beings are rational, strategic learners who work hard to make sense of the world around them.

Convinced that human cognition both could and should be a focus of study, Bruner and his colleague George Miller established and co-directed Harvard's Center for Cognitive Studies in 1960. Bringing together scholars from diverse disciplines (e.g., psychology, anthropology, linguistics, philosophy, mathematics), the

SEE ALSO *Cognitive Development; Constructivism; Information Processing Theory; Sociocultural Theories of Motivation.*

BIBLIOGRAPHY

WORKS BY

Bruner, J. S., Goodnow, J. J., & Austin, G. A. (1956). *A study of thinking.* New York: Wiley.

Bruner, J. S. (1960). *The process of education.* Cambridge, MA: Harvard University Press.

Bruner, J. S. (1966). *Toward a theory of instruction.* New York: W. W. Norton.

Bruner, J. S. (1983). *In search of mind: Essays in autobiography.* New York: Harper & Row.

Bruner, J. S. (1996). *The culture of education.* Cambridge, MA: Harvard University Press.

WORKS ABOUT

Olson, D. (2008). *Jerome Bruner: The cognitive revolution in educational theory.* London & New York: Continuum International.

Orlofsky, D. D. (2001). *Redefining teacher education: The theories of Jerome Bruner and the practice of training teachers.* New York: P. Lang.

Jeanne Ellis Ormrod

BULLIES AND VICTIMS

Bullying perpetration and victimization was brought to the attention of U.S. researchers by Dan Olweus, who spearheaded a nationwide Scandinavian campaign against bullying. Referring to bullies as "whipping boys" in the 1970s, Olweus set forth the following definition of bullying that continued to be consistently used into the early 2000s: "A student is being bullied or victimized when he or she is exposed, repeatedly and over time, to negative actions on the part of one or more students" (Olweus, 1993, p. 318). It often involves an imbalance of strength and power between the bully and the target and is repetitive in nature. Children and adolescents may experience isolated acts of aggression, but children who have been bullied live with the ongoing fear of the recurring abuse from the bully, which is usually more damaging than an isolated and unpredicted aggressive event. In the late 1990s and early 2000s, scholars have recognized that bullying can be verbal, physical, and social in nature. Smith and Sharp noted: "A student is being bullied or picked on when another student says nasty and unpleasant things to him or her. It is also bullying when a student is hit, kicked, threatened, locked inside a room, sent nasty notes, and when no one ever talks to him" (Sharp & Smith, 1991, p.1).

PREVALENCE

Bullying is thought to be one of the most prevalent types of school violence. Students assume roles, including bully, victim, bully/victim, and bystander. Estimates in the early 2000s suggest that nearly 30% of American students are involved in bullying in one of these capacities (Nansel et al., 2001). Specifically, findings from this nationally representative sample indicated that among sixth through tenth graders, 13% had bullied others (bullies), 11% had been bullied (victims), and 6% had both bullied others and been bullied (bully-victims). Worldwide incidence rates for bullying victimization in school-aged youth range from 10% of secondary students through 27% of middle school students who report being bullied often (Whitney & Smith, 1993). When peer, teacher, and self-reports were used to classify a sample of sixth graders (N = 1,985), the authors found 7% of the sample were bullies, 9% were victims, and 6% were bully-victims (Juvonen, Graham, & Schuster, 2003).

The delineation of these bully and bully-victim groups has direct implications for prevention and intervention efforts because these subgroups not only display different patterns of aggression, but they also have different emotional and psychological profiles. First, bullies exhibit a more goal-oriented aggression, entailing more control and planning. In contrast, bully-victims tend to display a more impulsive aggression with concurrent poor emotional and behavioral regulation, which is perceived as particularly aversive by their peers and contributes to their own victimization (Schwartz, Proctor, & Chien, 2001). Second, bully-victims are at-risk for greater social maladjustment than bullies and have been found to experience victimization in other domains, including childhood sexual abuse and sexual harassment (Holt & Espelage, 2005).

RISKS FOR BECOMING A BULLY, VICTIM, OR BULLY-VICTIM

Aggression, like other forms of behavior, is often conceptualized as emerging, being maintained, and modified as a result of a child's personality characteristics and the interactions between these characteristics and social contexts (e.g., peers, family, schools). This perspective has been called a social-ecological theory (Bronfenbrenner, 1979) and includes microsystems, which contains structures with which the child or adolescent has direct contact, including parents, siblings, peers, and schools. The mesosystem comprises the interrelations among microsystems, such as an adolescent's family and peers. For example, attachment to one's parents might contribute to a willingness to connect with a teacher at school. The social-ecological framework has been extended to predictive models of bullying victimization and perpetration, which are discussed briefly next.

Bullying can be verbal, physical, and social in nature. ©GIDEON MENDEL/CORBIS.

Individual Risk Factors. Certain individual characteristics heighten one's risk for being victimized or perpetrators. In demographic terms, boys are more often victimized and perpetrators than girls (Espelage & Holt, 2001), although this depends somewhat on the form of victimization; whereas boys are more likely to experience physical bullying victimization (e.g., being hit), girls are more likely to be targets of indirect victimization (e.g., social exclusion). In one of the few studies addressing the influence of race on bullying, Black students reported less victimization than White or Hispanic youth (Nansel et al., 2001). Juvonen and colleagues (2003) found that Black middle-school youth were more likely to be categorized as bullies and bully-victims than White students. Another study found that Hispanic students reported somewhat more bullying than Black and White youth (Nansel et al., 2001).

A wide range of personality characteristics has been associated with either pro-social behaviors or bullying victimization/perpetration. First, empathy is consistently negatively associated with aggression and positively associated with prosocial skills (Miller & Eisenberg, 1988). The inverse correlation between aggression and empathy was stronger in studies that focused on the emotional component of empathy rather than the cognitive aspects of empathy. This might be especially relevant in the case of bullying in which the aggressors might be able to understand others' emotional states without sharing the victims' feelings. Bullies' careful selection of victims who are vulnerable and disliked by their peers reflects good perspective-taking. However, the fact that they use violence to achieve their goals, disregarding the pain that they inflict on their victims suggests that perspective-taking (e.g., cognitive empathy) does little to inhibit aggression.

Second, a positive attitude toward bullying is often a strong predictor of bullying perpetration. Espelage and colleagues found that a positive attitude toward bullying partially mediated the relation between empathic concern and bullying for males, and the relation between perspective-taking and bullying for both males and females (Espelage, Mebane, & Adams, 2003). From a slightly different angle, Boulton and colleagues (2002) investigated children's general attitudes toward bullying and their impact on bullying. Investigators found significant positive correlations between pro-attitudes and self-reported involvement in bullying (Boulton, Trueman, & Flemington, 2002).

Contextual Influences. Family, peer, and school contexts can exert positive or negative influences on bullying involvement. With respect to the family context, bullies often report that their parents are authoritarian, condone fighting back, use physical punishment, lack warmth, and display indifference to their children (Baldry & Farrington, 2000). In addition, children who have insecure, anxious-avoidant, or anxious-resistant attachments when 18 months old were more likely than children with secure attachments to become involved in bullying at ages 4 and 5 (Troy & Sroufe, 1987). Similarly, middle school students classified as bullies and bully-victims indicated receiving substantially less social support from parents than students in the uninvolved group (Holt & Espelage, 2005). McFadyen-Ketchum and colleagues (1996) found aggressive children who experienced affectionate mother-child relationships showed significant decreases in aggressive-disruptive behaviors over time.

The peer context is another salient contributor to bullying behaviors. Several theories dominate the literature, including the homophily hypothesis, attraction theory, and dominance theory (for review, see Espelage, Wasserman, & Fleisher, 2007). According to the homophily hypothesis, adolescent peer group members tend to have similar levels of aggression. In addition, peer group bullying is predictive of individual youths' bullying behaviors over time, even after controlling for baseline levels of bullying, a finding that holds true for both males and females (Espelage, Holt, & Henkel, 2003). This might in part be due to deviancy training, a process by which values supportive of aggression are fostered. Peer groups can also have a positive influence on youth. Further, peers can promote positive social functioning among youth; adolescents with low levels of prosocial behaviors in sixth grade relative to their friends demonstrated improved prosocial behaviors at the end of eighth grade (Wentzel & Caldwell, 1997).

CLASSROOM AND SCHOOL FACTORS

One of the most salient and influential environments for children is the school (Eccles et al., 1993). A tremendous amount of research has tied schooling to both academic and personal outcomes. School contextual factors have been linked to children's mental health, achievement, self-concept, and ability to form social relationships. Understanding the school environment is an essential part of understanding a child's behavior. In addition, educators have long seen the classroom as having an important impact on children's well being. If a classroom does not meet the needs of a child, negative outcomes can occur and the child can be put at-risk for academic and social difficulties (Eccles et al., 1993).

Students involved in bullying reported more negative views of their school environment and positive school climate has been found to be vital to reducing bullying behaviors. Classroom practices and teachers' attitudes are also salient components of school climate that contribute to bullying prevalence. Aggression varies from classroom to classroom, and in some classrooms aggression appears to be supported. Bullying tends to be less prevalent in classrooms in which most children are included in activities, teachers display warmth and responsiveness to children, teachers respond quickly and effectively to bullying incidents (Newman, Murray, & Lussier, 2001), and parents are aware of their children's peers relationships (Olweus, 1993). It is well accepted that when school personnel tolerate, ignore, or dismiss bullying behaviors, they implicitly convey messages that students internalize. Conversely, if staff members hold anti-bullying attitudes and translate these attitudes into behaviors, the school culture becomes less tolerant of bullying.

Kasen and colleagues' 1994 study is perhaps the most comprehensive examination of the impact of school climate on changes in verbal and physical aggression, anger, and school problem indices. In this study, 500 children (and their mothers) across 250 schools were surveyed at the age of 13.5 and 16 years across a two-and-a-half year interval. A 45-item school climate survey included multiple scales assessing social and emotional features of the school environment, including a conflict scale (classroom control, teacher-student conflict), learning focus scale, social facilitation scale, and student authority scale (student has a say in politics and planning) as predictors. Outcome measures included a wide range of scales, including school problems, deviance, rebelliousness, anger, physical and verbal aggression, and bullying. School context can influence engagement in bullying and more positive social interactions. Results found that students in high-conflict schools had an increase in verbal and physical aggression, after controlling for baseline aggression. In contrast, attendance at schools that emphasized learning resulted in a decrease in aggression and other school-related problems. Of particular interest was the finding that schools high in informal relations had increases in bullying perpetration over the two-and-a-half year interval, and schools with high conflict and high informality combined had the highest increase in bullying over time.

RENEE'S STORY

As a high school mathematics teacher I have regretfully witnessed many bullying situations. It is of particular concern to me, because it can have such a profound impact on classroom performance. I am reminded of a student, Renee (pseudonym), that I recently had in one of my classes. Renee's story reflects many of the points raised in Espelage's entry on bullying.

As Espelage defined bullying in this chapter, two ideas emerged that are reflected in Renee's story. One was the idea that bulling is repeated over time, and often is not just a one time occurrence. The second idea is that bullying is not always a physical act; it also occurs via social interactions and dialogs between students. Both of these were apparent in the case of Renee. Renee was a student of mine in a freshman algebra class. She was in a unique situation because she was a sophomore. She had transferred from a different school and she was lacking her required algebra credit, so she was the only sophomore in the algebra class. Initially this did not seem to be a problem for Renee. She was a very happy and sociable student. She was friendly and would talk with everyone and she would laugh often. After several weeks it appeared she was developing some friendships. She was also an academically strong student; during class she was focused on the task at hand and she worked well with her classmates.

As the year progressed, there was a group of four boys that would commonly joke around with Renee. They would tease her by pretending that one of their group was dating her. They would say things like, "where are the two of you going tonight?" or "is your old boyfriend mad you left him for me?" These conversations usually occurred in the transition between classes and when I heard these comments, I quickly redirected the students to the tasks of the day. Renee would usually laugh at the group of boys and always seemed to have a quick-witted response. From my vantage point it genuinely seemed like a group of friends having fun and enjoying each others' company.

My feelings about the situation changed when I noticed Renee missing several class sessions. She did not turn in her homework, and when she did attend class she did not perform as well as she had previously. I investigated her poor performance and why she had been missing class, and I found that the boys were the reason. Renee told me she had

not been coming to class because she did not want deal with the groups of boys teasing her. Sometimes bullying is difficult for an outsider to detect. It is difficult to determine if kids are having good natured fun, or if someone is being victimized. As a teacher the best way I have seen to deal with these hard to distinguish situations is to build strong relationships with the students. The better you know the student the easier it will be to determine if they are actually being victimized. In Renee's case I did not see her as a victim of bullying initially, but her missing class and turning in poor work were immediate red flags.

After I realized that Renee was a victim of bullying by a peer group, I immediately confronted the four boys, called their parents, and notified the assistant principal of the situation. Renee began coming back to class and the boys seem more respectful toward her, but, on occasion, they would make the same type of comments to her, usually in the hallway before class so I was not aware. It was difficult to change the nature of the boys' interactions with Renee. On one occasion, I was working with a group of students and one of the boys made some remarks to Renee. I was unaware of the initial exchange, but I quickly noticed Renee aggressively react to their comments. She became extremely agitated and began yelling explicatives at the boys. As Espelage mentioned in this chapter, victims of bullying are often impulsive and lack behavior regulation, which can been seen in Renee's reactions.

The bullying between Renee and the boys was not immediately corrected but after time, consistent monitoring of interactions, parent conferences, and consultation with the assistant principal, the students developed a respectful relationship. Renee's performance returned to the level I had come to expect from her and the boys developed a more mature relationship with their classmate.

The bullying situation with Renee helped remind me, as a classroom teacher, that bullying is not always obvious, and that teachers have to know their students well to understand if bullying is occurring. As a teacher, it also is important to realize that bullying can profoundly influence a student's performance and achievement.

Anthony Durr

BULLIES AND VICTIMS ACROSS THE LIFESPAN

Victims, bullies, and bully-victims often report adverse psychological effects and poor school adjustment as a result of their involvement in bullying. For example, targets of bullying reveal more loneliness and depression, greater school avoidance, more suicidal ideation, and less self-esteem than their non-bullied peers (Hawker & Boulton, 2000).

Findings have been mixed about the stability of bullying behavior over time. In one study, bullying perpetration and victimization at age 8 were related to bullying perpetration and victimization at age 16, with particularly strong associations emerging for victimization patterns and for the experiences of boys (Sourander, Helstela, Helenius, & Piha, 2000). Similarly, in a later study, girls and boys classified as victims in Grade 4 were significantly more likely than their peers to be identified as victims in Grade 7 (Paul & Cillesen, 2003).

It does appear though that the psychological costs associated with involvement are not transient. Adults at the age of 23, who had been chronically victimized in their youth, had lower self-esteem and were more depressed than non-victimized members of their cohort who had not been bullied (Olweus, 1993). Whereas victims tend to report more internalizing behaviors, bullies are more likely than their peers to engage in externalizing behaviors, to experience conduct problems, and to be delinquent (Nansel et al., 2001). Furthermore, long-term outcomes for bullies can be serious; compared to their peers, bullies are more likely to be convicted of crimes in adulthood (Olweus, 1993). One study revealed that youth identified as bullies in school had a one in four chance of having a criminal record by age 30 (Eron, Huesmann, Dubow, Romanoff, & Yarnel, 1987). Finally, considerable research has documented that the most at-risk group of youth is bully-victims. Bully-victims demonstrate more externalizing behaviors, are more hyperactive, and have a greater probability of being referred for psychiatric consultation than their peers (Nansel et al., 2001).

CREATING BULLY-FREE ACADEMIC ENVIRONMENTS AND PROTECTING VICTIMS

Many school-based bullying prevention and intervention programs include training teachers to create bully-free environments. For example, bullying prevention programs generally encourage teachers to generate rules about bullying collaboratively with their students. These rules typically include variants of the following: (a) Bully is not allowed in the classroom; (b) If a child is being bullied, then students and teachers will help him or her; and (c) Students and teachers work to include students who are left out. These rules are often posted in the classroom. Students and teachers are also encouraged to generate potential sanctions for

violating the rules, including an individual talk with the bully, taking away a privilege, etc. Teachers are encouraged to hold class meetings to review the rules and sanctions in weekly class meetings in which students and teachers sit in a circle and discuss incidents of bullying. Teachers should also use praise when students engage in pro-social or caring acts.

Teachers are often encouraged then to incorporate a prevention program that more specifically teaches about bullying and helps children develop skills to minimize the risk of involvement with bullying. One program that is relatively inexpensive and easily adopted by elementary and middle school classroom teachers is Bully Busters (Newman, Horne, & Bartolomucci, 2000). Unlike many bullying prevention programs, Bully Busters has strong empirical support for its efficacy. For example, teachers who were trained to implement the program reported significantly higher levels of self-efficacy for managing bullying behavior, demonstrated greater knowledge of classroom behavior management, and had fewer classroom behavior problems and office referrals than comparison teachers (Newman-Carlson & Horne, 2004).

In this program, teachers are encouraged to do the following:

Develop a definition of bullying collaboratively with students. Exercises are used to facilitate a conversation among students about who is a bully, what is bullying, and where it happens.

Facilitate activities with students to recognize how their words/actions can be hurtful, and then role-play more constructive ways of interacting.

Discuss with students how bullying develops and the variety of forms it can take. Activities could include viewing movies or reading books in which characters are victims or bullies.

Engage in conversations with students about the effects of victimization and challenge myths about victims.

Encourage bystander intervention and encourage students to break the code of silence and create a safer climate for all students.

Teach empathy skills training, social skills training, and anger management skills.

Assist victims in becoming aware of their strengths, viewing themselves in a positive manner, and building skills and confidence in joining groups.

Identify how their attitudes and behaviors influence student behavior and how school-level factors relate to bullying.

School-based bullying perpetration and victimization develops and is maintained as a result of various factors, including a child's personality, home environment, peers, and experiences at school. Children and adolescents are at-risk for developing aggression or are at-risk for being involved in bullying because they have multiple risk factors and few protective experiences. However, research suggests that involvement in bullying can be prevented. For example, social support, teacher attachment, supportive friends, a positive school climate, involvement in extracurricular activities, all serve to protect or buffer children from both experiencing and expressing bullying, and these factors also serve to minimize the psychological impact over time.

SEE ALSO *Aggression.*

BIBLIOGRAPHY

Baldry, A. C., & Farrington, D. P. (2000). Bullies and delinquents: Personal characteristics and parental styles. *Journal of Community and Applied Social Psychology, 10,* 17–31.

Boulton, M. J., Trueman, L., & Flemington, J. (2002). Associations between secondary school student's definitions of bullying, attitudes towards bullying, and tendencies to engage in bullying: Age and sex differences. *Educational Studies, 28*(4), 353–370.

Bronfenbrenner, U. (1979). *The ecology of human development.* Cambridge, MA: Harvard University Press.

Eccles, J. S., Wigfield, A., Midgley, C., Reuman, D., MacIver, D., & Feldlaufer, H. (1993). Negative effects of traditional middle schools on students' motivation. *Elementary School Journal, 93,* 553–574.

Eron, L. D., Huesmann, L. R., Dubow, E., Romanoff, R., & Yarnel, P. W. (1987). Aggression and its correlates over 22 years. In D. H. Crowell & I. M. Evans (Eds.), *Childhood aggression and violence: Sources of influence, prevention, and control* (pp. 249–262). New York: Plenum Press.

Espelage, D., & Holt, M. K. (2001). Bullying and victimization during early adolescence: Peer influences and psychosocial correlates. *Journal of Emotional Abuse, 2,* 123–142.

Espelage, D. L., Holt, M. K., & Henkel, R. R. (2003). Examination of peer-group contextual effects on aggression during early adolescence. *Child Development, 74*(1), 205–220.

Espelage, D. L., Mebane, S., & Adams, R. (2004). Empathy, caring, and bullying: Toward an understanding of complex associations. In D. L. Espelage & S. M. Swearer (Eds.), *Bullying in American schools: A social ecological perspective on prevention and intervention* (pp. 37–61). Mahwah, NJ: Erlbaum.

Espelage, D. L., Wasserman, S., & Fleisher, M. (2007). Social networks and violent behavior. In D. J. Flannery, A. T. Vazsonyi, & I. Waldman (Eds.), *The Cambridge handbook of violent behavior.* New York: Cambridge University Press.

Hawker, D. S. J., & Boulton, M. J. (2000). Twenty years' research on peer victimization and psychosocial maladjustment: A meta-analytic review of cross-sectional studies. *Journal of Child Psychology and Psychiatry and Allied Disciplines, 41,* 441–455.

Holt, M., & Espelage, D. (2005). Multiple victimization of adolescents. In K. Kendall-Tackett & S. Giacomoni (Eds.), *Victimization of children and youth: Patterns of abuse, response strategies* (pp. 13–16). Kingston, NJ: Civic Research Institute.

Hoover, J. H., Oliver, R., & Hazler, R. (1992). *Causal attributions: From cognitive processes to collective beliefs.* Oxford: Blackwell.

Jvonen, J., Graham, S., & Schuster, M. A. (2003). Bullying among young adolescents: The strong, the weak, and the troubled. *Pediatrics, 112*(6), 1231–1237.

Kasen, S., Berenson, K., Cohen, P., & Johnson, J. G. (2004). The effects of school climate on changes in aggressive and other behaviors related to bullying. In D. L. Espelage & S. M. Swearer (Eds.), *Bullying in American schools: A social-ecological perspective on prevention and intervention* (pp. 187–210). Mahwah, NJ: Erlbaum.

McFadyen-Ketchum, S. A., Bates, J. E., Dodge, K. A., & Pettit, G. S. (1996). Patterns of change in early childhood aggressive-disruptive behavior: Gender differences in predictions from early coercive and affectionate mother-child interactions. *Child Development, 67*(5), 2417–2433.

Miller, P. A., & Eisenberg, N. (1988). The relationship of empathy to aggressive and externalizing/antisocial behavior. *Psychological Bulletin, 103,* 324–344.

Nansel, T. R., Overpeck, M., Pilla, R. S., Ruan, W. J., Simons-Morton, B., & Scheidt, P. (2001). Bullying behaviors among U.S. youth: Prevalence and association with psychosocial adjustment. *Journal of the American Medical Association, 285,* 2094–2100.

Newman, D. A., Horne, A. M., & Bartolomucci, C. L. (2000). *Bully busters: A teacher's manual for helping bullies, victims, and bystanders.* Champaign, IL: Research Press.

Newman, R. S., Murray, B., & Lussier, C. (2001). Confrontation with aggressive peers at school: Students' reluctance to seek help from the teacher. *Journal of Educational Psychology, 93*(2), 398–410.

Newman-Carlson, D., & Horne, A. (2004). Bully-busters: A psychoeducational intervention for reducing bullying behavior in middle school students. *Journal of Counseling and Development, 82,* 259–267.

Olweus, D. (1978). *Aggression in the schools: Bullies and whipping boys.* Washington, DC: Hemisphere.

Olweus, D. (1993). Bully/victim problems among schoolchildren: Long-term consequences and an effective intervention program. In S. Hodgins (Ed.), *Mental disorder and crime* (pp. 317–349). Thousand Oaks, CA: Sage Publications.

Schwartz, D., Proctor, L. J., & Chien, D. H. (2001). The aggressive victim of bullying, emotional and behavioral dysregulation as a pathway to victimization by peers. In J. Juvonen & S. Graham (Eds.), *Peer harassment in school: The plight of the vulnerable and victimized* (pp. 147–174). New York: Guilford Press.

Sharp, S., & Smith, P. K. (1991). Bullying in UK schools: The DES Sheffield Bullying Project. *Early Childhood Development and Care, 77,* 47–55.

Shields, A., & Cicchetti, D. (2001). Parental maltreatment and emotion dysregulation as risk factors for bullying and victimization in middle childhood. *Journal of Clinical Child Psychology, 30,* 349–363.

Sourander, A., Helstela, L., Helenius, H., & Piha, J. (2000). Persistence of bullying from childhood to adolescence: A longitudinal 8-year follow-up study. *Child Abuse & Neglect, 24,* 873–881.

Troy, M., & Sroufe, L. A. (1987). Victimization among preschoolers: Role of attachment relationship history. *Journal* of the American Academy of Child and Adolescent Psychiatry, 26, 166–172.

Wentzel, K. R., & Caldwell, K. A. (1997). Friendships, peer acceptance, and group membership: Relations to academic achievement in middle school. *Child Development, 68,* 1198–1209.

Whitney, I., & Smith, P. K. (1993). A survey of the nature and extent of bullying in junior/middle and secondary schools. *Educational Research, 35,* 3–25.

Dorothy L. Espelage

C

CALFEE, ROBERT C.
1933–

As of 2008 Robert C. Calfee was distinguished professor of education and professor emeritus at the University of California at Riverside, where he also served as dean of the College of Education from 1998 to 2003. The majority of his career (1969–1998) was spent as an associate professor and professor in the School of Education at Stanford University, where he worked following his first faculty position in the Psychology Department at the University of Wisconsin at Madison (1964–1969). Educational research was enriched immeasurably when Calfee joined Stanford's School of Education.

Calfee earned his BA, MA, and PhD (1963) in experimental psychology at the University of California at Los Angeles, working mostly on learning tasks, often with the psychologist Richard C. Atkinson. Early work on the reading process, much with the reading researcher Richard Venezky, brought Calfee into closer proximity with educational settings. When he turned full attention to the field of education he brought with him considerable knowledge about the psychology of reading, using the (then new) lens for the study of how individuals learn that was provided by cognitive psychology and information processing models of human learning. But he bought as well important methodological skills from his work in experimental psychology, and those interests subsequently influenced research design and assessment in educational research.

Education, in turn, gave Calfee a deeper understanding of school context and the organizational life of teachers, so that he gained deep knowledge of reading processes in the real world and respect for the difficulties of both teaching reading and learning to read in public school classrooms. Perhaps most important was his immersion in the Stanford environment, where both extraordinary faculty colleagues and a remarkable cadre of graduate students stretched his knowledge and were stretched by him as well.

From the 1980s on Calfee's career was more focused on applying cognitive psychology to reading and writing instruction and assessment; broad issues in educational policy but particularly reading policies; and school reform issues in California and across the United States. Much of this work was collaborative, with many of his students and co-authors going on to distinguished careers in reading research or related research areas. Calfee served the faculty at Stanford with turns as associate dean of research and director of the Stanford Center for Research and Development on Teaching. Subsequently he became director of Stanford's Teacher Education program and served as associate director of the Study of Stanford and the Schools, work that eventually transformed the nature of scholarship at Stanford. During this same period (the mid-1980s) Calfee also served as a member of the board of trustees of the Palo Alto Unified School District, marking him as an involved citizen/educator.

Calfee served as editor of the flagship journal in the field of educational psychology, the *Journal of Educational Psychology* (1985–1990), published by the American Psychological Association (APA). He also edited the journal *Educational Assessment* (1992–1998), and was co-editor of the first *Handbook of Educational Psychology*, published in 1996, by the Division of Educational Psychology of the APA. He served twice as a member of the board of directors of the National Society for the Study of Education (NSSE), and during these terms (1995–1998; 2000–2004) he chaired the board twice. Calfee was named to the California Reading Association Hall of Fame (1992) and the International Reading Association Hall of Fame (1993). In 2003 the National Reading Conference awarded him the Oscar Causey Award for Outstanding Contributions to Reading Research. His advisory work and consulting has been at the national, state, and local levels of education, and he served as chairperson of the educational advisory board for Leap-Frog Enterprises, an award-winning developer of educational products. As of 2008, Calfee was a Fellow of two divisions of APA, Experimental Psychology and Educational Psychology, and a Fellow of the Center for Advanced Studies in the Behavioral Sciences.

Calfee's interests evolved over three decades from a focus on the psychology of verbal learning to concerns about the assessment of beginning literacy skills and eventually to a concern with the broader reach of the school as a literate environment. His theoretical efforts were directed toward the nature of human thought processes and the influence of language and literacy in the development of problem-solving and communication. At home in theory and in practice, in running true experiments or design experiments, in the board-room or the classroom, and in working with policymakers or teachers, Calfee proves himself to be a unique scholar. As of 2008, he continued to have a productive and engaged career.

BIBLIOGRAPHY

Berliner, D. C., & Calfee, R. C. (1996). *Handbook of educational psychology.* New York: Macmillan.

Calfee, R. C. (1997). Assessing the development of learning over time. In J. Flood, S. B. Heath, & D. Lapp (Eds.). *Handbook for literacy educators: Research on teaching the communicative and visual arts.* New York: Macmillan.

Calfee, R. C. (1998). Leading middle-grade students from reading to writing. In R. C. Nelson, N., & Calfee, R. C. (Eds.), *The reading-writing connection (National Society for the Study of Education).* Chicago: Chicago University Press.

Calfee, R. C., & Norman, K. A. (in press). Psychological perspectives on the early reading wars: The case of phonological awareness. *Teachers College Record* (Special Issue).

Calfee, R. C., & Patrick, C. (1995). *Teach our children well.* Stanford, CA: Portable Stanford Series, Stanford Alumni Association.

Chambliss, M. J., & Calfee, R. C. (1998). *Textbooks for learning: Nurturing children's minds.* Malden, MA: Blackwell.

David C. Berliner

CARING TEACHERS

Literature over the last 30 years has increasingly documented the importance of supportive student-teacher relationships to improving student motivation, learning, and achievement (Davis, 2003). Research suggests caring, or supportive, teachers create qualitatively different classroom environments that feel warm, encourage student to behave in social responsible ways, and emphasize learning over performing. Students who perceive their teachers as caring tend to engage more with the content, take intellectual risks, and persist in the face of failure. Children who had caring, supportive teachers early in their schooling tend to evidence more adaptive academic and behavioral outcomes up through junior high school. Moreover, junior and senior high school students who perceive their teachers as caring are more likely to connect with classroom content and less likely to dropout of high school. Emerging from this literature are three different ways to think about what it means to be a caring teacher.

CARING GUIDES TEACHER ENGAGEMENT

Aaron Ben-Ze'ev thinks about care as reflecting an emotion state that motivates teachers to engage in different caring behaviors. From this perspective, the emotion of care arises as a function of teachers' making four distinct judgments about their students. These judgments, in turn, can result in them engaging in caring versus uncaring behaviors.

First, in order to care about a student, a teacher must judge the relationship to be important. However, judging importance is merely the first step in moving teachers from feeling care toward engaging in caring behavior. To engage in caring behavior, teachers must believe that without action their goals (either personal or instructional) might be undermined. They must believe they are in control, or responsible and they must judge themselves to be capable of managing the relationship. Within this framework for care, teachers can think about how they create boundaries, either implicitly or explicitly, around what they will care about. Teachers may consider which relationships they care the most about, whether they care equally for all students, and when they struggle to interact with a child do they care about the failure to try to understand what happened and to modify their approach (Muller, Katz, & Dance, 1994).

CARING AS A PROFESSIONAL DISPOSITION

Other scholars such as Nel Noddings (1988) and Lisa Goldstein conceptualize caring as a process; that is, something teachers do rather than something they feel. They argue caring is an ethic, or a moral value, that teachers communicate to students through their selection of curriculum, their planning of a lesson, their establishment of classroom norms, and their interactions with students. What teachers choose to teach communicates something to students about the content they care about. The norms

Students' perceptions of caring teachers

	Feeling understood	Feeling misunderstood
Locus/sense of responsibility	Teachers press students to develop relationships with them and with peers. Teachers want to 'know' each student and want students to 'know' them. Teachers create room for students to have voice in classroom.	Teachers distance themselves emotionally. Teachers develop differential relationships; Play favorites with some students in the class.
Orientation towards classroom climate, culture, and management	Teachers monitor their levels of unpleasant emotions. Teachers endorse humanistic orientations; Are supportive of students' autonomy. Teachers emphasize social negotiation; Emphasize natural consequences for disruptive behavior.	Teachers have high levels of unpleasant emotions. Teachers endorse custodial orientations; Are more controlling of student behavior Teachers emphasize law & order and may have severe consequences for mis-behavior.
Cultural synchronization	Teachers strive to be 'in sync' with interpreting and responding to student behavior.	Teachers and students are 'out of sync' and little attempt is made to understand student behavior.
	My understanding is important	My understanding is trivial
Academic content	Teachers create meaningful intellectual boundaries. Teachers press students to understand academic material. Teachers create space in the classroom for learning from mistakes/failure.	Intellectual boundaries seem arbitrary to students. Teachers press students to perform regardless of whether they understand. Students experience failure as an endpoint, something to be feared and avoided.
Role of student interest	Teachers cultivate student interest and strive to connect content to students' lives. Teachers identify authentic tasks or emphasize future value of tasks.	Student perceive their interest is subordinate to teachers' prescribed curriculum. Students perceive academic tasks as 'work'.
Expectations of success	Teachers hold attainable, high expectations for all students. Warm demander.	Teachers hold unreasonably high, low, or differential expectations for students. Demanding

Table 1 ILLUSTRATION BY GGS INFORMATION SERVICES. CENGAGE LEARNING, GALE.

they establish communicate to their students the values they care about and their frequency and quality of interactions with individual students communicates whom they care about. From this perspective, caring is not an entity that exists or does not exist in a classroom. Rather, educators can think of caring as a vector having a direction as well as a force, with teachers exhibiting caring about content, values, and relationships in different ways.

Identifying teacher candidates and socializing the value of caring has become a central task of most teacher preparation programs. Across the literature, several qualities have been identified as epitomizing a caring disposition. Beyond teaching content, caring teachers view schooling as serving either a liberating or marginalizing function. Caring teachers identify the ways in which society, in general, and schools, in particular, maintain existing social structures and incorporate in their lesson plans ways for students to identify these inequities, engage in social critique, and work for change. Caring teachers are oriented towards advocacy for all of their students, regardless of their cultural and economic background. Moreover, they are committed to being systematically and outwardly reflective about their

work as caring teachers (E. Davis, 2006). They are so because of the strong connection identified between self-reflection and change. Teachers who are willing to question their own practice in the face of failure, question the usefulness of their beliefs, and view change as a necessary component of growth are viewed as teachers who care about their teaching.

CARING AS A QUALITY STUDENTS PERCEIVE IN A RELATIONSHIP

Much literature on caring teachers, however, has less to do with actual teacher caring and more to do with students' perceptions of teacher caring. Table 1 organizes students' perceptions into two dimensions of caring: feeling understood and feeling that understanding is important.

Feeling Understood. First and foremost, students perceive teachers as caring when they make attempts to understand and connect with their students as individuals. Teachers who assume responsibility for developing individual relationships with students and who press them to develop relationships tend to be perceived as

NURTURE YOURSELF

■

Successful teachers not only need to care for their students, they need to care for themselves also.

Set aside relaxation time. Include rest and relaxation in your daily schedule. Don't allow other obligations to encroach. This is your time to take a break from all responsibilities and recharge your batteries.

Connect with others. Spend time with positive people who enhance your life. A strong support system will buffer you from the negative effects of stress.

Do something you enjoy every day. Make time for leisure activities that bring you joy, whether it be stargazing, playing the piano, or working on your bike.

Keep your sense of humor. This includes the ability to laugh at yourself. The act of laughing helps your body fight stress in a number of ways.

caring by their students. Caring teachers may employ strategies such as personal disclosure, where they share information about themselves as a way to create space for relationships in the classroom. They cultivate a climate in their classroom where students have an "authentic" voice (Oldfather & McLaughlin, 1993). In contrast, teachers who distance themselves emotionally or develop differential relationships (Babad, 1993), where they favor some students over others, are less likely to be viewed as caring teachers.

Teachers perceived as caring tend to endorse different orientations towards classroom management and establish distinctive types of classroom climates and cultures. Julianne Turner and colleagues (1998) suggest teachers perceived as caring tend to monitor the emotional climate of the classroom—particularly with regard to the experience of unpleasant emotions (i.e. anger, frustration) in themselves and their students. Teachers perceived as uncaring tend to express higher levels of unpleasant emotions and may, in fact, use the expression of unpleasant emotions (i.e. yelling, showing disappointment) as a way to regulate their students' behavior. In contrast, students tend to characterize caring teachers' classrooms as "warm" places. Again, it is not that caring teachers avoid expressing unpleasant emotions in their classroom, but they tend to be judicious about their expression of anger, frustration, and disappointment.

Teachers perceived as caring tend to endorse more humanistic orientations towards classroom management (Willower, Eidell, & Hoy, 1976). Caring teachers view students as able to learn responsibility for self-regulating their own behavior and view themselves as participating in the process of socializing necessary skills and values. The classroom becomes a place in which students learn about the value of rules and rule making and the teacher is a conduit for understanding social order. These classrooms tend to be more supportive of students' autonomy and emphasize the value of social negotiation (DeVries & Zan, 1996; see also Reeve, 2006). In contrast, teachers endorsing more custodial orientations tend to view undisciplined behavior as an indicator of irresponsibility and respond by increasing control and enforcing punitive sanctions. Sadly, a strong emphasis on law or order, without explicit rationales, may leave students feeling manipulated. Teachers perceived as caring do have some custodial elements in their classroom; not everything is negotiable and there are consequences for poor choices. However, caring teachers are willing to negotiate some elements of classroom life, they express clear expectations for students' self-management of behavior, and they are willing to endure somewhat more interpersonal conflict in the classroom.

CARING FOR ALL STUDENTS

This task of trying to understand students becomes challenging when students and teachers come from different cultural backgrounds. Jacqueline Irvine introduced the concept of cultural synchronization to describe the ways in which conflict is generated in relationships between students of minority backgrounds and their teachers when values, patterns of interaction, and ways of being are not aligned. In two seminal studies, Monroe and Obidah (2004) and Blackburn (2005) identified the ways in which majority teachers and minority students become out of sync with each other by misinterpreting each other's intentions and actions. From this perspective, caring teachers are those who seek to develop cultural competence when interacting with students from different backgrounds (Ladson-Billings, 2001) and strive to understand the perspectives of each student in their classroom.

STUDENTS FEEL THEIR UNDERSTANDING MATTERS

The perception of caring by students also has a strong instructional component. Teachers perceived as caring delineate intellectual boundaries, including what will be learned and the standards for mastery. Caring teachers are focused on cultivating student interest in the content they are teaching and employ a variety of strategies that connect content to their students' lives. Caring teachers set high expectations for all students in their classes and press their students to understand the material, not merely for the sake of performing on a test but to understand the world around them. Among teachers who push their students to excel, what distinguishes teachers perceived as caring is the quality of their interpersonal interactions with students. Across the literature, caring teachers have been defined as warm demanders, an idea conceived by Judith Kleinfeld (1975). Warm demanders exert influence on their students' learning through their relationship. They are not willing to let a child turn in lesser quality work or fail; instead, with compassion, they express their belief that their students can do better and are willing to work with students to improve their work.

IMPLICATIONS FOR TEACHERS

To be caring means to be willing to critically evaluate what and for whom one actively cares. Doing so entails being reflective of whether there is a match or mismatch between the things one cares about and the needs of one's students. To be caring means to be thoughtful about the scope of one's caring—including the extent to which one cares about maintaining or challenging the status quo, representing an authoritative view or allowing student conceptions to be at the forefront, and to create potential for what is personal to mingle with what is academic. To end here, however, would fail to acknowledge a tension in the caring teacher literature in that teachers who care more may be more prone to feeling emotional exhaustion, to becoming burnt out and to leaving the field (Sutton & Wheatley, 2003). Finally, to be a caring teacher inherently means to identify ways to care for oneself (Ben-Ze'ev, 2006); to create healthy intellectual and interpersonal boundaries and to identify sources of support for when the task of caring for a student, or a group of students, is beyond one's resources.

SEE ALSO *Classroom Environment; School Belonging.*

BIBLIOGRAPHY

Babad, E. (1993). Teachers' differential behavior. *Educational Psychology Review, 5,* 347–376.

Ben-Ze'ev, A. (2000). *The subtlety of emotions.* Cambridge, MA: MIT Press.

Blackburn, M. (2005). Talking together for a change: Examining positioning between teachers and queer youth. In J. A. Vadeboncoeur & L. P. Stevens (Eds.) *Re-constructing "the adolescent": Sign, symbol, and body* (pp. 250–270). New York: Peter Lang.

Davis, E. A. (2006). Characterizing productive reflection among pre-service elementary teachers. *Teaching and Teacher Education, 22,* 281–301.

Davis, H. A. (2003). Conceptualizing the role and influence of student-teacher relationships on children's social and cognitive development. *Educational Psychologist, 38,* 207–234.

Davis, H. A. (2006). Exploring the contexts of relationship quality between middle school students and teachers. *The Elementary School Journal: Special Issue on the Interpersonal Contexts of Motivation and Learning, 106,* 193–223.

DeVries, R., & Zan, B. (1996). A constructivist perspective on the role of the socio-moral atmosphere in promoting children's development. In C. T. Fosnot (Ed.), *Constructivism: Theory, perspectives, and practice* (pp. 103–119). New York: Teachers College Press. Goldstein, L. S. (1999). The relational zone: The role of caring relationships in the construction of mind. *American Educational Research Journal, 36,* 647–673.

Irvine, J. J. (1990). *Black students and school failure: Policies, practices, and prescriptions.* New York: Praeger.

Kleinfeld, J. (1975). Effective teachers of Eskimo and Indian students. *School Review, 83,* 301–344.

Moje, E. B. (1996). "I teach students, not subjects": Teacher-student relationships as contexts for secondary literacy. *Reading Research Quarterly, 31,* 172–195.

Monroe, C. R., & Obidah, J. E. (2004). The influence of cultural synchronization on a teacher's perceptions of disruption: A case study of an African American middle-school classroom. *Journal of Teacher Education, 5,* 256–268.

Muller, C., Katz, S., & Dance, L. (1999). Investing in teaching and learning. Dynamics of the teacher-student relationship from each perspective. *Urban Education, 34,* 292–337.

Noblit, G. (1993). Power and caring. *American Educational Research Journal, 30,* 23–38.

Noddings, N. (1988). An ethic of caring and its implication for instructional arrangements. *American Journal of Education, 96,* 215–230.

Oldfather, P., & McLaughlin, H. J. (1993). Gaining and losing voice: A longitudinal study of students' continuing impulse to learn across elementary middle level contexts. *Research in Middle Level Education, 17,* 1–25.

Pianta, R. C. (1999). *Enhancing relationships between children and teachers.* Washington, DC: American Psychological Association.

Reeve, J. (2006). Teachers as facilitators: What autonomy-supportive teachers do and why their students benefit. *Elementary School Journal, 106,* 225–236.

Sutton, R. E., & Wheatley, K. F. (2003). Teachers' emotions and teaching: A review of the literature and directions for future research. *Educational Psychology Review, 15,* 327–358.

Turner, J. C., Meyer, D. K., Cox, K. C., Logan, C., DiCintio, M., & Thomas, C. T. (1998). Creating contexts for involvement in mathematics. *Journal of Educational Psychology, 90,* 730–745.

Ward, J. R., & McCotter, S. S. (2004). Reflection as a visible outcome for pre-service teachers. *Teaching and Teacher Education, 20,* 243–257.

Ware, F. (2006). Warm demander pedagogy: Culturally responsive teaching that supports a culture of achievement for African American students. *Urban Education, 41,* 427–456.

Willower, D. J., Eidell, T. L., & Hoy, W. K. (1967). *The school and pupil control ideology.* Penn State Studies Monograph No. 24. University Park: Pennsylvania State University.

Heather A. Davis

CASE-BASED LEARNING

SEE *Constructivism: Case-Based Learning.*

CHEATING

Academic cheating appears in a variety of forms and at the heart of each is an attempt to convince others that one has higher academic skills, abilities, or potential, or

Cheating appears to be fairly prevalent at every educational level. **PHOTOS_ALYSON/TAXI/GETTY IMAGES.**

that one exerts more academic effort than is actually the case. Amid multitude of definitions for cheating, Garavalia, Olson, Russell, and Christensen noted that common components are the use or provision of unauthorized means of information in a setting in which there are assessment consequences for the performance. Cizek classified forms of cheating into four categories: the unapproved transfer of information between individuals, the use of unapproved materials, exploiting weaknesses in others, and plagiarism. Many cheating behaviors consist of elements from multiple categories. Cheating may be engaged in for one's own interest and also in the interest of others such as one's peers, students, or children.

PREVALENCE OF ACADEMIC CHEATING

The prevalence of cheating is difficult to estimate because few reliable sources for cheating information exist. Students have strong incentives to underreport their cheating and may have difficulty estimating the cheating that

occurs in their schools. Cheating that is not discovered obviously goes unrecognized by teachers and thus is not reported. Additionally, individuals may hold different definitions of cheating—staying home from school on the day of a test may be viewed differently from bringing a cheat sheet into a test. As Whitley concluded, in part due to these issues, reports of the percentage of students who cheat vary from 5 to 95%. However, some trends have been identified.

Cheating appears to be fairly prevalent at every educational level. According to Cizek, one-third of elementary students report having cheated and, according to Evans and Craig, just over 60% of middle school students report that they know when cheating occurs in their classes but rarely complain about cheating to peers or teachers. A nationally representative survey of youth conducted by the Josephson Institute of Ethics revealed that 38% of middle school students and 60% of high school students cheated on a test during the prior school year and approximately 24% of middle schools students and 33% of those in high school used unauthorized information from the Internet to complete out-of-class assignments. Both test cheating and plagiarism increase fairly steadily from grades 6 through 12.

Although widespread cheating also occurs in college, most of the available data suggest there is less academic dishonesty in higher education than in high school but in the 1990s and early 2000s rates appeared to increase. Self-reports of college cheating increased from 63% in 1963 to 70% in 1993 according to McCabe and Bowers. Investigations conducted by Newstead, Franklyn-Stokes, and Armstead, and separately by Schab revealed that college students report higher levels of cheating in science, technology, and math courses than in other domains. Compared to liberal arts majors and education majors, Baird found that business majors were more likely to report cheating on unit tests and to conceal professor errors and were less likely to disapprove of cheating. Similarly, McCabe, Butterfield, and Trevino found that graduate students in business reported cheating at a higher rate (56%) than graduate students in other fields (47%).

TYPICAL CHEATING METHODS

As reflected in a review of the research on cheating methods conducted by Garavalia and colleagues, the most comprehensive studies of the relative frequency of cheating methods have used samples of college students. When these authors asked college students how students cheat on graded work, more students listed at least one non-technological method than at least one technological method (84% versus 34%). Fifty-two percent of these students reported at least one method that did not require collaboration with others while 40% reported at least one method that did require collaboration.

Newstead and colleagues reported on the frequency of various specific behaviors at the college level. These data reveal multiple forms of plagiarism are common. Many students report having copied text from a source without a citation (42%), paraphrasing from a source without a citation (54%), inventing data (48%), allowing one's coursework to be copied by others (46%), and padding bibliographies (44%).

Students admitted to a number of coursework shortcuts. Many students reported copying other students' work with their knowledge (36%) or taking individual credit for collaborative work (18%). Students also cooperated by agreeing to mark peer-graded work too generously (29%) or doing others' work for them (16%). Frequently reported deceitful behaviors also included falsifying data (37%), hiding books or articles so peers cannot access them (32%), and lying about personal circumstances in order to get extensions or exemptions (11%). In testing situations, 13% of students copied exam answers from others without their knowledge. Relatively fewer students reported taking unauthorized

material into tests (8%), plotting in advance to get information on the exam (5%), or lying about circumstances to get special privileges by the examiner (4%).

Technological advances have increased the methods and opportunities for cheating. Students store and retrieve information in programmable calculators, MP3 players and cell phones during exams. They text message one another during exams and use portable electronic devices to illegally access the Internet. The World Wide Web has simplified plagiarism on take-home essay exams and papers, with numerous Web sites that will provide any sort of assignment for a price, and large volumes of easily accessible information that can be plagiarized.

PERCEPTIONS OF CHEATING SEVERITY

Evans and Craig found at the middle and high school levels, perceptions of cheating severity differ between students and teachers. According to Kohn, these perceptions also vary among teachers within a given school. For example, one teacher's assignments require collaboration in order to be completed, whereas another teacher will classify collaborative behavior as cheating. In a study of undergraduate students and instructors, Whitley and Keith-Spiegel (2002) found that other behaviors that are viewed as cheating by some and as honest by others include collaboration without specific permission, submitting a single paper for more than one class, and copying homework. However, there is general agreement that copying or using a cheat sheet during an exam and purchasing papers to submit as one's own work both qualify as cheating.

PREDICTORS OF CHEATING

In 1928, Hartshorne and May conducted the most well known study of dishonesty. Although the initial goal of the study was to determine the characteristics associated with people who made more or fewer moral decisions, their data revealed that people's behavior has little cross-situational consistency. Although many of the thousands of students they studied cheated on their schoolwork some of the time, few students cheated in every assessment situation and making the decision to be honest in the classroom was not always consistent with their behavior in other domains. Murdock and Stephens found that efforts to identify the profile of the moral student typically account for a small amount of the variance in students' actual behavior. As such, the view of as students' dishonesty as a resulting from the interaction between their personal choice and the specific environment permeates most theoretical models that have attempted to provide a framework for understanding cheating. Examples of such perspectives are Whitely's model of cheating as reasoned action, and Murdock and Anderman's motivational model of cheating.

INDIVIDUAL DIFFERENCE PREDICTORS OF ACADEMIC DISHONESTY

Findings from self-report suggest that students who engage in academic dishonesty differ in several ways from those who do not, including attitudes about cheating, views about themselves, and demographic characteristics. Whitley found that compared to those who do not cheat, cheaters in college hold more positive attitudes toward cheating and do not feel as strong a moral obligation to avoid cheating. They also view themselves as less generally honest, as lacking study skills, and as under pressure to achieve success. However, there are not strong achievement differences between cheaters and non-cheaters.

Miller, Murdock, Anderman, and Poindexter reported that college students are more likely to engage in academic dishonesty when they are younger or unmarried. In contrast, children in K-12 schools are more likely to cheat when they are older or in higher grade levels. Although researchers find no documented gender differences in cheating rates when actual cheating behavior is observed, men admit to more dishonesty when the information is self-reported. There are no such gender differences, however, when asked specifically about their cheating in the service of others.

CONTEXTUAL PREDICTORS OF ACADEMIC DISHONESTY

As described above, those who cheat also justify cheating more than those who do not. Several environmental factors influence perceived justifiability of cheating and whether cheating actually occurs, including peer norms, classroom factors, and facets of students' lives outside of school. Students may look to their peers for signs regarding whether cheating is justified. Whitely found students who cheat report that more of their peers cheat. Also, teachers' practices and interpersonal behaviors can influence cheating. Murdock, Miller, and Goetzinger found that students justify cheating based on poor pedagogy, testing practices, and student-teacher relationships.

The goals that teachers create for their classrooms can influence cheating. Interest or improvement objectives are more attainable than performance-related objectives. Anderman found that through assignments, assessments, and feedback, teachers who demonstrate that they are less concerned with learning or improvement and instead have set a predetermined standard for students to meet will increase the likelihood that their students will cheat. Similarly, Schraw and colleagues found that in contexts in which students work in order to earn a grade instead of to pursue an interest, students are more likely to cheat.

Clear instructional objectives in combination with active facilitation of students' progress towards those objectives improve the attainability of success and, according to Whitely and Keith-Spiegel (2002), reduce the likelihood of cheating. Through these and similar behaviors, teachers can convey respect and fairness toward students. Cheating is also reduced when these methods are reflected in tests that are aligned with the content being taught and that are not unreasonably difficult or long. Additionally, according to Anderman, cheating is less prevalent when scoring is criterion-referenced rather than norm-referenced (scored on a curve).

Finally, students' environments outside the classroom can influence the cheating that occurs inside the classroom. When students experience undue pressure to attain certain grades or when they have insufficient time to prepare for their courses, success becomes less attainable and cheating becomes more likely, according to Whitley.

PREVENTION OF CHEATING IN THE CLASSROOM

Cheating prevention research has been focused on college classrooms; however, the information gained from this work is likely applicable to other educational settings. While some schools implement formal honor codes, institutions' actual commitment to integrity is more important for reducing cheating than the existence of a code, according to McCabe and Trevino. Further, Whitely and Keith-Speigel (2001) found that institutions must model this commitment in order to minimize academic dishonesty. McCabe, Trevino, and Butterfield advocated communicating clear expectations for honest behavior, including explicit definitions of honesty; communicating clear consequences for dishonest behavior; and enforcing those consequences.

Clarity is also important in terms of educational objectives. Teachers must set and communicate clear objectives in order to reduce the likelihood of cheating. These objectives should drive instruction and assessment so that students can predict and prepare for tests instead of being surprised by test content. Also, students' progress towards these objectives should be supported through scaffolding and frequent assessments. Frequent assessments help ensure that students are progressing toward objectives at the expected pace, limiting the need for cramming before a major exam, and also result in more evaluations that contribute relatively less to the final grade, as opposed to one or two high-stakes exams.

As described above, students are less likely to cheat when they are interested in the content and are working to learn rather than to earn a grade. This can be accomplished through several means. First, teachers should seek student input into content or allow students to choose specific topics for projects or papers. Second, tasks and assignments should be constructed so that they are at levels of challenge appropriate for students. Finally, teachers should strive to create an atmosphere that is safe for and encouraging of student curiosity, risk-taking, and improvement.

In addition to pedagogical and interpersonal choices, teachers can take steps to reduce cheating through the way they format and administer exams. Multiple versions of the same test can be useful, but these versions must be carefully designed and implemented as students taking tests with scattered questions are able to cheat equally as well as students taking a single-version test, according to Houston. For multiple-choice tests, it is important to randomize question stems as well as answer options across versions. For open response tests, question order can be randomized and certain details of the questions, such as numbers, should be changed, if possible. Also for open response tests, teachers should distribute a blank piece of paper so students can cover their answers. Most exams that are delivered in online formats have features to reduce the likelihood of cheating such as set time limits and delivery of a random set of items and responses from a larger database. Without photographic or fingerprint identification, however, it is impossible to know who actually takes an online exam.

Teachers can take several steps to make cheating from multiple versions more difficult. When using multiple versions, it is important that the versions are not easily distinguishable. Also, depending on the space available, and thus how far apart students can be seated, two to four test versions may be necessary. Houston noted that assigning seating has the added benefit of preventing students from choosing cheating partners. Even with multiple test versions teachers must prevent students from accessing tests ahead of time. Cizek suggested that teachers create different sets of test versions for different administration days and times, keep paper copies locked or only keep electronic files of tests, and create new tests for every year.

Teachers can communicate respect to students to help reduce rates of cheating. While teachers may think that their own lax behavior during test sessions signifies respect, Cizek noted that it actually increases cheating and frustrates students who expect teachers to monitor the testing environment and are bothered if teachers are ignoring classmates' obvious cheating. Teachers can show students that they expect honest academic behavior by appearing aware of the class, noticing and acting on questionable behavior, and moving through the classroom during the test.

In addition to cheating on exams, plagiarism is another form of academic dishonesty that teachers can work to reduce. Just as multiple versions of a test can block attempts to cheat, creating new essay assignments can thwart plagiarism. Teachers can make widely available Internet essays useless by assigning less typical essays

and requiring students to tailor their essays to a particular context or to develop their own opinion. There are also commercially available tools, such as turnitin.com that check students' work against large-scale databases of other work and provide the instructor and student with a redundancy index.

As noted earlier, frequent assessments help eliminate cheating and requiring students to submit their work at several stages of progress can minimize plagiarism. For students who procrastinate or who are overscheduled, more frequent deadlines can reduce the need to anxiously complete an assignment during the days before the due date, possibly leading to drastic and dishonest measures. Also, feedback on students' progress supports their efforts to learn and helps clarify the objectives or requirements of the assignment, perhaps minimizing the perceived need to cheat.

SEE ALSO *Moral Development; Moral Education.*

BIBLIOGRAPHY

Anderman, E. M. (2007). The effects of personal, classroom, and school goal structures on academic cheating. In E. M. Anderman & T. B. Murdock (Eds.), *Psychology of academic cheating* (pp. 87–105). Burlington, MA: Elsevier.

Baird, J. S. (1980). Current trends in college cheating. *Psychology in the Schools, 17,* 515–522.

Cizek, G. J. (1999). *Cheating on tests: How to do it, detect it, and prevent it.* Mahwah, NJ: Erlbaum.

Evans, E. D., & Craig, D. (1990). Teacher and student perceptions of academic cheating in middle and senior high schools. *Journal of Educational Research, 84,* 44–52.

Garavalia, L., Olson, E., Russell, E., & Christensen, L. (2007). How do students cheat? In E. M. Anderman & T. B. Murdock (Eds.), *Psychology of academic cheating* (pp. 33–58). Burlington, MA: Elsevier.

Hartshorne, H., & May, M. A. (1928). *Studies in deceit.* New York: Macmillan.

Houston, J. P. (1983). Alternate test forms as a means of reducing multiple-choice answer copying in the classroom. *Journal of Educational Psychology, 75,* 572–575.

Josephson Institute of Ethics. (2006). *Youth ethics report card.* Retrieved April 10, 2008 from http://charactercounts.org/programs/reportcard/2006/index.html.

Kohn, A. (2007). Foreword. In E. M. Anderman & T. B. Murdock (Eds.), *Psychology of academic cheating* (pp. xi–xix). Burlington, MA: Elsevier.

McCabe, D. L., & Bowers, W. J. (1996). The relationship between student cheating and college fraternity or sorority membership. *NASPA Journal, 33,* 280–291.

McCabe, D. L., Butterfield, K. D., & Trevino, L. K. (2006). Academic dishonesty in graduate business programs: Prevalence, causes, and proposed action. *Academy of Management Learning and Education, 5,* 294–305.

McCabe, D. L., & Trevino, L. K. (1993). Academic dishonesty: Honor codes and other contextual influences. *Journal of Higher Education, 64,* 522–538.

McCabe, D., Trevino, L. K., & Butterfield, K. D. (1999). Academic integrity in honor code and non-honor code environments: A qualitative investigation. *Journal of Higher Education, 70,* 211–234.

Miller, A. D., Murdock, T. B., Anderman, E. M., & Poindexter, A. L. (2007). Who are all these cheaters? Characteristics of students who are academically dishonest. In E. M. Anderman & T. B. Murdock (Eds.), *Psychology of academic cheating* (pp. 9–32). Burlington, MA: Elsevier.

Murdock, T. B., & Anderman, E. M. (2006). Motivational approaches to classroom cheating: Towards an integrated model of academic dishonesty. *Educational Psychologist, 41,* 129–145.

Murdock, T. B., Miller, A. D., & Goetzinger, A. A. (2007). The effects of classroom context variables on university students' judgments of the acceptability of cheating: Mediating and moderating processes. *Social Psychology of Education, 10,* 141–169.

Murdock, T. B., & Stephens, J. M. (2007). Is cheating wrong? Students' reasoning about academic dishonesty. In E. M. Anderman & T. B. Murdock (Eds.), *Psychology of academic cheating* (pp. 229–253). Burlington, MA: Elsevier.

Newstead, S. E., Franklyn-Stokes, A., & Armstead, P. (1996). Individual differences in student cheating. *Journal of Educational Psychology, 88,* 229–241.

Schab, F. (1991). Schooling without learning: Thirty years of cheating in high school. *Adolescence, 26,* 839–847.

Schraw, G., Olafson, L., Kuch, F., Lehman, T., Lehman, S., & McCrudden, M. T. (2007). Interest and academic cheating. In E. M. Anderman & T. B. Murdock (Eds.), *Psychology of academic cheating* (pp. 58–85). Burlington, MA: Elsevier.

Whitley, B. E., Jr. (1998). Factors associated with cheating among college students: A review. *Research in Higher Education, 39,* 235–274.

Whitley, B. E., Jr., & Keith-Speigel, P. C. (2001). Academic integrity as an institutional issue. *Ethics and Behavior, 11,* 325–342.

Whitley, B. E., Jr., & Keith-Spiegel, P. (2002). *Academic dishonesty: An educator's guide.* Mahwah, NJ: Erlbaum.

Anne Beauchamp
Tamera B. Murdock

CHILDHOOD

SEE *Early Childhood Development.*

CLARK, KENNETH BANCROFT
1914–2005

Kenneth Bancroft Clark was born in 1914 in the Republic of Panama. Jones and Pettigrew note that he earned both a bachelor's and a master's degree from Howard University. In 1940 Clark became the first African American to obtain a Ph.D. in psychology from Columbia University. Through-

Kenneth B. Clark in his office, May 29, 1975. **HULTON ARCHIVE/GETTY IMAGES.**

out his career, Clark received honorary degrees from several colleges and universities, including Oberlin, Amherst, Haverford, Tuskegee, Columbia, and Princeton. Clark was the first African American president of the American Psychological Association (APA), a position he held from 1970 to 1971. According to Pickren and Tomes, Clark was instrumental in the establishment of the APA's Board of Social and Ethical Responsibility of Psychology, which was charged with a number of tasks, including monitoring discrimination by APA vendors, researching social problems, and developing ethical guidelines for research and assessment. He was the president of the Society for the Psychological Study of Social Issues from 1959 to 1960. Clark was also the director of Metropolitan Applied Research, Inc., and president of the Society for the Psychological Study of Social Issues from 1959 to 1960. In 1978 Clark received the first annual Distinguished Contribution to Psychology in the Public Interest Award from APA.

Clark taught psychology at Howard University from 1937 to 1938 and Hampton University from 1940 to 1941. Clark joined the faculty of City College of New York in 1942, becoming an assistant professor seven years later and, by 1960, a full professor—the first African American academic to be so honored in the history of New York's city colleges. He remained at City College until his retirement in 1975. Clark also served as a visiting professor at Columbia University, Harvard University, and the University of California at Berkeley. In 1962 Clark helped establish Harlem Youth Opportunities Unlimited, designed to help reduce unemployment, school dropout rates, and to prevent juvenile delinquency in the city. The *American Psychologist* notes that Clark was the president from its establishment in 1975 until 1986 of Clark, Phipps, Clark, and Harris, Inc., a consulting firm with a focus on affirmative action, human relations, and race relations.

Clark's most notable research collaborator was his wife, Mamie Phipps Clark (1917–1983). Together, Kenneth and Mamie Clark are best known for their focus on race relations and civil rights in education. Much of their work in this area concerned several experimental studies that explored racial identity and racial preferences in African American children. Among these studies are the line drawing tests and the more widely known "doll studies".

In 1939, for example, Kenneth and Mamie Clark designed a study to investigate the development of self and racial consciousness in African American preschool children. One hundred fifty African American children, ages three to five, were shown different combinations of line drawings of African American boys, Caucasian boys, and irrelevant objects, for example, a lion, a dog, a clown, and a hen. The young male participants were asked, "Show me which one is you. Which one is (name of subject)?" The young female participants were asked to identify a brother, cousin, or African American male playmate. As a whole, the African American participants chose the African American male line drawing more often than the Caucasian male line drawing. As age increased, the African American participants chose the African American male line drawing significantly more often than the Caucasian male line drawing. Also, the majority of participants chose a human line drawing significantly more than the irrelevant objects.

In that same year, Clark and his wife began examining racial preferences in African American children using African American and Caucasian dolls. A total of over 300 African American children between the ages of 3 and 9 were shown an African American and Caucasian doll. The dolls were identical except for skin color. The Clarks served as the primary investigators; they asked the participants a series of questions designed to probe the participants' racial and skin color preferences and, thus, provide insight into their racial identities. In particular, the participants were asked which doll they would like to play with, which doll was good, bad, nice, and which doll looked the most like them.

Over 90% of the children identified the African American doll as resembling themselves. However, over half of the children tested designated the Caucasian doll as the nice doll and the doll they wanted to play with. These same participants regarded the African American doll as the bad doll. Clark concluded that the children had suffered damage to their self-esteem and self-image due to segregation and the pervasive negative perception of African Americans. For the Clarks, the participants' choices were reactions to the pressures associated with being African American in the racially segregated South.

Clark's doll study results were integral to school desegregation during the 1950s. His testimony during the Supreme Court case, *Brown v. Board of Education, Topeka,*

Kansas, outlined the detrimental psychological effects of segregation on both African American and Caucasian children. While heralded for his significant contribution to the study of racial identity among African Americans, Phillips notes that Clark later was criticized for his advocacy for mainstream integration and for criticizing the Black Power movement. Kenneth Clark died May 1, 2005, at the age of 90.

SEE ALSO *Ethnic Identity and Academic Achievement.*

BIBLIOGRAPHY

WORKS BY

Clark, K. B. (1954). Some principles related to the problem of desegregation. *Journal of Negro Education, 23,* 339–347.

Clark, K. B. (1965). *Dark Ghetto.* New York: Harper & Row.

Clark, K. B. & Clark, M. P. (1939). The development of consciousness of self and the emergence of racial identification in negro preschool children. *Journal of Social Psychology, SPSSI Bulletin, 10,* 591–599.

Clark, K. B., & Clark M. P. (1939). Segregation as a factor in racial identification in Negro preschool children, a preliminary report. *Journal of Experimental Education, 8,* 161–163.

Clark, K. B. & Clark, M. P (1940). Skin color as a factor in racial identification of Negro preschool children. *Journal of Social Psychology, SPSSI Bulletin, 11,* 159–169.

Clark, K. B., & Clark, M. P. (1947). Racial identification preferences in Negro children. In E. Macoby, T. M. Newcomb, & E. H. Hartley (Eds.), *Readings in social psychology.* New York: Hold, Rinehart & Winston.

WORKS ABOUT

Distinguished contribution to psychology in the public interest award for 1978 (1979). *American Psychologist, 34,* 65–68.

Jones, J. M., & Pettigrew, T. F. (2005). Kenneth B. Clark (1914–2005) obituary. *American Psychologist, 60,* 649–651.

Phillips, L. (2000). Recontextualizing Kenneth B. Clark: An Afro-centric perspective on the paradoxical legacy of a model psychologist-activist. In Pickren, W. E. & Dewsbuury, D. A. (Eds.). *Evolving perspectives on the history of psychology.* Washington, DC: American Psychological Association.

Pickren, W. E. & Tomes, H. (2002). The legacy of Kenneth B. Clark to the APA: The board of social and ethical responsibility for psychology. *American Psychologist, 57*(1), 51-59.

Kenneth M. Tyler

CLASS SIZE

The consensus among many in education that smaller classes allow a better quality of teaching and learning has led to a policy of class size reductions (CSR) by a number of U.S. states, by the United Kingdom (UK) and Netherlands, and Asia Pacific countries as diverse as New Zealand and China. This policy is contentious, though: Some argue that the effects of CSR are modest and that there are other more cost-effective strategies for improving educational standards (Slavin, 1989; Rivkin, Hanushek, & Kain, 2000; Hattie, 2005).

Despite the important policy and practice implications of the topic, the research literature on the educational effects of class-size differences has not been clear. However, more recent research and reviews provide some answers, and this entry addresses whether class-size differences affect children's educational attainment and learning and classroom processes such as teaching and pupil behavior.

CLASS SIZE AND ACADEMIC ACHIEVEMENT

Overall, much previous research has not had designs strong enough to draw reliable conclusions (Blatchford, Goldstein, & Mortimore, 1998). It has long been recognized, for example, that simple correlational designs, which examine associations between a measure of class size or pupil-teacher ratios, on the one hand, and measures of pupil attainment on the other are misleading because researchers often do not know whether the results can be explained by another factor, for example, that poorer performing pupils are placed in smaller classes. To arrive at more valid evidence two kinds of research design have been used.

Experimental Studies. The frequent assumption that the problems of correlational research are best overcome by the use of experimental research or randomized controlled trials, offers one reason for the great attention paid to the Tennessee STAR project. A cohort of pupils and teachers at kindergarten through third grade were assigned at random to three types of class within the same school: a small class (around 17 pupils), a regular (typical) class (around 23 students), and a regular class with a teacher-aide. In brief, the researchers found that in both reading and mathematics pupils in small classes performed significantly better than pupils in regular classes, and children from minority ethnic group backgrounds benefited most from small classes (Finn & Achilles, 1999; Nye, Hedges, & Konstantopoulos, 2000). In fourth grade the pupils returned to regular classes and the experiment ended, but gains were still evident after the following three years, that is, grades 4–6 (Word, Johnston, Bain, & Fulton, 1990).

Longitudinal Studies. There are some difficulties (e.g., concerning validity) with experimental studies (Goldstein & Blatchford, 1998), and an alternative approach is to set up longitudinal studies that measure the full range of class sizes and account statistically for other possibly confounding factors, including pupil differences at an earlier point. This approach was adopted in a large-scale UK study (Class Size and Pupil Adult Ratio, CSPAR) project (Blatchford, 2003; Blatchford, Bassett, Goldstein, & Martin, 2003; Blatchford, Moriarty, Edmonds, &

Martin, 2002). This project tracked over 10,000 pupils in over 300 schools from school entry (at 4–5 years) to the end of the primary school stage (11 years). It used a multi-method approach and sophisticated multi-level regression statistical analyses.

The study found a clear effect of class size differences on children's academic attainment over the first year (4–5 years) in both literacy and mathematics. The effect size was comparable to that reported by the STAR project, and this trend is therefore supported by both experimental and non-experimental research designs. Small classes (fewer than 25) worked best in literacy for children with the lowest school entry scores who had most ground to make up. Effects of class size in the first year were still evident on literacy progress at the end of the second year of school, though by the end of the third year the effects were not clear. There were no clear longer-term effects of class size differences on mathematics achievement. Though this result indicates that the early benefits disappear after two years in school, there were no restrictions in terms of which size of class they moved to from year to year (in contrast with the STAR project).

The CSPAR's naturalistic design captured changes in class sizes from year to year. An important disruption effect on children's educational progress was found, that is, moving to a class of a different size, especially a larger class, had a negative effect on progress.

POSSIBLE EFFECTS OF CLASS SIZE ON TEACHERS AND PUPILS

Despite the widely held view that small classes will lead to a better quality of teaching and learning, the research evidence has not been clear. One reason is the often-anecdotal nature of much research. Finn, Pannozzo, and Achiles (2003) point out the need for systematic, preferably observational, research in this field. Overall, reviews of research suggest that class size effects are likely to be not singular but multiple, and that it is difficult in one study to capture all the complexities involved.

Effects on Teachers. Perhaps the most consistent finding is that class size affects individualization of teaching. The smaller the class, the greater the likelihood is that a teacher will spend more time with individual pupils. In smaller classes there also tends to be more teaching overall. Large classes present more challenges for classroom management, pupil control, and marking, planning, and assessment. Teachers are put under more strain when faced with large classes. Qualitative studies suggest that in smaller classes it can be easier for teachers to spot problems and give feedback, identify specific needs and gear teaching to meet them, and set individual targets for pupils. Teachers also experience better relationships with, and have more knowledge of, individual pupils.

Effects on Pupils. Finn, Pannozzo, and Achiles (2003) conclude that students in small classes in the elementary grades are more engaged in learning behaviors, and they display less disruptive behavior than do students in larger classes. The CSPAR study found in the case of four to five year old pupils more disengagement in large classes but no effects in 10 to 11 year old pupils, possibly because of assessment and curriculum pressures at that age. In large classes pupils were more likely to simply listen to the teacher while in smaller classes pupils interacted in an active way with teachers, by initiating, responding, and sustaining contact (Blatchford, Bassett, & Brown, 2005).

Curriculum Effects. Research shows a moderating role of school subject on relationships between class size and classroom processes. Rice (1999) found that in mathematics, but not science, as class size increased, less time was spent on small groups and individuals, innovative instructional practices, and whole group discussions. In the CSPAR study, the overall effects of class size on individualized attention were found in all subjects but English. One direction for future research is to identify more precisely ways in which class size effects vary in relation to particular school subjects and student age.

IMPLICATIONS FOR POLICY AND PRACTICE

Overall, results suggest that while small classes will not make a bad teacher a good one, they can allow teachers to be more effective; conversely, large classes inevitably present all teachers with difficulties and the need for compromises. Small classes can offer opportunities for teachers to teach better (Anderson, 2000) or, to use a different term, they can create facilitating conditions for teachers to teach and students to learn (Wang & Finn, 2000).

Age of Pupil. Research shows that the age of the child needs to be taken into account when class size effects are considered. There is a clear case for small class sizes in the first years of school. Results show where resources could be further targeted, that is, classes smaller than about 20 to 25 for those with most ground to make up in literacy skills. Another policy implication is to maintain smaller classes across years where possible.

Age versus Start Up Effect. Research also suggests that class-size reduction initiatives are best seen as a policy of prevention but not remediation, in the sense that the evidence supports the use of small classes immediately after entry to school, but there is little evidence that small classes introduced later in children's school lives are as

effective. However, there is still the possibility that smaller classes may be advantageous at later strategic points of transition in students' school lives, for example, in the first year of secondary education. Research evidence on this possibility is needed.

Implications for Practice. It has often been pointed out that teachers do not necessarily change the way they teach when faced with smaller classes, and this fact might well account for the relatively modest effects of class size on achievement. Blatchford, Russell, Bassett, Brown, and Martin (2007) have suggested several ways in which CSR can be accompanied by pedagogical changes to enhance beneficial effects for students, for example, taking advantage of the possibilities of increased individualization; adopting more adventurous and flexible teaching; and implementing more effective collaborative learning between pupils. Some have argued that teacher professional development is a better investment than CSR, but it is preferable not to see them in opposition. Rather, professional development should be used to help teachers see pedagogical opportunities in small classes and develop strategies for realizing educational objectives in small (and large) classes.

BIBLIOGRAPHY

Anderson, L. (2000). Why should reduced class size lead to increased student achievement? In M. C. Wang & J. D. Finn (Eds.), *How small classes help teachers do their best* (pp. 3–24). Philadelphia: Temple University Center for Research in Human Development and Education.

Biddle, B. J., & Berliner, D. C. (2002). What research says about small classes and their effects. Retrieved April 10, 2008 from http://www.wested.org/online_pubs/small_classes.pdf.

Blatchford, P. (2003). *The class size debate: Is small better?* Maidenhead: Open University Press.

Blatchford, P., Bassett, P., & Brown, P. (2005). Teachers' and pupils' behaviour in large and small classes: A systematic observation study of pupils aged 10–11 years. *Journal of Educational Psychology, 97*(3), 454–467.

Blatchford, P., Bassett, P., Goldstein, H., and Martin, C. (2003). Are class size differences related to pupils' educational progress and classroom processes? Findings from the Institute of Education class size study of children aged 5–7 years. In S. Gorrard, C. Taylor, & K. Roberts (guest eds.), special issue, *In Praise of Educational Research*, in *British Educational Research Journal, 29*(5), 709–730.

Blatchford, P., Goldstein, H., & Mortimore, P. (1998). Research on class size effects: A critique of methods and a way forward. *International Journal of Educational Research, 29*, 691–710.

Blatchford, P., Moriarty, V., Edmonds, S., & Martin, C. (2002). Relationships between class size and teaching: A multi-method analysis of English infant schools. *American Educational Research Journal, 39*(1), 101–132 (2002, Spring).

Blatchford, P., & Mortimore, P. (1994). The issue of class size in schools: What can we learn from research? *Oxford Review of Education, 20*(4), 411–428.

Blatchford, P., Russell, A., Bassett, P., Brown, P., and Martin, C. (2007). The effect of class size on the teaching of pupils aged 7–11 years. *School Effectiveness and Improvement, 18*(2), 147–172 (2007, June).

Cooper, H. M. (1989). Does reducing student-to-teacher ratios affect achievement? *Educational Psychologist, 24*(1), 79–98.

Ehrenberg, R. G., Brewer, D. J., Gamoran, A., and Willms, J. D. (2001). Class size and student achievement. *Psychological Science in the Public Interest, 2*(1) (May). Retrieved April 10, 2008, from http://www.psychologicalscience.org/journals/pspi/pdf/pspi2_1.pdf.

Finn, J. D., & Achilles, C. M. (1999). Tennessee's class size study: Findings, implications, misconceptions. *Educational Evaluation and Policy Analysis, 21*(2), 97–109.

Finn, J. D., Pannozzo, G. M., and Achiles, C. M. (2003). The 'why's' of class size: Student behaviour in small classes. *Review of Educational Research, 73*(3), 321–368.

Galton, M. (1998). Class size: A critical comment on the research. *International Journal of Educational Research, 29*, 809–818.

Grissmer, D. (1999). Class size effects: Assessing the evidence, its policy implications, and future research agenda. *Educational Evaluation and Policy Analysis, 21*(2), 231–248.

Hattie, J. (2005). The paradox of reducing class size and improving learning outcomes. *International Journal of Educational Research, 43*, 387–425.

Nye, B., Hedges, L. V., & Konstantopoulos, S. (2000). The effects of small classes on academic achievement: The results of the Tennessee class size experiment. *American Educational Research Journal, 37*(1), 123–151.

Rice, J. K. (1999). The impact of class size on instructional strategies and the use of time in high school mathematics and science courses. *Educational Evaluation and Policy Analysis, 21*(2), 215–229.

Rivkin, S. G., Hanushek, E.A., & Kain, J. F. (2000). Teachers, schools, and achievement. Retrieved April 10, 2008, from http://csab.wustl.edu/workingpapers/Hanushek_Kain_Rivkin_1.pdf.

Slavin, R. E. (1989). Class size and student achievement: Small effects of small classes. *Educational Psychologist, 24*, 99–110.

Wang, M. C., & Finn, J. D. (2000). Small classes in practice: the next steps. In M. C. Wang and J. D. Finn (Eds.), *How small classes help teachers do their best*. Philadelphia: Temple University Center for Research in Human Development.

Word, E. R., Johnston, J., Bain, H. P., & Fulton, B. D. (1990). *The state of Tennessee's student/teacher achievement ratio (STAR) project: Technical report 1985–90*. Nashville: Tennessee State University.

Peter Blatchford

CLASSICAL CONDITIONING

Associative learning occurs when an organism links two or more items of information. The simplest forms of associative learning are classical conditioning and instrumental conditioning. Classical conditioning is also known as Pavlovian conditioning in honor of Ivan Pavlov (1849–1936) who was the first person to conduct extensive research of this nature. In a typical experiment with dogs, Pavlov would present a neutral auditory stimulus such as a metronome immediately before applying sand or food powder to the dog's tongue, which produced salivation. After a number of these pairings, Pavlov presented the metronome alone, and the dog now salivated. Pavlov developed terminology for these components of classical conditioning: The dog experienced a relatively neutral stimulus or conditioned stimulus (CS, the metronome) in conjunction with a biologically significant stimulus or unconditioned stimulus (US, the food powder), which always produces an unconditioned response (UCR, salivation). After multiple CS-US pairings (i.e., acquisition), presentation of the CS alone elicited a response, the conditioned response (CR, also salivation), which is appropriate for its corresponding US. Following acquisition of the CR to the metronome CS, Pavlov also reported that presenting the CS alone a number of times would eventually eliminate the salivation CR, a procedure termed extinction.

Although most classical conditioning experiments have used nonhumans, classical conditioning readily occurs in humans (e.g., Hermans, Craske, Mineka, & Lovibond, 2006). With nonhumans, many model systems have been developed to explore classical conditioning, including conditioned eyeblink, conditioned taste aversion, and conditioned approach/avoidance (Domjan, 2003). Clearly, these have little classroom application, but the most common classical conditioning paradigm, conditioned emotional response, is applicable. Conditioned emotional reactions can be either positive or negative. A positive conditioned emotional response is produced by pairing a relatively neutral stimulus with a US that elicits a positive emotion such as happiness. For example, a parent may use the preferred taste of cheese to cover the flavor of broccoli. After a few meals of cheesy broccoli, a child will be more willing to eat broccoli by itself (for a review of food preference learning, see Capaldi, 1996). Although it is possible to produce positive emotional reactions, broad application of this methodology has not been implemented (other than in advertising when an attractive model is paired with a product). In practicality, it may be difficult for a teacher to spend substantial time during the earliest portions of class to pair their presence with a positively affective US. One can imagine only the youngest of children would not see through an instructor plying them with candy or treats on the first day of class.

Instead, the more commonly studied phenomenon, and the more likely classroom occurrence, is the negative conditioned emotional response. A classic example of conditioned fear in humans is the Little Albert Study conducted by Watson and Rayner (1920). Watson and Rayner examined if a phobia could be induced in a human, so they borrowed nine-month-old Albert from the nursery at Johns Hopkins University. After recording Albert's baseline responses to a range of stimuli such as animals and neutral objects, conditioning began two months later. During acquisition, a white rat was paired with a loud noise US (Watson clanged a steel bar with a hammer) seven times. Five days later, Albert was tested with a range of stimuli, including the white rat. Albert cringed and cried in response to the rat, behaviors that were quite different from his curiosity about the rat during the baseline phase. They tested long-term retention of fear 30 days later, and Albert was still scared of the white rat and other white objects such as a rabbit, white fur coat, and Santa Claus mask. In addition to demonstrating conditioned fear in humans, Watson and Rayner planned to examine the conditions necessary to extinguish Albert's fear. Unfortunately, on the day prior to the implementation of the extinction phase, Albert was released from the hospital with his fear intact.

CLASSROOM PHOBIAS AND TEST ANXIETY

Just as Albert learned to fear the white rat, the potential for students to learn a phobia to a neutral classroom or instructor is always present. Few instructors aim to produce a threatening or fearful situation, but a wrong answer or embarrassing situation may induce a negative emotion in the student and confer learning to the cues present at this time. As a result, the student may choose to miss class or decrease participation during class. A specific example comes from an advanced course in tests and measurements. Here, students are often given a short, timed, math ability test. Students frequently report experiencing anxiety during this exam. Some report their heart beating faster and harder, shortness of breath, and inability to concentrate because they cannot ignore the stopwatch used for timing. They often state "I hate math," or "I can't do math." Occasionally the anxiety is so strong, they stop in the middle of a problem and say, "I can't go on." When asked about their anxiety many trace its beginning to One Minute Arithmetic Tests in elementary school. In these tests, they had a sheet of arithmetic problems to complete correctly in one minute, or repeat the test until they did so. From a classical conditioning perspective, the CS is the arithmetic problems and the US is the time pressured testing situation that produces pressure and anxiety (the UCR) to both finish in a rapid time (one minute) and calculate problems correctly. After the CS-US pairing the CS (the math problems) alone produces anxiety (CR).

EXTINCTION AS NEW LEARNING

Because the student overcomes the anxiety enough to pass these tests, an instructor who has learned about conditioned fear might expect an extinction treatment has effectively eliminated the fear. A common miscon-

ception of extinction is that it is the equivalent of unlearning: Once a CS-US association has been learned, this association could be unlearned if the CS is frequently presented alone, like erasing a word from a blackboard so no trace remains. Yet, numerous studies have shown that extinction is not unlearning, but is actually new learning. Two extinction-related phenomena, spontaneous recovery and renewal, illustrate this interpretation. In spontaneous recovery, an organism experiences acquisition of the CS-US association, followed by CS-alone presentations (i.e., extinction). If the student is tested within a few days of the extinction trials, a weaker CR is observed. However, if CS testing is delayed for a few weeks (e.g., 21 days), a significantly stronger CR (anxiety reaction) is recorded. The fact that the CR returns without any additional training suggests that the original CS-US association is still intact (Rescorla, 2004). Indeed, some neuroscience studies suggest that the locus of the acquisition memory (CS-US association) is a different anatomical region from the locus of the extinction memory (CS-no US association) (e.g., Sotres-Bayon, Cain, & LeDoux, 2006). Thus it would not be unusual for a strong math anxiety reaction to recur spontaneously in students who had not experienced panic in quite some time.

THE RENEWAL EFFECT

Further support for this view comes from a second extinction-related phenomenon, the renewal effect (e.g., Bouton 2002; Bouton & King, 1983). The renewal effect is produced by alterations in the contexts of learning and extinction. For example, a control group will learn the CS-US association in an aqua room (A), experience CS alone experiences (i.e., extinction) in this aqua room (A), and then be tested with the CS in the same aqua room (A). Not surprisingly, following this order of experiences, members of Group AAA will show weak responding to the CS in the aqua room during testing. In contrast, the experimental group will receive learning in the aqua room (A), extinction in a blue room (B), and testing of the CS in the aqua room (A). Group ABA will show a significantly stronger response to the CS during testing than Group AAA. This outcome provides convergent evidence that the original CS-US association learned in the first (A) phase is still intact and can be retrieved if the contextual cues during testing are the same as during learning.

One might ask why some students develop test anxiety while others did not. In 2001, Bouton, Mineka, and Barlow proposed a modern learning theory approach to panic disorder that can be extrapolated to this anxiety. According to their model, during an experienced panic episode, various external or internal cues (CSs) can become associated with the negative emotion US. As individuals re-encounter these

CSs, they experience conditioned anxiety, and this may lead to a panic attack. Bouton and colleagues also argue that a major contributing factor to panic and conditioned anxiety is catastrophic misinterpretation of somatic symptoms. In the math test anxiety situation, the students experience panic during a testing situation, perhaps as an increasing heart rate or impaired recall or attention. These cues can lead to catastrophic thoughts, such as "I can't do math." There are a number of other cues that can serve as the CS in this situation. The contextual cues of the classroom are encountered in academic settings, the quiet shuffling of feet and the sound of pens scribbled on paper, the visual features of other individuals quietly hunched over their desks could be another cue. Importantly, a host of internal cues may be most salient, such as the heart rate and racing thoughts. If the students engage in catastrophic thinking at this stage, then they may increase their anxiety worrying that their performance on this test is the first step to career success or failure. Overall, this combination of events can then be generalized to a host of other testing situations because most tests will have common visual, auditory, or contextual conditions, these will be coupled with internal somatic sensations that seem unique to the situation, and even though the students have passed the previous exam, the current exam holds the same potential for life-long failure.

SEE ALSO *Applied Behavior Analysis; Connectionism; Operant Conditioning.*

BIBLIOGRAPHY

Bouton, M. E. (2002). Context, ambiguity, and unlearning: Sources of relapse after behavioral extinction. *Biological Psychiatry, 52,* 976–986.

Bouton, M. E., & King, D. A. (1983). Contextual control of the extinction of conditioned fear: Tests for the associative value of the context. *Journal of Experimental Psychology: Animal Behavior Processes, 9,* 248–265.

Bouton, M. E., Mineka, S., & Barlow, D. H. (2001). A modern learning theory perspective on the etiology of panic disorder. *Psychological Review, 108,* 4–32.

Capaldi, E. D. (Ed.). (1996). *Why we eat what we eat: The psychology of eating.* American Psychological Association, Washington, D.C.

Domjan, M. (2003). *The principles of learning and behavior* (5th ed.). Belmont, CA: Thomson-Wadsworth.

Hermans, D., Craske, M. G., Mineka, S., & Lovibond, P. F. (2006). Extinction in human fear conditioning. *Biological Psychiatry, 60,* 361–368.

Rescorla, R. A. (2004). Spontaneous recovery. *Learning and Memory, 11,* 501–509.

Sotres-Bayon, F., Cain, C. K., & LeDoux, J. E. (2006). Brain mechanisms of fear extinction: Historical perspectives on the contribution of prefrontal cortex. *Biological Psychiatry, 60,* 329–336.

Watson, J. B., & Rayner, R. (1920). Conditioned emotional reactions. *Journal of Experimental Psychology, 3,* 1–14.

W. Robert Batsell, Jr.
Robert W. Grossman

CLASSICAL TEST THEORY

Classical test theory (CTT) is both a philosophical argument in psychological science and a set of operations in mathematical statistics that focus on measuring mental attributes in humans. This broad description of CTT contains all the elements one needs to understand and appreciate it, both as a theory and in its operation in testing programs, but it does require an extended explanation. In the description, the phrases "philosophical argument in psychological science," "operations in mathematical statistics," and "measuring mental attributes" deserve particular attention because understanding them is the key to learning CTT. In this entry each term is explained in nontechnical language. Then CTT is discussed regarding its mathematical underpinnings, again presented nontechnically. In this second part, four formulas are explained that illustrate two essential aspects of CTT: reliability and standard error of measurement.

CTT is a scientific endeavor. In fact, realizing that CTT is science is an important step in learning about it. CTT meets all the criteria of any true science: It has a philosophical underpinning, a coherent methodology, and its methods are replicable by other scientists. Its place in science is so well established that it may be claimed that measuring mental attributes—the purpose of CTT—is psychology's greatest contribution to the world of science.

Even before exploring the terms listed in its description, however, it is useful to note the words that compose CTT: classical, test, and theory. *Classical* suggests something old as well as tried-and-true. CTT is classical in the sense that it is fundamental to measurement science, but it is not ancient. In fact, many persons are surprised to learn that the field of measurement science formed only in the mid-to-late 19th century with much of its development not until the 20th century, stemming from the groundbreaking work of Spearman, Binet, Thurstone, and later Thorndike, all persons with unusually high IQ. (For a history of the field, see the 1997 special issue of *Educational Measurement: Issues and Practices* or Sternberg's delightfully readable *Metaphors of Mind: Conceptions of the Nature of Intelligence* [1990].) The noun *test* is widely known, of course, meaning an instrument used to appraise, examine, or analyze. The last word in CTT, *theory,* is also descriptive and accurate. Theories are, by definition, ontologically unprovable; however, like most robust theories, CTT has provided over the years ample evidence that applying it appropriately yields meaningful and useful information.

The descriptive terms of CTT, "philosophical argument in psychological science," "operations in mathematical statistics," and "measuring mental attributes" need to be explained next. Regarding the philosophical argument supporting CTT, the ontological contention is made that there are certain malleable aspects to the fundamental being of humans—such as ability, proficiency, beliefs, attitudes, opinions, and probably, desire and intent, too. In psychological science these mental attributes are conceived of as cognitive processes and get hypothesized as *constructs*. Constructs are often more fully called *latent constructs* to emphasize that they are deeply embedded in human psyche and represent cognitive processes. Cognitive processes are malleable—after all, the very purpose of education is to develop them—but they are not directly observable. People cannot see *reasoning* even with sophisticated devices, although they can measure brain waves and quantify electrical and chemical actions. Still, despite not *seeing* into the brain, individuals perform myriad behavioral operations based on cognitive processes, such as reading or voting or expressing an opinion.

It follows that while latent constructs are not observable, the behaviors people use to express them are. For instance, people can observe an individual reading a story, reciting historical incidents, solving a mathematical or reasoning problem, or expressing a belief or an opinion. Hence, by observing behaviors they infer stimulation of a cognitive process. It is important to recognize that mental measurements of hypothesized latent constructs are only—and at best—inferences of more deeply seated cognitive processes.

Furthermore, people can reliably make distinctions between observations. That is, they can suggest that one person consistently comprehends more of a given passage in a text than is comprehended by another person or that a particular individual can reason through a problem more thoughtfully than another person or that one man or woman has an opinion that is more extreme than is the opinion expressed by others. In a 1904 foundational work on CTT, *Introduction to the Theory of Mental and Social Measurements*, Thorndike described the capacity to reliably make distinctions in behavioral observations as a concept called a *just noticeable difference*. In 1966, this just noticeable difference was given a mathematical structure in Fechner's law.

Putting the facts together that (1) observation of behaviors leads to inferences about cognitive activity, and (2) distinctions can be reliably made between degrees of a hypothesized construct gives us a test. A test—simply but significantly—standardizes the examinees' behavioral responses so that others can scale and score them and then make interpretations, usually by comparisons to peers or to

defined standards. In testing contexts, a test item or test exercise is considered to be a carefully prescribed *stimulus*.

However, the testing situation becomes complex when this basic idea is implemented with people. Several obvious reasons contribute to the complexity: (1) latent constructs are difficult to specify with precision, (2) the constructs are malleable, and (3) the stimuli meant to engender the examinee's behavioral response may be constructed such that an examinee's response does not completely or accurately engage the targeted construct (for example, in the case of a poorly crafted test item). All this adds up to imprecision in measurement—termed *measurement error*. Without measurement error, people would know the *true ability* for any individual on a given cognitive process. And the notion of true ability is a central feature of CTT. Of course, people never measure mental attributes without error.

Mathematically, the notion of measuring true ability in CTT is expressed in this famous formula:

$$X_{ij} = \tau_{ij} + \varepsilon \qquad (1)$$

where X is observed score,
τ is true score,
ε is error.

Formula 1 states that in CTT an observed score is the sum of a true score plus some error. While this is a logical supposition, expressing it as a mathematical formula allows testers to use it to model an individual's behavior in a testing context. Examining the CTT formula shows how this works.

Each term in the equation has a special meaning. The left-hand term (X) is a Roman letter indicating that this outcome is observed; namely, it is the test score of a given examinee. The first term on the right-hand side of the equation is the true score (τ *tau*) and denotes the structural part of the equation. That is to say, it represents the latency being measured. The error (ε *epsilon*) is called the stochastic part of the equation, from the Greek word for *aim* or *guess*. It is characterized by randomness in the population, an accurate description since no two individuals' true score is estimated with the same degree of precision. Greek letters are used for these terms to indicate that they apply globally; that is, everyone in the population has a true score (although it differs from person to person) and measuring always includes error.

The subscripts in the formula have meaning, too. The first subscripts specify that the observation is on a given item (i) and for a particular individual (j). There is no subscript for the error since it is not tied directly to any individual: again, the randomness of all measurement errors.

From the formula, it is easy to see that as the error decreases to a limit of zero (*attenuates*, in statistical language); the observed score grows closer to the value of the true score. In perfect measurement, they are the same: X = T. Unfortunately, measurements are never perfect, which explains the existence of the error term in CTT.

CTT often used to estimate the degree of error in a particular testing context. This application of the theory usually centers on two statistics: the standard error of measurement (SEM) and an index of the reliability of scores for a particular testing occurrence. Both concepts are mathematical estimations of measurement error, but they convey different information. In a global sense both measures indicate stability in measurement, or reliability. In fact, CTT is often called a theory of reliability, encompassing both indices.

Reliability means consistency of measurement. A perfectly reliable test is one that would yield the identical score (i.e., the examinee's true score) over many occasions, presuming no learning or other confounding factor intervened between the test administrations. But, of course, perfect reliability is never achieved in real-world scenarios. Were a test administered many times, any given examinee would likely not obtain the same score over and over again. Even with a carefully constructed test some variation in scores would occur. As illustration, in a case in which the raw score on a first testing occasion was 72, while on the second it was 74, and on the third a 68 was obtained, the inconsistency in scores is evidence of measurement error, or less than perfect reliability.

Given the improbable—but theoretically interesting—scenario in which a tolerant examinee took the test (or equivalent tests) a very large number of times and (also improbably) no learning or other factor such as fatigue influenced any attempt, the examinee would eventually have an entire distribution of scores that ranged from the examinee's lowest obtained score to the highest obtained score. From this theoretical distribution of scores, the mean is considered to be the examinee's true score, and the standard deviation is the SEM.

Thus, reliability and SEM are indicators of consistency in CTT, and there are methods for calculating various statistics that represent them. Of course, calculating indicators of consistency requires multiple occasions; with only one occasion, consistency cannot be determined. This point, while obvious, is important: For reliability estimation, regarding the test, there needs to be more than one item, and for the examinee, there needs to be more than one testing occasion.

To address this constraint it is necessary to introduce another important aspect of CTT, its additive character-istic. In CTT, tests are considered to be composed of some number of items that work together in an additive fashion. An additive function is one that conserves the addition operation, as shown for a test with n items in Equation 2.

$$f(x_1 + x_2 + \ldots + x_n) = f(x_1) + f(x_2) + \ldots f(x_n) \tag{2}$$

Essentially, this equation shows that in CTT the scores of individual items—which are often, but not always, dichotomous (meaning right or wrong)—can be summed to a cumulative whole, a test score. More technically, the overall test score is a linear combination of the individual test item scores. Working from the additivity rule, reliability is determined by calculating a consistent response among the items.

Traditional reliability strategies use one of two ways to estimate the consistency: either *temporal stability* or *internal consistency*. These are two routes to determine consistency of responses. Temporal stability is a family of techniques that gauge the extent to which a test yields consistent scores from one occasion to the next. It includes such strategies as test-retest and splitting the test in half (i.e., split-half) to produce an index of reliability. Internal consistency looks to the covariance structure of the item responses to produce an index of reliability. One popular measure of internal consistency is called Cronbach's alpha (α). By any of these means, however, reliability is theoretically conceived as the correlation of the observed score with the individual's true score, and it is expressed syntactically in Formula 3. In statistical contexts, a ρ (rho) symbolizes a correlation, and the subscripts denote the variables.

$$\rho_{XT} \tag{3}$$

This formula represents an index of reliability and applying it to any of the calculation strategies yields a coefficient. Coefficients in this context range from 0 to 1: no reliability (i.e., randomness) to perfect reliability.

Finally, as explained above, SEM indicates discrepancies between observed scores and true scores, and it too is a good indicator of reliability. Syntactically, it is the ratio of the standard deviation of the errors (expressed as sigma, σ) to the standard deviation of the observed scores, a shown in Formula 4. When the test's reliability is known, the SEM is easily calculated.

$$\frac{\sigma_\varepsilon}{\sigma_X} = \sqrt{(1 - \rho_{XT})} \tag{4}$$

In sum, CTT is clearly a powerful theory of measurement with a philosophical base and set of mathematics useful to implement it. From learning about them, people can readily appreciate why CTT is the most commonly used basis for educational and psychological tests.

SEE ALSO *Item Response Theory.*

BIBLIOGRAPHY

American Educational Research Association, American Psychological Association, and National Council on Measurement in Education. (1999). *Standards for educational and psychological testing.* Washington, DC: Author.

Fechner, G. T. (1966). *Elements of psychophysics.* New York: Holt, Reinhart, & Winston.

Thorndike, E. L. (1904). *Introduction to the theory of mental and social measurements.* New York: Teachers College, Columbia University.

Steven J. Osterlind

CLASSROOM ASSESSMENT

Classroom assessment is the process, usually conducted by teachers, of designing, collecting, interpreting, and applying information about student learning and attainment to make educational decisions. There are four interrelated steps to the classroom assessment process. The first step is to define the purposes for the information. During this period, the teacher considers how the information will be used and how the assessment fits in the students' educational program. The teacher must consider if the primary purpose of the assessment is diagnostic, formative, or summative. Gathering information to detect student learning impediments, difficulties, or prerequisite skills are examples of diagnostic assessment. Information collected on a frequent basis to provide student feedback and guide either student learning or instruction are formative purposes for assessment, and collecting information to gauge student attainment at some point in time, such as at the end of the school year or grading period, is summative assessment.

The next step in the assessment process is to measure student learning or attainment. Measurement involves using tests, surveys, observation, or interviews to produce either numeric or verbal descriptions of the degree to which a student has achieved academic goals. The third step is to evaluate the measurement data, which entails making judgments about the information. During this stage, the teacher interprets the measurement data to determine if students have certain strengths or limitations or whether the student has sufficiently attained the learning goals. In the last stage, the teacher applies the interpretations to fulfill the aims of assessment that were defined in first stage. The teacher uses the data to guide instruction, render grades, or help students with any particular learning deficiencies or barriers.

CLASSROOM ASSESSMENT CONCEPTS AND APPLICATIONS

Hundreds of books and articles on classroom assessment have been written, but most, if not all, ascribe to an assessment framework articulated in the 1930s and 1940s by Ralph Tyler (1949), who believed that assessment was an integral component of curriculum and instruction planning. Tyler developed a multistep model of curricular and instructional design that began with consideration of what the educator expected the student to be able to know and do after teaching had occurred. He termed these end results of education, "instructional objectives," which he stated should be crafted by considering both the mental skill, such as "applies" or "creates," and the subject matter content the student will develop. Good planning, according to Tyler, involved developing a table that specifies the body of objectives students will develop during the course of a school year, semester, or lesson.

After the instructional objectives are formulated, educational experiences can be developed that encompass the teaching materials and instructional opportunities that will be provided to students. Also during this planning stage, teachers must consider how they will determine if students have attained the instructional objectives. Indeed, good objectives are those that clearly define the type of activity the students will accomplish to indicate the degree to which the students have attained the objective. After students experience the learning opportunities provided by the teacher and after assessment has occurred, the teacher's task is to examine the assessment results and decide whether students have sufficiently reached the objectives. If they have not, the teacher can revise the educational experiences until attainment has occurred. Thus, Tyler's model of testing emphasized the formative role of classroom assessment.

Tyler did not organize the mental skills that make up objectives in any meaningful way. Benjamin Bloom, who earlier was a graduate student of Tyler at the University of Chicago, orchestrated a committee during the 1950s to develop a Taxonomy of Educational Objectives (Bloom et al., 1956). The committee organized mental, or intellectual, skills in a hierarchical fashion from the most basic levels, knowledge, and comprehension, to the most advanced levels, applications, analysis, synthesis, and evaluation. The Taxonomy has been widely used to organize the types of objectives students of all ages are expected to attain in schools worldwide.

Selected- and Constructed-response Formats. Teachers have an array of item formats upon which to measure student attainment of objectives (see Linn & Miller, 2005; Oosterhof, 2003). Assessment items can be classified into two categories: selected- and constructed-response formats. It is the student's duty in selected-response items to choose one or a few correct options among multiple alternatives. Examples of selected-response item formats include multiple-choice, ranking of options, interpretive exercises, matching, true-false, alternate-choice, embedded alternate-choice, sequential true-false, and checklists. In constructed-response items, students must supply an answer to a question prompt. Short answer and essay items are common constructed-response items. Essay items can require students to write either extended or restricted responses. Responses can be restricted by limiting the amount of space available to supply the answer, dictating the number of acceptable answers ("state three reasons …"), or by qualifying in the prompt the expected response length ("briefly describe …"). Restricted-response essays are useful for measuring student attainment of factual knowledge and basic comprehension. Extended-response essays are more appropriate if the goal is to measure students' skills at analyzing, synthesizing, constructing, or evaluating information because they offer students greater latitude in how to organize and present their thoughts.

Performance assessments are another type of constructed-response item. With this format, students are expected to perform an activity or set of activities. They can be asked to perform a process, such as delivering a public speech, or produce a product, such as a science notebook or work of art. Many performance assessments, but not all, attempt to represent real-life contexts or applications and are therefore considered authentic assessments. Because students perform activities during these assessment tasks, performance assessments can be integrated well with regular instructional activities.

Scoring. Constructed-response items must be scored by a judge, using either a norm- or criterion-referenced scoring procedure. In norm referencing, the teacher compares the quality of a student's response to a reference group, which might include the other students currently in the class or to prior students the teacher has taught. The teacher then assigns a score to the student's response based on how the response ranks or where it falls in the distribution of responses in the reference group. Criterion-reference scoring involves basing a student's score on the degree to which the student has demonstrated the attainment of specified knowledge or skills. Academic standards stipulate what students should know and be able to do, and performance standards specify the degree to which they have mastered the academic expectations.

The criteria or expectations often are defined in a scoring rubric, which provide descriptions of responses on a scale. Teachers can use either holistic or analytic scoring

rubrics to render criterion-referenced scores. An analytic rubric allows the teacher to score the constructed response on separate and multiple dimensions, such as organization, accuracy, and voice. For holistic scoring, the teacher produces one overall score. A holistic rubric could be based on multiple dimensions, but the teacher considers all of the dimensions simultaneously to yield the score. Analytic rubrics are more useful if the goal is to provide more extensive and deeper feedback to the student, because the student gets separate scores on multiple dimensions. Holistic scoring takes less time, typically, because only one score per response is made. It works, however, only when there is a high relationship among the dimensions for the responses. For example, if students who are high on organization also tend to be high on accuracy and voice, then holistic scoring can work effectively. If the dimensions are not correlated well (e.g., responses can be high on voice but low on accuracy), analytic scoring is more suitable.

Advantages and Limitations of Test Formats. There are advantages and limitations with each item format, and teachers should choose the format that best suits the purposes for assessment. If teachers have less time to score the assessments, selected-response questions are advantageous because they can be scored faster than constructed-response items. Selected-response items also are superior to constructed-response items if the goal is to measure basic levels of Bloom's Taxonomy, such as knowledge or comprehension. Students can respond more quickly to selected-response items, allowing the teacher to assess a broader range of objectives across a given timeframe. Selected-response items also are considered more objective than constructed-response questions because the latter items require teachers to score the responses, introducing rater error to the scores. Because reliability is increased by having more items with less error, selected-response items tend to yield more consistent scores relative to constructed-response items.

But given that selected-response items present both correct and incorrect options to students, those items are more prone to guessing than constructed-response items. The probability that students can guess correctly depends on the number of distracters for each question, the test-taking skills of the student, and the quality of the distracters. Constructed-response items also take less time to create, so if teachers have little time to construct an exam, they should consider including more of those items on the test. Crafting reasonable and high-quality distracters and selected-response items that are not prone to guessing is an arduous and time-consuming process. Also, because students must supply an answer for constructed-response items, the format is more suited for measuring more advanced levels of Bloom's Taxonomy in a direct manner. For example, if students are to demonstrate their evaluation skills or show that they can apply their knowledge in a novel situation, teachers must rely on constructed-response questions. Students would only be able to demonstrate that they can identify a proper application or accurate evaluation with selected-response items. Constructed-response items test the recall of information and actual demonstration of advanced skills, whereas selected-response items focus on mental recognition and serve, at best, as indirect indicators of advanced intellectual skills.

Report Card Grades. Teachers typically must assign grades indicating student performance based on assessment information. Often the types of grades to be assigned on report cards are determined by the district office. Many districts rely on letter grades, which require the teacher to report student performance in ordinal categories (e.g., A-E), while other districts use percentage grades (0–100), pass-fail marks, checklists, or narratives. It is not uncommon for report cards to consist of multiple grading methods (Guskey & Bailey, 2000). A relatively new form of grading is standards-based reporting. With this method, teachers report student performance on state or district academic standards using performance levels such as "Falls Below Expectations", "Approaches Expectations," "Meets Expectations," and "Exceeds Expectations." Many districts have moved to this newer method to encourage teachers to focus on academic standards and to provide students and parents with an alternative report on students' performance on the standards besides state achievement tests.

Though districts often determine the grading method, teachers usually have considerable freedom in deciding on how they will transform student performance into grades. Teachers can employ either norm-referenced or criterion referenced scoring procedures. Norm-referenced methods first require teachers to rank students from the highest to lowest performers. Curving is perhaps the most conventional normative method. After ranking students, teachers set thresholds between performance levels based on percentages that roughly follow the normal (i.e., bell-shaped) distribution. For example, the top 10 to 15 percent of students would be assigned A's, the next 20–30 percent of students would be assigned B's and so on. Teachers can modify curving by changing the proportions of students who receive various grades. Percentage scores can be administered based on norm referencing, that is, by assigning students percentage scores based on their percentile standing in the class distribution.

Many teachers have moved away from norm-reference grading because it encourages competition for a limited number of desirable grades and because it provides limited information regarding what students actually have learned. Most grading in classrooms in the early 2000s is based on criterion-reference scoring. The

point system probably is the most prevalent grading procedure used by teachers. This method involves assigning maximum possible points for each assignment or exam that comprises the final grade, allocating points for each of the assignments or exams for students based on their performance, and then tallying the total number of earned points for each student. If letter grades are used for reporting, teachers can assign A's to those students with 90 percent or greater of earned points, B's to students who earned between 80 and 90 percent of the points, and so on. Percentage grades also can be assigned by reporting the percent of total earned points per student. Other criterion-referenced methods can be used by teachers to produce standards-based grades (Ainsworth & Viegut, 2006).

CLASSROOM ASSESSMENT COMPARED TO EXTERNAL STANDARDIZED TESTING

Teacher classroom assessment commonly is compared to external achievement tests to articulate its strengths and weaknesses. Such comparisons, however, are misguided because the two types of assessment serve quite different purposes. Being standardized assessments, external achievement tests serve to compare the achievement levels of students across many schools, districts, states, or countries at discrete points in time (usually fall and spring) on broad knowledge and skills. Although these tests can serve a formative role, they typically are used for summative purposes. Classroom assessments usually are developed to reflect if students developed the knowledge and skills taught in a given classroom and, thus, are more focused on the specific curriculum and instruction delivered by the teacher. Assessment in the classroom also is an ongoing and continuous process, so its strength is the provision of formative information about student learning and teacher instruction.

Items on external achievement tests are subjected to extensive development and review processes. Items are carefully examined for content accuracy and lack of bias and other test flaws. Often external test items are field tested and statistically analyzed before they can be used operationally on test forms. Developers of external tests also expend considerable effort to systematize the scoring of constructed response items. Often they employ multiple judges who have received extensive training to calibrate their stringency levels and increase their reliability.

Teachers commonly develop their own items or use items provided in teachers' manuals that accompany textbooks. Items found on most classroom assessments, thus, have not been constructed with the same level of quality control compared to external tests. Further, teachers usually score constructed responses by themselves without applying preliminary procedures to reduce scorer error. Not only are external achievement tests developed with more deliberation, they typically contain more items than classroom final exams, quizzes, or graded assignments. For these reasons, scores from classroom assessments tend to be much less reliable than scores from external tests.

Besides yielding less reliable scores relative to external tests, scores across teachers often are not comparable. Teachers in the same school and teaching the same grade can administer tests that differ considerably in terms of item difficulty, cognitive demand, and scoring methods. Thus, students with the same levels of achievement can earn different grades in different classrooms. This situation would be unlikely if the students took the same standardized achievement test. Indeed, the lack of comparability across high school grades led to the development of standardized college admissions tests.

There are advantages, however, of assessments that are unique to classroom curriculum, instruction, and teacher expectations. Because most teacher tests are tailored to what students learned in the classroom, they usually provide teachers with richer information about student learning within the context of students' classroom experiences. This more targeted information can be used more effectively by the teacher to modify instruction to actual student needs. Teacher tests, therefore, likely produce more valid scores of the degree to which students attained the instructional objectives generated by the teacher.

Frequency of Testing. Though external tests contain more items than classroom assessments, the teacher has the opportunity to administer more items representing a far greater array of item formats during the school year. External tests typically are administered once or twice at most in a given year, and they usually contain one to three item formats. If teachers assess frequently and use an array of formats, they can collect a body of student information that has four major advantages.

First, frequent assessment allows the teacher to track student growth and to detect areas in need of more or different instruction. Second, assessing often yields learning information that teachers can use to give constructive feedback to students. Timely feedback focused on what students have mastered and where they need to improve has been linked to greater learning gains (Black & William, 1998). Third, if teachers base final grades on frequent small assessments containing items representing various formats, the final grades likely would be as or more reliable than external achievement tests, given teachers' opportunity to gather more information regarding student attainment than a single test administration. Finally, besides increasing reliability, this assessment approach yields more valid scores. As Campbell and Fiske (1959) noted, validity is delimited by relying on a sole item format or test method because scores are

influenced to some degree by those factors. By using various methods, including different item formats and paper-pencil as well as oral testing and observation, teachers can generate information about each student's learning that transcends the method type.

Ultimately, it is the prerogative of the teacher to maximize the strengths and limit the weaknesses of classroom assessments. Teachers must make a concerted effort to integrate testing into their teaching plans and practices. Research indicates that teachers who prioritize assessment and use test results to improve their instruction tend to be more effective instructors (Black & William, 1998). Unfortunately teachers vary greatly in the degree to which they value assessment. Some teachers are opposed to testing, while others assess in a haphazard manner. Still others use the same, favorite item format for all assessments, consequently limiting the validity of students' scores. By contrast, those teachers who systematize assessment and rely on it to guide their practice likely produce the highest quality of information available on student learning.

SEE ALSO *Criterion-Referenced Tests; Reliability; Validity.*

BIBLIOGRAPHY

Ainsworth, L., & Viegut, D. (2006). *Common formative assessments: How to connect standards-based instruction and assessment.* Thousand Oaks, CA: Corwin Press.

Black, P., & William, D. (1998). Assessment and classroom learning. *Assessment in education: Principles, policy, and practice, 5*(1), 1–34.

Bloom, B. S., Engelhart, M. D., Furst, E. J., Hill, W. H., & Krathwohl, D. R. (1956). *Taxonomy of educational objectives,* Book 1: *Cognitive domain.* New York: Longman.

Campbell, D., & Fiske, D. (1959). Convergent and discriminant validation by the multitrait-multimethod matrix. *Psychological Bulletin, 56,* 81–105.

Guskey, T. R., & Bailey, J. M. (2000). *Developing grading and reporting systems for student learning.* Thousand Oaks, CA: Corwin Press.

Linn, R. L., & Miller, M. D. (2005). *Measurement and assessment in teaching.* (9th ed.). Upper Saddle River, NJ: Merrill/Prentice Hall.

Oosterhof, A. (2003). *Developing and using classroom assessments.* Upper Saddle River, NJ: Merrill/Prentice Hall.

Tyler, R. W. (1949). *Basic principles of curriculum and instruction.* Chicago: University of Chicago Press.

Jerome V. D'Agostino

CLASSROOM ENVIRONMENT

Classroom environment encompasses a broad range of educational concepts, including the physical setting, the psychological environment created through social contexts, and numerous instructional components related to teacher characteristics and behaviors. The study classroom environment has been widespread across nearly all subspecializations of educational psychology. Researchers are interested in relationships between environment constructs and multiple outcomes, including learning, engagement, motivation, social relationships, and group dynamics. Early researchers recognized that behavior is a function of people's personal characteristics and their environment.

In the educational setting, Urie Bronfenbrenner's work on ecological contexts secured a place in educational research for studies of classroom environment. Bronfenbrenner's *Ecological Systems Theory* (Bronfenbrenner, 1977) encompasses the layered environmental system of microcosms in which human development takes place and emphasizes the importance of family, teachers, schools, and the larger sociocultural environment on the developmental process. Over the years this research has evolved from examining purely physical elements of the environment to more complex models of psychosocial relationships between students in the classrooms as well as between the teacher and students.

Research beginning in the mid-1990s has focused on one or more of these aspects and has associated classroom environment variables with numerous positive and negative student outcomes. In addition to the wide array of outcomes investigated in relationship to classroom environment, this area of study has also been of interest to methodologists as the data structure poses a unit of analysis dilemma; in terms of examining classroom variables in combination with student outcomes, researchers have had to determine if the data would be analyzed at the classroom level or at the student level. With the arrival in the 1990s of statistical methodologies capable of handling data collected from both levels, studies have been better able to include variables collected at both levels. Various methodologies, including survey, observations, and interviews have been used to capture aspects of the classroom environment from student, teacher, and observer perspectives. The Early Childhood group based at the University of Virginia has an extensive body of work that examines classroom environment as a validated observation system of multiple dimensions of the classroom.

THE PHYSICAL ENVIRONMENT
More frequently a focus in earlier studies of classroom environment, the physical environment has continued to appear in contemporary studies as an influence on behavioral and academic outcomes. Current studies of the physical environment have investigated aspects such as class composition, class size, and classroom management.

Class composition studies examine classroom grouping methods, including ability grouping of students, single-

sex classrooms and cooperative learning groups. Research has found that classrooms with highly cooperative groups appear to have students with more positive perceptions of fairness in grading, stronger class cohesion, and higher degree of social support, as well as higher achievement scores. Female students have been found to prefer collaborating with other students when studying and resolving problems, and they have a stronger preference for teacher support than male students. The primary school environments tend to use collaborative strategies more frequently and have higher levels of teacher involvement and support than is found in secondary schools. Research on single-sex classrooms has been more divided in terms of academic outcome research. Some studies found that girls do better in math and science particularly when separated from male students; other studies found no achievement differences between genders when either in single-sex or mixed-sex classrooms.

Studies about class size have examined how class size influences student and teacher behaviors. In general, smaller classes are associated with students who are less stressed and are more frequently on-task with fewer reported behavior problems than students in larger classes. Although teachers tend to use similar instructional strategies whether teaching large or small classes, there is some evidence to suggest that more class time is spent on administrative tasks for larger classes, leaving less time available for instruction. Some research has suggested that differences in academic outcomes based on class size are due to differences in student behaviors.

Overcrowded facilities, too many students in certain classes, and lack of teachers' assistants are three major issues cited as potentially creating problems due to increased stress levels of students and increased teacher-reported incidences of behavioral problems. These increased stress levels and behavior problems found in larger classrooms are frequently accompanied by lower levels of academic achievement.

Teacher-to-child ratios are also of interest to many researchers because the number of reported behavioral problems seem to increase as class size increases. Many researchers have observed that large classes, with 30 or more students, tend to have a larger number of students off task more often with fewer students engaged with the teacher than children in small classes of 20 students or less. Yet there may be a social cost for students in small classes; other researchers found that smaller classes also had high incidences of children engaging in asocial and exclusionary behavior. Whether students are engaging in on-task or disruptive behavior can also be influenced by effective classroom management instructions and consistency of teacher enforcement.

The timing of classroom management and organization also impacts students' perceptions of the teacher as an

CLASSROOM CLIMATE

Part of the larger focus on school improvement is School Climate or Educational Climate, which defines how teachers interact with each other and with administrators. This is different from Classroom Climate, which identifies relationships among students with each other, the teacher and how this translates into learning.

There are a number of tools available to determine Classroom Climate and then to use the results as part of the comprehensive plan for school improvement. Even the most sophisticated measurement tools rely heavily on opinion and perception. Opinion is generated from information, statistics on student and teacher performance, while perception is based on observation of the behaviors in the classroom and the school.

In determining Classroom Climate, it is important to apply information gathered from both opinion and perception to form a comprehensive picture of student success and to therefore create a meaningful school improvement plan.

Opinion is generated by reviewing student test scores, grades earned, attendance, health and family. Perception is formed by observation and by paper and pencil tools that evaluate Classroom Climate based on organization of the classroom, the attitude toward student achievement, the attitudes toward school, the attitudes toward peers, the degree of democracy experienced in the classroom, the acceptance of diversity, the range of learning experiences, the autonomy of the teacher, the competitiveness among students, the consistency of interpretation of rule infractions and their consequences.

Elizabeth Soby

spends in teaching organizational behaviors impacts the classroom environment. Researchers have found that students in classrooms that spent more time early in the school year on organizational instruction substantially increased the amount of time students spent in student-managed activities later in the academic year. Intentionally providing organizational instruction at the start of the academic year is a characteristic of an effective classroom environment manager.

THE PSYCHOLOGICAL ENVIRONMENT

Beyond the physical arrangement of a classroom a psychological environment is also created, based on the interaction of key players in the classroom, namely students and teachers. Research in this area has varied greatly and proliferated during the early twenty-first century. Studies have been particularly concentrated on student class participation rates, teacher support, and communication of learning goals.

Many teachers equate student engagement and on-task behavior with classroom participation, typically a top concern for teachers. Researchers support teachers' intuition of a difference in the participation style of the different genders. Whereas girls are more likely to participate as part of the relational responsibility they feel toward the teacher, boys tend to respond more often if they feel the class is interesting and less often if the class is perceived as boring—indicating that for these students, teachers may be equally responsible for the participation level and learning. Most studies have found that boys speak out in class about three times as frequently as girls do; however, both genders typically perceive girls as better class participants. Although responses vary when students are asked what participation consists of, the most common response, and one frequently examined by researchers, is that participation is defined as answering questions when specifically asked. Both boys and girls seem to indicate a need for relational aspects to be present in order for this type of participation to occur; however, whereas girls more frequently participate by responding to teachers' questions, boys are more likely to participate as a means of obtaining attention or being noticed by the teacher. Teachers who want to encourage development of relational aspects for both genders may need to utilize different acknowledgement techniques for male students to enhance their perceptions of feeling supported as a class participant.

The notion of feeling supported as students has also been extensively examined in the classroom environment literature. Helen Patrick and colleagues (Patrick, Ryan, & Kaplan, 2007) found that there is a strong, positive relationship between students' level of motivation and engagement and their perceptions of the classroom environment as being socially supportive. The perception of a climate of mutual respect is required in order for students to increase their use of effective study strategies and

effective manager. When students have been asked to describe effective classroom managers, researchers report that these are teachers who set clear expectations and consequences early in the year. They also describe teachers who consistently (and predictably) follow through with consequences, as opposed to merely threatening consequences. These characteristics appear essential in establishing good classroom environment in terms of social support and mutual respect. Additionally, the amount of time a teacher increase feelings of confidence about their ability to successfully complete assignments. Furthermore, when students perceive that they receive emotional support and encouragement from their teachers and academic support from their peers they are more likely to be on-task in the classroom and use self-regulated strategies.

Another large body of educational research has focused on the communication of learning goals to students in combination with the individual goals and expectations of students. Some students and classrooms are more focused on obtaining grades than on mastery of objectives; these students and classrooms are said to be performance oriented rather than mastery oriented. A multitude of studies have examined this social-cognitive aspect of classrooms and found that the classroom-level learning goal can be linked to both behavioral and academic outcomes. Students in classrooms where performance is emphasized are more likely to engage in cheating, avoid help-seeking, and exhibit lower levels of academic engagement. In contrast, students who are in a classroom where the focus is on learning and improvement demonstrate higher levels of self-efficacy and engagement as well as more positive affect. At the personal goal level researchers have found that whereas students who are more focused on grades tend to have higher grades, those students who are more focused on mastering objectives tend to engage in more academically challenging tasks and retain information learned for a longer period of time.

THE ROLE OF THE TEACHER IN THE CLASSROOM ENVIRONMENT

The third focus of many examinations of classroom environment has been on teacher behaviors, specifically teacher development and school culture and how these components affect classroom environment. Some research suggests that due to the complexity of cultivating an effective classroom environment, it may be beyond the developmental scope of the newly graduated teacher. Some researchers recommend that professional development for new teachers should include intense mentoring and teaching partnerships that reduce isolation and form productive and meaningful relationships with other adults in the school community.

Following the research studies on physical and psychological environment many suggestions for teachers have been presented in the literature, including classroom management plans and recommendations for building better relationships with students. Classroom rules and procedures should be introduced early in the school year and consequences should be enforced consistently across students and throughout the school year. Research has shown that routine and fairness have a positive impact on behavior as well as academic quality. It has been found that teachers who run respectful classrooms are in turn more respected by their students, and students believe that these teachers also hold higher learning expectations. Teachers are encouraged to focus more on the learning

task than on the outcome or grade assigned at the end of the task, although this becomes much more difficult if the emphasis in education is placed on accountability and high-stakes testing.

Although most classroom environment studies are by definition limited to classrooms, a few studies have investigated the impact of the school culture on classroom environment. Findings suggest that schools with an authoritative culture (e.g., clear direction, delegation of responsibilities, accountability to and from all) tend to be judged by students and teachers as being successful. Schools that lack leadership or have a culture of multiple micro-conflicts tend to be perceived by students and teachers as undermining educational gains.

MEASURING CLASSROOM ENVIRONMENT

In studies of classroom environment a plethora of measurement tools have been employed, including direct, objective observational measures as well as more subjective perceptions of the classroom environment. The types of items that have been used range from low inference (e.g., frequency counts of behavior) to high inference (e.g., classroom members' perceptions about meaning of behaviors). There has been a heavy reliance on perceptual measures in much of the literature, supported by the argument that observational measures tend to be low-inference based and are of a limited time period, whereas perception measures better capture high-inference constructs, and therefore better represent day to day experience in the environment. Moreover, advances in statistical analyses have allowed for better incorporation of multiple student observations in one classroom to be aggregated as a measure of classroom environment. In contrast, an objective observation tool is limited to a single opinion or an agreement statistics between two or three independent observers.

Some of the most extensive work on measuring classroom environment was completed in the 1970s by Rudolf Moos, resulting in the widely used Classroom Environment Scale (Moos, 1979). Moos's work, which has permeated the literature on classroom environment, is based on three essential areas of classroom environment: (1) Relationship dimension, which focuses on the interpersonal relationships between students and students and the teacher in a classroom; (2) Personal Development dimension, which centers on individual characteristics of the classroom member; and (3) System Maintenance and Change dimension which includes attributes such as classroom control and order as well as responsiveness to change. As delineated above, much of the research on classroom environment has also been attuned to these three dimensions or combinations thereof.

The mid-1990s was marked by a shift to more high-inference measures such as the What Is Happening In this Class (WIHIC) Questionnaire developed by Barry Fraser and colleagues (Fraser, 2002). This scale focuses entirely on student perceptions of a wide range of dimensions of the classroom, including student cohesiveness, teacher support, involvement, investigation, task orientation, cooperation, and equity. Each of the dimensions in the WIHIC can be mapped to three major dimensions of Moos's schema.

While these two measures continue to appear in the research literature, there are many other ways to measure classroom environment. As theories of learning continue to evolve the need to create and validate more measures of classroom environment continues to grow. Just as it is difficult to provide a concise definition of what classroom environment is, it is also difficult to define a measure of the construct, resulting in a multitude of varieties and variations in the literature.

IMPLICATIONS AND CONSIDERATIONS

Classroom environment is a broad term and the research in this area is far reaching and defined in many different ways according to theory as well as practice. Regardless of the definition, there are many important findings from the research as a whole that can impact students' learning and behavior. This is also an area of continued growth in research as changes in technology and social culture alter the dynamics of what is considered classroom environment.

One of these areas to consider is the environment beyond the classroom. There has been debate on the impact of school-wide environment on classroom environment. With an increased importance placed on school-wide performance in order to demonstrate school success in terms of annual academic progress of students, there is undoubtedly pressure on teachers to produce high scores on standardized state exams. This school-wide demand filters to the classroom and is communicated in various ways to students, directly impacting their experiences in the classroom. There is ongoing research to examine the implications of the high-stakes testing for the psychosocial dimension of the classroom as well as how this approach has influenced instructional strategies used by teachers in classrooms.

Furthermore, the definition of classroom environment continues to evolve with the development of online courses and increased use of technology in learning situations. Classrooms are now networked, expanding the environment beyond physical walls, enabling students to interact via email, video conferencing, and blogs. The addition of technology to the classroom has changed the environment, and research is only beginning to consider these new aspects and their impacts on classroom outcomes.

Information gained from ongoing studies of classroom environment continues to impact teachers' knowledge. Learning about factors that may shape students' perceptions of their learning environment, how teachers' actions appear to students, and how changes made to the learning environment may stimulate and encourage learning continue to be of the utmost importance to classroom teachers.

SEE ALSO *School Belonging.*

BIBLIOGRAPHY

Bronfenbrenner, U. (1977). Toward ecology of human development. *American Psychologist, 32,* 513–531.

Fraser, B. (2002). Learning environments research: Yesterday, today, and tomorrow. In S. C. Goh & M. S. Khine (Eds.), *Studies in educational learning environments: An international perspective* (pp. 1–26). Singapore: World Scientific.

Moos, R. (1979) *Evaluating educational environments: procedures, measures, findings and policy implications.* San Francisco: Jossey-Bass.

Patrick, H., Ryan, A., & Kaplan, A. (2007). Early adolescents' perceptions of the classroom social environment, motivational beliefs, and engagement. *Journal of Educational Psychology, 99,* 83–98.

Angela D. Miller
Kathryn Cunningham

CLASSROOM MANAGEMENT

This entry contains the following:

I. OVERVIEW
   Valerie A. Evans, Nina C. Wilde, Saul Axelrod

II. ASSERTIVE DISCIPLINE
   Rosetta F. Sandidge

III. PUNISHMENT
   T. Steuart Watson, Tonya S. Watson, Sarah Gebhardt

IV. RULES AND PROCEDURES
   Robert F. Putnam, Marcie W. Handler

V. TOKEN ECONOMIES
   Tonya N. Davis, Mark O'Reilly, Giulio Lancioni, Jeff Sigafoos, Wendy Machalicek

VI. WITHITNESS
   Edmund T. Emmer

OVERVIEW

Teacher enthusiasm, organization, and technical skill of instruction are almost all of the characteristics of an effective classroom leader. Almost. It is sophistication regarding classroom management that makes educated and enthusiastic teachers Classroom management encompasses all the components that impact upon the smooth delivery of education to students. These components include teacher behavior, student behavior, and the classroom's physical features. This entry reviews the most common factors that

Examples of simple data collection forms

Frequency Date:	Behavior: Call Out
Homeroom	JHT
Math	I
Art	
Gym	II
Lunch	
Music	I
Spanish	
Chemistry	I

Duration Date:	Behavior: Crying	
	Start time	Stop time
	9:27	9:43
	1:04	1:12

Figure 1 ILLUSTRATION BY GGS INFORMATION SERVICES. CENGAGE LEARNING, GALE.

may provoke problem behaviors for individual students or for an entire class, describes methods for determining why the problems are occurring, and suggests how to intervene effectively.

CHOOSING AND DEFINING BEHAVIORS TO MODIFY

Assessment and treatment of student behavior is time-consuming. Before a behavior is deemed a target for change, the teacher must first determine whether it is worth the time and effort to collect data, analyze function, and implement a treatment plan. If the behavior is a threat to the safety of the students, it should be addressed promptly. Examples of dangerous behavior are bullying, throwing furniture, running around the classroom, and engaging objects in a dangerous manner.

The impact of the behavior on the learning environment as a whole is another important consideration when deciding if a behavior is worth the time it takes to intervene. If the behavior is disruptive to the entire class (e.g., call-outs) or is incompatible with student participation (e.g., note-passing), then it warrants attention on the basis that the behavior is preventing the classroom from achieving its educational objectives. Once a behavior is chosen as a target for analysis and intervention, it must first be defined in specific and observable terms. The definition must be technical enough so that anyone may walk into the classroom, read the definition, and recognize whether the behavior of concern is occurring. Disruptive behavior, for example, is a broad behavior category in which many behaviors may be included. Out-of-seat behavior is much more specific and is very simple to define and measure. Specific definitions also make it easier for the student to understand, which should prove to be helpful during the intervention stage. Finally, it is important that the teacher prioritize treatment. Rather than feel overwhelmed by the immediate desire to have a classroom of orderly students,

the teacher should focus on one problem at a time and set realistic expectations.

DATA COLLECTION AND ANALYSIS

Teachers have many tasks to attend to each day. So they might wonder about the worth of adding another task, such as collection of data. Whether a teacher has chosen to work on an individual student's behavior or to work on class-wide performance, tracking progress allows the teacher to make informed decisions regarding whether intervention is necessary, and if so, if the intervention is resulting in desired outcomes. When a teacher identifies a target behavior to change, the teacher should begin with an initial assessment of behavior rates. This type of data is referred to as baseline. Before baseline data may be collected, the teacher must first choose which method of data collection is appropriate, given the nature of the behavior. There are measurement techniques that track the frequency, duration, rate, and latency of behavior (see Figure 1). The chosen data collection method should be both appropriate for the nature of the behavior and practical for the teacher to use.

During the baseline phase, another type of data should be gathered to further assess the variables correlated with the target behavior. These variables may be time of day, type of activities, and availability of certain preferred items (see Figure 2). Analysis of these data will provide the teacher with naturally occurring patterns that may indicate consistent precursors of behavior. For example, if students are reliably aggressive mid-morning, it may be due to hunger, the difficult math lesson that is presented at 10:00 each day, or agitation from being seated all morning. The effectiveness of intervention is highly correlated with the teacher's ability to critically analyze behavior trends with the data that were collected.

CONSEQUENCES OF STUDENT BEHAVIOR

In order to effectively treat students' behavior, the teacher must first understand it from the students' perspective. The

---

Sample of a data form that may be used to assess function

The example shows a pattern of all three episodes of behavior motivated by attention in the form of verbal interactions with the teacher and laughter from peers, as well as a possible concurrent motivation of escape from work tasks.

Antecedent (What was happening before the problem behavior?)	Behavior observed	Consequence (What happened after the problem behavior?)
Silent reading	Steven threw a book on the floor.	I asked him to pick the book up. Two other students laughed.
I asked the class to get out their homework.	Steven stood up and walked out of class.	I followed him into the hall and talked to him until he came back to class.
The class was walking in the hall to the lunchroom.	Steven began singing loudly.	I asked him to be quiet. Many students were laughing.

Figure 2 ILLUSTRATION BY GGS INFORMATION SERVICES. CENGAGE LEARNING, GALE.

---

teacher must always remember that the behavior of concern is adaptive and useful; otherwise, the students would not engage in it. Students engage in a particular behavior because it provides them with some valuable reinforcer. The reinforcer is any consequence that increases the probability or rate of the response in the future (Skinner, 1938). A consequence is anything that follows a behavior.

Consequences may be pleasant, unpleasant, or neutral. When the outcome of a behavior is something desirable, individuals are likely to engage in the behavior again. The pay-off, or reinforcer, for engaging in the behavior may not be readily apparent to others, but that does not mean it does not exist. "He just does it to annoy me" is a popular attitude of exasperated teachers, which is sometimes, but not always true. Concluding that "This is just a rambunctious group of students who cannot be controlled" will make any teacher feel better about not being effective but will do nothing to improve the situation for either teacher or students.

In order to improve the situation, the analysis of antecedents (events that occur before a behavior) and consequences of behavior will reveal the factors maintaining the undesired behavior and lead the educator toward effective intervention strategies. Understanding why students engage in the problem behavior (the function of the behavior) will indicate treatment options. For example, if disruptive students continually interrupt the lesson, it is likely that they are being disruptive to access attention from the teacher and peers. So in this case, the function is attention. An effective treatment will use attention as the reinforcer, as that is what motivates the students' behavior.

Understanding what motivates behavior is also useful in preventing accidental reinforcement of that behavior. For example, if students act up at school because they do not like attending school and the consequence is they are suspended for three days, the acting-out behavior was likely reinforced. It is very likely that these individuals will engage in the same undesirable behaviors in the future because it was those behaviors that gave them access to the desired consequence. In this case, if the school administrators referred to the suspension as a punisher, they would be mistaken.

Punishment is any consequence of behavior that decreases, rather than increases, the likelihood a behavior will occur again (Skinner, 1938). Both reinforcement and punishment are highly individualized per student and behavior. In the case of a student who acts out for peer and teacher attention, if the teacher were to give this student stage time at the end of the day for appropriate behavior, this would likely be an effective reinforcer. However, if stage time were given to a shy student, it would most likely act as a punishing consequence. These examples highlight why accurate assessment of the variables that maintain behavior are necessary before effective treatment may be designed and implemented.

OTHER CONSIDERATIONS

Some classroom problems may be influenced by physical characteristics of the environment or by the established teaching patterns and class schedule. According to Smith, Neisworth, and Greer (1978), a number of factors should be considered when arranging the instructional environment. These include several elements of physical design and organization, such as lighting, temperature, noise, visual distractions, colors, furniture, displays, and shelving. The seating arrangements, desks, and work and play areas should be designed so that the teacher is able to observe all the students in the room. This organization will allow the teacher to determine which students might need assistance, as well as what types of social interactions are occurring (Stainback, Stainback, & Froyen, 1987). A well-managed classroom also has a schedule and established classroom rules. These rules should be clearly stated and be visually accessible to the students throughout their school day. In addition, teachers should discuss with the students the consequences for both

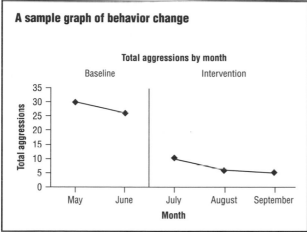

A sample graph of behavior change

Total aggressions by month

Baseline   Intervention

Figure 3 ILLUSTRATION BY GGS INFORMATION SERVICES. CENGAGE LEARNING, GALE.

rule following and rule breaking. The majority of teacher-student interactions should involve positive reinforcement of appropriate behavior. The teacher should move about the room, rather than remain seated at the desk. Doing so allows the teacher to deliver immediate prompts and reinforcers for appropriate behaviors. When students are actively engaged in instruction, they are less likely to exhibit be problematic behaviors.

Classroom schedules are another important consideration. Difficult or repetitive academic tasks should alternate with activities that are naturally reinforcing to the students. Minor classroom management problems might be addressed by making alterations in these areas, although it is important to note that these changes alone may not be sufficient to establish classroom order. Persistent issues with poor instructional control in the classroom will likely require some degree of more direct assessment of student and teacher performance and intervention by the teacher.

PROTOCOL DEVELOPMENT

The most effective protocols directly address the function of the target behavior. Just as the students learned to achieve their goals with an inappropriate behavior, they now learn how to achieve their goals with a socially acceptable behavior. The new socially acceptable way of achieving reinforcement is defined as an equivalent response; it serves the same function as the inappropriate behavior (Carr, McConnachie, Levin, & Kemp, 1993) but is an appropriate behavior. Simultaneously, the way in which teachers respond to the undesirable behavior may also need to change. The treatment plan is, simply, a protocol for changing the behavior patterns of both teacher and stu-

dents. If the plan is a success, the teacher will learn to reinforce appropriate student behavior and withhold reinforcement when undesirable behaviors occur.

The students will, in turn, learn to respond differently, based on the teacher's allocation of reinforcement. For example, if certain students shout out during class to gain the teacher's attention, the teacher will need to identify an equivalent response for gaining teacher attention. Hence, if the teacher instructs the students to raise their hands when they want attention, the teacher will need to provide more immediate and higher quality reinforcement for hand-raises than for call-outs. The students will quickly learn that hand raising is the most efficient way to receive attention from the teacher and will use hand raising in place of the call-outs. When a teacher chooses an appropriate equivalent response for a student, the new behavior must be at least as easy to perform for the student as the undesirable behavior. Hand raising is an appropriate equivalent response for call-outs. Writing a note to the teacher in place of call-outs would not be an appropriate equivalent response since writing notes is much more laborious than calling out. In the beginning of teaching equivalent responses, it is important that the teacher reinforce every appropriate response. As the student learns to raise his hand, the rate of reinforcement may be gradually thinned and the delivery of reinforcement can become less frequent and less immediate. Any effective intervention requires an investment of time and effort in the beginning stages, but soon pays off when the classroom comes under control.

MONITORING CHANGE

The data collection process should continue throughout intervention in order to monitor progress and to make informed decisions regarding intervention efforts. It is important to collect data and to display it in a graph that will allow the teacher to easily see progress or the lack of it. A visual display of data permits the teacher to see changes in behavior that may not have been expected or may not have otherwise been noticed. Graphing of data helps the teacher avoid over or underestimating behavior change. The simplest method of graphing is to draw a line graph by hand. The quantity of behavior(s) should be placed on the y-axis (ordinate), and time, such as days or weeks on the x axis (abscissa) (Figure 3). It is important to depict baseline and intervention data on the same graph. A vertical line should be inserted between all changes in condition. This arrangement allows the teacher to quickly scan graphs for treatment effects. Once the baseline and intervention data are graphed, the teacher may observe the effects of intervention. If the behaviors fail to respond to teacher interventions, it may be necessary to obtain assistance from a qualified behavior analyst.

Classroom management is an ongoing process that requires continual monitoring and adjustment. Knowledge of reinforcement and keen analytic skills are the most important tools for effectively managing a classroom. Many classroom problems may be prevented with careful attention to physical design and scheduling. When problems arise, analysis of the sequence of events leading up to and immediately following the behavior of concern will indicate strategies for effective treatment. Successful interventions are carefully planned and based upon the function of target behaviors. The time spent improving one's classroom management is an important investment toward a pleasant and productive working and learning environment for teachers and learners.

BIBLIOGRAPHY

Alberto, P. A., & Troutman, A. C. (2006). *Applied behavior analysis for teachers.* Upper Saddle River, NJ: Prentice Hall.

Axelrod, S., & Matthews, S. C. (Eds.). (2003). *How to improve classroom behavior series.* Austin, TX: ProEd.

The Behavior Analyst Certification Board. Retrieved April 11, 2008 from, http://www.bacb.com.

Carr, E. G., McConnachie, G., Levin, L., & Kemp, D. C. (1993). Communication-based treatment of severe behavior problems. In R. Van Houton & S. Axelrod (Eds.), *Behavior analysis and treatment* (231–267). New York: Plenum Press.

Cipani, E. (2003). *Classroom management for all teachers: 12 plans for evidence based practice.* Upper Saddle River, NJ: Prentice Hall.

Kerr, M. M., & Nelson, C. M. (2006). *Strategies for addressing behavior problems in the classroom.* Upper Saddle River, NJ: Prentice Hall.

Lewis, R. B., & Doorlag, D. H. (2005). *Teaching special students in general education classrooms.* Upper Saddle River, NJ: Prentice Hall.

Skinner, B. F. (1938). *Behavior of organisms.* New York: Appleton Century Crofts.

Smith, R. M., Neisworth, J. T., & Greer, J. G. (1978). *Evaluating educational environments.* Columbus, OH: Charles E. Merrill.

Stainback, W., Stainback, S., & Froyen, L. (1987). Structuring the classroom to prevent disruptive behaviors. *Teaching Exceptional Children 19*(4), 12–16.

United States Department of Education. (2004). Individuals with Disabilities Education Improvement Act of 2004. Retrieved April 11, 2008, from http://idea.ed.gov.

Wong, H. K., & Wong, R. T. (2004). *The first days of school: How to be an effective teacher.* Mountain View, CA: Harry K. Wong.

Valerie A. Evans
Nina C. Wilde
Saul Axelrod

ASSERTIVE DISCIPLINE

Assertive discipline is a structured, teacher-centered system designed to help educators manage student behavior in the classroom. Armed with the belief that teachers were ill prepared to address behavioral problems in their classrooms, Lee and Marlene Canter proposed a new discipline model in their 1976 book, *Assertive Discipline: A Take-Charge Approach for Today's Educators.* A straightforward model that was easy to understand and implement, assertive discipline gained rapid acceptance among teachers throughout the United States. The widespread popularity of the model became more evident with the growth of Canter and Associates, a firm designed to market books and resources on assertive discipline and provide assertive discipline training for school districts and educators across the country. It is estimated that well over 1 million teachers have received training in this packaged behavior management system since its inception in 1976 (Canter & Canter, 2002).

Over the years, the Canters published additional books that focused on assertive discipline for parents (1982) and assertive discipline strategies for difficult or challenging students (1993). The system was modified slightly over time as the Canters further developed aspects of the model. Perhaps the most notable change came with the publication of the third edition of *Assertive Discipline: Positive Behavior Management for Today's Classrooms* (2002), which stressed the importance of teachers building a caring and trusting relationship with students in addition to providing the classroom structure that was advocated in earlier works.

The overall premise of assertive discipline is that teachers must act assertively to ensure that their rights as teachers are met. The Canters believed that, traditionally, teachers had focused on student needs, in keeping with earlier theories espoused by Thomas Gordon (1918–2002), Sigmund Freud (1856–1939), Rudolph Dreikurs (1897–1972), and William Glasser (1925–), and ignored their own needs in the classroom (Canter & Canter, 1976, 1992). According to the Canters, teachers have the right to establish a classroom environment that facilitates student learning, determine expectations for student behavior in the classroom, expect student compliance with these expectations, and seek the support of parents and school administrators in implementing this system. Similarly, students have the right to have teachers who set boundaries for student conduct, provide support for appropriate behavior, and identify and enforce consequences for inappropriate behavior.

The Canters posit that teachers respond to student behaviors in an assertive, nonassertive, or hostile manner (Canter & Canter, 1992). To ensure that teacher and student needs are addressed, teachers must learn to respond assertively in the classroom. Assertive teachers clearly communicate their expectations to students and quickly administer positive recognition for appropriate student actions and consequences for inappropriate behaviors. Nonassertive teachers fail to specify to their students the behaviors they will or will not accept, threaten students with punishment for inappropriate behavior but do not follow through with their threats, and often ignore inappropriate behaviors altogether. Hostile teachers address students in an abusive manner, making sarcastic, demeaning, or mean-spirited comments that create feelings of embarrassment, fear, intimidation, and anger among their students.

PROCEDURES IN ASSERTIVE DISCIPLINE

Central to the assertive discipline model is a classroom discipline plan that is created by the teacher and implemented at the beginning of the school year or academic term. The plan includes three major components: a set of classroom rules, types of positive recognition for students who obey the rules, and a hierarchy of consequences for students who disobey the rules.

The Canters (1992) provide specific guidelines regarding the establishment of the classroom rules, the first component of the discipline plan. They recommend that teachers develop a limited number of rules, with five as a guideline, to allow students to easily learn and remember these expectations. These rules should focus on observable student behaviors and should apply at all times in the classroom. The rules should deal with behavior only and not address academic issues, such as homework.

The second component of the discipline plan includes identification of strategies for recognizing students who abide by the rules. The Canters (1992) believe that positive recognition of students who obey the rules encourages appropriate behavior, increases self-esteem, creates a positive learning environment, and establishes positive relationships within the classroom. Examples of positive recognition include praise, positive phone calls or notes sent home to parents or guardians, tangible rewards, and special privileges. In addition to individual student recognition, the Canters suggest that teachers also consider a classroom recognition system, which allows students to earn class-wide rewards for their on-task behaviors. When a predetermined number of points are earned by students in the class, the class is rewarded with a special party or event.

The third component of the discipline plan involves the development of a hierarchy of consequences that is administered to students who disobey the rules. The hierarchy includes approximately five consequences, with the first consequence a warning followed by additional consequences, which increase in severity. The more severe consequences involve referral to parents or guardians and school administrators. The hierarchy also identifies a severe clause specifying that students who commit

serious infractions be referred immediately to the school principal. The Canters (1992) recommend that teachers select age-appropriate consequences that students do not enjoy. Teachers should have a system in place to easily track the level of consequence for each student and administer the consequences calmly and quickly. To ensure that students learn from their previous mistakes and to motivate them to stay on task, each day the teacher begins administering the consequences at the lowest level of the hierarchy to give students a fresh start.

To ensure that students are familiar with the plan, the Canters (1992) recommend that teachers teach the plan to students by using the following procedures: explain why rules are needed, teach the rules, explain how positive recognition will be used, explain why consequences are needed, begin immediately reinforcing students who follow the rules, and review rules frequently. The plan should be posted in a prominent location in the classroom, and copies of the plan should be shared with school administrators and distributed to parents and guardians at the beginning of the school year or academic term.

EFFECTIVENESS OF ASSERTIVE DISCIPLINE

Both advocates and critics of assertive discipline have expressed strong opinions regarding its effectiveness in the classroom (Canter, 1988; Curwin & Mendler, 1988; Curwin & Mendler, 1989; McCormack, 1989; Render, Padilla, & Krank, 1989). Proponents indicate that the model is easy for students and parents to understand and for teachers to implement in the classroom, and practitioners point to benefits of the system in their own schools and classrooms (McCormack, 1989). Critics, however, suggest that the model does not teach students self-discipline and conflict resolution skills they need in the long term but rather relies on the use of consequences and rewards to secure student obedience to rules in the short term (Curwin & Mendler, 1988; Wade, 1997).

Much of the published literature on assertive discipline highlights the implementation of the model in particular settings (e.g., Malmgren, Trezek, & Paul, 2005; Wade, 1997) and reports the results of teacher survey data related to various aspects of the model (e.g., Ellis & Karr-Kidwell, 1995). There is, however, a scarcity of research on the effectiveness of assertive discipline in general, and the research that does exist is inconclusive. For example, two studies conducted in England examined the impact of assertive discipline on student behavior after teachers received assertive discipline training. The first study reported uneven implementation of the model across teachers in the school and no obvious positive impact on student behavior (Martin, 1994), while the second study reported improved rates of on-task behavior and a reduction in the numbers of disruptive incidents among students with emotional and behavioral problems as teachers increased their use of positive feedback and praise (Swinson & Cording, 2002). While some research appears to support the effectiveness of assertive discipline, the scope and quality of the research has been called into question. Render, Padilla, and Krank report in a 1989 study that the research is sparse and unsophisticated, that no generalizable data has resulted from the research, and that no study has compared the effectiveness of the model with other discipline models.

Clearly, given the widespread popularity and use of assertive discipline in classrooms, a need exists for additional research on the model. Many questions regarding the effectiveness of assertive discipline remain.

BIBLIOGRAPHY

Canter, L. (1988, October). Let the educator beware: A response to Curwin and Mendler. *Educational Leadership, 46,* 71–73.

Canter, L., & Canter, M. (1976). *Assertive discipline: A take-charge approach for today's educator.* Seal Beach, CA: Canter and Associates.

Canter, L., & Canter, M. (1982). *Assertive discipline for parents.* Los Angeles: Canter and Associates.

Canter, L., & Canter, M. (1992). *Assertive discipline: Positive behavior management for today's classroom.* Santa Monica, CA: Canter and Associates.

Canter, L., & Canter, M. (1993). *Succeeding with difficult students: New strategies for reaching your most challenging students.* Santa Monica, CA: Canter and Associates.

Canter, L., & Canter, M. (2002). *Assertive discipline: Positive behavior management for today's classroom* (3rd ed.). Bloomington, IN: Solution Tree.

Curwin, R. L., & Mendler, A. N. (1988, October). Packaged discipline programs: Let the buyer beware. *Educational Leadership, 46,* 68–71.

Curwin, R. L., & Mendler, A. N. (1989, March). We repeat, let the buyer beware: A response to Canter. *Educational Leadership, 46,* 83.

Ellis, D. W., & Karr-Kidwell, P. J. (1995). *A study of assertive discipline and recommendations for effective classroom management methods.* (ERIC Document Reproduction Service No. ED 379 207).

Malmgren, K. W., Trezek, B. J., & Paul, P. V. (2005). Models of classroom management as applied to the secondary classroom. *The Clearing House, 79*(1), 36–39.

Martin, S. C. (1994). A preliminary evaluation of the adoption and implementation of assertive discipline at Robinton High School. *School Organisation, 14*(3), 321–330.

McCormack, S. (1989, March). Response to Render, Padilla, and Krank: But practitioners say it works! *Educational Leadership, 46,* 77–79.

Render, G. F., Padilla, J. M., & Krank, H. M. (1989, March). What research really shows about assertive discipline. *Educational Leadership, 46,* 72–75.

Swinson, J., & Cording, M. (2002). Assertive discipline in a school for pupils with emotional and behavioural difficulties. *British Journal of Special Education, 29*(2), 72–75.

Wade, R. K. (1997, May). Lifting a school's spirit. *Educational Leadership, 54*(8), 34–36.

Rosetta F. Sandidge

PUNISHMENT

In common usage, punishment is typically conceptualized as a painful or otherwise unpleasant consequence that is delivered after an undesirable behavior. Punishment is usually associated with images of spankings, loud verbal reprimands, or loss of privileges. In applied behavior analysis, punishment is simply defined as any event that occurs after a behavior that results in a decrease in the frequency, intensity, duration, or latency of that behavior. There are two types of punishment: Type I punishment, also called positive punishment, involves the introduction of either an aversive stimulus or an aversive activity immediately following a behavior; Type II punishment, or negative punishment, involves the removal of a positive stimulus or preferred event immediately following a behavior. When used correctly, both Type 1 and Type 2 punishment procedures can be effective adjunctive methods for managing behavior in the classroom.

PUNISHMENT AS PART OF CLASSROOM MANAGEMENT

Type I punishments fall into two general categories: aversive activities and aversive stimuli. According to Brown-Chidsey and Steege (2004), the most common classroom application of aversive activities is overcorrection. Overcorrection takes place when a student is required to engage in an effortful behavior contingent on each incidence of a particular behavior. There are two components of overcorrection. The first, restitution, is a procedure whereby the student corrects what was damaged in the environment as a result of the behavior and restores the environment to a condition better than existed before the problem behavior. For example, a child who colors on her desk with a marker might be required to clean not only her desktop but also all the desktops in her row of desks. The second component of overcorrection is positive practice, in which a student, following a problem behavior, immediately engages in a correct version of appropriate behavior. For instance, a child who knocks over his chair and runs out the door to recess might be required to push his chair in appropriately and walk from his desk to the door ten times before joining his classmates at recess. Restitution and positive practice may be used singularly or in tandem, depending upon the circumstances of the situation.

The procedures most often used in the classroom that fall in the application of aversive stimuli category include verbal reprimands (e.g., telling a student "No"), negative social feedback, disapproving body language such as frowning or sending a negative letter home to parents. In some instances, teachers use these strategies in a systematic manner contingent upon specific behaviors. In many cases, teachers deliver these consequences without regard to their actual effect on behavior. Whatever the case, it is important to remember that, if delivery of aversive stimuli is going to be used as part of a classroom management, it should not be physically, psychologically, or emotionally harmful to the student.

There are several varieties of Type II punishment, or the removal of a reinforcer. The most effective form of Type II punishment is time-out, also known as time-out from positive reinforcement. Time-out involves removing a student from a reinforcing situation to a neutral or less reinforcing setting following the occurrence of problem behavior. The duration of a time-out may range from as little as thirty seconds to as much as five minutes. Although there are several different kinds of time-out, the ones most commonly used in schools are exclusionary and non-exclusionary time-out. Exclusionary time-out refers to situations in which the student is removed from the classroom and thus all possible sources of positive reinforcement are minimized or eliminated. Non-exclusionary time-out refers to instances in which the student remains in the room but does not have easy access to positive reinforcers (e.g., teacher and/or peer attention, activities, games). Non-exclusionary time-outs are often easier for a teacher to implement, as they do not require the teacher to leave the rest of the class unattended to escort the timed-out child to another setting. For example, if a student is being disruptive while the class is playing a math game to earn points, the teacher might ask the student to stop participating and stand by the flag at the back of the room for one minute. As mentioned earlier, a well planned and executed time-out procedure is one of the most effective behavior management tools available to teachers (Sterling & Watson, 1999).

Another regularly used form of Type II punishment is response cost. With the response cost procedure, a previously earned positive reinforcer is removed contingent upon the occurrence of an undesirable behavior. Response cost is most useful in classrooms in which teachers have some type of tangible reinforcement system (e.g., points, tokens, class money, coupons, or popsicle sticks) already in place. For example, teachers who reinforce academic work completion and appropriate social behavior with coupons that can be exchanged for small prizes at the end of the week may remove previously earned coupons when students either fail to do their work or exhibit inappropriate social behavior.

Attention extinction, or planned ignoring, is another effective form of Type II punishment when used correctly and in the appropriate situation. For example, a student who routinely asks questions of the teacher while she is giving directions may eventually stop if the teacher gives no indication that she is paying attention to the student's questions. However, planned ignoring would only work in this case if the attention being withheld by the teacher were actually reinforcing the behavior. That is, if the student's classmates laughed at the questions, it is unlikely that planned ignoring will result in a decrease in the ill-timed question-asking behavior.

While the types of misbehaviors that children exhibit invariably changes in topography and/or frequency, intensity, or duration as they age, teacher's preferred methods of discipline seem to remain fairly constant. As noted by Carter and Doyle (2006), verbal reprimands are sufficient for most mild misbehaviors that occur in early childhood and elementary classrooms. For more major forms of acting out, teachers usually prefer to use time-outs (most often some type of exclusionary time-out in which students are either removed from the classroom or sent home from school) or some other form of Type II punishment, such as restitution. Although misbehaviors among adolescents are much more complex and, if left unchecked, may be more likely to escalate into seriously disruptive behavior, verbal reprimands and time-outs are still the most common forms of punishment used even in secondary school settings (Emmer & Gerwels, 2006).

PROBLEMS WITH PUNISHMENT

Although punishment, by definition, is effective for reducing a behavior, the use of punishment as part of classroom management is controversial due to a number of problems associated with its use. First, punishment may result in a temporary increase in the undesirable behavior or the form of the behavior may change. Second, if the intensity of a punisher is gradually applied, students may tolerate very harsh forms of punishment. Third, some students may become physically aggressive when punishment is applied, particularly those students who are more prone to aggressive behavior. Fourth, punishment may produce unanticipated emotional side effects such as crying, general fearfulness, and social withdrawal. Fifth, students may model the behaviors exhibited by the adults who are delivering the punishment (e.g., yelling, finger pointing, rough handling). Sixth, there is a tendency of adults to over-rely on punishment strategies because it brings them temporary relief in the form of a brief escape from, or reduction in, a student's problematic behavior. Seventh, some educators are ethically opposed to the use of punishment, although this opposition is typically in response to the physically and emotionally harmful types of punishment. Eighth, teachers use punishment procedures every day, whether intentionally or unintentionally, without systematically evaluating the intended and unintended effects on behavior. Ninth, and perhaps most important, punishment does not teach a student what to do, it only teaches what not to do. Thus, any time a punishment procedure is used in the classroom, there should be a simultaneous plan in place that focuses on teaching and reinforcing a more appropriate behavior.

RECOMMENDATIONS FOR EFFECTIVE USE OF PUNISHMENT

Probably due to the negative consequences sometimes associated with, or produced by, punishment procedures, Landrum and Kauffman (2006) suggested that punishment should be reserved for serious misbehaviors and used only in the context of ongoing behavior management programs. The former suggestion is not necessarily true as using punishment for mild offenses can often prevent more serious infractions in the future. Prior to systematically using punishment as part of classroom management, several factors should be considered. First, teachers must be careful not to administer punishment in anger and use only a matter-of-fact tone of voice, not a threatening tone. Second, punishment should be fair, consistent, and an immediate response to problem behavior and, whenever possible, relevant to the misbehavior. Third, consistency is one of the most important factors in using punishment effectively. Teachers should pick a punisher that can be used frequently, is not physically or psychologically harmful, and then use the punishment in a systematic and planned manner in the classroom.

ALTERNATIVE APPROACHES TO DECREASING PROBLEM BEHAVIOR

Numerous procedures besides punishment can be used to decrease the occurrence of problem behavior in the classroom. Two of the most effective procedures involve implementing some type of positive reinforcement system and/or manipulating the antecedents of problem behavior. When using positive reinforcement to manage classroom behavior, the teacher should be clear as to which behavior will be reinforced and then provide reinforcement contingent on that behavior. Ideally, the behavior that is being reinforced is incompatible with the undesirable behavior. For example, if a student is running around the classroom disrupting other students, providing reinforcement for work completion should reduce the problem behavior. Completing work is likely to be incompatible with being out of one's seat disrupt-

ing others. Manipulating antecedents involves removing the triggers or cues for misbehavior (Watson & Steege, 2003). Although there are many methods for altering antecedents, the first step is to identify the variables that are actually triggering the problem behavior. After doing so, even small changes in these variables can have a significant impact on behavior. For example, if a teacher determines that difficult academic tasks reliably lead to problem behavior, she may a) decrease the difficulty of the task, b) provide additional instruction and modeling prior to assigning the work, c) assign a peer helper to assist with task completion, and/or d) intersperse very difficult problems with easier problems.

BIBLIOGRAPHY

Brown-Chidsey, R., & Steege, M. W. (2004). Punishment. In T. S. Watson & C. H. Skinner (Eds.), *Encyclopedia of school psychology* (pp. 258–261). New York: Kluwer Academic/ Plenum.

Carter, K., & Doyle, W. (2006). Classroom management in early childhood and elementary classrooms. In C. M. Evertson & C. S. Weinstein (Eds.), *Handbook of classroom management: Research, practice, and contemporary issues* (pp. 47–71). Mahwah, NJ: Erlbaum.

Emmer, E. T., & Gerwels, M. C. (2006). Classroom management in middle and high school classrooms. In C. M. Evertson & C. S. Weinstein (Eds.), *Handbook of classroom management: Research, practice, and contemporary issues* (pp. 47–71). Mahwah, NJ: Erlbaum.

Landrum, T. J., & Kauffman, J. M. (2006). Behavioral approaches to classroom management. In C. M. Evertson & C. S. Weinstein (Eds.), *Handbook of classroom management: Research, practice, and contemporary issues* (pp. 47–71). Mahwah, NJ: Erlbaum.

Sterling, H. E., & Watson, T. S. (1999). An empirically based guide for the use of time-out in the preschool and elementary classroom. *Psychology in the Schools, 36,* 135–148.

Watson, T. S., & Steege, M. W. (2003). *Conducting school-based functional behavioral assessments: A practitioner's guide.* New York: Guilford.

T. Steuart Watson
Tonya S. Watson
Sarah Gebhardt

RULES AND PROCEDURES

Classroom management is a problem that both impedes student learning and impacts teaching tenure. Approximately 46% of all new teachers in the United States leave the profession within five years of entering the classroom. Almost half of all teachers who leave the profession report problems with student behavior as the source of their dissatisfaction (U.S. Department of Education, 2002). Many schools and their classroom staff rely on discipline policies that are reactive, punitive, and exclusionary. In contrast, school-wide positive behavior support (SWPBS) is an empirically supported, preventive approach that teaches social skills to students across all school environments and all school personnel (Lewis, Sugai, & Colvin, 1998; Luiselli, Putnam, Handler, & Feinberg, 2005; Putnam, Luiselli, Handler, & Jefferson, 2003; Safran & Oswold, 2003; Sugai & Horner, 2002). Reductions in discipline concerns using these procedures at the school-wide level have been reported across a number of studies (Bohanon et al., 2006; Lassen, Steele, & Sailor, 2006; Luiselli, Putnam & Handler, 2001; Luiselli et al., 2005; McCurdy, Mannella & Eldridge, 2003; Rey et al., under review; Warren et al., 2006).

The use of class-wide behavior support practices (CWPBS) has also been shown to reduce problem behaviors in classrooms (Lambert, Cartledge, Heward & Lo, 2006; McCurdy, Mannella & Eldridge, 2003; Putnam et al., 2002). Utilizing a problem-solving model, teachers identify the problem(s) in their classrooms, validate the problem(s) using data, design solutions that include empirically supported practices, and then learn to implement and evaluate the solution(s). The development of a CWPBS program requires five components: (a) establishment of positive, class-wide behavioral expectations, (b) active teaching of these behavioral expectations to students, (c) methods to monitor student performance, (d) a system for reinforcing students, and, (e) managerial and instructional strategies to prevent and reduce problem behaviors.

Class-wide positive behavior support offers an approach that is very different from traditional discipline practices. The practices are designed to move from (a) reactive to proactive practices, (b) punitive to instructive practices, and (c) exclusionary to inclusionary practices. Reactive practices are used only after a student misbehaves, whereas proactive practices identify the challenging behaviors that students are displaying in school, and use this information to understand the areas in which students lack appropriate social skills and then teach these skills. Punitive discipline procedures punish students for acting inappropriately using a variety of events that are meant to serve as deterrents. However, research has shown that a punitive response to challenging behavior is ineffective for many students. In some cases, a punitive response can actually encourage inappropriate behavior, by providing the student with adult attention or with an escape from challenging academic tasks or social demands. In contrast, CWPBS employs an instructive approach to help students correct challenging behaviors. Often when students misbehave they are experiencing either a "skill deficit" or a "performance deficit." When students do not understand how and when to exhibit appropriate behavior or have not learned this behavior, they demonstrate a skill deficit. In this instance, the students will need to be taught new

Behavioral expectations – do's and don't's

Behavioral expectation	Examples	Non-examples
Compliance	• Follow the teacher's directions. • Do what the teacher asks after one request.	• Don't talk back or argue with teacher. • Don't take too long to do what you're told.
Preparation	• Have books, pencils & paper with you when you enter the classroom. • Bring completed homework to class.	• Don't forget your stuff. • Be ready for class.
Talking	• Ask questions and make comments relevant to the topic only. • Use quiet voices when working with groups or independently.	• Be polite and respectful to your peers. • No talking when the teacher is talking.
In class behavior	• Keep your hands and feet to yourself. • Leave your seat only with permission.	• Do your best! • No cheating, lying or stealing. • No gum, candy or soda in class.
Being on time	• Be in your seat before the bell rings. • Be in class with paper and pen out by 8 a.m.	• Don't be late
Transition behavior	• Remain in your seat while changing academic activities. • Line up quietly before walking to the next classroom.	• Don't leave before the bell. • No backpacks, coats or hats in the classroom.

Table 1 ILLUSTRATION BY GGS INFORMATION SERVICES. CENGAGE LEARNING, GALE.

behavioral skills. Sometimes students have been taught these skills but are not motivated to use them or have difficulty generalizing the skill across different locations, situations, peers, or adults. In this case, the students are demonstrating a performance deficit (i.e., they have the skill but do not consistently demonstrate it). In this instance, the students will need to be monitored and provided with feedback to reinforce their use of the new skill. The goal of a CWPBS is to address both sets of problems.

The first step in the development of an effective CWBSP is to define the behavioral expectations for the classroom or other area so that the students clearly understand how they should behave in the designated area. Overall, there are six different student performance areas that impact student learning and the functioning of the classroom: (a) compliance with requests, (b) preparation for learning, (c) talking in class, (d) in-classroom behavior, (e) being on time, and, (f) transition behavior. It is important to identify at least two behavioral expectations per rule (e.g., "bring homework to class"; "come prepared with books and pencils"). These expectations should be specific, observable, and measurable behaviors. They should be stated positively as behaviors to be performed. For example, teachers should identify the behavior that should be present rather than behaviors that should not occur. Table 1 lists some examples of these rules.

In the designing of rules and expectations, it is important to identify and address any environmental factors that could impact the successful implementation of those rules. It is also important to establish guidelines about how to manage and monitor all areas in the classroom, and how to arrange areas that are potentially problematic so students are prompted to meet the behavioral expectations.

Student behaviors can be frustrating, and it is sometimes easy to overlook the fact that students can get confused about what is expected of them. Too often, school staff assume that students know how to behave. Yet expectations tend to vary among different communities, teachers, parents, and administrators. The goal should be to have predictable routines to increase the likelihood that students can and will navigate through the class period successfully, toward a goal of independence and self-management.

Once the behavioral expectations have been developed it is essential to teach and review these behavior expectations. It is most effective to teach social skills to students in the same way academic skills are taught—through lesson plans. For example, teachers can teach students rules and behavioral expectations by (a) telling students the rules, (b) showing them the rules by modeling positive examples of how to follow the rules, (c) practicing—giving students opportunities to practice these new skills through role-play situations, written assignments, or actual situations, and assess whether students have mastered the rule, and (d) reinforcing—providing students with positive feedback on their understanding of the rule during their role-play or other assignments. Once the behavioral expectations have been taught they should be reviewed frequently and strategically. For example, these expectations should be actively reviewed before beginning or transitioning between classroom activities, after weekends and vacations, and particularly before activities or subjects that tend to have produced the most problematic behavior.

Another effective strategy within a CWBSP is proactively monitoring student behavior as a strategy to prevent problem behaviors from escalating, and minimizing attention to inappropriate behaviors. This entails three teacher behaviors: (a) moving—walking around the entire room, using proximity control to prevent problem behaviors; (b) looking—using frequent visual scans of the room, making eye contact with students; and, (c) interacting—reinforcing

students when they demonstrate positive behaviors, and correcting students when they break a rule.

Another major shift in classroom management is an active focus on recognizing students who follow the rules. Teachers should focus on positive behaviors more than negative behaviors to bring about a change in students. For the quickest change in behavior, teachers should aim for a 4:1 ratio of positive (reinforcing) to negative (corrective) statements. In addition to simple verbal and nonverbal feedback, teachers may want to use a more formal system to reward individual or groups of students for appropriate behavior.

Finally, there should be a system in place to correct inappropriate behaviors. The major emphasis should focus on being positive, proactive, and preventive. Then, teachers should follow a hierarchy of planned corrective responses, from least to most intrusive based on severity of problem behavior. Some students may continue to exhibit inappropriate behaviors despite a teacher's most creative attempts to provide positive reinforcement. In such instances teachers need to respond to inappropriate behavior by using corrective responses. Understanding students' motivations will help teachers establish consequences that do not inadvertently reinforce the inappropriate behavior. For example, if students cause trouble toward the end of lunch because they do not want to return to class, sending them to the office will not be effective. Instead, they should be sent directly to class.

Before planning corrective consequences, problem behaviors should be specifically defined. Next, the teacher should determine when problem behaviors occur—at the beginning of the day, during transitions, language arts, or during independent seatwork? Then the possible function of the behavior should be determined. For example, a student might act out to obtain attention or to avoid or escape undesirable activities, for example, a test.

Overall reductions in office discipline referrals and disruptive behavior have been observed in classrooms using this approach (Lambert, Cartledge, Heward, & Lo, 2006; McCurdy, Mannella, & Eldridge, 2003; Putnam et al., 2003a). Reductions in office discipline referrals or suspensions, or both, on playgrounds (McCurdy, Mannella, & Eldridge, 2003) and on buses (Putnam et al., 2003a) also have been demonstrated. Research published in 2003 by McCurdy, Mannella, and Eldridge reported that these interventions are particularly effective with students who come from challenging family and community circumstances and who display significantly disruptive behaviors.

Finally, the development of a CWBSP will not impact problem behavior in the classroom without the effective implementation of classroom behavior support interventions. A 2007 study by Sanetti, Luiselli, and Handler found that the provision of performance feedback on the implementation of the plan produced greater improvements in student behavior than when the plan was not implemented. Verbal plus graphic performance feedback was more effective than just verbal feedback in improving treatment integrity with the plan.

Teachers can improve their students' performance with the implementation of these procedures described above. Performance feedback may be helpful in assisting educational staff in the effective implementation of these procedures.

BIBLIOGRAPHY

Bohanon, H., Fenning, P., Carney, K., Minnis, M., Anderson-Harris, S., Moroz, K., et al. (2006). School-wide application of urban high school positive behavior support: A case study. *Journal of Positive Behavior Interventions and Supports, 8*(3), 131–145.

Hagermoser Sanetti, L.M., Luiselli, J. K., Handler, M. W. (2007). Effects of verbal and graphic performance feedback on behavior support plan implementation in a public elementary school. *Behavior Modification, 31,* 454–465.

Lambert, M. C., Cartledge, G., Heward, W. L., & Lo, Y-y (2006). Effects of response cards on disruptive behavior and academic responding during math lessons by fourth-grade urban students. *Journal of Positive Behavior Interventions, 8*(2), 88–99.

Lassen, S. R., Steele, M. M., & Sailor, W. (2006). The relationship of school-wide positive behavior support to academic achievement in an urban middle school. *Psychology in the Schools, 43,* 701–712.

Lewis, T. J., Sugai, G., & Colvin, G. (1998). Reducing problem behavior through a school-wide system of effective behavioral support: Investigation of a school-wide social skills training program and contextual interventions. *School Psychology Review, 27,* 446–459.

Luiselli, J. K., Putnam, R. F., & Handler, M. W. (2001). Improving discipline practices in public schools: Description of a whole-school and district-wide model of behavior analysis consultation. *The Behavior Analyst Today, 2,* 18–27.

Luiselli, J. K., Putnam, R. F., Handler, M. W., & Feinberg, A. (2005). Whole-school positive behavior support: Effects on student discipline problems and academic performance. *Educational Psychology, 25,* 183–198.

McCurdy, B., Mannella, M., & Eldridge, N. (2003). Positive behavior support in urban schools: Can we prevent the escalation of antisocial behavior? *Journal of Positive Behavior Interventions, 5,* 158–170.

Putnam, R. F., Handler, M., Rey, J., & O'Leary-Zonarich, C. (2002). *Classwide behavior support interventions: Using functional assessment practices to design effective interventions in general classroom settings.* Paper presented at the Annual Conference of the Association of Behavior Analysis. Toronto, Canada.

Putnam, R. F., Handler, M. W., Ramirez-Platt, C. M., & Luiselli, J. K. (2003a). Improving student bus riding behavior through a school-wide intervention. *Journal of Applied Behavior Analysis, 36,* 583–589.

Putnam R. F., Luiselli, J. K., Handler, M.W., Jefferson, G. L. (2003b). Evaluating student discipline practices in a public school through behavioral assessment of office referrals. *Behavior Modification, 27,* 505–523.

Rey, J., Their, K., Handler, H., & Putnam, R. *Primary prevention in urban schools: Are teachers 'Ready to Teach' prevention?* Manuscript submitted for publication.

Safran, S. P., & Oswald, K. (2003). Positive behavior supports: Can schools reshape disciplinary practices. *Exceptional Children, 69,* 361–373.

Sugai, G., & Horner, R. H. (2002). The evolution of discipline practices: School-wide positive behavior supports. *Child and Family Behavior Therapy, 24,* 23–50.

Sugai, G., Horner, R.H., Dunlap, G., Hieneman, M., Lewis, T., Nelson, C. M., et al. (2000). Applying positive behavior support and functional behavioral assessment in schools. *Journal of Positive Behavioral Interventions, 2*(3), 131–143.

U.S. Department of Education. (2002). *Schools and staffing survey, 1999–2000.* Washington DC: National Center for Education Statistics.

Warren, J. S., Bohanon-Edmonson, H. M., Turnbull, A. P., Sailor, W., Wickham, D., Griggs, P., & Beech, S. (2006). School-wide positive behavior support: Addressing behavior problems that impede student learning. *Educational Psychology Review, 18,* 187–198.

Robert F. Putnam
Marcie W. Handler

TOKEN ECONOMIES

In a classroom token economy, students earn tokens for appropriate behavior. Later, they exchange their earned tokens for back-up reinforcers. Back-up reinforcers could include a variety of preferred stimuli, such as extra time at recess or access to preferred activities. A token economy can represent a practical approach for achieving class-wide behavior management.

The basic principle underlying the token economy is the concept of generalized conditioned reinforcement. That is, tokens are intended to become generalized conditioned reinforcers by virtue of the fact that they can be exchanged for a variety of back-up reinforcers (Cooper, 1987). Conditioned reinforcers are items, which students do not automatically find rewarding, but after associating them with positive experiences, such as praise and privileges, become rewarding. Tokens are generalized conditioned reinforcers because they are exchanged for a variety of reward options, rather than one. In this respect, tokens are similar to money.

CLASSROOM IMPLEMENTATION

A token economy includes five components. These components need to be clearly outlined before implementing the system. A token economy can be successfully implemented provided that five basic elements are clearly defined: (a) target behaviors, (b) tokens, (c) token distribution, (d) backup reinforcers, and (e) the exchange system.

<table>
<tr><td colspan="2">**Examples of backup reinforcers**</td></tr>
<tr><td>**Natural**</td><td>**Items**</td></tr>
<tr><td>Attend special period with another class</td><td>Pencils</td></tr>
<tr><td>Be first in line</td><td>Pens</td></tr>
<tr><td>Care for class pets</td><td>Notebooks</td></tr>
<tr><td>Extra time with class games</td><td>Folders</td></tr>
<tr><td>Sit at the teacher's desk</td><td>Paper</td></tr>
<tr><td>Eat lunch in a special location</td><td>Small toys</td></tr>
<tr><td>Sit next to a friend</td><td>Stamps</td></tr>
<tr><td>Take shoes off</td><td>Stickers</td></tr>
<tr><td>Skip one homework assignment</td><td>Baseball cards</td></tr>
<tr><td>Special display of work</td><td>Markers</td></tr>
<tr><td>Spend time in another classroom</td><td>Gel pens</td></tr>
<tr><td>Tutor a younger student</td><td>Art supplies</td></tr>
<tr><td>Use the teacher's special pen</td><td>Erasers</td></tr>
<tr><td>Visit the principal (for praise)</td><td></td></tr>
<tr><td>Water class plants</td><td></td></tr>
<tr><td>Wear a hat to school</td><td></td></tr>
<tr><td>Extra computer time</td><td></td></tr>
</table>

Table 1 ILLUSTRATION BY GGS INFORMATION SERVICES. CENGAGE LEARNING, GALE.

TARGET BEHAVIORS

First, target behaviors are selected. Target behaviors must be distinct behaviors that a teacher can clearly identify as occurring or not occurring (Moore, Tingstrom, Doggett, & Carlyon, 2001). For example, having a nice attitude is not acceptable because one cannot observe a student's attitude. However, staying seated at the desk can be observed by the teacher. For starters, teachers ought to select a small number of behaviors for the token economy, adding more when students demonstrate success. The target behaviors should be positive social or academic skills that the teacher wishes to increase in the classroom.

TOKENS

Tokens fall into one of two categories, objects or symbols (Alberto and Troutman, 2006). Objects are actual items, such as poker chips, checkers, washers, marbles, or tickets. Symbols are representations, including check marks, tally marks, or holes punched into paper.

Good tokens meet several standards. First, the token must be safe, durable, and cost efficient. Also, tokens must be individualized and difficult, if not impossible, to counterfeit (Cooper, 1987). This is important to ensure that students do not unfairly acquire tokens by taking them from other students or creating their own tokens. For example, if a teacher used pennies as tokens in a class wide system, any student could bring pennies from home and accumulate unearned tokens. Counterfeit tokens can be prevented by selecting uncommon items as tokens or marking tokens with a special code, such as teacher initials. For example, if a teacher opted to use poker chips as tokens, a

special signature on the chips including the student's initials would help prevent counterfeit.

In addition, tokens must be easy to distribute. Tokens should be delivered immediately after the display of the target behavior, so they must be accessible to the teacher at all times, such as in a pocket. Ideally, tokens are delivered to a student with very little disruption to the class. Last, the appeal and value of the tokens themselves must be considered. Tokens should not be intrinsically valuable so that the students are unmotivated to exchange them. For example, if a teacher distributed scratch-and-sniff stickers as tokens, students might be less motivated to exchange them. Such stickers may also be distracting.

TOKEN DISTRIBUTION

Tokens must be distributed to students in a way that is rewarding, but not distracting. For example, teachers can whisper a word of praise or give a thumbs-up when distributing a token. Students must also have a place to store their tokens. A jar or cup placed on the student's desk is an easy storage method for object tokens. A container with a slotted lid would prevent students from playing with the tokens or spilling them. A small index card taped to students' desks is an easy method for collecting symbolic tokens. Placing token collections away from the students' desks, in the front of the classroom, may reduce distraction during distribution, but the rewarding effect of the token may be compromised. Last, there must be a plan for token collection when students are away from the classroom. Students may not be able to carry token jars when they leave the room; however, tokens can be awarded if there is a procedure in place, for example, students put tokens in pockets until they return to the classroom.

BACKUP REINFORCERS

Backup reinforcers are classified as activities or items that have positive value for the students (Alberto and Troutman, 2006). Activities are special events that occur naturally. They are ideal because they are free and relatively non-disruptive. Natural activities include acting as hall monitor, passing out papers, and a pass to the library. Actual items should also be included as backup reinforcers. However, it is unethical to withhold necessities and basic comforts, such as meals, air conditioning, heat, access to medical care, and educational activities (Cooper, 1987). (See Table 1 for more examples of activities and items that could be used as backup reinforcers.)

According to Alberto and Troutman (2006), backup reinforcers must meet several criteria. First, a wide variety of backup reinforcers should be available to ensure that each student will be motivated by at least one item. Also, the actual rewards or pictures of the rewards should be visible to the students at all times. In other words, a classroom store could be set up. If this is not possible, then a reward menu should be visible instead. Last, the cost system should be proportional to value. Smaller, cheaper items should cost fewer tokens than larger, more expensive items. For example, a pencil should cost fewer tokens than a teddy bear. This applies to naturally occurring activities as well. For example, if computer time was coveted by students more than a library pass, then computer time should cost more tokens than the library pass.

EXCHANGE SYSTEM

A clear routine for exchanging tokens must be established in order to prevent class disruption. When a token system is first implemented, students must be allowed to exchange tokens for backup rewards frequently, as much as four times per day. Frequent exchanges are necessary to teach the connection between tokens and rewards, thus increasing the value of tokens. As students learn the token economy, the duration between exchange opportunities can be increased. Younger students and students with disabilities may never benefit from infrequent exchanges; therefore, some token economies must maintain frequent exchanges. However, older children may eventually be able to manage a token system with only one exchange per week (Alberto and Troutman, 2006).

REVIEW OF THE RESEARCH

Research has shown that token economies can be successful in a variety of settings, including both general and special education classrooms. Token economies have been used with success in inclusive settings across ages (Carpenter, 2001; Filcheck, McNeil, Greco, & Bernard, 2004; Higgins, Williams, McLaughlin, 2001; Lannie & Martens, 2004). Several studies have demonstrated the success of token economies in special education settings, including resource rooms (Buisson, Murdock, Reynolds, & Cronin, 1995) and self-contained rooms (Cavalier, Ferretti, & Hodges, 1997; Truchlicka, McLaughlin, & Swain, 1998).

Token system success is also flexible across student characteristics and abilities. Token economies have been successful for typically developing children (Filcheck et al., 2004; Lannie & Martens, 2004). They have also been effective for students with disabilities, such as hearing impairments (Buisson et al., 1995), learning disabilities (Cavalier et al., 1997; Higgins et al., 2001), mental retardation (Carpenter, 2001), speech delays (Kahng, Boscoe, & Byren, 2003), attention deficit hyperactivity disorder (Bender & Mathes, 1995), and behavior disorders (Truchlicka et al., 1998).

Research has also demonstrated the success of token economies at managing a variety of target behaviors in school settings. Substantial research has shown the effectiveness of token systems in managing inappropriate or challenging behaviors (Buisson et al., 1995; Carpenter, 2001; Cavalier et al., 1997; Filcheck et al., 2004; Higgins et al., 2001). Furthermore, academic tasks such as math, reading, spelling, history, and language have been successfully improved using token systems (Lannie & Martens, 2004; Truchlicka et al., 1998) as well as social skills, such as sportsmanship and class participation (Boniecki & Moore, 2003; Hupp & Reitman, 1999).

In sum, the research on token systems has demonstrated that this is an effective strategy for increasing appropriate classroom behavior and managing inappropriate behavior across a variety of classroom settings and students.

BIBLIOGRAPHY

Alberto, P. A., & Troutman, A. C. (2006). *Applied Behavior Analysis for Teachers* (7th ed.). Upper Saddle River, NJ: Pearson Merrill Prentice Hall.

Bender, W. W., & Mathes, M. Y. (1995). Students with ADHD in inclusive classrooms: A hierarchical approach to strategy selection. *Intervention in School and Clinic, 30,* 226–234.

Boniecki, K. A., & Moore, S. (2003). Breaking the silence: Using a token economy to reinforce classroom participation. *Teaching of Psychology, 30,* 224–227.

Buisson, G. J., Murdock, J. Y., & Reynolds, K. E. (1995). Effects of tokens on response latency of students with hearing impairments in a resource room. *Education and Treatment of Children, 18*(4), 408–421.

Carpenter, L. B. (2001). Utilizing travel cards to increase productive student behavior, teacher collaboration, and parent-school communication. *Education and Training in Mental Retardation and Developmental Disabilities, 36*(3), 318–322.

Cavalier, A. R., Ferretti, R. P., & Hodges, A. F. (1997). Self-management within a classroom token economy for students with learning disabilities. *Research in Developmental Disabilities, 18*(3), 167–78.

Cooper, J. O. (1987). Token economy. In J. O. Cooper, T. E. Heron, & W. L. Heward (Eds.), *Applied Behavior Analysis.* Columbus, OH: Merrill.

Filcheck, H. A., McNeil, C. B., Greco, L. A., & Bernard, R. S. (2004). Using a whole-class token economy and coaching of teacher skills in a preschool classroom to manage disruptive behavior. *Psychology in the Schools, 4*(3), 351–361.

Higgins, J. W., Williams, R. L., McLaughlin, T. F. (2001). The effects of a token economy employing instructional consequences for a third-grade student with learning disabilities: A data-based case study. *Education and Treatment of Children, 42*(1), 99–106.

Hubb, S. D. A., & Reitman, D. (1999). Improving sports skills and sportsmanship in children diagnosed with attention-deficit/hyperactivity disorder. *Child and Family Behavior Therapy, 21*(3), 35–51.

Kahng, S. W., Boscoe, J. H., & Byrne, S. (2003). The use of escape contingency and a token economy to increase food acceptance. *Journal of Applied Behavior Analysis, 36,* 349–353.

Lannie, A. L., & Martens, B. K. (2004). Effects of task difficulty and type of contingency on students' allocation of responding to math worksheets. *Journal of Applied Behavior Analysis, 37,* 53–65.

Moore, J. W., Tingstrom, D. H., Doggett, R. A., Carlyon, W. D. (2001). Restructuring an existing token economy in a psychiatric facility for children. *Child and Family Behavior Therapy, 23*(3), 51–57.

Truchlicka, M., McLaughlin, T. F., & Swain, J. C. (1998). Effects of token reinforcement and response cost on the accuracy of spelling performance with middle-school special education students with behavior disorders. *Behavioral Interventions, 13,* 1–10.

Tonya N. Davis
Mark O'Reilly
Giulio Lancioni
Jeff Sigafoos
Wendy Machalicek

WITHITNESS

Withitness is a teacher characteristic that is evident when a teacher communicates awareness of a student's inappropriate behavior in a timely and accurate manner. A timely communication is one that occurs before the misbehavior has escalated or spread, and an accurate communication addresses the correct student. Thus, teachers who are *withit* detect inappropriate behavior promptly and let students know they are aware of it. Teachers who lack this skill either ignore inappropriate behavior or they fail to detect it until it is too late; that is, the inappropriate behavior has taken root and spread.

The term, *withitness*, was developed and operationalized by Jacob Kounin (1970) in a series of classroom studies. Kounin and his colleagues were interested in identifying how teachers dealt effectively with inappropriate student behavior. Initially they studied *desist* events (i.e., communications that are intended to stop some student behavior) to attempt to determine if properties of desists such as their clarity, firmness, or intensity had an impact on student work involvement or disruptive behavior. Unable to detect any significant effects for properties of desists, Kounin turned his attention to the timing of desists and their accuracy. Using videotapes of classrooms, a measure of teacher withitness was obtained by classifying desists according to whether each addressed the correct target and did so in a timely manner. The teachers' withitness scores (the percentage of desist events that were timely and accurate) were correlated moderately to highly with both student work involvement and freedom from deviancy in recitation settings (i.e., teacher led, whole class activities).

The concept of withitness is intuitively appealing. In common parlance, it is the measure of the "teacher with eyes in the back of her head." Kounin's great contribution was to develop a reliable observational measure of the concept and to demonstrate empirically its importance for the management of student behavior in group settings.

Some other research has provided support for the importance of withitness as a management skill. For example, in research on elementary and middle school classes, Evertson, Emmer, and Anderson operationalized withitness as a combination of effective teacher monitoring and stopping inappropriate behavior promptly. Their research found that teachers who were rated highly on these constituents of withitness had classes with higher levels of on-task behaviors and lower amounts of disruptive behaviors. In a study of physical education classes, Johnston found that desists that were accurate and prompt were successful in returning students to the task around 80 percent of the time, compared to 45 percent for desists that targeted the wrong students or were late.

An explanation for the effectiveness of withitness is that early detection of inappropriate behavior allows the teacher to communicate with the focus student before other students are involved. Waiting too long to address the problem or catching the wrong student risks escalation of the misbehavior. When such events occur frequently, the teacher ultimately has to use more intense interventions that take time and are distracting to other students. Typically the flow of classroom activities is disrupted, creating more opportunities for disorder to spread.

While it is tempting to conclude that withitness is directly causitive, affecting student behavior and related outcomes, several cautions should be noted. Withitness might be partly a function of the population served. In a classroom with large numbers of troublesome students, teachers might find it more difficult to exhibit withitness because they need to keep the activity moving. Too much attention to problem behaviors will distract student attention and interfere with instruction. Conversely, in a generally cooperative class, inappropriate behaviors stand out, making it easier for the teacher to detect and treat problems—in short, to be withit. Finally, withitness may be part of a more general teacher skill set so that other correlated skills contribute to the teacher's effectiveness.

The relationship between withitness and problematic student behaviors is likely to be recursive. Early in the school year, a teacher who exhibits withitness will obtain more appropriate student behavior, resulting in a more orderly setting; subsequently students are less likely to misbehave because their behavior has accommodated to the classroom norms and also because they know that they are more likely to be caught. A teacher who does not exhibit withitness in early encounters with students is likely to have more disorder, leading to greater difficulty displaying withitness and, as a consequence, further deterioration in student behavior.

BIBLIOGRAPHY

Emmer, E., Evertson, C., & Anderson, L. (1980). Effective management at the beginning of the school year. *Elementary School Journal, 80,* 219–231.

Evertson, C., & Emmer, E. (1982). Effective management at the beginning of the year in junior high school classrooms. *Journal of Educational Psychology, 74,* 485–498.

Johnston, B. D. (1995). "Withitness": Real or fictional? *The Physical Educator, 52*(1), 22–28.

Kounin, J. (1970). *Discipline and group management in classrooms.* New York: Holt, Rinehart, & Winston.

Edmund T. Emmer

COGNITIVE APPRENTICESHIP

Throughout most of history, teaching and learning have been based on apprenticeship. As Rogoff (1990) makes clear, children throughout the world learn how to speak, grow crops, and make clothes by apprenticeship. They do not go to school to learn these skills; instead, adults in their family and communities show them how and help them practice. Even in advanced societies, people learn through apprenticeship, such as gaining a first language, acquiring critical skills in a new job, and doctoral training for scientists. When people have the resources and a strong desire to learn, they often hire a coach to teach them by apprenticeship, because apprenticeship is a more effective for learning. But for most kinds of learning, schooling has replaced apprenticeship.

Collins, Brown, & Newman (1989) have argued that computer-based learning environments could provide students with apprenticeship-like experiences, providing the attention and feedback that are associated with apprenticeship. Their research builds on the ideas of Vygotsky (1978), whose view of how social interaction fosters cognitive development resembles apprenticeship, in which a novice works with an expert in the zone of proximal development.

FROM TRADITIONAL TO COGNITIVE APPRENTICESHIP

In her study of a tailor shop in Africa, Lave (1988) identified the central features of traditional apprenticeship. Learning is instrumental to the accomplishment of meaningful real-world tasks and embedded in a social and functional context. The apprentice observes the master modeling the target process. The apprentice then attempts to execute the process with coaching from the master. A key aspect is guided participation (Rogoff, 1990): the support that the master provides until the novice has acquired the needed skills. As the learner develops increasing skill, the master provides less help, eventually fading away completely.

Cognitive apprenticeship (Brown, Collins, & Duguid, 1989; Collins, Brown, & Newman, 1989) updated traditional apprenticeship to apply to subjects taught in school. The *cognitive* emphasizes that the focus is on cognitive skills, rather than physical ones. Traditional apprenticeship

---

KEY PRINCIPLES FOR COGNITIVE APPRENTICESHIP

■

CONTENT—TYPES OF KNOWLEDGE REQUIRED FOR EXPERTISE

Domain knowledge: subject matter specific concepts, facts, and procedures

Heuristic strategies: generally applicable techniques for accomplishing tasks

Control strategies: general approaches for directing one's solution process

Learning strategies: knowledge about how to learn new concepts, facts, and procedures

METHODS—WAYS TO PROMOTE THE DEVELOPMENT OF EXPERTISE

Modeling: teacher performs a task so students can observe

Coaching: teacher observes and facilitates while students perform a task

Scaffolding: teacher provides supports to help the student perform a task

Articulation: teacher encourages students to verbalize their knowledge and thinking

Reflection: teacher enables students to compare their performance with others

Exploration: teacher invites students to pose and solve their own problems

SEQUENCING—KEYS TO ORDERING LEARNING ACTIVITIES

Increasing complexity: meaningful tasks gradually increasing in difficulty

Increasing diversity: practice in a variety of situations to emphasize broad application

Global to local skills: focus on conceptualizing the whole task before executing the parts

SOCIOLOGY—SOCIAL CHARACTERISTICS OF LEARNING ENVIRONMENTS

Situated learning: students learn in the context of working on realistic tasks

Community of practice: communication about different ways to accomplish meaningful tasks

Intrinsic motivation: students set personal goals to seek skills and solutions

Cooperation: students work together to accomplish their goals

---

evolved to teach domains in which skills are visible. But students lack access to the cognitive processes of instructors as a basis for learning through observation. Cognitive apprenticeship is designed to bring these processes into the open, where students can observe and practice them.

There are two other major differences between cognitive apprenticeship and traditional apprenticeship. First, because traditional apprenticeship is set in the workplace, the tasks arise not from pedagogical concerns, but from the demands of the workplace. In cognitive apprenticeship tasks are sequenced to reflect the changing demands of learning. Second, whereas traditional apprenticeship emphasizes teaching skills in the context of their use, cognitive apprenticeship emphasizes generalizing knowledge, so that it can be used in many different settings.

A FRAMEWORK FOR COGNITIVE APPRENTICESHIP

Cognitive apprenticeship focuses on four dimensions that constitute any learning environment: content, method, sequence, and sociology.

Content. Experts have to master domain knowledge, the concepts, facts, and procedures associated with a specialized area. In the late twentieth and early twenty-first centuries, researchers have been identifying the strategic knowledge that supports people's ability to make use of these concepts, facts, and procedures to solve real-world problems:

1. Heuristic strategies are techniques for accomplishing tasks that might be regarded as tricks of the trade; they do not always work, but can be quite helpful. Most heuristics are tacitly acquired by experts, but there have been attempts to address heuristic learning explicitly (Schoenfeld, 1985).

2. Metacognitive strategies control the process of carrying out a task. Metacognitive strategies have monitoring, diagnostic, and remedial components; decisions about how to proceed in a task depend on one's current state relative to one's goals, on an analysis of current difficulties, and on the strategies available for dealing with difficulties.

3. Learning strategies pertain to learning domain knowledge, heuristic strategies, and control strategies. For example, Chi and her colleagues (1989) have identified strategies students should follow to learn how to solve math and science problems.

Method. The six teaching methods associated with cognitive apprenticeship fall roughly into three groups. The first three methods (modeling, coaching, and scaffolding) are the core of traditional apprenticeship. The next two methods (articulation and reflection) are designed to help students to generalize their learning. The final method (exploration) is aimed at encouraging learner autonomy.

1. Modeling involves an expert performing a task so that the students can observe the processes that are required to accomplish it. In cognitive domains, this requires externalization of internal processes. For example, a teacher might model reading in one voice, while verbalizing thoughts in another voice. In mathematics, Schoenfeld (1985) models problem solving when students bring him difficult problems to solve in class.

2. Coaching consists of observing students' work and offering hints, challenges, scaffolding, feedback, modeling, reminders, and new tasks aimed at more expert performance. In Palincsar and Brown's (1984) reciprocal teaching of reading, the teacher coaches the students while they ask questions, clarify their difficulties, generate summaries, and make predictions.

3. Scaffolding refers to the supports teachers provide to help students carry out tasks. These supports can take either the form of suggestions or hints, as in Palincsar and Brown's (1984) reciprocal teaching, or they can take the form of physical supports, as with the short skis used to teach downhill skiing. Fading involves the gradual removal of supports until students are on their own.

4. Articulation includes any method of getting students to explicitly state their knowledge and reasoning in a domain. Inquiry teaching (Collins & Stevens, 1983) is a strategy for questioning students to lead them to articulate their understanding.

5. Reflection involves enabling students to compare their own problem-solving processes with those of an expert or of other students. Reflection is enhanced by use of various techniques for replaying the performances of both expert and novice for comparison (Collins & Brown, 1988).

6. Exploration involves guiding students to problem solving on their own. Enabling them to do exploration is critical, if they are to learn how to frame interesting problems that they can solve. Exploration is the ultimate fading of support.

Sequencing. Cognitive apprenticeship provides principles to guide the sequencing of learning activities.

1. Increasing complexity. Tasks should be sequenced to include more and more of the skills and concepts necessary for expert performance. For example, in reading, students progress from relatively short texts

with simple syntax to longer texts with complex ideas that make interpretation difficult.

2. Increasing diversity. Tasks should be sequenced so that a wider variety of strategies or skills are required. As skills become well learned, it is important that the student learns to distinguish the conditions under which they apply.

3. Global before local skills. In tailoring (Lave, 1988) apprentices learn to put together a garment from pieces before cutting out pieces themselves. Having a model of the overall activity helps learners make sense of the portion they are carrying out, improving their ability to monitor progress and develop self-correction skills.

Sociology. Tailoring apprentices learn their craft in a busy shop, surrounded by masters and apprentices they can talk to and observe. They engage in activities that contribute directly to the production of garments. Hence, apprentices learn skills as applied to real-world problems, within a culture of expert practice. These considerations suggest several characteristics affecting the sociology of learning.

1. Situated learning. A critical element in fostering learning is having students carry out tasks in an environment that reflects the nature of such tasks in the world (Brown, Collins, & Duguid, 1989; Lave & Wenger, 1991). For example, Dewey created a situated-learning environment in his experimental school by having the students design and build a clubhouse, a task that emphasizes arithmetic and planning skills.

2. Community of practice. This refers to the creation of a learning environment in which the participants communicate about and engage in the skills involved in expertise (Lave & Wenger, 1991). Such a community develops a sense of ownership, personal investment, and mutual dependency.

3. Intrinsic motivation. It is important that students perform tasks, because they are intrinsically related to a goal of importance to them, rather than for some extrinsic reason, such as getting a good grade or pleasing the teacher.

4. Collaboration. Exploiting cooperation refers to having students work together in a way that fosters collaborative problem solving. Collaboration is a powerful motivator and a powerful mechanism for extending learning resources.

THEMES IN RESEARCH ON COGNITIVE APPRENTICESHIP

In the years since 1989 when cognitive apprenticeship was first introduced, there has been extensive research

toward developing learning environments that embody many of these principles.

Situated Learning. Goal-based scenarios (Schank et al., 1994) embody many of the principles of cognitive apprenticeship. Learners are given real-world tasks and the scaffolding they need to carry out such tasks. For example, in one computer-based scenario learners are asked to advise married couples as to whether their children are likely to have sickle-cell anemia, a genetically-linked disease. In order to advise the couples, learners must find out how different genetic combinations lead to the disease and run tests to determine the parents' genetic makeup. There are scaffolds in the system to support the learners, such as recorded experts who offer advice. Other goal-based scenarios support learners in a variety of challenging tasks, such as putting together a news broadcast or developing a computer-reservation system. Goal-based scenarios make it possible to embed cognitive skills and knowledge in the kinds of contexts where they are to be used.

Video and computer technology has enhanced the ability to create simulation environments where students are learning skills in context. A novel use of video technology is the Jasper series developed by the Cognition and Technology Group (1997) at Vanderbilt University to teach middle-school mathematics. In a series of 15- to 20-minute videos students are put into various problem-solving contexts: e.g., deciding on a business plan for a school fair or a rescue plan for a wounded eagle. The problems are quite difficult to solve and reflect the complex problem solving and planning that occurs in real life. Middle-school students work in groups for several days to solve each problem. Solving the problems develops a much richer understanding of the underlying mathematical concepts than the traditional school-mathematics problems.

Communities of Learners. In recent years there has developed a learning communities that approach builds on Lave and Wenger's (1991) concept of a community of practice. In a learning community the goal is to advance collective knowledge in a way to support the growth of individual knowledge (Bielaczyc & Collins, 1999).

Brown and Campione (1996) have developed a teaching model they call Fostering a Community of Learners (FCL) for grades 1 through 8. In the FCL model there are three research cycles per year. A cycle begins with shared activities to build a common knowledge base. Students then break into research groups that focus on a specific topic related to the central topic. For example, a class studying food chains may break into five groups that each focus on a different aspect, such as photosynthesis or consumers. Students research their subtopic as a group, with individuals majoring by pursuing their own research agendas within the subtopic.

Students engage in regular crosstalk sessions, in which the different groups explain their work, ask and answer questions, and refine their understanding. The research activities include reciprocal teaching (Palincsar & Brown, 1984), guided writing and composing, consultation with experts outside the classroom, and cross-age tutoring. Finally, students from each of the subtopic groups come together to form a jigsaw group (Aronson, 1978) in order to share their learning and work together on a consequential task. The consequential tasks require students to share knowledge across groups and serve as occasions for exhibition and reflection.

Scaffolding. Scaffolding helps learners carry out tasks that are beyond their capabilities. Quintana et al. (2004) suggest twenty specific strategies for designing scaffolds to support understanding, inquiry, articulation, and reflection in computer-based environments. In most situations, scaffolding naturally fades as learners are able to accomplish tasks on their own.

Sandoval and Reiser (2004) have developed a computer system called the Biology Guided Inquiry Learning Environment (BGuILE) that supports students in making scientific arguments in the context of population genetics. The system presents the students with a mystery concerning why many of the finches in the Galapagos Islands died during a drought. In order to solve the mystery, students have to analyze extensive data that were collected by scientists and come up with a reasoned conclusion as to why some finches died while others survived. The Explanation Constructor tool in the system prompts the students to put in all the pieces of a sound genetics-based argument, after they have decided what caused the finches to die. Hence, the system scaffolds students to articulate their argument in a much more explicit form than they would normally do.

The concept of scaffolding comes from Vygotsky's 1978 concept of the zone of proximal development, which described how adults support learners to accomplish tasks that they cannot accomplish themselves. The focus of research on scaffolding has been on supporting individuals, but Kolodner et al. (2003) point out that it is important to scaffold groups as well. So for example, in teaching science, they provide students with focused collaboration activities to solve simple problems, which they call launcher units. Engaging in these activities and reflecting on them helps students to collaborate more effectively and to understand the value of collaboration.

Articulation. In order to abstract learning from particular contexts, it is important for learners to articulate their thinking and knowledge. For example, Lampert (Lampert, et al., 1996) showed how fifth grade children can form a community of inquiry about important mathematical con-cepts. She engaged students in discussion of their conjectures and interpretations of each other's reasoning. Techniques of this kind have been successful with even younger children (Cobb & Bauersfeld, 1995) and may underlie the success of Japanese mathematical education.

A notable method for fostering articulation in science is the Itakura method developed in Japan (Hatano & Inagaki, 1991). First, students make different predictions about what will happen in a simple experiment, where they are likely to have different expectations. For example, one experiment involves lowering a clay ball into water and predicting what will happen. After students make their initial predictions, they discuss and defend why they think their predictions are correct. After any revisions in their predictions, the experiment is performed and discussion ensues as to why the result came out the way it did.

The Knowledge Forum environment developed by Scardamalia and Bereiter (1994) is an environment in which students articulate their ideas in writing over a computer network. The model involves students investigating problems in different subject areas over a period of weeks or months. As students work, they enter their ideas and research findings as notes in an on-line knowledge base. The software scaffolds students in constructing their notes through features such as theory-building scaffolds (e.g. "My Theory," "I Need to Understand") or debate scaffolds (e.g. "Evidence For"). Students can read through the knowledge base, adding text, graphics, questions, links to other notes, and comments on each other's work. When someone has commented on their work, the system automatically notifies them about it. The emphasis is on progress toward collective goals of understanding, rather than individual learning and performance.

Reflection. Reflection encourages learners to look back on their task performance and compare it to other performances, such as their previous performances and those of experts. One of the most effective ways to improve performance is for learners to evaluate how they did with respect to a set of criteria that determine good performance. For example, White and Frederiksen (1998) showed that students who evaluated their performance on science projects using a set of eight criteria learned much more than students who carried out the same tasks, but did not reflect on their performance. In fact, this reflection helped the weaker students much more than the stronger students.

The essential way people get better at doing things is by thinking about what they are going to do beforehand, by trying to do what they have planned, and by reflecting back on how well what they did came out. If they can articulate criteria for evaluating what they did, this will help them as they plan what they do on the next cycle. The wide availability of computers and other recording technologies makes performances easier to produce and to reflect upon. For example, students can now produce their own news broadcasts, musical performances, or plays, on audiotape or videotape. Furthermore, they can play these back, reflect upon them, and edit them until they are polished.

As these examples illustrate, there has been extensive research in recent years that has incorporated the principles of cognitive apprenticeship in the design of learning environments. As computer-based learning environments become more pervasive, there is likely to be continued development of new ways to embody these principles in their design.

SEE ALSO *Constructivism; Reciprocal Teaching.*

BIBLIOGRAPHY

Aronson, E. (1978). *The jigsaw classroom.* Beverly Hills, CA: Sage.

Bielaczyc, K., & Collins, A. (1999). Learning communities in classrooms: A reconceptualization of educational practice. In C. M. Reigeluth (Ed.), *Instructional-design theories and models: A new paradigm of instructional theory* (pp. 269–292). Mahwah, NJ: Erlbaum.

Brown, A., & Campione, J. (1996). Psychological theory and the design of innovative learning environments: On procedures, principles, and systems. In L. Schauble & R. Glaser (Eds.), *Innovations in learning: New environments for education* (pp. 289–325). Mahwah, NJ: Erlbaum.

Brown, J. S., Collins, A., & Duguid, P. (1989). Situated cognition and the culture of learning. *Educational Researcher, 18*(1), 32–42.

Chi, M. T., Bassok, M., Lewis, M. W., Reimann, P., & Glaser, R. (1989). Self-Explanations: How students study and use examples in learning to solve problems. *Cognitive Science, 13,* 145–182.

Cobb, P., & Bauersfeld, H. (Eds.). (1995). *The emergence of mathematical meaning: Interaction in classroom cultures.* Mahwah, NJ: Erlbaum.

Cognition and Technology Group at Vanderbilt. (1997). *The Jasper Project: Lessons in curriculum, instruction, assessment, and professional development.* Mahwah, NJ: Erlbaum.

Collins, A., & Brown, J. S. (1988). The computer as a tool for learning through reflection. In H. Mandl & A. Lesgold (Eds.), *Learning issues for intelligent tutoring systems* (pp. 1–18). New York: Springer.

Collins, A., Brown, J. S., & Newman, S. E. (1989). Cognitive apprenticeship: Teaching the crafts of reading, writing, and mathematics. In L. B. Resnick (Ed.), *Knowing, learning, and instruction: Essays in honor of Robert Glaser* (pp. 453–494). Hillsdale, NJ: Erlbaum.

Collins, A., & Stevens, A. L. (1983). A cognitive theory of interactive teaching. In C. M. Reigeluth (Ed.), *Instructional design theories and models: An overview* (pp. 247–278). Hillsdale, NJ: Erlbaum.

Hatano, G., & Inagaki, K. (1991). Sharing cognition through collective comprehension activity. In L. Resnick, J. Levine, & S. D. Teasley (Eds.), *Perspectives on socially shared cognition* (pp. 331–348). Washington, DC: American Psychological Association.

Lampert, M., Rittenhouse, P., & Crumbaugh, C. (1996). Agreeing to disagree: Developing sociable mathematical discourse. In D. R. Olson & N. Torrance (Eds.), *Handbook of education and human development* (pp. 731–764). Oxford: Blackwell.

Lave, J. (1988). *The culture of acquisition and the practice of understanding* (Report No. IRL88-0007). Palo Alto, CA: Institute for Research on Learning.

Lave, J., & Wenger, E. (1991). *Situated learning: Legitimate peripheral participation.* New York: Cambridge University Press.

Palincsar, A. S., & Brown, A. L. (1984). Reciprocal teaching of comprehension-fostering and monitoring activities. *Cognition and Instruction, 1*(2), 117–175.

Quintana, C., Reiser, B. J., Davis, E. A., Krajcik, J., Fretz, E., Duncan, R. G., et al. (2004). A scaffolding design framework for software to support science inquiry. *Journal of the Learning Sciences, 13*(3), 337–386.

Rogoff, B. (1990). *Apprenticeship in thinking: Cognitive development in social context.* New York: Oxford University Press.

Sandoval, W. A., & Reiser, B. J. (2004). Explanation-driven inquiry: Integrating conceptual and epistemic scaffolds for scientific inquiry. *Science Education, 88,* 345–372.

Scardamalia, M., & Bereiter, C. (1994). Computer support for knowledge-building communities. *Journal of the Learning Sciences, 3*(3), 265–283.

Schank, R. C., Fano, A., Bell, B., & Jona, M. (1994). The design of goal-based scenarios. *Journal of the Learning Sciences, 3*(4), 305–346.

Schoenfeld, A. H. (1985). *Mathematical problem solving.* Orlando, FL: Academic Press.

Vygotsky, L. S. (1978). *Mind in society: The development of higher mental processes.* Cambridge, MA: Harvard University Press.

White, B. Y., & Frederiksen, J. R. (1990). Inquiry, modeling, and metacognition: Making science accessible to all students. *Cognition and Instruction, 16*(1), 3–118.

Allan Collins

COGNITIVE DEVELOPMENT

This entry contains the following:

OVERVIEW

Methods of teaching are typically predicated on fixed assumptions about the mind of the child to be taught. Is the mind of the child a blank slate, upon which the lessons are written or engraved in wax? Or is the child an opening flower to be guided by the teacher as gardener? Is the development of the mind a simple build-up of habits, a continuous and gradual accumulation of information, or does the child progress through stage-like shifts in understanding, modifying information given to him or her in accordance with that level of understanding? Are those stages ordained by physiology, evolution, or genetics? Or is the mind of a child like an information-processing computer, with hardware capacity and speed of processing limitations, running software: cognitive strategies and procedures? Finally, there is the conception of the child as clay to be passively molded as contrasted with the child as active investigator, constructing reality inside his or her head with or without the help of caretakers, educational materials, cultural prescriptions and prohibitions. All of these views contain some truth, and each is also useful to educators. This entry provides an overview; specific classroom techniques can be found under the individual entry for each theory.

THE POWER OF HABIT: THE EMPIRICIST TRADITION

In *Some Thoughts Concerning Education* (Locke, 1693/1968), the British empiricist philosopher John Locke (1632–1704) provided the intellectual foundation for the dominant theory of cognitive development in England and the United States until the mid-20th century. Empiricism is the philosophy that all knowledge is ultimately based on sense experiences and cognitive reflection on those experiences. Thus, Locke's main childrearing and educational advice was to observe children behaving in their context and to be aware that they are observing their parents' behavior in turn. Rather than forcing children to memorize texts and rules and to beat them if they forgot, Locke recommended that a parent or tutor encourage practice of skills in carefully graduated steps matched to the age, experience, and temperament of the child. Children should be encouraged to work for the praise and good esteem of their parents, rather than to receive concrete bribes or to avoid punishment. Locke believed that children are born without innate ideas and thus are blank slates, but he said that each child has a unique natural temperament that once observed should be taken into account.

Thus in the empiricist school, practice followed by praise or punishment was thought to lead to a buildup of proper habits. At its best, the empiricist tradition promoted a sophisticated pragmatism. E. L. Thorndike (1874–1949), one of the founders of educational psychology at Teachers' College

at Columbia University in the early 20th century, believed that education did not expand general ability. Rather, he believed that every mental task could be decomposed into a series of discrete actions or thoughts that had met with success in particular tasks. Once a process had been trained to mastery in the classroom, only those elements that were the same between the training session and the new situation would transfer. This *identical elements* theory of education deemphasized massive rote learning in favor of taking care that habits should be explicitly useful in the world. For example, Thorndike suggested that quantities in all arithmetic word problems should be given with units of measurement (feet, inches, or pounds), and a child should never have to calculate 16/18ths of a dollar. No habits should be taught that would later have to be broken; thus, careful consideration should be given to the context where habits of thought would be used. Thorndike believed that once basic habits are learned so well as to be automatic, higher-level thinking would emerge. (Thorndike, 1910–1913).

Every time math problem sets are ordered so that the next problem is only slightly more complex than the previous one, the insights of this tradition are used. But the empiricists saw the child as relatively passive, and thus the brunt of learning fell on the teacher to rigorously prepare step-by- step materials. Their notion of learning as the gradual build-up of knowledge largely ignored qualitative developmental shifts in thinking. Much of the bad reputation of this method comes from the fact that its teacher-centered view was corrupted by the so-called factory school, the scale of which undermined Locke's cardinal principle of constantly observing child-teacher interactions, and instead encouraged one-way rote learning.

THE INFORMATION PROCESSING MODEL: THE MIND AS A COMPUTER

Philosophers, psychologists, and educators have frequently proposed metaphors based on the advanced technology of their times to understand the mind. Locke's view of the mind was really a mental chemistry model. Information processing theory sees the mind as a computer analyzing symbolic code data with strings of commands (software programs) through electronic computers with hardware components such as input devices, working memory, and long-term storage. This led to several findings concerning cognition and memory:

1. Adult memory can be characterized by a multistoried model: A vast amount of unanalyzed information is captured for a fraction of a second (visual) to a couple of seconds (auditory) in a sensory store. Attending to information captures it and moves it to a short-term store before it fades. Children as young as 5 have a similar sensory memory size but less attention

capability. Short-term memory, or working memory, holds 7 ±2 bits of information for a maximum of 30 seconds unless some strategy is used to remember it, such as chunking digits, or rehearsing, linking or grouping items in a meaningful way. Children in Western formal schools have deficiencies in these strategies (software programs) until about age 11 or 12, but they can be taught the strategies as young as first grade. Younger children who use these strategies remember more than their peers, but they may not transfer the useful strategies successfully to new settings. Use of such elaborative strategies sends information to long-term storage, which has large, indefinite size, and duration limits.

2. Elementary school children lack the ability to deploy memory and thinking strategies effectively, even though they would be helpful, because they lack *metamemory* or *metacognition*. That is, they may not accurately think about memory or think about thinking the relevant experience to know which strategies to use in which contexts, or find it very difficult to monitor their own thinking processes while using them. However, considerable research suggests that predicting what will come next in a paragraph, estimating how many things they might remember, or the end product of a math problem, helps them learn such skills. Similarly, summarizing, checking one's work, formulating questions about reading passages or other exercises in thinking about thinking promote metacognition, which can be conceptualized as higher order programs about how to deploy strategies and which tend to promote comprehension without endangering calculation or word decoding skills. One useful method is to coax the child to compare the results of using an effective strategy with one that is not effective, rather than the procedures themselves.

The child is seen as a more active learner in the information processing approach, but the major change in development is still the content in the child's head, in terms of meaningful knowledge about concepts, strategies, and metastrategies (strategies for using strategies). Hardware changes less than software and data. In this metaphor, children are also being compared with adults as the standard, rather than taken on their own terms. (For useful summaries of this position, see Klahr & Simon, 2002; Schneider & Pressley, 1997; Siegler, 1996.)

BIOLOGICAL THEORIES

With the advent of the science of brain physiology and the theory of evolution, strong biological theories were entertained beginning in the late 19th century, but lack of scientific knowledge of genetics, combined with race or

class biases in the scientists led at first to egregious errors in interpretation. Beginning with Darwin's cousin, Francis Galton (1869), racist or classist eugenicists believed that intelligence is not only heritable, but also unchangeable, so they argued that poor and minority children cannot or should not be raised up (see Gould, 1996).

This history of biological theories of cognition should remind us to be very careful about how and what conclusions are drawn from the latest biological or genetic information. It is now believed, for example, that racial differences were added far too late in evolution to have caused biologically based racial differences in intellectual capacity, and well-designed research supports this conclusion (e.g. Dickens & Flynn, 2006). But human cognition has undoubtedly been shaped by evolution, and some cognitive differences among children are heritable, at least in part. The role of evolution in cognitive development is examined in the new subfield of evolutionary developmental psychology, and the study of the inheritance of cognitive abilities is the field of behavioral genetics.

Evolutionary developmental psychologists have proposed a counterintuitive argument: that children's inability to think like adults-for a limited time in development—may actually help, rather than harm, their chances of survival (Bjorklund, 1997; Bjorklund & Green, 1992). They start with the fact that human children are more immature at birth than any other primate. Children are therefore more defenseless, but also more flexibly open to learn than the offspring of even their nearest evolutionary neighbors. Human children must learn a lot, and fast. Preschoolers are egocentric: they tend to reason from only their own perspective. Although not seeing others' viewpoints has some obvious disadvantages, it has advantages, too. It acts as a kind of cognitive tunnel vision, shutting out all but the most relevant information. Moreover, information relevant to one's own point of view is better remembered—even by adults—than personally irrelevant information, so egocentrism aids memory. Finally, egocentric preschoolers are likely to overestimate their cognitive abilities and are blissfully ignorant of others' performance, and are thus resistant to the negative effects of failure on their sense of ability to control the world.

Evolutionary developmental psychologists note that play, common to juveniles of most mammalian species, also has survival value (Pellegrini & Bjorklund, 2004). Children learn social roles, social interaction, physical coordination, cultural stories, and, through pretend play, symbol use and creativity. (A primate without built-in instincts needs creativity to survive in varied environments.)

Behavioral geneticists are concerned with biologically based individual differences among children in cognitive, emotional, or social behavior. It would be theoretically useful to know to what degree differences in, say, reading or math abilities are inherited. This work is technically complex and requires subtle interpretation. With the exception of a few specific single-gene disorders, scientists do not yet know the specific differences in a person's genotype (DNA sequences) that underlie differences in cognitive performance, and they strongly suspect that many genes are involved in any complex intellectual skill. Instead, they must infer their conclusions from giving intelligence, vocabulary, or standardized achievement tests to large groups of related individuals, and noting the correlated similarities in their scores. Identical twins share, at least at birth, 100% of their DNA, whereas fraternal twins (and other siblings) share about 50%. If identical twins have higher correlations in achievement test scores than fraternal twins or siblings, a degree of heritability is indicated for the tested cognitive skills. For example, a recent British longitudinal study of thousands of twins (Harlaar, Dale, & Plomin, 2007) has suggested that children's reading scores are stable across elementary school, and that a large proportion of that stability can be attributed to shared genes. And, children who are good in reading are statistically likely also to be good in math (Kovas & Plomin, 2007).

The correlations due to shared environment (shared homes, schools or teachers) are considerably lower, but still significant contributors to the scores (Harlaar, et al., 2007). But interestingly, the relative importance of a good environment is greater for poor families than affluent ones. If all of a sample of children is given every advantage offered by a culture, the differences among them in cognitive ability that remain to be measured are likely due to differences in their inheritance. Poor children still will benefit from enrichment in environmental circumstances to help them reach their full innate potential (Turkheimer, Haley, Waldron, D'Onofrio, & Gottesman, 2003). Finally, and most interestingly, behavioral geneticists have wondered about the role of nonshared environment: If all this is true, why are siblings so different (Plomin & Daniels, 1987; Turkheimer & Waldron, 2000)? Even twins from the same family have nonshared experiences, and they may even strive to be different from one another. This shows up in the data, but is hard to measure accurately, because different children will subjectively experience a teacher or parent differently, or demand different things from them for a host of different reasons. This could affect their cognitive development, but scientists are not sure exactly how. For teachers, a summary of this data might be: yes, cognitive abilities are inherited, but this does not mean that enriching an educational environment cannot also make a significant difference for every child. That something is inherited does not mean it is unchangeable.

CONSTRUCTIVISM: THE CHILD AS EPISTEMOLOGIST

Covered here so far, are those approaches that stress learning as a gradual filling up of habits, as in empiricism, or data and programs, as in information processing. Also touched on are nativist approaches, which rely on evolution to provide the timing for a gradual unfolding of capabilities. To Jean Piaget (1896–1980), learning was neither the mere acquisition of knowledge nor the unfolding of development. In his constructivist theory, children cannot merely copy and store what their teachers say, but they must act upon the world, first literally, by grasping it and sucking it, then symbolically, through language, and, finally, logically, through a combination of testing, experimenting, questioning, and reasoning, first with the concrete world and then with the formal logic of science and algebra. Piaget's theory is also a hierarchical stage theory. Each stage represents a qualitatively different, progressively more complex and abstract form of thought that is built on the stages that necessarily must come before it. Piaget was concerned not with child development but with the problem of epistemology, the branch of philosophy that deals with how knowledge of the world is constructed inside people's heads. Only by watching children can this process be seen from its genesis, its beginnings. Hence his theory's formal names: genetic epistemology or constructivism.

A baby cannot think aloud as adults do, because he has no language. A newborn has only senses, reflexes, limited motor activity, and the driving force of what might be called curiosity. Babies want to re-experience interesting and pleasant stimulations and gain control over them by repeating and varying certain actions. As they do so, the world becomes predictable and solid, and each baby's sense of self becomes differentiated from external experiences. Early consciousness in this sensorimotor period before the age of 2 is radically qualitatively different from that of older children and adults, and yet babies are still active, curious investigators, expanding through their own actions outward from an extreme point of egocentrism towards a self that interacts with the world. When they have constructed these self-object poles of existence, their perspective radically changes, and they cannot turn back. There is a radical shift in consciousness, passing into the preoperational period: toddlers can imitate actions that have happened in the past, integrating them into play-roles of cook or doctor, in both their play and their stories. They can name the now stable objects and people, and their language use takes off; their artwork has symbols of stick people, cartoon suns, and animals that do not look like what they are, but are labeled that way. These children assume that because they can control the world, other things are in the world because someone made them that way. They do not wait to explain the world until they understand it as adults do; they put forth the hypothesis that the sun shines because "God lighted it with a match!" Thus, the structure of reality is informed by the structure of their current state of knowledge. Each new piece of knowledge is interpreted in that light, not copied from the teacher.

Especially when explaining the major stage shifts of the elementary years (the concrete operational period) and later (formal operations), Piaget focused largely on the development of notions of space, time, objects, mathematics, logic, and scientific thinking. These areas of knowledge have a defined right answer in development, unlike those in the humanities. The details on early 20th-century research on these topics can found in other entries in this encyclopedia, but several general principles that are dealt with here.

1. Knowledge forms self-organizing structures. Whereas an empiricist might deal with addition and subtraction separately, Piaget suggested that these two mathematical actions form two halves of the same reversible operation, for example: 3 + 2 = 5–2 = 3. Teaching addition and subtraction as separate habits obscures this relationship. Moreover, in a sense, the structure wants to be completed; the child's mind is primed for addition by subtraction, and vice versa.

2. The child must invent to understand. Through manipulation of counters or mathematical objects, the child discovers these primed relationships through his own activity. However, it is useful to remember that children need not understand to invent; some of their inventions may be wrong, but fruitful.

3. Contradiction speeds development and widens the "grasp of consciousness"(Piaget, 1976). The self-constructed structures of knowledge are invariably challenged by how the world is: A preschooler who is so egocentric as to think that a doll on another side of a square table sees the same perspective as the child does, is challenged if instead the doll is another child who says, "That's not what I see!" The preschooler must change her hypothesis about points of view. A child who is so focused on counting to learn addition, can skip the step later in adding 2 + 3 and can later grab groups of 3's or 2's in multiplication. The grasp has widened from 1 by 1 to three 3's. Later, in algebra (formal operations), the variable x can stand for any number at all.

The teacher must guide (steer wild inventions away from blind alleys) and challenge (contradict to gently point out illogic) and explain (because the child wants and needs explanation for active understanding). According to Piaget, children do not discover properly or efficiently on their own. Children progress through the same major stages but not at the same rates, depending upon experience and skill of educators, but that is not all that matters. Piaget thus viewed

researchers who tried to disprove his theory by showing that younger children could accomplish a task, or who tried to accelerate development with disdain. Alluding to Thorndike and the behaviorist B. F. Skinner, Piaget dismissed this attempt to speed up children's growth as "The American Question" (Bringuier, 1980; general Piaget references: Gruber & Vonèche, 1977, McCarthy Gallagher & Reid, 1981; for the teacher's perspective, see Elkind, 1976, and Duckworth, 1996).

THE SOCIAL AND CULTURAL BASES OF COGNITION

Piaget's focus on the child's self-constructed structures of knowledge, from egocentrism to abstraction ignores a central truth, which is explored in the theory of the Russian, L. S. Vygotsky (1896–1934), variously called the dialectical, sociogenetic, or cultural-historical school of thought. Vygotsky also criticized the empiricist school and accepted the active role of the child in cognitive development, but children are not the only active players in the drama. In his view, children are social beings from birth, born into a culture with caretakers, peers, teachers, and social structures that actively help a child's growth and hinder his or her movement into culturally prohibited patterns of behavior. Their actions do not form an environmental layer on top of biological development, nor are they stored in the child; they come to constitute thought itself over time. Language and culture are tools of thought, allowing a child to learn, memorize, and reason in different and better ways than he could without them. There are several basic tenets of sociogenetic psychology:

1. Thought begins as social interaction and is then internalized (Vygotsky, 1978, 1986). For example, at the beginning of life, a parent must remind her child of virtually everything. Complex sequences of activity are kept in the parent's head, doled out step-by-step to the child. Simultaneously, the parent is teaching the child cultural practices such as putting the book bag by the door so that it will be remembered or, later, keeping a written list. Over time, as the child becomes responsible for larger chunks of activity, the parent might hear the child actually talking herself through the sequence aloud in private speech. The ultimate goal is for the child to use completely internalized, silent inner speech.

2. Children are capable of more advanced behavior with help than they are alone. More advanced peers or adults stand one step ahead of a child and act as a scaffold for more advanced behavior, by sequencing, breaking into smaller steps, reminding, demonstrating, physically guiding the hands, circumscribing, explaining, and prohibiting. At any given time, the number of tasks that a child can accomplish with help is far greater than

those she can accomplish alone. Intelligence, then, is partly social.

3. Language and culture are tools for thought. Children who can talk to themselves are capable of more complex activity than those who cannot. They can rehearse steps of a process or lists of items, state hypotheses to themselves and test them. Those who can write can revise to find out better what they want to say.

4. Culture and history are in every task, even internal cognitive ones. For example, mathematics does have an inner coherent structure, but it also has a social context. People who farm rice are expert in calculation and pricing of those quantities, but not in abstract calculation, although they can easily be taught. Eight-year-old candy sellers in Brazil are error free in complex calculations about candy that older children in formal schools cannot comprehend, but they have trouble carrying their one's (Nunes, Schliemann, & Carraher, 1993).

Thus, teachers in this school of thought promote internalization of higher cognitive processes not merely by lecturing, but by encouraging problem solving through external dialogue among peers of mixed levels of accomplishment in small groups. They model higher-level internalized thought (e.g. summarizing, predicting, questioning) negotiate meaning, referee disputes, keep children on track and generally serve as a guide through the culture of classroom learning, as attached to the larger cultures. Through reciprocal teaching, teachers gradually recede, handing over their tasks to students who take turns acting the role of teacher. Children who can teach have quite sophisticated metacognition: They can consider their audience, break down explanations into steps, ensure that students communicate effectively to one another, and form questions (or else be reminded by their friends that they are unclear). These methods have been used to promote reading comprehension (Palincsar & Brown, 1984; Tharp & Gallimore, 1991), math problem solving (Taylor & Cox, 1997), and science (Hoadley & Linn, 2000).

SEE ALSO *Constructivism.*

BIBLIOGRAPHY

Bjorklund, D. F. (1997). The role of immaturity in human development. *Psychological Bulletin, 122,* 153–169.

Bjorklund, D. F., & Green, B. L. (1992). The adaptive nature of cognitive immaturity. *American Psychologist, 47,* 46–54.

Bringuier, J. C. (1980). *Conversations with Jean Piaget.* Chicago: University of Chicago Press.

Dickens, W. T., & Flynn, J. R. (2006). Black Americans reduce the IQ gap: Evidence from standardized samples. *Psychological Science, 17,* 913–920.

Duckworth, E. (1996). *The having of wonderful ideas, and other essays on teaching and learning.* New York: Teachers College Press.

Elkind, D. (1976). *Child development and education: A Piagetian perspective.* New York: Oxford University Press.

Gould, S. J. (1996). *The mismeasure of man.* New York: Norton.

Galton, F. (1869). *Hereditary genius: An inquiry into its laws and consequences.* London: Macmillan.

Gruber, H. H., & Vonèche, J. J. (1977). *The essential Piaget.* New York: Basic Books.

Harlaar, N., Dale, P. S., & Plomin, R. (2007). From learning to read to reading to learn: Substantial and stable genetic influence. *Child Development, 78,* 116–131.

Hoadley, C. M., & Linn, M. C. (2000). Teaching science through online, peer discussions: SpeakEasy in the knowledge integration environment. *International Journal of Science Education, 22,* 839–857.

Klahr, D., & Simon, H. A. (2002). *Exploring science: The cognition and development of discovery processes.* Cambridge, MA: MIT Press.

Kovas, Y., & Plomin, R. (2007). Learning abilities and disabilities: Generalist genes, specialist environments. *Current Directions in Psychological Science, 16,* 285–288.

Locke, J. (1968). Some thoughts concerning education. In J. L. Axtell (Ed.), *The educational writings of John Locke.* Cambridge, U.K.: Cambridge University Press. (Original work published 1693).

McCarthy Gallagher, J., & Reid, D. K. (1981). *The learning theory of Piaget and Inhelder.* Monterey, CA: Brooks/Cole.

Nunes, T., Schliemann, A. D., & Carraher, D. W. (1993). *Street mathematics and school mathematics.* Cambridge, U.K.: Cambridge University Press.

Palincsar, A. S., & Brown, A. L. (1984). Reciprocal teaching of comprehension-fostering and comprehension-monitoring activities. *Cognition and Instruction, 1,* 117–175.

Pellegrini, A. D., & Bjorklund, D. F. (2004). The ontogeny and phylogeny of children's object and fantasy play. *Human Nature, 15,* 23–43.

Piaget, J. (1976). *The grasp of consciousness: Action and concept in the young child.* Cambridge, MA: Harvard University Press.

Plomin, R. & Daniels, D. (1987). Why are children in the same family so different from one another? *Behavioral and Brain Sciences, 10,* 1–60.

Schneider, W., & Pressley, M. (1997). *Memory development between two and twenty.* Mahwah, NJ: Erlbaum.

Siegler, R. S. (1996). *Emerging minds: The process of change in children's thought.* New York: Oxford University Press.

Taylor, J., & Cox, B. D. (1997). Microgenetic analysis of group-based solution of complex two step mathematical word problems. *Journal of the Learning Sciences, 6,* 183–226.

Tharp, R. G., & Gallimore, R. (1991). *Rousing minds to life: Teaching, learning and schooling in social context.* New York: Cambridge University Press.

Thorndike, E. L (1910–1913). *Educational psychology.* 3 vols. New York: Teachers College Press.

Turkheimer, E., Haley, A, Waldron, M., D'Onofrio, B., & Gottesman, I. I. (2003). Socioeconomic status modifies heritability of I. Q. in young children. *Psychological Science, 14,* 623–628.

Turkheimer, E. & Waldron, M. (2000). Nonshared environment: A theoretical, methodological, and quantitative review. *Psychological Bulletin, 126,* 79–108.

Vygotsky, L. S. (1978). *Mind in society: Development of the higher psychological processes.* Cambridge, MA: Harvard University Press.

Vygotsky, L. S. (1986). *Thought and Language* (Rev. ed., A. Kozulin, Trans. & Ed.) Cambridge MA: MIT Press. Original work first published in English in 1962.

Brian D. Cox

BIOLOGICAL THEORIES

In the fields of biology and psychology, the theory of evolution is used to help to better understand how biological influences on growth interact with experiences to shape developing traits. Examples of this approach are provided by the work of Mary Jane West-Eberhard for the field of biology and David Bjorklund and Anthony Pellegrini for the field of psychology. When applied to people, the basic idea is that there are biases and constraints on the types of knowledge children easily acquire during development, as well as an ability to learn evolutionarily novel and culturally specific knowledge. The corresponding area of evolutionary educational psychology was introduced by David Geary (1995, 2007) and represents an attempt to understand how evolved learning biases interact with the learning of evolutionarily novel knowledge in school.

COGNITIVE EVOLUTION

One basic assumption is that natural selection has resulted in the evolution of cognitive competencies and learning biases that facilitated the survival and reproduction of human ancestors. Evolutionary psychologists such as Leda Cosmides and John Tooby argue that most of these competencies are modular and domain specific; that is, they are supported by brain and cognitive systems that are designed to process only certain types of information. There are, as an example, dedicated brain and cognitive systems that process basic language sounds (e.g., *ba, pa*) and different brain and cognitive systems that process other types of information, such as the visuospatial information involved in navigating from one place to the next. The extent to which these modular competencies are *plastic* or modifiable by experiences during development is vigorously debated and not well understood as of 2008.

Whatever the degree of plasticity, modular systems are organized around the domains of folk psychology, folk biology, and folk physics, as exemplified by the work of Scott Atran, Frank Keil, Roger Shepard, and Steven Pinker, among others. The cognitive modules associated with folk psychology appear to be organized around knowledge about the self and about other people. The competencies that allow people to interact with others include language, theory of mind (e.g., being able to make inferences about the intentions of other people), and abilities that allow people to interpret the body language and facial expressions of others. The competencies associated with folk biology include the ability to classify flora and fauna in the local ecology and learn about the associated growth and behavioral patterns. These are underdeveloped abilities in modern societies, but people in hunter-gather societies have extensive knowledge about the plants and animals in their local area. Folk biological knowledge enables people in these traditional cultures to classify and categorize local species, hunt some of these species, and use plants as medicines, for food, and in social rituals. Folk physics refers to the competencies that allow people to engage the physical world, including the ability to navigate in three-dimensional space, remember the location of objects in the environment, and use objects (e.g., stones) to make tools.

In addition to folk competencies, there are more general cognitive systems that coordinate and integrate the workings of these specialized systems. Alan Baddeley's central executive component of working memory provides a good summary. The central executive is expressed as attention-driven control of information represented by one or several of the more specialized systems, such as the language system. The focusing of attention results in the information being represented in working memory and thus available to conscious awareness. An example is the intentional verbal repetition of information to be remembered, such as a phone number. The central executive also includes mechanisms for inhibiting irrelevant information from intruding into conscious awareness and for integrating information represented in different specialized systems. An example of the latter is integrating the symbol *5* with the sound *five* and with the conceptual knowledge that these represent a set of *five items.*

EVOLUTION, DEVELOPMENT, AND THE BRAIN

The long development of humans has a clear risk—death before the age of reproduction—and thus could only evolve if there were substantial benefits. In cross-species analyses of the relation between length of the developmental period, brain size, and potential factors that may have influenced their co-evolution, Tracey Joffe and many others have identified social complexity as the most important evolutionary pressure. Basically, a long developmental period is found in all social mammals and the length of this period increases with increases in the complexity of the species' social system. These patterns suggest that one purpose of childhood is to practice and refine folk psychological competencies, such as language and other social skills, although learning about other species and the physical world is also

---

COMPETING PERSPECTIVES ON COGNITIVE DEVELOPMENT

In 2005 Harvard president Lawrence Summers made a statement that would ignite controversy in academic establishments around the world. Women, he suggested, may not be pursuing careers in engineering because they are intellectually inferior to their male counterparts. Summers pointed to possible biological differences between men and women as the culprit of such intellectual differences. Summers' comments brought to light a debate that has perpetually riddled social scientists: are humans primarily the product of nature (biology) or nurture (experience)?

Jean Piaget and Lev Vygotsky were two of the first theorists to examine human development in a learning context. The two have often been pitted against one another as competing for arguments that nature or nurture primarily impact human development. Over the last several decades, researchers have explored and developed these competing arguments. Importantly, even the definitions of "cognition" and "development" have evolved. Development can be understood as any process of change that is organized and adaptive. Cognition can be described as the process of making meaning of information. Cognitive development, then, is an organized, adaptive change that improves our ability to make meaning of information provided by the world around us. It should be clear from this definition that cognitive development relies both on biology and on experience. As a result, social scientists are exploring which aspects of cognitive development are indeed biological and which can be influenced by experience.

One important strand of research focuses on children's development of concepts. A concept is a mental representation of a category (e.g. people, pens, puppets) that helps recognize and organize new information. Concept researchers disagree about whether concepts are in-born or emerge from experience, but they agree that even infants must have some capacity to recognize and organize information. A second strand of research focuses on the timing of experience and its role in cognition. They ask: Does early childhood experience impact cognitive capacity more than later experience? Many argue it does. Partially based on this idea, programs such as Head Start have emerged for low-income pre-school-aged children to ensure they have access to social educational environments early. The "Mozart Effect" (coined by Alfred Tomatis), which refers to the notion that use of classical music can improve psychological disorders, has also been connected to the timing paradigm. Although peer-reviewed research does not support the idea that playing classical music for a fetus in-utero improves IQ, the practice that grew out of early 1990s theory seems to have maintained popularity through the early 2000s.

In addition to theoretical advances, technological breakthroughs have enabled psychologists to examine brain differences among people who exhibit typical and atypical behaviors. One such development has been the functional Magnetic Resonance Image (fMRI), which can highlight active areas in the brain during specific thoughts or behaviors. Although the technology is new, researchers hope it will help shed light on the possible biological causes of disorders such as Attention Deficit Disorder and Autism. Because the human brain is heavily influenced by genetic heritage, many believe brain research connects much of who people are to their genetic inheritance rather than their experiences. As Lawrence Summers discovered, however, researchers continue to disagree.

Sarah Kozel Silverman

---

important, especially for children who are growing up in traditional societies.

Play, social interactions, and exploration of the environment and objects appear to be the ways emerging folk competencies are practiced and refined during development. Child-initiated social play, exploration, and so fourth are intimately linked to cognitive and brain development, in that these activities provide experiences with the social, biological, and physical world. These experiences interact with the inherent but skeletal structure of folk modules and ensure their normal development and adaptation to local conditions. In this view, children are biologically prepared to learn about other people and the biological and physical world and are inherently motivated to seek out experiences that will facilitate this learning.

It is important to note that this is a different perspective than that of Jean Piaget. Piaget proposed that children's inherent curiosity and engagement of the world resulted in broad stages of general reasoning abilities. From an evolutionary perspective, children's curiosity, play, and other developmental activities are not general but rather focused on fleshing out specific competencies in the domains of folk psychology, biology, and physics. Their interests and motivations are expected to be particularly strong when it comes to social relationships.

NATURE AND NURTURE

For evolutionary developmental biology and psychology, the developing individual and most of the associated traits emerge from an interaction between nature (genetically based programs that guide development) and nurture (experiences that influence how and when these programs are expressed). As described by Sandra Scarr and Kathleen McCartney, the relative contributions of heritable and environmental effects on children can vary from infancy through adolescence. During infancy, the environments children experience are largely controlled by their parents and thus nurture should outweigh nature. As children grow, the influence of parents begins to decline and heritable influences are more strongly expressed. These influences are expressed as children seek their own experiences and build their own niches in their peer groups and in the wider world. In other words, nature influences, to some extent, how children react to other people, how other people react to them, and how interested they are in learning about the biological and physical world, among other traits.

The result is that many estimates of heritable influences on developing traits become larger as people develop into adolescence and adulthood. However, it is not yet fully understood how the expression of heritable influences is influenced by evolutionarily expectant experiences. As described by William Greenough, James Black, and Christopher Wallace, evolution has resulted in a linking of brain development and the expected experiences that will ensure that brain, cognitive, and social development is normal for the species. As an example, human language emerges naturally, that is, without instruction, and is dependent on the maturation and functioning of an integrated system of brain regions. Though heavily dependent on nature, language will not be normal unless the child is exposed to language and social discourse: The natural language systems need experience to develop normally. Variation in language competencies may be partly heritable, but the expression of these heritable differences may also be related to differences in the types of experiences children seek as these competencies emerge.

EVOLUTIONARY EDUCATIONAL PSYCHOLOGY

The cognitive competencies that compose the folk domains have evolved to allow humans to function in and adapt to the social conditions and ecologies of their ancestors. In some cases, as with language, these competencies are just as

useful in the 21st century as they were at earlier points in human evolution. Other competencies, such as those involved in categorizing flora and fauna, may be less useful for many people today. A more central concern in modern society is children's learning of evolutionarily novel competencies, such as reading, writing, and complex arithmetic. Evolutionary educational psychology is the study of the relation between folk knowledge as these influence academic learning in evolutionarily novel cultural contexts, such as schools and the industrial workplace. One core goal of schools and schooling is to organize the activities of children so that they acquire competencies, such as the ability to read, that are important in the wider culture but have no evolutionary history.

David Geary (1995) referred to language and other evolved folk competencies as biologically primary abilities, and skills that build upon these primary abilities but are principally cultural inventions, such are reading, as biologically secondary abilities. The mechanisms by which primary systems are adapted to produce secondary competencies are not yet fully understood, but appear to involve simultaneous activation of the frontal areas of the brain that control attention and working memory and the areas of the brain that support folk competencies.

To illustrate how these interactions might occur, consider the relation between language, a primary ability, and reading, a secondary ability. As proposed by Paul Rozin, the acquisition of reading-related abilities (e.g., word decoding) appears to involve the modification of primary language and language-related systems, among others (e.g., visual scanning). Consistent with this proposal, individual differences in the fidelity of kindergarten children's phonological processing systems, which are basic features of the language domain, are strongly predictive of the ease with which basic reading skills (e.g., word decoding) are acquired in first grade. In other words, the evolutionary pressures that selected for phonological processing systems, such as the ability to segment language sounds, were unrelated to reading, but these systems are can be modified to form the sound-letter and sound-word associations that are important components of reading ability.

Implicit knowledge is also built into the organization of folk systems. Sometimes this knowledge can aid in learning and at other times it can interfere with learning. As an example of the former, consider that the initial development of geometry as an academic discipline may have been based on access to knowledge implicit in the primary systems that support navigation in the physical world. The implicit understanding that the fastest way to get from one place to another is to go "as the crow flies," was made explicit in the formal Euclidean postulate, that a line can be drawn from any point to any point. From an evolutionary perspective, the former reflects an implicit understanding of how to quickly get from one place to another and is knowledge that is built into the brain and cognitive systems that support navigation. The latter was discovered, that is, made explicit, by Euclid. Once explicit, this knowledge was integrated into the formal discipline of geometry and became socially transmittable and teachable.

An example of how implicit knowledge and inferential biases that are part of folk systems can interfere with learning in school is provided by people's naïve understanding of motion. When asked about the forces acting on a thrown baseball, most people believe there is a force propelling it forward, something akin to an invisible engine, and a force propelling it downward. The downward force is gravity, but there is in fact no force propelling it forward, once the ball leaves the player's hand. The concept of a forward-force, called *impetus*, is similar to pre-Newtonian beliefs about motion prominent in the 14th to 16th centuries. The idea is that the act of starting an object in motion, such as throwing a ball, imparts to the object an internal force—impetus—that keeps it in motion until this impetus gradually dissipates. Although adults and even preschool children often describe the correct trajectory for a thrown or moving object, reflecting their implicit folk competences, their explicit explanations reflect this naïve understanding of the forces acting upon the object.

Careful observation, use of the scientific method (secondary knowledge itself), and use of inductive and deductive reasoning, are necessary to move from an intuitive folk understanding to scientific theory and other forms of secondary knowledge. Isaac Newton did just this, and in fact he noted: "I do not define time, space, place and motion, as being well known to all. Only I must observe, that the vulgar conceive those quantities under no other notions but from the relation they bear to sensible objects" (1995, p. 13). The "vulgar" individuals only understand physical phenomena in terms of folk knowledge, and Newton intended to and did go well beyond this. Newton corrected the pre-Newtonian beliefs about the forces acting on objects. In doing so, he helped to create the evolutionary novel field of scientific physics. These discoveries, as well as those of many others before and since Newton, have created a gap between children's intuitive, folk understanding of the physical world and modern understanding of these same phenomena. Teaching the latter is made all the more difficult by evolved human biases.

EVOLUTION AND THE MOTIVATION TO LEARN

One important implication is that the motivation to acquire school-taught secondary abilities is based on the requirements of the larger society and not on the inherent interests of children. Given the relatively recent advent of near universal schooling in contemporary societies, there is no reason to believe that the skills that are taught in school are inherently interesting or enjoyable for children to learn. In other words, one important difference between primary and secondary cognitive abilities is the level and source of motivation to engage in the activities that are necessary for their acquisition. This does not, however, preclude the self-motivated engagement in some secondary activities.

Even though reading is a secondary ability, many children and adults are motivated to read. The motivation to read, however, is probably driven by the content of what is being read rather than by the process itself. In fact, the content of many stories and other secondary activities (e.g., video games, television) might reflect evolutionarily relevant themes that motivate engagement in these activities, such as social relationships and social competition. Furthermore, the finding that intellectual curiosity is a basic dimension of human personality suggests there will be many intellectually curious individuals who will pursue secondary activities. Euclid's investment in formalizing and proving the principles of geometry and Newton's work on motion and gravity are examples. However, this type of discovery typically reflects the activities and insights of only a few individuals, and the associated advances spread through the larger society only by means of informal (e.g., newspapers) and formal education. The point is that the motivation to engage in the activities that will promote the acquisition of secondary abilities is not likely to be universal.

EVOLUTION AND INSTRUCTION

The combination of inherent, built-in brain and cognitive systems and children's inherent motivation to seek out evolutionarily expectant experiences, for example through social play, ensures the appropriate development of biologically primary folk systems. In contrast, there is no inherent structure supporting the acquisition of secondary abilities, nor are most children inherently motivated to engage in the activities that are necessary for all of the different aspects of secondary learning that are necessary for functioning in modern societies. From this evolutionary perspective, one essential goal of schooling is to provide content, organization, and structure to the teaching of secondary abilities, features that have been provided by evolution to primary abilities.

Furthermore, it cannot be assumed that children's inherent interests, such as social relationships, and preferred learning activities, such as play, will be sufficient for the acquisition of secondary abilities, even though they appear to be sufficient for the fleshing out of primary abilities. Instruction must, therefore, involve engaging children in activities that facilitate the acquisition of secondary abilities, whether or not children are inherently interested in engaging in such activities. This does not mean that play and social activities cannot be used to engage children in some forms of secondary learning. It does, however, mean that it is very unlikely that the mastery of many secondary domains (e.g., reading or algebra) will occur with only these types of primary activities.

In fact, research in cognitive and educational psychology indicates that some forms of secondary learning will require activities that differ from those associated with the fleshing out of primary abilities. These would include, among others, direct instruction, in which teachers' provide the goals, organization, and structure to instructional activities and explicitly teach basic competencies, such as how to sound out unfamiliar words or manipulate algebraic equations. The mastery of secondary domains also requires extensive exposure to the material, distributed over many contexts and oftentimes over many years, as well as extensive practice in using any associated procedures (e.g., to solve mathematics problems). Extensive exposure and practice also appear to be needed for the development of primary abilities, but this exposure and practice automatically occur as children engage in social discourse, play, and exploration. In contrast, most children will not automatically engage in the practice needed to master secondary domains, and, as a result, this practice needs to be built into instructional activities. For some domains, such as in the biological and physical sciences, mastery will also require many hands-on activities, as in conducting experiments, although more traditional methods will be needed as well (e.g., learning basic facts and principles, such as the theory of evolution).

In summary, the core assumption of a biological perspective on children's learning is that evolution has provided a basic brain and cognitive structure to a suite of primary domains. These primary abilities allow people to negotiate social relationships (folk psychology) and the biological (folk biology) and physical (folk physics) world. Children have an inherent bias to seek out and engage in the experiences, such as social play, that will adapt these domains to the nuances of their social group and biological and physical world. However, humans also have an evolved ability to create evolutionarily novel knowledge and to pass this knowledge from one generation to the next (e.g., through books). The cross-generational accumulation of this biologically secondary knowledge has created a gap between knowledge represented by folk domains and that needed to function in modern-day society. Schools emerged in these societies to help children to bridge this gap. In school settings, it cannot be assumed that the cognitive, motivational, and activity biases that support the fleshing out of primary abilities during development will be sufficient for the learning of secondary abilities in school.

SEE ALSO *Brain and Learning; Information Processing Theory.*

BIBLIOGRAPHY

Atran, S. (1988). Folk biology and the anthropology of science: Cognitive universals and cultural particulars. *Behavioral and Brain Sciences, 21,* 547–609.

Baddeley, A. D. (1986). *Working memory.* Oxford: Oxford University Press.

Bjorklund, D. F., & Pellegrini, A. D. (2002). *The origins of human nature: Evolutionary developmental psychology.* Washington, DC: American Psychological Association.

Cosmides, L., & Tooby, J. (1994). Origins of domain specificity: The evolution of functional organization. In L. A. Hirschfeld & S. A. Gelman (Eds.), *Mapping the mind: Domain specificity in cognition and culture* (pp. 85–116). New York: Cambridge University Press.

Euclid. (1956). *The thirteen books of "The Elements."* (T. L. Heath, Trans.). New York: Dover. (Original work published c. 300 BCE).

Geary, D. C. (1995). Reflections of evolution and culture in children's cognition: Implications for mathematical development and instruction. *American Psychologist, 50,* 24–37.

Geary, D. C. (2007). Educating the evolved mind: Conceptual foundations for an evolutionary educational psychology. In J. S. Carlson & J. R. Levin (Eds.), *Educating the evolved mind* (pp. 1–9). Greenwich, CT: Information Age.

Joffe, T. H. (1997). Social pressures have selected for an extended juvenile period in primates. *Journal of Human Evolution, 32,* 593–605.

Keil, F. C. (1992). The origins of an autonomous biology. In M. R. Gunnar & M. Maratsos (Eds.), *Modularity and constraints in language and cognition: The Minnesota symposia on child psychology* (Vol. 25, pp. 103–137). Hillsdale, NJ: Erlbaum.

Newton, Isaac. (1995). *The principia.* (A. Motte, Trans.). Amherst, NY: Prometheus Books. (Original work published in 1687).

Piaget, Jean. (1952). *The origin of intelligence in children.* New York: International University Press.

Pinker, Steven. (1997). *How the mind works.* New York: Norton.

Rozin, Paul. (1976). The evolution of intelligence and access to the cognitive unconscious. In J. M. Sprague & A. N. Epstein (Eds.), *Progress in psychobiology and physiological psychology* (Vol. 6, pp. 245–280). New York: Academic Press.

Scarr, S., & McCartney, K. (1983). How people make their own environments: A theory of genotype–environment effects. *Child Development, 54,* 424–435.

Shepard, R. N. (1994). Perceptual-cognitive universals as reflections of the world. *Psychonomic Bulletin & Review, 1,* 2–28.

West-Eberhard, M. J. (2003). *Developmental plasticity and evolution.* New York: Oxford University Press.

David C. Geary

INFORMATION PROCESSING THEORIES

Information processing theory explains human thinking by relating cognitive processes to the workings of a computer. The model presents the basic components of a computer as mechanical representations of the components of the human mind used in thinking. The basic components in information process are the sensory receptors, the working memory, and the long-term memory. These relate to the computer's data input device, the data processing area, and the data storage, respectively. Along with these components are the executive functions, such as metacognition, related to the computer's operating system. Research in information processing has helped to develop improved strategies for learning and memory.

Robert Sternberg (1987) claims that information processing is an improvement over traditional views of intelligence because it resolves some long-standing issues. Through information processing theory, any observed deficit in intelligence, such as learning and reasoning ability, can be identified at a process level and improved through training. Deanna Kuhn (2006) recognizes that information processing is an improvement over Piagetian theory because information processing explains how children acquire strategies.

Ann Brown (1997), a sociocultural theorist, integrates ideas from information processing theory. She claims information processing addresses the issue of "what it is that children are ready to learn easily and what (it is that) is resistant to ... instruction (however) exquisitely designed" (Brown, 1997, p. 400). She emphasizes that information processing explains Vygotsky's *zone of proximal development* in which children can perform beyond their developmental abilities if they are given the proper instruction for strategies. Children do not lack the capacity of learning at a higher level than their stage. Often, they are not effectively using the capacity they have. They need education to understand what strategies they have and how to apply them effectively.

INFORMATION PROCESSING THEORY APPLIED TO DEVELOPMENTAL ISSUES

Piagetian theory and information processing theories agree on several points. Both view a child as an active agent in development and learning. Both approaches recognize age-related differences in cognitive abilities and try to explain these differences. Both are concerned with how later advanced understandings can develop from the earlier rudimentary ideas. Finally, both recognize that current understanding can either aid or hinder the development of new understanding.

Differences in the two approaches are based on the explanations of the age-related changes. One of the ways that information-processing theorists account for age-related differences focuses on the increased capacity of the working memory. Kail (2003) notes that "Age-related change in working memory contributes to improved rea-

soning and problem solving during infancy, childhood, and adolescence" (p. 74). Contrary to this, Piaget felt that changes in performance are due to qualitative changes in developmental stages. Piaget attributed little value to repeated exposures or the capacity of memory. Although later in his research career Piaget conceded that there is a relation between memory and strategies, for most of his career he tried to separate memory from understanding.

Piaget emphasized the need to study children's reasoning as exemplified by the broad strategic changes in their approach to problem solving. He felt that older children, having grown into a higher developmental stage, have better logical frameworks and strategies. He did not associate the older children's greater knowledge base and more associations with their improved performance.

Many information processing theorists hold that much developmental change can be explained by greater use of memory strategies, including faster and more efficient diagnosis of memory tasks and monitoring of strategies. Greater task-relevant knowledge also improves the performance based on age. Maturation and experience play an interactive role in the age-related differences observed by information processing theorists (Kail, 2003).

INFORMATION PROCESSING AND DEVELOPMENTAL CHANGES

Some of the key concepts of information processing used to explain developmental changes include the processes involved in memory, thinking, and metacognition. Memory has the functions of encoding, storage, and retrieval. Thinking involves forming concepts and solving problems. Metacognition constitutes the functions bringing about a continuous analysis of one's thinking.

Research in age-related differences conducted from an information processing perspective has discovered phenomena similar to those described by Piagetian theorists. However, there are some new discoveries about children's abilities from information processing research that challenge the Piagetian perspectives. Information process researchers have shown that some skills are developed earlier than suggested by Piaget. Also, some developmental changes previously thought to be qualitative in nature have been shown by information process researchers to progress quantitatively.

An important process of memory is encoding—fitting information into long-term memory so it can be retrieved when needed. The age-related differences in encoding involve children's use and application of attention. From infancy until school age, there are distinct differences in the degree to which children are willing or able to attend to an event or activity. Infants quickly habituate to a familiar stimulus; they lose interest in the familiar and look for something new. Infants demonstrate their processing of information by recognizing that a stimulus is familiar. Infants need change and novelty. Toddlers are also interested in novelty and are not focused very long on any one discovery.

From age 3 on, children spend more time in an activity or challenge that holds their interest. However, the preschool child is easily distracted from an activity by something more sensory arousing than the essential aspects of the task. The child at this age cannot always distinguish the relevant from the irrelevant. In listening to a story or solving a puzzle, children at this age may focus on some inconsequential aspect, distracting them from the essential. After the age of 6 or 7, the child is more efficient at focusing on the relevant characteristics of a task or challenge. Also, at this age children become less distracted and more easily stay on task in their activities. Developmentalists and information processing theorists attribute this change to a cognitive control of attention. The information processing approach explains that the child is learning the importance of developing strategies for concentrating and focusing mental resources.

The grade school child is more efficient at attention tasks than the preschool child because the older child is more likely to plan an effort in maintaining attention. The activities that older children are involved in at school help them recognize the need for organization. When younger children are taught the attentional strategies, they have been able to apply them effectively. However, they do not usually apply them spontaneously. Older children, through experience or maturation, learn to use their minds actively and effortfully. They learn that investing resources produces better results than a passive effort to retrieve available information.

Another age-related difference in encoding is the use of rehearsal, the act of repeating information in the working memory to keep it from fading. Children discover this technique around the age of 5. Before this age, rehearsal is not usually observed. Even when children below the age of 5 are taught this strategy, they usually do not apply it effectively. After the age of 7, children recognize that rehearsal is not the most effective technique for learning and remembering important information. They tend to use it less except in specific circumstances such as remembering a phone number until they can write it down. Information processing theorists explain that the mental effort involved for the younger child is not worth the small return. In addition, younger children who are successful with rehearsal often do not recognize that their success is due to the strategy. Children older than 7 recognize the inefficiency of rehearsals because they have a better repertoire of strategies for remembering, including depth of processing and elaboration.

Elaboration is the mental process of taking new concepts and relating them to personal examples or other meaningful knowledge or experiences. Elaboration gives the new information more meaning and value. This makes retrieving the information more easy because the memory trail is more distinct. In trying to recover information from long-term memory, encoded among a multitude of code, the memory with the distinct code will be easier to find.

There is a developmental pattern in the use of elaboration. Adolescents tend to use it spontaneously when motivated to remember or learn something new. However, grade school children are not likely to apply it in most circumstances. Grade school children may apply elaboration if they are taught the strategies for a given subject, but will not generalize the skill beyond the given subject. According to Pressley (1982), second graders and fifth graders show little difference in learning vocabulary words without elaboration. With elaboration, the second graders can improve more than 2 ½ times and fifth graders nearly 3 ½ times.

Constructing images is a form of elaboration in which a child creates a mental picture of a concept being learned or remembered. Children 9 years old and older benefit more from being encouraged to use constructing images as a learning strategy than younger children do. Encoding is more effective through organization. Organization involves recognizing and categorizing information based on a hierarchy of the most important characteristics. Organization can be compared to a network in which multiple connections are established based on categories and subcategories of characteristics, properties, and abilities. These various connecting points to a concept can be used as retrieval cues. Children show increased use of organization in middle and late childhood. As with many other strategies, the younger children are much less likely than the older children to apply organization strategies even when taught. Furthermore, the quality of groupings tends to be better among the older children. This is another strategy that is not effort-effective for younger children. "Knowledge (based on networks) can aid memory because it provides special codes that simplify memorization ... Children's growing knowledge ... provides more retrieval cues ... alternative ways to gain access to a concept" (Kail, 2003, p. 72).

Memory time frames are measures of how long relevant information can be retained in sensory and working memory. Sensory memory holds the information from the sensory receptors for only a brief period. Because this information is fleeting it has to be encoded to be saved. A comparison of children's time frame to adult's time frame reveals that adults encode sensory information only relatively faster than children do. However, the small advantage that adults have over children multiplied by the huge amount of information produces an extremely different cumulative effect.

Short-term memory, also known as *working memory*, has a limited capacity. Most researchers prefer the latter term because the processes are actively applied (as implied by "working") rather than passively stored (as implied by "short-term"). Information is retained for about 30 seconds in the working memory if not preserved through strategies or encoded to long-term memory. Age-related differences in working memory are attributed to an increased capacity in the working memory and an increased speed of processing. Measures of working memory capacity demonstrate that the increase is based on age. However, there is a wide range of variability at every age because of individual differences. Before age 5, all children are slow at processing. From 5 years old through about 15 years old, speed is closely correlated with age.

Reading is a skill that relies on the working memory. Each word read must be saved in the working memory until the whole sentence is scanned, putting all the words together to form a coherent concept. Kail (2003) notes that "age-related changes in working memory are due primarily to age-related increases in the speed with which children can execute basic cognitive processes" (p. 74).

In a 1989 study by Siegel and Ryan, reading ability and capacity of the working memory were shown to be related. Normal readers and problems readers from age 7 to 13 years old were given a task of working memory. Both groups increased their working memory performance at the same rate, as a function of age. However, they maintained their original group differences in performance gaps.

There is little age-related difference in the capacity of the long-term memory. However, retrieval rates increase with age based on more effective encoding and retrieval strategies. Kail (2003) says "As the capacity of working memory increases with age, children have more resources available to storing and processing operations during reasoning and problem solving resulting in improved performance" (p. 74).

The research into the development of a theory of mind in young children is of interest for various fields of psychology. The finding that a preoperational child can understand another person's point of view contradicts Piaget's theory of egocentrism in the preoperational child. Furthermore, researchers have shown a continuous age-related function in acquiring a theory of mind. This means a change more quantitative than the qualitative change that Piaget expected. That there is a wide range of variability in the age that one acquires a theory of mind implies that the change is a function of maturation interacting with experience. Information processing theory takes into consideration the maturation influences and experiential influences more completely than Piaget's theory does. As with many

other strategies and developmental tasks, the child's spontaneous application is limited by the working memory. However, the child's effectiveness can advance based on important experiences or strategy instruction.

Robert Siegler's 1976 work demonstrates that the application of rules is an age-related function. In solving a problem, young children between the ages of 5 and 9 focus on the most basic rule incorporating only the most visible influence. Children in late childhood recognize that there can be more than one influence but do not necessarily allow for the interaction of influences. Adolescents recognize the influences and the interaction of influences, but rely on guessing in unfamiliar settings. Adolescents stop short of developing and applying a formula that could guarantee success. There is a relationship between the "relative difficulty of the problem-types" and the "developmental trends in performance on them" (Siegler, 1976, p. 518). Illustrative of this is the "balance scale task." To determine if the arm of a scale balanced on a fulcrum will tip to the right or the left or will balance, the child has to have a concept of the influence of not only the weight of both sides but also the distance of the weight from the fulcrum. The weight of each side multiplied by the distance from the fulcrum determines whether the scale will tip or balance. In reaching a decision young children will only consider the equality of weight on both sides. Older children understand the influence of the distance from the fulcrum but do not fully apply this understanding. Adolescents will apply the influence of the weight and the distance effectively except when one side has more weight and the other side has more distance; they will then guess. Interestingly, the adolescents who have had experience calculating weight by distance will not necessarily apply this solution if they have not had previous experience with this type of scale (Siegler, 1976).

RESEARCH INSPIRED BY INFORMATION PROCESSING THEORY

Among many lines of research that have been inspired by information processing theory, three that are relevant to education include (1) metacognition, (2) critical thinking, and (3) classroom applications.

Kuhn (2006) stresses there is more to know about metacognition and its contribution to improved thinking and reasoning. She notes that Flavell's seminal research on metacognition in the late 1970s was focused on the underlying strategies that make up memory tasks. However, research since that time has expanded the understanding of the concept of metacognition and increased the theoretical implications needed to be tested. There is still so much that is not known about the development of strategies relying on metacognitive process. Research needs to study metacognition processes because they help to "explain how and why cognitive development both occurs and fails to occur" (Kuhn, 2006, p. 68). Research has to be increased even in areas in which metacognition has been shown to increase efficiency, such as text comprehension, problem solving, reasoning, and memory. Research in the early 21st century focuses mostly on the effects of metacognition. Kuhn proposes more research on the actual application of metacognition in the process of acquiring new knowledge. Since it is established that individuals change existing ideas to accommodate new knowledge, research should identify the metacognitive processes involved in evaluating the components of the existing ideas in comparison with the components of the new information (Kuhn, 2006).

Critical thinking is another increasing area of research in which the principles of information processing can be applied. Critical thinking involves the active evaluation of the incoming information, questioning the accuracy of information, and verifying the authority of those making the salient statements. Critical thinking leads to more complete analysis of information which in turn leads to (1) a comparison of principles and strategies across domains, (2) an elaboration of information expanded by analogies, richer associations and a hierarchy of accuracy; (3) a willingness to receive and consider the opinions of others, and (4) a higher level of questioning. Other benefits include an intellectual curiosity, effective planning and accurate understanding (Santrock, 2006).

An interesting classroom application of information processing principles is Ann Brown's 1997 Community of Learners. This program incorporates strategies of metacognition and strategic thinking. The Community of Learners is designed to foster reflection and discussion. Three basic strategies that the students use include teaching each other, consulting with experts through email, and using adults to model how to think and reflect. Students teach each other by sharing insights on the material being studied and seeking more understanding from the others. The experts that the children interact with online encourage the students to think more deeply about the study material through stimulating questions and intriguing discussions. When a visiting expert is expected, the children draw up a number of questions to ask; the teacher helps them organize the questions according to topics and subtopics. Brown's work is based on the information processing principles she has recognized in her sociocultural research. She has been motivated to help passive students learn strategies to become active agents in their own learning. In addition, she has wanted to demonstrate how learning strategies can be generalized across domains.

SEE ALSO *Information Processing Theory.*

BIBLIOGRAPHY

Brown, A. (1997). Transforming schools into communities of thinking and learning about serious matters. *American Psychologist, 52,* 399–409.

Kuhn, D. (2006). Metacognitive development. In Karen L. Freiberg (Ed.), *Annual editions: Human development* (34th ed.). Dubuque, IA: McGraw-Hill.

Kail, R. V. (2003). Development of memory in children. In John H. Byrne (Ed.), *Learning and Memory* (2nd ed). New York: Macmillan.

Pressley, M. (1982). Elaboration and memory development. *Child Development, 53,* 296–309.

Santrock J. W. (2004). *Child development* (10th ed.). New York: McGraw-Hill.

Siegler, R. S. (1976). Three aspects of cognitive development. *Cognitive Psychology, 8,* 481–520.

Siegel, L. S., Ryan, E. B. (1989). The development of working memory in normally achieving and subtypes of learning disabled children. *Child Development, 60,* 973–980.

Sternberg, R. J. (1987). Information processing. In R. L. Gregory (Ed.), *The Oxford companion to the mind.* New York: Oxford University Press.

Ray Brogan

PIAGET'S THEORY

Jean Piaget (1896–1980), a Swiss psychologist, centered his work on cognitive developmental processes such as perceiving, remembering, believing, and reasoning in children. Piaget was influenced by his experience in the Paris laboratory of Alfred Binet (1857–1911) where he worked on standardizing a French version of a British intelligence test. His studies at the Sorbonne in abnormal psychology, epistemology, mathematics, and the history of science are reflected in his approach to understanding how children think. Piaget used observational methods as well as experimental methodology in developing his theory of intelligence.

Piaget defined intelligence as the individual's ability to cope with the changing world by continuing to organize and reorganize experiences. He believed that the mental structures necessary for intellectual development are genetically determined and include both the nervous system and sensory organs. These structures set limits on what a child may do at each stage of development. Children are born without logic and construct their own intellectual development based on what they learn at an earlier stage through their informal experiences with the environment. Adaptation, according to Piaget, is the most important principle of human functioning and involves two major processes: assimilation and accommodation. Assimilation occurs when children take in new information from the environment and fit it into a preconceived notion or plan. Babies assimilate food by

Jean Piaget in a classroom. BILL ANDERSON / PHOTO RESEARCHERS, INC.

licking and chewing, but they must also open their mouths to accommodate the size and shape of a spoon. If children once ride on a hobbyhorse and then, in play, use a broom as a hobbyhorse, then assimilation has occurred. However, if children sweep the floor with the broom, then accommodation has occurred. Through accommodation, children adjust to new and changing conditions in the environment. Pre-existing patterns of behavior are changed or modified in order to deal with new situations. Thus, individuals achieve equilibration, a regulatory process whereby a balance is achieved based on the demands of assimilation and accommodation.

STAGES OF A CHILD'S INTELLECTUAL DEVELOPMENT

Piaget conceived of intellectual development as a series of fixed and sequential stages that all children pass through. Although children may go through these stages at different rates, no stage is skipped. The ages at which each stage is entered and completed, however, is somewhat arbitrary. A child, for example, may be in transition—in one stage in language usage and at another stage in the understanding of mathematical concepts.

STAGE ONE—SENSORY-MOTOR STAGE: BIRTH TO AGE 2

The first stage, the sensory-motor stage, consists of six substages. In substage one, random and reflex actions (birth to one month), the newborn uses innate reflexes such as sucking, grasping, blinking, crying, vocalizing, and random movements of arms and legs. Babies may suck their own fingers or even one of a baby near him. Gradually, these movements become more refined and directed, displaying rudimentary intelligence as when babies grasp a rattle and shake it, rub a blanket, tug at their ear, and suck on a nipple when hungry, rather than on a pacifier.

In sub stage two, primary circular reactions (1 to 4 months), babies discriminate among shapes and forms. They may stare at a mobile or mother's face with interest but do not reach out for the mobile to touch the dangling objects. They may not recognize their hands as part of their bodies. If they drop a rattle, they may not search for it. Only later, around 8 months, will the baby search for the rattle, signifying that a lost object is no longer out of mind.

In sub stage three, secondary circular reactions (4 to 8 months), their strategies become more complex and

196

repetitive. Senses become sharper. Infants may gaze at an unfamiliar object for an extended period of time. They can imitate more complex actions and repeat new sounds. Although they may gaze at their mother's face, they do not purposefully reach for it to touch it. As they advance in age, an important feature of this stage gradually occurs called object permanency, the ability to recognize that when an object is moved from it visual field, the object continues to exist.

During sub stage four, coordination of secondary schemata (8 to 12 months), intentional behavior begins. If babies swat at a mobile hanging over their crib and repeat this act and the mobile moves, a connection is made. The next time they try to reach for the mobile, they do so in a more coordinated way, and a plan or schema for striking at the mobile is formed. Movements become a means to an end. The rattle or bottle may be retrieved if it falls. The notion of object permanency is now a regular part of the babies' intellectual repertoire; it is no longer so easy to divert their attention from something they find desirable. In being able to recall objects even when they are not visible, babies show that their symbolic thought is developing. Babies at this stage smile when their mother approaches the crib; they know she coming to feed or play with them.

In substage five, tertiary circular reactions (12–18 months), babies increase their capacity to explore the environment, constantly inventing new plans if old schemata do not work. Thus, if they want an object outside of the playpen, they may learn to tilt the object to get it between the bars. If they drop food on the floor, they are interested in seeing where this drops. They find it empowering to let go of the food and to repeat this act again much to their parents' consternation. Nesting blocks and shape sorters begin to interest babies who are constantly poking, pulling, pushing objects, testing their strength and trying to make sense out of the environment.

Finally, in substage six, invention of new means through mental combinations (18–24 months), toddlers start to think before they act. Some of the information they have assimilated through trial and error in the previous stages can now result in new acts. Limited speech and gestures can convey that they are thinking about a problem and about what they want and intend to do.

Play for toddlers is sensory-motor, the pleasure of using their senses, sucking, biting, touching, and moving toes, fingers, arms and legs. They babble and enjoy listening to sounds of others' voices. They imitate expressions of others such as opening their mouths, imitating hand gestures, and body movements. Ritualistic play or practice play begins in which they repeat acts for pleasure such as swatting at the mobile over the crib or dropping items into a basket. Toward the end of the end of the second year, they can use a substitute object for an item as when they use a small stick to symbolize a doll or truck. Symbolic imitation in the form of simple play occurs around this time when they attempt, as early as eighteen months, to feed a doll or toy bear.

STAGE TWO—PREOPERATIONAL STAGE: AGES 2 TO 7

The term *preoperational* signifies that the toddler has not developed the mental structures to think logically or in abstract terms. There are two substages in this period of preoperational thought, preconceptual (ages 2 to 4 years) and perceptual or intuitive thought (ages 4 to 7 years). During the preconceptual phase, children use rudimentary language and mental images and generalize in illogical ways. In the stage of perceptual or intuitive thought, they solve problems based on intuition and on appearances rather than on judgment or reasoning. This mode of thinking is called transductive reasoning—reasoning from one particular idea to another idea without any logical connection between them. If the train has a whistle, that makes the train move. This cause-and-effect relationship is a distortion of thought.

Preoperational children in the preconceptual phase may also be egocentric, acting on the assumption that the world centers on them. If their food is hot, then everyone's food is hot. If they are cold, then mother must also be cold. Moreover, it is difficult for children in this stage to recognize the difference between reality and fantasy. They believe in animism. The stuffed animals and dolls to which children talk are deemed alive and are given personalities. Sometimes they even become imaginary companions. Preoperational children also believe in artificialism. For example, they may believe that a pond is a giant's footprint that has been filled with rainwater, or that human beings created the moon, sun, stars, and the natural features of the earth.

In terms of language, children who are beginning to talk use echolalia, repeating words that others say and using sounds for pleasure. In this stage they use monologues, a running commentary on what they are doing, without listening or replying to their companions. They also engage in collective monologues: Children will talk at the same time as they sit or play beside each other but not necessarily respond appropriately to each other. Onomatopoeia is often used by preoperational children who enjoy the sounds or noises that objects make such as "choo-choo," "bow-wow," or "meow," long before they can say the actual words that designate the train, dog, or cat. Children in this period have difficulty with centering, the child's tendency to center or concentrate its attention on one aspect of an object at a time and its inability to shift its attention to other aspects of a situation. They do not relate parts of an object to the whole. A doorknob is a doorknob when attached to the door, but if found on the table, the child may not be able to relate it to its actual purpose. Words are taken literally; these children may interpret "blackmail" to mean that letters and envelopes are the color black, or if a father said he was "tied up" at work, they may envision him with ropes around his legs or arms. They ask many questions but may not expect an answer, or they may answer the questions themselves.

Children in the preoperational stage have difficulty with the concept of conservation of quantity, volume, and size when there are changes in their appearance. For example, when there are two rows of the same quantity of pennies placed one above the other, they look like they contain the same number to a child, but if one row is spread out, the child thinks this row has more pennies than the one that is not spread out. In the same way, two identical glasses filled with equal amounts of water will appear equal, but if one glass is emptied into a taller narrower glass, it will appear to contain more water than the original glass next to it. Two balls made of the same amount of clay look equal to children in this stage, but if one ball is spread out and flattened, the child who cannot conserve believes there is more clay in this elongated clay. Thus, perception rules over logic for the preoperational child. Adults can make the same mistake. For example, a large package of napkins may look as if it contains more napkins than a nearby compressed package. The packages may contain the same number, but adults may need to rely on the label for that information.

The preoperational child's conception of space is topological. Children can distinguish between open and closed figures, but when asked to copy a triangle or square, children in this stage will draw a circle. If shown open figures of a triangle or square, they will draw an open circle. They think that a bowl is like a dish, but a cup is like a doughnut because they both contain holes.

When preoperational children draw objects, they represent them in two dimensions and only later are able to draw using three dimensions. Young children also have difficulty recognizing and discriminating between two different perspectives of the same object, believing that theirs is the only perspective, termed spatial egocentrism by Piaget. In setting out silverware from the opposite side of a table, they may place all objects on the table from their point of view (upside down) rather than understanding that silverware must be arranged according to the view of the person who will sit at that place setting and use it.

Time is a difficult concept for preoperational children. If it takes one hour to get to a place by airplane, it must be closer in distance from their perspective than if it takes two or more hours by car. Time also is judged by a concrete action. Suppertime and bedtime are designated as periods of time without their knowing clock time. Age is confused with height. A taller child must be older than the smaller child even if they are, in fact, the exact same age.

Imaginative play is at its peak for the preconceptual child and is designated by Piaget as symbolic play. Three- and 4-year-olds engage in pretend or make-believe play and can take on many roles, doctor, prince, queen, or mail carrier. Younger children may play beside their friends without interacting, which is called parallel play, but older preconceptual children enjoy social play by interacting and conversing with each other.

STAGE OF CONCRETE OPERATIONS—AGES 7 THROUGH 11

Children at this stage of intellectual development can form interiorized mental operations. In terms of counting, they know that numbers stand for actual objects, and they develop one-to-one correspondence. Numbers are not simply recited in a rote manner, but actually stand for discrete quantities. Gradually, adding, subtracting, multiplying, and dividing are performed mentally. Time has more meaning for them, and some children begin to learn how to tell time. One characteristic of children in this stage is reversibility: Numbers can be counted forwards and backwards; children can trace their path to school and home again; and emotionally, they can put themselves in another's place and feel empathy.

Classification of objects by color, size, and shape is possible. Demonstrating the ability called seriation, children can arrange objects by size or by weight. Children begin to understand part-whole relationships and can classify using two or more aspects of an entity. For example, they may understand that beads can be both wooden and also be of two colors, white or brown, as in Piaget's experiments. Thus they can classify by different aspects of an object.

Euclidean geometry can be comprehended in this stage as children learn about different shapes and angles. In this stage of concrete operations, they can coordinate perspectives and rotate surfaces. They can draw a straight line without using an edge. They can understand the difference between curvilinear and rectilinear shapes. They recognize and draw circles, squares, triangles, rectangles, and hexagons.

Children are now capable of conservation, which was difficult in the previous stage; children understand that objects or quantities remain the same even if there is a change in their physical appearance. Piaget carried out various experiments to test children's awareness of changes in number, substance (mass), area, weight, and volume.

Socialized speech begins and children may use adapted information, an exchange of opinions and ideas in conversation with another child or adult. In this stage, children also begin to use criticism usually based on emotion rather than on logic or reasoning. In this way these youngsters exert their superiority over others. Commands, threats, and requests occur whereby children attempt to influence others. Children enjoy punning, making jokes, and playing with long words. They are capable of argument and use logic and facts to back up their positions.

According to Piaget in the stage of concrete operations, games with rules are enjoyed. Children may still bend the rules, but they are capable of abiding by them, insisting on fair play, and enforcing punishment if rules are broken. Play continues in all of its forms, sensory-motor, imitation, practice, symbolic, and games with rules even into adulthood. Adults use sensory-motor while playing with sand or water at the beach, practice play when trying out a golf swing of an expert, following rules in chess or bridge, and they continually use symbolic play through writing poetry or fiction, acting in a community theater, and engaging in games of pageantry.

STAGE OF FORMAL OPERATIONS— AGES 11 THROUGH 16

Piaget's final stage of intelligence coincides with the beginnings of adolescence. Adolescents can think abstractly, use deductive reasoning, and are flexible, rational, and can approach a problem in a systematic way. They can think about space and time in a more abstract manner and are capable of doing more complex mathematics, even physics and chemistry; students can think scientifically. They are capable of mental operations such as drawing conclusions and can construct tests to evaluate hypotheses. The logical or formal operations include theoretical reasoning, combinatorial reasoning, functionality and proportional reasoning, control of variables, and probabilistic thinking. According to Piagetian theory most students in high school are able to exhibit these reasoning patterns. However, research studies (Huitt & Hummel, 2003) have shown that many students have not developed these reasoning abilities. About two-thirds of all people do not develop this form of reasoning fully enough for it to become their normal mode for cognition, and so they remain, even as adults, concrete operational thinkers.

In terms of morality, the adolescent develops an inner values system. Previously, in the premoral stage, toddlers had no obligation to follow rules. Very young children believe in immanent justice: Objects have within themselves the power to punish. Obeying rules literally occurs in the moral conventional stage from about age 4 to 7 when adults are seen as powerful and can inflict punishment. In the autonomous stage, 7- to 12-year-olds

consider the purposes of rules and their consequences if not obeyed. Adolescents, however, understand the appropriateness of punishment, expect others to be fair, and adapt a codification of rules understood by all players and by society as a whole.

PIAGET AND VYGOTSKY

Piaget believed that children construct their knowledge by their own actions on the environment, whereas Lev Vygotsky (1896–1934) placed a greater emphasis on understanding as originating in the social/cultural aspects of society. A Russian educational psychologist, Vygotsky proposed the theory that social interaction and cultural influences lead to a continuous change in children's thought and behavior. Vygotsky disagreed with Piaget's assumption that development could not be impeded or accelerated through instruction. While Piaget believed that concepts should not be taught until a child is in the appropriate developmental stage, Vygotsky suggested that adults could help children learn through scaffolding, reaching a higher level in a subject through being sensitive to their capabilities. He coined the term *proximal development* to refer to that zone or range of tasks that children cannot perform alone but can accomplish with the help of skilled partners, parents, or teachers. Vygotsky criticized Piaget's link between psychology and philosophy. He believed that Piaget was not scientific enough in his methodology. Play was important to Vygotsky who believed that children learn through play, since play is a way of dealing with culture and is necessary for self-regulation and control of behaviors. According to Vygotsky, play also serves to separate thought from actions, thus promoting symbolic thinking. While Piaget discussed play in its many forms, he did not deal adequately with the influence of culture and the social environment on play as Vygotsky did.

EVALUATIONS OF PIAGET

In a scholarly article (1996), Lourenço and Machado rebut criticisms of Piaget's theories; the authors suggest that many writers misinterpret Piaget's conclusions and fail to appreciate the central issues of his theory. Lourenço and Machado also contend that critics do not recognize the post-1970 modifications of Piaget's theories. Lourenço and Machado present in detail ten areas of criticism and their arguments against each. Concepts reviewed in their article include competence in children; age norms concerning when children are able to complete particular tasks; what critics call Piaget's negative view of children; his neglect of cultural and social influences on children; his failure to adequately explain his theory of cognitive development; the descriptive rather than explanatory quality of his work; and finally, his ignoring postadolescent development. Examples of some of the studies that are critical of Piaget appear below.

George Butterworth (1977) and Rene Baillargeon and colleagues (1985) conducted experiments with babies to demonstrate that object permanence occurs much earlier than Piaget believed. Babies appeared to understand that objects continue in existence, but they did not know what to do to find them. Andrew Meltzoff and M. Keith Moore (1983) asserted that babies can imitate human facial expressions as early as two to three weeks of age and imitate movements of others even when they do not see these movements on their own bodies. The discovery of "mirror neurons" (the same regions in the brain that control action also support perception) may be a neurophysiological explanation for these developmental behaviors (Jaffe, 2007). Jean Mandler (1990) found that babies can determine boundaries of objects (separating a cup from a saucer) and can deal with figure and ground experiments at an earlier age than Piaget indicated. Merry Bullock and Rochel Gelman (1979) demonstrated through their studies that children in the preoperational stage could understand cause and effect earlier than Piaget had predicted but are not able to use verbal explanations. These studies suggest that babies are social from birth and that a key way to learn is by observing others, a point more in line with Vygotsky's premise.

Jean Piaget's theory, despite many studies that find fault with it, remains into the 21st century an important theoretical explanation of the emergence of logical thought in the development of children.

BIBLIOGRAPHY

Baillargeon, R., Spelke, S., & Wasserman, S. Object permanence in five-month-old infants. *Cognition, 20,* 191–208.

Bullock, M., & Gelman, R. (1979). Preschool children's assumptions about cause and effect: Temporal ordering. *Child Development, 50,* 89–96.

Butterworth, G. (1977). Object disappearance and error in Piaget's stage IV task. *Journal of Experimental Psychology, 23,* 391–501.

Huitt, W., & Hummel, J. (2003). Piaget's theory of cognitive development. *Educational Psychology Interactive.* Valdosta, GA: Valdosta State University. Retrieved April 14, 2008, from http://chiron.valdosta.edu/whuitt/col/cogsys/piaget.html.

Jaffe, E. (2007). Mirror neurons: How we reflect on behavior. *Association for Psychological Science, 20* (5), 22–25.

Lourenço, O., & Machado, A. (1996). In defense of Piaget's theory: A reply to 10 common criticisms. *Psychological Review, 103* (1), 143–164.

Mandler, J. (1990). A new perspective on cognitive development in infancy. *American Scientist, 78,* 236–243.

Meltzoff, A., & Moore, M. K. (1983). Newborns imitate adult facial gestures. *Child Development, 54,* 702–709.

Piaget, J. (1955). *The language and thought of the child.* Cleveland, OH: World Publishing.

Piaget, J. (1962). *Play, dreams, and imitation in childhood.* New York: Norton.

Piaget, J. (1963). *The origins of intelligence in children.* New York: Norton.

Piaget, J. (1965). *The child's conception of the world.* Totowa, NJ: Littlefield, Adams.

Piaget, J. (1965). *The moral judgment of the child.* New York: Free Press.

Singer, D. G., & Revenson, T. A. (1996). *A Piaget primer: How a child thinks* (Rev. ed.). New York: Penguin Group/Plume.

Vygotsky, L. S. (1978). *Mind in society.* Cambridge, MA: Harvard University Press.

Dorothy G. Singer

VYGOTSKY'S THEORY

The Russian psychologist Lev Semenovich Vygotsky (1896–1934) introduced a theoretical approach that emphasizes the contributions of the social and cultural world to cognitive development. In this theory, basic mental functions, which are regulated by maturation, are distinguished from higher mental functions, which integrate basic mental functions and are used to carry out purposeful, goal-directed action. For Vygotsky, higher mental functions develop from experience in the social and cultural context. He was especially interested in how more experienced cultural members help children learn about the world through the use of cultural tools and symbol systems that support and extend thinking.

For Vygotsky, social and cultural experiences transform cognitive development in that they create thought processes that would not be possible without these experiences. For instance, the cultural practice of literacy transforms the way that people approach memory-related tasks. As the developing child adopts the tools and ways of thinking of the culture, the child's thought and action become increasingly aligned with the values and practices of their community. To understand how cultural values and practices become integrated with cognitive development, Vygotsky was particularly interested in social interactions involving more and less experienced cultural members. In these interactions, the more experienced partner assists the less experienced partner in ways that support the learner's engagement in intelligent activities that extend beyond his or her current capabilities. This process is most effective when it is aimed at the learner's zone of proximal or potential development or the region of sensitivity for learning. For Vygotsky, what people do and learn in the course of collaborative cognitive activity is the foundation of cognitive development.

CORE CONCEPTS

Four core concepts of Vygotsky's theory are the distinction between elementary and higher mental functions, the role of mediational means in higher psychological functioning, the importance of social and cultural experience in the development of these mediational means, and the significance of the developmental approach to understanding human cognition.

Elementary and Higher Mental Functions. Vygotsky distinguished two general types of mental functions: elementary and higher-level functions. Elementary mental functions are biologically based and they carry out discrete and basic cognitive functions. Higher mental functions emerge from social and cultural experience, and they are complex in that they integrate many elementary cognitive abilities. Higher mental processes are not simply more complex versions of elementary functions; they are qualitatively distinct in that they also incorporate historical properties of the culture in which cognitive development occurs. These historically based properties are instantiated in the symbol systems (e.g. language, mathematics) and material artifacts (e.g., literacy, technology) of the culture and they are passed onto children by more experienced cultural members. For example, memory has both an elementary and a higher form. The elementary form, which is constructed of images and impressions of events, is similar to perception in that it is unintentional and the environment directly influences its content. In contrast, the higher form of memory involves the intentional use of signs to carry out goal-directed action. For example, when literacy is used to elaborate on or extend the natural memory function it enables a person to carry out an activity that would not be possible without this mediational means. The signs and tools that are used to mediate higher mental functions are conveyed to children through other people in their culture who are experienced with these representational systems and artifacts.

Mediational Means and Higher Psychological Functioning. The use of cultural signs and tools to mediate mental functioning was, for Vygotsky, the single distinguishing feature of human intelligence. Whereas other primates, and human beings when they use basic mental functions, react to and use external features of the world to guide action, human beings are capable of creating signs, such as language and number systems, and tools, such as navigational systems and computer technology, that affect or mediate how people think and interact with the world. Moreover, human beings create and live in an organized social unit called culture, which devises signs and tools that support and extend human thinking and action. Culture passes these systems of representation and cognitive artifacts across generations and, thereby, creates the historical basis of human cognition.

An important part of Vygotsky's theory is the idea that signs and tools are not merely external forces or stimuli to which children learn to respond. Rather, signs and tools carry meaning and it is the meaning that is learned and adopted by children. By participating in this meaning system, the child is able to engage with others in goal-directed behaviors as well as interpret and act upon the world in ways that make sense to other people in their developmental context. Children come to understand and use cultural signs and tools largely through social interaction, especially with more experienced cultural members. Cultures also provide institutions and formal social settings, such as rituals, and less formal social settings, such as storytelling routines, which provide children with access to valued mediational forms. More experienced cultural members play significant roles in this process. They are the most immediate participants in children's lives who use the mediational means of their culture to support thinking. More experienced cultural members guide children in the development and use of these cultural systems and they model the use of these systems in their own actions.

Language plays a central role in Vygotsky's theory. The acquisition and use of language is a primary component of children's developing intellectual abilities because it provides children with access to the ideas and understandings of other people. Language also enables children to convey their own ideas and thoughts to others in meaningful ways. With development, language, which is a cultural product, comes to mediate individual mental functioning. Therefore, as children learn to use language, the cultural system of meaning is gradually incorporated into their thought processes and, as a result, it both facilitates and constrains thinking.

Researchers have studied several social processes that promote children's learning of culturally valued skills, such as observational learning, the social regulation of attention, deliberate efforts to transfer knowledge from more to less experienced partners, social coordination during joint cognitive activity, and cognitive socialization through conversation and joint narratives. Taken together, this research suggests that social opportunities for children's learning appear in many forms and that culture determines the frequency and manner with which these processes occur.

Development of Mediational Means. To examine social and cultural contributions to intellectual growth, Vygotsky focused on social interactions involving children and more experienced cultural members. In his view, these interactions provide children with opportunity to practice, and thereby develop, cognitive skills under the tutelage of more experienced partners. Because these interactions introduce children to higher-level cognitive processes, Vygotsky saw children's participation in these interactions as a better index of children's potential development than individual performance, which describes what children already are capable of doing. Vygotsky was less concerned with children's individual intellectual capabilities at any particular point in time than he was with their potential for intellectual growth through social experience.

To assess this potential and to understand how intellectual development occurs, Vygotsky proposed the notion of the *zone of proximal development* (ZPD), defined as the difference between a child's actual developmental level as revealed in independent problem solving and the child's potential level of development when solving the problem with adult guidance or in collaboration with a more capable peer. For instance, a child learning how to count may be able to count to 10, but not beyond 10, on her own. When she tries to count the small collection of coins that she has saved, which exceeds 10 coins, she will not be able to do so on her own. In order to count the coins, the child may enlist an older sibling or parent to help her, or perhaps the sibling or parent may recognize the child's need and offer help. The interaction that ensues will help the child find out how many coins she has, which is her goal, while at the same time it will provide her with a chance to learn about, and practice, counting above 10. During the interaction, the more experienced partner may rely on many different techniques, such as modeling how to count the coins, suggesting ways to organize the coins to make counting easier, and instructing the child in number terms and numerical sequence.

For Vygotsky, the important features of this interaction for cognitive development are (a) the child would not be able to reach the goal of counting all her coins without the help of a more experienced partner, (b) the child is a full participant in the interaction, albeit a participant who has less understanding and skill at the task than does the more experienced partner; (c) the child's participation provides her with access to and experience with the thinking of the more experienced partner, and (d) the child is introduced to a way of solving the problem (counting beyond 10) that is valued in the culture in which the child will eventually be expected to function as a mature member. The reason this interaction helps the child advance in her understanding of counting is not solely due to the input of the more experienced partner, however. The child is able to participate in this interaction and, thereby, learn from it because she is actively engaged in the learning and is intellectually ready to embrace the new level of understanding that is introduced. In other words, the interaction is targeted at the child's zone of proximal or potential development. In contrast, if the more experienced partner were to insist that the child count up to 20 on her own before the partner provided help, the child would be unable to do so and the opportunity to learn, previously described, would not occur.

The concept of the zone of proximal development is twofold. First, it represents an alternative approach to the assessment of intelligence—examining children's intellectual potential under optimal conditions, that is, conditions that are tailored to the child's specific learning needs and that build on the child's present capabilities. These ideas were especially relevant to Vygotsky's research on the learning needs of children with disabilities and mental retardation. Second, the zone of proximal development represents a way of understanding how cognitive development occurs through social interaction with more skilled partners. As such, it builds bridges between the mind of the individual child and the minds of others.

According to Vygotsky, working within a child's zone of proximal development—that is, with the assistance of an adult or more experienced peer—allows the child to participate in the environment in more complex and competent ways. In other words, in social interaction targeted toward the child's zone of proximal development, a child has the opportunity to engage in more advanced cognitive activities than the child could undertake alone. This is because more experienced partners are able to arrange an activity in a way that makes it more accessible to the learner. More experienced partners also help the learner by modeling new strategies for solving the problem and supporting the learner's involvement in the more complex components. For Vygotsky, the most significant aspect of social interaction for cognitive development is the fact that social experiences convey to children the mediational means for adapting basic cognitive abilities to higher cognitive functions.

Importance of the Developmental Approach. Vygotsky considered the developmental method critical to psychological study. His interest in development led him to focus on dynamics of change, both within an individual, as captured in the idea of the zone of proximal development, and in a culture, expressed in the signs and tools that are used to organize and guide intelligent action.

Vygotsky was interested in four different ways in which history contributes to the development of higher mental functions: general cultural history, ontological history, the history of higher psychological functions, and the history of a particular learning experience. General cultural history includes aspects of human social life that are passed across generations and represent collective means of acting and thinking, such as material resources or tools that support thinking and socially organized activities and institutions in which intelligent actions occur. Ontological history is a person's individual or life history, and it includes the integration of biological processes that regulate the development of basic mental functions and sociocultural processes that regulate the development of higher mental functions. The history of higher psychological functions examines how specific mental functions, such as remembering, have changed over human history as they have adapted to the circumstances and environments in which people live. The history of a particular learning experience includes change at the microanalytic level and is captured in the process described in the notion of the zone of proximal development.

Vygotsky did not believe that any single factor could explain all of mental functioning and its development. He was critical of reductionist views of his time, such as behaviorism, as well as theories that were broader in scope but nonetheless posited single explanatory forces for psychological functioning, such as Gestalt psychology with its emphasis on structural forms. Vygotsky emphasized the multiple forces underlying psychological phenomena and he argued that these forces were only apparent when they were in the process of change or development.

VIEWS ON COGNITIVE DEVELOPMENT

Vygotsky proposed that cognitive development is a product of social and cultural experience. He saw social interaction, in particular, as a critical force in intellectual development. Through the assistance provided by others, children gradually learn to function intellectually as individuals. Vygotsky defined the sociocultural environment of cognitive development in very broad terms, including social interaction, the values and practices of the culture, and the tools and symbol systems that people use to support and extend thinking. However, Vygotsky did not view individual psychology or human cognition as socially determined. He proposed that cognitive development is socially constructed. In other words, individual psychological functioning is an emergent property of the sociocultural experiences of the human organism. During social interaction that supports cognitive development, the child participates in and learns ways of thinking and acting that were not previously available to the child. The cognitive growth that emerges is initially intermental—it occurs between two or more individuals. Following the interaction, if the child's thinking and understanding change so as to resemble what occurred during the interaction, the resulting cognitive change or development is intramental or psychological. Because the child's own capabilities, interests, and goals contribute to the social interaction, what develops is not a duplicate of the partner's understanding. Rather, it emerges as the partners work and think together.

Vygotsky considered cognitive development as a process of qualitative change. He focused on changes that occur when elementary mental functions, such as involuntary memory, are transformed into higher mental functions, such as voluntary memory. For Vygotsky, higher mental functions are the result of the transformation of basic cognitive abilities into mental processes that are capable, with the aid of mediational means, of devising and carrying out conscious, goal-directed actions. To this end, he concentrated on changes in the mediational means that an individual uses to understand and act upon the world, and social phenomena are instrumental in this process.

Vygotsky was interested in a range of mediational means, both symbolic and material, including language, mathematics, mnemonic devices, artistic symbols, and literacy. For Vygotsky, when children learn how to use and eventually adopt signs and tools that support thinking, the fundamental nature of thinking changes. Furthermore, these mediational means not only support and extend an individual's intellectual functioning; they connect the individual's thinking and action with the social and cultural context in which development occurs.

RELATION TO PIAGETIAN THEORY

In contrast to Jean Piaget's emphasis on individual functioning, Vygotsky stressed the relation between individual cognitive development and the sociocultural environment in which this development occurs. Although Piaget did consider some aspects of the social environment in his theory, in particular peer interaction, Vygotsky defined the social environment in much broader terms. Like Piaget, Vygotsky was a constructivist. However, Piaget concentrated on constructive processes in the individual's mind, whereas Vygotsky emphasized the socially constructed nature of cognitive development.

Another distinction between Piaget and Vygotsky is in their views on the relation of thought and language. For Vygotsky, thought and speech are independent in early development, but around the second year of life they join together when children begin to use words to label objects. Within a year, speech assumes two forms: social or communicative speech and egocentric or private speech. Vygotsky's view of egocentric speech differs markedly from Piaget's concept of the same name. For Vygotsky, egocentric speech is a form of self-directed "dialogue" that the child uses as a guide in solving problems. As such, egocentric speech becomes a tool for intellectual growth. By age 7 or 8, this form of speech becomes internalized in the thought process and becomes inner speech, an internal monologue that guides intelligent action.

For Piaget, egocentric speech reflects a limitation of the preoperational stage in which the child's self-focused way of thinking leads children to explain natural phenomena in reference to the self, for example by claiming that the moon follows the child home at night. Unlike Piaget, who thought that egocentric speech served no useful cognitive function, Vygotsky considered egocentric speech as one step in the path of the development of internalized knowledge. Finally, Piaget suggested that egocentric speech diminishes at the end of the preoperational period, as the child's perspective-taking abilities improve, whereas Vygotsky thought that this kind of speech becomes internalized as thought. Much of the research evidence tends to favor Vygotsky's position; for example, children use more private or self-speech when encountering a difficult cognitive task and, as a result, their performance improves.

INFLUENCE ON LATER DEVELOPMENTALISTS

At the time of his death from tuberculosis in 1934 at the age of 37, Vygotsky was a prominent psychologist in Russia with a large following of students and colleagues. However, in 1936 his influence was threatened when the Stalinist regime banned his writings. Two of Vygotsky's close colleagues, A. R. Luria and A. N. Leont'ev, who also went on to become prominent psychologists, helped to sustain and advance Vygotsky's ideas during this time. In 1953 Stalin died and by 1956 Vygotsky's writings were again available in Russia. In the early 1960s, the influence of his ideas extended beyond Russia when the first English translations of his writings appeared in the book *Thought and Language*. Since then many other translated works have followed, and these ideas have inspired much theoretical, empirical, and applied research on cognitive development. Vygotsky's ideas are especially influential in some contemporary approaches to cognitive development, such as the sociocultural perspective and cultural psychology.

Vygotsky's theory has had considerable impact in both developmental psychology and education. His ideas have inspired much research on the contributions of adult-child and peer interaction to cognitive development. The form of instruction known as scaffolding was inspired by Vygotsky's ideas. Scaffolding is the process by which the more experienced partner or teacher adjusts the amount and type of support provided for the learner in relation to changes in the learner's needs over the course of the interaction. The concept of guided participation, introduced by B. Rogoff as a way of describing children's informal learning experiences outside of school, was also informed by Vygotsky's ideas.

Since the late 1980s educational programs that draw on Vygotsky's ideas have increased. In these programs more knowledgeable people, especially teachers, play critical roles in arranging and supporting children's learning using techniques like scaffolding, collaboration, and the provision of tools that support learning and thinking. In the method of reciprocal teaching, developed by A. Palinscar and A. L. Brown, the idea of the zone of proximal development is used as the basis of a tutoring program for children in reading comprehension. Another classroom application is the community of learners model, introduced by A. L. Brown and J. Campione. In this approach, the teacher uses the technique of scaffolding to support children's learning, and the students, who vary in knowledge and ability, actively help each other learn through their interchanges.

CRITIQUE AND CONTRIBUTIONS

Vygotsky's theory emphasizes the culturally organized and socially mediated nature of cognitive development. This theory offers a view of cognitive development that respects the contexts in which this development occurs and, as such, it overcomes limitations in theories that focus solely on the individual or on the environment. Vygotsky's theory has made developmental psychologists more aware of the importance of the immediate social contexts of learning and it has increased appreciation of the importance of culture in cognitive development. This theory also provides a way of conceptualizing how cultural symbol systems and tools get passed across generations as they are incorporated into the developing mind. The shortcomings of the theory include lack of specification regarding age-related changes in cognition and how other aspects of development, such as physical, social, and emotional capabilities, contribute to cognitive change.

Vygotsky left developmental psychology a unique and valuable legacy of ideas. His approach to cognitive development has helped steer the field toward an important set of questions that are not found in other contemporary theories. His emphasis on mediational means as central to intellectual development provides a cornerstone for contemporary research in a wide range of areas including language development, social cognition, problem solving, educational psychology, child socialization, and cultural psychology.

SEE ALSO *Communities of Learners; Guided Participation; Reciprocal Teaching; Scaffolding.*

BIBLIOGRAPHY

Chaiklin, S. (2003). The zone of proximal development in Vygotsky's analysis of learning and instruction. In A. Kozulin, B. Gindis, V. S. Ageyev, & S. M. Miller (Eds.), *Vygotsky's educational theory in cultural context: Learning in doing* (pp. 39–64). New York, NY: Cambridge University Press.

Daniels, H. (2005). *An introduction to Vygotsky* (2nd ed.). New York, NY: Routledge.

Daniels, H., Cole, M., & Wertsch, J. V. (2007). *The Cambridge companion to Vygotsky*. New York, NY: Cambridge University Press.

Gauvain, M. (2001). *The social context of cognitive development.* New York, NY: Guilford Press.

John-Steiner, V., & Holbrook, M. (2003). Sociocultural contexts for teaching and learning. In W. M. Reynolds & G. E. Miller (Eds.), *Handbook of psychology: Educational psychology, Vol. 7* (pp. 125–151). Hoboken, NJ: John Wiley and Sons.

Kozulin, A. (1990). *Vygotsky's psychology. A biography of ideas.* Cambridge, MA: Harvard University Press.

Kozulin, A. (2005). *The concept of activity in Soviet psychology: Vygotsky, his disciplines and critics.* New York, NY: Routledge.

Luria, A. R. (1978). *The making of mind: A personal account of Soviet psychology.* Cambridge, MA: Harvard University Press.

Maynard, A. E., & Martini, M. I. (2005). *Learning in cultural context: Family, peers, and school.* New York, NY: Kluwer Academic/Plenum.

Moll, L. C. (1990). *Vygotsky and education: Instructional implications and applications of sociohistorical psychology.* New York: Cambridge University Press.

Palinscar, A. S. (2005). *Social constructivist perspectives on teaching and learning.* New York, NY: Routledge.

Rieber, R. W., Robinson, D. K., Bruner, J., Cole, M., Glick, J., Ratner, C., & Stetsenko, A. (2004). *The essential Vygotsky.* New York, NY: Kluwer Academic/Plenum.

Rogoff, B. (1990). *Apprenticeship in thinking: Cognitive development in social context.* New York: Oxford University Press.

Scribner, S. (1985). Vygotsky's uses of history. In J. V. Wertsch (Ed.), *Culture, communication, and cognition: Vygotskian perspectives.* Cambridge, UK: Cambridge University Press.

Tudge, J., & Scrimsher, S. (2003). Lev S. Vygotsky on education: A cultural-historical, interpersonal, and individual approach to development. In B. J. Zimmerman & D. H. Schunk (Eds.), *Educational psychology: A century of contributions* (pp. 207–228). Mahwah, NJ: Erlbaum.

Van der Veer, R., & Valsiner, J. (1991). *Understanding Vygotsky: A quest for synthesis.* Oxford, UK: Basil Blackwell.

Vygotsky, L. S. (1978). *Mind in society: The development of higher psychological processes.* Cambridge, MA: Harvard University Press.

Vygotsky, L. S. (1987). *The collected works of L. S. Vygotsky, Vol. 1: Problems of general psychology* (R. W. Rieber & A. S. Carton, Eds.). New York: Plenum.

Wertsch, J. V. (1985). *Vygotsky and the social formation of mind.* Cambridge, MA: Harvard University Press.

Wertsch, J. V., & Tulviste, P. (2005). *L. S. Vygotsky and contemporary developmental psychology.* New York, NY: Routledge.

Mary Gauvain

COGNITIVE LOAD THEORY

Cognitive load theory (CLT) can provide guidelines to assist in the presentation of information in a manner that encourages learner activities that optimize intellectual performance. Central to CLT is the notion that human cognitive architecture should be a major consideration when designing instruction. This cognitive architecture consists of a limited working memory (WM), which interacts with a comparatively unlimited long-term memory (LTM). The limited WM carries the risk of learners being cognitively overloaded when performing a high-complexity task. According to the theory, the limitations of working memory can be circumvented by coding multiple elements of information as one element in cognitive schemata, by automating rules, and by using more than one presentation modality.

COGNITIVE ARCHITECTURE: MEMORY AND SCHEMAS

WM is what people use when engage in activities such as reading. The text is a stimulus that enters the sensory register through attention and recognition. WM is used for all conscious activities and is the only memory that can be monitored. Everything else—content and function—is concealed until brought into working memory. A problem, especially for instructional designers, is that WM is limited to about seven new items or elements of information at any one time when the information merely has to be remembered (Miller, 1956; Baddeley, 1992). Furthermore, when this new information is also used to organize, contrast, compare or work on, only two or three items of information can be processed simultaneously (Cowan, 2000). Finally, WM is not one monolithic structure, but rather a system embodying at least two mode-specific components: a visuo-spatial sketchpad and a phonological loop coordinated by a central executive.

In contrast, LTM is what people use to make sense of and give meaning to activities such as reading. People are not directly conscious of LTM. It is the repository for more permanent knowledge and skills and includes all things in memory that are not currently being used but which are needed to understand (Bower, 1975). Most cognitive scientists believe that the storage capacity of LTM is unlimited and is a permanent record of everything that a person has learnt.

Human cognition thus places its primary emphasis on the ability to store seemingly unlimited amounts of information, including large, complex interactions and procedures, in LTM. Human intellect comes from this stored knowledge and not from long, complex chains of reasoning in working memory. Because of its capacity limitation, WM is incapable of such highly complex interactions using new information elements not previously stored in LTM. It follows, that instruction (and instructional design) that require learners to engage in complex reasoning processes involving combinations of unfamiliar information elements are likely to present problems and not work well. Instruction, thus, must consider how this information is stored and organized in LTM so that it is accessible when and where it is needed.

According to schema theory, after being processed in WM, new knowledge is stored in LTM in schemas. A schema is essentially a mental framework for understanding and remembering information. For example, "the existence of a cognitive schema for the letter *a* allows us to treat each of the infinite number of printed and hand-written variants of the letter in an identical fashion" (Sweller, 2002, p. 3). Schemas categorize information elements according to how they will be used (Chi, Glaser & Rees, 1982). When new schemas are formed or existing schemas altered, learning occurs. Schemata can integrate information elements and production rules and become automated, thus requiring less storage and controlled processing. Skilled performance and increasing expertise consists of building increasing numbers of increasingly complex schemas by combining elements consisting of lower level schemas into higher-level schemas. Although, WM can process only a limited number of new elements at a time, the size, complexity, and sophistication of known elements—the schemata—is unimportant, because a schema can be treated as a single entity. In summary, schema construction aids the storage and organization of information in LTM and reduces the risk of a learner being overloaded by an instruction.

COGNITIVE LOAD

As a result of the WM limitation instruction should be designed so that WM is capable of processing the instruction (i.e., the information that constitutes the instruction). The instruction, because of its information elements that have to be processed, as well as the way it is designed, imposes a cognitive load (CL) on a learner. For understanding to commence, the load should not exceed the capacity of the limited WM. Thus CLT is concerned with measures that can be taken to control the cognitive load and the construction of schemata, that is, learning. The challenge for the instructional designer is to ensure that the limits of the learner's WM load are not exceeded when he or she is processing instruction.

Both causal and assessment factors affect CL (Paas and Van Merriënboer, 1994a; see figure 1). Causal factors can be characteristics of the subject (e.g., cognitive abilities such as expertise), the task (e.g., task complexity), the environment (e.g., noise), and their mutual relations. Assessment factors include mental load, mental effort, and performance as the three measurable dimensions of CL. Mental load is the portion of CL that is imposed exclusively by the task and environmental demands. Mental effort refers to the cognitive capacity actually allocated to the task. The subject's performance is a reflection of mental load, mental effort, and the aforementioned causal factors (Kirschner, 2002).

WM load is affected by the inherent nature of the instruction (intrinsic CL) and by the manner in which the instruction is presented (extraneous and germane CL). The following (Kirschner, 2002) is a short explication of these three aspects of CL.

Intrinsic cognitive load is a direct function of performing the task, in particular, of the number of elements that must be simultaneously processed in working memory

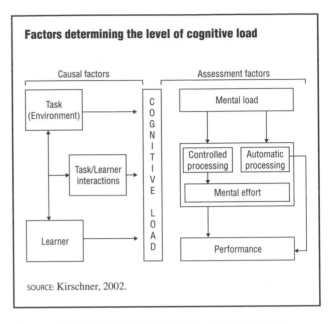

Figure 1 ILLUSTRATION BY GGS INFORMATION SERVICES. CENGAGE LEARNING, GALE.

(element interactivity). A task with many constituent skills (a high-complexity task) that must be coordinated yields a higher intrinsic load than a task with less constituent skills (a low-complexity task) that need to be coordinated. Cerpa, Chandler, and Sweller (1995) give the following example. Learning basic operations on cells in a spreadsheet program, such as selecting a cell or group of cells, entering data into a cell or modifying data already in a cell are low-complexity tasks with low element interactivity. Each operation can be learned independently with minimal reference to any other operations. By contrast, creating formulas requires learning that cells are intersections of rows and columns, identifying and manipulating them, learning that formulas consist of a number of cells and operations/operators (i.e., equals/=, add/+, subtract/-), all of which must be learned and understood in conjunction with each other.

Extraneous cognitive load is the extra load beyond the intrinsic CL, mainly resulting from poorly designed instruction. For instance, if learners must search in their instructional materials for the information they need to perform a learning task (e.g., searching for data needed in a cell somewhere else in the spreadsheet or determining what the value of a variable in a cell might be while the task is to learn how to use a spreadsheet), this search process itself does not directly contribute to learning and thus causes extraneous CL.

Germane cognitive load is related to processes that directly contribute to learning, in particular to schema construction and rule automation. For instance, consciously connecting new information with what is already known, rather than focusing on task details (e.g., making explicit that the operator in a specific cell is very much like a different one already learned, but varies with respect to a specific characteristic), is a process that yields germane CL.

Intrinsic, extraneous, and germane CL are additive in that, if learning is to occur, the total load of the three together should not exceed the WM capacity. A basic assumption of CLT is that an instructional design that results in unused working memory capacity due to low extraneous CL because of appropriate instructional procedures may be further improved by encouraging learners to engage in conscious cognitive processing directly relevant to learning, that is, germane CL (Paas & Van Merriënboer, 1994b). Consequently, the greater the proportion of germane CL created by the instructional design, the greater the potential for learning.

According to CLT the limitations of working memory are rarely taken into account in conventional instruction. Conventional instructions tend to impose a high extraneous CL on WM, whereas learning something requires shifting from extraneous to germane CL. CLT states that the instructional interventions cannot change the intrinsic CL because this is *ceteris paribus* intrinsic to the material being dealt with. Extraneous and germane CL, however, are determined by the instructional design (Sweller, 1994). Appropriate instructional designs decrease extraneous CL but increase germane CL, provided that the total CL stays within the limits of WM capacity.

MEASURING COGNITIVE LOAD

Measuring CL can be done with several assessment techniques, subjective, physiological, and task- and performance-based (Paas, Tuovinen, Tabbers, & Van Gerven, 2003). Subjective techniques are based on the assumption that people are able to assess the amount of mental effort they expended. A frequently used measuring instrument in this category of techniques is the one-dimensional ninth-grade symmetrical category scale developed by Paas (1992), in which learners have to rate their perceived mental effort after completing a task on a 9-point rating scale ranging from "very, very low mental effort" to "very, very high mental effort." Physiological techniques are based on changes in cognitive functioning that are reflected in physiological measurements like heart rate or eye activity. Task- and performance-based techniques consist of primary task measurements, which is the actual task performance, and of secondary task measurements, based on the performance of a second task, which is performed concurrently with the primary task. Some of these techniques have been combined to give a relative indication of the acceptable level of cognitive load. A good example of such a combination is

the instructional efficiency measurement developed by Paas and van Merrienboer (1993), which combines primary performance with the subjective mental effort rating scale developed by Paas to obtain information on the relative mental efficiency of instructional conditions.

EFFECTS GENERATED BY CLT

CLT research has led to the development of a number of instructional formats primarily meant to decrease extraneous CL. These have enabled freed up WM capacity to be used for effective learning, and therefore studies have been conducted in which germane CL was increased when it was considered directly relevant to schema construction (Sweller, 1999). The basic assumption in these studies is that an instructional design that results in unused WM capacity because of a low intrinsic CL imposed by the instructional materials, and/or low extraneous CL due to appropriate instructional procedures, may be further improved by encouraging learners to engage in conscious cognitive processing that is directly relevant to schema construction. Clearly, this approach can only work if the total CL of the instructional design (the combination of intrinsic CL, extraneous CL, and germane CL) is within working memory limits. This is the new frontier of instructional design.

An exhaustive overview of CLT-based instructional formats and their empirical base is given by Sweller, van Merriënboer, and Paas (1998); Paas, Renkl, and Sweller (2003); and Van Merriënboer and Sweller (2005). Six of the most researched instructional techniques are (a) the goal-free effect, (b) the worked examples effect, (c) the completion effect, (d) the split-attention effect, (e) the modality effect, and (f) the redundancy effect.

The goal-free effect occurs when a learner receiving a conventional, goal-specific problem learns less than when he or she receives a non-specific or goal-free problem to solve. Novice learners with a specific learning goal focus primarily on the goal and therefore pay no attention to other information. They compare the current state of a problem (i.e., where they are) to the goal state (i.e., where they want to get to, the solution), and the difference between them is divided up into a series of sub-goals that will have to be achieved to reach the goal, using their own limited repertoire of operators. This so called means-ends analysis approach (Newell & Simon, 1972) operates on the principle of trying to reduce differences between the goal state and problem givens, but it is a weak approach to problem solving, because it is an approach or strategy independent of a particular problem and causes a high extraneous CL. Consequently, it is detrimental to learning. In goal-free problems, a problem solver has no other option than to focus on the information provided (the given data) and to use it where possible, automatically inducing a forward-working solution path similar to that generated by expert problem solvers. Such forward-working solutions impose very low levels of extraneous CL and facilitate learning.

The worked examples effect involves using known and resolved examples, which diminish extraneous CL and improve comprehension. A worked example consists of a problem and the steps to its solution. Reviewing worked examples eliminates the need to use means-end analysis because, since the solution is provided, it is no longer necessary to search for an operator to reduce the difference between the current state and the goal state. Presenting the problem solution allows the learner to focus on individual problem states, the problem solving moves associated with them, and the problem states resulting from these moves. Because this is the type of information contained in a problem-solving schema it was hypothesized that worked examples would help in schema acquisition and automation as well as in reducing working memory load since they deconstruct a problem solution into its parts.

The completion effect has a similar rationale and effect as that of the worked examples. Instead of providing a completely worked out example followed by a problem, the learner is provided with partially completed worked examples. Such examples provide enough guidance to reduce problem solving search and extraneous CL while problem completion ensures that learners are motivated to continue working.

The split-attention effect occurs when learners are forced to process and integrate multiple and separated sources of information. Many instructional materials make use of both a pictorial component and a textual component of information. Often, the pictorial component (i.e., a graphic) is presented with the associated text above, below, or at the side of it. This manner of presentation introduces a split-attention effect in which the learner must attend to both the graphic and the text, because neither alone provides sufficient information for solving the problem. Learning and understanding can only occur after mental integration of the different sources of information. WM capacity needed for integrating the graphic information and the textual information is subsequently unavailable for processes that foster learning. Good instructional design incorporates (i.e., physically integrates) the graphical and textual information, thus reducing the need for the learner to do this and thus freeing up WM for learning. This is the traditional spatial split-attention effect. In addition, there is also a temporal split-attention effect that holds that learning from mutually referring information sources is facilitated if these sources are not separated from each other in time but, rather, are presented simultaneously.

The modality effect occurs when information is presented in two different sensory modalities, for example when textual information is presented in auditory form and diagrammatic information is presently visually. By making use of both auditory and visual channels, effective WM capacity is increased. This expanded WM can be used to reduce mental workload and results in better learning than equivalent, single-mode presentations that only use visual information (Tabbers, Martens, & van Merriënboer, 2004).

The redundancy effect holds that the multiple processing of the same information that is presented more than once—such as when a presenter projects a slide and then reads it aloud to the audience—has a negative effect on comprehension since it increases extraneous CL. This effect sounds counter-intuitive because most people think that the presentation of the same information will have a neutral or even positive effect on learning. However, the presentation of redundant information causes learners to unnecessarily attend to individual bits of repeated information that can be understood in isolation. Also, learners must first process the information to determine whether the information from the different sources is actually redundant. These cognitively demanding processes do not contribute to meaningful learning.

EFFECTS OF CLT RESEARCH ON INSTRUCTIONAL DESIGN

In their book Van Merriënboer and Kirschner (2007) discuss how good instructional design can control CL and by doing so increase and/or facilitate learning. The CL associated with performing learning tasks is controlled in two ways. First, intrinsic CL is managed by organizing the learning tasks in easy-to-difficult task classes. For learning tasks within an easier task class, less elements and interactions between elements need to be processed simultaneously in WM. As the task classes become more complex, the number of elements and interactions between the elements increases. Second, extraneous CL is managed by providing a large amount of support and guidance for the first learning task(s) in a task class, thus preventing weak-method problem solving and its associated high extraneous CL. This support and guidance decreases as learners gain more expertise ("scaffolding").

Because supportive information typically has high element interactivity, it is preferable not to present it to learners while they are working on the learning tasks. Simultaneously performing a task and studying the information would almost certainly cause cognitive overload. Instead, supportive information is best presented before learners start working on a learning task. In this way, a cognitive schema can be constructed in LTM that can subsequently be activated in WM during task performance. Retrieving the already constructed cognitive schema is expected to be less cognitively demanding than activating the externally presented complex information in working memory during task performance.

Procedural information consists of cognitive rules and typically has much lower element interactivity than supportive information. An example of procedural information is knowing that a voltmeter needs to be attached to a circuit in parallel while an ammeter must be attached in series. Furthermore, the development of cognitive rules requires that relevant information is active in WM during task performance so that it can be embedded in those rules. Studying this information beforehand has no added value; therefore, procedural information should be presented precisely when learners need it. This is, for example, the case when teachers give step-by-step instructions to learners during practice, becoming in effect like an assistant looking over the learners' shoulders.

Finally, part-task practice automates particular recurrent aspects of a complex skill. In general, an over-reliance on part-task practice is not helpful for complex learning. But the automated recurrent constituent skills may decrease the CL associated with performing the whole learning tasks, making performance of the whole skill more fluid and decreasing the chance of making errors due to cognitive overload.

SEE ALSO *Constructivism; Information Processing Theory.*

BIBLIOGRAPHY

Baddeley, A. D. (1992). Working memory. *Science, 255,* 556–559.

Bower, G. H. (1975). Cognitive psychology: an introduction. In W. K. Estes (Ed.), *Handbook of learning and cognitive processes: Vol. 1, Introduction to concepts and issues.* Hillsdale, NJ: Erlbaum.

Cerpa, N., Chandler, P., & Sweller, J. (1995). *Some consequences of training strategies when learning a computer application.* Paper presented at the 1995 Australian Association for Research in Education conference, Hobart, Australia. Retrieved April 15, 2008, from http://www.aare.edu.au/95pap/cerpn95385.txt.

Cowan, N. (2000). The magical number 4 in short-term memory: A reconsideration of mental storage capacity. *Behavioral and Brain Sciences, 24,* 87–114.

Fletcher, S. (1997a). *Designing competence-based training* (2nd ed.). London: Kogan Page.

Fletcher S. (1997b). *Analysing competence: Tools and techniques for analysing jobs, roles and functions.* London: Kogan Page.

Kirschner, P. A. (2002). Cognitive load theory: Implications of cognitive load theory on the design of learning. *Learning and Instruction, 12*(1), 1–10.

Kirschner, P. A., van Vilsteren, P., Hummel, H., & Wigman, M. (1997). A study environment for acquiring academic and professional competence. *Studies of Higher Education, 2*(22), 151–171.

Miller, G. A. (1956). The magical number seven, ± two: Some limits on our capacity for processing information. *Psychological Review, 63,* 81–97.

Newell, A., & Simon, H. (1972). *Human problem solving.* Englewood Cliffs, NJ: Prentice-Hall.

Paas, F. (1992). Training strategies for attaining transfer of problem-solving skill in statistics: A Cognitive-load approach. *Journal of Educational Psychology, 84,* 429–434.

Paas, F., & van Merriënboer, J. (1993). The efficiency of instructional conditions: An approach to combine mental-effort and performance measures. *Human Factors, 35,* 737–743.

Paas, F., & van Merriënboer, J. (1994a). Instructional control of cognitive load in the training of complex cognitive tasks. *Educational Psychology Review, 6,* 51–71.

Paas, F., & van Merriënboer, J. (1994b). Variability of worked examples and transfer of geometrical problem-solving skills: A cognitive-load approach. *Journal of Educational Psychology 86,* 122–133.

Paas, F., Renkl, A., & Sweller, J. (2003). Cognitive load theory and instructional design: Recent developments. *Educational Psychologist, 38,* 1–4.

Paas, F., Tuovinen, J., Tabbers, H., & van Gerven, P. (2003). Cognitive load measurement as a means to advance cognitive load theory. *Educational Psychologist, 38,* 63–71.

Sweller, J. (1994). Cognitive load theory, learning difficulty and instructional design. *Learning and Instruction, 4,* 295–312.

Sweller, J. (1999). *From cognitive architecture to instructional design.* Paper presented at the inaugural seminar of Professor J. G. van Merriënboer, Heerlen, The Netherlands.

Sweller, J. (2002). Visualisation and instructional design. Paper presented at the International Workshop on Dynamic Visualisations and Learning. Knowledge Media Research Center, Tübingen, Germany. Retrieved April 15, 2008, from http://www.iwm-kmrc.de/workshops/visualization/sweller.pdf.

Sweller, J., van Merriënboer, J., & Paas, F. (1998). Cognitive architecture and instructional design. *Educational Psychology Review, 10*(3), 251–296.

Van Merriënboer, J., & Kirschner, P. A. (2007). *Ten steps to complex learning.* New York: Taylor and Francis.

Van Merriënboer, J., & Sweller, J. (2005). Cognitive load theory and complex learning: recent developments and future directions. *Educational Psychology Review, 17,* 147–177.

Paul A. Kirschner
Femke Kirschner
Fred Paas

COGNITIVE STRATEGIES

A cognitive strategy is a mental process or procedure for accomplishing a particular cognitive goal. For example, if students' goals are to write good essays, their cognitive strategies might include brainstorming and completing an outline. The cognitive strategies that students use influence how they will perform in school, as well as what they will accomplish outside of school. Researchers have found that effective learners and thinkers use more effective strategies for reading, writing, problem solving, and reasoning than ineffective learners and thinkers.

SOME IMPORTANT DISTINCTIONS

Cognitive strategies can be general or specific (Pressley & Woloshyn, 1995). General cognitive strategies are strategies that can be applied across many different disciplines and situations (such as summarization or setting goals for what to accomplish), whereas specific cognitive strategies tend to be more narrow strategies that are specified toward a particular kind of task (such as drawing a picture to help one see how to tackle a physics problem). Specific strategies tend to be more powerful but have a more restricted range of use. Effective learners use both general and specific strategies.

Strategies have been distinguished from skills. Although skills are similar to strategies, they are different in that they are carried out automatically, whereas strategies usually require individuals to think about what strategy they are using (Alexander, Graham, & Harris, 1998). Effective learners develop the ability to use strategies automatically while also reflecting upon those strategies when necessary. People who are able to reflect upon their own cognition and cognitive strategies are said to have metacognitive awareness.

One factor that determines whether students use a strategy is whether students know what the strategy is and how to use it. Strategy use can be influenced both by knowledge of what the strategy is and how to use it, and by belief in the effectiveness of the strategy (Chinn, 2006). One reason why students may not use an effective strategy is that they do not know about it. For example, students who study simply by reading a textbook chapter a second time may not know that more effective strategies include actively trying to summarize the text and trying to explain challenging ideas to themselves. A second reason why students do not use strategies is that they may not believe the strategy is effective or worthwhile. The student who is encouraged to summarize the chapter may not believe it will really improve learning, or the student may agree that it will improve learning but that the amount of additional learning is not worth the time that summarizing takes.

STRATEGY USE AND THEORIES OF LEARNING AND DEVELOPMENT

The role of effective strategies in learning and thinking is emphasized by most theories of learning and development. Information processing theorists treat strategies as procedures that act on information in working memory in ways that improve memory and understanding through better interconnections with existing knowledge. For example, elaborating information is an effective strategy because it integrates new information with other information retrieved from long-term memory.

Constructivists emphasize the role of strategies as learners construct new knowledge. Strategies such as identifying problems with one's own understanding can help learners construct new understandings. Students who learn effectively will have a wide range of effective strategies for constructing knowledge at their disposal.

Lev Vygotsky (1896–1934) developed a sociocultural theory of development that emphasizes the role of groups in enabling learners to master strategies. Learners internalize strategies after first encountering them in group conversations. For instance, students may internalize the strategy of critiquing their own writing after participating in collaborative discussions in which peers critique each other's writing.

Social cognitive theorists emphasize the role of efficient strategy use in becoming a self-regulated learner. Self-regulated learners are those who are adept at controlling their own learning processes without outside supervision or help. Self-regulated learners are able to set goals for learning (e.g., study for an exam), select strategies to achieve these goals (e.g., outline each chapter and make sure each main idea is understood), monitor whether they are achieving these goals (ask themselves questions about whether everything makes sense), and make adaptations if goals are not being achieved (e.g., going back and rereading some hard-to-understand sections).

IMPORTANCE OF COGNITIVE STRATEGIES IN LEARNING AND THINKING

There are several lines of research that support the importance of cognitive strategies in learning and thinking. One prominent line of research compares experts with novices or proficient students with less proficient students (e.g., Chan, Burtis, Scardamalia, & Bereiter, 1992; Chi, Bassok, Lewis, Reimann, & Glaser, 1989). Researchers using these methods have found significant differences in strategy use between more and less proficient learners, reasoners, and problem solvers.

A second line of research experimentally examines the effects of training students to learn by employing a strategy or set of strategies (e.g., Graham, MacArthur, & Schwartz, 1995). Many such studies have demonstrated that students who learn the new strategies outperform those who did not learn the strategies.

A third line of research comes from long-term classroom experiments or quasi-experiments (Brown, Pressley, Van Meter, & Schuder, 1996; Guthrie et al., 2004). These studies usually last many months, often a whole school year. They contrast a traditional school curriculum that does not focus much on strategy instruction with curricula that teach students many different cognitive strategies. These studies have shown that with carefully designed instruction, students' performance on measures of learning, reasoning, and/or problem solving improves.

Finally, researchers have compared high-performing schools with low-performing schools to see if they differ in their emphasis on strategy instruction (e.g., Langer, 2001). A number of studies have found that higher-performing schools do in fact focus more on helping students learn effective cognitive strategies than lower-performing schools do.

Much of the research on cognitive strategies has sought to identify particular strategies that are effective on different kinds of tasks. The remainder of this entry will examine strategies that have proven to be effective in comprehension, writing, problem solving, and reasoning, and discuss several effective domain-general strategies for general self-regulation.

COMPREHENSION STRATEGIES

Comprehension strategies are strategies that help students understand and remember material such as texts and lectures. Most of the research on comprehension strategies has focused on learning from reading texts. Five strategies that have been found to be useful for enhancing comprehension are monitoring, using text structure, summarizing, elaborating, and explaining.

One widely studied comprehension strategy is monitoring (Markman, 1979). When students monitor their understanding, they review as they read in order to check that they comprehend what they are reading or learning. This skill develops with age as students' reading proficiency increases. Many unsuccessful learners mistakenly believe that they understand ideas that they do not in fact understanding; they have not mastered the strategy of accurately monitoring their understanding.

The strategy of using text structure involves utilizing the organization of a text in order to enhance comprehension (Meyer & Rice, 1984). The structure of a text refers to how ideas are organized. For example, textbooks are often organized by main concepts with several paragraphs of supporting details and peripheral concepts. Editorials are organized as a claim followed by arguments intended to persuade people that the claim is true. Compare-and-contrast essays are organized around a series of points and counterpoints. Authors use cues such as topic sentences, headings, transition words, and underlined or bold-faced font, to highlight their particular text structure as they write. These cues are used by proficient readers to help them organize the ideas they are learning. Ineffective learners make little or no use of text structure cues.

Three other important comprehension strategies are summarization, elaboration, and explaining. When students summarize, they choose the most important concepts from the text and express them in their own words. Summarization is not an easy task for students (Dole, Duffy, Roehler, & Pearson, 1991). Poor readers often generate summaries with too much detail and too little focus on key points. In addition to summarization, effective learners elaborate, which means connecting new information to information that they already know (Gagné, Weidemann, Bell, & Anders, 1984). Elaboration is different from mere paraphrasing. When students paraphrase, they simply reinterpret, in their own words, the text that they have read. In contrast, when students elaborate, they actively link the new information to old information. A student who contrasts a text about democracy to information learned earlier about dictatorships has elaborated, as has the student who connects the text about democracy to the student's own personal experiences serving on student council. Finally, when students explain ideas, they ask themselves "why" questions and then attempt to answer these questions. For instance, as students read a book on U.S. pioneers, they could try to explain why the pioneers risked so much to travel west. Studies have shown that generating explanations is a highly effective means of learning (Chi, de Leeuw, Chiu, & LaVancher, 1994).

PROBLEM-SOLVING STRATEGIES

Problems occur when a person has a goal but does not immediately see how to achieve that goal. The person must then apply problem-solving strategies to try to achieve the goal.

The mathematician George Polya (1887–1985) devised four effective problem-solving strategies: understanding the problem, developing a plan for a solution, carrying out the plan, and looking back to see what can be learned. In addition to looking back to see what can be learned, learners can check to make sure that the solution makes sense. If a math problem asks how many 40-seat buses are needed to take 120 students on a field trip, the answer 4,800 does not make sense. Ineffective problem solvers often generate solutions such as this that show little or no reflection on what the problem means.

In addition to these strategies, there are other strategies that researchers have found to be highly effective for problem solving. These strategies include representing the problem, identifying sub goals, and noticing commonalities and differences.

When representing the problem, problem solvers develop a clear picture of the problem. Sometimes this means literally making a drawing or a diagram. Sometimes it means creating a mental vision of the problem situation. Useful problem representations (a) are complete, (b) embed initial inferences that can be drawn from the problem information, and (c) exclude irrelevant information.

Real-world problems tend to be complex; they cannot be solved with a simple one-step solution. As a consequence, problem-solvers must set sub goals that must be achieved on the way to achieving the overall goal (Thevenot & Oakhill, 2006). Effective problem solvers learn to establish sub goals that effectively break down complex problems into manageable steps.

Examining and reflecting on contrasting problems can be an effective way to learn how to solve future problems better. By noticing how a difference in problem conditions affects the best solution (e.g., how a change in the wording of a mathematical word problem changes the solution method), problem solvers gain knowledge that can help them solve problems more efficiently in the future.

WRITING STRATEGIES

Writing can be viewed as an ill-structured problem—a problem with numerous potential solutions but no specifically defined criteria for deciding what counts as a good solution. Therefore, strategies that are useful in writing will be strategies that are more likely to be useful for other ill-structured tasks (such as designing a house or developing a campaign plan) than for well-structured problems with agreed-upon solution procedures.

In a 1986 study John Hayes and Linda Flower developed an influential model of writing that has guided thinking about effective writing strategies. Hayes and Flower identified three basic writing processes: planning, sentence generation, and revising. Planning and revising have been the subject of the most research.

When students plan, they think about what they are going to write about and organize these ideas before they start writing (Kellogg, 1988). Effective planners both *generate* ideas and *organize* those ideas. Effective writers typically generate more ideas than they need; this gives them a reservoir of ideas from which to choose. Organization involves ordering ideas and selecting which to include and which to exclude. Planning can fail either because the writers generate too few ideas or because the writers do a poor job of combining the ideas into a well-integrated fabric. Effective writers spend substantially more time planning than less successful writers. They often start by working at a more general level before fleshing out their ideas with many details. Effective writers are more likely than ineffective writers to make major changes to their plans as they are planning, or even later when they begin writing.

Effective student writers tend use a planning strategy called *knowledge transformation*, by which they take their existing ideas and fashion them anew into new ideas and new structures of thought (Bereiter & Scardamalia, 1987). Ineffective writers (and younger writers, as well) use a strategy called *knowledge telling*. Knowledge tellers do little or no planning, and they certainly do not fashion their current ideas into new structures. Instead, they write down ideas on paper exactly in the order that they think of them.

Once a draft is composed, effective writers revise their work (Hayes & Flower, 1986). Good writers spend more time revising than poor writers do. But they also differ from poor writers in the quality of their revisions. Poor writers may simply lightly proofread their work, if they do anything at all. More successful writers often make major revisions, perhaps choosing to make major changes to the structure of the paper or rewriting a paragraph to make it more understandable for the reader. Good writers also take the audience into consideration throughout the writing process.

REASONING STRATEGIES

Reasoning strategies are strategies that help people decide what they believe to be true or correct and what they believe to be false or incorrect. There are several strategies that differentiate more successful reasoners from less successful reasoners: generating arguments and counterarguments, fair-mindedness in evaluating evidence, considering control or comparison groups, sourcing, and seeking corroboration.

Generating counter-arguments refers to the ability to come up with arguments that *oppose* one's own argument. Most adolescents and adults can generate two to three times more arguments than counter-arguments; even the number of arguments generated for one's own claim tends to be fairly low. Researchers have argued that an important reasoning strategy is therefore to learn to consider alternative positions and arguments more carefully (Kuhn, 1991).

Ineffective reasoners tend to be biased when evaluating evidence. For instance, they will discount studies that oppose their position by pointing out many flaws in the study, but when they read a similarly flawed study that supports their position, they seem not to notice the flaws at all (Chinn & Brewer, 2001).

Effective reasoners tend to consider relevant comparison groups (Stanovich, 1999). If shown data that students who attended a test prep center increased their test scores by 20% in 2 months, they will not jump to the conclusion that the center improves test scores. They will notice the lack of a comparison group and will wonder whether students who did not attend the center also improved their test scores over 2 months.

A fourth reasoning strategy used by effective reasoners is sourcing (considering the source of the information when evaluating it). Students reading historical documents typically fail to consider—or even pay attention to—who wrote the document (Wineburg, 1991). Thus, they will not notice important issues such as whether the source might have been biased. This is an especially important concern because of the Internet; many sources on the Internet are not credible, yet many poor reasoners do not recognize or consider the credibility of the source.

Finally, effective reasoners employ the strategy of corroboration, which refers to consulting different sources of information to try to verify what is learned from one source with supporting information from another source (Wineburg, 1991). For example, a historian would be more likely to believe a former president's account of how a legislative battle was won if this account is corroborated in important details by documentary evidence.

GENERAL SELF-REGULATION STRATEGIES

General self-regulation strategies are strategies that can be used in almost any learning, problem solving, or reasoning situation. Researchers have stressed the importance of a number of general self-regulation strategies (Zimmerman, 1998). Prominent among these are goal setting, self-monitoring and self-evaluation, time management, and executive control.

When students set goals, they are recognizing and identifying what exactly they want to accomplish. Students can set long-term, intermediate-term, or short-term goals. Effective learners will use all three of these types of goals, but pay particular attention to short-term goals as steps toward longer-term goals. Research also supports the value of focusing on process goals (such as the goal of using the summarization strategy effectively) rather than just focusing on outcome goals (such as the goal of getting an *A* on the test) (Zimmerman & Kitsantas, 1999).

Monitoring has been discussed earlier as a comprehension strategy. As a general self-regulation strategy, self-monitoring, together with self-evaluation, refers more generally to the observing and taking note of the activities that one is engaged in. As students self-monitor, they are evaluating their progress toward achieving their goals. Self-monitoring includes deciding what standards one will use to judge one's own progress (e.g., deciding how to judge whether good progress has been made while conducting a science experiment). It also requires students to determine whether they have attained the goals that they have set. If they find that they are not making good progress toward their goals, they will need to develop a revised plan that will lead to better progress.

Effective time management requires students to organize their time effectively in order to accomplish goals. Proficient learners tend to manage their time more effectively than their less proficient peers.

Lastly, effective outcomes demand that the learner be skilled at controlling and managing different strategies and using them when appropriate. When learners can manage strategies effectively in this way, they have achieved executive control over the strategies.

EDUCATIONAL IMPLICATIONS

This entry has briefly reviewed some of the main cognitive strategies that enhance comprehension, problem solving, writing, and reasoning. It has also examined several of the many general-purpose self-regulation strategies that can be used on any kind of learning or thinking task.

Because less successful learners frequently use less effective strategies, teachers can help students learn by identifying strategies that students are using (assessing strategy use) and, if necessary, helping them learn more effective strategies (strategy instruction).

One method for assessing strategy use is to administer formal or informal self-report questionnaires to determine what strategies students themselves say they are using. One type of self-report questionnaire used by teachers is a cognitive strategy questionnaire (such as the widely used *Motivated Strategies for Learning Questionnaire* (MSLQ), developed by Paul Pintrich and colleagues), which asks students about their strategy use. A disadvantage of self-report measures is that students might not answer truthfully, they might misunderstand the questions, or they might lack the metacognitive awareness needed to answer accurately. An advantage of self-report measures is that they can be administered quickly to many students.

The second general way that teachers can assess strategy use is by listening to the strategies students are using as they speak in class discussions and group work or what they write in their assignments. The teacher can also listen to students' strategy use when working with students individually. Teachers can encourage their students to "make their thinking public" by thinking out loud as they are reading a text, solving a problem, writing, or reasoning. By listening to what students say in these contexts, teachers can gain an understanding of their students' strategy use. This will enable teachers to set instructional goals to help students learn more effective strategies that will help them become better learners and thinkers.

SEE ALSO *Critical Thinking; Metacognition.*

BIBLIOGRAPHY

Alexander, P. A., Graham, S., & Harris, K. (1998). A perspective on strategy research: Progress and prospects. *Educational Psychology Review, 10,* 129–154.

Bereiter, C., & Scardamalia, M. (1987). *The psychology of written composition.* Hillsdale, NJ: Erlbaum.

Brown, R., Pressley, M., Van Meter, P., & Schuder, T. (1996). A quasi-experimental validation of transactional strategies instruction with low-achieving second-grade readers. *Journal of Educational Psychology, 88,* 18–37.

Chan, C. K. K., Burtis, J., Scardamalia, M., & Bereiter, C. (1992). Constructive activity in learning from text. *American Educational Research Journal, 29,* 97–118.

Chi, M. T. H., Bassok, M., Lewis, M. W., Reimann, P., & Glaser, R. (1989). Self-explanations: How students study and use examples in learning to solve problems. *Cognitive Science, 13*, 145–182.

Chi, M. T. H., de Leeuw, N., Chiu, M., & LaVancher, C. (1994). Eliciting self-explanations improves understanding. *Cognitive Science, 18*, 439–477.

Chinn, C. A. (2006). Learning to argue. In A. M. O'Donnell, C. Hmelo-Silver, & G. Erkens (Eds.), *Collaborative learning, reasoning, and technology* (pp. 355–383). Mahwah, NJ: Erlbaum.

Chinn, C. A., & Brewer, W. F. (2001). Models of data: A theory of how people evaluate data. *Cognition and Instruction, 19*, 323–393.

Dole, J. A., Duffy, G. G., Roehler, L. R., & Pearson, P. D. (1991). Moving from the old to the new: Research on reading comprehension instruction. *Review of Educational Research, 61*, 239–264.

Gagné, E. D., Weidemann, C., Bell, M. S., & Anders, T. D. (1984). Training thirteen-year-olds to elaborate while studying text. *Human Learning: Journal of Practical Research & Applications, 3*, 281–294.

Graham, S., MacArthur, C., & Schwartz, S. (1995). Effects of goal setting and procedural facilitation on the revising behaviors and writing performance of students with writing and learning problems. *Journal of Educational Psychology, 87*, 230–240.

Guthrie, J. T., Wigfield, A., Barbosa, P., Perencevich, K. C., Taboada, A., Davis, M. H., et al. (2004). Increasing reading comprehension and engagement through concept-oriented reading instruction. *Journal of Educational Psychology, 96*, 403–423.

Hayes, J. R., & Flower, L. S. (1986). Writing research and the writer. *American Psychologist, 41*, 1106–1113.

Kellogg, R. T. (1988). Attentional overload and writing performance: Effects of rough draft and outline strategies. *Journal of Experimental Psychology: Learning, Memory, and Cognition, 14*, 355–365.

Kuhn, D. (1991). *The skills of argument.* Cambridge, England: Cambridge University Press.

Langer, J. A. (2001). Beating the odds: Teaching middle and high school students to read and write well. *American Educational Research Journal, 38*, 837–880.

Markman, E. M. (1979). Realizing that you don't understand: Elementary school children's awareness of inconsistencies. *Child Development, 50*, 643–655.

Meyer, B. J. F., & Rice, G. E. (1984). The structure of text. In P. D. Pearson, R. Barr, M. L. Kamil & P. Mosenthal (Eds.), *Handbook of reading research* (pp. 319–351). New York: Longman.

Pressley, M., & Woloshyn, V. (1995). *Cognitive strategy instruction that really improves children's academic performance* (2nd ed.). Cambridge, MA: Brookline.

Stanovich, K. E. (1999). *Who is rational? Studies of individual differences in reasoning.* Mahwah, NJ: Erlbaum.

Thevenot, C., & Oakhill, J. (2006). Representations and strategies for solving dynamic and static arithmetic word problems: The role of working memory capacities. *European Journal of Cognitive Psychology, 18*, 756–775.

Wineburg, S. S. (1991). Historical problem solving: A study of the cognitive processes used in the evaluation of documentary and pictorial evidence. *Journal of Educational Psychology, 83*, 73–87.

Zimmerman, B. J. (1998). Academic studying and the development of personal skill: A self-regulatory perspective. *Educational Psychologist, 33*, 73–86.

Zimmerman, B. J., & Kitsantas, A. (1999). Acquiring writing revision skill: Shifting from process to outcome self-regulatory goals. *Journal of Educational Psychology, 91*, 241–250.

Clark A. Chinn
Lisa M. Chinn

COLLABORATIVE LEARNING

Collaborative learning (also known as cooperative learning) occurs when small groups of students, called collaborative groups, work together to complete an academic task. As its name suggests, in order for collaborative learning to be successful, students must *collaborate* productively and work together on a task, sharing ideas and learning from one another. Researchers have found that if collaborative learning is designed properly, students learn more than when working individually. Conversely, poorly designed collaborative learning does not promote learning goals effectively.

GOALS AND OBSTACLES

For many researchers and educators, the ultimate goals of collaborative learning include the following:

- Each individual in the group effectively learns the academic content, such as gaining a conceptual understanding of photosynthesis or the Great Depression.

- Each individual becomes more proficient in the use of cognitive strategies such as comprehension, problem solving, and reasoning strategies.

- Each individual develops valued social skills, such as engaging in prosocial behavior and the ability to work well in group settings. These are skills that are needed to work effectively in teams as adults.

- All individuals learn to value and respect their peers, to appreciate diversity, and to develop friendships.

Some researchers advocate goals not only at the level of individual learning but also at the level of the overall class. For example, in their 2006 article, Marlene Scardamalia and Carl Bereiter advocate a view of learning, or knowledge building, in which the goal is for the class as a whole to generate knowledge. For example, a class might generate knowledge that is new to them about photosynthesis by reading a variety of sources, conducting their own experiments, and posting their ideas on a shared computer space. The collaborative learning process is valuable to the extent that the class collectively generates ideas new to most or all students on this shared space.

However, there are common obstacles to achieving these goals (O'Donnell & O'Kelly, 1994; Salomon & Globerson, 1989). First, students in groups may waste time in *off-task behavior*. Second, students in collaborative groups may engage in *social loafing*, in which some of the students in a group do little or none of the work, relying instead on others to do the work for them. Third, *unequal interactions* can occur, in which some students talk most of the time, and/or some students participate very little or not at all. Fourth, *negative interactions* among students can occur (e.g., criticism, ridicule, or harassment). Fifth, there may be *no interactions* at all; although the teacher intends for the students to work together, they may instead work independently. Sixth, even if there are interactions, the interactions may be of *low quality*; students may not engage in the kinds of talk that can drive learning forward. Finally, there is the problem of *social status differences*, in which group work can exacerbate existing status differences among students (e.g., students viewing others as more or less intelligent) (Cohen, 1994b).

PRODUCTIVE GROUP PROCESSES

Researchers investigating different ways of organizing collaborative learning have identified a number of collaborative learning formats that promote the goals described above (Barron, 2003; Cohen, 1994a, 1994b; D. Johnson & Johnson, 1990; D.W. Johnson & R.T. Johnson, 1991; Slavin, 1996; Webb, 1982; Webb & Farivar, 1994). These formats promote a number of interactive processes that are conducive to learning. The first of these processes is *engagement*. When groups are engaged in the task at hand and interested in the task, they are naturally less likely to fall into off-task behavior or social loafing. Second, David and Roger Johnson have emphasized the importance of *positive interdependence*, which occurs when students can only complete a task by working together; the task cannot be completed as effectively or at all when working individually. Effective positive interdependence is likely to result in *joint attention* to the tasks at hand (Barron, 2003). This means that students are focused on the same task, often literally looking at the same information and certainly talking about a common topic. Students will also be more likely to work effectively if they have *mutual respect* for one another. Mutual respect will also reduce negative feelings and discriminatory feelings. Effective groups are also marked by *balanced participation*. When balanced participation occurs, all students in a group are contributing to the discussion. As they listen to each other, they display frequent *uptake*

of ideas. Uptake refers to responding to peers' ideas by accepting and building on them through further discussion, or by engaging in constructive argumentation when students are not in agreement. Finally, students in collaborative learning groups should also engage in *high-quality strategy use*, which includes both social strategies and cognitive strategies.

A great deal of research has focused on cognitive strategy use in groups. Generally, students who use high-level cognitive strategies such as elaboration, explanation, and coordinating theories with evidence learn more from collaborative work than students who do not employ these strategies. Noreen Webb (Webb, 1982; Webb & Farivar, 1994; Webb, Farivar, & Mastergeorge, 2002) and her colleagues have produced a very influential body of work that has emphasized the importance of giving and receiving explanations during group work. For example, if students are working on mathematics problems in groups, when a student explains to another how to do a problem, or how to carry out some of the steps in the problem, the giver of the explanation typically benefits. The receiver of the explanation may benefit if the explanation is sufficiently elaborated and if the receiver proceeds to apply what was learned. In contrast, when one student simply tells another student the answer (this is called *terminal help*), this can even be harmful to the learning of the student who receives terminal help. Webb's research has pointed to the importance of designing collaborative learning formats in ways that increase the frequency of explanations in group work and decrease the frequency of terminal help.

Another class of highly productive strategies is providing alternative perspectives on issues and advancing reasons and evidence (Chinn, 2006). Students benefit from encountering ideas that are different from their own, and they gain a deeper understanding of ideas they are learning when they consider how claims are related to evidence for and against those claims.

INSTRUCTIONAL FORMATS

Researchers have developed many instructional formats intended to promote instructional goals by achieving most or all of the productive group processes discussed above. This section provides an overview of several of these: methods incorporating reward structures, guided questioning, and complex tasks.

Methods Incorporating Reward Structures. Robert Slavin (Slavin, 1990, 1996) is the most well-known proponent of the use of reward structures to promote learning in groups. Slavin has distinguished between three methods for assigning rewards to a group. The first is that the entire group can receive a reward for its performance (e.g., each group member receives the same grade on a group project). This method does not encourage positive interdependence; the most skilled student may do all the work to ensure a high grade. Other students may loaf or be excluded. In a second method, students work together in a group but receive individual grades. This method discourages social loafing because each group member is individually evaluated, but it provides no reason for students to work together. Lastly, students can receive group rewards based on individual improvement on quizzes or worksheets over class periods. For example, students might receive a group reward based on the average individual improvement on a math quiz to be taken after the collaborative work. This provides incentive for students to help each other. The more proficient students will want to help the less proficient students because their reward depends partly on the performance of those students on the quiz. The less proficient students have an incentive to collaborative in order not to let the group down. Slavin has recommended that the rewards for average group improvement not be grades but rewards such as class points that can be exchanged for free time, computer times, or stationery items.

The use of rewards in group work is controversial because many researchers have argued that tangible rewards undermine intrinsic motivation (David W. Johnson & Roger T. Johnson, 1991). Researchers investigating group rewards for average individual performance have typically not included measures of motivation. In addition, the learning tasks that have been investigated have typically been relatively simple tasks such as the straightforward study of textbook material for a quiz, rather than more complex tasks. Rewards may not be needed for more complex, authentic problem-solving tasks that are more intrinsically interesting (Cohen, 1994b).

Guided Cooperation. In *guided cooperation*, students are directed to use specific cognitive strategies, such as summarization or elaboration. There are many kinds of guided cooperation, including scripted cooperation, peer-assisted learning strategies (PALS), guided peer questioning, and reciprocal teaching. Research has supported the efficacy of all of these methods.

In *scripted cooperation* (O'Donnell, 1999), students (usually working in pairs) are given specific instructions to summarize texts and evaluate each other's summaries. PALS is a guided cooperation method in which pairs work together to improve reading comprehension (Fuchs, Fuchs, Mathes, & Simmons, 1997). One of its core components is a form of scripted cooperation. The stronger reader reads the text for five minutes while the weaker reader acts as a tutor, responsible for correcting any mistakes the reader makes. After the reader finishes reading, the tutor asks the reader to explain what he or she has learned and fills in any missing information.

Then, the students switch roles. In *guided peer questioning* (King, 2002), students are given a series of questions with blanks, such as "How is _____ different from _____ that we learned about before?" Students in pairs question each other with questions that they construct from these question stems. Answers require students to use strategies such as elaboration and explanation. In *reciprocal teaching* (Palincsar & Brown, 1984), students typically work in groups of three or four. Students take turns being the group leader. All students read the passage and then the leader summarizes the passage and asks questions based on the passage, which the entire group should discuss. Then the leader offers a prediction or asks for a prediction about the next part of the text. All of these guided cooperation methods seek to promote learning goals by creating explicit demands for students to employ high-quality cognitive strategies in their conversations.

Complex Tasks. Many researchers have called for the use of more complex tasks in collaborative group work, such as writing skits, conducting research, creating multimedia presentations, investigating scientific questions, and solving real-life problems (Cohen, 1994b). These tasks can take hours, days, or weeks to complete and require much higher-level and complex strategies and thinking. Complex tasks require the use of multiple strategies and diverse knowledge; it is critical that no student has enough knowledge to complete the task individually. Many researchers support the production of public artifacts (such as posters presented in a poster fair) in complex tasks to promote engagement and adoption of high standards for work.

There are several specific approaches to the use of complex tasks that have strong research support. In *Group Investigation* (Sharan & Sharan, 1992), the class begins with a broad topic provided by the teacher. Groups of students choose and investigate specific topics of their choice within this topic. Students work out how to divide the work and work toward a presentation for the whole class.

Constructive Controversy is a method in which students engage in argumentation about a topic. Students work together to discuss reasons or evidence supporting an argument but remain open-minded about changing their minds. In one version of this approach, pairs of students first explore one side and then another side of an issue, interleaving pair work with work in groups of four. Students ultimately work out their final position in groups of four (D. W. Johnson & Johnson, 1995).

In *Complex Instruction* (Cohen, Lotan, Scarloss, & Arellano, 1999), students work collaboratively, moving to different stations in the classroom. For example, in a unit on feudal Japan, students might perform tasks such as preparing a skit addressing life in feudal Japan or developing a model showing patterns of social stratification in a castle town (Lotan, 1997).

Interventions to reduce status differences are very important in Complex Instruction. One such intervention is the multiple-ability treatment, in which the teacher emphasizes to students that in order to complete complex tasks, the group needs many different cognitive abilities, such as problem solving, writing, planning, public speaking, and hypothesizing. Then the teacher must make it very clear to the students that *"None of us has all of these abilities; Each one of us has some of these abilities"* (Cohen, 1994a, p. 128, italics in original). Complex tasks for which this is true are thus essential to Complex Instruction. A second intervention is providing separate instruction to the lower-status students so that they can become experts on the task and teach it to the higher-status students. Teachers also highlight the contributions of students who make contributions to the groups.

Knowledge Forum provides students with a computer environment in which they can jointly explore issues, posting their ideas and responding to peers ideas (Scardamalia & Bereiter, 2006). The goal of knowledge forum is to create classrooms in which the class taken as a collective whole is engaged in constructing knowledge that is new to all of the students. This simulates real-world knowledge creation that occurs in real settings such as research teams in universities, task forces in government, or design teams in corporations.

SCAFFOLDING COLLABORATIVE WORK ON COMPLEX TASKS

Students will need scaffolding to complete complex tasks successfully. Scaffolding refers to a variety of different kinds of help that enable students to complete tasks that they could not have completed on their own. Scaffolds may be provided by the teacher or built into the supporting materials such as texts, worksheets, or computer software that students are using.

One method of scaffolding is *preteaching needed knowledge and strategies.* Teachers might provide instruction into how to construct arguments before asking students to complete tasks involving written argumentation. Another method, *task decomposition* occurs when teachers break tasks down into smaller parts. Teachers could help students break the process of conducting their own original science investigation into a series of steps such as generating a question, designing an experiment, and so on.

A heavily investigated method of scaffolding is the use of *cognitive prompts,* which are questions or directions to use specified strategies or to reflect on particular issues. For example, students learning about history from original sources could be prompted to consider whether authors of documents might be biased. One kind of prompt asks students to construct diagrams, such as diagrams of how evidence supports or contradicts a theory.

Researchers have also employed *social and cognitive roles.* A role in collaborative work consists of instructions to focus on a particular kind of task. An example of a social role is to be the discussion leader. Another social role is to take responsibility for making sure that everyone gets the opportunity to talk. An example of a cognitive role is the role of "explainer," who might be responsible for making sure that the group develops complete explanations for its ideas.

Hints can be provided when students are having difficulty. A number of researchers have developed computer-based learning environments that are capable of providing hints to students at times of difficulty. Researchers generally recommend that the provider of the hint—whether a teacher or a computer—provide the least possible amount of help to enable students to solve the problem on their own.

Self-evaluation is a powerful scaffolding method that encourages students to regulate their own learning processes. In self-evaluation, groups of students evaluate their own performance along criteria provided by a teacher or developed by themselves (Sharan & Sharan, 1992; Webb & Farivar, 1994). Self-evaluations help students learn the criteria by which high levels of performance are identified. For example, in their 1998 study White and Frederiksen had students evaluate their performance along criteria that included "being systematic" and "writing and communicating well."

An important principle of scaffolding, regardless of which form of scaffolding is used, is that scaffolds should be *faded* over time. This means that students are given less and less help until they can complete the task on their own.

All of these scaffolding methods are designed to facilitate productive group processes as students work together in groups. Many scaffolding methods are particularly focused on promoting effective use of high-level strategies as students work on complex tasks. The complex tasks themselves are designed to encourage engagement, positive interdependence, and a desire to work well with peers to solve a challenging problem that requires all of their knowledge and abilities to solve.

PREPARING STUDENTS FOR GROUP WORK

Before dividing students into collaborative groups and assigning them tasks, teachers must make sure that they prepare students for group work first so that they can work in groups effectively and productively. One way teachers can do this is through team building exercises to encourage mutual respect and caring among students and sometimes also to show that working in a group can be more productive than working individually. A second way teachers prepare students is by providing group norms for students to use as a guideline for working in groups. The norms are usually posted in visible places in the classroom to remind students to treat each other with respect, to listen to one another's opinions open-mindedly, and to engage in positive interactions.

THE TEACHER'S ROLE

Research on the teacher's role in collaborative learning provides mixed recommendations. Most agree that the teacher needs to be attentively listening to the students and evaluating the quality of the interactions. However, some researchers believe that teachers should be quite active and should intervene frequently and help groups when they need it, whereas others believe that teachers should actively walk around and listen carefully but should interact with the groups only minimally. There is relatively little research on this important issue.

GROUP SIZE AND COMPOSITION

The ideal group size varies according to the task. Many effective implementations of collaborative learning (such as guided cooperation) have employed pairs. Others have used larger groups, typically no larger than six, however. Groups of about four may be best when working on complex tasks such as Group Investigation.

In composition, groups can be heterogeneous (composed of students of different genders, abilities, and ethnic backgrounds) or homogenous (composed of students who are similar to one another in these dimensions). Researchers have not identified a single ideal type of group composition. In addition, the idea of making groups heterogeneous along dimensions such as gender and ethnicity carries with it a major disadvantage: When students see that groups are always mixed in gender and ethnicity, this makes gender and ethnicity highly salient. If a class is made up of 25% of students from a minority group, it would be highly undesirable always to put a single minority student in every group of four, never allowing students from this minority group to work together. A good alternative to any fixed way of assigning groups is to use flexible grouping so that students form different groups on different days, depending on their interests, on who needs to work on a particular skill, or based on diversity of background knowledge relevant to a task.

Collaborative learning is potentially a highly effective method of instruction. However, it is not the case that any way of doing it will be effective, or even that most ways used commonly by teachers are effective. Only those methods that promote productive group processes and provide needed support to students as they engage in complex tasks are likely to be effective.

SEE ALSO *Cognitive Strategies; Constructivism.*

BIBLIOGRAPHY

Barron, B. (2003). When smart groups fail. *The Journal of the Learning Sciences, 12*(3), 307–359.

Chinn, C. A. (2006). Learning to argue. In A. M. O'Donnell, C. Hmelo-Silver & G. Erkens (Eds.), *Collaborative learning, reasoning, and technology* (pp. 355–383). Mahwah, NJ: Erlbaum.

Cohen, E. G. (1994a). *Designing groupwork: Strategies for the heterogeneous classroom* (2nd ed.). New York: Teachers College Press.

Cohen, E. G. (1994b). Restructuring the classroom: Conditions for productive small groups. *Review of Educational Research, 64*, 1–35.

Cohen, E. G., Lotan, R. A., Scarloss, B. A., & Arellano, A. R. (1999). Complex instruction: Equity in cooperative learning classrooms. *Theory Into Practice, 38*, 80–86.

Fuchs, D., Fuchs, L. S., Mathes, P. G., & Simmons, D. C. (1997). Peer-assisted learning strategies: Making classrooms more responsive to diversity. *American Educational Research Journal, 34*, 174–206.

Johnson, D., & Johnson, R. (1990). Cooperative learning and achievement. In S. Sharan (Ed.), *Cooperative learning: Theory and research* (pp. 23–37). New York: Praeger.

Johnson, D. W., & Johnson, R. T. (1991). *Learning together and alone: Cooperative, competitive, and individualistic learning.* Englewood Cliffs, NJ: Prentice Hall.

Johnson, D. W., & Johnson, R. T. (1995). *Creative controversy: Intellectual challenge in the classroom* (3rd ed.). Edina, MN: Interaction Book.

King, A. (2002). Structuring peer interaction to promote high-level cognitive processing. *Theory Into Practice, 41*, 33–39.

Lotan, R. A. (1997). Complex Instruction: An introduction. In E. G. Cohen & R. A. Lotan (Eds.), *Working for equity in heterogeneous classrooms: Sociological theory in practice* (pp. 15–27). New York: Teachers College Press.

O'Donnell, A. M. (1999). Structuring dyadic interaction through scripted cooperation. In A. M. O'Donnell & A. King (Eds.), *Cognitive perspectives on peer learning* (pp. 179–196). Mahwah, NJ: Erlbaum.

O'Donnell, A. M., & O'Kelly, J. (1994). Learning from peers: Beyond the rhetoric of positive results. *Educational Psychology Review, 6*, 321–349.

Palincsar, A. S., & Brown, A. L. (1984). Reciprocal teaching of comprehension-fostering and comprehension-monitoring activities. *Cognition and Instruction, 1*, 117–175.

Salomon, G., & Globerson, T. (1989). When teams do not function the way they ought to. *International Journal of Educational Research, 13*, 89–99.

Scardamalia, M., & Bereiter, C. (2006). Knowledge building. In R. K. Sawyer (Ed.), *The Cambridge handbook of the learning sciences* (pp. 97–115). Cambridge, England: Cambridge University Press.

Sharan, Y., & Sharan, S. (1992). *Expanding cooperative learning through group investigation.* New York: Teachers College Press.

Slavin, R. E. (1990). Research on cooperative learning: Consensus and controversy. *Educational Leadership*, 52–54.

Slavin, R. E. (1996). Research on cooperative learning and achievement: What we know, what we need to know. *Contemporary Educational Psychology, 21*, 43–69.

Webb, N. M. (1982). Student interaction and learning in small groups. *Review of Educational Research, 52*, 421–445.

Webb, N. M., & Farivar, S. (1994). Promoting helping behavior in cooperative small groups in middle school mathematics. *American Educational Research Journal, 31*, 369–395.

Webb, N. M., Farivar, S. H., & Mastergeorge, A. M. (2002). Productive helping in cooperative groups. *Theory Into Practice, 41*, 13–20.

White, B. Y., & Frederiksen, J. R. (1998). Inquiry, modeling, and metacognition: Making science accessible to all students. *Cognition and Instruction, 16*, 3–118.

Clark A. Chinn
Lisa M. Chinn

COMMUNICATION WITH PARENTS TO ENHANCE LEARNING

In its broadest sense, school communication with parents includes all the information that flows—intentionally or not—from teachers, the school, the district, and the student to the parents (including, for the purposes of this entry, persons fulfilling the role of parent in the child's life outside of school). This entry, however, focuses on features of intentional school-to-parent communication that may increase parents' involvement in schools and improve student learning and motivation, with an emphasis on strategies for individual teachers. The considerations and strategies are presented in the context of written communication, but they are relevant to other forms of communication as well.

A FRAMEWORK FOR PARTNERSHIPS

Increasing parents' positive involvement in their children's education is one short-term goal for most school-to-parent communication. Epstein's framework of school, family, and community partnership comprises six types of involvement: parenting, communicating, volunteering, learning at home, decision making, and collaborating with community. Epstein's model acknowledges challenges for each type of involvement and identifies potential results of each type of involvement for students, parents, and teachers. Because school-to-parent communication is often a means for promoting other types of involvement, illustrative practices for each of the six types of involvement are presented in Table 1. These activities are not intended as to-do list. Teachers, schools, and districts choose one or several of these activities or develop their own activities, depending on their needs, resources, and goals. These efforts may have both short- and long-term goals.

Research suggests that school-to-parent communication can promote productive parental involvement, and that productive parental involvement in schools can, in turn, have a positive impact on student achievement (Henderson & Mapp; Jeynes). Because of limitations in financial and human resources and because ineffective attempts at parental communication may result in educators' abandoning rather than refining their efforts, it is important for every school-to-parent communication effort to be as effective as possible. How can teachers, schools, and districts effectively communicate with parents to promote the positive parental involvement that may result in improved student achievement?

OUTSIDE ASSISTANCE FOR SCHOOL-TO-PARENT COMMUNICATION

There are alternatives to traditional do-it-yourself school-to-parent communication efforts. Some educators have access to a communications department or public relations professional within their school districts to help them assess their needs, develop a communications plan, draft documents, and similar tasks. The National School Public Relations Association includes school communications professionals who support the communication efforts of schools and districts. Organizations such as the National Network of Partnership Schools offer extensive resources and comprehensive support for schools and districts whose goals include developing a strong parent involvement program. The school- or district-wide commitment required for participation, however, could present a barrier for teachers lacking the broad-based support required for participation in most networks.

Educators taking the do-it-yourself route may supplement their own work with print materials from professional organizations or commercial providers. The International Reading Association, for example, offers booklets and brochures for parents in both English and Spanish at a minimal cost. Commercial providers' products include audio compact disks for parents, videos, web content, and print materials, many of them in several languages. Even for educators who have access to outside support and resources, however, developing effective school-to-parent communications requires more than joining a network or selecting commercial products and sending them home. Effective school-to-parent communication requires consideration of parents as an audience for the school's information.

AUDIENCE AWARENESS FOR SCHOOL-TO-PARENT COMMUNICATION

According to McIntyre, Kyle, Moore, Sweazy, and Greer (2001), the efforts of parents and teachers gain synergy

Six types of involvement in school, family, and community partnership and examples of related activities

Type	Examples of related activities
Parenting	Assist families with parenting and child-rearing skills, understanding child and adolescent development, and setting home conditions that support children as students at each grade and level. Assist schools in understanding families.
Communicating	Communicate with families about school programs and student progress through effective school-to-home and home-to-school communications.
Volunteering	Improve recruitment, training, work, and schedules to involve families as volunteers and audiences at the school or in other locations to support students and school programs.
Learning at home	Involve families with their children in learning activities at home, including homework and other curriculum-linked activities and organizations.
Decision making	Include families as participants in school decisions, governance, advocacy through PTA/PTO, school councils, committees, other parent organizations.
Collaborating with the community	Coordinate resources and services for families, students, and the school with businesses, agencies, and other groups, and provide services to the community.

SOURCE: National Network of Partnership Schools, retrieved from http://www.csos.jhu.edu/p2000/sixtypes.htm.

Table 1 ILLUSTRATION BY GGS INFORMATION SERVICES. CENGAGE LEARNING, GALE.

when they know one another and are aware of one another's efforts. McIntyre and his colleagues suggest that teachers who know more about the child's experiences at home are better able to provide classroom instruction suited to the child's needs. Similarly, teachers who know their students' parents or at least know about their students' parents can tailor both the format and content of their messages to meet parents' needs.

Presumably when educators have information to convey to parents, they choose the most effective medium (or media) available, but limited resources mean limited choices. Commercial media, such as radio and television, are not among the media options for most educators, particularly teachers working independently. Most school-to-parent communication involves some form of text—printed in a newsletter, posted on a Web site, or sent in an e-mail—created with the expectation that parents will not only receive the message but also read and understand it. To increase the chances of that occurring, educators must meet parents' needs as an audience. Important audience awareness features include parents' literacy levels, their cultural differences, their need for specific information, and their prior experiences with schools.

COMPREHENSIBILITY

Any form of written communication requires selecting or composing text for an audience of parents. Educators routinely consider readability when choosing or creating text for students, and similar considerations are important when composing writing for an audience of parents. A widely cited reference in medical literature asserts that patient education materials should be written at a sixth-grade level to reach 75% of the U.S. adult population and a third-grade level to reach 90% of the same population (Doak,

Doak & Root). Most word processing programs apply one or more readability formulas, weighing such factors as sentence length, the frequency of multi-syllable words, and the use of unusual words, enabling educators to revise text so the audience has an opportunity to understand the message.

Words with specialized meanings in different contexts, such as fluency and factor, pose a special challenge for educators. Teachers and students likely know what these words mean, but will parents know what they mean in the education context? Educators can provide context clues defining specialized terminology to help parents understand text that might otherwise be not only confusing but also off-putting to frustrated readers. As noted previously, teachers should describe their intended meaning for vague words, such as read and master. Finally, educators must attempt to communicate with parents in a language the parents understand. When translation services are not available, the educator may need to enlist the help of a student, teacher, or community member who can translate text reliably, or he or she may need to rely on commercially available products until resources for translation can be located.

CULTURAL DIFFERENCES

Cultural differences between educators and parents may affect the way a parent perceives information provided by the school. For example, a culture-based preference for collectivity and interdependence in the home may conflict with a school culture that values individuality and autonomy (Torrez, 2004; Van Velsor & Orozco, 2007). These differences may result in mutual concern and confusion over the roles of parents, teachers, schools, and the community in children's education. Parents' volunteering in schools and personally participating in their children's formal education may be another source of concern and confusion for some parents. Far from being cultural universals, these concepts are unfamiliar to some parents. Educators who know more about their students, their parents, and their cultures are more likely to understand these differences and be able to communicate in ways that promote positive parent participation at home and at school while minimizing conflicts between the culture of the school and the cultures of their students' homes.

SPECIFICITY

Even when parents can read the information and there are no apparent cultural barriers, parents' lack of familiarity with instructional processes may present a challenge to their cooperating with teachers' requests. In a case study involving two urban elementary students, their parents, and their teachers, Musti-Rao and Cartledge found that teacher communication lacking specific instructions for parents may result in frustration for both the parents and the teacher. For example, a teacher may try to encourage parents to read with their children by sending home information about the benefits of practice: "Children who read more become better readers." She may even go a step further: "Please read with your child for ten minutes every day." The teacher has made what she perceives as a specific request, but without a definition of "read with," do these statements tell the parents precisely what the teacher wants them to do? Some parents would have questions: "How much do I read during each session? How do I structure these readings? What should I look for when we are reading? How do I know he is making progress? How can I measure this progress? Would you show me how I should read to/with him?" (Musti-Rao & Cartledge, 2004, p. 16).

Based on the case studies, Musti-Rao and Cartledge suggest that the parent who does not know how to comply with the teacher's request may perceive vagueness as a reflection of indifference or insensitivity to the parent's needs. When the parent does not comply, the teacher perceives the noncompliance as indifference on the part of the parent. In this scenario, what started as a well-intended suggestion resulted in a mutual perception between the parent and the teacher that the other is indifferent to the child's needs. If the teacher provides specific instructions, parents will know—or at least have a better idea of—how to help: "One way you can help your child develop her reading skills is to read (this book) out loud to her for two minutes and then have her read (this book) out loud to you for two minutes for a total of ten minutes every day." The message could be tailored with suggestions for follow-up activities to address the students' needs while respecting the parents' ability to comply. If a written explanation is too

daunting, a video explanation and demonstration could accomplish the same purpose.

PARENTS' PREVIOUS EXPERIENCES WITH SCHOOLS

In contrast to problems that arise from parents' unfamiliarity with classroom processes, some problems arise from parents' familiarity with schools and programs. Many parents have had negative experiences with schools, both as parents and as students themselves. As suggested by McBride, Bae, & Blatchford (2003), parents whose school experiences were negative may be less likely to respond positively to a school's communication with them as parents than parents whose own school experiences were generally positive.

To appeal to members of their audience whose negative experiences present a barrier, educators should make a particular effort to present sincere and accessible information these parents will perceive is important and relevant to them and their children. Whitaker and Fore propose replacing "the traditional open-house program in which parents are urged to come to school to listen to teachers explain rules and expectations for the school year" (2001, p. 31) with interaction between parents and teachers, establishing a relationship on which further positive communication could be built.

BROADER APPLICATIONS

As suggested by Epstein's framework, some school-to-parent communication aims to inform parents about matters other than academic endeavors. Audience awareness considerations discussed in this entry apply to these types of parent communication, too. For example, a group of teachers may want to address their concerns that parents do not believe their actions can affect their children's behavior or performance at school. The educators may be aware of Shumow and Lomax's finding that parental efficacy, "the extent to which parents believed that they could influence the context in which their adolescents were growing up" (2002, 127–128), among parents of adolescents predicted parental involvement and monitoring, and that parental involvement and monitoring predicted adolescents' academic and social-emotional adjustment.

Shumow and Lomax do not claim the study demonstrates a causal connection between parental efficacy and particular outcomes for children; nevertheless, educators who become aware of this research could reasonably decide to act on it. Deciding how to act on this or other important research would be challenging, however. Sending parents an abstract of the study's methodology and findings would not address most parents' needs: few parents would find the information accessible and relevant in that format. If the information were presented in a comprehensible, culturally sensitive way, however, it is reasonable to expect that many parents would perceive such information as important and relevant to them as parents, at least as compared to information about classroom rules.

SEE ALSO *Discussion Methods.*

BIBLIOGRAPHY

Adams, K. S., & Christenson, S. L. (2000). Trust and the family-school relationship: Examination of parent-teacher differences in elementary and secondary grades. *Journal of School Psychology, 38,* 477–497.

Boyd, B. A., & Correa, V. I. (2005). Developing a framework for reducing the cultural clash between African American parents and the special education system. *Multicultural Perspectives, 7*(2), 3–11.

Dearing, E., Kreider, H., Simpkins, S., & Weiss, H. B. (2006). Family involvement in school and low-income children's literacy: Longitudinal associations between and within families. *Journal of Educational Psychology, 98*(4), 653–664.

Doak, C. C., Doak, L. G., & Root, J. H. (1996). *Teaching patients with low literacy skills* (2nd ed.). Philadelphia: Lippincott.

Eccles, J., & Harold, R. (1993). Parent-school involvement during early adolescent years. *Teachers College Record 94,* 568–587.

Epstein, J. L. (1995) School/family/community partnerships: Caring for the children we share. *Phi Delta Kappan, 76,* 701–712.

Fan, X. (2001). Parental involvement and students' academic achievement: A growth modeling analysis. *Journal of Experimental Education 70*(1), 27–61.

Henderson, A. T., & Mapp, K. (2002). *A new wave of evidence: The impact of school, family, and community connections on student achievement.* Austin, TX: Southwest Education Development Lab.

Jeynes, W.H. (2005) A meta-analysis of the relation of parent involvement to urban elementary school student academic achievement. *Urban Education, 40,* 237–269.

Machen, S. M., Wilson, J. D., & Notar, C. E. (2005). Parental involvement in the classroom. *Journal of Instructional Psychology 32*(1), 13–16.

McBride, B. A., Bae, J., & Blatchford, K. (2003). Family-school-community partnerships in rural pre-K at-risk programs. *Journal of Early Childhood Research, 1*(1), 49–72.

McIntyre, E., Kyle, D., Moore, G., Sweazy, R. A., & Greer, S. (2001). Linking home and school through family visits. *Language Arts, 78*(3), 264–272.

Musti-Rao, S., & Cartledge, G. (2004). Making home and advantage in the prevention of reading failure: Strategies for collaborating with parents in urban schools. *Preventing School Failure, 48*(4), 15–21.

National Network of Partnership Schools. Epstein's six types of involvement. Retrieved April 16, 2007, from http://www.csos.jhu.edu/p2000/sixtypes.htm.

Shumow, L., & Lomax, R. (2002). Parental efficacy: Predictor of parenting behavior and adolescent outcomes. *Parenting: Science and Practice, 2*(2), 127–150.

Torrez, N. (2004). Developing parent information frameworks that support college preparation for Latino students. *High School Journal, 87*(3), 54–62.

Van Velsor, P., & Orozco, G. L. (2007). Involving low-income parents in the schools: Community centric strategies for school counselors. *Professional School Counseling, 11*(1), 17–24.

Whitaker, T., & Fiore, D.J. (2001). *Dealing with difficult parents (and with parents in difficult situations).* Larchmont, NY: Eye on Education.

Kim Walters-Parker

COMMUNICATION WITH STUDENTS TO ENHANCE LEARNING

For much of the 20th century, instructional communication researchers (who study human communication processes and related messages as they occur in instructional contexts across subject matter, grade levels, and types of settings) have relied on a teacher-centric rhetorical framework—acknowledging that the primary difference between knowing and teaching is communication (Hurt, Scott, & McCroskey, 1978). The teacher-centric perspective provides a manageable framework from which to understand communication within any instructional context because, (1) roles are generally restricted and adhered to carefully, (2) a majority of classroom communication is concerned with dispensing information and creating understanding, (3) the primary focus is on improving student competencies, and (4) evaluation is a major component of most educational environments. Within these parameters, it is possible to understand how teacher communication behaviors and strategies can enhance student learning. A comprehensive review of three decades of social scientific research focusing on the role and effects of communication in instructional settings is beyond the scope of the current review but is available in the *Handbook of Instructional Communication* (Mottet, Richmond, & McCroskey, 2006). The purpose here, however, is to summarize what is known about teacher communication competencies, focusing especially on teacher concerns, teacher immediacy, teacher clarity, and content relevance as rhetorical strategies for improving teacher communication in ways that promote student motivation, equity in the classroom, and effective classroom management.

TEACHER COMMUNICATION COMPETENCIES

In his review integrating research from education and communication literature intended to isolate effective teacher behaviors, Nussbaum (1992) cautioned against the creation of prescriptive lists because teacher effectiveness is largely dependent upon such dimensions as timing, context, content, and student ability. Effective teachers must have the ability to adapt to each particular context they encounter. There are general competencies, however, that are applicable across contexts. The National Communication Association (the oldest and largest national organization to promote communication scholarship and education) has outlined five broad teacher communication competencies regarding informative, affective, imaginative, ritualistic, and persuasive instructional messages. Effective teachers should demonstrate competencies in sending and receiving messages that (1) give or obtain information, (2) express or respond to feelings, (3) speculate or theorize, (4) maintain social relationships and facilitate interaction, and (5) seek to convince or influence (Cooper, 1988). Beyond these competencies, several teacher communication behaviors and strategies have been demonstrated to enhance student learning.

TEACHER CONCERNS

The original model for examining general teacher concerns (e.g., assessing student progress, excessive non-instructional duties) was provided by Fuller (1969) in her framework for examining three major categories of teacher concerns that teachers experience at different developmental stages in their career: (a) concern about self (concern about how one is perceived as a teacher); (b) concern about task (concern about instructional duties); and (c) concern about impact (concern about student learning). According to the model, teacher socialization occurs as a natural flow from concerns about self to concerns about task (teaching) followed by concerns about impact (student learning). Every teacher will have concerns in all three areas but the balance among the three can significantly affect the learning climate in the classroom. Borich (1994) cautions that when teachers are unaware of a preponderance of self concerns to the exclusion of task and impact concerns, they run the risk of unintentionally creating a learning climate that may be contrary to the goals of instruction.

Since the late 1970s communication researchers have chosen to narrow the focus of Fuller's original model by focusing specifically on teachers' communication concerns (e.g., ability to adequately present ideas and required material) and the resulting behaviors in an effort to discover how a teacher's communication strategies and tactics affect classroom interaction and impact the overall climate for learning (Staton & Hunt, 1992; Staton-Spicer,1983; Staton-Spicer & Bassett, 1979; Staton-Spicer & Darling, 1986; Staton-Spicer & White, 1981; Feezel & Myers, 1997). The results of this research program provide support for Fuller's original dimensions and indicate that teachers express communication concerns about their individual communication abilities (self), their ability to communicate with their

students (task), and the effects of their messages and communication behaviors to increase student learning (impact).

Self concerns. Communication concerns about self are primarily related to establishing credibility as a teacher and achieving flexibility in teaching. Teachers attempt to establish credibility through self-disclosure behaviors that communicate that they are human, that they have good intentions, and that they are competent. Learning student names also allows teachers to be perceived as personable. Teacher concerns about flexibility are most apparent in assignment and schedule changes, re-teaching of course concepts, and in-class digressions.

Task concerns. Determining the best way to make abstract concepts concrete and finding the most appropriate teaching strategies are the two most critical communication task concerns expressed by teachers. The use of numerous examples and the integration of guest speakers have been demonstrated as effective communication strategies for making abstract concepts more concrete for students. Teachers are also genuinely concerned about their ability to lead an effective discussion, lecture, and employ other appropriate teaching strategies. Unfortunately, the choice of any instructional teaching strategy seems to be more a function of comfort than appropriateness.

Impact concerns. The two primary communication concerns about impact are related to facilitating student understanding and establishing a non-threatening instructional environment. Teacher communication behaviors that provide a clear and organized structure for lectures (i.e., define, restate, elaborate, and provide an example) and discussions (i.e., teacher asks a question, student responds, teacher paraphrases, elaborates, and provides a clear example) are more successful in facilitating student understanding. Non-threatening environments are established when teachers use reinforcement, self-disclosure, comprehension checks, and convey clear expectations. Teachers are more successful managing communication concerns about impact when they use comprehension checks to encourage student questions and elicit feedback, ask questions, give examples, and use classroom technology (e.g., chalkboard, handouts, computer presentations) to provide graphical representations that clearly communicate course concepts (for additional examples see Angelo & Cross, 1993).

Results of instructional communication research have provided a clear link between teacher communication concerns and actual classroom behavior. Teachers communicate differently depending upon whether they are concerned with (1) being accepted, credible, liked, and respected (self communication concerns), (2) teaching performance (task communication concerns), or (3) student learning and establishing a non-threatening

Effective communication between teachers and students includes much more than simple knowledge transmission. WILL & DENI
MCINTYRE/PHOTO RESEARCHERS, INC.

climate (impact communication concerns). Prospective teachers express more self than task or impact concerns whereas student teachers express more task than impact concerns. Likewise, in-service teachers express more impact than self or task concerns and prospective teachers express more self concerns than student or in-service teachers. Finally, student teachers express more task concerns than prospective or in-service teachers, and in-service teachers express more impact concerns than prospective or student teachers. Taken together, the results demonstrate that teacher classroom communication concerns direct and affect classroom communication behavior that, in turn, serves to either enhance or hinder student learning.

TEACHER IMMEDIACY

Teacher immediacy was defined from a communication perspective by Andersen (1979) as a set of verbal and nonverbal behaviors that reveal a teacher's willingness to approach and be approached by students. The use of teacher immediacy behaviors enhances closeness and generates positive attitudes by decreasing the physical and/or

psychological distance between communicators (Mehrabian, 1969). Teachers who exhibit immediate behaviors reduce psychological distance by recognizing individual student ideas and viewpoints, incorporating student input into course and class design, and communicating availability and willingness to engage in one-to-one interactions.

Nonverbal immediacy behaviors include behaviors demonstrating variety in vocal pitch, loudness, and tempo, smiling, leaning toward a person; face-to-face body position, decreasing physical barriers (such as a podium or a desk) between themselves and their students, overall relaxed body movements and positions, spending time with students, and informal but socially appropriate attire. Verbal immediacy includes a teacher's use of humor, praise, actions and/or comments that indicate willingness to converse with students both in and out of the classroom, teacher self-disclosure, using inclusive pronouns (i.e., "we," "us," "our") when referring to coursework, willingness to provide feedback, and asking students about their perceptions about assignments and due dates.

Teachers using verbal behaviors and nonverbal immediacy behaviors appear more human and accessible to their students. In turn, student-teacher interaction contributes to the quality of the overall learning experience. Findings from a significant amount of instructional communication research have demonstrated the profound effects of teachers immediacy behaviors to positively impact student achievement (for a complete review see Richmond, Lane, & McCroskey, 2006). Results provide a clear and substantial link between teacher immediacy and student favorable attitudes toward course content and the instructor, as well as improvement in student attention, concentration, retention, and recall. In addition, teacher immediacy increases student interaction and student motivation while decreasing student resistance. Finally, teachers who exhibit verbal and nonverbal immediacy behaviors are perceived as more competent communicators and receiver higher course and teacher evaluations.

TEACHER CLARITY

Teachers who are content experts must also possess specific communication competencies that allow them to transfer the cognitive dimensions of teaching into visible instructional behaviors that are clear, organized, understandable, and effective. Teacher clarity, therefore, is the teacher's ability to effectively stimulate the desired meaning of course content and processes in the minds of students through the use of appropriately structured verbal and nonverbal messages (Chesebro, 2002). Instructional clarity has also been defined as an instructional message variable that constitutes a cluster of teacher behaviors that contributes to the fidelity of instructional message (Chesebro & Wanzer, 2006). Put simply, teachers who present knowledge in a way that students understand are perceived as clear. As such, clarity functions to connect content and pedagogy. Students tend to judge a teacher's effectiveness based largely on perceptions of teacher clarity. In fact, researchers have demonstrated a fairly robust positive relationship among teacher clarity, student satisfaction, student motivation, and student achievement.

Teacher clarity is a multidimensional construct that includes three broad behavior clusters: (1) presentation or verbal clarity (e.g., verbal fluency, explanations, and examples); (2) structural or message clarity (e.g., previews, organization, transitions, summaries, outlines, illustrations and visual aids); and (3) instructional process clarity (e.g., stresses important aspects of the content, assesses and responds to perceived deficiencies in student understanding, connects and integrates specific concepts into course curriculum, provides content relevance, communicates classroom policies and violation consequences).

Inexperienced teachers (because of self and task concerns) have a tendency to focus too heavily on detailed content and, as a result, create cognitive overload by trying to cover too much information. When inexperienced teach-

ers are worried about whether they are perceived as credible they inadvertently provide too much information (TMI) to their students. Unfortunately, students don't seem to care about the leaves on the trees in the forest until they know what the forest is and where it is located relative to other places with which they are familiar. Clarity increases as teachers develop and as impact become more salient. That is, clear teachers will begin to "essentialize" and "chunk" the curriculum using a deductive strategy that focuses on the most important information presented in a logical sequence—before providing specific details. Teacher clarity can best be understood using a jigsaw puzzle example. Clear teachers first provide students with a jigsaw puzzle box top so students have a complete picture (clear direction for learning). Next, clear teachers extract and assemble the edge pieces to distinguish the border clearly before requiring students to focus on any individual puzzle piece (color, shape, possible location). Finally, clear teachers provide the details of the puzzle pieces and provide a context for which they can be organized.

Results across three decades of research demonstrate that teacher clarity, as it occurs in each of the three broad clusters of instructional behaviors (presentation, message, and process) is relatively stable across varied populations and academic contexts. Clear teaching reduces student anxiety, increases student motivation, improves student affect for both instructors and course material and ultimately functions positively to enhance student achievement.

CONTENT RELEVANCE

Content relevance was originally defined by Keller (1983) as a student's perception of whether the course instruction and its content, or both, satisfied personal needs, personal goals, and career goals. As is readily demonstrated by the teacher classroom behaviors explicitly related to teacher concerns, immediacy, and clarity, perceptions of content relevance can be enhanced when teachers make a conscious effort to make the content of their instructional messages relevant to students' personal and career goals. However, just as teacher effectiveness is largely dependent upon such dimensions as timing, context, content, and student ability, content relevance is influenced by teacher characteristics (e.g., credibility, competence, immediacy), message characteristics (e.g., clarity, structure), and by individual student characteristics (e.g., aptitude, interests, etc.).

There are six types of strategies that can be implemented by teachers to increase the likelihood that more of their students will perceive their instructional messages as personally relevant (Keller, 1987). However, because instruction does not take place in a vacuum, the implementation of any strategy to increase content relevance will obviously require that teachers have some knowledge and understanding of their students. Included in the six types of strategies are

(1) experience (state explicitly how the instruction builds on the learner's existing skills, relate learner's interests to instruction, build on common student experiences); (2) present worth (provide examples of how the content is meaningful and important, have students relate course concepts to personally interesting contexts); (3) future usefulness (state explicitly how instruction relates to future learner activities, ask learner to relate instruction to personal future goals); (4) need matching (link content to specific student needs); (5) modeling (use guest speakers, alumni, or tutors to demonstrate the value and relevance of course content; and (6) choice (provide meaningful alternative assignments, provide personal choices for organizing work (Keller, 1987).

It seems logical to conclude that student motivation to study is positively related to whether students are able to connect course content presented by their teacher to their personal needs and career goals. Research comparing students on the dimensions of content relevance support this claim and consistently demonstrate that students who perceive instructional activities as having increased value and as something worthy of their effort, report increased affect for teachers and subject material, a sense of greater empowerment in the classroom, and higher levels of achievement and state motivation (Frymier & Shulman, 1995; Frymier, Shulman, & Houser, 1996; Frymier, 2002).

IMPLICATIONS FOR EDUCATORS

What teachers need to know obviously goes beyond how to enhance self-presentation, how to keep students on task, and how to manage student resistance. Effective communication includes much more than simple knowledge transmission. There are critical moral and intellectual dimensions of teaching that supersede concerns for technique, climate, and control. In addition, because of the scope of the current review is relatively narrow, it does not include research focused on student characteristics (e.g., students' motives for communicating with teachers, student immediacy and nonverbal influence, or student resistance) or research from a more relational perspective (e.g., teacher caring, power, humor, and affinity seeking). What researchers know (from a teacher-centric rhetorical framework) is that teachers who are interested in improving their communication with students can integrate knowledge gleaned from three decades of research about teacher concerns, immediacy, clarity, and relevance to promote student motivation and enhance student achievement.

BIBLIOGRAPHY

Andersen, J. (1979). Teacher immediacy as a predictor of teaching effectiveness. In D. Nimmo (Ed.), *Communication Yearbook 3* (pp. 543–559). New Brunswick, NJ: Transaction Books.

Angelo, T. A., & Cross, P. (1993). *Classroom assessment techniques: A handbook for college teachers* (2nd ed.). San Francisco: Jossey-Bass.

Borich, G. D. (1994). *Observation skills for effective teaching* (2nd ed.). New York: Macmillan.

Cooper, P. (1988). *Communication competencies for teachers.* Annandale, VA: Speech Communication Association.

Chesebro, J. L. (2002). Teaching clearly. In J. L. Chesebro and J. C. McCroskey (Eds.), *Communication for teachers* (pp. 93–103). Boston: Allyn and Bacon.

Chesebro, J. L. & Wanzer, M. B. (2006). Instructional message variables. In T. P. Mottet, V. P. Richmond, and J. C. McCroskey (Eds.), *Handbook of instructional communication: Rhetorical and relational perspectives* (pp. 89–116). Boston: Allyn and Bacon.

Feezel, J. D. & Myers, S. A. (1997). Assessing graduate assistant teacher communication. *Communication Quarterly, 45(3),* 110–124.

Frymier, A. B. (2002). Making content relevant to students. In J. L. Chesebro and J. C. McCroskey (Eds.), *Communication for teachers* (pp. 93–103). Boston: Allyn and Bacon.

Frymier, A. B., & Shulman, G. M. (1995). "What's in it for me?": Increasing content relevance to enhance students' motivation. *Communication Education, 44,* 40–50.

Frymier, A. B., & Shulman, G.M., & Houser, M. (1996). The development of a learner empowerment measure. *Communication Education, 45,* 181–199.

Fuller, F. F. (1969). Concerns of teachers: A developmental conceptualization. *American Educational Research Journal, 2,* 207–226.

Hurt, H. T., Scott, M. D., & McCroskey, J. C. (1978). *Communication in the classroom.* Reading, MA: Addison-Wesley.

Keller, J. M. (1983). Motivational design of instruction. In C. M. Reigeluth (Ed.), *Instructional design theories: An overview of their current status* (pp. 383–434). Hillsdale, NJ: Erlbaum.

Keller, J. M. (1987). Strategies for stimulating the motivation to learn. *Performance and Instruction, 26(8),* 1–7.

Mehrabian, A. (1969). Some referents and measures of nonverbal behavior. *Behavioral Research Methods and Instrumentation, 1,* 213–217.

Mottet, T. P, Richmond, V. P., & McCroskey, J. C. (2006). *Handbook of instructional communication: Rhetorical and relational perspectives.* Boston: Allyn and Bacon.

Nussbaum, J. F. (1992). Effective teacher behaviors. *Communication Education, 41,* 167–180.

Richmond, V. P., Lane, D. R., & McCroskey, J. C. (2006). Teacher immediacy and the teacher-student relationship. In T. P. Mottet, V. P. Richmond, and J. C. McCroskey (Eds.), *Handbook of instructional communication: Rhetorical and relational perspectives* (pp. 167–193). Boston: Allyn and Bacon.

Staton, A. Q., & Hunt, S. L. (1992). Teacher socialization: Review and conceptualization. *Communication Education, 41,* 109–137.

Staton-Spicer, A. Q. (1983). The measurement and further conceptualization of teacher communication concern. *Human Communication Research, 9,* 158–168.

Staton-Spicer, A. Q., & Bassett, R. E. (1979). Communication concerns of preservice and inservice elementary teachers. *Human Communication Research, 5,* 138–146.

Staton-Spicer, A. Q., & Darling, A. L. (1986). Communication in the socialization of preservice teachers. *Communication Education, 35,* 215–230.

Staton-Spicer, A. Q., & Marty-White, C. R. (1981). A framework for instructional communication theory: The relationship between communication concerns and classroom behavior. *Communication Education, 30,* 354–366.

Derek R. Lane

COMMUNITIES OF LEARNERS

In the early 1990s the Fostering a Community of Learners' classrooms (FCL) research project became renowned for modeling the practical instantiation of a set of theoretically grounded "first principles" of learning and teaching. When Jerome Bruner and Courtney Cazden, among others, visited FCL classrooms, they witnessed students talking, writing, thinking, and using technology in the service of both science understanding and literacy skills in a classroom environment specifically designed to support such activity. They saw formerly disenfranchised students, who typically had little exposure to advanced science curricula or sophisticated literacy tasks, become active participants in their own learning. Cazden, reflecting on FCL's 1990s efforts, has said:

> FCL ... became one of the most visible school reform programs in the U.S.—well documented for the quantitative achievements of its students over successive years on both standardized literacy tests and criterion-referenced tests in both literacy and science developed within the program, and also discussed in the writings of numerous academic visitors. (Cazden, 2005, p. 1)

The origins of FCL lie with Ann Brown and her closest collaborator and husband Joe Campione. The couple had moved from the University of Illinois, Champagne Urbana, to the University of California Berkeley's Education in Mathematic Science and Technology Department in 1988. They immediately established a research team of faculty, graduate students, postdoctoral scholars, and skilled technical staff to design classroom *communities of learners* in the Berkeley/Oakland area. Brown (1992) described the FCL classroom design in this way: "I attempt to engineer innovative educational environments and simultaneously conduct experimental studies of those innovations" (p. 141).

Their goal was to put theory into practice in visible, equitable, and intellectually honest ways. The FCL project encompassed K-8 classrooms, in several schools, including a multigrade spiraling curriculum in John Swett Elementary School and Sequoia Middle School, both in East Oakland. The goal was to design robust classroom learning environments in which everyone (students, teachers, researchers) learned to "use their minds

---

First Principles

- Active, strategic nature of learning
- Metacognition
  - Awareness and understanding
  - Intentional learning, self-selection, and direction
  - Self monitoring and other-monitoring for common good
  - Reflective practice
- Multiple zones of proximal development
  - Multiple expertise, multiple roles, multiple resources
  - Mutual appropriation
  - Guided practice, guided participation
- Dialogic base
  - Shared discourse, common knowledge
  - Seeding, migration, and appropriation of ideas
- Legitimating of differences
  - Diversity, identity and respect
  - Creation of community and individual identity
  - Multiple access, multiple ways in
  - Peripheral of full participation
- Community of Practice
  - Communities of practice with multiple overlapping roles
  - Sense of community with shared values
  - Element of ownership and choice
  - Community beyond the classroom wall
- Contextualized and situated
  - Theory and practice in action
  - Repeatable participant structures
  - Fantasy and sociodramatic play (being a researcher, being a scientist)
  - Intellectually honest curriculum
  - Responsive transparent assessment.

SOURCE: Adapted from Brown & Campione, 1994, p. 237.

Table 1 ILLUSTRATION BY GGS INFORMATION SERVICES. CENGAGE LEARNING, GALE.

---

well." Learning and teaching were viewed as a social process within which mutual appropriation is facilitated by talk, gesture, drawing, computers, and text (Brown & Campione, 1994). FCL promoted dialogic modes of communication in ordinary classrooms.

The underlying principles (Brown & Campione, 1994) are listed in Table 1.

Brown and Campione's first principles were influenced by branches of psychology, linguistics, anthropology, sociology and out of school learning, and by the leading scholars of the time, including Bruner (1990), Cazden (1984), Cole and the Laboratory of Comparative Human Cognition (1998), Heath (1991); Latour & Wolgar (1986), Lave & Wenger (1991), Rogoff (1994), and Wertsch (1991) among others. FCL design was grounded in sociocultural views of learning and teaching, especially Vygotsky's (1978) concept of the *zone of proximal development* (ZPD). Disciplinary content goals were predicated on Bruner's views of learning and development. As Bruner put it, "We begin with the hypothesis that any subject can be taught effectively in some intellectually honest form to any child at any stage of development" (Bruner, 1996, p. 33).

Participant structures

Participant structure	Configuration of participants	Frequency	Purpose
Research rotations	Research teams were divided into 3 activities: research, Reciprocal Teaching, computer use.	Daily, when there is no benchmark/cross-talk	**Decompose** content into researchable units.
Cross-talk	Whole class; students presented emerging research ideas and stances.	As needed, about once a week	**Synthesize** across different research group expertise areas.
Benchmark lesson	Whole class activity where important content or process ideas were introduced.	As needed, about every two weeks	**Infuse foundational knowledge**; establish common knowledge and practices.
Jigsaw	Reconfigure in jigsaw groups to teach other classmates the content of their work.	At the end of every unit, or as needed	**Recombine content** into a whole; synthesize across expertise areas.
Dilemma	Whole and small group; aim was to use new knowledge to collectively solve an ecological dilemma.	At the end, or during, a learning unit; also months later	**To assess transfer** of ways of reasoning and ability to use ideas from jigsaws, benchmarks and cross-talks.

SOURCE: Adapted from Rutherford & Ash (2008).

Table 2 ILLUSTRATION BY GGS INFORMATION SERVICES. CENGAGE LEARNING, GALE.

The life science content was chosen for its "high appeal and engaging qualities to motivate students to learn to read, write, and talk and reason about important ideas" (Rutherford & Ash, in press, p. 5). The life science content was chosen also because high-quality science teaching and learning is less commonly available to the students who most need it. Several in-depth discussions of scientific reasoning in FCL classrooms are available (Ash, 2008; Engle & Conant, 2004; Ricco & Shulman, 2004); these focus on adaptation and interdependence, core principles of FCL's life sciences disciplinary content.

Anne Marie Palincsar, a collaborator with and colleague of Brown said of FCL:

> Fostering a Community of Learners ... had an amazing synthetic quality, both in substance and form ... a diverse array of participant structures in which students—engaged as collaborative researchers—pursued deep understanding of content knowledge and domain-specific reasoning in the biological sciences. (Palincsar, 1999, p. 33)

One key aspect of FCL's success was translating Vygotsky's (1978) zone of proximal development to practical classroom design. The ZPD is the distance between current levels of comprehension and levels that can be accomplished in collaboration with people or powerful artifacts; such interpretations emphasize readiness to learn, "where upper boundaries are seen not as immutable but as constantly changing with the learner's increasing independent competence at each successive level" (Brown et al., 1993, p. 35). Brown designed the classroom to contain multiple and overlapping ZPDs by carefully selecting specific participant structures (involving people, computers, books, videos, TV programs, and other mediational means) encompassing

various goals (content knowledge, computer tech savvy, reading comprehension) in different social configurations.

Students were expected to know different things; they shared this distributed expertise within dialogically based, ritualized participant structures (Brown et al., 1993; Rutherford & Ash, in press), such as reciprocal teaching (Palincsar & Brown, 1984), jigsaw teaching (Aronson, 1978), and whole-group discussion. Such participant structures are now commonly used in many classrooms across the United States.

Schoenfeld (2004) has argued that such classroom design is marked by:

> A carefully delineated set of classroom practices, among them decomposing and recombining the topic under discussion into interlocking subtopics that can be studied by subgroups of students and then can be taught to other students. For FCL to succeed, then, the big ideas of the curriculum need to be identified and 'jigsawed' in ways that are suitable to the intended organization of classroom practices. (p. 243)

In actual FCL practice, "decomposing and recombining" was reflected in a basic research cycle of research (decompose content); jigsaw teach (recombine content); and consequential task (transfer content) (Brown et al., 1993; Brown & Campione, 1994, 1996).

In most FCL classrooms teams of five to six students researched, talked about, and wrote a collaborative research report, which they would use to teach other students in jigsaw groups. Students were socialized into these patterns of expected participation with particular participation structures such as Benchmarks, Research Rotations, Jigsaw groups,

Cross-talk groups, and Dilemmas. Table 2 lists some participant structures' configuration, frequency and purpose.

Cazden (2005) has described particular FCL participant structures in this way:

- *Research rotations* through several activities: (a) individual research, reading, and note-taking; (b) working at the computer to find new resources, e-mailing each other and outsiders or working on their team's report and conferencing about it with the teacher; (c) participating, initially under the teacher's guidance.

- *Reciprocal Teaching* (RT) comprehension discussions of texts—from books, the Internet, or sections of their student reports.

- *Jigsaw groups:* Periodically, as research teams became more knowledgeable about their subtopics, a student from each team met in an ad hoc group with a member of each of the other teams and taught them.

- *Cross-talk:* When the students themselves realized that Jigsaw teaching required them to know all about their team's topic, not just their individual sub-topic, they initiated an intra-team version of Jigsaw that they named Cross-talk. (Cazden, 2005, p. 8).

THE IMPORTANCE OF COMMUNITY OF LEARNERS

FCL design has been extensively cited, reviewed, transformed, borrowed, critiqued, and expanded over the past 15 years. A Google search for the phrase FCL cross-referenced with Ann Brown produced approximately 5,000 sites. A brief scan of the first 50 or so Google pages reveals that researchers and practitioners alike have adapted FCL principles and practices to multiple disciplines and at many levels of the educational system, from elementary to university). The special issue of the *Journal of Curriculum Studies* (2004) illustrates FCL implementation in several disciplines: English language arts, mathematics, science, and social studies. Such work has underscored both the benefits and limitations of the FCL curricular reform.

Perhaps more telling is the fact that FCL principles and practices have influenced leading scholars and researchers in the learning sciences. Scholars from many disciplines have subsequently explored a variety of FCL-influenced research agendas, including Disciplinary Perspectives on Fostering a Community of Teachers as Learners (Special Issue of the *Journal of Curriculum Studies*, edited by Shulman & Sherin, 2004); *Instructional Psychology: Past, Present, and Future Trends* (de Corte & Verschaffel, 2006), *Thinking Practices in Mathematics and Science Learning* (Greeno & Goldman, 1998), *Inside Japanese Classrooms: The Heart of Education* (Sato, 2004), *Design Research: Theoretical and Methodological Issues* (Collins, Joseph & Bielaczyc, 2004), to name just a few. The research agendas of these scholars

inevitably have relied, at least in part, on FCL first principles and the notion of design experiments.

There have also been criticisms. Lehrer & Schauble (2004) suggested these limitations:

> ... two questions about FCL remain open. The first concerns the utility of principles as a way to both describe and spread new educational programs. ... A second major question about FCL is whether it is a good idea for school science to be so exclusively focused on the reading and integration of textual information.

Lehrer & Schauble have accurately suggested that a central challenge in FCL (or any) dissemination is transporting and translating principles and practices, as both are essential. Brown herself was wary of "lethal mutations" particularly when practices, without the principles that informed them, were blindly copied. Brown and Campione argued instead that specific choice of participant structure or content, or form of transfer task, depended on particular contexts, as well as how first principles were specifically interpreted within them. Campione has said that he and Brown:

> saw their work as going from laboratory research to learning principles to the design of a learning environment. Then based on their analysis of the learning environment, they would make modifications and additions to the learning principles, which in turn led to modifications of the learning environment and new laboratory experiments. (Collins, Josephs, & Bielaczyc, 2004, p.16).

The emphasis, then, was on the reciprocal interplay between the "first principles" and real-world classroom practices; they saw dissemination itself as "implementation with evolution." They viewed such principles as constantly evolving as further instantiation of the project took place.

The second limitation mentioned by Lehrer and Schauble (2004), lack of hands-on materials (other than texts, computers, and experts), was accepted by Brown and Campione within this complex FCL intervention model. Brown has argued often and convincingly that the students in her classroom practiced science as many scientists practiced it over the centuries, as natural historians, using observation and thought experiment, rather than direct experimentation, as the basis for their reasoning.

Erik de Corte's 2000 study has noted perhaps the biggest challenge to wide-scale dissemination of FCL-like projects, "[the] methodological problem of the confounding of variables in design research, echoing a major criticism of the protagonists of randomized field trials" (p. 6). Such validity arguments have become more common over the past decade in a current climate of standardized tests and accountability.

Regarding the long-term curricular reform potential of projects such as FCL, Rutherford and Ash (2008) have written:

> In the early 1990s, we had more latitude to develop our own curriculum, schedule our day, and embed literacy practices into all our work.... Such choices are not so readily available to teachers in current environments. New state and national standards and testing guidelines have narrowed teachers and researchers' choices. But before we say that we cannot create such learning communities in the 2000s, let us take seriously Ann's caution about not throwing the baby out with the bath water and revisit her first principles of learning from the perspective of "possible worlds," to borrow Bruner's (1986) phrase.

Finally the following comment about FCL should be noted:

> [It is the] one program discussed in detail by Jerome Bruner in his book, *The Culture of Education,* [in which he calls for a] "more intimate perspective" of what we have learned about how teachers teach and how students learn. Bruner speaks of Brown as "perhaps the leading figure in this advance." (Bruner, 1996, p. 86, cited in Cazden, 2005. p. 8)

SEE ALSO *Constructivism; Design Experiment.*

BIBLIOGRAPHY

Brown, A. L. (1992). Design experiments: Theoretical and methodological challenges in creating complex interventions in classroom settings. *The Journal of Learning Sciences, 2*(2), 141–178.

Brown, A. L. (1994) The advancement of learning. *Educational Researcher, 23*(8), 4–12.

Brown, A. L., Ash, D., Rutherford, M., Nakagawa, K., Gordon, A., & Campione, J. (1993). Distributed expertise in the classroom. Saloman, G. (Ed.). *Distributed Cognitions.* New York: Cambridge University Press.

Brown, A. L., & Campione, J. C. (1990). Communities of learning and thinking or a context by any other name. In D. Khun (Ed.), *Contributions to Human Development, 21,* 108–125.

Brown, A. L., & Campione, J. C. (1994). Guided discovery in a community of learners. In K. McGilly (Ed.), Classroom lessons: Integrating cognitive theory and classroom practice (pp. 229–270). Cambridge, MA: MIT Press/Bradford Books.

Brown, A. L., & Campione, J. C. (1996). Psychological learning theory and design of innovative environments: On procedure, principles and systems. In: L. Schauble & R. Glaser (Eds.), *Contributions of instructional innovation to understanding learning* (pp. 86–102). Hillsdale, NJ: Erlbaum.

Bruner, J. (1996). *The culture of education.* Cambridge, MA: Harvard University Press.

Cazden, C. B. (2001) *Classroom discourse: The language of teaching and learning* (2nd ed.). Portsmouth, NH: Heinemann.

Cazden, C. (2005, September). *Agency, collaboration, and learning in a middle-school program for science and literacy.* Paper presented at the Charles Darwin Symposium, Imagining childhood: Children, culture and community, Alice Springs, Australia.

Cole, M. (1998). Can cultural psychology help us think about diversity? *Mind, Culture, and Activity 5,*(4) 291–304.

Collins, A., Joseph, D., & Bielaczyc, K. (2004). Design Research: Theoretical and Methodological Issues. Special Issue: Design-Based Research: Clarifying the Terms. *Journal of the learning Sciences 13* (1) 15–42.

De Corte, E. (2000, November). High-powered learning communities: a European perspective. Keynote address to the First Conference of the Economic and Social Research Council's Research Programme on Teaching and Learning. Leicester, England.

Lehrer, R., & Schauble, L. (2004). Modeling natural variation through distribution. *American Educational Research Journal,* 41(3), 635–679.

Palincsar, A. S., & Brown, A. L. (1984). Reciprocal teaching of comprehension-fostering and monitoring activities. *Cognition and Instruction, 1*(2), 117–175.

Rogoff, B. (1994). Developing understanding of the idea of communities of learners. *Mind, Culture, and Activity, 1*(4), 209–229.

Rutherford, M., & Ash, D. (2008). The Ann Brown fostering a community of learners legacy: Still learning after all these years. In J. Campione, A. Palincsar & K. Metz (Eds.) *The legacy of Ann Brown* (pp. 222–249). Mahwah, NJ: Erlbaum.

Schoenfeld, A. (2004). Multiple learning communities: Students, teachers, instructional designers, and researchers. *Journal of Curriculum Studies, 36*(2), 237–255.

Vygotsky, L. S. (1978) *Mind in society: The development of higher psychological processes.* (M. Cole, V. John-Steiner, S. Scribner, & E. Souberman, Eds. and Trans.). Cambridge, MA: Harvard University Press.

Doris B. Ash

COMPETITION

Competition is most commonly associated with sports or athletic events in which individuals or teams of individuals compete for some reward or accolade. Competition is also seen in classroom settings, where either individualistically or in teams or small groups, students strive to win by being the smartest or fastest on an academic task. Studies on the influence of competition in classrooms have looked at it from multiple perspectives. An earlier one studied forms of classroom competition that involved small groups of students competing with one another, much like what is seen on the field or in a gym. Here, researchers examined cooperative versus competitive learning in small group formats and the impact on motivation and achievement. Subsequent classroom research on competition shifted from a focus on groups to a focus on the individual and the ways in which classroom structures impact students' level of competitiveness. From this perspective, competition is constructed as a personal attribute that students bring to the classroom setting. Thus, researchers examine classroom goal structures and individual goal orientations to understand what competitive orientations bring resultant motivation and academic outcomes. Additionally, developmentalists have examined how competitive strivings unfold over time and how they vary according to gender, culture, and age.

COOPERATION AND COMPETITION IN SMALL GROUPS

During the 1970s and 1980s, when small group learning was at its height in popularity, researchers studied the nature and function of small group formats for enhancing student motivation and learning. Researchers wanted to understand the trade-offs of having students work alone versus work in small groups and whether working together (cooperatively) or working to outperform others (competitively) was more effective. A review of this literature reveals that cooperative small group learning activities were largely more successful for student learning and motivation than competitive ones, whether individuals or small groups were involved (Johnson et al., 1981).

Data also suggest that age, group size, and type of learning task matter such that the benefits of cooperation are stronger for younger students than for older students, and for smaller group sizes than larger ones. Further, cooperation is more beneficial for problem solving and other types of higher processing tasks, whereas competition is more effective for rote learning (e.g., Johnson et al., 1981; Johnson, Skon, & Johnson, 1980). Cooperation is also linked to students' positive attitudes towards teachers, the belief that teachers care about them, and feeling liked and accepted by teachers in grades 2 through 12 (Johnson & Ahlgren, 1976). Thus, when it comes to small group formats, activities that promote cooperation are generally more beneficial socially, motivationally, and academically than competitive ones.

GOALS, GOAL STRUCTURES, AND COMPETITION

Throughout the 1980s, and as cognitive processing models emerged, researchers became more interested in students' cognitive orientations (goals) toward schooling and the ways in which they interpreted classroom activities. The focus shifted among motivational researchers from small group settings to a greater concern for individual perspectives about learning. Achievement goal theory emerged as the dominant approach for studying these processes (Ames, 1992; Elliott & Dweck, 1988).

Achievement goal theorists organize individuals' cognitive attributes according to two types of goal orientations that are referred to as *mastery* or *performance*. Students with a mastery goal orientation adopt learning goals that are about mastering the task at hand for the sake of gaining competence or increased knowledge. Performance goals, by contrast, pertain to social comparisons of ability. Performance goals are consistent with notions of competition because competition is about the "relative ability comparisons among students in the classroom" (Ryan & Patrick, 2001, p. 442). Data suggest that students who hold performance oriented goals and who are largely more preoccupied with their achievement performance as it compares to others tend to have less adaptive motivational dispositions and attitudes.

Classroom goal structures have also been studied to understand how teacher-created tasks impact students' attitudes towards learning. Classroom goal structures are communicated to students throughout the many layers of the teaching process, including the type of tasks assigned (difficulty, variety), the nature of student evaluations (norm-based or criterion-based), and the way teacher authority is communicated (e.g., Ames, 1992; Blumenfeld, 1992). Tasks promote competition when they prompt students to compare their abilities with those of other students. Similarly, evaluation systems (i.e., grades, achievement feedback) that stress social comparisons in achievement are associated with performance goal classroom structures, as are authority systems or classroom management techniques that restrict student autonomy and control. Thus, classroom structures that emphasize academic comparisons among students tend to be more maladaptive to student motivation than structures that emphasize academic progress or mastery (see Anderman, 2007).

COMPETITION AND CHARACTERISTICS OF STUDENTS

Research from the developmental literature suggests that competitive natures vary according to gender, race, and age. In terms of gender, most research suggests that males tend to be more competitive than females. Similarly, students from cultures that emphasize individualism such as European Americans tend to be more competitive than students from cultures that emphasize collectivism (such as Latin Americans and African Americans). However, some research has revealed more complexity in these generalizations according to a multidimensional view of competition. Schneider, Woodburn, del Pilar Soteras del Toro, and Udvari (2005) examined competitiveness among a cross-cultural group of seventh graders. They defined competition according to four main types: (a) hypercompetitiveness, the need to win at all costs that is expressed by hostility and disregard for the opponent, (b) non-hostile social comparisons, the comparison of achievements without hostility, aggression, or jealousy, (c) enjoyment of competition, which gauges the amount of positive affect toward the experience of competition and (d) avoidance of competition. Schneider and colleagues (2005) found cultural and gender-based differences in competitive orientations. Specifically, Canadian boys were more hypercompetitive and emotionally competitive, but Canadian girls were more competitive when it came to making social comparisons. However, the sample from the Costa Rican culture showed the opposite pattern, namely that boys had more social comparison competitiveness than did girls. By contrast, in Cuba girls were more likely to avoid competition all together. Thus, additional research was thought to be needed to explore the manner in which student characteristics interact with one another in order to determine attitudes regarding competition.

Another interesting consideration of competition involves examining whether winning means diminishing the opponent's chances of getting any rewards. Referred to as *interference competition*, researchers tested whether females and males differ according to the manner in which they competed. Data suggest that boys are more likely than girls to harm another's chances of getting rewards or status when they compete (e.g., Knight & Kagan, 1981; Roy & Benenson, 2002). This gender difference appears at all ages and in various contexts. For example, in naturalistic observations of children's play, researchers find that boys are more likely to engage in interference competition than girls in their choice of games such as football or basketball on the playground. By contrast, girls typically engage in games in which one can maximize one's own potential without having to interfere with someone else's potential (Lever, 1978).

Importantly, interference competition emerged only in certain contexts. Roy and Benenson (2002) found that fourth-grade girls tend to avoid competitive interference in conditions of plenty—when there were enough rewards to go around. By contrast, they did engage in interference competition when the rewards were scarce. However, fourth-grade boys and kindergartners (both boys and girls) used interference competition to the same extent under conditions of scarcity and plenty. One explanation may be that girls learn over time about strategically using interference competition when the stakes are high (or rewards are scarce). The growing trend in girls' use of indirect aggression against one another may point to a form of interference competition they have learned over time where spreading rumors, backstabbing, and excluding become a form of competitive behavior, the goal of which is to undermine another's popularity status.

NEGATIVE IMPACT OF COMPETITION

Good and Brophy (2008) summarize several ways in which classroom competition may negatively impact students' development, learning, and motivation. For example, if students become preoccupied with winning or losing the competitive activity, they may lose sight of important instructional objectives and content. From the student's perspective, performance takes precedence over learning. Further, inherent in the practice of competition is the necessity for someone to lose. If the same students lose over and over despite their best efforts, they may come to see the world as unfair and are likely to give up when faced with challenging academic tasks, as they have learned that failure will be the outcome no matter how hard they try to succeed. Such students may think, "Why should I put forth the effort or invest in the activity if I'm probably just going to lose anyway?" These students will evaluate themselves negatively and will see school as a threatening place in which to be; these students also may be rejected or evaluated negatively by peers, as classmates are unlikely to be willing to work with a person perceived to be a loser.

Conversely, students who routinely win at competitive tasks may lose interest in the instructional material and over time may put forth the minimal amount of effort required to outperform other students, rather than maximizing effort in order to master the task or material. These students might think, "Why should I try my hardest when I can beat the other students by simply going through the motions? Sure I don't learn as much as I would if I invested 100% in the activity, but I still win the competition, and isn't that what's most important?"

Findings from numerous research studies support these ideas. For example, Johnson and colleagues (1981) conducted a meta-analysis examining the effects of competitive goal structures on academic achievement, as compared to cooperative and individual tasks. Results suggest that across studies, students completing academic tasks under cooperative conditions were likely to perform at higher levels than students completing tasks under either competitive or individual conditions. Interestingly, students in competitive and individual conditions were likely to perform similarly to one another.

More contemporary investigations of competition are based on goal orientation and motivation research and attempt to identify explanations for the negative influence of competition. For example, theoretical and research-based perspectives suggest that competition may promote the development of performance goals rather than mastery goals. As previously noted, this means that under competitive conditions, students approach tasks with a desire to succeed in order to appear competent in front of others or to outperform peers (i.e., performance orientation), rather than approaching tasks with a desire to expand their knowledge and skills (i.e., mastery orientation). As explained by Ames (1992), students with a mastery orientation are more likely to attribute successful learning outcomes to effort, which increases the likelihood of continued motivation and is associated with the development of self-regulation skills. Conversely, students adopting a performance orientation are more likely to attribute success to ability, which may or may not encourage continued motivation. So how do these concepts relate to competition? If students come to learn that winning at competitive activities will lead to rewards, they may adopt performance goal orientations rather than mastery goal orientations. The goal is to win (or to avoid failure) by outperforming their peers rather than to develop their competence by mastering the task; completing the task becomes a means to an end (i.e., winning) rather than valued as a way of building competence (e.g., Bergin & Cooks, 2000).

Similarly, competition and performance goals may decrease intrinsic motivation towards academic tasks because students rely on rewards from others to motivate them to complete tasks, rather than completing tasks for the reward of building competence and skills. Competition in the classroom also might distract students from learning: they become so focused on performing better than peers that they get distracted from learning or anxious about losing. A review by Meece, Anderman, and Anderman (2006) concluded that many students are not motivated by competitive classroom activities, which is probably especially true for students who perform poorly in comparison to peers. Classrooms that emphasize competition among students are likely to promote the development of performance goals, as students learn that outperforming other students is valued more than learning. Further, the authors present evidence that tasks or activities that require students to enhance their knowledge and skills (i.e., mastery-oriented tasks) are likely to promote motivation and effort among students, as they strive for greater understanding. In this way, teachers' use of competition in the classroom can influence the types of goal orientations that students adopt, which in turn can influence their motivation towards learning.

PERCEIVED BENEFITS OF COMPETITION

Competition is not without its advocates, and several reasons for this are offered in the literature. First, competition may generate interest and excitement in topics or tasks that would otherwise be of limited interest to students. Team-based competitive approaches (e.g., class-wide games) may be especially effective at making instructional material more enjoyable and engaging. Good and Brophy (2008) suggest that competitive classroom activities may be appropriate if all students have a chance to win, and when a team approach is used rather than individually based evaluations. These practices may reduce the likelihood that the same students are always the winners and losers, in which the losers become embarrassed and demoralized. Further, competition between groups (using a team-based approach) may increase cooperation within groups, as students are unified in working towards a common goal (i.e., outperforming the other teams).

Second, competitive approaches may be appropriate within the context of behavior management, such as when the teacher is attempting to reduce disruptive behaviors and increase positive behaviors. For example, interventions such as the Good Behavior Game and its variations (Tingstrom, Sterling-Turner, & Wilczynski, 2006) use team-based competition to motivate students and modify their behaviors. These approaches provide examples of effective uses of competition in the classroom, as they often result in reduced disruptive behaviors and increased on-task and prosocial behaviors among large numbers of students. These interventions often involve either providing a predetermined reward (e.g., free time, tangibles, spending time with teachers or other adults) to the team with the fewest behavioral infractions over a certain time period or providing a reward to all teams that earn fewer than a predetermined number of behavioral infractions over a certain time period. Such competition-based behavior management strategies can also increase academically relevant behaviors such as work completion. Third, some argue that competition in the classroom will prepare students for competition in their lives beyond school (i.e., the workplace). The reasoning behind this argument is that if all classroom tasks are cooperative, students may become overly dependent on their classmates when completing academic tasks and may be unable to perform in competitive or individual contexts in the future.

In the early 2000s school reform efforts seem to be maximizing potential for competition in learning environments. Under the 2002 No Child Left Behind Act (NCLB), students' academic performance is regularly publicized and scrutinized and used for making significant decisions about teachers and their students. This chronic public accounting of student performance creates a climate that maximizes the likelihood that students will be known primarily in terms of their test score achievement (Nichols & Berliner, 2007). Therefore, NCLB virtually mandates that students compete with one another to demonstrate their achievement as measured by standardized test scores.

Educators would be wise to encourage students to focus on mastering tasks and making improvements in performance on an individual basis rather than to focus on who is scores the highest. Competition is probably rewarding and motivating for students who win regularly, but what about those who do not? With this in mind, educators are encouraged to be mindful when deciding whether to use competition in the classroom and to be able to articulate a well-reasoned rationale for using competition, just as they would for any other instructional decision. Specifically, they ought to be able to explain how making a particular task or activity competitive will enhance students' learning and motivation. They ought to consider how using competition may be harmful to students in this situation. They ought to be able to identify instructional benefits to using competition. They ought to consider from the students' perspective what the stakes involved in winning and losing are. Addressing these considerations will likely help educators apply competition appropriately in the classroom.

SEE ALSO *Goal Orientation Theory.*

BIBLIOGRAPHY

Ames, C. (1992). Classrooms: Goals, structures, and student motivation. *Journal of Educational Psychology, 84,* 261–271.

Anderman, E. M. (2007). The effects of personal, classroom, and school goal structures on academic cheating. In E. M. Anderman & T. B. Murdock (Eds.), *The psychology of academic cheating* (pp. 87–106). New York: Elsevier.

Bergin, D. A., & Cooks, H. C. (2000). Academic competition among students of color: An interview story. *Urban Education, 35* (4), 442–472.

Blumenfeld, P. C. (1992). Classroom learning and motivation: Clarifying and expanding goal theory. *Journal of Educational Psychology, 84,* 272–281.

Elliott, E., & Dweck, C. (1988). Goals: An approach to motivation and achievement. *Journal of Personality and Social Psychology, 54,* 5–12.

Good, T. L., & Brophy, J. E. (2008). *Looking in classrooms* (10th ed.). Boston: Pearson Education.

Johnson, D. W., & Ahlgren, A. (1976). Relationship between student attitudes about cooperation and competition and attitudes toward schooling. *Journal of Educational Psychology, 68,* 92–102.

Johnson, D. W., Maruyama, G., Johnson, R., Nelson, D., & Skon, L. (1981). Effects of cooperative, competitive, and individualistic goal structures on achievement: A meta-analysis. *Psychological Bulletin, 89,* 47–62.

Johnson, D. W., Skon, L., & Johnson, R. (1980). Effects of cooperative, competitive, and individualistic conditions on children's problem-solving performance. *American Educational Research Journal, 17,* 83–93.

Knight, G. P., & Kagan, S. (1981). Apparent sex differences in cooperation-competition: A case of individualism. *Developmental Psychology, 17,* 783–790.

Lever, J. (1978). Sex differences in the complexity of children's play and games. *American Sociological Review, 43,* 471–483.

Meece, J. L., Anderman, E. M., & Anderman, L. H. (2006). Classroom goal structure, student motivation, and academic achievement. *Annual Review of Psychology, 57,* 487–503.

Nichols, S. L., & Berliner, D. C. (2007). *Collateral damage: How high-stakes testing corrupts America's schools.* Cambridge, MA: Harvard Education Press.

Roy, R., & Benenson, J. F. (2002). Sex and contextual effects on children's use of interference competition. *Developmental Psychology, 38*(2), 306–312.

Ryan, A. M., & Patrick, H. (2001). The classroom social environment and changes in adolescents' motivation and engagement during middle school. *American Educational Research Journal, 38,* 437–460.

Schneider, B. H., Woodburn, S., del Pilar Soteras del Toro, M., & Udvari, S. J. (2005). Cultural and gender differences in the implications of competition for early adolescent friendship. *Merrill-Palmer Quarterly, 51*(2), 163–191.

Tingstrom, D. H., Sterling-Turner, H. E., & Wilczynski, S. M. (2006). The good behavior game: 1969–2002. *Behavior Modification, 30,* 225–253.

Sharon L. Nichols
Jeremy R. Sullivan

COMPREHENSIVE SCHOOL REFORM FOR HIGH-POVERTY SCHOOLS

Since its inception in 1965, the Federal Title I Program has provided billions of dollars in aid to high-poverty schools, hoping to help these schools narrow the achievement gap with advantaged students. Extensive research on the effects of Title I funding has found that while there are generally benefits to the schools, they are quite small and variable (see Borman, Stringfield, & Slavin, 2001). Yet it has long been observed that individual schools often make outstanding gains using Title I resources in innovative ways to improve the functioning of the entire school. Beginning with the 1988 reauthorization, these findings led the U.S. Congress to progressively reform rules for the use of Title I funding in the highest-poverty schools to allow them to use these monies for professional development, materials, and personnel to improve teaching and learning schoolwide, not just (as had been the case previously) for group remedial services to individual low achievers.

PROGRAMS DEVELOPED IN 1980S AND 1990S

The movement toward schoolwide projects in Title I schools encouraged a flowering of whole-school innovations in high-poverty schools. Much of this innovation has taken place in individual schools and districts, without any intention to make changes on a broader scale, but there arose in the late 1980s and early 1990s a set of programs, explicitly designed by university researchers and non-profit organizations not only to improve whole schools but also to be replicable, to eventually offer large numbers of schools well-developed alternatives to current practices. These programs came to be known as *Comprehensive School Reform* (CSR). CSR sees the school as the primary unit of change in education. It seeks to implant effective practices in all of the central areas of school functioning most likely to affect student achievement: Curriculum, instruction, assessment, grouping, accommodations for struggling students, parent and community involvement, school organization, and professional development (see Stringfield, Ross, & Smith, 1996; ERS, 1998; CSRQ, 2006a, 2006b; Borman, Hewes, Overman, & Brown, 2003). In 1998 the U.S. Department of Education defined comprehensive school reform as innovative programs that include all of the following elements:

1. Coordination of resources: The program identifies how all resources (federal/state/local/private) available to the school will be utilized to coordinate services to support and sustain the school reform effort;

2. Effective, research-based methods and strategies: A comprehensive school reform program employs innovative strategies and proven methods for student learning, teaching, and school management that are based on reliable research and effective practices, and have been replicated successfully in schools with diverse characteristics;

3. Comprehensive design with aligned components: The program has a comprehensive design for effective school functioning, including instruction, assessment, classroom management, professional development, parental involvement, and school management, that aligns the school's curriculum, technology, and professional development into a schoolwide reform plan designed to enable all students to meet challenging state content and performance standards and addresses needs identified through a school needs assessment;

4. Professional development: The program provides high-quality and continuous teacher and staff professional development and training;

5. Measurable goals and benchmarks: A comprehensive school reform program has measurable goals for student performance tied to the state's challenging content and student performance standards, as those

standards are implemented, and benchmarks for meeting those goals;

6. Support within the school: The program is supported by school faculty, administrators, and staff;

7. Parental and community involvement: The program provides for the meaningful involvement of parents and the local community in planning and implementing school improvement activities;

8. External technical support and assistance: A comprehensive reform program utilizes high-quality external technical support and assistance from a comprehensive school reform entity (which may be a

Summary of research on comprehensive school reform models

	Number of studies	(Third party)
Strongest evidence of effectiveness		
Success for All	41	(25)
Direct Instruction	40	(38)
School Development Program	9	(5)
Highly promising evidence of effectiveness		
Roots & Wings	5	(4)
Expeditionary Learning/Outward Bound	4	(3)
Modern Red Schoolhouse	4	(3)
Promising evidence of effectiveness		
Accelerated Schools	3	(2)
America's Choice	1	(1)
ATLAS Communities	2	(2)
Montessori	2	(2)
Paideia	3	(3)
The Learning Network	1	(1)
Greatest need for additional research		
Audrey Cohen	1	(1)
Center for Effective Schools	0	(0)
Child Development Project	2	(0)
Coalition for Essential Schools	1	(1)
Community for Learning	0	(0)
Community Learning Centers	1	(1)
Co-Nect	5	(4)
Core knowledge	6	(6)
Different Ways of Knowing	1	(1)
Edison	3	(3)
High Schools That Work	4	(0)
High/scope	3	(2)
Integrated Thematic Instruction	1	(1)
Microsociety	1	(0)
Onward to Excellence II	0	(0)
Talent Development High School	1	(0)
Urban Learning Centers	0	(0)
All CSR models	145	(109)

SOURCE: Adapted from Borman, Hewes, Overman, & Brown (2003)

Table 1 ILLUSTRATION BY GGS INFORMATION SERVICES. CENGAGE LEARNING, GALE.

university) with experience or expertise in school-wide reform and improvement;

9. Evaluation strategies: The program includes a plan for the evaluation of the implementation of school reforms and the student results achieved.

Ideally, a comprehensive school reform model is one in which each of the elements is carefully integrated around a shared conception of how students will learn and develop. Most CSR models require that staff members vote to adopt the model, and most require a supermajority in favor (say, 80%). The idea is to engage the energies and enthusiasm of a given school staff around a common vision and a common set of strategies, but not to ask the staff to completely design its own reform model. Comprehensive school reform designs are provided by organizations (mostly nonprofits) that provide professional development, teacher and student materials, and perhaps most importantly a network of like-minded schools around the country that share similar visions and support one another's efforts.

In schools implementing CSR designs, teachers have colleagues who are working toward similar objectives, sharing a vision and a language to describe that vision and sharing practical strategies for achieving the vision. Almost all CSR models include a facilitator or coach within the school who visits teachers' classes, organizes opportunities for teachers to work with one another, facilitates discussions about data, student work, classroom teaching practices, and other elements, ensures coordination among program elements, and acts as a communication link between the principal and the teachers. Comprehensive school reform takes the view that genuine, lasting change takes place in supportive groups of like-minded professionals, and that schools are capable of establishing norms of practice and expectations for continuous improvement that would be difficult to establish on a teacher by teacher basis.

Comprehensive school reform grew explosively in the 1990s, helped first by the 1991 appearance of the New American Schools Development Corporation (NASDC), a coalition of large corporations that funded the development and scale-up of CSR models (Kearns & Anderson, 1996). A second major boost came from the 1997 Obey-Porter Comprehensive School Reform legislation, which made grants available to high-poverty schools to adopt "proven, comprehensive" CSR models. By 2001 there were an estimated 6,000 schools, mostly high-poverty elementary schools, using CSR models, with or without Obey-Porter funding. A lack of support for CSR in the second administration of President George W. Bush ended Obey-Porter and slowed the growth of CSR, but there are still thousands of schools implementing CSR programs. Further, perhaps no edu-

CSRQ center report on elementary school comprehensive reform models	
Model	**Number of studies rated "conclusive"**
Moderately strong evidence of positive effects	
Success for All	34
Direct Instruction (full immersion)	11
Moderate evidence of positive effects	
America's Choice	6
Accelerated Schools PLUS	3
Core Knowledge	3
School Development Program	3
School Renaissance	1
Limited evidence of positive effects	
National Writing Projects	5
Literacy Collaborative	2
Co-Nect	2
ATLAS Communities	1
Integrated Thematic Instruction	1
Different Ways of Knowing	0
Modern Red Schoolhouse	0
Ventures Initiative and Focus System	0
Zero evidence of positive effects	
Breakthrough to Literacy	0
Coalition of Essential Schools	0
Community for Learning	0
Comprehensive Early Literacy Learning	0
Expeditionary Learning	0
First Steps	0
Onward to Excellence II	0
SOURCE: Adapted from CSRQ, 2006a	

Table 2 ILLUSTRATION BY GGS INFORMATION SERVICES. CENGAGE LEARNING, GALE.

cation reform initiative in history has been as thoroughly researched as CSR, and this research continues.

RESEARCH ON COMPREHENSIVE SCHOOL REFORM PROGRAMS

Comprehensive school reform models have been extensively evaluated in large-scale quantitative as well as qualitative studies. A review of experimental research on comprehensive school reform models was published by Borman, Hewes, Overman, and Brown (2003), who categorized programs according to the numbers of well-designed experiments on each and the consistency of positive achievement effects. A simplified adaptation of their main results appears in Table 1. Reviews using somewhat different procedures were carried out by the Comprehensive School Reform Quality Center (CSRQ, 2006a, 2006b) at the American Institutes for Research. The CSRQ reviews, summarized in Tables 2 and 3, emphasized the number of "conclusive" studies done on each program and the proportion of significantly positive findings. The following sections discuss research on some of the most prominent of the CSR models.

Success for All. Success for All (Slavin & Madden, 2001) is the most widely used and extensively evaluated of the CSR models. It provides schools with specific curriculum materials and extensive professional development in reading, writing, and language arts, along with detailed assessment, cross-grade grouping strategies, within-school facilitators, and other school organization elements. The program gives one-to-one tutoring to primary-grades children who are struggling in reading, and extensive outreach to parents. It provides detailed teacher's manuals and about 26 person-days of on-site professional development to enable schools to engage in a substantial retooling process. Originally focused on elementary school, prekindergarten to grade 6, Success for All now has a middle school (grades 68) program as well (Chamberlain et al., 2007). Programs in mathematics, science, and social studies were also developed, and the term *Roots & Wings* was used to describe schools using all of these elements (Slavin, Madden, Dolan, & Wasik, 1994). However, most schools, including many of those categorized as Roots & Wings in the Borman et al. (2003) review, use only the reading program, and the Roots & Wings term is no longer used. Research on Success for All and Roots & Wings are combined for discussion in this chapter.

Borman and colleagues (2003) identified a total of 46 experimental-control comparisons evaluating Success for All, 31 of which were carried out by third-party investigators. A mean effect size of +0.20 (combining Success for All and Roots & Wings) was obtained across all studies and measures. A longitudinal study by Borman & Hewes (2003) found that students who had been in Success for All elementary schools were, by eighth grade, still reading significantly better than former control group students and were about half as likely to have been retained or assigned to special education.

Comprehensive School Reform Quality Center (CSRQ) (2006a) rated the strength of evidence for the Success for All elementary program as "moderately strong," the highest rating given to any program (one other, Direct Instruction, also received this rating). A total of 34 studies were rated as "conclusive." CSRQ (2006b) rated the evidence for the Success for All middle school as "moderate," with two conclusive studies.

Since the review by Borman and colleagues, a number of additional studies of Success for All have been carried out. Most importantly, a national randomized evaluation of Success for All was reported by Borman and colleagues (2007). A total of 35 schools were randomly assigned to use Success for All either in grades K-2 or in grades 3-5. The primary grades in 3-5 schools were used as controls, as were the intermediate grades in K-2 schools. By the end of the

CSRQ center report on middle and high school comprehensive school reform models	
Model	**Number of studies rated "conclusive"**
Moderate evidence of positive effects	
America's Choice	5
Success for All Middle School	2
School Development Program	2
Talent Development High School	2
First Things First	1
Limited evidence of positive effects	
KIPP	1
Middle Start	1
Project GRAD	1
More Effective Schools	0
Expeditionary Learning	0
Zero evidence of positive effects	
Accelerated Schools PLUS	0
Atlas Communities	0
Coalition of Essential Schools	0
High Schools That Work	0
Making Middle Grades Work	0
Modern Red Schoolhouse	0
Onward to Excellence II	0
Turning Points	0
SOURCE: Adapted from CSRQ, 2006b	

Table 3 ILLUSTRATION BY GGS INFORMATION SERVICES. CENGAGE LEARNING, GALE.

study, Success for All second graders were scoring significantly better than controls on all reading measures (Borman, Slavin, Cheung, Chamberlain, Madden, & Chambers, 2007). Taken together, there are now more than 50 experimental-control studies of Success for All involving more than 200 schools throughout the United States. Since 1998 Success for All has been developed and disseminated by the non-profit Success for All Foundation, and is currently working in about 1,200 schools in 48 states in the United States, and 100 schools in England.

Direct Instruction. Direct Instruction (DI) (Adams & Engelmann, 1996), once known as DISTAR, is an elementary school program originally designed to extend an effective early childhood curriculum into the early elementary grades, in a federal program called Follow Through. Like Success for All, DI is primarily intended to help high-poverty schools succeed with all students, and the program is even more systematically specified for teachers.

The DI reading and math programs have long been marketed by SRA, a division of the McGraw Hill publishing company, under the titles "Reading Mastery" and "Connecting Math Concepts." The publisher provides limited professional development with the program, but schools can contract with providers of professional development, primarily the National Institute for Direct Instruction (NIFDI) at the University of Oregon. Such schools receive approximately 32 person-days of professional development in their first year, similar to the services provided in the Follow Through studies. Research on DI has overwhelmingly focused on the model with extensive professional development, not on use of the books alone, and research findings for DI should therefore be assumed to apply only to the program with professional development. Certainly only this form could be considered a comprehensive reform model.

Borman and colleagues (2003) identified 40 experimental-control studies of DI, of which 38 were third party. The mean effect size was +0.15. CSRQ (2006a) rated DI's evidence of positive effects as "moderately strong," with 11 "conclusive" studies.

School Development Program. James Comer developed one of the earliest of the comprehensive reform models, the *School Development Program* (SDP) (Comer, Haynes, Joyner, & Ben-Avie, 1996). The focus of SDP is on the whole child. Rather than focusing on specified curricula and instructional methods, SDP concentrates on building a sense of common purpose among school staff, parents, and community, working through a set of teams in each school that develop, carry out, and monitor reforms tailored to the needs of each school. A school planning and management team develops an overall plan, and mental health and parent teams focus on issues beyond the classroom.

Borman and colleagues (2003, p. 155) listed SDP as one of three CSR programs with "strongest evidence of effectiveness." A set of three high-quality third-party evaluations described mixed evidence of the program's impact. One, a randomized evaluation in Prince George's County, Maryland, found poor implementation and no achievement effects (Cook et al., 1999), but a partially randomized study in Chicago (Cook, Murphy, & Hunt, 2000) and a matched study in Detroit (Millsap, Chase, Obeidallah, Perez-Smith, & Brigham, 2000) found small but positive impacts on achievement. CSRQ (2006a, 2006b) rated the evidence for SDP as "moderate," with three "conclusive" studies at the elementary level and two at the secondary level.

America's Choice. America's Choice (AC) (NCEE, 2003) is a comprehensive reform model that focuses on standards and assessments, instruction aligned with standards, extensive professional development, and parent involvement. In particular, the program mandates a core curriculum in literacy and mathematics, tutoring for struggling students, and a school leadership team to coordinate implementation.

Borman and colleagues (2003) included only one study of the America's Choice design, but more recently researchers at the Center for Policy Research in Education at the University of Pennsylvania have carried out several evaluations. A longitudinal matched study in Rochester, New York, found that America's Choice students made greater gains than other students from 1998 to 2003 in reading and math (May, Supovitz, & Perda, 2004). A matched study in Duval Co., Florida (Supovitz, Taylor, & May, 2002) compared America's Choice and other schools on state tests, and results favored the AC schools in writing and, to a small degree, in math (but not reading). A 1-year matched study (Supovitz, Poglinco, & Snyder, 2001) also compared matched AC and control schools in Plainfield, New Jersey, and found greater gains for the AC students on the state English Language Arts test. CSRQ (2006a) rated the evidence of positive effects for America's Choice as "moderate" at the elementary level, with six "conclusive" studies, and also "moderate" at the secondary level, with five "conclusive" studies (CSRQ, 2006b).

Modern Red Schoolhouse. Modern Red Schoolhouse (Heady & Kilgore, 1996) is a program that emphasizes standards-based teaching, appropriate uses of technology, and frequent assessment. It provides customized professional development to help schools build coherent curriculum aligned with state standards and then implement aligned practices. In recent years, Modern Red Schoolhouse has begun to focus more on district reform and leadership.

Borman and colleagues (2003) identified four experimental-control studies of Modern Red Schoolhouse, with an average effect size of +0.17. CSRQ (2006a) rated the evidence for Modern Red Schoolhouse as "limited" at the elementary level.

Accelerated Schools. Accelerated Schools (Hopfenberg, Levin, & Chase, 1993; Levin, 1987) is a process-oriented school reform model that emphasizes high expectations for children and giving students complex and engaging instruction. Each school staff designs its own means of putting into practice the basic principles: High expectations, powerful learning based on constructivist principles, and avoidance of remediation.

Borman and colleagues (2003) identified three studies of Accelerated Schools with a mean effect size of +0.21. CSRQ (2006a) rated Accelerated Schools as "moderate" in research evidence, with three studies rated "conclusive."

Expeditionary Learning/Outward Bound. Expeditionary Learning (Campbell et al., 1996, p. 109) is a design built around "learning expeditions," which are "explorations within and beyond school walls." The program is affiliated with Outward Bound and incorporates its principles of active learning, challenge, and teamwork. It makes extensive use of project-based learning, cooperative learning, and performance assessments.

Borman and colleagues (2003) identified four experimental-control evaluations of Expeditionary Learning, which had positive effects. However, CSRQ (2006a, 2006b) did not rate any studies of Expeditionary Learning as "conclusive."

The experience of comprehensive school reform shows the great potential of whole-school reform for high-poverty schools. Research on CSR has clearly established that fundamental reforms can be introduced, implemented with quality, and maintained over many years. The longstanding belief dating back to the Rand Change Agent study of the 1970s (McLaughlin, 1990) that every school has to create its own approach to reform was conclusively disproved. Not all CSR approaches have been adequately researched, but in particular those with well-specified designs, clear expectations for what teachers and students will do, and extensive teacher and student materials, have been repeatedly found to be effective, scalable, and sustainable in a broad range of circumstances. Quality of implementation matters, of course (Aladjem & Borman, 2006), but it has been demonstrated that high-quality implementations of CSR can be achieved and that in such schools, children benefit.

BIBLIOGRAPHY

Adams, G. L., & Engelmann, S. (1996). *Research on Direct Instruction: 25 years beyond DISTAR*. Seattle, WA: Educational Achievement Systems.

Aladjem, D.K., & Borman, K.M. (Eds.) (2006). *Examining comprehensive school reform*. Washington, DC: Urban Institute Press.

Borman, G., Slavin, R. E., Cheung, A., Chamberlain, A., Madden, N. A., & Chambers, B. (2007). Final reading outcomes of the national randomized field trial of Success for All. *American Educational Research Journal, 44*(3), 701–739.

Borman, G., & Hewes, G. (2003). Long-term effects and cost effectiveness of Success for All. *Educational Evaluation and Policy Analysis, 24*(2), 243–266.

Borman, G.D., Hewes, G. M., Overman, L. T., & Brown, S. (2003) Comprehensive school reform and achievement: A meta-analysis. *Review of Educational Research, 73*(2), 125–230.

Borman, G. D., Stringfield, S. C., & Slavin, R. E. (2001). *Title I: Compensatory education at the crossroads*. Mahwah, NJ: Erlbaum.

Campbell, M., Cousins, E., Farrell, G., Kamii, M., Lam, D., Rugen, L. & Udall, D. (1996). The Expeditionary Learning Outward Bound design. In S. Stringfield, S. Ross, & L. Smith (Eds.), *Bold plans for school restructuring: The New American Schools designs,* 109–138. Mahwah, NJ: Erlbaum.

Chamberlain, A., Daniels, C., Madden, N., & Slavin, R. (2007). A randomized evaluation of the Success for All Middle School reading program. *Middle Grades Research Journal, 2*(1), 1–21.

Comer, J. P., Haynes, N. M. Joyner, E. T., & BenAvie, M. (1996). *Rallying the whole village: The Comer process for reforming education*. New York: Teachers College Press.

Comprehensive School Reform Quality Center (2006a). *CSRQ center report on elementary school comprehensive school reform models (revised)*. Washington, DC: American Institutes for Research.

Comprehensive School Reform Quality Center (2006b). *CSRQ Center report on middle and high school comprehensive school reform models*. Washington DC: American Institutes for Research.

Cook, T. D., Habib, F.-N., Phillips, M., Settersten, R. A., Shagle, S. C., & Degirmencioglu, S.M. (1999). Comer's School Development Program in Prince George's County, Maryland: A theory-based evaluation. *American Educational Research Journal, 36*(3), 543–597.

Cook, T. D., Murphy, R. F., & Hunt, H. D. (2000). Comer's School Development Program in Chicago: A theory-based evaluation. *American Educational Research Journal, 37*(2), 535–597.

Educational Research Service (1998). *Comprehensive models for school improvement: finding the right match and making it work*. Arlington, VA: Author.

Heady, R., & Kilgore, S. (1996). The Modern Red Schoolhouse. In S. Stringfield, S. Ross, & L. Smith (Eds.), *Bold plans for school restructuring: The New American Schools designs,* 139–178. Mahwah, NJ: Erlbaum.

Herman, R. (1999). *An educator's guide to schoolwide reform*. Arlington, VA: Educational Research Service.

Hopfenberg, W. S., Levin, H. M., & Chase, C. (1993). *The Accelerated Schools resource guide*. San Francisco: Jossey-Bass.

Kearns, D. T., & Anderson, J. L (1996). Sharing the vision: creating New American Schools. In S. Stringfield, S. Ross, & L. Smith (Eds.) *Bold plans for school restructuring: The New American Schools,* 9–24. Mahwah, NJ: Erlbaum.

Levin, H. M. (1987). Accelerated schools for disadvantaged students. *Educational Leadership, 44*(6), 19–21.

May, H., Supovitz, J. A., & Perda, D. (2004). *A longitudinal study of the impact of America's Choice on student performance in Rochester, New York, 1998–2003*. Philadelphia: Consortium for Policy Research in Education.

McLaughlin, M.W. (1990). The Rand change agent study revisited: Macro perspectives and micro realities. *Educational Researcher, 19*(9), 11–16.

Millsap, M. A., Chase, A., Obeidallah, D., Perez-Smith, A., & Brigham, N. (2002) *Evaluation of Detroit's Comer schools and family initiative. Final report*. Cambridge, MA: Abt Associates.

National Center for Education and the Economy (2003). *America's Choice: Program overview*. Washington, DC: Author. Retrieved April 16, 2008, from http://www.ncee.org/acsd.

Slavin, R. E. (in press). Comprehensive school reform. In C. Ames, D. Berliner, J. Brophy, L. Corno, & M. McCaslin (Eds.), *21st Century Education: A Reference Handbook*. Thousand Oaks, CA: Sage.

Slavin, R. E., & Madden, N. A. (Eds.) (2001). *One million children: Success for all*. Thousand Oaks, CA: Corwin.

Slavin, R. E., Madden, N. A., Dolan, L. J., & Wasik, B. A. (1994). Roots & Wings: Inspiring academic excellence. *Educational Leadership, 52*(3), 10–13.

Stringfield, S., Ross, S., & Smith, L. (Eds.) (1996). *Bold plans for school restructuring: The New American Schools designs*. Mahwah, NJ: Erlbaum.

Supovitz, J., Poglinco, S., & Snyder, B. (2001). *Moving mountains: Successes and challenges of the America's Choice comprehensive school reform design.* Philadelphia: Consortium for Policy Research in Education.

Supovitz, J., Taylor, B., & May, H. (2002). *Impact of America's Choice on student performance in Duval County, Florida.* Philadelphia: Consortium for Policy Research in Education.

Robert E. Slavin

CONCEPT DEVELOPMENT

Whether finding a classroom, meeting a new teacher, learning to add, or reading a story, children understand the world through their concepts. Concepts are crucial for understanding the world because they represent current experiences as belonging to a category of similar experiences. By having a concept chair, a student who sees a new chair at his desk need not re-discover whether it is alive, whether he should write with it or sit on it, or what the teacher means by "take your seat" when pointing at the new chair. In this way, the concept of chairs—rather the sight of a particular chair—allows the mapping of an open-ended number of appropriate reactions and inferences about chairs onto an open-ended number of particular chairs.

Central concept acquisition is key to cognitive development, and children learn actually many concepts. The most conservative estimate of children's concepts would be the number of words for which they know the meaning—roughly 40,000 by age 10 and 60,000 by age 19, which over the first two decades of life is roughly one new concept every 90 waking minutes (Anglin, 1993; Bloom, 2000; Miller, 1996). In truth, this figure radically underestimates the rate of concept acquisition because words often denote separate concepts (e.g., the mole found in the ground is not the same mole found working for an intelligence agency), and many concepts are expressed in word-combinations (bunk bed, riverbed, flowerbed), in predicates (e.g., old enough to run for president), and in morphemes (e.g., -*ed* in the English past tense or -*s* in the English plural). Further, judging from non-human animals', infants', and languageless adults' performance on learning and memory tasks, many non-verbal concept-like representations (subject, agency, action, cause, consequence, more/less, near/far) appear to exist in absence of language (Fodor, 1975; Furth, 1966; Hauser, 2000; Spelke, 1994). Clearly, even the most ambitious adult could not teach children even a small portion of the concepts that they actually acquire by age 10.

As might be expected, then, most concepts are learned not through direct instruction but through children's experiences. As they encounter the who, what, where, when, why, how, and how many of everyday events, children accumulate information about categories of people, objects, locations, time, causes, functions, and numbers. Although development of concepts pertaining to each of these categories deserves special treatment, certain common trends have also emerged. Three general trends in conceptual development are described below.

WEIGHTING DEFINING FEATURES

First, children increasingly weight defining features of nominal kinds. Although it is difficult for most adults (and even dictionaries) to list necessary and sufficient features for natural kind concepts such as *oak, octopus,* and *onyx,* adults find it easier to define nominal kind concepts, such as *odd number, uncle,* and *island.* Unlike natural kind concepts, nominal kind concepts follow simple rules, for example, "A number is odd if and only if it is not evenly divisible by two" (Schwartz, 1977). Development of nominal kind concepts was particularly interesting to developmental psychologists because concepts presented such a straightforward test of Vygotsky's idea that "grouping of objects on the basis of maximum similarity is superseded by grouping on the basis of a single attribute" (1986, pp. 136–137) and of Piaget's idea that children's initial categories group things on the basis of accidental rather than essential features (Inhelder & Piaget, 1964).

To test this idea, Keil (1989) presented children with descriptions of nominal kinds that lacked defining features of the category but possessed characteristic features or that lacked the characteristic features of the category but possessed the defining features. For example, when testing children's concept of *island,* Keil found that kindergartners typically said that a "place that sticks out of land like a finger" with coconut trees and palm trees was an island—despite lacking defining features of an island, whereas a "place that is surrounded with water on all sides" and covered in snow was not an island—despite possessing defining features of an island. In contrast, second graders typically recognized that palm trees and snow were inessential characteristics of islands and based their judgment of island-hood strictly on the defining features. Moreover, Keil found this age-difference across most of the nominal kind concepts tested, with young children variously averring that "pancakes can't be lunch" (even if eaten at noon) and that 2-year-olds cannot be uncles (even if brothers of somebody's mother).

Although the "characteristic-to-defining features shift" is an important trend in development of nominal kind concepts, subsequent research showed that the shift does not accompany qualitative changes in conceptual representation that Vygotsky and Piaget theorized. First, although adults' knowledge of definitions might allow them to categorize atypical category members (e.g., whales as mammals; Armstrong et al., 1983), even adults can be swayed by characteristic features for conjunctive concepts. For example, definitions imply propositions like "Rover is a dog-and-pet [the conjunctive concept] because Rover has the defining features of dogs and pets." Yet, when making judgments about conjunctives, adults typically weight characteristic over defining features (e.g., judging chess as a game-and-sport but not a sport; Hampton, 1997). Also, even 5-year-olds make surprisingly philosopher-worthy judgments regarding such moral concepts as *lying* and *stealing* (e.g., by recognizing that a boy unpopular for his goodness is still lying when he pretends—uncharacteristically—to be bad; Keil, 1989). These observations are not consistent with Vygotsky's and Piaget's broader claims about conceptual development.

SENSITIVITY TO STATISTICAL STRUCTURE

Second, children become increasingly sensitive to the statistical structure of the environment. By their nature, concepts store information about correlations among features, and for good reason: Features well correlated with a category are more reliable cues to category-membership (e.g., wagging tail, furry, barking are correlated with dogs) than features that are not well correlated with the category (e.g., brown-colored is not very well correlated with being a dog since many non-dogs are brown and many dogs are not brown). Barking, for example, would have higher *cue validity* than being brown-colored, and sensitivity to this cue validity would allow recognition of category-membership most reliably. This principle applies to natural and nominal kind concepts. For example, being older-than-2-years-old would not be a feature of uncle because many non-uncles are older-than-2-years-old.

Children of all ages (even infants) are sensitive to the statistical distribution of features over natural categories (Quinn & Eimas, 1996; Rosch et al., 1976), and this fact explains many aspects about infants' perceptual categories and older children's concepts. For example, basic-level categories (dog, table, and car) possess features with higher cue validities than both superordinate categories (animal, furniture, and vehicles), which have few features in common, and subordinate categories (collie, coffee-table, and Corvette), which have many features in common with contrasting subordinate categories (Rosch et al., 1976). This is important for conceptual development: Children learn basic-level categories most easily (Horton & Markman, 1980), learn names of basic-level categories earlier than names of superordinate and subordinate categories (Anglin, 1977), are most likely to interpret novel words as basic level categories (Callanan, 1989), and are most likely to generalize novel properties over basic level categories (Gelman & O'Reilly, 1988). Further,

category-members differ in the number of features that have high cue validity for that concept, with prototypical category-members having the most such features. For example, robins are more prototypical birds than are ostriches because robins fly and flight has high cue validity for the bird category. Again, this difference in cue validity is important in the development of category recognition, with younger children typically claiming that robins are birds (but ostriches are not). Older children and adults show a similar effect of cue validity: robins are recognized as birds more quickly than ostriches (Rips et al., 1973). Finally, even infants as young as 3 months can rapidly form category prototypes from brief experiences with novel categories (Bomba & Siqueland, 1983), and adults judge even abstract categories to have prototypical members (e.g., judging 7 a better example of "odd number" than 23; Armstrong et al., 1983).

Although infants and young children are initially quite sensitive to the statistical distribution of many features, much of the statistical structure of the world passes beneath their notice and requires intervention by adult experts. This is especially true of features that are not perceived, either because the feature is perceptible in principle but not in actuality (e.g., because it is too subtle to notice, too small, or too far away) or because the feature is abstract and not even perceptible in principle (e.g., the fairness of a rule, the truth of a statement, or the product of two quantities). Toddlers notoriously overlook subtle properties (such as wicks on candles) when categorizing objects, unless an experimenter explains how the property correlates with its function (Tversky & Hemenway, 1984; Banigan & Mervis, 1988).

The ability to notice correlations among imperceptible properties is especially important in mathematical and scientific reasoning. For example, although children cannot see the movement of plants (because they move too slowly to be perceived), knowing abstractly that plants move helps older children realize that plants are living things like animals (Opfer & Gelman, 2001; Opfer & Siegler, 2004). One cannot directly perceive torque (the product of the weight of an object and its distance from the fulcrum), yet torque tells us which of two sides of a balance beam will go down, and sensitivity to the correlation between torque and balance increases quite dramatically with age and education (Siegler, 1976). Finally, many features are relative (e.g., having more bristles than eyes), and when learning artificial categories, recognition of cue validity of relative features improves with development (Sloutsky, Kloos, & Fisher, 2007).

SENSITIVITY TO CAUSAL STRUCTURE

Third, children become increasingly sensitive to the causal structure of the environment. Beyond representing information about the statistical structure of the world, concepts also retain information about causal structure. Children do not simply know that birds build nests and can fly and have feathers and are bird-offspring, they also know that birds build nests because they can fly, can fly because they have feathers, and have feathers because they are bird-offspring. Acquiring causal information is important for learning, memory and generalization (Murphy & Medin, 1985).

Children show early evidence of their sensitivity to the causal structure of the environment, allowing them to better learn and remember categories. Provided with a causal theory explaining how the features of fictitious animals were related to their behaviors (e.g., "wugs need armor for fighting" and "gillies need big ears for hiding"), 4-year-olds better remembered the feature/category associations than those who only learned that wugs have armor and gillies have big ears but not why (Krascum & Andrews, 1998). The implication is that children provided with causal information explaining why features co-occur remember categories better than if they have only learned what features co-occur.

Older children become increasingly sensitive to the relative importance of causal similarities. In one study, preschoolers were asked to label, infer novel properties, and project future appearances of a novel animal that varied in two opposite respects: (1) how much it looked like another animal whose name and properties were known, and (2) how much its parents looked like parents of another animal whose name and properties were known. When origins were known, preschoolers generalized to animals with similar origins rather than with similar appearances; when origins were unknown, preschoolers generalized to animals with similar appearance. Results imply that preschoolers actively choose the similarities that best predict accurate generalization (Opfer & Bulloch, 2007). This ability also improves over time. For example, when told that "pizers" have "blickem" in their blood that causes them to have small lungs and purple skin, 9-year-olds are more likely to use causal features, such as "blickem," to judge category membership than to use an effect, such as purple skin or small lungs (Ahn et al., 2000).

Sensitivity to the causal structure of the world also leads children to hold essentialist beliefs, that is, an idea that categories in the world are based on a true nature that gives an object its identity (Gelman, 2003). These essentialist beliefs can be helpful in leading preschoolers to realize that a pig's insides are more like that of a cow than a piggy bank (Gelman & Wellman, 1991). However, they can also lead to mistaken beliefs about an underlying true nature for social groups and genders (Heyman & Gelman, 2000; Gelman, Collman & Maccoby, 1986).

At times, young children express funny beliefs that can take them many years to overcome, such as the notion that "pancakes can't be lunch", that "plants are not alive," and that pink barrettes can turn a boy into a girl. From these examples, it is tempting to think that children's concepts differ qualitatively from those of adults. Errors such as these can be viewed instead as part of continuous trends in conceptual development, a process that neither begins nor ends at the driveway of their schoolhouse.

SEE ALSO *Concept Learning.*

BIBLIOGRAPHY

Ahn, W., Gelman, S. A., Amsterlaw, J. A., Hohenstein, J., & Kalish, C. W. (2000). Causal status effect in children's categorization. *Cognition, 76*(2), B35–B43.

Anglin, J. M. (1977). *Word, object, and conceptual development.* New York: Norton.

Anglin, J. M. (1993). Vocabulary development: A morphological analysis. *Monographs of the society for research in child development, 238*(58) 10.

Armstrong, S., Gleitman, L., & Gleitman, H. (1983). What some concepts might not be. *Cognition, 13*(3), 263–308.

Banigan, R. L., & Mervis, C. B. (1988). Role of adult input in young children's category evolution: II An experimental study. *Journal of child language, 15*(3), 493–504.

Bloom, P. (2000). *How children learn the meaning of words.* Cambridge, MA: MIT Press.

Bomba, P. C., & Siqueland, E. R. (1983). The nature and structure of infant from categories. *Journal of Experimental Child Psychology, 35,* 294–328.

Callanan, M. A. (1989). Development of object categories and inclusion relations: Preschoolers; hypotheses about word meanings. *Developmental Psychology 25*(2), 207–16.

Eimas, P. D., & Quinn, P. C. (1994). Studies on the formation of perceptually based basic-level categories in young infants. *Child Development, 65*(3), 903–917.

Fodor, J. A. (1975). *The language of thought.* New York: Crowell.

Furth, H. G. (1966). *Thinking without Language. Psychological implications of deafness.* New York: Free Press.

Gelman, S. A. (2003). *The essential child: Origins of essentialism in everyday thought.* New York: Oxford University Press.

Gelman, S. A., & Markman, E. M. (1986). Categories and induction in young children. *Cognition, 23*(3), 183–209.

Gelman, S. A., & O'Reilly, A. W. (1988). Children's inductive inferences within superordinate categories: The role of language and category structure. *Child Development, 59*(4), 876–887.

Gelman, S. A., & Wellman, H. M. (1991). Insides and essences: early understandings of the non-obvious. *Cognition 38*(3), 213–44.

Gelman, S. A., Collman, P., & Maccoby, E. E. (1986). Inferring properties from categories versus inferring categories from properties: The case of gender. *Child Development, 57*(2), 396–404.

Hampton, J.A. (1997) Associative and similarity-based processes in categorization decisions. *Memory and Cognition, 25*(6), 625–640.

Hauser, M. (2000). *Wild minds: What animals really think.* New York: Holt.

Heyman, G. D., & Gelman, S. A. (2000). Preschool children's use of novel predicates to make inductive inferences about people. *Cognitive Development, 15*(3), 263–280.

Horton, M. S., & Markman, E. M. (1980). Developmental differences in the acquisition of basic and superordinate categories. *Child Development, 51*(3), 708–719.

Inhelder, B., & Piaget, J. (1964). *The early growth of logic in the child.* New York: Norton.

Keil, F. (1989). *Concepts, kinds and cognitive development.* Cambridge, MA: MIT Press.

Krascum, R. M., & Andrews, S. (1998). The effects of theories on children's acquisition of family-resemblance categories. *Child Development, 69*(2), 333–346.

Mervis, C., & Crisafi, M. (1982). Order of acquisition of subordinate-, basic- and superordinate-level categories. *Child Development, 53*(1), 258–266.

Miller, G. A. (1996). *The science of words* (Rev. ed.). New York: Freeman.

Murphy, G., & Medin, D. (1985). The role of theories in conceptual coherence. *Psychological Review, 92*(3), 289–316.

Opfer, J. E., & Bulloch, M. J. (2007). Causal relations drive young children's induction. *Cognition, 105*(1), 206–217.

Opfer, J. E., & Gelman, S. A. (2001). Children's and adults' models for predicting teleological action: The development of a biology-based model. *Child Development 72*(5), 1367–1381.

Opfer, J. E., & Siegler, R. S. (2004). Revisiting preschoolers' living things concept: A microgenetic analysis of conceptual change in basic biology. *Cognitive Psychology, 49*(4), 301–332.

Quinn, P. C., & Eimas, P. D. (1996). Perceptual organization and categorization in young infants. *Advances in Infancy Research 10,* 1–36.

Quinn, P. C., Eimas, P. D., & Rosenkrantz, S. L. (1993). Evidence for representations of perceptually similar natural categories by 3- and 4-month-old infants. *Perception, 22,* 463–475.

Rips, L. J., Shoben, E. J., & Smith, E. E. (1973). Semantic distance and the effect of semantic relations. *Journal of Verbal Learning and Verbal Behavior 12*(1), 1–20.

Rosch, E., & Mervis, C. B. (1975). Family resemblances: Studies in the internal structure of categories. *Cognitive Psychology, 7*(4), 573–605.

Rosch E., Mervis, C. B., Gray, W. D., Johnson, D., and Boyes-Braem, P. (1976). Basic objects in natural categories. *Cognitive Psychology, 8*(3), 382–439.

Schwartz, S. P. (1977). *Naming, necessity, and natural kinds.* Ithaca, NY: Cornell University Press.

Siegler, R. S. (1976). Three aspects of cognitive development. *Cognitive Psychology, 8*(4), 481–520.

Sloutsky, V. M., Kloos, H., & Fisher, A. V. (2007). When looks are everything: Appearance similarity versus kind information in early induction. *Psychological Science 18*(2), 179–185.

Spelke, E. S. (1994). Initial knowledge: Six suggestions. *Cognition, 50*(11), 431–445.

Tversky, B., & Hemenway, K. (1984). Objects, parts, and categories. *Journal of Experimental Psychology: General 113*(2), 169–97.

Vygotsky, L. (1986). *Thought and language.* Cambridge, MA: MIT Press. (Originally published in 1934).

John E. Opfer
Megan J. Bulloch

CONCEPT LEARNING

A concept is the way in which a category or class of objects is represented mentally. Concepts allow individuals to discern class membership or non-membership, relate different classes of objects, and provide context for learning new information about classes and class membership. There is wide debate about the way in which categories and classes are mentally represented and defined. The way in which concepts are learned can depend on the age of the learner, whether or not explicit instructions are provided, and the type of category or class the concept represents.

TYPES OF CONCEPTS

Concepts can be learned about categories that include people, events, objects, or even ideas. Various divisions have been made between different types of concepts. Concepts can be divided into groups based on the concreteness of the items involved. Concrete concepts have aspects or dimensions that are easily seen, heard, or touched. Examples of concrete concepts include fruit, dogs, and houses. Concepts can also be categorized as semi-concrete. Semi-concrete concepts are those which are have roughly equal aspects that are concrete and not concrete. An example of a semi-concrete concept is a firefighter. The concept firefighter is defined along some concrete terms, such as wears a fire hat, and along some less concrete terms such as risks his or her life, and protects the public. Concepts that are not easily comprehended with the senses are abstract concepts. Abstract concepts include justice, freedom, and love. These concepts are often the most difficult to explain and have the most complex rules or explanations for determination. Abstract concepts are often very difficult for younger children, and as development progresses, increasingly complex abstract concepts are mastered.

Other differentiations can also be made between different types of concepts. Some concepts are natural concepts. Natural concepts are those that occur in the environment naturally without human intervention. This type of concept includes water, eggs, and monkeys.

THEORIES ABOUT CONCEPTS

There are many different theories about how concepts are learned, what information people have when they have mastered a concept, and how information about new items is related to previously learned concepts.

The Classical View. The classical view of concepts is based on the idea that concepts are defined by lists of rules. It is the first view on record about the idea of concepts, and dates back to Aristotle (384–322 BCE). Each concept is believed to be defined by a list of relevant rules or characteristics, all of which are necessary for the object or instance to be a member of that category or class. For instance, the concept "mug," includes the rule "is able to hold water," meaning that a mug must necessarily be able to hold water in order or be classified as a mug. All of the rules taken together that govern a category are sufficient to make something identifiable as a member of that category or class.

The view of concepts as defined by relevant necessary characteristics was the main basis for thought and research about categorization and category learning until the 1950s. At that time, cognitive psychologists and philosophers began to question whether it was a good representation of the way people actually think about categories, especially when they are using them to make judgments in daily life. In the 1970s a series of studies was done, many by Eleanor Rosch, that demonstrated that people did not hold lists of attributes when deciding category membership. Instead, she found that individuals had a mental picture or belief about what made up an example of a member of a class, not a list of well-defined rules (Rosch & Mervis 1975).

Prototype Theory. The prototype idea of concept learning was built on the research done by Rosch and her colleagues. Central to this idea is the concept of a prototype that exists as the ideal example of each category or class for which a concept has been learned. A prototype is an object or item that is the most typical of that concept. There is some debate about whether the prototype is a real example that has been seen or experienced, or it if is an amalgamation of various examples of the concept. If it is an abstract amalgamation it can actually be seen as being more typical of a concept than any actual instance of that concept could be. To determine category membership or non-membership of novel items, each new item is compared with the prototype and the degree of similarity reviewed. Proponents of the prototype theory also often believe that information about examples are organized as being more or less similar to the prototype.

A fairly broad body of evidence developed in the 1970s and afterward in support of the prototype theory. Studies found that participants responded faster to questions about category membership when the item in question was a more typical member of the category than when it was not (McCloskey & Glucksberg, 1979). For example, participants would have responded more quickly to the question, "Is an oak a tree?" than to the question, "Is a bonsai a tree?" Although the developing evidence supported the prototype theory much more strongly than the classical theory, some problems with prototype theory became apparent. Researchers began to find that participants judged items to be more typical of a category in some situations than in others, which prototype theory had difficulty explaining. Also, prototype theory did not explain

cases in which an item was very typical of a certain category but was identified as a member of a different category of which it was less typical. For example, although cottage cheese is more typical of pudding than cheese, it is clearly categorized as a cheese.

Exemplar Theory. The exemplar theory of concept learning states that specific examples of concepts are learned, instead of a generalized or prototypical example or a list of specific required characteristics. Proponents of this view believe that although not every example that an individual comes across is stored in the memory, many examples are retained. In this way novel items or circumstances can be compared to examples that are stored in the memory. Novel items that are not similar to any of the stored exemplars are therefore very difficult for people to put into any specific category. Some people believe that the more typical of a category a specific example is, the more likely it is to be stored as an exemplar of that category.

The exemplar view explains many of the results found during research on concept learning and categorization. As discussed above, participants tend to respond more quickly when asked about the category membership of items that are typical of the category in question. This is because these items are more likely to be stored exemplars or more similar to stored exemplars. The exemplar theory also has problems explaining some things. It is not clear how many exemplars are stored or how the determination of storage is made. Another objection frequently raised is that it requires that individuals store many different exemplars for each concept, taking up vast quantities of long-term memory, more so than a single prototype would require.

ACQUIRING CONCEPTS

Views on how people acquire concepts are guided in large part by which theory of concept determination is believed. Research on acquisition of concepts is often seemingly contradictory because individuals use different types of strategies depending on the situation, the type of information involved, and any beliefs about what the structure of the underlying concept is. Concept acquisition is probably a complex process with a number of strategies available depending on the perceived situation.

When individuals are trying to form a concept, and feedback is given about group membership or non-membership, the individuals tend to form and test hypotheses. J. S. Bruner and his colleagues did significant work on this in 1956, examining the way that participants tried to identify a concept provided by the researchers. The participants chose cards and were told whether each card chosen was a member of the group or not. All the participants formed hypotheses and then tested them, but the strategy to achieve this differed across participants. Some participants picked a card that was a member of the group and then tested cards that differed by it in only one respect to determine which aspects of the cards were critical and which were not. Other participants created complex hypotheses and then chose cards that would test the most attributes at once. A third set of participants formed a number of hypotheses but tested them one at a time (Bruner et al., 1956).

Although the above strategies may work when individuals are given feedback about each successive item, this is not particularly likely to occur in day-to-day life. Instead, other strategies for concept acquisition must be used. When individuals have to determine two categories and then assign novel items to one category or the other, different strategies may be used. According to the classical theory, individuals would create a set of rules for each category that were necessary and sufficient for group membership and then apply those rules to each new item. According to the prototype theory, individuals would form a prototype for each category by examining as many of the example items as possible, and then classify novel examples by comparing them to the two prototypes and determining similarity. According to the exemplar theory, examples from each of the two categories would be memorized, and then novel items would be compared to the memorized exemplars for similarity.

The research indicates that individuals use a variety of these approaches, and that no one approach is completely correct. It appears that the various approaches serve different functions, and may be found to be more effective in different situations. Students use a variety of these techniques as different educational concepts are learned. In some cases the expectation of concept formation is made clear and regular feedback is received, in which case the student may be more likely to use hypothesis generation and testing. In other cases the formation of a prototype may appear to be the most effective method for concept attainment. In some cases, especially when the criteria are dictated by the educator, the classical view may be used. In some cases, especially if the student is not completely clear on the underlying concept, exemplars may be memorized to aide in class membership determination.

TEACHING CONCEPTS

There are many different ways in which concepts can be taught, and there is some debate about which methods are the most effective. In general, methods differ depending on the desired outcome of the educational experience, the age of the learner, and the difficulty or abstractness of the concept being taught.

The most basic way of teaching concepts is by determining a rule or set of rules for the concept and having the students memorize them. The students can then apply the memorized rule or rules when prompted to make decisions about class membership of novel items. Although this does achieve some objectives of concept learning (i.e., allowing the student to make judgments about class membership), it does not necessarily provide a solid foundation for comparing the concept to previously learned concepts, a basis for learning new concepts, or a strong likelihood that the rule will be applied in novel situations when the student is not prompted.

To provide students with a more solid understanding of the concept, additional information is often useful. Students can be provided with items that are similar to the concept but that differ on one or more dimensions, making them non-members of the category in question. For example, the concept "peninsula" may be defined as "a body of land surrounded by water on three sides." Relevant examples, such as Florida, may be shown to help give the concept a visual dimension. To achieve more complete student mastery of the concept, students and the educator can discuss what makes other similar items non-members of the class. For example, an island is not a peninsula because it is completely surrounded by water instead of only on three sides. Students can also be shown members of the concept that differ significantly but are still category members, such as the Korean peninsula and a small, local peninsula. Although Florida, the Korean peninsula, and small local peninsulas differ drastically in size and location, they are all members of the category "peninsula." This can help students create a rich and complex understanding of the concept being studied.

An alternative to teaching concepts through memorization of rules provided by the educator is a more student-centered, hands-on approach. This approach may be more helpful when teaching concepts that do not have simple definitions to older students with more advanced critical thinking skills. Having students decide on the defining characteristics or most ideal examples of a class or category can provide an understanding of a concept deeper than that provided by memorization. Students may be provided with a number of examples of members of a category or class and then be prompted to vocalize their reasoning in categorizing those examples. For more abstract concepts, such as "justice," or "freedom," students can be prompted to think critically and debate between themselves why some examples are members of the class when other seemingly similar examples are not. Additionally, the teacher may provide new examples, and the students can discuss where they believe the examples fit, and why they classify them in that way.

PROBLEMS IN CONCEPT LEARNING

Many concepts are a challenge to learn, and are learned slowly as more examples and rules are integrated and information is sorted into more straightforward units. All students learn concepts at different rates, and a student who demonstrates mastery of one concept very quickly may find another particularly challenging. However, some students have more than the expected amount of difficulty learning concepts. Students with learning disabilities often have an especially difficult time learning concepts. Although the degree of difficulty and the types of concepts that commonly present problems differ depending on the learning disability, the degree of disability, and the individual child, some problems are common. Basic math concepts, time concepts including time sequencing, and reading concepts are especially likely to present significant challenges. Students with such problems learning concepts may benefit from additional educational strategies to help prevent the student falling behind as additional information and concepts are built upon concepts that were not completely mastered.

Children and adolescents often bring a lot of information into the classroom. Unfortunately, information gathered through life and experiences outside the classroom is not always completely accurate. Many children have previously conceived notions of concepts before being exposed to them in a classroom setting. When mastering a concept in the classroom involves conceptual change, that is replacing a previously held concept with a new one, students can encounter unexpected difficulties. It is important to identify situations in which previously held concepts are at conflict with the concept being taught, because different educational strategies may be appropriate.

Much of the literature about the difficulties encountered in conceptual change has involved the sciences. This is because students often have ideas about natural phenomena, such as what causes rain, and why it is dark at night, before learning about them in school. In these situations educator-led investigation and discussion may not be the most effective road to concept learning. This is because it may be difficult for students who believe they understand something to think outside that understanding or to accept different ideas presented by other students. In this case, teacher-provided rules and critical criteria can help a student overcome a previously believed, but incorrect, concept. Teaching conceptual change can also be accomplished by discussing student preconceptions about a concept, discussing evidence contrary to the preconceived concept, and guiding the student through a changing understanding to mastery of the correct concept.

SEE ALSO *Concept Development.*

BIBLIOGRAPHY

Barton, M. E. & Komatsu, L. K. (1989). Defining features of natural kinds and artifacts. *Journal of Psycholinguistic Research, 18,* 433–447.

Bruner, J. S., Goodnow, J. J. & Austin, G. A. (1956). *A study of thinking.* New York: Wiley.

Haygood, R. C. (1975). *Concept learning.* Morristown, NJ: General Learning Press.

McCloskey, M. & Glucksberg, S. (1979). Decision processes in verifying category membership statements: Implications for models of semantic memory. *Cognitive Psychology, 11,* 1–37.

Merrill, D. M., Tennyson, R. D. & Posey, L. O. (1992). *Teaching concepts: An instructional design guide.* Englewood Cliffs, NJ: Educational Technology Publications.

Rosch, E. & Lloyd, B. B. (Eds.). (1978). *Cognition and categorization.* Hillsdale, NJ: Erlbaum.

Rosch, E. & Mervis, C. B. (1975). Family resemblances: Studies in the internal structure of categories. *Cognitive Psychology, 7,* 573–605.

Helen Davidson

CONCEPT MAPS

Concept mapping is the technique used by individuals and groups to organize, represent, and visualize knowledge and ideas in graphical formats. It is used to develop a structured framework in order to plan or evaluate various types and sizes of projects. Sometimes called knowledge maps, the graphical technique is based on graphically describing topics within one concept and/or relationships found among different concepts.

The diagram used to visualize these relationships among various concepts is called a *concept map.* Within a concept map, networks are drawn that consist of nodes, which represent concepts. Connecting lines, or links, represent a particular relationship between two concepts. Linking words, phrases, and symbols, used to describe relationships between nodes, often appear on the links.

Concept maps are generally, but not always, created so they are read from the top downward. Some concept maps are simple designs that examine one central theme and only a few associated topics. Other concept maps contain complex structures that describe multiple themes and relationships.

HISTORICAL BACKGROUND

The concept map is a relatively new way to visualize complex subject matter. The technique of concept mapping was first developed in the 1960s and 1970s by American educator and research scientist Joseph D. Novak (1930–) while at Cornell University, in Ithaca, New York. During this time, Novak, a professor of education and biological sciences, developed an effective way to strengthen the process for his students performing research. Novak discovered that representing thoughts visually often helped students to effectively associate ideas without being inconvenienced by writing them down in lengthy formats. His students, Novak found, could represent newly learned information by first defining a concept, adding related topics, and linking similar ideas. Such an arrangement helped to organize research information and formulate educational theses.

Novak's work was based on the cognitive learning theory first developed by educational psychologist David Ausube in the 1960s. Also known as the theory of meaningful learning and assimilation theory, Ausube's theory became a tool for structuring information in an easy-to-recognize way. He found that students learned new material based on prior knowledge. According to Ausube, by visualizing past knowledge, students were better able to control the learning process and, consequently, learned new information faster and more efficiently.

The concept map itself is founded in a learning theory called constructivism, which states that humans learn from previously acquired knowledge. Swiss developmental psychologist Jean Piaget (1896–1980) is generally recognized as the first scientist to formalize constructivism into scientific structure.

Later, the theory of concept mapping developed by Novak, and first published in 1977, helped to guide educational research and instruction. Since that time, concept mapping has been widely applied to science, education, business, and government.

COMPONENTS OF NETWORKS

There are several components used when teaching and applying concept mapping. The concept map is generally represented in a defined order, with members arranging parts of the concept map according to a pre-determined ranking. The more general concepts are usually positioned at the top, and the more specific concepts, along with examples, images, and other describers, placed underneath. Networks are drawn, consisting of *nodes* usually enclosed in boxes but also represented by points, circles, or other figures. Nodes represent various concepts, with a concept defined as a perceived regularity in, or record of, some event or object.

Nodes are joined together with *connecting lines,* or links, which represent a particular relationship between two concepts. Nodes are always labeled, while links are usually labeled. Links can be nondirectional (with no arrows), unidirectional (with an arrow at one end), or bidirectional (with an arrow at both ends).

Linking words, phrases, and symbols are used to demonstrate the relationship or connection between concepts. Besides words and phrases, symbols such as +, -, and = are sometimes used. A *proposition* is the term used when two or more concepts are connected with linking lines and linking words, phrases, or symbols to form a meaningful statement.

Cross-links are long connections, which consist of connecting lines with linking words, phrases, and symbols, between concepts in different themes (domains) of the concept map. Cross-links are usually used to help identify how various domains are related.

VARIETY OF CONCEPT MAPS

Three types of concept maps are generally recognized by professionals who have researched and developed the theory behind concept mapping. *Spider concept maps* place the main topic in the center of the map and related themes are linked around it—thus, the map is shaped like a spider's body with its many legs. Spider concept maps are often developed when only one concept is being used. For instance, a single node might state "National Football League" and linked around it could be the various teams of the NFL.

Hierarchical concept maps place the most general, or most important, concept at the top of the map and the more specific, or less important but related, topics below it. For instance, the most important concept contained in a specific hierarchical concept map might be "Sally Ride," and below it the specific, but related, topics of "astronaut," "physicist," "writer," and "businesswoman."

Flow chart concept maps represent a sequence or a process in a linear format. Flow charts are frequently used in businesses and organizations to analyze the steps involved in completing tasks. For instance, a computer manufacturing company might use a flow chart concept map as a guide to assembling its laptops, using such terms as "motherboard," "graphics card," and "hard drive." Alternatively, mathematicians often use flow chart concept maps when analyzing a complicated mathematical equation.

RESEARCH IN SUPPORT

Concept mapping is designed to help students and others clear up ambiguities and clarify misconceptions in information (which often arise in the learning process), along with strengthening the memory and retention process after the learning is accomplished. Such improvements in education with the use of concept maps have been proven by scientific studies.

When performing such scientific studies, researchers want to ask a multitude of questions relating to concept mapping. Some of these questions include: What aspects of achievement and learning can be bettered? How much improvement can be achieved? How do these improvements compare with other approaches? Do all students (including special needs students) benefit? How do different grade levels compare in their benefits? Do gender, racial, socioeconomic and other differences affect the benefits? Do students and educators like or dislike the process? And how much training is necessary for implementation?

Research scientists have found that concept mapping is very effective in educational settings. The use of concept maps was reported in studies to have the largest positive effect at the university level; however, modest and consistent improvements were also seen at the elementary, middle school, and high school levels.

Numerous studies have found that students with and without disabilities benefit equally from concept mapping. For instance, improvements in verbal and written abilities, reading and comprehension abilities, and other such capacities were increased when students with learning disabilities used concept mapping.

In addition, research studies have found that the use of concept maps during reading lessons early in the educational life of a student were exceptionally beneficial. Other areas in which researchers found a positive correlation between the use of concept maps and educational learning include science, social studies, mathematics, and language arts. Using concept maps to learn mathematics, for instance, was found very useful in teaching a sometimes-difficult subject.

Besides these specific fields of study, researchers discovered that concept mapping is useful to prepare students for their studies. Such areas as taking notes and organizing question-and-answer responses were shown to work well with concept mapping. Many times researchers found that students took less notes in class but were more effective in learning and retaining the information when they used concept maps.

A study funded by the Office of Special Education Programs, within the U.S. Department of Education, showed a slight but consistent improvement in comprehension and a moderate improvement in vocabulary when students used concept mapping during their general studies. The students were tested using such measures as written summaries, traditional tests, concept acquisition tests, and grammar tests, along with the widely used Stanford Diagnostic Reading Test.

The ability and knowledge of educators to implement concept mapping is important to the process. An 11-year study, for instance, showed that learning results in students were more positive when teachers properly instructed them on the use of concept maps, along with providing realistic, informative, and positive ways to use them. It was also learned that computer-based methods to present concept mapping can be effective for the learning and application of educational materials In addition, searching on the Web was shown to improve students' abilities to develop more detailed and complicated maps.

A paper written in 2006 by Josianna Basque and Marie-Claude Lavoie, of the LICEF Research Center (Montreal, Canada), discussed the conclusions of 39 research studies conducted between the late 1980s and early 2000s. The studies were performed on the theory, methodology, and results of *collaborative concept mapping* (CCM), a process in which students construct concept maps in small groups. Basque and Lavoie's conclusion praised the collaborative learning style of concept maps.

Extensive research has also been conducted supporting the use of concept maps for business and organizational settings. Several classic research papers explain the research performed on the development of concept mapping. Some of these historic articles include "An Introduction to Concept Mapping for Planning and Evaluation," by American social research scientist William Trochim, and "Concept Mapping For Evaluation and Planning," a compilation of articles edited by Trochim.

In addition, the "Concept Mapping Resource Guide" Web site of the Web Center for Social Research Methods provides additional information on many of the important articles written about concept mapping.

Research has found that six general steps are involved in developing and implementing any concept map. Step one, the preparation step, involves the selection of participants and the development of the basic reason for the project. A broad range of people are sometimes involved because their various areas of expertise will be valuable in the development of a complex project. In other groups, a random sampling of people from a total population might be selected. Small groups are more easily managed when developing a concept map, but larger groups may be needed when the complexity of the project is immense.

Statements are discussed and recorded during the second step. Usually a brainstorming session, or other type of idea-generating meeting, is initiated to produce as many statements as possible. Later, during the third step, these statements are ranked and sorted based on the project's requirements. Participants are often asked to distinguish each item as to importance and how likely each item will affect the final conclusion.

The most difficult part in planning or evaluating a project is conceptualization. How well a project is accomplished is often based on how well it is initially organized. Thus, it is important that all members recognize the project's major goals, resources, and capabilities; and place them at levels of most to least important.

In the fourth step, the concept map is physically generated by using symbols, words, phrases, and pictures to represent the statements developed earlier. Each statement is given a position (node) within the developing concept map. Closely related statements are positioned physically nearer to one another than are less related statements.

The interpretation of the concept map is the primary focus in step five. All of the parts of the concept map are grouped, ranked, classified, and generally interpreted for use within the final concept map.

The sixth step involves the utilization of the concept map. It is used as a guide to actually carry out the various details of the project such as planning meetings; developing products, procedures, or services; and assessing results.

Research has found that the use of concept mapping—with its easy-to-read and interpret structure of symbols, pictures, and phrases—helps members to remember the primary mission of the project. Major ideas and concepts are easily visible, making it easier to accomplish goals and coordinate the activities of individuals and the group as a whole.

GLOBAL APPLICATIONS

Concept mapping has been proven to provide meaningful learning in the educational setting by offering clear structure and detailed organization during the process by which students gain knowledge.

Concept mapping does not replace traditional educational systems; it only provides a conduit for better learning, wider discussions, and more positive advancements within those environments. Teachers use concept maps to better assess knowledge gained by their students. Traditional testing, such as with essay, multiple-choice, and fill-in-the-blank questions, is a valuable way to test students.

However, the practice of having students construct concept maps to determine their level and quality of learning has been found to be more effective in showing how well students understand important concepts recently learned. In fact, according to the researchers in the Department of Education at Stanford University, California, teachers and other educators find concept mapping an easy-to-use and effective method for evaluating the progress of their students.

In addition, concept mapping has been found to be conducive to the quantity and quality of material learned based on long-term memory. This relationship is partly based on the work of Australian educational psychologist John Sweller and his cognitive load theory first proposed in the late 1980s. He created the theory based on the research of many earlier scientists including American psychologist George A. Miller from Princeton University, New Jersey.

Sweller stated within his theory that the ability of long-term memory within a person is best when it is not overloaded. He found that long-term memory, when it is

used for problem solving, reasoning, and thinking, is optimized when humans can make clear and direct connections between previously learned materials and newly learned information. Sweller stated it is essential for educators and designers of educational materials not to overload a person's memory with large amounts of information.

Instead, Sweller recommended using smaller segments during the learning process. Concept mapping is ideal for such "piece-work" learning because it helps students to easily make the connection between what was previously learned and what was just learned, and not to forget the information in the future. Concept maps accomplish Sweller's ideas by physically organizing information into small groupings so as not to overload students with too much information at any given time.

Primarily, concept mapping provides for applications within the planning process, the learning process, and the assessment process. Even before students learn material, concept mapping is a valuable tool used by educators to organize the material they want to teach their students during the planning stage. Often, educators have difficulty creating both a comprehensive and an understandable teaching program. However, with concept mapping, they are much more likely to be able to create and implement effective teaching curriculum (including concepts, ideas, and images) that will be communicated more effectively to their students and better comprehended by their students.

During the learning stage, concept mapping is a very important learning tool because it facilitates the learning of material in a meaningful and structured way, by organizing information piece by piece so that it is easy for students to comprehend.

After students learn material, concept mapping is also used to test the learning of students during the assessment stage. It can easily and effectively track, document, and evaluate learning and knowledge gained during the educational process.

More than 40 years of research, development, and application has resulted in the inclusion of concept mapping within many businesses and organizations, large and small, throughout the world. In the United States, Concept Systems, Inc., is one of the leading companies that provide computer software and consulting services in the area of concept mapping. Its clients include national and regional associations, nonprofit organizations, government agencies, and private businesses.

The Web Center for Social Research Methods is an important academic resource in the applied social research and evaluation of concept mapping. It provides introductory materials, research, and case studies involving concept maps.

There are many reasons why concept maps are generated in the first place. They are used within an established business, such as taking simple notes at a department meeting and remembering important concepts at a board of director's meeting. A new business might use concept mapping to identify its employees' knowledge base. Computer programmers often use concept maps to design complicated computer programs, such as for creating Web sites and video games. Large organizations often use concept maps to communicate complex ideas to their employees or to the general public.

Lawyers use concept maps to illustrate arguments on both sides of complex issues. Educators frequently use concept maps to help students learn new material, retain historic material, and integrate the two together. Problem solvers use concept maps to better understand and diagnose problems. A troubled company, for example, might use concept mapping to create a shared direction to improve employee morale or increase its customer base.

BIBLIOGRAPHY

Basque, J., & Lavois, M-C. (2006). *Collaborative concept mapping in education: Major research trends.* Institute for Human and Machine Cognition. Retrieved April 24, 2008, from http://cmc.ihmc.us/cmc2006Papers/cmc2006-p192.pdf.

Birbili, M. (2006). Mapping knowledge: Concept maps in early childhood education. *Early Childhood Research & Practice, 8*(2). Retrieved May 4, 2008, from http://ecrp.uiuc.edu/v8n2/birbili.html.

Concept mapping resources guide. Web Center for Social Research Methods. Retrieved April 16, 2008, from http://www.social researchmethods.net/mapping/mapping.htm.

Concept systems, incorporated. Retrieved April 16, 2007, from http://www.conceptsystems.com/.

Concept-mapping software: How effective is the learning tool in an online learning environment? Department of Education, Stanford University. Retrieved April 16, 2008, from http://www.stanford.edu/dept/SUSE/projects/ireport/articles/concept_maps/Concept MapsOnlineLearningEnvironment.pdf.

Derbentseva, N., Safayeni, F., & Cañas, A. J. (2006). Concept maps: Experiments on dynamic thinking. *Journal of Research in Science Teaching, 44(3)*.

Novak, J. D. (1998). *Learning, creating, and using knowledge: Concept maps as facilitative tools in schools and corporations.* Mahwah, NJ: Erlbaum Associates.

Novak, J. D., & Cañas, A. J. *The theory underlying concept maps and how to construct them.* Pensacola., FL: Florida Institute for Human and Machine Cognition. Retrieved May 6, 2008, from http://cmap.ihmc.us/Publications/ResearchPapers/TheoryCmaps/TheoryUnderlyingConceptMaps.htm.

O'Donnell, A., Dansereau, D., & Hall, R. H. (2002). Knowledge maps as scaffolds for cognitive processing. *Educational Psychology Review, 14,* 71–86.

Preszler, R. W. (2004). Cooperative concept mapping improves performance in biology. *Journal of College Science Teaching, 33,* 30–35.

Strangman, N., Hall, T., & Meyer, A. *Universal design for learning: graphic organizers with UDL.* Center for Applied Special Technology. Retrieved April 16, 2008, from http://www.cast.org/publications/ncac/ncac_goudl.html.

Trochim, W. M. K. *Concept Mapping: An Introduction to Structured Conceptualization.* Web Center for Social Research Methods. Retrieved April 16, 2008, from http://www.social researchmethods.net/mapping/Concept%20Mapping%20 Presentation,%20Jan05.ppt.

Trochim, W. M. K. *An introduction to concept mapping for planning and evaluation.* Web Center for Social Research Methods. Retrieved April 16, 2008, from http://www.socialresearchmethods.net/research/epp1/epp1.htm.

Trochim, W. M. K. *Concept mapping for evaluation and planning.* Web Center for Social Research Methods. Retrieved April 16, 2008, from http://www.socialresearchmethods.net/research/Concept %20Mapping %20for%20Evaluation%20and%20 Planning.PDF.

Web Center for Social Research Methods. Retrieved April 16, 2008, from http://www.socialresearchmethods.net/.

William Arthur Atkins

CONCEPTUAL CHANGE

In representational theories of mind, concepts are mental units that are bearers of meaning and that can be mapped onto single words such as *dog, animal, grow,* and *die.* They are used to form beliefs, such as *Fido is a dog* or *Dogs can die,* guide inference and organize knowledge of the world. Conceptual change occurs when there is change in what these mental units are and how they are articulated within larger conceptual systems. Although there are obviously different degrees of conceptual change, ranging from adding a new concept that fits within an existing conceptual system (e.g., learning about a new type of dog) to changing the organizing principle of an entire classification system (e.g., recognizing species as interbreeding populations of individuals that change over time rather than as unchanging ideal types), the term *conceptual change* has typically been reserved for forms that involve significant restructuring. These changes are notoriously difficult to make because they involve coordinated changes in multiple concepts, rather than simple additions or elaborations. For example, if children say "A lamp is alive," "The Earth is flat," or "This piece of clay weighs nothing at all," they may be expressing beliefs that are true from the perspective of their conceptual systems. Changing their beliefs involves more than telling them they are wrong or providing new information; it involves helping them develop different concepts of the Earth, alive, or weight. An important challenge is to identify cases of learning that involve significant restructuring and to understand how it occurs.

In his influential book, *The Structure of Scientific Revolutions* (1962), Thomas Kuhn (1922–1996) challenged

250

the view of science as the steady accumulation of knowledge by describing the profound shifts in the meaning of concepts that have occurred when scientists have moved from one dominant paradigm to another. He argued that scientists' work is governed by a paradigm shared by members of that community—a complex structure of theory and laws, preferences about instrumentation, and more general assumptions about what kinds of entities exist and what form laws should take—that helps fix the meaning of common vocabulary, as well as provide the rules for problem solving in a given domain. He distinguished between normal science, periods that involve routine puzzle solving for problems defined by a paradigm, and revolutionary science, periods of crisis during which a dominant paradigm fails to solve key problems and is eventually overthrown by a new paradigm that gains allegiance from the community of scientists. The changes in worldview and commitments about what entities exist and how they interact can be so great when scientists switch paradigms that Kuhn argued that members of the community effectively no longer speak the same language.

In the 1980s George Posner and colleagues (1982) brought these ideas of conceptual change to the science education community. Challenging the prevailing model of learning in which students were seen as gradually accumulating new beliefs based on generalizing from observation, he and his colleagues proposed that in learning current scientific theories, students needed to undergo conceptual revolutions that in many ways were analogous to the paradigm shifts Kuhn had identified in the history of science. They called for a new "conceptual change" model of learning that acknowledged the powerful role children's ideas play in observing, defining problems, and making sense of new information. Indeed, researchers were discovering that adolescents brought a wealth of ideas to the science classroom. Many were strongly held ideas that proved to be extremely resistant to instruction, and some resembled earlier theories in the history of science—for example, the impetus theory in mechanics (McCloskey, 1983) or the source-recipient model of heat (Wiser, 1988).

At the same time Susan Carey (1985) brought the ideas of conceptual change to the developmental psychology community. This group was already keenly aware that development involved *qualitative* shifts in children's ideas about number, physical quantities, space, time, mind, and life, thanks to the pioneering work of Bärbel Inhelder (1913–1997) and Jean Piaget (1896–1980). However, there was growing dissatisfaction with Piaget and Inhelder's explanations of these changes in terms of the progressive construction of more powerful *domain-general thinking structures* (i.e., shifts from sensori-motor, to pre-operational, concrete operational and finally formal operational thought) in part because children's

thinking did not show the kinds of consistency expected on these accounts. Carey proposed that it would be more fruitful to think of children's thought as constrained by *domain specific structures* (intuitive theories akin to Kuhnian paradigms). In her view, even preschoolers and elementary school students have implicit intuitive theories in which their everyday explanatory concepts are embedded and play a role, which guide their patterns of inference and problem solving, and which can be fundamentally revised in the face of new information from their culture. Thus, conceptual change came to be seen not only as occurring in mature scientists and students receiving explicit science instruction, but also in younger children in the normal course of their development.

LEARNING CAN INVOLVE CONCEPTUAL CHANGE

Not all aspects of learning or cognitive development involve conceptual change. Much learning fills in the gaps and elaborates on a given conceptual structure rather than radically restructures it. Change may also involve units other than concepts; for example, beliefs, mental models, strategies, and event scripts. Further, not all aspects of cognitive development involve learning; some profound changes may depend primarily on maturational processes.

However, there are now a number of cases in which change does seem to involve a fundamental restructuring of concepts. In each case, researchers have provided detailed analysis of the changing structure of the concepts across two conceptual systems, empirical evidence that children show the kinds of systematicity expected on these analyses, and evidence that learning shows significant resistance to change. These cases span changes that occur for students during the elementary school years to cases that only rarely occur even among college students. Most of the work has focused on science concepts, but there are some well worked out examples in mathematics and other fields. Indeed, in a couple of cases, relevant conceptual changes in science and mathematics may be linked.

One of the first cases examined was children's concept of the Earth. Joseph Nussbaum (1985) found that how children think about the shape of the Earth has implications for their concepts of space and gravity. Initially children think of the Earth as flat, space as bounded, with an absolute up/down orientation, and objects as falling down to earth. As children come to accept that the Earth is a sphere, they re-conceptualize space as unbounded, extending in all directions from the Earth, with gravity acting towards its center. Stella Vosniadou and William Brewer (1992, 1994) extended this analysis by showing how children's initial Earth concept was constrained by the presuppositions of a larger framework theory—a naïve physics in which the Earth was seen as a kind of flat, stationary, physical object. They found that children invent many synthetic models of the Earth (such as the flat disc and dual Earth models) in an attempt to reconcile the new information that the Earth is round with their initial presuppositions. Coming to understand the earth as spherical, moving, and unsupported involves constructing and assigning the Earth to a new ontological category—astronomical object—with distinctive properties; this in turn changes the framework they can use for explaining the causes of day/night or the seasons.

The development of children's concepts of matter, weight, and density is another case that may involve restructuring a network of concepts. Carol Smith (2007) found evidence for an initial conceptual system that uses an undifferentiated concept of weight/density (one that unites the elements heavy and heavy for size) and a later system in which weight and density are fundamentally different kinds of quantities that figure in different generalizations. That is, weight is an extensive quantity whose magnitude varies with the amount of matter, whereas density is an intensive quantity whose magnitude is independent of amount of matter. Movement from conceptual system one to two involves coordinated changes in multiple concepts: representing weight and volume as measured quantities mapped to number rather than as perceptual magnitudes, representing matter as a fundamental constituent that occupies space and has weight rather than something that can be seen, felt, and touched; and coordinating weight and volume in a new concept of density. There was evidence of coherency in reasoning patterns among children who failed to differentiate weight and density as well as those who successfully did. In teaching studies, there was both evidence of resistance to change among some children and coordinated patterns of change among multiple concepts for those who were more successful.

The conceptual restructuring that occurs in children's intuitive matter theory may be related to a profound restructuring that occurs in mathematics. During the early years, children develop and entrench a rich concept of counting numbers, positive integers as represented by the integer list and that participate in operations of addition and subtraction. For each positive integer, there is an answer to the question "Which is the next one?" It is the next word in the count list. Later, they are exposed to new entities—fractions and decimals. To develop an understanding that fractions and decimals are numbers, children must restructure their concept of number from count number to rational number and make a host of changes, including developing a mathematical understanding of division. They must also rethink many core assumptions about what numbers are. For example, in

the count list, there are no numbers between the integers, but for rational numbers there are. Various reflections of conceptual understanding of fractions develop in parallel across samples of children (Gelman, 1991). Researchers have also found evidence of resistance to change, as children initially try to assimilate fractions to their concept of counting number. Finally, understanding rational number was strongly related to understanding weight as a continuous property of matter (Smith et al., 2005).

There are other cases in which the current scientific theories are deemed even more wildly counter-intuitive and fail to be understood by most adults. Coming to understand Newtonian dynamics, thermal physics, and Darwinian theory of natural selection are prime examples. For example, Andrew Shtluman (2006) identified two contrasting frameworks for understanding evolution: a transformationist framework (that characterized most students) and the variational framework of Charles Darwin (1809–1882). Students think of species as having essences, leading them to downplay variation within species and to think of evolution as a directed process of *transforming* the species essence over time. In contrast, Darwin thought of species as populations of inter-breeding individuals, making individual variation more important and salient, with evolution involving the two-step process of production of new variations followed by selection. Most individuals reasoned about six diverse phenomena in ways that were consistent with a given framework. Further, there was evidence of resistance to change, as students were actually asked to answer as they thought Darwin would.

Researchers have also characterized the contrasting frameworks for understanding knowledge acquisition in science, ranging from simpler knowledge-unproblematic epistemologies in which knowledge is seen as accumulating through observation, to more complex knowledge-problematic epistemologies in which conceptual frameworks guide inquiry. Movement from one framework to the other involves making fundamental differentiations (e.g., differentiating ideas from evidence, theories from hypotheses) as well as reanalyzing the meaning of concepts (e.g., scientific truth; scientific model). Studies have shown some consistency in student reasoning across tasks, as well as considerable resistance to change. Most college students still embrace a limited knowledge-unproblematic epistemology, although significant conceptual restructuring can occur with unusual science teaching experiences in elementary school (Smith et al., 2000).

WHAT CHANGES WHEN CONCEPTUAL CHANGE OCCURS

Most theorists see conceptual change as involving change at multiple interacting levels. First, there are changes in the *internal structure* of concepts: changes in the attributes represented in a concept and the weighting of those attributes. For example, movement to a differentiated weight concept involves adding a representation of weight as a measured quantity mapped to number, making this new representation central to the meaning, moving felt weight from core to periphery, and removing heavy for size as a relevant attribute of weight at all. Second, there are changes in the *external structure* of concepts: the collection of beliefs stated using the concept, including the relations formulated between concepts and ways that concepts are used in explanations. For example, as children differentiate weight and density, they can explicitly state their relation and use these concepts in separate generalizations.

In addition, many conceptual change researchers and developmental psychologists argue that there are multiple interacting levels of external structure. More specifically, some have proposed a distinction between *larger framework theories* and the more *specific intuitive theories* that can be formulated within a given framework theory (Wellman & Gelman, 1992), inspired by a similar distinction made by philosophers and historians of science. Framework theories delimit different domains of human reasoning by identifying the important classes of entities that need to be considered in the domain (its *ontology*) and the kinds of causal relations that are expected to occur among those entities. For example, preschool children may have at least three framework theories: a naïve physics (centered on *physical objects* that interact via mechanical causality), a naïve psychology (centered on *people* whose actions are caused by their goals, intentions and desires), and the beginnings of a naïve biology (centered on *animals* whose growth and development is governed by innate potential and whose movement and health is powered by vital forces). The existence of framework theories explains how children are able to make certain classes of inferences readily, often in the face of limited data, and why new beliefs, concepts, mental models, and even specific theories can be formed relatively quickly and fluidly when consistent with a framework theory. In contrast, more radical forms of conceptual restructuring involve changes in the larger framework theory. These changes are difficult because they involve changing basic ontological and epistemological assumptions, as well as expectations about types of causal patterns that will occur.

Not all conceptual change researchers embrace the notion that children's concepts are embedded in intuitive theories. Micheline Chi (2008) acknowledges the critical importance of ontological categories in organizing concepts, but describes them more generally as schemas rather than as part of theories. Andrea diSessa (1993) acknowledges the explanatory component to children's concepts, but suggests that children's explanatory ideas

are too shallow and uncoordinated with each other to be well described as a systematic theory, at least in their naïve mechanics. The framework theory proposal, however, may capture the abstract level at which there is consistency in children's thought while leaving room for children to be ignorant about the details needed for a well worked out specific theory, and for much fluidity in children's thought.

Researchers have also considered what stays the same in conceptual change. Carey (2008) notes that not all concepts are reworked even in conceptual revolutions; some survive and serve as sources of stability. DiSessa identifies subconceptual elements, or phenomenological primitives, such as "balancing" or "overcoming," that he thinks are as close as one gets to stable elements of thought and that are the explanatory bedrock of intuitive thought. He sees conceptual change as shifts in salience and cuing priorities among these elements, not replacing or eliminating these elements. Indeed a main contribution of his research program is to call attention to the productive resources within intuitive thought and the ways they continue to be used in later, more well structured theories.

CONTRASTING THEORIES OF HOW CHANGE OCCURS

If student learning is constrained by the assumptions of their guiding framework theory, how can new framework theories be learned? Instructional texts often focus on refuting specific beliefs. But if the faulty student belief stems from a faulty ontology, then refutation at that level will not be that effective. Instead, students will discount the data in numerous ways as they reinterpret it within their existing views rather than perceive it as anomalous (Chinn & Brewer, 1993). Even if they recognized an anomaly, they would not know what they needed to change to resolve it.

Chi argues that instruction in these cases would be more effective if the student were directly taught a new (more appropriate) ontological category. For example, she argues that many of the mistaken beliefs students develop about forces, heat, electricity, light, and magnetism stem from their assigning these concepts to the ontological category of "substance-kind entities" or "direct causal processes," and that these scientific concepts can be better understood if thought of as "emergent causal processes." Because students do not initially have such a category, she advocates directly teaching it by telling students the ways that emergent causal processes are different from direct causal processes. She found that college students who had a brief (1-hour) introduction to the category of emergent causal process, explained with some computer animations and several worked examples, had improved conceptual understanding of electricity in a follow-up unit compared to controls (Slotta & Chi, 2006).

Carey (2008) argues that conceptual change often rests on multi-step, iterative bootstrapping processes. One step involves the (culture's) introduction of a network of external symbols that function as (at best) partially interpreted *placeholders* (e.g., a drawing of a number line, or children being told "You need to eat to grow and stay alive"). These new networks of symbols may initially be learned by rote, where their meaning is captured more by their relations to each other than to prior knowledge. A second step involves coming to *interpret* the placeholders, using a variety of non-deductive modeling processes (e.g., analogies, thought experiments, inference to best explanation) that allow children to build connections with prior knowledge and observations in the world.

Both John Clement (2008) and Nancy Nersessian (1992) have studied how modeling processes work, both in students and in scientists, and how they can lead to the construction of fundamentally new representations. Crucially, models draw on people's everyday capacity to run mental simulations of events, in which they can both *simplify* their representations of events (by selectively abstracting away from surface details) and *enrich* them (by adding in depictions of unseen entities and processes, such as moving and colliding atoms, that help explain how things work). In creating these representations, individuals combine elements from diverse analogies, visual images and sensori-motor schemes in novel ways. Overall, Clement sees engaging students in incremental cycles of generating, evaluating, and revising explanatory models as at the heart of conceptual change.

Reasoning about models, of course, does not occur in a vacuum, but depends critically on social discourse and argumentation (e.g., dialogue about whether the model makes sense and explains the phenomena in question) and on using a wide variety of external symbols, inscriptions, and cultural artifacts. For this reason, many have extended analyses to include the study of how different discourse practices, participant structures, and cultural tools contribute to learning in conceptual change.

Finally, there is increasing recognition of the active role of students in regulating their own learning (Sinatra & Mason, 2008), guided by personal goals, interests, values, metacognitive understandings, and epistemic ideals.

EXAMPLES OF SUCCESSFUL INSTRUCTION

Successful instruction calls for the careful orchestration of multiple practices that actively engage students' initial ideas and help them restructure them in order to build a better understanding of their world. There is much art in this orchestration, as well as much that is domain specific. There are a number of examples of instructional sequences that have led to conceptual change in different domains.

Jim Minstrell, a high school physics teacher, is one of the pioneers in crafting a high school physics curriculum that helps students to build a deeper understanding of the core concepts in Newtonian mechanics (Minstrell, 1984). His instruction combines diagnostic quizzes that engage students in making predictions about everyday events and explaining their reasoning, classroom discussion of these predictions that leads to outlining a range of views, classroom demonstrations and experiments that often produce discrepant events, followed by further discussion to sort out and interpret findings in terms of a network of concepts. It also involves the careful sequencing of benchmark lessons and revisiting ideas throughout instruction. More accessible ideas are built up first so they can be used as resources for building other ideas later through logical arguments.

Jim Stewart collaborated with high school teachers to develop modules in genetics, evolution, and observational astronomy that are attentive to student starting ideas and that develop student understanding through engaging them in model-based inquiry (Stewart, Cartier, & Passmore, 2005). All modules start with activities that promote explicit understanding of a model as a conceptual structure used to explain data and guide inquiry, because they found students enter thinking of models only as representations and need a better framework for later discussions. In the evolution module, students contrast three models of species adaptation and diversity: the model of intelligent design, created by William Paley (1743–1805) the model of acquired characteristics, developed by Jean-Baptiste Lamarck (1744–1829), and the model of natural selection, created by Darwin. Contrasting these models was an effective way of helping them sort out what Darwin was claiming from what he was not, thus avoiding many common misconceptions about natural selection. Students then extend their understanding of natural selection through applying this model to make sense of real data sets. The other modules also develop and inter-relate multiple models in a carefully sequenced manner.

Others have successfully engaged elementary and middle school students in model-based inquiry that simultaneously promotes conceptual change and greater metacognitive understanding of science. For example, Barbara White's ThinkerTools curriculum (1993) involved sixth grade students in constructing, testing, and revising models of force and motion, through designing and carrying out investigations with computer microworlds and real-world experiments. As students moved through the curriculum, the microworlds became more complex (e.g., progressively adding in effects of friction, mass, and gravity), allowing them to sequentially build up more complex conceptual models. Microworlds have been used productively as additional resources in promoting conceptual change in a variety of domains (Snir & Smith, 1995; Wiser & Amin, 2001). Finally, some educators have redesigned their whole approach to teaching grades 1 to 6 science (Hennessey, 2003) or science and math (Lehrer, Schauble, Strom, & Pligge, 2001) with a focus on engaging children with model building in the service of developing and testing their own ideas. These complex curricula not only have successfully built domain specific understandings, but showed that elementary school students can develop insights about the conceptual change process and the role of frameworks in inquiry that elude many adults!

BIBLIOGRAPHY

Carey, S. (1985). *Conceptual change in childhood*. Cambridge, MA: MIT Press.

Carey, S. (2008). *The origin of concepts*. New York: Oxford University Press.

Clement, J. (2008). *Creative model construction in scientists and students: The role of analogy, imagery, and mental simulation*. Dordrecht, The Netherlands: Springer.

Chi, M. (2008). Three types of conceptual change: Belief revision, mental model transformation, and categorical shift. In S. Vosniadou (Ed.), *International Handbook of Research on Conceptual Change*. Boca Raton, FL: Routledge.

Chinn, C. A., & Brewer, W. F. (1993). The role of anomalous data in knowledge acquisition: A theoretical framework and implications for science instruction, *Review of Educational Research, 63(1)*, 1–49.

diSessa, A. A. (1993) Toward an epistemology of physics. *Cognition and Instruction, 10(2/3)*, 105–225.

Gelman, R. (1991). Epigenetic foundations of knowledge structures: Initial and transcendent constructions. In S. Carey and R. Gelman (Eds.), *The epigenesis of mind: Essays on biology and cognition* (pp. 293–322). Hillsdale, NJ: Erlbaum.

Hennessey, M.G. (2003). Probing the dimensions of metacognition: Implications for conceptual change teaching-learning. In G. Sinatra & P. Pintrich (Eds.), *Intentional conceptual change* (pp. 103–132). Mahwah, N.J.: Lawrence Erlbaum Associates.

Kuhn, T. (1962). *The structure of scientific revolutions*. Chicago: University of Chicago Press.

Lehrer, R., Schauble, L., Strom, D., & Pligge, M. (2001) Similarity of form and substance: Modeling material kind. In S. Carver & D. Klahr (Eds.), *Cognition and instruction: Twenty-five years of progress* (pp. 39–74). Mahwah, NJ: Lawrence Erlbaum Associates.

McCloskey, M. (1983). Naïve theories of motion. In D. Gentner & A.L. Stevens (Eds.), *Mental models* (pp. 299–324). Hillsdale, NJ: Erlbaum.

Minstrell, J. (1984). Teaching for the development of understanding of ideas: Forces on moving objects. In C. Anderson (Ed.), *AETS Yearbook: Observing Classrooms: Perspectives from Research and Practice* (pp. 55–73). Columbus: Ohio State University.

Nersessian, N. (1992). Constructing and instructing: The role of 'abstraction techniques' in developing and teaching scientific theories. In R. Duschl & R. Hamilton (Eds.), *Philosophy of Science, Cognitive Science, & Educational Theory and Practice* (pp. 48–68). Albany, NY: SUNY Press.

Nussbaum, J. (1985). The Earth as a cosmic body. In R. Driver, E. Guesne, & A. Tiberghien (Eds.), *Children's ideas in science* (pp. 170–192). Philadelphia: Open University Press.

Posner, G. J., Strike, K. A., Hewson, P. W., & Gertzog, W.A. (1982). Accommodation of a scientific conception: Toward a theory of conceptual change. *Science Education, 66(2)*, 211–227.

Shtulman, A. (2006) Qualitative differences between naïve and scientific theories of evolution. *Cognitive Psychology, 52*, 170–194.

Sinatra, G., and Mason, L. (2008) Beyond knowledge: Learner characteristics influencing conceptual change. In S. Vosniadou (Ed.), *International Handbook of Research on Conceptual Change*. Boca Raton, FL: Routledge.

Smith, C., Maclin, D., Houghton, C. & Hennessey, M.G. (2000). Sixth graders' epistemologies of science: The impact of school science experiences on epistemological development. *Cognition and Instruction, 15(3)*, 317–393.

Smith, C., Solomon, G., & Carey, S. (2005). Never getting to zero: Elementary school students' understanding of the infinite divisibility of matter and number. *Cognitive Psychology 51*, 101–140.

Smith, C. (2007). Bootstrapping processes in the development of students' commonsense matter theories: Using analogical mappings, thought experiments, and learning to measure to promote conceptual restructuring. *Cognition and Instruction, 25(4)*, 337–98.

Snir, J., & Smith, C. (1995) Constructing understanding in the classroom: Integrating laboratory experiments, student and computer models, and class discussion in learning scientific concepts. In D. Perkins, J. Schwartz, M. West, & S. Wiske (Eds.), *Software goes to school* (pp. 233–254). Oxford, England: Oxford University Press.

Stewart, J., Cartier, J. & Passmore, C. (2005). Developing understanding through model-based inquiry. In M. S. Donovan and J. D. Bransford (Eds.), *How Students Learn: Science in the Classroom* (pp. 515–565). Washington, DC: The National Academies Press.

Thagard, P. (1992). *Conceptual revolutions*. Princeton, NJ: Princeton University Press.

Vosniadou, S., & Brewer, W. (1992). Mental models of the Earth: A study of conceptual change in childhood. *Cognitive Psychology, 24*, 535–585.

Vosniadou, S., & Brewer, W. (1994). Mental models of the day/night cycle. *Cognitive Science, 18*, 123–183.

Welman, H., & Gelman, S. (1992). Cognitive development: Foundational theories of core domains. *Annual Review of Psychology, 43*, 337–375.

White, B. (1993). Thinkertools: Causal models, conceptual change, and science instruction. *Cognition and Instruction, 10*, 1–100.

White, B., & Frederickson, J. (1998). Inquiry, modeling, and metacognition: Making science accessible to all students. *Cognition and Instruction, 16(1)*, 3–117.

Wiser, M. (1988). The differentiation of heat and temperature: History of science and the novice-expert shift. In S. Strauss (Ed.), *Ontogeny, phylogeny, and historical development* (pp. 28–48). Norwood, NJ: Ablex Publishing Company.

Wiser, M., & Amin, T. (2001). Is heat hot? Inducing conceptual change by integrating everyday and scientific perspectives on thermal phenomena. *Learning & Instruction, 11,* 331–355.

Carol L. Smith

CONFLICT RESOLUTION

Conflicts may be resolved or managed. A conflict exists whenever incompatible activities occur (Deutsch, 1973). An activity that is incompatible with another activity is one that prevents, blocks, or interferes with the occurrence or effectiveness of the second activity. Conflict resolution is solving the problem so the conflict is ended. Conflict management is handling the conflict so it is under control. Conflicts are constructive to the extent they (a) result in an agreement that allows all participants to achieve their goals, (b) strengthen the relationship among participants, and (c) strengthen the ability of participants to resolve their future conflicts constructively (Deutsch, 1973; Johnson & F. Johnson, 2006).

Whether constructive or destructive outcomes result from conflict depends largely on the context in which the conflict occurs. In situations dominated by cooperation, conflicts tend to be viewed as problems to be solved. Individuals tend to communicate effectively, accurately perceive the other person and his or her position, trust and like the other, recognize the legitimacy of the other's interests, and focus on their own and others' well being. In situations dominated by competition conflicts are viewed as "win-lose" situations. Individuals tend to focus on gaining an advantage at the expense of others, communicate misleading information, misperceive the other person's position and motivation, be suspicious of and hostile toward others, and deny the legitimacy of others' goals and feelings.

CONFLICT RESOLUTION PROGRAMS

Conflict resolution programs are aimed primarily at teaching students the competencies they need to regulate their own and their classmates' behavior so that conflicts may be resolved constructively. Conflict resolution and peer mediation programs have been generated by (a) researchers in the field of conflict resolution, (b) groups committed to nonviolence, (c) anti-nuclear war groups, and (d) lawyers.

Mean weighted effect sizes for peacemaker studies

Dependent variable	Mean	Standard deviation	Number of effects
Learned procedure	2.25	1.98	13
Learned procedure—retention	3.34	4.16	9
Applied procedure	2.16	1.31	4
Application—retention	0.46	0.16	3
Strategy constructiveness	1.60	1.70	21
Constructiveness—retention	1.10	0.53	10
Strategy Two-concerns	1.10	0.46	5
Two-Concerns—retention	0.45	0.20	2
Integrative negotiation	0.98	0.36	5
Quality of solutions	0.73	0	1
Positive attitude	1.07	0.25	5
Negative attitude	−0.61	0.37	2
Academic achievement	0.88	0.09	5
Academic retention	0.70	0.31	4

SOURCE: Reprinted with permission from: Johnson, R., & Johnson, D. W. (2002). *Teaching students to be peacemakers: A meta-analysis.* Paper presented at the Annual Convention of the American Educational Research Association, New Orleans, April.

Table 1 ILLUSTRATION BY GGS INFORMATION SERVICES. CENGAGE LEARNING, GALE.

While there are numerous programs, some of the most historic and important are discussed below.

Research Theory-Based Programs. The Teaching Students to Be Peacemakers Program (TSP) was developed in the mid-1960s at the University of Minnesota by researchers in the field of conflict resolution (Johnson, 1970, Johnson & Johnson, 2005). Beginning in 1966, teachers were trained to teach students how to resolve conflicts constructively. The Peacemaker Program trains all students in the school in the value of conflict, the five strategies for managing conflicts, the integrative negotiation procedure, and the peer mediation procedure. The training may be integrated into curriculum units. It is repeated every year at an increasingly higher level of sophistication as a 12-year spiral curriculum. The Peacemaker Program has been implemented in schools throughout North America, and in numerous countries in Europe, the Middle East, Africa, Asia, and Central and South America.

Columbia University's International Center for Cooperation and Conflict Resolution (ICCCR) focuses primarily on research and training in conflict resolution (Coleman & Fisher-Yoshida, 2004). Their program is implemented by training school mediators, placing conflict resolution concepts and skills into the curriculum, using cooperative learning and constructive controversy as pedagogical methods, changing the school culture from competitive to cooperative, and involving the broader community in the program.

The Conflict Resolution Model (Davidson & Wood, 2004) was developed in Australia. It consists of four components: (a) developing expectations for "win-win" solutions by teaching that cooperation is the most effective means of managing conflict, (b) identifying each party's interests, (c) brainstorming creative options, and (d) combining options into win-win solutions.

The Constructive Controversy Program, which was first taught in the early 1970s, consists of teaching students how to engage in intellectual conflict, either in academic or group decision making situations (Johnson & Johnson, 1979, 2007). Constructive controversy occurs when one person's ideas, information, conclusions, theories, and opinions are incompatible with those of another and the two seek to reach an agreement. Students are trained to prepare the best case possible for their position, give a persuasive presentation to convince others to agree with them, engage in an open discussion in which they attempt to refute opposing positions while rebutting attacks on their position, engage in perspective reversal in which they present the best case for the opposing position, and then reach a joint consensual decision based on their best reasoned judgment. The program has been implemented in schools and universities throughout North America and in many countries in Europe, the Middle East, Africa, Asia, and Central and South America.

Nonviolence Advocacy Groups. In the early 1970s, Quaker teachers in New York City became interested in conducting nonviolence training with their students. Their efforts, known as the New York Quaker Project on Community Conflict, resulted in the founding of the Children's Creative Response to Conflict in 1972 (Prutzman, Stern, Burger, & Bodenhamer, 1988). Priscilla Prutzman was named its first director. Weekly workshops in public schools are given to teach that the power of nonviolence lies in justice, love and caring, and the desire for personal integrity.

Anti-Nuclear War Groups. In 1985, in partnership with the New York City public schools, the Educators for Social Responsibility began the Resolving Conflict Creatively Program (RCCP) (Selfridge, 2004). The program is aimed at implementing (a) a 10-unit curriculum with lessons on intergroup relations, cooperative learning, and dispute resolution procedures; (b) 20 hours of training in how to be a peer mediator, and (c) 10 4-hour workshops for parents.

Lawyers. In 1977 trial lawyer Ray Shonholtz established the Community Boards in San Francisco to mediate conflicts in neighborhoods. In mediating conflicts among adults, the mediators had to teach conflict resolution

skills. Considering prevention, Shonholtz approached local schools with the idea of beginning a peer mediation program in schools. In 1982 Helena Davis wrote a conflict manager curriculum for elementary schools that was piloted in 1984. In the 1985–1986, middle and high school curricula were developed and implemented. The curriculum has been extended and modified by Gail Sadalla (Sadalla, Holmberg, & Halligan, 1990).

Large-Scale Implementation. The Ohio Commission on Dispute Resolution and Conflict Management and the Ohio Department of Education created a statewide model of teaching conflict resolution education (Batton, 2002). Each school year, they award competitive grants to Ohio's K-12 public schools to design, implement, and evaluate conflict resolution programs. They also make training, technical assistance, and age-appropriate lesson plans and resource materials available to grantee schools. In 2002 more than 1,400 public schools in 380 or more of Ohio's 612 school districts reported having a conflict resolution program.

Age-Appropriate Implementation. Some conflict resolution programs are aimed at specific age levels such as elementary or high schools. Other programs are aimed at all ages. There are developmental differences that the programs have to take into account. Young children may be more rule oriented, less able to be empathetic, less able to understand concepts such as reciprocity, and less able to engage in higher-level reasoning. There are also individual differences in self-efficacy, self-regulation, and other characteristics that influence how individuals of all ages manage their conflicts.

Meta-analysis of academic controversy studies: weighted effect sizes

Dependent variable	Controversy/ concurrence seeking	Controversy/ debate	Controversy/ individualistic efforts
Achievement	0.68	0.40	0.87
Cognitive reasoning	0.62	1.35	0.90
Perspective taking	0.91	0.22	0.86
Motivation	0.75	0.45	0.71
Attitudes toward task	0.58	0.81	0.64
Interpersonal attraction	0.24	0.72	0.81
Social support	0.32	0.92	1.52
Self-esteem	0.39	0.51	0.85

SOURCE: Reprinted with permission from: Johnson, D. W., & Johnson, R. (1995). *Creative controversy: Intellectual conflict in the classroom.* Edina, MN: Interaction Book Company.

Table 2 ILLUSTRATION BY GGS INFORMATION SERVICES. CENGAGE LEARNING, GALE.

CLASSIFYING CONFLICT RESOLUTION PROGRAMS

There are at least three ways to describe conflict resolution and peer mediation programs in schools. First, the programs can be described as either cadre or total student body programs. The cadre approach emphasizes training a small number of students to serve as peer mediators. The total student body approach emphasizes training every student in the school to manage conflicts constructively. Second, conflict resolution programs may be divided into pre-planned lessons that teachers take and teach or a conceptual framework that teachers use to plan lessons specially adapted for their students. Third, conflict resolution programs may be divided into skills-oriented approaches in which students are taught the interpersonal and small group skills needed to resolve conflicts constructively; academically oriented approaches in which students can be taught the intellectual procedures and cognitive skills for managing conflicts; and structural change approaches which emphasize changing the school structure to provide a cooperative context for the management of conflict.

While these and many other programs are being implemented, there may be only two conflict programs that are (a) based on principles formulated from theory, (b) extensively and systematically validated by research, and (b) integrated into academic lessons to enhance achievement. These programs are the Teaching Students to Be Peacemakers Program and the Constructive Controversy Program.

Teaching Students To Be Peacemakers. The Peacemaker Program begins with twenty lessons of thirty minutes each. These lessons may be divided into six parts (Johnson & Johnson, 2005). First, students learn the nature of conflict and the potential constructive consequences of conflict. Second, students learn that in conflict they should focus on two concerns: achieving their goals and maintaining a good relationship with the other person. The importance of the goals and relationship determine whether a person should withdraw (giving up one's goal and relationship), force (achieving one's goal while giving up relationship), smooth (giving up one's goal to enhance relationship), compromise (giving up part of one's goal and relationship), or negotiate to solve the problem (achieve one's goal while maintaining relationship). All five strategies have their place, but the most important is problem-solving negotiations, which form part three of the program. The procedure consists of (a) describing what one wants, (b) describing how one feels, (c) describing the reasons for one's wants and feelings, (d) taking the other's perspective, (e) inventing three optional plans to maximize joint benefits, and (f) choosing one option and formalizing the agreement.

Fourth, students learn how to mediate schoolmates' conflicts by (a) ending hostilities and cooling off disputants, (b) ensuring disputants are committed to the mediation process (introducing mediation and setting the ground rules of agreeing to solve the problem: no name calling, no interrupting, be as honest as possible, abide by the agreement made, keep anything said in mediation confidential); (c) helping disputants successfully use the problem-solving negotiation procedure, and (d) formalizing the agreement (disputants sign a Mediation Report Form and shake hands as a commitment to implement the agreement and abide by its conditions).

Fifth, the peacemaker program is implemented. Once these initial lessons are completed, the peer mediation program is implemented. Each day two class members serve as mediators. The role of mediator is rotated so that all students have the opportunity to mediate. If peer mediation fails, the teacher mediates the conflict. If teacher mediation fails, the teacher arbitrates by deciding who is right and who is wrong. If that fails, the principal mediates the conflict. If that fails, the principal arbitrates.

Finally, teachers continue to teach the problem-solving negotiation and peer mediation procedures to refine and upgrade students' skills, integrating them into academic lessons. Each year, the program is retaught in an increasingly sophisticated and complex way.

Benefits of the Peacemaker Program. Eighteen studies have been conducted on the effectiveness of the Peacemaker Program in eight different schools in two countries (Johnson & Johnson, 2005). The studies included students from kindergarten through ninth grades and were conducted in rural, suburban, and urban settings in the United States and Canada involving both majority and minority students. In most of the studies, students were randomly assigned to conditions and teachers were rotated across conditions. Sixteen of the studies were included in a meta-analysis.

Before training, students tended either to force the other to concede or withdraw. The training resulted in the students learning the negotiation and the mediation procedures and retaining their knowledge up to a year after the training had ended (see Table 1). After training, students applied the procedures almost perfectly and were still quite good at them months later. As a result, the number of discipline problems teachers had to deal with decreased by about 60% and referrals to administrators dropped about 90%. The attitudes of trained students toward conflict became more positive. Students used the negotiation and mediation procedures in classrooms, hallways, lunchrooms, playgrounds, and family settings. Teachers, administrators, and parents tended to perceive the peacemaker program as constructive and helpful.

The Peacemaker training was integrated into both English literature and history academic units to determine its impact on academic achievement. Students who received the Peacemaker training as part of an academic unit tended to score significantly higher on achievement and retention tests than did students who studied the academic unit only. Students not only learned the factual information contained in the academic unit better, they were better able to interpret the information in more insightful ways.

Constructive Controversy Program. Teaching students how to engage in constructive controversy begins with randomly assigning students to cooperative learning groups of four members (Johnson & Johnson, 1979, 2007). The groups are given an issue on which to write a report and pass a test. Each cooperative group is divided into two pairs. One pair is given the con-position on the issue and the other pair is given the pro-position. Each pair is given the instructional materials needed to define their position and point them towards further information. The cooperative goals of reaching a consensus on the issue and writing a quality group report are highlighted. Students then (a) prepare the best case possible for their assigned position, (b) present and advocate their position to the opposing pair, (c) participate in an open discussion in which they attempt to refute the opposing position while defending their own, (d) reverse perspectives and present each other's positions, and (e) synthesize and integrate the best evidence and reasoning from both sides into a joint position. They finalize the report (the teacher evaluates reports on the quality of the writing, the logical presentation of evidence, and the oral presentation of the report to the class), present their conclusions to the class (all four members of the group are required to participate orally in the presentation), individually take the test covering both sides of the issue (if every member of the group achieves up to criterion, they all receive bonus points), and process how well they worked together and how they could be even more effective next time.

The process of constructive controversy is most effective within a certain set of conditions. The more cooperative the context, the more skilled the students are in engaging in the constructive controversy procedure, and the more able students are in engaging in rational argument, the more constructively the controversy will be resolved.

Research Results. A meta-analysis was conducted on the 28 studies involving elementary, intermediate, and college students that were conducted to assess the effectiveness of constructive controversy programs (Johnson and Johnson, 2007) (see Table 2). The results of the research indicate that compared with concurrence-seeking, debate, and individualistic efforts, constructive controversy tends to result in higher-quality decisions (including decisions that involve ethical dilemmas) and higher-quality solutions to complex problems for which different viewpoints can plausibly be developed. Controversy programs tend to promote more frequent use of higher-level reasoning strategies, more accurate and complete understanding of opposing perspectives, more continuing motivation to learn about the issue, and more liking for the task. In addition, constructive controversy has been found to promote greater liking, greater social support, and higher self-esteem than debate, concurrence-seeking, or individualistic efforts.

Conflicts may be resolved so that an agreement is reached that solves the problem or manages it so that the conflict is controlled. Whether constructive or destructive outcomes result from conflict depends largely on the context in which the conflict occurs and the competencies of disputants. Conflict resolution and peer mediation programs have their roots in research in the field of conflict resolution, advocates of nonviolence, antinuclear war activists, and lawyers. While numerous conflict resolution programs are being implemented, the two that have been most thoroughly researched and validated (as well as implemented most widely) are the Teaching Students to Be Peacemakers and Constructive Controversy Programs.

SEE ALSO *Aggression; Egocentrism; Moral Development.*

BIBLIOGRAPHY

Batton, J. (2002). Institutionalizing conflict resolution education: The Ohio model. *Conflict Resolution Quarterly, 19*(4), 479–494.

Coleman, P., & Fisher-Yoshida, B. (2004). Conflict resolution at multiple levels across the lifespan: The work of the ICCCR. *Theory Into Practice, 43*(1), 31–38.

Davidson, J., & Wood, C. (2004). A conflict resolution model. *Theory Into Practice 43*(1), 6–13.

Deutsch, M. (1973). *The resolution of conflict.* New Haven, CT: Yale University Press.

Johnson, D. W. (1970). *Social psychology of education.* New York: Holt, Rinehart, & Winston.

Johnson, D. W., & Johnson, F. (2006). *Joining together: Group theory and group skills* (9th ed.). Boston: Allyn & Bacon.

Johnson, D. W., & Johnson, R. (1979). Conflict in the classroom: Controversy and learning. *Review of Educational Research, 49,* 51–61.

Johnson, D. W., & Johnson, R. (2005). *Teaching students to be peacemakers.* Edina, MN: Interaction Book.

Johnson, D. W., & Johnson, R. (2007). *Creative controversy: Intellectual challenge in the classroom.* Edina, MN: Interaction Book.

Prutzman, P., Stern, L., Burger, M. L., & Bodenhamer, G. (1988). *The friendly classroom for a small planet.* Philadelphia: New Society Publishers.

Sadalla, G., Holmberg, M., & Halligan, J. (1990). *Conflict resolution: An elementary school curriculum.* San Francisco: Community Boards.

Selfridge, J. (2004). The Resolving Conflict Creatively Program: How we know it works. *Theory into Practice, 43*(1), 59–67.

David W. Johnson
Roger T. Johnson

CONNECTIONISM

Connectionism is the study of artificial neural networks. These networks are designed to emulate the neural circuits that are found in real nervous systems, although the similarities are sometimes only superficial. As a broad set of concepts and research techniques, connectionism can be divided into two major approaches. First, researchers in psychology, neuroscience, linguistics, and related disciplines use connectionist models to simulate cognitive processes such as perception, memory, learning, and motor skill. Second, researchers in computer science, engineering, and mathematics study the formal properties of connectionist models and also use these models to analyze and solve complex real-world tasks (e.g., pattern recognition, robot planning and control, and non-linear function approximation).

HISTORICAL BACKGROUND

The perceptron, one of the most basic types of artificial neural networks, was proposed by Frank Rosenblatt in 1958. As Figure 1A illustrates, the perceptron includes two layers of simulated neurons: a layer of input units, which is analogous to a simple sensory system (e.g., tactile skin receptors, retinal neurons), and a layer of output units, which is analogous to a simple motor system (e.g., muscle fibers). Each unit in the network can be interpreted as corresponding to a neuron, whose activity level (i.e., simulated firing rate) is influenced by its connections to other units in the network. A given network's architecture is determined by the particular pattern of connections among the units in the network. For example, the perceptron is a two-layer feed-forward network because the activity at the input layer propagates forward and influences activity at the output layer (e.g., from sensory input to motor output). Like real synapses, the connections between units in an artificial neural network can vary in strength, causing each receiving unit either to increase or decrease its activity (i.e., excitation or inhibition).

Rosenblatt's 1958 work helped to highlight an important feature of artificial neural networks: With an appro-

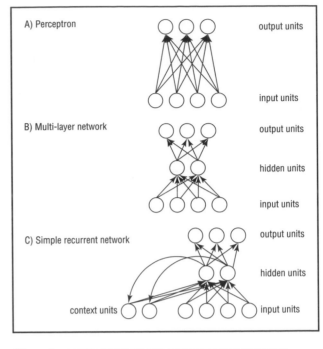

Figure 1 ILLUSTRATION BY GGS INFORMATION SERVICES. CENGAGE LEARNING, GALE.

priate set of weighted connections, a network can be used to transform a given set of input patterns into a desired set of output patterns. For example, imagine that the four input units in Figure 1A are retinal sensors whose activity varies from 0 to 1, depending on the intensity of light stimulating each unit. Similarly, imagine that the units in the output layer either (1) drive an eye movement to the left or right, or (2) maintain the fixation point, depending on which of the three units is most active. With the correct set of connection weights, this network would then be able to perform a simple orienting response, which shifts its gaze laterally toward bright objects in its visual field.

The initial success of Rosenblatt's perceptron was challenged by Marvin Minsky and Simon Papert (1969), who published a critical analysis of two-layer networks. Their critique demonstrated by mathematical proof that the perceptron was severely limited in the kinds of input-output mappings or functions that it could compute. As a result, research on artificial neural networks stalled for more than a decade.

However, in 1986 David Rumelhart and James McClelland published a landmark two-volume text that both revived interest in the study of artificial neural networks and, more importantly, provided a comprehensive response to Minsky and Papert's criticisms. In particular, Rumelhart and McClelland proposed a set of relatively modest changes to the perceptron. One of these changes, as Figure 1B illustrates, was to insert a new layer of units between the input and output layers. This set of units is called the hidden layer, as it is hidden from the external environment (i.e., only the input and output units make direct contact with the environment). Surprisingly, Rumelhart and McClelland's multilayer networks are able to approximate all of the input-output functions that Minsky and Papert proposed, and under the appropriate set of conditions, they can also be broadly interpreted as universal function approximators.

LEARNING IN ARTIFICIAL NEURAL NETWORKS

Rumelhart and McClelland also promoted the idea that neural networks can learn. More specifically, the connections in a network can be modified by a set of mathematical rules called a learning algorithm. For example, in a Hebbian network, the connection between two units is strengthened when both are active at the same time. Thus, an artificial neural network can "learn" in the sense that as it is repeatedly presented with one or more input patterns, it adjusts or modifies its connection weights, which gradually changes the pattern of output produced by the network.

One of the most common learning algorithms is back-propagation-of-error, which belongs to a set of methods called supervised learning algorithms. These methods are supervised in the sense that after an input pattern is presented to the network, the model-builder compares the output produced by the network to a desired pattern. The network's connection weights are then adjusted so that the output is moved closer to the desired pattern. Thus, a fundamental assumption of supervised learning is that a "teacher" not only is available, but also provides highly specific feedback during the learning process. It is important to note, however, that there are alternative methods for simulating learning in artificial neural networks that do not require explicit feedback from a teacher (e.g., reinforcement learning, unsupervised learning; for a recent review, see Schlesinger & Parisi, 2004).

The learning algorithm back-prop, as it is typically called, derives its name from the fact that in a standard network, activation flows forward, from the input layer to the output layer. In contrast, when the connection weights are modified, the training signal propagates in reverse: Changes are first made to the connections at the output layer, followed by changes to the connections at the hidden layer. While this bi-directional flow of information is a mathematical requirement, it has been challenged as biologically implausible. Indeed, a growing number of researchers advocate for designing artificial neural networks that more accurately represent both the structure and function of the brain (e.g., Sejnowski, Koch, & Churchland, 1988).

APPLICATIONS TO LEARNING AND COGNITION

There are numerous examples of connectionist models that may be relevant to the study of classroom learning. While these models are designed to simulate learning within a particular knowledge domain (e.g., grammar learning, numerical cognition, etc.), they also suggest more general principles that are broadly applicable across domains.

The Importance of Starting Small. Jeff Elman (1993) modified the standard 3-layer architecture to study how a network learns the structure of a small artificial language. As Figure 1C illustrates, the unique feature of this simple recurrent network is that activation from the hidden layer both propagates forward to the output layer and projects back to a set of context units in the input layer. These context units provide a type of short-term memory trace that allows the network to differentiate between two identical input patterns that occur within different contexts (e.g., "I read the book" vs. "They will book a room").

Elman presented the network with sentences from the artificial language—one word at a time—and trained it to predict the next word in each sentence. Initially, the network was unable to learn the task. Next, he trained a new network that started with limited short-term memory (this was implemented by clearing the memory trace after every few words), which gradually increased during training. In contrast to the first network, the network with limited short-term memory succeeded on the learning task. Elman used these findings to argue that modest limitations on information processing (e.g., memory, attention, etc.) during early learning may be an advantage for novices who are acquiring a new skill.

Growing New Connections. Another important innovation in connectionist models was proposed by Tom Shultz (2003), who conducts simulations with a learning algorithm called cascade correlation. What makes the cascade correlation algorithm unique is that, in contrast to standard multilayer networks that have a fixed architecture, cascade correlation networks are able to generate new hidden units as they learn.

One of the tasks that Shultz has studied with the cascade correlation algorithm is the balance-scale task. This task was first investigated by Jean Piaget (1896–1980), who asked children to predict which side of the scale will tip when weights are hung on each side; Piaget discovered that children pass through four stages as they learn to master the balance scale. Shultz first simulated the task with a fixed 3-layer network and found that the network was only able to reach stage three. He then trained a second network with cascade correlation and found that as new hidden units were generated, the network reached stage four on the balance scale task.

Shultz proposes that while networks with a fixed architecture learn by a process comparable to rote memorization, dynamic networks "grow" new units and connections and are thus able to actively reorganize what is being learned. Walter Schneider and David Graham (1992) suggest that traditional classroom learning can benefit from this research by exploiting both styles or modes: conventional memorization-based learning, balanced with self-directed or problem-based learning.

BIBLIOGRAPHY

Elman, J. (1993). Learning and development in neural networks: The importance of starting small. *Cognition, 48,* 71–99.

Minsky, M., & Papert, S. (1969). *Perceptrons.* Cambridge, MA: MIT Press.

Rosenblatt, F. (1958). The perceptron: A probabilistic model for information storage and organization in the brain. *Psychological Review, 65,* 386–408.

Rumelhart, D., & McClelland, J. (1986). *Parallel Distributed Processing: Explorations in the Microstructure of Cognition.* Cambridge, MA: MIT Press.

Schlesinger, M., & Parisi, D. (Eds.). (2004). Beyond backprop: Emerging trends in connectionist models of development. [Special section]. *Developmental Science, 7,* 131–132.

Schneider, W., & Graham, D. (1992). Introduction to connectionist modeling in education. *Educational Psychologist, 27,* 513–530.

Sejnowski, T., Koch, C., & Churchland, P. (1988). Computational neuroscience. *Science, 241,* 1299–1306.

Shultz, T. (2003). *Computational Developmental Psychology.* Cambridge, MA: MIT Press.

Matthew Schlesinger

CONSTRUCTIVISM

This entry contains the following:

OVERVIEW

The term constructivism has played a dominant role in educational literature for a number of decades. While educators generally agree on several core aspects of constructivism, significantly different interpretations, perspectives, and approaches exist regarding the details of constructivist learning and teaching. This section discusses (a) the historical roots of constructivism, (b) perspectives on constructivism as epistemological theory, learning theory, and pedagogy; (c) the continuum of constructivist perspectives from individual to social, (d) evidence for the efficacy and adoption of constructivism, (e) the key assumptions about constructivist learning and instruction, and (f) introductions to several instructional approaches involving constructivist designs.

HISTORICAL ROOTS OF CONSTRUCTIVISM

Constructivism, although relatively new in its current form, has deep historical roots. At their core, constructivist perspectives focus on how learners construct their own understanding. Some philosophers, such as Socrates, focused on helping students construct meanings on their own rather than having authority figures transmit information to them. Immanuel Kant (1724–1804) built upon this by recognizing that the way learners perceive stimuli from their environment shapes their understanding of the world. In the early 20th century, John Dewey (1859–1952) proposed that education should work with students' current understanding, taking into account their prior ideas and interests. Later, Jean Piaget (1896–1980) defined accommodation and assimilation as ways for new knowledge to build upon previous knowledge. The ideas of Lev Vygotsky (1896–1934) also influenced constructivism. He helped increase awareness of the interactions between the individual, interpersonal, and cultural historical factors that affect learning.

CONSTRUCTIVISM AS EPISTEMOLOGICAL THEORY, LEARNING THEORY, AND PEDAGOGY

The term constructivism can refer to one of many different but related concepts. More specifically, constructivist perspectives can focus on epistemological theory, learning theory, and pedagogy.

As an epistemological theory, constructivism focuses on how bodies of knowledge come to be. This perspective is important to note even though this view of constructivism is not discussed in the educational literature as frequently as other views. Constructivism as an epistemological theory holds that disciplines, such as history and mathematics, are constructed by human interactions and decisions. For some disciplines, such as literature, this idea is fairly well accepted; there are certain books that most people agree are worth reading and others that are purposefully forgotten. For disciplines such as science and mathematics, however, the idea that people (and not nature) construct the bounds of the disciplines and the concepts within them remains contentious.

More commonly, educators view constructivism as a learning theory. Some educators use the term constructivist simply to indicate a non-behaviorist learning theory. While constructivist learning theories are non-behaviorist, constructivism involves much more than simple opposition to a previous learning theory. From the perspective of constructivism, learners construct knowledge based on what they already understand as they make connections between new information and old information. Students' prior ideas, experiences, and knowledge interact with new experiences and their interpretations of the environment around them. Research by Savery & Duffy (1995) suggests that learning how to use constructivist theories involves many interactions between the content, the context, the activity of the learner, and the goals of the learner.

Cognitive conflict drives this knowledge-building process. Cognitive conflict occurs for learners when they encounter and recognize discrepancies between what they already know and new persuasive information that brings their current understanding into question. These discrepancies cause cognitive tension requiring adjustment to reduce the discrepancies. When students resolve these discrepancies they actively figure out ways to reconcile their prior knowledge or understanding with the new information. Students may construct new knowledge from pieces of prior knowledge or restructure prior knowledge. Thus the resolution of cognitive conflict drives learning.

Finally, based on the core ideas of constructivist learning theory, constructivist pedagogy proposes that instruction must take students' prior ideas, experiences, and knowledge into account while providing opportunities for students to construct new understanding. Constructivist pedagogies are discussed in greater detail below, in the sections titled Assumptions about Constructivist Learning and Instruction, and Instructional approaches with constructivist designs.

CONSTRUCTIVIST PERSPECTIVES FROM INDIVIDUAL TO SOCIAL

While the general principles discussed above apply to most constructivist theories and pedagogies, significantly different interpretations have evolved regarding the details. One key distinction, discussed by Phillips (2000) and other educators, among constructivist perspectives involves the continuum of interpretations in terms of where the construction of knowledge takes place. Radical

constructivism anchors one end of this continuum and social constructivism anchors the other. Most educators' theoretical commitments fall somewhere between these two perspectives.

RADICAL CONSTRUCTIVISM

Radical constructivism proposes that the construction of knowledge takes place solely in the learner's mind and on an individual level. Ernst von Glasersfeld (1917–) refined many of the core ideas of radical constructivism. McCarty and Schwandt (2000) explain that according to radical constructivism, concepts form through the learner's experiences with objects or events as the learner notes similarities and differences among the experiences and gradually builds up a concept relating to that object or event.

Radical constructivism is similar in many ways to Jean Piaget's perspectives on assimilation and accommodation and to theories of information processing. Both Piagetian and information processing theories view learning as a cognitive activity through which individuals actively incorporate new information and experiences into the information and understandings already stored in memory. Piaget explains these processes in terms of assimilation, in which learners add new information into their existing knowledge frameworks, and accommodation, in which the new information causes cognitive conflict that results in the reorganization of learners' knowledge frameworks. Information processing theory uses a computer metaphor to explain how knowledge construction works. The learner perceives various stimuli, encodes them into useful information, and then stores the information for later use. The learner is able to modify previous knowledge or strategies in order to help with current problem solving and develop more sophisticated knowledge. In alignment with radical constructivist perspectives, therefore, both perspectives focus on how the individual processes and relates new information to information already in the mind.

Radical constructivism holds serious implications for learning and teaching. Most importantly, from the perspective of radical constructivism, a person cannot ascertain that what other people have constructed in their minds is exactly the same as what he or she has constructed. In spite of this paradox, teachers must act "as if there were a world about which meanings were shared" (Howe & Berv, 2000, p. 33).

SOCIAL CONSTRUCTIVISM

Social constructivism represents the other end of the continuum. Social constructivism, heavily influenced by Vygotsky and sociocultural theory, proposes that learning takes place in the interaction between people and their

CONTROVERSY OVER THE EFFICACY OF CONSTRUCTIVISM

While significant evidence supports the efficacy of constructivist approaches, other evidence suggests that other forms of instruction offer important advantages depending on context. Research by Kirschner, Sweller, and Clark, for example, suggests that many constructivist-based approaches do not work as well as direct instruction in changing long-term memory. Part of their argument hinges on findings from cognitive science that limit the amount of information that can exist in working memory at one time. In addition, constructivist methods commonly involve problem solving situations where the learning is self-directed, which unchecked can lead to potential misconceptions. Furthermore, research by Elby suggests that different theoretical views about what misconceptions are (either stable entities or cued responses based on context) lead to dramatically different student outcomes. Teachers who are able to recognize productive elements in students' intuitive understanding may be more successful in constructive pedagogies. A further issue limiting the efficacy of constructivist approaches involves the fact that many teachers have not received sufficient training to effectively support their students in constructivist learning activities. More research on the efficacy of constructivism would be useful and would help educators focus on specific pedagogical methods and the limitations and advantages of each.

environment. An extreme social constructivist view developed by Kenneth Gergen proposes no strict boundary between the mind and the environment or between language and reality. This view further proposes that a person's understanding of the world cannot be removed from the way he or she uses language to describe it, view it, and discuss it with others.

Less extreme social constructivist perspectives propose simply that students construct knowledge through an interaction with their surroundings rather than in isolation from them. Social interactions play an important part in knowledge construction because they support the introduction and resolution for the cognitive conflict at the heart of constructivist learning perspectives. Although moderate social perspectives acknowledge the

role of people's prior knowledge in the evolution of their understanding, moderate perspectives propose that knowledge structures evolve socially through observation and interaction with other people and the environment. Sociocultural theories and perspectives emphasize the importance of learners' interactions with their social environment in order to determine what should be learned and how it should be learned. Also, being able to discuss developing ideas with others helps learners determine how to modify their ideas.

Different flavors of social constructivism have different emphases for learning and instruction. Some emphasize cognitive skills and strategies for learning while others emphasize the big ideas or concepts in a discipline. Some social constructivists propose three fundamental commitments for teaching and learning: treat the discipline with respect, treat students' ideas with respect, and view the discipline as a "collective intellectual endeavor situated within a community" (Ball & Bass, 2000, p. 197). From this perspective, instruction should involve a democratic process in which students and the teacher discuss what represents publicly shared knowledge and what does not. Instruction should focus on this publicly shared knowledge in order to allow all the students to build upon what they know and to help the teacher understand what steps need to be taken in order to achieve certain goals.

EFFICACY AND ADOPTION OF CONSTRUCTIVISM

Constructivist teaching, introduced by Piaget in the early 1930s, has found increasingly wide acceptance by researchers and educators since the early 1980s. Although widely accepted, however, constructivism remains less widely practiced. A study by Moussiaux and Norman (1997) involving 49 schools and 289 teachers in Michigan found that only 28% to 50% of teachers claimed to use constructivist methods. Furthermore, as noted by Jones and Carter (2007), many teachers who believe they enact constructivist methods do not actually use methods in alignment with constructivist theories. Teachers should be aware of not just the instructional strategies they are implementing but also the theoretical reasons behind those strategies and how they can be used in different ways. Abbott and Fouts found that only 17% of 669 classrooms in 34 schools in Washington actually incorporated constructivism into instruction.

Barron and colleagues (1998) suggest that constructivist approaches remain underimplemented and underutilized because constructivist teaching practices are foreign to students and teachers, and difficult to apply. Many people in the general public remain suspicious when teaching methods differ from the forms of instruction they experienced in school. High-stakes testing represents another obstacle to wider implementation of constructivist instruction. Although state education standards usually include constructivist goals, these standards and goals often do not align with the high-stakes tests or the preparation for those tests. A review by Jones and Carter (2007) suggested that wider implementation of constructivist approaches will require changes in teacher attitudes and beliefs in addition to educational reform.

While authentic constructivist pedagogies remain relatively uncommon in classrooms, many studies support the potential efficacy of constructivist approaches. Abbot and Fouts (2003), for example, found a significant correlation between constructivist teaching and higher achievement. Different constructivist approaches appear, however, to vary in their levels of efficacy. Research on guided discovery learning and pure discovery learning demonstrates that students engaging in guided discovery learning activities outperform students in pure discovery curricula (Shulman & Keisler (1966), Kittel (1957), and Mayer (2004)). In summary, studies have shown that constructivist approaches have great potential but require authentic implementation in order to achieve that potential.

ASSUMPTIONS ABOUT CONSTRUCTIVIST LEARNING AND INSTRUCTION

Although constructivist instruction can take many forms based on the instructor's theoretical commitments, constructivist teaching at its core focuses on students' active role in their own learning as they build and organize their knowledge. Constructivist instructional frameworks, such as those discussed by Lebow (1993), often focus on the following attributes: personal relevance, the opportunity to generate new knowledge, personal autonomy, active engagement, collaboration, the opportunity to reflect on learning, and pluralism. In addition, Langer and Applebee (1987) discuss how the core goals of constructivist teaching often include promoting democratic learning environments and student-centered instruction. As a result, "teachers are apt to feel comfortable in this role only if they view uncertainty and conflict as natural and potentially growth producing for members of the learning community" (Prawat & Floden, 1994, p. 40).

To create personal relevance, learners need to understand the benefits and importance of the curriculum for their own interests. Teachers can promote this relevance by incorporating real-life situations and experiences into their students' classroom learning. To give students an opportunity to be involved in creating knowledge, the learner should be involved not in activities in which the goal is to memorize facts but in problem-solving activities. For instructional design geared toward radical con-

structivism, students should be provided with personal autonomy in which individual work is part of the instructional framework. Also, students should be part of the process of designing the problem as well as dictating the process for working on that problem. Furthermore, to actively engage students, "the teacher's role should be to challenge the learner's thinking—not to dictate or attempt to proceduralize that thinking" (Savery & Duffy, 2001, p. 5). For instruction geared toward social constructivism, collaboration provides opportunities for students to interact and teach one another in small group work.

INSTRUCTIONAL APPROACHES WITH CONSTRUCTIVIST DESIGNS

While many pedagogical approaches integrate key constructivist assumptions about learning and instruction discussed above, five approaches currently receive significant attention. These include (a) case-based learning, (b) discovery learning, (c) inquiry-based learning, (d) problem-based learning, and (e) project-based learning.

Case-based learning, as Herreid (1997) explains, uses real-life examples to build knowledge by resolving questions about a specific case. Usually these questions have no single right answer. Generally, case-based learning focuses on small groups and the interactions between the participants. The teacher facilitates the students' interactions while the students choose analysis techniques and work toward solutions of the open-ended problem. Under this pedagogical approach, students learn content while exposed to real-life issues. Students benefit from this type of instruction because they are given an opportunity for decision making as part of their learning process and because they experience and address different viewpoints.

Discovery learning engages learners in problem solving to make a discovery, as described by Mayer (2004). According to Seymour Papert, "The role of the teacher is to create the conditions for invention rather than provide ready-made knowledge" (Papert, 1980). The instructional design of discovery learning provides students with a problem and the opportunity for exploration to formulate solutions to the problem. The teacher guides the development of problem-solving skills and the creativity of the students. Discovery learning works on the assumption that students are more likely to retain knowledge if they discover it on their own. Students benefit from this type of instruction because it fosters curiosity and creativity.

As discussed by Edelson, Gordin, and Pea (1999), inquiry-based learning places the responsibility for learning and understanding concepts on the student. In other words, inquiry learning requires students to determine the content, the learning process, and the assessment of learning. Inquiry-based methods use questions to guide instruction rather than predetermined topics. Usually this instructional design begins with a general theme that serves as a starting point for learning. Then the instruction builds upon the responses and interactions of the students. Teachers monitor the students' learning process through interviews, journaling, and group discussions. Students benefit from this instructional approach because they develop meta-cognitive learning skills and research skills upon which they can build toward future educational experiences.

Similar to case-based learning, problem-based learning teaches students to think critically, analyze problems, and use appropriate resources to solve real-life problems. Through this process, students identify the nature of the problem and determine what resources they need to utilize to solve the problem, as described by Boud & Feletti (1997). The teacher offers scaffolding by providing examples of how to approach the problem. A study by Wood (1993) suggests that students benefit as they integrate analytical skills with content knowledge as a member of a team.

Project-based learning also harnesses the process of investigation to encourage understanding. This method, as described by Polman (2000), engages students in a long-term project based on a real-life problem. These activities typically involve a wide range of interdisciplinary skills, including math, language, art, geography, science, and technology. This instructional design has less structure than traditional instruction because the students organize their own work. Generally, this approach involves collaborative learning. The teacher provides guidelines (such as checklists) for the students as they progress toward the completion of their project. By providing students with an authentic problem, project-based learning offers students a meaningful experience that promotes the development of research skills.

SEE ALSO *Cognitive Development: Piaget's Theory; Information Processing Theory; Sociocultural Theory.*

BIBLIOGRAPHY

Abbott, M. L., & Fouts, J. T. (2003). Constructivist teaching and student achievement: The results of a school-level classroom observation study in Washington. *Technical Report #5.* Lynnwood, WA: Washington School Research Center.

Ball, D. L., & Bass, H. (2000). Making believe: The collective construction of public mathematical knowledge in the elementary classroom. In D. C. Phillips (Ed.), *Constructivism in education: Opinions and second opinions on controversial issues* (pp. 193–224). Chicago: National Society for the Study of Education.

Barron, B. J. S., Schwartz, D. L., Vye, N. J., Moore, A., Petrosino, A., Zech, L., et al. (1998). Doing with understanding: Lessons from research on problem- and project-based learning. *Journal of the Learning Sciences, 7*(3/4), 271–311.

Boud, D., & Feletti G. (1997) *The challenge of problem-based learning.* London: Routledge.

Edelson, D. C., Gordin, D. N., & Pea, R. D. (1999). Addressing the challenges of inquiry-based learning through technology and curriculum design. *Journal of the Learning Sciences 8*(3/4), 391–450.

Elby, A. (2000). What students' learning of representations tells us about constructivism. *Journal of Mathematical Behavior 19*(4), 481–502.

Herreid, C. F. (1997). What makes a good case? Some basic rules of good storytelling help teachers generate student excitement in the classroom. *Journal of College Science Teaching, 27*(3), 163–165.

Howe, K. R., & Berv, J. (2000). Constructing constructivism, epistemological and pedagogical. In D. C. Phillips (Ed.), *Constructivism in education: Opinions and second opinions on controversial issues* (pp. 19–40). Chicago: National Society for the Study of Education.

Jones, G., & Carter, G. (2007). Science teacher attitudes and beliefs. In S. K. Abell & N. G. Lederman (Eds.), *Handbook of research on science education* (pp. 1067–1104). Mahwah, NJ: Erlbaum.

Kirschner, P. A., Sweller, J., & Clark, R. E. (2006). Why minimal guidance during instruction does not work: An analysis of the failure of constructivist, discovery, problem-based, experiential, and inquiry-based teaching. *Educational Psychologist, 41*(2), 75–86.

Kittel, J. E. (1957). An experimental study of the effect of external direction during learning on transfer and retention of principles. *Journal of Educational Psychology, 48,* 391–405.

Langer, J., & Applebee, A. N. (1987). *How writing shapes thinking: A study of teaching and learning.* Urbana, IL: National Council of Teachers of English.

Lebow D. (1993). Constructivist values for systems design: Five principles toward a new mindset. *Educational Technology Research and Development, 41,* 4–16.

Mayer, R. (2004). Should there be a three-strikes rule against pure discovery learning? The case for guided methods of instruction. *American Psychologist, 59*(1), 14–19.

McCarty, L. P., & Schwandt, T. A. (2000). Seductive illusions: Von Glasersfeld and Gergen on epistemology and education. In D. C. Phillips (Ed.), *Constructivism in education: Opinions and second opinions on controversial issues* (pp. 41–85). Chicago: National Society for the Study of Education.

Moussiaux, S. J., & Norman J. T. (1997). Constructivist teaching practices: Perceptions of teachers and students. Proceedings of the Annual International Conference of the Association for the Education of Teachers in Science (Cincinnati, OH), January 9-12, 1997.

Papert, S. (1980). *Mindstorms: Children, computers, and powerful ideas.* New York: Basic Books.

Phillips, D. C. (2000). An opinionated account of the constructivist landscape. In D. C. Phillips (Ed.), *Constructivism in education: Opinions and second opinions on controversial issues* (pp. 1–16). Chicago: National Society for the Study of Education.

Polman, J. L. (2000). *Designing project-based science: Connecting learners through guided inquiry.* New York: Teachers College Press.

Prawat, R. S., & Floden, R. E. (1994). Philosophical perspectives on constructivist views of learning. *Educational Psychology,* 29(1), 37–48.

Savery, J. R., & Duffy, T. M. (1995). Problem based learning: An instructional model and its constructivist framework. *Educational Technology, 35*(5), 31–38.

Shulman, L. S., & Keisler, E. R. (1966). *Learning by discovery.* Chicago: Rand McNally.

von Glasersfeld, E. (1995). *Radical constructivism: A way of knowing and learning.* London: Falmer Press.

Wood, E. J. (1993). Problem-based learning. *Biochemical Education 21*(4), 169.

Cynthia M. D'Angelo
Stephanie Touchman
Douglas B. Clark

CASE-BASED LEARNING

Case-based instructional methods are used in a variety of disciplines, including medicine, law, business, and education. Cases provide analogs of personal experience; they include a representation of a situation, how the situation was dealt with, and what the consequences were of dealing with it in that way (Kolodner, 1997). Cases describe an interesting story that will generate alternative perspectives from learners. Cases should provoke alternative ideas and require decision making (Herreid, 2008). There are a variety of methods for using cases in the context of instruction. Collaborative discussions among students about the case are common. Students are expected to bring their knowledge and perspectives to the consideration of the case, engage in argumentation about the interpretation of the case with their peers, and deepen their understanding of the issues at hand. In doing so, students use their prior experiences and knowledge to construct new knowledge and understandings.

The various disciplines that use cases as part of their instruction vary in how they define cases. It is difficult to distinguish a case from an example or a problem. Cases are used in various disciplines for different functions. In law schools, students study cases from the past and learn to use them as examples of judicial reasoning (Herreid, 2008). In medicine, cases are examples of previous medical decision making. In both law and medicine, the consequences of the particular decisions made are clear. In education, cases are used in preservice teacher education to illustrate theoretical ideas or to practice decision making. However, the consequences of one set of actions rather than another are much less clear in education than in other domains.

The use of cases in teacher education has the potential to bridge the gap between the declarative knowledge acquired in coursework and the procedural and condi-

tional knowledge developed through practice. Many of the writings available about cases appeal to this potential (e.g., Doyle, 1990; Shulman, 1992). Because cases (e.g., a particular problem in a teacher's class) have face validity as representations of classrooms, teaching by using cases is often touted as a preferred teaching method (Silverman, Welty, & Clark, 1996). However, in 1996 K. K. Merseth noted: "the collective voice of its proponents [the use of cases] far outweighs the power of existing empirical work" (p. 722).

The use of cases for instruction also has the potential to provide a window on developing expertise. More and less experienced individuals can be expected to respond to cases in different ways, providing instructors with insight into how cases are understood. There is some evidence that the use of cases can result in the development of theoretical and practical knowledge (Lundeberg, Levin, & Harrington, 1999). Case discussions can promote reflection and metacognition (Harrington, 1995; Levin, 1995). Much of the research on the use of cases in teacher education has been conducted within the context of college classrooms, and the designs of such research are typically pre- and posttest designs within specific courses that show an increase in the number and kind of theoretical constructs included in the posttest case analysis. Although this kind of research has yielded useful and important information, it is unclear whether the effects are due to the case method *per se* or simply to the exposure to the content of the course. Lundeberg and colleagues (1999) and Levin (1995) call for more systematic research on the use of cases in teacher education.

Students vary in their responses to case-based instruction. In a small study of nine veterinary students, students who had high levels of self-regulatory skills perceived the format of the instruction to be relevant and effective, whereas those students with low self-regulatory skills did not (Ertmer, Newman, & MacDougall, 1996). The degree to which participants engage in discussions related to a case also influences the quality of their thinking about the case (Levin, 1995).

The research on the use of cases has not been programmatic nor are the results systematically organized. It is difficult to draw conclusions about the effectiveness of case-based instruction and learning when there are different criteria across disciplines for what constitutes a good case, how effectiveness is assessed, and how research is conceptualized.

SEE ALSO *Cognitive Apprenticeship; Scaffolding.*

BIBLIOGRAPHY
Doyle, W. (1990). Case methods in the education of teachers. *Teacher Education Quarterly, 17, 1–16.*

Ertmer, P., Newby, T., & MacDougall, M. (1996). Students' responses and approaches to case-based instruction: The role of reflective self-regulation. *American Educational Research Journal, 33,* 719–752.

Harrington, H. L. (1995). Fostering reasoned decisions: Case-based pedagogy and the professional development of teachers. *Teaching and Teacher Education, 11,* 203–214.

Herreid, C. F. (2008). What makes a good case? Some basic rules of good storytelling help teachers generate student excitement in the classroom. Retrieved April 17, 2008, from http://ublib.buffalo.edu/libraries/projects/cases/teaching/good-case.html.

Kolodner, J. L. (1997). Educational implications of analogy: A view from case-based reasoning. *American Psychologist, 52,* 57–66.

Levin, B. (1995). Using the case method in teacher education: The role of discussion and experience in teachers' thinking about cases. *Journal of Teaching and Teacher Education, 11,* 63–79.

Lundeberg, M. A., Levin, B. B., & Harrington, H. L. (1999). *Who learns from cases and how: The research base for teaching and learning with cases.* Mahwah, NJ: Erlbaum.

Merseth, K. K. (1996). Cases and case methods in teacher education. In J. Sikula (Ed.), *Handbook of research on teacher education* (2nd ed., pp. 722–744). New York: MacMillan.

Silverman, R., Welty, W. M., & Clark, S. (1996). From teaching incident to case. *Innovative Higher Education, 2,* 23–37.

Shulman, J. H. (Ed.). (1992). *Case methods in teacher education.* New York: Teachers College Press.

Angela M. O'Donnell

DISCOVERY LEARNING

Discovery learning is an instructional method in which students are free to work in a learning environment with little or no guidance. For example, discovery learning is the method of instruction when students are given a math problem and asked to come up with a solution on their own, when students are given a scientific problem and allowed to conduct experiments, or when students are allowed to learn how a computer program works by typing commands and seeing what happens on a computer screen. The early 21st-century interest in discovery learning has its roots in Jerome Bruner's (1961) eloquent call for discovery methods of instruction and is echoed in Seymour Papert's (1980) focus on discovery methods for teaching computer programming and Deanna Kuhn's (2005) focus on discovery methods for teaching scientific thinking.

Constructivism is a theory of learning in which learners build knowledge in their working memory by engaging in appropriate cognitive processing of mental representations during learning. Richard Mayer (2008) identified three major cognitive processes in this view of learning as knowledge construction: (a) selecting, attending to relevant information that enters the cognitive system through the eyes and ears, (b) organizing, mentally arranging the selected material into coherent cognitive structures, and (c) integrating, mentally integrating the incoming material with prior knowledge activated from long-term memory. The role of active cognitive processing during learning has its roots in the constructivist theories of Frederick Bartlett (1932) and Jean Piaget (1970).

THE RELATIONSHIP BETWEEN CONSTRUCTIVISM AND DISCOVERY

What is the relation between constructivism as a theory of learning and discovery learning as a method of instruction? In a review of research in the learning sciences, John Bransford, Ann Brown, and Rodney Cocking (1999) showed how constructivism has become the dominant view of how people learn. Importantly, they noted that "the revolution in the study of the mind that has occurred in the last three or four decades has important implications for education" (Bransford, Brown, & Cocking, 1999, p. 3). Richard Mayer (2004) has shown how it might be tempting for educators to equate a constructivist vision of active learning (i.e., the idea that deep learning occurs when learners engage in active cognitive processing during learning) with a seemingly corresponding vision of active methods of instruction (i.e., instructional methods emphasizing learning by doing such as discovery learning). Mayer (2004, p. 15) refers to this confusion as the constructivist teaching fallacy, namely the idea that active learning requires active teaching. Instead, the goal of constructivist-inspired teaching methods is to prime appropriate cognitive activity during learning—a goal that does not necessarily require behavioral activity during learning. In short, Mayer (2004, p. 17) argues that "the formula *constructivism = hands-on activity* is a formula for educational disaster."

In educational research, it is customary to compare the effects of pure discovery methods (in which learners receive little or no guidance while working on an educational task), guided discovery methods (in which learners receive substantial guidance while working on an educational task), and direct instruction (in which learners are presented with the to-be-learned material). The overwhelming pattern of results shows that pure discovery methods result in poorer learning than guided discovery or direct instruction. In their landmark book, *Learning by Discovery: A Critical Appraisal,* Lee Shulman and Evan Keiser concluded that research conducted during the 1960s did not favor pure discovery as an effective method of instruction: "there is no evidence that supports the

Conducting experiments is one type of discovery learning. MAURO FERMARIELLO/PHOTO RESEARCHERS, INC.

proposition that having students encounter a series of examples ... and then having them induce the rule is superior to teaching the rule first and asking students to apply it" (1966, p. 191). More than 30 years later, John Sweller came to the same conclusion in comparing learning to solve math problems via worked examples versus via learning by doing: "worked examples proved superior to solving equivalent problems" (1999, p. ix).

DISCOVERY LEARNING

In a review of research on teaching children how to solve Piagetian conservation tasks conducted mainly in the 1970s, C. J. Brainerd (2003) reported that children learned better when given heavy amounts of specific guidance than when left to learn on their own through hands-on discovery. In *Teaching and Learning Computer Programming*, edited by Richard Mayer (1988), research-

ers working in the 1980s reported that students learned the LOGO programming language better through guided discovery or direct instruction than through pure discovery. Subsequently, Klahr and Nigam (2004) found that students who learned to test scientific hypotheses by being given guidance on how to carry out controlled comparisons learned to reason scientifically better than students who learned through using hands-on pure discovery.

In their provocative review, "Why Minimal Guidance During Instruction Does Not Work," Paul Kirschner, John Sweller, and Richard Clark (2006, p. 75) concluded: "although unguided or minimally guided instructional approaches are very popular and intuitively appealing ... these approaches ignore both the structures that constitute human cognitive architecture and evidence from empirical studies over the past century that consistently indicate that minimally guided instruction is less effective than instructional approaches that place a strong emphasis on guidance of the student learning process." Similarly, in "Should There Be a Three-Strikes Rule against Pure Discovery Learning?" Richard Mayer demonstrated that "there is sufficient research evidence to make any reasonable person skeptical about the benefits of discovery learning—practiced under the guise of . . . constructivism—as a preferred instructional method" (2004, p. 14). Overall, in the educational research conducted between 1965 and 2005 across many different learning tasks, discovery methods (i.e., methods of instruction that emphasize hands-on activity without adequate guidance) have consistently been shown to be less effective than more guided methods of instruction.

Theories of learning in the early 2000s provide the theoretical rationale for providing guidance during learning. Based on John Sweller's (1999) cognitive load, Richard Mayer (2001) notes that discovery methods of instruction can encourage learners to engage in extraneous cognitive processing—cognitive processing that does not support the instructional goal. Because cognitive resources are limited, when a learner wastes precious cognitive capacity on extraneous processing, the learner has less capacity to support essential cognitive processing—to mentally represent the target material—and generative cognitive processing—to mentally organize and integrate the material. Guidance—in the form of scaffolding, coaching, modeling, or providing direct instruction—is effective when it helps guide the learner's essential and generative processing during learning while minimizing extraneous processing. In short, discovery learning is particularly ineffective when students do not naturally engage in appropriate cognitive processing during learning—a situation that characterizes most novice learners.

SEE ALSO *Cognitive Apprenticeship; Scaffolding.*

BIBLIOGRAPHY

Bartlett, F. C. (1932). *Remembering.* Cambridge, U.K.: Cambridge University Press.

Brainerd, C. J. (2003). Jean Piaget, learning research, and American education. In B. J. Zimmerman & D. H. Schunk (Eds.), *Educational psychology: A century of contributions.* Mahwah, NJ: Erlbaum.

Bruner, J. S. (1961). The act of discovery. *Harvard Educational Review, 31,* 21–32.

Kirschner, P. A., Sweller, J., & Clark, R. (2006). Why minimal guidance during instruction does not work: An analysis of the failure of constructivist, discovery, problem-based, experiential and inquiry-based teaching. *Educational Psychologist, 42,* 99–107.

Klahr, D., & Nigam, M. (2004). The equivalence of learning paths in early science instruction: Effects of direct instruction and discovery learning. *Psychological Science, 15,* 661–667.

Kuhn, D. (2005). *Education for thinking.* Cambridge, MA: Harvard University Press.

Mayer, R. E. (Ed.). (1988). *Teaching and learning computer programming.* Mahwah, NJ: Erlbaum.

Mayer, R. E. (2001). *Multimedia learning.* New York: Cambridge University Press.

Mayer, R. E. (2004). Should there be a three-strikes rule against pure discovery learning? *American Psychologist, 59,* 14–19.

Mayer, R. E. (2008). *Learning and instruction* (2nd ed.). Upper Saddle River, NJ: Pearson Merrill Prentice Hall.

Papert, S. (1980). *Mindstorms: Children, computers, and powerful ideas.* New York: Basic Books.

Piaget, J. (1970). *Science of education and psychology of the child.* New York: Oxford University Press.

Shulman, L. S., & Keislar, E. R. (Eds.). (1966). *Learning by discovery: A critical appraisal.* Chicago: Rand McNally.

Sweller, J. (1999). *Instructional design in technical areas.* Camberwell, Australia: Australian Council for Educational Research.

Richard E. Mayer

INQUIRY-BASED LEARNING

Research in education and psychology that addresses the development of reasoning typically acknowledges the difficulty children (and adults) have in mastering this form of thinking. Constructivist teaching practice, particularly inquiry-based learning, seeks to mediate the learning process and make this kind of cognition an object of classroom instruction. Through inquiry learning, students play the role of scientists, a role that is familiar to researchers, as it is modeled on the authentic inquiry activities of professional scientists. Their tasks include formulating questions, designing informative investigations, analyzing patterns, drawing inferences, accessing evidence in responding to questions, formulating explanations from evidence, connecting explanations to knowledge, and communicating and justifying claims and explanations. The focus on inquiry learning originated with the work of Jean Piaget (1896–1980) on the development of adolescent reasoning skills, particularly his focus on the discontinuous, or abrupt, transition from concrete to formal operational thought during adolescence.

Piaget advanced an image of children at the early stages of development as intuitive scientists, actively engaged in understanding their environment and forming theories that they seek to support with evidence from their experience. The construction of these theories is driven by their exercise in informal experimentation, although this is not necessarily how people commonly understand experimentation in the work of professional scientists. Frequently, children's theories are hampered by bias, specifically toward confirmation of their existing theories and flawed efforts to integrate new information with existing knowledge, a limitation one would not characterize as typical of scientific reasoning. Although Piaget focused on the development of children's understanding, he emphasized that their strategies of knowledge acquisition exhibit developmental trajectories as well. Research since Piaget has demonstrated that the developmental path he envisioned as discrete stages is more continuous in nature. Abandoning inefficient strategies of knowledge acquisition actually overlaps with adoption of more efficient strategies. One of the primary difficulties students have in evaluating evidence is understanding that their theories exist and can (and most of the time should) be revised by new information. Without some form of intervention to support this development, many students will not achieve this sophisticated level of thinking, and their adult thinking will continue to be characterized by inconsistent, inefficient strategy use.

USE OF INQUIRY-BASED LEARNING

Inquiry-based learning has come to be most frequently used in and associated with science instruction. Preeminent science educators in the United States identify inquiry as the preferred and prescribed method of teaching science. In fact, the first science teaching standard developed by the National Research Council requires science teachers to plan an inquiry-based science program for their students. The National Science Teachers Association (NSTA) has adopted these standards and proclaims itself an integral part of their dissemination and implementation. Typically, the procedure they advocate includes five distinct phases that reflect the scientific process:

Phase 1: engagement with a scientific question, event, or phenomenon connected with their current knowledge, though at odds with their own ideas, which motivates them to learn more;

Phase 2: exploration of ideas through hands-on experiences, formulating and testing hypotheses, problem-solving, and explaining observations;

Phase 3: analysis and interpretation of data, idea synthesis, model building, and clarification of concepts and explanations with scientific knowledge sources (including teachers);

Phase 4: extension of new understanding and abilities and application of learning to new situations (transfer);

Phase 5: review and assessment of what they have learned and how they have learned it (metacognition).

Although receiving most attention in science, inquiry skills have been cited as integral to virtually all subjects taught in K-12 schools. Professional organizations governing instruction in most subjects, from language arts to social studies to music education, include these skills in standards for their disciplines. According to these standards, then, students in K-12 schools can and should be expected to master the skills of inquiry in all areas.

PRINCIPLES OF INQUIRY-BASED LEARNING

The most common components of comprehensive approaches to inquiry-based learning are characterized by close adherence to authentic scientific inquiry as modeled by researchers and scientists themselves. Inquiry-based learning can take multiple forms depending on the task at hand: open, guided, coupled, or structured inquiry. The goals of each approach are dependent upon whether the learning objective involves conceptual or procedural knowledge or some combination of the two. Whether engaging in open or structured inquiry, students may perform most, if not all, components of reasoning, including generating hypotheses, designing experiments, gathering and evaluating evidence, and drawing conclusions based on evidence. The tasks they complete may involve investigation of an actual physical system or of a computer simulated system, an increasingly common practice given its cost-effectiveness and the ubiquitous availability of classroom technological tools. Relations between variables in these systems typically include some that reflect a student's prior beliefs and some that do not. Performance measures in these tasks can be numerous, ideally addressing all components of the process and in multiple forms with feedback to further inform student learning.

Most empirical studies of scientific investigation show significant age differences in performance, with adults typically outperforming children. Researchers have suggested that the development of metacognitive reasoning accounts for these weaknesses, specifically with regard to understanding false beliefs, growing awareness of the sources of personal knowledge, and differentiating and coordinating theory and evidence. The effective use of inquiry requires meta-level understanding of why a particular strategy works, suggesting that the goal of reasoning instruction in general, and inquiry learning methods in particular, should take particular account of metacognition.

EVIDENCE SUPPORTING THE USE OF INQUIRY-BASED LEARNING

Though not the only method of instruction, inquiry-based learning remains a clearly effective method for teaching the skills of inquiry and ensuring their long-term retention and transfer to new domains. Other instructional methods are appropriate complements to inquiry-based learning, particularly when the goals of instruction are conceptual rather than procedural. There is a great deal more to learn in inquiry than just the control of variables strategy that has been the focus of research. Most research on scientific thinking, in fact, has been strictly focused on the control of variables strategy without consideration of the more complex metacognitive awareness required for its consistently successful use. This lack of concern with the meta-level of understanding has resulted in exclusive emphasis on the performance level, i.e., strategy execution. More critically, students must develop explicit models of inquiry procedures that include not just the reasoning process itself but also its value in acquiring knowledge.

SEE ALSO *Cognitive Apprenticeship; Scaffolding.*

BIBLIOGRAPHY

Kuhn, D. (2006) *Education for thinking.* Cambridge, MA: Harvard University Press.

Inquiry and the national science education standards: A guide for teaching and learning. (2000). Washington, DC: NRC, National Academy Press.

Lehrer, R., & Schauble, L. (2006). Cultivating model-based reasoning in science education. In K. Sawyer (Ed.), *Cambridge handbook of the learning sciences* (pp. 371–388). New York: Cambridge University Press.

Zimmerman, C. (2007). The development of scientific thinking skills in elementary and middle school. *Developmental Review, 27,* 172–223.

David Dean, Jr.

PROBLEM-BASED LEARNING

Problem-based Learning (PBL) is an approach to instruction that situates learning in guided experience solving complex problems, such as medical diagnosis, planning instruction, or designing a playground. Developed initially for use in medical schools it has expanded to other settings such as teacher education, business, engineering, and K-12 instruction (Barrows, 2000; Hmelo-Silver, 2004; Torp & Sage, 2002).

PBL is considered a constructivist approach to instruction because in PBL, students are actively engaged in learning content, strategies, and self-directed learning skills through collaboratively solving problems, reflecting on their experiences, and engaging in self-directed inquiry. The role of the teacher is to facilitate the students' learning by providing opportunities for learners to engage in constructive processing. The students take responsibility for their own learning and for the collective progress of their collaborative group.

PRINCIPLES OF PROBLEM-BASED LEARNING

PBL was designed with five instructional goals (Barrows, 1985): to help students (1) construct flexible knowledge, (2) develop effective problem-solving skills, (3) develop self-directed learning skills, (4) become effective collaborators, and (5) become motivated to learn. Major factors in the effectiveness of PBL are having good problems that allow for extended engagement, a student-centered tutorial process, and a facilitator to help guide the learning process.

To foster learning and engagement, good PBL problems have several characteristics. They need to be complex, open-ended, and multiple solution paths; they must be realistic, connect with the learners' experiences, and allow free inquiry. Good problems require multidisciplinary solutions and provide feedback that allows students to evaluate the effectiveness of their knowledge, reasoning, and learning strategies. Problems should be rich enough to promote conjecture and discussion. They should motivate the students' need to learn and apply their new knowledge (Savery, 2006). As learners generate and support their ideas, they publicly express their current understanding, thus enhancing knowledge construction and preparing them for future learning.

Each problem requires a final product or performance that allows the learners to display their understanding. For example, in their 2000 study, Hmelo, Holton, and Kolodner used PBL to help middle-school students learn life science by designing artificial lungs. The students conducted experiments and used a variety of other resources to learn about breathing. Their final products were models of their designs. In teacher education, the final product might be a lesson design, whereas in medical education, it is often an explanation of underlying mechanisms that cause a patient problem.

The heart of PBL is the small group tutorial process. A PBL tutorial begins by presenting a group of students with some information about a complex problem. From the outset, students need to obtain additional problem information through engaging in inquiry. They may gather this information from problem simulations, for example from a patient record database in medical education or from a classroom video in teacher education (Derry, Hmelo-Silver, Nagarajan, Chernobilsky, & Beitzel, 2006); they may also gather facts by doing experiments or other research. At several points, students pause to reflect on the data they have collected so far, generate questions about that data, and ideas about solutions. Students identify concepts they need to learn more about to solve the problem. After considering the problem with their current knowledge, learners divide and independently research the learning issues identified. They then come back together to share what they learned and re-evaluate their ideas. When completing the task, they reflect on the problem to consider the lessons learned, as well as how they performed as self-directed learners and collaborative problem solvers.

As part of the tutorial process, students use white-boards to help guide their learning and problem solving. The whiteboard is divided into four columns that help structure their activity by reminding the learners of the problem-solving process. The whiteboard serves as a focus for group discussions. The *Facts* column holds information that the students obtain from the problem statement and from their inquiry into the details of the problems. The *Ideas* column serves to keep track of their evolving hypotheses about solutions, such as difficulty breathing might be caused by asthma, a common respiratory ailment. The students place their questions for further study into the *Learning Issues* column. They use the *Action Plan* column to keep track of plans for resolving the problem or obtaining additional information. It should be noted that although this is a typical white-board, some schools using PBL use only the first three columns. Other schools that use PBL use *KWL charts* in which students indicate what they *Know*, what they *Want* to learn, and what they *Learned.*

The facilitator is a key factor in an effective PBL tutorial. In PBL, facilitators (also called tutors or coaches) are expert learners, able to model good learning and reasoning strategies, rather than providing content expertise. The facilitator helps move students through the various stages of PBL and monitors group dynamics, ensuring that all students are involved and encouraging them both to articulate their own thinking and to comment on one another's thinking. The facilitator plays an important role in modeling the thinking skills needed when self-assessing reasoning and understanding. It is important to note that the facilitator's moves build on students' thinking to maintain a student-centered learning process. For example, the facilitator encourages students to explain and justify their thinking as they propose solutions to problems. Facilitators guide the tutorial largely through the use of open-ended questions. Their questions help model the use of particular reasoning strategies as they encourage students to connect their inquiry to hypotheses, explain their thinking, and realize the limits of their understanding. Facilitators progressively reduce their support as students become more experienced with PBL until the facilitators' questioning role is largely adopted by the students. However, the facilitators continue to actively monitor the group, making moment-to-moment decisions about how to facilitate the PBL process using a repertoire of different strategies (Hmelo-Silver & Barrows, 2006).

RESEARCH ON PROBLEM-BASED LEARNING

Of the five goals for PBL, much of the research has focused on knowledge construction, problem-solving skills, and self-directed learning skills. There is less evidence about collaboration and motivation. The majority of the research has been conducted in the medical school context. In a 2003 analysis across many studies of PBL in medical education, Dochy and colleagues found that students in a PBL curriculum were better at applying their knowledge than students in a traditional curriculum and that there were no differences on fact-based measures. A few studies have been conducted outside the medical venue and these show some positive effects but there are too few studies to draw firm conclusions (see Hmelo-Silver, 2004 for a review).

BIBLIOGRAPHY

Barrows, H. S. (1985). *How to design a problem-based curriculum for the preclinical years.* New York: Springer.

Barrows, H. S. (2000). *Problem-based learning applied to medical education.* Springfield IL: Southern Illinois University Press.

Derry, S. J., Hmelo-Silver, C. E., Nagarajan, A., Chernobilsky, E., & Beitzel, B. (2006). Cognitive transfer revisited: Can we exploit new media to solve old problems on a large scale? *Journal of Educational Computing Research, 35,* 145–162.

Dochy, F., Segers, M., Van den Bossche, P., & Gijbels, D. (2003). Effects of problem-based learning: A meta-analysis. *Learning and Instruction, 13,* 533–568.

Hmelo, C. E., Holton, D., & Kolodner, J. L. (2000). Designing to learn about complex systems. *Journal of the Learning Sciences, 9,* 247–298.

Hmelo-Silver, C. E. (2004). Problem-based learning: What and how do students learn? *Educational Psychology Review, 16,* 235–266.

Hmelo-Silver, C. E., & Barrows, H. S. (2006). Goals and strategies of a problem-based learning facilitator. *Interdisciplinary Journal of Problem-based Learning, 1,* 21–39.

Savery, J. R. (2006). Overview of PBL: Definitions and distinctions. *Interdisciplinary Journal of Problem-based Learning, 1,* 9–20.

Torp, L., & Sage, S. (2002). *Problems as possibilities: Problem-based learning for k-12 education* (2nd ed.). Alexandria VA: Association for Supervision and Curriculum Development.

Cindy E. Hmelo-Silver

PROJECT-BASED LEARNING

The use of projects in learning has a long history, dating back to the 1918 work of William Heard Kilpatrick (1871–1965). In this initial formulation, project-based learning was the idea of "whole-hearted purposeful activity proceeding in a social environment." Thus, many elements of project-based approaches of the twenty-first century are present in this early conception. A goal of using projects is to provide opportunities for students to become engaged in their own learning as they create meaningful artifacts. These may include reports, physical models, computer models, exhibits, Web sites and other concrete products that provide opportunities for students to demonstrate their understanding. Project-based learning (PBL) is a constructivist approach to learning because students are involved in constructing deep understanding as they engage with the ideas needed for their projects.

University of Michigan researchers Krajcik and Blumenfeld (2006) have contributed to articulating the key features of designs for PBL:

1. Learners start with a driving question, such as "What's in our water?"

2. They explore the driving question by engaging in inquiry. For example, they may study changes in water quality at a local stream. In this process, they learn to apply key disciplinary ideas.

3. Learners work collaboratively to address the driving question.

4. Learning technologies support the learners' inquiry and allow them to participate in authentic activities that might otherwise be beyond their reach.

5. Learners create artifacts to address the driving question such as a computer model of a local water source.

The driving question helps learners see the relevance of what they are learning. This is important as learners are engaged in inquiry over a prolonged time period rather than the typical short-term laboratory experiences. Students need scaffolding for their inquiry, which is accomplished through teacher modeling and feedback as well as through technology-based scaffolding. A key feature of many PBL approaches is the use of technology as cognitive tools that support planning, collaboration, data collection and analysis, modeling, visualization, and information gathering. Examples of these approaches are found in the work of Linn and Slotta with the Web Integrated Science Environment (2006) and the Center for Learning Technology in Urban Schools (Krajcik & Blumenfeld, 2006). Although the research on the effectiveness of PBL overall is limited, according to Krajcik and Blumenfeld, there is growing evidence that project-based science is effective in improving student achievement and motivation.

PBL has similarities to problem-based learning and case-based learning as Savery has noted. All situate learning in real-situations that provide contexts for applying ideas (Hmelo-Silver, 2004). In case-based learning, cases are used as illustrations with a variety of different instructional strategies. There is no signature student-centered pedagogy in case-based instruction though such approaches tend to be oriented toward promoting knowledge application and critical thinking skills. There is a fine line between problem- and project-based learning. Both may involve creating artifacts, but this is not necessarily the case in problem-based learning. In problem-based learning, the problem may be more complex than in project-based learning. There are also differences in the activity structures that are used. The role of the teacher is similar in both approaches because they both build on student thinking. In both approaches, the teacher builds on student thinking, but in a project-based approach, the teacher may also provide benchmark lessons and play a larger role in setting learning goals than in problem-based learning.

BIBLIOGRAPHY

Hmelo-Silver, C. E. (2004). Problem-based learning: What and how do students learn? *Educational Psychology Review, 16,* 235–266.

Kilpatrick, W. H. (1918). The project method. *Teachers College Record, 19,* 319–33.

Krajcik, J. S., & Blumenfeld, P. C. (2006). Project-based learning. In R. K. Sawyer (Ed.), *Cambridge Handbook of the Learning Sciences* (pp. 317–333). New York: Cambridge University Press.

Linn, M. C., & Slotta, J. D. (2006). Enabling participants in online forums to learn from each other. In A. M. O'Donnell, C. E. Hmelo-Silver, & G. Erkens (Eds.), *Collaborative learning, reasoning, and technology* (pp. 61–98). Mahwah, NJ: Erlbaum.

Savery, J. R. (2006). Overview of PBL: Definitions and distinctions. *Interdisciplinary Journal of Problem-based Learning, 1,* 9–20.

Cindy E. Hmelo-Silver

CONCEPT-ORIENTED READING INSTRUCTION (CORI)

SEE *Learning and Teaching Reading.*

COOPERATIVE LEARNING

SEE *Collaborative Learning.*

CORI (CONCEPT-ORIENTED READING INSTRUCTION)

SEE *Learning and Teaching Reading.*

CORRELATIONAL RESEARCH

Correlational research is an important form of educational and psychological research. Some knowledge of correlational methods is important for both the consumption and conduct of research. The purpose of this entry is to (a) define quantitative research methods as a way of framing correlational research, (b) consider multivariate extensions of the bivariate correlation, including statistical methods for analyzing correlational research data, (c) provide some relevant examples of correlational research, (d) discuss the role of correlational research, and (e) mention some key issues associated with correlational research.

DEFINITIONS OF QUANTITATIVE METHODS OF RESEARCH

Research in education and psychology can be roughly divided into quantitative research, qualitative research, and historical research. Quantitative research methods can be categorized as descriptive research, correlational research, and experimental research.

Descriptive research describes the phenomena being studied. Data are gathered and descriptive statistics are then used to analyze such data. Thus descriptive research considers one variable at a time (i.e., univariate analysis), and is typically the entry-level type of research in a new area of inquiry. Descriptive research typically describes what appears to be happening and what the important variables seem to be.

The purpose of correlational research is to determine the relations among two or more variables. Data are gathered from multiple variables and correlational statistical techniques are then applied to the data. Thus correlational research is a bit more complicated than descriptive research; after the important variables have been identified, the relations among those variables are investigated. Correlational research investigates a range of factors, including the nature of the relationship between two or more variables and the theoretical model that might be developed and tested to explain these resultant correlations. Correlation does not imply causation. Thus correlational research can only enable the researcher to make weak causal inferences at best.

In experimental research, the researcher manipulates one or more independent or grouping variables (e.g., by comparing treatment conditions, such as an intervention group vs. a control group) and then observes the impact of that manipulation on one or more dependent or outcome variables (e.g., student achievement or motivation). The statistical method of analysis is typically some form of the analysis of variance. Experimental research includes (a) true experiments (in which individuals are randomly assigned to conditions or groups, such as method of instruction or counseling) and (b) quasi-experiments (in which individuals cannot be randomly assigned as they are already in a condition or group, such as gender, socioeconomic status, or classroom). The basic question to be posed in experimental research concerns what extent a particular intervention causes a particular outcome. Thus experimental studies are those in which strong causal inferences are most likely to be drawn.

MULTIVARIATE EXTENSIONS AND RELEVANT STATISTICAL TECHNIQUES

There are a number of different methods in which correlations can be considered. Each of these methods is directly tied to a particular statistical technique (with names and dates of their initial development). Thus these methods and statistical techniques can be considered together. At the most basic level is a bivariate correlation (contributions by Galton, 1888; Edgeworth, 1892; Pearson, 1900), which examines the correlation or relation between two variables (hence the terms co-relation and bivariate). In some cases one variable is known as an independent variable (or input variable) and the second variable as a dependent variable (or outcome variable). In other cases there are two variables without any such designation. Bivariate correlations provide information about both the strength of the relationship (from uncorrelated, when the correlation is zero, to perfectly correlated, when the correlation is positive or negative one), and the direction of the relationship (positive or negative). A bivariate correlation can only consider two variables at a time. However, there are a number of multivariate extensions to the bivariate correlation in which more than two variables can be simultaneously analyzed.

Regression analysis (1805) of Adrien-Marie Legendre (1752–1833) is a method for using one or more independent variables or predictors to predict a single dependent variable or outcome. The relations among the variables are used to develop a prediction model. Because only one dependent variable can be considered, regression analysis can only be used to test simple theoretical models. A related method, created by George Udny Yule (1871–1951), is that of the multiple correlation (1897);

it represents the correlation between multiple independent variables and a single dependent variable. The multiple correlation is a direct extension of the bivariate correlation for situations involving multiple independent variables. Path analysis (1918), created by Sewall Wright (1889–1988), is an extension of regression analysis for more than a single dependent or outcome variable. Here more complex theoretical models can be tested, as the relations among multiple independent variables and multiple dependent variables can be simultaneously considered.

Canonical correlation analysis (1935), created by Harold Hotalling (1895–1973) is used to determine the correlation between the linear combination of two sets of variables. Statistically this process is superior to examining a multitude of bivariate correlations (both within and across sets). For example, there may be one set of independent variables and a second set of dependent variables. This method takes the best linear combinations from each set of variables and generates a canonical correlation between the combinations of the two sets. Obviously this method represents an extension of the bivariate correlation and the multiple correlations for situations involving multiple independent variables and multiple dependent variables (or simply for two separate sets of variables).

The previously described methods examine the relations among what are known as observed variables. For example, the Stanford-Binet IQ measure is an instrument that produces an observed measured variable (or score) than can be used to infer intelligence. Latent variables (also known as constructs or factors) are variables that are not directly observed or measured but can be indirectly measured or inferred from a set of observed variables. The Stanford-Binet is one possible observed measure of the latent variable intelligence.

The following methods use both observed variables and latent variables. Factor analysis (Spearman, 1904; Thurstone, 1931) and principal component analysis (Pearson, 1901; Hotelling, 1933) are related multivariate correlational methods. Their purpose is to reduce a set of correlated variables into a smaller set of linear combinations of those variables, known as latent factors or components. For example, with a battery of intelligence tests, one can determine how many factors underlie the data (e.g., a single general intelligence factor, specific performance and verbal intelligence factors, etc.).

Structural equation modeling (Joreskog, 1973; Keesling, 1972; Wiley, 1973) combines factor analysis with path analysis to test theoretical relations among latent variables. Here models can range from simple to complex in nature in that any number of variables of any type can be involved (i.e., observed, latent, independent, and/or dependent variables). The incorporation of factor analysis

in structural equation modeling allows the researcher to use multiple measures of each latent variable instead of a single measure, thereby enabling better measurement conditions (i.e., reliability and validity) than with a single measure, for example, determining the relationship between an intelligence latent variable and an achievement latent variable, in which each latent variable is measured through multiple indicator variables.

EXAMPLES OF CORRELATIONAL RESEARCH

What follows are a few prototypical examples of correlational research that educational and psychological researchers have investigated. Bivariate correlations determined the relations between math anxiety measures and teacher confidence measures (Bursal & Paznokas, 2006). Their results indicated that low math-anxious pre-service teachers were more confident in teaching math and science than high math-anxious pre-service teachers. Regression analysis was used to predict student exam scores in statistics (dependent variable) from a series of collaborative learning group assignments (independent variables) (Delucchi, 2006). The results provided some support for collaborative learning groups improving statistics exam performance, although not for all tasks. Multiple correlations were computed between a nonverbal test of intelligence (dependent variable) and various ability tests (independent variables) (Domino & Morales, 2000). The nonverbal test was significantly correlated with grade point average and ability test scores for Mexican American students.

In a path analysis example, Walberg's theoretical model of educational productivity was tested for fifth-through eighth-grade students (Parkerson et al., 1984). The relations among the following variables were analyzed in a single model: home environment, peer group, media, ability, social environment, time on task, motivation, and instructional strategies. All of the hypothesized paths among those variables were shown to be statistically significant providing support for the educational productivity model. A canonical correlation analysis study examined battered women who killed their abusive male partners (Hattendorf, Ottens, & Lomax, 1999). There were two sets of variables: (1) frequency and severity of posttraumatic stress disorder (PTSD) symptoms, and (2) severity of types of abuses inflicted. The set of symptom variables were found to be highly related to the set of abuse variables, thus indicating a strong relationship between PTSD symptoms and severity of abuse. Another more general example involves the relation between a set of student personality variables and a set of student achievement variables.

In terms of factor analysis and principal component analysis, early examples considered the structure underlying different measures of intelligence (subsequently developed into theories of intelligence). Similar work has examined the dimensions of the Big Five personality assessments.

Finally, two examples of structural equation modeling involving both latent and observed variables can be given here. Kenny, Lomax, Brabeck, and Fife (1998) examined the influence of parental attachment on psychological well being for adolescents. In general, maternal attachment had a stronger effect on well being for girls, while paternal attachment had a stronger effect on well being for boys. Shumow and Lomax (2002) tested a theoretical model of parental efficacy for adolescent students. For the overall sample, neighborhood quality predicted parental efficacy, which predicted parental involvement and monitoring, both of which predicted academic and social-emotional adjustment.

ROLE OF CORRELATIONAL RESEARCH

Correlational research has played an important role in the history of educational and psychological research. Early on, the bivariate correlation was used in heredity research and then eventually expanded into all areas of educational and psychological inquiry. Subsequently more sophisticated multivariate extensions enabled researchers to examine multiple variables simultaneously. Correlational research has had and will continue to have an important role in quantitative research in terms of exploring the nature of the relations among a collection of variables. In part, unrelated variables can be eliminated from further consideration, thereby allowing the researcher to give more serious consideration to related variables.

Correlational research can also play an important role in the development and testing of theoretical models. Once the nature of bivariate relations has been determined, this information can then be used to develop theoretical models. The idea here is to attempt to explain the nature of the bivariate correlations rather than to simply report them. At this point, methods such as factor analysis, path analysis and structural equation modeling can come into play.

ISSUES IN CORRELATIONAL RESEARCH

When consuming or conducting correlational research, there are a number of issues to consider, with some issues being positive and others negative in nature. On the positive side, once descriptive research has helped to identify the important variables, correlational research can then be used to examine the relations among those important variables. For example, researchers may be interested in determining which variables are most highly related to a particular outcome, such as student achievement. This can then lead into experimental research in which the causal relations among those key variables can be examined under more tightly controlled conditions. Here one independent variable can be manipulated by the researcher (e.g., method of instruction), with other related variables being controlled in some fashion (e.g., grade, level of school funding). This then leads to a determination of the impact of the independent variable on the outcome variable, allowing a test of strong causal inference.

On the negative side, a limitation of correlational research is that it does not allow tests of strong causal inference. For example, if researchers find a high bivariate correlation between amount of instructional time (X) and student achievement (Y), then they may ask if this correlation necessarily implies that more instructional time causes higher achievement. The answer is not necessarily. Two variables X and Y can be highly correlated for any of the following reasons and others: (a) X causes Y; (b) Y causes X; (c) Z causes both X and Y, but X and Y are not causally related; (d) X and Y both cause Z, but X and Y are not causally related; and (e) many other variables might be involved. In addition, for a causal relationship X must occur before Y. Thus a bivariate correlation coefficient gives information about the nature of the relations between two variables, but not why they are related. Theoretical models of educational and psychological phenomena tend to be rather complex, certainly involving more than simply two variables. More sophisticated correlational methods, such as factor analysis, path analysis, or structural equation modeling, have the ability to examine the underlying relations among many variables and can, therefore, be used as a basis to argue for causal inference.

Another limitation of correlational methods is they commonly suggest that the variables are linearly related to one another. For example, variables X and Y can be shown to have a linear relationship if the data can be nicely fitted by a straight line. When variables are not linearly related, correlational methods will reduce the strength of the relationship (in other words, the linear relation will be closer to zero). Therefore, nonlinear relationships will result in smaller linear correlations, possibly misleading the researcher and the field of inquiry. Outliers, observations that are quite a bit different from the remaining observations, will also reduce the strength of the relationship. It is wise for researchers to examine their data to see if (a) variables are linearly related (e.g., by the use of scatterplots), and (b) there are any influential observations (i.e., outliers).

A final limitation of correlational research occurs when a researcher seeks to consider the relations among every possible variable. The idea is if researchers examine the relations among enough variables, then certainly some variables will be significantly related. While there is an exploratory consideration here, in terms of seeing which variables are related, there is a statistical consideration as well. That is, if researchers examine enough bivariate correlations, they will find some variables that are significantly related by chance alone. For example, if they examine 100 correlations at the .05 level of significance, then they expect to find five correlations that appear to be significantly different from zero, even though these correlations are not truly different from zero. In this case, the more sophisticated multivariate correlational methods can be useful in that fewer tests of significance tend to be done than in the bivariate case.

Correlational methods of inquiry have been popular in educational and psychological research for quite some time in part because they are foundational in nature in terms of their ability to examine the relations among a number of variables. Also, correlational methods can be used to develop and test theoretical models (e.g., factor analysis, path analysis, structural equation modeling). Despite the limitations of correlational research described here, these methods will continue to be used. Additional information on correlational methods can be found in Grimm and Yarnold (1995, 2000), Lomax (2007), and Schumacker and Lomax (2004).

SEE ALSO *Experimental Research; Research Methods: An Overview.*

BIBLIOGRAPHY

Bursal, M., & Paznokas, L. (2006). Mathematics anxiety and pre-service teachers' confidence to teach mathematics and science. *School Science & Mathematics, 106,* 173–180.

Delucchi, M. (2006). The efficacy of collaborative learning groups in an undergraduate statistics course. *College Teaching, 54,* 244–248.

Domino, G., & Morales, A. (2000). Reliability and validity of the D-48 with Mexican American college students. *Hispanic Journal of Behavioral Sciences, 22,* 382–389.

Grimm, L.G., & Yarnold, P. R. (Eds.) (1995). *Reading and understanding multivariate statistics.* Washington, DC: APA.

Grimm, L.G., & Yarnold, P. R. (Eds.) (2000). *Reading and understanding more multivariate statistics.* Washington, DC: APA.

Hattendorf, J., Ottens, A. J., & Lomax, R. G. (1999). Type and severity of abuse and posttraumatic stress disorder symptoms reported by battered women who killed abusive partners. *Violence Against Women, 5,* 292–312.

Kenny, M. E., Lomax, R. G., Brabeck, M. M., & Fife, J. (1998). Longitudinal pathways linking maternal and paternal attachments to psychological well-being. *Journal of Early Adolescence, 18,* 221–243.

Lomax, R. G. (2007). *An introduction to statistical concepts* (2nd ed.). Mahwah, NJ: Erlbaum.

Parkerson, J. A., Lomax, R. G., Schiller, D. P., & Walberg, H. J. (1984). Exploring causal models of educational achievement. *Journal of Educational Psychology, 76,* 638–646.

Schumacker, R. E., & Lomax, R. G. (2004). *A beginner's guide to structural equation modeling* (2nd ed.). Mahwah, NJ: Erlbaum.

Shumow, L., & Lomax, R. G. (2002). Parental efficacy: Predictor of parenting behavior and adolescent outcomes. *Parenting: Science and Practice, 2,* 127–150.

Richard G. Lomax
Jian Li

CREATIVITY

Creativity, of particular interest in Europe and North America, has been defined in many ways over time, reflecting era and culture. Most definitions frame creativity as involving shaping novel possibilities using imagination, recognizing the originality and value of outcomes that are thus generated.

A clear historical evolution of distinctive approaches researching creativity can be documented (Ryhammar & Brolin, 1999; Sternberg, 2003), many earlier approaches being clearly visible even in 2007, as, in common perhaps with many fields of study, intellectual fragmentation of discourse occurs.

HISTORICAL EXPLANATIONS FOR CREATIVITY

The idea of creativity as inspiration produced by a higher power is found far back in Greek, Judaic, Christian, and Muslim traditions, the driving idea being that creativity comes from a mysterious, even divine source. Such ideas are still found in the early 2000s in attempts to understand the mystery of intuition, particularly in the arts (Bannerman et al., 2006; Ghiselin, 1985).

The Romantic era in mid-19th century Europe spawned a very different view, with creativity seen as emerging from human creative capacity for genius expressed as originality, insight, and feeling. Inspiration was seen during this period as being expressed artistically, with a core role given to the subjectivity of feeling. Subsequently many disciplines have contributed to the study of creativity, including psychology, which grew, by the end of the 19th century, to be perhaps the most dominant.

EARLY PSYCHOLOGICAL PERSPECTIVES ON CREATIVITY

From the late 19th century, and rooted in the Romantic conceptions of creativity, psychological explorations focused initially on genius, with the first systematic study undertaken in 1869 by Sir Francis Galton (1822–1911), leading to around a hundred studies well into the 1920s, exploring creativity as achievement acknowledged in the wider public arena.

Approaches from the early 1900s through the first half of the 20th century were characterized by a broadly deductive, philosophical approach within psychology, dominant threads being psychoanalytic, cognitive, and humanistic traditions.

The psychodynamic tradition in the early twentieth century saw the unconscious as playing a significant role in behavior and subjective experience. The work of Sigmund Freud (1856–1939) (1908, 1910) offered insights born of his therapeutic practice-derived psychoanalytic theory, that great creators are driven to do what they do to satisfy unconscious desires. Others, such as Donald Woods Winnicott (1896–1971), followed, with psychodynamic theories of creativity as fundamental and intrinsic to human nature, as closely linked to play and necessary to development.

By the mid-20th century, creativity was seen as associated with science as well as with art; pragmatic approaches were also increasingly adopted as a global economy based on knowledge increasingly required creativity as a core capability (Haste, 2008). Also emerging from therapeutic practice, humanistic approaches to creativity in the later 20th century saw creativity as self-realization, or self-actualization (Rogers, 1954, 1961; Maslow, 1971).

COGNITIVE APPROACHES TO CREATIVITY

But by far the most influential tradition has been the cognitive one, searching both conceptually and empirically, for models to describe creative behavior. This tradition generated many models, including seminal work by Graham Wallas (1926) of the creative process (preparation, incubation, illumination, verification), Mednick's 1962 associative process model, Finke's 1995 exploration of generative to exploratory thought, and Hudson's recognition (1968) that both divergent and convergent thought are involved in creativity.

From the 1950s, building from the cognitive tradition and launched by Guilford's 1950 work on limitations of intelligence testing, came perhaps more deductive, empirically based approaches than hitherto. Some focused on pragmatic strategies to increase individual and collective creativity. These included de Bono's 1993 creative thinking strategies, Buzan's mind mapping techniques (e.g., Buzan, 2006), and Osborn-Parnes' "creative problem solving," triggered by Osborn's early work (1953). Others emphasized psychometric testing (e.g., Torrance, 1969, 1974). Studies proliferated exploring individual and social traits of creative persons and groups, with a

remarkable degree of correlation (Brolin, 1992), leading to perspectives on creativity as inherently collaborative (John-Steiner, 2000). Researchers in Europe and North America sought to contribute to developing the creative organization (e.g., Amabile, 1988; Ekvall, 1996; Isaksen & Lauer, 2002).

Evolutionary approaches to creativity (e.g., Campbell, 1960; Perkins, 1995; Simonton, 1999) also developed, seeking to understand evolution in ideas and identifying two basic steps: first, blind variation (generativity), then, selective retention (novelty judged as valuable), the most creative possibilities surviving.

As the twentieth century drew to a close, many studying creativity began to recognize that multiple components must converge in a confluence approach. These include Amabile's work (1982, 1996, 1999) on intertwining intrinsic motivation, domain knowledge, and creativity skills, also the evolving-systems model generated by Gruber (1981, 1989) integrating knowledge, purpose, and affect, as well as documenting "networks of enterprise" surrounding creative practitioners. Mihaly Csíkszentmihályi (1988, 1996), too, proposed a systems approach, comprising dynamic interaction between individual, domain, and field.

The late 20th century saw a shift from measuring to characterizing, from simple to complex, from individual to collective, from universalized to situated (Jeffrey & Craft, 2001). Researchers began to see creativity as life-wide and domain-wide (Craft, 2005; Claxton, 2006), and as democratic (NACCCE, 1999).

Since the mid-1990s, creativity in applied contexts has experienced unprecedented resurgence globally as an area of scholarship, policymaking and practice, in the classroom, the workplace and personal life. Embedded is the assumption of everyday creativity as necessary and feasible, life-wide and lifelong, a distinctly different perspective to previous ones, which had emphasized the extraordinary, *big c* or high creativity.

The resurgence spans Northern, Central, and Southern Europe, the Middle and Far East and Australasia and North America, expanding the research discourse pool well beyond the earlier North-American community. Such international re-engagement with creativity reflects the relationship perceived at policy level between fostering everyday creativity within education, and economic competitiveness (Jeffrey and Craft, 2001; Craft, 2005). Research methodology shifted, from positivist, large-scale studies aiming to measure creativity, toward ethnographic, qualitative research (Jeffrey & Craft, 2001). Early 21st century studies of creativity in education increasingly emphasize cultural dimensions of creativity, in particular discontinuities between universalized and marketized North American creativity discourse and Asian perspectives

(Craft, Cremin, & Burnard, 2008; Craft, Gardner, & Claxton, 2008).

In the first decade of the 21st century conceptual work examined the ethical dimension of creativity (Craft, 2005; Craft, Gardner, & Claxton, 2008), asking how creativity engages with wisdom and trusteeship, in a world facing unprecedented global problems (Craft, Gardner, & Claxton, 2008).

Approaches to fostering creativity reflect the perspectives discussed earlier. Creativity in education is increasingly linked both to the economy, and, in England in particular, to cultural development, reflecting several rhetorics (Banaji & Burn, 2006). Pedagogical developments include working in partnership with those beyond the classroom, initially recommended by the National Advisory Committee on Creative and Cultural Education (NACCCE, 1999) and then by later government reviews (e.g. Roberts, 2006; Department for Culture, Media and Sport, 2006).

How organizations and societies handle the spectrum of creative and cultural development in the learning age is a contested area spanning psychological, social, and economic theory. Richard Florida (2002) offers such a theory, suggesting, controversially, that urban and economic regeneration correlate with growth in "the creative class" (high-tech workers, artists, musicians, gay men, and bohemians), generating open, dynamic professional and personal activity. While critiqued (Malanga, 2004), the theory remains influential.

MEASURING CREATIVITY

Knotty problems yet to be adequately tackled, include how creativity is assessed. Challenge exists in acknowledging how creativity is recognized and valued in different cultures, particularly where Eastern and Western perspectives are concerned (Craft, 2005; Ng & Smith, 2004). Such is the case because ways in which creativity is assessed imply an underpinning model of creativity.

Some of the most influential and widely used tests of creativity (Torrance, 1969, 1974) can be seen as being based on a temporally located Westernized model of creativity as individualized and involving the generating of a product-outcome. The Torrance Tests of Creativity (TTCT) drew directly on Guilford's 1967 characteristics of divergent production, that is, fluidity, flexibility, originality, and elaboration. Torrance saw creativity as an ability to notice omissions or gaps, to propose solutions to problems, to produce original ideas, to recombine these, and to be able to detect novel relationships between ideas. His figural and verbal tests of creativity imply creativity involves producing outcomes, triggered by challenges focused on exploring consequences of questions, improving ideas, considering unusual uses for artifacts, and imagining what might be, as well as involving figural invention, elaboration, and departure from structure. Responses to the tests are judged to be creative in terms of the following features:

fluency (number) of appropriate or relevant responses

flexibility in types of responses

originality in terms of novelty of responses

elaboration in terms of details that embellish or extend responses.

The Torrance tests, however, take no account of context or of how judgments are made. Amabile's Consensual Assessment Technique, or CAT, (1982, 1996) addresses this by recognizing creativity is embedded in its cultural context, thus a product may be considered to be creative when appropriate judges (familiar with the field) agree that it is so.

Amabile's CAT contrasts with Torrrance's in being contextually dependent but also because the field of judges may include those who have generated the creative products. The CAT process involves judges rating products in a random order by level of creativity a five-point scale, from very uncreative to very creative. Amabile's work with Hennessey (Hennessey & Amabile, 1999) suggests it is not only tangible products that may be assessed using CAT, but any open task that has multiple potential outcomes, leading to what might be seen as a relativist perspective on what constitutes creativity and one which is culturally sensitive (Cheng, 2008).

Attempts to explore assessment of creativity in a learning context include those acknowledging teacher stance in relation to learner stance (Craft, Cremin, Burnard, & Chappell, 2008).

SEE ALSO *Gifted Education.*

BIBLIOGRAPHY

Amabile, T. M. (1982). Social psychology of creativity: A consensual assessment technique. *Journal of Personality and Social Psychology, 43,* 997–1013.

Amabile, T. M. (1988). A model of creativity and innovation in organizations. In B. M. Staw & L. L. Cunnings (Eds.), *Research in organizational behavior.* Vol. 10. Greenwich, CT: JAI.

Amabile, T. M. (1996*). Creativity in context.* Boulder, CO: Westview Press.

Banaji, S., & Burn, A. (2006). *The rhetorics of creativity.* London: Arts Council England.

Bannerman, C., Sofaer, J., & Watt, J. (Eds.). (2006). *Navigating the unknown: The creative process in contemporary performing arts.* London: Middlesex University Press.

Brolin, C. (1992). Kreativitet och kritiskt tandande. Redsckap for framtidsberedskap [Creativity and critical thinking. Tools for preparedness for the future], *Krut, 53,* 64–71.

Buzan, T. (2006). *Use your head.* Rev. ed. London: BBC Active.

Campbell, D. T. (1960). Blind variation and selective retention in creative thought and other knowledge processes. *Psychological Review, 67,* 380–400.

Cheng, V. M. Y. (2008). Consensual assessment in creative learning. In Craft, A., Cremin, T., & Burnard, P. (Eds.), *Creative learning* (pp. 3–11). Stoke-on-Trent, U.K.: Trentham Press.

Claxton, G. (2006). Creative glide space. In Bannerman, C., Sofaer, J., & Watt, J. (Eds.), *Navigating the unknown.* London: Middlesex University Press.

Craft, A. (2005). *Creativity in schools: Tensions and dilemmas.* Abingdon, U.K.: Routledge.

Craft, A., Cremin, T., & Burnard, P. (Eds.). (2008). *Creative learning* (pp. 3–11). Stoke-on-Trent: Trentham Press.

Craft, A., Cremin, T., Burnard, P., & Chappell, K. (2007). Teacher stance in creative learning: A study of progression. *Thinking Skills and Creativity, 2*(1) 136–147.

Craft, A., Gardner, H., & Claxton, G. (Eds.). (2008). *Creativity, wisdom and trusteeship.* Thousand Oaks, CA: Corwin Press.

Csíkszentmihályi, M. (1988). Society, culture and person: A systems view of creativity. In R. J. Sternberg (Ed.), *The nature of creativity* (pp. 325–339). Cambridge, U.K.: Cambridge University Press.

De Bono, E. (1993). *Serious creativity.* New York: HarperBusiness.

Department for Culture, Media and Sport. (2006). *Government response to Paul Roberts' report on nurturing creativity in young people.* London: Author.

Ekvall, G. (1996). Organizational climate for creativity and innovation. *European Work and Organizational Psychology, 5,* 105–123.

Finke, R. A. (1995). Creative insight and preinventive forms. In R. J. Sternberg & J. E. Davidson (Eds.), *The nature of insight* (pp. 225–280). Cambridge, MA: MIT Press.

Florida, R. (2002). *The rise of the creative class: And how it is transforming work, leisure, community and everyday life.* New York: Perseus Books Group.

Freud, S. (1908). The relation of the poet to daydreaming. In J. Riviere (Ed. & Trans.) *Collected papers* (Vol. 4, pp. 173–183). New York, London [etc.]: The International Psycho-analytical Press, 1924–50.

Freud, S. (1910). *Leonardo da Vinci and a memory of his childhood* (J. Strachey, Ed. & Trans.). (1989). New York: Norton.

Galton, F. (1869). *Hereditary genius: An inquiry into its laws and consequences.* London: Macmillan.

Ghiselin, B. (Ed.). (1985). *The creative process: A symposium.* Berkley: University of California Press.

Gruber, H. (1981). *Darwin on man: A psychological study of scientific creativity* (2nd ed.). Chicago: University of Chicago Press. (Original work published 1974).

Gruber, H. (1989). The Evolving Systems Approach to Creative Work. In Wallace, D.E. and Gruber H., *Creative People at Work: Twelve Case Studies*: 3–24. Oxford: Oxford University Press.

Guilford, J. P. (1950). Creativity. *American Psychologist, 5,* 444–454.

Guilford, J. P. (1967). *The nature of human intelligence.* New York: McGraw-Hill.

Haste, H. (2008). Good thinking: The creative and competent mind. In Craft, A., Gardner, H., & Claxton, G. (Eds.),

Creativity, wisdom, and trusteeship: Exploring the role of education. Thousand Oaks: Corwin Press.

Hennessey, B., & Amabile, T. M. (1999). Consensual assessment. In M. Runco (Ed.), *Encyclopedia of creativity* (Vol. 1, pp. 347–359). San Diego: Academic Press.

Isaksen, S.G. & Lauer, K. J. (2002). The Climate for Creativity and Change in Teams *Creativity and Innovation Management* 11 (1), 74–86.

John-Steiner, V. (2000). *Creative collaboration.* New York: Oxford University Press.

Malanga, S. (2004, January 19). The curse of the creative class. *Wall Street Journal.* Retrieved April 18, 2008 from http://www.opinionjournal.com/extra/?id=110004573.

Maslow, A. H. (1971). *The farther reaches of human nature.* New York: Viking Press. (An Esalen book).

Mednick, S. A. (1962). The associative basis of the creative process. *Psychological Review, 69,* 220–232.

National Advisory Committee on Creative and Cultural Education (NACCCE). (1999). *All our futures: Creativity, culture and education.* London: Department for Education and Employment.

Ng, A. K., & Smith, I. (2004). The paradox of promoting creativity in the Asian classroom: An empirical investigation. In Sing, L., Hui, A., & Ng, G. (Eds.), *Creativity: Where East meets West.* Singapore: World Scientific.

Osborn, A. F. (1953). *Applied Imagination.* New York: Charles Scribner's Sons.

Perkins, D. N. (1995). *Outsmarting IQ: The emerging science of learnable intelligence.* New York: Free Press.

Roberts, P. (2006). *Nurturing creativity in young people. A report to government to inform future policy.* London: Department Culture, Media, and Sport.

Rogers, C. R. (1954). Towards a theory of creativity. *ETC: A Review of General Semantics 11,* 249–260.

Rogers, C. R. (1961). *On becoming a person: A therapist's view of psychotherapy.* Boston: Houghton.

Ryhammar, L., & Brolin, C. (1999). Creativity research: historical considerations and main lines of development. *Scandinavian Journal of Educational Research, (43)*3: 259–273.

Simonton, D. K. (1999). Talent and its development: An emergenic and epigenetic mode. *Psychological Review, 106,* 435–457.

Torrance, E. P. (1969). Originality of imagery in identifying creative talent in music. *Gifted Child Quarterly.* (13), 3–8.

Torrance, E. P. (1974). *Torrance tests of creative thinking.* Lexington, MA: Ginn & Company.

Wallas, G. (1926). *The art of thought.* New York: Harcourt, Brace.

Winnicott, D. W. (1971). *Playing and reality.* London: Tavistock.

Anna Craft

CRITERION-REFERENCED TESTS

A *criterion-referenced test* is a test that provides a basis for determining a candidate's level of knowledge and skills in relation to a well-defined domain of content. Often one or more performance standards are set on the test score scale to aid in test score interpretation. Criterion-referenced tests, a type of test introduced by Glaser (1962) and Popham and Husek (1969), are also known as domain-referenced tests, competency tests, basic skills tests, mastery tests, performance tests or assessments, authentic assessments, objective-referenced tests, standards-based tests, credentialing exams, and more. What all of these tests have in common is that they attempt to determine a candidate's level of performance in relation to a well-defined domain of content. This can be contrasted with *norm-referenced tests*, which determine a candidate's level of the construct measured by a test in relation to a well-defined reference group of candidates, referred to as the norm group. So it might be said that criterion-referenced tests permit a candidate's score to be interpreted in relation to a domain of content, and norm-referenced tests permit a candidate's score to be interpreted in relation to a group of examinees. The first interpretation is content-centered, and the second interpretation is examinee-centered.

CRITERION-REFERENCED TESTS AND NORM-REFERENCED TESTS

Because these two types of tests have fundamentally different purposes, it is not surprising that they are constructed differently and evaluated differently. Criterion-referenced tests place a primary focus on the content and what is being measured. Norm-referenced tests are also concerned about what is being measured but the degree of concern is less since the domain of content is not the primary focus for score interpretation. In norm-referenced test development, item selection, beyond the requirement that items meet the content specifications, is driven by item statistics. Items are needed that are not too difficult or too easy, and that are highly discriminating. These are the types of items that contribute most to score spread, and enhance test score reliability and validity. With criterion-referenced test development, extensive efforts go into insuring content validity. Item statistics play less a role in item selection though highly discriminating items are still greatly valued, and sometimes item statistics are used to select items that maximize the discriminating power of a test at the performance standards of interest on the test score scale.

Some scholars have argued that there is little difference between norm-referenced tests and criterion-referenced tests, but this is not true. A good norm-referenced test is one that will result in a wide distribution of scores on the construct being measured by the test. Without score variability, reliable and valid comparisons of candidates cannot be made. A good criterion-referenced test will permit content-referenced interpretations and this means that the content domains to

which scores are referenced must be very clearly defined. Each type of test can serve the other main purpose (norm-referenced versus criterion-referenced interpretations), but this secondary use will never be optimal. For example, since criterion-referenced tests are not constructed to maximize score variability, their use in comparing candidates may be far from optimal if the test scores that are produced from the test administration are relatively similar (see Hambleton & Zenisky, 2003).

RELIABILITY AND VALIDITY ASSESSMENT

Because the purpose of a criterion-referenced test is quite different from that of a norm-referenced test, it should not be surprising to find that the approaches used for reliability and validity assessment are different too. With criterion-referenced tests, scores are often used to sort candidates into performance categories. Consistency of scores over parallel administrations becomes less central than consistency of classifications of candidates to performance categories over parallel administrations. Variation in candidate scores is not so important if candidates are still assigned to the same performance category. Therefore, it has been common to define reliability for a criterion-referenced test as the extent to which performance classifications are consistent over parallel-form administrations. For example, it might be determined that 80% of the candidates are classified in the same way by parallel forms of a criterion-referenced test administered with little or no instruction in between test administrations. This is similar to parallel form reliability for a norm-referenced test except the focus with criterion-referenced tests is on the decisions rather than the scores. Because parallel form administrations of criterion-referenced tests are rarely practical, over the years methods have been developed to obtain single administration estimates of decision consistency (see, for example, Livingston & Lewis, 1995) that are analogous to the use of the corrected split-half reliability estimates with norm-referenced tests.

With criterion-referenced tests, the focus of validity investigations is on (1) the match between the content of the test items and the knowledge or skills that they are intended to measure, and (2) the match between the collection of test items and what they measure and the domain of content that the tests are expected to measure. The "alignment" of the content of the test to the domain of content that is to be assessed is called *content validity evidence*. This term is well known in testing practices.

Many criterion-referenced tests are constructed to assess higher-level thinking and writing skills, such as problem solving and critical reasoning. Demonstrating that the tasks in a test are actually assessing the intended higher-level skills is important, and this involves judgments and the collection of empirical evidence. So, construct validity evidence too becomes crucial in the process of evaluating a criterion-referenced test.

SETTING PERFORMANCE STANDARDS

Probably the most difficult and controversial part of criterion-referenced testing is setting the performance standards, i.e., determining the points on the score scale for separating candidates into performance categories such as "passers" and "failers." The challenges are great because with criterion-referenced tests in education, it is common on state and national assessments to separate candidates into not just two performance categories, but more commonly, three, four, or even five performance categories. With four performance categories, these categories are often called *failing, basic, proficient,* and *advanced.*

What makes the setting of performance standards on criterion-referenced tests controversial is that the process itself is highly judgmental, and the implications are far-reaching. Candidates who fail the test may be denied a high school diploma or a license to practice in the profession they trained for. Teachers and administrators can lose their jobs if student test performance does not meet the performance standards. Perceptions of the quality of education in a state can be affected by large percentages of students being assigned to the failing or basic performance categories. With international assessments such as Trends in Mathematics and Science Study (TIMSS), the educational reputations of countries are based on criterion-referenced test performance.

The process of setting performance standards proceeds through many steps (see Cizek, 2001; Hambleton & Pitoniak, 2006). First, it is common to set a policy about the composition of the panel that will set the performance standards. Here, decisions about the demographic make-up of the panel, such as gender, ethnicity, years of experience, geographical distribution, role (e.g., teachers, administrators, curriculum specialists, parents), are usually considered, as well as other factors. Then a plan is put in place to draw a representative panel to meet the specifications.

Another big decision concerns the choice of standard-setting method. There are probably 10 to 20 major methods, and large numbers of variations of each. The methods include Angoff, Ebel, Nedelsky, contrasting groups, borderline groups, direct consensus, item cluster, booklet selection, extended Angoff, bookmark, and more.

Prior to the meeting of the panel to set the performance standards it is common for a different panel to prepare performance category descriptions. These descriptions lay out for the standard-setting panel what it means to be a failing student, a basic student, and so on. The descriptions provide a basis for the standard-setting panel to carry out its work of determining just how well candidates must perform on the test to demonstrate basic, proficient, and advanced level performance. The descriptions are also helpful in communicating what the expectations are for students in the performance categories, and at the time of score reporting.

Next, the panel is brought together and the chosen method is applied to produce performance standards. A typical panel meeting often begins with discussion of the purpose of the test and exposure to the performance category descriptions. Having the panelists take a portion or even the entire test is another activity that is included as part of the training. Then the method is introduced, and practice is given prior to the panel starting on its task of setting the standards.

The meeting continues, and often two to three days are needed for the panelists to work through the method and related discussions until a final recommended set of performance standards is produced. Validity evidence is compiled about the process and the panelists' impressions of it, a technical manual is often written, and then all of the information is forwarded to a board for setting the final performance standards for the criterion-referenced test. If multiple tests are involved (e.g., mathematics, reading, and science tests at several grade levels), the task of making the complete set of performance standards across subjects and grades consistent or coherent is especially challenging.

USES

Criterion-referenced tests are used in many ways. Classroom teachers use them to monitor student performance in their day-to-day activities. States find them useful for evaluating student performance and generating educational accountability information at the classroom, school, district, and state levels. The tests are based on the curricula, and the results provide a basis for determining how much is being learned by students and how well the educational system is producing desired results. Criterion-referenced tests are also used in training programs to assess learning. Typically pretest-posttest designs with parallel forms of criterion-referenced tests are used. Finally, criterion-referenced tests are used in the credentialing field to determine persons qualified to receive a license or certificate. There are hundreds of credentialing agencies in the United States that are using criterion-referenced tests to make pass-fail credentialing decisions.

SEE ALSO *Classroom Assessment.*

BIBLIOGRAPHY

Cizek, G. (Ed.). (2001). *Setting performance standards: Concepts, methods, and perspectives.* Mahwah, NJ: Erlbaum.

Glaser, R. (1963). Instructional technology and the measurement of learning outcomes. *American Psychologist, 18,* 519–521.

Hambleton, R. K., & Pitoniak, M. (2006). Setting performance standards. In R. L. Brennan (Ed.), *Educational measurement* (pp. 433–470). Westport, CT: American Council on Education.

Hambleton, R. K., & Zenisky, A. (2003). Issues and practices of performance assessment. In C. Reynolds and R. Kampaus (Eds.), *Handbook of psychological and educational assessment of children* (pp. 377–404). New York: Guilford.

Livingston, S., & Lewis, C. (1995). Estimating the consistency and accuracy of classifications based on test scores. *Journal of Educational Measurement, 32,* 179–180.

Popham, W. J., & Husek, T. R. (1969). Implications of criterion-referenced measurement. *Journal of Educational Measurement, 6,* 1–9.

Ronald K. Hambleton

CRITICAL THINKING

One of the most challenging and yet rewarding experiences in teaching any college course occurs when the professor is faced with dispelling a popular myth or misconception that students hold in their belief system. It is challenging because beliefs are part of an entire system of understanding, and the process of changing a belief typically requires considerable effort by both professor and students. Ideally, beliefs are based on solid reasoning and good data, so changing a belief may mean changing the way someone reasons and the data that are accepted as valid. In changing a belief, educators need to understand how students explain events. For example, if someone is thinking about a friend and the friend calls him moments later, is this evidence of chance or a premonition? It is not easy to get most people to consider all of the people they think about everyday and realize that, just by chance, sometimes they will get a phone call from the very person who occupied their thoughts in the last few minutes.

The reward for the professor occurs when students can understand faulty reasoning patterns and distinguish good data from poor data. The deconstruction and rebuilding of a belief system requires critical thinking. The term critical thinking refers to the use of those cognitive skills or strategies that increase the probability of a desirable outcome. It is purposeful, reasoned, and goal directed. It is the kind of thinking involved in solving problems, formulating inferences, calculating likelihoods, and making decisions. When people think critically, they are evaluating the outcomes of their thought processes—how good a decision is or how well a problem is solved. Critical thinking also involves evaluating the thinking process—the reasoning that went into the conclusion arrived at or the kinds of factors considered in making a decision.

Professors who teach introductory courses (e.g., introduction to psychology, critical thinking, and life span and human development) are often faced with common misconceptions. Examples of misconceptions include the credibility and use of astrological readings, belief in the power of healing crystals, and reliance on shoddy research to justify a belief in products such as the use of shark oil to cure cancer or copper bracelets to relieve the pain of arthritis. Students must engage with new information in a conscious and critical manner for these misconceptions to be replaced with a new belief system.

CRITICAL THINKING

Critical thinking is one type of thinking. Other types are the use of random methods to arrive at a conclusion, rote memorization, day and night dreaming, and sloppy thinking. Critical thinking is not a new idea. The philosopher John Dewey, who wrote about this topic at the turn of the 20th century, advocated for teaching skepticism, reflective inquiry, and tolerance for ambiguity, while working to reduce uncertainty. Students must be taught to consider evidence, from multiple sources, in order to solve problems. What is now thought of as critical thinking had a place in Dewey's basic writings. For Dewey, schools act as a repair organ for society, and it is through education that students can learn to think critically so that society can work toward self-improvement.

Diane Halpern (2003) notes that different types of information can be held or processed by different cognitive processes. For example, information in the form of speech is processed differently than visual information. In fact, these are examples of the two preferred modes of thought; silent speech and imagery. Based on these two types of processing information, different cognitive strategies are used during the critical thinking process.

The notion of different cognitive processes dealing with different information is related to the definition of critical thinking. Halpern defines the term as follows:

> Critical thinking is the use of those cognitive skills or strategies that increase the probability of a desirable outcome. It is used to describe thinking that is purposeful, reasoned, and goal directed—the kind of thinking involved in solving problems, formulating inferences, calculating likelihoods, and making decisions, when the

thinker is using skills that are thoughtful and effective for the particular context and type of thinking task (2003, p. 6).

The student who believes in astrological readings may focus on those outcomes that confirm the predictions made in the readings, which are always vague enough that almost anyone can find confirmation for the predictions. Another key element to critical thinking is an awareness of one's own thinking. Metacognition, or knowledge about what a person knows and how the person thinks is a key concept in the critical thinking literature because students need to have an awareness of the process and outcome of their thinking in order to consciously improve how they think.

A MODEL OF INTELLECTUAL DEVELOPMENT

Critical thinking is a developmental process that can begin at an early age. When thinking about critical thinking, people need to keep their definitions developmentally appropriate so that what constitutes critical thinking in the elementary school grades will differ from what is expected of an adult. William Perry conducted a survey of the thinking processes of students at Harvard University and Radcliffe College in 1953. Perry later (1968) devised an intellectual development model based on his analysis of survey responses. Although Perry's model was not designed to describe the development of critical thinking, it does describe many of the characteristics of a critical thinker such as open-mindedness, flexibility, willingness to self-correct, and pursuit of consensus (Halpern, 2003). The authors have broken Perry's model into four stages, with progression through the stages in a linear fashion. Perry's model can help educators understand how important aspects of critical thinking develop.

The first stage of Perry's (1968) model is called basic duality. This type of thinking is best illustrated by someone who believes there is only one truth and the authority of the truth is not to be questioned. Students who are functioning at this level will strictly memorize material with little critical thinking about the material. Some students in this stage will begin to question authority figures but will only identify those whom they believe are frauds. They will start to perceive information as limited truths. The second stage is called multiplicity pre-legitimate. A student's thinking about information changes from the notion that there is an absolute truth with correct/incorrect information to the notion that the truth remains to be known. At this stage, students' thinking processes change in that they understand that work is needed to provide evidence for opinions, including their own, for what may be the truth and that there may be multiple truths in the world.

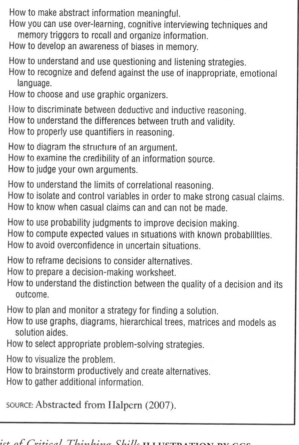

How to make abstract information meaningful.
How you can use over-learning, cognitive interviewing techniques and memory triggers to recall and organize information.
How to develop an awareness of biases in memory.

How to understand and use questioning and listening strategies.
How to recognize and defend against the use of inappropriate, emotional language.
How to choose and use graphic organizers.

How to discriminate between deductive and inductive reasoning.
How to understand the differences between truth and validity.
How to properly use quantifiers in reasoning.

How to diagram the structure of an argument.
How to examine the credibility of an information source.
How to judge your own arguments.

How to understand the limits of correlational reasoning.
How to isolate and control variables in order to make strong casual claims.
How to know when casual claims can and can not be made.

How to use probability judgments to improve decision making.
How to compute expected values in situations with known probabilities.
How to avoid overconfidence in uncertain situations.

How to reframe decisions to consider alternatives.
How to prepare a decision-making worksheet.
How to understand the distinction between the quality of a decision and its outcome.

How to plan and monitor a strategy for finding a solution.
How to use graphs, diagrams, hierarchical trees, matrices and models as solution aides.
How to select appropriate problem-solving strategies.

How to visualize the problem.
How to brainstorm productively and create alternatives.
How to gather additional information.

SOURCE: Abstracted from Halpern (2007).

List of Critical Thinking Skills ILLUSTRATION BY GGS INFORMATION SERVICES. CENGAGE LEARNING, GALE.

The third stage is called relativism correlate, competing or diffuse. In this stage of development, students begin to understand that truth is contextual. Furthermore, they see that validity is an important issue that must be addressed in accepting that all knowledge may be relative but not equally valid. Another important aspect of the thinking process is the realization that theories are more like metaphors for the real world and are not to be accepted as absolute truths. With the realization of information being relative and the idea of validating information, students can become disoriented and starts to question the self. There is a realization that decisions need to be made in an uncertain world, a difficult process to go through. The final stage of Perry's model is called commitment foreseen. The students who reach this stage have come to the conclusion that commitments for how knowledge is obtained, used, and created needs to be made carefully.

The commitments made in the final stage influence personal values and career decisions. More importantly, students realize a balance must be made in assessing and accepting new information. Students become more flexible in respecting others' values and are aware that they must be open-minded and ready to learn new information while still maintaining their own values. The key element to this stage of thinking is that the student realizes that the process of acquiring, analyzing, and making a decision about new information is an iterative process. It is a process that requires much knowledge about one's own thinking while allowing for acquiring new information. This process has come to be known as metacognition.

METACOGNITION

Metacognitive processes are central to understanding critical thinking. John Flavell (1979) introduced four basic components to self-knowledge: metacognitive knowledge, metacognitive experiences, goals, and strategies. They are often referred to as ease of learning judgments. The ease of learning judgment is an initial assessment by the student of how easy or difficult it will be to acquire the new information. In making these judgments, critical thinkers will devise a plan for the best way to obtain new information. Critical thinkers also recognize the potential cognitive strategies and skills that may be required. The quality of learning judgment is a monitor of how well the information is being learned. Critical thinkers assess if any changes in their learning process need to be changed by using different cognitive strategies or skills. The feeling of knowing judgment is a check on how well information is known. During this time in the thinking process, critical thinkers will seek consensus to determine if information has been conceptualized correctly. If the information turns out to be false, critical thinkers are willing to self-correct.

The degree of confidence judgment is a monitor for how confident the student is in giving an answer. Many errors can occur in the process of making this judgment. Asher Koriat, Sarah Lichtenstein, and Baruch Fischhoff (1980) found that people are susceptible to ignoring evidence that contradicts their answers and tend to favor positive evidence when compared to negative evidence. It is crucial that students are willing to self-correct while judging how confident they are in a belief. Metacognition is an important component in the critical thinking process in that people need to be aware of their own knowledge in the cognitive strategies and skills that are at their disposal. It is during the process of thinking about their own thinking that students assess the quality of the data or other evidence that supports their conclusion and how closely related the data are to the conclusion.

COGNITIVE STRATEGIES AND SKILLS

The instruction of critical thinking has been transitioning from teaching students to critically think in a content driven course to courses designed exclusively to teach critical thinking. The latter approach allows the students to become explicitly aware of their thinking by providing them with both academic and real-world examples in demonstrating the cognitive strategies and skills associated with critical thinking. Halpern's taxonomy of critical thinking allows students to develop a critical thinker attitude by engaging in real-world, practical examples as opposed to the more traditional approach of dialectical reasoning.

Halpern's critical thinking taxonomy is designed from a skills based approach. The skills are broken down into ten primary categories as follows: critical thinking framework, memory, language and thought, reasoning, analyzing arguments, hypothesis testing, likelihood and uncertainty, decision making, problem solving skills, and creativity. The skills taught are geared toward the student becoming accustomed to thinking at the highest levels of Bloom's taxonomy, which include evaluating, designing, and creating knowledge.

The critical thinking framework includes the skills for framing the problem and recognizing the goal. Skills in memory include mnemonics and the recognition that memory is a mediator of thought. The relationship between language and thought is important for students to understand, and they need to gain skills in recognizing emotional language, the use of vagueness, ambiguity, and reification. Other basic skills include recognizing anchoring and framing effects, thinking in terms of probability and likelihood, and working backwards to find a solution to a problem.

Understanding arguments and the concept of hypothesis testing are both important for people to be effective critical thinkers. The skills that come in understanding arguments include recognizing the components of an argument and recognizing typical fallacies that people use in arguments. For hypothesis testing, the necessary skills include being able to distinguish between inductive and deductive reasoning, knowing the difference between an independent variable and dependent variable, and the importance of random assignment.

The accumulation and combination of these skills, along with many others, are what create a critical thinker. Critical thinking is not a single skill that can be used over and over in a rote fashion; this sort of conceptualization is antithetical to the very idea of a critical thinker. A critical thinker has the ability to use any and all strategies as appropriate and maybe even to create some new strategies in developing a solution to a problem.

CRITICAL THINKING ASSESSMENT

There are two primary critical thinking assessments. The first assessment, the Watson-Glaser Critical Thinking Appraisal (WGCTA), is designed to evaluate a critical thinker's ability to solve problems, reason deductively, evaluate arguments, make inferences, and conduct interpretations. The second is the Halpern Critical Thinking Assessment (HCTA). Similar to Halpern's taxonomy, this assessment is designed to test students' critical thinking skills within the context of real-world situations. For example, test takers might be asked to evaluate an argument that if the Immigration Office changes one country's immigration quota, then it will have to change the immigration quota for all other countries. The objective of this particular example is to see if the person recognizes the slippery slope fallacy being used by the Immigration Office.

Critical thinking is a process that requires the conscious awareness of a person's ability to recognize the cognitive strategies and skills that he or she can use appropriately. Metacognition is the monitoring of one's own cognition and capabilities. In explicitly teaching students critical thinking strategies through a skills-based approach, they will be directed through the developmental stages of intellectual development. The result is a critically conscious citizen whose decisions will have a higher probability rate of being informed and judicious.

SEE ALSO *Cognitive Strategies; Reasoning.*

BIBLIOGRAPHY

Dewey, J. (1916). *Democracy and education: an introduction to the philosophy of education.* New York: Macmillan. Retrieved April 18, 2008 from http://www.ilt.columbia.edu/Publications/dewey.html.

Flavell, J. H. (1979). Metacognition and cognitive monitoring: a new area of cognitive-developmental inquiry. *American Psychologist, 34*(10), 906–911.

Halpern, D. F. (2007). The nature and nurture of critical thinking. In R. Sternberg, R. Roediger, & D. F. Halpern (Eds.). *Critical Thinking in Psychology* (pp. 1–14). Cambridge, MA: Cambridge University Press.

Halpern, D. F. (2003) *Thought and knowledge: An introduction to critical thinking.* Mahwah, NJ: Erlbaum.

Koriat, A., Lichtenstein, S., & Fischhoff, B. (1980). Reasons for confidence. *Journal of Experimental Psychology: Human Learning and Memory, 6*(2), 107–118.

Perry, W. G. (1968). *Forms of intellectual and ethical development: in the college years.* New York: Holt, Rinehart and Winston.

Shepard, R. N., & Metzler, J. (1971). Mental rotation of three-dimensional objects. *Science, 171*(3972), 701–703.

Diane F. Halpern
Clayton L. Stephenson
Patrick B. Williams

CRONBACH, LEE J(OSEPH)
1916–2001

Lee Joseph Cronbach was born in 1916 in Fresno, California. He graduated from high school at the age of 14 and from college at the age of 18. He earned a Bachelor of Arts degree from Fresno State's teacher's college, and a master's degree from the University of California.

After a fast-paced doctoral training in educational psychology at the University of Chicago, he joined the psychology faculty at Washington State College in 1940, where he taught his first courses in evaluation and measurement, and wrote the first edition of *Essentials of Psychological Testing* (1949). During World War II he worked as a research psychologist at the U.S. Navy's sonar school in San Diego. In 1948 he accepted a joint appointment in education and psychology at the University of Illinois, Urbana. He returned to California in 1964 to join the faculty of Stanford's School of Education, where he remained until his retirement in 1980. He died on October 1, 2001, at the age of 85.

Cronbach was president of the American Educational Research Association, the American Psychological Association, and the Psychometric Society. He was a member of the National Academy of Sciences, the National Academy of Education, the American Philosophical Society, and the American Academy of Arts and Sciences. He received many honorary degrees.

ISSUES IN MEASUREMENT

Cronbach's early work on measurement led to the "Coefficient Alpha" paper (Cronbach, 1951), which provided a widely used formula for estimating the reliability of test scores. Later he developed generalizability theory (Cronbach, Gleser, Rajaratnam, & Nanda, 1972) that examined systematic variations in test performance, and provided techniques for assessing the relative influences of various aspects or facets of the testing procedure. The theory provided important guidance for test developers on matters such as the number of items or the optimal allocation of raters.

Cronbach and Meehl's 1955 study established the centrality of validity considerations in testing, and "construct validity" as a unifying theme for interpreting test scores. Whereas traditional approaches to test validity were limited to examining test content or simple correlations with other variables, construct validation was to build a firm, rigorous theoretical basis for score interpretation. Cronbach also drew attention to the plurality of points of view, values, and beliefs for test developers, users, and policy-makers as essential ingredients in the process of test validation.

THE INTERACTIONIST APPROACH

Cronbach (1957, 1975) argued that the rift between experimental and correlational psychologies artificially separated the learner from the learning environment. He maintained that aptitudes—individual differences in response to educational treatments—were as important to understanding and improving educational programs as the typical response or average program effect. In earlier work (Cronbach & Gleser, 1957) on personnel-decision theory he and his colleague concluded that optimal placements must acknowledge the interaction of personal characteristics and job demands. His work on aptitude-treatment interactions (ATI) sought to demonstrate the potential benefits of matching the right type of instruction to students' abilities, motivations, and interests (Cronbach & Snow, 1977; Corno, et al., 2002). His efforts to discover general propositions about who would benefit from alternative methods of teaching and how learning environments could be designed to maximize benefits for all students, led him almost two decades later to suggest a radical shift in the goals of social science research toward a more contextualized inquiry (Cronbach, 1975). He sharpened the sensitivity of educational researchers to the ways different learners cope with the demands and affordances imbedded in different learning environments, and he advocated the use of intensive local studies and field methods that produced rich narratives of teaching and learning.

PROGRAM EVALUATION

Cronbach built on the ideas of Ralph W. Tyler (1902–1994), about how teachers should fashion their instruction to fit their students' needs, to pioneer the movement of "formative evaluation"—the idea that assessment is not a yardstick against which students should be measured and ranked but a feedback tool to stimulate teachers' efforts to improve instruction. He saw the evaluator as an educator informed by empirical studies rather than as an impartial observer submitting a verdict and drafting a correctional order. For him, evaluation was a pluralist, inclusive, and open-ended inquiry, sensitive to unexpected issues or unforeseeable events, even if such real-time adjustments spoiled the scientific elegance of the study.

Cronbach led the Stanford Evaluation Consortium, a multidisciplinary group whose work was summarized in a volume published in 1980 (Cronbach and associates, 1980). Two years later, Cronbach published his own book on program evaluation (Cronbach, 1982), in which he argued that the academic study of human affairs is not an exercise in abstraction. Research programs, he claimed, are valuable to the extent they serve the purpose of improving some aspect of the social reality.

SEE ALSO *Reliability.*

BIBLIOGRAPHY

WORKS BY

Corno, L., Cronbach, L. J., Kupermintz, H., Lohman, D. F., Mandinach, E.B., Porteus, A.W., et al. (2001). *Remaking the concept of aptitude: Extending the legacy of Richard E. Snow.* Mahwah, NJ: Erlbaum.

Cronbach, L. J. (1949). *Essentials of psychological testing.* New York: Harper.

Cronbach, L. J. (1951). Coefficient alpha and the internal structure of tests. *Psychometrika, 16,* 297–334.

Cronbach, L. J. (1957). The two disciplines of scientific psychology. *American Psychologist, 12,* 671–684.

Cronbach, L. J. (1975). Beyond the two disciplines of scientific psychology. *American Psychologist, 30,* 116–127.

Cronbach, L. J. (1982). *Designing evaluations of educational and social programs.* San Francisco: Jossey-Bass.

Cronbach, L. J., et al. (1980). *Toward reform of program evaluation.* San Francisco: Jossey-Bass.

Cronbach, L. J., & Gleser, G. C. (1957). *Psychological tests and personnel decisions.* Urbana: University of Illinois Press.

Cronbach, L. J., Gleser, G. C., Nanda, H. & Rajaratnam, N. (1972). *The dependability of behavioral measurements.* New York: Wiley.

Cronbach, L. J., & Meehl, P. E. (1955). Construct validity in psychological tests. *Psychological Bulletin, 52,* 281–302.

Cronbach, L. J., & Snow, R. E. (1977). *Aptitude and instructional methods.* Irvington, New York.

Haggai Kupermintz

CROSS-SECTIONAL RESEARCH DESIGNS

When psychologists want to investigate age differences between groups of children, they frequently use a cross-sectional design (Creasey, 2006; Miller, 2006). In a cross-sectional design different children at different ages are assessed at the same time. For instance, if one were interested in the development of arithmetic abilities, different groups of children at ages 4, 5, 6, and 7 could be given tests that assess addition and the strategies children use to arrive at their answers. In a very brief time the test giver would have an idea of how this important skill changes with age. (If the researcher used a longitudinal design, in which the same children were tested repeatedly over time, it would take them four years to get the same information.) The intent of a cross-sectional design is to allow psychologists to efficiently describe change over time and to identify the various mechanisms associated with those changes.

Cognitive strategies—the deliberate plans children use to organize their problem solving—have been studied extensively in developmental psychology using cross-sectional designs (Bjorklund, 2005). For example, Jane Gaultney (1998) investigated the use of memory strategies in third-, fourth-, and fifth-grade students with and without learning disabilities. Specifically, she examined the degree to which children organized their recall of related items (e.g., sorting and later recalling together items from the same semantic category) and the extent to which such strategy use benefited their memory performance. She found that typically developing children benefited more from the use of strategies than children with learning disabilities. This difference increased with age and was due to the lack of progress by older children with learning disabilities. Her research also showed that children with learning disabilities experienced more benefit when they used strategies to study items for later recall, whereas typically developing children benefited most from strategies when actually recalling the items. Such an approach identifies potentially important age differences in children quickly and provides some insights into the specific problems children of different ages and abilities have.

CONDUCTING RESEARCH FROM A DEVELOPMENTAL PERSPECTIVE

The use of cross-sectional designs in education implicitly involves a concern for age differences, and this awareness implies an interest in development. A developmental-psychological perspective is concerned with age-related changes and the factors associated with those changes. The deeper issues of how, when, and ultimately why psychological change takes place shape the formulation of research questions, which in turn influence the methods chosen to answer these questions.

While the importance of measuring age-related change should not be underestimated, it is often the normative, or perhaps even more critical, non-normative influences associated with change that most interest developmental and educational psychologists. A broad holistic view of development leads to questions about children's thinking in both social and academic environments that can lead to techniques for enhancing education (Teti, 2006; Bergman et al., 2000).

FACTORS INVOLVED IN CONDUCTING CROSS-SECTIONAL STUDIES

Several factors must be taken into account in conducting a study using a cross-sectional design. For instance, if researchers are interested in the development of scientific reasoning in school-age children, they can design a study in which groups of children are given problems to solve requiring reasoning associated with (a) developing an hypothesis, (b) deciding how to test the hypothesis, (c) collecting data, and (d) evaluating the hypothesis. Questions immediately surface regarding how they might go

about conducting such a study and what pitfalls they must avoid in order to make sure the results of their study are interpretable.

In such a study researchers must ensure that each age and experimental group is balanced in terms of important demographic characteristics. For example, in the study of scientific reasoning, they may give children in grades 3 through 8 different types of science instruction or different textbooks to read. They would need to balance the age and instruction groups for gender. They would need to consider if children from different age groups are from different schools, and if so if the schools differ in any important way, such as socio-economic status (SES) or quality of instruction. Also, they would consider if the children in the various grades or instruction groups differ in academic abilities, motivation, or previous knowledge of the subject matter in any systematic way. Academic and developmental differences are often associated with gender, SES, motivation, and a host of other factors. Researchers may be interested in how these factors affect scientific reasoning, but in order to interpret unambiguously any age or instruction differences they may find in their study, they have to insure that their groups are balanced, as much as reasonably possible, in terms of demographic and related factors.

Another consideration when doing cross-sectional research is the tasks children in each group perform. These tasks should be age-appropriate, so they are not too difficult for the youngest children or too easy for the oldest. Researchers must check that the wording of the problems is comprehensible to children of all ages to be tested. Once they have decided what tasks they are going to give children, they have to decide how to administer them. Children in each group should be tested in a similar fashion. However, because of differences in the social, emotional, and particularly cognitive abilities of children of different ages, it may not be possible to use the identical procedures with all children. What is important is that children of all ages understand the task and what they are supposed to do. As a result, testing procedures may have to be varied to ensure that both younger and older children understand the tasks, but not varied so much as to make the tasks qualitatively different for children of different ages. For example, it is possible to read or rephrase directions, or even use pictorial representations of the directions, to help younger children understand the expectations of the task. Robust results from research are predicated on ensuring that attention is given not only to the design of the study, but also to the manner in which the research design is implemented.

USING CROSS-SECTIONAL DESIGNS AND OTHER RESEARCH METHODS

Cross-sectional designs can be used in conjunction with both experimental and correlational studies. Experimental research is the gold standard for answering questions about cause-and-effect relationships. Experimental studies involve the manipulation of one or more factors, or variables, and observation of how these manipulations change the behavior under investigation. For example, Schwenck, Bjorklund, and Schneider (2007) were interested in factors that influence memory strategy development in groups of first- and third-grade children. To assess these factors, they gave some children instruction in strategy use on some trials, whereas others received no such instruction. They also varied the type of materials that children were asked to remember, including items that were either typical of their category (e.g., shirt, dress, pants for clothes) or atypical of their category (e.g., (e.g., socks, tie, belt for clothes). They found age differences not only in how well children of different ages remember, but also in children's abilities to benefit from strategy training. For instance, older compared to younger children required less explicit prompting to use a strategy, were more likely to use a strategy when atypical category items served as stimuli, and generalized a strategy to new sets of words. They also identified differences in children's tendencies to use a strategy but not to experience any benefit in recall, termed a utilization deficiency, something important to educators concerned with teaching strategies in the classroom.

In correlational studies researchers make comparisons between two or more variables. Keep in mind that identifying a relationship between two variables does not imply causation, but if a relationship does exist, further understanding may be gained by pinpointing the nature of the relationship and then conducting experimental studies. Cross-sectional designs have been used in correlational studies leading to understanding about different developmental trends in the use of reading strategies for children with different levels or styles of learning aptitudes (see Gaultney, 1998). For example, in one study (Siegel & Ryan, 1988), researchers compared the phonological processing (specifically, reading pronounceable pseudowords such as blurt) of 7- to 14-year-old children with and without reading disabilities. Both groups of children showed marked improvement in pseudoword reading with age, although at each age tested, children with reading disabilities performed significantly worse than typically developing children. In fact, the pseudoword reading of 13- to 14-year-old reading-disabled children was comparable to that of their 7- to 8-year-old typically developing peers.

CONTRIBUTIONS TO TEACHER PRACTICE USING CROSS-SECTIONAL DESIGNS

A prominent myth exists that practitioners, most notably teachers, have no need for an understanding of research. The poor transfer of scientific research findings to application in the classroom creates a void between empirical inquiry and classroom-based practices. In short, teachers must be able to understand the meaning of research findings and how to incorporate the results into pedagogical practices. This transfer of knowledge poses a challenge for many teachers who may need more than simple exposure to the research literature in order to make fundamental change. The challenge to teach essential knowledge and foster skill development in children is the primary responsibility of the classroom teacher. It is critical that teachers be able to pose and ultimately answer questions about important aspects of the teaching and learning process. Evaluating the outcomes of schooling based solely on students' abilities to engage in particular skills is clearly an inadequate approach to gain an understanding of the entire schooling process. There is no paucity of variables one must take into account when investigating why and how children make academic and social progress, and equally as important are the factors that account for failure to make adequate progress. A holistic view of the full teaching and learning process is necessary to account for the mechanisms underlying learning, and this often involves an ability to interpret the findings of developmental/educational research and sometimes to perform simple studies.

Research is not the enemy of teachers, and it is possible to structure research that can help answer some of the most salient questions about teaching and learning. There is common ground between researchers and teachers. Each group desires to answer questions about children's ability to learn content and develop skills. For many teachers, the daily grind of classroom instruction is reason enough to shy away from any sort of formal inquiry into the teaching and learning process, but it is exactly these daily routines that provide a rich source of potential issues from which to gain further insight. The cross-sectional design is a relatively accessible approach that can be used in the classroom to answer questions about how children change with age in regard to a particular ability or process and how children of different ages respond to different types of instruction. The following paragraphs provide an example of a cross-sectional study that a classroom teacher could conceivably implement, beginning with the formulation of a research question to the execution of the project.

EXAMPLE OF A CROSS-SECTIONAL STUDY

Formal inquiry begins with the generation of questions about instruction and student learning. From here, the challenge is to isolate a particular aspect of the process that warrants attention. Research is most easily facilitated with a clear focus. For example, a teacher may wonder about how students benefit from the use of reading-comprehension strategies to recall information from a science textbook. Perhaps there are age differences in children's ability to benefit from using reading-comprehension strategies that can be traced using a cross-sectional design.

After formulating the research question, it is then necessary to identify groups of children to participate in the study and to determine what, if any, experimental groups teachers want to include. They may decide based on the science curriculum at their school that children much below grade 3 would be too young and children much beyond middle school would be too old for the questions they wish to ask. In the present example, they may include at each grade tested an experimental group that gets special reading-comprehension strategy instruction, as well as a control group that gets standard classroom instruction or perhaps some extra time with the teacher to balance for the amount of teacher-time children in both groups receive. (They may also want to test special groups of children, such as those with learning disabilities, slow readers, or those from less-advantaged homes, and compare them to typically developing children, but the design can be kept simple for this example.) When identifying groups of participants, it is important to recruit approximately equal numbers of boys and girls and to ensure that the different ages and instructional groups are balanced for other factors that may influence children's performance, such as academic achievement and SES.

The next step is to determine the measurement for the study. In this case, the teachers would need to develop or identify a reading-comprehension strategy that they could teach to their participants (likely obtained from the research literature) and a measure to identify whether using such a strategy works, that is, enhances recall of science-text content. They may be able to use tasks already used in the classroom, for instance, questions taken from the science text or teacher-made questions. They want to make sure that the questions are age-appropriate and that the testing methods are similar across ages.

Based on such an experiment, they may find that whereas third-grade children can implement the reading-comprehension strategy, the students tend not to generalize it to new texts and perhaps experience only minimal improvement in recall from its use. In contrast, older children not only use the strategy but also generalize it to new texts and experience substantial recall benefits from

its use. Such findings would help in the development of different types of instruction for children of different ages and perhaps cause teachers to ask more questions about what it is about the reading-comprehension instruction that works (or does not work) for children of different ages. Of course, there are a number of possible outcomes from such a study, but the point here is that one is able to get an idea of how strategy use is developed and then make a determination of which strategies to use and when.

Cross-sectional designs permit researchers or teachers to collect quickly information about age changes in some ability. However, in order to assess true developmental change, longitudinal approaches, which test the same children over time, are necessary. Such studies are not out of the question for classroom teachers. For example, the assessment of reading-comprehension strategy instruction on children's recall of science information could be performed once in November and again in May to see if individual children make improvements over the course of the school year.

Research has not always been held in high regard or maintained a prominent place in the typical classroom. This does not have to be the case if research studies are designed to be easily understood and implemented in the classroom. Teachers typically reflect on the teaching and learning process, and the use of research designs simply allows these questions to be tested and better understood.

SEE ALSO *Longitudinal Research; Research Methods: An Overview.*

BIBLIOGRAPHY

Bergman, L. R., Cairns, B., Nilsson, L-G., & Nystedt, L. (Eds.). (2000). *Developmental Science and the holistic approach.* Mahwah, NJ: Erlbaum.

Bjorklund, D. F. (2005). *Children's thinking: Cognitive development and individual differences* (4th ed.). Belmont, CA: Thomson.

Bronfenbrenner, U. (1979). *The ecology of human development: Experiments by nature and design.* Cambridge, MA: Harvard University Press.

Creasey, G. L. (2006). *Research methods in lifespan development.* Boston: Pearson.

Gaultney, J. F. (1998). Utilization deficiencies among children with learning disabilities. *Learning and Individual Differences, 10,* 13–28.

Miller, S. A. (2006). *Developmental research methods* (3rd ed.). London: Sage.

Siegel, L. S., & Ryan, E. B. (1988). Development of grammatical-sensitivity, phonological, and short-term memory skills in normally achieving and learning disabled children. *Developmental Psychology, 24,* 28–37.

Teti, D. M. (Ed.). (2006). *Handbook of research methods in developmental science.* Malden, MA: Blackwell.

Charles Dukes
David F. Bjorklund

CTT

SEE *Classical Test Theory.*

CULTURAL BIAS IN TEACHING

Cultural bias in teaching can be described as teachers and administrators holding the belief that the dominant or mainstream (presumably European and North American) cultural ways of learning and knowing are superior to ways of learning and knowing that do not reflect such a culture. Historically, the research on cultural bias in teaching and learning can be traced back to the research of Lev Vygotsky (1896–1934) and Alexander Luria (1902–1977). Both psychologists launched research programs determining the cultural bias inherent in evaluators' critique of young children's problem-solving strategies.

Throughout their work, it was uncovered that many mainstream evaluators would render impoverished Soviet children's responses to cognitive tasks incorrect (Vygotsky, 1978). However, according to Vygotsky and Luria, this evaluation oftentimes reflected the evaluator's cultural frame of reference. That is, the evaluation of the correct response was found to be a) biased towards a set of culturally aligned ways of thinking, knowing, and problem-solving, and b) biased against alternative, cultural ways of thinking, knowing, and problem-solving. Work in the late 1990s and early 2000s has shown that cultural bias continues to inform the ways individuals evaluate student performance (Baker, 2005; Ndura, 2004).

PREVALENCE OF CULTURAL BIAS IN EDUCATION

For many education researchers, cultural bias in teaching is evidenced within various academic texts and modules across multiple academic domains (Baker, 2005, Loewen, 2007). Particularly in the United States, several researchers agree that most contributions to academic subject matter (i.e., history and social and natural sciences) are made by members of the majority race or culture (American Psychological Association, 2003; Gay, 2000; Rogoff, 2003) and much of the text throughout this subject matter is used to reinforce the superiority of this group (Loewen, 2007). Loewen (2007), for example, offers that most elementary and secondary U.S. history textbooks offer a romanticized view of the Europeans' experience in the United States whereas most of the experiences of Native Americans and/or Africans in these same lands are either misrepresented or underrepresented. He and others have also noted that many of these texts have continued to marginalize the achievements and significant traditions of many ethnic minority populations living in the United States (Howard, 1999; Loewen, 2007). Other works have shown that additional academic domains such as the natural sciences and English also promote a U.S./European ideological focus (e.g., Solano-Flores & Nelson-Barber, 2001).

In addition to cultural bias found throughout public school curricula and standardized testing, cultural bias is believed to be salient throughout the instructional practices promoted and executed by school teachers and administrators (Boykin, Tyler, & Miller, 2005; Gay, 2000; Nieto, 2001). Here, cultural bias beliefs sanction as appropriate certain forms of classroom behavior, including the manner in which a student is to perform and learn during class time. An example of cultural bias in classroom practices is reflected in the belief that learning must occur in a controlled environment, where students are seated independently and working quietly on a singular task and are only to interact and correspond to the instructor (Gay, 2000). For many, these activities reflect a mainstream cultural perspective (Gay, 2000; Howard, 1999; Nieto, 2001).

These same works have also claimed these learning behaviors and activities are inconsistent with the varied and cultural-laden learning experiences many ethnic minority students have outside the classroom. Some of these experiences reflect communalism or interdependence along with verve or the presence of and adherence to multiple and simultaneous activities (Boykin, Tyler, Watkins-Lewis, & Kizzie, 2006; Gay, 2000). Despite the salience of these learning activities that display an alternative cultural worldview, many classroom teachers continue to promote learning and instructional practices that reveal an adherence to a mainstream ideology or worldview (Boykin, Tyler, Watkins-Lewis, & Kizzie, 2006; Tyler, Boykin, & Walton, 2006).

Thus, cultural bias in teaching occurs when classroom instruction, learning activities, materials, and lessons largely reflect the contributions and/or cultural values and perspectives of the majority race or culture. In the United States, that race is White, Caucasian, or European American, and the culture is largely mainstream oriented (Strickland, 2000). In most classrooms with predominantly ethnically and culturally diverse students, cultural bias is also presented as an inherent promotion of the perceived superiority and effectiveness of mainstream cultural modes of learning, thinking, and performing (APA, 2003).

An explicit example of cultural bias in classroom learning and thinking is found in the work of Perry and Delpit (1998). The researchers report a study in which African American students' responses to test items were evaluated. One test item showed a man standing, wearing a suit and carrying a briefcase. Students in the study were asked about the destination of the man in the picture. Perry and Delpit (1998) reported that the test writers concurred that the correct answer was that he was going to his place of work or business. It was reported, however, that many of the African American children thought the man was going to church.

Perry and Delpit (1998) argued that the African American students' response reflected aspects of their cultural background. Specifically, within their communities, men dressed in suits and carrying briefcases are typically going to church. Yet, from a mainstream cultural perspective, this response is deemed incorrect. Students were to observe that the suited man carrying a brief case is going to work and not church. For Perry and Delpit (1998), however, marking the African American students' responses incorrect reveals bias toward a knowledge base rooted in a North American or mainstream cultural value system. It also shows bias against knowledge emerging from an alternative, albeit equal cultural value system. Other works support these claims (Baker, 2005).

CULTURAL DISCONTINUITY

What results from these culturally biased beliefs is an in-school cultural socialization process in which ethnically and culturally diverse students are exposed to instructional practices and learning activities that do not reflect their cultural-laden modes of learning and knowing. In fact, their adherence to more mainstream culture-based classroom practices is oftentimes, imposed and coerced. Some evidence exists to support each of these claims (Tyler, Boykin, Miller, & Hurley, 2006; Boykin, Tyler, Watkins-Lewis, & Kizzie, 2006; Tyler, Boykin, & Walton, 2006). The result of this in-school socialization process is cultural discontinuity.

Cultural discontinuity is defined here as a school-based behavioral process in which teachers and administrators are a) active in promoting adherence to classroom curricula and classroom learning and instruction that reflect mainstream or European and/or North American cultural values, and b) active in diminishing preferences for and practices of learning modes and practices that reflect the indigenous cultures of ethnically and culturally diverse students. While Ogbu (1982) charged that all

students experience home-school discontinuities throughout their schooling experiences, such discrepancies are considered more pronounced for ethnically and culturally diverse students (Gay, 2000; Nieto, 2001). For these students, home-school cultural discontinuity emerges from cultural bias in teaching.

In particular, the values and behavioral preferences of many ethnically and culturally diverse students are discontinued in classrooms because of a) the bias held for mainstream cultural norms and values in public school classrooms, and b) the bias held against those cultural norms and values brought to such classrooms by ethnically and culturally diverse students. Specifically, it has been suggested that most ethnic minority students emerge from households that maintain several culturally aligned practices and behaviors that do not reflect a mainstream ideology, but rather aspects of their indigenous cultures (Gay, 2000; Howard, 1999; Nieto, 2001; Vygotsky, 1978). For these students, it is often difficult and undesirable to abide by a set of behaviors that do not reflect their indigenous culture or cultures (Boykin et al., 2006).

Yet due to cultural bias in teaching, where there is an apparent adherence to mainstream forms of thinking, learning, and behaving (Howard, 1999; Loewen, 2007), ethnically and culturally diverse students often have to discontinue learning behaviors and activities that reflect aspects of their home or indigenous culture. In fact, they are often told to replace these indigenous cultural value-laden behaviors with classroom practices and behaviors reflective of mainstream cultural values. Not doing so often leads to misperceptions of students' learning abilities and in some cases, recommendations for in-school remediation and/or psychological services (Baker, 2005).

RESEARCH ON CULTURAL BIAS AND CULTURAL DISCONTINUITY

Some research corroborates the claims that cultural bias beliefs and cultural discontinuity practices are part of the classroom realities for ethnically and culturally diverse students (Gay, 2000; Nieto, 2001). Regarding low-income African American students, research conducted by Wade Boykin and associates has determined that many classroom teachers are biased toward mainstream ways of learning and instruction. For example, in one study, classroom teachers were asked to respond to a questionnaire assessing their endorsement of mainstream and alternative ethnocultural classroom practices. Teachers reported significantly higher reports of classroom practices that reflected mainstream cultural values (i.e., competition and individualism) than those practices that reflected students' alternative ethnocultural values such as communalism and verve (Boykin, Tyler, Watkins-Lewis, & Kizzie, 2006).

Another study asked teachers to report their perceptions of the academic motivation and achievement of hypothetical students displaying either mainstream or alternative ethnocultural classroom practices. Teachers read a scenario depicting a student engaged in classroom learning in one of four culturally aligned ways. Teachers then completed a scale assessing their perceptions of the student's motivation and academic performance. Motivation and achievement ratings were significantly higher for hypothetical students displaying mainstream cultural classroom practices than those students displaying alternative ethnocultural classroom practices (Tyler, Boykin, & Walton, 2006). Together, these two studies show that many teachers of low-income African American students hold biases for mainstream cultural practices in the classroom. Moreover, the findings indicate that such biases also inform how teachers perceive and evaluate students displaying alternative ethnocultural values.

In addition to research illuminating the presence of cultural bias towards mainstream cultural values and practices, other work has determined that many ethnically and culturally diverse students experience cultural discontinuity throughout their schooling experiences (Gay, 2000; Nieto, 2001; Rogoff, 2003). Some evidence suggests that low-income African American students actually prefer classroom learning in ways that reflect their indigenous cultural values (Tyler, Boykin, Miller, & Hurley, 2006). Other works have determined, however, that these students are not allowed to carry out academic tasks in these culturally specific ways.

For example, in one qualitative study, 21 classroom teachers maintained classroom practices and instructional styles that largely reflected mainstream cultural values. Observations of classroom practices reflecting alternative ethnocultural values were marginal (Boykin, Tyler, & Miller, 2005). In another study, African American students reported that they would be disciplined at school for displaying classroom behaviors reflecting alternative ethnocultural values. The cultural values in question were communalism or interdependence and verve or simultaneity. These same behaviors and values, though not allowed in school, were permissible in their households (i.e., working in groups or listening to music while working). Moreover, the participants indicated that they would not be disciplined at school for displaying classroom behaviors reflective of mainstream cultural values. These students did, however, indicate that they would get in trouble for displaying mainstream cultural values at home (Tyler, Boykin, Miller, & Hurley, 2006). Together, these and other works corroborate the claim that cultural discontinuity is part of the classroom learning experiences of many ethnically and culturally diverse students, particularly African American students (Gay, 2000; Nieto, 2001; Rogoff, 2003)

REDUCING CULTURAL BIAS IN TEACHING AND CULTURAL DISCONTINUITY

Although the specific effects of cultural bias and cultural discontinuity on student outcomes have not been studied empirically, the literature is replete with examples of ways to reduce cultural bias and cultural discontinuity. To begin, a reduction of cultural bias and cultural discontinuity requires teachers to establish and maintain classroom environments in which the emotional, social, cognitive and cultural needs of all students are met (Brown, 2004). The term *culturally responsive teaching* is commonly used by researchers to describe an environment in which teachers respond appropriately to the diverse learning experiences and culturally situated behavioral preferences of learners in their classroom (Brown, 2004).

One of the major factors emphasized in achieving a culturally responsive classroom is that teachers and administrators examine their own biases regarding what is and is not appropriate classroom behavior. Prior to acknowledging and using the cultural values and belief systems of ethnically and culturally diverse students, teachers may profitably engage in self-reflection in order to gain understanding of their own cultural biases in teaching (APA, 2003). Also integral to this reflective process is the teachers' understanding of how these biases towards mainstream culture may impact the type of instruction they engage in, the classroom learning activities they sanction, and the evaluation of their students.

For many, reducing cultural bias in teaching requires teachers to become more aware of themselves as cultural beings (APA, 2003). Teachers must be more cognizant of their own biases towards specific cultural values before they begin to acknowledge and use the cultural values of others. Such self-reflection aids in the development of positive attitudes towards the cultural values and learning styles of ethnically and culturally diverse students. These positive attitudes, then, become the precursor to aligning curricula and classroom activities with the cultural values and behaviors of ethnically and culturally diverse students. For example, Phuntsog (2001) found that teacher attitudes toward cultural value diversity were important factors in their willingness to create culturally responsive classrooms. Indeed, self-reflection of the culturally based teaching practices and beliefs is considered an essential first step toward establishing a culturally responsive learning environment and reducing cultural bias in teaching (Gay, 2000).

TEACHER CARING

In addition to self-reflection as a way to reduce cultural bias in teaching, some researchers have suggested more interactive practices that can help teachers respond more appropriately to culturally and ethnically diverse students. One such practice is *teacher caring*, a term that refers to a set of teacher-initiated practices that promote strong interpersonal bonds between teachers and their students (Rogers & Webb, 1991). Research has shown that students' reports of teacher caring contribute to perceptions of teacher effectiveness, academic effort, and academic success (Perez, 2000; Ware, 2006). In a study of classroom management strategies and culturally responsive teaching, Brown (2004) identified a caring attitude as a major teacher-centered characteristic that facilitated the interaction with ethnically and culturally diverse students. For many, a teacher who cares about students will not display biases against the students' distinct cultural values. In 'ead, the teacher finds ways to use these cultural values throughout classroom practice (APA, 2003; Gay, 2000; Nieto, 2001; Rogoff, 2003).

One way that teacher caring is demonstrated with ethnically and culturally diverse students is through the adoption of warm demander pedagogical styles. A teacher who is a warm demander maintains a classroom environment in which students feel respected and are respectful of the instructor's directions and rules. That is, the teacher cares about the students and does so in a manner that maintains the teacher's position in the classroom as the authority figure (Ware, 2006). Warm demander characteristics displayed in the classroom have been shown to enhance the social and academic experiences of ethnically and culturally diverse students, particularly low-income African American students (Gay, 2000). These characteristics also reflect the typical caretaker-child dynamic many ethnically and culturally diverse students are exposed to during their out-of-school socialization (Brown, 2004). Regarding African American students, promoting warm demander pedagogy has been shown to enhance their schooling experiences, particularly by reducing their exposure to classroom-based cultural discontinuity practices (Ware, 2006).

In addition to teacher-based characteristics and activities that can reduce cultural bias and cultural discontinuity at school, some research has shown that incorporating aspects of ethnically and culturally diverse students' cultural values into academic tasks and lessons actually facilitates their performance (Serpell, Boykin, Madhere, & Nasim, 2006). Other works have shown that utilizing these cultural values can foster greater communication in the classroom, greater task engagement, increased responsiveness to teacher expectations and instruction, and enhanced academic performance (Gay, 2000; Nieto, 2001; Rogoff, 2003).

In all, these studies provide practical suggestions that teachers can use to reduce cultural bias and cultural discontinuity in their classrooms. For instance, constructing classroom lessons and activities that build upon the cultural values of ethnically and culturally diverse students reduces cultural discontinuity as students are no longer asked to forego their culturally aligned learning practices and preferences. Many of the cited research studies have indicated that these culturally aligned practices enhance student performance outcomes. Thus, classroom teachers can use these in an effort to reduce cultural discontinuity and promote optimal performance among ethnically and culturally diverse students.

Moreover, the demonstrated effectiveness of these culturally situated practices aids in the reduction of cultural bias in teaching. Specifically, classroom teachers using culturally responsive pedagogical practices are exposed to instructional practices and learning activities that do not solely reflect a mainstream cultural value system. Rather, many of these practices reflect the cultural values and customs of many ethnically and culturally diverse students. The fact that these practices and activities have proven to be beneficial to these students gives teachers alternative instructional practices to consider in class. Using them can result in the broadening of classroom teachers' understanding of what works best for this student population. Considering alternative instructional practices and knowledge sources also reduces cultural bias in teaching.

SEE ALSO *Cultural Bias in Testing; Culturally Relevant Pedagogy; Vygotsky, Lev Semenovich.*

BIBLIOGRAPHY

American Psychological Association. (2003). Guidelines on multicultural education, training, research, practice, and organizational change for psychologists. *American Psychologist, 58*(5), 377–401.

Baker, P. B. (2005). The impact of cultural biases on African American students' education: A review of research literature regarding race based schooling. *Education and Urban Society, 37*(3), 243–256.

Boykin, A. W., Tyler, K. M., & Miller, O. A. (2005). In search of cultural themes and their expressions in the dynamics of classroom life. *Urban Education, 40*(5), 521–549.

Boykin, A. W., Tyler, K. M., Watkins-Lewis, K. M., & Kizzie, K. (2006). Culture in the sanctioned classroom practices of elementary school teachers serving low-income African American students. *Journal of Education of Students Placed At-Risk, 11*(2),161–173.

Brown, D. F. (2004). Urban teachers' professed classroom management strategies: Reflections of culturally responsive teaching. *Urban Education, 39*(3), 266–289.

Gay, G. (2000). *Culturally responsive teaching: Theory, research, and practice.* New York: Teachers College Press.

Howard, G. R. (1999). *We can't teach what we don't know: White teachers, multiracial schools.* New York: Teachers College Press.

Loewen, J. W. (2007). *Lies my teacher told me: Everything your American history textbook got wrong.* New York: Simon & Schuster.

Ndura, E. (2004). ESL and cultural bias: An analysis of elementary through high school textbooks in the Western United States of America. *Language, Culture and Curriculum, 17*(2), 143–153.

Nieto, S. (2001). *The light in their eyes: Creating multicultural learning communities.* New York: Teachers College Press.

Ogbu, J. U. (1982). Cultural discontinuities and schooling. *Anthropology and Education Quarterly, 13*(4), 290–307.

Perez, S. (2000). An ethic of caring in teaching culturally diverse students. *Education, 121*(1), 102–105.

Perry, T., & Delpit, L. (1998). *The real Ebonics debate: Power, language, and the education of African-American children.* Boston: Beacon.

Phuntsog, N. (2001). Culturally responsive teaching: What do selected United States elementary school teachers think? *Intercultural Education, 12*(1), 51–64.

Rogers, D., & Webb, J. (1991). The ethic of caring in teacher education. *Journal of Teacher Education, 42*(3), 173–181.

Rogoff, B. (2003). *The cultural nature of cognitive development.* New York: Oxford University Press.

Serpell, Z. N., Boykin, A. W., Madhere, S., & Nasim, A. (2006). The significance of contextual factors in African American students' transfer of learning. *Journal of Black Psychology, 32*(4), 418–441.

Solano-Flores, G., & Nelson-Barber, S. (2001). On the cultural validity of science assessments. *Journal of Research in Science Teaching, 38*(5), 553–573.

Strickland, B. R. (2000). Misassumptions, misadventures, and the misuse of psychology. *American Psychologist, 55*(3), 331–339.

Tyler, K. M., Boykin, A. W., Miller, O. A., & Hurley, E. A. (2006). Cultural values in the home and school experiences of low-income African American students. *Social Psychology of Education, 9,* 363–380.

Tyler, K. M., Boykin, A. W., & Walton, T. R. (2006). Cultural considerations in teachers' perceptions of student classroom behavior and achievement. *Teaching and Teacher Education, 22,* 998–1005.

Vygotsky, L. S. (1978). *Mind in society: The development of higher psychological processes* (M. Cole, V. John-Steiner, S. Scribner, & E. Souberman, Eds.). Cambridge, MA: Harvard University Press.

Ware, F. (2006). Warm demander pedagogy: Culturally responsive teaching that supports a culture of achievement for African American students. *Urban Education, 41*(4), 427–456.

Kenneth M. Tyler
Ruby J. Stevens
Aesha L. Uqdah

CULTURAL BIAS IN TESTING

Any book that focuses on psychology is incomplete without a discussion of testing, including the topic of test bias. Psychologists, more than professionals in other disciplines, are the primary administers of intelligence tests,

with schools being the primary user. In the high-stakes testing of the early 2000s, employment opportunities, high school graduation, grade promotion, college admission, gifted education placement, and special education placement rely extensively on test results. Thus, the discussion of how tests impact the decisions of test users and the opportunities of those tested is by no means insignificant. Stated another way, "an intelligence test is a neutral, inconsequential tool until someone assigns significance to the results derived from it. Once meaning is attached to a person's score, that individual will experience many repercussions, ranging from superficial to life changing. These repercussions will be fair or prejudiced, helpful or harmful, appropriate or misguided—depending on the meaning attached to the test score" (Gregory, 2004, p. 240).

Regarding intelligence tests, this entry presents an overview of issues surrounding test bias primarily related to African Americans. It defines bias, gives examples of test bias, and recommends ways to reduce bias. Two caveats are in order. First, clearly test bias is not unique to African Americans, but the bulk of research and discussions focus on this group. Thus, the focus here on African Americans is not a slight to other culturally and linguistically diverse (CLD) groups. Second, different types of tests exist beyond intelligence tests—aptitude, achievement, career/vocational—and they are not exempt from discussions about bias. However, the focus here is specifically on bias regarding intelligence tests, as this is the most controversial type of test. One complication is that intelligence tests and the meaning attached to the word *intelligence* carry more significance than those associated with achievement tests. Intelligence tests (also called cognitive ability and ability tests) are often associated with genetic endowment and capacity, while achievement tests are more often associated with learning opportunities and educational experiences—the environment—and their effect on test performance. As Gregory (2004) noted, beyond a doubt, no practice in modern psychology has been more assailed than psychological testing. Commentators reserve a special and often vehement condemnation for ability testing in particular. Additionally, Jensen (1980) contended that test bias is the most common rallying point for critics.

The test bias controversy and debate has its origins in the observed differences in average IQ scores between various racial groups (Blacks) and ethnic groups (immigrants) in the early 1900s (Cole & Zieky, 2001). Specifically, several studies indicate that African Americans score, on average, 15 points lower than their White counterparts on traditional intelligence tests—tests with high linguistic/verbal and cultural loadings (Flanagan & Ortiz, 2001). This finding of differential group test score performance in intelligence heightened the controversy over test bias (Gregory, 2004). Under scrutiny have been all versions and editions of traditional intelligence tests, including the Wechsler tests (e.g., WISC-IV, WAIS, WPPSI), the Binet tests (e.g., Stanford-Binet, Binet-IV), Otis Lennon School Aptitude Test, and Peabody Picture Vocabulary Test. Non-verbal intelligence tests have also been examined for bias (e.g., Ravens Progressive Matrices; Naglieri Non-Verbal Intelligence Test) (e.g., Bracken & Naglieri, 2003).

In addition to coming under professional scrutiny, intelligence tests have been challenged legally. One of the most famous cases is *Larry P. v. Wilson Riles* (1979) in which 9th U.S. District Judge Robert F. Peckham in California ruled that intelligence tests used for the assessment of Black children for special education classes for the educable mentally retarded are culturally biased. One year later, Judge John F. Grady in Illinois ruled in *Parents in Action in Special Education v. Joseph P. Hannon* that intelligence tests are not racially biased; they do not discriminate against Black children. Set one year apart, the opposing positions of these two cases helped to create or sustain the debates that continued into the early 2000s.

POSITION 1: INTELLIGENCE TESTS ARE BIASED

Opponents of using intelligence tests with Black and other CLD groups often focus on the social and educational consequences—fairness and disparate impact. The primary argument and belief is that persons from backgrounds other than the culture in which the test was developed will always be penalized; they will likely score lower on the test and, thus, have their opportunities limited and face misinterpretations about their worth and potential (academically, as students, as employees, etc.). They argue that too few intelligence tests have been normed with representative numbers (not just percentages) of CLD populations. Therefore, the test scores are not valid and reliable for them, rendering the test inappropriate to use. This argument or position also applies to topics other than race and ethnicity. For example, if few in the norming group are low income or linguistically diverse, then the test is viewed as inappropriate and potentially useless and harmful to that group. Further, if few gifted students or students with learning disabilities were in the norming group, the test's usefulness for them is questionable (Ford, 2004, 2007).

Recognizing that Black students in particular were and are negatively affected by their test performance or scores, the Association of Black Psychologists (Williams, 1970) charged that Black students were/are subsequently denied many educational opportunities; they charged that intelligence tests are not valid measures for Black students and that they are more harmful than helpful.

This notion of tests being harmful goes against the principles of fair and equitable testing, a key feature of professional testing standards (e.g., American Psychological Association, American Educational Research Association, National Council on Measurement in Education, 1999). Simply put, tests should be used to help not harm; they should benefit the test taker.

POSITION 2: INTELLIGENCE TESTS ARE NOT BIASED

Proponents of intelligence tests maintain that tests are valid and reliable tools for all groups. According to Armour-Thomas and Gopaul-McNicol (1998), support for this position falls into at least three categories or assumptions: (1) tests are culturally fair and items do not favor a particular cultural group; (2) the tasks assess the cognitive abilities underlying intellectual behavior for all groups; and (3) the tests accurately predict performance for all groups.

It is also important to note that test construction is grounded in the assumption of homogeneity and equal opportunity to learn and acquire knowledge and experiences (Armour-Thomas & Gopaul-McNicol, 1998; Flanagan & Ortiz, 2001), meaning that (a) the test items measure the everyday experiences of populations and (b) everyone has had an equal opportunity to learn and be exposed to the tasks in the tests and its format (Ford, 2004). Essentially, it is believed that tests are not discriminatory.

TEST BIAS DEFINITIONS: TECHNICAL AND SOCIAL DEFINITIONS

It is important to keep in mind that tests are often viewed as being biased against Black and other culturally and linguistically diverse groups, and against low-income students, but biased in favor of White and middle class students. Gregory (2004) defined test bias as "objective statistical indices that examine the patterning of test scores for relevant subpopulations" (p. 242). He adds that consensus exists about the statistical criteria that indicate when a test is biased. A review of definitions indicates that test bias can be categorized in two ways: technically and socially. Technically, test bias refers to differential validity for definable, relevant subgroups of persons (Sattler, 1992, p. 616). Hence, a test would be considered biased if the scores from subpopulations did not fall upon the same regression line or a relevant criterion.

Bias is present when a test score has meanings or implications for a relevant, definable subgroup of test takers that are different from the meanings or implications for the remainder of test takers. Thus, bias is the differential validity of a given interpretation of a test score for any definable, relevant subgroup of test takers (Cole & Moss, 1998, cited in Gregory, 2004, p. 242). When a test is biased, from a social or social values viewpoint, the concern relates to denial of opportunity and the false negative hypothesis. Two other terms or concepts are relevant to discussions regarding testing CLD groups. It can be argued that while a test might not be biased technically, it can still be unfair (see Cole & Zieky, 2001). Test fairness is fundamentally about the social consequences of test results (Gregory, 2004, p. 249; Hunter & Schmidt, 1976). Test fairness is the extent to which the social consequences of test usage are considered fair or unfair to relevant subgroups; test fairness is especially important to consider when used for selection or placement decisions. From a legal point of view, this is related to the notion of disparate impact (see *Griggs v. Duke Power*, 1971). If a test negatively affects opportunities for a group to participate in, for example, gifted education, then it has a disparate impact and should not be used. Out of *Griggs v. Duke Power* came the fundamental question: "If a group consistently performs poorly on a test, why do we continue to use it?"

TYPES OF BIAS

Fundamentally, all concerns about bias relate to differential performance between and among groups. Why does one group perform differently than another group (Black /CLD or White, female or male, high income or low income) on a consistent basis? Attempts to account for differential performance target the individual characteristics of examinees, the testing environment, and/or characteristics of the test or test items (Scheuneman, 1985). Four types of bias are often discussed.

Bias in Construct Validity. Bias in construct validity is present when a test is shown to measure different hypothetical constructs or traits for one group than another; this type of bias also exists when the test measures the same trait for groups but with differing degrees of accuracy. Statistics regarding factor structure are often employed here. Specifically, a biased test will show different factor structures across subgroups. There will be a lower degree of similarity for the factor structure and the rank or item difficulty across groups (Sattler, 1992). The basic question here is: Does the item or test measure what it is intended to measure? A key illustration relates to language. Testing a student in English who has yet to become proficient in English is problematic. An intelligence test then becomes a language test. Certain students or groups may have the knowledge and experiences needed to answer the item correctly but cannot do so if they do not understand the question due to language barriers.

Bias in Content Validity. Bias in content validity is present when an item or subscale is relatively more difficult for members of one groups than another after the general ability level of the two is held constant. For example, if asked the question, "How are soccer and football alike?" a student or group who has never played or watched or had discussions about soccer is at a disadvantage. Lack of exposure and experience place them at a disadvantage. Reynolds (1998) defined content bias in this way: "an item or subscale of a test is considered biased when it is demonstrated to be relatively more difficult for members of one group than another when the general ability of both groups is held constant and no reasonable theoretical rationale exists to explain group differences on the item or subscale in question" (cited in Gregory, 2004, p. 243). Reynolds (1998) lists three examples of content bias:

> The items ask for information that minority persons have not had equal opportunity to learn;
>
> The scoring of the item is inappropriate, because the test author/developer had arbitrarily decided on the only correct answer and minority groups are inappropriately penalized for given answers that would be correct in their own culture;
>
> The wording of questions in unfamiliar, and minority groups who may know the answer may not be able to respond because they do not understand the question(s) and/or are unfamiliar with the test format.

Bias in item Selection. Bias in item selection is present when the items and tasks selected are based on the learning experiences and language of the dominant group. This bias is closely related to content validity, but addresses more directly concerns regarding the appropriateness of individual items. While the overall test may not be biased statistically, a few items in them can be. Essentially, this issue concerns how an item gets included in a test but another item does not.

Bias in Predictive or Criterion-Related Validity. Bias in predictive or criterion-related validity is present when the inference drawn from the test score is not made with the smallest feasible random error or when there is constant error in an inference or prediction as a function of membership in a particular group. The overarching question here is: "Does the test scores accurately predict how the student or group will perform on a task in the future?" It is often presumed that a high intelligence score predicts a high grade point average and success in college and on the job, and so much more. A concern of opponents is that intelligence tests are given too much power, and if a student or group scores low on an intelligence test, there is a high probability that they will be denied an opportunity to access a program or service because expectations for them are low. In other words, a test is considered "unbiased if the results for all relevant subpopulations cluster equally well around a single regression line ... an unbiased test predicts performance equally for all groups, even though their means may be different" (Gregory, 2004, p. 244).

NON-DISCRIMINATORY ASSESSMENT: SOME RECOMMENDATIONS FOR REDUCING BIAS

In newer editions of intelligence test, most producers endeavor to ensure that their tests are low in bias, and their manuals address such efforts. No matter how diligent these efforts are, there is no such thing as a bias-free test; nonetheless, we must aim for bias-reduced tests. Some suggestions for achieving this goal are as follows:

Translate tests into the language of the examinee;

Use interpreters to translate test items for examinees;

Examine all test items/tasks to see if groups perform differently and eliminate those items/tasks;

Eliminate items that are offensive to examinees;

When interpreting test scores, always consider the examinee's background experience;

Do not support the assumption of homogeneous experience or equal opportunity to learn; groups have different backgrounds and experiences that affect their test performance;

Never base decisions on one test and/or one score. One piece of information or lone score cannot possibly be useful in making effective and appropriate decisions;

Do not interpret test scores in isolation; collect multiple data and use this comprehensive method to make decisions;

When an individual or group scores low, consider that the test may be the problem; it may be inappropriate and should be eliminated;

If a group consistently performs poorly on an intelligence test, explore contributing factors and the extent to which it is useful/helpful for that group (Griggs Principle);

Always consider the technical and social merits of tests. A test can be technically unbiased and simultaneously unfair (i.e., have a disparate impact);

Review norming data and sample sizes; while diverse groups can be proportionally represented in the standardization sample, their actual numbers may be too small to be representative, which hinders generalizability;

Include culture-fair or culture-reduced tests in the assessment or decision making process; these tests are designed to minimize irrelevant influences of cultural learning and social climate and, thereby, produce a clearer separation of ability or performance from learning opportunities; non-verbal intelligence tests fall into this category, with their reduced cultural and linguistic loadings (see Bracken & Naglieri, 2003; Flanagan & Ortiz, 2001);

Always use and interpret test scores with testing principles and standards in mind, such as those published by the American Psychological Association and others (1999), which address professional responsibility and ethics, as well as working effectively with culturally diverse populations (Ford & Whiting, 2006; Whiting & Ford, 2006).

As of 2004, culturally diverse students comprised some 43% of the U.S. public school population, and demographers predicted that this percentage would increase. Given the rapid changes in school demographics and the ever-increasing reliance on tests for decision-making purposes, the discussion of test bias was anticipated to continue. Testing is here to stay, and high-stakes testing is on the rise as of the early 2000s. Thus, the power of tests to open or close doors is increasing and of increasing concern.

While test developers increasingly work to decrease biases in their tests and, in effect, to increase the usefulness of their measures, controversy continues. It has been argued that tests in and of themselves are harmless tools, a philosophical viewpoint that often fails to hold true in actual practice. "Unfortunately, the tendency to imbue intelligence test scores with inaccurate and unwarranted connotations is rampant ... Test results are variously over-interpreted or under-interpreted, viewed by some as a divination of personal worth but devalued by others as trivial and unfair" (Gregory, 2004, p. 240). While not intended for this purpose, in practice, tests do serve as gatekeepers, often resulting in closed doors and limited options for Black and other diverse groups (Ford & Joseph, 2006). Moreover, if misuse and misinterpretation were not problematic, there would be no need for task forces and standards to hold educators accountable (see works by Association of Black Psychologists, and the joint testing standards of APA, AERA, and NCME, 1999).

Despite the best intentions to develop tests that are low or reduced in bias, human error—stereotypes and prejudice—undermine test administration, interpretation, and use. More often than not, African American and other culturally diverse students are the recipients of this inequity.

SEE ALSO *Ability Grouping; Culturally Relevant Pedagogy.*

BIBLIOGRAPHY

American Educational Research Association (AERA), American Psychological Association (APA), and National Council on Measurement in Education (NCME). (1999). *Standards for educational and psychological testing.* Washington, DC: American Psychological Association.

Armour-Thomas, E., & Gopaul-McNicol, S. (1998). *Assessing intelligence: Applying a bio-cultural model.* Thousand Oaks, CA: Sage.

Bracken, B. A., & Naglieri, J. A. (2003). Assessing diverse populations with nonverbal tests of general intelligence. In C. R. Reynolds & R. W. Kamphaus (Eds.), *Handbook of psychological and educational assessment of children* (2nd ed.). New York: Guilford.

Cole, N. S., & Zieky, M. J. (2001). The new faces of fairness. *Journal of Educational Measurement, 38*(4), 369–382.

Ford, D. Y. (2004). *Intelligence testing and cultural diversity: Concerns, cautions, and considerations.* Storrs, CT: University of Connecticut, National Research Center on the Gifted and Talented.

Ford, D. Y. (2007). Intelligence testing and cultural diversity: The need for alternative instruments, policies, and procedures. In VanTassel-Baska, J. L. (Ed.), *Alternative assessments with gifted and talented students* (pp. 107–128). Waco, TX: Prufrock Press and the National Association for Gifted Children.

Ford, D. Y., & Joseph, L. M. (2006). Non-discriminatory assessment: Considerations for gifted education. *Gifted Child Quarterly, 50*(1), 41–51.

Ford, D. Y., & Whiting, G. W. (2006). Under-representation of diverse students in gifted education: Recommendations for nondiscriminatory assessment (part 1). *Gifted Education Press Quarterly, 20*(2), 2–6.

Gregory, R. J. (2004). *Psychological testing: History, principles, and applications.* Boston: Allyn & Bacon.

Jensen, A. R. (1980). *Bias in mental testing.* New York: Free Press.

Reynolds, C. R. (1998). Cultural bias in testing of intelligence and personality. In A. Bellack & M. Hersen (Series Eds.) & C. Belar (Vol. Ed.), *Comprehensive clinical psychology: Sociocultural and individual differences.* New York: Elsevier Science.

Sattler, J. M. (1992). *Assessment of children* (3rd ed.). San Diego: Jerome M. Sattler.

Scheuneman, J. (1985). Exploration of causes of bias in test items. *GRE Board Professional Report GREB No. 81–21P, ETS Research Report 85–42.* Princeton, NJ: Educational Testing Service.

Whiting, G. W., & Ford, D. Y. (2006). Under-representation of diverse students in gifted education: Recommendations for nondiscriminatory assessment (part 2). *Gifted Education Press Quarterly, 20*(3), 6–10.

Williams, R. (1970). Danger: Testing and dehumanizing Black children. *Clinical Child Psychology Newsletter, 9*(1), 5–6.

Gilman W. Whiting
Donna Y. Ford

CULTURAL DEFICIT MODEL

In attempting to explain the widespread underachievement among students of color and students from lower socioeconomic strata in schools, many teachers, administrators, school agents and others locate the problem within the students, their families and communities. This cultural deficit model attributes students' lack of educational success to characteristics often rooted in their cultures and communities. That is, research grounded in a deficit perspective blames the victims of institutional oppression for their own victimization by referring to negative stereotypes and assumptions regarding certain groups or communities. This perspective overlooks the root causes of oppression by localizing the issue within individuals and/or their communities. Because this model frames the problem as one of students and families, the remedies informed by deficit perspectives created to ameliorate student underachievement and failure often fail meaningfully to address problems within schools or society at large that combine to depress the performance of certain groups of students. Under the cultural deficit model, schools are, at least in part, absolved from their responsibilities to educate all students appropriately, and this charge is shifted almost entirely to students and their families.

CHARACTERISTICS OF THE CULTURAL DEFICIT MODEL

The cultural deficit model stems from negative beliefs and assumptions regarding the ability, aspirations, and work ethic of systematically marginalized peoples. It asserts that students of color and low-income students often fail to do well in school because of perceived "cultural deprivation" or lack of exposure to cultural models more obviously congruent with school success. Consequently, according to this perspective students of color and poor students often enter school with a lack of "cultural capital" (Bourdieu, 1997), cultural assets that are affirmed by schools and often shared by school agents and therefore considered valuable. In addition, there is a popular assumption that the families of students of color and socioeconomically disadvantaged students do not value education in the same ways that their middle- and upper-class White counterparts do. Conversely, upper-

and middle-class students, according to the theory, are more likely to do well in school because they possess more cultural capital. Much of the deficit-centered literature also suggests that a lack of involvement among families living in poverty is in part responsible for the educational outcomes of this community.

Deeply embedded in the fabric of schools, the deficit perspective is often disseminated through educational research and within teacher training programs (Trueba 1988; Valencia, 1997; González, 2005). For example, Ruby Payne's 2001 *Framework for Understanding Poverty*, a widely disseminated text with significant popularity within school districts, has been critiqued for promoting classist, deficit-centered theories to explain the underachievement of youth in poverty (Gorski, 2006). The results of the deficit perspective can be devastating and are manifested in multiple forms, making school a "subtractive" experience for many youth (Valenzuela, 1999). One of the most deleterious impacts is supported by research which suggests that students of color continue to be overrepresented in special education and in the less academically rigorous, non college-prep tracks of their schools (Russo & Talbert-Johnson, 1997; Patton, 1998; Coutinho & Oswald, 2000; Noguera, 2001; Oakes, 2005; Conchas, 2006). The negative impact of deficit perspectives is also evidenced by disproportionately high drop out or "push out" rates among students of color and poor students. Moreover, the negative beliefs regarding students of color and poor students can also result in stereotype threat (Steele, 1997), resulting in depressed academic performance.

ALTERNATIVES TO DEFICIT PERSPECTIVE

In spite of its pervasive influence, deficit perspective research has been discredited by an emerging body of literature. One area of critique notes that deficit perspectives fail to consider the fact that traditional avenues for parental participation in schools are closed off to many low income families and families of color. In a 2001 ethnographic study of Latino/a families, Concha Delgado-Gaitán (2001) found that almost all the teachers in her study believed parental involvement was extremely important, yet they also asserted that the majority of Latino/a parents were not sufficiently involved in their children's education. Nitza Hidalgo (1997, 2000) explored the contributions Latino/a parents make to the educational experiences of their children. The findings from her study suggest that Latino/a parents, and the extended familial social networks that they develop, contribute to the educational experiences of their children in meaningful ways that often remain unrecognized by schools. In their study of academically successful Puerto Rican students in the mid-

western United States, René Antrop-Gonzalez, William Vélez and Tomás Garrett (2005) found that students' families, and particularly their mothers, played a large role in fostering academic success, helping their children with schoolwork, locating resources to help support their learning, serving as mentors, and guiding them through the learning process. Similarly, research examining the role of parental involvement among African Americans demonstrates that parents have high participation in school programs when program themes emphasize empowerment, outreach, and valuing community resources (Abdul-Adil & Farmer, 2006).

Also contributing to debunking the myth that low-income families and families of racially and ethnically diverse backgrounds are apathetic about education, Gerardo Lopez's 2001 study cogently argues that the Latino low-income family in his study was highly involved in what he refers to as the "transmission of sociocultural values" (p. 430). That is, the family taught their children the value of hard work and underscored the importance of getting an education in part by taking their children with them to do physically demanding agricultural work, explicitly "giving their children the 'choice' to work hard at school or work hard in the fields" (p. 420).

By locating the causes for student underachievement within students and communities, the cultural deficit model fails to examine institutional barriers (i.e., school funding, racial and ethnic segregation) that can also potentially influence student achievement. It also fails to acknowledge the relationships between school practices, the sociopolitical factors that shape these efforts, and student outcomes. Much of the deficit-centered literature fails to explain or account for students who come from families and communities with the same alleged limitations yet succeed in school. The 2006 work of Gilberto Conchas highlights the voices of successful students of color in urban schools and examines the support structures that facilitated their success. In an effort to counter deficit perspectives and "RicanStruct" the discourse regarding urban Latino students, research by Jason Irizarry and René Antrop-González (2007) critically examines the characteristics of a group of exemplary teachers and academically successful students and puts forward a theory for culturally responsive pedagogy for this group. Similarly, Katie Haycock summarizes research that documents how entire schools that serve so-called culturally deprived students are as successful as many high-achieving schools in more affluent communities (Haycock, 2001).

This growing body of research urges schools to acknowledge the social and cultural capital present in communities of color and poor communities (Moll & Greenberg, 1990; Gonzalez, 2005; Yosso, 2005). Tara

Yosso (2005), for example, critiques static notions of cultural capital that fail to recognize what she refers to as "community cultural wealth"—characteristics, such as resiliency, that students of color and poor students often bring to school that should be recognized and built upon. Similar research by Wenfan Yan (1999) suggests that academically successful African American students bring unique forms of social capital with them into the classroom that are distinct from white, middle-class cultural models and that African American parents tended to contact their children's schools regarding their teens' future career aspirations and experiences in schools more than White parents. As this body of research continues to develop, schools and school agents may abandon deficit perspectives, affirm the cultural richness present in these communities, and implement more culturally responsive approaches aimed at improving the educational experiences and outcomes for students of color and students from lower socioeconomic strata.

SEE ALSO *Cultural Bias in Teaching; Cultural Bias in Testing; Culturally Relevant Pedagogy; Stereotype Threat.*

BIBLIOGRAPHY

Abdul-Adil, J. K. & Farmer, A.D. (2006). Inner-city African American parental involvement in elementary schools: Getting beyond urban legends of apathy. *School Psychology Quarterly, 21*(1), 1–12.

Antróp-González, R., Vélez, W., Garrett, T. (2005). ¿Donde están los estudiantes puertorriqueños/os exitosos? [Where are the academically successful Puerto Rican students?]: Success factors of high-achieving Puerto Rican high school students. *Journal of Latino/as and Education, 4*(2), 77–94.

Bourdieu, P. 1997. The forms of capital. In A.H. Halsey, H. Lauder, P. Brown, and A. S. Wells (Eds.), *Education: Culture, economy, and society* (pp. 40–58). Oxford, England: Oxford University Press.

Conchas, G. Q. (2006). *The color of school success: Race and high-achieving urban youth.* New York: Teachers College Press.

Coutinho, M. J., & Oswald, D. P. (2000). Disproportionate representation in special education: A synthesis and recommendations. *Journal of Child and Family Studies, 9*(2), 135–156.

Delgado, Gaitán, C. (2001). *The power of community: Mobilizing for family and schooling.* Lanham, MD: Rowan and Littlefield.

Haycock, K. (2001, March). Closing the achievement gap. *Educational Leadership,* 6–11.

Hidalgo, N. M. (1997). A layering of family and friends: Four Puerto Rican families' meaning of community. *Education and Urban Society, 30*(1), 20–40.

Hidalgo, N. M. (2000). Puerto Rican mothering strategies: The role of mothers and grandmothers in promoting school success. In S. Nieto (Ed.), *Puerto Rican students in U.S. schools* (pp. 167–196). Mahwah, NJ: Erlbaum.

González, N. (2005). Beyond culture: The hybridity of funds of knowledge. In N. González, L. C. Moll & C. Amanti (Eds.), *Funds of knowledge* (pp. 29–46). Mahwah, NJ: Erlbaum.

Gorski, P. (2006). The classist underpinnings of Ruby Payne's framework. *Teachers College Record.* Retrieved April 21, 2008, from http://www.tcrecord.org/content.asp?contentid=12322.

Irizarry, J. G. & Antrop-González, R. (2007). RicanStructing the discourse and promoting school success: Extending a theory of culturally responsive pedagogy to DiaspoRicans. *Centro Journal of the Center for Puerto Rican Studies, 20*(2), 3–25.

Lopez, G. R. (2001). The value of hard work: Lessons on parent involvement from an (im)migrant household. *Harvard Educational Review, 71*(3), 416–437.

Moll, L. C. & Greenberg, J. B. (1990). Creating zones of possibilities: Combining social contexts for instruction. In L. C. Moll (Ed.), *Vygotsky and education: Instructional implications and applications of sociohistorical psychology* (pp. 319–348). New York: Cambridge University Press.

Noguera, P. (2001). Racial politics and the elusive quest for excellence and equity in education. *Education and Urban Society, 34*(1), 18–41.

Oakes, J. (2005). *Keeping track: How schools structure inequality* (2nd ed.). New Haven, CT: Yale University Press.

Patton, J. M. (1998). The disproportionate representation of African-Americans in special education: Looking behind the curtain for understanding and solutions. *Journal of Special Education, 32*(1), 25–31.

Payne, R. K. (2001). *A framework for understanding poverty.* Highlands, TX: aha! Process.

Russo, C. J. & Talbert-Johnson, C. (1997). The overrepresentation of African American children in special education: The resegregation of educational programming? *Education and Urban Society, 29*(2), 136–148.

Steele, C. M. (1997). A threat in the air: How stereotypes shape intellectual identity and performance. *American Psychologist, 52,* 613–629.

Trueba, E. H. T. (1988). Culturally based explanations of minority students' academic achievement. *Anthropology & Education Quarterly, 19*(3), 270–287.

Valencia, R. R. (Ed.). (1997). *The evolution of deficit thinking: Educational thought and practice.* Washington, DC: Falmer Press.

Valenzuela, A. (1999). *Subtractive schooling: US–Mexican youth and the politics of caring.* Albany: State University of New York Press.

Yan, W. (1999). Successful African American students: The role of parental involvement. *The Journal of Negro Education, 68*(1), 5–22.

Yosso, T. (2005). Whose culture has capital? A critical race theory discussion of community cultural wealth. *Race, Ethnicity and Education, 81,* 69–91.

Jason G. Irizarry

CULTURALLY RELEVANT PEDAGOGY

During the last three decades of the 20th century, teacher preparation addressed diversity as a critical component in effective teacher interaction with students in an increasingly multicultural population. In 1972 the American

Association of Colleges and Teacher Education published "No One Model American," the aim of which was to "build an effective and humane society through the betterment of teacher education" ("No one model", 1972). The resulting Commission on Multicultural Education endorsed three premises: (1) Cultural diversity is a valuable resource, (2) multicultural education preserves and extends the resource of culture diversity rather than merely tolerating it or making it "melt away," and (3) a commitment to cultural pluralism should permeate all aspects of teacher preparation programs (Cochran-Smith, 2008, p. xv).

This commitment to multiculturalism expanded in 1976, when teacher preparation institutions had to provide evidence that their candidates had received adequate opportunities to interact with issues concerning teaching diverse populations (Gollnick, 1992). However, in spite of the ever-increasing terminology to encompass the changing faces of students in the classroom—multicultural, diverse, culturally responsive, diversity in race, ethnicity, gender, sexual orientation, socio-economic, linguistic, disability— Eurocentric attitudes often persisted. Nonetheless, effective teachers strive to acknowledge the kaleidescope of background experiences students bring to the classroom and to ensure the materials and methods are representative of this ever-growing diversity. They aim to provide students with opportunities to connect their learning experiences to their own lives.

In 2002, No Child Left Behind (NCLB) emphasized that high-quality teachers were essential for student success. However, Ardila-Rey points out that NCLB's "definition of what it means to be a highly qualified teacher ... does not provide any provisions on ... cultural requirements.... Only a handful of states have developed policies or standards for teacher preparation and credentialing that address issues to diverse populations" (Ardila-Rey, 2008, p. 341). This is cause for concern because teacher preparation institutions and other entities involved with ongoing professional development are responsible to "prepare educators who have the competencies and dispositions to work effectively with diverse students" (Anstrom, 2004, p. viii), address issues of theories and practices for effective learning, to include "experiences, knowledge, skills, and attitudes to successfully promote the educational success of all children" (Nevárez-La Torre, Sanford-DeShields, Soundy, Leonard, & Woyshner, 2008, p. 270), and include competencies in which teachers "learn, reflect, introspect and incorporate ... new ideas into pre-service and in-service teachers' actions in their classrooms" (p. 277). With these goals in mind, teacher preparation and professional programs are being restructured so that candidates acquire the competencies to meet the challenges of educating a diverse student population (Phuntsog, 1999). However, despite con-

tinuing efforts to attract a balanced representation of teachers from various cultures, there is minimal diversity among teachers and the numbers who do exist are dwindling. According to Gay (2003):

> It is increasingly a cross-cultural phenomenon, in that teachers are frequently not of the same race, ethnicity, class, and language dominance as their students. This demographic and cultural divide is becoming even more apparent as the number of individuals in teacher preparation and active classroom teaching dwindle. (p.1)

PREPARING TEACHERS FOR CULTURALLY RELEVANT PEDAGOGY

Culture has been defined as "The system of values, beliefs, and ways of knowing that guide communities of people in their daily lives" (Trumbull, 2005, p. 35). Effective teacher preparation addresses the need for teachers to acknowledge students' diversity and incorporate their pluralistic backgrounds and experiences into the learning experiences and classroom environment. In "culturally relevant pedagogy" (Ladson-Billings, 2001), "culturally responsive teaching" (Gay, 2000) (and other similar terms) teachers "develop the knowledge, skills, and predispositions to teach children from diverse racial, ethnic, language, and social class backgrounds" (Weinstein, Curran, & Tomlinson-Clarke, 2003, p. 270). Kirkland (2003) commented that "good multicultural teaching honors our diverse cultural and ethnic experiences, contributions and identities" (p. 131) and emphasized that teachers need to "understand the experiences and perspectives [students] bring to educational settings and be responsive to the cultures of different groups in designing curriculum, learning activities, classroom climated, instructional materials and techniques, and assessment procedures" (p. 134).

According to Hackett, teachers need to develop a "strong cultural identity [so as to be] responsible for teaching the whole child by teaching values, skills, knowledge for school success and participation in society, linking classroom teaching to out-of-school personal experiences and community situations" (Hackett, 2003, p. 329). Ambrosio emphasizes the importance of multiculturalism for the teacher:

> Teaching is learning—a process of slowly integrating knowledge into practice. ... The most important aspect of teaching is developing the mental habit of reflecting on your instructional practice and of altering your practice according to what you discover about how students learn best. Knowledge of multicultural theory and practice will give you the reflective space, the necessary

reservoir of cultural insight, to intelligently address pedagogical issues as they arise in your everyday practice. (Ambrosio, 2003, p. 37)

Gay (2006) echoed one recurring response to the need to ensure high-quality teacher preparation:

U.S. society is becoming increasingly diverse, and that diversity is reflected in its classrooms. Creating a respectful, productive classroom environment is always a challenge; this challenge is even greater when students and teachers come from different cultural backgrounds, or when students differ in terms of race, ethnicity, socioeconomic status, cultural and linguistic background, sexual orientation, ableness, and academic aptitude. Unless teachers have the knowledge, skills, and disposition to effectively guide diverse groups of children, they are likely to face classes characterized by disrespect and alienation, name-calling and bullying, disorder and chaos. (pp. 365–366)

Moreover, Gay advised that "teachers must be multicultural themselves before they can effectively and authentically teach students to be multicultural" (Gay, 2003, p. 4) and proposed that "culturally responsive teachers … validate, faciltiate, liberate and empower ethnically diverse students by simultaneously cultivating their cultural integrity,individual abilities, and academic success" (Gay, 2000, pp. 43–44).

Culturally relevant pedagogy aims to ensure that educators acknowledge and honor the diverse viewpoints of their student population and refrain from promoting homogeneous perspectives as universal beliefs. Glanzer (2008) referenced Hunter (2000) in that "the unspoken imperative of all moral education is to teach only those virtues, principles, and other moral teachings about which there is no disagreement in American society" (p. 525). Glanzer proposed that "schools should show fairness to diverse visions of the good life and not merely replace them with neutered and safe substitutes" (p. 526). Dingus (2003) further emphasized the importance of this perspective: "No student should have to sacrifice cultural heritage, ethnic identity, and social networks in order to obtain an education" (p. 99).

CHARACTERISTICS OF A CULTURALLY RESPONSIVE CLASSROOM

For more than five decades, teachers have developed strategies to comply with the responsibility to accommodate diverse students in an inclusive classroom; these challenges are compounded by the increasing diversity among the student population. Although teachers must be competent in the subject area they are assigned to teach ("Highly qualified teachers," 2006), the main focus in teaching has switched from the "What"—that is, content in the curriculum—to the "Who":- who is the learner in the classroom. Teachers are responsible for teaching their students and for ensuring they all learn. It is critical that educators use their knowledge of students' background and incorporate what they know about these learners into quality learning experiences. Culturally responsive teaching involves incorporating into learning experiences components of what is known about students' knowledge of their cultures, their prior experiences both in their countries of origin and their current living situations, as well as the learning styles of diverse students, to make learning more appropriate and effective for them (Gay, 2000). "Culture is central to learning. It plays a role not only in communicating and receiving information, but also in shaping the thinking process of groups and individuals. A pedagogy that acknowledges, responds to, and celebrates fundamental cultures offers full, equitable access to education for students from all cultures" ("Culturally Responsive Teaching," 1994).

Ambrosio (2003) referred to Freire's (1970) premise that "Rather than seeing students as empty vessels, to be filled with the expert knowledge of teachers … students must make their own meanings; they must be producers of knowledge themselves" (p. 31). Moreover, he advised that teachers consider "students as creators rather than consumers of knowledge, as makers of meaning rather than passive recipients of socially sanctioned truths" (p.34). Ambrosio advocated a "pedagogy that uses the personal knowledge and experiences of students to reflect critically on issues presented from a variety of perspectives" (p. 34), advising that teachers should commit themselves to developing classrooms based on a "cultural democracy, to creating learning experiences and opportunities that allow students from diverse cultural groups to see themselves in … curriculum, instructional practices, and classroom climate" (p. 34). Pratt (2008) supported a student-centered curriculum, which "appreciates diverse abilities and interests and adapting teaching to allow for these differences" (p. 517). Students succeed when academic tasks include themes representative of their own culture (Boykin, Tyler, & Miller, 2005). Ironically, practices that give students choices about what they learn and how they learn are misaligned with standards-based curriculum and accountability through testing.

Culturally relevant pedagogy is a component in the foundation of competencies effective teachers require. Ladson-Billings (Summer, 1995) commented about this concept:

But that's just good teaching! Instead of some "magic bullet" or intricate formula and steps for instruction, some members of my audience are shocked to hear what seems to them like some routine teaching strategies that are a part of good teaching. (p. 159)

These "routine strategies for good teaching" are the criteria for effective teaching and learning. It is with this repertoire of theories, skills, and practices that effective teachers are able to create environments conducive to achieving the goal of education. That goal is to facilitate the development of intelligent, life-long learners who possess the strategies and metacognitive processes to make meaningful connections with their knowledge basis and transfer their skills to (and beyond) the challenges they encounter in their daily life. Teachers are obligated to "prepare students to become effective and critical participants in the world" (Nieto, 1999, p. 143). Effective educators are cognizant of the components necessary for learning to occur and are able to delve into their "toolbox" of theories and practices, strategies and perceptions, to ensure that all of their students will succeed. This is the more critical as the information and skills students learn will often be outdated by the time they exit the school environment.

Gay (2003) acknowledged, "much is said about the necessity and value of variety in teaching styles or using multiple means to achieve common learning outcomes" (p.2). When teachers plan for successful learning, they make a concerted effort to deliberately plan for classroom experiences in which all learners can be reached at multiple points throughout the learning experiences. Teachers who plan deliberately for an environment conducive to learning for all students ensure differentiation by incorporating various learning styles, multiple intelligences, cooperative learning, and "the diversity of learning styles, histories, cultures, and experiences that ethnically different students bring to the classroom" (p. 2).

Ambrosio (2003) emphasized that "multicultural education places a high value on critical thinking, on the personal truth making that enables students to challenge the moral and intellectual authority of the dominant culture" (p. 36).

Cooperative Learning. When a classroom incorporates the tenets of Cooperative Learning, the environment promotes maximal learning (Kagan, 2001). Ladson-Billings' (1994) notion of culturally relevant classrooms provided Craviotto and Heras (1999) with the concept that when a classroom is designed around culturally relevant principles, there is significant interaction between students as well as between students and the teacher. They explained that, "Classroom dialogue is a fundamental aspect of classroom discourse. ... [and the] classrooms are framed as an inviting space for exploration, learning, and dialogue among peers, students, and adults" (np). Rothstein-Fisch and Trumbull (2008) referenced Mar-

zano (2003) to promote classrooms where expectations include actions based on mutual respect. They support their premise with Slavin's (2006) endorsement that an advantage of cooperative learning situations reinforces students' responsibility for their own learning.

Classroom Management from a Cultural Perspective. The competencies for effective teaching include creating an environment conducive to learning. Effective classroom techniques are critical for each and every student to receive the learning experiences to which they are entitled (Weinstein et al., 2003). Culturally responsive pedagogy helps teachers achieve the goal of culturally responsive classroom management (CRCM) when they develop their management plan with an awareness of the diversity in their classrooms. Weinstein and colleagues (2003) outlined three premises by which to achieve the goal of CRCM:

1. *Recognize that we are all cultural beings, with our own beliefs, biases, and assumptions about human behavior.* At the same time, as it is incumbent that the educator incorporate the values "implicit in the western, White, middle-class orientation of U.S. schools, such as the emphasis on individual achievement, independence, and efficiency... By bringing cultural biases to a conscious level, we are less likely to misinterpret the behaviors of our culturally different students and treat them inequitably;

2. *Acknowledge the cultural, racial, ethnic, and class differences that exist among people.* People must acquire "cultural content knowledge." They must learn, for example, about their students' family backgrounds, their previous educational experiences, their culture's norms for interpersonal relationships, their parents' expectations for discipline, and the ways their cultures treat time and space, and use acquired cultural knowledge as a way of demonstrating an openness and willingness to learn about the aspects of culture that are important to students and their families;

3. *Understand the ways that schools reflect and perpetuate discriminatory practices of the larger society.* This involves an understanding of how differences in race, social class, gender, language background, and sexual orientation are linked to power (p. 270).

Weinstein and colleagues proposed that, "Culturally responsive classroom managers work to create a sense of community. This means anticipating the cultural conflicts that are likely to arise and promoting positive relationships among students" (p. 273).

Rothstein-Fisch and Trumbull (2008) emphasized that teachers be trained in techniques of classroom management from a cultural perspective in that "cultural values and beliefs are at the core of all classroom organization and management decisions" (p.xiii). They acknowledged the continuing concern that "School culture is relatively consistent across the United States and reflects the individualistic values of the dominant, European American culture" (p.xiii).

Cultivating Caring, Respectful Relationships. The ultimate goal of an effective teacher preparation program is to develop and hone the skills educators require to create learning environments that acknowledge, respect and are representative of the social world of all students (Noddings,1992). "When teachers and students come from different cultural backgrounds, planned efforts to cross social borders and develop caring, respectful relationships are essential" (Weinstein et al., 2003, p. 272). When teachers create an environment which is based on caring and concern, and in which each student is valued, the result is that students become more motivated and learn more (Stipek, 2002).

Pratt (2008) identified "caring" as a central dimension of effective teaching. He advised:

> Sometimes it is important to put aside the research journals, political commentaries, and popular news about the state of education and stop long enough to listen to the voice of a 9-year-old. ... You can learn a lot about classrooms just by listening to the kids who inhabit them. (p. 515)

Teacher Reflection as a Standard of Effective Teaching. In the standards for effective teaching, reflective practice is a criterion for all teachers—pre-service, novice, and veteran. Teachers' ability to reflect on student achievement is a critical component in teacher preparation as well as in continuing professional development. Teachers who reflect on their own teaching ensure students are successful in their learning (Hoffman-Kipp, 2003; Ladson-Billings, 1995, 1999). Howard (2003) recommended teacher reflection as a means of incorporating issues of equity and social justice into teaching thinking and practice.

THE INFLUENCE OF THE TEACHER IN THE CLASSROOM: A THOUGHT FOR EDUCATORS

Diversity in the classroom encompasses many categories, among them ethnicity, culture, learning needs, and other issues. For all of these, educators have to hone their pedagogical skills to differentiate instructional practices to meet the varying needs of the population in the general classroom. The significant shift in the balance of diverse students—the multicultural panorama of 21st-century school environment—is no longer an exception to the world outside of the classroom, but a direct reflection of

it. Effective educators incorporate culturally relevant pedagogy to ensure that all students succeed. Sroka (2006) summarized the essential qualities of effective teachers in the criteria that teachers be nonjudgmental—that students' opinions are welcomed and respected and that teachers have a passion for the content they teach.

Ginott (1995) made a powerful statement when he described the overpowering influence the teacher has in the classroom:

> I have come to a frightening conclusion. I am the decisive element in the classroom. It is my personal approach that creates the climate. It is my daily mood that makes the weather. As a teacher I possess tremendous power to make a child's life miserable or joyous. I can be a tool of torture or an instrument of inspiration. I can humiliate or humor, hurt or heal. In all situations, it is my response that decides whether a crisis will be escalated or de-escalated, and a child humanized or de-humanized. (p.302)

A KALEIDOSCOPE EFFECT

Effective teachers are equipped with a repertoire of teaching strategies designed to meet the educational needs of all students in the classroom. The components of their repertoire can be likened to a kaleidoscope that contains a multitude of prisms, which are dynamic and ever changing. Just as the kaleidoscope creates images using the diversity of color, shape, and sizes from the composite of the prisms, so, too, do successful educators develop an environment for optimal learning for the diverse student population.

SEE ALSO *Cultural Bias in Teaching; Cultural Bias in Testing; Cultural Deficit Model; Multicultural Education.*

BIBLIOGRAPHY

Ambrosio, John. (2003). We make the road by walking. In Geneva Gay (Ed.), *Becoming multicultural educators: Personal Journey toward professional agency* (pp. 17–41). San Francisco: Jossey-Bass.

Anstrom, K. (2004). Introduction. In K. Anstrom, J. Glazier, P. Sanchez, V. Sardi, P. Schwallie-Giddis & P. Tate. (Eds.), *Preparing all educators for student diversity: Lessons for higher education* (pp. vii–xvii). Washington, DC: Institute for Education Policy Studies, Graduate School of Education and Human Development, The George Washington University.

Ardila-Rey, A. (2008). Language, culture, policy, and standards in teacher preparation. In M. E. Brisk (Ed.), *Language, culture, and community in teacher education* (pp. 331–351). Mahwah, NJ: Erlbaum.

Boykin, A., Tyler, K., & Miller, O. (2005). In search of cultural themes and their expressions in the dynamics of classroom life. *Urban Education, 40*(5), 521–549.

Cochran-Smith, M. (2008). Foreword. In M. E. Brisk. (Ed.), *Language, culture, and community in Teacher Education* (p. xv). Mahwah, NJ: Erlbaum.

Craviotto, E. & Heras, A. (1999). *Characteristics of culturally relevant classrooms*. Retrieved April 18, 2008, from http://www.ncrel.org/sdrs/areas/issues/content/cntareas/reading/li4lk57.htm.

"Culturally responsive teaching" (1994). Retrieved April 18, 2008, from http://www.alliance.brown.edu/tdl/tl-strategies/crt-principles.shtml/.

Dingus, J. (2003). Making and breaking ethnic masks. In G. Gay (Ed.), *Becoming multicultual educators: Personal journey toward professional agency* (pp. 91–116). San Francisco: Jossey-Bass.

Freire, P. (1970). *Pedagogy of the oppressed*. New York: Continuum.

Gay, G. (2000). *Culturally responsive teaching: Theory, research, and practice*. New York: Teachers College Press.

Gay, G. (2003). Introduction: Planting seeds to harvest fruits. In G. Gay (Ed.), *Becoming multicultual educators: Personal journey toward professional agency* (pp. 1–16). San Francisco: Jossey-Bass.

Gay, G. (2006). Connections between classroom management and culturally responsive teaching. In C. M. Evertson & C.S. Weinstein (Eds.), *Handbook of classroom management: Research, practice, and contemporary issues.* (pp. 343–370). Mahwah, NJ: Erlbaum.

Ginott, H. (1995). *Teacher and child*. New York: Collier.

Glanzer, P. L. (March, 2008). Harry Potter's provocative moral world: Is there a place for good and evil in moral education. *Kappan, 89*(7), 525–528.

Gollnick, D. (1992). Multicultural education: Policies and practices in teacher education. In H. Baptise, M. Baptiste, & D. Gollnick (Eds.), *Multicultural teacher education: Preparing teacher educators to provide educational equity* (Vol. 1). Washington, DC: American Association of Colleges for Teacher Education (AACTE).

Hackett, T. (2003). Teaching them through who they are. In G. Gay (Ed.), *Becoming multicultual educators: Personal journey toward professional agency* (pp. 315–340). San Francisco: Jossey-Bass.

Highly qualified teachers for every child. (August, 2006). Retrieved April 18, 2008, from http://www.ed.gov/nclb/methods/teachers/stateplanfacts.html.

Hoffman-Kipp, A. (Summer, 2003). Beyond reflection: teacher learning as praxis. *Theory Into Practice, 42*(3), 167–178.

Howard, T. C. (Summer, 2003). Culturally relevant pedagogy: Ingredients for critical teacher reflection. *Theory Into Practice, 42*(3), 195–202.

Hunter, J. D. (2000). *The death of character: Moral education in an age without good and evil*. New York: Basic.

Kirkland, K. (2003). Steppin' up and representin'. In G. Gay (Ed.), *Becoming multicultual educators: Personal journey toward professional agency* (pp. 117–142). San Francisco: Jossey-Bass.

Ladson-Billings, G. (1994). *The dreamkeepers: Successful teachers of African-American teachers*. San Francisco: Jossey-Bass.

Ladson Billings, G. (Summer, 1995). But that's just good teaching! The case for culturally relevant pedagogy. *Theory into Practice 34*(3), 159–165.

Ladson-Billings, G. (Autumn, 1995). Toward a theory of culturally relevant pedagogy. *American Educational Research Journal, 31*(3), 465–491.

Ladson-Billings, G. (1999). Preparing teachers for diverse student populations: A critical race theory perspective. *Review of Research in Education, 24*, 211–247.

Ladson-Billings, G. (2001). *Crossing over to Canaan: The journey of new teachers in diverse classrooms*. San Francisco: Jossey-Bass.

Marzano, R. J. (2003). *Classroom management that works: Research-based strategies for every teacher*. Alexandria, VA: Association for Supervision and Curriculum Development.

Marzano, R., & Kendall, J. (2006). *The new taxonomy of educational objectives*. Thousand Oaks, CA: Corwin Press.

Nevárez-La Torre, A., Sanford-DeShields, J., Soundy, C., Leonard, J., & Woyshner, C. Faculty perspectives in integrating linguistic diversity into an urban teacher education program. In M. E. Brisk (Ed.), *Language, culture, and community* (pp. 267–312). Mahwah, NJ: Erlbaum.

Nieto, S. (1999). *The light in their eyes: Creating multicultural learning communities*. New York: Teachers College Press.

Noddings, N. (1992). *The challenge to care in schools: An alternative approach to education*. New York: Teachers College Press.

No One Model American. (1972). American Association of Colleges and Teacher Education (AACTE). Retrieved April 18, 2008, from http://www.aacte.org/About_Us/multiculturaledstatement.pdf.

PDK 2008 International Summit. *Kappan, 89* (7), 546.

Phuntsog, N. (Summer, 1999). The magic of culturally responsive pedagogy: In search of the genie's lamp in multicultural education. *Teacher Education Quarterly, 26*(3), 97–111.

Pratt, D. (March, 2008). Lina's letters: A 9-year-old's perspective on what matters most in the classroom. *Kappan, 89*(7), 515–518.

Rothstein-Fisch, C., & Trumbull, E. (2008). *Managing Diverse Classrooms*. Alexandria, VA: Association for Supervision and Curriculum Development.

Slavin, R. (2006). *Educational psychology: theory and practice* (8th ed.). Boston: Pearson.

Sroka, S. (January, 2006). Listening to the whole child. *ASCD Education Update, 48(1),* 1, 8.

Stripek, D. (2002). *Motivation to learn: Integrating theory and practice* (4th ed.). Boston: Allyn and Bacon.

Trumbull, E. (2005). Language, culture, and society. In E. Trumbull & B. Farr (Eds.). *Language and learning: What teachers need to know* (pp.33–72). Norwood, MA: Christopher-Gordon.

Weinstein, C., Curran, M., & Tomlinson-Clarke, S. (2003). Culturally responsive classroom management: Awareness into action. *Theory Into Practice, 42*(3), 269–276.

Gilda Oran

D

DEAF AND HARD OF HEARING

Hearing loss is common, and its incidence increases with age. For the most part hearing loss is mild and has no serious effect on the development of spoken language and communication. The number of children for whom hearing loss has implications for the classroom and for general communication is relatively small, and profound hearing loss, or deafness, constitutes a low-incidence condition. In general, two categories are used to describe hearing loss: hard of hearing and deaf, with no clear demarcation between the two. Roughly, hard of hearing children are characterized as having incomplete or limited access to the spoken word, either with or without augmented hearing. Deaf children have no functional access to the spoken word, either with or without augmented hearing. The hard of hearing category may be subdivided into two categories, mild and moderate, and deafness into another two, severe and profound. Numbers decrease with the severity of the hearing loss, with one school-age child in 2,000 exhibiting a profound hearing loss (Gallaudet Research Institute, 2005). Approximately 80,000 deaf and hard of hearing children in the United States have been identified as receiving education services (Mitchell, 2004).

ASSESSMENT OF HEARING

The most significant development in assessment of hearing has been the spread of neonatal hearing screening. Close to 95% of newborn children are screened in the hospital. Until the implementation of neonatal screening, the average age of identification of hearing loss was 2 1/2 years. The two most common types of tests used are Automatic Auditory Brainstem Response (AABR) and Transient Evoked Otoacoustic Emissions (TEOAE) (Wrightstone, 2007). In the AABR test electrodes are placed on the forehead, mastoid, and nape of the neck of the infant, and the infant is fitted with a disposable earphone. The stimulus is a click or series of clicks. In the TEOAE test a microphone is placed in the external ear and a series of clicks tests the infant's response. In both cases, in order to reduce the number of false positives, a follow-up test is recommended for infants who do not pass the first screening.

Hearing testing, or audiometric assessment, can be accomplished in a variety of ways. Most frequently it is done by a trained audiologist using an audiometer, a device that emits tones at various frequencies and at different levels of loudness. The testing usually is conducted in a soundproof room. The person being tested wears a set of headphones or a headband and each ear is tested separately. The results are shown on an audiogram, a graph that represents hearing levels from low to high frequencies. The hearing is measured in units called decibels. Normal speech patterns are around 30 to 50 decibels. Hard of hearing individuals would have difficulty with much of spoken language and deaf individuals would have no access to it through audition.

CHARACTERISTICS OF DEAF AND HARD OF HEARING CHILDREN

Deaf and hard of hearing children, with some exceptions, reflect the general American school-age population. The exceptions are due to factors such as heredity, etiology, extent of hearing loss, and age of onset of a hearing loss.

309

Deaf students talking in the computer lab at Gallaudet University on November 3, 2006 in Washington, DC. **ANDY NELSON/THE CHRISTIAN SCIENCE MONITOR/GETTY IMAGES.**

For approximately half of American deaf and hard of hearing children, the hearing loss is caused by genetic factors (Moores, 2001).

Predominantly, genetic hearing loss is of a recessive nature, typically meaning that both parents, although they are able to hear, carry a gene for hearing loss. In a smaller number of cases, one parent may be deaf or hard of hearing and pass the gene along to the child in 50% of the cases. There are a small number of incidences of sex-linked hearing loss in which the hearing mother may pass the gene along to male children. This is possibly a partial explanation of why males constitute slightly more than half of the school age deaf and hard of hearing population. With a few exceptions, children with a genetic etiology do not possess disabilities; they are normal intellectually, physically, and emotionally.

Non-genetic factors play a decreasing but still important role. For generations, and perhaps for hundreds of years, worldwide maternal Rubella would double the number of deaf children born in particular periods of time. For large numbers of children, the results would include hearing loss, visual impairment, heart conditions, neurological disorders and physical frailness. The development of a Rubella vaccine has eliminated Rubella as a cause of hearing loss. Mother-child blood incompatibility is another cause of hearing loss that has been brought under control, at least in developed countries. Childhood meningitis, however, presents a somewhat different picture. In the past a very young child who contracted meningitis might die, whereas an older child might survive but with profound hearing loss. In the 21st century it is more likely that the older child would be cured without any hearing loss and the younger child survive but with multiple disabilities. Hearing loss may also occur as a consequence of premature birth, with the possibility of additional disabilities. Again, medical advances can lead to survival, but with concomitant conditions. Miller (2006) has argued that there are essentially two distinguishable categories of children with hearing loss: those who are normal intellectually and physically and those with overlays of disability.

There are some differences in the racial/ethnic make up of the school age deaf and hard of hearing population as compared to the hearing population. According to information compiled by the Gallaudet Research

Institute (2005), 50% of the deaf and hard of hearing school-age population is classified as White, 15% as Black/African American, and 25% as Hispanic/Latino, with the remaining 10% being classified as Asian/Pacific, American Indian, Other, or Multi-ethnic. The disparity is with the Hispanic/Latino category. A larger percentage of Hispanic/Latino children are in programs for deaf and hard of hearing children than in the general school population. The reasons for this are not clear.

CURRENT EDUCATIONAL AND INSTRUCTIONAL PRACTICES

Historically, there have been three interrelated major points of contention concerning the education of deaf and hard of hearing children and educational practices: Where should the children be taught, what should the children be taught, and how should the children be taught? (Moores & Martin, 2006). Complex sets of demographic changes, medical developments, societal expectations, and federal legislation have had major impacts on each of these questions.

Traditionally, deaf and hard of hearing children were taught either in residential school or in separate day-school programs in large cities. The situation began to change after World War II, due to the baby boom and population explosion. State legislatures were not willing to commit extra money for the construction of new residential facilities, and increasing numbers of deaf and hard of hearing children attended public schools, often in separate classes in schools with a majority of hearing children. The trend continued with the last major Rubella epidemic in the 1960s, at a time when the baby boom was over and there were empty rooms in the schools. The passage in 1975 of the Education of all Handicapped Children Act, which has undergone extensive amendment over time, including the Individuals with Disabilities Education Improvement Act Amendments (IDEA) of 2004, was the impetus for the acceleration of the movement of special education children to mainstream or integrated settings. The law requires a Free Appropriate Public Education (FAPE) for all disabled children, with each child receiving an Individualized Education Plan (IEP). Children are to be educated in the Least Restrictive Environment (LRE), and placement with non-disabled children is viewed as desirable. The concept of integration has been replaced with that of inclusion, by which modifications of instruction are expected to adapt to the needs of the child rather than placing the onus on the child. This is the expectation in theory, but it is not necessarily realized.

Amendments of IDEA lowered the age at which disabled children could be served until services are available at birth. For very young children there is an empha-

sis on serving the family as a whole system; instead of an individual education plan for the child, a family plan is developed. Coupled with universal neonatal screening there has been an increase of programs for children from birth to 3 years of age. Unfortunately, many states have not developed effective systems for follow-up once a hearing loss is identified, so there is often a lack of appropriate response.

Approximately half of deaf and hard of hearing children are placed in a regular classroom setting with hearing children, and may be served, depending on the IEP, by an itinerant teacher of the deaf or other professional. An estimated 40% of deaf and hard of hearing children in regular class settings receive sign interpreting services (Gallaudet Research Institute, 2005).

The question of what deaf and hard of hearing children should be taught has been influenced by changes in school placement and by federal legislation. The curricula for deaf and hard of hearing children used to emphasized speech training, speech recognition, and English, with relatively little attention devoted to content areas such as math, science, and social studies. However, as more and more children were educated in regular classrooms the regular education curriculum of the particular school district took precedence.

The enactment of the No Child Left Behind (NCLB) legislation in 2001 brought education of deaf and hard of hearing children into even more close alignment with regular education. Among other things, the law mandates that each state must establish high standards of learning for each grade and that the states develop rigorous, grade-level assessments to document student progress. Results are reported at school, school district, and state levels. Results are also reported at each level for all students and disaggregated by race/ethnicity, speakers of languages other than English, poverty (as demonstrated by free or reduced lunch eligibility), and disability. Annual goals are established for each category, and schools, school districts, and states must show annual yearly progress (AYP). Any achievement gaps among racial/ethnic, income, language, or disability groups must be closed so that by 2014 100% of American children will demonstrate academic proficiency, as measured by grade-level standardized state-administered tests. Only a small number of profoundly impaired children are exempt. All others, including deaf and hard of hearing students, must take the tests and, by 2014, have a 100% pass rate.

This poses an enormous challenge. Deaf and hard of hearing children in regular classrooms are already being exposed to the curricula of their home school districts, and most day and residential programs have adopted or adapted general education curricula. However, many, if not most, deaf and hard of hearing children start school, even after early intervention and preschool experiences, without the English skills and word knowledge that most children have acquired before the start of formal schooling. They are therefore unable to use English fluency as a tool to acquire academic knowledge and skills. For many deaf and hard of hearing children English is a barrier to learning that must be overcome. The curriculum must be modified to help deaf and hard of hearing children develop some of the skills that hearing children already have at the start of their education. Only a small percentage of high school-age deaf children achieve at grade level at the same level as their hearing peers (Moores & Martin, 2006) and the goal of 100 percent success in demonstrated academic proficiency will not be achieved by 2014.

The third issue, how to teach deaf children, deals with the oral-manual controversy, which has been raging for more than a century. In the first American schools for the deaf, which enrolled a substantial number of late deafened and hard of hearing students, instruction was through either a natural sign language, the precursor of American Sign Language (ASL), or through a system of signs modified by means of the American manual alphabet to represent English and presented in English word order. This method predated English-based signed systems that may be presented in coordination with spoken English. Oral-only education was introduced in the last third of the nineteenth century and quickly became dominant in the large city day schools and in some private residential schools. In the state residential schools a system evolved in which children up to around age 12 were taught orally and then tracked into either oral or manual classes (Winzer, 1993).

The situation began to change in the 1960s because of dissatisfaction with results of oral-only early intervention programs. A philosophy called Total Communication quickly grew in popularity. Theoretically, it involved the use of any means of communication to meet individual needs: speech, ASL, English-based signing, writing, gesture, or speech-reading. It reality it usually involved English-based signing in coordination with speech, and was known as simultaneous communication (Sim Com). During the 1990s a movement developed to employ ASL as the main mode of classroom instruction, with an additional concentration on written English. The approach was labeled Bi-BI, or bilingual-bicultural. Early 21st-century data indicates that 50% of deaf and hard of hearing children are taught through oral-only communication, 40% through sign and speech, and 10% through sign-only communication (Gallaudet Research Institute, 2005).

There has been growing interest in multichannel cochlear implants for deaf and hard of hearing children. The surgical procedure involves removing part of the mastoid bone and inserting a permanent electrode array into the cochlear. The procedure has been more common in Australia (Lloyd & Uniake, 2007) and Western European countries such as Sweden (Preisler, 2007), where as many as 80% of young deaf and hard of hearing children have received implants. Implantation has increased in the United States and in some areas approaches 50% of the deaf and hard of hearing population. Cochlear implants are designed to bring a more clear representation of the spoken word to deaf and hard of hearing children. There have been anecdotal reports of dramatic improvements in hearing in some children, but systematic reports of the extent to which it helps children with different characteristics are not available.

ASSESSMENT AND INSTRUCTION

In is important to keep in mind that the purposes of assessment for each child can include facilitating educational placement decisions, evaluating progress, determining educational approaches to be used, improving educational and intervention strategies, monitoring progress for individualized education plans, or family education plans (Miller, 2006). Although the situation is improving, attempts to provide meaningful and valid assessments for deaf and hard of hearing children have met with limited success. Miller points out that there is difficulty getting agreement in the field about which tests require "deaf norms" and which tests should use "hearing norms." When separate norms are desired there is the additional question of who should be included in the normative sample—all deaf children, deaf children without disabilities, deaf and hard of hearing children, children with disabilities, and so forth.

Miller states that in establishing an assessment framework assessment specialists must keep in mind the normal course of development of a typical deaf or hard of hearing child who has no disabilities and who has been in a linguistically enriched environment from birth. Other deaf and hard of hearing children should be compared to this ideal prototype or model of development and measured in ways that can estimate their similarities to or differences from the ideal. The template of developmental norms for deaf and hard of hearing children should be the model for all deaf and hard of hearing children even if such children comprise a minority of the population under consideration. Some of the key variables to be considered include age of onset of the hearing loss, age of identification and beginning of educational services, home and school linguistic environment, presence or absence of disabling conditions, use of and benefit from auditory amplification, and consistency of the communication approach over the years.

Considering these variables, the assessment specialist should be able to identify those children with hearing loss only, those with disabilities who have received excellent programming from an early age, and those who have received little or inappropriate educational services. The need is for assessment specialists to redouble efforts to develop meaningful, relevant, and linguistically and culturally appropriate assessment batteries that make the most sense in practical terms for deaf and hard of hearing children and their families.

SEE ALSO *Special Education.*

BIBLIOGRAPHY

Gallaudet Research Institute. (2005). *Report of data from the 2004–2005 annual survey of deaf and hard of hearing children and youth.* Washington, DC: Gallaudet University.

Lloyd, K., & Uniake, M. (2007). Deaf Australians and the cochlear implant. In L. Komesaroff (Ed.), *Surgical consent, bioethics and cochlear implantation* (pp. 174–194). Washington, DC: Gallaudet University Press.

Miller, M. S. (2006). Individual assessment and educational planning. In D.F. Moores & D. S. Martin (Eds.), *Deaf learners: Developments in curriculum and instruction* (pp.161–176). Washington, DC: Gallaudet University Press.

Mitchell, R. E. (2004). National profile of deaf and hard of hearing students in special education from weighted results. *American Annals of the Deaf, 149,* 336–349.

Moores, D. F. & D. S. Martin. (Eds.). (2006). *Deaf learners: Developments in curriculum and instruction.* Washington, DC: Gallaudet University Press.

Preisler, G. (2007). The psychosocial development of deaf children with cochlear implants. In L. Komensaroff (Ed.), *Surgical consent: Bioethics and cochlear implantation* (pp. 120–136). Washington, DC: Gallaudet University Press.

Winzer, M. (1993). *The history of special education: From isolation to integration.* Washington, DC: Gallaudet University Press.

Wrightstone, A. S. (2007). Universal newborn hearing screening. *American Family Physician, 76,* 1349–1356.

Donald Moores
Margery Miller

DECISION MAKING

Researchers generally assume that people engage in a small set of cognitive processes when they make decisions. These processes include (a) evaluating a set of options that could be implemented to attain a goal and (b) choosing one of these options. For example, a student who wants to do well on a test (a goal) may decide to study for it by making flash cards (option 1) instead of rereading relevant textbook chapters (option 2) or reviewing notes (option 3). Decision-making processes are instigated whenever an individual wants to accomplish something and realizes that there are several different ways to accomplish this goal. Defined in this way, it should be clear that people make numerous decisions every day (e.g., when to wake up in the morning; what

to wear; what to eat for breakfast). The definition suggests that decision processes are not involved when only one option is possible; similarly, they are not involved when people decide to pursue a particular goal always the same way and never attempt to consider alternatives.

Given the pervasiveness of choices in daily life and the fact that some of these choices are rather important (e.g., choice of spouse; which job offer to accept; whether to have surgery; whether to purchase a new house; whether to drink and drive), decision-making should be of interest in its own right as a focus of research. In reality, however, most of the psychological studies of decision-making have generated interest because of their implications regarding the limits of human reasoning and the extent to which adults routinely violate the norms of rationality.

In particular, philosophers have argued that some of the hallmarks of rational behavior include the tendencies to (a) take full account of all options that may be available in a given situation, (b) act in accordance with one's beliefs and values, and (c) maintain a rank-ordering of evaluated options across situations (e.g., if option 1 is rated higher than option 2 at a given time, the former should always be selected over the latter in all other situations as well). These and other characteristics comprise the so-called *normative model of decision-making* because they describe what people should do rather than what they actually do. Beginning in the 1950s, psychological researchers conducted carefully controlled laboratory experiments on decision making and began to discover that adults often fail to demonstrate one or more of these presumed characteristics of rationality. In response to such findings, researches began to wonder if people are fundamentally irrational, a question that generated considerable interest and controversy in the field of psychology. The arguments on either side of this issue have filled entire volumes and special issues of scholarly journals. In addition, the frequent deviations from the normative model prompted theorists to devise theoretical models that capture what decision-makers actually do, rather than what they should do. These so-called *behavioral decision theories* contrasted with the normative models.

LEADING FIGURES IN THE FIELD

Herbert Simon (1916–2001), who was associated with Carnegie Mellon University, was one of the first to point out the limits of human reasoning as it relates to decision-making. He argued against the normative model using the tenets of Information Processing theory and proposed the construct of *bounded rationality,* which specifies that the human mind is incapable of processing all aspects of all possible options in a given situation. Instead, the mind must simplify the process by reducing the number of options that are considered (e.g., five or less) and the number of attributes of these options (e.g., just the price, gas mileage, and color of potential cars to buy). He argued further that decision makers have a tendency to engage in "satisficing" when they think about their options; that is, instead of waiting to choose an option until all options have been carefully and exhaustively considered, decision makers consider options one by one in sequence until they reach one that is good enough. Once this good enough option is encountered, none of the remaining options is examined. This tendency to satisfice runs against the prescriptions of the normative model because it is possible that the best option that should have been selected was among those that were not yet evaluated. The notion of bounded rationality was extremely influential because of its applicability across disciplines. Scholars in the field of economics were particularly enamored with this notion and eventually nominated Simon for the Nobel Prize in economics (which he subsequently was awarded).

Simon's application of Information Processing theory to decision making influenced several generations of decision theorists that came along in the 1970s and 1980s. The idea that decision makers engage in *cognitive shortcuts* soon became pervasive in the literature. In some of the seminal studies in this area, Daniel Kahneman of Princeton University and the late Amos Tversky of Stanford University proposed a series of cognitive heuristics that people use when they process information relevant to decisions. These heuristics, in turn, produce systematic biases to respond in particular ways, and these biases affect their choices. For example, the so-called representativeness heuristic is operative whenever people are presented with a category of things (e.g., cars) or events (e.g., random sequences). All categories have prototypical instances that are assumed to be highly representative of the categories (e.g., the sequence 3, 19, 26, 29, 34, 40 in a lottery drawing for random events), as well as instances that are assumed to be less representative (e.g., the sequence 1, 2, 3, 4, 5, 6; in reality, both sequences are equally probable). Incorrect or not, the assumption that an instance is representative prompts people to think it is more likely to occur than the less representative instance. In the case of random number sequences, the representativeness heuristic may make gamblers decide to place a large bet right after observing the occurrence of a less representative sequence because the occurrence of the less probable sequence makes them think that the more probable sequence will occur next.

Kahneman and Tversky also gained prominence for discovering the fact that people will make different choices regarding the same information depending on how it is *framed* (e.g., "400 out of 1000 people will be saved by a drug" versus "600 will die") and for their Prospect Theory. Other prominent scholars who have examined the prevalence and consequences of these and other reasoning biases on decision making are Baruch Fischhoff of Carnegie Mellon, Paul Slovic of Decision Research in Oregon, Jonathan Baron of the University of Pennsylvania, Hal Arkes of Ohio State University, Valerie Reyna of Cornell University, and Keith Stanovich of the Ontario Institute for Studies in Education.

In addition to stressing constructs such as memory limitations and cognitive shortcuts, the Information Processing (IP) approach also emphasizes other important aspects of performance that have a bearing on decisions such as cognitive strategies and metacognition. To illustrate one of these further applications, John Payne and James Bettman of Duke University examined the systematic strategies people use when they examine a number of options that are placed before them (e.g., 20 possible apartments that could be rented). The IP approach eventually developed a natural affinity to the idea that many aspects of human cognition (including cognitive shortcuts) were selected via evolutionary processes because of their adaptive value. Thus, the field took a 180-degree turn away from the original assumption that deviations from the normative model were a bad thing to the subsequent claim that these deviations were actually adaptive and likely to lead to environmental success.

Scholars such as Gerd Gigerenzer argued that in many situations, processing too many things could lead to serious negative consequences. For example, emergency room (ER) doctors could look for quite a number of symptoms when a cardiac patient enters the ER, but three particular signs are highly diagnostic of a heart attack. Spending time collecting data on the other less diagnostic symptoms would surely lead to an increase in ER deaths. Gigerenzer argued further that the most useful cognitive processes that people engage in during decisions operate at an unconscious level. Engaging in the conscious, systematic consideration of options would either be a waste of time or lead to lower levels of goal attainment, according to Gigerenzer.

Between the 1960s and 1990s, researchers who studied decision making in adults frequently were confronted with the criticisms that (a) much of the experimental work in decision making utilizes laboratory tasks that have little relevance to the real world, and (b) the IP inspired approaches seem to neglect the potentially important role of motivational or emotional factors in decision making. Perhaps in response to these criticisms, many of the most prominent figures in the field refocused their energies on explaining real world phenomena (e.g., actual home buyers assessing the risk of living near a nuclear reactor), and several also developed new theoretical models that give a more prominent role to emotions. Examples include Fischhoff, Slovic, Baron, and Arkes.

The portrait that has emerged since the 1990s is that of an adult decision maker who relies on cognitive short-cuts and emotional processing to make many ordinary decisions in ways that often lead to goal attainment. These same shortcuts and emotional responses can, however, lead to poor decisions in some circumstances. For example, there are times when it is a good idea to consider options more fully and not be distracted or misled by transient emotional states.

THE DEVELOPMENT OF DECISION MAKING

There are far fewer studies of the development of decision making in children and adolescents than studies of decision making in adults. Nevertheless, it is possible to draw some tentative conclusions about age changes that have the potential to affect the quality of decisions made by children and adolescents. Before doing so, however, it is important to note that developmentalists have not been concerned with age changes in the extent to which children make decisions (i.e., all children make many decisions per day at all ages), but rather, with age changes in the quality of children's decisions. Charting age changes in quality, of course, requires that one have a working model of what decision making competence entails.

Because of important shortcomings in the aforementioned normative model, some scholars have shifted from using the normative model as a guide to evaluating decision quality and moved towards defining decision competence in terms of environmental success. In particular, these scholars argue that a skilled decision maker is someone who knows the difference between options that are likely to lead to goal attainment (good options) and options that are unlikely to lead to goal attainment (not-so-good options). If so, the question then becomes one of identifying characteristics of decision makers that help them recognize or discover good options in a particular situation.

Some of the characteristics that have been proposed are (a) knowledge and experience (i.e., more knowledgeable individuals are likely to correctly predict the consequences of particular actions), (b) the tendency to seek advice from the right people when personal knowledge is lacking, (c) the tendency to pursue adaptive goals that are likely to promote physical health, emotional health, or financial well-being, (d) the tendency to prefer options that satisfy multiple goals as opposed to options that satisfy only a single goal (e.g., find a car that is attractive, relatively inexpensive, and reliable), (e) the tendency to learn from decision-making successes and failures, (f) the tendency to engage in effortful and thorough examination of options and consequences for important decisions, but not expend considerable effort considering options for unimportant decisions, and (g) the ability to regulate one's emotional and impulsive tendencies in ways that keep these tendencies from interfering with appropriate consideration of options and consequences.

Although, as of the early 2000s, the evidence was still emerging regarding age differences in such characteristics, some studies suggested that older adolescents and adults are more likely than younger adolescents and children to (a) understand the difference between options likely to satisfy multiple goals and options likely to satisfy only a single goal, (b) anticipate a wider array of consequences of their actions, (c) evaluate their options in systematic ways and apply effortful strategies only for important decisions, and (d) learn from their decision-making successes and failures. Unfortunately, adolescents have also been found to seek advice less often from knowledgeable individuals than children, and they are more likely to pursue goals that could negatively affect their physical health, emotional health, or financial well-being (e.g., smoking cigarettes; drinking and driving).

MODERATING FACTORS

Earlier in this entry, it was noted that emotionality and impulsivity could have negative effects on decision-making. Some scholars argue that these tendencies should be considered moderating factors because people tend to make better decisions when they are calm and reflective than when they are emotionally aroused and impulsive. Generally speaking, these tendencies cause problems whenever they keep decision makers from fully considering the consequences of their actions and discovering better options than those that they implemented. Scholars such as Lawrence Steinberg and Ronald Dahl argue that adolescents are particularly vulnerable to the influences of emotions and impulsivity, and they argue that this vulnerability has a neural basis in their brain. As the brain continues to mature into adulthood, Steinberg and Dahl argue that decision makers gain the capacity to regulate their emotions and impulsivity. As with most other developmental claims regarding decision-making competence, however, the evidence supporting this view is relatively sparse and open to multiple interpretations. More research is needed to substantiate all of the age trends reported here.

INSTRUCTIONAL APPROACHES TO IMPROVE DECISION MAKING

In light of the rise in problem behaviors during adolescence (e.g., cigarette smoking, alcohol use, etc.), university researchers and policy makers in school systems have implemented a number of interventions to improve the quality of decision making in adolescents. Some of these interventions focus on general characteristics of good decision-making (e.g., seek advice from knowledgeable individuals when you do not know what to do) while others specifically target particular problem behaviors (e.g., illicit drug use). Those who implement the general approaches hope that students will apply the principles to all decisions, including those related to problem behaviors. The standard by which a program should be judged to be effective is that it both alters the manner in which decisions are made and reduces the incidence of problem behaviors. Proving the latter requires the application of rigorous methodological approaches such as randomly assigning teens to intervention and control conditions, measuring decision making and problem behaviors before and after the intervention, and using valid measures of decision making and problem behaviors. Reviews of the literature reveal that few studies meet these standards of quality. Many studies show that teens can learn the content of a program, but few show that their actual decision-making changed as a result. The studies that do meet the standards have been found to be more effective when (a) they are more comprehensive (i.e., they target multiple causes of the problem behavior), (b) the teens themselves learn the information in an active rather than passive manner, and (c) the participants engage in peer-to-peer instruction.

SEE ALSO *Impulsive Decision Making; Problem Solving; Reasoning.*

BIBLIOGRAPHY

Baron, J. (2000). *Thinking and deciding.* New York: Cambridge University Press.

Byrnes, J. P. (1998). *The nature and development of decision making: a self regulation model.* Mahwah, NJ: Erlbaum.

Byrnes, J. P. (2002). The development of decision making. *Journal of Adolescent Health, 31,* 208–215.

Jacobs, J. E., & Klaczynski, P. A. (Eds.). (2005). *The development of judgment and decision making.* Mahwah, NJ: Erlbaum.

Gigerenzer, G. (2004). Fast and frugal heuristics: The tools of bounded rationality. In D. J Koehler & Nigel Harvey (Eds.), *Blackwell handbook of judgment and decision making* (pp. 62–88). Malden, MA: Blackwell.

Koehler, D. J., & Harvey, N. (Eds.). (2007). *Blackwell handbook of judgment and decision making.* Malden, MA: Blackwell.

Stanovich, K. E. (1999). *Who is rational? Studies of individual differences in reasoning.* Mahwah, NJ: Erlbaum.

James P. Byrnes

DESIGN EXPERIMENT

Improving classroom teaching and learning is the primary goal of research in education, educational psychology, and the learning sciences. However, a common complaint about traditional research using experimental and quasi-experimental design points at the gap between

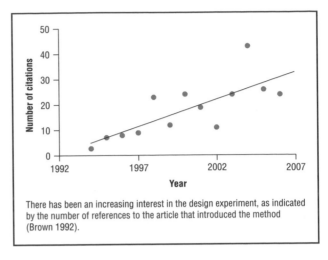

There has been an increasing interest in the design experiment, as indicated by the number of references to the article that introduced the method (Brown 1992).

Figure 1 ILLUSTRATION BY GGS INFORMATION SERVICES. CENGAGE LEARNING, GALE.

educational research and educational practice. Introduced in 1992 to address the theoretical and methodological challenges in creating complex interventions in classrooms (Brown 1992), design experiment, an initially unorthodox method, was eventually adopted quite widely as the method of choice for studying teaching and learning in the classroom setting. Between 1992 and the early 2000s, there was increasing interest in this research method, as shown by the increasing number of citations to Brown's article listed in Thompson's ISI Web of Knowledge (Figure 1). The success likely derives from the fact that the design experiment combined two existing functions of educational psychology: explanation and guidance of practice (Solomon 1996). Although Ann L. Brown and others credit Allan Collins for coining the term, it is through Brown's work generally and through her introductory article in the *Journal of the Learning Sciences* specifically that learning scientists have come to know about this method. There has been an increasing interest in the design experiment, as indicated by the number of references to the article that introduced the method (Brown 1992).

DEFINITION

The term *design experiment* was modeled on the design sciences aeronautics and artificial intelligence, in which research and development are combined. It refers to interventions in which educational environments are engineered and where experimental studies of those innovations are conducted simultaneously. Design experiments differ from classical laboratory experiments and quasi-experiments in that the intervention itself is changed in response to problems that the ongoing (interpretative, qualitative, ethnographic) research reveals. Design experimenters focus on understanding teaching and learning in complex, designed settings rather than reduce them to their constituent building blocks: The ultimate purpose of a design experiment is to bring about a lasting instructional change, which it can only achieve, as experience has shown, when the intervention is adapted to the contingencies of each setting. Thus, design experiments aim at arriving both at (a) the best possible form of the intervention in each setting, that is, instruction and learning, and (b) theoretical articulations that delineate why an intervention works across settings and thus makes it consistently repeatable.

USERS

An analysis of ISI Web of Science focusing on the authors and journals that cite Brown's article on the design experiment shows that the method is particularly of interest to learning scientists—*Journal of the Learning Sciences, Cognition and Instruction*, and *Educational Psychologist* account for over 20% of the citations—and science educators (three science education journals) and educational technology/instructional science account for another 16% and 7% of the citations, respectively. The common allegiance of the researchers is to the idea of research and development as design rather than to a particular epistemology, though a quick survey of articles citing Brown (1992) shows that the most common commitments are to social constructivist (constructionist), sociocultural, and cultural-historical theories of knowing and learning. This common allegiance may explain the large proportion of designers of (computing) technology-based learning environments—with their cultural-historical practices of design, testing, and revising alpha, beta, and gamma versions of their artifacts—among those who employ the design experiment as method.

DESIGN VERSUS CLASSICAL EXPERIMENTS

Structure of Experimental and Quasi-Experimental Designs. Design experiments are useful for moving instructional design through all the phases of development and implementation and especially in the final, gamma phase of designing instructional reform, that is, the widespread use with minimal support, which is a measure of reform longevity. Despite the increasing interest and use of design experiments, there continues to exist a lack of clarity concerning its methodological and epistemological features (Bell, 2004).

Classical laboratory experiments test hypotheses about relations that causally link independent and dependent variables. Causation can be established only when the variance between treatment and control group (different

or no treatment [placebo]) is reliably attributable to the treatment. Random assignment to treatment and control conditions has the function of drawing participant samples that (a) are representative of the target population and (b) are comparable, both within the limits of sampling error (Cook & Campbell, 1979). Whereas random assignment is possible in psychological laboratory experiments, which often have the problem that their results do not translate into real settings, educational research in real classroom settings, though more realistically addressing the context of learning, generally cannot randomly assign students to treatments and control. A common quasi-experimental design has the following structure

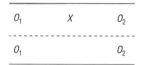

where the O_1 refers to observations (e.g., literal observations, written tests, or responses in computer presented tasks) and X refers to the treatment (e.g., "using computers" or "using peer teaching"). In other words, there are two groups (one above, one below the dotted line), which are observed/tested at one point in time (O_1). One group receives treatment ("X") the other does not. After the treatment has ended, both groups are observed again (O_2). Everything else being equal, any post-treatment differences can be attributed to the treatment. This structure addresses the comparability of non-equivalent control groups by collecting relevant information (e.g., pre-tests) that allows researchers to statistically adjust for the possible non-equivalence of experimental and control groups that may exist at the outset of the research. Although different quasi-experimental designs differ in their weaknesses and strengths, a creative mixture of designs within the same study may significantly increase confidence in the causes underlying the phenomena under study.

Structure of Design Experiments. Design experiments differ substantially from traditional psychological experiments and quasi-experiments because these systematically vary the interventions, using each iteration as an experiment that assists in evolving and testing theory in a naturalistic setting. Rather than having a previously specified constant treatment, design experiments change the intervention on the basis of emergent understandings so that the X (treatment) in the structure of the experiment no longer is the same from the beginning to the end of the intervention. It is therefore no longer possible to establish causal relations between, for example, particular interventions—for example, Brown's reciprocal teaching—with other interventions. This does not prevent design researchers from conducting experimental (laboratory) studies within their design experiments to test hypotheses about causal relations. Design researchers frequently choose to deepen the study of emergent aspects by means of formal laboratory studies or classroom studies with random assignment of students to conditions (treatments). Such studies, then, allow the establishment of cause and effect but always relative to the theoretically interesting features that emerge in the course of the larger study.

This feature of design experiments is associated, for many psychologists, with substantial drawbacks (weaknesses) because it substantially alters the conception of what constitutes relevant knowledge and how it is derived. However, the design experiment can be understood through the analogy with an interrupted time series design because researchers go through considerable efforts in documenting learning prior to, during, and following the changes in instructional design. Design experiments therefore are characterized by the structure

$$O_1 \quad O_2 \quad X \quad O_3 \quad O_4 \quad X' \quad O_5 \quad X'' \quad O_6 \quad O_7 \quad O_8 \quad \ldots$$

where each "O" represents an observation and each "X" an intervention. Note that the treatment changes in the course of the experiment (X becomes X' becomes X'' and so on) based on the information collected during the observations. However, in contrast to interrupted time series in which treatment episodes follow non-treatment episodes (to verify that the treatment rather than something else makes the difference), design research does not withdraw treatment but continually seeks to improve teaching (i.e., the treatment) and therefore learning. This structure of the design experiment, however, provides opportunities for a Bayesian approach. In a Bayesian approach, the already-generated quantitative and qualitative information is combined between the phases of the implementation to generate adjusted estimates of the success of the intervention in the future (Gorard, Roberts, & Taylor, 2004). These adjusted predictions are better estimates for the impact of future interventions because they explicitly take into account previous findings. Clearly, design experiments play into the hands of those interested in optimizing the learning environment by acting upon contingently emerging problems and understandings.

Criticisms and Responses. Even critics recognize that the strengths of design experiments lie in their ability to generate and test theories in situ, to cross the theory-practice gap by adaptively changing the intervention of interest. But the data generated before and during the

intervention generate immense datasets, which frequently leads authors to use narrative forms that do not and cannot provide the kinds of warrants required for establishing the veracity of claims made (Shavelson, Phillips, Towne, & Feuer, 2003). Here Brown's introductory article countered some common objections to design experiments. For example, the very specificity of learning predictable in design experiments makes them immune to false claims due to the Hawthorne effect (positive effects merely because of attention researchers pay to research participants rather than because of treatment in and of itself). More so, addressing what Brown called the reality principle (the continued positive effects [shelf life] of an intervention), design experiments tend to achieve longevity and widespread adoption with minimal additional intervention. Such interventions that are the products of good design experiences are adaptive and fit the contingencies of the different settings. Design experiments, much more than other inventions of the past, have lasting and widespread effect because of the close collaboration of participants and researchers.

TWO PROTOTYPICAL EXAMPLES

By their very nature, design experiments require researchers to become familiar with and understand the setting, encouraging them to become ethnographers interested in how particular cultures make sense. Students tend to become researchers responsible for defining relevant expertise, and teachers tend to become researchers. It is not surprising that (a) teachers become design experimenters, (b) researchers become teachers to ascertain that a best-case scenario is studied, or (c) university-based design researchers become interested in the social agendas of students and teachers that their designs support. Two prototypical examples of design research are provided below that illustrate the first and third types of design research.

Teachers as Design Researchers. In the learning sciences literature, there are numerous examples of design experiments that involve researchers who not only observe but also teach during the intervention; there are also examples in which teachers themselves legitimately conduct design research. The present example is of the second kind, involving two science teachers investigating the implementation of an open-inquiry science curriculum (e.g., Roth & Bowen, 1995) that used the same guiding principles that also motivated the design work of Brown and Collins during the late 1980s and early 1990s—that is, cognitive apprenticeship and community of learners. Students are provided opportunities to enact cognitive practices that have a high degree of family resemblance with the practices of professionals. With respect to the sciences, this means that students learn to pose research questions, collect data for answering them, and use mathematical representations for analyzing the data and for representing the data in reports to substantiate research claims. In this model, the two teachers, both with graduate degrees in the natural sciences, were experts who scaffolded students' efforts. They did so on a need-to-know and just-in-time basis, that is, precisely when knowing something significantly would advance students in their work (Pea, 1997).

The two teachers set out to study (a) problem posing and solution finding, (b) mathematization and other representational practices of science, (c) the relationship between culture, practices, and cognitive resources, and (d) differences in mathematical practices arising from open inquiry versus school tasks. They planned a cognitive anthropological study in which mathematical representations and mathematical practices oriented data collection. They videotaped all lessons in one eighth-grade class and collected all students' field notebooks, laboratory reports, unit tests, end of semester test, and final examination in both participating classes. A third eighth-grade class taught differently served as the control group. The researchers collected student responses to standard instruments such as the Constructivist Learning Environment Scale; and they interviewed, using open-ended and structured protocols, about 25% of the participating students concerning different aspects of the intervention. Their substantial database allowed the researchers to evaluate knowing and learning in quantitative and qualitative ways and correlate achievement with other measures collected as part of the research.

The researchers transcribed all videotapes in an ongoing manner with less than 48-hour delays between recording tapes and conducting initial analyses. This allowed them to (a) design particular curricular strategies when problems became evident and (b) frame tentative hypotheses, which subsequently were tested experimentally. For example, the researchers framed the hypothesis that students' choice of mathematical representations was a function of the data set: Students were more likely using graphs to find trends in large data sets, whereas they were more likely to seek trends by visual inspection of the raw data. The researchers designed three forms of a task and randomly assigned pairs of students to one of the three conditions. Based on this experiment, the researchers rejected the hypothesis. A second part of the experiment, which compared the degree of mathematization that the eighth-grade students achieved to teachers in training with at least a BSc revealed statistically reliable differences: The eighth-grade participants in open-inquiry used more-abstract representations with a reliably higher frequency than the future science teachers (Roth, McGinn, & Bowen, 1998). The experiment also proved valuable because the researchers videotaped students during their work on the assigned, textbook-like tasks. As a

result, the researchers were able to study the differences between eighth-grade students' solving data analyses practices when students designed their own problems versus when the teacher-researchers set the problems.

This study shows the adaptive nature of design research both with respect to the intervention and research, thereby bettering the intervention and getting better data for understanding how students learn in an open-inquiry learning environment.

Critical Design and Social Change. Instead of simply building an artifact to help individuals accomplish a particular task or to meet a specific standard, critical design experiments focus on the development of social, technology-enhanced structures that facilitate human subjects individually and collectively in critiquing and improving themselves and the societies in which they function. Critical design experimenters agree that this substantially changes the roles of researchers, teachers, students, and administrators involved. Their point is to change the world (for the better) rather than merely to understand it. It may come as little surprise that some design researchers, as those in the example featured here, explicitly support or engage themselves in social agendas using what they come to understand for the purpose of increasing the participants' control over attendant conditions.

Quest Atlantis is a multi-user virtual environment that allows children to learn academic and social skills and to evolve social agendas as they assist the council of Atlantis in recovering the lost forms of knowledge and wisdom of the culture (Barab, Dodge, Thomas, Jackson, & Tuzun, 2007). The environment was designed to support the development of seven social commitments—personal agency, diversity affirmation, healthy communities, social responsibility, environmental awareness, creative expression, and compassionate wisdom—through (a) Quests targeted toward individual commitment and (b) the technical infrastructure of the software. Changes to the original design were based on the concept of participatory design, a Scandinavian model for bringing together computer scientists and professionals to evolve more appropriate workplaces.

On the instructional side, Quest Atlantis situates itself at the intersection of education, a set of social commitments, and entertainment. The virtual world consists of worlds, each divided into three thematically related villages associated with up to 25 Quests. The themes include healthy bodies, community power, global issues, and waterways. There were five steps to the design experiment: the study (a) initially built rich understandings, (b) focused on developing critical commitments, (c) reified commitments into the design, (d) targeted the expansion of the impact, and (e) generated theoretical claims.

To build a rich understanding, the researchers conducted a 12-month ethnographic effort including more than 200 site visits and more than 500 pages of data entries in field notebooks. They conducted open-ended interviews with children individually and collectively and carried out semistructured interviews. The participating children built personal documents, including narratives and images (photographs). Finally, the researchers themselves kept diaries designed to record a day in the life of a particular participant. The researchers conducted laboratory studies with factorial ANOVA designs to test, among others, the impact of computing tools (3D vs. 2D) and collaboration (singles vs. dyads) on the ability to transfer skills to distal-level standardized items. Such experiments demonstrated that the Quest Atlantis software supports learning; other parts of the four-year study produced theoretical conjectures, including an expanded taxonomy of motivations involved while children learn through playing games.

As a result of their work, the researchers found to have been building "petite generalizations." Petite generalizations are refined understandings of the patterns that researchers have encountered and that others in the field may likewise encounter. Most importantly, the ultimate product expanded its impact as it was redesigned, fitted, and adapted, together with the users, to the contingencies of each local setting.

The design experiment offers many advantages to the psychologist interested in designing and studying complex interventions in their naturalistic settings. Design experiment may be understood as an integrated approach to research and development that includes qualitative and quantitative approaches. This, then, allows design scientists to simultaneously (a) adapt interventions by taking into account local contingencies and (b) test hypotheses in a scientifically rigorous way that allows weeding out chance variations from true cause-and-effect relations. Design experiments thereby provide opportunities to meet the two major goals educational psychologists and learning scientists have set themselves: understanding knowing and learning scientifically and developing interventions that have a long shelf life because they meet the needs of the participants.

BIBLIOGRAPHY

Barab, S., Dodge, T., Thomas, M. K., Jackson, C., & Tuzun, H. (2007). Our designs and the social agendas they carry. *Journal of the Learning Sciences, 16,* 263–305.

Bell, P. (2004). On the theoretical breadth of design-based research in education. *Educational Psychologist, 39,* 243–253.

Brown, A. L. (1992). Design experiments: Theoretical and methodological challenges in creating complex interventions in classroom settings. *Journal of the Learning Sciences, 2,* 141–178.

Cook, T. D., & Campbell, D. T. (1979). *Quasi-experimentation: Design and analysis issues for field settings.* Boston, MA: Houghton Mifflin.

Gorard, S., Roberts, K., & Taylor, C. (2004). What kind of creature is a design experiment? *British Educational Research Journal, 30,* 577–590.

Pea, R. D. (1997). Learning and teaching with educational technologies. In H. J. Walberg & G. D. Haertel (Eds.), *Educational psychology: Effective practices and policies* (pp. 274–296). Berkeley, CA: McCutchan.

Roth, W.-M., & Bowen, G. M. (1995). Knowing and interacting: A study of culture, practices, and resources in a grade 8 open-inquiry science classroom guided by a cognitive apprenticeship metaphor. *Cognition and Instruction, 13,* 73–128.

Roth, W.-M., McGinn, M. K., & Bowen, G. M. (1998). How prepared are pre-service teachers to teach scientific inquiry? Levels of performance in scientific representation practices. *Journal of Science Teacher Education, 9,* 25–48.

Shavelson, R. J., Phillips, D. C., Towne, L., & Feuer, M. J. (2003). On the science of education design studies. *Educational Researcher, 32* (1), 25–28.

Solomon, G. (1996). Unorthodox thoughts on the nature and mission of contemporary educational psychology. *Educational Psychology Review, 8,* 397–417.

Wolff-Michael Roth

DEVELOPMENT OF CORE KNOWLEDGE DOMAINS

From where does knowledge come? Scholars interested in this question have delineated three possible sources: experience, culture, and evolution. Knowledge obtained through experience is knowledge derived from one's own observation and exploration of the physical world. Knowledge obtained through culture is knowledge initially derived by someone other than oneself but acquired through the process of cultural transmission. Knowledge obtained through evolution is knowledge of a genetic origin, endowed in humans by natural selection due to its utility to our prehominid ancestors.

Although few would dispute the claim that humans acquire knowledge through experience and culture, many have disputed the claim that humans have acquired knowledge through evolution. Indeed, this claim has remained controversial since its origins in ancient Greek philosophy and its revival in eighteenth-century Enlightenment philosophy (Stich, 1975), though, in recent years, it has gained substantial support from empirical studies of infant cognition and animal cognition. Drawing on the findings of such studies, Spelke (2000) has proposed that innate knowledge, or "core knowledge," can be identified by three defining features: (1) domain-specificity, or a restriction on the types of objects and relations the system can represent; (2) task-specificity, or a restriction on the goals and objectives the system can accomplish; and (3) encapsulation, or operational independence from other systems of knowledge.

Core knowledge is thought to guide learning in a variety of ways, from guiding the interpretation of one's early experiences to constraining the scope of one's early inferences to providing the foundations of one's future knowledge. Although there is some controversy as to what domains of knowledge are innate and what domains are not, scholars have pointed to at least five possibilities: (1) the domain of objects and their physical properties, (2) the domain of agents and their psychological properties, (3) the domain of space and its geometric properties, (4) the domain of number and its arithmetic properties, and (5) the domain of living things and their functional properties.

Evidence of early emergence, cross-species homology, and cross-cultural universality are stronger for some domains (e.g., the domain of number) than for others (e.g., the domain of living things). Nevertheless, there is ample evidence that all five domains emerge prior to formal instruction. Below are charted the development of three such domains: the domain of space, the domain of number, and the domain of living things. For each domain, characterizations are provided of (a) the domain's initial knowledge state, and (b) the domain's first major restructuring. Following these characterizations, this entry discusses general similarities and dissimilarities among the early transitions within each domain.

THE DOMAIN OF SPACE

Spatial cognition consists of a variety of competencies, including navigation, depth perception, landmark encoding, and reorientation. Here, the focus is on reorientation, or the process of realigning one's mental representation of the environment with the environment itself, as there is much evidence that reorientation involves an evolutionarily ancient mechanism present in both human and nonhuman animals.

The earliest studies of reorientation were conducted with rats (Cheng, 1986; Margules & Gallistel, 1988). In these studies, food-deprived rats were shown food being hidden in one of four corners of a rectangular enclosure. The rats were then removed from the enclosure and disoriented via rotation. Upon their return to the enclosure, the rats searched for the hidden food in either the correct corner or the geometrically equivalent corner, that is, the corner diagonal to the correct corner, which shares with the correct corner the property of being to the left of a short wall and to the right of a long wall (or vice versa, depending on the particular hiding location). Amazingly, the disoriented rats did not use the nongeometric properties of their enclosure, like wall color or wall odor, to guide their search, even though these properties uniquely specified the food's location and were readily used as navigational cues by fully oriented rats. Similar results have since been obtained with monkeys (Gouteux, Thinus-Blanc, & Vauclair, 2001), fish (Sovrano, Bisazza, & Vallortigara, 2002), and chicks (Sovrano & Vallortigara, 2006).

Studies of reorientation in humans have revealed striking similarities between how disoriented children search for hidden toys and how disoriented rats search for hidden food (Hermer & Spelke, 1994; 1996). In these studies, children aged 18 to 24 months were shown a toy being hidden in the corner of a rectangular room and were then disoriented by being spun around with their eyes closed. Following disorientation, children tended to search for the toy in one of two locations: the correct corner or the geometrically equivalent corner. This behavior persisted even in rooms where the location of the toy was uniquely specified by a distinctive nongeometric cue: a blue wall. Thus, children, like rats, do not initially take nongeometric information into consideration when reorienting themselves, and they continue to ignore such information until around the age of 7 (Hermer-Vazquez, Moffet, & Munkholm, 2001).

Children's sensitivity to geometric information—and only geometric information—in reorientation tasks appears to be limited to a particular kind of geometry: the geometry of extended, three dimensional surfaces. Studies that have explored children's reorientation behavior in open space have found that children do not reorient by the geometry of moveable objects within that space (Gouteux & Spelke, 2001). Moreover, studies that have explored children's reorientation behavior in different kinds of enclosures have found that children who fail to reorient by differences in wall color will nonetheless reorient by differences in wall shape (Wang, Hermer, & Spelke, 1999). The fact that children's reorientation is sensitive to some features of the environment (i.e., wall location, wall shape) but not others (i.e., wall color, object locations) suggests that the mechanism responsible for this behavior attends only to stable features of the environment unlikely to change from day to day or from season to season.

As mentioned previously, older children (and adults) do not reorient like rats. Instead, they reorient by both geometric information (e.g., wall location) and nongeometric information (e.g., wall color). What allows older children, but not younger children, to use such information? One hypothesis, suggested by Hermer & Spelke (1996), is that remembering the location of an object relative to nongeometric features of the environment requires encoding such relationships in language. In support of this hypothesis, Hermer-Vazquez and colleagues (2001) have shown that children's production of the words *left* and *right* is highly correlated with their use of nongeometric information in reorientation tasks. More-over, Hermer-Vazquez, Spelke, and Katsnelson (1999) have shown that adults' use of nongeometric information in these same tasks is significantly impaired when adults are required to listen to and repeat a tape recording of continuous speech, thereby preventing them from pro-ducing phrases like "left of the blue wall." These data imply that the development of spatial cognition is tied to the acquisition of spatial language, though the exact nature of this relationship has yet to be determined.

THE DOMAIN OF NUMBER

Numerical cognition, like spatial cognition, appears to be ubiquitous throughout the animal kingdom (Gallistel, 1990), and evidence of numerical cognition in humans can be found as early as six months of age. For instance, habituation studies have shown that 6-month-old infants can discriminate visual arrays of 8 dots from visual arrays of 16 dots (Xu & Spelke, 2000). Infants of this age have also been shown to discriminate auditory sequences of 8 tones from auditory sequences of 16 tones (Lipton & Spelke, 2005). By 9 months of age, infants are not only able to keep track of different numerosities but are also able to add and subtract those numerosities (McCrink & Wynn, 2004). That is, if they see five objects go behind a screen followed by another five objects, they expect to see ten objects when the screen is lowered, not five, as evidenced by a difference in how long they look at each outcome.

How do infants' number representations compare to the number representations of children and adults? Although some (e.g., Gallistel & Gelman, 2003) have argued that infants' representations form the basis of all subsequent mathematical knowledge, others (e.g., Le Corre, Van de Walle, Brannon, & Carey, 2006) have argued that these representations are too imprecise to support an understanding of integers and the operations defined over them. Evidence of such imprecision comes from the finding that although 6-month-old infants can discriminate 8 dots from 16 dots and 8 tones from 16 tones, they cannot discriminate 8 dots from 12 dots or 8 tones from 12 tones. Imprecision of this nature decreases with age, but it never disappears altogether (Barth, Kanwisher, & Spelke, 2003), which has lead many to posit the existence of two distinct systems for represent-ing number: (1) a nonverbal system capable of represent-ing approximate numerosity, present from infancy through adulthood and shared with many nonhuman animals, and (2) a verbal system capable of representing exact numerosity, unique to humans and acquired around the age of 3 in the form of counting.

Because counting involves the mastery of a represen-tational system not supported by core knowledge, learn-ing how to count is not easy. In fact, studies of how children learn to count have revealed that children acquire this ability in a succession of small, discrete steps (Wynn, 1990; Carey, 2004). First, children learn their language's "count list," or their language's list of words used to denote sets of increasing numerosity (e.g., "one," "two," "three"). Second, they learn how to apply this list to an array of objects by labeling each object in the array with one, and only one, word in the count list. Third, they learn that, when applying the count list to an array of objects, the last number word reached when counting corresponds to the cardinal value of the set. In other words, they learn that the word *four* refers not only to the fourth object encountered during the counting rou-tine but also to the total number of objects encountered up to that point.

Evidence that children learn these three skills in stages, rather than in tandem, comes from dissociations in children's performance on simple numerical reasoning tasks. For instance, children are able to recite the count list long before they are able to apply it consistently to an array of objects. Likewise, children are able to apply the count list to an array of objects long before they realize that the last word reached when counting constitutes an answer to the question, "How many are there?" In fact, children go through a 6- to 9-month period during which time they are able to count a collection of objects but are not able to retrieve a particular number of objects from the collection. That is, when asked to retrieve a particular number of objects, they grab a handful at random and make no attempt to coordinate their knowl-edge of counting with their estimation of numerosity.

Of crucial importance to learning how to count is being exposed to a count list. Some cultures, such as the Pirhaha and Munduruku tribes of the Amazon rain forest, do not have count lists, and the members of those cultures cannot therefore keep track of exact numerosities (Gor-don, 2004; Pica, Lemer, & Izard, 2004). For instance, when shown a collection of objects and asked to select a particular number (indicated nonverbally with fingers or sticks), Piraha adults tend to produce a close match, but not an exact match, to the requested number, implying that the only system they have for representing numerosity is the imprecise system they inherited via evolution.

THE DOMAIN OF LIVING THINGS

Evidence for a core knowledge of living things comes not from studies of infant cognition or animal cognition but from studies of cross-cultural universals. These studies have revealed that, across cultures, children's early under-standing of animals appears to be structured around three metaphysical commitments: (1) vitalism, or the belief that living things require energy in order to function; (2) essentialism, or the belief that living things possess an internal "essence" that determines their outward appearance and behavior; and (3) taxonomic relatedness, or the belief that living things can be organized into inferentially rich, multilevel hierarchies.

An early-developing commitment to vitalism is evident from studies of children's understanding of digestion, respiration, and circulation (e.g., Inagaki & Hatano, 1993; Morris, Taplin, & Gelman, 2000). In these studies, 5- and 6-year-old children are presented a variety of explanations for an activity like eating and are asked to select the best one. Although adults tend to prefer mechanistic explanations (e.g., we eat food "because we take the food into our body after the food is changed in our stomach"), children tend to prefer to vitalistic ones (e.g., we eat food "because our stomach takes in energy from the food"), regardless of their cultural upbringing. In line with these findings, preschool-aged children recognize that animals, but not artifacts, grow (Rosengren, Gelman, Kalish, & McCormick, 1991) and that consuming food is necessary for growth (Inagaki & Hatano, 1996).

Studies demonstrating an early-developing commitment to essentialism have focused not on children's understanding of metabolic processes but on their understanding of inheritance (Gelman & Wellman, 1991; Sousa, Atran, & Medin, 2002). In these studies, 3- and 4-year-old children are told stories about a baby animal who was raised by adult animals of a different species (e.g., a cow raised by pigs) and are asked to predict which properties it would possess as an adult: the biological properties of its birth parents (e.g., a straight tail and a diet of grass) or the biological properties of its adopted parents (e.g., a curly tail and a diet of slop). Regardless of cultural upbringing, children tend to predict that the baby animal will grow to possess the biological properties of its birth parents, not its adopted parents.

Evidence of a universal commitment to taxonomic relatedness comes from studies of how individuals from different cultures categorize the flora and fauna of their local ecologies (Atran, 1990; Berlin, 1992). These studies have found that individuals the world over classify living things into hierarchies that typically include the ranks of "kingdom" (e.g., plants, animals), "life form" (e.g., trees, birds), "generic species" (e.g., oaks, parrots), and "folk-specific species" (e.g., white oaks, African Gray parrots). These ranks constrain a variety of biological inferences—from inferences about how to extend known properties to novel organisms to inferences about how to extend novel properties to known organisms—for children and adults alike. Indeed, children as young as 2 consistently use their knowledge of taxonomic relations to constrain their extension of known properties to novel animals (Gelman & Coley, 1990).

Despite the above evidence for an early-developing conception of living things, children have been shown to experience great difficulty grasping other aspects of biological knowledge, including the very meaning of the words *alive* and *dead* (Piaget, 1929; Carey, 1985). For instance, when children aged 8 and younger are quizzed on their knowledge of what is alive and what is not, they classify many things that are alive (e.g., flowers, tress, bugs, worms) as "not alive" and many things that are not alive (e.g., the sun, the wind, clocks, fire) as "alive." Moreover, children of this age are reluctant to extend properties true of all living things (e.g., has cells, has babies, gets sick) to plants and insects.

These misconceptions suggest that children do not initially understand life as a process of maintaining and regulating bodily functions and death as the cessation of that process. Consequently, they confuse life with animacy, observability, or functionality, and they confuse death with inanimacy, unobservability, or nonfunctionality. Acquiring a correct conception of life appears to be tied to acquiring a mechanistic conception of biological functioning. Support for this claim comes from a study by Slaughter and Lyons (2003), in which children were questioned on their beliefs about death both before and after a teaching intervention designed to impart a mechanistic understanding of the internal workings of the human body. Before the teaching intervention, children revealed a number of misconceptions about the nature of death (e.g., that death can be avoided, that death can be reversed). After the teaching intervention, these same children revealed significantly fewer misconceptions, even though the intervention itself did not broach the topic of death.

TRANSCENDING CORE KNOWLEDGE

Each of the developmental transitions described above share at least two commonalities. First, all three transitions involve overcoming structural limitations in the architecture of core knowledge, whether they be limitations in the information used to reorient oneself in the environment, limitations in the precision with which numerosities are represented, or limitations in the properties used to identify living things. Second, all three transitions involve the acquisition of culturally constructed knowledge, whether it be knowledge of the words *left* and *right*, knowledge of a count list, or knowledge of the inner workings of the human body.

Commonalities aside, each developmental transition exemplifies a slightly different type of knowledge acquisition. For instance, children's transition from geometry-based reorientation to landmark-based reorientation is more strategic than conceptual in nature, for this transition involves learning to attend to a spatial relationship that had previously been neglected (i.e., "left of the blue wall") rather than learning to conceptualize space in an entirely new way. Children's transition from a vitalistic biology to a mechanistic biology, on the other hand, is more conceptual than strategic in nature, for this transition involves learning to conceptualize living things in an entirely new way (i.e., as self-sustaining, self-regulating machines) rather than learning to attend to a particular property of living things that had previously been neglected. The transition from an approximate representation of number to an integer-based representation of number also exemplifies a conceptual change, though the kinds of concepts that change within the domain of number (i.e., nominal-kinds concepts) are very different from the kinds of concepts that change within the domain of biology (i.e., natural-kinds concepts). Whether, and how, such a difference matters to the process of conceptual change itself has yet to be determined.

SEE ALSO *Concept Development; Theory of Mind.*

BIBLIOGRAPHY

Atran, S. (1990). *Cognitive foundations of natural history.* Cambridge, England: Cambridge University Press.

Atran, S., Medin, D., Lynch, E., Vapnarsky, V., Ucan Ek', E., & Sousa, P. (2001). Folkbiology doesn't come from folkpsychology: Evidence from Yukatek Maya in cross-cultural perspective. *Journal of Cognition and Culture, 1(1),* 3–42.

Barth, H., Kanwisher, N., & Spelke, E. (2003). The construction of large number representations in adults. *Cognition, 86,* 201–221.

Berlin, B. (1992). *Ethnobiological classification.* Princeton, NJ: Princeton University Press.

Carey, S. (1985). *Conceptual change in childhood.* Cambridge, MA: MIT Press.

Carey, S. (2004). Bootstrapping and the origin of concepts. *Daedalus,* 59–60.

Cheng, K. (1986). A purely geometric module in the rat's spatial representation. *Cognition, 23,* 149–178.

Gallistel, C. R. (1990). *The organization of learning.* Cambridge, MA: MIT Press.

Gallistel, C. R., & Gelman, R. (2003). Nonverbal numerical cognition: From reals to integers. *Trends in Cognitive Sciences, 4(2),* 59–65.

Gelman, S. A., & Coley, J. D. (1990). The importance of knowing a dodo is a bird: Categories and inferences in 2-year-old children. *Developmental Psychology, 26(5),* 796–804.

Gelman, S. A., & Wellman, H. M. (1991). Insides and essences: Early understanding of the nonobvious. *Cognition, 38,* 213–244.

Gordon, P. (2004). Numerical cognition without words: Evidence from Amazonia. *Science, 306,* 496–499.

Gouteaux, S., & Spelke, E. S. (2001). Children's use of geometry and landmarks to reorient in an open space. *Cognition, 81,* 119–148.

Gouteaux, S., Thinus-Blanc, C., & Vauclair, J. (2001). Rhesus monkeys use geometric and nongeometric information during a reorientation task. *Journal of Experimental Psychology: General, 130,* 505–519.

Hermer, L., & Spelke, E. S. (1994). A geometric process for spatial orientation in young children. *Nature, 370,* 57–59.

Hermer, L., & Spelke, E. S. (1996). Modularity and development: The case of spatial reorientation. *Cognition, 61,* 195–232.

Hermer-Vazquez, L., Moffet, A., & Munkholm, P. (2001). Language, space, and the development of cognitive flexibility in humans: The case of two spatial memory tasks. *Cognition, 79,* 263–299.

Hermer-Vazquez, L., Spelke, E. S., & Katsnelson, A. (1999). Source of flexibility in human cognition: Dual-task studies of space and language. *Cognitive Psychology, 39,* 3–36.

Inagaki, K., & Hatano, G. (1993). Young children's understanding of the mind-body distinction. *Child Development, 64(5),* 1534–1549.

Inagaki, K., & Hatano, G. (1996). Young children's recognition of commonalities between animals and plants. *Child Development, 67,* 2823–2840.

Le Corre, M., Van de Walle, G., Brannon, E. M., & Carey, S. (2006). Revisiting the competence/performance debate in the acquisition of the counting principles. *Cognitive Psychology, 52(3),* 130–169.

Lipton, J. S., & Spelke, E. S. (2003). Origins of number sense: Large number discriminations in human infants. *Psychological Science, 14(5),* 396–401.

Margules, J., & Gallistel, C. R. (1988). Heading in the rat: Determination by environmental shape. *Animal Learning & Behavior, 16(4),* 404–410.

McCrink, K., & Wynn, K. (2004). Large number addition and subtraction by 9-month-old infants. *Psychological Science, 15(11),* 776–781.

Morris, S. C., Taplin, J. E., & Gelman, S. A. (2000). Vitalism in naïve biological thinking. *Developmental Psychology, 36(5),* 582–595.

Piaget, J. (1929). *The child's conception of the world.* London: Routledge and Kegan Paul.

Pica, P., Lemer, C., & Izard, V. (2004). Exact and approximate arithmetic in an Amazonian indigene group. *Science, 306,* 499–503.

Rosengren, K. S., Gelman, S. A., Kalish, C., & McCormick, M. (1991). As time goes by: Children's early understanding of biological growth. *Child Development, 62,* 1302–1320.

Slaughter, V., & Lyons, M. (2003). Learning about life and death in early childhood. *Cognitive Psychology, 46,* 1–30.

Sousa, P., Atran, S., & Medin, D. (2002). Essentialism and folkbiology: Evidence from Brazil. *Journal of Cognition and Culture, 2(3),* 195–223.

Sovrano, V. A., Bisazza, A. & Vallortigara, G. (2002). Modularity and spatial reorientation in a simple mind: Encoding of geometric and nongeometric properties of a spatial environment by fish. *Cognition, 85,* B51–B59.

Sovrano, V. A., & Vallortigara, G. (2006). Dissecting the geometric module: A sense linkage for metric and landmark information in animals' spatial reorientation. *Psychological Science, 17(7),* 616–621.

Spelke, E. S. (2000). Core knowledge. *American Psychologist, 55,* 1233–1243.

Stich, S. (1975). *Innate ideas.* Berkeley, CA: University of California Press.

Wang, R. F., Hermer, L., & Spelke, E. S. (1999). Mechanisms of reorientation and object location by children. *Behavioral Neuroscience, 113(3),* 475–485.

Waxman, S., Medin, D., & Ross, N. (2007). Folkbiological reasoning from a cross-cultural developmental perspective: Early essentialist notions are shaped by cultural beliefs. *Developmental Psychology, 43(2),* 294–308.

Wynn, K. (1990). Children's understanding of counting. *Cognition, 36,* 155–193.

Xu, F., & Spelke, E. S. (2000). Large number discrimination in 6-month-old infants. *Cognition, 74,* B1–B11.

Andrew Shtulman

DEWEY, JOHN
1859–1952

It is fair to say that the philosopher John Dewey, who was born before the Civil War in 1859 and died in 1952 just before the Eisenhower administration, has had the greatest single impact on American education of any scholar in

Portrait of John Dewey. COLUMBIANA COLLECTION, COLUMBIA UNIVERSITY LIBRARIES.

history. Dewey, more than anyone else, is associated with the alternative to traditional education known as child- or learner-centered education. Dewey's contribution to education was part and parcel of his contribution to shaping the intellectual life of the time in which he lived.

Dewey took the discipline of philosophy more seriously than most, borrowing five hundred dollars from an aunt after graduating from the University of Vermont in 1897 to pursue a doctorate at Johns Hopkins University—this at a time when most philosophers at colleges were ministers with seminary degrees. Dewey's first academic job was at the University of Michigan, which was headed by a family friend. He spent 10 fruitful years in Ann Arbor, laying the groundwork for an approach to philosophy that he was able to apply to education in 1894 when he moved to the newly founded University of Chicago. Dewey was lured away from Chicago in 1904 and spent the remainder of his long career at Columbia University, retiring from that institution in 1930 but continuing to serve as an active professor emeritus until shortly before his death in 1952 at the age of 92.

There are at least three key ideas associated with John Dewey's approach to education that continue to resonate with progressive or, in current usage, *constructivist* U.S. educators. In fact, all three of the great reform movements in U.S. education, in the 1930s, 1960s, and 1990s, highlighted variations on these three themes: Individualism, the notion that it is up to the individual child, with guidance from the teacher, to make sense of his or her own experience; readiness, the notion that the child will learn when he or she is ready to learn; and pragmatism, the notion that the worth of learning lies in its instrumental value.

Individualism has repeatedly been central to reform efforts as a reliance on the pedagogy of personal experience, a belief that individuals must be the instigators of their own learning. The teacher, according to this view, works within the students' own experiential workspace as it were. The goal here, it should be emphasized, is a specific type of conceptual learning, the type that individual students induce from their own particular or discrete experience. The teacher, it is thought, in this child- or learner-centered approach, can at best only indirectly influence the inferential process of induction, pointing out to the learner patterns in particular data that become concepts and suggesting names for these patterns in a facilitative rather than a controlling way.

The second tenet of reform-oriented education in the United States is a corollary to the first: This is the need for the teacher to be watchful in fulfilling the facilitative role often described as being a *guide on the side*. Because student need is thought to drive the process of induction, of rethinking personal experience, teaching is an opportunistic enterprise that depends on attentiveness to student needs. This idea, that students learn best when they are ready to learn, became in important curricular principle in 1966: Jerome Bruner's notion of the spiral curriculum, the idea that the way to handle differences in students' readiness to learn is to spiral back on important content that thus reappears throughout the elementary and middle school years. This principle derived from Dewey explains why curriculum content in the United States is organized in a block rather than hierarchical way as is the case in other countries, especially those where students perform better on international measures of achievement. Student achievement, particularly in mathematics and science, appears to be enhanced in countries where the content priorities at each grade level are made clear.

The third tenet, pragmatism, is part and parcel of the way Americans view knowledge. The key idea behind pragmatism is deceptively simple; the value of knowledge is a function of its usefulness or relevance. In the hands of Dewey-oriented educational progressives, this view of knowledge shifted the evaluative focus from content-oriented outcomes to so-called child- or learner-centered outcomes. In U.S. education, this process involves the substitution of measures of content knowledge for those that are thought to tap directly into student thinking processes. The issue here, a clear legacy of John Dewey, is whether process is viewed as being in service of content (the traditional view) or whether the opposite holds, namely, that content is viewed as being in service of process.

John Dewey enjoyed a long and fruitful career: His collected works, thirty-seven volumes in all, are divided into *The Early Works, 1882–1898* (five volumes), *The Middle Works, 1899–1924* (fifteen volumes), and *The Later Works, 1925–1953* (seventeen volumes). The bulk of Dewey's writing on education occurred in the first half of his career; his mature work in philosophy mostly dates from the second half of his career. One important debate, which goes beyond the scope of this entry, relates to the extent to which changes in his philosophical views after mid-career render many, if not most, of his earlier educational views obsolete. The specific issue is whether Dewey abandoned his earlier emphasis on inductionism in education, which he shared with William James, and adopted instead a more complex, realist view of learning and teaching derived from the philosophy of Charles Sanders Peirce (1839–1914). In brief, this view of learning assigns a major role to what can best be described as creative intelligence in the discovery of new ideas in the disciplines. Teaching thus is largely about getting students to look *with* ideas, not *for* ideas, as is the case in the early 2000s in the common alternative to traditional education.

BIBLIOGRAPHY

WORKS BY

Dewey, J. (1916). *Essays in experimental logic*. Chicago: University of Chicago Press.

Dewey, J. (1986a). How we think: A restatement of the relation of reflective thinking to the educative process. In J. A. Boydston (Ed.), *John Dewey: The later works, 1925–1953*, Vol. 8 (pp. 105–352). Carbondale: Southern University Press. (Original work published 1933)

Dewey, J. (1986b). The need for a philosophy of education. In J. A. Boydston (Ed.), *John Dewey: The later works, 1925–1953*, Vol. 9 (pp. 194–204). Carbondale: Southern University Press. (Original work published 1934)

Dewey, J. (1986c). Logic: The theory of inquiry. In J. A. Boydston (Ed.), *John Dewey: The later works, 1925–1953*, Vol. 12. Carbondale: Southern University Press. (Original work published 1938)

WORKS ABOUT

Prawat, R. S. (2003). The nominalism versus realism debate: Toward a philosophical rather than a political resolution. *Educational Theory, 33*(3), 275–311.

Prawat, R. S., & Schmidt, W. H. (2006). Curriculum coherence: Does the logic underlying the organization of subject matter matter? In S. J. Howie & T. Plomp (Eds.), *Contents of learning mathematics and science: Lessons learned from TIMSS*. Lisse, Netherlands: Routledge/Falmer.

Richard S. Prawat

DIRECT INSTRUCTION

Direct instruction, as a general approach to instruction, involves explicit explanations, small learning steps, frequent review, frequent teacher-student interactions, and choral responses. This approach described by Rosenshine and Stevens (1984) is usually referred to with lower-case letters, *di*. Direct Instruction (with capital *DI*) is generally recognized in education as referring to the specific procedures and instructional material authored by Siegfried Engelmann (1931–) and his colleagues. The instructional material is designed according to the principles presented in Engelmann and Carnine's *Theory of Instruction* (1982) and is supported by practices designed to control the details that affect student learning and that are under the schools' control—procedures for managing students, for placing them in the instructional sequences, for correcting errors, for scheduling instruction, and for training teachers.

The DI model was introduced in the mid-1960s at the University of Illinois and achieved impressive results with at-risk preschoolers, raising the children's IQs an average of 24 points and teaching them reading and math (Engelmann, 1970).

The DI model is guided by the basic principle that if children are not learning, the fault lies with the instruction, not the children. DI programs are repeatedly tried out and revised before being published. Because DI instructional programs are referenced to the observed performance and deficiencies of at-risk preschoolers, the programs teach skills that have traditionally not been taught—the language of instruction for example. The DI beginning language curriculum teaches prepositional concepts, actions, plurals, and parts of common objects. The program provides sufficient practice for children to learn the concepts thoroughly. The DI beginning reading program was the first to introduce phonemic-awareness skills (practice of blending and rhyming with orally presented words), completely decodable stories composed entirely of words that had been taught, and explicit instruction in comprehension skills (Engelmann & Bruner, 1969).

Each program is designed so that (a) it did uses language familiar to the children, and (b) it provides ample examples of each concept being taught. DI focuses on one concept at a time and then integrates the newly taught concept into applications that are familiar to the children. The instructional design principles of DI are based on logical analysis. One of the principles is that if what is presented to students is consistent with more than one interpretation, some students will learn the unintended interpretation. For example, if all the examples of "blue" the teacher presents are circular, some students will not learn that blue is a color, but a shape or a combination of a color and a shape. Another principle is that learners have the built-in ability to generalize from a set of examples that clearly demonstrates a concept.

Early applications of DI showed that preschoolers learned faster when the teacher used exactly the same wording in an explanation, rather than varying wording from one example to another (Carnine, 1980). DI provides a script that indicates the precise wording teachers are to say in connection with examples. The script specifies both student responses and correction procedures for more common mistakes. DI programs were the first to have scripted teacher presentations (Engelmann, 2007).

Other principles of effective instruction that emerged from the early DI efforts include the need for frequent checking of student learning, the need for adjusting the rate of new instruction according to the rate of student mastery, and the need for cumulative reviews to demonstrate to students that everything that is taught is reviewed and applied. Principles based on behavior analysis are also applied to DI teaching, including the need for students to receive plenty of reinforcement for correct responses, as well as for appropriate behavior.

DI programs are designed so that children learn only about 10% new material on each lesson. This approach assures that students who are correctly placed in an instructional sequence will learn everything taught in the sequence. The approach also assures that students will be aware of their achievements and will tend to be more motivated to learn new material.

INSTRUCTIONAL COMPONENTS AND ACTIVITIES OF DIRECT INSTRUCTION

The published DI curricula in reading, language, math, and spelling are designed for preschool level through middle-school level with remedial programs for older students. For students to succeed they must be tested and placed into the DI curriculum where they belong. Instructional groups must be homogeneous so that all students in that group will succeed starting at the same spot in the instructional sequence. Although the activities and instructional components vary according to the content and skills the program addresses, some common features emerge, such as lessons designed so that each may be completed in a period. This provision makes it easier to measure the performance of children at any time during the year. If an average group started the program on the first lesson and has been in school 84 days, the group should be close to lesson 84 in the program and should be at mastery on all skills taught by lesson 84.

Another design feature is that lesson events are arranged so that more-reinforcing activities occur late in each lesson, not near the beginning. This feature ensures that students will work hard to get through the less reinforcing parts quickly so they "earn" the more-reinforcing activities.

In the beginning levels of the DI reading program, for instance, students start each lesson with work on the sounds different letters and letter combinations make. Next they read several new words, and words or word families that have been introduced in the last one to three lessons. The next activity is story reading. This is more reinforcing to the students than working on sounds or words in lists. Finally, students do independent work. This activity is also reinforcing.

DI introduces very little homework. The program assumes that there is a sufficient amount of time in the school day for students to do everything they need to do. What little homework is assigned is governed strictly by the rule that students must be able to perform without error at school on the same kind of assignment that they are expected to do at home before they are assigned to do it as homework. DI programs are built on the understanding that parents, particularly low-income parents, cannot be expected to teach their children at home.

DI MODEL COMPARED TO OTHER MODELS

Prevailing educational models variously called child-centered, progressive, or constructivist focus on how to teach, leaving the content up to the individual teacher, often based on student interest. The constructivist model assumes that if learners are placed in settings that provide autonomy and developmentally appropriate practices, students will learn naturally (Bruner, 1961). For example, balanced literacy proponents feel that the motivating power of "authentic" literature will help children learn to read faster than carefully constructed "decodable" stories. The frequently dismal outcomes of these approaches are what led to the creation of DI (see American Institutes for Research, *An Educator's Guide to Schoolwide Reform* [1999] for a review of intervention outcomes).

The DI model has several features in common with behavior analysis. Both behavior analysis and DI focus on how to teach and how to respond to what students do, so that some behaviors are reinforced and others are extinguished. Both behavior analysis and DI analyze tasks and use the information to insure that pre-skills for these tasks are taught before the tasks are presented. But the DI analysis goes beyond tasks to concepts and families of related information. The result is that the manner in which the material is introduced and sequenced is more sophisticated in DI than it is in behavior analysis.

Mastery Learning might be considered by some to be another educational model similar to DI; however, it is not as complete as Direct Instruction's model. Mastery Learning is based on the goal of bringing students to mastery of a series of objectives in sequence. Those students who achieve mastery with less practice engage in enrichment activities until the others have caught up. Then all begin work together on the next objective.

The DI model tries to arrange groups so all children in a group perform at the same level. In this way the faster students are not slowed by those who require more practice. Slower homogeneous groups progress through the lesson sequences more slowly than students who require less practice. DI also attempts to design the sequences so that mastery is achievable. Mastery Learning does not specify details of the teaching or how to sequence objectives efficiently.

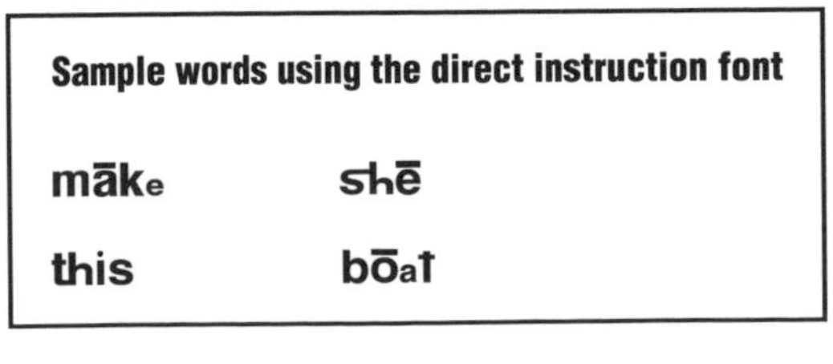

Figure 1 ILLUSTRATION BY GGS INFORMATION SERVICES. CENGAGE LEARNING, GALE.

REVIEW OF DI CURRICULUM

Over the years many different curricula have been developed using the DI model. Two main classes of curricular sequences have emerged: developmental and remedial. The developmental curricula are designed to begin in kindergarten or first grade, teach a broad range of objectives, provide an unbroken sequence of skills across six year-long levels, and culminate in skills necessary for middle school. The remedial curricula are designed for older students (fourth grade through high school). These programs address narrower objectives. For example, the DI corrective reading strand that focuses on decoding addresses decoding problems poor readers typically have and provides specific remedies for the various problems. One problem is that students use generically different strategies for reading words in lists than they use for reading stories. The program addresses this problem through a dog that talks but becomes flustered when excited and says strings of unrelated words, such as "of for to do from go." This technique requires students to apply the strategy they use for reading lists to read connected sentences.

DI has developmental curricula in reading, math, language and spelling. These programs are published by SRA/McGraw-Hill. More information can be found at their website under the Direct Instruction "product family." The most complete developmental reading program is *Reading Mastery.* Designed to begin in kindergarten, *Reading Mastery* teaches beginning reading by teaching blending and a sounding-out strategy before introducing words. Also, the program has letter combinations that are joined, macrons to mark long vowels, and words with tiny letters that are not to be sounded out. (See Figure 1.) As students become proficient at reading words written with these font conventions, the letters are progressively changed until the font has no unusual features.

Connecting Math Concepts, the DI developmental program in math, teaches a broad range of math topics. As in other DI programs, concepts and strategies are taught in a series of lessons then reviewed and used in subsequent lessons and levels. Provided students are brought to mastery, the longer they use DI programs, the easier it becomes for them as well as for the teacher. The developmental programs in language include a three-year sequence, *Language for Learning, Language for Thinking,* and *Language for Writing,* as well as a six-level program called *Reasoning and Writing. Language for Learning* was developed initially to respond to the language deficits seen in at-risk preschoolers and is used in kindergartens primarily. There is also a six-level spelling program entitled *Spelling Mastery.* It, too, represents an unbroken sequence of skills from beginning levels up through middle-school spelling skills and includes unique curricular analyses such as learning morphographs—word parts which retain meaning and spelling across words.

Funnix is a CD reading program based on the *Horizons* reading series that has 120 lessons for the beginning level and 100 lessons for the following level. The program is used for tutoring or small-group instruction. The remedial reading program has two strands, *Corrective Reading Decoding* and *Corrective Reading Comprehension*. Each strand presents a three-year sequence that covers skills from those that are elementary to the middle-school level. Often the corrective reading programs are appropriate for lower-performing students in regular secondary classrooms. The *Corrective Math* series addresses remedial needs of students in math computation by focusing on an operation at a time: *Addition; Subtraction; Multiplication; Division; Basic Fractions; Fractions, Decimals and Percents;* and *Ratios and Equations*. The remedial spelling program is entitled *Spelling Through Morphographs*. More information can be found at the web site supported by Funnix.

RESEARCH BASE FOR DIRECT INSTRUCTION

The Direct Instruction research base is extensive and thorough. As stated in *An Educators' Guide to Schoolwide Reform*, "Direct Instruction has a lengthy and rich base of empirical research" (American Institutes for Research, 1999, p. 64). The *Educators' Guide* gave Direct Instruction its highest rating. Research has been conducted on individual Direct Instruction programs, different components of the Direct Instruction methodology, and schoolwide implementations. A meta-analysis of published empirical studies is presented in Adams and Engelmann's monograph, *Research on Direct Instruction: 25 Years Beyond DISTAR* (1996). The analysis was based on 34 studies that met a strict set of criteria for analysis, including pretest scores, comparison group research designs, and use of appropriate statistical measures. The analysis disclosed that 32 of the 34 studies' effect-size scores were positive, with a mean effect size of 0.87 (Adams & Engelmann, 1996, p. 43). The monograph indicates that "effects of .75 and above are rare in educational research" (p. 42), which makes the results of the meta-analysis "overwhelmingly favorable" (p. 48).

Direct Instruction achieved impressive results in Project Follow Through (1968–1976), the largest educational experiment in history. Of the 22 models that participated in Follow Through, the Direct Instruction model displayed the highest impact on student learning in all academic subjects measured, including reading, mathematics, language, and spelling. DI also had the highest effect in all learning domains measured (basic skills, cognitive-conceptual skills, and affective measures). The Direct Instruction model was the only model in

Follow Through in which the average student score was above the 40th percentile in all academic subjects measured (Stebbins, St. Pierre, Proper, Anderson, and Cerva, 1977).

Follow-up studies indicated a lasting positive effect of Direct Instruction. Students who were in the first cohort of students in the Direct Instruction model in Williamsburg, South Carolina, had a significantly higher school graduation rate than the comparison group (Darch, Gersten, & Taylor, 1987). Students in the Direct Instruction model in New York City had significantly higher college application and acceptance rates as well as school graduation rates than the comparison group (Meyer, Gersten, & Gutkin, 1983).

Subsequent studies continue to confirm the effectiveness of the Direct Instruction model. In a 2000–2001 study of 40 schools in Houston (with a combined student population of nearly 10,000), Carlson, Francis, and Ferguson (2001) found that those schools implementing Direct Instruction outperformed the control schools significantly. Specifically, the authors concluded that the Direct Instruction implementation accelerated students' development of pre-reading and word reading skills in kindergarten and first grade, and students maintained a large lead in terms of skill acquisition over comparison students in the second grade. Students who stayed in the program longer achieved considerably better results by the end of first grade: 60% to 74% of the students at the DI schools scored above the 50th percentile on the SAT-9 Reading tests, but only 43% to 53% of the students at the control schools scored above the 50th percentile (Carlson, Francis, & Ferguson, 2001, pp. 5–7).

Since 2001, the Association for Direct Instruction has published the *Journal of Direct Instruction*. Archived articles from the journal are available via the Association's web site.

SEE ALSO *Applied Behavior Analysis; Behavioral Objectives; Constructivism: Overview; Feedback in Learning; Mastery Learning.*

BIBLIOGRAPHY

Adams, G. L., & Engelmann, S. (1996). *Research on direct instruction: 25 years beyond DISTAR.* Seattle, WA: Educational Achievement Systems.

American Institutes for Research. (1999). *An educator's guide to schoolwide reform.* Arlington, VA: Educational Research Service.

Bereiter, C., & Engelmann, S. (1966). *Teaching disadvantaged children in the preschool.* Englewood Cliffs, NJ: Prentice-Hall.

Bruner, J. S. (1961). The act of discovery. *Harvard Educational Review, 31*(1), 21–32.

Carlson, C., Francis, D., & Ferguson, C. (2001). *RITE Program External Evaluation 2000–2001.* Houston: Texas Institute for Measurement, Evaluation, and Statistics.

Carnine, D. W. (1980). Relationships between stimulus variation and the formation of misconceptions. *Journal of Educational Research, 74,* 106–110.

Darch, C., Gersten, R., & Taylor, R. (1987). Evaluation of Williamsburg County Direct Instruction program: Factors leading to success in rural elementary programs. *Research in Rural Education, 4,* 111–118.

Engelmann, S. (2007). *Teaching needy kids in our backward system: 42 years of trying.* Eugene, Oregon: ADI Press.

Engelmann, S. (1970). The effectiveness of Direct Instruction on IQ performance and achievement in reading and arithmetic. In J. Hellmuth (Ed.), *Disadvantaged child: Vol. 3. Compensatory education: A national debate* (pp. 339–361). New York: Brunner/Mazel.

Engelmann, S., & Bruner, E. C. (1969). *DISTAR Reading I: Teacher's guide,* Chicago: Science Research Associates.

Engelmann, S., & Carnine, D. (1982). *Theory of instruction: Principles and applications.* New York: Irvington.

Engelmann, S., & Colvin, G. (2006). *Rubric for identifying authentic Direct Instruction programs.* Eugene, OR: Engelmann Foundation.

Meyer, L. A., Gersten, R., & Gutkin, J. (1983). Direct Instruction: a Project Follow Through success story in an inner-city school. *Elementary School Journal, 84,* 241–252.

Rosenshine, B., & Stevens, R. (1984). Classroom instruction in reading. In P. D. Pearson (Ed.), *Handbook of reading research* (pp. 745–798). New York: Longman.

Stebbins, L. B., St. Pierre, R. G., Proper, E. C., Anderson, R. B., & Cerva, T. R. (1977). *Education as experimentation: A planned variation model* (Vol. IV-A). Cambridge, MA: Abt Associates.

Donald Crawford
Kurt E. Engelmann
Siegfried Engelmann

DISCOVERY LEARNING

SEE *Constructivism: Discovery Learning.*

DISCUSSION METHODS

Discussion methods are a variety of forums for open-ended, collaborative exchange of ideas among a teacher and students or among students for the purpose of furthering students' thinking, learning, problem solving, understanding, or literary appreciation. Participants present multiple points of view, respond to the ideas of others, and reflect on their own ideas in an effort to build their knowledge, understanding, or interpretation of the matter at hand. Discussions may occur among members of a dyad, small group, or whole class and be teacher-led or student-led. They frequently involve discussion of a written text, though discussion can also focus on a problem, issue, or topic that has its basis in a "text"

in the larger sense of the term (e.g., a discipline, the media, a societal norm). Other terms for discussions used for pedagogical purposes are *instructional conversations* (Tharp & Gallimore, 1988) and *substantive conversations* (Newmann, 1990).

A defining feature of discussion is that students have considerable agency in the construction of knowledge, understanding, or interpretation. In other words, they have considerable "interpretive authority" for evaluating the plausibility or validity of participants' responses. To illustrate, the following excerpt is taken from a discussion between a teacher and a small-group of second-grade students (from Eeds & Wells, 1989). They are discussing the short story, "Me and Neesie," by Eloise Greenfield. The story is about a girl, Janell, and her imaginary friend, Neesie, and the teacher and students are trying to understand why Neesie is at school with Janell for the day.

Austin: But nobody knew about her but Janell. And how could the teacher put her name down on the thing outside for her to be in the classroom if she didn't know about her?

Ashley: Well, actually, if only Janell could see her, why would Neesie be in the other classroom if Janell was the only one that could see her?

Austin: But what if she didn't go to school when Janell did?

Beth: But she did go to school when Janell did.

Chad: And nobody can see her, only Janell.

Ashley: Yeah, but why would they be in different classes if Janell's the only one that can see her? Why would she be in a different class?

Austin: I know.

Teacher: I think you're all agreeing, really, that the question doesn't make sense.

Justin: But the one who put her in the class can't see her.

Ashley: Yeah, but just Janell can.

Austin: The teacher wouldn't know about her.

Justin: I know! She would have snuck in–if she's invisible.

The discourse is marked by many contributions from students and frequent student-to-student exchanges without interruption by the teacher. In this example, the only contribution from the teacher is to summarize the students' contributions. For the most part, students are responsible for constructing an understanding of why the imaginary friend, Neesie, is in school with Janell and why the fictional teacher allows Neesie to attend class for the day. The students ask questions they are genuinely interested in exploring and that evoke a variety of responses ("authentic questions"), they build on each other's responses by incorporating previous responses into their questions ("uptake"), and they challenge each other's views in a collective effort to make sense of the text. Students' contributions largely shape the discourse.

DISCUSSION VERSUS RECITATION

Discussions stand in contrast to a more traditional classroom event called *recitation,* so called because it provides a forum for the students and/or the teacher to recite what is known, usually from the reading of a written text. The defining feature of recitations is that the teacher controls the talk and has complete interpretive authority. To illustrate, the following excerpt comes from an 11th grade English classroom (adapted from Langer, 1993, pp. 36–37). The teacher and the students have read the short story, "Tularecito," by John Steinbeck and they are talking about the character Pancho.

> **Teacher:** Who's Pancho?
>
> **Mario:** The employee.
>
> **Teacher:** An employee, okay. Do you know anything else about Pancho?
>
> **Mariloo:** He's a Mexican Indian.
>
> **Teacher:** He's a Mexican Indian.
>
> **Tarek:** He's always sober.
>
> **Teacher:** What else?
>
> **Rock:** When he's not in jail.
>
> **Teacher:** When he's not in jail, okay.
>
> **Matt:** He doesn't drive when drunk.
>
> **Teacher:** All right. That's good.
>
> **John:** When he arrives at work he's always sleepy.
>
> **Teacher:** Yeah, and that's important. Do you think he fools around? What gives you that impression?

In this case, the teacher contributed most to the talk. Indeed, in recitations, teachers typically talk about two-thirds of the time (Cazden, 2001). The discourse is marked by a pattern called the IRE (Mehan, 1979) or IRF (Sinclair & Coulthard, 1975): the teacher *initiates* a topic by asking a question (e.g., "Who's Pancho?"); students *respond* to the question with an answer (e.g., "The employee"); and the teacher *evaluates* the student's response or gives *feedback* (e.g., "An employee, okay"). The questions are intended to test or stimulate recall of what had been read ("known answer" or "test questions"). The teacher determines the nature of the questions, the order of the questions, and the correctness of students' responses. Although the students offer their own responses,

the teacher does not allow them to explain what they mean about the character Pancho. Instead, she steers the talk in the direction she wants the students to take. The teacher has the ultimate interpretive authority and controls the discourse.

A criticism of recitation and the IRE/IRF pattern of discourse is that they can restrict student talk in ways that are counter-productive to the collaborative construction of knowledge, understanding, and interpretation. Students' responses are typically no longer than two- or three- word phrases and teachers rarely acknowledge the value of students' contributions by incorporating their responses into subsequent questions. Recitation can play a useful role in classroom pedagogy (Mercer, 1995) and there are ways of using the IRE/IRF to good effect (see Hicks, 1995; O'Connor & Michaels, 1996; Wells, 1993). Nevertheless, the oft-cited concern is that this traditional interactional cycle constrains students' contributions and gives them little responsibility for shaping their own learning.

The relative incidence of discussion versus recitation is difficult to determine as there are few surveys of these classroom events that draw from nationally representative samples of classes, at least in the United States. Moreover, most of the research on recitation has been conducted at the secondary level. The best available reports indicate the discussions are rare in classrooms. A 1998 study by Commeyras and Degroff surveyed the pedagogical practices of a random sample of 1,519 K-12 literacy teachers and related professionals in the United States. They found that only 33% of respondents reported that they frequently or very frequently had students meet in small groups to discuss literature in their classrooms. They also found that such discussions were more common in elementary and middle school classes than they were in high school classes. Nystrand (1997) observed the instructional practices in 58 eighth-grade and 54 ninth-grade language arts and English classes in eight Midwestern communities in the United States. He found that open-ended, whole-class discussion averaged only 52 seconds per class in eighth grade and only 14 seconds per class in ninth grade. By contrast to these figures, recitation has a long and well-established history in U.S. classrooms (see Nystrand, 2006) and anecdotal reports suggest that it is still a pervasive phenomenon (Almasi, 1994; Cazden, 2001; Goldenberg, 1992; Tharp & Gallimore, 1988; Worthy & Beck, 1995).

METHODS AND DIMENSIONS

Discussion methods vary on a number of dimensions. Roby (1988) classifies types of discussions primarily on a continuum that relates to whether the teacher or students, or both, have interpretive authority. A secondary dimension is the content of the discussion. Using these dimensions, he identifies three types of discussion. *Problematical* discussions focus on the solutions to either complex or simple problems in which the teacher is dominant in the discussions. *Dialectical* discussions focus on expressing, comparing, and refining students' (and the teacher's) points of view, and the students play a dominant role in the discussions. *Informational* discussions focus on controversial issues within an accepting atmosphere, and students have considerable freedom to bring up issues they wish to discuss. At the extremes are two types of what Roby calls "quasi-discussions": *Quiz Shows* and *Bull Sessions.* In the former, the teacher determines the questions to be asked and has almost all the interpretive authority; in the latter, the students have control over the topic and almost all the interpretive authority. In their 1949 study, Axelrod, Bloom, Ginsburg, O'Meara, and Williams, which was one of the first empirical investigations of discussion, also placed discussions on a continuum that related to whether the teacher or students had interpretive authority.

Gall and Gall (1976) classify discussions according to the instructional objectives: to achieve subject mastery, to bring about a change in attitude or opinion about an issue, or to solve a problem. An example of a subject-mastery discussion method is Manzo and Casale's (1985) *Listen-Read-Discuss Strategy.* In this method, the students listen to the teacher give a short lecture on the material to be learned, they read the pages of the text on which the lecture was based, and they then discuss questions raised by the text. An example of an issue-oriented discussion method is found in Roby (1983): *Devil's Advocate Strategy.* In this method, students articulate their positions on an issue and then take an opposing position and argue against themselves. An example of a problem-solving discussion method is Maier's (1963) *Developmental Discussion Strategy.* In this method, the teacher and students identify a problem, break it into manageable parts, and work on the parts in small groups. The small groups then reconvene as a whole class to discuss their solutions with the teacher.

Discussions about and around texts vary on a large number of dimensions. These approaches serve various purposes depending on the goals teachers set for their students, defined in terms of the stance towards the text: to acquire and retrieve information (an efferent stance), to make spontaneous, emotive connection to the text (an aesthetic or expressive stance), or to interrogate or query the text in search of the underlying arguments, assumptions, worldviews, or beliefs (a critical-analytic stance). Each approach comprises some type of instructional frame that describes the role of the teacher, the nature of the group, type of text, and so forth. Although the goals of these approaches are not identical, all have the potential to help students develop high-level thinking and comprehension of text.

Most variation across text-based discussion approaches is in the degree of control exerted by the teacher versus the students in terms of who has control of topic, who has interpretive authority, who controls turns, who chooses the text, and the relative standing on the three stances. Moreover, there is a relationship between degree of control exercised by teachers versus students and the stance toward the text. Discussions in which students have the greatest control tend to be those that give prominence to an aesthetic or expressive stance. These approaches are *Book Club* (Raphael & McMahon, 1994), *Grand Conversations* (Eeds & Wells, 1989), and *Literature Circles* (Short & Pierce, 1990). These discussions are often peer-led. Conversely, discussions in which teachers have the greatest control tend to be those that give prominence to an efferent stance. These approaches are *Instructional Conversations* (Goldenberg, 1992), *Questioning the Author* (Beck & McKeown, 2006; Beck, McKeown, Hamilton, & Kucan, 1997), and *Junior Great Books shared inquiry* (Great Books Foundation, 1987). It should be noted that *Questioning the Author* is the only discussion approach that was designed specifically to help students grapple with the meaning of informational text. Finally, discussions in which students and teachers share control tend to give prominence to a critical-analytic stance. In these approaches, the teacher has considerable control over text and topic, but students have considerable interpretive authority and control of turns. The approaches that fall into this category are *Collaborative Reasoning* (Anderson, Chinn, Waggoner, & Nguyen, 1998), *Paideia Seminars* (Billings & Fitzgerald, 2002), and *Philosophy for Children* (Sharp, 1995).

Other approaches to text-based discussion, not included in the above, are less easy to classify and there is less research on them. These are *Conversational Discussion Groups* (O'Flahavan, 1989), *Dialogical-Reading Thinking Lesson* (Commeyras, 1993), *Idea Circles* (Guthrie & McCann, 1996, and *Point-Counterpoint* (Rogers, 1990). There are also text-based discussions that have less consistency of application, so they cannot be readily labeled. These include the general class of literature discussion groups based on reader-response theory (see Gambrell & Almasi, 1996), discussion-based envisionments of literature (Langer, 1993, 1995, 2001), and instructional integrations of writing, reading, and talk (Nystrand, Gamoran, & Carbonaro, 2001; Sperling & Woodlief, 1997). *Accountable talk* is another approach to conducting intellectually stimulating discussions that, although not specifically designed for discussions about text, has applicability for promoting reading comprehension (Wolf, Crosson, & Resnick, 2004). It comprises a set of standards for productive conversation in academic contexts and forms part of the New Standards Project developed by Lauren Resnick and colleagues at the University of Pittsburgh.

Another dimension on which discussions vary is small-group versus whole-class discussions. In a 1991 study of 58 12th grade students, Sweigart found that student-led small-group discussions produced greater effects on students' recall and understanding of essays they had read than did lecture or whole-class discussion. Morrow and Smith, in a 1990 study of kindergarten students who engaged in discussions of stories that were read aloud, reported similar benefits of small-group discussions compared to one-on-one discussions with the teacher or whole-class discussions. Smaller groups provided more opportunities for students to speak, interact, and exchange points of view. Taking into account all available evidence, the best generalization that can be made is that smaller groups are better but they should not be so small as to limit the diversity of ideas necessary for productive discussions (Wiencek & O'Flahavan, 1994).

Yet another dimension is teacher-led versus student-led discussions. The relative merits of these formats have been the subject of debate and some research. On the one hand, the teacher can play an important role in discussion by keeping students on topic and modeling and scaffolding the talk to enhance the quality of their learning opportunities (O'Flahavan, Stein, Wiencek, & Marks, 1992; see also Wells, 1989). On the other hand, student-led discussions can enable students to collectively explore topics more fully and to have more control and interpretive authority (Almasi, 1994). Most probably the question as to who should lead the group is the wrong question. The issue is not so much who leads the group but how much structure and focus is provided while giving students the flexibility and responsibility for thinking and reasoning together (Mercer, 1995). Productive discussions need to be structured and focused, but flexible enough to foster generative learning—and these can be teacher-led or student-led.

DISCUSSION AND STUDENT ACHIEVEMENT

Nystrand and Gamoran conducted possibly the largest study ever of the relationship between discussion and student achievement (Gamoran & Nystrand, 1991; Nystrand, 1997; Nystrand & Gamoran (1991). As described earlier, they observed the practices used in 58 eighth-grade and 54 ninth-grade language arts and English classes in eight Midwestern communities in the United States. They observed each class four times per year and assessed students' understanding and interpretation of literature at the end of each year, collecting data on over 1,895 students. Their results indicated that the features of open-ended, whole-class discussion were positively associated with students' reading comprehension,

as measured by both recall and depth of understanding, as well as response to aesthetic aspects of literature.

These results were largely replicated in a 2003 follow-up study by Applebee, Langer, Nystrand, & Gamoran of 974 students in 64 middle- and high-school English classrooms. Results showed that discussion-based practices, used in the context of academically challenging tasks, were positively related to students' reading comprehension and literature achievement.

Other correlational studies have shown similar benefits of discussion. A 2001 study by Langer, for example, studied the characteristics of instruction that accompanied student achievement in 25 schools, involving 44 teachers and 88 classes. She found that whole-class and small-group discussion was one of the characteristics of instruction in schools that showed higher than expected achievement in reading, writing, and English.

In a quasi-experimental study, Fall, Webb, and Chudowsky (2000) analyzed 10th-grade students' performance on language arts tests in which students either discussed or did not discuss a story they were required to read and interpret. Results showed that allowing students to engage in a 10-minute discussion of the story in three-person groups was positively related to students' understanding of the story.

Murphy, Wilkinson, Soter, Hennessey, and Alexander (2007) conducted a meta-analysis of quantitative studies that provided evidence of the effects of different approaches to text-based discussions on measures of teacher and student talk and/or of individual student comprehension and reasoning outcomes. Included were single-group pretest-posttest design studies and multiple-group studies. Three major findings emerged from the meta-analysis. One major finding was that the approaches to discussion differentially promoted high-level comprehension of text. Many of the approaches were highly effective at promoting students' comprehension, especially those that were more efferent in nature, namely *Questioning the Author*, *Instructional Conversations*, and *Junior Great Books shared inquiry*. Moreover, some of the approaches were effective at promoting students' critical-thinking, reasoning, argumentation, and metacognition about and around text, especially *Collaborative Reasoning* and *Junior Great Books*.

A second major finding was that increases in student talk did not necessarily result in concomitant increases in student comprehension. Rather, it seemed that a particular kind of talk was necessary to promote comprehension. This is consistent with observations from other research that the success of discussion hinges not on increasing the amount of student talk *per se*, but in enhancing the quality of the talk (Wells, 1989). A third major finding was that effects varied by students' academic ability. Results showed that the approaches exhibited greater effects when employed with below-average and average ability students and weaker effects with above-average students. It appears that above-average ability students could understand a text and think independently about the nuances of meaning even without participating in discussion.

Possibly the most stringent test of the benefits of discussions come from experimental and quasi-experimental studies that have examined the effects of a discussion approach, relative to a control condition, on commercially available, standardized measures (rather than researcher-developed measures). Murphy and colleagues (2007) found only five such studies: Mizerka's 1999 study of the effects of *Literature Circles*, Bird's (1984) study of the effects of *Junior Great Books*; and Banks (1987), Chamberlain (1993), and Lipman's (1975) studies of the effects of *Philosophy for Children*. Among these studies, the strongest effect was found by Lipman for *Philosophy for Children*, as measured by students' comprehension scores on the Iowa Test of Basic Skills, with an effect size of 0.55. The effect sizes for the other studies averaged approximately 0.20.

An important finding from research on discussion methods is that they can benefit both fluent and limited-English-proficient (LEP) students. Saunders and Goldenberg (1999) conducted an experimental study of the effects of *Instructional Conversations*, in combination with literature logs, on 116 fourth and fifth grade LEP and English-proficient students. Results showed both fluent and LEP students who participated in the *Instructional Conversations* + literature logs condition scored significantly higher on factual and interpretive comprehension than did students in other conditions. Other studies of *Instructional Conversations* have reported similar benefits for LEP students. Nystrand (2006) noted a number of studies that provided evidence of the benefits of discussions for L2 as well as L1 speakers.

SEE ALSO *Collaborative Learning; Questioning.*

BIBLIOGRAPHY

Almasi, J. F. (1994). The nature of fourth graders' sociocognitive conflicts in peer-led and teacher-led discussions of literature. *Reading Research Quarterly 30*, 314–351.

Alvermann, D. E., Dillon, D. R., & O'Brien, D. G. (1987). *Using discussion to promote reading comprehension*. Newark, DE: International Reading Association.

Anderson, R. C., Chinn, C., Chang, J., Waggoner, J., & Nguyen, K. (1998). Intellectually stimulating story discussions. In J. L. Osborn & F. Lehr (Eds.), *Literacy for all: Issues in teaching and learning* (pp. 170–186). New York: Guilford Press.

Applebee, A., Langer, J., Nystrand, M., & Gamoran, A. (2003). Discussion-based approaches to developing understanding: Classroom instruction and student performance in middle and high school English. *American Educational Research Journal, 40*, 685–730.

Axelrod, J., Bloom, B. S., Ginsburg, B. E., O'Meara, W., & Williams, J. C. Jr. (1949). *Teaching by discussion in the college program*. Chicago: University of Chicago.

Banks, J. C. R. (1987). *A study of the effects of the critical thinking skills program, philosophy for children, on a standardized achievement test*. Unpublished doctoral dissertation, Southern Illinois University, Edwardsville.

Beck, I. L., McKeown, M. G., Hamilton, R. L., & Kucan, L. (1997). *Questioning the author: An approach for enhancing student engagement with text*. Newark, NJ: International Reading Association.

Beck, I. L., & McKeown, M. G. (2006). *Improving comprehension with questioning the author: A fresh and expanded view of a powerful approach*. New York: Scholastic.

Billings, L., & Fitzgerald, J. (2002). Dialogic discussion and the paideia seminar. *American Educational Research Journal, 39*(4), 907–941.

Bird, J. B. (1984). *Effects of fifth graders' attitudes and critical thinking/reading skills resulting from a junior great books program*. Unpublished doctoral dissertation, Rutgers, The State University of New Jersey, New Brunswick.

Bloom, B. (1954). The thought processes of students in discussion. In S. J. French (Ed.), *Accent on teaching: Experiments in general education* (pp. 23–46). New York: Harper.

Bridges, D. (1979). *Education, democracy, and discussion*. Winsor, England: NFER Publishing.

Cazden, C. B. (2001). *Classroom discourse: The language of teaching and learning* (2nd ed.). Portsmouth, NH: Heinemann.

Chamberlain, M. A. (1993). *Philosophy for children program and the development of critical thinking of gifted elementary students*. Unpublished doctoral dissertation, University of Kentucky, Lexington.

Chinn, C. A., Anderson, R. C., et al. (2001). Patterns of discourse in two kinds of literature discussion. *Reading Research Quarterly, 36*, 378–411.

Commeyras, M. (1993). Promoting critical thinking through dialogical-thinking reading lessons. *The Reading Teacher, 46*(6), 486–494.

Commeyras, M., & DeGroff, L. (1998). Literacy professionals perspectives on professional development and pedagogy: A national survey. *Reading Research Quarterly, 33*, 434–472.

Dillon, J. T. (1984). Research on questioning and discussion. *Educational Leadership, 42*, 50–56.

Eeds, M., & Wells, D. (1989). Grand conversations: An exploration of meaning construction in literature study groups. *Research in the Teaching of English, 23*(1), 4–29.

Fall, R., Webb, N. & Chudowsky, N. (2000). Group discussion and large-scale language arts assessment: Effects on students' comprehension. *American Educational Research Journal, 37*(4), 911–942.

Gall, J. P., & Gall, M. D. (1990). Outcomes of the discussion method. In W. W. Wilen (Ed.), *Teaching and learning through discussion* (pp. 25–44). Springfield, IL: Thomas.

Gall, M. D. (1987). Discussion methods. In M. J. Dunkin (Ed.), *The international encyclopedia of teaching and teacher education* (pp. 232–237). Oxford, England: Pergamon.

Gall, M. D., & Gall, J. P. (1976). The discussion method. In N. L. Gage (Ed.), *Psychology of teaching methods. National Society for the Study of Education. Seventy-Fifth yearbook, Part 1* (pp. 166–216). Chicago: University of Chicago Press.

Gall, M. D., & Gillett, M. (1980). The discussion method in classroom teaching. *Theory into Practice, 19*, 98–103.

Gambrell, L. B., & Almasi, J. F. (Eds.). (1996). *Lively discussions! Fostering engaged reading.* Newark, DE: International Reading Association.

Gamoran, A., & M. Nystrand (1991). Background and instructional effects on achievement in eighth-grade English and social studies. *Journal of Research on Adolescence 1,* 277–300.

Goldenberg, C. (1992). Instructional conversations: Promoting comprehension through discussion. *The Reading Teacher, 46*(4), 316–326.

Great Books Foundation. (1987). *An introduction to shared inquiry.* Chicago: Author.

Guthrie, J. T., & McCann, A. D. (1996). Idea circles: Peer collaboration for conceptual learning. In L. B. Gambrell and J. F. Almasi (Eds.), *Lively discussions! Fostering engaged reading* (pp. 87–105). Newark, DE: International Reading Association.

Hicks, D. (1995). Discourse, learning and teaching. In M. Apple (Ed.), *Review of research in education, Vol. 21* (pp. 49–95). Washington, DC: American Educational Research Association.

Hoetker, J., & Ahlbrand, W. Jr. (1969). The persistence of the recitation. *American Educational Research Journal, 6,* 145–167.

Langer, J. (1993). Discussion as exploration: Literature and the horizon of possibilities. In G. E. Newell & R. K., Durst (Eds.), *Exploring texts: The role of discussion and writing in the teaching and learning of literature* (pp. 23–43). Norwood, MA: Christopher-Gordon.

Langer, J. A. (1995). *Envisioning literature: Literary understanding and literature instruction.* Newark, DE: International Reading Association.

Langer, J. A. (2001). Beating the odds: Teaching middle and high school students to read and write well. *American Educational Research Journal 38,* 837–80.

Lipman, M. (1975). *Philosophy for children.* Monclair, NJ: Monclair State College.

Maier, N. R. F. (1963). *Problem solving discussions and conferences: Leadership methods and skills.* New York: McGraw-Hill.

Manzo, A. V., & Casale, U. P. (1985). Listen-read-discuss: A content heuristic. *Journal of Reading, 28*, 732–734.

Mehan, H. (1979) *Learning lessons.* Cambridge, MA: Harvard University Press.

Mercer, N. (1995). *The guided construction of knowledge: talk amongst teachers and learners.* Clevedon, England: Multilingual Matters.

Mizerka, P. M. (1999). *The impact of teacher-directed literature circles versus student-directed literature circles on reading comprehension at the sixth-grade level.* Unpublished doctoral dissertation, University of Illinois, Urbana-Champaign.

Morrow, L. M., & Smith, J. K. (1990). The effects of group size on interactive storybook reading. *Reading Research Quarterly, 25,* 213–231.

Murphy, P. K., Wilkinson, I. A. G., Soter, A., Hennessey, M. N., & Alexander, J. F. (2007) *Examining the effects of classroom discussion on students' high-level comprehension of text: A meta-analysis.* Unpublished manuscript. State College, PA: Pennsylvania State University.

Newmann, F. (1990). Higher order thinking in teaching social studies: A rationale for the assessment of classroom thoughtfulness. *Journal of Curriculum Studies, 22,* 41–56.

Nystrand, M. (1997). *Opening dialogue: Understanding the dynamics of language and learning in the classroom.* New York: Teachers College Press.

Nystrand, M. (2006). Research on the role of discussion as it affects reading comprehension. *Research in the Teaching of English, 40*(4), 392–412.

Nystrand, M., & Gamoran, A. (1991). Instructional discourse, student engagement, and literature achievement. *Research in the Teaching of English, 25*(3), 261–290.

Nystrand, M., Gamoran, A., & Carbonaro, W. (2001). On the ecology of classroom instruction: The case of writing in high school English and social studies. In P. Tynjala, L. Mason, and K. Lonka (Eds.), *Writing as a learning tool: Integrating theory and practice* (pp. 57–81). Dordrecht, The Netherlands: Kluwer.

O'Connor, M. C., & Michaels, S. (1996). Shifting participant frameworks: Orchestrating thinking practices in group discussion. In D. Hicks (Ed.), *Discourse, learning and schooling* (pp. 63–103). New York: Cambridge University Press.

O'Flahavan, J. F. (1989). *Second-graders' social, intellectual, and affective development in varied group discussions about narrative texts: An exploration of participation structures.* Unpublished doctoral dissertation, University of Illinois, Urbana-Champaign.

O'Flahavan, J. F., Stein, S., Wiencek, J., & Marks, T. (1992). *Interpretive development in peer discussion about literature: An exploration of the teacher's role.* Urbana, IL: Final report to the trustees of the National Council of Teachers of English.

Raphael, T. E., & McMahon, S. I. (1994). Book club: An alternative framework for reading instruction. *The Reading Teacher, 48*(2), 102–116.

Roby, T. (1983). *The other side of the question: Controversial turns, the devil's advocate, and reflective responses.* Paper presented at the annual meeting of the American Educational Research Association, Montreal, Canada.

Roby, T. (1988). Models of discussion. In J. T. Dillon (Ed.), *Questioning and discussion: A multidisciplinary study* (pp. 163–191). Norwood, NJ: Ablex.

Rogers, T. (1990). A point, counterpoint response strategy for complex short stories. *Journal of Reading, 34*(4), 278–282.

Saunders, W. M., & C. Goldenberg (1999). Effects of instructional conversations and literature logs on limited- and fluent-English-proficient students' story comprehension and thematic understanding. *The Elementary School Journal 99,* 277–301.

Sharp, A. M. (1995). Philosophy for children and the development of ethical values. *Early Child Development and Care, 197,* 45–55.

Short, K. G., & Pierce, K. M. (Eds.) (1990). *Talking about books: Creating literature communities.* Portsmouth, NH: Heinemann.

Sinclair, J., & Coulthard, M. (1975). Toward an analysis of discourse: The English used by teachers and pupils. London: Oxford University Press.

Sperling, M., & Woodlief, L. (1997). Two classrooms, two writing communities: Urban and suburban tenth graders learning to write. *Research in the Teaching of English, 31,* 205–239.

Sweigart, W. (1991). Classroom talk, knowledge development, and writing. *Research in the Teaching of English, 25,* 497–509.

Tharp, R. G., & Gallimore, R. (1988). *Rousing minds to life: Teaching, learning, and schooling in social context.* Cambridge, England: Cambridge University Press.

Wells, G. (1989). Language in the classroom: Literacy and collaborative talk. *Language and Education, 3,* 251–273.

Wells, G. (1993). Reevaluating the IRF sequence: A proposal for the articulation of theories of activity and discourse for the analysis of teaching and learning in the classroom. *Linguistics and Education, 5,* 1–38.

Wiencek, J., & O'Flahavan, J. F. (1994). From teacher-led to peer discussions about literature: Suggestions for making the shift. *Language Arts, 71,* 488–498.

Wolf, M. K., Crosson, A. C., & Resnick, L. B. (2004). Classroom talk for rigorous reading comprehension instruction. *Reading Psychology, 26,* 27–53.

Worthy, J., & Beck, I. L. (1995). On the road from recitation to discussion in large-group dialogue about literature. In K. Hinchman & C. Kinz, (Eds.), *Perspectives on literacy research and practice: Forty-fourth yearbook of the national reading conference* (pp. 312–324). Chicago: The National Reading Conference.

Ian A. G. Wilkinson

DISTRIBUTED COGNITION

Proponents of distributed cognition argue that the distribution of cognition across the brain extends to material settings and artifacts, to social interaction, and across time. A cognitive process involves representational states—in the world and in the head—that are brought into coordination with one another. This coordination may be strictly internal, but it more typically involves interaction with one or more technologies, interactions among multiple persons, and/or incorporation of products of past cognitive activity.

Because cognitive processes may extend beyond the head of the individual, researchers of distributed cognition use a broader unit of analysis when studying cognitive systems. Depending on the goals of the analysis, the boundary of the cognitive system may be defined around a person working with a tool or artifact, a team of people and their tools, or the skull of a single individual. To avoid over-attribution of internal states, distributed cognition researchers prefer to work outside-in, using analysis of visible activity to set constraints on what must be happening in the internal cognitive system.

HUTCHINS'S VIEW OF DISTRIBUTED COGNITION

Distributed cognition is most closely associated with the work of the cognitive anthropologist Edwin Hutchins (1948–) at the University of California, San Diego, and with his students and colleagues. In his groundbreaking research, Hutchins studied the work of a navigation team on a navy ship. The team used specialized tools and coordinated activity to accomplish more than could be done by any individual thinker. This study led Hutchins to broaden his definition of what constituted the cognitive system and to argue that cognition is distributed in three fundamental ways: across the individual and aspects of the material environment; across multiple individuals interacting and communicating in an organized way; and across time, in that products of earlier cognitive processes change the nature of later cognitive tasks.

Material Distribution of Cognition. A cognitive task as mundane as multiplying two-digit numbers is rarely done in the head; instead, multiplication commonly involves a written representation of the problem or the use of a calculating device. Many familiar cognitive activities are impossible without such artifacts: clocks, for example, are manufactured precisely to support time telling, and much instruction in the early grades is devoted to learning to read clock times. In complex domains such as ship navigation, specialized tools and procedures have been developed over centuries to solve important, frequently recurring problems such as determining the ship's location or speed. Mastering their use is essential to becoming an expert navigator.

While such artifacts seem to amplify natural cognitive abilities—a written list, for example, augments memory—the most powerful cognitive artifacts transform tasks so that complex computations can be carried out through simple manipulation and perception. One example is the nautical slide rule, which can be used to solve distance-rate-time problems by moving dials, aligning marks, and reading numbers, all far simpler than applying algebra and arithmetic, even with the aid of paper and pencil or a calculator. The slide rule method is also less prone to error: The computational relations among distance, rate, and time are built into the structure of the artifact, locking out many possible errors. The use of the slide rule is easily learned, and the system of person plus artifact is powerful and reliable although not readily generalizable to other task settings. Like the slide rule, most cognitive artifacts are linked to specific practices, in which they enable humans to use simple abilities to produce sophisticated outcomes.

From the perspective of distributed cognition, a person using one or more cognitive artifacts constitutes a cognitive functional system for solving a particular problem. The user is the glue that binds this system together—the one who coordinates the various resources, internal and external, to produce the desired result. Different functional systems can be computationally equivalent—that is, they can start from the same inputs and produce the same outputs—yet vary greatly in the demands they place on the person. For example, multiplying two-digit numbers through mental arithmetic is difficult and prone to error. Writing a multiplication problem in a conventional form and applying a school algorithm helps keep track of intermediate results but still demands accurate recall of the procedure and the multiplication tables. Punching a sequence of buttons on a calculator or looking up the answer in a table is simple to do but requires that the specialized tool be ready at hand—more likely in a work setting where tasks often repeat. These distinct methods use different resources, place different demands on memory and mental processes, and have different propensities for error, yet all accomplish the same computation.

In real-world activity, a cognitive functional system is dynamically instantiated to solve a current problem and then dissipates as soon as the problem-solving event is over. In unusual situations, the functional system may be wholly improvised and quickly forgotten; in more familiar situations, the functional system is likely to be highly conventionalized, although always fitted to the particular circumstances. Such conventional functional systems constitute a significant portion of the curriculum in schools, universities, and trade and professional training programs.

Social Distribution of Cognition. Through orchestrated group activity, humans accomplish tasks that would overwhelm any individual, while social institutions distribute labor and expertise across groups, sustaining complex societies. From sports to science, nearly every human endeavor depends on the social coordination of activity, whether among people in close proximity or widely dispersed in time and space. How social groups are organized, how work is divided, how knowledge is distributed, and how information is communicated all have important cognitive consequences.

Fundamental to distributed cognition is the idea that a group may have cognitive properties that differ from those of the individual. A group may have greater knowledge and processing capacity and speed, enabling it to accomplish a task too complex for a single person, especially under severe time pressure. In Hutchins's study of ship navigation, the team had to fix the position of the ship and project its future position at three-minute intervals; when the circumstances were most harrowing, the interval was reduced to one minute. The team succeeded by distributing subtasks into local functional systems

(individuals with specialized tools) like those discussed above and coordinating the flow of information between these systems through a distinct pattern of social interaction. This arrangement produced a global functional system for navigation that operated rapidly and reliably and that proved to be robust in the face of changing circumstances.

How work is divided across the members of a social group matters because some divisions are more productive and robust than others. In organizing group work, it is beneficial to maximize parallel effort without violating sequential dependencies in the task (what must be done before what). If some group members are idle or must undo or redo what has already been done by others, then the system will operate inefficiently. It may also be useful to divide activity in a way that provides mutual access and monitoring, both to catch errors and to promote learning—for which some modest yet non-catastrophic rate of error is beneficial. Or it may be useful to isolate some parts of the system from potential distraction or disruption. How activity is distributed across the group partially determines how the system adapts to change, making it more flexible or brittle; a modular arrangement, for example, makes it easier to alter some parts of the system without impacting others. Social organization and the distribution of labor—both physical and cognitive—crucially affect the success of the global functional system.

Other critical social factors include the distribution of knowledge and the pattern of communication among members of a group. Overlapping knowledge supports error detection, increasing the robustness of the system, while different patterns of communication can lead to different outcomes. In Hutchins's study, the promotion of quartermasters to new jobs paralleled the flow of information during the navigation task. The result was that those performing more critical parts of the task understood how the information they received had been generated since they themselves used to perform that portion of the task. Sensory activities such as sighting landmarks through a special telescope fed integrative and evaluative activities such as fixing the ship's location, projecting its future position, and assessing the quality of the fix. The operation of this socially distributed system thus parallels conventional descriptions of individual cognition.

Finally, in systems of socially distributed cognition, it is not necessary, nor is it always efficient, to have a central executive or overseer who coordinates the activities of the group; instead, the group can operate interdependently. Computational dependencies can be turned into social dependencies, so that one group member relies on another's output to perform his portion of the task; this dependence keeps the system from halting prematurely. However, there may be times when it is helpful to have an experienced observer watch the group's activities and recommend ways to help the system operate more efficiently. Here the observer is engaged in a different activity: representing and evaluating the performance of the system—a metacognitive function.

Temporal Distribution of Cognition. Human cognition incorporates products of past activity, distributing cognition over time. Environments for human cognition are highly artificial, crafted to support certain activities, and riddled with representations. These activities follow conventional social practices and incorporate artifacts provided by others often unknown or long since deceased. The residua of past cognition—material and conceptual—become structuring resources for new cognitive functional systems. Human cognition is thus inherently cultural, where culture is a process that accumulates partial solutions to frequently encountered problems.

In addition to increasing the sophistication of human cognitive accomplishments over many generations, the temporal distribution of cognition also provides an immediate benefit: It reduces cognitive load by spreading complexity over time. A navigation chart, for example, represents the results of centuries of work by navigators and cartographers; this precomputation turns the chart into a powerful computational tool. A line drawn on the chart gains an immediate relation to all the information represented there; drawing two intersecting lines executes a computation that connects a navigator to the ages.

Here in the temporal distribution of cognition, the material, social, and conceptual come together. Every moment of practice resonates on three vastly different timescales: the conduct of the activity, the development of the practitioner, and the development of the practice. This intersection explains why researchers who study distributed cognition are drawn to studying cognition in real-world settings, to what Hutchins calls "cognition in the wild."

HOW DISTRIBUTED COGNITION DIFFERS FROM INDIVIDUAL VIEWS OF COGNITION

The cognitive revolution that led to information processing psychology and artificial intelligence was founded on the idea that the mind, like a computer, is a symbol processing system: The senses transduce perceptual input into symbols which are operated on by an internal logic engine, producing other symbols that are programs for action. Distributed cognition preserves the view that humans are users of symbols and that cognition is computation but dispenses with internal symbol processing as the fundamental architecture of cognition. Cognition is

computation accomplished through the propagation of representational states across representational media, which may be internal or external to the individual. Representational states are propagated by bringing the media into coordination with one another. Broadening the unit of analysis to socio-technical systems actually helps make the idea of cognition as computation plausible: Inputs are transformed into outputs through the operation of cognitive functional systems. The operation of these distributed systems is what is modeled by formal systems such as computers—not internal symbol processing in the head.

IMPLICATIONS OF DISTRIBUTED COGNITION FOR EDUCATION

Because distributed cognition focuses on activity in real-world settings, most research has investigated learning in the context of work; domains include ship navigation, fleet fishing, air traffic control, and commercial aviation. Despite the limited availability of classroom-based research, distributed cognition does offer a perspective on learning that can inform classroom instruction, both for mastering conventional systems and for supporting innovation.

Distributed cognition views learning as adaptive reorganization in a functional system. This definition covers organizational learning (the activity of groups) as well as individual learning, so long as some parts of the system adapt, or are adapted, to structure in other parts. Learning may involve changes internal to the individual, changes in the world (in representations, tools, and settings), and/or changes in social interaction. Changes internal to the individual have been the focus of traditional learning theories, probably because it is the person who brings the media into coordination to accomplish the task. A broader unit of analysis, however, entails a broader understanding of what counts as learning in a cognitive system.

For students, mastering conventional systems means more than developing simple literacy and numeracy; it means learning to compose and use functional systems to reliably perform culturally valued activities. Learning to tell time from the display of hands on a clock, for example, involves learning to coordinate ideas of number, shape, and motion with structures on the clock face and with the conventions of the system of time measurement. During instruction, a teacher guides this coordination through talk, gestures, and manipulations of objects. With practice, the student becomes able to perform without this guidance. With further practice, the student begins to recognize familiar patterns and to shift strategies, for example, from counting to directly naming times; this adaptation yields a different but computationally equivalent functional system that operates more efficiently. To help students master conventional systems, familiar teaching practices of modeling, scaffolding, and reinforcement work well, the fading of material and social supports coinciding with the encouragement of independent practice.

Innovating is different in that the individual or group must use the resources at hand to compose a functional system to accomplish a novel task, where the method for doing so may not be readily apparent. In Hutchins's study, the navigation team suffered the loss of the gyrocompass while the ship was navigating a narrow channel; the team was forced to invent new procedures immediately as the ship faced the danger of running aground. At first, the team's activity was driven almost entirely by the environment—by whatever information happened to be coming in. As individuals made changes to simplify their own activity, others adapted to these changes. Eventually, the system settled into a stable pattern—a new functional system that dissipated as soon as the crisis was over. To help students innovate, teaching practices that introduce variability into established systems or that pose novel problems are likely to work best. These should be followed by comparison and analysis of different approaches, paying particular attention to the representations used, their coordination, and any adaptations that had to be made. Other topics to discuss include the specificity or generality of the approach, its propensity for error, and the demands it places on the person using it. Distributed cognition provides a useful framework for guiding such discussion.

SEE ALSO *Constructivism; Information Processing Theory; Situated Cognition.*

BIBLIOGRAPHY

Educational Psychology Review, 10(1). 1998 special issue on distributed cognition.

Hutchins, E. (1995). *Cognition in the wild.* Cambridge, MA: MIT Press.

Hutchins, E. (1995). How a cockpit remembers its speeds. *Cognitive Science, 19,* 265–288.

Journal of Interactive Learning Research, 13(1). 2002 special issue on distributed cognition.

Salomon, G. (Ed.) (1993). *Distributed cognitions: psychological and educational considerations.* New York: Cambridge University Press.

Robert F. Williams

DROPPING OUT OF SCHOOL

An important focus in education research is the occurrence of high school non-completion. The work of defining, measuring, and reporting on students who drop out of school permeates the research. Theorists and policy makers utilize varying methods of counting and reporting those students who do not complete their high school education. In addition, tracking families who opt for private school or change schools or districts and students who choose to complete requirements for a General Education Diploma further complicates the process of making accurate estimates regarding attrition.

The two prominent reporting agencies, the National Center for Educational Statistics (NCES) and the United States Bureau of the Census (Census), report on different aspects of the outcome performance. One focuses on high school completers, whereas the other focuses on non-enrolled and non-completing people who are aged 16 to 24. According to the Census, dropout estimates from 1967 to 2003 showed a decrease from 17% to 10%; however, NCES reported high school completion rates ranging between 65% to 75% for roughly the same time period (1967–2002) (Warren & Halpern-Manners, 2007). This phenomenon needs more uniform definition and measurement. The Interdivisional Task Force on School Dropout Prevention, created in response to the American Psychological Association's 1996 call for increased research and understanding into the educational outcome of dropping out, revealed that the majority of prior research did not focus on intervention and prevention programs (Doll & Hess, 2001). Much is known, however, about the individual characteristics and other factors that place students at-risk of dropping out of school.

RISK FACTORS AND PREVALENCE

Most research on the phenomenon of dropping out focuses on a deficit model, on what students are lacking. The personal characteristics that have been consistently identified as placing students at-risk for educational failure and subsequent dropout include: minority group status, low socioeconomic status/families receiving welfare, exceptionalities and disabilities, English as a second language, low test scores and grades, misbehavior/suspension, grade retention, over age for grade, absenteeism, multiple school moves, single parent homes, large urban schools, poor neighborhoods, low parental/mother education, and student emotional/behavior disorders (Nowicki, Duke, Sisney, Stricker, & Tyler, 2004; Suh, Suh, & Houston, 2007). Of the dropouts in 2005, 65% were over age for grade; 61% were minorities; 58% were male; 33% were from low-income families; and 17% were second generation or less immigrants (NCES, 2005). Researchers have increasingly moved away from deficit models of academic failure to more positively focused models such as examining environmental and instructional factors that facilitate students' resiliency (see Freeman, Leonard, & Lipari, 2007, for a review).

Inconsistent findings across dropout prevention programs highlight the problem of using deficit models, in that programs are only effective for some students, but no program has been able to improve the outcome for all at-risk students (Dynarski & Gleason, 2002). In light of the government-mandated move to increased academic accountability and performance standards on standardized tests (No Child Left Behind Act, 2002), research efforts have increasingly focused on the multi-level influences that contribute to students either being pushed out, dropping out, or persisting in school. The theoretical underpinnings of most of this work utilize Urie Bronfenbrenner's ecological systems theory as a starting point to identify obstacles and protective factors in students' environments (Cassidy & Bates, 2005; Gallagher, 2002).

CONTEXTUAL ANTECEDENTS OF DROPPING OUT

According to Bronfenbrenner, changes within and between the microsystems (school, family), exosystem (neighborhood, extended family), and the macrosystem (culture, government) can influence an individual's development, as well as the person's choices in terms of staying in school. More specifically, such administrative issues as harsh discipline policies and grade retention have been shown to be related to students' decision to dropout of school (Cassidy & Bates, 2005; Stearns, Moller, Blau, & Potochnick, 2007). Furthermore researchers and theorists have highlighted that leaving school early is not a sudden occurrence, but a process that occurs over time and results from certain interactions between student, family, and school (Christenson & Thurlow, 2004). Theorists have also emphasized that some students may begin disengaging from school as early as elementary school (Finn, 1989); whereas the documented decrease in achievement motivation that occurs during the transition into middle school (Anderman, Maehr, & Midgley, 1999) further complicates students' progress to high school completion. Beyond the demographic predictors that place students at risk of dropping out, researchers have identified how certain psychosocial factors tend to co-occur.

PSYCHOSOCIAL PREDICTORS

Research evidence from multiple theoretical and methodological approaches supports the relational nature of students' motivation and academic achievements, including high school completion (Finn, 1989; Whelage, 1989). Qualitative evidence from both dropouts and school staff members (principals, teachers, counselors) identifies the psychological and social aspects of students' decisions to withdraw from school (Anderson, Kerr-Roubicek, & Rowling, 2006; Gallagher, 2002). Such variables as feelings of alienation, perceptions of teacher caring, feeling a sense of school belonging/community, academic valuing, academic identity, locus of control, future optimism, self-esteem, disengagement, and participation are some factors shown to be related to the outcome of dropping out (Anderson et al., 2006; Gallagher, 2002; Kemp, 2006; Nowicki et al., 2004; Osborne & Walker, 2006; Reschly & Christenson, 2006; Stearns et al., 2007; Su, Su, & Houston, 2007).

The demographic characteristic of minority group status alters how such psychological and social variables influence students' academic trajectories; this correlation has stimulated research on minority students' developmental processes. For example, Osborne and Walker found that minority students who had a high level of academic identification and subsequent high levels of academic success were more likely to withdraw from school than their Caucasian counterparts. Thus, other psychosocial variables such as stereotype threat (Steele, 1992), in which case the threat of confirming a negative stereotype negatively impacts minority students' academic performance, also play a role in students' reasons for not completing school, as well as their motivation in continuing to pursue positive academic goals. Likewise, students from low income families have been shown to greatly benefit from having an internal locus of control and higher levels of self esteem (Nowicki et al., 2004). Research has shown multiple determinants for dropping out of school and each student's trajectory may be different based on the student's personal and social circumstances. Once students have formally withdrawn from school, they face many challenges associated with the adult world of work and survival.

CONSEQUENCES OF DROPPING OUT

As emphasized in reports on Project Head Start, students identified as at-risk who receive early intervention seem to escape the negative life paths associated with dropping out of school. Some of the most noted consequences of being a high school drop out are lower economic status, higher rates of delinquency, greater reliance on government sponsored programs, higher rates of criminality (75% of inmates are high school dropouts), lost local and state tax revenues, four times higher unemployment rates, lower self-esteem (Edmonson & White, 1998), increased drug use (Dynarksi & Gleason, 2002), and higher incidence of mental health problems (Brewster & Bowen, 2004). Given the gravity of these negative life outcomes, the need for intervention and prevention programs is obvious.

SUCCESSFUL INTERVENTIONS

Many dropout programs promote academic success, improved self-esteem, psychosocial skill development, mentoring, adult behavior management training, and increased student participation in school activities. Other program initiatives focus on creating more intimate environments and helping students to overcome personal, family, and social barriers (Cassidy & Bates, 2005; Dynarski & Gleason, 2002; Prevatt & Kelly, 2003). Overall, dropout prevention/intervention programs that take a multifaceted approach appear to be the most effective in helping at-risk students complete their high school education. According to Christenson and Thurlow, successful interventions typically first address students' personal-affective needs and then address their academic needs. They also stress supportive connections between the students and their families and the teachers and student peers.

IMPLICATIONS FOR TEACHERS

Understanding both individual and environmental factors that cause students to drop out can help teachers break the negative processes that can lead to students disengaging from school and eventually withdrawing altogether. Across intervention programs, teachers who are perceived as creating caring, respectful, and relevant educational environments and experiences are the ones who tend to facilitate academic resiliency, giving students the chance at more adaptive life outcomes after high school graduation.

SEE ALSO *At-risk Students; Bronfenbrenner, Urie; Stereotype Threat.*

BIBLIOGRAPHY

Anderman, E. M., Maehr, M. L., & Midgley, C. (1999). Declining motivation after the transition to middle school: Schools can make a difference. *Journal of Research and Development in Education, 32,* 131–147.

Anderson, S., Kerr-Roubicek, H., & Rowling, L. (2006). Staff voices: What helps students with high mental health support needs connect to school? *Australian Journal of Guidance & Counseling, 16,* 1–13.

Christenson, S., & Thurlow, M. L. (2004). School Dropouts: Prevention considerations, interventions, and challenges. *Current Directions in Psychological Science, 13,* 36–39.

Doll, B., & Hess, R. S. (2001). Through a new lens: Contemporary psychological perspectives on school completion and dropping out of high school. *School Psychology Quarterly, 16,* 351–356.

Dynarski, M., & Gleason, P. (2002). How can we help? What we have learned from recent federal dropout prevention evaluations. *Journal of Education for Students Placed at Risk, 7,* 43–69.

Finn, J. D. (1989). Withdrawing from school. *Review of Educational Research, 59,* 117–142.

Freeman, T. M., Leonard, L. M., & Lipari, J. (2007). The social contextual nature of resiliency in schools: Organizational structures that facilitate positive school climate. In D. Davis (Ed.), *Resiliency Reconsidered: Deconstructing the Policy Implications of the Resiliency Movement* (pp. 15–30). Greenwich, CT: Information Age.

Gallagher, C. J. (2002). Stories from the strays: What dropouts can teach us about school. *American Secondary Education, 30,* 36–60.

Nowicki, S., Duke, M. P., Sisney, S., Stricker, B., & Tyler, M. A. (2004). Reducing the dropout rates of at-risk high school students: The effective learning program (ELP). *Genetic, Social, and General Psychology Monographs, 130* (3), 225–239.

Osborne, J. W., & Walker, C. (2006). Stereotype threat, identification with academics, and withdrawal from school: Why the most successful students of colour might be most likely to withdraw. *Educational Psychology, 26,* 563–577.

Stearns, E., Moller, S., Blau, J., & Potochnick, S. (2007). Staying back and dropping out: The relationship between grade retention and school dropout. *Sociology of Education, 80,* 210–240.

Steele, C. M. (1992). Race and the schooling of black Americans. *Atlantic Monthly, 269,* 68–78.

Suh, S., Suh, J., & Houston, I. (2007). Predictors of categorical at-risk high school dropouts. *Journal of Counseling and Development, 85,* 196–203.

Warren, J. R., & Halpern-Manners, A. (2007). Is the glass emptying or filling up? Reconciling divergent trends in high school completion and dropout. *Educational Researcher, 36,* 335–343.

Whelage, G. G. (1989). Dropping out: Can schools be expected to prevent it? In L. Weis, E. Farrar, & H. Petrie (Eds.), *Dropouts from school.* Albany: State University of New York Press.

Tierra M. Freeman
Makini L. King
Rachel B. Kirkpatrick

DUAL CODING THEORY

Dual coding theory is a general theory of cognition and mind. It originated in the 1960s to explain the powerful effects that mental imagery has on memory, and it has been extended since to account for increasingly more mental phenomena. Dual coding theory has inspired much research and debate in psychology, and it has played a major role in stimulating a modern resurgence of interest in mental imagery and its role in mind. It has been described as "one of the most influential theories of cognition this century" (Marks, 1997). It has been directly applied to education in several fields. The major volumes that detail the theory, its extensions, and its empirical base are Paivio (1971, 1986, 1991, 2007), Paivio and Begg (1981), and Sadoski and Paivio (2001).

Dual coding theory is sometimes referred to as a theory of mental imagery, particularly visual imagery. However, the theory is more than that. From an historical perspective, it is the first systematic, scientific attempt to bridge two traditions in philosophy and psychology: the imagery tradition and the verbal tradition. The imagery tradition can be traced to the emphasis on concrete experience and thought in Aristotle, the Renaissance educators' slogan of "things not words," the pragmatism of George Herbert Mead and John Dewey, and aspects of the cognitive revolution in modern psychology. The verbal tradition emphasized the abstract and can be traced to the idealist philosophy of Plato, Peter Ramus's epitome of linear verbal organization, Immanuel Kant's transcendental idealism, and the exclusive emphasis on language in behaviorist psychology. The historical tension between these traditions is recounted in Yates (1966), Carruthers (1993), Paivio (1971, 2007), and Sadoski and Paivio (2001). The implications of bridging these two traditions are far reaching but remain controversial in the early 2000s.

BASIC PRINCIPLES OF DUAL CODING THEORY

The core ideas of dual coding theory can be stated succinctly: The theory assumes that cognition involves the activity of two qualitatively different mental codes, a verbal code specialized for dealing with language in all its forms and a nonverbal code specialized for dealing with nonlinguistic objects and events in the form of mental images. These coding systems are separate but interconnected so that they can operate independently, in parallel, or through their interconnections. The linguistic, or verbal, code dominates in some tasks, the nonverbal code dominates in others, and both systems are frequently used together. The great diversity and flexibility of cognition all comes from activity within and between these codes. No deeper, abstract code is assumed.

Dual coding theory is based on the common assumption of a continuity between perception and memory. External experiences occur through the stimulation of people's senses and are encoded in memory traces that retain some of their original, concrete qualities as words and things. The theory is, therefore, multimodal because both verbal and nonverbal experiences can occur in different sense modalities, including vision, hearing, and touch (Braille) in the case of language, and all five senses in the case of mental images. Theories of working memory that propose different, modality-specific memory stores are generally consistent with dual coding theory. For example, the working memory theory of Baddeley and Hitch (1974) proposes a phonological loop for rehearsing inner speech and a visuospatial sketchpad for manipulating visual images. Dual coding theory assumes that long-term memory is modality specific as well.

Dual coding theory also assumes innate contributions to cognition and individual differences because all human nature is the product of the interaction of genes and the environment. More layers of complexity are built on these basic assumptions, including accounts of meaning, memory, knowledge organization, and learning. One direct implication of the theory is that pictures or concrete language (e.g., juicy hamburger) should be understood and recalled better than abstract language (e.g., basic assumption), a consistent research finding.

APPLICATIONS AND EXTENSIONS OF DUAL CODING THEORY

Perhaps the most productive application of dual coding theory has been to literacy. The theory offers empirically supported accounts of all aspects of literacy, including decoding, comprehension, and response in reading (Sadoski & Paivio, 1994, 2001, 2004, 2007), written composition (Sadoski & Paivio, 2001), and spelling (Sadoski, Willson, Holcomb, & Boulware-Gooden, 2005). A large-scale instructional program to improve reading comprehension by teaching students to visualize while reading text was successfully applied in urban schools (Sadoski & Willson, 2006). Another application used kinesthetic imagery in teaching reading comprehension strategies such as how to locate the main idea (Block, Paris, & Whiteley, in press). An extensive review of applications to literacy is found in Sadoski and Paivio (2001, Chapter 8). A review of applications to other aspects of education is found in Clark and Paivio (1991).

The use of mental imagery and language in learning psychomotor skills also has been extensively studied. The procedure typically takes the form of guided relaxation followed by mentally imagining physical acts in detail from a verbally presented description. Two meta-analyses of experimental studies found substantial overall effects (Feltz & Landers, 1983; Driskell, Copper, & Moran, 1994). Studies employing heavily cognitive tasks (touching intersections on a grid) had larger effects than more purely motor tasks (tennis shot) or strength tasks (bench press). These techniques have been used to teach medical students to draw blood and perform basic surgery (Sadoski & Sanders, in press).

The most ambitious extension of dual coding theory is its explanation of the evolution of mind (Paivio, 2007). In this view, hominid intelligence evolved from a primeval nonverbal base into a more recent period that incorporated language. Verbal and nonverbal thought have been synergistically bound since. Mental images from memory represented perceptually absent events whether past, present, future, possible, or impossible. In turn, language provided an increasingly sophisticated system of signs for efficient thought and communication between and within our human ancestors. This combination of imagination and language is seen as the evolutionary power source of all human progress (cf. Bronowski, 1978).

CHALLENGES AND CONTROVERSIES

Dual coding theory can be contrasted with theories which assume that all cognition has a common, abstract code in the form of schemata or propositions (Sadoski, Paivio, & Goetz, 1991). This mentalese is assumed to be computational in nature, built into the brain like a computer's built-in machine code (Pylyshyn, 2003). Proponents believe that this conception is more elegant and parsimonious than dual coding theory, and some aspects of cognition have been modeled in computers to a degree (Seidenberg, 2005). However, Paivio (2007) responded that such theories lack elegance because of the complexity of their programming, and they cannot account for findings involving mental imagery, concreteness effects, and neuropsychological evidence. These debates remain unresolved and challenging.

SEE ALSO *Memory; Providing Explanations.*

BIBLIOGRAPHY

Baddeley A. D., & Hitch, G. J. (1974). Working memory. In G. A. Bower (Ed.), *The psychology of learning and motivation* (pp. 47–89). New York: Academic Press.

Block, C. C., Parris, S. R., & Whiteley, C. (in press). CPMs: Helping primary grade students self-initiate comprehension processes through kinesthetic instruction. *Reading Teacher.*

Bronowski, J. (1978). *The origins of knowledge and imagination.* New Haven, CT: Yale University Press.

Carruthers, Mary J (1993). *The book of memory: A study of memory in medieval culture.* New York: Cambridge University Press.

Clark, J. M., & Paivio, A. (1991). Dual coding theory and education. *Educational Psychology Review, 3,* 149–210.

Driskell, J. E., Copper, C., & Moran, A. (1994). Does mental practice enhance performance? *Journal of Applied Psychology, 79,* 481–492.

Feltz, D. L., & Landers, D. M. (1983). The effects of mental practice on motor skill learning and performance: A meta-analysis. *Journal of Sport Psychology, 5,* 25–57.

Marks, D. F. (1997). Paivio, Allan Urho. In N. Sheehy, A. J. Chapman, & W. A. Conroy (Eds.), *Biographical Dictionary of Psychology* (pp. 432–434). New York: Routledge.

Paivio, A. (1971). *Imagery and verbal processes.* New York: Holt, Rinehart, and Winston.

Paivio, A. (1986). *Mental Representations: A Dual Coding Approach.* New York: Oxford University Press.

Paivio, A. (1991). *Images in mind: The evolution of a theory.* Sussex, U.K.: Harvester Wheatsheaf.

Paivio, A. (2007). *Mind and its evolution: A dual coding theoretical approach.* Mahwah, NJ: Erlbaum.

Paivio, A., & Begg, I. (1981). *The psychology of language.* Englewood Cliffs, NJ: Prentice-Hall.

Pylyshyn, Z. (2003). *Seeing and visualizing: It's not what you think.* Cambridge, MA: MIT Press.

Sadoski, M., & Paivio, A. (1994). A dual coding view of imagery and verbal processes. In R. R. Ruddell & M. R. Ruddell (Eds.), *Theoretical models and processes of reading* (4th ed.), pp. 582–601. Newark, DE: International Reading Association.

Sadoski, M., & Paivio, A. (2001). *Imagery and text: A dual coding theory of reading and writing.* Mahwah, NJ: Erlbaum.

Sadoski, M., & Paivio, A. (2004). A dual coding theoretical model of reading. In R. R. Ruddell & N. J. Unrau, (Eds.), *Theoretical models and processes of reading* (5th ed.), pp. 1329–1362. Newark, DE: International Reading Association.

Sadoski, M., & Paivio, A. (2007) Toward a unified theory of reading. *Scientific Studies of Reading, 11,* 337–356.

Sadoski, M., Paivio, A., & Goetz, E. T. (1991). A critique of schema theory in reading and a dual coding alternative. *Reading Research Quarterly, 26,* 463–484.

Sadoski, M., & Sanders, C. W. (in press). Mental imagery in clinical skills instruction: A promising solution to a critical problem. *Annals of Behavioral Science and Medical Education.*

Sadoski, M., & Willson, V. L. (2006). Effects of a theoretically based large-scale reading intervention in a multicultural urban school district. *American Educational Research Journal, 43,* 137–154.

Sadoski, M., Willson, V. L., Holcomb, A., & Boulware-Gooden, R. (2005). Verbal and nonverbal predictors of spelling performance. *Journal of Literacy Research, 36,* 461–478.

Seidenberg, M. S. (2005). Connectionist models of word reading. *Current Directions in Psychological Science, 14,* 238–242.

Yates, F. A. (1966). *The art of memory.* London: Routledge and Kegan Paul.

Mark C. Sadoski

DWECK, CAROL S(USAN)
1946–

Carol Susan Dweck is a leading expert on achievement motivation. She has investigated variables that impact individuals' adaptive versus maladaptive responses to academic challenges. Dweck received her BA from Barnard College, Columbia University in 1967, graduating magna cum laude with honors in psychology. She continued her education at Yale University, where she was a National Science Foundation Fellow (1967–1971) and earned a PhD in psychology in 1972. Dweck began her academic career in the Department of Psychology at the University of Illinois at Urbana-Champaign, first as an assistant professor (1972–1977) and then as an associate professor (1977–1981), and returned there later as a professor (1985–1989). From 1981 to 1985 she was a professor at Harvard University in the Laboratory for Human Development. From 1989 to 2004 she was on the faculty of Columbia University, where she was the William B. Ransford Professor of Psychology. Since 2004 Dweck has been the Lewis and Virginia Eaton Professor of Psychology at Stanford University.

ACHIEVEMENT MOTIVATION PATTERNS

Based on extensive research, Dweck has identified two major achievement motivation patterns. In each, individuals' implicit theory of intelligence (i.e., their beliefs about the nature of intelligence), goal orientation, and response to academic challenges are associated. Those with an entity theory view their intelligence as a fixed trait that cannot be developed. They tend to endorse performance goals that focus on obtaining a positive evaluation of their ability and avoiding a negative evaluation. When they experience failure they typically show a helpless response characterized by blaming failure on lack of ability, decreasing the sophistication of problem solving strategies, abandoning the task completely, and displaying negative emotion. In contrast, those with an incremental theory view their intelligence as a malleable quality with potential to be developed. They pursue learning goals that focus on increasing their skills. When faced with a challenge they demonstrate a mastery-oriented response that includes blaming failure on lack of effort, increasing the sophistication of problem-solving strategies, and displaying positive emotion. Notably, these motivation patterns impact responses to academic challenge regardless of individuals' intellectual ability (e.g., those with either low or high ability may show helplessness).

RELATIONS OF ACHIEVEMENT MOTIVATION PATTERNS TO ACADEMIC PERFORMANCE AND EDUCATIONAL PRACTICE

Research has indicated that beginning in junior high school, when academic challenges increase, achievement motivation patterns are related to student outcomes. For example, seventh grade students who endorsed an incremental theory earned higher grades in math over the next two years than students with an entity theory, even when controlling for prior achievement (Blackwell, Trzesniewski, & Dweck, 2007). College students' endorsement of learning goals positively predicted their grade in a chemistry course, as well as grade improvement across the semester (Grant & Dweck, 2003).

Dweck (2007) provides a motivation-based explanation for gender differences in math and science achievement. Girls, particularly bright girls, are especially vulnerable to a loss of confidence and helpless behavior when they encounter confusing material (Licht & Dweck, 1984). Given that math and science typically involve new concepts and skills that may cause confusion, girls' greater likelihood for maladaptive responses to such challenges may contribute to their poorer achievement in these areas.

Dweck's findings have important applications for educational practice. To promote adaptive student functioning, the classroom climate should encourage incremental

theories, learning goals, and effort-based attributions. In an intervention study, Blackwell, Trzesniewski, and Dweck (2007) taught seventh grade students that intelligence is malleable and can be developed. The intervention group exhibited stable performance in math, whereas the control group showed a steady decline. These results suggest that promoting an incremental theory generated greater motivation in the classroom. Emphasizing learning goals (and minimizing a focus on performance goals) is also a strategy for increasing mastery-oriented behavior (Elliott & Dweck, 1988). Another effective approach involves teaching students to attribute their failures to lack of effort rather than lack of ability. Effort attributers are more persistent when challenged (Dweck, 1975). Finally, although teachers frequently use praise to encourage achievement, Mueller and Dweck (1998) have shown that focusing praise on students' ability tends to have negative consequences for motivation. Specifically, those praised for their intelligence tend to care more about performance goals and show more helpless responding when challenged. Thus, educators should be careful to direct praise to students' efforts. This ultimately encourages students to value learning opportunities and persistence.

Throughout her career, Dweck has collaborated with dozens of graduate students and post-doctoral fellows.

SEE ALSO *Achievement Motivation; Goal Orientation Theory; Theories of Intelligence.*

BIBLIOGRAPHY

WORKS BY

Blackwell, L. S., Trzesniewski, K. H., & Dweck, C. S. (2007). Implicit theories of intelligence predict achievement across an adolescent transition: A longitudinal study and an intervention. *Child Development, 78*, 246–263.

Dweck, C. S. (1975). The role of expectations and attributions in the alleviation of learned helplessness. *Journal of Personality and Social Psychology, 31*, 674–685.

Dweck, C. S. (1999). *Self-theories: Their role in motivation, personality, and development.* New York: Psychology Press.

Dweck, C. S. (2006). *Mindset: The new psychology of success.* New York: Random House.

Dweck, C. S. (2007). Is math a gift? Beliefs that put females at risk. In S. J. Ceci & W. M. Williams (Eds.), *Why aren't more women in science: Top researchers debate the evidence* (pp. 47–56). Washington, DC: American Psychological Association.

Dweck, C. S., & Leggett, E. L. (1988). A social-cognitive approach to motivation and personality. *Psychological Review, 95*, 256–273.

Elliott, E. S., & Dweck, C. S. (1988). Goals: An approach to motivation and achievement. *Journal of Personality and Social Psychology, 54*, 5–12.

Elliott, E. S., & Dweck, C. S. (Eds.). (2005). *Handbook of competence and motivation.* New York: Guilford Press.

Grant, H., & Dweck, C. S. (2003). Clarifying achievement goals and their impact. *Journal of Personality and Social Psychology, 85,* 541–553.

Heckhausen, J. & Dweck, C. S. (Eds.). (1998). *Motivation and self-regulation across the life span.* New York: Cambridge University Press.

Licht, B. G., & Dweck, C. S. (1984). Determinants of academic achievement: The interaction of children's achievement orientations with skill area. *Developmental Psychology, 20,* 628–636.

Mueller, C. M., & Dweck, C. S. (1998). Praise for intelligence can undermine children's motivation and performance. *Journal of Personality and Social Psychology, 75,* 33–52.

Cynthia A. Erdley

DYNAMIC ASSESSMENT

A procedure that attempts to modify performance, via examiner assistance, in an effort to understand learning potential, is called dynamic assessment (DA). Dynamic assessment determines whether substantive changes occur in examinee behavior if feedback is provided across an array of increasingly complex or challenging tasks. This procedure contrasts with traditional models of assessment in which there is no feedback from the examiner on student performance.

GOALS

Several authors suggest that traditional intelligence or aptitude tests (i.e., tests that measure unassisted performance on global measures of academic aptitude) underestimate general ability. That is, traditional approaches to the assessment of aptitude typically provide little feedback or practice prior to testing; therefore, performance on such measures often reflects the individual's misunderstanding of instructions more than his ability to perform the task. One possible alternative or supplement to traditional assessment is to measure an individual's performance when given examiner assistance. The goals of DA are to (a) provide a better estimate of ability, (b) measure new abilities, and (c) improve mental efficiency when compared to static testing procedures (see Embretson, 1987).

DIFFERENT MODELS

Models or variations of DA include learning potential assessment (e.g., Budoff, 1987a), testing-the-limits (Carlson & Wiedl, 1979; Swanson, 1995a), mediated assessment (e.g., Feuerstein, 1980), and assisted learning and transfer (e.g., Bransford, Delclos, Vye, Burns, & Hasselbring, 1987; Campione, Brown, Ferrara, Jones, & Steinberg, 1985). Although DA is a term used to characterize a number of distinct approaches, two common features of this approach are to determine the learner's potential for

change when given assistance and to provide a prospective measure of performance change independent of assistance. Unlike traditional testing procedures, score changes due to examiner intervention are not viewed as threatening task validity. In fact, some authors argue that construct validity increases (e.g., Budoff, 1987b; Carlson & Wiedl, 1979). To obtain information about an individual's responsiveness to hints or probes, DA approaches require the interaction of an examiner and the examinee. When a student is having difficulty, the examiner attempts to move the student from failure to success by modifying the format, providing more trials, providing information on successful strategies, or offering increasingly more direct cues, hints, or prompts. The intensity of the intervention ranges from several sessions to brief intensive prompts in one session. Thus, potential for learning new information (or accessing previously presented information) is measured in terms of the distance, difference between, and/or change from unassisted performance to a performance level with assistance.

TYPE OF MEASURES

A major goal of dynamic assessment models is to measure modifiability (Embretson, 1987; Grigorenko & Sternberg, 1998; Swanson & Lussier, 2001). A major issue is the type of scores necessary to measure modifiability (see Embretson, 1987 for a review). For example, Campione and Brown (1987) measured modifiability as the number of hints needed to solve a problem that has been failed. The fewer the hints, the more modifiability the examinee possesses. Embretson (1987) has suggested that this score merely provides a better estimate of initial ability (see p. 149). Another method to measure modifiability is to bring scores to an asymptotic level (under the probing conditions) and then obtain a measure on the test again after the probes have been removed. The basic rationale is to eliminate performance differences due to different strategies or unfamiliarity with the laboratory procedures. As yet, there is no agreed upon measure of cognitive modifiability (Grigorenko & Sternberg, 1998; Swanson & Lussier, 2001)

Several authors consider the first area of focus in DA, however, to be one of improving the processing of information. For example, utilizing Vygotsky's (1978) "zone of proximal development," Brown and French (1979) make a distinction between an individual's proximal potential and actual level of performance. In the area of child development, for example, they make a distinction between a child's actual development, that is, her completed development as might be measured on a standardized test, and her level of potential development, the degree of competence she can achieve with aid.

An assessment of the examinee's "zone of potential" (i.e., ability to access available information) typically involves three steps (see Swanson, 1995a, 1995b, for a review). First, the examinee is administered a battery of items on a particular test. Second, if the examinee fails to retrieve the item information, the examiner provides a series of progressive probes based upon the information that was forgotten. The number of probes or hints necessary to achieve maximal performance is considered the width of the individual's zone of potential. Third, the items at which the examinee achieved the highest level of performance are readministered at a later point in time. This maintenance activity is important in assessment because it reflects the examinee's ability to benefit from the aids or probes provided by the examiner. The ability of the examinee to maintain behavior provides valuable assessment information about the potency of the aids that help the examinee access information.

LIMITATIONS

Although DA has been suggested as an alternative and/or supplement to traditional assessment, only a few critical reviews of such procedures have been published (e.g., Grigorenko & Sternberg, 1998; Swanson & Lussier, 2001). A comprehensive review of DA procedures as of 2007 was the qualitative analysis conducted by Grigorenko and Sternberg (1998). Their study reviewed the strengths and weaknesses of five different dynamic testing models: Feuerstein and colleagues' model of structural cognitive modifiability (e.g., Feuerstein, Miller, Hoffman, Rand, Mintzker, & Jensen, 1981; Feuerstein & Schur, 1997), Budoff's learning potential testing model (1987a, 1987b), Campione and Brown's transfer model (Campione, 1989, Campione & Brown, 1987), Carlson's testing-the-limits model (Campbell & Carlson, 1995; Carlson & Wiedl, 1979), and an information processing framework as conceptualized by the Swanson Cognitive Processing Test (S-CPT, Swanson, 1995a, 1995b).

Their review questioned whether DA increased the comparability of performance among students from differing backgrounds and handicapping conditions when compared to static (traditional) conditions. That is, when compared with static measures, DA has not been shown to equate the performance among children with differing learning abilities (i.e., level the playing field). In addition, Grigorenko and Sternberg (1998) suggested that cognitive modifiability (a psychological construct frequently referred to in DA literature) has not been shown to be independent of initial learning ability. Likewise, their review questions whether changes in mental processing come about because of DA or merely reflect artifacts related to retesting. That is, they argue that approximately 30% of children improve to a statistically significant extent simply because of retesting (see p. 104). Thus, changes in performance may be unrelated to DA procedures.

Swanson and Lussier (2001) used meta-analytic techniques to address some of the issues raised in Grigorenko and Sternberg's (1998) qualitative review. Their results provide a metric to compare the magnitude of the differences between DA and other approaches. Higher effect sizes are considered better than lower effect sizes. Swanson and Lussier's analysis showed that effect sizes (ES) when using DA procedures varied significantly as a function of ability group (under achievers yielded higher and children with learning disabilities yielded lower ESs than average, hearing impaired, and mentally retarded participants), chronological age (younger yield higher ESs than older ages), sample size (studies with moderate sample sizes yield larger ESs than studies with small or large sample sizes), and type of assessment procedure (testing the limits yielded larger ESs than mediated assessment). The magnitude of the ES was best predicted by the type of outcomes measure (ESs are higher on visual-spatial than verbal measures).

EDUCATIONAL APPLICATIONS

DA has direct application to the context of classroom assessment and instruction. Measuring responsiveness of an individual's performance to feedback has long been viewed as an alternative to traditional (static) ability assessment. Dynamic assessment has been suggested to teachers as a means to enhance children's performance and tap potential which might otherwise be undiscovered by traditional static approaches. For example, children with identical performance on static tests may profit differentially from feedback. An example is that children with learning problems but with the same aptitude as average achieving children may need more feedback to improve their performance than average achievers.

SEE ALSO *Classroom Assessment; High Stakes Testing; Meta-Analysis; Scaffolding; Standardized Testing.*

BIBLIOGRAPHY

Bransford, J. C., Delclos, J. R., Vye., N.J., Burns, M., & Hasselbring, T. S. (1987). State of the art and future directions. In C. S. Lidz (Ed.), *Dynamic assessment: An interactional approach to evaluating learning potential* (pp. 479–496). New York: Guilford Press.

Brown, A., & French, L. (1979). The zone of proximal development: Implications for intelligence in the year 2000. *Intelligence, 11,* 61–75.

Budoff, M. (1987a). Measures for assessing learning potential. In C. S. Lidz (Ed.), *Dynamic Testing* (pp. 173–195). New York: Guildford Press.

Budoff, M. (1987b). The validity of learning potential. In C. S. Lidz (Ed.), *Dynamic Testing* (pp. 52–81). New York: Guildford Press.

Campbell, C., & Carlson, J. S. (1995). The dynamic assessment of mental abilities. In J.S. Carlson (Ed.), *Advances in*

Cognition and Educational Practice: Vol. 3, *European Contributions to Dynamic Assessment.* London: JAI Press.

Campione, J. C. (1989). Assisted assessment: A taxonomy of approaches and an outline of strengths and weaknesses. *Journal of Learning Disabilities, 22,* 151–165.

Campione, J. C., & Brown, A. L. (1987). Linking dynamic testing with school achievement. In C. S. Lidz (Ed.), *Dynamic Testing* (pp. 82–115). New York: Guilford Press.

Campione, J. C., Brown, A. L., Ferrara, R. A., Jones, R. S., & Steinberg, E. (1985). Breakdowns in the flexible use of information: Intelligence-related differences in transfer following equivalent learning performance. *Intelligence, 9,* 297–315.

Carlson, J. S., & Wiedl, K. H. (1979). Toward a differential testing approach: Testing the limits employing the Raven matrices. *Intelligence, 3,* 323–344.

Embretson, S. E. (1987). Toward development of a psychometric approach. In C. Lidz (Ed.), *Dynamic assessment: Foundations and fundamentals* (pp. 141–172). New York: Guilford.

Feuerstein, R. (1980). *Instrumental enrichment: An intervention program for cognitive modifiability.* Baltimore, MD: University Park Press.

Feuerstein, R., Miller, R., Hoffman, M. B., Rand, Y., Mintzker, Y., & Jensen, M. R. (1981). Cognitive modifiability in adolescence: Cognitive structure and the effects of intervention. *Journal of Special Education, 15,* 269–287.

Feuerstein, R. & Schur, Y. (1997). Process as content in regular education and in particular in education of the low functioning retarded performer. In A. L. Costa & R. M. Liebmann (Eds.), *Envisioning process as content: Toward a renaissance curriculum.* Thousand Oaks, CA: Corwin Press.

Grigorenko, E. L., & Sternberg, R. J. (1998). Dynamic testing. *Psychological Bulletin, 124* (1), 75–111.

Swanson, H. L. (1995a). *Swanson-Cognitive Processing Test (S-CPT).* Austin, TX: Pro-Ed.

Swanson, H. L. (1995b). Using the Cognitive Processing Test to assess ability: Development of a dynamic measure. *School Psychology Review, 24,* 672–693.

Swanson, H. L., & Lussier, C. (2001). A selective synthesis of the experimental literature on dynamic assessment. *Review of Educational Research, 71,* 321–363.

Vygotsky, L. S. (1978). Interaction between learning and development. In M. Cole, V. John-Steiner, S. Scribner, & E. Souberman (Eds.), *Mind in society: The development of higher psychological processes* (pp. 79–91). Cambridge, MA: Harvard University Press (original work published 1935).

H. Lee Swanson

E

EARLY CHILDHOOD DEVELOPMENT

Early childhood development is defined as "a set of concepts, principles, and facts that explain, describe and account for the processes involved in change from immature to mature status and functioning" (Katz, 1996, p. 137). Development is generally divided into three broad categories: physical development, cognitive development, and social emotional development (Berk, 2000). Physical development addresses any change in the body, including how children grow, how they move, and how they perceive their environment. Cognitive development pertains to the mental processes (e.g., language, memory, problem solving) that children use to acquire and use knowledge. Emotional and social development addresses how children handle relationships with others, as well as understand of their own feelings.

Early childhood development is generally divided into three age categories (Bredekamp & Copple, 1997). The first age category includes infants and toddlers who are between the ages of birth and 3 years of age. According to Lally and colleagues (1997), the most important factor for young infants (birth to 8 months) is security with primary caregivers. Between the ages of 9 to 18 months, mobile infants are mostly concerned with exploration and between 18 and 36 months, the central focus of development is identity, and children become more independent. The second age category of early childhood development includes preschoolers who are 3 to 5 years of age. According to Bredecamp and Copple (1997), this period of development is characterized by rapid gross motor development (e.g., jumping, hopping, skipping),

refined movement of small muscles for object manipulation, major increases in vocabulary and use of language, abstract representation of mental constructs, and the development of relationships with other young children. The final category of early childhood development includes those children in the primary grades who are between 6 and 8 years of age. Bredekamp and Copple (1997) describe highlights in primary-aged children's development during this time: Gross and fine motor development is characterized by children's ability to perform controlled movements and sequence motor skills. Greater reasoning, problem solving, and assimilation also characterize children's cognitive development at this stage. During the primary years, children's vocabulary increases at a rapid pace. In addition, their written communication skills develop. Socially, primary-aged children begin to understand others' perspectives, are concerned with fairness, and monitor their own behavior.

INFLUENCES ON EARLY CHILDHOOD DEVELOPMENT

Practices for enhancing children's development are influenced most by child development theories. Berk defines a theory as "an orderly, integrated set of statements that describes, explains, and predicts behavior" (2000, p. 6). Generally speaking there are four broad theoretical perspectives that guide practice in early childhood development: behaviorism and social learning theory, cognitive-developmental theory, sociocultural theory, and ecological systems theory.

B. F. Skinner (1904–1990) is most noted for his theory of behaviorism or more specifically operant conditioning theory, which is based on the premise that children's behavior can be increased based on the presentation of reinforcers and decreased through punishment (Berk, 2000). Social learning theory, created by Albert Bandura (b. 1925), expands on operant conditioning by adding the idea that imitation or observational learning increases the chances that children will learn new behaviors. Generally speaking, behaviorists believe that children's development is outside of their own influence, that it is shaped by environmental stimuli (Daniels & Shumow, 2003).

Jean Piaget (1896–1980) is credited with the cognitive-developmental theory that "views the child as actively constructing knowledge and cognitive development as taking place in stages" (Berk, 2000, p. 21). According to his constructivist theory, Piaget asserted that children pass through four distinct stages of development, including the sensorimotor stage (birth to 2 years), preoperational stage (2 to 7 years), concrete operational stage (7 to 11), and formal operational stage (11 and beyond). Piaget believed that reasoning deepens in children as they grow, engagement in the physical and social world enhances development, and "conceptual change occurs through assimilation and accommodation" (Daniels & Shumow, 2003, p. 497).

Lev Vygotsky (1896–1934) saw child development as a kind of social constructivism, in which development is determined by culture. According to Berk and Winsler (1995) there are a number of tenets that are unique to social constructivism. First, because children's culture influences the activities, language, and education to which children are exposed, these variables affect children's development. Second, while some development is innate or influenced by biology, higher level development is affected by culture. Finally, the theory incorporates the zone of proximal development, that is, the range in children's development between their ability to perform a task independently and their ability to perform a skill with the assistance of a more competent member of the their culture (adult or older child).

The ecological systems theory was originated by Urie Bronfenbrenner (1917–2005) who believed that children developed "within a complex system of relationships affected by multiple levels of the environment" (Berk, 2000, p. 26). Bronfenbrenner described four systems that influence child development. The microsystem involves those that are part of children's most immediate environment, including the child's parents and other primary caregivers. Interactions between the child and those adults impact children's development. The second system is the mesosystem and involves systems that interact with the people in the microsystem, including child care programs and schools. Exosystems are places in which children do

not spend time but which still impact children's development, including the parents' workplace policies. Finally, the macrosystem consists of "the values, laws, customs, and resources of a particular culture" (Berk, 2000, page 29). For example a culture's beliefs about the importance of high quality childcare impact children's development.

Child development theories generally guide teaching practices of children from birth to 8 years of age. Daniels and Shumow (2003) describe differences in instructional practices based on theoretical orientation. Teachers who espouse behaviorist theory generally follow more teacher-directed instructional practices, including didactic instruction with emphasis on acquisition of basic skills. Other child development theories emphasize child-centered practices. Teachers who support the constructivist theory provide child-choice, guided discovery, and cooperative learning. They emphasize critical thinking, problem solving, and intrinsic motivation. Social constructivists build their practices around a community of learners, instructional conversation, and authentic tasks, and emphasize cultural literacy, collaboration, and metacognition. Teachers emphasizing the ecological systems theory in their classrooms stress parent and community involvement, out-of-school activities, and cultural instruction. They teach social cognition, cultural awareness, and adaptive habits of coping.

PRACTICES

Many early childhood development experts believe that knowledge of child development theory should guide educational practices of children from birth to 8 years of age (Katz, 1996). Katz questions "if we do not know enough about the relationship between early experience and the ultimate competencies necessary for effective participation in democratic processes, how can we design effective educational practice?" (1996, p. 141). Theories are useful in helping researchers and teachers guide their observations (Stott & Bowman, 1996). It is from this point of view that practices for supporting the development of children from birth to 8 years of age originate. Developmentally appropriate practices are a set of standards for providing high quality early care and education experiences (Goldstein, 1997) to children, birth to 8, which are based on knowledge about "how children develop and learn" (Bredekamp & Copple, 1997, p. 9).

The National Association for the Education of Young Children (NAEYC) describes specific educational practices to which those working with young children should adhere (Bredekamp & Copple, 1997). These include: a) creating a caring community of learners; b) teaching to enhance development and learning; c) creating appropriate curriculum; d) assessing children's learning and development; and e) establishing relationships with families. Detailed information about the application of these practices to specific age groups can be found in Bredekamp and Copple (1997). The following section provides an overview of each of these practices, empirical support for the practice, and some challenges educators face in implementing the practice in the current educational context.

Creating a Caring Community of Learners. The community in which children spend time involves both the physical and social environment and their influence impact children's development. Specific variables in early care and education settings that influence how children grow and learn include low staff/child ratios, positive social interactions between children and between children and adults, appropriate classroom arrangements, and safe and healthy practices. According to Kontos and colleagues (2002), there is evidence that the presence of these specific variables in early care and education settings are "those where children are more likely to thrive, as determined by their attachment to the teacher, their peer relations, and their verbal ability" (p. 240).

Measures are available that evaluate the physical and social environments in which children to birth to 8 spend time (i.e., Infant/Toddler Environmental Rating Scale - Revised–Birth to 3; Early Childhood Environmental Rating Scale - Revised–preschool; and Assessment of Practices in Early Elementary Classrooms–primary). Evidence of studies that have examined the community of learners has found disturbing results in some cases. In a study of Kentucky's early care and education system, Grisham-Brown and colleagues (2005) found that young children from low social-economic backgrounds and those of minority status were more likely to participate in low quality early care and education programs than their counterparts. Similarly, a study of primary classrooms by Buchanan and colleagues (1998) found that those classrooms most likely to use developmentally inappropriate practices were those serving the largest number of children who receive free lunch. Incidentally, these same classrooms had larger class sizes than their counterparts who were engaged in developmentally appropriate practices.

Teaching to Enhance Development and Learning. Teaching practices for young children include opportunities for choice, hands-on learning, promotion of collaboration between children, use of a variety of teaching strategies, individualization, and self-regulation (Bredekamp & Copple, 1997; Buchanan et al., 1998). There is evidence that these practices support the development of young children. Kontos and colleagues (2002) found that preschool aged children experience more complex interactions with peers when engaged in creative activities than other types of activities (e.g., language arts or gross

motor). In Kontos, et al., the creative activities were those that were open ended without a finished product expected. McCormick and colleagues (2003) evaluated the 25 top-performing primary programs in Kentucky and found that one variable that differentiated those classrooms from the lowest performing classrooms was the provision of choice in selection of materials and activities. This study supports that the use of developmentally appropriate practices in primary classrooms positively impacts child outcomes.

A challenge in defining developmentally appropriate teaching strategies has been the emphasis on child-centered approaches. Whereas child-centered approaches originate from constructivist theory, didactic or teacher-directed instruction originates from a behaviorist perspective (Stipek, 2004). Because of the theoretical orientation from which child-centered practices derive, some have viewed them as synonymous with developmentally appropriate practices. However, Bredekamp and Rosegrant (1995) indicate that developmentally appropriate teaching strategies, in fact, fall along a continuum from those that are non-directive (acknowledgement) to those that are directive (direct instruction). Stipek (2004) found that teachers serving large numbers of low achieving children were more likely to use direct instruction than child-centered instructional techniques. Grisham-Brown, Hemmeter, and Pretti-Frontczak (2005) argue that in blended programs where teachers encounter groups of children with wide ability levels, it is appropriate for teachers to employ the full continuum of teaching behaviors. This view is certainly in keeping with the ideas of response to intervention, as set forth by Pretti-Frontczak and colleagues (2008) whereby children's needs are addressed using more intentional, direct instruction. By using the full continuum of optional teaching strategies, those working with young children are, in fact, addressing the individualization ideas associated with developmentally appropriate practice.

Constructing Appropriate Curriculum. According to Pretti-Frontczak and colleagues (2007) there are four parts to a curriculum framework: 1) assessment for gathering information about children; 2) scope and sequence or the developmental/content areas that will be addressed; 3) activities and instruction or the contexts and strategies for teaching; and 4) progress monitoring or methods for determining success of the instruction. Bredekamp and Copple (1997) indicate that developmentally appropriate curricula should address all areas of the children's development and all content areas, bearing in mind the child's age and considering children's cultural, linguistic, and ability differences. Grisham-Brown and colleagues (2005) indicate that collaboration between educators, families, and other support personnel is essential for implementing a high quality curriculum for children in blended classrooms.

One key issue shaping curriculum design is the development of learning standards. Although states have had learning standards for K-12 programs since the early 1990s, early learning standards for children five and under were only developed in the mid-2000s (Scott-Little, Kagan, & Frelow, 2006). As of 2008, over 40 states and the District of Columbia have developed pre-kindergarten standards, many across all areas of development (Neuman & Roskos, 2005). The arrival of standards into programs serving children from birth to 8 years of age has challenged those who want to ensure the implementation of developmentally appropriate practices during a standards-based climate that emphasizes accountability. In the late 2000s, leading researchers in early childhood education were beginning to provide guidance for ensuring that the needs of young children are appropriately addressed within this context. Goldstein found in a qualitative study that kindergarten teachers could address content standards in a developmentally appropriate manner by "recognizing and building on the curricular stability in kindergarten, employing instructional approaches that accommodate the children's developmental needs, setting limits, acquiescing to demands for developmentally inappropriate practices and materials, engaging in proactive education and outreach, accepting additional responsibilities, and making concessions" (2007, p. 51). Grisham-Brown (2008) and Gronlund (2006) have proposed that curricula driven by early learning standards can be appropriate, if standards are addressed at different levels, depending on the needs of the children.

Assessing Children's Learning and Development. Specific guidelines are available regarding children's development. The National Association for the Education of Young Children (NAEYC) and the Division for Early Childhood (DEC) advocate the use of authentic assessment practices as the primary approach for assessing young children (Division for Early Childhood, 2007; National Association for the Education of Young Children and National Association of Early Childhood Specialists in State Departments of Education, 2003). Authentic assessment strategies involve documenting learning and development of children during real-life activities and routines by familiar adults (Losardo & Notari-Syverson, 2001; Neisworth & Bagnato, 2004). Research has shown that many teachers prefer authentic assessment approaches over more traditional assessment methods (Gao, 2007; McNair et al., 2003), and there are positive relationships between the use of authentic assessment practices, other classroom practices, and child outcomes (Bagnato, 2005; Meisels et al., 2003).

Appropriate assessment practices for young children have been compromised by the accountability climate in education in the early 2000s. Early childhood leaders have advocated the use of authentic assessment approaches for accountability purposes, indicating that these methods are more appropriate for young children (Meisels et al., 2003; Neisworth & Bagnato, 2004; Grisham-Brown, 2008). Emerging research shows that authentic assessment approaches, used for accountability purposes, can yield technically adequate assessment data (Grisham-Brown, Pretti-Frontczak, & Hallam, in press), thereby not compromising the results of high-stakes assessment.

Establishing Reciprocal Relationships with Families. Indicators of active family involvement in programs serving young children should involve collaboration and communication. Bredekamp and Copple (1997) indicate that programs should collaborate with families as they design early experiences for their children using two-way communication strategies. Unlike other practices in early childhood education, family involvement has been an enduring value that few have challenged (Hoover-Dempsey & Sandler, 1995) primarily because of the positive benefits on children's development. For example, family literacy practices have been positively linked to children's ability to read successfully (Gambrell & Mazzoni, 1999). Grisham-Brown and colleagues (2005) provide specific examples of how to involve families in child assessment, selection of children's priorities, and curriculum development.

The period of development between birth and 8 is unique in a child's life. Some have argued that there are critical periods of time by which children should learn specific skills, if they are to learn them (Shore, 1997). In one compelling article, Bailey argues that there should be a shift from emphasis on critical periods to critical experiences. Bailey questions: "What are the experiences that are absolutely necessary for all children to maximize school success, mental health, and social development?" (2002, p. 290). Clearly the practices that early childhood educators implement with children from birth to 8 have the greatest impact on child outcomes. Knowledge of those practices and the underlying theoretical orientation that supports them is essential in order for young children to receive "critical experiences."

BIBLIOGRAPHY

Bagnato, S. (2005). The authentic alternative for assessment in early intervention: An emerging evidence-based practice. *Journal of Early Intervention, 28*(1), 17–22.

Bayley, D. B. (2002). Are critical periods critical for early childhood education? The role of timing in early childhood pedagogy. *Early Childhood Research Quarterly, 17,* 281–294.

Berk, L. E. (2000). *Child development* (5th ed.). Needham Heights, MS: Allyn & Bacon.

Berk, L. E., & Winsler, A. (1995). *Scaffolding children's learning: Vygotsky and early childhood education.* Washington, DC: National Association for the Education of Young Children.

Bredekamp, S., & Copple, C. (Eds.) (1997). *Developmentally appropriate practice in early childhood programs* (Rev. ed.). Washington, DC: National Association for the Education of Young Children.

Bredekamp, S., & Rosegrant, T. (Eds.) (1995). *Reaching potentials: Transforming early childhood curriculum and assessment* (Vol. 2). Washington, DC: National Association for the Education of Young Children.

Buchanan, T. K., Burts, D. C., Bidner, J., White, V. F., & Charlesworth, R. (1998). Predictors of the developmentally appropriateness of the beliefs and practices of first, second, and third grade teachers. *Early Childhood Research Quarterly, 13,* 459–483.

Daniels, D. H., & Shumow, L. (2003). Child development and classroom teaching: A review of the literature and implications for educating teachers. *Applied Development Psychology, 23,* 495–526.

Division for Early Childhood. (2007). *Promoting positive outcomes for children with disabilities: recommendations for curriculum, assessment, and program evaluation.* Missoula, MT: Author.

Gambrell, L. B., & Mazzoni, S. A. (1999). Emergent literacy: What research reveals about learning to read. In C. Seefeldt (Ed.), *The early childhood curriculum: Current findings in theory and practice* (pp. 80–105). New York: Teachers College Press.

Gao, X. (2007). *Validity of an authentic assessment in order to report young children's accountability data on early language, literacy and pre-math areas.* Unpublished doctoral dissertation. University of Kentucky, Lexington, Kentucky.

Goldstein, L. S. (1997). Between a rock and a hard place in the primary grades: The challenge of providing developmentally appropriate early childhood education in an elementary school setting. *Early Childhood Research Quarterly, 12,* 3–27.

Goldstein, L. S. (2007). Beyond the DAP versus standards dilemma: Examining the unforgiving complexity of kindergarten teaching in the United States. *Early Childhood Research Quarterly, 22,* 39–54.

Grisham-Brown, J. (2008). Best practices in implementing standards in early childhood education. In A. Thomas & J. Grimes (Eds.), *Best practices in school psychology V* (pp. 1025–1042). Washington, D.C.: National Association of School Psychologists. Texas: Psychological.

Grisham-Brown, J., Cox, M., Barbee, A., & Antle, B. (2005). *KIDS NOW evaluation report.* Lexington: University of Kentucky and the Kentucky Department of Education.

Grisham-Brown, J. L., Hemmeter, M. L., & Pretti-Frontczak, K. (2005). *Blended Practices in Early Childhood Education.* Baltimore: Brookes.

Grisham-Brown, J. L., Pretti-Frontczak, K., & Hallam, R. (in press). Measuring child outcomes using authentic assessment practice. *Journal of Early Intervention.*

Gronlund, G., (2006). *Make early learning standards come alive: Connecting your practice and curriculum to state guidelines.* St. Paul, MN: Redleaf Press.

Hoover-Dempsey, K. V., & Sandler, H. W. (1995). Parental involvement in children's education: Why does it make a difference? *Teachers College Record, 97*(2), 310–331.

Katz, L. G. (1996). Child development knowledge and teacher preparation: Confronting assumptions. *Early Childhood Research Quarterly, 11,* 135–146.

Kontos, S., Burchinal, M., Howes, C., Wisseh, S., & Galinsky, E. (2002). An eco-behavioral approach to examining the contextual effects of early childhood classrooms. *Early Childhood Research Quarterly, 17,* 239–258.

Lally, J. R., Griffin, A., Fenichel, E., Segal, M., Szanton, E., & Weissbourd, B. (1997). Developmentally appropriate practice for infants and toddlers. In S. Bredekamp & C. Copple (Eds.), *Developmentally appropriate practice in early childhood programs* (Rev. ed., pp. 55–94). Washington, DC: National Association for the Education of Young Children.

Losardo, A., & Notari-Syverson, A. (2001). *Alternative approaches to assessing young children.* Baltimore: Brookes.

McCormick, K., Grisham-Brown, J., Nellis, L., Anderman, L., Privett, N., & Williams, A. (2003). *Characteristics and attributes of effective primary schools and classrooms.* Lexington: University of Kentucky and the Kentucky Department of Education.

McNair, S., Bhargava, A., Adams, L., Edgerton, S., & Kypros, B. (2003). Teachers speak out on assessment practices. *Early Childhood Education Journal, 31*(1), 23–32.

Meisels, S. J., Atkins-Burnett, S., Xue, Y., Bickel, D. D., & Son, S. (2003). Creating a system of accountability: The impact of instructional assessment on elementary children's achievement test scores. *Education Policy Analysis Archives, 11*(9), 1–18.

NAEYC and NAECS/SDE. (2003). *Early childhood curriculum, assessment, and program evaluation building an effective, accountable system in programs for children birth through age 8.* Retrieved April 21, 2008, from http://www.naeyc.org/about/positions/cape.asp.

Neisworth, J., & Bagnato, S. J., (2004). The mismeasure of young children: The authentic assessment alternative. *Infants and Young Children, 17,* 198–212.

Neuman, S. B., & Roskos, K. (2005). The state of state pre-kindergarten standards. *Early Childhood Research Quarterly, 20,* 125–145.

Pretti-Frontczak, K., Jackson, S., Goss, S. M., Grisham-Brown, J., Horn, E., Harjusola-Webb, S., et al. (2007). A curriculum framework that supports quality early childhood education for all young children. *Young Exceptional Monograph Series,* No.9, 16–28.

Pretti-Frontczak, K., Jackson, S., McKeen, L., & Bricker, D. (2008). Supporting quality curriculum frameworks in early childhood programs. In A. Thomas & J. Grimes (Eds.), *Best practices in school psychology V* (pp. 1249–1259). Washington, DC: National Association of School Psychologists. Texas: Psychological.

Scott-Little, C., Kagan, S. L., & Frelow, V. S. (2006). Conceptualization of readiness and the content of early learning standards: The intersection of policy and research? *Early Childhood Research Quarterly, 21,* 153–173.

Shore, R. (1997). *Rethinking the brain: New insights into early development.* New York: Families and Work Institute.

Stipek, D. (2004). Teaching practices in kindergarten and first grade: Different strokes for different folks. *Early Childhood Research Quarterly, 19,* 548–568.

Eccles, Jacquelynne S.

Stott, F. & Bowman, B. (1996). Child development knowledge; A slippery base for practice. *Early Childhood Research Quarterly, 11,* 169–183.

Jennifer Grisham-Brown

ECCLES, JACQUELYNNE S.
1944–

Jacquelynne S. Eccles (1944–) is one of the leading educational and developmental psychologists in the world. Her prolific scholarship has focused on gender-role socialization, social and motivational development in family and school contexts, and gender and ethnic identity development. Eccles received her bachelor's degree in social psychology from the University of California at Berkeley in 1966, and then taught in the Peace Corps in Ghana from 1966 to 1968. She received her Ph.D. in psychology from the University of California at Los Angeles in 1974. She was assistant professor of psychology at Smith College (1973–1976), and then moved to the University of Michigan, where she rose through the ranks to full professor between 1976 to 1988. She was professor of psychology at the University of Colorado-Boulder from 1988 to 1992, and then returned to Michigan. As of 2008, she is the McKeachie Collegiate Professor of Psychology at the University of Michigan. She has won numerous awards for her scholarship from major research societies.

Some of Eccles's research focuses on how children's self-beliefs and values are socialized at home and in school and how these beliefs and values predict young people's choices of activities to pursue and their performance in them. Another major purpose of this line of work is to investigate gender differences in choice and performance, with particular reference to gender differences in participation in math and science education and careers. Eccles and her colleagues, including Carol Kaczala, Judith Meece, Carol Midgley, and Allan Wigfield, developed the expectancy-value theoretical model of motivated choice and performance that provides the theoretical foundation for their work. This model has been highly influential in the field. They and other colleagues (including Pamela Davis-Kean, Constance Flanagan, and Janis Jacobs) have conducted several major longitudinal studies testing this model.

Major conclusions from this work include the following: 1) children's competence beliefs and expectancies for success are the strongest predictors of subsequent performance, and children's achievement values are the strongest predictor of achievement choice, even when previous performance is controlled; 2) gender differences in children's competence beliefs and values indicate that males have more positive beliefs and values for math and sports, and girls for English and music; 3) children's beliefs and values for different academic and non-academic activities decline across the school years, with some variation in the pattern of decline for boys and girls; and 4) parents' beliefs and stereotypes, and children's perceptions of them, predict children's own beliefs and values.

A second major area of research that builds on this work is Dr. Eccles's investigations of how school environments influence the development of children's competence-related beliefs and values for different activities and their identity development. She has collaborated in this work with Bonnie Barber, Carol Midgley, David Reuman, Rob Roeser, and Arnold Sameroff, among others. Eccles began this work with middle school students, making the compelling case that there is not a good fit between middle school students' developmental stage and the school environments they typically experience. At a time when children are maturing cognitively, desire to have more control over the activities they do, and enjoy interacting with others in learning and other environments, the kinds of school environments they encounter often provide fewer of these opportunities. Eccles initially documented this mismatch in a large scale study of Midwest middle schools. Her study showed that (compared to elementary school teachers) middle school teachers believe they are less effective in teaching their students, have less close relations with them, and provide fewer opportunities for student decision-making. She and her colleagues expanded this work to a large school district in the East that has a majority African American student population. As part of both studies Eccles and her colleagues examined the effects of puberty on teacher-child and parent-child relations. They also included measures of other important psychological factors, such as self-esteem, gender and racial identity, and indicators of psychological well-being and distress. Thus, they extended their expectancy-value model in important ways.

Much of Eccles's research has been longitudinal, and in two of her major studies she and her colleagues followed children into young adulthood. They used the most sophisticated data analytic tools available and were able to provide a clear picture of the development of children's beliefs and values. In a later work Eccles studied how the opportunity structures provided by parents and other socializers and children's involvement in extracurricular activities influence their development, both with respect to their performance and choice and their evolving identities.

SEE ALSO *Expectancy Value Motivational Theory.*

PSYCHOLOGY OF CLASSROOM LEARNING

BIBLIOGRAPHY

WORKS BY

Downey, G., Eccles, J. S. & Chatman, C. (2005). *Navigating the future: social identity, coping, and life tasks.* New York: Russell Sage.

Eccles (Parsons), J. et al. (1983). Expectancies, values and academic behaviors. In J. Spence (Ed.), *Achievement and achievement motives* (pp.75–146). San Francisco: W. H. Freeman.

Eccles, J. S. (1993). School and family effects on the ontogeny of children's interests, self-perceptions, and activity choice. In J. E. Jacobs (Ed.), *Nebraska Symposium on Motivation, 1992: Developmental perspectives on motivation* (pp. 145–208). Lincoln: University of Nebraska Press.

Eccles, J. S., Barber, B. L., Stone, M., & Hunt, J. (2003). Extracurricular activities and adolescent development. *Journal of Social Issues, 59,* 865–889.

Eccles, J. S., & Gootman, J. (2002). *Community Programs to Promote Youth Development.* Washington DC: National Academy Press.

Eccles, J. S., Wigfield, A., & Schiefele, U. (1998). Motivation. In W. Damon (Series Ed.) and N. Eisenberg (Volume Ed.), *Handbook of child psychology,* (Vol. 3, 5th ed., pp. 1017–1095). New York: Wiley.

Jacobs, J. E., Hyatt, S., Osgood, W. D., Eccles, J. S., & Wigfield, A. (2002). Changes in children's self-competence and values: Gender and domain differences across grades one through twelve. *Child Development, 73*(2), 509–527.

Mahoney, J. L., Larson, R. W., & Eccles, J. S. (2005). *Organized activities as contexts of development: extracurricular activities, after-school and community programs.* Mahwah, N.J.: Lawrence Erlbaum.

Wigfield, A. L., & Eccles, J. S. (2001). *Development of Achievement Motivation.* San Diego, CA: Academic Press.

Allan Wigfield

EGOCENTRISM

Egocentrism, a concept derived from Jean Piaget's (1951) theory of cognitive development, refers to a lack of differentiation between some aspect of self and other. The paradigm case is the failure of perspective-taking that characterizes young children who are unable to infer what another person is thinking, feeling, or seeing. Unable to infer accurately the perspective of others, the egocentric child attributes to them his or her own perspective instead. The inability to decenter from one's own perspective results in egocentric confusion of social perspectives.

But egocentrism is a broader concept that encompasses a number of additional curiosities of early cognitive development, including realism (the confusion of objective and subjective), animism (confusion of animate and inanimate), and artificialism (confusion of human activity or intentions with natural causes). What these forms of egocentrism have in common is the inability to differentiate subjective and objective perspectives. Children project subjective qualities onto external objects or events; are unable to *decenter* from their own perspective, or else assimilate objective reality to their subjective schemas, deforming reality as a result. So the child who believes that dreams take place in one's room at night (realism), that moving objects have life and consciousness (animism), or that the moon follows them because it wants to (artificialism), is displaying egocentrism just as surely as the child who is unable to differentiate self-other perspectives. Piaget suggested that egocentrism was a primary characteristic of children's thought processes until around 6 to 7 years of age, or when they are able to form mental representations during problem solving. However, while egocentrism is regarded typically as a problem of early cognitive development, such seemingly childish thought may not be entirely absent even in later periods of development.

EGOCENTRISM AND DEVELOPMENT

Elkind (1967) famously reconstructed Piaget's four broad stages of cognitive development to show that each stage is imbued with a form of egocentrism. In the sensori-motor period, for example, egocentrism is evident when the infant stops looking for hidden objects, almost as if objects no longer exist if out of sight. The sensori-motor child is egocentric with respect to objects to the extent that object permanence is confused with object perception. Sensori-motor egocentrism is overcome when children are able to form mental representations of absent objects, an ability that emerges with the symbolic functions of preoperational thought, the next stage of cognitive development. At this stage objects have permanent existence, even when not perceived, because they exist symbolically as cognitive representations.

Although preoperations liberate the child from sensori-motor egocentrism, it ensnares the child in a form of egocentrism with respect to symbols. Indeed, most of the classic examples of egocentrism are linked to this stage of cognitive development. Hence children in early childhood are unable to infer accurately the cognitive, affective, or visual perspective of others. Their thinking is prone to realism, animism, and artificialism. They fail conservation problems. They are unable to differentiate between symbols and their referents; they confuse make-believe play and reality. This preoperational egocentrism is overcome by the emergence of concrete operations, the next stage of cognitive development. At concrete operations the child can hold two mental representations at once (e.g., symbol and referent, objective and subjective) and thereby distinguish between them.

Although concrete operations liberate the child from preoperational egocentrism, the child nonetheless falls prey to a form of egocentrism all its own.In middle childhood, children fail to differentiate the products of their cognition—their convictions and claims about the world—from empirical reality. It is almost as if children believe that their perspective has a certain felt necessity which renders alternative perspectives nonsense or contrary evidence inadmissible. It is not until the emergence of the final stage of cognitive development—formal operations—that this form of egocentrism is surmounted. At formal operations, adolescents can think theoretically, entertain contrary-to-fact propositions, generate logical possibilities, formulate hypotheses, and systematically test them. This ability to entertain multiple possibilities minimizes the felt necessity that attaches to one's own perspective. Moreover, the capacity for scientific reasoning disposes the adolescent to consider claims in light of the evidence.

But the transition to formal operations involves its own variant of egocentrism—what Elkind (1967) termed "adolescent egocentrism." Here adolescents fail to differentiate between what is the object of their concern (which is the *self*) from what is the concern of others. Hence teenagers beset by adolescent egocentrism believe that others are as concerned about them as they are about themselves. They construct imaginary audiences of peer critics and admirers for whom they must perform, although being the object of so much (imagined) attention also leaves the adolescent craving privacy and vulnerable to feelings of heightened self-consciousness, shame, shyness, and embarrassment.

Adolescent egocentrism also encourages the construction of personal fables that showcase the self relative to others. Three fables capture the egocentrism of adolescence. First, adolescents are convinced of their personal uniqueness. Second, often as a result of their uniqueness, adolescents evaluate risks in a way that emphasizes a sense of invulnerability. Third, egocentric adolescents revel in subjective omnipotence, believing the self to be a source of unusual influence or power within their peer network. Personal fables are differentially related to adaptation in adolescence (Aalsma, Lapsley & Flannery, 2006). For example, personal uniqueness predicts internalizing symptoms, especially in girls. Invulnerability predicts risk behavior but counterindicates internalizing symptoms. Omnipotence predicts mastery coping and indices of positive adjustment.

EGOCENTRISM IN SOCIAL AND ACADEMIC DOMAINS

The transition to concrete operations after age 7 brings with it new cognitive abilities that diminish egocentrism. For example, a young school-age child is able to decenter from his or her own perspective so that it can be reversed with the perspective of another, yielding a reciprocal form of role-taking ("I think that you think . . ."). By the end of childhood simultaneous role-taking is a possibility so that

the child can reflect upon the self from the perspective of others. The suite of concrete operational abilities hence allow the child to be a better mind-reader, that is, allows the child to infer the intentions and perspectives of others. This ability clearly matters for communicative competence, moral reasoning, and interpersonal understanding, which are three areas that have attracted the most research on egocentrism in childhood. For example, egocentric speech is characterized by the child's use of monologue without any clear audience or in the presence of an audience but without considering that audience's view or contribution. In contrast, socialized speech involves the child responding to other's questions, adding information to the thoughts of others, or attempting to influence others through requests or commands. Piaget suggests that egocentric speech peaks at around 6 years of age, but then declines around 7 or 8 years. In the moral domain, egocentrism makes it difficult for the preschool child to understand the reason for rules other than what serves self-interest. Moral judgment and prosocial behavior require taking into account the life circumstances and perspectives of others, which is only possible when advances in perspective-taking diminish egocentric thought. Finally, egocentrism is a barrier to friendships and intimate relationships insofar as it inhibits the ability to see things from the perspective of the other. Growth of perspective-taking skills brings forth a capacity for authentic, other-regarding friendship.

Egocentrism also constrains performance on skills that are crucial to academic achievement, including understanding of number and scientific concepts. The preoperational child is incapable, for example, of hierarchical classification, seriation, multiplication of classes. The child has difficulty conserving transformations of the substance, amount, weight, and volume of objects. This skill must await the decentered, reversible thought of concrete operations.

INDIVIDUAL AND CONTEXTUAL DIFFERENCES

The role of egocentrism in cognitive development has been qualified greatly by early 21st-century research. Nobody believes that egocentrism is a pervasive cognitive failure of young children. In the social domain, for example, young children clearly are empathically sensitive and responsive to the distress of others, and they engage in prosocial behavior. Alongside egocentrism, then, is an ability to orient to the needs of others. Moreover, young children appear to show more evidence of perspective-taking when tasks require assuming the perspective of age-mates and peers rather than the perspective of adults and strangers. Similarly, whether intellectual competence or egocentrism is observed in young children appears to vary with the nature of the tasks presented to them. Tasks that are simplified to reduce inordinate performance requirements or extensive demand on memory, for example, often reveal less egocentric responding. There is some evidence that children with learning disabilities present with role-taking deficits, indicating that such students might profit from interventions that improve social skills.

SUGGESTIONS FOR TEACHERS

For Piaget, the engine that drives cognitive development is the experience of *disequilibration,* that is, a sense of cognitive conflict that results when current cognitive schemes are incapable of resolving contradiction. Disequilibration is induced in classrooms that are marked by robust peer activities. Piaget and others have suggested that children learn how to take the perspectives of others better through interacting with their peers than with adults. Hence classroom activities that emphasize cooperative learning, peer group discussion, and cross-age teaching are well-suited to introduce instances of cognitive conflict that require better appreciation of the perspective of others.

SEE ALSO *Cognitive Development: Overview; Piaget, Jean.*

BIBLIOGRAPHY

Aalsma, M., Lapsley, D. K., & Flannery, D. (2006). Narcissism, personal fables, and adolescent adjustment. *Psychology in the Schools. 43,* 481–491.

Elkind, D. (1967). Egocentrism in adolescence. *Child Development, 38,* 1025–1034.

Piaget, J. (1951). *The child's conception of the world.* London: Routledge & Kegan Paul.

Patrick L. Hill
Daniel K. Lapsley

EI

SEE *Emotional Intelligence.*

ELEMENTARY SCHOOL, TRANSITION TO

SEE *School Transitions: Elementary School.*

EMOTION REGULATION

An extensive body of literature indicates that children's school success is critical to their development. Students must overcome numerous challenges to perform well in school, and it is clear that many do not. Educational researchers initially focused heavily on curricula, classroom structure, teacher-child ratios, whereas more recently, investigators have begun to focus on children's social and emotional functioning as important contributors to school success. Many teachers believe that social skills are the most important characteristic necessary for school readiness and success and that many children lack these skills (Lewit & Baker, 1995). This situation is problematic because there is evidence that emotion regulation is a better predictor of school readiness than IQ (Blair & Razza, 2007).

This entry describes (1) key theoretical issues involved in the study of children's emotion regulation and especially effortful control (EC), an index of regulatory abilities, (2) methods of measuring EC, (3) what is known about if, and why, EC is related to students' academic competence, (4) socialization correlates of EC and how educators might work to improve children's EC, and (5) strategies for classroom management.

THEORETICAL ISSUES IN THE STUDY OF EMOTION REGULATION

Emotion-related regulation is defined as "processes used to manage and change if, when, and how (e.g., how intensely) one experiences emotions and emotion-related motivational and physiological states, as well as how emotions are expressed behaviorally" (Eisenberg, Hofer, & Vaughan, 2007, p. 288). This definition is purposely broad to accommodate the assumption that emotion regulation can occur before, during, and after the onset of emotion.

Often researchers use effortful control (EC), defined as "the efficiency of executive attention—including the ability to inhibit a dominant response and/or to activate a subdominant response, to plan, and to detect errors" (Rothbart & Bates, 2006, p. 129), as an index of children's regulatory abilities. Individuals high in EC can control their attention and are able to avoid or engage in behavior to accomplish a goal, even if the individual would prefer to engage in another set of behaviors. Although EC is willful, it often may be executed automatically without much thought, and children are not always aware that their thoughts or actions are regulating emotion or behavior. Key to the study of academic competence, EC is hypothesized to regulate attention, emotion, and behavior (Rothbart & Bates, 2006). The authors of a National Academy of Sciences report noted that "self-regulation is a cornerstone of early childhood development that cuts across all domains of behavior" (Shonkoff & Phillips, 2000, p. 3).

Basic regulatory processes begin early in life and become more complex as children age. Infants mostly rely on caregivers to soothe their distress and are not able to actively engage the caregiver until approximately six months of age. In general, self-soothing and looking away from a stress inducing stimulus are quite common methods of regulation among 5- to 18-month-olds, and by 20 months toddlers' use of avoidance and self-distractions become more common (see Eisenberg et al., 2007). By 48 months of age, children often use more complex regulatory strategies and are more proficient at willfully inhibiting behavior and focusing and shifting attention, and there is a marked decline in external forms of regulation. In addition to undergoing rapid development early in life, there is evidence that components of effortful control improve, albeit more slowly, throughout childhood and even into adulthood (Williams, Ponesse, Schachar, Logan, & Tannock, 1999).

ASSESSMENT OF EMOTION REGULATION

Investigators typically measure EC and related regulatory capacities with questionnaires and structured laboratory tasks. As with all methods of assessment, each approach has both advantages and disadvantages. The focus here is on measurement issues that seem most important to the advancement of the study of EC and academic competence (see Rothbart & Bates, 2006 for a review of issues related to the measurement of EC).

A benefit of assessing EC and related constructs via questionnaires is that one can obtain information from the child and parents and teachers who witness the child's behavior in multiple contexts; however, such information is subject to self-presentation biases and error due to inaccurate perceptions and problems created by the difficulty of describing complex interactions or behaviors with relatively simple wording. The Child Behavior Questionnaire is a commonly used questionnaire for assessing children's attention focusing, attention shifting, and inhibitory control—all aspects of EC (Rothbart, Ahadi, Hersey, & Fisher, 2001). Less commonly used is the Brief, but it has the advantage of assessing components of behavioral regulation such as inhibition, attention shifting, and emotional control, as well as working memory and organization of materials (Gioia, Espy, & Isquith, 2003). When behavioral measures are considered, it is common to assess inhibitory control—and to some extent attention—using measures such as the peg task (Diamond & Taylor, 1996). To complete this task, children are directed to tap a peg once on a table when an experimenter taps twice and to tap twice when experimenter taps once. In doing so, participants must inhibit the desire to mimic the experimenter and use attentional skills to remember the rule of responding. Kochanska and colleagues have contributed several tasks that are appropriate for assessing the ability to delay. For exam-

ple, in a M&M task, children must wait for the experimenter to ring a bell prior to eating the candy that is placed under a clear cup (see Kochanska, Coy, & Murray, 2001). Investigators interested in assessing attention and memory would find the forward and backward Digit Span tasks quite useful. In the backward Digit Span, the experimenter lists numerical digits, for example 4, 9, 3 and the participant responds in reverse: 3, 9, 4. A paper by Carlson contains a more complete summary of frequently used measures of EC and related constructs (Carlson, 2005).

THE RELATIONS BETWEEN EMOTION REGULATION AND ACADEMIC COMPETENCE

Theory and data suggest that cognitive and emotional systems are interconnected and that promoting emotion-related skills, including effortful control, can promote academic achievement. Findings indicating that attentional regulation is positively related to measures of school readiness support this conclusion (NICHD Early Child Care Research Network, 2003). Evidence indicates that the measures of regulation predict later levels of academic competence, even when the effects of cognitive variables are controlled (Blair & Razza, 2007), and long-term evidence suggests that preschoolers' ability to delay gratification, a component of EC, predicts their verbal and quantitative SAT scores (Shoda, Mischel, & Peake, 1990).

Children's EC probably is linked to their academic competence both directly and indirectly. More specifically, the attentional and planning components of EC may be directly related to academic competence, whereas the delay and inhibitory control components of EC relate to children's social and motivational processes, which in turn relate to academic competence. Indeed, many of the explanations offered for why relations exist implicate the role of students' relationships with their peers and teachers. Findings from the developmental, social, and clinical psychological literatures suggest that students high in self-regulation are likely to build relationships with teachers and peers that foster academic competencies, whereas less-regulated children are at risk for more turbulent relationships (Rothbart & Bates, 2006; Valiente, Lemery-Chalfant, Swanson, & Reiser, in press). Developing a supportive teacher-child relationship may buffer children from some risk factors associated with poor performance, perhaps because teachers are more likely to provide extra assistance to children with whom they have a positive relationship. Maintaining a good relationship with the teacher is important because declines in the nurturant teacher-child relationship precede declines in achievement, and evidence indicates that teacher-reported negativity in the teacher-child relationship is related to achievement test scores even when controlling for verbal IQ (Hamre & Pianta, 2001).

As children age, a crucial developmental task is to become integrated into peer groups and to maintain friendships. Poor-quality friendships or a lack of friendships is hypothesized to interfere with academic competence as early as preschool and kindergarten, but it likely becomes more important with age because social competence and peer acceptance are posited to promote social inclusion and resources that promote academic success. For example, Welsh, Parke, Widaman, and O'Neil (2001) found children's prosocial behaviors were reciprocally related to academic competence. Initial findings indicate that the quality of the teacher-child relationship and children's social competence partially mediate relations between children's EC and grade point average (Valiente et al., in press).

HOW PARENTS AND TEACHERS CAN PROMOTE EC

Given the importance of emotion-related regulation to the formation of relationships and academic skills, it is somewhat surprising that only since 1995 has the development of EC been a focus of study. Although EC is a component of temperament and it is hypothesized to have a biological basis, many believe it is influenced by the environment (Rothbart & Bates, 2006). A number of scholars have argued that regulatory abilities are developed in relationships and can be learned. Consistent with these ideas, Eisenberg, Spinrad, and Cumberland (1998) argued that parents socialize their children's emotion regulation by (1) their reactions to children's emotions, (2) their discussion of emotion, (3) their expression of emotion, and (4) their selection or modification of situations. According to Eisenberg and colleagues, when socializing behaviors are positive and supportive they promote learning about emotions and their regulation, but when parental actions are harsh and punitive, children are likely to experience overarousal, which undermines opportunities to learn about emotions and their regulation.

Numerous cross-sectional studies demonstrate associations between parenting and EC, but longitudinal studies that are sensitive to change and that contain rich measures of both constructs are needed to determine if parenting influences children's EC. As of 2007, there were few studies of this type. For example, parents who are high in warmth and positive, as opposed to negative, have children who are rated by parents and teachers as high in EC (Valiente et al., 2006). Data from other research laboratories are consistent with the premise that positive parenting predicts growth in children's persistence across four years (Halverson & Deal, 2001). Evidence that Indonesian parents' expressions of negative

emotion and Chinese parents' style of parenting predict measures of children's EC in the theoretically expected ways suggests that relations are somewhat similar in other cultures (see Eisenberg et al., 2007).

Significantly, most theories predict reciprocal relations between parenting and children's EC. Although not all findings are consistent (Valiente et al., 2006), Eisenberg and colleagues (1999) found that 6- to 8-year-olds' regulation predicted their parents' punitive responses two years later, which, in turn, predicted 10- to 12-year-olds' regulation. This area of research needs additional theoretical and empirical attention.

Regarding relations between EC and academic competence, experimental evidence shows that teachers can improve children's inhibitory control, attentional control, and delay of gratification. In the Tools of the Mind Preschool Program, teachers embed social, emotional, and cognitive self-regulation throughout all aspects of the curricula. In a pilot evaluation where children were randomly assigned to either the Tools condition or a control condition, those in Tools performed significantly better than controls in two different EC tasks. In addition, children in Tools either met or exceed state and national standards in literacy and math (Diamond, Leong, & Bodrova, 2006). These results are consistent with Greenberg and colleagues' findings that participation in PATHS, a intervention designed to promote self-control, emotional awareness, and interpersonal problem-solving skills, leads to improvements in self-control, emotional understanding, and the ability to plan (Greenberg, Kusche, Cook, & Quamma, 1995).

STRATEGIES FOR TEACHING CHILDREN WHO ARE LOW IN REGULATION

Every teacher is likely to have at least one child in the classroom who is relatively dysregulated. To facilitate learning for all students in the class, teachers and students need to have a positive and reassuring relationship. For the classroom to run efficiently, a limited number of rules, typically less than eight, must be set by the end of the first week by both the teacher and the students (Lindberg & Swick, 2002). When the rules are violated, teachers should use discipline that is related to the violation. For example, if a student writes on the desk, that student should clean the desks. For more disruptive situations, teachers may find exchanging time-outs with colleagues effective so that they can send a child to another room to calm down for 15 to 20 minutes. It is important to note that rewards are often more effective than punishments, and the implementation of activities such as having lunch with the teacher, calling the child's parents to praise specific activities, or a token system where students earn play money that allows them to purchase desirable gifts/activities often prevents many undesirable behaviors, even for children prone toward dysregulation (see Lindberg & Swick, 2002).

Helping children succeed in school is critical for individual students and for society. This entry touches on some of the theoretical and methodological issues involved in studying EC and academic competence. The existing body of research supports the hypothesis that EC is positively related to young children's academic competence; however, the majority of data are correlational, and there are only a handful of studies involving students beyond fifth grade. Clearly, additional longitudinal findings and data from interventions are needed before drawing firm conclusions. A promising avenue for future research involves obtaining a variety of assessments of the components of EC utilizing a variety of methodologies. By assessing EC in a variety of ways, one would be in a good position to test the hypothesis that relational processes mediate the associations between the inhibitory components of EC, but the attentional- and memory-related components of EC are both directly and indirectly related to academic competence.

SEE ALSO *Classroom Management; Peer Relationships; Special Education.*

BIBLIOGRAPHY

Blair, C., & Razza, R. P. (2007). Relating effortful control, executive function, and false belief understanding to emerging math and literacy ability in kindergarten. *Child Development, 78,* 647–663.

Carlson, S. M. (2005). Developmentally sensitive measures of executive function in preschool children. *Developmental Neuropsychology, 28,* 595–616.

Diamond, A., Leong, D., & Bodrova, E. (2006). *Helping children become masters of their own behavior: A preschool curriculum that improves executive functions.* Paper presented at the Society for Research in Child Development, Boston, MA.

Diamond, A., & Taylor, C. (1996). Development of an aspect of executive control: Development of the abilities to remember what I said and to "Do as I say, not as I do." *Developmental Psychobiology, 29,* 315–334.

Eisenberg, N., Fabes, R. A., Shepard, S. A., Guthrie, I. K., Murphy, B. C., & Reiser, M. (1999). Parental reactions to children's negative emotions: Longitudinal relations to quality of children's social functioning. *Child Development, 70,* 513–534.

Eisenberg, N., Hofer, C., & Vaughan, J. (2007). Effortful Control and Its Socioemotional Consequences. In J. J. Gross (Ed.), *Handbook of Emotion Regulation* (pp. 287–306). New York: Guilford Press.

Eisenberg, N., Spinrad, T. L., & Cumberland, A. J. (1998). The socialization of emotion: Reply to commentaries. *Psychological Inquiry, 9,* 317–333.

Gioia, G., A., Espy, K. A., & Isquith, P. K. (2003). *Brief: Behavior rating inventory of executive function.* Lutz, FL: Psychological Assessment Resources.

Greenberg, M. T., Kusche, C. A., Cook, E. T., & Quamma, J. P. (1995). Promoting emotional competence in school-aged children: The effects of the PATHS curriculum. *Development and Psychopathology, 7,* 117–136.

Halverson, C. F., & Deal, J. E. (2001). Temperamental change, parenting, and the family context. In T. D. Wachs & G. A. Kohnstamm (Eds.), *Temperament in context* (pp. 61–79). Mahwah, NJ: Erlbaum.

Hamre, B. K., & Pianta, R. C. (2001). Early teacher–child relationships and the trajectory of children's school outcomes through eighth grade. *Child Development, 72,* 625–638.

Kochanska, G., Coy, K. C., & Murray, K. T. (2001). The development of self-regulation in the first four years of life. *Child Development, 72,* 1091–1111.

Lewit, E. M., & Baker, L. S. (1995). School readiness. *Future of Children, 5,* 128–139.

Lindberg, J. A., & Swick, A. M. (2002). *Common-sense classroom management: Surviving September and beyond in the elementary classroom.* Thousand Oaks, CA: Corwin Press.

NICHD Early Child Care Research Network. (2003). Do children's attention processes mediate the link between family predictors and school readiness? *Developmental Psychology, 39,* 581–593.

Rothbart, M. K., Ahadi, S. A., Hersey, K. L., & Fisher, P. (2001). Investigations of temperament at three to seven years: The children's behavior questionnaire. *Child Development, 72,* 1394–1408.

Rothbart, M. K., & Bates, J. E. (2006). Temperament. In W. Damon (Series Ed.) & N. Eisenberg (Vol. Ed.) (Eds.), *Handbook of Child Psychology.* Vol. 3. *Social, emotional, personality development* (6th ed., pp. 99–166). New York: Wiley.

Shoda, Y., Mischel, W., & Peake, P. K. (1990). Predicting adolescent cognitive and self-regulatory competencies from preschool delay of gratification: Identifying diagnostic conditions. *Developmental Psychology, 26,* 978–986.

Shonkoff, J. P., & Phillips, D. A. (2000). *From neurons to neighborhoods: The science of early childhood development.* Washington, D. C.: National Academy Press.

Valiente, C., Eisenberg, N., Spinrad, T. L., Reiser, M., Cumberland, A., Losoya, S. H., et al. (2006). Relations among mothers' expressivity, children's effortful control, and their problem behaviors: A four-year longitudinal study. *Emotion, 6,* 459–472.

Valiente, C., Lemery-Chalfant, K., Swanson, J., & Reiser, M. (in press). Prediction of children's academic competence from their effortful control, relationships, and classroom participation. *Journal of Educational Psychology.*

Welsh, M., Parke, R. D., Widaman, K., & O'Neil, R. (2001). Linkages between children's social and academic competence: A longitudinal analysis. *Journal of School Psychology, 39,* 463–482.

Williams, B. R., Ponesse, J. S., Schachar, R. J., Logan, G. D., & Tannock, R. (1999). Development of inhibitory control across the life span. *Developmental Psychology, 35,* 205–213.

Carlos Valiente
Nancy Eisenberg

EMOTIONAL/BEHAVIORAL DISORDERS

Emotional disturbance (ED, here called emotional or behavioral disorder or EBD) is one of the categories of disability included under the Individuals with Disabilities Education Improvement Act, also known as IDEA, 2004. Every teacher will have at least one student who is extraordinarily difficult because of his or her behavior, simply due to the fact that most students with EBD have not been identified and placed in special education. Most of the students who are the topic of this entry are in general education classrooms, where they typically cause serious and legitimate concern for their teachers and often for their classroom peers and school administrators as well. This has been true throughout the history of compulsory education, as James Kauffman and Timothy Landrum (2006) have observed.

A frequent misunderstanding is that students with EBD are just chronically difficult—irritating to teachers but not really disabled. However students can be both disturbed and disturbing, have EBD, and irritate the teacher. Some irritating students do not have EBD. Nevertheless, most students are neither particularly irritating nor have EBD. Moreover, a student who is consistently irritating is at high risk of acquiring EBD if he or she does not already have such a disability, and such a student is likely also to bring out the worst in others.

Another misunderstanding is that students with EBD exhibit their problematic behavior all the time. Such disorders tend to be episodic, highly variable, and sometimes situation-specific (for example, exhibited only when demands are placed on the student to perform or exhibited only outside the home or family). Understanding the episodic nature of EBD is critical. Expecting someone with EBD to exhibit problem behavior all the time is somewhat like expecting a person with a seizure disorder to have constant seizures. Because EBD is typically episodic, an observer may miss incidents that cause a teacher, who sees the student throughout the day and week, enormous and legitimate concern.

DEFINITION OF EBD

Defining EBD is fraught with difficulty, and the federal definition of this category of disability is seriously flawed. Distinguishing "emotional disturbance" from "behavioral disorder" is impossible. Steven Forness and Jane Knitzer recounted problems in the definition in IDEA (the federal special education law first enacted in 1975) and proposed an alternative formulated by the National Mental Health and Special Education Coalition, a coalition of more than thirty national organizations concerned with children's mental health. Although many definitions have been proposed, Daniel Hallahan, James Kauffman, and Paige Pullen conclude that all definitions contain these common elements:

- extreme behavior (not just slightly different from the usual)
- a chronic problem (constant and on-going, which does not resolve quickly)
- violation of social or cultural expectations

Most teachers understand that many students exhibit minor behavior problems and that some students exhibit serious problems that nonetheless fall short of disability. However, most teachers also understand that serious, persistent violations of behavioral expectations that are appropriate for a student's social and cultural context are debilitating.

A major controversy regarding definition is the exclusion in the IDEA definition of students who are socially maladjusted but not emotionally disturbed. Sometimes identification of a student with EBD is resisted because the family or community is said to have failed to teach the individual appropriate behavior, and the problem is therefore judged to be social maladjustment, not emotional disturbance. However, exclusions based on presumed or known causes are neither logically nor morally defensible. For example, one does not conclude that a student is not blind because his or her lack of sight was caused by X (e.g., disease, accident, or genetic process). Blind simply means one cannot see, regardless of the cause. Likewise, EBD simply means a serious, persistent problem behavior regardless of cause.

The exclusion of students who are judged to be socially maladjusted is essentially uninterpretable and indefensible for two other reasons. First, it is inconsistent with the intention and writing of Eli Bower, who provided the federal definition without the exclusion. Second, the EBD most likely to be interpreted as social maladjustment (conduct disorder, which includes various forms of antisocial behavior and is closely linked to poor socialization) is one of the most serious disabilities in the EBD category (Kauffman and Landrum, 2009). Thus the exclusion of social maladjustment is both illogical, given the federal definition, and inconsistent with the IDEA principle of identifying and serving all students with disabilities.

PREVALENCE OF EBD

According to the U.S. Department of Education (2005) and the National Research Council (2002), about 1% of students in public schools in the United States receive special education under the ED (EBD) category. The Department of Health and Human Services (2001) as well as data from other studies (Costello, Egger, & Angold,

2005; Kauffman & Landrum, 2009) strongly suggest that the actual prevalence of EBD is at least five times greater (about 5%).

Students with EBD typically are rated as having behavior problems far more often than their peers and are directly observed to exhibit problems far more often than other students. Nevertheless, as Kauffman has suggested, in most cases students with EBD are not identified until their problems are severe and protracted, often because educators are afraid of labeling or of being accused of making a mistake in identification. Educators appear to be far more willing to decide that the student should be identified as having a learning disability (LD) than they are to identify a student as having EBD. As a consequence, students with EBD are often ignored or mislabeled. After reviewing the literature on identification of EBD, Costello and her colleagues concluded: "Substantively, we can say with certainty that only a small proportion of children with clear evidence of functionally impairing psychiatric disorder receive treatment" (p. 982). These children pose a heavy burden on public health, not to mention a serious problem for schools and schooling.

ASSESSMENT AND IDENTIFICATION

There is no standardized test for EBD as there is for intelligence or academic achievement. Standardized behavior rating scales and procedures for observing and evaluating problem behavior are available, but EBD is a matter of judgment that the student's behavior is seriously problematic and in need of change. In essence, teachers and other educators are the tests for EBD, as Michael Gerber suggested is the case for LD. That is, their judgments, based on comparisons to other students they have taught, comprise the test.

Assessment of internal states through projective testing and other psychoanalytic means is not a reliable basis for identification of students as having EBD. Although sometimes unconscious or internal states may be assessed by psychologists or psychiatrists, the direct observation and rating of behavior by school personnel is a better basis for judgment.

CHARACTERISTICS, VARIATIONS, AND SUBGROUPS

As a group, students with EBD tend to be lower than average in IQ and to be lower in academic achievement than most students, although there are a few high IQ and high-achieving students with EBD. Because students with EBD are typically not intellectually highly able and high-achieving, it is understandable that many would be identified as having LD. In fact, there is a substantial overlap in the characteristics of students with LD and those with

EBD, as Janine Stichter, Maureen Conroy, and James Kauffman as well as other writers (e.g., Hallahan, Kauffman & Pullen, 2009; Kauffman & Hallahan, 2005a) have noted.

Students with EBD are generally divided into two subcategories: those with externalizing behavior and those with internalizing behavior. Externalizing behavior includes aggression, disruption, and other forms of acting out; internalizing behavior includes such problems as depression, anxiety, and social withdrawal, in which the primary difficulty is private or internal. The most frequent problems observed by teachers are externalizing. However, internalizing problems can be debilitating, and students can have both types of problems, showing both types at the same time or alternating between the two.

Besides the two broad subcategories of externalizing and internalizing problems, EBD includes many other types of disorders. Kauffman and Landrum (2009) describe several subcategories of difficulty: attention and activity disorders, conduct disorders (which may be overt aggression or covert antisocial behavior), special problems of adolescence (which include delinquency, substance abuse, and early sexual activity), anxiety, depression, and schizophrenia. Many types of disorders can occur together. A case in which a particular individual exhibits simultaneous occurrence of disorders is described as comorbid. In fact, multiple or comorbid disorders are more common than are single difficulties.

Most students with EBD are not what most people would consider psychotic—unable to tell the difference between reality and unreality. However, a few students with EBD have schizophrenia, a major thought disorder that often includes hallucinations and delusions. For these students, antipsychotic medication, as well as appropriate education, is extremely important.

INTERVENTIONS AND INSTRUCTION

Intervention based on behavior principles is the most effective way of responding to EBD, as explained by Hallahan and Kauffman (2009), Kauffman and Landrum (2006, 2009), Stichter and colleagues (2008), and Hill Walker, Elizabeth Ramsey, and Frank Gresham (2004). Other interventions may appeal to one's intuition or tradition, but they tend to be less reliable and may make problems worse. Behavior principles emphasize instruction in how to behave, support for desirable behavior, and other primarily positive interventions, although effective, nonviolent, and appropriate punishment procedures may sometimes be necessary. Application of these behavior principles in teaching is also described by James Kauffman, Mark Mostert, Stanley Trent, and Patricia Pullen (2006), by Mary M. Kerr and C. Michael Nelson (2006), and by Landrum and Kauffman (2006). A behavioral approach relies primarily on using consequences to change behavior, although instruction, talking to students, and correcting environmental factors that set the stage for misconduct are also important. Skillful application of these principles should address the problems of students with EBD, as Hill Walker, Steven Forness, and colleagues (1998) have suggested.

Appropriate academic instruction plays a primary role in programming for students with EBD and in classroom management. In fact, Kauffman, Mostert, Trent, and Pullen suggest that a teacher who is having difficulty with a student's behavior should first consider academic instruction. Joseph Witt, Amanda VanDerHeyden, and Donna Gilbertson, as well as Kathleen Lane, emphasize the importance of educators having instruction in academic skills in helping students with EBD.

Psychopharmacology plays an increasingly important role in managing EBD. The role of drugs can be overplayed or misunderstood, but medication is clearly important not only in managing such problems as attention deficit hyperactivity disorder (ADHD), depression, bi-polar disorder, and schizophrenia but also in making students with these disorders more accessible to instruction (see Steven Forness & Kelli Beard; Steven Forness, Stephanny Freeman, & Tanya Paparella; and Dean Konopasek & Steven Forness).

ISSUES IN ASSESSMENT AND EDUCATION

A major problem in assessment is fear of false identification. In fact, this fear is so common that students with EBD typically are known to have serious problems for years before they are identified, and the evidence for EBD must be so overwhelming that almost no one can argue that the identification is unjustified. Of course, such fear kills any hope of prevention, as Kauffman has pointed out.

No one suggests letting behavior problems fester until they become severe, protracted, and nearly insurmountable, yet that is what typically happens, as Kauffman, Walker and his colleagues (2004) and Phillip Wang and his associates (2005) have observed. In fact, Glen Dunlap and his colleagues present the consensus of researchers in the field that early identification of children with challenging behavior (EBD) is possible and more effective than later intervention. Moreover, Wang and his fellow researchers wrote that "long periods of untreated illness may also be harmful to those with less severe disorders" and that "most people with 1 disorder progress to develop comorbid disorders and such comorbidity is associated with an even more persistent and severe clinical course" (pp. 610–611). Thus, the case for early identification and prevention has been made

clearly, yet prevention is not typically put into practice (see Dunlap & colleagues; Kauffman). Early identification and prevention are not controversial ideas; however, when they are put ingot practice, controversy can arise. Complications regarding labeling, privacy, disproportionate identification of children by ethnic or color group, and doubt about misdiagnosis result in inaction.

Violence in schools is recognized as a serious problem; however, few schools use what is known about violence prevention. Get-tough policies and harsh punishment for aggression, the usual responses, are mostly counterproductive. The best approaches include school-wide behavior monitoring and behavior management procedures that emphasize careful monitoring, clear expectations, reward for desirable behavior, and nonviolent negative consequences for behavioral infractions, which have been described by Walker and his colleagues (2004) and by Kerr and Nelson (2006). However, although some EBD students commit violent acts, most do not.

The placement of students with EBD has been a matter of special concern and controversy in the context of movement toward full inclusion, the idea that all students should be placed in general education classes in their neighborhood school regardless of their disabilities (see Kauffman and Hallahan, 2005b). The placement in general education classrooms of many students with EBD is not feasible, as James Kauffman, John Lloyd, Teresa Riedel, and John Baker have suggested. The idea of basing all services for all students with EBD in the communities where they live is appealing, and community-based services are clearly feasible for some. However, closing all hospitals and residential placements for students with severe EBD and attempting to provide all services in the community has not proven feasible (Hallahan & Kauffman; Kauffman & Landrum, 2009). Effective programs for students with EBD are expensive, and inclusionary programs and community-based services promise savings for taxpayers. The anticipated cost saving makes inclusionary, community-based programs popular, although research does not show them to be particularly effective.

Adolescents and young adults with EBD are among the most frequently unemployed individuals with disabilities. Helping students with EBD make the transition from high school to work or to further education is among the most difficult tasks in special education, as Douglas Cheney and Michael Bullis have noted. Programs for the transition of students with EBD have been criticized as unsuccessful, but they are often criticized for other reasons as well. Critics may claim that they represent consignment of students to second-class citizenship or that they emphasize vocational skills when they should be focused on academic preparation for higher education.

In fact, any schooling different from that for students headed for college is vulnerable to charges that its expectations are too low.

Students who are members of ethnic minority groups in the United States, particularly African Americans, are disproportionately identified as having EBD. Although the reasons for disproportionality have not been identified unambiguously by research, multicultural special education is considered essential (Hallahan, Kauffman & Pullen, 2009). That is, special education teachers need to be sensitive to and respectful of cultural differences, but they may not understand how to do so and much of the education literature is unclear on the subject. James Kauffman, Maureen Conroy, Ralph Gardner, and Donald Oswald have suggested that effective, evidence-based education is culturally neutral and that culturally sensitive education demands attention to the individual student from a scientific perspective. Although science itself has been criticized as culturally biased, that criticism has been resoundingly rejected by many special educators, exemplified by *Challenging the Refusal of Reasoning in Special Education*, edited by Mark Mostert, Kenneth Kavale, and James Kauffman. About ethnicity, Kauffman, Conroy, Gardner, and Oswald concluded that "first and foremost we must recognize that the most culturally responsive practices are empirically validated instructional strategies.... At this point the data seem to suggest that this applies to all children, regardless of their ethnicity."

SEE ALSO *Special Education.*

BIBLIOGRAPHY

Bower, E. M. (1982). Defining emotional disturbance: Public policy and research. *Psychology in the Schools 19,* 55–60.

Cheney, D., & Bullis, M. (2004). The school-to-community transition of adolescents with emotional and behavioral disorders. In R. B. Rutherford, M. M. Quinn, and S. R. Mathur (Eds.), *Handbook of Research in Emotional and Behavioral Disorders.* New York: Guilford.

Costello, E. J., Egger, H. H., & Angold, A. (2005). One-year research update review: The epidemiology of child and adolescent psychiatric disorders: I. methods and public health burden. *Journal of the American Academy of Child and Adolescent Psychiatry 44,* 972–986.

Dunlap, G., Strain, P. S., Fox, L., Carta, J. J., Conroy, M., Smith, B. J., et al. (2006). Prevention and intervention with young children's challenging behavior: Perspectives regarding current knowledge. *Behavioral Disorders 32,* 29–45.

Forness, S. R., & Beard, K. Y. (2007). Strengthening the research base in special education: Evidence-based practice and interdisciplinary collaboration. In J. M. Crockett, M. M. Gerber, & T. J. Landrum (Eds.), *Achieving the radical reform of special education: Essays in honor of James M. Kauffman.* Mahwah, NJ: Lawrence Erlbaum Associates.

Forness, S. R., Freeman, S., & Paparella, T. (2007). Recent randomized clinical trials comparing behavioral interventions and psychopharmacologic treatments for school children with EBD. *Behavioral Disorders 31,* 284–296.

Forness, S. R., & Knitzer, J. (1992). A new proposed definition and terminology to replace "serious emotional disturbance" in individuals with disabilities act. *School Psychology Review 21,* 12–20.

Gerber, M. (2005). Teachers are still the test: Limitations of response to instruction strategies for identifying children with learning disabilities. *Journal of Learning Disabilities 38,* 516–524.

Hallahan, D. P., Kauffman, J. M., & Pullen, P. (2009). *Exceptional learners: Introduction to special education* (11th ed.). Boston: Allyn & Bacon.

Kauffman, J. M. (1999). How we prevent the prevention of emotional and behavioral disorders. *Exceptional Children 65,* 448–468.

Kauffman, J. M., Conroy, M., Gardner, R., & Oswald, D. Cultural sensitivity in the application of behavior principles to education. *Education and Treatment of Children.* in press.

Kauffman, J. M., & Hallahan, D. P. (2005a). *Special education: What it is and why we need it.* Boston: Allyn & Bacon.

Kauffman, J. M., & Hallahan, D. P. (Eds.). (2005b). *The illusion of full inclusion: A comprehensive critique of a current special education bandwagon* (2nd ed.). Austin, TX: PRO-ED.

Kauffman, J. M., & Landrum, T. J. (2006). *Children and youth with emotional and behavioral disorders: A history of their education.* Austin, TX: Pro-Ed.

Kauffman, J. M., & Landrum, T. J. (2009) *Characteristics of emotional and behavioral disorders of children and youth* (9th ed.). Upper Saddle River, NJ: Prentice Hall.

Kauffman, J. M., Lloyd, J. W., Riedel, T., & Baker, J. (1995). Inclusion of all students with emotional or behavioral disorders? Let's think again. *Phi Delta Kappan 76,* 542–546.

Kauffman, J. M., Mostert, M. P., Trent, S. C., & Pullen, P. L. (2006). *Managing classroom behavior: A reflective case-based approach* (4th ed) Boston: Allyn & Bacon.

Kerr, M. M., & Nelson, C. M. (2006). *Strategies for addressing behavior problems in the classroom* (5th ed.). Upper Saddle River, NJ: Prentice Hall.

Konopasek, D. E., & Forness, S. R. (2004). Psychopharmacology in the treatment of emotional and behavioral disorders. In R. B. Rutherford, M. M. Quinn, & S. R. Mathur (Eds.), *Handbook of Research in Emotional and Behavioral Disorders.* New York: Guilford.

Landrum, T. J., & Kauffman, J. M. (2006). Behavioral approaches to classroom management. In C. Evertson & C. Weinstein (Eds.), *Handbook of classroom management: research, practice, and contemporary Issues.* Mahwah, NJ: Lawrence Erlbaum Associates.

Lane, K. L. (2004). Academic instruction and tutoring interventions for students with emotional and behavioral disorders. In R. B. Rutherford, M. M. Quinn, & S. R. Mathur (Eds.), *Handbook of research in emotional and behavioral disorders.* New York: Guilford.

Mostert, M. P., Kavale, K. A., & Kauffman, J. M. (Eds.). (2008) *Challenging the Refusal of Reasoning in Special Education.* Denver, CO: Love.

National Research Council. (2002). *Minority students in special and gifted education.* M. S. Donovan & C. T. Cross. (Eds.) Washington, DC: National Academy Press, Division of Behavioral and Social Sciences.

Stichter, J. P., Conroy, M. A., & Kauffman, J. M. (2008). *An introduction to students with high-incidence disabilities.* Upper Saddle River, NJ: Merrill-Prentice Hall.

U. S. Department of Education. (2005). *27th annual report to Congress on the implementation of the Individuals with Disabilities Education Act, 2004.* Washington, DC: Author.

U. S. Department of Health and Human Services. (2001). *Report of the surgeon general's conference on children's mental health: A national action agenda.* Washington, DC: Author.

Walker, H. M., Forness, S. R., Kauffman, J. M., Epstein, M. H., Gresham, F. M., Nelson, C. M., et al. (1998). Macro-social validation: Referencing outcomes in behavioral disorders to societal issues and problems. *Behavioral Disorders, 24,* 7–18.

Walker, H. M., Ramsey, E., & Gresham, F. M. (2004). *Antisocial Behavior in School: Strategies and Best Practices* (2nd ed). Belmont, CA: Wadsworth.

Wang, P. S., Berglund, P., Olfson, M., Pincus, H. A., Wells, K. B., & Kessler, R. C. (2005). Failure and delay in initial treatment contact after first onset of mental disorders in the national comorbidity survey replication. *Archives of General Psychiatry 62,* 603–613.

Witt, J. C., VanDerHeyden, A. M., & Gilbertson, D. (2004). Instruction and classroom management: prevention and intervention research. In R. B. Rutherford, M. M. Quinn, & S. R. Mathur (Eds.), *Handbook of Research in Emotional and Behavioral Disorders.* New York: Guilford.

James M. Kauffman

EMOTIONAL DEVELOPMENT

Along with physical and cognitive development, every child progresses through phases of emotional development. Arguably, all children differ in their individual development. Studies have shown that parents admit to having little information on emotional development, even though they also admit that their actions have great influence on their children's emotional development.

Emotions are not as easy to study or recognize as cognition, and for many decades the study of emotional development lagged behind study in other areas of child development. However, by the early twenty-first century researchers had developed several theories on emotional development.

EMOTIONAL DEVELOPMENT DEFINITION

Emotional development is the emergence of a child's experience, expression, understanding, and regulation of emotions from birth through late adolescence. It also comprises how growth and changes in these processes concerning emotions occur. Emotional development does not occur in isolation; neural, cognitive, and behav-

ioral development interact with emotional development and social and cultural influences, and context also play a role. Various emotional development theories are proposed, but there is general agreement on age-related milestones in emotional development.

Social and emotional development are strongly linked and sometimes studied or reported in tandem. Parents and other caregivers play an important role in emotional development, but as a child's world expands, other people in the social context also play a part in emotional development.

Debate continues as to exactly when emotions appear in infants. For example, smiles occur early, but the earliest ones are more likely reflexive than social. A smile may express emotion as early as 6 weeks of age but it is not until about age 6 months that a smile can be considered more emotional and social in nature. Crying is a powerful emotion for infants and may be used as a communication tool. Distress, pleasure, anger, fear, and interest are among the earliest emotions that infants express. Laughter begins at about 3 to 4 months of age. Eliciting laughter in babies at this age often involves an action that deviates from the norm, such as peek-a-boo games provoke. Development of negative emotions probably follows soon after, with anger still winning over sadness to express negative feelings. Fear begins to emerge, and infants often follow the emotions of their caregivers and form strong attachment to them.

By toddlerhood and early childhood, children begin to develop more of a sense of self. Emotions such as pride, shame, and self-recognition begin to emerge. These developments are facilitated partly by the rapid maturation of a toddler's frontal lobes and limbic circuit in the brain. These emotional developments lead to the strong sense of independence and defiance that often characterize the toddler years. Of course, toddlers also are becoming more independent physically, having developed skills such as walking. They may begin to play independently too. The self-recognition brings new levels of emotional development. For example, toddlers will begin to respond to negative signals from caregivers and others. It is at the toddler stage, or at least by age 2, that children also begin showing empathy, which is a complex emotional response to a situation. Feeling empathy requires that a child not only read emotional clues from others but understand the distinction between self and others. Actually putting one's self in the other's position also is required for empathy.

Emotional expression is still largely nonverbal, although some emotional language may develop by age 20 months. For the most part, facial expressions, crying or other vocal expressions, and gestures still express many of toddlers' emotions. In early childhood, verbal skills develop and with them, verbal reasoning. Children also are able to talk about their feelings as they learn how to express themselves verbally. As young children enter preschool, they may be able to label their emotions and learn about them by understanding family discussions and actions concerning emotions. For example, a child may be able to say, "I am mad," or "I am sad," instead of simply expressing the emotion through actions such as crying, stomping, or yelling. This is not to say that tantrums do not occur; between toddlerhood and school age, children still express anger in the form of tantrums. Because emotions have become important to young children, they talk about them often in conversation.

Preschoolers begin to understand the rules of family, school, and society concerning how they express some of their emotions. They also can recognize nonverbal cues of emotion from one another. Preschoolers begin to distinguish between negative emotions such as sadness, anger, and fear. Although these young children have empathy, their knowledge of others' feelings generally is limited to people and situations with which they are familiar. Development of this emotional capacity also depends on positive, culturally acceptable emotional exchanges with peers. Negative emotional influences of family life that are common and harsh, particularly in the child's discipline model, can lead to problems with emotional development and even psychopathology.

ENTERING SCHOOL

As children enter school, they gain a greater sense of self and an understanding of how specific situations can lead them to experience emotions. Children may experience shame, even in reaction to emotions expressed. They also can begin to understand how an event can lead to mixed emotions. Research has shown that by about age 6, children may appreciate that people can experience one emotion, then a completely different emotion immediately after the first. The understanding of simultaneous and even conflicting emotions soon follows.

As children move into later childhood, they learn the "rules" of displaying emotion, which is a form of social and emotional development. For example, if children have been taught to do so, they may, out of politeness or respect, be able to avoid showing disappointment in a gift or the failure of an adult to fulfill a promise. As they understand the emotional states of those around them, children realize that these states are not as simple as they might have once imagined.

School-aged children begin developing emotional coping skills, even if those skills are at very basic levels. For example, children may rationalize situations and behaviors or reconstruct scenarios to make them seem less upsetting emotionally. The ability to suppress negative emotions is a factor of normal development, as well as other influences, such as gender, the specific situation, cultural influences, and the person likely to receive the expressed emotion.

In adolescence emotions still are developing. In face, the adolescent years often are considered an emotional period of development. Although adolescents begin to develop independence from their parents and begin to display social signs of independence by gaining employment, driving, and other activities, their emotional autonomy is represented by conflict and often negative emotions. One reason for the negative emotions may be cognitive development of abstract thinking abilities. Because adolescents can imagine all sorts of complex and theoretical scenarios for romance or in response to other relationships, they may suffer resulting emotional distress. In turn, social problems become more complex, and adolescents look to their peers to help provide a basis for how to manage the emotions they feel.

Family issues and struggles over becoming independent, with curfews, academic pressure, and romantic and other peer interactions, all place a great deal of pressure on adolescent emotions. Strong self-perceptions from earlier childhood may give way to self-doubt or feelings of worthlessness. As adolescents realize that their emotions are separate from their parents' emotions, a process called "emotional autonomy" begins. Adolescents may feel pulled between the close emotional ties they have with their parents and a need to develop independent emotional responses. If depression is going to occur, it generally begins during adolescence and is more common in girls than in boys.

EMOTIONAL REGULATION

A major part of emotional development in children and adolescents is how children recognize, label, and control the expression of their emotions in ways that generally are consistent with cultural expectations. This is called *emotional regulation*. In short, development of an emotion almost is dependent on regulation. The exact definition and models of emotional regulation have been debated. But what is apparent in the study of child and adolescent development and the development of positive instructional strategies is the complex interaction of emotional regulation and development of emotions.

Self-regulation of emotions includes recognition and delineation of emotions. Once a child can articulate an emotion, the articulation already has a somewhat regulatory effect. Children may be able to use various techniques to self-regulate as they develop and mature. Children begin learning at a young age to control certain negative emotions when in the presence of adults, but not to control them as much around peers. By about age 4, children begin to learn how to alter how they express emotions to suit what they feel others expect them to express. The ability to do so is what psychologists call *emotional display rules*.

By about age 7 to 11 years, children are better able to regulate their emotions and to use a variety of self-regulation skills. They have likely developed expectations concerning the outcome that expressing a particular emotion to others might produce and have developed a menu of behavioral skills to control how they express their emotions. By adolescence, they adapt these skills to specific social relationships. For example, older children may express negative emotions more often to their mothers than to their fathers because they assume their fathers will react negatively to displays of emotion. Adolescents also have heightened sensitivity to how others evaluate them. Their self-consciousness and the culture-specific nature of guidelines concerning the appropriateness of emotional expression make this a particularly difficult time to learn when and how to express or regulate many emotions.

Several emotional development models and perspectives present views on emotional regulation. The functionalist perspective emphasizes that emotions serve a function of focusing action to achieve personal goals. Self-regulation is critical to emotional development because it marks a progressive ability to regulate emotions according to demands of the physical and social worlds. Actions match the demands of the situation and each family of emotions provides a range of behavior-regulatory, social-regulatory, and internal-regulatory functions for an individual.

The perspective of emotions as discrete states is based on understanding emotions as patterns of configurations in the brain, as demonstrated in cognitive neuroscientific studies. Neurochemical processes result in subjective feeling states, with accompanying automatic changes in bodily function and behavior. These give rise to basic emotions. Specific sections of the brain are associated with particular emotions. For example, the right prefrontal cortex is associated with negative affect and withdrawal. Theorists propose a maturational timetable for emergence of these basic emotions, beginning in infancy. Emotional development and regulation are dependent on cognition for the most part; cognitive development leads to new abilities to understand and self-regulate basic emotions.

Process viewpoints, also known as systems perspectives, do not disclaim the functional utility of emotions or their grounding in discrete feeling states. But the perspectives focus on how emotions emerge from one's tendency to self-organize various interacting components. These components include felt experiences, cognitive appraisals, motivations, functions, and control elements. This perspective leaves emotional regulation dynamic and open to transformation, as emotions are complex and specific to situations. They also help form the basis of one's self and personality. Like functional and discrete state perspectives, systems theories maintain that emotions can serve adaptive functions for a child, especially in social situations.

EMOTIONS AT SCHOOL

The interplay of emotional development, social development, and academic performance is complex. C. Cybele Raver's 2002 research has established a strong link between social/emotional development and behavior and school success, particularly in the first few years of schooling. If a child's academic tasks are interrupted by problems with peers, following directions, or controlling negative emotions, the child will have trouble learning to read or staying on task in other educational activities. Research also has linked antisocial behavior with decreased academic performance.

Emotional understanding can positively relate to adaptive social behavior, yet it can negatively relate to internalizing behavior. This may lead to feelings of anxiety, depression, and loneliness. Knowledge of emotion can affect verbal ability, and in turn, academic competence. Verbal and prosocial skills are critical to academic achievement. For example, a child must be able to communicate with his or her teacher, which includes reading emotional cues. Children who do not learn to regulate emotions and who display disruptive behavior in school spend less time on tasks and receive less instruction and less positive feedback.

ASSESSING EMOTIONAL DEVELOPMENT

Taking a preventive approach to challenging behaviors by designing programs that engage students and teach them new social skills may ward off some challenging behaviors. Others may continue in spite of quality programming. Although the emotional-related behaviors may be obvious, it is important to gather some data to assess the child's emotional development or atypical development and to aid in developing a plan to improve the behavior.

Assessment begins with deciding which behavior is the most challenging and needs immediate intervention. Considerations include whether or not the behavior is harmful to the child or others, how the behavior might interfere with learning or participation in learning activities, and if the behavior will hinder development of positive social relationships. Detailed explanations of behaviors are most helpful at this stage. The second step is to conduct a functional assessment. This involves conducting interviews with parents and others to determine what precipitates the behavior and what the consequences of the behavior are. An ABC chart of columns can help with observation.

Next is the step of developing hypothesis statements based on behavioral patterns that emerge from the functional assessment information. A support plan follows, with proposed changes to the antecedent events that lead to the behaviors and inappropriate emotional expressions. Finally, professionals can implement, evaluate, and modify the plan. Baseline rates of challenging behaviors and appropriate replacement skills should be noted and later compared.

RISK AND PROTECTION IN EMOTIONAL DEVELOPMENT

Dr. Carolyn Saarni, professor of counseling at Sonoma State University (California) has discussed two rules of emotional display, prosocial and self-protective. With prosocial rules, a child alters his or her displays of emotion to protect another's feelings. In self-protective display, the child masks emotions to avoid embarrassment or to protect himself or herself from potentially negative consequences. Research on which of these self-regulation strategies emerges first is mixed. Throughout a child's life, however, the risks of displaying emotion persist, probably most blatantly in adolescence, when peer pressure works on emotional regulation. Gender also plays a role in the types of emotions children, and adolescents, in particular, feel comfortable displaying. Boys are less likely than girls to express fear in times of stress, for example, for fear of belittlement. For the most part, self-protection and prosocial rules aid in positive emotional development.

RESEARCH ON CLASSROOM STRATEGIES

A framework that promotes positive relationships in the classroom helps prevent and address challenging behaviors. The pyramid model developed by Fox, Dunlap, Hemmeter, Joseph, and Strain in 2003 begins with positive, supportive relationships from parents, teachers, and other professionals. Many professionals agree that students with an emotional disturbance need a structured leaning environment and inclusive schooling. However, data from the Special Education Elementary Longitudinal Study (SEELS) and the National Longitudinal Transition Study-2 (NLTS2), reported in 2006, showed that elementary and middle school students with emotional disturbances tended to spend more time in special education classes than other students with disabilities. The study also showed that 75% of students with emotional disturbances were receiving extra time to complete academic tests. A low percentage were receiving mental health services.

The issue of violence has taken an elevated importance in schools. Concern has been expressed that discipline provisions in the Individuals with Disabilities Education Improvement Act (IDEA), such as the "stay-put" rule and cumulative 10-school-day limit on suspensions would promote school violence by unfairly protecting students with disabilities who exhibit disruptive or violent behaviors. In 2001, the General Accounting Office reported that students with and without disabilities generally were disciplined in the same manner and that IDEA played a limited role in affecting schools' ability to properly discipline students.

SEE ALSO *Anxiety; Emotion Regulation; Evaluation (Test) Anxiety.*

BIBLIOGRAPHY

Corso, R.M. (2007). Practices for enhancing children's social-emotional development and preventing challenging behavior. *Gifted Child Today, 30*(3), 51–56.

Kern, L. Recommended practices: addressing persistent challenging behaviors. Retrieved April 21, 2008, from http://challengingbehavior.fmhi.usf.edu/resources.html#handouts.

Moissinac, L. (2003). Affect and emotional development. In J. W. Guthrie (Ed.), *Encyclopedia of education* (2nd ed., Vol. 1, pp. 58–61). New York: MacMillan Reference.

Raver, C. (2002). *Ready to enter. Emotions matter. Making the case for the role of young children's emotional development for early school readiness among three-and four-year-old children.* New York: National Center for Children in Poverty.

Skarbek, D. (2005). Are children with special needs more likely to commit school violence? In K. Hudson (Ed.), *Contemporary issues companion: school violence.* San Diego: Greenhaven Press.

Smith, B. J. Recommended practices. Linking social development and behavior to school readiness. Retrieved April 21, 2008, from http://challengingbehavior.fmhi.usf.edu/resources.html#handouts.

Trentacosts, C., & Izard, C. (2006). Emotional development. In N. Salkind (Ed.), *Encyclopedia of human development* (Vol. 1, pp. 456–458). Thousand Oak, CA: Sage Reference.

Wagner, M., Friend, M., Bursuck, W. D., Kutash, K., Duchnowski, A. J., Sumi, W. C., et al. (2006). Educating students with emotional disturbances. A national perspective on school programs and services. *Journal of Emotional and Behavioral Disorders, 14*(1), 12–30.

Teresa Odle

EMOTIONAL INTELLIGENCE

The term *emotional intelligence* (EI), first introduced in the 1990s by Peter Salovey of Yale University and John (Jack) Mayer of the University of New Hampshire, refers to how thinking about emotion and integrating emotion into cognitive processes both facilitate and enhance reasoning. Similar to conceptualizations of intelligence, EI involves the capacity to engage in abstract reasoning, but about emotions in particular. According to the Salovey and Mayer model, there are individual differences in EI, such that individuals who are more skilled at perceiving, using, understanding, and managing emotions are more successful at accomplishing many learning and social tasks than those who are less skilled.

BACKGROUND

In the 1980s, the concept of intelligence was broadening to include an array of mental abilities. Most notably, Howard Gardner, who was primarily interested in helping educators to appreciate students with diverse learning styles and potentials, advised practitioners and scientists to place a greater emphasis on the search for multiple intelligences such as interpersonal intelligence. At the same time, psychologists and cognitive scientists began revisiting the Stoic idea that emotions made humans irrational and self-absorbing; specifically, they considered the alternative viewpoint that emotions could enhance cognitive tasks and social interactions.

Influenced by and active participants in these movements, psychologists Salovey and Mayer began integrating the scientific evidence showing that emotions facilitate reasoning into their theory of EI. Intelligence and emotion, prior to their theorizing, generally identified divergent areas of research.

To understand the relevance of EI, it is important to grasp the critical role emotions play in social interactions and human behavior. Research conducted by Charles Darwin in the late 1800s, Silvan Tomkins in the 1960s, Paul Ekman from the 1970s into the early 2000s, and many others show that the experience and expression of emotion communicates important information about one's relationships. For example, anger signifies that someone or something is blocking one's goal, and fear signifies that someone or something in the environment poses a threat. There is scientific evidence that these emotion signals are universal, that is, broadly understood by cultures around the world. Emotions also appear to be essential to thinking and decision making. Work by neuroscientist Antonio Damasio demonstrates that the ability to integrate emotional information with rational decision-making and other cognitive processes is essential for people to manage their daily lives. Individuals unable to attend to, process, or experience emotion due to damage to specific brain areas (i.e., prefrontal lobe area) make decisions that put themselves at risk.

THE ABILITY MODEL OF EI

The Ability Model of EI proposed by Salovey and Mayer includes four relatively distinct emotion-related abilities:

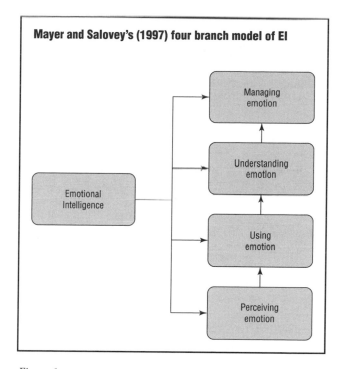

Figure 1 ILLUSTRATION BY GGS INFORMATION SERVICES. CENGAGE LEARNING, GALE.

perceiving, using, understanding, and managing emotion. Their model is depicted in Figure 1.

Perceiving Emotion. Perceiving emotion involves identifying and differentiating emotions in one's physical states (including bodily expressions), feelings, and thoughts, and in the behavioral expressions of others (such as facial expressions, body movements, voice), as well as in the cues expressed in art, music, and other objects. Persons skilled in perceiving emotion are adept at differentiating between the range of emotion expressions (frustration, anger, and rage) in themselves and in others.

Using Emotion. Using emotion to facilitate thought refers to the use of emotion both to focus attention and to think more rationally, logically, and creatively. For example, positive emotions such as joy and amusement are more useful in stimulating creative thought while slightly negative moods such as sadness are more conducive to engaging in deductive reasoning tasks. Persons skilled at using emotions are better able to generate specific emotional states to carry out a task effectively.

Understanding Emotion. Understanding emotion is the ability to label emotions accurately with language and to know the causes and consequences of emotions, including how emotions combine, progress, and shift from one to the other (e.g., in some situations, fear and anger combine to create jealousy). Persons skilled in this area have a rich feelings vocabulary and are knowledgeable about what causes various emotions and what behaviors or thoughts may result from their occurrence.

Managing Emotion. Managing emotion is the ability to regulate moods and emotions and involves attending and staying open to pleasant and unpleasant feelings as well as engaging in or detaching from an emotion depending on its perceived utility in a particular situation. To manage emotions effectively, persons must garner the other skill areas of EI: They must be able to accurately monitor, discriminate, and label their own and others' feelings, believe that they can improve or modify these feelings, assess the effectiveness of these strategies, and employ strategies that will alter these feelings. By effectively managing emotions, persons can accomplish situational goals, express socially appropriate emotions, and behave in socially acceptable ways.

EI theory hypothesizes that these four abilities have developmental trajectories. There are various skills within each domain that evolve from more basic to more advanced. For example, in the domain of perceiving emotion, basic skills involve accurately recognizing an emotional expression in others and more advance skills entail expressing emotions in adaptive ways and discriminating between honest and false emotional expressions in others. EI theory also specifies that the four abilities are hierarchical in structure such that perceiving emotion is at the foundation, followed by using emotion and understanding emotion, with managing emotion at the top of the hierarchy.

The Ability Model of EI is measured by the Mayer-Salovey-Caruso Emotional Intelligence Test (MSCEIT) and the MSCEIT-Youth Version for children. These tests require respondents to perform emotion-related tasks in order to measure their abilities within and across each of the four areas. For example, to assess perception of emotion, respondents examine a photograph of a person's face and indicate the extent to which each of four emotions is present in the expression. To assess managing emotion, respondents rate the effectiveness of different strategies to reduce a particular emotion in order to achieve a specified goal. The correctness of responses is compared to those provided by normative sample and a sample of emotion experts.

OTHER MODELS OF EI

In 1995 the concept of emotional intelligence was made wildly popular by the publication of Daniel Goleman's book, *Emotional Intelligence: Why It Can Matter More than IQ*. In the ensuing years, myriad models of EI were

created. The ability model of EI proposed originally by Salovey and Mayer was published prior to Goleman's book and stands in contrast to other models which incorporate a wide variety of personality traits and other characteristics such as optimism, happiness, and self-awareness. Proponents of these so-called *mixed* or *trait models* of EI (i.e., models that mix abilities with personality and other characteristics) typically use self-report scales instead of performance-based assessments to measure EI (i.e., respondents indicate the extent to which they believe they are able to regulate their emotions as opposed to identifying effective strategies to solve emotion-laden problems). Self-report EI scales in general overlap considerably with personality assessments (i.e., they do not measure a construct significantly distinct from existing personality scales). Responses to self-report EI scales typically do not correspond with performance on the MSCEIT, and MSCEIT scores generally are more predictive of important outcomes than self-report EI scales.

EI AND CLASSROOM LEARNING

The abilities and knowledge areas captured by the EI ability framework contribute to students' academic achievement, ability to maintain quality social relationships, psychological and physical well-being, and later life success. A meta-analysis of more than 250 studies conducted by Roger Weissberg and Joseph Durlak at the Collaborative for Social and Emotional Learning (CASEL) reveals that the average student enrolled in school-based programs that promote emotion and social skills performs significantly better on achievement tests and has better grades than non-participants. Emotionally skilled students, for example, are better able to identify the causes of their anxiety and may anticipate that an upcoming test is causing them to feel distress. To manage the distress, these students are more likely to engage in proactive behaviors such as asking teachers for help in studying and ensuring they have sufficient time and resources to prepare for the exam.

There is ample scientific evidence that the skills of EI are related to social competence (see work by Nancy Eisenberg and by Susanne Denham for examples. Students who recognize emotions in others and understand, label, express, and regulate their own emotions effectively have good social skills, strong friendships, and high opinions from peers. These positive social outcomes enhance academic achievement. For example, compared to others, students with strong friendships feel more comfortable in the school environment, receive better academic support from teachers, get more social support from peers, and develop healthier attachments to school.

The skills of EI also are related to psychological well-being and to anxiety and depression (in the expected directions). Students with lower EI, especially boys, are more likely to engage in behaviors that put their health and well-being at risk, including drinking, smoking, using drugs, and engaging in violent behaviors. The incidence of anxiety and depression and of these behaviors interferes with learning.

In their research Brackett and Rivers found relationships between EI with teacher ratings of students' leadership skills, study skills, and their ability to adapt to changes. They also found that students with greater EI were less likely to experience (according to teacher evaluations) problems that include aggression, anxiety, conduct problems, hyperactivity, and learning difficulties.

TEACHING EMOTION SKILLS AND KNOWLEDGE IN SCHOOLS

Schools and classrooms provide an ideal place for teaching emotion skills and knowledge. For many children, school is the first opportunity for continued and stable social interactions, and it is difficult for many children to develop their emotion skills solely within the home when, more and more, both parents are working full-time and often have multiple jobs. CASEL researchers contend that "Schools and classrooms in which adults are nurturing, supportive, and caring furnish the best contextual opportunities for social emotional learning programs to be introduced, sustained and effectively provided" (Elias et al., 1997, p. 75).

With their collaborators, Brackett and Rivers have developed a series of programs to teach students how to recognize, understand, and label accurately both their own and others' emotions, appropriately express their thoughts and feelings, and regulate their emotions effectively, as well as to appreciate the significance of these skills in the academic, social, and personal lives. These programs, titled "Emotional Literacy in the Classroom" (ELC) are grounded in theory and scientific evidence, are field-tested, and are integrated easily into existing school curricula. These programs leverage reading, language arts, and social studies instruction to teach emotion knowledge using an innovative multi-faceted approach. The programs complement the regular school-day curriculum and adhere to both state and national standards. The ELC programs, which have been adopted by and tested in school districts across the United States and abroad, address the particular social and emotional needs of students and help create a caring and challenging classroom environment that fosters effective and enduring academic learning. Accompanying profession development and training programs for teachers and administrators provides educators with the skills and support they need to effectively teach emotion knowledge and skills to students.

SEE ALSO *Intelligence: An Overview.*

BIBLIOGRAPHY

Brackett, M. A., Kremenitzer, J. P., Maurer, M., Carpenter, M. D., Rivers, S. E., & Katulak, N. A., (Eds.). (2007). *Emotional literacy in the classroom: Upper elementary.* Port Chester, NY: National Professional Resources.

Denham, S. A. (1998). *Emotional development in young children.* New York: Guilford Press.

Eisenberg, N., Fabes, R. A., Murphy, B., et al. (1995). The role of emotionality and regulation in children's social functioning: A longitudinal study. *Child Development, 66,* 1360–1384.

Elias, M. J. Zins, J. E., Weissberg, R. P., Frey, K. S., Greenberg, M. T., et al. (1997). *Promoting social and emotional learning: Guidelines for educators.* Alexandria, VA: Association for Supervision and Curriculum Development.

Matthews, G., Zeidner, M., & Roberts, R. D., (Eds.) (2007). *The science of emotional intelligence: Knowns and unknowns.* New York: Oxford University Press.

Mayer, J. D., & Salovey, P. (1997). What is emotional intelligence? In P. Salovey & D. J. Sluyter, (Eds.), *Emotional development and emotional intelligence: Educational implications.* New York: Basic Books.

Salovey, P., & Mayer, J. D. (1990). Emotional intelligence. *Imagination, Cognition and Personality 9,* 185-211.

Zins, J. E., Weissberg, R. P., Wang, M. C., & Walberg, H. J. (Eds.). (2004). *Building academic success on social and emotional learning: What does the research say?* New York: Teachers College Press.

WEB SITES

Collaborative for Academic, Social, and Emotional Learning (CASEL). Retrieved April 21, 2008, from www.casel.org. Report by Weissberg, R. & Durlak retrievedApril 21, 2008, from http://casel.org/downloads/metaanalysissum.pdf.

Emotionally Intelligent Schools (EI-Schools). Retrieved April 21, 2008, from www.ei-schools.com.

Health, Emotion, Behavior Laboratory (HEB Lab). Retrieved April 21, 2008, from http://research.yale.edu/heblab/.

Marc A. Brackett
Susan E. Rivers

EPISTEMOLOGICAL BELIEFS

Epistemology is the branch of philosophy that investigates what knowledge is and how people know whether they know something (BonJour, 2002). It addresses questions such as: What is knowledge? How do people know if they really have knowledge? What provides a justification for any knowledge that they have? For example, on what grounds are people justified in believing that electrons have negative charge or that an accused robber is guilty? Are people convinced by sensory evidence, by testimonial evidence, by strong intuitions, or by some other means?

Epistemologists, of course, have developed many ideas about how to answer questions such as these. In recent years, psychologists have become interested in whether people other than philosophers have ideas about what knowledge is and how knowledge is justified. In other words, psychologists have wondered if people have beliefs about epistemological questions (called *epistemological beliefs* or *personal epistemological beliefs*) and whether these beliefs affect in any way their learning or reasoning.

To see why these issues are important, consider the following hypothetical students, both eighth graders learning science:

- Emily believes that the scientific knowledge she is trying to master typically has a very *complex* structure with rich and numerous interconnections. Sharon, on the other hand, believes that scientific knowledge has a very *simple* structure, consisting of lists of unrelated facts.

- Emily believes that people know that scientific knowledge is true on the basis of observational evidence. In contrast, Sharon believes that people know that scientific knowledge is true because the textbook and her teacher say so.

- Emily believes that scientific theories are fallible; she knows that there are often competing theories, and it sometimes takes years to work out which theories explain the observational evidence better. Sharon, however, thinks that there is only one scientific theory on any idea, and this theory is absolutely and forever true.

In summary, Emily and Sharon differ in their beliefs about the *complexity of knowledge*, the *source of knowledge* (observation versus the authority of the teacher and text), the *certainty* of knowledge, and whether there can be (and are) *competing theories* attempting to explain the same data.

Emily's and Sharon's ideas for learning and reasoning in science have several possible implications:

1. When studying cellular processes, Emily expects to find rich interrelations among ideas, and she tries to understand them when she finds them. Sharon, on the other hand, simply tries to memorize each concept separately, never realizing that the processes are interrelated in interesting ways. In this way, beliefs about the *structure* of knowledge can influence learning.

2. When conducting an experiment on seed germination, Emily finds that the seeds sprout and grow for a while even when they are kept in the dark. She realizes that when the textbook says that "plants need sunlight to grow," this must not apply to seeds. She

decides that perhaps seeds contain their own energy for initial growth. Sharon, however, assumes that she did something wrong in her experiment, because she takes her textbook at its word, and the textbook says that plants need sunlight to grow. Thus, beliefs about the *source* of knowledge (observations versus textbooks) affect how students reason about new evidence.

3. When Emily reads a magazine article about conflicting studies regarding the role of carbohydrate consumption on weight control and health, she understands that much more evidence will probably be needed before matters are more fully understood. She decides to adopt a medium-carbohydrate diet, but she is aware that later evidence may make it necessary for her to change her mind. In contrast to Emily, Sharon is sure that her current ideas about the superiority of a low-carbohydrate diet are absolutely correct, because she learned about these ideas on a website written by an important doctor. She is puzzled why a magazine article would not just state the one correct theory. On this topic, it is clear that students' ability to understand competing ideas as well as how they act in response to these ideas can be affected by beliefs about the certainty of knowledge.

These examples illustrate that epistemological beliefs may have powerful effects on learning and reasoning. A growing body of research supports that such effects do exist (Mason & Boscolo, 2004; Qian & Alvermann, 1995; Schommer, 1990; Songer & Linn, 1991).

EMERGENCE OF PSYCHOLOGICAL RESEARCH ON EPISTEMOLOGICAL BELIEFS

Contemporary psychological research on learners' epistemological conceptions has its roots in the work of William Perry (1968/1999), who investigated the development of male Harvard students' ideas about knowledge during the college years. Other researchers, including Mary Belenky, Patricia King and Karen Kitchener, Marcia Baxter Magolda, and Deanna Kuhn have also investigated changes in epistemological ideas over time. This research has generally aimed to make claims about broad, overall epistemological stances expressed by individuals. For example, in Kuhn's scheme (Kuhn & Weinstock, 2002), children move from a realist epistemology (assertions are copies of reality) to an absolutist epistemology (assertions are correct or incorrect facts), and later to a multiplist epistemology (assertions are opinions, and everyone has a right to their own opinion), and finally (in some but not all people) an evaluativist epistemology (assertions are judgments based on weighing arguments on different sides of a question).

In the late 1980s, Marlene Schommer (Schommer, 1990) and others argued for an alternative approach to conceptualizing people's epistemologies. Schommer argued that epistemologies might be separable into independent beliefs. Schommer proposed three beliefs that would be called epistemological beliefs: a belief in how complex knowledge is (ranging from complex to simple), a belief in how certain knowledge is (ranging from highly certain to highly uncertain), and a belief in the source of knowledge (e.g., knowledge coming from authority). These beliefs were independent of each other. For instance, a person could believe in complex but certain knowledge, complex but uncertain knowledge, simple and certain knowledge, or simple but uncertain knowledge.

Methodologically, Schommer advanced an influential way to measure epistemological conceptions. In contrast to developmental work, which had relied principally on interviews and, to a lesser extent, on written, open-ended questions, Schommer developed a questionnaire called the Epistemological Questionnaire. Several different items were intended to measure the same underlying dimension. For example, two of the items that were intended to measure *certain knowledge* were (1) "Truth is unchanging" and (2) "Nothing is certain, but death and taxes." Respondents rated agreement to each statement on a Likert scale.

Other researchers have developed analogous scales tapping overlapping but not identical sets of epistemological beliefs. For example, Barbara Hofer (2000) developed a questionnaire with items that addressed four epistemological beliefs. The questionnaire was also designed so that the questions referred to a specific field. That is, the questions did not refer to knowledge in general but to knowledge in a specific field such as science or mathematics. The first two epistemological beliefs were about the nature of knowledge:

- Certainty. This belief refers to the extent to which the respondent thinks that knowledge is certain versus fallible and subject to change.

- Simplicity. This refers to the extent to which the respondent believes that knowledge is structured and organized in simple ways with a single right answer rather than in more complex ways with more than one right answer.

The third and fourth beliefs address how a person comes to "know" something.

- Source of knowledge. This belief references where knowledge comes from—from oneself (and one's own experiences) or from others (such as the teacher, the textbook writer, or experts in a field).

QUESTIONS TO ASSESS EPISTEMOLOGICAL BELIEFS

Epistemological beliefs have been measured educational psychologists in different ways and for different reasons. One variation depends on how epistemology is understood. This can range from very narrow to extremely broad theoretical concepts.

There are also many methods for measurement that are not necessarily related to one's theoretical understanding of epistemology. These methods vary according to the preference of the researcher, trends in educational research, and the compatibility of the method to the field and/or context.

Some of the qualitative methods have depended on case studies in which a general question such as: "What stands out to you about the year so far?" is posed to a sample of students. In other quantitative instances, researchers measure specific factors in surveys such as, "belief scales," where students indicate, on a scale of one to five, how much they agree with the statement: "Hard work can increase one's ability to do math."

The context of each study provides another degree of precision. Epistemological beliefs are researched in subject or grade specific contexts, from comparative and multi-cultural perspectives, and within discourse of race, class, and gender. This large variety of subject matter denotes the especially broad and important nature of the study of epistemological beliefs in education and beyond.

Samuel Rocha

- Justification of knowledge. Closely related to the source of knowledge, this belief is about the kinds of justifications that are offered in support of knowledge. Justifications might be on the basis of personal experience or the authority of experts.

Other researchers have used items from these scales and have developed their own items to construct new measures.

Though inspired by the philosophical literature, research by psychologists and educational psychologists on epistemological beliefs has not been tightly linked to the philosophical literature. There are relatively few citations of the epistemological literature in psychological and educational articles about epistemological beliefs. There has been somewhat more connection to the philosophical literature by researchers in the epistemological development tradition, especially in the seminal work of William Perry.

In a 2005 study Clark Chinn and Ala Samarapungavan (have argued that closer attention to philosophical research would suggest many other kinds of epistemological beliefs that could be explored by researchers. For example, psychologists have not explored people's beliefs about social processes of knowledge construction (e.g., are processes such as peer review or interactive argumentation conductive to arriving at true ideas?) or people's beliefs about evidence (what exactly counts as evidence? How should one respond to anomalous evidence?)

EPISTEMOLOGICAL BELIEFS VERSUS BELIEFS ABOUT LEARNING

One issue that has arisen with respect to measures of epistemological beliefs is the need to distinguish between epistemological beliefs and beliefs about learning. Barbara Hofer and Paul Pintrich (1997) argued that researchers have sometimes confused these two related but distinct sets of beliefs. An epistemological belief is a belief about the nature of knowledge or how one comes to believe that it is knowledge. A belief about learning is a belief about how people come to understand and remember ideas—regardless of whether they believed them or not. For example, the belief that "knowledge is complex" is a belief about the nature of knowledge but says nothing about how people learn that knowledge. In contrast, the belief that one can learn ideas quickly is not a belief about what knowledge is or how one comes to know or believe it, but rather a belief about how one comes to *learn* the ideas. Indeed, one can learn something which is not viewed as knowledge at all (e.g., one can learn about astrology while believing it to be bunk). One can believe that knowledge is justified on the basis of observational evidence collected by experts (an epistemological belief) yet believe that the best way to learn that knowledge is by having a teacher explain it quickly (a learning belief). Learning is about understanding and remembering. Epistemology is about the criteria for deciding that something is true.

RESEARCH ON EPISTEMOLOGICAL BELIEFS

During the growth of research on epistemological development and epistemological beliefs by educational and developmental psychologists, a second body of research on epistemological beliefs was being conducted by science educators. Most science educators have characterized their research as investigating students' beliefs or ideas about the *Nature of Science* (NOS). Research on

NOS has been growing rapidly since the 1970s and 1980s. Two figures important in inspiring research on NOS were Richard Duschl and Norman Lederman. Duschl made a compelling claim that work by philosophers of science was highly relevant to many aspects of science education; he argued that science educators should align their ideas about the goals and practices of science with what was being learned by philosophers and historians of science. Science educators have responded to this call by investigating the understanding of NOS by both scientists and by students. Science educators have also linked their work more explicitly than educational psychologists have to the philosophical literature, especially to the work of Thomas Kuhn (1922–1996).

Research on students' understanding of NOS has, as one would expect, focused on epistemological issues related to science. The VNOS (Views of Nature of Science Questionnaire) was developed by Lederman and has been since refined by a number of others, including Fouad abd-el-Khalick. In its most recent version, a few of the questions are:

- What makes science different from other disciplines of inquiry (e.g., religion, philosophy)?

- Does the development of scientific knowledge require experiments? Why or why not?

- After scientists have developed a scientific theory (e.g., atomic theory, evolution theory), does the theory ever change? Why or why not? Give examples.

- Is there a difference between a scientific theory and a scientific law? Give examples.

- Science textbooks often represent the atom as a central nucleus composed of protons (positively charged particles) and neutrons (neutral particles) with electrons (negatively charged particles) orbiting the nucleus. How certain are scientists about the structure of the atom? What specific evidence do you think scientists used to determine what an atom looks like?

These questions are centered around what science is, whether scientific knowledge changes, what scientific knowledge is based on (e.g., experiments), and so on. Other questions address how social and cultural values influence science. Another frequently used interview protocol has been developed by Carol and colleagues (Smith, Maclin, Houghton, & Hennessey, 2000).

Interestingly, at about the same time that educational psychologists began to rely less on interview measures and more on written questionnaire measures of epistemological beliefs, science educators moved in the opposite direction. Whereas early investigations of students' understanding of

NOS tended to use questionnaires, more recent work has favored interviews and open-ended written questions of the sort presented above.

INFLUENCES OF EPISTEMOLOGICAL BELIEFS ON LEARNING AND REASONING

Most researchers would probably argue that promoting more sophisticated epistemological beliefs is a worthy educational goal in its own right. This is particularly true of science educators, as national and state standards explicitly say that part of learning science is coming to understand the nature of science. Most researchers would also agree that developing more sophisticated epistemological beliefs can also benefit other aspects of learning. A large research effort has been devoted to investigating correlations between epistemological beliefs and performance on learning and reasoning tasks. Although a comprehensive summary of findings is beyond the scope of this entry, here are a few typical findings: (1) Students who believe that knowledge is certain write essays that reach unqualified conclusions, even when there is evidence supporting different viewpoints, as well (Schommer, 1990). (2) Students who believe that knowledge consists of ideas that are interconnected (rather than a disconnected series of facts) are better able to understand texts that present alternative positions on controversial ideas (Kardash & Scholes, 1996). (3) Students with more sophisticated epistemological beliefs were better able to learn from an inquiry-based learning environment (Windschitl & Andre, 1998).

These findings should not be interpreted as showing that there are always strong relationships between measure of epistemological beliefs and measure of learning and reasoning. Some have found little relationship, for example, between reasoning and beliefs about the nature of science, and students who exhibit strong progress in reasoning better may show no gains at all in epistemological beliefs (Sandoval & Morrison, 2003). In addition, correlations between epistemological beliefs and measures of learning and reasoning are often relatively low.

HOW PEOPLE FORM EPISTEMOLOGICAL BELIEFS

Many researchers investigating learners' epistemologies have proceeded on the assumption that people do in fact have at least tacit beliefs about knowledge that they can express. Other researchers have questioned this assumption. David Hammer and his colleagues (Hammer & Elby, 2002, 2003) are among those who have argued that most people (other than philosophers) probably do not think about knowledge at all. On the other hand, even if people do not have actual beliefs about knowl-

edge, they do make decisions about what counts as knowledge and what they believe. These decisions are guided by epistemological commitments which are wholly tacit, and which cannot be readily expressed. Alternatively, one can view people as engaged in epistemic practices even if they do not have explicit epistemological beliefs. The term *epistemic* indicates that an activity is oriented to deciding what to believe and why to believe it. A child who decides that bugs have six legs because she has just picked up a bug and counted the legs has engaged in an epistemic activity of forming a belief that bugs have six legs on the basis of her personal observations.

People *do* form beliefs, and by examining the basis on which they form beliefs, researchers can identify their epistemological commitments or epistemic practices. Ala Samarapungavan (1992) conducted a study in which she assessed children's epistemological commitments by observing the theory choices they made. She gave children different theories to consider and different configurations of evidence bearing on those theories. She found that even seven year olds preferred logically consistent to logically inconsistent theories. They also preferred theories that explained more evidence (as opposed to less evidence) and theories that were not inconsistent with any evidence. Through this study, Samarapungavan was able to show that even young children share some of the epistemological commitments often attributed to scientists—a preference for simplicity, consistency with the evidence, and coverage of the broadest possible scope of evidence.

DOMAIN-SPECIFICITY OF EPISTEMOLOGICAL BELIEFS

Researchers interested in personal epistemologies have investigated the extent to which epistemological beliefs and epistemic practices are domain-specific. A domain-specific belief is one that is limited to a particular domain (such as mathematics, physics, and so on). For instance, a person might believe that knowledge is certain in math but not in other disciplines. A domain-general belief is one that applies generally to all or many domains. A person who believes that all knowledge in all domains is certain has a domain-general belief.

Researchers have found evidence that epistemological beliefs are domain-specific. For example, Hofer (2000) compared undergraduates' beliefs about knowledge in science with their beliefs about knowledge in psychology. The undergraduates believed that knowledge was more certain and more attainable in science than in psychology. Knowledge in psychology was justified on more personal bases than knowledge in science, which was viewed as based more on authority.

Hammer and his colleagues (Hammer & Elby, 2002, 2003; Rosenberg, Hammer, & Phelan, 2006) have argued for a much more radically contextual view of personal epistemologies. They argue that epistemologies shift very rapidly from one context to another. For instance, students who are working in a science class may at one moment view knowledge about the rock cycle as *propagated stuff* (information told to them by a textbook or a teacher) consisting of meaningless, isolated facts, and one or two minutes later, the same students working on the same topic may shift dramatically to viewing the same knowledge as *fabricated stuff* (ideas that they are creating themselves) composed of meaningful ideas that they are trying to make sense of. Radical shifts in epistemic practices can be triggered very quickly by shifts in environmental cues. In this view, people do not have stable epistemologies at all.

Research on personal epistemologies is thriving, with alternative theories being advanced and tested and a new measurement tools being developed. The steady increase in the number of researchers investigating this topic suggests that ideas about epistemologies and epistemological development will play an important role in theorizing about how people learn and reason.

SEE ALSO *Epistemological Development.*

BIBLIOGRAPHY

BonJour, L. (2002). *Epistemology: Classic problems and contemporary solutions.* Lanham, Maryland: Rowman & Littlefield.

Chinn, C. A., & Samarapungavan, A. (2005, July). *Toward a broader conceptualization of epistemology in science education.* Paper presented at the biennial meeting of the International History, Philosophy, and Science Teaching Conference, Leeds, United Kingdom.

Hammer, D., & Elby, A. (2002). On the form of a personal epistemology. In B. K. Hofer & P. R. Pintrich (Eds.), *Personal epistemology: The psychology of beliefs about knowledge and knowing* (pp. 169–190). Mahwah, NJ: Erlbaum.

Hammer, D., & Elby, A. (2003). Tapping epistemological resources for learning physics. *Journal of the Learning Sciences, 12,* 53–90.

Hofer, B. K. (2000). Dimensionality and disciplinary differences in personal epistemology. *Contemporary Educational Psychology, 25,* 378–405.

Hofer, B. K., & Pintrich, P. R. (1997). The development of epistemological theories: Beliefs about knowledge and knowing and their relation to learning. *Review of Educational Research, 67,* 88–140.

Kardash, C. M., & Scholes, R. J. (1996). Effects of preexisting beliefs, epistemological beliefs, and need for cognition on interpretation of controversial issues. *Journal of Educational Psychology, 88,* 260–271.

Kuhn, D., & Weinstock, M. (2002). What is epistemological thinking and why does it matter? In B. K. Hofer & P. R. Pintrich (Eds.), *Personal epistemology: The psychology of beliefs about knowledge and knowing* (pp. 121–144). Mahwah, NJ: Erlbaum.

Mason, L., & Boscolo, P. (2004). Role of epistemological understanding and interest in interpreting a controversy and in topic-specific belief change. *Contemporary Educational Psychology, 29,* 103–128.

Perry, W., G., Jr. (1968/1999). *Forms of intellectual and ethical development in the college years: A scheme.* San Francisco, CA: Jossey-Bass.

Qian, G., & Alvermann, D. (1995). Role of epistemological beliefs and learned helplessness in secondary school students' learning science concepts from text. *Journal of Educational Psychology, 87,* 282–292.

Rosenberg, S., Hammer, D., & Phelan, J. (2006). Multiple epistemological coherences in an eighth-grade discussion of the rock cycle. *Journal of the Learning Sciences, 15,* 261–292.

Samarapungavan, A. (1992). Children's judgments in theory choice tasks: Scientific rationality in childhood. *Cognition, 45,* 1–32.

Sandoval, W. A., & Morrison, K. (2003). High school students' ideas about theories and theory change after a biological inquiry unit. *Journal of Research in Science Teaching, 40,* 369–392.

Schommer, M. (1990). Effects of beliefs about the nature of knowledge on comprehension. *Journal of Educational Psychology, 82,* 498–504.

Smith, C. L., Maclin, D., Houghton, C., & Hennessey, M. G. (2000). Sixth-grade students' epistemologies of science: The impact of school science experiences on epistemological development. *Cognition and Instruction, 18,* 349–422.

Songer, N. B., & Linn, M. C. (1991). How do students' views of science influence knowledge integration? *Journal of Research in Science Teaching, 28,* 761–784.

Windschitl, M., & Andre, T. (1998). Using computer simulations to enhance conceptual change: The roles of constructivist instruction and student epistemological beliefs. *Journal of Research in Science Teaching, 35,* 145–160.

Clark A. Chinn

EPISTEMOLOGICAL DEVELOPMENT

Epistemology, historically the province of philosophers, concerns the origin, nature, limits, methods, and justification of human knowledge. From a psychological perspective, *personal epistemology* refers to individual conceptions of knowledge and knowing and how people develop, interpret, evaluate and justify knowledge (Hofer & Pintrich, 1997, 2002). Knowledge and knowing appear to develop in a patterned sequence across the life span. Understanding the trajectory of epistemological development and how it relates to learning and education can be useful for teachers, students, and educational researchers.

TRAJECTORY OF EPISTEMOLOGICAL DEVELOPMENT

Research on epistemological development began with the work of William Perry, who conducted longitudinal interviews with several classes of Harvard students beginning in the mid-1950s, asking them a set of open-ended questions at the end of each academic year. Perry was interested in how individuals responded to the intellectual and moral relativism encountered in a pluralistic university. At the outset of his research he expected that the differences he had observed in undergraduates' views about learning and teaching were likely to be related to personality. For example, a dichotomous view of knowledge as right or wrong and to be transmitted from an all-powerful authority would be evidence of an authoritarian personality, a construct of considerable interest to psychologists in the era following World War II. What he and his research staff found, however, was that the way in which students thought about knowledge and knowing changed during the college years, and most important, this change occurred in an ordered and predictable sequence of intellectual and ethical development.

The trajectory that Perry and his colleagues identified suggested that over time individuals transformed their views of knowledge and knowing from a position of dualistic thinking (a world viewed in absolutist polar binary terms of black and white, right and wrong) toward more contingent, relativistic thought. Thus the perception of knowledge as objective and certain was not a personality characteristic, but something malleable and apparently influenced by education. Perry's research resulted in a nine-point scheme of development that became the precursor for a significant body of research and the foundation for a wide range of ideas about educational implications of epistemological development.

Other similar schemes of intellectual development with epistemological components followed, all based on Perry's work. These models include reflective judgment, developed by Patricia King and Karen Kitchener; women's ways of knowing, developed by Mary Belenky, Blythe Clinchy, Nancy Goldberger, and Jill Tarule; and epistemological reflection, developed by Marcia Baxter Magolda. Additionally, Deanna Kuhn, in her research on the skills of argument, outlined a set of epistemological assumptions that further refined into a pattern of epistemological development with colleagues Richard Cheney and Michael Weinstock. Overall, each of these approaches involves a stage-like progression of from three to nine positions, but the components and the trajectory are remarkably similar.

Typically, individuals in any of these studies, primarily of college students and adults, are perceived as beginning with absolutism, a worldview marked by dualism and certainty: knowledge is black or white, right or wrong, highly certain, composed of discrete facts, and handed down from authorities unquestioningly. This position is modified as individuals come to recognize the legitimacy of other viewpoints. A midpoint on most schemes is characterized by multiplism, the idea that one opinion is equally valid as any other, that knowledge is highly uncertain, and that there is no agreed-upon means for justification. Advancement from this subjective state to a position of evaluativism (or commitment within relativism, as Perry called it) is marked by a growing realization that there are means for justification of various positions and that this enables an individual to assert some positions with confidence even if knowledge is evolving and contingent. Individuals who see the world from the upper levels of development are able to evaluate expertise, reconcile theory and evidence, provide support for their claims, and re-evaluate those claims in the light of new evidence.

EXPANDING THE SCOPE OF EPISTEMOLOGICAL DEVELOPMENT

Although the original scheme of development was based on Perry's study of males at an elite post-secondary institution in the United States in the 1950s and 1960s, the research was later extended to include broader populations: females, older adults, individuals not attending college, children and adolescents, and individuals in diverse cultures. One particularly important expansion of Perry's work in the decades that followed was the inclusion of women in the research sample and more deliberate attention to the perceptions of women, as in the women's ways of knowing study, or on gender-related patterns in the epistemological reflection research.

Belenky and her colleagues determined it important to study women only, as a means of understanding how women in particular approached knowledge and knowing. One of their contributions was in their attention to women's perceptions of the source of knowledge—whether knowledge was viewed as external and received, entirely internal, or constructed in interaction with the environment. In the fourth level of a 5-point scheme, called procedural knowing, individuals may be either separate knowers who are detached, critical, and skeptical, or connected knowers, who are empathic and trusting, valuing understanding over judgment. The final stage, constructed knowing, involves integration of these two approaches, a more complex recognition of the relation between the knower and the known and a tolerance for contradiction and ambiguity.

The epistemological reflection model, derived from longitudinal interviews of both male and female college students, suggests that some patterns of knowing may be gender-related but not gender-specific, as had been hypothesized by the authors of the women's ways of knowing study. At various stages in a five-point scheme that culminates in contextual knowing, women are more likely than men to be described as received knowers rather than mastery knowers, interpersonal rather than impersonal, and inter-individual rather than individual.

Such findings about gender-related patterns may need to be placed in the historical context of research conducted primarily in the 1980s. Little work in the 2000s has been done to assess the continuing validity of gender-related patterns of epistemological development and to determine whether changes in child-rearing or increased successes of females in education at all levels may have had an influence on epistemic worldviews. Continued research is needed in this area, and any application of gender-specific findings from these early studies should be made with caution. As with any group-level findings, generalizing from group differences to the individual is not recommended.

In addition to expanding epistemological research to include women, researchers have pursued epistemological development prior to the college years, an area that as of 2008 also needed further study. The early research on college students posited a trajectory beginning in absolutism, which implied that younger individuals simply viewed the world in absolutist terms until their beliefs were challenged in college. Surprisingly little longitudinal research has been conducted prior to college, but researchers such as Michael Boyes and Michael Chandler, who have assessed epistemological development in adolescence, have identified parallel stages similar to those in the college years. Chandler and others have thus raised questions about whether development might be recursive: Perhaps individuals move through the stages repeatedly, with enhanced understanding at each passage. In general, research on adolescence would indicate that high school students can exhibit post-absolutist perspectives, but more work is needed to distinguish this from the more nuanced perspectives of advanced college students. An established trajectory of epistemological development prior to the college years was as of 2008 not available.

Research from the late 1990s and early 2000s on young children began to illuminate the origins of epistemological development and to connect it to cognitive development. Very young children appear to begin at a state of egocentric subjectivity, a period in which the only perspective available is the knower's own. The attainment of theory of mind, a cognitive development between 3 and 5 years of age that involves a growing awareness of the beliefs, desires, and intentions of others, creates the potential for advancement toward an early sense of epistemic objectivity. Typically assessed through false belief tasks, theory of mind allows a child to know that another

individual can believe something erroneously. This cognitive awareness of multiple perspectives on knowing, and of the sense that one person can be right and another wrong, provides the foundation for absolutism.

Other researchers have been interested in understanding whether the developmental trajectory evidenced in U.S. studies is consistent in other cultures, or whether it might be an artifact of western education. In one cross-cultural study of Perry's scheme, Li-Fang Zhang found that students in Beijing, unlike those in the United States, became more dualistic during their college education, perhaps as result of an educational system that at the time of the study permitted few opportunities for individual decision making. Results of this and other studies suggest the need for sensitivity to cultural context and for more explorations of the interaction between educational environment, cultural context, and epistemological development.

DOMAIN SPECIFICITY

Much of the research on epistemological development is based on a presumption that a general cognitive framework guides one's views of knowledge and knowing across domains. Thus an individual who believes that there is one right answer and that authorities are the sole source of knowledge would believe this regardless of the area in question. By contrast, research on epistemic beliefs has been examined both generally and in regard to specific disciplines, such as math, science, or history. Students have been found to hold differing beliefs about disciplines, for example, that knowledge in chemistry is more certain than knowledge in psychology, as well as beliefs specific to disciplines, for example, that knowing history means learning dates. Math and science educators have extensively pursued an understanding of students' epistemic beliefs within these particular disciplines, exploring such conceptions as the nature of science. This area had as of 2008 seldom been investigated developmentally, however, although Ala Samarapungavan, Erik Westby, and George Bodner found that the epistemic development of chemistry students was influenced by aspects of their research experience and engagement with expert researchers.

Within the paradigm of epistemological development, some researchers began to explore domain differences, but little of this research focused on disciplines. In one such report, King and Kitchener (2004) noted in their overview of research on reflective judgment that there is a high rate of consistency in the use of epistemic assumptions in reasoning about ill-structured problems, regardless of domain. Other research on domain differences in epistemological development addressed domains not as disciplines, but in regard to judgment domains, such as taste, morality, aesthetics, values, or facts. In their study of individuals from second grade through adulthood, Kuhn, Cheney, and Weinstock found that individuals can be at different epistemological levels depending on the domain, with individuals, for example, accepting multiple viewpoints in regard to personal taste before they accept them in regard to objective facts. The movement from multiplism to evaluativism is more likely to occur first in regard to objective facts, where warrants for claims begin to supersede individual opinions.

Domain differences have also been explored in studies of young children by Cecilia Wainryb and her colleagues, who found that even 5-year-olds display evidence of relativism in some domains more than others. Children can be expected at a fairly early age, for example, to know and accept that a friend prefers a different flavor of ice cream but can be quite certain that hitting is wrong. What this continued line of research suggests is both that epistemological development varies by judgment domain and that it is possible for aspects of multiplism to occur much younger than might have been predicted in the pioneering studies of college students.

METHODS OF INVESTIGATING EPISTEMOLOGICAL DEVELOPMENT

The original research on epistemological development was inherently phenomenological, with open-ended interviews that prompted meaning-making on the part of the student being interviewed. Perry, for example, began his end-of-semester interviews by asking "What stands out for you about this year?" Some of the researchers who followed Perry continued to use open-ended interviews, and others have posed ill-structured problems as a means of eliciting epistemological assumptions. For example, reflective judgment interviews involve responding to questions about issues such as the dangers of chemical additives in food, e.g., "Can you ever know for certain that your position on this is correct? How? Why not?" and "How is it possible that experts in the field could disagree about this subject?" Similarly, research on the epistemological aspects of argumentation employed questions about the certainty and justification of knowledge on topics such as reasons for criminal recidivism and other topics for which there are not likely to be simple, agreed-upon answers. Other studies on epistemological development involved asking individuals about the possible causes for a fictitious war or required a simulation of juror reasoning. Research interviews with young children, particularly in regard to domains of judgment, have been more likely to involve puppets and other props or vignettes with illustrated depictions of the scenario involved.

Interviews that require individuals to respond to ill-structured problems are called production tasks, as the interviewee is asked to produce a response. The transcribed protocols that result are complicated to score and typically require trained raters. Although this method provides rich data and affords a complex understanding of participants' thinking, it is also an expensive and time-consuming approach. The need for measures that can be administered and scored more easily led to the design of written instruments, typically aimed at providing some means for scoring developmental level. These are more likely to involve recognition tasks, in which individuals indicate the similarity of prepared responses to their own understanding. For example, participants indicate how similar a statement such as the following is to their own thinking: "It is my perspective that what researchers conclude is just their own opinion." These instruments make it possible to conduct larger studies more quickly, but there is also concern about validity, reliability, and reductionism, as complex developmental phenomena are reduced to recognition of simple statements, potentially inflating individual scores.

EDUCATIONAL IMPLICATIONS

Epistemological development has significant implications for the ways individuals consider and approach knowing and learning in a wide range of contexts, across the life span. Individuals often need to make considered judgments on a wide range of issues from personal health to global environmental concerns, and these judgments typically require weighing of evidence and evaluation of competing knowledge claims. Yet research on epistemological development suggests that the skills required to do this, evidenced in the position of evaluativism, are not all that common and that adults in the United States are more likely to be either absolutists, convinced one position must be right, or, more often, multiplists, basing decisions on personal judgments and viewing opinions as equally valid. Kuhn and others have argued that epistemological understanding matters and that preparation of an educated citizenry requires more attention to this process within the educational system at all levels.

A number of researchers who work within the developmental tradition assert that the higher levels of epistemological development are consistent with the skills of critical thinking and adaptive complexity. Thus epistemological development has been viewed by some as one of the aims of education and as a potential outcome measure for a college education. Accordingly, a number of studies have evaluated students' progressions toward higher stages of the various schemes, particularly during the college years. Longitudinal interview studies conducted in college and in some cases beyond suggest that college does have a small but measurable impact on epistemological development and that graduate school may advance this further, particularly in terms of higher stages of reflective judgment. Cross-sectional studies generally show a correlation between education and level of development and also between expertise and epistemological development.

Epistemological stance can also lead students to have different views of education, classroom tasks, and expectations of teachers. For example, absolutists would be likely to want teachers to provide objective truth, multiplists might have difficult understanding how teachers could make the judgments they do, and evaluativists would expect substantiated support for various positions. Educators' awareness of these general schemes can help them understand student reasoning and responses to particular aspects of education and to enable them to provide support for developmental transitions. The relation between education and development can also be viewed as reciprocal, with individuals interpreting learning through a current lens that is also being transformed in the process.

Overall, educators may wish to help students make a progression toward competence in evaluating multiple truth claims and understanding how knowledge is constructed, supported, and evolving. Research on epistemological development suggests that teachers need to attend to thinking skills and cognitive development as well as the mastery of content. Teachers can provide students with opportunities to discuss ill-structured problems, for example, and to recognize that not all problems have one right answer. Educators might also structure assignments so that students learn to gather support for particular positions, consider opposing viewpoints, coordinate theory and evidence, and evaluate expertise and authority. These are challenging tasks, but they are critically important in helping students develop intellectual skills.

SEE ALSO *Cognitive Strategies; Epistemological Beliefs; Metacognition; Theory of Mind.*

BIBLIOGRAPHY

Baxter, M.. (1992). *Knowing and reasoning in college: Gender-related patterns in students' intellectual development.* San Francisco: Jossey Bass.

Belenky, M. F., Clinchy, B. M., Goldberger, N. R., & Tarule, J. M. (1986). *Women's ways of knowing: The development of self, voice, and mind.* New York: Basic Books.

Boyes, M. C., & Chandler, M. (1992). Cognitive development, epistemic doubt, and identity formation in adolescence. *Journal of Youth and Adolescence, 21*(3), 277–303.

Chandler, M. J., Hallett, D., & Sokol, B. W. (2002). Competing claims about competing knowledge claims. In B. K. Hofer & P. R. Pintrich (Eds.), *Personal Epistemology: The Psychology of Beliefs about Knowledge and Knowing* (pp. 145–168). Mahwah, NJ: Erlbaum.

Hofer, B. K., & Pintrich, P. R. (1997). The development of epistemological theories: Beliefs about knowledge and knowing and their relation to learning. *Review of Educational Research, 67,* 88–140.

Hofer, B. K., & Pintrich, P. R. (Eds.). (2002). *Personal epistemology: The psychology of beliefs about knowledge and knowing.* Mahwah, NJ: Erlbaum.

King, P. M., & Kitchener, K. S. (1994). *Developing Reflective judgment: Understanding and promoting intellectual growth and critical thinking in adolescents and adults.* San Francisco: Jossey-Bass, 1994.

King, P. M., & Kitchener, K. S. (2004). Reflective judgment: Theory and research on the development of epistemic assumptions through adulthood. *Educational Psychologist, 39,* 5–18.

Kuhn, D. (1991). *The skills of argument.* Cambridge: Cambridge University Press.

Kuhn, D., Cheney, R., & Weinstock, M. (2000). The development of epistemological understanding. *Cognitive Development, 15,* 309–328.

Perry, W. G. (1970). *Forms of intellectual and ethical development in the college years: A scheme.* New York: Holt, Rinehart, and Winston.

Samarapungavan, A., Westby, E. L., & Bodner, G. M. (2006). Contextual epistemic development in science: A comparison of chemistry students and research chemists. *Science Education, 90*(3), 468–495.

Wainryb, C., Shaw, L. A., Langley, M., Cottam, K., & Lewis, R. (2004). Children's thinking about diversity of belief and in the early school years: Judgments of relativism, tolerance, and disagreeing persons. *Child Development, 75,* 687–703.

Zhang, L-F. (1999). A comparison of U.S. and Chinese university students' cognitive development: The cross-cultural applicability of Perry's theory. *Journal of Psychology, 133,* 425–439.

Barbara K. Hofer

ERIKSON, ERIK
1902–1994

Erik Erickson (1902–1994), noted psychoanalyst and student of Anna Freud, is not a figure who immediately comes to mind when one thinks about the great contributors to understanding of the psychology of classroom learning. Erikson stands out among Freudians as one of the first to use a psychoanalytic perspective with children and to develop play therapy techniques for counseling. His work with World War II U.S. veterans experiencing shell shock helped solidify his understanding of the mechanisms of identity, and his famous 1968 publication, *Identity: Youth in Crisis,* helped explain the generational, social, and racial tensions of his day. The central question of his work had to do with identifying factors that affect personality.

Erik Erikson in his home study, March 4, 1975. **TED STRESHINSKY/TIME** & **LIFE PICTURES/GETTY IMAGES.**

ERIKSON'S CONTRIBUTION TO THE FIELD

Erikson's contribution to the field of educational psychology may be subtler than the mainstays of school-related research pertaining to learning and achievement. It lies not in the products of schooling, but in helping people understand the importance of interactions between teachers and students.

Erikson's work is likely to be known in many areas outside educational psychology, and any casual student of identity is familiar with his theory. His description of identity development and the mechanisms associated with this interpersonal milestone are familiar to most teachers of adolescents either through personal experience or through observation. In this context, Erikson made two important contributions regarding classroom interaction: (a) recognition that adolescence is a time when individuals search for the standards and truths that really matter, and (b) adults, and especially teachers, play an important role in adolescents' identity development. These two contributions provide insight into effective

strategies teachers can use when interacting with their adolescent students.

IDENTITY AND STANDARDS

The first contribution has to do with how Erikson understood ego and identity. Erikson agreed with Sigmund Freud's triadic model of the human psyche (id, ego, super-ego). Unlike Freud, who focused on the conflict between id and superego and the mediating role of the ego, Erikson described the work of the ego in terms of differentiating itself from the superego. In Erikson's view, each stage of psychosocial development, from birth to old age, involves some form of differentiation of self from others.

Differentiation of the ego has to do with the degree to which a person is what others tell him versus how much a person controls what he is. During the stage of psychosocial development associated with adolescence, the work of identity formation involves examination of social standards or values and selection of those that the adolescent believes are truly important. If choices are not actively made, the person's identity is in a state of foreclosure. If adolescents are actively involved in searching, but have not yet chosen standards, identity can be described as being in a state of moratorium, the condition most often associated with adolescence.

ROLE OF ADULTS

Given Erikson's perspective on identity development, the second important contribution is his description of the role that adults play in adolescents' identity development. This description is particularly relevant for educators. During the time of adolescent moratorium, adults can facilitate identity development in two ways. The first way is by being a "sanctioner of capabilities." (Erikson, 1968, p. 87) To adolescents, adults are the bearers of society's standards. In this generational role, adults should be clear about the standards they hold, exhibit behaviors consistent with stated beliefs, and use those standards to judge adolescents. By using society's standards to judge, adults communicate with adolescents about their capabilities and help clarify their selection of standards. Judged in an honest fashion, adolescents learn about their capabilities for adult roles. The second way adults assist with identity development is by providing an environment in which identity can be explored. During the time of moratorium, adolescents need opportunity to scrutinize society's standards and try on identities in a setting that does not impose an uncritical choice.

IDENTITY DEVELOPMENT AND TEACHER-STUDENT INTERACTIONS

Adults, and especially teachers through their generational role, can contribute to adolescents' identity development by being sanctioners of capabilities and by providing a safe environment in which adolescents can deal with their identity crisis. In his understanding the dynamics of schools and classrooms, Erikson believed these two actions are keys for effective interactions between teachers and adolescent students. Teachers who are honest about their beliefs, consistent in their actions, and who find capabilities in adolescents to sanction are, according to Erikson, more likely to sustain adolescents' initiative and elicit their cooperation in academic matters.

SEE ALSO *Classroom Environment; Identity Development; Self-Determination Theory of Motivation.*

BIBLIOGRAPHY

WORKS BY

Erikson, E. (1993). *Childhood and Society* (3rd ed.), New York: Norton.

Erikson, E. (1968). *Identity: Youth and Crisis,* New York: Norton.

Erikson, E. (1994). *Identity and the Life Cycle* (3rd ed.), New York: Norton.

WORKS ABOUT

Burston, D. (2007). *Erik Erikson and the American psyche: ego, ethics, and evolution.* Lanham, MD: Jason Aronson.

Friedman, L. J. (1999). *Identity's architect: a biography of Erik H. Erikson.* New York: Scribner.

Hoare, C. H. (2002). *Erikson on development in adulthood: new insights from the unpublished papers.* New York: Oxford University Press.

Hoover, K. R. (Ed.). (2004). *The future of identity: centennial reflections on the legacy of Erik Erikson.* Lanham, MD: Lexington Books.

Welchman, K. (2000). *Erik Erikson: his life, work, and significance.* Buckingham, PA: Open University Press.

Doug Hamman

ETHNIC IDENTITY AND ACADEMIC ACHIEVEMENT

This entry provides an overview of the concept of ethnic identity, with a focus on its relevance for ethnic minority adolescents' academic development. Researchers and educators increasingly have recognized the important role of race-related beliefs and experiences in the academic achievement of ethnic minority children and adolescents. Various explanations have been offered to explain ethnic minority achievement and underachievement, and most implicate the role of youths' *ethnic identity* beliefs, or their self-constructed definitions of the relevance and meanings associated with being a member of their ethnic group. Ethnic minority groups face many social and

structural risks and challenges in the United States, and a stronger identification with an ethnic minority identity has been related to perceiving more ethnic group barriers and discrimination and having a higher awareness of group stigma and stereotypes. Because of this, some have suggested that a stronger ethnic group identity necessarily places youth at risk for decreased academic engagement. However, there is more support from emerging theory and research that a strong, positive sense of racial identity relates to more positive achievement values and may help adolescents maintain positive academic motivation and engagement when they perceive group barriers or have negative race-related experiences. The literature reviewed in this entry suggests a number of implications for education. One is that schools can play important roles in supporting youths' development of a positive sense of ethnic identity. Furthermore, moving away from a "colorblind" approach and recognizing youths' distinct ethnic identities as potential assets can improve schools' and educators' abilities to create truly inclusive settings.

ETHNIC IDENTITY: DEFINITION AND SIGNIFICANCE

During adolescence, individuals begin to construct a general sense of their identity, or their personal definitions of who they are, what is important to them, and appropriate ways to think and behave. During this period, youth also differentiate their various social identities, the self-constructed definitions of who they are in relation to the social groups to which they belong. A sense of ethnic identity becomes salient for many ethnic minority adolescents as they explore the significance of their ethnic group membership in defining who they are (Spencer & Markstrom-Adams, 1990; Phinney, 1990). Ethnic identity has multiple components, including individuals' views of the importance of their ethnic group to their self-definitions, the meanings they attach to their ethnic group, and their thinking about how their ethnic group affects their position in society. Thus, ethnic identities are descriptive (e.g., "I am a Mexican American"; "I am an African American"), affective ("I feel positively about being an African American"; "I think others regard my ethnic group positively"), as well as prescriptive ("I know how Chinese Americans act"; "I know how African Americans act"). Adolescents' understandings of the meanings of their social identities influence their adaptations and responses within domains in which those identities are salient. Because race and ethnicity often are salient in the domain of education, adolescents' ethnic identities may be particularly relevant in shaping how youth interpret and respond to their social and classroom contexts at school.

ETHNIC IDENTITY DURING ADOLESCENCE

Relative to younger children, adolescents have more highly developed cognitive abilities related to understanding themselves and their experiences in more complex, abstract, and indirect ways, and this period also involves intensification of particular social-cognitive attributes, e.g., heightened awareness of how they are viewed by others. Thus, they become more cognizant of the relevance of race and ethnicity in society and have a higher likelihood of perceiving experiences in terms of race and ethnicity (Spencer, Dupree, & Hartmann, 1997).

In addition to individual differences in social cognition, cultural, structural, and social influences during adolescence may affect the development of ethnic identity beliefs. Information youth appraise from interactions in their primary social contexts influences how they develop understandings of themselves in relation to the social groups to which they belong (Harter, 1990; Spencer, Dupree, & Hartmann, 1997). Adolescents' ethnic identity beliefs derive in large part from their understanding and internalization of socialization messages they receive from their families and communities about their ethnic group's history and values (Hughes & Chen, 1999). Other important influences on ethnic identity development include the social and economic opportunities and constraints youth perceive as available to members of their group in their families and communities. Finally, adolescents' increased exposure to personal and societal racism (Garcia Coll et al., 1996; Greene, Way, & Pahl, 2006) influences their ethnic identity development.

ETHNIC IDENTITY AND ETHNIC MINORITY ACADEMIC ACHIEVEMENT

Academic engagement requires linking one's personal identity to the roles of student and learner (Garcia & Pintrich, 1994), showing sustained curiosity and interest in class, and displaying intense efforts in learning tasks (Connell, Spencer, & Aber, 1994; Skinner & Belmont, 1993). Adolescents' academic engagement has been linked to social identities that are made salient in the academic domain (Garcia & Pintrich, 1994). The academic domain is one in which race often is salient for many ethnic minority adolescents. For instance, entry into secondary schools is associated with increased racial cleavage, social comparison, and heightened salience of racial and ethnic stereotypes (Fisher, Wallace, & Fenton, 2000). Thus, it is likely that minority adolescents' levels of academic engagement are influenced, in part, by their ethnic identity beliefs. Theory and research suggests that ethnic identity may serve as a risk factor for lower academic motivation and achievement as well as promote academic motivation and achievement. The risk and promotion approaches are described below.

RACIAL IDENTITY AS AN ACADEMIC RISK FACTOR APPROACH

Within several well-known theoretical models, ethnic minority identity has been posited to place individuals at risk for decreased academic engagement through the influence of their heightened awareness of the negative status of their racial group in society (e.g., Aronson, 2002; Fordham & Ogbu, 1986; Fordham, 1988; Mickelson, 1990; Steinberg, Dornbusch, & Brown, 1992). The Cultural-Ecological framework of ethnic minority achievement offered by Fordham and Ogbu (1986), for instance, asserts that because African American populations immigrated to the United States under conditions of oppression and opportunity constraint, they developed a collective group identity that rejects institutions that are dominated by the oppressive mainstream culture, including the American educational system. As a consequence, youth's identification with a Black identity came to entail a rejection of a pro-achievement orientation, including attitudes and behaviors associated with being successful in school.

Fordham (1988) expanded on this framework, positing that sustained school success for high-achieving African American students entails minimizing their connectedness to their racial identity in exchange for mainstream attitudes and values that are better aligned with an academic identity, a process termed as becoming "raceless." A similar theme within educational research is the notion that having a "colorblind" perspective is the best way to ameliorate racial group differences in achievement. Within the education field, the majority of teachers are white, from backgrounds that differ from those of their students of color, and often have had limited multicultural training (Ford & Harris, 1996). A common ideology among teachers entering their professions and classrooms is that it is best to simply not see race or racial group differences at all but view students only as individuals (Markus, Steele, & Steele, 2000; Rousseau & Tate, 2003). However, the underlying presumption is that minority youth must de-emphasize their ethnic/cultural backgrounds in order to develop a positive academic identity and emphasize thinking and acting in ways more consistent with White middle-class norms (Delpit, 1995; Ladson-Billings, 1995; McAllister & Irvine, 2000).

Other theoretical perspectives viewing ethnic identity as a risk factor for achievement have focused on the stigma associated with identifying with an ethnic minority group in the United States. This work suggests that African American and Hispanic youth disidentify with school and academics because the academic domain is one in which their ethnic group is regarded negatively (e.g., Crocker & Major, 1989; Osborne, 1997). While this coping strategy is theorized to protect individuals' self-concept from the negative impact of perceiving group-based discrimination and devaluation, it inhibits the motivational attitudes and behaviors that lead to good school performance. Similarly, stereotype threat theory posits that African American students' academic underperformance result from fears or apprehensions around supporting racial stereotypes related to intellectual ability, and, over time, these threat experiences lead to less personal identification with academics and engagement in the learning process (Aronson, 2002; Steele, 1997). Implicit across these perspectives is that individuals who perceive societal discrimination or stigma for their ethnic group disengage with the educational process, and those who emphasize their ethnic minority identity are particularly vulnerable to the negative effects of this discrimination and stigma on academic engagement.

LIMITATIONS OF THE ETHNIC IDENTITY AS RISK APPROACH

A major limitation of the ethnic identity-as-risk approach to understanding ethnic minority academic achievement is that there is very little empirical evidence in support of the major assertions of the approach. First, there have been few studies directly assessing the relationship between ethnic identity attitudes and academic engagement in African Americans. The few studies that have been used to support the approach do not directly address the question of whether identifying with one's race and perceiving racial barriers explains individual differences in African American students' levels of academic engagement. For instance, in the widely cited ethnographic study of urban African American high school students (Fordham & Ogbu, 1986), although low-achieving students perceived particular behaviors associated with school success—e.g., spending time in library studying, reading and writing poetry, being on time—as inconsistent with their personal identities, students were not asked about their racial identities nor did the youth mention ethnicity or race when discussing their academic identities (e.g., youth connected pro-achievement behaviors to being a nerd or "brainiac," not necessarily as being inconsistent with a Black identity).

Other evidence used in support of the risk approach include studies showing smaller associations between African American adolescents' self-concept and their academic grade performance relative to other ethnic groups (e.g., Demo & Parker, 1987; Osborne, 1997) and lower academic task performance for ethnic minority college students for whom racial stereotypes are made salient (e.g., Steele & Aronson, 1995). None of these studies, however, directly assessed youths' ethnic identity beliefs and thus are unable to fully demonstrate the presumed links between ethnic identity and academic engagement.

ETHNIC IDENTITY AS PROMOTING ACADEMIC ACHIEVEMENT

Although the identity-as-risk approach has received a great deal of attention, ethnic minority identity also has been conceptualized as an important psychologically protective set of beliefs that individuals have developed to buffer against the impact of racial discrimination and stigmatized status (e.g., Cross, Helms, & Parham, 1998). Researchers have begun to conceptualize racial/ethnic identity as an important resilience resource in the normative development of African American youth (e.g., Cross et al., 1999; Spencer, Cunningham, & Swanson, 1995; Spencer et al., 1997). This view of ethnic identity, while recognizing the significant challenges that confront African American youth, also acknowledges the fact that many youth are resilient in the face of those challenges. An approach that views a strong, positive sense of ethnic identity as promoting achievement is consistent with a historical view of both Black and Hispanic immigrant communities that recognizes that because the groups were denied opportunities for education and advancement (during and after slavery for African Americans) or came to the United States because of the lack of opportunities in their countries of national origin (for many Hispanic and Asian American groups), they often placed a stronger emphasis on the importance of learning and education as the primary route to mobility (Chavous, et al., 2003).

Thus, ethnic identity can relate to a meaning-making process that affords members of historically oppressed ethnic minority groups an opportunity to define their racial membership in such a way that academic success can be seen as valuable despite structural- and individual-level barriers (such as stigma and racial discrimination) to academic success. For instance, findings from a study by Altschul, Oyserman, and Bybee (2006) indicate that African American middle school students who felt more connected to their Black identity and who linked their Black identity to a value for achievement were more academically motivated and performed better than youth who identified less with their ethnic group and who didn't view academic achievement as connected to their ethnic group identity. Chavous and colleagues (2003) also found that African American high school students who had a strong ethnic group identity accompanied by group pride and awareness of societal discrimination had more positive academic attitudes and showed higher academic persistence and postsecondary educational attainment than youth who de-emphasized their ethnic identities, felt less group pride, and who were less conscious of the potential for bias against their group.

Also, there is growing evidence that having a strong, positive sense of ethnic identity may protect minority adolescents from the negative psychological and academic impacts of perceiving ethnic group barriers or experiencing interpersonal discrimination based on their ethnic group. For instance, in a 2006 study, Sellers and colleagues found that Black youth having an ethnic identity characterized by feelings of strong group connection and group pride showed more positive psychological well being when experiencing racial discrimination compared to those adolescents with less strong feelings of connection to and positive attitudes about their ethnic group. Wong and colleagues in their 2003 study found that African American adolescents who held a strong connection to and pride in being Blacks were protected from the negative impact on academic attitudes and performance of experiencing racial discrimination at school relative to those with less of a strong, positive connection with their ethnic group.

IMPLICATIONS FOR SCHOOLS AND EDUCATORS

Although ethnic identity may be influenced by and reflect the languages, customs, cultural values, and experiences deriving from youths' homes and communities, there is evidence that school settings can play important roles in youths' ethnic identity development. Researchers find that ethnic minority adolescents frequently report experiences related to race and ethnicity within their school settings (e.g., Fisher et al., 2000; Rosenbloom & Way, 2004; Wong et al., 2003). In particular, the secondary school context provides classroom and social structures that can result in heightened racial salience and more awareness of racial group differences, including stereotypes. For instance, entry into secondary schooling is associated with more ethnic cleavage in classes and peer social groups. Teachers and class curricula often emphasize social comparison more than in elementary grades, resulting in more attention to group differences in achievement and performance (Seidman, Allen, Aber, Mitchell, & Feinman, 1994).

At school, ethnic minority adolescents are likely to have White teachers from middle-class backgrounds, even in urban schools, and teachers in general are unlikely to have received extensive training in multicultural education (Ford & Harris, 1996). Additionally, ethnic minority youth report racially biased treatment within the classroom and peer contexts at school as common occurrences, e.g., perceiving that they received poor grades or evaluations from teachers and other adults at school or harsher discipline due to race, and social exclusion or harassment due to race (Fisher et al., 2000; Romero & Roberts, 1998). Thus, schools may contribute to youths' development of ethnic identities and the extent to which youth perceive their group identity as consistent with schooling and achievement.

Teacher training practices are not necessarily designed to equip teachers to work in multicultural class settings

(Delpit, 1995; Irvine, 1986; Ladson-Billings, 1995). This will continue to be a problem as the ethnic minority population continues to rise in the United States. As noted, a perspective prevalent among educators and in professional training of teachers is the "colorblind" ideology (Delpit, 1995; Markus, Steele, & Steele, 2000). However, ethnic identity research presents growing evidence that such a perspective does not relate to positive academic outcomes for ethnic minority youth and in fact may lead to increased cultural tensions and miscommunications. The research concerning the positive influences of a strong, positive ethnic identity on youth achievement outcomes suggest that the colorblind approach (or a de-emphasis on group membership and emphasis on conforming to mainstream values) may hinder teachers from seeing the needs of their ethnic minority students and may result in students not being acknowledged in ways that facilitate their achievement. Furthermore, while teachers may not be formally trained in theory and research related to race and education, many teachers enter their classrooms with some familiarity of the most prevalent perspectives on race in education. Unfortunately, they are most likely to be familiar with the notion that certain ethnic minority youth and their families devalue educational achievement and define their ethnic identity as inconsistent with achievement (or "acting White"), while the values of other youth and families include embracing education. Such misinformation may lead to making erroneous attributions and conclusions when students show lower performance and experience academic difficulty.

Thus, school practitioners must receive training about the development of youth from multicultural backgrounds. This training should not only acknowledge the unique risks associated with membership in ethnic minority groups in the United States but also consider how youths' ethnic identities can serve as cultural assets in relation to their achievement and how to use this information to create inclusive classroom contexts for all students. Without such training, it is likely that teaching approaches and practices will be based on popular views of common sense approaches not supported by empirical research. Additionally teachers should be mindful of endorsing their own ethnic identity beliefs in the class contexts they create.

SEE ALSO *Identity Development.*

BIBLIOGRAPHY

Altschul, I., Oyserman, D., & Bybee, D. (2006). Racial-ethnic identity in mid-adolescence: Content and change as predictors of academic achievement. *Child Development, 77*(5), 1155–1169.

Aronson, J. (2002). Stereotype threat: Contending and coping with unnerving expectations. In J. Aronson (Ed.), *Improving* academic achievement: *Impact of psychological factors on education* (pp. 279–301). San Diego, CA: Academic Press.

Chavous, T. M., Bernat, D., Schmeelk-Cone, K., Caldwell, C., Kohn-Wood, L. P., & Zimmerman, M. A. (2003). Racial identity and academic attainment among African American adolescents. *Child Development, 74*(4), 1076–1091.

Connell, J. P., Spencer, M. B., & Aber, J. L. (1994). Educational risk and resilience in African American youth: Context, self, action, and outcomes in school. *Child Development, 65*(2), 493–506.

Crocker, J. & Major, B. (1989). Social stigma and self-esteem: The self-protective properties of stigma. *Psychological Review, 96*(4), 608–630.

Cross, W. E., Parham, T. A., & Helms, J. E. (1998). Nigrescence revisited: Theory and Research. In R. L. Jones (Ed.), *African American identity development: Theory, research, and intervention.* Hampton, VA: Cobb & Henry.

Cross, W. E., Strauss, L., & Fhagen-Smith, P. (1999). African American identity development across the life span: Educational implications. In R. H. Sheets & E. R. Hollins (Eds.), *Racial and ethnic identity in school practices: Aspects of human development* (pp. 29–48). Mahwah, NJ: Erlbaum.

Delpit, L. (1995). *Other people's children: Cultural conflict in the classroom.* New York: New Press.

Fisher, C., Wallace, S., & Fenton, R. (2000). Discrimination distress during adolescence. *Journal of Youth and Adolescence, 29*, 679–695.

Ford, D., & Harris, J. (1996). Perceptions and attitudes of Black students toward school, achievement, and other educational variables. *Child Development, 67*(3), 1141–1152.

Fordham, S. (1988). Racelessness as a factor in Black students' school success: Pragmatic strategy or pyrrhic victory? *Harvard Educational Review, 58*(1), 54–84.

Fordham, S., & Ogbu, J. (1986). Black students' school success: Coping with the "burden of acting White." *Urban Review, 18*, 176–206.

Garcia, T., & Pintrich, P. R. (1994). Regulating motivation and cognition in the classroom: The role of self-schemas and self-regulatory strategies. In D. Schunk & B. J. Zimmerman (Eds.), *Self-regulation of learning and performance* (pp. 127–154). Hillsdale, NJ: Erlbaum.

Garcia Coll, C., Lamberty, G., Jenkins, R., Pipes McAdoo, H., Crnic, K., Hanna Wasik, B., & Vazquez Garcia, H. (1996). An integrative model for the study of developmental competencies in minority children. *Child Development, 67*(5), 1891–1914.

Greene, M., Way, N., & Pahl, K. (2006). Trajectories of perceived adult and peer discrimination among Black, Latino, and Asian American adolescents: Patterns and psychological correlates. *Developmental Psychology, 42*(2), 218–238.

Harter, S. (1990). Issues in the assessment of the self-concept of children and adolescence. In A.M. LaGreca (Ed.), *Through the eyes of the child: Obtaining self-reports from children and adolescents* (pp. 292–325). Boston: Allyn & Bacon.

Hughes, D., & Chen, L. (1999). The nature of parents' race-related communications to children: A developmental perspective. In L. Bater & C. S. Tamis-LeMonda (Eds.), *Child psychology: A handbook of contemporary issues* (pp. 467–490). Philadelphia: Taylor & Francis.

Irvine, J. (1986). Teacher-student interactions: Effects of student race, sex, and grade level. *Journal of Educational Psychology, 78*(1), 14–21.

Ladson-Billings, G. (1995). But that's just good teaching: The case for culturally relevant pedagogy. *Theory into Practice, 34*(3), 159–165.

Markus, H., Steele, C., & Steele, D. (2000). Colorblindness as a barrier to inclusion: Assimilation and nonimmigrant minorities. *Daedelus, 129*(4), 233–263.

Mickelson, R. (1990). The attitude-achievement paradox among Black adolescents. *Sociology of Education, 63*, 44–61.

McAllister, G., & Irvine, J. (2000). Cultural competency and multicultural teacher education. *Review of Educational Research, 70*(1), 3–24.

Osborne, J. W. (1997). Race and academic disidentification. *Journal of Educational Psychology, 89*, 728–735.

Phinney, J. S. (1990). Ethnic identity in adolescents and adults: Review of research. *Psychological Bulletin, 18*(3), 499–514.

Rosenbloom, S. R., & Way, N. (2004). Experiences of discrimination among African American, Asian American, and Latino adolescents in an urban high school. *Youth & Society, 35*(4), 420–451.

Romero, A., & Roberts, R. (1998). Perception of discrimination and ethnocultural variables in a diverse group of adolescents. *Journal of Adolescence 21*(6), 641–647.

Rosenbloom, S. R., & Way, N. (2004). Experiences of discrimination among African American, Asian American, and Latino adolescents in an urban high school. *Youth & Society, 35*(4), 420–451.

Rousseau, C., & Tate, W. (2003). No time like the present: Reflecting on equity in school mathematics. *Theory into Practice, 42*(3), 210–216.

Seidman, E., Allen, L., Aber, J. L., Mitchell, C., & Feinman, J. (1994). The impact of school transitions in early adolescence on the self-system and perceived social context of poor urban youth. *Child Development, 65*(2), 507.

Sellers, R. M., Linder, N. C., Martin, P. P., & Lewis, R. L. (2006). Racial identity matters: The relationship between racial discrimination and psychological functioning in African American adolescents. *Journal of Research on Adolescence, 16*(2), 187–216.

Skinner, E. A., & Belmont, M. J. (1993). Motivation in the classroom: Reciprocal effects of teacher behavior and student engagement across the school year. *Journal of Educational Psychology, 85*(4), 571–581.

Spencer, M. B., & Markstrom-Adams, C. (1990). Identity processes among racial and ethnic minority children in America. *Child Development, 61*, 290–310.

Spencer, M. B., Cunningham, M., & Swanson, D. P. (1995). Identity as coping: Adolescent African American males' adaptive responses to high risk environments. In H. W. Harris, H. C. Blue, & E. H. Griffith (Eds.), *Racial and ethnic identity* (pp. 31–52). New York: Routledge.

Spencer, M. B., Dupree, D., & Hartmann, T. (1997). A phenomenological variant of ecological systems theory (PVEST): A self-organization perspective in context. *Development and Psychopathology, 9*(4), 817–833.

Steele, C. M. (1997). A threat in the air: How stereotypes shape intellectual identity and performance. *American Psychologist, 52*, 613–629.

Steele, C. M., & Aronson, J. (1995). Stereotype threat and the intellectual test performance of African Americans. *Journal of Personality and Social Psychology, 69*(5), 797–811.

Steinberg, L., Dornbusch, S., & Brown, B. (1992). Ethnic differences in adolescent achievement: An ecological perspective. *American Psychologist, 47*(6), 723–729.

Wong, C. A., Eccles, J. S., & Sameroff, A. (2003). The influence of ethnic discrimination and ethnic identification on African American adolescents' school and socioemotional adjustment. *Journal of Personality, 71*(6), 1197–123.

Tabbye M. Chavous

EVALUATION (TEST) ANXIETY

In the era of the No Child Left Behind legislation there is a growing concern that high-stakes testing may have a negative impact on student learning and performance. Mulvenon, Stegman, and Ritter (2005) noted that a cursory review of the academic literature and national news sources on the impact of standardized testing reveals a plethora of anecdotal cases of students experiencing illness, anxiety, and heightened levels of stress. Furthermore, numerous studies have surveyed teachers regarding the impact of standardized tests, producing findings that low performance on these tests is correlated with increased levels of anxiety and stress. Mulvenon and colleagues conducted a survey and concluded that most of the dangers of standardized testing are overstated and that most students, parents, principals, and counselors do not report increased levels of stress or anxiety. Nevertheless, there remains a nationwide concern that an increase in high-stakes testing and test anxiety is harming students.

Test anxiety (TA) is a feeling of apprehension and discomfort accompanied by cognitive difficulties during a test. There is general consensus that it involves at least two components: (a) a pattern of physiological hyperarousal (i.e., increased heart rate, blood pressure, etc.) that may include physical changes and complaints, and (b) a cognitive obstruction or disorganization of effective problem-solving and cognitive control, including difficulty in thinking clearly (Friedman & Bendas-Jacobs, 1997). These two factors have also been termed *emotionality* (nervousness about the test situation) and *worry* (a cognitive aspect which involves concern over one's performance). A proposed third factor that has received less attention is social humiliation, referring to one's concern and awareness that others may negatively view the test performance. This third factor could easily be subsumed by the worry or cognitive component.

Test anxiety is similar to math anxiety in that both involve physiological and worry components. However,

Low performance on standardized tests has been correlated with increased levels of anxiety and stress. ©WILL & DENI MCINTYRE/ CORBIS.

math anxiety can occur during math instruction and homework, whereas test anxiety only occurs in testing environments. Public speaking anxiety is also characterized by the cognitive and emotionality components, but much of the anxiety occurs before the event and tapers off after the first minute of the speech. TA is thought to persist throughout the testing experience, and its onset occurs at the start of the test.

TA has been studied as a construct for more than 50 years (Mandler & Sarason, 1952). Whether test anxiety causes poor test performance or whether previous poor test performance causes TA is unclear. Tobias (1985) proposed the latter causal relationship where previous low test scores are caused by inadequate study skills and/or poor test-taking skills, which in turn cause text anxiety. Research investigating the cause of TA has led to two models: the interference model and the skills deficit model (Birenbaum, 2007). The interference model states that high TA students are plagued by worry and distracting thoughts that interfere with their ability to retrieve information during a test. The skill deficit model states that high TA students' problems occur before the test—in the form of inadequate learning that results in poor performance. Thus, TA is simply an emotion that results from an awareness of being unprepared for the test. The former model stresses reducing TA whereas the latter model stresses an irrelevant role for TA and thus increasing learning strategies. Naveh-Benjamin and colleagues (1987) combined these models and distinguished between two types of TA students. One knows the material well but has trouble retrieving it, whereas the other has poor understanding of the material and thus cannot retrieve it. This entry refers to debilitating test anxiety, rather than facilitating test anxiety. The latter has been demonstrated in both early (Yerkes & Dodson, 1908) and subsequent (Alpert & Haber, 1960) studies where a small amount of anxiety actually improves test performance.

In this entry, normative data is provided on rates of anxiety levels, various correlates of TA are described, and evaluation and assessment of TA are discussed as are methods for helping students manage TA.

CORRELATES OF TEST ANXIETY

An excellent meta-analysis conducted by Hembree (1988) is the source of many of the conclusions presented here, and Hembree source gives a more complete coverage of TA. Where appropriate, these conclusions are updated with more recent research findings.

Normative data on rates of TA are difficult to estimate because as of 2008 large-scale studies have not been conducted. However, a study by Methia (2004) found that more than one-third of school age children experience at least some TA. As mentioned earlier, it is assumed that TA has increased in the early 2000s, possibly due to an increased emphasis on testing in schools. Whatever the precise prevalence rate may be, it is clear that TA remains a concern for educators.

Not surprisingly, TA has been found to be negatively correlated with tests of IQ and various types of achievement and aptitude (Hembree, 1988). Again, these data are correlational and not causal. Thus, it is as plausible that low achievement causes TA as it is to say that TA causes low achievement. In terms of motivational factors, although there is a negative correlation between need for achievement and TA in the elementary years, there appears to be no relationship during the high school and college years. There is a strong negative correlation between self-esteem and TA. Moreover, students with high TA tend to have an external locus of control (i.e., feeling as if they have little control over the events of their lives). TA is positively related with defensiveness

and both general state and trait anxiety, whereas it is negatively related with dominance.

One study tested the hypothesized negative impact of cognitive TA in the test preparation, performance, and reflection phases (Cassady, 2004). Students with high-cognitive TA reported lower study skills, rated tests as more threatening, and prepared less effective test notes. The high-anxiety students performed worse on tests and reported higher levels of emotionality. Cassady concluded that cognitive TA is associated with detrimental perceptions and behaviors in all phases of the learning-testing cycle.

Females typically are more prone to TA than are males, with the difference peaking during grades 5 through 10, and declining thereafter. However, this difference is not associated with lower test performance. In one study investigating differences between males and females, Chappell and colleagues (2005) found a small inverse relationship between TA and GPA in both groups. Low-test-anxious female graduate students had significantly higher GPAs than high-test-anxious female graduate students, but there were no GPA differences between low- and high-test-anxious male graduate students. Female undergraduates had significantly higher TA and higher GPAs than male undergraduates, and female graduate students had significantly higher TA and higher GPAs than male graduate students.

Both African American (in elementary school) and Hispanic students exhibit higher TA than do Caucasian students. Later-born children exhibit higher TA than do first-borns. Some researchers have proposed that TA among minority students may be partly explained by the stereotype threat hypothesis (Steele & Aronson, 1995). Based on the perception that there are negative stereotypes regarding certain groups' performance on standardized tests, group members experience higher anxiety on tests due to fear of being stereotyped or confirming the negative group stereotype. According to some, this hypothesis may help to explain why girls perform worse than boys on high-stakes math tests and why African American and Hispanic students perform worse on achievement tests than do Caucasian and Asian-American students (Osborne, 2007).

MEASURING TEST ANXIETY

Many scales are used for measuring test anxiety. Sarason's 1984 Reaction to Tests (RTT) questionnaire consists of four 10-item scales: two that measure the cognitive component (worry and test irrelevant thinking) and two that measure the emotional component (emotionality and bodily symptoms). The Friedban Scale (Friedman & Bendas-Jacob, 1997) of TA has 23 items covering three subdimensions: social derogation (eight items, e.g., "If I fail a test, I am afraid I shall be rated as stupid by my friends."), physical tenseness (six items, e.g., "I am very tense before a test, even if I am well prepared."), and cognitive obstruction (nine items, e.g., "In a test, I feel like my head is empty, as if I have forgotten all I have learned."). Internal consistency reliability coefficients for the three subscales in one study were .93, .88, and .94, respectively (Sawyer & Hollis-Sawyer, 2005), indicating satisfactory levels of internal consistency. The Test Anxiety Inventory for Children and Adolescents (Lowe & Lee, 2005) is a 45-item self-report measure for grades 4 through 12. Coefficient alphas for the TAICA have ranged from .81 to .94. There is also the Test Anxiety Inventory (Spielberger, 1980) used solely with adults. For a shorter scale that can be also be used with older students, the Westside Test Anxiety Scale (Driscoll, 2007) has 10 items covering self-assessed anxiety impairment and cognitions that can impair performance and is designed to identify students with anxiety impairments who may benefit from an anxiety-reduction intervention.

TREATING TEST ANXIETY

Most early treatments of TA were behavioral and mainly systematic desensitization—a process in which the person is trained in relaxation techniques in the presence of increasing levels of the aversive, anxiety-producing stimulus (here testing environments). Unfortunately, although the early treatments were successful in reducing TA, they were less successful in improving test performance (Allen, Elias, & Zlotlow, 1980). Tryon (1980) suggested that students also need study counseling combined with desensitization to improve test performance. However, Hembree (1988) concluded that TA reduction programs generally result in higher test performance and GPA. Ergene (2003) conducted a meta-analysis that synthesized results from TA reduction programs. The most effective treatments appear to be those that combine skill-focused approaches with behavior or cognitive approaches. Individually conducted programs, along with programs that combined individual and group counseling formats, have produced the greatest changes. More research is needed to clarify the causal role TA reduction programs may have with regard to achievement and test performance.

Regardless of its prevalence and severity, TA will continue to be a concern of parents and educators. In an era of heightened school accountability, schools (especially administrators and teachers) will be interested in ways to reduce TA in students so as to enhance test performance. Merely treating TA by desensitizing students to the testing situation may not improve their test performance because some students' struggles may be simply due to inadequate preparation. It is important to assess both TA and academic preparedness before deciding on an intervention program. Interventions that provide training in study skills

and test taking, combined with reducing the emotionality of the testing situation, are likely to be more successful in facilitating test performance.

SEE ALSO *Anxiety; Student Emotions.*

BIBLIOGRAPHY

Allen, G., Elias, M., & Zlotlow, S. (1980). Behavioral interventions for alleviating test anxiety: A methodological overview of current therapeutic practices. In I. G. Sarason (Ed.), *Test anxiety: Theory, research, and applications* (pp. 155–185). Hillsdale, NJ: Erlbaum.

Alpert, R., & Haber, R. N. (1960). Anxiety in academic achievement situations. *Journal of Abnormal and Social Psychology, 61,* 207–215.

Birenbaum, M. (2007). Assessment and instruction preferences and their relationship with test anxiety and learning strategies. *Higher Education, 53,* 749–768.

Cassady, J. C. (2004). The influence of cognitive test anxiety across the learning-testing cycle. *Learning and Instruction, 14,* 569–592.

Chapell, M. S., Blanding, Z. B., Silverstein, M. E., Takahashi, M., Newman, B., Gubi, A., et al. (2005). Test anxiety and academic performance in undergraduate and graduate students. *Journal of Educational Psychology, 97,* 268–274.

Driscoll, R. (2007). *Westside Test Anxiety Scale validation: Abstract.*. Retrieved April 21, 2008, from http:// www.eric.ed.gov/ERICDocs/data/ericdocs2sql/ content_storage_01/0000019b/80/28/06/7b.pdf.

Ergene, T. (2003). Effective interventions on test anxiety reduction: A meta-analysis. *School Psychology International, 24,* 313–328.

Friedman, I. A., & Bendas-Jacob, O. (1997). Measuring perceived test anxiety in adolescents: A self-report scale. *Educational and Psychological Measurement, 57,* 1035–1046.

Hembree, R. (1988). Correlates, causes, effects and treatment of text anxiety. *Review of Educational Research, 58,* 47–77.

Lowe, P. A., & Lee, S. W. (2005). *The test anxiety inventory for children and adolescents.* Lawrence: University of Kansas Press.

Mandler, G., & Sarason, S. (1952). A study of anxiety and learning. *Journal of Abnormal and Social Psychology, 47,* 166–173.

Mulvenon, S. W., Stegman, C. E., & Ritter, G. (2005). Test anxiety: A multifaceted study on the perceptions of teachers, principals, counselors, students, and parents. *International Journal of Testing, 5,* 37–61.

Osborne, J. W. (2007). Linking stereotype threat and anxiety. *Educational Psychology, 27,* 135–154.

Sawyer, T. P., & Hollis-Sawyer, L. A. (2005). Predicting stereotype threat, test anxiety, and cognitive ability test performance: An examination of three models. *International Journal of Testing, 5,* 225–246.

Spielberger, C. D. (1980). *Test anxiety inventory.* Palo Alto, CA: Consulting Psychologists Press.

Steele, C. M., & Aronson, J. (1995). Stereotype threat and the intellectual test performance of African Americans. *Journal of Personality and Social Psychology, 69,* 797–811.

Tobias, S. (1985). Test anxiety: Interference, defective skills, and cognitive capacity. *Educational Psychologist, 20,* 135–142.

Tryon, G. (1980). The measurement and treatment of test anxiety. *Review of Educational Research, 50,* 353–372.

Yerkes, R. M., & Dodson, J. D. (1908). The relation of strength of stimulus to rapidity of habit formation. *Journal of Comparative and Neurological Psychology, 18,* 459–482.

Daniel H. Robinson

EXPECTANCY VALUE MOTIVATIONAL THEORY

Between 1980 and the early 2000s, Jacquelynne Eccles and colleagues studied the motivational and social factors influencing such long and short-range school-related goals and behaviors as school grades, course selections, and high school graduation. They elaborated a comprehensive theoretical model linking achievement-related choices to two sets of beliefs: the individual's expectations for success and the importance or value the individual attaches to the various options perceived by the individual as available (see Eccles, Wigfield, & Schiefele, 1998). In this model, they also specified the relation of these beliefs to cultural norms, experiences, aptitudes, and to those personal beliefs and attitudes that are commonly assumed to be associated with achievement-related activities (Eccles et al., 1998). In particular, they linked achievement-related beliefs, outcomes, and goals to interpretative systems such as causal attributions and other meaning-making beliefs linked to achievement-related activities and events, to the input of parents, peers, and teachers, to various social roles and other culturally based beliefs about both the nature of various tasks in a variety of achievement domains and the appropriateness of participation in such tasks, to self-perceptions and self-concepts, to perceptions of the task itself, and to the processes and consequences associated with identity formation.

For example, regarding engagement in school learning, they believe people will be most likely to engage fully in school-based learning activities if they have confidence in their ability to do well and place high value on doing well in school. High confidence in one's academic potential results from a history of doing well in school, as well from strong messages that one is academically competent from one's parents, teachers, and peers (Wigfield et al., 2006). Similarly, the personal value one attaches to learning in school is influenced by several factors: Does the person enjoy doing the subject material? Is the learning activity seen as instrumental in meeting one of the individual's long- or short-range goals? Is the person anxious about his or her ability to successfully master the learning material being presented? Does the person think that the learning task is appropriate for people like him or her?

Do the person's parents and teachers think doing well in school is important and have they provided advice on the utility value of school success for various future life options? Finally, does taking the working on the learning task interfere with other more valued options?

At the most basic psychological level, the Eccles and colleagues expectancy-value model reduces to two fundamental motivational questions: "Can I do the task?" and "Do I want to do the task?" If students answer no to the question "Can I do the task?" then they are unlikely to fully engage in the learning opportunities provided in school. But even if the answer to the first question is yes, full and sustained engagement in school learning depends on the answer to the question, "Do I want to do the task?" If the answer to this question is no, then it is also unlikely that the students will engage the learning opportunities at school.

ASKING "CAN I DO THE TASK?"

Research supports the hypothesis that a yes answer to the question, "Can I do the task?" predicts better performance and more motivation to select more challenging tasks (Wigfield et al., 2006). Importantly, confidence in one's ability to master academic work is a strong predictor of school achievement among academically struggling students (NRC, 2004). Unfortunately, negative racial, ethnic, gender, and social class stereotypes can lead teachers and school districts to communicate low expectations for the academic achievements of some groups of students through a variety of mechanisms, including differential teacher-student face-to-face daily interactions, tracking into low ability groups coupled with providing inferior educational experiences in these groups, failure to provide encouragement for high educational aspirations, and failure to provide high quality educational experiences that promote both current achievement levels and confidence and lay the groundwork for continued success in future courses (see Eccles, 2007).

ASKING "DO I WANT TO DO THE TASK?"

Fully engaging learning at school requires a desire to do the task (Wigfield et al. 2006). Eccles and colleagues argue that the perceived value of school work is determined by four related constructs: (1) the enjoyment one expects to experience while engaging in the task—intrinsic interest; (2) the extent to which engaging in the task is consistent with one's self-image or identity—attainment value; (3) the value of the task for facilitating one's long range goals or in helping one obtain immediate or long range external rewards—utility value; and (4) the perceived cost of engaging in the activity.

Intrinsic Value. Eccles and colleagues use the term *intrinsic value* to refer to either the enjoyment one feels when doing the task or the enjoyment one expects to experience while one is engaged in the task. This construct is most closely related to two related constructs: the idea of intrinsic motivation as developed by E. Deci and R. Ryan and the idea of interest as developed by theorists such as A. Krapp, A. Renniger, and U. Schefiele. According to Deci and Ryan, intrinsic motivation is highest when individuals are doing tasks that they enjoy, as well as when they are doing tasks that are personally meaningful (somewhat like *attainment value*). Interest theorists argue that engagement will be highest when individuals are doing interesting tasks. According to these theorists, interest value results from either inherent characteristics of the task (called *situational interest*) or personal characteristics of the individuals doing the task (called *personal interest*). Individual interest is considered a relatively stable evaluative orientation towards certain domains that one enjoys; situational interest is an emotional state aroused by specific features of an activity or a task. Evidence is quite strong that interests, intrinsic motivation, and intrinsic value predict greater academic engagement and learning (see Eccles et al., 1998; Wigfield et al., 2006).

Some educational psychologists are interested in individual differences in trait-like individual differences in what might be referred to as the desire to learn (e.g., Gottfried, Harter, Hidi, and Schiefele). These researchers define this enduring learning orientation in terms of three components: (1) preference for hard or challenging tasks, (2) learning that is driven by curiosity or interest, and (3) striving for competence and mastery. Empirical findings suggest that the three components are highly correlated and that high levels of a trait-like desire to learn is related to a mastery-oriented coping style for dealing with academic failure, high academic achievement, both comprehension and deep-level learning, and the use of appropriate self-regulated learning strategies in academic tasks (see Wigfield et al., 2006). Some scholars believe the component of interest should be considered as an influence on attainment value.

Situational learning is more transitory because it is based in the nature of the academic curriculum and materials themselves. The following task features arouse situational interest: personal relevance, both familiarity and novelty, high activity level, and comprehensibility (see Wigfield et al., 2006). These characteristics facilitate both engagement and learning. We classify this construct under intrinsic value.

Attainment and Utility Value. Eccles and colleagues use the term *attainment value* to refer to the link between tasks and individuals' own identities and preferences. As they grow up, individuals develop an image of who they

are and what they would like to be. This image is made up of many parts, including (1) conceptions of one's personality and capabilities, (2) long range goals and plans, (3) schema regarding the proper roles of men and women in one's culture group, (4) instrumental and terminal values, (5) motivational sets, (6) ideal images of what one should be like; (7) stable personal interests, and (8) social scripts regarding proper behavior in a variety of situations. Eccles and colleagues conceptualize attainment value in terms of these needs, personal interests, and personal values that an activity fulfills. Those parts of an individual's self-image that are central or critical to self-definition should influence the value the individual attaches to various activities such as school-based learning activities versus other activities. These differential values, in turn, should influence the individual's desire to engage fully in school-based learning activities. For example, if doing well in school and being a good student is a central part of an individual's self-image, then that person should place higher value on investing time and energy in doing well in school than in other pursuits because doing well in school has high attainment value for this individual.

Utility value is determined by how well a task fits into an individual's goals and plans or fulfills other basic psychological needs. For example, if students plan to become engineers then mastering arithmetic in elementary school and doing well in challenging mathematics and science courses in secondary school will have high utility value because it will allow them to take college track mathematics in secondary school and then get into college training programs in engineering. If not, then the value of doing the work necessary to succeed in these courses may be too low to motivate their effort.

Regarding what might influence the attainment value and utility of doing well and being engaged in school, J. Connell and colleagues proposed three basic human needs that should influence the attainment value of any task or situation: the needs for competence, relatedness, and autonomy. They argue that people's motivation to engage in the demands of any particular situation or setting is influenced by the extent to which the setting provides opportunities to experience autonomy, social relatedness, and a sense of competence. If schools and classrooms do not provide these opportunities, then individuals will not become engaged in school learning and will try to disengage by whatever means are available to them. In contrast, if classroom experiences provide opportunities for students to fulfill these basic needs, then the attainment value of fully engaging in the learning agenda of school should be increased.

The importance of competence needs, in particular, has received a great deal of attention in the achievement literature. This research has shown that early school failure predicts disengagement from school (Eccles et al., 1998; Wigfield et al., 2006). Given this evidence, it is essential that teachers set up their instructional practices in ways that allow all children to experience success at their mastery attempts, particularly at critical school transitions when academic failure may precipitate a downward spiral of disengagement leading to school drop out. Researchers in the area of achievement goal theory (e.g., Maehr & Midgley) have explored the importance of mastery-oriented classrooms. These researchers hypothesize that school learning tasks vary along at least two important dimensions: (1) the extent to which mastery or improvement is stressed (i.e., a mastery focus); and (2) the extent to which doing better than others is stressed (i.e., a performance focus). They argue that the greater the focus on mastery instead of performance, the greater the likelihood that all students will feel competent and will have repeated experiences of mastery. Their research supports this hypothesis.

Evidence also supports the importance for school engagement. For example, several researchers (e.g., Goodenow, Patrich, Roeser, Ryan, & Wentzel), have shown that feelings of belongingness in classrooms and schools, as well as a sense of being part of a supportive learning community, predict increased engagement and school learning. In addition, one of the major benefits of both cooperative learning structures and Catholic schools is that they increase all students' sense of belonging in their classroom's and school's agenda (see Eccles, 2007).

In contrast, experiences of racial, ethnic, religious, linguistic, and gender discrimination are likely to undermine minority and female students' sense of belonging at school. For example, C. Wong and her colleagues showed that experiences of racial discrimination predicted declines in school achievement. Similarly, C. Steele and his colleagues argue that students who believe that their teachers have low expectations for their academic performance will disidentify with school learning as a way of coping with experiences of racial and ethnic discrimination at school (see Eccles, 2007).

Deci, Ryan, and their colleagues have done most of the work on the importance of support for autonomy in classrooms for students' motivation to fully engage the learning agenda of the classroom. They argue that individuals need to feel personally responsible for their behavior and their goals. To the extent that teachers create opportunities for this to be the case, students are more motivated to do their school work and learn the material better.

Eccles and colleagues believe that people need to feel that they are considered valuable contributors to their social groups and institutions. This need is likely to become especially salient during adolescence. One intervention study was done based on this need: the Coca Cola study (see Eccles, 2007). In this project, at-risk adolescents were asked to provide cross-age peer tutoring in reading to first graders. Those adolescents who had this experience over an extended period of time showed an increased commitment to their own academic performance as evidenced by increases in their grades and high school graduation rates.

Individual differences in school motivation are also likely to be linked to individual differences in self-schema and both personal and social goals and identities. As noted above, these differences should be directly related to the perceived attainment value of various activities. The work of Eccles and colleagues on gender differences in high school math and science course enrollment illustrates the importance of the perceived utility value of various course options. Using longitudinal methods, they demonstrated that gender differences in students' decisions to enroll in advanced mathematics are mediated primarily by gender differences in the value that the students' attached to mathematics. More specifically, their findings indicate that young women are less likely than the young men to enroll in advanced high school mathematics and physics courses primarily because they feel that math and physical science are less important, less useful, and less enjoyable than do young men. Furthermore, young women tend to think that advanced math and physics are less important and enjoyable than the many other advanced high school courses they could be taking instead. Interestingly, interventions based on making physics more interesting to females by using more human biological examples of physical principles have been quite successful at increasing females' engagement in physics classes.

Perceived Cost. The value of a task also depends on a set of beliefs that can best be characterized as the cost of participating in the activity. Cost is influenced by many factors, such as anticipated anxiety, fear of failure, fear of the social consequences of success, such as rejection by peers or anticipated racial discrimination, or anger from one's parents or other key people, and fear of loss of a sense of self-worth.

This conceptualization of cost is similar to the kinds of dynamics discussed by M. Covington in his self-worth theory. Covington defined the motive for self-worth as the desire to establish and maintain a positive self-image or sense of self-worth. Because children spend so much time in classrooms and are evaluated so frequently there, Covington argued that protecting one's sense of academic competence is likely to be critical for maintaining a positive sense of self-worth. However, school evaluation, competition, and social comparison can make it difficult for some children to maintain the belief that they are competent academically. Covington outlined various strategies children develop to avoid appearing to lack ability, including procrastination, making excuses, avoiding challenging tasks, and not trying. Therefore, if failure seems likely, some children will not try, precisely because trying and failing threatens their ability self-concepts.

Avoiding challenging tasks is a good way to avoid or minimize failure experiences. Similarly, work by R. Newman and his colleagues demonstrated that students may be reluctant to ask for help in classrooms because they think that this will make them appear to be stupid.

Cost can also be conceptualized in terms of the loss of time and energy for other activities. People have limited time and energy. They cannot do everything they would like. They must choose among activities. Eccles and colleagues asserted that cost is especially important to choice and that socio-cultural processes linked to social identity formation and cultural socialization should have a big influence of the perceived cost of the various activities competing for young people's time and energy. Schools need to provide young people with genuine reasons for attaching higher subjective task value to engaging in school work than in engaging in the variety of tasks associated with other aspects on their daily lives.

As noted above, the expectancy-value model focuses attention on two fundamental motivational questions: "Can I do the task?" and "Do I want to do the task?" The first question illustrates the expectancy component. If students answer no to this question, then they will be unlikely to fully engage in the learning opportunities provided in school. But even if the answer to this question is yes, full and sustained engagement in school learning depends on the answer to the question "Do I want to do the task?" This question illustrates the value component of the model. If the answer to this question is no, then it is also unlikely that the students will engage the learning opportunities at school. It is critical that school environments provide students will the kinds of experiences that will allow them to answer yes to both of these questions.

SEE ALSO *Eccles, Jacquelynne S.; Goal Orientation Theory; School Belonging; Teacher Expectations.*

BIBLIOGRAPHY

Eccles, J. A. (2007). Motivational perspective on school achievement: Taking responsibility for learning and teaching. In R. J. Sternberg and R. F. Subotnik (Eds.), *Optimizing student success in schools with the new three Rs* (pp. 199–202). Charlotte, NC: Information Age.

Eccles, J. S., Wigfield, A., & Schiefele, U. (1998). Motivation. In N. Eisenberg (Ed.), *Handbook of child psychology* (Vol. 3, 5th ed.). New York: Wiley.

National Research Council. (2003). *Engaging schools.* Washington, DC: National Academy Press.

Wigfield, A., Eccles, J. S., Schiefele, U., Roeser, R. W., Davis-Kean, P. (2006). The development of achievement motivation. In N. Eisenberg (Ed.), *Handbook of child psychology* (Vol. 3, 6th ed.). New York: Wiley.

Jacquelynne S. Eccles

EXPERIMENTAL RESEARCH

Suppose teachers wished to determine which of two methods of reading instruction was most effective—one that involved 20 minutes of direct instruction in phonics each day throughout the academic year in grade 1 or one that involved the current practice of having the teacher read a book to the class for 20 minutes each day throughout the year in grade 1. Similarly, suppose they wished to determine whether children learn better in a small class (i.e., with 15 students) or a large class (i.e., with 30 students). Finally, suppose they wished to determine whether requiring students to take a short quiz during each meeting of a college lecture class would result in better performance on the final exam than not giving quizzes.

Each of these situations can be examined best by using experimental research methodology in which investigators compare the mean performance of two or more groups on an appropriate test. In experimental research, it is customary to distinguish between the independent variable and the dependent measure. The independent variable is the feature that is different between the groups—for example, whether 20 minutes of time each day is used for phonics instruction or reading aloud to students, whether the class size is small or large, or whether a short quiz is given during each class meeting. The dependent measure is the score that is used to compare the performance of the groups—for example, the score on a reading test administered at the end of the year, the change in performance on academic tests from the beginning of the year to the end of the year, or the score on a final exam in the class. When researchers compare two or more groups on one or more measures, they use experimental research methodology.

EXPERIMENTAL RESEARCH DEFINED

Experimental research is based on a methodology that meets three criteria: (a) random assignment—the subjects (or other entities) are randomly assigned to treatment groups, (b) experimental control—all features of the treatments are identical except for the independent variable (i.e., the feature being tested), and (c) appropriate measures—the dependent measures are appropriate for testing the research hypothesis. For example, in the class size example, random assignment involves finding a group of students and randomly choosing some to be in small classes (i.e, consisting of 15 students) and some to be in large classes (i.e., consisting of 30 students). The researcher cannot use pre-existing small or large classes because doing so would violate the criterion of random assignment. The problem with violating random assignment is that the groups may systemically differ; for example, students in the smaller classes may be at more wealthy schools that also have more resources, better teachers, and better-prepared students. This violation of the random assignment criterion, sometimes called *self-selection*, is a serious methodological flaw in experimental research.

In the class size example, the criterion of experimental control is reflected in having the classes equivalent on all relevant features except class size. That is, large and small classes should have teachers who are equivalent in teaching skill, students who are equivalent in academic ability, and classrooms that are physically equivalent; they should also have equivalence in support services, length of school day, percentages based on gender, English language proficiency, ethnicity, and so on. If the groups differ on an important variable other than class size, determining whether differences in test performance can be attributed to class size will be difficult. This violation of the experimental control criterion, called *confounding*, is a serious methodological flaw in experimental research.

Finally, in the class size example, the dependent measure should test the research hypothesis that class size affects academic learning, so an appropriate measure would be to give an achievement test covering the curriculum at the start and end of the year. The appropriate measures criterion would be violated if the dependent measure were a survey asking students how well they enjoyed school this year or an ungraded portfolio of their artwork over the year. When a test does not measure what is intended, the test lacks *validity*; invalid tests represent a serious methodological flaw in experimental research.

BENEFITS AND LIMITATIONS OF EXPERIMENTAL RESEARCH

Experimental research is generally recognized as the most appropriate method for drawing causal conclusions about instructional interventions, for example, which instructional method is most effective for which type of student under which conditions. In a careful analysis of educational research methods, Richard Shavelson and Lisa Towne concluded that "from a scientific perspective, randomized trials (we also use the term experiment to refer to causal studies that feature random assignment) are the ideal for establishing whether one or more factors caused change in an outcome because of their strong ability to enable fair comparisons" (2002, p. 110). Sim-

ilarly, Richard Mayer notes: "experimental methods—which involve random assignment to treatments and control of extraneous variables—have been the gold standard for educational psychology since the field evolved in the early 1900s" (2005, p. 74). Mayer states, "when properly implemented, they allow for drawing causal conclusions, such as the conclusion that a particular instructional method causes better learning outcomes" (p. 75). Overall, if one wants to determine whether a particular instructional intervention causes an improvement in student learning, then one should use experimental research methodology.

Although experiments are widely recognized as the method of choice for determining the effects of an instructional intervention, they are subject to limitations involving method and theory. First, concerning method, the requirements for random assignment, experiment control, and appropriate measures can impose artificiality on the situation. Perfectly controlled conditions are generally not possible in authentic educational environments such as schools. Thus, there may be a tradeoff between experimental rigor and practical authenticity, in which highly controlled experiments may be too far removed from real classroom contexts. Experimental researchers should be sensitive to this limitation, by incorporating mitigating features in their experiments that maintain ecological validity.

Second, concerning theory, experimental research may be able to tell that one method of instruction is better than conventional practice, but may not be able to specify why; it may not be able to pinpoint the mechanisms that create the improvement. In these cases, it is useful to derive clear predictions from competing theories so experimental research can be used to test the specific predictions of competing theories. In addition, more focused research methods—such as naturalistic observation or in-depth interviews—may provide richer data that allows for the development of a detailed explanation for why an intervention might have a new effect. Experimental researchers should be sensitive to this limitation, by using complementary methods in addition to experiments that provide new kinds of evidence.

EXPERIMENTAL DESIGNS

Three common research designs used in experimental research are between subjects, within subjects, and factorial designs. In between-subjects designs, subjects are assigned to one of two (or more) groups with each group constituting a specific treatment. For example, in a between-subjects design, students may be assigned to spend two school years in a small class or a large class. In within-subjects designs, the same subject receives two (or more) treatments. For example, students may be assigned to a small class for one year and a large class

RANDOMIZED TRIALS IN EDUCATIONAL RESEARCH

Experimental research helps test and possibly provide evidence on which to base a causal relationship between factors. In the late 1940s, Ronald A. Fisher (1890–1962) of England began testing hypotheses on crops by dividing them into groups that were similar in composition and treatment to isolate certain effects on the crops. Soon he and others began refining the same principles for use in human research.

To ensure that groups are similar when testing variables, researchers began using randomization. By randomly placing subjects into groups that say, receive a treatment or receive a placebo, researchers help ensure that participants with the same features do not cluster into one group. The larger the study groups, the more likely randomization will produce groups approximately equal on relevant characteristics. Nonrandomized trials and smaller participant groups produce greater chance for bias in group formation. In education research, these experiments also involve randomly assigning participants to an experimental group and at least one control group.

The Elementary and Secondary Education Act (ESEA) of 2001 and the Educational Sciences Reform Act (ERSA) of 2002 both established clear policies from the federal government concerning a preference for "scientifically based research." A federal emphasis on the use of randomized trials in educational research is reflected in the fact that 70% of the studies funded by the Institute of Education Sciences in 2001 were to employ randomized designs.

The federal government and other sources say that the field of education lags behind other fields in use of randomized trials to determine effectiveness of methods. Critics of experimental research say that the time involved in designing, conducting, and publishing the trials makes them less effective than qualitative research. Frederick Erickson and Kris Gutierrez of the University of California, Los Angeles argued that comparing educational research to the medical failed to consider social facts, as well as possible side effects.

Evidence-based research aims to bring scientific authority to all specialties of behavioral and clinical medicine. However, the effectiveness of clinical trials can be marred by bias from financial interests and other biases, as evidenced in recent medical trials. In a 2002 Hastings Center Report, physicians Jason Klein and Albert Fleischman of the Albert Einstein College of Medicine argued that financial incentives to physicians should be limited. In 2007 many drug companies and physicians were under scrutiny for financial incentives and full disclosure of clinical trial results.

BIBLIOGRAPHY

CONSORT Transparent Reporting of Trials. (2008). Retrieved April 22, 2008, from http://www.consort-statement.org.

Constas, M. A. (2007). Reshaping the methodological identity of education research. *Evaluation Review, 31*(4), 391–399.

Erickson, F., & Gutierrez, K. (2002). Culture, rigor, and science in educational research. *Educational Researcher, 31*(8), 21–24.

Healy, B. (2006, September 11). Who says what's best? *U.S. News and World Report, 141.9.* 75.

Klein, J.E., & Fleischman, A.R. (2002). The private practicing physician-investigator: ethical implications of clinical research in the office setting. *Hastings Center Report, 32*(4), 22–26.

Kopelman, L. M. (2004). Clinical trials. In S. Post (Ed.) *Encyclopedia of bioethics* (3rd ed.), pp. 2334–2343. New York: MacMillan Reference USA.

National Cancer Institute. (2006). Clinical trials: questions and answers. Retrieved February 11, 2008, from http://www.cancer.gov/cancertopics/factsheet/Information/clinical-trials.

Teresa Odle

for the next year, or vice versa. Within-subjects designs are problematic when experience with one treatment may spill over and affect the subject's experience in the following treatment, as would likely be the case with the class size example. In factorial designs, groups are based on two (or more) factors, such as one factor being large or small class size and another factor being whether the subject is a boy or girl, which yields four cells (corresponding to four groups). In a factorial design it is possible to test for main effects, such as whether class size affects learning, and interactions, such as whether class size has equivalent effects for boys and girls.

Finally, a quasi-experiment has the trappings (and some of the advantages) of an experiment but may not fully meet all of the criteria, such as a study in which matched groups are used (rather than randomly assigned groups) or a study that compares people based on a characteristic (such as differences between boys and girls or high and low-achieving students).

COMPARISON TO OTHER RESEARCH METHODS

In educational research, it is customary to distinguish between experimental and observational research methods, quantitative and qualitative measures, and applied versus basic research goals.

First, if experimental methods are preferred for testing causal hypotheses, what is the role of observational methods, in which a researcher carefully describes what happens in a natural environment? Observational methods can be used in an initial phase of research, as a way of generating more specific hypotheses to be tested in experiments, and observational methods can be used in conjunction with experiments to help provide a richer theoretical explanation for the observed effects. However, a collection of observations, such as portions of transcripts of conversations among students, is generally not sufficient for testing causal hypotheses. An important type of observational method is a correlational study, in which subjects generate scores on a variety of measures. By looking at the pattern of correlations, using a variety of statistical techniques, it is possible to see which factors tend to go together. However, controlled experiments are required in order to determine if the correlated factors are causally related.

Second, should educational research be based on quantitative measures (e.g., those involving numbers) or qualitative measures (e.g., those involving verbal descriptions)? Experiments may use either type of measure, depending on the research hypothesis being tested, but even qualitative descriptions can often be converted into quantitative measures by counting various events.

Third, should educational research be basic or applied? In a compelling answer to this question, Donald Stokes argues for "use-inspired basic research" (1997, p. 73). For example, in educational research, experimental researchers could examine basic principles of how instruction influences learning, that is, experiments aimed at the basic question of how to help people learn within the practical setting of schools.

HISTORICAL OVERVIEW AND 21ST-CENTURY TRENDS

Applying experimental research methods to questions about human behavior is recognized as one of the greatest scientific advances of the 20th century. Between 1975 and 2005, in particular, experimental research methodology has enabled an explosion of educationally relevant findings on how to design effective instruction in subject areas such as reading, writing, mathematics, and science.

In spite of these advances, Peggy Hsieh and colleagues (2005) found that the percentage of articles based on randomized experiments declined from 40 percent in 1983 to 26 percent in 2004 in primary educational psychology journals and from 33 percent in 1983 to 4 percent in 2004 in primary educational research journals. The authors conclude that "the use of experimental methodology in educational research appears to be on the decline" (Hsieh et al., 2005, p. 528). They characterize the decline as "unfortunate" especially in light of growing concerns about "the untrustworthiness of educational research findings" (Hsieh, et al., 2005, p. 528). In a slightly earlier report to the National Research Council, Shavelson and Towne also noted the consensus view that the "reputation of educational research is quite poor" (2002, p. 23). The decline in training in experimental research methods in schools of education can be seen as an example of the deskilling of educational researchers, marginalizing one of the most powerful and productive research methodologies and ultimately marginalizing educational researchers as well.

Valerie Reyna notes that, as a reaction against the perceived low quality of educational research, members of the U.S. Congress passed bills that were signed into law in 2001 and 2002 requiring that educational practices in the United States be based on "scientifically-based research" (2005, p. 30) Reyna shows that the definition of scientifically based research includes research using "experimental or quasi-experimental designs in which individuals ... are assigned to different conditions and with appropriate controls to evaluate the effects of the condition of interest" and using "measures ... that provide reliable and valid data" (2005, p. 38). According to Reyna "two landmark pieces of legislation were passed that could substantially change educational practice" not by endorsing a particular program or policy but rather by calling for educational researchers to "embrace ... the scientific method for generating knowledge that will govern educational practice in classrooms" (2005, p. 49). Similarly, in their report to the National Research Council, Shavelson and Towne call for "evidence-based research" in education—the fundamental principle of science that hypotheses should be tested against relevant empirical evidence rather than ideology, opinion, or random observation (2002, p. 3).

Early 21st-century trends in experimental research include the use of effect size, meta-analysis, randomized field trials, and net impact.

The Use of Effect Size. Effect size is a measure of the strength of an effect in an experiment. Jacob Cohen (1988) suggested a simple measure of effect size—referred to as Cohen's *d*—in which the mean of the control group is subtracted from the mean of the treatment group and this difference is divided by the pooled standard deviation of the groups. According to Cohen, effect sizes can be classified as small ($d = .2$), medium ($d = .5$) and large ($d = .8$). Use of effect size allows educational policy makers to determine if an instructional treatment causes a statistically significant effect and if it has a practical effect. Hsieh et al. reported an increase in studies reporting effect size in educational psychology journals between 1995 and 2005, starting with 4 percent in 1995 to 61 percent in 2004, whereas the rate remained steady at about 25 percent from 1995 to 2004 for a primary educational research journal (2005).

The Use of Meta-analysis. The effect size measure allows for a particular instructional effect to be compared across experiments using a common metric, yielding a new kind of literature synthesis called meta-analysis. In meta-analysis, researchers tally the effect sizes of the same comparison across many different experiments, yielding an average effect size. For example, Gene Glass and Mary Smith (1978) reported a pioneering meta-analysis of research on class size revealing small positive effects of smaller class size. In the early 2000s meta-analysis is commonly used to review and summarize experimental research.

The Use of Randomized Trials. Randomized field trials (RFT), randomized clinical trials (RCT) and randomized trials (RT) refer to a particularly rigorous form of experimental research in which students (or other entities) are randomly assigned to treatments within an authentic field setting. Gary Burtless states that "a randomized field trial ... is simply a controlled experiment that takes place outside a laboratory setting" (2002, p. 180).

Although randomized trials have been used in medical research and research on public policy, they are rarely used in educational research. However, there are some notable exceptions such as a study of effects of class size conducted in Tennessee, reported by Jeremy Finn and Charles Achilles (1999). As part of the study, 11,600 students in 79 schools across the state were assigned along with their teachers to small classes (13–17 students), regular classes (22–26 students), or regular classes with full-time teacher aides. Students stayed in the program from kindergarten through third grade, and then all were returned to regular classes. Importantly, the study showed that students in the small classes outperformed those in the regular classes, with or without aides, and the effects were greatest for minorities. Frederick Mosteller called the Tennessee class size study "one of the most important educational investigations ever carried out" (1995, p. 113) In the foreword to *Evidence Matters* by Fredrick Mosteller and Robert Boruch, the authors observe, "When properly conducted, randomized field trials—often called the gold standard in research involving human subjects—allow for fairly precise estimates of

programmatic effects" (2002, p. vi). Using an appropriate unit of measure (for example, individual students, classrooms, or schools) is an important consideration in research using randomized field trials.

Net Impact. Judith Gueron (2002, p. 18) distinguishes between an intervention's outcomes (e.g., the percentage of students graduating from a school or passing a certification test) and its net impact (e.g., the percentage who graduate or who pass a certification test who would not have without the intervention). Gueron argues that "administrators often know and tout their program's outcomes, but they rarely know the program's net impacts" (p. 18). When administrators focus on the question, "Is the new intervention effective?" they focus only on outcomes. When they focus on the question, "Does the new intervention have more impact than the current practice?" they focus on net impact. In order to determine an intervention's net impact, experimental researchers compare the outcomes with current practice (e.g., current instructional method) to the outcomes with the new intervention (e.g., the new instructional method). In short, Gueron argues that the question "Compared to what?" is an important and profound issue in experimental research.

In their analysis of educational research methodologies, Shavelson and Towne note: "decisions about education are sometimes instituted with no scientific basis at all, but rather are derived from ideology or deeply held beliefs" (2002, p. 17). In contrast, experimental research methodology has the potential to be a tool for promoting effective change in education in which decisions about instructional interventions are guided by scientific evidence and grounded in research-based theory. In the preface to Gary Phye, Daniel Robinson, and Joel Levin's *Empirical Methods for Evaluating Educational Interventions*, Gary Phye observed: "we are on the cusp of a reaffirmation that experimental research strategies provide the strongest evidence" for testing the effects of educational interventions (2005, p. xi). Finally, Robert Boruch quotes Walter Lippman who, in the 1930s, said: "Unless we are honestly experimental, we will leave the great questions of society and its improvement to the ignorant opponents of change on the one hand, and the ignorant advocates of change on the other" (2005, p. 189). In short, the experimental research methodology that fueled an explosion of scientific research about humans in the 1900s remains a powerful and indispensable tool for educational researchers in the new millennium.

SEE ALSO *Research Methods: An Overview.*

BIBLIOGRAPHY

Burtless, G. (2002). Randomized field trials for policy evaluation: Why not in education? In F. Mosteller & R. Boruch (Eds.),

Evidence matters: Randomized trials in educational research (pp. 179–197). Washington, DC: Brookings Institution Press.

Boruch, R. (2005). Beyond the laboratory or classroom: The empirical basis of educational policy. In G. D. Phye, D. H. Robinson, & J. Levin (Eds.), *Empirical methods for evaluating educational interventions* (pp. 177–192). San Diego: Elsevier Academic Press.

Cohen, J. (1988). *Statistical power analysis for the behavioral sciences.* 2nd ed. Mahwah, NJ: Erlbaum.

Finn, J. D., & Achilles, C. M. (1999). Tennessee's class size study: Findings, implications, misconceptions. *Educational Evaluation and Policy Analysis, 21,* 97–109.

Glass, G. V., & Smith, M. L. (1978). *Meta-analysis of research on the relationship of class size and achievement.* San Francisco: Far West Laboratory of Educational Research and Development.

Gueron, J. M. (2002). The politics of random assignment: Implementing studies and affecting policy. In F. Mosteller & R. Boruch (Eds.), *Evidence matters: Randomized trials in educational research* (pp. 15–49). Washington, DC: Brookings Institution Press.

Hsieh, P., Acee, T., Chung, W., Hsieh, Y., Kim, H., Thomas, G. D., et al. (2005). Is educational intervention research on the decline? *Journal of Educational Psychology, 97,* 523–530.

Mayer, R. E. (2005). The failure of educational research to impact educational practice: Six obstacles to educational reform. In G. D. Phye, D. H. Robinson, & J. Levin (Eds.), *Empirical methods for evaluating educational interventions* (pp. 67–81). San Diego: Elsevier Academic Press.

Mosteller, F. (1995). The Tennessee study of class size in the early school grades. *The Future of Children, 5,* 113–127.

Mosteller, F., & Boruch, R. (2002). *Evidence matters: Randomized trials in educational research.* Washington, DC: Brookings Institution Press.

Phye, G. D., Robinson, D. H., & Levin, J. (Eds.). (2005). *Empirical methods for evaluating educational interventions.* San Diego: Elsevier Academic Press.

Reyna, V. F. (2005). The no child left behind act, scientific research, and federal education policy: A view from Washington, D.C. In G. D. Phye, D. H. Robinson, & J. Levin (Eds.), *Empirical methods for evaluating educational intervention* (pp. 29–52). San Diego: Elsevier Academic Press.

Shavelson, R. J., & Towne, L. (Eds.). (2002). *Scientific research in education.* Washington, DC: National Academy Press.

Stokes, D. E. (1997). *Pasteur's quadrant: Basic science and technological innovation.* Washington, DC: Brookings Institution Press.

Richard E. Mayer

EXPERT-NOVICE STUDIES

Expert-novice studies involve natural contrasts between individuals at *relatively* high performance levels in a given domain (academic discipline or profession or hobby) and individuals at a *relatively* low performance level in that given domain. The word "relatively" is emphasized because expertise is a continuum rather than two discrete states and a given study usually just compares two points along the continuum. For example, one classic study compared physics faculty (experts) against physics graduate students (novices), whereas another classic study compared undergraduates who had performed very well in an introductory course (experts) against undergraduates who performed much less well in that same course (novices).

Some researchers use the terms *expert* and *novice* in a more restricted, absolute way. For example, expert, for these researchers, is applied to individuals having spent at least 10 years of focused practice in a domain. This categorization method is called the 10-year-rule. It is based on the empirical observation that world-class expertise in a domain generally takes at least 10 years of focused practice, whether that domain be game playing, sports, writing, music composition, music playing, or scientific research (Hayes, 1985). The term novice, in the absolute sense, applies to individuals who have just learned the basics of the given domain but have not had an opportunity to practice. In other words, they can do basic tasks in the domain (unlike completely uninformed individuals), but only at a very low level of performance.

In general, experts are much faster and more accurate than novices in typical tasks in the domain of expertise being examined. Expert-novice studies have examined many different possible factors underlying this large performance difference, including differences in memory ability (how much of a problem is remembered), facts/chunks (how many example situations are known), representations/schemas (what features of problems are perceived), and procedures/strategies (what solution methods are used). Expert-novice differences have been found for all of those factors, although particular expert-novice studies tend to focus on only a subset of these dimensions, as illustrated in the following prototypical studies.

PROTOTYPICAL STUDIES

Chase and Simon (1973) recruited three participants of varying chess skill for their study (one master chess player, one Class A player, and one beginner). Each participant completed two different tasks involving side-by-side chessboards with a divider between them. The left board presented a different configuration each trial, and the right board was used by the participants to make responses. For the perception task, the participants were asked to recreate 14 game configurations, completing each as quickly and accurately as possible. For the memory task, the participants viewed an additional 14 game configurations for only five seconds and needed to recreate each configuration from memory. Each configuration was repeated until the participant correctly recreated the configuration. The game configurations varied by whether they were selected from the middle of a game or the end of the game and whether they were actual game configurations or random organizations of the pieces (i.e., unlikely to occur in a game).

Chase and Simon found that recall ability increased with chess skill ability. This relationship only occurred in recreations of actual configurations, not with random configurations. Chase and Simon hypothesized that the expert memory advantage was specific to actual configurations because experts saw chessboards in terms of familiar chunks, and random configurations did not have familiar chunks. Chase and Simon empirically estimated chunk size by using the time intervals between the placements of each chess piece as participants were recreating the configurations. Using this information to parse the chunks for each participant, they found that master chess players indeed had more chunks and larger chunks than the less skilled players. Even though the chunk size was larger, the chunks still fit within the accepted memory span—that is to say, chess masters did not have better memory ability, just bigger chunks.

Another classic expert-novice study involved the study of representations rather than chunks. Chi, Feltovich, and Glaser (1981) recruited 16 participants of varying physics knowledge (eight experts included advanced PhD students from the physics department and eight novices included undergraduates who had just completed a semester of mechanics). Each participant sorted 24 physics problems selected from eight chapters of a physics textbook that were copied onto note cards. They were instructed to make their categorizations based on the similarities of the solutions. After the sorting process, they explained why they chose to group certain problems.

While there were no differences in the number of categories the experts and novices used in the sorting task, there was very little overlap in the category labels used by the experts and novices. From both the categorizations and the explanations, it was clear that novices grouped by what the problems looked like (e.g., incline planes or pulley problems) and experts grouped by the major physics principle necessary to solve each problem (e.g., conservation of energy problems or Newton's second law).

ROLE OF EXPERT-NOVICE STUDIES IN EDUCATIONAL RESEARCH

Expert-novice studies have many important roles in educational research. First, they define the educational end point. The core of educational research is about defining how to structure teaching and learning rather than in defining what should be taught or learned, at least with respect to the end point of learning. From somewhere else, there must be input on the appropriate targets of learning. Expert-novice studies are a very important method of specifying those targets, and they are a method that has systematic advantages over simply asking disciplinary experts to list the target knowledge. The reason is that one hallmark of expertise is that much of the knowledge is tacit and situationally evoked (Patel, Arocha, & Kaufman, 1999)—experts don't know all the things they know and do, and it is hard to systematically extract the things they do know.

Second, expert-novice studies define the educational start point. Young children are remarkably adept at some things (e.g., extracting patterns from statistics in the environmental input) and young adults are remarkably weak at other things (e.g., reasoning about confounded variables in very simple situations). Research on where novices sit with respect to experts establishes empirically where the biggest gains need to be made by the learner.

This start-to-endpoint view of expert-novice studies connects with a knowledge decomposition view of curriculum design: what are all the individual knowledge and skill components that make up the goals of educational interventions (Gagne, 1962)? Here the assumption is that expertise is made up of many independent skills and knowledge, and instruction must cover each of these skills and knowledge in some logical order.

A variation of this decomposition perspective, derived from expertise research that emphasized the contextualized nature of knowledge and skills, is that experts not only know facts and have separable skills but are also better able to selectively and appropriately apply facts and skills in particular contexts (Lemaire & Siegler, 1995). For example, the early expertise studies on chess suggested that experts had tens of thousands of chess chunks, but the research also showed that experts had associated moves with these chunks that allowed them to quickly "see" which moves were worth considering. The educational implication is that students must learn these connections with the correct contexts (and perhaps break connections with the wrong contexts).

A third important use of expert-novice studies for educational research is to provide models of some form of education that was clearly successful. Expertise research has generally ruled out the genetic or talent perspective on expertise, which makes especially salient the question of what environmental factors were in place to develop that expertise (Ericsson, Krampe, & Tesch-Roemer, 1993). That is, can we develop better models for instruction on the basis of these success stories? For example, some researchers have considered the ways in which experts and novices interact in many settings that lead to high levels of expertise (e.g., in a professional or sport setting), namely apprenticeship. The observation is that novices are asked to participate in authentic disciplinary activities from the beginning (e.g., playing in full basketball games), and move gradually from peripheral, supporting roles to central, independent roles (Collins, Brown, & Newman, 1989). Another important educational implication from this angle on expertise research is the central importance of focused practice: expertise is developed through thousands of hours of focused, regular practice, and curricula that devote much less time to an important topic are unlikely to be successful (Ericsson et al., 1993).

A fourth focus involves the importance of some expertise for learning in addition to performance. For example, research on learning by analogy has found that more expert students are better able to find relevant features in examples and learn by analogy to these examples than more novice students, who tend to encode problems in more superficial ways (Novick, 1988). This kind of research suggests which knowledge and skills should be placed earlier in the curriculum because they enable or accelerate later learning.

EXPERT-EXPERT EXTENSIONS OF EXPERT-NOVICE RESEARCH

Expertise is often treated as a single dimension, such that there is only one way of being more expert in a given domain. However, expertise is actually more nuanced than that single dimension view, and individuals can be more or less expert on different dimensions. For example, a person might be an expert on facts of a domain, but not expert in the skills of a domain, such as in the case of a U.S. Civil War buff with no training in historical thinking. Another person might have considerable training in the skills relevant to a particular domain but relatively little knowledge of the facts relevant to that domain, such as in the case of a physics researcher working on biology research. Studies that compare different kinds of experts allow for some teasing apart of the importance of different kinds of knowledge or skill on performance in different kinds of circumstances. For example, Voss, Tyler, and Yengo (1983) compared political scientists with expertise in the Soviet Union against political scientists with expertise on other regions, as well as comparing them to chemistry faculty and undergraduates. They found that some aspects of reasoning performance (on a problem relating to solving a political science problem involving the Soviet Union) depended upon training in political science in general whereas other aspects of reasoning performance depended specifically on being an expert on that exact region.

Most importantly for educational research, expert-expert studies can address the central educational question of generality and transfer of knowledge. A tension in curriculum design is the extent to which reasoning skills can be taught outside of a context or in some arbitrary context, or whether reasoning skills must be taught specifically in the context in which they will be later used. An example would be statistics or research methods. These are often stand-alone courses, with the idea that students will later be able to apply the skills learned in those courses to

whatever later contexts they need to apply them in, even if those contexts involve reasoning *about* very different content. The alternative approach is to teach only more specialized reasoning courses that are specific to subgroups of students' goal reasoning domain, or maybe have them take many such courses if they are unsure about their target domain. The general reasoning course approach is more efficient, but depends upon there being successful transfer. Expert-expert studies help address this question methodologically: if an expert in one domain can successfully solve problems in another domain, then the general training approach is a viable one. In fact, some recent studies have found generality to many aspects of training (e.g., Schunn & Anderson, 1999).

STATISTICAL ANALYTICAL TECHNIQUES USED IN EXPERT-NOVICE RESEARCH

Although expertise is really a continuum rather than true categorical stages as the term "expert-novice" implies, expert-novice studies tend to focus on extreme group comparisons. Thus, the independent variables tend to be categorical. Dependent variables used in expert-novice research can be quite diverse, ranging from simple quantitative performance measures (such as accuracy or solution time) to more qualitative measures such as protocol analysis. In the case of simple performance metrics, basic univariate statistics such as ANOVA and t-tests are commonly used. In the case of protocol analysis, statistical techniques relevant to analysis of frequencies are used (e.g., Chi-Squared or other non-parametric tests). Because experts are often hard to find in large quantities, the minimum N assumptions of many statistical tests are not met, and low N variations of those tests are required (e.g., Fisher-exact instead of Chi-Squared).

STRENGTHS AND WEAKNESSES OF EXPERT-NOVICE RESEARCH

In abstract terms, expert-novice research generally involves high external validity at the cost of low internal validity. To be more specific, expert-novice contrasts tend to involve participants similar to ultimate situations of interest working on tasks of ultimate interest, in contrast to using participants of convenience working on highly simplified tasks with questionable levels of motivation to perform the given experimental tasks. However, the downside is that the statistical power of the studies is often low because experts are hard to find and the statistical method is by necessity the lower powered, between-subjects method. There are also many confounded variables bundled with expertise because one cannot randomly assign participants to expertise. Thus, expert-novice research is an excellent methodological tool that should work in conjunction with other techniques that have better statistical power and methodological control but perhaps lower external validity.

Another important methodological feature of expert-novice research involves confirmatory versus exploratory research. Because expertise is a natural variable rather than an experimentally controlled one, expertise research tends to be more exploratory. Exploratory research has the advantage of being able to provide many unexpected findings, but it often involves looking at many possible dependent variables to find which of the many complex ways in which expertise could express itself is relevant to the given domain/task being studied. This "fishing expedition" nature of data analysis in expert-novice studies is why qualitative data is so often collected—it allows the researcher to explore many different dimensions of behavior after the data is collected. It also explains why expert-novice studies are slow to be analyzed and published.

SEE ALSO *Expertise.*

BIBLIOGRAPHY

Chase, W. G., & Simon, H. A. (1973). Perception in chess. *Cognitive Psychology, 4,* 55–81.

Chi, M. T. H., Feltovich, P. J., & Glaser, R. (1981). Categorization and representation of physics problems by experts and novices. *Cognitive Science, 5,* 121–152.

Collins, A., Brown, J. S., & Newman, S. E. (1989). Cognitive apprenticeship: Teaching the crafts of reading, writing, and arithmetic. In Resnick, L. B. (Ed.), *Knowing, learning, and instruction: Essays in honor of Robert Glaser* (pp. 453–494). Hillsdale NJ: Erlbaum.

Ericsson, K. A., Krampe, R. T., & Tesch-Roemer, C. (1993). The role of deliberate practice in the acquisition of expert performance. *Psychological Review, 100*(3), 363–406.

Gagne, R. (1962). Military training and principles of learning. *American Psychologist, 17,* 263–276.

Hayes, J. R. (1985). Three problems in teaching general skills. In S. Chipman, J. W. Segal, & R. Glaser (Eds.), *Thinking and learning skills* (Vol. 2, pp. 391–406). Hillsdale, NJ: Erlbaum.

Lemaire, P., & Siegler, R. S. (1995). Four aspects of strategic change: Contributions to children's learning of multiplication. *Journal of Experimental Psychology: General, 124*(1), 83–97.

Novick, L. R. (1988). Analogical transfer, problem similarity, and expertise. *Journal of Experimental Psychology: Learning, Memory, & Cognition, 14*(3), 510–520.

Patel, V. L., Arocha, J. F., & Kaufman, D. R. (1999). Expertise and tacit knowledge in medicine. In R. J. Sternberg & J. H. Horvath (Eds.), *Tacit knowledge in professional practice: Researcher and practitioner perspectives* (pp. 75–99). Mahwah, NJ: Erlbaum.

Schunn, C. D., & Anderson, J. R. (1999). The generality/ specificity of expertise in scientific reasoning. *Cognitive Science, 23*(3), 337–370.

Voss, J. F., Tyler, S. W., & Yengo, L. A. (1983). Individual differences in the solving of social science problems. In R. F. Dillon & R. R. Schmeck (Eds.), *Individual differences in cognition* (Vol. 1, pp. 205–232). New York: Academic Press.

Christian D. Schunn
Melissa M. Nelson

EXPERTISE

The notion of expertise underlies many facets of the educational process. Educators look to subject matter experts to inform the selection of content and establish levels of optimal performance against which student performance can be compared. Expert teachers are highly valued and actively sought out to serve as mentors and master teachers for those who are less experienced in the classroom. It is also hoped that students acquire expertise in some area so that they may be successful in their future academic and professional endeavors. Despite the centrality expertise in education, however, there are substantial challenges that exist in defining it.

DEFINITIONS OF EXPERTISE

Expertise is difficult to define with precision. Generally, experts are expected to outperform non-experts consistently on tasks in a specific domain. However, scholars disagree about the most effective means by which to identify these individuals. K. Anders Ericsson (1948–) argues that experts are those individuals who reliably excel on specific key tasks that are central to performance in a domain (Ericsson & Smith, 1991). In contrast, Robert Sternberg (1949–) suggests that such narrowly bounded criteria are inauthentic and do not represent expertise as it occurs in professional settings (Sternberg & Horvath, 1995, 1998; Sternberg, Gigorenko, & Ferrari, 2002). Rather than relying on a static list of necessary and sufficient characteristics for expertise, he advocates a "family resemblance" approach in which the central tendencies of expertise (proficiency, experience, etc.) may manifest differently among different experts within and across domains.

It is also an open question in some domains whether or not it is possible to be an expert. James Shanteau (1943–) reports that the reliability of expert evaluations and predictions varies significantly by domain. For example, expert weather forecasters are almost perfectly consistent ($r=0.98$) in their predictions when presented with the same information on different occasions (Shanteau, 2000; Shanteau, Weiss, Thomas, & Pounds, 2002). In contrast, expert stockbrokers ($r=0.40$) and expert pathologists ($r=0.50$) are fairly inconsistent. Similarly, the level of agreement between experts in a field varies between domains and is closely related to rates of internal consistency. Shanteau suggests that evidence of unreliability in expert judgment does not inherently invalidate claims of expertise. In some cases, experts may discern multiple valid paths to reach a desired goal and evaluate the information at hand in that context. In other cases, the scientific knowledge base that supports experts' decision-making may itself be underdeveloped—as is the case in social sciences such as economics, psychology, and education. Experts in these domains may apply the best available knowledge of the field consistently and effectively but need to fill knowledge gaps with personal judgments that are less reliable.

In contrast, Robyn Dawes (1936–) argues that expertise can exist only in fields for which advanced training and accumulated experience lead to higher reliability and success rates. His 1994 book, *House of Cards*, analyzed the fields of clinical psychology and psychotherapy and found that licensed practitioners were no more successful in helping their clients than laypeople with minimal training. Further, supposed experts in the field were no more accurate than novices when interpreting the results of psychological tests (e.g., Rorschach and sentence completion tests) or predicting the future behaviors of the individuals whom they evaluated. His conclusion was that expertise could not exist in the domain.

The problem of defining expertise increases for fields in which there is little agreement on desired outcomes or best practices. In the field of education, for example, identifying and expert teachers and training novices to become experts are considered to be crucial. The early work of David Berliner (1938–) and others observed that teachers considered to be experts typically had a superior understanding of relevant factors impacting classroom dynamics, were better able to improvise during lessons to adapt to their students' abilities, and more successfully managed competing demands for their limited attentional resources (Berliner, 1986, 1987; Carter, Sabers, Cushing, Pinnegar, & Berliner, 1987; Carter, Cushing, Sabers, Stein, & Berliner, 1988; Sabers, Cushing, & Berliner, 1991).

However, in his recent work, Berliner (2005) suggests that two major issues prevent an adequate understanding of expertise in teaching. First, there are multiple standards of "good teaching" that are dependent upon cultural norms. Second, there is persistent disagreement on the desired outcomes of public education and appropriate ways to measure student success in relation to them. Thus, an expert teacher would need to be both a "good" teacher in a cultural sense by implementing commonly embraced practices and an "effective" teacher in terms of measured student learning outcomes (Berliner, 1987, 2005). The fact that teaching effectiveness must be evaluated on the basis of students' achievement rather than the actions of the teachers themselves further problematizes the concept of the expert pedagogue, because cultural, contextual, and personal factors impact student performance and are beyond the control and/or professional responsibility of an individual teacher.

RESEARCH FINDINGS ON EXPERTISE

Research stemming from the field of cognitive psychology in the 1970s and 1980s has yielded a sizeable body of evidence for common traits across domains of expertise. The seminal book by Michelene Chi, Robert Glaser, and Marshall Farr, *The Nature of Expertise* (1988), compiled examinations of data from typewriting, restaurant orders, mental arithmetic, computer programming, judicial decision-making, and medicine. The overview chapter listed seven primary attributes that characterize the performance of most experts across domains. These observations have helped to shape the development of the field:

1. Experts excel mainly in their own domains;

2. Experts perceive large meaningful patterns in their domain;

3. Experts are fast; they are faster than novices at performing the skills of their domain, and they quickly solve problems with little error;

4. Experts have superior short-term and long-term memory;

5. Experts see and represent a problem in their domain at a deeper (more principled) level than novices; novices tend to represent a problem at a superficial level;

6. Experts spend a great deal of time analyzing a problem qualitatively;

7. Experts have strong self-monitoring skills.

When performing in their domains, experts rely on their highly refined mental models to represent and solve the problems they encounter. These schemas allow experts to identify the problem type and respond using efficient and effective strategies that leverage their deep understanding of the problem structure (Chi, Feltovich, & Glaser, 1981). Using known strategies, they are able to proceed directly toward the desired outcome. Referred to as "forward reasoning," this process differs sharply from novices' approaches to problem solving, which typically involve reasoning backward from the desired outcome to identify appropriate intermediate steps (Chi, Glaser, & Rees, 1982).

In addition to these characteristics, studies from various domains suggest that experts typically have at least 10 years of experience in their fields. In a major review of the research, Ericsson and his colleagues (Ericsson, Krampe, & Tesch-Römer, 1993) analyzed many studies of training outcomes across a wide range of tasks (e.g., Morse Code operation, musical performance, Olympic sporting events) and found strong evidence that years of experience alone was not sufficient for explaining performance outcomes. Replicating these findings, their own study demonstrated that in some cases expert professional pianists had up to six fewer years of experience than their less-skilled amateur counterparts.

To explain this discrepancy, Ericsson proposes that those individuals who become experts engage in focused and intensive training during their years of experience known as *deliberate practice* that is qualitatively different than other types of experience within the domain. Defined as "the individualized training activities especially designed by a coach or teacher to improve specific aspects of an individual's performance through repetition and successive refinement [that includes] monitor[ing] their training with full concentration, which is effortful and limits the duration of daily training" (Ericsson & Lehmann, 1996, pp. 278–279), deliberate practice is not considered to be inherently motivating. It is specifically intended to refine performance and remediate any facet of relevant skills in which there is room for improvement (Ericsson & Charness, 1994).

Ericsson characterizes experts' performance as demonstrating maximal adaptation to task constraints. In simpler terms, this means that experts have shaped their skills to maximize the efficiency of their actions within the structural context of their domains as they solve relevant problems. Such adaptations can take the form of "shortcuts" that would not be feasible for non-experts but produce superior results when employed appropriately. For example, expert athletes learn to anticipate changing conditions rapidly and respond effectively before the new condition has actually formed (e.g., anticipating the gunshot that starts a race). Likewise, chess masters can visualize the ways in which a particular move may prevent or allow an opening several moves later in a game and make preemptive decisions on that basis.

When task constraints change, however, some experts are unable to adapt successfully to the new situation while others retain their high levels of performance. Giyoo Hatano (1936–2006) characterized members of these respective groups as *adaptive* and *routine* experts (Hatano, 1982). Adaptive experts typically understand why their skills are effective under normal circumstances and successfully modify them to fit the new situation or invent new procedures as necessary (Hatano & Inagaki, 1986, 2000). However, it is challenging to reliably identify adaptive experts. Studies of expert bridge players, electronics troubleshooters, and others have found that changing task constraints (e.g., point values in bridge) or introducing highly unusual situations often leads to weak performance by

---

EXPERTISE AND IQ

Expertise is often attributed to high levels of intelligence. However, studies of expertise consistently find that there is no correlation between IQ and experts' performance. Ericsson (1998; Ericsson & Charness, 1994; Ericsson & Lehmann, 1996) investigated reports of child prodigies who are reputed to perform feats rivaling top experts' abilities. However, in instances where these abilities have been sufficiently documented to permit independent validation, the prodigies consistently have approximately 10 years of deliberate practice that was initiated and supported by parents, tutors, or coaches as young as 18 months old. The available evidence indicates that even those abilities typically attributed to innate talent (e.g., perfect pitch, exceptional memory, reflexes, muscle strength and endurance, etc.) can be fostered through environmental factors and training experiences for children who are highly motivated to succeed in these tasks.

---

individuals who typically demonstrate high levels of expertise in their domains under routine conditions.

DIFFERENT PERSPECTIVES ON THE DEVELOPMENT OF EXPERTISE

As discussed above, Ericsson's findings across domains indicate that world-class performers tend to require about 10 years of deliberate practice prior to attaining that status. However, other research from various fields suggests that other factors may also play a role. Dean Keith Simonton (1948–) argues that those experts who demonstrate adaptive expertise through creative innovations in their respective fields typically score higher on personality measures of nonconformity, independence, openness to experience, ego strength, introversion, and aggressiveness. They are also significantly more willing to take risks than routine experts in their fields (Simonton, 1999, 2000). Additional research also suggests that highly creative experts tend to have broader interests than their less creative counterparts (Simonton, 1976).

Simonton's analyses also indicate that several assumptions of the deliberate practice hypothesis are not borne out with regard to experts in creative fields like music composition and scientific discovery. He argues that if deliberate practice were the sole factor affecting the development of expertise, then the best experts ought to be those with the most years of deliberate practice. However, his (1991a, 1991b) studies of 120 classical composers and 2,026 scientists and inventors indicated that those who were most productive and considered to be most eminent in their respective fields trained for fewer years and made major contributions sooner after their first accomplishments than those considered to be less important contributors. Further, the career trajectories of creative experts tend to peak and then decline, despite ongoing deliberate practice, and the odds of generating a creative success do not change significantly over the course of a career (Simonton, 1985, 1986, 1997).

Ericsson (1998, 2004) suggests that practice which becomes rote rather than deliberate may limit the development of expertise in this way. Research in cognitive skill development indicates that as people practice new skills, they typically require less and less conscious attention directed to their actions while maintaining a consistent level of performance. For example, learning to read or drive a car is typically highly effortful, slow, and halting when it is first learned. However, with continued practice, performance becomes fluent with little or no attention directed to the component skills (e.g., pronunciation or word recognition during reading; shifting gears or stepping on the brake pedal while driving). This *automaticity* of skills results in performance that is very fast and consistent. It may also lead to people being unaware of how they perform those skills—and even whether or not the skills were used in a particular situation. As skills automate, they demand fewer cognitive resources, so attention can be redirected to other tasks.

What is done with surplus attention during practice and performance is likely a critical factor in the development of advanced and creative expertise. In deliberate practice, this attention is reinvested to continually monitor and improve performance. However, when spare attention is allocated to unrelated activities (e.g., talking on a cellular phone while driving), skill development plateaus.

For this reason, Ericsson argues that automaticity should be avoided as individuals seek to become experts. However, research on skill acquisition and expertise from cognitive science indicates that automaticity in fundamental domain skills is necessary to make available the attentional resources required to develop and execute more sophisticated strategies. Spare attention during performance is especially important for adaptive experts, because they must allocate their cognitive resources to recognizing and understanding novel or unusual aspects of a task and the implications of resulting atypical constraints. Therefore, those routine skills that are directly applicable to the new task must not demand conscious attention that would compete with these needs.

David Feldon (1975–) suggests that what differentiates adaptive experts who are able to leverage their automaticity from routine experts whose flexibility is limited by it is the number and relevance of the decision points in their procedures (Clark, Feldon, van Merriënboer, Yates, & Early, 2008; Feldon, 2007a). As skills automate and basic skills combine to form more complex procedures, consciously mediated decision points remain where details of the specific situation determine which of several possible strategies will be the best to employ from an expert's repertoire in that instance. Thus, the training most likely to lead to adaptive expertise presents learners with a wide variety of practice scenarios to support the development of appropriately placed decision points and to avoid inappropriate automatization of requisite skills (Clark, Feldon, Howard, & Choi, 2006; Feldon, 2007b).

IMPLICATIONS OF RESEARCH ON EXPERTISE FOR INSTRUCTION

Conventional wisdom suggests that if a learner needs to know how to do something well, the best instructor would be an expert in the field. However, research indicates that this is not always the case. Trends in the findings on experts' instructional abilities indicate that, overall, experts are (1) inaccurate in their assessments of learners' knowledge and abilities relevant to learning procedures in an expert's field, and (2) inaccurate in their explanations of how they accomplish tasks within their domains.

Pamela Hinds' studies of experts as instructors demonstrate that experts are significantly worse than nonexperts in predicting the amount of time that it would take novices to learn presented material within the experts' domain of expertise. Further, debiasing techniques that are often effective in improving the accuracy of non-experts' preliminary assessments of novices did not improve their predictions (Hinds, 1999). In another study, Hinds compared the efficacy of one-on-one instruction between novices and experts with one-on-one peer instruction among novices. She found that when novices taught other novices how to perform a task, the students were better able to perform the procedure correctly than when experts provided the instruction. However, if the novice learners were asked to complete a task that required adjustments to the procedure that was taught, those who learned from the experts performed better (Hinds, Patterson, & Pfeffer, 2001).

These findings indicate that the explanations of experts offer an advantage, because their sophisticated mental models of their domains allowed them to structure the information that they provided to be broadly applicable. This differed from the overly specific explanations of novices, which were based solely on their experiences with the single task in the study. However, it seems that experts excluded specific information which would have been helpful to learners as they attempted to perform the task. This may have occurred (1) because the experts overestimated learners' pre-existing knowledge bases, (2) because they could not successfully explain the automated skills they themselves use, or (3) for a combination of both reasons.

Feldon's investigations of experts' self-report accuracy (2004, 2007a, 2007c) indicate that automaticity does play a role in limiting their abilities to fully describe their own problem-solving processes. Analysis of experts' explanations of their actions during a recorded task revealed that inaccuracies represented both omissions of relevant steps in their activities and statements that directly contradicted their actions. If the only reason for experts' inaccurate explanations was an overestimation of students' abilities, then only errors of omission would be expected. However, the presence of errors of commission indicates that experts' may lack an awareness of their own actions that would limit the accuracy and completeness of their explanations to others.

Research on ways to maximize the benefits of experts' knowledge for instruction has identified techniques that appear to avoid the limitations of experts' limited self-awareness within their domains. Collectively known as *cognitive task analysis* (CTA), these techniques involve intensive, highly structured interviews with multiple experts to identify and collectively validate complete explanations of effective ways to perform a specific task within the domain of expertise. Instructors then incorporate these protocols into their course materials to supplement or replace their own explanations of the skills to be learned. Controlled studies of CTA-based instruction consistently demonstrate dramatic effect sizes favoring its use over more traditional unscaffolded explanations by experts in diverse domains including medicine, electronic systems troubleshooting, and spreadsheet applications (Clark et al., 2008; Feldon, 2007a; Feldon & Clark, 2006).

SEE ALSO *Expert-Novice Studies.*

BIBLIOGRAPHY

Berliner, D. C. (1986). In pursuit of the expert pedagogue. *Educational Researcher, 15,* 5–13.

Berliner, D. C. (1987). Simple views of effective teaching and a simple theory of classroom instruction. In D. C. Berliner & B. Rosenshine (Eds.), *Talks to teachers* (pp. 93–110). New York: Random House.

Berliner, D. C. (2005). The near impossibility of testing for teacher quality. *Journal of Teacher Education, 56*(3), 205–213.

Carter, K., Sabers, D., Cushing, K., Pinnegar, S., & Berliner, D. C. (1987). Processing and using information about students: A study of expert, novice, and postulant teachers. *Teaching and Teacher Education, 3,* 147–157.

Carter, K., Cushing, K., Sabers, D., Stein, P., & Berliner, D. C. (1988). Expert-novice differences in perceiving and processing visual classroom information. *Journal of Teacher Education, 39*(3), 25–31.

Chi, M. T. H., Feltovich, P. J., & Glaser, R. (1981). Categorization and representation of physics problems by experts and novices. *Cognitive Science, 5,* 121–152.

Chi, M. T. H., Glaser, R., & Rees, E. (1982). Expertise in problem solving. In R. J. Sternberg (Ed.), *Advances in psychology of human intelligence* (Vol. 1, pp. 7–75). Hillsdale, NJ: Erlbaum.

Chi, M. T. H., Glaser, R., & Farr, M. (1988). *The Nature of Expertise.* Hillsdale, NJ: Erlbaum, 1988.

Clark, R. E., Feldon, D. F., Howard, K., & Choi, S. (2006). Five critical issues for web-based instructional design research and practice. In H. F. O'Neil, Jr., & R. S. Perez (Eds.), *Web-based learning: Theory, Research and Practice* (pp. 343–370). Mahwah, NJ: Erlbaum.

Clark, R. E., Feldon, D., van Merriënboer, J. J. G., Yates, K., and Early, S. (2008). Cognitive task analysis. In J. M. Spector, M. D. Merrill, J. J. G. van Merriënboer, & M. P. Driscoll (Eds.). *Handbook of research on educational communications and technology* (3rd ed., pp. 577–593). New York: Routledge.

Dawes, R. M. *House of cards.* New York: Free Press.

Ericsson, K. A. (1998). The scientific study of expert levels of performance: General implications for optimal learning and creativity. *High Ability Studies, 9*(1), 75–100.

Ericsson, K. A. (2004). Deliberate practice and the acquisition and maintenance of expert performance in medicine and related domains. *Academic Medicine, 79*(10), S70–S81.

Ericsson, K. A., & Charness, N. (1994). Expert performance: Its structure and acquisition. *American Psychologist, 49*(8), 725–747.

Ericsson, K. A., Krampe, R. T., & Tesch-Römer, C. (1993). The role of deliberate practice in the acquisition of expert performance. *Psychological Review, 100,* 363–406.

Ericsson, K. A., & Lehmann, A. C. (1996). Expert and exceptional performance: Maximal adaptation to task constraints. *Annual Review of Psychology, 47,* 273–305.

Ericsson, K. A., & Smith, J. (1991). *Towards a general theory of expertise: Prospects and limits.* New York: Cambridge University Press.

Feldon, D. F. (2004) *Inaccuracies in expert self report: Errors in the description of strategies for designing psychology experiments.* Unpublished doctoral dissertation, Rossier School of Education, University of Southern California, Los Angeles.

Feldon, D. F. (2007a). Implications of research on expertise for curriculum and pedagogy. *Educational Psychology Review, 19*(2), 91–110.

Feldon, D. F. (2007b). Cognitive load in the classroom: The double-edged sword of automaticity. *Educational Psychologist, 42*(3), 123–137.

Feldon, D. F. (2007c, April). *Experimental design and analysis strategies: What experts do but fail to report.* Paper presented at the Annual Meeting of the American Education Research Association, Chicago.

Feldon, D. F., & Clark, R. E. (2006). Instructional implications of cognitive task analysis as a method for improving the accuracy of experts' self-report. In G. Clarebout & J. Elen (Eds.), *Avoiding simplicity, confronting complexity: Advances in studying and designing (computer-based) powerful learning environments* (pp. 109–116). Rotterdam, The Netherlands: Sense.

Hatano, G. (1982). Cognitive consequences of practice in culture specific procedural skills. *Quarterly Newsletter of the Laboratory of Comparative Human Cognition, 4,* 15–18.

Hatano, G., & Inagaki, K. (1986). Two courses of expertise. In H. Stevenson, H. Asuma & K. Hakauta (Eds.). *Child development and education in Japan* (pp. 262–272). San Francisco: Freeman.

Hatano, G. & Inagaki, K. (2000, April). *Practice makes a difference: Design principles for adaptive expertise.* Paper presented at the Annual Meeting of the American Education Research Association, New Orleans, LA.

Hinds, P. (1999). The curse of expertise: The effects of expertise and debiasing methods on predictions of novice performance. *Journal of Experimental Psychology: Applied, 5,* 205–221.

Hinds, P. J., Patterson, M., & Pfeffer, J. (2001). Bothered by abstraction: The effect of expertise on knowledge transfer and subsequent novice performance. *Journal of Applied Psychology, 86*(6), 1232–1243.

Sabers, D. S., Cushing, K. S., & Berliner, D. C. (1991). Differences among teachers in a task characterized by simultaneity, multidimensionality, and immediacy. *American Educational Research Journal, 28*(1), 63–88.

Shanteau, J. (2000). Why do experts disagree? In B. Green, R. Cressy, F. Delmar, T. Eisenberg, B. Howcroft, M. Lewis, et al. (Eds.), *Risk behaviour and risk management in business life* (pp. 186–196). Dordrecht, Netherlands: Kluwer Academic Press.

Shanteau, J., Weiss, D. J., Thomas, R. P., & Pounds, J. C. (2002). Performance-based assessment of expertise: How to decide if someone is an expert or not. *European Journal of Operational Research, 136,* 253–263.

Simonton, D. K. (1976). Biographical determinants of achieved eminence: A multivariate approach to the Cox data. *Journal of Personality and Social Psychology, 33,* 218–226.

Simonton, D. K. (1985). Quality, quantity, and age: The careers of 10 distinguished psychologists. *International Journal of Aging and Human Development, 21,* 241–254.

Simonton, D. K. (1986). Aesthetic success in classical music: A computer analysis of 1935 compositions. *Empirical Studies of the Arts, 4,* 1–17.

Simonton, D. K. (1991a). Career landmarks in science: Individual differences and interdisciplinary contrasts. *Developmental Psychology, 27,* 119–130.

Simonton, D. K. (1991b). Emergence and realization of genius: The lives and works of 120 classical composers. *Journal of Personality and Social Psychology, 61,* 829–840.

Simonton, D. K. (1997). Creative productivity: A predictive and explanatory model of career trajectories and landmarks. *Psychological Review, 104,* 66–89.

Simonton, D. K. (1999). Talent and its development: An emergenic and epigenetic model. *Psychological Review, 106,* 435–457.

Simonton, D. K. (2000). Creative development as acquired expertise: Theoretical issues and an empirical test. *Developmental Review, 20,* 283–318.

Sternberg, R. J., Gigorenko, E. L., & Ferrari, M. (2002). Fostering intellectual excellence through developing expertise. In M. Ferrari (Ed.), *The pursuit of excellence through education* (pp. 57–83). Mahwah, NJ: Erlbaum.

Sternberg, R., & Horvath, J. (1995). A prototype view of expert teaching. *Educational Researcher, 24*(6), 9–17.

Sternberg, R. J., & Horvath, J. A. (1998). Cognitive conceptions of expertise and their relations to giftedness. In R. C. Friedman & K. B. Rogers (Eds.), *Talent in context* (pp. 177–191). Washington, DC: American Psychological Association.

David F. Feldon

F

FEEDBACK IN LEARNING

Feedback occurs when the output of a system becomes an input to the same system, causing the system to respond dynamically to its previous productions. In learning, feedback can occur when consequences or products of a learner's behavior or cognition indicate the degree to which a goal or expectation is left unmet. Such information allows learners to check and improve the quality of their understanding, their application of knowledge and skill, and the processes by which they acquire new capabilities. In order for the consequences of behavior or cognition to influence further learning (and thus operate as feedback), at least three conditions must be met:

- A learner with implicit or explicit learning goals or expectations

- An environment that makes the consequences of action or cognition observable

- The ability of the learner to note and interpret the consequences of action or cognition.

In educational contexts, feedback appears in various guises, often tailored by an agent in the learner's environment with the specific intent of altering or nurturing some aspect of the learning process. In interpersonal interactions, feedback can appear in dialogues between a teacher and student or in the discourse of students engaged in collaboration. Feedback can be a smile or a frown, verbal corrections and explanations, or a display of expert performance after a novice attempt. A teacher can provide feedback to students about whether specific performance

criteria have been met in formative assessments. Feedback can appear in myriad mediated forms—paper-based workbooks and programmed instruction, computer-based tutorials, and computer-based simulations—where students check their answers or study informative consequences (e.g., the correct answer, suggestions for improvement, and simulation results). Many inquiry and project-based educational programs rely on learners to test hypotheses and gain new knowledge from analysis of experimental results. The capable, independent learner can find feedback in all sorts of interactions with the learning context if the learner has clear goals and expectations and abilities to perceive and interpret relevant consequences of action and cognition.

A BRIEF HISTORY OF FEEDBACK

In the early twentieth century, the term *feedback* referred to electrical systems used in audio broadcast. For example, feedback was brought to public attention in a notorious series of lawsuits over a patent for a circuit that would amplify radio signals by feeding back the signal into the circuit in rapid oscillations. Engineers came to use feedback to refer to products of a mechanical or electrical system that allowed the system to regulate itself. For example, if a heating system warms air temperature beyond a specified point, a thermostat can switch the system off and restart the heating system once the air temperature cools. Feedback became an explicit and crucial engineering concern as industry and the military sought to increasingly automate during World War II.

In 1948 *Cybernetics: Control and Communication in the Animal and the Machine*, by Norbert Wiener (1894–1964) made an enormously influential articulation of the role of feedback in the operation of all varieties of mechanical, biological, psychological, and social systems. Coining the term cybernetics from the Greek for *steersman*, Weiner conceived of a new science to investigate how feedback and information dissemination regulate systems. With ideas both persuasive and prescient, Weiner imagined how feedback systems could be linked to complex calculating machines to create mechanical brains that demonstrate artificial intelligence, the machine learning and action that is responsive to dynamic features of a changing environment.

Simultaneous with conceptualizations of feedback in engineering, behaviorism emerged as a psychological paradigm which emphasized the consequences of an organism's behavior as the primary determinant of future behavior. Simply put, behaviorism argued that certain behavioral consequences act as reinforcers, increasing the subsequent frequency of behaviors that produce them. A child might increase, for example, the frequency of behaviors that lead to acquiring candy. Some consequences act as punishment, dramatically reducing the frequency of a behavior that produces them. Without reinforcing or punishing consequences, a behavior extinguishes, diminishes to some baseline frequency.

However, behaviorism struggled to account for the operation of some behavioral consequences and learning phenomena. How might it explain behaviors that persist in spite of punishment or which seem indifferent to reinforcement? How might behaviorism account for one-time learning and sudden insight, early acquisition of the grammar of a language, creativity, and actions that seem guided by abstract concept, not perceptible stimuli? Such phenomena implied the operation of some mental apparatus that could perform interpretative transformations on stimuli and produce new capabilities that are not so directly derived from simple behavior-consequence contingencies.

The combined influence of the cybernetics paradigm, weaknesses in behaviorism's account of learning, and developments in computer technology made psychology and education ripe for a so-called cognitive revolution. A new paradigm of humans as processors of information, borrowed from computing, supplanted behaviorism. Perceptible stimuli were no longer only considered cues or consequences for behavior, but informative signals that could be interpreted by mental apparatus, stored in meaning-preserving ways in memory, and used to inform future goal-directed action. The consequences of that action could then be fed back into the interpretive mental processor.

CONTEMPORARY VIEWS OF INSTRUCTIONAL FEEDBACK

At the beginning of the twenty-first century, the information-processing paradigm still provides a standard conceptualization of instructional feedback. For example, for the influential instructional psychologist, Robert Gagné (1916–2002), learning is the encoding of information from short-term into long-term memory storage. In subsequent practice, newly stored knowledge is retrieved and applied. Feedback, the consequences of knowledge applications, re-enters the cognitive system, causing potential alterations in goals, learning processes, and stored knowledge.

Feedback's conceptualization has evolved in two significant ways. First, the source of feedback is no longer presumed to be a teacher or even external consequences. Butler and Winne, for example, emphasize the importance of internal sources of feedback generated through self-monitoring as a critical engine of self-regulated learning. In the absence of teacher-provided feedback, capable learners could interpret the consequences of their actions and cognitions in light of learning goals and thus provide feedback to themselves.

Second, some researchers distinguish among types of feedback. Bangert-Drowns, Kulik, Kulik, and Morgan suggested that feedback can provide information about knowledge retrieval and application, emotional and motivational states, and strategic management of learning. It could indicate whether a performance is correct, explain the nature of an error, provide prototypical responses, or simply display the consequences of actions. Each of these likely requires different features to be optimally effective. Hattie and Timperley, extending Kluger and DeNisi's suggestion that feedback loops can be hierarchically nested one in another, proposed four levels of feedback: about the quality of task performance, about the cognitive processes used to accomplish the task, about the ways in which a learner could better manage learning engagement, and about the self. Evidence suggests that these different kinds of feedback will be differentially effective according to different standards; for example, information about the self may not provide effective performance enhancements because it does not indicate specific ways in which knowledge or learning processes can be adjusted.

OPTIMIZING FEEDBACK FOR LEARNING

Feedback in learning is difficult to research. It has been found to inform learners about the following:

The accuracy or efficiency of knowledge and its retrieval or application

The quality of mental operations applied to information

The quality of psychomotor performance

The viability of a hypothesis or expectation

The emotional or motivational state of the learner

The efficiency or quality of learning processes employed in a learning task

The efficiency or quality of learning processes employed in a learning task

The management of learning processes

Enduring qualities and goals of self

The nature of relationships with co-learners and teachers.

Different feedback features might be differentially effective for different learners and different aspects of learning. Even apparently straightforward feedback depends on the interpretation of a learner. A learner could interpret the response "incorrect" as indicating a need to revise knowledge, a personal rejection, the confirmation of a hypothesis, or a hint to work harder.

Despite these difficulties, some generalities about feedback effects are possible. Kulhavy suggested—and Bangert-Drowns, Kulik, Kulik, and Morgan supported—that if feedback is available before a learner actively attempts to perform a task (presearch availability), the learner may not be cognitively and motivationally prepared to effectively use the feedback. Kulhavy also suggested—and subsequent research corroborates—that response certitude, the degree to which learners feel most sure of their knowledge, makes disconfirming corrective feedback more salient and thus more influential in learning. Kluger and DeNisi suggest that feedback most effectively enhances performance when it directs attention to motivational and task-specific goals, not self-related goals. Research on the timing of externally provided instructional feedback—immediate or delayed after some learner performance—has yielded highly varied results. Hattie and Timperley suggest that this variation might be accounted for by level of feedback; immediate task feedback might most benefit task performance, but delayed processing feedback might most enhance cognitive processing of information.

Clearly, feedback is a critical, ubiquitous, and complex feature of learning processes guided by teachers or directed by learners themselves. Educators would do well to create environments that support challenging standards and goal-setting and provide informative feedback. Students can also benefit from assistance regarding how to look for and use feedback and how to provide feedback for themselves. Future research will continue to clarify conditions that optimize feedback effects for different tasks and learners.

SEE ALSO *Behaviorism; Gagné, Robert Mills; Information Processing Theory; Operant Conditioning; Rewards; Self-Regulated Learning.*

BIBLIOGRAPHY

Bangert-Drowns, R. L., Kulik, C.-L. C., Kulik, J. A., & Morgan, M. T. (1991). The instructional effect of feedback in test-like events. *Review of Educational Research, 61*(2), 213–238.

Butler, D. L., & Winne, P. H. (1995). Feedback and self-regulated learning: A theoretical synthesis. *Review of Educational Research, 65*(3), 245–281.

Gagné, R. M., Briggs, L. J., & Wager, W. W. (1992). *Principles of Instructional Design.* New York: Harcourt Brace Jovanovich.

Hattie, J., & Timperley, H. (2007). The power of feedback. *Review of Educational Research, 77*(1), 81–112.

Kluger, A. N., & DeNisi, A. (1996). The effects of feedback interventions on performance: A historical review, a meta-analysis, and a preliminary feedback intervention theory. *Psychological Bulletin, 119*(2), 254–284.

Kulhavy, R. W., & Stock, W. A. (1989). Feedback in written instruction: The place of response certitude. *Educational Psychology Review, 1*(4), 279–308.

Lewis, F. L. (1992). *Applied optimal control and estimation.* Paramus, NJ: Prentice-Hall.

Twelve-year quarrel. (1928, November 26). *Time.* Retrieved April 18, 2008, from http://www.time.com/time/magazine/article/0,9171,732133,00.html.

Wiener, N. (1948). *Cybernetics or control and communication in the animal and the machine.* Cambridge, MA: MIT Press.

Robert L. Bangert-Drowns

FIRST (PRIMARY) LANGUAGE ACQUISITION

The term *first language acquisition* refers to children's natural acquisition of the language or languages they hear from birth. It is distinguished from second language acquisition, which begins later, and from foreign language learning, which typically involves formal instruction.

First language acquisition is a rapid process. In the span of just a few years, newborn infants who neither speak nor understand any language become young children who comment, question, and express their ideas in the language of their community. This change does not occur all at once. First, newborns' cries give way to coos and babbles. Then, infants who coo and babble start to show signs of comprehension such as turning when they hear their name. Infants then become toddlers who say "bye-bye" and "all gone" and start to label the people and objects in their environment. As their vocabularies continue to grow, children start to combine words. Children's first word combinations, such as "all gone juice" and "read me," are short and are missing parts found in adults' sentences. Gradually children's immature sentences are replaced by longer and more adultlike sentences. As children learn to talk, their comprehension abilities also develop, typically in advance of their productive speech. As children master language, they also become masters at using language to communicate. One-year-olds who can only point and label become 2-year-olds who comment, question, and command, and 4-year-olds who can carry on coherent conversations. Studies of middle-class, typically developing children acquiring English have documented that by four years of age children are nearly adult like in phonological properties of their speech; they have vocabularies of several thousand words, and they produce most of the types of structures observable in the speech of adults (Hoff, 2008).

THEORIES OF FIRST LANGUAGE ACQUISITION

First language acquisition is a robust process. Despite differences among cultures in the kind of early language experience provided to children, all normal children in anything remotely approximating a normal environment learn to talk (Hoff, 2006a). The rapidity and robustness of first language acquisition, along with its status as an accomplishment unique to humans, suggests to some that first language acquisition is supported by language specific innate knowledge. Language, according to this view, is encoded in the human genome—as are stereoscopic vision and bipedal locomotion. Another argument for the position that language has significant innate support comes from analyses of the nature of language knowledge in both the adult and child. Once language is acquired, speakers and hearers have the capacity to produce and understand an infinite number of novel sentences. This productivity of language poses a challenge to efforts to account for language acquisition on the basis of experience. Somehow children go beyond what they have experienced and construct a grammar that allows them to produce an infinite number of different sentences from a finite inventory of words. The argument for innate linguistic knowledge is also supported by evidence that very young children are sensitive to structural properties of language for which there is no obvious explanation in terms of infants' experience (Lidz, 2007).

INFANT ATTENTION TO AND RECOGNITION OF ENVIRONMENTAL SPEECH

Although it is not possible at this point to fully explain how language could be acquired without language-specific innate knowledge, there is mounting evidence that children can and do learn a great deal from their environments. Infants come to the language learning task equipped with attentional biases and learning capacities that operate on the experience their environments provide. Infants are biased to attend to speech over other environmental noises, and they pay particular attention to speech that has the exaggerated rhythm and intonation contour that characterizes the speech addressed to infants. Infants are excellent at extracting patterns from input, and this capacity for what is

termed statistical learning may make a substantial contribution to the language acquisition process (Gerken, 2007). For example, infants learn which acoustic features tend to co-occur in the speech they hear, with the result that their speech perception becomes tuned to the particular speech sounds used in the language they hear (Maye, Werker, & Gerken, 2002). A side effect of this tuning to the native language is a decline in the ability to hear sound contrasts that are not used in the ambient language. Thus, the basis for the foreign accent that is characteristic of late-acquired second languages is laid in infancy (Kuhl, Conboy, Padden, & Pruitt, 2005).

Infants also detect patterns among speech sounds. In experimental testing, it has been demonstrated that eight-month-old infants can detect patterns of co-occurring syllables in a stream of sound that they were exposed to for only two minutes (Saffran, Aslin, & Newport, 1996). These pattern learning abilities allow infants to recognize many familiar sound patterns in their language before they have learned the meanings associated with them. By nine months, infants have learned that some sound sequences are typical of their language and others are not. For example, American and Dutch nine-month-olds can discriminate English from Dutch words based on differences between them in what are allowable sound sequences (Jusczyk, Friederici, Wessels, Svenkerud, & Jusczyk, 1993; Gerken & Aslin, 2005).

Pattern learning may also provide children the basics of grammar. In experimental testing, 1-year-old children have demonstrated the ability to learn the patterns among words in word strings that they hear such that they later can distinguish sequences that violate this pattern from other sequences that are grammatical (Gomez & Gerken, 1999). It has been suggested that children may also learn the grammatical categories of their language (e.g., noun and verb) by noticing distributional regularities (e.g., all the words that are nouns are frequently preceded by "the"). Noticing co-occurrences also is one source of information about word meanings. When children hear the same word in many different contexts, they can use information about what is constant across those situations to narrow down the possible meanings of the word.

USING A COMMUNICATION SYSTEM TO MAKE CONTACT

Language acquisition is not solely a matter of learning the sounds, the words, and the grammar of language. In acquiring language children acquire a system that is used to communicate. Human infants are social beings, and the basic human desire to make contact with others is part of the foundation of language acquisition. (Children with autism seem not to have this desire to the same degree as typically developing children, and this difference is thought to be one root of the language disturbances that are characteristic of autism.) An important

Reading to a child encourages language development. © BRIAN MCENTIRE, 2008. USED UNDER LICENSE FROM SHUTTERSTOCK.COM.

social-cognitive ability that contributes to communicative interaction and to language development is the capacity for joint attention. Around the age of 10 months, children become able to actively engage their parents (and other individuals) while simultaneously focusing on an object of interest. In the first two years of life, language interaction that occurs in episodes of joint attention seems to be particularly useful to the language learning process (Baldwin & Meyer, 2007). More specifically, children as young as 18 months can use speakers' eye gaze as a clue to the referent of the words the speaker is producing. Children's non-linguistic, cognitive understandings also support word learning because a great deal of word learning consists of mapping sound sequences onto concepts children already understand nonlinguistically (Poulin-Dubois & Graham, 2007).

Many properties of children's language learning experience support the process of language acquisition. When adults (and older children) talk to infants they speak more slowly, clearly, at a higher pitch, and with exaggerated intonation. This special register for talking to children has been called *motherese*. Infants have been shown to prefer to listen to motherese over adult-directed speech, even when the speech is in another language. The properties of motherese may also be beneficial for language acquisition. Vowel sounds are more consistent in infant-directed speech, and the stress patterns that indicate word and phrase boundaries are exaggerated. Mothers and other adults also tend to provide labels and information about things that they present to children, which aids children in vocabulary building. Infant and child-directed speech is characterized by repeating and expanding on the words and phrases children produce, which also may help children learn word meanings and sentence structure (Hoff, 2008).

FACILITATING FIRST LANGUAGE ACQUISITION

Although all normal children acquire language, there are large individual differences in the rate at which children acquire language and therefore in the language skills children possess when they enter school (Hoff, 2006b; 2006c). These individual differences in oral language skill are predictive of success in acquiring literacy. Some of these individual differences may be the result of differences among children in language learning ability, but to a significant degree, variance among children in their language skills reflects variability in the language learning experiences they have had (Hoff, 2003a). Studies of children within the United States have shown that children who experience more one-to-one conversation with adults have more rapid language development. Thus, a supportive environment for language acquisition is one that is characterized by a great deal of verbal engagement with the child (Huttenlocher et al., 1991; Hart & Risley, 1994). The quality of the speech children hear also matters.

Contrary to the view that children require simple input, speech that uses a rich vocabulary and long, information-containing utterances has been found to promote language development (Hoff & Naigles, 2002; Pan, Rowe, Singer, & Snow, 2005). Children who hear a more diverse vocabulary develop larger vocabularies themselves—even at age 2 (Hoff & Naigles, 2002; Pan et al., 2005). Thus, successful and optimal language acquisition is contingent upon the richness of language input a child is exposed to. In addition, grammatical development seems to be accelerated when child-directed speech repeats and expands on a phrase or utterance a child attempts to produce (Hoff-Ginsberg, 1985, 1986). Studies of children in the United States suggest that book reading with an adult is a positive activity that provides children with a great deal of language input. Studies show that mothers produce more speech during book reading time than during toy play time, and this speech is richer than that produced during play time. Object labeling is also frequent during book reading, which may facilitate lexical development (Hoff, 2003b).

BILINGUAL FIRST LANGUAGE ACQUISITION

First language acquisition can be the acquisition of more than one language. The term bilingual first language acquisition has been used to refer to the circumstance in which a child acquires two languages from birth (Genesee & Nicoladis, 2007). (There has been very little research on the acquisition of more than two languages.) In the case of bilingual first language acquisition, the course of language development is largely unaffected by bilingualism. Infants seem to have the ability to distinguish two different types of sound streams based on the acoustic characteristics of the languages, and they are able to build two separate language systems. The rate of development in each language depends on the amount of exposure children receive. Typically, bilingually developing children show more rapid development in the language that they hear more (Pearson, 2008).

In sum, the human infant brings a social inclination, powerful learning abilities, and perhaps language-specific innate knowledge to the language learning task. In order for language acquisition to occur, the environment must meet those abilities by providing children with communicative experience. Linguistically rich and responsive communicative environments promote optimal language development.

SEE ALSO *Second Language Acquisition.*

BIBLIOGRAPHY

Baldwin, D., & Meyer, M. (2007). How inherently social is language? In E. Hoff & M. Shatz (Eds.), *Blackwell handbook of language development* (pp. 87–106). Malden, MA: Blackwell.

Genesee, F., & Nicoladis, E. (2007). Bilingual first language acquisition. In E. Hoff & M. Shatz (Eds.), *Blackwell handbook of language development* (pp. 324–342). Malden, MA: Blackwell.

Gerken, L. (2007). Acquiring linguistic structure. In E. Hoff & M. Shatz (Eds.), *Blackwell handbook of language development* (pp. 173–190). Malden, MA: Blackwell.

Gerken, L., & Aslin, R. N. (2005). Thirty years of research on infant speech perception: The legacy of Peter W. Jusczyk. *Language, Learning and Development, 1,* 5–21.

Gomez, R. L., & Gerken, L. (1999). Artificial grammar learning by 1-year-olds leads to specific and abstract knowledge. *Cognition, 70,* 109–135.

Hart, B., & Risley, T. R. (1994). *Meaningful differences in the everyday experience in young American children.* Baltimore, MD: Paul H. Brookes.

Hoff, E. (2003a). The specificity of environmental influence: Socioeconomic status affects early vocabulary development via maternal speech. *Child Development, 74,* 1368–1378.

Hoff, E. (2003b). Causes and consequences of SES-related differences in parent-to-child speech. In M. H. Bornstein & R. H. Bradley (Eds.), *Socioeconomic status, parenting, and child development* (pp.147–160). Mahwah, NJ: Erlbaum.

Hoff, E. (2006a). How social contexts support and shape language development. *Developmental Review, 26,* 55–88.

Hoff, E. (2006b). Language experience and language milestones during early childhood. In K. McCartney & D. Phillips (Eds.), *Blackwell handbook of early childhood development* (pp. 233–251). Malden, MA: Blackwell.

Hoff, E. (2006c). Environmental supports for language acquisition. In D. K. Dickinson & S. B. Neuman (Eds.), *Handbook of early literacy research* (Vol. 2, pp. 163–172). New York: Guilford Press.

Hoff, E. (2008). *Language development,* 4th ed. Farmington Hills, MI: Wadsworth.

Hoff, E., & Naigles, L. (2002). How children use input to acquire a lexicon. *Child Development, 73,* 418–433.

Hoff-Ginsberg, E. (1985). Some contributions of mothers' speech to their children's syntax growth. *Journal of Child Language,* 12, 367–385.

Hoff-Ginsberg, E. (1986). Function and structure in maternal speech: Their relation to the child's development of syntax. *Developmental Psychology, 22*, 155–163.

Huttenlocher, J., Haight, W., Bryk, A., Seltzer, J., & Lyons, T. (1991). Early vocabulary growth: Relation to language input and gender. *Developmental Psychology, 27*, 236–248.

Jusczyk, P. W., Friederici, A. D., Wessels, J. M., Svenkerud, V. Y., & Jusczyk, A. M. (1993). Infants' sensitivity to the sound patterns of native language words. *Journal of Memory & Language, 32*, 402–420.

Kuhl, P. K., Conboy, B., Padden, D. N. T., & Pruitt, J. (2005). Early speech perception and later language development: Implications for the "critical period." *Language Learning and Development, 1*, 237–264.

Lidz, J. (2007). The abstract nature of syntactic representations: Consequences for a theory of learning. In E. Hoff & M. Shatz (Eds.), *Blackwell handbook of language development* (pp. 277–303). Malden, MA: Blackwell.

Maye, J., Werker, J. F., & Gerken, L. (2002). Infant sensitivity to distributional information can affect phonetic discrimination. *Cognition, 82*, B101–B111.

Pan, B. A., Rowe, M. L., Singer, J. D., & Snow, C. E. (2005). Maternal correlates of growth in toddler vocabulary production in low-income families. *Child Development, 76*, 763–782.

Pearson, B. Z. (2008). *Raising a bilingual child*. New York: Random House.

Poulin-Dubois, D., & Graham, S. A. (2007). Cognitive processes in early word learning. In E. Hoff & M. Shatz (Eds.), *Blackwell handbook of language development* (pp. 191–211). Malden, MA: Blackwell.

Saffran, J. R., Aslin, R. N., & Newport, E. L. (1996). Statistical learning by 8-month-old infants. *Science, 274*, 1926–1928.

Erika Hoff
Kelly Bridges

FLOW THEORY

Flow theory was proposed by Mihalyi Csikszentmihalyi to describe the experiences of intrinsically motivated people, those who were engaged in an activity chosen for its own sake (Csikszentmihalyi, 1975, 1997). Such activities were viewed as worth doing just for the sake of doing them rather than as means to another end. While other research on intrinsic motivation focused on behavioral outcomes, Csikszentmihalyi attempted to describe the quality of subjective experience, or how intrinsic motivation felt. Further, he sought to explain the characteristics of activities that people were intrinsically motivated to pursue, and why such activities were rewarding.

Under certain conditions, people's experiences are optimal. Csikszentmihalyi (1975, 1997) and his colleagues, Rathunde, Whalen and Nakamura, defined optimal experiences as those that were accompanied by a merging of action and awareness, strong concentration on the task at hand, and a loss of awareness of time. At such times, people concentrate so hard on the current task that they forget about time and the world around them: They are thoroughly engrossed. Further, these activities are accompanied by positive emotions. They termed this quality of experience "flow."

The experience of flow is possible under certain circumstances: when individuals find the activities challenging and also believe they have the skills to accomplish them. Optimal experience, or flow, occurs when a person perceives the challenges in a certain situation and the skills brought to it as both balanced and above average. In contrast, when challenges and skills are unbalanced, such as when challenges outpace skills, an activity could evoke anxiety. The various ratios of challenges and skills are predicted to be associated with different qualities of experience: flow with high challenges and skills, apathy with low challenges and low skills, anxiety with high challenges and low skills, and boredom or relaxation with low challenges and high skills. The original classification scheme based on level of challenge and skill, described above (flow, relaxation, anxiety, and apathy) has been further refined into an eight-category scheme, and a twenty-four-category scheme. All schemes are based on the tenet that levels of challenge and skill interact to affect the quality of experience.

The idea of optimal challenge is not new to the field of education. Indeed, both Lev Vygotsky, a Russian psychologist (1896–1934), and Jean Piaget, a Swiss psychologist (1896–1980), contended that learning best occurs when people engage in activities that are at the peak of their abilities, when they have to work to their full potential to accomplish a task. However, the study of the experience of optimally challenging activities and the method of study are unique to flow theory.

MAJOR RESEARCH METHODS

Flow theorists not only study those who are intrinsically motivated to participate in an activity, but also individuals engaged in everyday activities. Csikszentmihalyi developed the Experience Sampling Method (ESM) to explore how individuals experience activities throughout their daily lives. The ESM involves randomly alerting individuals to answer questions about what they are currently doing, as well as their emotions, motivation, concentration, and thoughts associated with the task. Alerting methods have included beepers, watches, or PDAs set to randomly alert throughout a given time period. In this way, researchers can gain access to the thoughts and feelings during an activity as individuals are engaged in it. Other methods require individuals to recall how they felt or what they were thinking during prior activities, relying on memory.

The standard use of the Experience Sampling Method is to electronically beep students randomly during the day and ask that they complete a questionnaire (the Experience

Sampling Form, ESF, validated by Csikszentmihalyi and Larson). The first items on the ESF ask individuals to describe the activity in which they are currently engaged, followed by a series of questions to assess levels of motivation, cognition, and affect associated with the activity. These are Likert-type items (in which responses can range from 1 = not at all to 9 = very much) that resemble, for example: "Was this activity important to you?" "How hard were you concentrating?" "How do you feel about the challenges of the activity?" "How did you feel about your skills in the activity?" An additional thirteen semantic-differential items measure emotion during the activity (e.g., happy-sad, excited-bored, and sociable-lonely). Each activity can then be classified into the flow categories as determined by the level of perceived challenge and skill—above or below average.

With such a method, researchers are able to determine (a) the amount of time spent in different types of activities throughout a day, week, or month, (b) which individuals spent more or less time in certain activities, (c) how different activities were experienced (both cognitively and emotionally) and which were most or least enjoyed, (d) characteristics of the environment or context that best contribute to optimal experiences and (e) which individuals were more likely to enjoy different activities.

While this method is often used to gain an understanding across all the activities in everyday life, some researchers have specified the types of activities they want to study. For example, some researchers, such as Schweinle and colleagues and Shernoff and Hoogstra, have limited the random alerts to times when participants are in school or completing homework. In this way, they gain information about the experience of different school and homework activities, such as whole-class instruction, group projects, watching videos, taking tests or quizzes, etc.

One drawback to the ESM is that it can be expensive and time consuming. Further, it requires using a large number of participants to get a broad range of experiences. It is also difficult in educational settings where teachers may not be amenable to some students randomly stopping their activity to complete questionnaires. Some researchers have adapted the ESM to assess the experience of specific activities without random beeps. For example, Schweinle and colleagues were interested in elementary students' experience of mathematics classes. Rather than beeping students randomly throughout their math classes, they asked students to complete ESFs at the end of twelve different math classes across a school year. This type of method provided information specific to activities during math class rather than a cross-section of activities in everyday life. One drawback, though, was that it required students to recall their math class and respond with a general sense of how they experienced the whole class rather than specific points throughout the math class. Using the tradi-

tional ESM or modified versions, researchers have learned about how students experience school and academic activities and the environments that contribute to the most optimal academic experiences.

FACTORS INFLUENCING FLOW AND MOTIVATIONAL CONSEQUENCES

One benefit of flow theory is that it presumes that motivation, cognition, and affect are situational. Whereas much research in motivation has focused on relatively decontextualized individual psychological processes, flow theory presumes that these psychological processes are made meaningful by the environment. The ESM allows for study of both the environment and the persons within the setting. For example, researchers have used the ESM to determine how students spend their days and how they experience those activities. In one study, Shernoff, Knauth, and Makris found that high school students spend most of their classroom time paying attention to the teacher lecture (23%) or performing individual tasks such as writing notes or completing homework assignments (23%). Only about 8% of students' time was spent in interactive activities, including classroom discussion (5%) and group tasks or laboratory experiments (3%). In short, students were engaged in intellectually challenging tasks for more than half of the day; however, roughly one-third of their time was spent passively listening to the teacher lecture or observing a video.

Using the ESM, Shernoff and colleagues were also able to determine the quality of the students' experiences while engaged in each of these activities. Specifically, while students enjoyed watching videos and TV in class, they viewed these activities as the least challenging. Students also enjoyed individual work, which they reported most positively in terms of academic challenge, affect, control, and motivation. Lecture was viewed as unchallenging and was met with negative affect and lower levels of control. Considering that students spend approximately one-third of their time in the classroom passively listening to teachers or video, students may not be adequately challenged or motivated to learn.

Further, researchers have examined the quality of the experience as it relates to the balance of the challenge and skill of the activities. Researchers have for years extolled the benefits of high challenge matched with skill level, or optimal challenge. Vygotsky explained that the highest levels of learning occur when students are pushed to perform just beyond their current ability levels. As their skill levels increase, so must the level of challenge, maintaining an optimal balance that encourages continuous learning.

Flow theory further contends that, not only do activities with high challenge matched with high skill offer the best opportunities for learning, but they also provide an optimal environment for positive affect and intrinsic motivation. (It should be mentioned that not all activities with high challenge and high skill elicit flow states. However, flow states can only occur when high challenge is coupled with high skill.) If students believe that they have the skills to produce the desired results, positive affect is more likely to be experienced. When challenges and skills are optimal and balanced, students can experience higher levels engagement, attention, concentration and interest, according to Shernoff and his colleagues, as well as higher levels of positive affect, interaction with the class, efficacy, and value of the material, according to Schweinle and her colleagues (2006).

Interestingly, it is still possible to have positive affect if skill exceeds challenge. In fact, Schweinle and colleagues (in press) found that a student's skill level, rather than the perceived challenge of the activity, was the most significant factor in predicting positive affect and efficacy. While students may feel more positive if they believe they can succeed whether or not the challenge is high, only activities with high levels of challenge will also provide opportunities to learn. Phrased another way, students must have high to moderate levels of efficacy to demonstrate a preference for challenge. Teachers can use these tenets of flow theory to provide for optimal learning as well as positive affect and motivation to learn.

IMPLICATIONS FOR TEACHERS

Teachers encourage flow and intrinsic motivation by creating an environment that fosters enjoyable learning experiences. Ideally, to encourage optimal experiences, teachers must provide optimal challenge and support for competence (or skill). Schweinle and colleagues also found that, in classrooms where students reported high positive affect, efficacy and value of the material, teachers balanced levels of challenge and skill as well as (a) provided immediate, constructive feedback, (b) encouraged students to persist, (c) encouraged cooperation rather than competition, (d) supported student autonomy, (e) ensured that new challenges were tempered with support to match students' skill, (f) emphasized the importance of the material, and (g) pressed students to understand the principles rather than memorize algorithms.

Csikszentmihalyi (1997) argues that when teachers provide immediate, informational feedback regarding student performance, students become more interested and persistent with goal setting. Additionally, intrinsic motivation and self-efficacy increases in students. If a student receives non-constructive feedback, such as evaluating an individual's trait, motivation will decrease and negative affect may occur.

In addition to providing effective feedback, teachers can also increase intrinsic motivation and classroom experience by supporting student autonomy. Students become more involved when instructional activities are perceived as important and when students perceive themselves as autonomous and in control over their environment, according to Shernoff, Schneider, and Csikszentmihalyi. Schools can promote autonomy by minimizing external controls to facilitate conceptual understanding, allowing students to set goals and choose their own activities. In such a way, students are more likely to feel in control of their goals. However, if teachers provide a controlling environment by inflicting deadlines, stressing grades and performance, and demanding specific solutions rather than creativity, a decrease in affect, interest, and motivation could occur.

Positive affect may be one of the most powerful predictors of intrinsic motivation. Humor, expressions of enjoyment towards the subject matter, and utilizing kindness and sensitivity can produce a positive atmosphere in the classroom. In contrast, if teachers use threats, sarcasm, and directives, students may become less motivated and may experience negative affect. In addition to providing a positive atmosphere, teachers should also encourage social relationships. Schweinle's research suggests that teachers who allow students to work with their peers will help build cooperation in the classroom and an increased commitment and interest in the subject matter.

Challenge and feeling competent are important for optimal experiences. Teachers support this when they use students' errors as learning opportunities and provide chances for students to show their skill levels. The students' skill levels should match the challenge of class activities to encourage flow experiences. The difficulty level of tasks should increase as student skills increase. If a student maintains low skills and perceives the task as highly challenging, then the student may become anxious and experience negative feelings. To provide an ideal level of challenge, teachers can scaffold tasks, provide adequate time for students to complete tasks, and reduce long-term goals into smaller units, which follows Vygotsky's principles. This could increase the enjoyment of math, lessen anxiety, increase feelings of success, and ultimately create an environment conducive to optimal experiences.

Optimal experience in classrooms is important for students' learning and motivation at the present and also for their future educational plans. Shernoff and Hoogstra found that when students experience cognitive and emotional engagement with a specific topic, the resulting feelings may guide post-high school plans, such as college courses or majors. Further, interest and enjoyment with certain topics were essential factors for highly engaged students when making career decisions.

In sum, flow theory addresses how students experience educational contexts and how this experience influences learning and motivation. Activities that challenge students, but are still within their ability to accomplish, set the stage for optimal emotional and motivational experiences as well as optimal learning. Within the context of balanced challenge and skill, teachers can also improve the chances of positive experience by supporting autonomy; providing immediate, constructive feedback; encouraging cooperation among students; supporting positive affect; and pressing understanding rather than rote learning.

SEE ALSO *Interest; Intrinsic and Extrinsic Motivation; Piaget, Jean; Vygotsky, Lev Semenovich.*

BIBLIOGRAPHY

Csikszentmihalyi, M. (1975). *Beyond boredom and anxiety.* San Francisco: Jossey-Bass.

Csikszentmihalyi, M. (1997). Intrinsic motivation and effective teaching: A flow analysis. In J. J. Bass (Ed.), *Teaching well and liking it: Motivating faculty to teach effectively* (pp. 72–89). Baltimore, MD: Johns Hopkins University Press.

Csikszentmihalyi, M., & Larson, R. (1987). Validity and reliability of the experience-sampling method. *Journal of Nervous and Mental Disease, 175,* 526–536.

Csikszentmihalyi, M., & Nakamura, J. (1989). The dynamics of intrinsic motivation. In R. Ames & C. Ames (Eds.), *Handbook of motivation theory and research* (Vol. 3, pp. 45–71). New York: Academic Press.

Csikszentmihalyi, M., Rathunde, K., & Whalen, S. (1993). *Talented teenagers: The roots of success and failure.* Cambridge, UK: Cambridge University Press.

Delle Fave, A., & Bassi, M. (2000).The quality of experience in adolescents' daily lives: Developmental perspectives. *Genetic, Social, and General Psychology Monographs, 126*(3), 347–367.

Massimini, F., & Carli, M. (1988). The systematic assessment of flow in daily experience. In M. Csikszentmihalyi & I. S. Csikszentmihalyi (Eds.), *Optimal experience: Psychological studies of flow in consciousness* (pp. 166–287). Cambridge, UK: Cambridge University Press.

Piaget, J. (1952). *The origins of intelligence in children.* New York: Norton.

Schweinle, A., Turner, J. C., & Meyer, D. K. (2006). Striking the right balance: Students' motivation and affect in upper elementary mathematics classes. *Journal of Educational Research, 99*(5), 271–293.

Shernoff, D. J., Csikszentmihalyi, M., Schneider, B., & Shernoff, E. S. (2003). Student engagement in high school classrooms from the perspective of flow theory. *School Psychology Quarterly, 18*(2), 158–176.

Shernoff, D. J., & Hoogstra, L. (2001). Continuing motivation beyond the high school classroom. In M. Michaelson & J. Nakamura (Eds.), *Supportive frameworks for youth engagement* (pp. 73–87). New York: Jossey Bass.

Shernoff, D., Knauth, S., & Makris, E. (2000). The quality of classroom experience. In M. Csikszentmihalyi & B. Schneider (Eds.), *Becoming adults: How teenagers prepare for the world of work* (pp. 141–164). New York: Basic Books.

Vygotsky, L. (1978). *Mind in society.* Cambridge, MA: Harvard University Press.

Amy Schweinle
Andrea Bjornestad

FLYNN EFFECT

SEE *Misdiagnoses of Disabilities.*

FOREIGN LANGUAGES, LEARNING AND TEACHING

SEE *Learning and Teaching Foreign Languages.*

FORMATIVE AND SUMMATIVE ASSESSMENT

Assessment is the use of a variety of procedures to collect information about learning and instruction. Formative and summative assessment represent two classifications of assessment, each with a distinct purpose. Formative assessment is commonly referred to as assessment for learning, in which the focus is on monitoring student response to and progress with instruction. Formative assessment provides immediate feedback to both the teacher and student regarding the learning process. Summative assessment is commonly referred to as assessment of learning, in which the focus is on determining what the student has learned at the end of a unit of instruction or at the end of a grade level (e.g., through grade-level, standardized assessments). Summative assessment helps determine to what extent the instructional and learning goals have been met. Formative and summative assessment contribute in different ways to the larger goals of the assessment process.

PROCEDURES USED IN FORMATIVE ASSESSMENT

Formative assessment includes a variety of procedures such as observation, feedback, and journaling. However, there are some general principles that constitute effective formative assessment. Key requirements for successful formative assessment include the use of quality assessment tools and the subsequent use of the information derived from these assessments to improve instruction. The defining characteristic of formative assessment is its interactive or cyclical nature (Sadler, 1988). At the classroom level, for example, teachers collect information about a student's learning, make corresponding adjustments in their instruction, and continue to collect information. Formative assessment can result in significant learning gains but only when the assessment results are used to inform the instructional and learning process (Black & William, 1998). This condition requires the collection, analysis of, and response to information about student progress.

The most common procedures of formative assessment include the following.

Feedback. A teacher provides oral or written feedback to student discussion or work. For example, a teacher responds orally to a question asked in class; provides a written comment in a response or reflective journal; or provides feedback on student work.

Curriculum-based measurement (CBM). This set of standardized measures is used to determine student progress and performance (Deno, 2001). An example is the use of oral reading fluency (the number of words a student can read correctly during a timed reading of a passage) as an indicator of a student's overall reading ability (Fuchs et al., 2001).

Self-assessment. Students reflect on and monitor their progress. This activity may be performed in conjunction with a CBM, in relation to predetermined academic and behavioral goals, or with learning contracts.

Observation. A teacher observes and records a student's level of engagement, academic and/or affective behavior; develops a plan of action to support that student; implements the plan; and continues to record observations to determine its effectiveness.

Portfolios. A growth portfolio can be used to create a record of student growth in a number of areas. For example, a teacher may use writing portfolios to collect evidence of a student's progress in developing writing skills.

PROCEDURES USED IN SUMMATIVE ASSESSMENT

Summative assessment also employs a variety of tools and methods for obtaining information about what has been learned. In this way, summative assessment provides information at the student, classroom, and school levels. Defining characteristics of effective summative assessment

include a clear alignment between assessment, curriculum, and instruction, as well as the use of assessments that are both valid and reliable. When objectives are clearly specified and connected to instruction, summative assessment provides information about a student's achievement of specific learning objectives.

Summative assessments (or more accurately, large-scale, standardized assessments) are frequently criticized for a variety of reasons: 1) they provide information too late about a student's performance (Popham, 1999); 2) they are disconnected from actual classroom practice (Shepard, 2001); 3) they suffer from "construct underrepresentation" (Messick, 1989), meaning that one assessment typically cannot represent the full content area, so only those areas that are easily measured will be assessed, and hence, taught; and 4) they have a lack of "consequential validity" (Messick, 1989), meaning that the test results are used in an inappropriate way. This last concern is related to state accountability systems because high stakes, such as student retention or teacher performance pay, are attached to performance on state assessment systems, yet most of these assessments have not been designed for the broad and numerous purposes they serve (Baker & Linn, 2004). Nevertheless, summative assessments can provide critical information about students' overall learning as well as an indication of the quality of classroom instruction, especially when they are accompanied by other sources of information and are used to inform practice rather than to reward or sanction. Examples of summative assessment include the following.

End of unit tests or projects. When assessments reflect the stated learning objectives, a well-designed end of unit test provides teachers with information about individual students (identifying any student who failed to meet objectives), as well as provides an overall indication of classroom instruction.

Course grades. If end of course grades are based on specified criteria, course grades provide information on how well a student has met the overall expectations for a particular course.

Standardized assessments. Tests that accurately reflect state performance and content standards provide an indication of how many students are achieving to established grade-level expectations.

Portfolios. When used as part of an evaluation of student learning, portfolios provide evidence to support attainment of stated learning objectives.

Although formative and summative assessments serve different purposes, they should be used ultimately within an integrated system of assessment, curriculum, and instruction. To be effective in informing the learning process, assessments must be directly integrated with theories about the content, instruction, and the learning process (Herman et al., 2006) and must be valid and reliable for the purposes for which they are used. Summative assessments should be created prior to instruction to capture and identify both the content and process of learning that represent the desired outcomes. In this way, summative assessment can serve as a guide for directing the curriculum and instruction. Performance on summative assessments must serve as a valid inference of instructional quality. For example, teacher grades generally have strong validity when compared to student performance on other academic measures (Hoge & Colardarci, 1989).

Formative assessments are more informal in nature but must also serve as valid indicators of student performance if they are to be useful in informing the teaching process. Curriculum-based measurement represents a standardized process of formative assessment that relies on the use of valid measures of student progress in a given academic area. Additionally, a strong evidence base supports the use of interactive feedback (Black & William, 1998) to increase student achievement.

HOW OUTCOMES INFORM INSTRUCTION AND EDUCATIONAL PRACTICES

A consistent feature of the research findings on formative assessment is that attention to the interactive nature of formative assessment can lead to significant learning gains (Black & William, 1998; Herman et al., 2006). Reviews of research on formative assessment processes support the use of questioning, observation, and self-assessment. Similarly, research has demonstrated positive effects on student achievement with the use of CBM (Stecker et al., 2005). Frequent monitoring of student progress to a determined goal and performance level results in higher achievement for students, particularly when teachers use the data collected to inform their instructional practices (Stecker et al., 2005).

Formative assessment can be most directly used at the individual student level because it measures how a particular student is progressing in the instructional program and identifies where support may be needed. The focus on individual students provides immediate feedback on their progress within the curriculum. Formative assessment may also be evaluated at the classroom level to inform teaching practices because it reveals how many students may be experiencing difficulty. If several students are having difficulty, then perhaps a more general change in instruction is needed. CBM in particular serves in these dual roles, but other types of formative assessment such as portfolios and journals can be used in a similar way.

Summative assessment informs instructional practices in a different yet equally important way as formative assessment.

Critics of large-scale assessments argue that they adversely affect the classroom and remain disconnected from instruction (Shepard, 2001) to the extent that they are not useful in the instructional process. However, summative assessment can serve both as a guide to teaching methods and to improving curriculum to better match the interests and needs of the students. A primary use of assessment data is in planning curricula. For example, if a school's performance on a state assessment indicates high percentages of students who do not meet standards in writing, then the school could collect more information on its writing curricula, student writing performance (through portfolios or other classroom work), and professional development needs for its teachers. After collecting such information, the school may then review and adopt new writing curricula as well as provide professional development to its teachers in order to support stronger student achievement in writing. Ongoing evaluation of the writing program would be conducted through the use of formative and summative assessment. In this manner, when summative and formative assessments are aligned, they can inform the instructional process and support both the daily instructional practices of teachers as well as the longer-term planning of curricula and instruction.

Assessment entails a collection of procedures that inform the learning process. Formative and summative assessment entail integrated components of the larger process of assessment, instruction, and curriculum. However, an ample research base suggests that practitioners have difficulty implementing formative assessments (Marsh, 2007) and responding to data collected through summative assessments (Popham, 1999). When formative assessments are used in conjunction with summative assessment, the potential exists to improve outcomes for all students (Stiggins, 2002), both those meeting a minimum performance standard and all other students across the spectrum. Assessments can only serve this purpose, however, when teachers are supported to implement and respond to the procedures through corresponding adjustments in their instruction (Herman et al., 2006; Marsh, 2007).

SEE ALSO *Criterion-Referenced Tests; Standardized Testing.*

BIBLIOGRAPHY

Baker, E. L., & Linn, R. L. (2004). Validity issues for accountability systems. In S. H. Fuhrman & R. F. Elmore (Eds.), *Redesigning accountability systems for education* (pp. 47–72). New York: Teachers College Press.

Black, P., & William, D. (1998). Assessment and classroom learning. *Assessment in Education, 5*(1), 7–74.

Cronin, J., Gage Kingsbury, G., McCall, M. S., & Bowe, B. (2005). *The impact of the No Child Left Behind Act on student achievement and growth: 2005 edition.* Technical Report. Northwest Evaluation Association.

Deno, S. L. (2001). Curriculum-based measures: Development and perspectives. Retrieved April 18, 2008, from http://www.progressmonitoring.net/CBM_Article_Deno.pdf.

Fuchs, L. S., Fuchs, D., Hosp, M. K., & Jenkins, J. R. (2001). Oral reading fluency as an indicator of reading competence: A theoretical, empirical, and historical analysis. *Scientific Studies of Reading, 5,* 239–256.

Herman, J. L., Osmundson, E., Ayala, C., Schneider, S., & Timms, M. (2006). The nature and impact of teachers' formative assessment practices. *CSE Technical Report #703.* National Center for Research on Evaluation, Standards, and Student Testing (CRESST).

Hoge, R. D., & Coladarci, T. (1989). Teacher-based judgments of academic achievement: A review of literature. *Review of Educational Research, 59*(3), 297–323.

Marsh, C. J. (2007). A critical analysis of the use of formative assessment in schools. *Educational Research and Policy Practice, 6,* 25–29.

Messick, S. (1989). Validity. In R. L. Linn (Ed.), *Educational measurement* (3rd ed., pp. 13–103). New York: Macmillan.

Popham, W. J. (1999). Where large scale assessment is heading and why it shouldn't. *Educational Measurement: Issues and Practice, 18*(3), 13–17.

Sadler, D. R. (1988). Formative assessment: Revisiting the territory. *Assessment in Education, 5,* 77–84.

Shepard, L. A. (2001). The role of classroom assessment in teaching and learning. In V. Richardson (Ed.), *Handbook of research on teaching* (4th ed., pp. 1066–1101). Washington, DC: AERA.

Stecker, P. M., Fuchs, L. S., & Fuchs, D. (2005). Using curriculum-based measurement to improve student achievement: Review of research. *Psychology in the Schools, 42,* 795–819.

Stiggins, R. J. (2002). Assessment crisis: The absence of assessment for learning. Phi Delta Kappan International. Retrieved April 18, 2008, from http://www.pdkintl.org/kappan/k0206sti.htm.

Evelyn S. Johnson
Joseph R. Jenkins

FRIENDSHIPS
SEE *Peer Relationships: Friendships.*

G

GAGE, NATHANIEL LEES
1917–

Nathaniel Lees Gage is one of the most highly regarded educational psychologists of his time, the editor of the first *Handbook of Research on Teaching* (1963a), the champion of the scientifically based assertion in the field of education (Gage, 1978; 1985), and the "proud papa" of some of the most productive educational psychologists working since the late twentieth century in the United States and Canada.

N. L. Gage was born in New Jersey in 1917, one of two sons of Polish emigrants determined to raise their children as intellectuals. After departing the east coast as a junior in college, Gage completed his bachelors degree at the University of Minnesota, where he majored in psychology and worked in the lab of B. F. Skinner (1904–1990). Upon graduating college in 1938, Gage enrolled in a then new educational psychology doctoral program at Purdue University to work with a professor named H. H. Remmers. Gage and Remmers collaborated for many years until Gage completed his doctorate in 1947.

The career of Gage since that time spans his tenure as assistant and then associate professor at the University of Illinois beginning in 1948, through his presidency of the educational psychology division (Division 15) of the American Psychological Association (APA) in 1960, and his presidency of the American Educational Research Association (AERA) in 1962, to his long and acclaimed university teaching as the Margaret Jacks Professor of Education at Stanford University, where he retired Emeritus in 1987 at age 70. Throughout his career Gage was known to his students as a warm, engaging man, always present with a smile and a twinkle in his eye. Many of those students simply called their esteemed professor "Nate."

Three contributions for which Gage is perhaps most widely known are his highly commended editing of the first *Handbook of Research on Teaching*, his ability to produce some of the most prominent professors in immediately succeeding generations of educational psychologists, and his strong writing on the scientific basis of research on teaching. Each of these achievements deserves some elaboration.

The *Handbook*, as it came to be called by students who dog-eared its pages between its publication date of 1963 and the appearance of the second *Handbook* a decade later, is a masterful collection of chapters written by established scholars in education that reshaped the landscape of educational research. The *Handbook* organized a heretofore scattered field both substantively and methodologically, with Gage's (1963b) own chapter on "Paradigms for Research on Teaching" as a guide. The *Handbook* provided cogent criticism of extant research methods in the field of education and models for addressing key issues in sampling, design, measurement, and data analysis; some chapters of the volume, such as that of Campbell and Stanley on experimental design, were developed into books. It was Gage who secured funding for the *Handbook*, selected its topics and authors, and meticulously edited each and every page. Widespread attention to the *Handbook* gave new promise to diligent empirical work in education, inspiring a generation of scholars to take up the gauntlet in their own careers.

Gage's own chapter in the *Handbook*, which was translated into German, encouraged him to focus his own research efforts into the 1970s on classroom research on teaching. Working at the Stanford Center for Research and Development in Teaching, which he helped to found in 1965, Gage was able to secure federal funding to build and sustain a research team that labored over the next two decades to move from correlational to experimental methods in assessing the validity of process-product models connecting teacher behavior to student learning outcomes in a variety of field-based samples (e.g., Gage, 1967). Gage had a knack for finding promising graduate students to direct and form his teams. Directors were Christopher Clark and John Crawford, who with their teams and Gage produced papers published in archived journals demonstrating the important influence of particular combinations and sequences of instructional behavior in influencing student classroom learning. Some of the students on those teams who have gone on to become APA Division 15 and AERA presidents in their own right, deans of schools of education, and endowed chairs at major research universities in the United States and Canada, include Ronald Marx, Penelope Peterson, Dale Schunk, and Philip Winne.

Other projects Gage completed with prominent educational psychologists include a textbook, co-authored with David Berliner, for teaching educational psychology that ran to six editions (Gage & Berliner, 1998), and book chapters and reports with Theodore Coladarci, Torsten Husen, Barak Rosenshine, and Albert Yee. Gage's closest professional colleague at Stanford was Richard Snow. All of the students mentioned had early successes stemming, in part, from Gage's steady influence Gage, and many have contributed chapters to one or more of the subsequent three handbooks of research on teaching.

The books that Gage wrote arguing cogently for evidence-based assertions in the field of education are often cited as background for a resurgence of this view since 2002. The first book (Gage, 1978), written as a series of sponsored lectures at Teachers College, Columbia University, has been on the basic reading list of doctoral courses in research on teaching since its publication.

Following his retirement, Gage continued to be active in conceptualizing and writing, working on a theoretical extension of his ideas on the "hard gains" still to be made in the field of educational psychology. Gage sought a theory of research on teaching that had solid empirical evidence as a basis, a theory that explained in technical terms how teachers can make a real difference in the lives of their students. In 1985 Gage wrote *Hard Gains in the Soft Sciences,* and since then he has penned articles in several other refereed journals confronting important issues that continue for research on teaching, always championing the warranted assertion,

always defending the usefulness of research to the practicing field of education. This is one teacher who *did* make a difference in the lives of his students; perhaps that explains Gage's lasting commitment to a theory of teacher effectiveness.

BIBLIOGRAPHY

WORKS BY

Gage, N. L. (Ed.) (1963a). *The handbook of research on teaching.* Chicago: Rand McNally.

Gage, N. L. (1963b). Paradigms for research on teaching. In N. L. Gage (Ed.), *The handbook of research on teaching* (pp. 94–141). Chicago: Rand McNally.

Gage, N. L. (1967). A factorially designed experiment on teacher structuring, soliciting, and reacting. *Journal of Teacher Education, 27,* 35–38.

Gage, N. L. (1978). *The scientific basis of the art of teaching.* New York: Teachers College Press.

Gage, N. L. (1985). *Hard gains in the soft sciences.* Bloomington, IN: Phi Delta Kappa.

Gage, N. L., & Berliner, D. C. (1998). *Educational psychology* (6th ed.). Boston: Houghton Mifflin.

Lyn Corno

GAGNÉ, ROBERT MILLS
1916–2002

Robert Mills Gagné, an education psychologist best known for his book *The Conditions of Learning,* was born in 1916. He received his BA from Yale University in 1937 and went on to earn a PhD (1940) in experimental psychology from Brown University. During a career of 50 years, Gagné held both academic and research and development positions in military training and in human performance. In 1940 he held a position at Connecticut College for Women. He taught at Princeton University from 1958 to 1962 and from 1966 to 1969 at the University of California, Berkeley. Next he taught at Florida State University from 1969 to 1985. During a hiatus from teaching from 1962 to 1966, Gagné served as director of research at the American Institute for Research in Pittsburgh, Pennsylvania. He died in 2002.

As a graduate student in 1964 it was the privilege of this writer to read *The Conditions of Learning* in manuscript. This book was first published in 1965 and appeared in three additional editions (1970, 1977, and 1985). It became perhaps the most important work in instructional design, laying the foundation for a theory- and research-based approach to the design of instructional materials. Gagné's unique approach was was founded first in behavioral psychology and later in cognitive processing. The prescriptions Gagné advocated were all based on theory supported by research in the psychology of learning. This book and the friendship this writer developed with Gagné throughout the reminder of his life had a profound influence on this writer's career in instructional technology.

Many would acknowledge Robert M. Gagné as the father of instructional design, in which area he made three major contributions. First, regarding cumulative learning theory and learning hierarchies, Gagné advocated starting with the final task to be acquired and asking, "What must the learner do to accomplish this task given only directions?" This hierarchical analysis is repeated for each subsequent task until all the prerequisite skills for a given task have been identified. The resulting learning hierarchy provides a map for the subsequent instruction.

Second, Gagné identified five varieties of learning and the internal (cognitive) and external (instructional design) conditions necessary to promote effective and efficient acquisition of each of these different kinds of knowledge and skill. The categories Gagné identified were modified with each edition of *The Conditions of Learning*. The last list included the following intellectual skills: discriminations, concrete concepts, defined concepts, and rules; cognitive strategies; verbal information; problem solving; motor skills; and attitudes. When these conditions of learning are implemented in instructional materials, research shows that the resulting learning is more efficient and effective. Most instructional designers are also familiar with Gagné's third contribution, his nine events of instruction, and have used them as a guide to designing effective lessons. These events are: gaining attention, informing the learner of the objective, stimulating the recall of prior learning, presenting the stimulus, providing learner guidance, eliciting the performance, giving informative feedback, assessing performance, and enhancing retention and transfer.

Jointly Gagné and this writer proposed the notion of integrative goals, bringing together into an integrated whole the different varieties of learning. This author's own work continued into the early 2000s to build on Gagné's contributions with the identification of first principles of instruction, including problem-centered instructional design. An important collection of Gagné's papers and a brief summary of his life can be found in *The Legacy of Robert M. Gagné* (2000), edited by Rita Richey.

BIBLIOGRAPHY

WORKS BY

Gagné, R. M. (1941). *Some interrelations of excitation, inhibition, and retention in a conditioned operant response.* Lancaster, PA: Lancaster Press.

Gagné, R. M. (1961). *Abilities and learning sets in knowledge acquisition.* Washington: American Psychological Association.

Gagné, R. M. (ed.). (1962). *Psychological principles in system development.* New York: Holt, Rinehart & Winston.

Gagné, R. M. (1965). *The Conditions of Learning* (1st ed.). New York: Holt, Rinehart & Winston.

Gagné, R. M. & Briggs, L. J. (1974). *Principles of instructional design.* New York, Holt, Rinehart & Winston.

Gagné, R. M. & Driscoll, M. P. (1988). *Essentials of learning for instruction* (2nd ed.). Englewood Cliffs, NJ: Prentice Hall.

Gagné, R. M. & Medsker, K. L. (1996). *The conditions of learning. Training applications.* Fort Worth: Harcourt Brace College Pub.

Gagné, R. M. et al. (2005). *Principles of instructional design* (5th ed.). Belmont, CA: Thomson/Wadsworth.

WORKS ABOUT

Merrill, M. D. (2002). First principles of instruction. *Educational Technology Research and Development, 50*(3), 43–59.

Richey, R. C. (Ed.). (2000). *The Legacy of Robert M. Gagné.* Syracuse, NY: ERIC Clearinghouse.

M. David Merrill

GARDNER, HOWARD
1943–

Howard Gardner, a professor at the Harvard Graduate School of Education, is a developmental psychologist best known for his theory of multiple intelligences. The author of more than twenty books and several hundred journal articles, he has also conducted research in fields ranging from arts education to creativity to socially responsible work.

Born in 1943, Gardner grew up in Scranton, Pennsylvania, the son of German-Jewish immigrants who fled Germany prior to World War II. Gardner was an excellent student as well as a talented pianist. He gave up formal study of the piano as an adolescent in order to focus on academics, but his interest in music and the arts has remained an important part of his life and has also influenced his academic pursuits. Gardner graduated from Harvard College in 1965 where he studied with the renowned Erik Erikson, and then he earned his doctorate at Harvard in developmental psychology, during which time he worked with Roger Brown, Jerome Bruner, and Nelson Goodman, among others. Gardner is one of the founding members and remains a senior director of Harvard's Project Zero, a research group established in 1967 and dedicated to the study of cognition, creativity, and the arts. From 1971 to 1991 he also carried out a research program in neuropsychology at the Boston Veterans' Administration Medical Center. In 1986, he was named the John H. and Elizabeth A. Hobbs

Howard Gardner JAY GARDNER ©2003.

Professor of Cognition and Education at the Harvard Graduate School of Education.

Gardner's earliest books such as *The Arts and Human Development* (1973) and *The Shattered Mind* (1975) draw on his empirical investigations in the fields of developmental psychology and neuroscience. He is best known for his 1983 publication *Frames of Mind: The Theory of Multiple Intelligences*. In this work, Gardner laid out his theory that human intelligence is better understood as a multiple rather than unitary construct. Gardner originally conceived of seven distinct intelligences: linguistic, logical-mathematical, bodily-kinesthetic, spatial, musical, interpersonal, and intrapersonal. In the 1990s he added an eighth intelligence: naturalist intelligence. Gardner's work on multiple intelligences has been controversial in the psychology world, but has been enthusiastically embraced by many in the educational community. Multiple intelligences schools, which shape their mission and curricula around the eight intelligences, have sprung up around the world. Hundreds of books have been written in numerous languages about incorporating multiple

intelligences theory into the curriculum. In 2005, Danfoss Universe, a multiple intelligences science and adventure park, opened in Denmark. For his work, Gardner received a MacArthur Genius Prize in 1981 and became the first American to win the University of Louisville's Grawemeyer Award in Education in 1990. He has also received honorary degrees from more than twenty universities in the United States, Ireland, Italy, Israel, Chile, and Korea.

In 1995 with colleagues Mihaly Csikszentmihalyi and William Damon, Gardner began the Good Work Project, which seeks to identify individuals and institutions that carry out work that is excellent in equality, socially responsible, and meaningful to its practitioners, as well as the forces that support and inhibit such efforts. The project has investigated good work in the fields of journalism, medicine, theater, business, law, education, philanthropy, and genetics; its findings have been described in numerous books and papers (see goodwork project.org). Books co-authored by Gardner that have come out of the Good Work Project include *Good Work: When Excellence and Ethics Meet* (2001), *Making Good: How Young People Cope with Moral Dilemmas at Work* (2004), and *Responsibility at Work* (2007). In 2005 Gardner and several other researchers developed a Good Work toolkit that includes activities and moral dilemmas designed to encourage high school and university students to think critically about what constitutes high quality and meaningful work. Numerous secondary schools and universities have used the toolkit in a variety of ways to encourage reflection about good work.

In 2000 Gardner, Kurt Fischer, and others colleagues at the Harvard Graduate School of Education developed a master's program in Mind, Brain and Education, thought to be the first such program in the world. Since then, similar programs have been founded both in the United States and abroad. Gardner has also continued to write about the mind/brain. In 2004 he published *Changing Minds*, a work about the seven levers of mind-change. In 2007 he published *Five Minds for the Future*, a policy book about the five types of minds Gardner regards as essential for success in the 21st century. As of 2007 he continues to write and speak about the theory of multiple intelligences as well.

SEE ALSO *Intelligence: An Overview; Multiple Intelligences.*

BIBLIOGRAPHY

WORKS BY

Fischman, W., Solomon, B., Greenspan, D., & Gardner, H. (2004). *Making Good: How Young People Cope with Moral Dilemmas at Work.* Cambridge: Harvard University Press.

Gardner, H. (1973). *The Arts and Human Development.* New York: John Wiley.

Gardner, H. (1975). *The Shattered Mind.* New York: Vintage.

Gardner, H. (1983). *Frames of Mind: The Theory of Multiple Intelligences.* New York: Basic Books.

Gardner, H. (1995). The Good Work Project, www.goodwork project.org.

Gardner, H., Csikszentmihalyi, M., & Damon, W. (2001). *Good Work: When Excellence and Ethics Meet.* New York: Basic Books.

Gardner, H. (2004). *Changing Minds: The Art and Science of Changing Our Own and Other People's Minds.* Boston: Harvard Business School Press.

Gardner, H. (2007a). *Five Minds for the Future.* Boston: Harvard Business School Press.

Gardner, H. (2007b). *Responsibility at Work.* San Francisco: Jossey Bass.

Scott Seider

GENDER BIAS IN TEACHING

A common response from teachers when asked about gender inequity in classrooms is that they treat all their students the same. There are two problems with this statement. First, students are diverse and have different learning issues, thus treating all students in the same way means that some students will have a better learning experience than their peers. Second, teachers may be ignoring their unconscious gender biases towards their students, their schools and themselves. If ignored, these gender biases, which may have developed from cultural norms, may lead to bias in the classroom.

Gender bias occurs when people make assumptions regarding behaviors, abilities or preferences of others based upon their gender. Because there are strong gender role stereotypes for masculinity and femininity, students who do not match them can encounter problems with teachers and with their peers. For example, the expectation is that boys naturally exhibit boisterous, unruly behavior, are academically able, rational, and socially uncommunicative, whereas girls are quiet, polite, and studious. Girls are also expected to possess better social skills than boys and to excel at reading and the language arts. So girls who present discipline problems for teachers, or quiet, studious boys, may encounter a lack of understanding from peers and teachers. Within the classroom, these biases unfold in students' practices and teachers' acceptance of certain behaviors from one student or another based upon the students' gender. Also, bias due to a person's gender is not mutually exclusive of other social categories such as race, ethnicity, class, religion, and language. For example, some teachers may perceive African American or other Black girls as loud and uncontrollable because the girls do not exhibit the feminine behaviors associated with White women, such as quiet, self-effacing and malleable.

Gender bias can occur within subject areas and school activities. For example, in subjects such as mathematics and the sciences, there are different participation patterns for girls and boys. Gender bias promulgates a myth that boys are naturally better at mathematics and science than girls. The implications are that if girls succeed in these subjects it is due to their hard work, not their intelligence, whereas boys' success is credited to their natural talent. There are some signs that gender bias in schools may be decreasing in some areas. The percentage of girls participating in science has increased and achieved parity with boys in biology, chemistry and algebra. However, subjects that are prerequisites for college majors such as engineering or physics remain dominated by men. Only 25% of high school students enrolled in physics are female. Moreover, there has been little increase in the percentage of women in engineering programs.

Males are also more likely than females to be in remedial programs, and students' race also impacts these patterns. For example, African American males are more likely than White or female peers to enroll in remedial reading and mathematics courses. And non-White students have a higher representation in vocational and non-college preparatory courses than their White peers. Teachers are critical components in challenging gender bias in schooling, but they also can be major contributors to it as well, through their pedagogical practices, curriculum choices, and assessment strategies.

GENDER BIAS IN TEACHERS

Teachers' unconscious gender biases can produce stereotypic expectations for students' success and participation in the classroom. Teachers view male students' domination of the classroom and their time as typical masculine behavior. However, these biases have consequences for the students and the classroom climate. More than two decades ago, researchers identified and named groups of students who dominated the teacher's time and the classroom resources as "target students" (Tobin & Gallagher, 1987). Target students were typically white and male. They answered most of the teacher's questions and also asked most of the questions. This behavior pattern was particularly insidious in mathematics and science classrooms because teachers did not expect girls to have competent knowledge in these subject areas. Classroom observations documented that target students typically called out answers to the teacher's questions, thus denying other students the opportunity to engage in dialogue with the teacher or get to grips with the subject matter. Furthermore, because boys are perceived as having natural talent in science, teachers asked boys harder and more complicated questions than girls. If girls attempted to answer more difficult questions than boys and faltered, teachers often repeated the question and asked that another student, typically a boy, provide the answer. However, if a boy failed to answer correctly, teachers reframed the question or broke it into a series of simpler questions that could help the student find the answer. Teachers' unconscious stereotyped gender bias that boys are smarter than girls, especially in mathematics and the sciences, meant they were willing to work with boys to reach the answer because they perceived boys were capable of achieving that goal but girls were not. Conversely, teachers of subjects perceived as feminine will spend more time engaged with girls.

Teachers' gendered perceptions of students' ability is also reflected in the type of praise and expectations they have of their students. Teachers often give girls less meaningful and less critical praise than boys. Boys' work is described as unique or brilliant, while girls' work is often undervalued, critically ignored, and praised for its appearance. This aspect of teachers' behavior is particularly detrimental to girls because it means they do not receive feedback on their work that could help them develop deeper understandings of concepts (Liu, 2006).

Teachers also use target students to maintain the tempo and pace of classroom instruction. For example, in a lecture or whole class discussion when a teacher is posing questions to the class, he or she may encourage target students to call out answers in order to keep the lesson moving, rather than wait for the other students to process the question and provide an answer. This short "wait time" may be detrimental to learning. More than three decades ago, researchers found that if teachers waited three to five seconds before accepting a student's answer, more students became engaged in the classroom and also improved their understanding of the content. Moreover, the longer wait time meant that teachers began to ask more cognitively challenging questions. However, the existence of target students in classes who often call out answers without direction from teachers meant that fewer students, especially girls, engaged in the lessons. In the absence of proactive teacher intervention, these patterns in which males dominate classroom interactions also occur in mixed-gender, small groups.

Target students dominate classroom interactions and exchanges at all education levels. In the early 2000s, researchers identified these same patterns of engagement in a professional development program for science teachers. When alerted to the invasive behaviors of the male teachers in the cohort, faculty began using overt breaching strategies to stop the target students calling out answers, dominating the human and materials resources of the classroom, and showing disrespect to their peers (Martin, Milne & Scantlebury, 2006).

Teachers' gender bias towards students can also extend to their response to students who challenge their authority. Such risk-taking behavior in boys is expected and at times praised, but assertiveness in girls is viewed negatively and labeled unfeminine. Similarly, boys who do not exhibit stereotypic masculine behaviors may be ridiculed (Renold, 2006).

Teachers use gender expectations as a means of maintaining classroom control. For example, teachers will seat undisciplined boys next to girls as a classroom management strategy. Further, teachers use the gendered expectation that girls' nurturing characteristics will lead them to place others' needs before their own. In other words, teachers often ask girls to assume mothering roles towards students who have fallen behind with learning because of inattentiveness, absenteeism through truancy, or in-school disciplinary procedures, and often those students are male.

PEDAGOGICAL CHOICES AND ASSESSMENT PRACTICES

Girls and boys have different educative experiences in classrooms. Target students can dominate lecture-style classes, and most students prefer to learn in groups, using hands-on activities. Group work can engage more students, but teachers must monitor the interactions between students in those groups to ensure all students are participating and that one student is not dominating the group. Students, especially girls, dislike lectures, worksheets and 'busy' work assignments, preferring to study subjects and topics that they perceive as relevant to their lives. However, girls are often relegated to passive roles in the class and in performance-based assessments. Whereas boys use equipment and complete the tasks, girls read the instructions and record results (Scantlebury & Baker, 2007).

Although publishers have reduced gender bias in textbooks, girls are often depicted in passive roles with boys as active participants. Teachers can help to counteract this bias by reviewing classroom texts from a gender perspective and analyzing the hidden curriculum promulgated by these books. Moreover, they can also counteract this message about girls' passivity by highlighting girls' and women's achievements. They can also asking students to critically examine texts for these subtle gender stereotypic messages.

Teachers often use girls as a civilizing influence on male students. Disruptive boys are reassigned to sit near or with girls. Yet little thought is given to the impact that this strategy has on girls' learning or students' attitudes towards the classroom environment. Rather than expecting boys to exhibit self-control and regulation, when teachers use this practice it reinforces the stereotype that boys are undisciplined, whereas girls are cooperative and orderly. It also implies that boys need looking after, and the girls are cast in a maternal role to do just that.

Gender bias can also occur with the style and type of assessments teachers use. For example, teachers often use multiple choice questions as the primary format in assessments. Girls are not encouraged to explore risk-taking behaviors and often do not venture a guess on a multiple choice test, even if they are not penalized for incorrect answers. Girls are therefore less likely to complete multiple-choice exams than their male peers because if boys are uncertain or do not know, they will guess an answer. However, when high-stakes tests use a variety of question types, for example, short answer, problem solving, and multiple choice, often gender differences in student achievement disappear (Kahle, 2004).

EFFECTS OF GENDER BIAS

Gender bias can impact students' attitudes towards learning and their engagement with the subject. If affected by gender bias, girls will tend to believe that any success they have is due to hard work rather than any innate talent or intelligence. Boys may be encouraged to believe that success in science and mathematics should come easily to them because of their gender. Some males report dropping out of college science and mathematics programs because they no longer perceive these subjects as easy. Overall, teachers have lower expectations for girls' academic success compared to boys, and their attitudes are shown through the type and quality of the student-teacher interaction. The type and quality of critique teachers give their students can also have an impact. Teachers' comments on girls' work focuses on its appearance but with boys' work teachers focus on the content. Girls often do not receive substantive comments or criticism from teachers from which they could improve their ability to learn. During the many hours spent in classrooms, girls receive less time and attention from teachers than their male peers. Teachers usually ask girls easier questions than they ask boys. Typically, girls receive fewer opportunities to engage in classroom discourse, use equipment and assert their knowledge in classrooms.

REDUCING GENDER BIAS

Gender bias in education is a series of microinequities whose impact is cumulative and often ignored. Girls are rewarded and praised for compliant behavior. Teachers do not challenge girls with questions and rarely offer criticisms of their work. Teachers can reduce and challenge gender bias through an examination of their peda-

gogical practices and by posing simple questions about their practices. For example, which students do they frequently interact with? Are target students evident in their classroom? If so, how does the teacher deal with those students? What questioning techniques does the teacher use to engage students? Does the teacher ask complicated questions to girls as well as boys? Does the teacher use a variety of pedagogical and assessment practices? Which students are engaged with the curriculum?

Another way of reducing gender bias would be for teachers to videotape their classes and review their interactions with the students. Or they could invite a colleague to watch their teaching and record which students are being asked questions and what type of questions. However, teachers must also prepare for the consequences of changing their practices. Girls are conditioned to receiving less of the teacher's attention, and they do not usually cause discipline problems if they are not receiving their fair share, but boys can react negatively to losing the teacher's attention, causing disruption to lessons and becoming discipline problems. Moreover, research has also shown that boys avoid written work and often have poor communication skills when asked to work in single-sex groups.

However, the gains in reducing gender bias in education may disappear with the requirements of high-stakes testing required by No Child Left Behind (NCLB). NCLB requires that states report academic achievement data in most social categories, except gender (Kahle, 2004). This may result in less attention being placed on gender bias and less data that might reveal it. Continued monitoring of gender bias is necessary to minimize its impact on students' opportunities for learning and achievement.

SEE ALSO *Cultural Bias in Teaching.*

BIBLIOGRAPHY

Kahle, J. B. (2004). Will girls be left behind? Gender differences and accountability. *Journal of Research in Science Teaching, 41*(10), 961–969.

Liu, F. (2006). School culture and gender. In C. Skelton, B. Francis, & L. Smulyan (Eds.), *The SAGE Handbook of Gender and Education* (pp. 425–438). Thousand Oaks, CA: Sage.

Martin, S., Milne C. E., & Scantlebury, K. (2006). Eyerollers, jokers, risk-takers and turn sharks: Target students in a professional science education program. *Journal of Research in Science Teaching, 43*(8), 819–851.

Renold, R. (2006). Gendered classroom experiences. In C. Skelton, B. Francis, & L. Smulyan (Eds.), *The SAGE Handbook of Gender and Education* (pp. 439–452). Thousand Oaks, CA: Sage.

Tobin, K., & Gallagher, J. J. (1987). The role of target students in the science classroom. *Journal of Research in Science Teaching, 24*(1), 61–75.

Kathryn Scantlebury

GENDER IDENTITY

Gender identity refers to an individual's identification with a particular gender category; the term encompasses the sense of belonging, attitudes, and values associated with that gender. It can be considered one part of an individual's greater identity or the enduring sense of who one is and what one wants to do. Gender identity is different from sex, which is determined by physiological characteristics of a male or female; it is also different than gender, which is a social determination of what it means to be a man or a woman. In other words, an individual may be biologically female and viewed by society as a woman but may not necessarily identify strongly with the roles, attitudes, and values that most people in society associate with being a woman.

MODELS OF GENDER IDENTITY

Much of the work on gender identity borrows heavily from research on gender roles and gender schema theory, associated with Sandra Lipsitz Bem. In Bem's theory, strong sex role identification leads to the acquisition of attitudes and behaviors in line with that role. Within this theory, individuals of either gender can take on masculine or feminine roles. Moreover, some individuals display a combination of masculine and feminine roles, while others do not identify with either set of roles. Bem would refer to the former group as androgynous and to the latter group undifferentiated.

Similarly, Janet Taylor Spence refers to differences between instrumental traits and expressive traits, which are similar in concept to Bem's masculinity and femininity, respectively. Spence argued, however, that such a unidimensional view was not enough to fully capture gender identity. She advocated instead for a multidimensional view of gender identity, with each dimension having unique developmental components and correlates. Further work on such a multidimensional conceptualization, by Susan Egan and David Perry, identified four factors based on previous gender research: knowledge of membership in a gender category, feelings of compatibility with gender, feelings of pressure to act in accordance with the gender's roles, and ingroup bias toward the gender. Knowledge of membership refers to the individual identifying of oneself as a man or a woman. Compatibility refers to the extent an individual feels like a typical member of one's gender and even the extent to which one feels content with the gender assignment. Pressure refers to the extent to which an individual perceives parents, peers, and self as wanting the individual's self to conform to gender stereotypes. Finally, ingroup bias refers to the extent to which individuals prefer the gender with which they identify opposed to the other.

DEVELOPMENTAL CHANGES IN GENDER IDENTITY

Much of the research on the development of gender identity focuses on the development of gender constancy or sustained knowledge of one's sex. Between the ages of two and a half years and six years, children develop a sense of gender constancy. This means that by the age of six, children are able to answer the question, "are you a boy or a girl?" and realize that this answer does not change over time or with differences in appearance (e.g., a boy who wears a pink dress is not suddenly a girl).

Views on the development of additional characteristics of gender identity vary depending on whether one takes a unidimensional or multidimensional perspective on the construct. With a unidimensional view, the understanding of sex roles comes from the discovery of gender constancy, as children learn what is and is not appropriate for their gender. This view of learning and internalizing sex roles is addressed thoroughly using social cognitive theory. It is more difficult to summarize the development of specific dimensions of gender identity in the multidimensional perspective because each dimension has its own trajectory of growth and correlates.

Regardless of which perspective one takes when discussing gender identity, its development remains a salient issue among adolescents. Traditionally, during adolescence individuals begin coming to terms with their overall identities. As adolescents begin assessing who they are and what their roles in the world will be, they have questions regarding the extent to which they are aligned or not with gender-stereotypic behaviors. Just as research shows the importance of a strong general identity in positive psychosocial development, a strong gender identity is also associated with positive psychosocial outcomes. Gender identity need not be sex-stereotypical to be strong; rather, individuals with strong, positive gender identities are confident in who they are and have social support for their identity.

GROUP DIFFERENCES IN THE DEVELOPMENT OF GENDER IDENTITY

The general pattern of gender identity development may differ across groups. Most notably, several theorists have focused specifically on the development of gender identity among women. The work of Carol Gilligan on identity development in females, while not specifically related to gender identity, has several implications in this area. Gilligan's theory states that as girls enter adolescence, they must come to terms with the silent role of women in the social world. Often, this is accompanied in adolescence by a time when girls silence their thoughts and identity. Several theorists have similarly proposed models, specifically for the development of gender identity among women, referred to as feminist or womanist identity theories. These theories focus on the importance of reconciling negative social views of women with individual attitudes and values.

In addition, several studies have concentrated on the extent that race and ethnicity moderate the development of gender identity. Much of this work focuses on African American children and adolescents and has found that negative stereotypes associated with being a Black boy or girl are a risk to positive gender identity development. Some researchers have amplified these general findings by asserting more specifically that stereotypes of the perfect boy or the perfect girl are often White; therefore, the negative outcomes among racial-minority adolescents come from a desire to oppose this standard. Positive identity development is achieved by guiding these adolescents toward more prosocial ways of opposing this standard of perfection.

Another line of research focusing on racial/ethnic variation in the development of gender identity addresses the relationship between gender identity and positive psychosocial outcomes. One such study found that several dimensions of gender identity related to positive psychosocial development for White adolescents were not related for African American adolescents. Among Hispanic students, stronger gender identity was related to negative development for females but related to positive development for males. More research in this area is needed to understand why these differences occur.

GENDER IDENTITY AS RELATED TO SCHOOL OUTCOMES

Compared to the literature on gender differences in school outcomes, research specifically related to gender identity is lacking. However, the consideration of gender identity is important for more fully understanding observed gender differences in many school-related outcomes.

One line of research relating gender identity to academic outcomes focuses on achievement motivation, and in particular on self-efficacy and stereotype threat. First relating to self-efficacy, some research shows that students with more masculine or androgynous orientations have higher levels of general and academic self-efficacy than do students with feminine or undifferentiated orientations, regardless of gender. Other studies suggest that this relationship between gender identity and self-efficacy may be more subject-specific. For example, some research has found that feminine-oriented students hold higher self-efficacy in writing.

The consideration of gender identity in relation to achievement motivation also has implications for research on stereotype threat or the decrease in achievement when faced with the possibility of confirming a negative belief about one's ingroup. Studies find that female students' mathematics performance diminished when confronted with a threatening gender-related stereotype. Together, research on self-efficacy and stereotype threats approach gender differences in performance as due to enhanced efficacy or anxiety resulting from the requirement of characteristics that are supposedly like or unlike the individual. Improving performance then becomes a matter of persuading students that they can succeed in any subject regardless of their gender.

Additional research focuses on the interaction between students' gender identities and their identities as students. According to research in this area, students view the perfect male and female students differently. The ideal female student is beautiful and does not have to work too hard at being smart; the ideal male student is loud and funny. At the same time, ideal male and female students are good at different subjects, with the ideal male student excelling in the sciences and the idea female student excelling in the arts. Male students hold the most gendered views of good students and are less likely to report liking non-conforming students. This line of research has implications for understanding both how the social context of schools shape gender identities and how students with non-conforming gender identities perform and are accepted in school.

SEE ALSO *Gender Role Stereotyping.*

BIBLIOGRAPHY

Bem, S. L. (1981). Gender schema theory: A cognitive account of sex typing. *Psychological Review, 88,* 369–371.

Choi, N. (2004). Sex role group differences in specific academic, and general self-efficacy. *Journal of Psychology, 138*(2), 149–159.

Corby, B. C., Hodges, E. V. E., & Perry, D. G. (2007). Gender identity and adjustment in Black, Hispanic, and White preadolescents. *Developmental Psychology, 43*(1), 261–266.

Egan, S. K., & Perry, D. G. (2001). Gender identity: A multidimensional analysis with implications for psychosocial adjustment. *Developmental Psychology, 37*(4), 451–463.

Gilligan, C. (1982). *In a different voice: Psychological theory and women's development.* Cambridge, MA: Harvard University Press.

Hoffman, R. M. (2006). Gender self-definition and gender self-acceptance in women: Intersections with feminist, womanist, and ethnic identities. *Journal of Counseling and Development, 84,* 358–372.

Isom, D. A. (2007). Performance, resistance, caring: Racialized gender identity in African American boys. *Urban Review, 39*(4), 405–423.

Kessels, U. (2005). Fitting into the stereotype: How gender-stereotyped perceptions of prototypic peers relate to liking for school subjects. *European Journal of Psychology of Education, 20*(3), 309–323.

Neuville, E., & Croizet, J. C. (2007). Can salience of gender identity impair math performance among 7–8 years old girls? The moderating role of task difficulty. *European Journal of Psychology of Education, 22*(3), 307–316.

Niemi, N. S. (2005). The emperor has no clothes: Examining the impossible relationship between gendered and academic identities in middle school students. *Gender and Education, 17*(5), 483–497.

Pajares, F., & Valiante, G. (2001). Gender differences in writing motivation and achievement of middle school students: A function of gender orientation? *Contemporary Educational Psychology, 26,* 366–381.

Spence, J. T. (1993). Gender-related traits and gender ideology: Evidence for a multifactorial theory. *Journal of Personality and Social Psychology, 64*(4), 624–635.

Carolyn Barber

GENDER ROLE STEREOTYPING

Gender role stereotyping occurs when a person is expected to enact a series of norms or behaviors based upon their sex. Gender is a social construction, and other social categories such as race, ethnicity, class, religion, and language also influence that construction. In most European and North American societies, gender roles divide through male and female behavioral norms. Certain types of behaviors are categorized as masculine or feminine. However, gender as a continuum is social and relational, rather than categorical. In other words, gender only exists as a comparative quality (if people are "less masculine" than others, they are also "more feminine" than those same others, even if their biological sex is the same). Thus gender role stereotyping occurs when individuals are expected to enact certain practices or behaviors because of their gender.

Although girls' schooling experiences vary depending upon their socioeconomic status, geographic location, ethnicity, and/or disability (AAUW, 1998), many schools, and other educational institutions, reinforce and support gender stereotyped roles. Moreover, schools operate through the interactions of groups and individuals, and how students and teachers construct gender in the classroom impacts the learning environment. Two decades after Title IX of the Elementary and Secondary Education Act legislation banned sex discrimination in education programs and activities, public schools still exhibited bias against girls. In 2005, comments by the then-president of Harvard University Lawrence Summers suggesting that innate sex differences may contribute to fewer female faculty in the sciences resulted in national and international discussions on how cultural factors are more likely to explain women's participation in science than biological differences between females and males.

The gender role stereotypes that schools help to reproduce include the notion that girls are caring, nurturing, quiet, helpful, considerate of others, and place others' needs before their own. Academically able girls' achievements are attributed to their hard work, whereas successful boys are considered naturally gifted. In contrast, underachieving male students are considered lazy, whereas underachieving girls are regarded as not capable. Boys are viewed as rational, logical, unemotional, and strong and are also expected to be outgoing, smart, and naturally academically talented. Thus in schools, gender role stereotypes attribute males' academic success to innate intelligence and girls' achievements to hard work. Moreover, these gender differences are explained through biological differences without any consideration of the impact of social environment on students' learning, achievement, motivation and attitudes.

GENDER ROLE STEREOTYPES AND STUDENT-TEACHER INTERACTIONS

Gender role stereotypes also influence classroom interactions between teachers and students. First, students who dominate the classroom, answering and asking most of the questions, and using the available resources, are called target students. Regardless of the schooling level, target students are typically White males. Teachers predominantly ask White male students more and harder questions than any other group of students because these students are viewed as inherently smart. If a target student fails to answer a question, teachers will often reword or reconstruct the question, breaking a difficult question into a series of simpler questions to attain the answer. If other students are unable to answer a question teachers typically move on, usually to a target student.

Overall, boys are more likely than girls to answer teachers' questions. Often they call out answers, a risk-taking behavior expected of males, and seek the teacher's attention. In contrast, girls are more likely to receive criticism rather than praise for such risk-taking behavior. Teachers reward girls for being compliant, quiet, and helpful, which are stereotypic feminized behaviors. These behaviors in girls are also associated with White culture. Thus African American girls, whose socialization encourages assertive behavior, are often at odds with teachers who deem practices such as asking questions before being acknowledged, and non-compliance, as unfeminine.

INFLUENCE OF GENDER ROLE STEREOTYPES ON SCHOOL SUBJECTS

The accepted and encouraged assertive behavior in males that produces target students also enables boys to control other resources. For example, in science classes boys dominate equipment and relegate girls to roles such as data recorder, reading instructor, or cleaning up the work area. Girls' stereotyped views of science as a masculine endeavor may mean they prefer these passive roles. However, laboratory work can be an important facet of learning science and if girls are disengaged or relegated to peripheral roles they may not fully focus on the subject matter.

Recent data shows that there are equal numbers of girls and boys enrolled in high school science classes, with the exception of physics and Advanced Placement science courses (Scantlebury, 2006). Girls prefer studying subjects that they perceive as having value, being connected to people or other living things and having relevance in their lives. Often science is taught without an emphasis on how the subject connects to the "real" world. Boys are viewed as less able than girls in reading and the language arts, subjects that are stereotyped as feminine.

MOTIVATIONAL AND BEHAVIORAL CONSEQUENCES OF STEREOTYPING

The acceptance of gender-stereotyped roles as normal behaviors, with boys being rewarded for assertive behavior, uniqueness, and risk-taking, and girls for nurturing, conformity, and placing others' needs before their own, is often invisible to students and teachers. Moreover, participants in classrooms do not notice how the subtle inequities that are the outcomes of these behaviors impact students' motivations and behaviors. For example, the expectation that girls place others before themselves has consequences regarding their attitudes towards success in school. Girls' motivation for succeeding in school is often related to pleasing others, such as parents and teachers, rather than themselves. They report doing well in classes because of a personal, positive connection with their teachers. However, that personal connection is often missing in first-year, college-level classes when they become merely one student in classes of several hundred. As young college women they may struggle with their studies because there is no one person to achieve for, and they are not used to achieving for themselves.

Girls' preference for a positive, personal connection with their teachers can also influence their course selection. For example, young women may avoid advanced mathematics or science because they dislike the teacher. Another consequence of gender stereotyping for girls is learned helplessness. When girls struggle with learning material, teachers often give them the answer, promulgating a status of learned helplessness. In other words, because they are given the answers, girls learn that they are not capable of learning.

For females, placing others first is an important characteristic of a caring, nurturing person. A consequence of this practice is girls' fear of success. Girls often may not succeed in their academic achievements because to do so may be viewed as unfeminine, which may reduce their attractiveness to boys.

For males whose achievement is attributed to their natural intelligence, problems arise when this natural ability is no longer a guarantee of success. They perceive themselves as failures and often change majors instead of addressing their fear of failure by re-examining study habits and patterns.

Gender role stereotyping impacts students' perceptions of their abilities and their achievements. Similarly, research has shown that teachers' and parents' expectations of students' abilities, achievements and behaviors are influenced by gender role stereotyping. Gender role stereotyping is usually subtle, and often unrecognized or unchallenged. The assumption that girls should assume feminine traits in school such as caring for others, and quiet and unassertive behavior, can mean that they set aside their own learning needs for others. For boys, the masculine gender role stereotype suggests that they should have natural talent to achieve, and that they are expected to exhibit rationality and logic as well as loud, domineering behaviors.

Gender role stereotypes remain strong influences in society, schools and the daily life in classrooms. Yet inequities because of gender issues are often rendered invisible to students and teachers by their very pervasiveness in classrooms. A major challenge for educators is to establish classroom environments that do not favor one group of students to the detriment of another group, and recognize that gender role stereotypes remain a major influence on schools' organization, teachers' practices and students' attitudes and behaviors.

SEE ALSO *Gender Bias in Teaching; Stereotype Threat.*

BIBLIOGRAPHY

American Association of University Women Educational Foundation (AAUW). (1993). *Hostile hallways: The AAUW survey on sexual harassment in America's schools.* Washington, DC: Author.

American Association of University Women Educational Foundation (AAUW). (1998). *Gender gaps: Where schools still fail our children.* Washington, DC: Author.

Scantlebury, K. (2006). Gender. In K. Tobin (Ed.), *Teaching and learning science: A handbook* (pp. 201–206). Praeger Publishing.

Kathryn Scantlebury

GIFTED EDUCATION

In the most recently released federal report, as of 2007, titled *National Excellence, A Case for Developing America's Talent* (O'Connell-Ross, l993), a quiet crisis is described related to the education of gifted and talented students in the United States. The report asserts: "Despite sporadic attention over the years to the needs of bright students, most of them continue to spend time in school working well below their capabilities. The belief espoused in school reform that children from all economic and cultural backgrounds must reach their full potential has not been extended to America's most talented students. They are underchallenged and therefore underachieve" (p. 5).

DEFINING GIFTEDNESS

For many years, psychologists and psychometricians, following in the footsteps of Lewis Terman in 1916, equated giftedness with high IQ. In the early 2000s, this legacy is beginning to dissipate, but in some states, giftedness is still defined as an IQ of 130 or above, and this type of score is required for identification of gifted students. Research, however, from 1975 to 2005 supports a broadened conception of giftedness (Sternberg & Davidson, 1986; 2005). Most of these researchers define giftedness as a combination of multiple qualities; in addition to intellectual factors, such features as motivation and creativity are considered key qualities in many of these broadened conceptions of giftedness.

Bloom and his associates at the University of Chicago engaged in a study of the development of talent in children, examining the processes by which young people under 35 who reached the highest levels of accomplishment in academics, the arts, and sports developed their capabilities. Bloom and his associates found that the following factors play a role in the development of talent: the home environment, which develops the work ethic and the importance of doing one's best at all times; the encouragement of parents in a highly approved talent field; the involvement of families and teachers; and the presence of achievement and progress, which are necessary to maintain a commitment to talent over a decade of increasingly difficult learning (Bloom, 1985, pp. 508–509).

The importance of development throughout the life-span of the individual is reinforced by most developmental and educational psychologists who study giftedness, as is the domain-specific nature of giftedness. Gifted individuals are seen as those who can excel usually in one domain, providing that the environmental factors enable this excellence to develop.

Joseph Renzulli's (1978) three-ring definition of gifted behavior is a widely recognized example of a multifaceted and expanded conceptualization of giftedness. Renzulli (1978; 1986; 2005) defines gifted behaviors as composed of three components as follows.

Gifted behavior consists of behaviors that reflect an interaction among three basic clusters of human traits—above average ability, high levels of task commitment, and high levels of creativity. Individuals capable of developing gifted behavior are those possessing or capable of developing this composite set of traits and applying them to any potentially valuable area of human performance. Persons who manifest or are capable of developing an interaction among the three clusters require a wide variety of educational opportunities and services that are not ordinarily provided through regular instructional programs (Renzulli & Reis, 1997, p. 8).

The U.S. government subscribed to a multifaceted approach to giftedness as early as 1972 when the Marland Report definition was passed (Public Law 91–230, section 806) (Marland, 1972). This U.S. Department of Education definition has dominated most states' definitions of giftedness and talents. As of 2007 the federal definition, cited in *National Excellence*, the national report on the status of gifted and talented education, is as follows:

> Children and youth with outstanding talent perform or show the potential for performing at remarkably high levels of accomplishment when compared with others of their age, experience, or environment. These children and youth exhibit high performance capability in intellectual, creative, and/or artistic areas, possess an unusual leadership capacity, or excel in specific academic fields. They require services or activities not ordinarily provided by the schools. Outstanding talents are present in children and youth from all cultural groups, across all economic strata, and in all areas of human endeavor. (O'Connell-Ross,1993, p. 26)

Though many school districts adopt this or other broad definitions as their district's operational definition, most focus solely on intellectual ability when both identifying and serving students, and few provide programs for students with talents and gifts in the areas of creativity, the arts, leadership, and specific academic fields.

Common themes that emerge in any discussion of how to define giftedness include the need to identify the domain that serves as the basis of one's definition, whether individual or societal; the essential role that cognitive abilities and motivation play in giftedness; the importance of the developmental course of one's talents for whether or how they are expressed; and the inevitability of how one's abilities emerge and interact with educational, societal, and chance factors.

ASSESSMENT AND IDENTIFICATION OF GIFTEDNESS

Assessment and identification of gifted and talented students occurs using various methods and instruments that vary from state to state. Students are usually identified for gifted programs based on assessments of their abilities and achievement, and their creativity and motivation are often considered as well. In most school districts, an attempt is made to use multiple criteria for identification of students involving nationally normed standardized tests, as well as other measures of academic achievement, creativity, and motivation.

Classroom teachers usually nominate students for gifted programs, and children are usually referred on an ongoing basis. In addition to teacher nomination, many districts accept nominations from the student (self-referral), the parent, a peer, or from others, such as a psychologist, community members, principal, or a gifted students' coordinator. The following are usually used for assessment: group aptitude or achievement tests; various assessments of creativity or motivation; individually administered tests; auditions or performances; displays of work; and teacher of parent checklists or rating scales.

Identification of students for gifted and talented programs is usually completed using a comprehensive assessment of the child's abilities and potentials rather than simple IQ testing. The rationale for assessment typically centers on the need for developing an understanding of a child's relative strengths and how these relate to educational settings and matching children's strengths with appropriate educational programs.

There are usually three stages in the identification process. The first is nomination, which includes gathering student data from a variety of sources, including teacher, parent, and peer nominations; grades; portfolios; observations; review of student records; and outstanding products or performances. All students are involved in the pre-assessment pool to ensure equal access to screening and further assessment by all district children, including culturally or linguistically diverse children, children from low socioeconomic backgrounds, children with disabilities, and children for whom English is a second language.

The second stage is usually screening when the data gathered from the pre-assessment stage is examined to

Behavioral manifestations of giftedness according to Renzulli's "Three-ring" definition of gifted behaviors

Above average ability (general)
- high levels of abstract thought
- adaptation to novel situations
- rapid and accurate retrieval of information

Above average ability (specific)
- applications of general abilities to specific area of knowledge
- capacity to sort out relevant from irrelevant information
- capacity to acquire and use advanced knowledge and strategies while pursuing a problem

Task commitment
- capacity for high levels of interest, enthusiasm
- hard work and determination in a particular area
- self-confidence and drive to achieve
- ability to identify significant problems within an area of study
- setting high standards for one's work

Creativity
- fluency, flexibility and originality of thought
- open to new experiences and ideas
- curious
- willing to take risks
- sensitive to aesthetic characteristics

SOURCE: Adapted from Renzulli & Reis, 1997, p. 9.

Table 1 ILLUSTRATION BY GGS INFORMATION SERVICES. CENGAGE LEARNING, GALE.

determine if additional assessment is necessary. In making decisions about additional assessment, existing test data for students is not the sole determining criterion. School personnel examine all available information about a student to determine if an evidence of possible giftedness exists for that student, and they conduct necessary additional assessment.

The third stage is final identification, when additional assessment has been completed, the data obtained throughout the stages of identification are evaluated, the identification decision is made, and student's educational needs are determined. The most important part of identification is to consider the purposes for identification and the match with the resulting program.

CHARACTERISTICS OF GIFTEDNESS

Multiple lists of characteristics of giftedness exist but the most common characteristics are summarized below using Renzulli's definition of giftedness in Table 1.

PROCEDURES TO MEET THE NEEDS OF GIFTED AND TALENTED STUDENTS

Renzulli and Reis (1997) recommend the development of a continuum of services to challenge the diverse learning and affective needs of gifted and talented students. This continuum provides services that range from general enrichment across all grade levels, to curriculum differentiation opportunities for both enrichment and acceleration, to advanced classes and individualized research, as well as counseling and other services to meet affective needs. Two considerations exist when a district-wide continuum of services for academically and artistically gifted and talented students is developed.

The first consideration is organizational, relating to where and when students will be provided with services to meet their advanced learning needs and how and when different grade level students will be grouped together in or across different schools. For example, gifted and talented students can be grouped by instructional level in both elementary and middle schools. They can be cluster grouped in one or more content areas across classrooms and assigned to classes with teachers who have had professional development and use strategies to meet their learning needs. Separate classes can be provided for gifted students at any grade level. Interventions to attempt to reverse underachievement can be incorporated into counseling options either during or after school at the high school level. Students can have opportunities for advanced project work after school or during a time that their curriculum has been compacted. The second consideration in the development of a district-wide continuum of services relates to curriculum and learning opportunities, as decisions must be made about what will be taught and why and whether acceleration opportunities will be made available. Other questions to consider include whether the regular curriculum will be extended with enrichment or whether it will be compacted and replaced with teacher-selected advanced content and whether students will have the opportunity to pursue their personal interests using independent study.

Both of these considerations should be addressed as a continuum of services is developed. If organizational structures are the only component addressed in a district-wide continuum of services, little thought will have been extended to essential instructional and curricular decisions. For example, if students are grouped into a separate class for gifted students without any advanced or accelerated curriculum or instruction, little justifiable reason exists for that instructional grouping. If a large percentage of gifted students are underachieving and are not able to participate in advanced classes or are dropping out of school, an expansion of a district continuum of services should be considered to include more affective and counseling services.

Establishing opportunities for enrichment across the grade levels and differentiation in all classrooms are one way to begin the development of a continuum of services that range from some level of service in the regular classroom setting to a separate school or center for gifted learners. School-based gifted programs should offer a diverse set of learning opportunities. Resource room programs enable teachers to send out students from their regular classrooms to spend time with other high potential students to enable them to work on in-depth, advanced independent study projects and group projects in their interest areas. In some districts, students have the opportunity to travel to a center one day each week to work with other identified gifted and talented students on advanced curriculum or to pursue individual interests.

Curriculum compacting and differentiation is also suggested to accommodate the learning needs of advanced students. In a national study on compacting, the use of compacting to differentiate curriculum and eliminate previously mastered work was used with hundreds of gifted and high-ability students. Compacting is one component of the Schoolwide Enrichment Model (SEM) (Renzulli, 1977; Renzulli & Reis, 1985, 1997) that is widely implemented as an enrichment program used with academically gifted and talented students. This talent development approach provides enriched learning experiences and higher learning standards for all children through three goals; developing talents in all children, providing a broad range of advanced-level enrichment experiences for all students, and follow-up advanced learning for children based on interests. This SEM focuses on enrichment for all students through engagement, in enjoyable, challenging learning experiences and enhancement of students' interests.

Renzulli Learning, a 2006 innovation to challenge gifted and talented learners in classrooms and in separate gifted programs, is an online system designed to use strength-based assessment and differentiated learning experiences for gifted and talented students. The online assessment, which takes about 30 minutes, results in a printed profile that highlights individual student strengths and is accompanied by a differentiation search engine that selects hundreds of resources that relate specifically to each student's interests, learning styles, and product styles.

VARIATIONS IN GIFTEDNESS

Unfortunately, the majority of young people participating in gifted and talented programs across the country continue to represent the majority culture, most likely because identification and selection procedures may be ineffective and inappropriate for the identification of these young people (Frasier & Passow, 1994). Limited referrals and nominations of students who are minorities or from other unrepresented groups affect their eventual placement in programs. Test bias and inappropriateness have been mentioned as reasons for the continued reliance on traditional identification approaches.

In addition to students from economically disadvantaged populations, variations in gifted students include students from minority and cultural groups, as well as gifted students with various disabilities such as learning disabilities, visual and hearing impairments, and physical handicaps. Special programs, strategies, and identification procedures have been suggested for many of these groups; however, much progress still remains to be made to achieve equity for these underrepresented groups. Baum (1990) has identified four important approaches for handling gifted students with learning disabilities: encourage compensation strategies, encourage awareness of strengths and weaknesses, focus on developing the child's gift, and provide an environment that values individual differences.

Underachieving gifted learners, especially young people with high ability, whose performance fall noticeably short of potential, present the most bewildering and perhaps the most frustrating of all challenges to teachers and parents. One cause of underachievement in gifted or high potential students is the inappropriate curriculum and content which some of them encounter on a daily basis. The hundreds of hours spent each month in classrooms in which students rarely encounter new or challenging curriculum, the boredom of being assigned routine tasks mastered much earlier, the low levels of discussion, and the mismatch of content to students' ability lead to frustration on the parts of many of the brightest students. Reis and McCoach (2000) identified specific characteristics of gifted underachievers and recommended numerous strategies that can be used to reverse underachievement of gifted and talented students. This research may provide helpful insights for educators regarding the performance of some of their underachieving gifted students.

SEE ALSO *Intelligence: An Overview; Special Education.*

BIBLIOGRAPHY

Bloom, B. S. (Ed.). (1985). *Developing talent in young people.* New York: Ballantine Books.

Frasier, M. M., & Passow, A. H. (1994). *Toward a new paradigm for identifying talent potential* (Research Monograph No. 94112). Storrs, CT: National Research Center on the Gifted and Talented.

Marland, S. P., Jr. (1972). *Education of the gifted and talented:* Vol. 1, *Report to the Congress of the United States by the U.S. Commissioner of Education.* Washington, DC: U.S. Government Printing Office.

O'Connell-Ross, P. (1993). *National excellence: A case for developing America's talent.* Washington, DC: U. S. Department of Education, Government Printing Office.

Reis, S. M., & McCoach, D. B. (2000). The underachievement of gifted students: What do we know and where do we go? *Gifted Child Quarterly, 44*(3), 152–170.

Renzulli, J. S. (1977). *The enrichment triad model.* Mansfield Center, CT: Creative Learning Press.

Renzulli, J. S. (1978). What makes giftedness? Reexamining a definition. *Phi Delta Kappan, 60*(5), 180–184.

Renzulli, J. S. (1986). The three-ring conception of giftedness: A developmental model for creative productivity. In R. J. Sternberg & J. E. Davidson (Eds.), *Conceptions of giftedness* (pp. 53–92). New York: Cambridge University Press.

Renzulli, J. S., & Reis, S. M. (1985). *The schoolwide enrichment model: A comprehensive plan for educational excellence.* Mansfield Center, CT: Creative Learning Press.

Renzulli, J. S., & Reis, S. M. (1997). *The schoolwide enrichment model: A comprehensive plan for educational excellence* (2nd ed.). Mansfield Center, CT: Creative Learning Press.

Sternberg, R. J., & Davidson, J. E. (Eds.). (1986). *Conceptions of giftedness.* New York: Cambridge University Press.

Sternberg, R. J., & Davidson, J. (Eds.). (2005). *Conceptions of giftedness* (2nd ed.). New York: Cambridge University Press.

Sally M. Reis
Joseph S. Renzulli

GILLIGAN, CAROL
1936–

Carol Gilligan, the author of *In a Different Voice*, is noted for her work in moral reasoning, gender differences, and feminine psychology. She was born in New York City in 1936, the daughter of William Friedman, a successful lawyer, and Mabel Caminez Friedman, a humanitarian. After attending the prestigious Walden School throughout grade school and high school, she studied literature at Swarthmore and graduated *magna cum laude.* She went on to Radcliff University to earn a master's degree in clinical psychology. At age 28 she earned her PhD in social psychology from Harvard with a dissertation entitled "Responses to Temptation in Analysis of Motives."

NOTABLE COLLABORATORS

Gilligan taught as an adjunct professor at the University of Chicago while her husband finished medical school. Years later, she returned to Harvard to work with Erik Erikson. She appreciated Erikson's concern that social scientists should contribute to the social issues of the day. However, she was frustrated that he, like so many other researchers of the day, felt that the feminine perspective had to be ignored because of the complications of mixed gender studies. In working with Lawrence Kohlberg, Gilligan recognized the seriousness of ignoring the feminine perspective. She noted

Carol Gilligan © JERRY BAUER.

that although Kohlberg's research on moral development and his stage theory of moral development, justice, and rights was impressive, the conclusions could only be applied to the population of privileged boys and men that Kohlberg's sample represented. After establishing her theory of gender differences in moral reasoning, Gilligan collaborated with Lyn Mikel Brown in developing the Harvard Project on Women's Psychology and Girls' Development and in writing the book *Meeting at the Crossroads: Women's Psychology and Girls' Development.* Brown has since become recognized as an expert on feminine psychology, particularly aggression in girls.

MAJOR CONTRIBUTIONS TO THE FIELD OF EDUCATIONAL PSYCHOLOGY

Gilligan has made two major contributions to the field of educational psychology. First is her discovery of a moral reasoning based on the ethics of care, which complements Kohlberg's morality based on the ethics of justice. Her second contribution is identifying the self-silencing of a young person's authentic voice in surrender to the expectations of society.

The recognition of a morality of care and responsibility grew out of Gilligan's work with Kohlberg. Gilligan recognized that the participants in Kohlberg's norming groups were all privileged males. This meant that any viewpoints of female participants would be compared to a collective male perspective. Gilligan noticed that when a woman, in analyzing moral dilemmas, voiced a judgment based on caring for others, her response was rated lower than a man's response based on justice. Gilligan noticed a pattern in the women's responses that was divergent from the pattern of male responses. The males in the study were focused on justice, an adherence to law emphasizing the rights of individuals. The females in the study were focused on compassion, an awareness of relationships emphasizing a responsibility toward others. Although later researchers have not found the gender differences in moral reasoning that Gilligan did, the concept of an *ethic of care* is well accepted and found in moral reasoning regardless of gender.

Gilligan discovered and validated over many years that girls tend to lose their authentic voice, the true expression of their ideals, during puberty. At age 11, a girl will tell her point of view no matter how controversial, but by age 15, she has learned to suppress it. Gilligan attributes this tendency to the young woman's confrontation with the "patriarchy," the male-dominant society. In studies with boys, Gilligan has found that boys also suppress their authentic voice but at a younger age.

MAJOR IMPACT

The major impact of Gilligan's work on psychological research is the inclusion of women as participants in studies generalized to a mixed-gender population. This has led to increased interest in feminine psychology and the inclusion of gender differences as an important part of all psychological studies. Gilligan's work has brought about a revolution in psychological research so complete that it is hard to remember a time when studies with only males as the participants were used to generalize to women's situations.

SEE ALSO *Moral Development.*

BIBLIOGRAPHY

WORKS BY

In a different voice: Psychological theory and women's development. (1982). Cambridge, MA: Harvard University Press.

Mapping the moral domain: A contribution of women's thinking to psychological theory and education. (1989). Cambridge, MA: Harvard University Press.

Making connections: The relational worlds of adolescent girls at Emma Willard School. (1990). Cambridge, MA: Harvard University Press.

Meeting at the crossroads: Women's psychology and girls' development. (1992). Cambridge, MA: Harvard University Press.

Between Voice and Silence: Women and Girls, Race and Relationships. (1997). Cambridge, MA: Harvard University Press.

WORKS ABOUT

Prose, F. (1990, January 7). *Confident at 11, confused at 16.* New York Times. Retrieved, April 9, 2008, from http://query.nytimes.com/gst/fullpage.html?res=9C0CE2D91030F934A35752C0A966958260 &sec=&spon=&pagewanted=1.

Santrock, J. W. (2004). *Child development* (10th ed.). New York: McGraw-Hill.

Woolfolk, A. (2007). *Educational psychology* (10th ed.). Boston: Allyn and Bacon.

Ray Brogan

GOAL ORIENTATION THEORY

Goal orientation theory is a social-cognitive theory of achievement motivation. Goal theory originated early in the 20th century but became a particularly important theoretical framework in the study of academic motivation after 1985. Whereas other motivational theories (e.g., attribution theory) examine students' beliefs about their successes and failures, goal orientation theory examines the reasons why students engage in their academic work. Although goal orientation theory is predominantly studied in the domain of education, it also has been used in studies in the domains of sports psychology, health psychology, and social psychology.

TERMINOLOGY

In order to understand the basic properties of goal orientation theory, it is important to understand how goals are conceptualized in the research literature (Pintrich, 2000). First, in this framework, goals fall in two major classes. These classes have been referred to by various names in the literature, but for the sake of simplicity, two terms are used in this entry. The first type is called a mastery goal. Students hold mastery goals (also referred to as being mastery-oriented) when their goal is to truly understand or master the task at hand; students who are mastery-oriented are interested in self-improvement and tend to compare their current level of achievement to their own prior achievement. In contrast, the second type is called a performance goal. Students hold performance goals (also referred to as being performance-oriented) when their goal is to demonstrate their ability compared to others. Students who are performance-oriented are

interested in competition, demonstrating their competence, and outperforming others; they tend to use other students as points of comparison, rather than themselves.

Second, mastery and performance goals are each divided into approach and avoid goals. In terms of mastery goals, mastery-approach oriented students are interested in truly mastering an academic task; in contrast, mastery-avoid oriented students are interested in avoiding misunderstanding the task. In terms of performance goals, performance-approach oriented students are interested in demonstrating that they are more competent than other students (i.e., have more ability than others); in contrast, performance-avoid oriented students are interested in avoiding appearing incompetent or stupid. Below are examples for each type of goal orientation:

Mastery approach: Jennifer's goal in French class is to become fluent in the language because she is interested in the language and wants to be able to converse with others and read French literature.

Mastery avoid: Jason's goal in French class is to avoid misunderstanding the grammatical lessons presented by his teacher.

Performance approach: Haley's goal in French class is to demonstrate to her teacher and to other students that she is better at speaking French than many of her classmates.

Performance avoid: T.J.'s goal in French class is to avoid appearing incompetent at speaking or reading French.

It is important to note that students can hold multiple goals simultaneously; thus it is possible for a student to be both mastery-approach oriented and performance-approach oriented; such a student truly wants to learn and master the material but is also concerned with appearing more competent than others.

In addition, some researcher have operationalized performance goals somewhat differently and referred to them as "extrinsic goals" (Anderman & Johnston, 1998; Pintrich & de Groot, 1990). When students hold an extrinsic goal, their reasons for engaging in academic tasks are to either earn a certain reward (e.g., a good grade) or to avoid a punishment.

Third, students' goals can be conceptualized at differing organizational levels. Personal goals refer to students' individual, personally held goals; the types of mastery and performance goals described above are examples of personal goals. In contrast, classroom goal structures refer to students' beliefs about the goals that are emphasized by their teachers in their classrooms. Most researchers distinguish between a classroom mastery goal structure and a classroom performance classroom goal structure; however, most do not make the approach/avoid distinction with classroom goal structures. When students perceive a classroom mastery goal structure, they believe that instruction in the class is characterized by emphases on improvement, learning new material to a level of mastery, and self-comparisons; when students perceive a performance goal structure, they believe that the class is characterized by competition, an emphasis on grades and relative ability, and outperforming others.

Some researchers also discuss school-level goal structures. A school can be perceived by students as being mastery oriented (i.e., the culture of the school focuses on learning, improvement, and task mastery) or as being performance-oriented (i.e., the culture of the school focuses on grades, achievement, competitiveness, and outperforming others).

MAJOR RESEARCH METHODS AND MEASUREMENT TOOLS USED TO TEST GOAL THEORY

Much research examining goal orientations has used self-report survey instruments. Students are asked to complete surveys that assess students' personal goals, and their perceptions of classroom and/or school goal structures. Some researchers collect survey data at one point in time in order to get a snapshot of students' goal orientations, whereas others collect survey data at multiple time points, in order to examine changes in goals and perceived goal structures.

There are many existing survey-based measures of goal orientations. One of the most commonly used measures is the Patterns of Adaptive Learning Survey (PALS; Midgley et al., 1998). The PALS contains measures of students' personal goals, as well as their perceptions of classroom goal structures. These measures have been used with a wide range of age groups, including young children, adolescents, and college-aged students. Other measures, such as the AGQ of Elliot and colleagues (Conroy, Elliot, & Hofer, 2003) and measures developed by Dweck (e.g., Dweck, 1999) also can be used to measure students' goal orientations across a variety of domains. Most survey measures of achievement goals assess students' reasons for engaging in academic tasks; however, Nichols and his colleagues conceptualized their measures of goal orientations in terms of how students feel about learning (Nicholls, 1989).

Some researchers have used other methodologies to examine goals. For example, Patrick, L. Anderman, and their colleagues developed an observational instrument that can be used by observers to assess goal structures in classrooms (Patrick, Anderman, Ryan, Edelin, & Midgley, 2001). Turner, Meyer, and their colleagues have examined transcripts of teacher-student discourse to examine how goals are communicated to students by teachers (Turner et al., 2002).

INDIVIDUAL AND CONTEXTUAL INFLUENCES ON DEVELOPMENT OF GOALS

Motivation researchers who study goal orientations acknowledge that both students' individual characteristics and contextual influences affect the types of goals that students adopt in various learning environments. Studies indicate that the environments in which students learn influence students' goal orientations in important ways.

Individual Differences Studies that have examined gender differences in goal orientations have produced mixed results. Many studies that have examined gender have found that males tend to report being more performance-oriented than do females (L. H. Anderman & E.M. Anderman, 1999; Roeser, Midgley, & Urdan, 1996); however, other studies have found no gender differences (e.g., Midgley & Middleton, 1997).

Fewer studies as of 2008 have examined ethnic differences in goal orientations. Results from studies that have been conducted are inconclusive. Much additional research in this area is needed. In one large-scale study, Midgley and Middleton (1997) compared goal orientation using a sample of European American and African American adolescents. Although no differences were found for performance-approach or avoid goals, African American adolescents reported somewhat higher mastery goals than did European American students. In a longitudinal study, Freeman and her colleagues found that across eight waves of data collection, African American students reported overall being more mastery oriented and more extrinsically oriented than did European American students (Freeman, Gutman, & Midgley, 2002). In a qualitative study of African American students' goal orientations, Edelin (1998) found that when students were asked to discuss their achievement goals during interviews, most of the students talked about holding extrinsic goals. Interestingly, students occasionally mentioned mastery goals, but rarely mentioned performance goals (i.e., outperforming others).

One area that has received additional attention in the literature is the relation of students' beliefs about intelligence to goal orientations. Dweck and her colleagues indicate that students who hold incremental beliefs about intelligence (i.e., they believe that intelligence is modifiable) tend to adopt mastery goals. In contrast, students who hold entity theories of intelligence (i.e., they believe that one's intelligence is a fixed entity that can not be changed) tend to adopt performance goals (Dweck, 1999).

ARE PERFORMANCE GOALS BAD?

Are performance goals bad? If studies have shown that performance-approach goals are related to higher achievement, whereas few studies have shown a direct relation between mastery goals and achievement, then shouldn't teachers structure classrooms so students are challenged to reach optimal achievement as measured against "average?" While it appears clear that performance-avoidance goals result in few benefits, mounting evidence indicates performance-*approach* goals may have adaptive value—e.g., they have been positively associated with task value, academic self-concept, effort, and achievement (Harackiewicz, *et al.*, 2002).

In a series of studies, Elliot, Shell, Bouas Henry, and Maier (2005) divided students into groups of performance-approach, performance-avoidance, or mastery conditions. The result? When students believed their work would result in future opportunities to reap rewards, students in the performance-approach group out achieved those in the mastery group. And when they thought there was no future contingency hanging on their work? They performed *just as well* as those in the mastery group. In other words, there appeared to be no penalty for being in an environment that encouraged performance-approach—indeed, there appeared to be benefits.

In another study, Barron and Harackiewicz (2003) examined achievement goals in a small undergraduate psychology classroom that promoted critical thinking, writing, oral presentation skills, and participation—a setting the authors felt would have been conducive to a mastery orientation. Students who adopted higher levels of performance-approach goals at the outset were more likely to earn a higher grade—but, to also have less interest by the end of the semester, whereas those adopting mastery goals tended to demonstrate increased interest. In order to succeed in this setting, students taking a performance-approach orientation would have had to go beyond mere memorization of facts and adopt deeper processing strategies. The results of this study suggest that it could be that performance-approach and mastery goals serve two ends for the student—achievement *and* interest.

However, others have questioned the benefits of encouraging performance-approach goals as they may not

be effective across educational settings. If students are encouraged to evaluate their performance against norms, then inevitably some will be left out. For every student who achieves above the norm, one falls below it. Under such circumstances, those who already have a sense of academic efficacy will be motivated to engage in academic tasks—those who have experienced failure may avoid them. Midgley, Kaplan, and Middleton (2001) noted that performance goals may be most advantageous if one is male, older, and in a competitive class where mastery goals are also encouraged, adding that school settings already tend to be predominantly performance oriented. Since the time of their writing, *No Child Left Behind* has been signed into law—it is not likely classrooms have become any more mastery oriented during the intervening years.

So, are performance goals bad? While it appears that performance-approach may be adaptive for students in some situations, certainly further study is needed. One thing that appears to be clear is that the greater learning context needs to be considered in answering this question—including teachers' and students' long- and short-term goals for learning, the school and larger societal settings, and the individual characteristics of the student.

BIBLIOGRAPHY

Barron, K. E., & Harackiewicz, J. M. (2003). Revisiting the benefits of performance-approach goals in the college classroom. Exploring the role of goals in advanced college courses. *International journal of Education Research, 39,* 357–374.

Elliot, A. J., Shell, M. M., Bouas Henry, K., & Maier, M. A. (2005). Achievement goals, performance contingencies, and performance attainment: An experimental test. *Journal of Educational Psychology, 97(4),* 630–640.

Harackiewicz, J. M., Barron, K. E., Pintrich, P. R., Elliot, A. J., & Thrash, T. M. (2002). Revision of achievement goal theory: Necessary and illuminating. *Journal of Educational Psychology, 94(3),* 638–645.

Midgley, C., Kaplan, A., & Middleton, M. (2001). Performance-approach goals: Good for what, for whom, under what circumstances, and at what cost? *Journal of Educational Psychology, 93(1),* 77–86.

Michael S. Yough

Contextual Influences Research suggests that in addition to student characteristics, social contexts are also influential in determining students' goal orientations. More specifically, the instructional practices that are used in classrooms and schools have an impact on the types of goal orientations that students adopt (Maehr & Anderman, 1993; Maehr & Midgley, 1996; Roeser et al., 1996; Turner et al., 2002). In a given classroom, if a teacher talks about and truly focuses on mastery, improvement, and self-comparisons, then students are quite likely to adopt mastery goals and to perceive a mastery goal structure in that classroom; in contrast, if a teacher constantly talks about grades, test scores, and who is doing the best (or the worst) in class, then students are likely to adopt performance goals and to perceive a performance goal structure in that classroom.

In addition, practices that are used by the school as a whole can influence the adoption of mastery or performance goals. For example, many schools place much emphasis on the importance of the honor roll. In many schools, students' names are placed on the honor roll when they receive certain grades (e.g., an A average). Additionally, in many schools, the honor roll hangs on a highly visible bulletin board or is projected on a television monitor, where it is viewed daily by students, teachers, and visitors. When schools emphasize ability differences in this and similar ways, students are likely to adopt performance goals and to perceive that the school is performance-oriented.

Parents can also influence students' goal orientations. Parental emphasis on the importance of grades and high test scores may lead offspring to become performance-oriented students. In contrast, parental emphasis on learning and mastery encourages offspring to become mastery-goal students.

RELATIONS OF GOALS TO EDUCATIONAL OUTCOMES

Mastery and performance goals are related to various educational outcomes in important ways. When students adopt either mastery or performance goals, predictable outcomes often result.

Research frequently indicates that mastery goals are related to adaptive outcomes (see Anderman & Wolters, 2006, for a review). When students report being mastery oriented, they persist longer at academic tasks, they are more engaged with their work, they use more effective cognitive processing strategies, they report lower levels of self-handicapping behaviors, and they choose to continue to engage with tasks in the future when those tasks become optional (e.g., choosing to enroll in an additional course after the completion of a current course). Interestingly, few studies indicate that the adoption of mastery goals is related directly to increased academic performance (i.e., higher grades or test scores). As of the early 2000s, many researchers had studied mastery-approach goals but had not examined mastery avoid goals.

The connections between performance goals and various educational outcomes are more complex. Prior to the mid 1990s, researchers often measured performance approach and avoid goals within the same scales, thus confounding these measures; later measures clearly distinguished between approach and avoid performance goals.

In general, results indicate that performance avoid goals are not related to adaptive outcomes; more specifically, studies indicate that performance-avoid goals are related to poor academic performance, low levels of academic engagement, and avoidant behaviors such as self-handicapping (Urdan, Ryan, Anderman, & Gheen, 2002).

Studies examining the connections of performance-approach goals to various educational outcomes yield somewhat mixed results. Some research indicates that the adoption of performance approach goals is related to persistence at academic tasks, whereas other studies do not indicate a relation between performance approach goals and persistence. Similarly, some studies indicate that performance-approach goals are related to the use of adaptive cognitive and metacognitive strategies, whereas other studies do not yield these findings. In addition, some research indicates that the adoption of performance-approach goals is related to maladaptive outcomes, such as the avoidance of help-seeking (Ryan, Hicks, & Midgley, 1997). Despite these mixed results, several studies do indicate that there is a positive connection between course grades and performance-approach goals in college students and sometimes in younger students (see Anderman & Wolters, 2006, for a review).

Studies examining the relations of classroom goal structures to educational outcomes yield similar results. Perceptions of a mastery goal structure are generally related to adaptive outcomes, whereas perceptions of performance goal structures are often related to maladaptive outcomes. Studies examining the relations of perceived performance goal structures to academic achievement yield mixed results, with some studies indicating that performance goal structures are related negatively to achievement (E. M. Anderman & Midgley, 1997), and other studies indicating that mastery goal structures are either unrelated to achievement or related positively to achievement (Midgley & Urdan, 2001).

THE DEBATE ABOUT PERFORMANCE GOALS

Debate in the educational psychology literature regarding performance approach goals has focused on revisions to goal orientation theory (involving approach and avoid goals) in the late 1990s. Some researchers argue that performance approach goals are adaptive and can be beneficial for students, particularly when they are paired with mastery goals (Harackiewicz, Barron, Pintrich, Elliot, & Thrash, 2002). In contrast, other researchers argue that there are few benefits to performance approach goals (Midgley, Kaplan, & Middleton, 2001). These debates have important implications for the design of educational environments and for school reform. As noted by Roeser (2004), part of this debate emanates from the fact that some goal theory researchers (e.g., Midgley et al.) primarily have been concerned with issues of reforming school learning environments, whereas others (e.g., Harackiewicz et al.) have been concerned with developing theoretical models to enhance and explain individual student motivation. Interestingly, despite the debate about performance goals, the vast majority of goal theory researchers converge on the benefits of mastery goals for educational outcomes.

IMPLICATIONS FOR EDUCATORS

Nearly two decades of research from about 1985 into the early 2000s on achievement goal orientations offered educators a number of practical implications for classrooms. As educators think more critically about the types of goals that teachers and schools foster in their students, they may be better able to shape the motivational patterns adopted by children and adolescents in school settings.

One of the basic tenets of goal orientation theory is that students' goals, as well as classroom and school goal structures, can be changed. Goals can change across different social contexts. In addition, teachers and administrators can deliberately alter instructional practices to affect the social contexts of schools and classrooms.

Maehr, Midgley, and their colleagues engaged in extensive work in the early 1990s, using goal orientation theory to guide school reform. Specifically, in a series of studies of both elementary and middle grades schools, they demonstrated that the instructional practices used in schools could be changed, using goal orientation theory as a guiding framework, to make practices focus more on mastery and improvement and less on performance and ability differences. A team of researchers (including both university faculty and graduate students, several of whom had experience as classroom teachers) met with a team of school-connected adults (i.e., teachers, administrators, and parents) to critically examine the practices of the schools using goal orientation theory. These collaborative teams worked to identify practices that encouraged either mastery or performance goals. Then, over a three-year period, the teams worked to eliminate some of the

instructional practices that focused on performance goals and to enhance and increase the strategies that fostered the adoption of mastery goals. Results indicated that these changes could be successfully implemented in school settings and that student motivation was enhanced as a result of these changes (Maehr & Midgley, 1996).

Several researchers have suggested that educators can use TARGET a means of examining and realigning instructional practices according to goal orientation theory. Developed by Joyce Epstein (1989), the TARGET acronym refers to six aspects of the learning environment that are strongly related to academic motivation: tasks, authority, recognition, grouping, evaluation, and time. Several researchers have demonstrated that instructional practices can be restructured using TARGET as a guiding framework (Ames, 1990; Maehr & Anderman, 1993). Tasks can be examined and altered so that they encourage students to focus on mastering the task, regardless of the performance of other students on the task. Authority refers to how much control students have over tasks: Students will be more likely to adopt mastery goals when they have at least some choice/control over some aspects of their work. Recognition refers to how and why students are acknowledged in the classroom (i.e., for their personal accomplishments or for their performances compared to others).

Grouping refers to how students are organized socially for instruction; if students are grouped by ability, this may support the endorsement of performance goals in some students, whereas if students are grouped according to their interests, they may be more likely to adopt mastery goals. Evaluation simply refers to how students are assessed; evaluations can be based on mastering a task or on how quickly or accurately one student completes a task compared to others. Finally, time refers to how time is used in classrooms; some educators use time and structure their classes so that students can master tasks and spend the necessary time on complex tasks, whereas others structure time more rigidly and may limit the amounts of time that students can spend on tasks. If students feel rushed when working on a complex task, they may become more performance oriented and start comparing their performance to that of other students.

SEE ALSO *Social Goals.*

BIBLIOGRAPHY

Ames, C. (1990, April). *The relationship of achievement goals to student motivation in classroom settings.* Paper presented at the American Educational Research Association, Boston, MA.

Anderman, E. M., & Johnston, J. (1998). Television news in the classroom: What are adolescents learning? *Journal of Adolescent Research, 13*(1), 73–100.

Anderman, E. M., & Midgley, C. (1997). Changes in achievement goal orientations, perceived academic competence, and grades across the transition to middle-level schools. *Contemporary Educational Psychology, 22*(3), 269–298.

Anderman, L. H., & Anderman, E. M. (1999). Social predictors of changes in students' achievement goal orientations. *Contemporary Educational Psychology, 25*, 21–37.

Conroy, D. E., Elliot, A. J., & Hofer, S. M. (2003). A 2 x 2 achievement goals questionnaire for sport: evidence for factorial invariance, temporal stability, and external validity. *Journal of Sport and Exercise Psychology, 25*(4), 456–476.

Dweck, C. S. (1999). *Self-theories: Their role in motivation, personality, and development.* Philadelphia: Taylor & Francis.

Freeman, K. E., Gutman, L. M., & Midgley, C. (2002). Can achievement goal theory enhance our understanding of the motivation and performance of African American young adolescents? In C. Midgley (Ed.), *Goals, goal structures, and patterns of adaptive learning* (pp. 175–204). Mahwah, NJ: Erlbaum.

Harackiewicz, J. M., Barron, K. E., Pintrich, P. R., Elliot, A. J., & Thrash, T. M. (2002). Revision of achievement goal theory: Necessary and illuminating. *Journal of Educational Psychology, 94*(3), 638–645.

Maehr, M. L., & Anderman, E. M. (1993). Reinventing schools for early adolescents: Emphasizing task goals. *Elementary School Journal, 93*(5), 593–610.

Maehr, M. L., & Midgley, C. (1996). *Transforming school cultures.* Boulder, CO: Westview Press.

Midgley, C., Kaplan, A., & Middleton, M. J. (2001). Performance-approach goals: Good for what, for whom, under what circumstances, and at what cost? *Journal of Educational Psychology, 93*(1), 77–86.

Midgley, C., Kaplan, A., Middleton, M. J., Maehr, M. L., Urdan, T., Anderman, L. H., et al. (1998). The development and validation of scales assessing students' achievement goal orientations. *Contemporary Educational Psychology, 23*(113–131).

Midgley, C., & Urdan, T. (2001). Academic self-handicapping and achievement goals: A further examination. *Contemporary Educational Psychology, 26*(1), 61–75.

Nicholls, J. G. (1989). *The competitive ethos and democratic education.* Cambridge, MA: Harvard University Press.

Patrick, H., Anderman, L. H., Ryan, A. M., Edelin, K. C., & Midgley, C. (2001). Teachers' communication of goal orientations in four fifth-grade classrooms. *Elementary School Journal, 102*(1), 35–58.

Pintrich, P. R. (2000). An Achievement Goal Theory Perspective on Issues in Motivation Terminology, Theory, and Research. *Contemporary Educational Psychology, 25*(1), 92–104.

Pintrich, P. R., & de Groot, E. V. (1990). Motivational and self-regulated learning components of classroom academic performance. *Journal of Educational Psychology, 82*(1), 33–40.

Roeser, R. W., Midgley, C., & Urdan, T. (1996). Perceptions of the school psychological environment and early adolescents' psychological and behavioral functioning in school: The mediating role of goals and belonging. *Journal of Educational Psychology, 88*, 408–422.

Ryan, A. M., Hicks, L. H., & Midgley, C. (1997). Social goals, academic goals, and avoiding seeking help in the classroom. *Journal of Early Adolescence, 17*(2), 152–171.

Turner, J. C., Midgley, C., Meyer, D. K., Gheen, M. H., Anderman, E. M., Kang, Y., et al. (2002). The classroom environment and students' reports of avoidance strategies in mathematics: A multimethod study. *Journal of Educational Psychology, 94*(1), 88–106.

Urdan, T., Ryan, A. M., Anderman, E. M., & Gheen, M. (2002). Goals, goal structures, and avoidance behaviors. In C. Midgley (Ed.), *Goals, goal structures, and patterns of adaptive learning* (pp. 55–83). Mahwah, NJ: Erlbaum.

Eric M. Anderman

GOAL SETTING

Goal setting is an important component of students' motivation, self-regulation, and achievement in academic settings. A goal is a behavior or outcome that one is consciously trying to perform or attain. Goal setting refers to the process of establishing that behavior or outcome to serve as the aim of one's actions. Goals can exert positive effects in achievement settings by directing learners' attention to important activities and away from distractions and by mobilizing their effort and persistence directed toward goal attainment. Given the centrality of goals to classroom learning, it is important that students set goals that are likely to have desirable effects.

TYPES OF GOALS

Simply having a goal does not automatically benefit a student's academic performance. Researchers such as Bandura (1986) and Locke and Latham (1990, 2002) have identified various goal properties and have investigated how different goals link with achievement outcomes.

Goals may be cast as absolute or normative. An absolute goal has a fixed standard, such as reading one chapter in a book in one hour. A normative goal is relative to the attainments of others, such as being the first one in class to finish an assignment.

Goals can be distinguished according to how far they extend into the future. Goals may be relatively close at hand (proximal) such as reading one chapter tonight, or more long term (distant) such as reading one chapter by the end of the current week. Proximal goals lead to higher motivation directed toward goal attainment than do long-term goals (Bandura, 1986). Proximal goals are especially beneficial for children because they have short time frames of reference and are not fully developmentally capable of representing long-term outcomes in thought.

Goals also can be distinguished according to the specificity of their performance standards. Goals that incorporate specific standards (e.g., complete 20 problems in one hour) are more likely to enhance motivation and learning than are general goals (e.g., do your best) because specific goals better describe the amount of effort needed to succeed. Motivational benefits are not as great with general goals because almost any level of perform-ance satisfies the standard (Locke & Latham, 2002).

An important goal property is difficulty, or how hard it is to attain the goal. In general, difficult goals (e.g., read a 30-page chapter tonight) boost motivation better than do easier goals (e.g., read five pages tonight), because students persist longer and expend greater effort when they pursue difficult goals. However, goal difficulty and motivation do not bear an unlimited positive rela-tion with one another. Students are not motivated to attempt goals that they believe are impossible to attain. Difficult goals do not raise motivation and learning in the absence of the skills needed to attain them. Goals are motivating when learners view them as challenging but attainable (Locke & Latham, 2002).

Another way to differentiate goals is according to students' level of commitment to attain them. Goals do not affect performance in the absence of commitment (Locke & Latham, 1990). The goal properties identified above can help foster commitment. Students typically are more committed to attempt goals when they are specific, proximal, and moderately difficult, than when they are general, distant, and either overly easy or difficult.

Finally, goals can be distinguished by what students ultimately are trying to accomplish. A process or learning goal refers to what knowledge, behavior, skill, or strategy students are trying to acquire. An outcome or perform-ance goal denotes what task students are trying to com-plete. While working on algebra homework, a student may have a goal of learning how to solve two equations in two unknowns (process) or a goal of finishing the home-work assignment (outcome). Although both types of goals can motivate behavior, they can have different effects on learners' beliefs and cognitive processes. As Pintrich has shown, process goals focus attention on the skills needed to learn. Students often evaluate their prog-ress in learning, and the belief that one is learning can enhance motivation. In contrast, outcome goals focus attention on completing tasks. These goals can lead learners to compare their work with that of others, which can lower motivation among students who are not mak-ing adequate progress.

GOAL SETTING EFFECTS ON ACHIEVEMENT OUTCOMES

To explain why goals affect achievement behaviors, researchers have advanced different theories. Locke and Latham (1990) proposed that the key components are goal choice and commitment. Goal choice includes the goal people are trying to obtain and the level at which they are trying to attain it. Goal commitment refers to how enthu-siastic people are about a goal or how determined they are to achieve it. Locke and Latham identified several factors

that affect goal choice and commitment, including per-sonal-individual factors such as skill level and previous performance and social-environmental factors such as group norms and the nature of authority and feedback. Because this theory was developed and tested in organiza-tional settings, it places strong emphasis on external factors.

Bandura's social cognitive theory (1986) posits that human functioning results from reciprocal interactions among personal factors (e.g., cognitions, emotions), behaviors, and environmental conditions. There are two primary cognitive sources of motivation (personal fac-tors): goals and expectations. Goals help to focus and sustain effort toward task completion. As people work on tasks they compare their performances with their goals. Positive self-evaluations of progress raise self-efficacy (dis-cussed below) and sustain motivation. The perception of a discrepancy between present performance and the goal can create dissatisfaction and raise motivation for goal attainment.

Bandura's theory identifies two types of expecta-tions. Outcome expectations are beliefs about the likely consequences of actions. Based on their past experiences and observations of models in their environments people form beliefs about the likely consequences of given actions. People are likely to act in ways that they believe will lead to desired outcomes. Outcome expectations can motivate behavior over long periods when people believe that their actions will eventually result in success.

Efficacy expectations, or self-efficacy, refers to personal beliefs about one's capabilities to learn or perform actions at designated levels (Bandura, 1997). Self-efficacy is not the same as an outcome expectation. Students may believe that studying diligently for an exam will produce a high grade (positive outcome expectation) but may doubt their capa-bilities to study diligently (low self-efficacy). Often, how-ever, self-efficacy and outcome expectations are related. Students with high self-efficacy for doing well in school expect to receive good grades for their coursework. Both types of expectations can affect motivation.

Bandura (1997) noted that people gauge their self-efficacy from their performances, observations of models, forms of social persuasion, and physiological indexes (e.g., heart rate). Actual performances offer the best source of information; successes generally raise and failures may lower self-efficacy. Students receive information about their capabilities by observing others perform. Observing similar others succeed can raise observers' self-efficacy. Social per-suasion, such as when a teacher tells a student "I know you can do this," can raise self-efficacy, but this increase will not last long if students perform poorly. Physiological symp-toms can be informative of self-efficacy. When students

Effective athletic training places a strong emphasis on both proximal and process goals. ©RICHARD HAMILTON SMITH/CORBIS.

notice that they are less anxious studying for an exam, they may feel more self-efficacious about performing well on it.

Bandura's social cognitive theory (1986) contends that learners set goals that they feel self-efficacious about attaining and believe that when attained will result in positive outcomes. They evaluate their goal progress as they work on the task. Their self-efficacy and motivation are strengthened when they believe that they are making progress toward their goals. Self-efficacy is further enhanced when learners attain their goals, as well as their motivation to set and pursue new goals.

Goal setting also is a key component of self-regulation, or the process by which students activate and sustain cognitions, behaviors, and affects systematically oriented toward the attainment of goals. Zimmerman's three-phase model of self-regulation (2000) includes forethought, performance/volitional control, and self-reflection. The forethought phase precedes performances and refers to processes that set the stage for action. The performance/volitional control phase includes processes that occur during learning and affect motivation and action. During the self-reflection phase, learners reflect

on their performances and determine whether changes in behaviors or strategies are needed.

Goals and self-efficacy are active throughout the model. In the forethought phase, learners set goals and have a sense of self-efficacy for attaining them. As they work on the task they mentally compare their performances with their goals to determine progress. Their self-efficacy is sustained when they believe that they are making goal progress. During self-reflection learners determine whether their present approach is effective. If they feel self-efficacious for succeeding but believe that their present strategy is not working well enough, they may alter their strategy by working harder, persisting longer, deciding to use a different method, or seeking help from others. These self-regulatory processes promote learning, motivation, and self-efficacy.

GOAL SETTING RESEARCH IN EDUCATION

Goal setting research in education has established the importance of specific, proximal, and moderately challenging goals as beneficial for motivation and learning. Schunk has conducted several studies investigating these variables. In these studies, elementary school children received instruction on arithmetic operations and opportunities to practice solving problems. In one study some children received a specific goal denoting the number of problems to complete, whereas others were given a general goal of working productively. Compared with the general goal, the specific goal promoted higher self-efficacy and mathematical achievement.

Bandura and Schunk conducted a similar study investigating goal proximity. Over several sessions children received instruction that explained and demonstrated subtraction operations and opportunities to practice solving problems. Proximal-goal children were asked to complete a portion of the instructional material during each session; distant-goal children were told to complete all of the material by the end of the last session. Proximal goals raised motivation during the sessions, as well as children's self-efficacy and subtraction achievement, better than distant goals.

Schunk's research also has addressed goal difficulty during school learning. In one study, children received long-division instruction and practice opportunities. All children received the same instruction and practice time. Some children were given a more difficult goal (higher number of problems to complete), whereas others received an easier goal (lower number to complete). Difficult goals led to higher motivation during learning, self-efficacy, and skill acquisition.

Goal progress feedback provides information about progress toward goals and can promote self-efficacy and motivation when students cannot derive progress information on their own. It often is difficult for children to know whether their reading comprehension or their written expression is improving. Research by Schunk and Rice with children with reading difficulties showed that giving children feedback on how well they were learning to use a comprehension strategy improved their reading comprehension self-efficacy and achievement. Schunk and Swartz obtained comparable results in writing achievement and found that self-efficacy and achievement gains generalized to different types of writing assignments and maintained themselves over time.

Researchers have addressed how process and outcome goals affect motivation, learning, and self-regulation. In the Schunk and Rice study, children were taught a comprehension strategy. Some received a process goal of learning to use the strategy to answer comprehension questions, whereas others were given an outcome goal of answering questions. The process goal, coupled with progress feedback on how well the children were using the strategy, promoted self-efficacy and achievement the best. With college students, Schunk and Ertmer found that a process goal of learning computer applications led

to higher self-efficacy, self-judged learning progress, and strategy use, compared with an outcome goal of performing the applications.

Research by Zimmerman and Kitsantas found benefits from shifting from process to outcome goals. High school students were taught a writing revision strategy. Some students received a process goal (following steps in the strategy) or an outcome goal (number of words in sentences). Others initially were given a process goal but then were advised to shift to an outcome goal. Learners who changed goals as their revision skills developed demonstrated higher self-efficacy and skill than students who pursued either the process or the outcome goal.

IMPLICATIONS FOR EDUCATORS

Goal-setting research in school settings shows that students' learning, motivation, and self-regulation can be improved when students pursue goals that are specific, proximal, and moderately difficult, receive feedback on their goal progress, focus their attention on learning processes, and shift their focus to outcome goals as their skills develop. These points have implications for educators who desire to use goal setting systematically.

Much educational planning is based on proximal, specific, and moderately challenging goals. Teachers typically plan daily lessons around specific student learning outcomes. Content difficulty usually is low initially to ensure that students acquire skills but increases as students become more proficient.

Students may need to be taught how to set goals that are proximal, specific, and moderately difficult. Many students are not realistic about the steps involved in completing a project or about how much time is required to complete those steps. Goal-setting research suggests that the key to completing a long-term task is to divide it into short-term goals. Educators who work with high school students who have to write a research paper can help them subdivide this task into proximal and specific steps, such as deciding on the topic, doing library and Internet research, outlining the paper, and writing the first draft. Timelines can be established for the subgoals. As students gain experience with goal setting, they will be able to set realistic goals on their own.

Educators can help students focus on process goals by providing feedback that stresses processes, such as how well students are using a strategy, budgeting their time, and completing subgoals. However, as the research by Zimmerman and Kitsantas showed, outcome goals can be highly motivating and lead to skill gains once students have acquired some competence. Teachers can shift students to focusing on outcome goals that are self-referenced such as how well students are doing currently compared with how they did previously, rather than socially referenced such as how well they are doing compared with how classmates are doing. These social comparisons will not raise self-efficacy among students who perceive that they are performing worse than their peers.

Finally, goal setting theory and research underscore the importance of developmental factors. Because children have short time frames of reference, immediate goals are motivating, whereas long-term goals are not. Short, focused lessons reflect this idea. With development, students are better able to cognitively represent long-term outcomes. Teachers can work with students to help them break long-term goals into short-term subgoals, establish timelines, and assess their progress toward their goals. Teachers also can assist students in evaluating their capabilities to engage in these tasks, which will help to develop their self-regulatory competencies. Students who graduate from high school with a mindset that includes the importance of setting goals and assessing progress will be well prepared to meet future educational and life challenges.

SEE ALSO *Expectancy Value Motivational Theory; Self-Efficacy Theory; Self-Regulated Learning.*

BIBLIOGRAPHY

Bandura, A. (1986). *Social foundations of thought and action: A social cognitive theory.* Englewood Cliffs, NJ: Prentice Hall.

Bandura, A. (1997). *Self-efficacy: The exercise of control.* New York: Freeman.

Bandura, A., & Schunk, D. H. (1981). Cultivating competence, self-efficacy, and intrinsic interest through proximal self-motivation. *Journal of Personality and Social Psychology, 41,* 586–598.

Locke, E. A., & Latham, G. P. (1990). *A theory of goal setting and task performance.* Englewood Cliffs, NJ: Prentice Hall.

Locke, E. A., & Latham, G. P. (2002). Building a practically useful theory of goal setting and task motivation: A 35-year odyssey. *American Psychologist, 57,* 705–717.

Pintrich, P. R. (2000). Multiple goals, multiple pathways: The role of goal orientation in learning and achievement. *Journal of Educational Psychology, 92,* 544–555.

Schunk, D. H. (1991). Goal setting and self-evaluation: A social cognitive perspective on self-regulation. In M. L. Maehr & P. R. Pintrich (Eds.), *Advances in motivation and achievement* (Vol. 7, pp. 85–113). Greenwich, CT: JAI Press.

Schunk, D. H., & Ertmer, P. A. (1999). Self-regulatory processes during computer skill acquisition: Goal and self-evaluative influences. *Journal of Educational Psychology, 91,* 251–260.

Schunk, D. H., & Rice, J. M. (1991). Learning goals and progress feedback during reading comprehension instruction. *Journal of Reading Behavior, 23,* 351–364.

Schunk, D. H., & Swartz, C. W. (1993). Goals and progress feedback: Effects on self-efficacy and writing achievement. *Contemporary Educational Psychology, 18,* 337–354.

Zimmerman, B. J. (2000). Attaining self-regulation: A social cognitive perspective. In M. Boekaerts, P. R. Pintrich, & M. Zeidner (Eds.), *Handbook of self-regulation* (pp. 13–39). San Diego: Academic Press.

Zimmerman, B. J., & Kitsantas, A. (1999). Acquiring writing revision skill: Shifting from process to outcome self-regulatory goals. *Journal of Educational Psychology, 91,* 241–250.

Dale Schunk

GRADING

Grading is an evaluative practice that assigns letters, marks, numbers, or descriptions that indicate the level of student performance. It is carried out to provide meaningful feedback to students and parents about what a student has learned. Grading requires professional judgments and evaluations of student work. As such, grading practices can vary significantly from one teacher to another. There is also considerable variability in what is included in determining grades (i.e., student achievement, effort, participation, cooperation). These differences have been documented with research that shows that, in the main, teachers' grading tends to include a hodgepodge of various factors (Brookhart, 1994; McMillan, 2007). There is little consistency in grading practices across school and teachers, even within the same school, resulting in the use of different inputs and judgments.

PURPOSE OF GRADING

Grades have been used to serve three purposes: (1) ranking students, (2) reporting what students have learned and are able to do, and (3) providing feedback to improve learning and motivate students (Brookhart, 2004). In the past, one of the main reasons for grading students was to show how a student's performance compared to that of other students. This kind of comparison is called *norm-referenced.* With this approach, higher grades (As and Bs) are awarded to students who perform best in comparison with the performance of other students, and lower grades (D and F) are given to students whose relative standing is the worst. Students in the middle are "average," with a C grade. This approach has been called *grading on the curve.*

Knowing which students are the best or highest is an important function of schooling, but many contend that the competitiveness among students that results is detrimental to learning and interpersonal relationships (O'Connor, 2002). If ranking is used exclusively, students are more interested in outdoing one another than learning, and this encourages the designation of "winners" and "losers." Most importantly, grades determined by ranking may not indicate how much students have learned. It is possible that students learning little are given high grades because their performance is better than students who learn very little.

The primary reason for grading is to give students, parents, and teachers information about the achievement of goals, objectives, and standards (Marzano, 2006; McMillan, 2008; Stiggins, 2008). Grades are awarded based on student performance that is compared to pre-established levels of competence. This kind of grading has been called *criterion-referenced, standards-based, mastery,* or *absolute.* The focus is on what students know and can do rather than relative standing. Theoretically, all students can obtain the highest grade, and all students can also get a low grade.

A key component of standards-based grading is the determination of what determines designations such as mastery, proficient, or passing. This requires clarity in the criteria that are used to judge student performance and depends on who establishes the criteria. An important development is the use of several levels of performance or benchmarks that can be used to give specific feedback and to rank students (Guskey, 2008; Guskey & Baily, 2001). This kind of grading results in a much more supportive learning environment that fosters positive relationships among students and teachers.

FEEDBACK TO STUDENTS

Grades can be used to provide feedback to students about their performance by showing the ways in which proficiency was demonstrated, and what is needed for a higher grade. This is important for student learning because students have a better understanding of why they received the grade. When provided in sufficient detail, feedback can tell students where there were mistakes, areas of strength and weaknesses, and what subsequent steps are needed to improve their understanding. Feedback is usually provided with prepared narratives that accompany grades, and/or with specific, individualized teacher comments. When feedback is specific, individualized, ongoing, and immediate it has the greatest impact on student learning. In using what is called *formative assessment* feedback is an essential component to help students become more proficient as they learn. General comments such as "good job" or "very good" are not very helpful.

A key distinction with feedback is whether it is primarily evaluative or descriptive (Brookhart, 2004). *Evaluative feedback* is provided in the form of rewards, praise, and positive expressions and non-verbal messages. For young children (grades K–2) these may take the form of stickers, "smiley faces," or treats. For older students (grades 3–12) evaluative feedback is given primarily through letter grades. *Descriptive feedback* is structured to provide the student with information that relates specifically to the learning objectives or standards. This consists of specific, targeted praise and verbal and written messages that show students what they have learned and what remains to be learned, sometimes with an emphasis on student self-assessment and suggestions for further learning.

Many teachers use both kinds of feedback (Brookhart, 2004; McMillan, 2007). For early grades (K-2) students are usually rated with a simple scale, such as satisfactory/unsatisfactory or needs improvement/partially proficient/proficient. When these ratings are used there is usually further information that is more specific. Older students typically receive letter grades, though the trend is for giving more descriptive feedback in addition to letter grades. The standards-based trend in American education has emphasized evaluative grading of all students, regardless of age (McMillan, 2008). Students of all ages can learn to use descriptive feedback to improve learning.

GRADING AND STUDENT MOTIVATION

In one way or another, grading affects student motivation. If grades are viewed as extrinsic rewards students tend to be motivated more by doing what is needed to obtain the reward (or avoid the punishment) than by improving their understanding of the content. In contrast, when the reinforcement focuses on improving knowledge, understanding, or skills, getting the extrinsic reward is viewed as secondary to the intrinsic reward of learning and motivation. This is a mastery orientation. Students with this type of motivation see the value in what is learned, prefer challenging tasks, stay engaged longer, display independent learning, and have positive attitudes toward learning.

EFFORT AND IMPROVEMENT

A longstanding issue in grading is whether to use student effort and improvement as factors that effect final ratings and letter grades. Effort is often assessed by participation, completion of work, extra credit, and teacher observation. It is problematic to include effort as part of a grade that purportedly represents achievement, primarily because it is difficult to measure accurately, and because if included in grades it distorts the meaning of the grade. But effort is important in learning, so it needs to be considered. The recommended approach to assessing effort is to grade and report it separately from achievement (Brookhart, 2004; Guskey & Bailey, 2001; Stiggins, 2008).

Improvement is also difficult to incorporate into grades. While actual learning is represented by how much students' achievement changes, grades typically do not include this factor. However, improvement is often considered in an anecdotal manner and may affect the grade, especially for students who initially demonstrate low performance.

In summary, grading is important for several reasons and will continue to be used. Teacher judgment is always an important factor; there is no completely objective approach. The relationship of grading to learning and motivation is important. Standards-based education models have promoted grades that reflect primarily student achievement, with little or no reflection of effort or improvement. The validity and fairness of grading depends on the match between what grades are claimed to represent and what is actually included in the grade. Feedback is an essential aspect of grading that can have positive benefits for both learning and motivation.

SEE ALSO *Classroom Assessment.*

BIBLIOGRAPHY

Brookhart, S. M. (1994). Teachers' grading: Practice and theory. *Applied Measurement in Education,* 7(4), 279–301.

Brookhart, S. M. (2004). *Grading.* Upper Saddle River, NJ: Pearson Merrill Prentice-Hall.

Guskey, T. R. (Ed.) (2008). *Practical solutions for serious problems in standards-based grading.* Thousand Oaks, CA: Corwin Press.

Guskey, T. R., & Bailey, J. M. (2001). *Developing grading and reporting systems for student learning.* Thousand Oaks, CA: Corwin Press.

Marzano, R. J. (2006). *Classroom assessment and grading that work.* Alexandria VA: Association of Supervision and Curriculum Development.

McMillan, J. H. (2007). *Classroom assessment: Principles and practice for effective instruction* (4th ed.). Boston: Allyn & Bacon.

McMillan, J. H. (2008). *Assessment Essentials for Standard-Based Education* (2nd ed.). Thousand Oaks, CA: Corwin Press.

O'Connor, D. (2002). *How to grade for learning: Linking grades to standards* (2nd ed.). Arlington Heights, IL: SkyLight.

Stiggins, R. (2008). *Introduction to student-involved assessment for learning* (5th ed.). Upper Saddle River, NJ: Prentice-Hall.

James H. McMillan

GRAHAM, SANDRA (HALEY)
1945–

In 1982 Sandra Haley Graham completed her doctorate in educational psychology at the University of California, Los Angeles. Before coming to Los Angeles, Graham graduated from Barnard College (B.A., 1969) and from Columbia University (M.A., 1970). Graham then taught junior high school in Newton, Massachusetts, for three years. Curious about the behavior and academic orienta-

tion of some of her junior high school students, she began to consider the unique socio-cultural experiences and needs of minority children, particularly African American boys.

At UCLA Graham worked with social psychologist Bernard Weiner on attribution theory. Graham's early research used attribution theory as a framework to understand individual, contextual, and interpersonal factors influencing children's achievement motivation. Her research examined how others consciously and unconsciously may send messages to students that may undermine their own sense of self. Graham recalled having such an experience as a college freshman during final exams week. She got a note from the professor urging her to attend an extra help session, and immediately Graham began to doubt herself, wondering why the professor had singled her out for help. She realized at that point that unsolicited offers of help can undermine a person's self-concept by communicating a message of perceived low ability. In *Communicating Low Ability in the Classroom: Bad Things Good Teachers Sometimes Do* (1990), Graham describes how praise and well-intentioned yet unsolicited assistance communicates perceptions of low ability that may reduce children's beliefs in their own efficacy and undermine achievement motivation.

Graham was a pioneer in examining the relationship between the social context and behaviors and how they are linked to children's academic engagement. Research has consistently supported that even the most capable and supported students likely will not achieve their potential if they are not engaged in their academic lessons. Graham noticed that during her work in classrooms that many students who were not engaged academically had behavior problems and were identified as aggressive by their peers and teachers. More troubling, she noticed that these students' predicaments were only negatively amplified by the time spent in principals' offices. Continuing her focus on children's attributions, Graham incorporated into her repertoire an examination of the determinants of aggression among minority male youth. Consistent with her hypothesis, Graham found a link between attribution, affect and action in that aggressive males were more likely than non-aggressive males to assume that a peer's negative behaviors were intentional, become angered, and respond with aggression of their own.

Graham recognized that in order to address the needs of an increasingly diverse population, diversity must be represented and valued in the literature. This lack of diversity was the impetus for her article "Most of the Subjects Were White and Middle Class: Trends in Published Research on African Americans in Selected APA Journals" (1992). This work highlighted the lack of ethnic representation in research of the time and was a call for more representation in research.

Graham never lost sight of her ultimate goals for her research. Her next tasks involved bridging theory and practice by designing and conducting a hostile-attribution retraining program in collaboration with her former student Cynthia Hudley. This line of intervention work included Best Foot Forward, a 32-lesson curriculum focused on enhancing social and academic motivational skills. The social skills component was comprised of two sections, impression management and attributions of intent. The academic motivation component was divided into sections covering intermediate risk taking, goal setting, task focus, and failure attributions. This curriculum has had an overall positive impact on aggressive participants: There were increased adaptive responses to conflict and decreased hostile attributions. Academically, participants made fewer external attributions for failure and evinced more adaptive goal setting. Additionally, teacher ratings of cooperation/motivation and persistence increased significantly for intervention participants. This work highlights the value of theory-guided, multi-method, student-focused research in education.

Graham's research has included topics ranging from students' achievement values, affirmative action, peer victimization and harassment, to the cognitive competence of juvenile offenders. Her 2006 work with Janna Juvonen focused on a longitudinal investigation of the importance of school and classroom ethnic compositions for students' social-psychological adjustment and peer relationships both within middle and high school as well as across the school transition. The body of research from this data identifies requirements for optimal learning and socialization for all students, ethnic minority and non-minority alike. Findings support that ethnic diversity in classrooms and schools reduces students' feelings of victimization and vulnerability as a result of a balance of power among ethnic groups. Contrary to what one might expect, in non-diverse classrooms, victimized students who are members of the ethnic group that is the numerical majority are particularly vulnerable for maladaptive and destructive self-appraisals.

Graham received an Independent Scientist Award funded by the National Institute of Mental Health and an Early Contribution Award from Division 15 (Educational Psychology) of the American Psychological Association. She is a former Fellow at the Center for Advanced Study in the Behavioral Sciences in Stanford, California. As of 2008, Graham was a professor in the Graduate School of Education and Information Studies at the University of California, Los Angeles.

BIBLIOGRAPHY

WORKS BY

Graham, S. (1992). Most of the subjects were white and middle class: Trends in reported research on African-Americans in selected APA journals, 1970–1989. *American Psychologist, 47,* 629–639.

Graham, S. (1994). Motivation in African Americans. *Review of Educational Research, 64,* 55–117.

Graham, S., & Juvonen, J. (1998). Self-blame and peer victimization in middle school: An attributional analysis. *Developmental Psychology, 34,* 587–599.

Graham, S., & Lowery, B. (2004). Priming unconscious racial stereotypes about adolescent offenders. *Law and Human Behavior, 28,* 483–504.

Juvonen, J., Nishina, A., & Graham, S. (2006). Ethnic diversity and perceptions of safety in urban middle schools. *Psychological Science, 17,* 393–400.

April Z. Taylor

GUIDED PARTICIPATION

Guided participation refers to the process by which children actively acquire new skills and problem-solving capabilities through their participation in meaningful activities alongside parents, adults, or other more experienced companions. Guided participation emphasizes the active role of the child in learning and cognitive growth and the complementary role of parents and other caring adults in supporting, assisting, and guiding the child's intellectual development. Support includes both explicit verbal and non-verbal guidance as well as more subtle direction through the arrangement and organization of children's interactions with the environment. Guided participation occurs throughout the course of childhood as children progress from a peripheral and dependent role to one of increased autonomy and responsibility while they strive to master the challenges posed by the surrounding social and cultural milieu (Rogoff, 1990,1998; Gauvain, 2001).

Casual observations of parents interacting with their young children typically offer many examples of guided participation. In the grocery store 3-year-old Alberto holds the shopping list for his mother and studies a box of Cheerios as he sits in the shopping cart. Alberto's older brother, who is 7, is searching for a can of soup that says "tomato." When he has found the soup and they move on to the next aisle, his mother will have another job for each of them. Alberto's mother is skillfully engaging her boys with the shopping, and the children are enjoying themselves in an activity with their mother, feeling competent with the tasks she sets for them as they learn about their social world.

The term guided participation was introduced by the neo-Vygotskian, Barbara Rogoff, in her book *Apprenticeship in Thinking* (Rogoff, 1990) to clarify the nature of children's cognitive development within the framework of sociocultural theory. Vygotsky claimed that the ability to engage in higher mental functions, the distinguishing feature of human psychology, is rooted in social inter-action. Thinking emerges from early social interactions in which the child works with others to solve problems. To insure children's success, more experienced partners direct their assistance to the child's *zone of proximal development* or potential development. This is defined as "the distance between the actual developmental level as determined by independent problem solving and the level of potential development as determined through problem solving under adult guidance or in collaboration with more capable peers" (Vygotsky, 1978, p. 86.). This approach differed from prevailing views of cognitive development since the focus was not on what the child could do alone, but was future oriented, focusing on what could be done with help from others.

The notion of zone of proximal development offered a new way of thinking about verbal interactions and cognitive growth. Because language plays an important role in struc-turing social interactions language and communication pat-terns serve as one type of "scaffold" supporting the child's developing capabilities. A number of researchers looked for evidence demonstrating that appropriate talk on the part of adults supports children's problem-solving success (Berk & Winsler, 1995; Diaz, Neal & Amaya-Williams, 1990; Wood, Bruner, & Ross, 1976).

Guided participation expands upon adult talk as a scaffold by broadening the social context and emphasiz-ing the role of the child in relation to the adult. Gauvain (2001) notes that in this view, "the child is not merely a learner, or a naïve actor who follows the instructions or prompts of the more experienced partner. Rather, the child is a full participant, albeit a participant of a specific type characterized by individual and develop-mentally related skills, interests and resources" (p. 38). Children's participation in the organized routines and practices of the social community as well as engagement in more didactic experiences are all essential to cognitive development.

Some of the most compelling illustrations of guided participation are evident in parents' interactions with young children. These show that guided participation includes two focal processes: "creating bridges" to make connections to new ideas and skills and "structuring children's participation" in activities by creating oppor-tunities for their involvement and through social support and challenge in activities and roles valued in their com-munity (Rogoff et al., 1998).

While examples of adult-child interactions can be found anywhere people interact in meaningful activity, schools are critical contexts for guided participation. Particularly good illustrations can be found in child-centered or learner-centered classrooms where children are actively engaged in learning activities that have been carefully planned by the teacher, as the following exam-ple shows.

Sasha is one of the less skilled writers in her first-grade class. She has completed a drawing and the teacher would like her to write something underneath the com-pleted picture but she doesn't seem to know how to start. Sasha's teacher uses a technique that relies on graphic mediators to support children's early writing attempts. "Let's write something about your picture," the teacher says. Sasha replies, "They are eating at McDonalds." The teacher writes the five words Sasha has dictated on a strip of paper she has placed under the picture. "Do you see what I wrote? I wrote exactly what you said!" The teacher then takes another strip of paper and draws five horizon-tal lines along the edge, one for each of Sasha's words. Then she re-reads the sentences, pointing to the lines. Sasha will copy the sentence, one word on each line.

As Sasha becomes more confident of her writing the teacher will decrease the support she provides. Rather than provide the model, the teacher may simply draw the lines, one for each word, to help Sasha remember her sentence and to guide the spacing of her words. With further practice Sasha will be able to write a sentence independently. Sasha's teacher has supported her partic-ipation in the writing activity through sensitive and indi-vidualized guidance, adjusting the help she offers in response to the needs she observes in Sasha. Sasha and her teacher working together illustrate a child learning in the zone of proximal development.

THE CHILD IN A SOCIAL CONTEXT

The sociocultural view of the Vygotskians and neo-Vygotskians (including the notion of guided participa-tion) differs from more familiar American and western European approaches to learning and development. This is most evident in the assumptions about the nature of the individual as a learner and the nature of the environ-ment in which learning occurs. Classical learning theories such as behavioral analysis or social learning theory emphasize a strong distinction between the learner and the environment. According to these mechanistic perspec-tives, individual learning results from some action of the environment on the individual. For example, the learner is rewarded for new behavior or the learner responds to a model in the environment. The learner is passive, awaiting direction for the environment. Conversely, the environment can be fully planned, and if done correctly, fully shape and direct behavior.

A second view, also at odds with the Vygotskian notion of guided participation, is the organismic approach of many developmental psychologists, including Jean Piaget (1896–

A COMPARISON OF GAGNÉ'S COMPONENT SKILLS APPROACH WITH GUIDED PARTICIPATION APPROACH TO LEARNING

Both Gagné's component skills approach and Rogoff's guided participation approach focus on learning through varied instruction. However, influenced by behaviorism and information processing theories, Gagné suggests that the skills needed for a task could be analyzed and taught as separate components in a hierarchical order from lower skills to higher ones. Indeed, he defines instruction as "the set of planned external events which influence the process of learning and thus promote learning" (1974, p.5). Yet, it still maintains the concept of knowledge acquired by learner, which Rogoff's notion of guided participation shares. Bringing Piaget's cognitive learning and Vygotsky's sociocultural learning theories together, Rogoff views instruction as an interactive process in which the learners participate in the activity guided by sociocultural values and systems. A more skilled peer or adult who jointly participate in the process gradually transfers the responsibility of activity to the learner. Yet, there is no external sequential instruction planned and applied either by instructor or learner. Because guided participation approach is drawn from cross-cultural community contexts, it has been widely applied to natural learning settings in early childhood and occupational learning fields, whereas Gagné's component skills approach has been utilized by instructional and curricular design in both educational and technical-military settings.

BIBLIOGRAPHY

Gagné, R. M. (1974). Educational technology and the learning process. *Educational Researcher, 3(1)*, 3–8.

Rogoff, B. (1995). Observing sociocultural activity in three planes: Participatory appropriation, guided participation and apprenticeship. In J. V. Wertsch, P. del Rio, & A. Alvarez (Eds.), *Sociocultural studies of mind.* Cambridge, UK: Cambridge University Press.

Zeynep Isik-Ercan

1980). From this vantage point, changes within the developing child are critical for understanding changes in children's behavior. These "within child" changes include physical as well as mental structures, and until they are formed learning is constrained. For example, children's expressive language capabilities result from developing physical characteristics, and these are largely separate from environmental or experiential factors.

Both of these orientations assume that the individual and the environment are separable, a notion at odds with guided participation. Rather than focusing on the learner and the guiding "other" as independent, with one being active and the other passive, from a guided participation perspective, both the child and the environment (particularly the social environment) are active. The individuals and the social context in which they function are always linked, and the appropriate focus is the dyadic interaction within the real world. How learning processes work can be understood only by contextualizing the learning activity (see Gauvain, 2001, and Rogoff, 1990, for excellent discussions).

ORIGINS OF GUIDED PARTICIPATION CONCEPT

The construct of guided participation is grounded in the work of Russian psychologist Lev Vygotsky and the approach to cognitive development attributed to him in the early 20th century. This approach is known as the sociocultural perspective. Vygotsky and his colleagues were deeply influenced by the Marxist foundations of the new Soviet Union. One of the early goals of the Soviet regime was to bring literacy to the masses. Language and literacy are both tools of culture, and their use transforms mental capabilities. Vygotsky and his contemporaries were interested in understanding the impact of this effort as well as other aspects of the social environment on children's learning.

Although Vygotsky himself did not use the term guided participation, it shares several key notions with his work. The early socioculturalists were interested in the processes of social mediation and mind. They downplayed the idea of the individual knower separated from a social context; instead, they emphasized the role of the dyad or social group embedded in "activity." At the time, the field of psychology was still in its infancy and very little was known about the mind, society, and the influences of culture upon thinking.

The work of the Russian psychologists was barely known to western European and American scholars. Some of their work was censored within Russia and much of it was not translated into English until the 1970s and 1980s. At the same time American psychologists were looking for alternative ways to conceptualize cognitive development. The shortcomings and limitations of Piaget's model of cognitive development were becoming evident to some. New findings from cross-cultural psychology were raising new questions about the universality of cognitive structures, an idea at the core of Piaget's theory. However, it was not clear how new findings in cross-cultural psychology should be interpreted. Cognitive psychology, rooted in information processing, was also becoming popular, but many researchers were unhappy with the excessively mechanistic, "machine-like" models of human functioning the early information processing models offered.

At the same time that Vygotsky's later work was appearing in the United States other cultural approaches to the study of human behavior were emerging. Some of this work was being conducted by anthropologists. This work was done outside university laboratories and relied instead upon ethnographic and field-based methodologies. These approaches focused on studying behavior as it is situated or as it occurs in the context of the real world. Knowledge was viewed as a highly valued social practice rather than something "in the head" (Lave, 1991). The workplace and communities, and the practices, routines, and talk that occurs within them were an important focus of study because they reveal the understandings and representations of participants (Heath, 1991; Wertsch, 1985).

An illustration of this is the work of Jean Lave. Lave worked in Africa, studying everyday cognition among workers in a tailor shop. She studied the rich repertoire of cognitive skills deployed by tailors in their work at the shop and studied the processes by which novices learn their craft. Tailors are trained through an apprenticeship. The apprentices learn their craft in a busy shop, not in a learning environment separated from world (as is school). They are surrounded by masters and other apprentices all engaged in the target skills at varying levels of expertise. They are expected to participate in activities that contribute directly to the production of actual garments, advancing quickly toward independent, skilled production (Collins, 2006, p. 32).

Lave & Wenger (1991) emphasize the movement of the learner from a peripheral position to a central position in activity. As Collins notes, guided participation and coaching are especially powerful forces for learning in the tailor shop. In the tailor shop, learners were mastering complex tasks that occurred with a web of memorable associations, all in highly meaningful contexts. Learning and teaching were highly situated and highly focused on the specific skills needed for the task.

Apprentices learn domain-specific skills through observation, coaching, and practice. The apprentice then attempts to execute the process with guidance and help from a master through a process of coaching. Collins explains this as follows:

> A key aspect of coaching is guided participation: the close responsive support which the master provides to help the novice complete an entire task, even before the novice has acquired every

skill required. As the learner masters increasing numbers of the component skills the master reduces his or her participation, providing fewer hints and less feedback to the learner. Eventually, the master fades away completely when the apprentice has learned to smoothly execute the whole task. (Collins, 2006, p. 48)

ILLUSTRATIONS OF GUIDED PARTICIPATION

Some educators and cognitive psychologists have extended the ideas of Lave and Wenger (1991) to the design of instructional models useful in elementary and secondary education (Collins, 2006). Developmental psychologists have focused on issues in children's learning and cognitive development, often with a focus on parent-child interactions and the influences of these processes on higher mental capabilities (Cole, 2006; Gauvain, 2001; Rogoff, 1998; Wood, 1998).

Rogoff notes that while Vygotsky was primarily interested in the development of the mind through interpersonal interaction, he placed a great deal of emphasis on the relationship between language and thinking. Rogoff argued that the child was capable of developing thinking even when the culture placed less emphasis upon language and writing. She demonstrated this in her research with Mayans in Mexico, many of whom did not write or engage in excessive amounts of verbal interaction (Rogoff, 1998).

Gauvain (2001) notes that guided participation offers a fuller account of the child's active role in cognitive change, along with the significance of social interactional context. Guided participation can include notions such as scaffolding, coaching, and tutoring, but it also extends to broader views of supportive context for learning and development beyond the adult or more experienced partner. Such a context includes the myriad ways in which adults structure experiences for children and hence enable children to move from positions of peripheral involvement to full involvement within the community (Lave & Wenger, 1991).

Finally, an essential component of guided participation is the notion of *intersubjectivity*. This is the process by which two individuals achieve a joint focus on a problem. Intersubjectivity must be mutual, but even young infants participate in the process. Research shows that infants as young as 3 months can shift focus and visual engagement with their mothers. This type of interaction provides the starting point for intersubjectivity (Bruner, 1985; Tronick, 1982). While adults can establish general goals for children, and the adult can direct and scaffold children's performance, fine tuning and adjustment to the mutual needs of the particular individuals participating in the interaction is needed for optimal learning and meaning making.

CONTRAST WITH TRADITIONAL VIEWS OF LEARNING

The first way guided participation differs from traditional views of learning concerns the assumptions about the nature of the learner. Learning in the traditional sense assumes that the learner can be clearly differentiated from the environmental setting. Instead, it is assumed that children's activity is intimately linked with the social context in which it is occurring. Guidance can be provided in many different ways, close at hand (e.g., the parent leading the child through a game) or more distal, as when a teacher has carefully selected and arranged materials for small groups of children to use in a learning center. In both cases, the adult begins with a general plan, but then adapts and fine tunes the plan in response to the child. The adult works to achieve a level of intersubjectivity with the child. This allows the adult to adjust and fine tune to meet the child optimally. One metaphor is to view the learner as following a path to an endpoint or destination specified by the adult. The child discovers the path. The adult posts trail markers if and when they are needed along the way. The adult cannot post the markers before the journey because the precise path the child will try to pursue is not known.

Second, unlike traditional views of learning, it is assumed that the meaning of behavior for the child will change over time. First efforts may look like play, or childish imitations. Yet these early attempts are the first steps towards mature, independent, self-directed activity. With time, and the appropriate environmental support, children will be able to carry out the behavior more independently. Later, children will carry out the behavior with a different understanding of why they are doing it, why it works, and how it is understood by others.

For example, children's first attempts at writing may be scribbles on a page, following a period of observing others writing with crayons on paper. Later, children will understand that these marks on paper can be used to communicate with others. Initially the action of "writing" is an exploration of the physical world (crayons on paper) and a way to become part of the group of other children marking on papers with the adult. In another year or two, the children will sit at their tables and writing, but it will have an entirely different meaning. Perhaps they will be writing their names.

Third, while traditional views approach learning as a strictly cognitive process, guided participation unifies the cognitive, social, and emotional dimensions of behavior. The focus is the whole person; the social and the emotional cannot be separated from the cognitive (see

Rathunde & Csikszenthemihalyi, 2006). The interpersonal relationship between the partners supports the give and take necessary for children to appropriate and acquire new competencies. While the more knowledgeable partner sets broad goals for the interaction, adaptations to the needs of the individuals must be made. Again, this is particularly evident in parent-child interactions with young children.

PREVALENCE OF GUIDED PARTICIPATION CROSS CULTURALLY

Rathunde & Csikszenthmihalyi (2006) note that the basic processes of guided participation are universal. In all cultural settings, parents and children must arrive at a mutual interpretation of a situation that allows intersubjectivity, or a common focus of attention and shared presuppositions. This is substantiated by findings from cross-cultural research comparing parent-toddler dyads from four cultural settings: Utah; Mayans in Mexico; Turkey; and India. Results demonstrate striking similarities, as well as distinctive differences, across these settings (Rogoff, Mistry, Goncu & Mosier, 1993; Packer, 1993).

The benefits of guided participation are grounded in maintaining the child/learner in the zone of proximal development (Rathunde & Csikszenthmihalyi, 2006; Vygotsky, 1978). A number of studies confirm that guided participation is beneficial to children's development. They note that parents' use of guided participation has been linked to infants' and toddlers' communicative competence, to improvement in children's seriation skills, and to greater exploration of novel objects by 3- to 7-year-olds. Wood and Middleton (1975) note that when mothers adjusted their instruction to their children's needs by guiding at a slightly challenging level and adapting their behavior based upon their children's successes, children performed more successfully on a complex building task. Importantly, it was not the number of interventions the mother made but the quality of the interventions that was important (Rathunde & Csikszenthmihalyi, 2006, p. 498).

Some illustrative examples of guided participation are evident in the research reported by Rogoff and her colleagues (Rogoff, Mistry, Goncu, & Mosier, 1993) comparing U.S. mother-child dyads with Mexican Mayan mother-child dyads. All mother-child dyads were observed in their homes as they interacted with selected materials, such as a baby doll, nesting dolls (a set of wooden dolls that were seriated in size and fit one inside the other) and play dough. Past work has shown that middle-class U.S. parents and others with similar schooling experiences appear to place a greater emphasis on explicit, declarative statements, in contrast to tacit, procedural, and more subtle forms of verbal and non-verbal instruction which are more evident in other cultures.

These differences were evident in a comparison of the mother-child pairs Rogoff and her colleagues studied. They describe a 20-month-old and mother from both communities. Both were first-born boys who played with the nesting dolls in a skilled and interested manner. Both included a counting routine as they interacted with their mothers. For both communities, the interaction was extreme in similar ways: Counting routines are not usual with this toy in either community, and both mothers seemed more concerned with their children's perform-ance than other mothers from their communities. As Rogoff and colleagues (1993) note, the most extreme differences between these two dyads concerned status roles. The American mother would get on the child's level, playing with or teaching her child. The Mayan mother also assisted the child but maintained a difference of status. They also differed in responsiveness and in the subtlety of their verbal and non-verbal communication. The difference is consistent with the American child "being treated as the object of teaching and the Mayan child being responsible for learning" (Rogoff, 1993, p. 246). The researchers comment that Mayan mothers showed readiness to aid in their children's efforts to learn whereas the American caregivers acted as teachers and playmates (see Rogoff et al., 1993, pp. 246–247 for full examples).

EXAMPLES OF INSTRUCTIONAL APPLICATIONS

Guided participation is most evident in interactions involving an adult or other skilled individual with an individual child or a small group of children. Examples can be found across a variety of areas including some early childhood programs (Golbeck, 2001). Detailed dis-cussion for programs in specific practices include *Tools of the Mind* (Bodrova & Leong, 1996), one museum-based science education project (Gelman, Massey & McManus, 1991), several mathematics programs (e.g., Lampert, Rit-tenhouse & Crumbaugh, 1996; Cobb, Wood & Yackel, 1993), and a technique called reciprocal teaching (Palin-scar, Brown & Campione, 1993) which has been used in early reading instruction and elsewhere.

In their discussion of *Tools of the Mind* (an early childhood curriculum), Bodrova and Leong (1996) iden-tify the "structuring of situations" as an illustration. The teacher (or other adult expert) structures tasks into differ-ent levels or sub-goals. Sub-goals are broken down fur-ther or changed as the child and adult are engaged in interaction or in exploring the zone of proximal develop-ment. Guided participation occurs as the adult and child

work together on a problem. The expert may repeat directions or model actions several times. If the teacher is teaching counting, she may limit the number of objects to count or choose objects of only one type to help simplify or structure the task. When the child cannot count ten objects the teacher may drop back to counting only five objects. Such structuring helps the child per-form at the highest level of the zone of proximal develop-ment. The changes the teacher makes cannot be fully planned ahead of time. They occur in response to the child and the assistance the child needs at a particular point in time.

A CLASSROOM ILLUSTRATION

The following is an example of a guided participation approach to teaching within the context of a preschool classroom. Four children and their teacher are sitting at a table in the writing center. They are working together on a book for a child in the class who is in the hospital. Every child will contribute a page and then the pages will be bound together. The children differ in age, previous writing experience, language development, vocabulary knowledge, and fine motor capabilities. The teacher has helped the children individually define writing goals, and the children have told the group of their writing plans. Because the teacher knows each child's independent capabilities she knows how she might extend their writ-ing and help them reach their optimal performance. These children all know one another quite well and they look to one another for help, at least occasionally. The most accomplished writer is proud to help others in this context.

As the teacher chats with the children she is attend-ing closely to their work. One child consistently fails to allow enough room on the paper for his writing. She makes a mark on his paper and suggests he start at that point. She points to the left edge of the paper, near the mark, and says that if he starts near this side he will have plenty of space to write. Another child is a much more sophisticated writer than the others. He requests help spelling. The teacher tells herself she must get a dic-tionary within reach of the writing center. Another child is frustrated with the writing process. The teacher was about to suggest he make a drawing to illustrate his written message, planning to have him return to the writing after he completes a drawing. But before she got the words out, another child turned to him express-ing interest in his work and asked him what he was writing to their friend in the hospital. The frustrated child calmed down and said he was writing about the new truck in the block area. He returned to writing the word "truck" which he was copying from an index card written earlier by the teacher.

One more child is sitting on the teacher's lap. This child is developmentally delayed and functions at the cognitive and emotional level of a toddler. This child has had far less writing experience than the other children. He watches the others. Then the teacher hands him the crayon and they make eye contact. She points to a paper she has placed within his reach, and he drags his crayon across the paper in a slow, careful scribble. He smiles and looks at the teacher. She smiles warmly and says, "We will put this in the book too."

In this example, the teacher is working with the children to create opportunities for guided participation in different ways and at different levels of proximity to the children. She has organized the environment and has helped children identify a broad goal (making the book). This is an important and meaningful activity. She helps individual children define goals for themselves within this larger task. She has arranged the writing center with appropriate materials and brought together a small group of children, creating a social environment of peers as well as herself. She is reaching out beyond the classroom and school world with this activity by reminding the children about their classmate's situation. (They will talk more about the hospital and what it is like to be in the hospital later in the day.) The teacher is also individualizing guidance by sitting at the table watching the children's activity, coaching them as needed and keeping notes on their progress.

SEE ALSO *Cognitive Development: Vygotsky's Theory; Sociocultural Theory.*

BIBLIOGRAPHY

Berk, L. & Winsler, A. (1995) *Scaffolding children's learning: Vygotsky and early childhood education.* Washington D.C.: National Association for the Education of Young Children.

Bodrova, E. & Leong, D.J. (1996). *Tools of the mind: The Vygotskian approach to early childhood education.* Englewood Cliffs, NJ: Merrill.

Bruner, J.S. (1985). Vygotsky: A historical and conceptual perspective. In J.V. Wertsch (Ed.). *Culture, communication and cognition: Vygotskian perspectives* (pp. 21–34). Cambridge, UK: Cambridge University Press.

Cobb, P., Wood, T. & Yackel, E. (1993). Discourse, mathematical thinking and classroom practice. (Ch. 4. pp. 91–119). In E.A. Forman, N.Minnick, & C.A. Stone (eds.). *Contexts for learning: Sociocultural dynamics in children's development.* New York: Oxford University Press.

Cole, M. (2006). Culture and cognitive development in phylogenetic, historical and ontogenetic perspective. In D. Kuhn & R. Siegler (eds.) *Handbook of child psychology, Vol 2, Cognition, perception, and language, 6th ed.* (pp. 636–686). NY: John Wiley & Sons.

Collins, A. (2006). Cognitive apprenticeship. (Ch. 4). In R.K. Sawyer (Ed.). *The Cambridge handbook of the learning sciences.* (pp. 47–60). New York: Cambridge University Press.

Diaz, R.M., Neal, C.J., & Amaya-Williams, M. (1990). The social origins of self-regulation. In L.C. Moll (ed.) *Vygotsky and education: Instructional implications and applications of sociohistorical psychology.* (pp. 127–54). New York: Cambridge University Press.

Gauvain, M. (2001). *The social context of cognitive development.* New York: Guilford Press.

Gauvain, M. & Perez, S. (2005). Parent-child participation in planning children's activities outside of school in European and Latino families. *Child Development, 76*(2), 371–383.

Gelman, R., Massey, C.M., & McManus, M. (1991). Characterizing supporting environments for cognitive development: Lessons from children in a museum. In L.B. Resnick, J.M. Levine, & S.D. Teasley (Eds.), *Perspectives on socially shared cognition* (pp. 226–256). Washington, DC: American Psychological Association.

Golbeck, S. (2001). Instructional models for preschool education: In search of a child regulated/teacher guided pedagogy. In S. Golbeck (Ed.), *Psychological Perspectives on Early Childhood Education: Reframing dilemmas in research and practice.* (pp. 3–34). Mahwah, NJ: Erlbaum Press.

Heath, S. (1991). "It's about winning!" In L. Resnick, J. Levine & S. Teasley (eds.) *Perspectives on socially shared cognition.* (pp. 101–124). Washington DC: American Psychological Association.

Lampert, M., Rittenhouse, P. & Crumbaugh, C. (1996). Agreeing to disagree: Developing sociable mathematical discourse. (Ch. 31, pp. 731–764). In D.Olson & N. Torrance (eds.) *The handbook of education and human development.* Malden, MA: Blackwell Publishers.

Lave, J. (1991). Situated learning. In L. Resnick, J. Levine & S. Teasley (eds.) *Perspectives on socially shared cognition.* (pp. 63–82). Washington DC: American Psychological Association.

Lave, J. & Wenger, E. (1991). *Situated learning: Legitimate peripheral participation.* Cambridge England, Cambridge University Press.

Packer, M.J. (1993). Away from internalization. In E.A. Forman, N. Minnick & C.A.Stone (Eds.) *Contexts for learning: Sociocultural dynamics in children's development.* (pp. 254–267). NY: Oxford University Press.

Palincsar, A.S., Brown, A.L. & Campione, J. (1993). First-grade dialogues for knowledge acquisition and use. (Chapter 2). In E.A. Forman, N. Minnick & C.A. Stone (Eds.) *Contexts for learning: Sociocultural dynamics in children's development.* (pp. 43–57). New York: Oxford University Press.

Piaget, J. (1967/1971). *Biology and Knowledge,* Chicago: University of Chicago Press. Originally published in French, 1967.

Rathunde, K. & Csikszentmihalyi, M. (2006). The developing person: An experiential perspective. Ch. 9. In R. Lerner (ed.). *Handbook of child psychology, Vol 1, Theoretical models of development, 6th ed.* (pp. 465–515). New York: John Wiley & Sons.

Rogoff, B. (1990). *Apprenticeship in thinking: Cognitive development in social context.* New York: Oxford University Press.

Rogoff, B. (1998). Cognition as a collaborative process. In W. Damon (Series Ed.) & D. Kuhn & R.S. Siegler (Vol.Eds.), *Handbook of Child Psychology: Cognition, perception, and language, 5th ed.* (pp. 679–744). New York: Wiley.

Rogoff, B., Mosier, C., Mistry, Jayanthi, & Goncu, A. (1993). Toddlers guided participation with their caregivers in cultural activity. (Ch. 10). In In E.A. Forman, N.Minnick & C.A.Stone (Eds.) *Contexts for learning: Sociocultural dynamics in children's development*. (pp. 230–253). New York: Oxford University Press.

Rogoff, B., Mistry, J., Goncu, A. & Mosier, C. (1993). Guided participation in cultural activity by toddlers and caregivers. *Monographs of the Society for Research in Child Development,* 58 (Serial No. 236).

Rogoff, B., Matusov, E. & White, C. (1996). Models of teaching and learning: Participation in a community of learners (Ch. 18). In D.R. Olson & N. Torrance (eds.) *The handbook of education and human development*. (pp. 388–414) Malden MA: Blackwell Press.

Tronick, E.Z. (Ed.) (1982). *Social interchange in infancy: Affect, cognition, and communication*. Baltimore: University Park Press.

Vygotsky, L. (1978). *Mind in society: The development of higher mental processes*, eds. & trans. M.Cole, V. John-Steiner, S. Scribner & E. Souberman. Cambridge MA: Harvard University Press.

Vygotsky, L. (1934/1986). Thought and language, trans. A. Kozulin, Cambridge, MA: MIT Press.

Wertsch, J. (1985). *Vygotsky and the social formation of mind*. Cambridge MA: Harvard University Press.

Wood, D. (1998). *How children think and learn, 2nd ed*. Malden MA: Blackwell Publishing.

Wood, D., Bruner, J. & Ross, G. (1976). The role of tutoring in problem solving. *Journal of Child Psychology and Psychiatry, 17;* 89–100.

Wood, D.J. & Middleton, D. (1975). A study of assisted problem solving. *British Journal of Psychology, 66,* 181–191.

Susan L. Golbeck

H

HARD OF HEARING

SEE *Deaf and Hard of Hearing..*

HELP-SEEKING

Students commonly seek help in classrooms and elsewhere when they have difficulty learning new material or completing assignments. They ask questions of teachers during whole group activity, of peers when working in small groups, and of family members when completing homework assignments. The help-seeking process in instructional contexts involves cognitive and emotional challenges that are most often public and that arise from the need for students to constantly learn more difficult curricular material. Thus it is important to understand the process and the factors that influence whether students ask for help, as well as responses to such requests, which can determine whether students continue to struggle or ultimately succeed. The explication of help-seeking begins with drawing critical distinctions between seeking help in ways considered more versus less adaptive. The term adaptive help-seeking refers to an action, namely, requesting assistance that both increases the likelihood of immediate success, such as solving a math problem, and that decreases the need for help subsequently (e.g., by learning now to solve such problems). Adaptive help-seeking also can provide short-term stress reduction and the long-term development of healthy self-system resources, such as self-efficacy, self-reliance, and perceived control, which are important for coping with future academic difficulties (Skinner & Zimmer-Gembeck, 2007).

Resources required for adaptive help-seeking (also described as instrumental, strategic, or autonomous; Butler, 1998; Karabenick, 1998; Newman, 2000) include:

1. cognitive competencies—knowing when help is necessary and knowing how to formulate linguistically a specific question that yields exactly what is needed;

2. social competencies—knowing which instructors and classmates are more knowledgeable and can potentially help them and knowing how and when to approach helpers and how and when to thank them;

3. affective-motivational resources—academic and social goals, self-beliefs, and emotions that allow the student to tolerate difficulty and uncertainty and the ego strength required to withstand possibly negative perceptions in the eyes of classmates; and

4. contextual and interpersonal resources—classroom and home affordances such as teachers' goals, grading system, collaborative activities, rules of student-teacher engagement, and teachers' and parents' expectations for the student that support the student's cognitive and social competencies and affective-motivational resources.

Help-seeking can also be viewed as a social strategy of self-regulation that is part of the resources of cognitively, behaviorally, and emotionally engaged learners (e.g., Butler, 1998; Karabenick, 2003, 2004; Karabenick & Knapp, 1991; Karabenick & Newman, 2006; Nelson-Le Gall & Resnick, 1998; Newman, 2000). Any learning strategy or tool can be used more or less effectively. Less adaptive help-seeking (also described as expedient, excessive, or executive) is characterized as effort-avoidant and unnecessary (Nelson-Le Gall & Resnick, 1998); students requesting this sort of assistance typically put forth little effort, ask for help immediately or, for example, want others to supply the answers just before their homework is due. Because learning is not the objective, this form of help-seeking can encourage dependency. Just as seeking help that is excessive may not be in students' long-term best interests, avoiding seeking help when that help is truly necessary also can be non-adaptive (Marchand & Skinner, 2007). The distinction between more and less strategic, or adaptive, forms of help-seeking must be kept in mind when a teacher examines the personal characteristics and features of the learning context that influence its use

FACTORS THAT INFLUENCE THE INCIDENCE AND FORMS OF HELP-SEEKING

Help-seeking has been extensively examined through the lens of achievement goal theory, which distinguishes between mastery-focused and performance-focused approaches to learning (Butler, 1998; Butler & Neuman, 1995; Karabenick, 2003, 2004; Pintrich, 2000; Ryan, Hicks, & Midgley, 1997). Consistently, mastery-oriented students, whose goal is to develop competence, are more likely to seek adaptive help or to work independently when that would be more effective (Butler, 1998). Performance-oriented students, who are concerned about appearing incompetent, are less likely to seek adaptive help. If such students do seek help, it is often for expedient or executive reasons—to avoid work rather than to learn and improve (e.g., Karabenick, 2004).

Students' achievement goals at any point in time are a function both of past experiences and features of the contemporaneous learning context. Achievement goal structure refers to how students construe their classrooms and courses of study in terms of the contextual emphasis on mastery and/or performance goals (Midgley, 2002). Studies using hierarchical modeling have consistently found that students' perceptions of their classes' achievement goal structure influence their tendencies to seek or to avoid seeking help (Midgley, 2002). In elementary school classes, which students collectively judge as more focused on mastery, students are less likely to avoid seeking needed help (Turner, Midgley, Meyer, Gheen, Anderman, Kang, et al., 2002). Although young children are concerned about not appearing incompetent by asking for help, not until middle school do such concerns influence whether they will make a request (Newman, 2000). Presumably as a consequence of increased evaluation pressures that begin with the transition to middle school, performance goal-related classroom characteristics, in addition to perceived classroom mastery goals, affect middle school students' tendencies to seek or to avoid

seeking help (Ryan, Gheen, & Midgley, 1998). By the time students are in college, evidence suggests that classroom performance goals are more relevant than are mastery goals. Students in classes with a focus on performance-avoid goals, in which students are more concerned about not looking incompetent, are likely not to seek needed help; or, if they do seek help, they are likely to be motivated by expedient reasons (Karabenick, 2004).

Cultural factors, in particular, the degree of stress on individualism versus collectivism (Triandis, 1994) can also influence whether and in what situations students seek help. Learners in the United States especially are socialized to idealize individualism and deplore dependency (Fischer & Torney, 1976), values that typically add to the threat posed by help-seeking. In early theories of achievement motivation, seeking help was considered incompatible with individualistic values and, more specifically, an achievement motive (Nelson-Le Gall & Resnick, 1998). Learners in collectivist societies presumably are not as subject to the same prohibitions and should accordingly be less reluctant to seek help. This prediction was verified in that students raised in collectivistic-oriented Israeli kibbutz cultures were more likely to seek help than those socialized in individualistic-oriented cities (Nadler, 1998). Such cultural influences extend to learning and performance in the workplace as well. Evidence indicates that collectivistic (as opposed to individualistic) norms facilitate help-seeking due to the perceived safety that results from collectivist organizational norms (Sandoval & Lee, 2006).

When teachers examine the effects of culture on help-seeking, however, it is important for them to avoid essentialist generalizations. Doing so entails taking into consideration specific characteristics of tasks and learning contexts, such as whether the help is sought in public (as in classrooms), in relative privacy (after class or in faculty offices), or in complete privacy (e.g., delivered by a computer) (Karabenick & Knapp, 1988a). Thus, the cultural differences found by Nadler (1998) depended on whether students worked on tasks individually or in groups. In another example, Japanese collectivistic acculturation stresses cooperation, dependency, and empathy, which facilitate college students' seeking assistance from peers outside the classroom. Due to culturally induced deference to authority in the form of relationships with instructors, however, college students are hesitant to ask their instructors questions in class (Shwalb & Sukemune, 1998). Situational influences have also been demonstrated with U.S. and Australian college students. According to Volet and Karabenick (2006), the more that students are culturally different from their peers, the less likely they are to approach them for needed academic assistance. Importantly, this cultural effect was moderated by classroom factors: The negative relation between cultural difference and help-seeking was less strong when instructors supported intercultural interaction among the students in their classes. This is but one way in which teachers can promote help-seeking in culturally diverse settings.

FOSTERING ADAPTIVE HELP-SEEKING IN THE CLASSROOM

Help-seeking in the classroom is a social transaction (Newman, 1998a). Teachers establish—and students internalize—patterns of classroom discourse. It has been argued that teachers who respond to requests for help with hints and contingent instruction rather than direct and controlling answers help students both to accomplish difficult tasks and to learn that questioning is an invaluable academic strategy. In contrast, teachers who take on the role of expert (e.g., who present to the class an explanation without discussion and then expect students simply to practice) are likely to support overly dependent executive/expedient help-seeking. Moreover, when teachers personally demonstrate that uncertainty can be tolerated—and perhaps even transformed into intellectual challenge—students are likely to realize it is normal not to be able to solve all problems independently. It is expected that when teachers scaffold learning experiences and socialize the normalcy of academic difficulty, need for collaboration, and expectation of answers to their questions, students internalize a personal sense of empowerment and voice (Nelson-Le Gall & Resnick, 1998).

Ideally, students learn in their classrooms the value, usefulness, and skills of questioning that are important for monitoring, diagnosing, and fixing misconceptions. The frequency with which teachers call on students, the amount of time they wait for a response, and the amount and type of praise they give vary from student to student (Eccles & Wigfield, 1985). Teacher feedback helps students know when they need help. Giving no more assistance than is necessary may help students learn the difference between adaptive and non-adaptive (i.e., expedient) help-seeking. Encouraging students to go back to an incorrect problem and try to re-solve it may convince them of the importance of determining if they need further assistance. Additionally, it may be instrumental in students' coming to appreciate the function of questioning and help-seeking in the ongoing process of self-monitoring and learning (Newman, 1998a).

ESTABLISHING CLASSROOM GOALS

Teachers are responsible for establishing classroom goals. When both classroom and personal goals emphasize learning and developing competence, students are especially likely to

seek help adaptively, whereas when both types of goals emphasize performance, students are reluctant to do so. When students who are concerned about grades and looking smart are placed in a learning-goal classroom, they may tend to overcome—and compensate for—their personal tendencies to avoid help. Thus, by being attuned to individual students' personal goals, teachers can assist those who otherwise might give up in the face of adversity (Newman, 1998b). Teachers can also try to accommodate students' social goals (e.g., social affiliation, social status) that influence help-seeking (Ryan et al., 1997). The task of goal-coordinator is not easy, as multiple personal and classroom goals can complement or conflict with one another. Circumstances become even more complex when one considers that teachers' approaches to teaching, in terms of their own achievement goals, can influence how supportive they are perceived to be by students (Butler, 2007). Responsive teachers try to support student autonomy while at the same time satisfying their own personal achievement-related and social goals and need for autonomy within the constraints of public school settings (Butler, 2006).

In classrooms in which teachers share with children their time, energy, and nurturance, students tend to be attentive, effortful, self-expressive, and interested in learning. Teachers who are interpersonally involved with students and attuned to their goals typically establish classrooms that facilitate adaptive help-seeking. When teachers and students are aligned, teachers are especially able to take the student's perspective and understand his or her thinking regarding academic tasks and, based on this understanding, appropriately guide the student's learning. Teachers who are perceived as friendly and caring tend to demonstrate democratic interaction styles, with lines of communication open to students; they listen, ask questions, inquire if students need help, make sure students understand difficult material, and provide help in a non-threatening way (Wentzel, 1997). When they experience this type of communication, students learn that teachers are trustworthy helpers. Low achievers, who often have poor self-perceptions of ability and low self-esteem, typically are reluctant to seek academic help in class (Karabenick & Knapp, 1988b, 1991). For these students, especially, teachers who believe their responsibility is to attend to students' social and emotional as well as academic needs can counter student disengagement (Ryan et al., 1998).

POSITIVE AND NEGATIVE TEACHER INVOLVEMENT

Teacher involvement forms the basis of students' beliefs and feelings about the benefits and costs of help-seeking. Early elementary-age students generally feel comfortable approaching their teacher for assistance because of global, affective traits of the teacher such as niceness and kindness. By the middle of elementary school, students tend to view teachers as helpful when they show an awareness of their problems and give them advice, time, energy, and encouragement to ask questions in class (Newman & Schwager, 1993). In classes in which teachers are perceived as supporting collaboration, student questioning, teacher fairness, respect and caring, middle and high school students are especially likely to seek adaptive help. The same is true at the college level (Karabenick & Sharma, 1994). Just as positive teacher involvement can foster help-seeking, negative involvement can do just the opposite. As early as grade 2, students often are fearful of teachers' negative reactions (e.g., "I think she might think I'm dumb") if they ask for help (Newman & Goldin, 1990). Perceived costs are heightened when teachers are unwilling to help (e.g., "if you had paid attention, you wouldn't need to ask that question"). Children weigh relative benefits and costs of help-seeking, with the integration process becoming increasingly complex over the school years, whereas older students increasingly struggle in deciding what to do when they need academic assistance (Newman, 1990).

In sum, a critically important task for teachers is to help students become self-regulated learners. Clearly, students must learn how to cope with academic difficulty. Teachers can enhance students' personal beliefs about the usefulness of help-seeking as a strategy of self-regulated learning. As noted earlier, when teachers stress the intrinsic value of learning in their classrooms and emphasize understanding and improvement rather than just getting good grades or avoiding bad grades, students are most likely to seek help in an adaptive way. Sensitive and responsive teachers buffer students from factors, such as potential embarrassment, that typically inhibit them from seeking the help they need. How teachers coordinate multiple forms of achievement and social goals, how they accommodate students' personal and interpersonal needs, how they structure task activity, and how they actually engage students through instruction can affect help-seeking and maximize the likelihood of student success.

BIBLIOGRAPHY

Butler, R. (1998). Determinants of help-seeking: Relations between perceived reasons for classroom help-avoidance and help-seeking behaviors in an experimental context. *Journal of Educational Psychology, 90,* 630–644.

Butler, R. (2006). An achievement goal perspective on student help-seeking and teacher help giving in the classroom: Theory, research, and educational implications. In S. A. Karabenick & R. S. Newman (Eds.), *Help-seeking in academic settings: Goals, groups, and contexts* (pp. 15–44). Mahwah, NJ: Erlbaum.

Butler, R. (2007). Teachers' achievement goal orientations and associations with teachers' help-seeking: Examination of a novel approach to teacher motivation. *Journal of Educational Psychology, 99*(2), 241–252.

Butler, R., & Neuman, O. (1995). Effects of task and ego achievement goals on help-seeking behaviors and attitudes. *Journal of Educational Psychology, 87,* 261–271.

Eccles, J. S., & Wigfield, A. (1985). Teacher expectations and student motivation. In J. B. Dusek (Ed.), *Teacher expectations* (pp. 185–226). Hillsdale, NJ: Erlbaum.

Fischer, P. L., & Torney, J. V. (1976). Influence of children's stories on dependency: A sex-typed behavior. *Developmental Psychology, 12*(5), 489–490.

Karabenick, S. A. (2003). Help-seeking in large college classes: A person-centered approach. *Contemporary Educational Psychology, 28,* 37–58.

Karabenick, S. A. (2004). Perceived achievement goal structure and college student help-seeking. *Journal of Educational Psychology, 96,* 569–581.

Karabenick, S. A. (Ed.) (1998). *Strategic help-seeking: Implications for learning and teaching.* Mahwah, NJ: Erlbaum.

Karabenick, S. A., & Knapp, J. R. (1988a). Effects of computer privacy on help-seeking. *Journal of Applied Social Psychology, 18*(6), 461–472.

Karabenick, S. A., & Knapp, J. R. (1988b). Help-Seeking and the need for academic assistance. *Journal of Educational Psychology, 80,* 406–408.

Karabenick, S. A., & Knapp, J. R. (1991). Relationship of academic help-seeking to the use of learning strategies and other instrumental achievement behavior in college students. *Journal of Educational Psychology, 83*(2), 221–230.

Karabenick, S. A., & Newman, R. S. (Eds.) (2006). *Help-seeking in academic settings: Goals, groups, and contexts.* Mahwah, NJ: Erlbaum.

Karabenick, S. A., & Sharma, R. (1994). Perceived teacher support of student questioning in the college classroom: Its relation to student characteristics and role in the classroom questioning process. *Journal of Educational Psychology, 86,* 90–103.

Marchand, G., & Skinner, E. (2007). Motivational dynamics of children's academic help-seeking and concealment. *Journal of Educational Psychology, 99,* 65–82.

Midgley, C. (Ed.) (2002). *Goals, goal structures, and patterns of adaptive learning.* Mahwah, NJ: Erlbaum.

Nadler, A. (1998). Relationship, esteem, and achievement perspectives on autonomous and dependent help-seeking. In S. A. Karabenick (Ed.), *Strategic help-seeking: Implications for learning and teaching* (pp. 61–93). Mahwah, NJ: Erlbaum.

Nelson-Le Gall, S., & Resnick, L. (1998). Help-seeking, achievement motivation, and the social practice of intelligence in school. In S. A. Karabenick (Ed.), *Strategic help-seeking: Implications for learning and teaching* (pp. 39–60). Hillsdale, NJ: Erlbaum.

Newman, R. S. (1990). Children's help-seeking in the classroom: The role of motivational factors and attitudes. *Journal of Educational Psychology, 82,* 71–80.

Newman, R. S. (1998a). Adaptive help-seeking: A role of social interaction in self-regulated learning. In S. A. Karabenick (Ed.), *Strategic help-seeking: Implications for learning and teaching* (pp. 13–37). Mahwah, NJ: Erlbaum.

Newman, R. S. (1998b). Students' help-seeking during problem solving: Influences of personal and contextual achievement goals. *Journal of Educational Psychology, 90,* 644–658.

Newman, R. S. (2000). Social influences on the development of children's adaptive help-seeking: The role of parents, teachers, and peers. *Developmental Review, 20,* 350–404.

Newman, R. S., & Goldin, L. (1990). Children's reluctance to seek help with schoolwork. *Journal of Educational Psychology, 82,* 92–100.

Newman, R. S., & Schwager, M. T. (1993). Student perceptions of the teacher and classmates in relation to reported help-seeking in math class. *Elementary School Journal, 94,* 3–17.

Pintrich, P. R. (2000). An achievement goal theory perspective on issues in motivation terminology, theory, and research. *Contemporary Educational Psychology, 25,* 92–104.

Ryan, A., Gheen, M., & Midgley, C. (1998). Why do some students avoid asking for help? An examination of the interplay among students' academic efficacy, teachers' social-emotional role, and classroom goal structure. *Journal of Educational Psychology, 90,* 528–535.

Ryan, A. M., Hicks, L., & Midgley, C. (1997). Social goals, academic goals, and avoiding help in the classroom. *Journal of Early Adolescence, 17,* 152–171.

Sandoval, B. A., & Lee, F. (2006). When is seeking help appropriate? Now norms affect help-seeking in organizations. In S. A. Karabenick & R. S. Newman (Eds.), *Help-seeking in academic settings: Groups, goals, and contexts* (pp. 151–173). Mahwah, NJ: Erlbaum.

Shwalb, D. W., & Sukemune, S. (1998). Help-seeking in the Japanese college classroom: Cultural, developmental, and social-psychological influences. In S. A. Karabenick (Ed.), *Strategic help-seeking: Implications for learning and teaching* (pp. 141–170). Mahwah, NJ: Erlbaum.

Skinner, E., & Zimmer-Gembeck, M. (2007). The development of coping. *Annual Review of Psychology, 58,* 119–144.

Triandis, H. (1994). Theoretical and methodological approaches to the study of collectivism and individualism. In U. Kim, H. Triandis, C. Kagitcibasi, C., S-C. Choi, & G. Yoon (Eds.), *Individualism and collectivism: Theory, method and applications: Cross-cultural research and methodology series* (pp. 41–51). Thousand Oaks, CA: Sage.

Turner, J. C., Midgley, C., Meyer, D. K., Gheen, M., Anderman, E. M., Kang, Y., et al. (2002). The classroom environment and students' reports of avoidance strategies in mathematics: A multimethod study. *Journal of Educational Psychology, 94,* 88–106.

Volet, S., & Karabenick, S. A. (2006). Help-seeking in cultural context. In S. A. Karabenick & R. S. Newman (Eds.), *Help-seeking in academic settings: Groups, goals, and contexts* (pp. 117–150). Mahwah, NJ: Erlbaum.

Wentzel, K. R. (1997). Student motivation in middle school: The role of perceived pedagogical caring. *Journal of Educational Psychology, 89,* 411–419.

Stuart A. Karabenick
Richard S. Newman

HIGH SCHOOL, TRANSITION TO

SEE *School Transitions: High School.*

HIGH STAKES TESTING

High stakes testing is so named because the test outcomes are used to make important, often life-altering decisions. Such decisions may include the denial of a high school diploma, the repetition of a grade, the labeling of students and schools in pejorative ways, the withholding of funding, and even the closing of a school. Students who may do well in school all year but fail a high stakes test may be required to attend summer school and take the test again or spend another year in the same grade. Local newspapers routinely publish the results of high stakes tests, which can cause a range of reactions from pride to shame among students, school staffs, and parents.

ORIGINS

High stakes testing in schools had its origin in the 1980s with the publication of *A Nation at Risk* (National Commission on Excellence in Education, 1983) issued by the Reagan administration. The report stated that public schools in the United States lacked rigorous standards and were failing. It also attacked the social promotion of students. The Business Roundtable (BRT) initiated a campaign to return curriculum to the so-called basics (such as phonics), require schools to meet high standards, and be held accountable. These reforms were to be guided by experts from the business world who understood the economy (Johnson, Johnson, Farenga, & Ness, 2008).

When the Louisiana state legislature appointed a School Accountability Advisory Committee in 1998, the state became the first in the nation to inaugurate high stakes testing with harsh consequences. Fourth- and eighth-graders were targeted for testing, and students who did not score at predetermined performance levels were to spend another year in the same grade. Low performing schools were to be sanctioned with increasingly severe measures. Within a few years, 7 states based grade promotion on a statewide test score, and by 2008, 24 states were anticipated to require passing a statewide test to graduate from high school (Education Week, 2006). Additional consequences of test results include monetary rewards to high-test-performing schools in 16 states; turning allegedly failing schools over to private managers in 14 states; sanctioning, with varying penalties, low-performing schools in 28 states; and allowing closure of low-performing schools in 10 states (Johnson & Johnson, 2006).

Public Law 107–110, called the No Child Left Behind (NCLB) bill, was signed into law on January 8, 2002, by President George W. Bush. All children, regardless of physical or mental challenges, race, socioeconomic status, or English language proficiency are to have an equal and significant opportunity to attain a high-quality public education. NCLB mandates the annual testing—using each state's achievement test—of every child in grades three through eight. The law requires that by 2014, every child

461

must achieve proficiency in reading and math as measured by the high stakes tests, but it leaves the definition of proficiency to each state. NCLB links standardized test performance to sanctions for public schools that fail to make adequate yearly progress (AYP) by each subgroup of students based on special needs, minority status, English language proficiency, and socioeconomic status. Sanctions include the requirement that every school make public the achievement scores of each student subgroup. Schools that do not achieve AYP must help their students, who wish to do so, transfer to another school and pay the students' transportation costs. Schools are required to provide special tutoring for low-performing students, typically done through contracts with private tutoring firms. In extreme cases, sanctions may call for the replacement of an entire school staff (Schrag, 2007). No Child Left Behind has become synonymous with high stakes testing even though other elements of the law focus on teacher qualifications and professional development.

ARGUMENTS OF HIGH STAKES TESTING PROPONENTS

High stakes testing, as exemplified by NCLB, is highly controversial. Proponents of NCLB claim that the law has focused a spotlight on the plight of underserved, mostly minority, high poverty students. Holding schools accountable for all children, pinpointing failing schools, and allowing poor children to have access to amenities such as private tutoring, is sensible and just. The testing allows teachers to discuss low-performing students and subgroups and generate instructional improvements (Gunning, 2008). Proponents of high stakes testing believe that high standards and high stakes tests are essential to motivate students, teachers, and administrators to work ever harder to boost achievement. High stakes testing, proponents believe, will ensure that high school graduates will have the academic skills requisite for success in the workplace. For high stakes testing to be effective, the consequences of low achievement must be severe—hence, the use of sanctions such as repeating a grade, withholding a high school diploma, or school closure.

ARGUMENTS OF HIGH STAKES TESTING CRITICS

Critics of high stakes testing contend that NCLB mandates for proficiency in reading and mathematics have meant the de-emphasis or elimination of art, music, oral language, history, science, physical education, and even recess in many public schools, especially in low-performing, underserved schools. Creativity, innovation, critical thinking, discussion, and debate are things of the past in these schools, having been replaced by lock-step, repetitive test-preparation activities. The Center for Education Policy

(Dillon, 2006) reports that 70% of the nation's school districts have eliminated courses to make more time for math and reading.

High stakes test opponents argue that test scores are more likely related to socioeconomic status than to school test preparation. Standardized tests punish poor, minority, special education, and non-English-speaking students in underfunded schools who must compete with middle class and wealthy students in well-funded schools on the same high stakes tests. Children who never have traveled, have few books and resources in their homes, are hungry, ill-clad, in pain or in poor health, and who live with violence cannot be expected to make the same progress or be at the same test level as children whose life circumstances are the opposite. With high stakes testing, less privileged students must endure unwarranted stress and humiliation while being denied a well-rounded education such as that enjoyed by students in affluent or private schools (Johnson et al., 2008).

Measurement issues have been another cause for concern about high stakes testing. Group standardized tests inaccurately assess individual strengths and weaknesses, and the results are unreliable. Flaws in test design and scoring have created serious problems and have led to the recall of test results in Massachusetts, Nevada, and Georgia. A scoring error on PRAXIS, a teacher certification exam, failed 4,100 prospective teachers nationwide (Johnson & Johnson, 2006).

There is ample evidence that what is measured on state high stakes tests often does not transfer to other measurements or situations (Amrein & Berliner, 2002). Learning that does not transfer from one situation to another frequently is shallow learning.

A comparison of percentages of students achieving proficiency on state tests with the federally administered National Assessment of Educational Progress (NAEP) shows wide disparities by state. On the Mississippi state test, nearly 90% of test takers were judged proficient, but on the NAEP, fewer than 20% were shown to be proficient. In Missouri, the gap between the state and NAEP results was only 2% (Wallis & Steptoe, 2007). Such disparities illuminate the lack of transfer but also the variability in state standards and state test expectations.

Lower state standards and lower target scores to determine proficiency give the appearance that a state is doing well. In 2005, 19 states reported that 80% or more test takers scored at the proficient level on the state tests. In contrast, in only one state, Massachusetts, did more than 40% of test takers score at the proficiency level on the NAEP. Critics question what proficiency under NCLB really means. High stakes testing is corrupting American education according to Berliner and Nichols (2007), who provide examples of administrators and teachers cheating by falsifying test data.

When school staffs' reputations, salaries, and job retention are related to student test performance, such corruption sometimes happens.

Other criticisms of high stakes testing and NCLB include the increasing numbers of school dropouts as schools focus on the middle range of students to the neglect of the lowest performers (Viadero, 2007). High stakes testing has been pushed on ever younger children, including preschoolers and, under the Bush administration, Head Start children. State and federal mandated testing has led to a financial bonanza for corporations in the testing, tutoring, and publishing industries as billions of dollars are spent to raise test scores.

High stakes testing has prompted extraordinary practices. In Florida, where test secrecy is sacrosanct, a 12-year-old who gained access to a test was charged with a felony (*Education Week*, 2004). In Louisiana a multiple-district pep rally for the state test included 800 band members, 400 cheerleaders, and a flyover by Navy pilots (Nelson, 2003). The New York City school district inaugurated a plan to pay students up to $500 for doing well on mandated tests (Medina, 2007).

While proponents and opponents of high stakes testing do battle with each other, the testing continues, and as of 2008, No Child Left Behind remains the law of the land. Only time will tell if the education pendulum swings away from the standards, testing, and accountability movement.

SEE ALSO *Accountability.*

BIBLIOGRAPHY
Amrein, A. L., & Berliner, D. C. (2002). High-stakes testing, uncertainty, and student learning. *Education Policy Analysis Archives, 10*(18), 1–69.

Berliner, D. C., & Nichols, S. L. (2007). *Collateral damage: How high-stakes testing corrupts America's schools.* Cambridge, MA: Harvard Education Press.

Dillon, S. (2006, March 26). Schools cut back subjects to push reading and math. *New York Times,* 1, 22.

Education Week (2004, March 17). Fla. student charged with crime for having copy of state test, 4.

Education Week (2006, January 5). *Quality counts 2006: A decade of standards-based education.* Bethesda, MD: Education Week.

Gunning, T. J. (2008). *Creating literacy instruction for all students* (6th ed.). Boston: Pearson.

Johnson, D. D., & Johnson, B. (2006). *High stakes: Poverty, testing, and failure in American schools* (2nd ed.). Lanham, MD: Rowman & Littlefield.

Johnson, D. D., Johnson, B., Farenga, S. J., & Ness, D. (2008). *Stop high-stakes testing: An appeal to America's conscience.* Lanham, MD: Rowman & Littlefield.

Medina, J. (2007, June 19). New York City schools plan to pay for good test scores. *New York Times,* A21.

National Commission on Excellence in Education. (1983). *A nation at risk: The imperative for educational reform.* Washington, DC: U.S. Government Printing Office.

Schrag, P. (2007). Schoolhouse crock: Fifty years of blaming America's educational system for our stupidity. *Harper's Magazine, 315*(1888), 36–44.

Viadero, D. (2007, August 1). Study: Low, high fliers gain less under NCLB. *Education Week,* 7.

Wallis, C., & Steptoe, S. (2007, June 4). How to fix No Child Left Behind. *Time Magazine,* pp. 34–41.

Dale D. Johnson
Bonnie Johnson

HOME–SCHOOL DISSONANCE

Students experience home-school dissonance when their integrity and adequacy are threatened by real or perceived differences between home/self and what is valued within the school context. Home-school dissonance includes both cognitive and affective components. It incorporates an awareness of real or perceived discrepancies between home culture—a reflection of who one is—and what is valued in the school context and the negative emotional reaction that accompanies this awareness (Kumar, 2006). Phelan and colleagues (Phelan, Davidson, & Yu, 1998) defined these discrepancies as borders between students' selves—thoughts, feelings and adaptation strategies—and the worlds of home, school, and peers, all located within students' larger community. Each "world" is characterized by values, beliefs, expectations, actions, and emotional responses that may be consonant or dissonant across contexts. Not all differences necessarily lead to feelings of conflict and dissonance. It is the threat to self posed by perceived cultural differences and discrepancies, not the differences *per se* that arouses dissonance.

ANTECEDENTS OF HOME-SCHOOL DISSONANCE

Home-school dissonance is often a consequence of contact between the school culture, reflecting mainstream culture, and home or community culture. Dissonance results from the differing demands placed on students as they negotiate the norms, values, and behavior expectations of both contexts (Kumar, 2006; Phelan, Davidson, & Yu, 1998). Many immigrant and minority children, and adolescents from ethnically and economically diverse backgrounds, perceive differences between home and school cultures as insurmountable (Suarez-Orosco & Suarez-Orosco, 2002). Others may negotiate the boundaries between the two even when norms, values, and behavior expectations are dissonant—though this may come at great psychological cost (Gibson, 1991; Arunkumar, Midgley, & Urdan, 1999; Phelan, Davidson, & Yu, 1998).

Adolescents' feeling of home-school dissonance is a function of the degree of polarization in values and normative expectations between contexts (Ward, Bochner, & Furham, 2001). Adolescents' subjective culture—including, among others, beliefs about parents' academic and behavioral expectations, occupational aspirations, and normative attributions for school success and failure—shapes their behavioral choices and motivational orientation toward learning and achievement. Immigrant and minority adolescents may find such choices problematic when family culture does not align with what is considered normative in mainstream culture.

Home-school dissonance often arises because adolescents feel that qualities they possess are devalued in school and society (Graham & Hudley, 2005). For example, the cultural markers associated with African American youth—dress, music, and language—are often equated with poor performance (Ladson-Billings, 1995) and classroom misbehavior (Spencer. 1999). Along similar lines, several European countries look upon *hijab* (head scarves worn by Muslim girls and women) with disfavor and preclude students from wearing *hijab* in schools. Sometimes students belonging to groups that are numerical minorities in school or whose phenotypic characteristics differ from mainstream society feel marginalized because they do not "fit in" with peers and others (Brewer, 2003).

By studying acculturation patterns of immigrant minorities to host societies, researchers highlight the importance of intercultural relations within the school context to understand adolescents' experiences of home-school dissonance (Montreuil & Bourhis, 2004). Group membership is the lens through which individuals in a culturally pluralistic society view one another. Thus when students categorize themselves as minority or others within the school context, the probability of stereotyping, ethnocentrism, intergroup clashes, and competition increases (Tajfel & Turner, 1979). Mainstream members are more likely to adopt a segregationist orientation toward immigrants whose culture differs considerably from the mainstream. Ethnic group relations in schools parallel ethnic and minority immigrant group inclusion or exclusion within American society (Montreuil & Bourhis, 2004). In fact, cultural minority students in more integrated school environments report greater exclusion and ostracism than students in more homogenous school environments. Friendship patterns in schools are also based on the inclusion or exclusion of a student's racial, ethnic, or national group.

While some experiences of home-school dissonance are tied closely to students' racial, ethnic, religious, and socioeconomic background, others cut across cultural lines. Students often feel marginalized when not performing well in school and when they feel disengaged from an environment designed to promote learning (Kumar, Gheen, & Kaplan, 2002). Kumar (2006) conducted a growth-curve study examining stability and change in adolescents' experiences of home-school dissonance during the elementary-to-middle school transition and found that dissonance increases when students perceive an evaluative classroom environment and move into middle schools that encourage social comparison and competition among students. These findings are supported by interviews conducted with seventh-grade students who reported high home-school dissonance. No two students experienced dissonance for all the same reasons. Interviews indicated that lack of material resources and cultural affiliations promoted feelings of dissonance in many students. Additionally, students described school factors, including emphasis on relative ability in the classroom and the nature of student-teacher relationships, as contributing to home-school dissonance.

Beliefs and behaviors of significant others in both contexts may also trigger feelings of home-school dissonance among students. Teachers' attitudes toward students, together with the ways they communicate expectations, influence students' beliefs about themselves, motivations and behaviors (Oakes, 1985). Evidence indicates that teachers reflect society's deep ambivalence toward minority and immigrant students in their attitudes towards these students (Suarez-Orosco & Suarez-Orosco, 2002). If teachers view cultural minority students as lazy, less intelligent, and more prone to trouble, such expectations may exert a profound effect on students' beliefs about school, motivation and behavior—thereby exacerbating feelings of dissonance.

PSYCHOLOGICAL CONSEQUENCES OF HOME-SCHOOL DISSONANCE

There is a psychological cost associated with feeling caught between two cultures, marginalized, powerless, and socially alienated (Rosenberg, 1962; Ward, Bochner, & Furham, 2001). High-dissonance fifth-grade students reported feeling angrier, engaged in more self-deprecation, had lower self-esteem, were less hopeful about the future, felt less academically efficacious, and had a lower GPA than low-dissonance students. Additionally, high-dissonance students experienced a greater decline in GPA and smaller decline in anger than low-dissonance students when moving from elementary school to the larger, more complex middle-school environment (Arunkumar et al., 1999). Home-school dissonance, controlling for ethnicity, is also a significant predictor of skeptical beliefs about the value of school (Kumar, Gheen, & Kaplan, 2002) and lower levels of school belonging (Kumar, 2006). Poor intercultural adjustment is associated with depression, anxiety, and poor emotion regulation among students of different ages (Buddington, 2002).

For some adolescents and young adults from immigrant and minority groups the sociocultural differences between classroom and family culture norms interfere with their ability to adjust to school environments (Lafromboise, Hardin, Coleman, & Gerton, 1993). Tharp and his colleagues (Vogt, Jordan, & Tharp, 1993) demonstrated that traditional American classroom structure (independent seat work, whole-class instruction) interfered with Hawaiian students' learning. Changes in classroom structure that incorporated group learning centers and peer collaboration similar to their community's emphasis on sharing, cooperation, and group needs facilitated adjustment to school. Gibson's ethnography (1991) demonstrated that Punjabi adolescents not joining majority-dominated school activities were made to feel culturally inferior by their peers. Ogbu (1987) attributes poor school performance, low motivation, and high dropout rate among African Americans and non-immigrant Latinos as resistance to mainstream institutions. Research also indicates that the aggressive coping attitude of African American youth results from the dilemma posed by competing allegiances and socialization contexts that are daily stressors. This reactive coping mechanism is seen as a response to negative peer and teacher perceptions and an inferred, undervalued sense of self (Spencer, 1999).

Both negative and positive stereotyping regarding group intellectual capacity contribute to dissonance. Experimental studies on stereotype threat demonstrate that awareness of negative stereotypes regarding one's groups' intellectual capacity results in disidentification with academic achievement (Steele 1997) and dropping out of school (Osborne & Walker, 2006), because group members perceive these attributes as stable, internal, and uncontrollable (Reyna, 2000). It is equally likely that the "model minority" stereotype associated with Asian American adolescents often sets them up for failure. Many low-performing, model-minority adolescents feel ashamed of poor performance and inability to fulfill the stereotype. Consequently, they are reluctant to seek academic support, thereby perpetuating their academic struggles (Lee, 1996).

AMELIORATING DISSONANCE IN SCHOOL AND CLASSROOM PRACTICES

Schools and teachers who want to promote the well-being of students at risk for experiencing dissonance need to face the challenge of minimizing the saliency of differences among students and work to foster learning within an inclusive and empowering environment. This can be accomplished at the individual level by requiring teachers and school personnel to examine their own beliefs and behaviors toward culturally diverse students and at the systems level by restructuring school practices in ways that help ameliorate home-school dissonance.

For quite some time educators have stressed the need to encourage teachers to critically examine, and overcome their personal prejudices and biases so that they may be fair and equitable in their dealings with students. As early as 1971 Geneva Gay, a prominent multicultural education scholar, developed a model for educating prospective teachers. The model included three components for multicultural education: *knowledge*, whereby "teachers become literate about ethnic group experiences" (p. 34); *attitudes* "to help teachers examine their existing attitudes and feelings towards ethnic, racial, and cultural differences" (p. 43); and *skills* "to translate their knowledge and sensitivities into school programs, curricular designs, and classroom instructional practices" (p. 48). The 2006 revisions of the National Council for Accreditation of Teacher Education (NCATE) guidelines advocate the deliberate articulation of multicultural values into all the standards that define quality teaching; a focus on the ideals of fairness; the utilization of teaching and learning strategies that permit all students to learn; and the application of knowledge as it relates to students, families, and communities.

The social reconstructionist view of multicultural education takes a systems approach and calls for major school policy reform that will promote equity among students (Banks & Banks, 1997). It urges schools to dismantle policies and practices promoting inequality—such as tracking and ability grouping—and replace them with policies and practices that empower students to acquire the knowledge and skills necessary to function effectively. This, according to Banks & Banks (1997), requires integration of multicultural curricula into all subject areas; an understanding among teachers that all knowledge is culturally constructed (and thus necessitates the adoption of culturally relevant pedagogical approaches); and the reduction of prejudice and improvement of inter-group relationships in the learning context. In essence, social reconstructionists' vision of education through equity pedagogy and culturally responsive teaching requires redefinition of school culture that students find empowering, validating, and inclusive.

The understanding of school and classroom culture in a way that can help ameliorate home-school dissonance and foster a sense of belonging to school, can be advanced by achievement goal theory, a social cognitive theory of motivation that conceptualizes the relationships between school learning environments and students' motivational, emotional, and academic well-being. Achievement goal theory defines school practices that encourage intellectual development through effort and engagement in challenging activities as "mastery-focused," and describe school practices in which comparison and competition are the norm as "performance-focused" (Maehr & Midgley, 1996). For instance, practices such as public honor rolls or special privileges based upon academic standing send important messages to students regarding what constitutes success in a given school (Maehr & Midgley, 1996). In a performance-focused school environment, the nature of the task is not the issue; rather, the focus is on student performance, particularly relative to others. Thus, one of the main distinctions between mastery- and performance-focused environments is a focus on self-improvement versus a focus on the self in comparison to others in the environment.

Mastery-focused learning environments are designed to create a community of learners in an atmosphere of mutual respect. An environment that promotes respect for and openness toward others' ideas and ways of thinking is more likely to encourage students and teachers to be less judgmental of others whose ideas, values, and cultural norms are different from theirs. Thus, a mastery-focused academic culture, unlike a performance-focused one, is beneficial for students at risk of experiencing home-school dissonance (Kumar, 2006).

Research across disciplines indicates that home-school dissonance produces negative consequences. Though not all minority students experience home-school dissonance, they are at risk if they perceive insurmountable discrepancies between the two contexts. Nevertheless, mastery-focused school and classroom environments can be created that ameliorate feelings of home-school dissonance and emphasize differences as a source of opportunity. This is best done exposing students to multiple cultural perspectives and contrasting systems of thought and affect, thus creating cognitive flexibility and tolerance.

SEE ALSO *Bilingual Education; Multicultural Education; School Belonging.*

BIBLIOGRAPHY

Arunkumar, R., Midgley, C., & Urdan, T. (1999). Perceiving high or low home-school dissonance: Longitudinal effects on adolescent emotional and academic well being. *Journal of Research on Adolescence, 4,* 441–466.

Banks, J., & Banks, M. C. (1997). Equity pedagogy and multicultural education. In J. A. Banks (Ed.), *Educating citizens in a multicultural society* (pp. 78–87). New York: Teachers College Press.

Brewer, M. B. (2003). Optimal distinctiveness, social identity, and the self. In M. R. Leary & J. P. Tangney (Eds.), *Handbook of self and identity* (pp. 480–491). New York: Guilford Press.

Buddington, S. (2002). Acculturation, psychological adjustment (stress, depression, and self-esteem) and academic achievement of Jamaican immigrant college students. *International Social Work, 45,* 447–464.

Gay G. (1971). Ethnic minority studies: How widespread? How successful? *Educational Leadership, 29,* 108–112.

Gibson, M. A. (1991). Minority and schooling: Some implications. In M. A. Gibson & J. U. Ogbu (Eds.), *Minority Status and schooling: A comparative study of immigrant and involuntary minorities* (pp. 357–381). New York: Garland.

Graham, S., & Hudley, C. (2005). Race and ethnicity in the study of motivation and competence. In A. J. Elliot & C. S. Dweck (Eds.), *Handbook of competence and motivation* (pp. 392–413). New York: Guilford Press.

Kumar, R. (2006). Students' experiences of home-school dissonance: The role of school academic culture and perceptions of classroom goal structures. *Contemporary Educational Psychology, 31,* 253–279.

Kumar, R., Gheen, M. H., & Kaplan, A. (2002). Goal structures in the learning environment and students' disaffection from learning and schooling. In C. Midgley (Ed.), *Goals, Goal Structures, and Patterns of Adaptive Learning* (pp. 142–173). Hillsdale, NJ: Erlbaum.

Ladson-Billings, G. (1995). But that's just good teaching! The case for culturally relevant pedagogy. *Theory into Practice, 34,* 159–165.

Lafromboise, T., Coleman, H. L. K., & Gerton, J. (1993). Psychological impact of biculturalism: Evidence and theory. *Psychological Bulletin, 114,* 395–412.

Lee, S. J. (1996). *Unraveling the "model minority" stereotype: Listening to Asian American youth.* New York: Teachers College Press.

Maehr, M. L., & Midgley, C. (1996). *Transforming school cultures.* Boulder, CO: Westview, Harper Collins.

Montreuil, A., & Bourhis, R. Y. (2004). Acculturation orientations of competing host communities toward valued and devalued immigrant. *International Journal of Intercultural Relations, 6,* 507–532.

Oakes, J. (1985). *Keeping track: How schools structure inequality.* New Haven: Yale University Press.

Ogbu, J. U. (1987). Variability in minority school performance: A problem in search of an explanation. *Anthropology and Education Quarterly, 18,* 312–334.

Osborne, J. W., & Walker, C (2006). Stereotype threat, identification with academics, and withdrawal from school: Why the most successful students of color might be most likely to withdraw. *Educational Psychology, 26,* 563.

Phelan, P. K., Davidson, A. L., & Yu, H. C. (1998). *Adolescents' worlds: Negotiating family, peer, and school.* New York: Teachers College Press.

Reyna, C. (2000). Lazy, dumb, or industrious: When stereotypes convey attribution information in the classroom. *Educational Psychology Review, 12,* 85–110.

Rosenberg, M. (1962). The dissonant religious context and emotional disturbance. *American Journal of Sociology, 78,* 1–10.

Spencer, M. B. (1999). Social and cultural influenced on school adjustment: The application of an identity-focused cultural perspective. *Educational Psychologist, 34,* 43–57.

Steele, C. M. (1997). A threat in the air: How stereotypes shape intellectual identity and performance. *American Psychologist, 52,* 613–629.

Suarez-Orosco, C., & Suarez-Orosco, M. M. (2002). *Children of immigration.* Cambridge, MA: Harvard University Press.

Tajfel, H., & Turner, J. C. (1979). An integrative theory of intergroup conflict. In W.G. Austin & S. Worschel (Eds.), *The social psychology of intergroup relations* (pp. 33–47). Monterrey, CA: Brooks/Cole.

Vogt, L. A., Jordan, C., & Tharp, R. G. (1993). Explaining school failure, producing school success: Two cases. In E. Jacob & E.

Jordan (Eds.), *Minority education: Anthropological perspectives* (pp. 53–65). Norwood, NJ: Ablex.

Ward, C., Bochener, S., & Furnham, A. (2001). *The psychology of culture shock.* London: Routledge.

Revathy Kumar

HOME SCHOOLING

Home schooling is a term used to refer to the education of children by their parents or guardians in a setting other than a public or private school, most often in their homes. Home schooling styles vary substantially; there is no typical home schooling day. Methods of instruction include, but are not limited to the parent directly instructing the child, the child watching a video recording or satellite feed of an actual classroom, completing self-study workbooks or computer programs, some types of online instruction, or reading literature (Clements, 2004). Additional activities may include field trips, volunteering, scouting, organized sports, or taking classes through a home school cooperative in which parents teach groups of students. There is a practice often described as unschooling in which no traditional educational activities are employed, but students are encouraged to learn through life experiences (Clements, 2004). An example might be learning geometry, physics, drawing, and economics through the planning and construction of a structure such as a cabin or small home.

THE EMERGENCE OF HOME SCHOOLING

Parents' right to direct the education of their children is founded on the Fourteenth Amendment to the U.S. Constitution as interpreted in *Pierce v. Society of Sisters.* In 1925, after the state of Oregon adopted a law requiring all children to be educated in public schools, the U.S. Supreme Court ruled in *Pierce v. Society of Sisters* that private schools have the right to exist and that parents have the right to direct the upbringing and education of their children (Bloom, 2003). This decision has been commonly used to support home schooling, as have several legal opinions since (e.g., *Troxel v. Granville,* decided June 5, 2000, as cited in Bloom, 2003).

State legislatures, influenced by repeated legal challenges from home schooling families, gradually changed their laws to permit the practice of home schooling as it grew in popularity during the 1980s. By 1993 home schooling had become legal in all 50 states in one form or another. The increased availability of home schooling as an educational option and reduced stigma toward home schooling since the 1980s partially explains its

estimated annual growth rate of 15 to 20 percent during the 1990s (Lines, 2000). As of 2003 home schoolers constituted approximately 2.2 percent of the total school-age population (National Center for Education Statistics [NCES], 2006). However, attempts to pin down the actual number of home schooled children found that 2 to 3 percent of the school-age population remained unaccounted for in either home school or traditional school reporting, so the number could actually be closer to 5 percent. Because not all states require registration of home school families, the exact number of children being home schooled is difficult to determine (Lines, 2000).

Home schoolers have traditionally been thought to consist primarily of very conservative or very liberal families. Religiosity is significantly associated with both private schooling and home schooling. Evangelical Protestant parents are more likely to home school than are other groups of parents, but do not constitute the majority of home schoolers (Isenberg, 2007). Since the rapid increase in home schooling during the 1980s and 1990s, families from many religious and political persuasions are found among those home schooling (Reich, 2002; Romanowski, 2001). The typical home schooled child comes from a two-parent household in which parents have an above-average level of education, according to the *U.S. Department of Education Trends in Schools from 1993–1999* (NCES, 2003). Compared with private school children, however, home school children tend to come from less affluent and more rural households.

PARENTS' REASONS FOR HOME SCHOOLING

After completing an empirical study investigating parents' reasons for home schooling, Green and Hoover-Dempsey stated, "Homeschool parents appear to decide to homeschool not so much because they believe that public schools cannot educate their children but because they believe that they are personally responsible for their child's education and they are capable of educating their children well in ways consistent with their priorities" (2007, p. 278). According to Brian Ray (2006), president of the National Home Education Research Institute [NHERI], primary goals prompting families to home school include the following:

Teach a particular set of values, beliefs, and worldview

Accomplish more academically than in schools

Customize or individualize the curriculum and learning environment for each child

Use pedagogical approaches other than those typical in institutional schools, enhance family relationships between children and parents and among siblings

In a typical home schooling scenario, the lessons for each child are tailored to that particular child. **BRIDGET BESAW GORMAN/AURORA/ GETTY IMAGES.**

Provide guided and reasoned social interactions with youthful peers and adults

Provide a safer environment for children and youth, given problems in schools with physical violence, drugs and alcohol, psychological abuse, and improper and unhealthy sexuality

The National Home Education Network publication *Reasons to Home School* listed spending more time together as a family as the number one reason to home school. In 1999 and 2003, the National Household Education Surveys Program (NHES) collected responses from a nationally representative sample regarding reasons people choose to home school. The top reasons were "concerns about the environment" of other schools (31%), "to provide religious or moral instruction" (30%), and "dissatisfaction with academic instruction" at other schools (16%, NCES, 2004, p. 2). Isenberg (2007), by combining several sources of data on reasons for home schooling, supported the idea that approximately 30% of parents home school primarily for religious reasons (25% to

52%, depending on the year of data collection) but that educational reasons are more often cited as reasons for home schooling. These include dissatisfaction with current public schools as well as disability or exceptionality of the child being home schooled.

Many parents who choose to home school cite a weakening of emphasis on the teaching of traditional school subjects such as writing and mathematics in public schools and a promotion of certain social constructs such as tolerance. For example, as states enact legislation that mandates teaching tolerance regarding such controversial subjects as homosexuality, parents who object to those subjects being taught to their children become more likely to remove their children from public schools. This exodus from schools, seen as many educators as sheltering children from developing a broader world view, is seen by home schooling parents as a chance to both teach children their own world view and protect their children from indoctrination with competing views.

THE EFFECTS OF HOME SCHOOLING

There is abundant evidence that home school students tend to be quite successful academically and socially. Home schoolers' average test scores have been well above that of their public and private school counterparts on average. In fact, as of 2008, no study indicated lower achievement (Lincs, 2000) or poorer adjustment of home-schooled children. However, just as there is difficulty obtaining an accurate number of children being home schooled, there is difficulty ensuring the representativeness of data reporting on the effectiveness of home schooling. It is possible that those parents who are more successful at home schooling are also more likely to respond to surveys, report achievement data, have their children participate in standardized testing, and have children who apply for college admission.

Home Schooling and Achievement. In 1998 Lawrence Rudner of the University of Maryland conducted a study of 20,760 home schooled children who took the Iowa Tests of Basic Skills or the Tests of Achievement and Proficiency. Among the findings were the following:

The median scores for every subtest at every grade (most in the 70th to 80th percentile) were well above those of public and private school students.

Almost 25 percent of home school students were enrolled one or more grades above their age-level peers in public and private schools.

On average, home school students in grades 1 to 4 performed one grade level above their age-level public/private school peers.

The achievement test score gap between home school students and public/private school students widens from grade 5 upwards.

Students who have been home schooled their entire academic lives have higher scholastic achievement test scores than students who also have attended other educational institutions.

Rudner's findings are not atypical. An earlier study by Ray (1997) showed higher standardized test scores among home school students than among the general population. A separate study found that home school children in the state of Washington consistently scored above the national average in reading, language, math, and science. Of course, these are data from children who participated in these assessments. Nothing is known about children who were not tested.

In a survey of adults aged 18 to 24 who had been home schooled, more than 74 percent have taken college-level courses—as compared with 46 percent for the general U.S.

population. An overwhelming majority of them report that they are glad they were home schooled (Ray, 2006). In a related study, it was found that, while the potential for success in college did not differ significantly between home school graduates and conventional-school graduates, home school students did earn higher scores on the ACT English subtest (Ensign, 1997).

Perceptions of home schoolers applying for college admission became more favorable between 1993 and 2008. As of 2004, approximately 75 percent of institutions had a home school admission policy, and the vast majority of college admissions officers responding to the survey reported that they expected home-schooled students to do as well or better than non-home schooled students. In fact, no significant differences are typically found between home schooled and traditionally schooled first-year college students on ACT score, GPA, or retention.

The home schoolers' achievements that have gained the most public attention have been spelling and geography bee wins. In 2001, the winner of the National Spelling Bee was the third winner in five years to have been home schooled. Ten percent of the 2001 spelling bee contestants were home schooled (which is significant given that home schoolers made up less than 5 percent of the student population with some estimates as low as 2 percent). In 2000, eight of the finalists had been home schooled, with home schoolers taking the top three places.

Home Schooling and Socialization. The primary concern expressed about home schooling does not involve academic achievement, but tends to be related to students' socialization or more accurately lack of socialization. Those concerned envision home schoolers as being isolated with their parents, having little cultural exposure, little opportunity to interact with other children, and having minimal contact with the world beyond their homes. In truth, for many home schoolers the opposite is true. Some have such an excess of social and extracurricular activities that having time to complete their studies can be challenging. Many, if not most home schooling parents supplement academic material with extracurricular activities such as music lessons, sports, scouting, church activities, and other endeavors that engage children with their peers (Clements, 2004).

Not only are findings about socialization of home-schooled children not negative, several researchers have found an overwhelmingly positive picture of the socialization of home school students (see, for example, Medlin, 2000). Home schoolers are provided opportunities that foster positive interaction and they also are protected from many sources of negative socialization (Lines, 2000; Romanowski, 2001; Shyers, 1992). Richard Medlin of Stetson University found that self-concept was higher for home school students than for public school students, and in a blind, controlled study comparing 70 home school with 70 non-home school children, the former had fewer behavioral disorders (Lines, 2000).

Home Schooling and Homogenization. One goal of public education is to provide common experiences for children with the goal being some degree of homogenization of citizens. Along with fears about lack of socialization in home schoolers, an additional criticism involves an alleged lack of homogenization of home school children. Some, such as Rob Reich (2002) of Stanford University, believe that children should be exposed to a common set of ideas and have a common set of experiences. He sees a civic peril in insulating children from certain ideas. However, the same argument could be leveled against public schools. The practice of prohibiting the expression of religion in public schools—particularly Christianity—is an example. It is unlikely that a child whose parents have never introduced him or her to Christian beliefs would learn about them in public school. The argument for exposing the child to a broad range of ideas thus breaks down. Reich goes on to argue that children should learn decency, civility, and respect. However, the perceived absence of these values in the public school environment is a common reason that parents remove their children from public schools in favor of home schooling.

Some Explanations for the Success of Home Schooling. Available data suggest a number of hypotheses as to why home-schooled children excel academically. These include parental involvement, the education level of the parents, and the benefits of one-on-one instruction. Romanowski of Ohio Northern University and Hoxby of Harvard, among others, attribute home schooled students' success to the high degree of parental involvement. There has been a great deal of research supporting the benefits of parental involvement in children's education. In fact, teacher training programs and schools routinely recommend techniques for soliciting parents' involvement within public and private schools for this reason.

A second possible explanation for the academic success of home schoolers is that home-schooled children tend to have more educated parents (Romanowski, 2001). As mentioned, home schooling families tend to have parents with more years of education than public and private school families. Either the value placed on education or the intelligence that enabled those parents to complete more education could contribute to their children's academic success.

An additional reason for the success of home schooling is that one-on-one instruction has traditionally been thought to be more effective than traditional group schooling. In a typical home schooling scenario, a parent may teach only one or may teach multiple children, but the lessons for each child are tailored to that child. This is of particular benefit to children who learn more rapidly or more slowly than most children in their age group. In group schooling teachers usually teach to the majority which tends to be composed of children achieving at the average rate, leaving slow learners behind and causing rapid learners to lose interest. One-on-one instruction has also been found to be beneficial to children with attention deficits. Having fewer people in the learning environment reduces distractions, thereby helping the student to stay focused on learning.

THE AVAILABILITY OF THE OPTION TO HOME SCHOOL

Research has accumulated over several decades showing numerous benefits of home schooling; however, it is not possible for all families who would like to home school their children to do so. Most, but not all, of these reasons are economic. Families who must have two incomes or families in which a single parent is the only income earner have difficulty home schooling. However, there are non-economic reasons as well. There are families in which the parent or parents do not have the education or temperament to be able to effectively home school (Clements, 2004). For these, a group schooling setting may be their only option.

BIBLIOGRAPHY

Bloom, I. (2003). The new parental rights challenge to school control: Has the Supreme Court mandated school choice? *Journal of Law & Education, 32*(2), 139–183.

Clements, A. D. (2004). Homeschooling: A research-based how-to manual. Lanham, MD: ScarecrowEducation.

Ensign, J. (1997). *Homeschooling gifted students: An introductory guide for parents.* ERIC Digest #543 (No. EDO-EC-95–6). ERIC Clearinghouse on Disabilities and Gifted Education, Council for Exceptional Children, 1920 Association Drive, Reston, VA 20191-1589.

Green, C. L., & Hoover-Dempsey, K. V. (2007). Why do parents homeschool? A systematic investigation of parent involvement. *Education and Urban Society, 39,* 264–285.

Hoxby, C. M. (2001). Rising tide. *Education Next, 1*(4), 68–74.

Houston, P. D. (2003). Time to re-public the republic. *School Administrator, 60*(8), 10–12.

Isenberg, E. J. (2007). What have we learned about homeschooling? *Peabody Journal of Education, 82*(2–3), 387–409.

Jones, P., & Gloeckner, G. (2004). A study of admission officers' perceptions of and attitudes toward homeschool students. *Journal of College Admission, (185),* 12–21.

Lines, P. M. (2000). Homeschooling comes of age. *Public Interest, 140,* 74–85.

National Home Education Network. (n.d.). *Reasons to homeschool.* Retrieved April 17, 2008, from http://www.nhen.org.

National Center for Education Statistics. (2003, May). *Trends in school choice 1993 to 1999: Statistical analysis report.* U.S. Department of Education: Institute of Education Sciences (Report No. NCES 2003–031).

National Center for Education Statistics. (2004, July). *Issue brief: 1.1 million homeschooled students in the United States in 2003.* U.S. Department of Education. Institute of Education Sciences, NCES 2004–115.

National Center for Education Statistics. (2006, February). *Homeschooling in the United States: 2003: A statistical analysis report.* U.S. Department of Education. Institute of Education Sciences, NCES 2006–042.

Ray, B. (1997). *Strengths of their own: Home Schoolers across America: Academic achievement, family characteristics, and longitudinal traits.* Salem, OR: National Home Education Research Institute.

Ray, B. (2006, July). *Research facts on homeschooling.* Salem, OR: National Home Education Research Association. Retrieved April 17, 2008, from http://www.nheri.org.

Reich, R. (2002). The civic perils of homeschooling. *Educational Leadership, 59*(7), 56–59.

Romanowski, M. H. (2001). Common arguments about the strengths and limitations of home schooling. *Clearing House, 75*(2), 79–83.

Shyers, L. E. (1992). A comparison of social adjustment between home and traditionally schooled students. *Home School Researcher, 8*(3), 1–8.

Andrea D. Clements

HOMEWORK

Homework can be defined as tasks assigned to students by teachers that are intended to be carried out during nonschool hours. This definition excludes (a) in-school guided study (although homework is often worked on during school); (b) home study courses, and (c) extracurricular activities such as sports teams and clubs.

VARIATIONS IN HOMEWORK

According to Harris Cooper (2007), the most common variation in homework assignments relates to its content or subject matter. Independent of content, homework assignments also vary in their purpose or goal. Practice homework assignments ask students to go over material already presented in class so as to reinforce learning and facilitate mastery of specific skills. Preparation assignments introduce material that will be presented in future lessons. These assignments aim to help students obtain the maximum benefit when the new material is covered in class. Extension homework involves the transfer of previously learned skills to new situations, such as asking students to apply their mathematics knowledge to construct a household budget. Finally, integration homework requires the student to apply separately learned skills to produce a single product, such as reading a book and writing a report on it.

Homework also can serve purposes that do not relate directly to instruction. Homework can be used to (a) establish communication between parents and children, (b) fulfill directives from school administrators, (c) punish students, and (d) inform parents about what is going on in school. Most homework assignments have elements of several different purposes.

Assignments can vary in many other ways, including the skill area covered (e.g., reading, writing, math), the level of difficulty, and the time required for completion. With regard to the latter, the amount of homework students are assigned can best be thought of in terms of (a) the frequency, or how often, homework is assigned and (b) the duration of each assignment, or how long it takes to complete each assignment. For example, two students doing four hours of homework a week might be having very different homework experiences. One might be doing one hour of homework on each of four nights while the other is doing two hours of homework on just two nights.

POSITIVE AND NEGATIVE EFFECTS OF HOMEWORK

The most direct positive effect of homework is that it can improve the retention and understanding of academic material. More indirectly, homework can improve students' study skills and attitudes toward school (by showing how skills that are learned in school have application to activities students enjoy doing outside school) and can teach students that learning can take place anywhere, not just in school buildings. The nonacademic benefits of homework include fostering independent and responsible character traits. Finally, homework can involve parents in the school process, enhancing their appreciation and understanding of what goes on in the classroom and allowing them to express positive attitudes toward the value of school success.

Homework can have negative effects as well. It can lead to boredom with schoolwork if students are required to spend too much time on academic material. Homework can deny students access to leisure time and community activities that also teach important life skills. Parent involvement in homework can turn into parent interference. For example, parents can confuse their child if the instructional techniques they use at home differ from those used by teachers. Homework can lead to the acquisition of undesirable character traits if it promotes cheating, either through the copying of assignments or if the student receives help with homework that goes beyond tutoring. Finally, homework could accentuate existing social inequities. Diane Scott-Jones has argued that children from disadvantaged homes may have more difficulty completing assignments than their middle-class counterparts.

Homework can reinforce concepts taught in the classroom. ANDY SACKS/STONE/GETTY IMAGES.

RESEARCH ON HOMEWORK

Research on homework generally supports the notion that it helps students learn academic material, but with important qualifications. Cooper, Jorgianne Robinson, and Erika Patall have conducted, since 1984, six studies that used two groups of students who were on average as similar as possible—by randomly assigning students to groups, statistically controlling for student differences, or matching a student in one group with a similar student in the other group while eliminating students who did not have a good match—and then manipulated whether students did or did not receive homework assignments. These studies provide a clear picture that homework can be effective in improving students' scores on unit tests (the class tests that come at the end of a topic unit). Students doing homework in second grade did better on number places, third and fourth grade did better on English skills and vocabulary, fifth grade on social studies, high school on American history, and twelfth graders on Shakespeare. Across five studies, the average (50th percentile) student doing homework had a higher unit test score than 73% of students not doing homework.

A second type of study supports the conclusion that students who do homework perform better on tests. This type simply asked students (or one of the students' parents) how much homework the students did; no manipulation of homework assignments was involved. However, these studies attempted to statistically equate students on other characteristics that might be associated with homework and achievement and therefore might account for any relationship between the two. Because they do not purposively manipulate homework, these studies can never lead to as confident a conclusion about homework's direct effect on achievement. However, they do typically involve large nationally representative samples of students such as the National Educational Longitudinal Study. Also, these studies typically use broader measures of achievement than unit tests, such as cumulative grades and standardized test scores. Twelve such studies have tested more than 30 different statistical models. The other factors that might influence achievement (and time on homework) that were controlled for in the statistical models included numerous student factors (for example, sex, ethnicity, ability, motivation), family factors (for example, wealth, parent involvement), school factors (for example, subject matter, teacher training, class size), and other student behaviors (for example, TV watching, extracurricular activities and jobs, absences from school). Achievement was measured for all sorts of content areas using all types of achievement measures. In 11 of the 12 samples, the link between time on homework and achievement was positive.

A third type of study that looked at homework involved no attempt to purposively vary homework or to equate students on other characteristics that might explain any relationship. Thus, these correlational studies can make no claims about a causal link between homework and achievement. Though not conclusive, this type of evidence can give important clues about when, where, and for whom homework might be more or less effective. In 35 samples of students used in correlational studies, 27 found the link between homework and achievement was a positive one; in 8, it was negative.

The correlational results were noticeably different depending on the grade level of the students. The average correlation between time spent on homework and achievement was substantial for secondary school students but for elementary school students, it hovered around no relationship at all. There are several possible explanations for this finding. First, cognitive psychologists Dana Plude, James Enns, and Darlene Broudeur suggest that younger children are less able to tune out distractions. It is easy to imagine that the distractions present in a younger student's home would make studying there less effective for them than for older students. Second, a study by Annette Dufresne and Akira Kobasigawa suggests that younger students have less well-developed study habits. Their study showed that older students spend more time than younger ones working on harder items. Older students were also more likely to use self-testing strategies to monitor how much of the material they have learned.

Other explanations for the weak correlation between homework and achievement in early grades are possible. A study by Laura Muhlenbruck, Cooper, Barbara Nye, and James Lindsay found evidence suggesting teachers in early grades may assign homework more often to develop young students' management of time—a skill rarely measured on standardized achievement tests or graded in class. This study also provided some evidence that young students who are struggling in school take more time to complete homework assignments. Thus, while it seems highly likely that age difference in attention span and study habits can be applied to the homework situation, it is also likely that poor-achieving young children spend more time on homework simply because it is more difficult for them.

APPROPRIATE AMOUNTS OF HOMEWORK

Based on these results and the experience of teachers, consensus has emerged regarding rough guidelines for the amount of homework that should be assigned to students in different grade levels. The National PTA and the NEA suggest that homework for children in grades K-2 is most effective when it does not exceed ten to twenty minutes each day. In grades 3 through 6, children can benefit from 30 to 60 minutes per day. Junior high and high school students can benefit from more time on homework and the amount might vary from night to night. These recommendations are consistent with the conclusions reached by studies of the effectiveness of homework.

In conclusion, homework can be an effective instructional device. However, both experience and research suggest that the relationship between homework and achievement is influenced greatly by the students' developmental level. Expectations for homework's effects, especially in the short term and in earlier grades, must be modest. Further, homework can have both positive and negative effects depending on how it is used, with whom, and in what context.

BIBLIOGRAPHY

Cooper, H. (2007). *The Battle over Homework: Common Ground for Administrators, Teachers, and Parents* (3rd ed.). Thousand Oaks, CA: Corwin Press.

Cooper, H., Robinson, J., & Patall, E. (2006). Does homework improve academic achievement?: A synthesis of research, 1987–2003. *Review of Educational Research, 76,* 1–62.

Dufresne, A., & Kobasigawa, A. (1989). Children's spontaneous allocation of study time: Differential and sufficient aspects. *Journal of Experimental Child Psychology, 42,* 274–296.

Mulhenbruck, L., Cooper, H., Nye, B., & Lindsay, J. (1999). Homework and achievement: Explaining the different strengths of relation at the elementary and secondary school levels. *Social Psychology of Education, 3,* 295–317.

National Parent Teacher Association and National Education Association. *Help Your Student Get the Most Out of Homework.* Retrieved April 17, 2008, from http://www.nca.org/parents/homework.html.

Plude, D., Enns, J., & Brodeur, D. (1994). The development of selective attention: A life-span overview. *Acta Psychologica, 86,* 227–272.

Scott-Jones, D. (1984). Family influences on cognitive development and school achievement. In E. Gordon (Ed.), *Review of Research in Education,* Vol. 11. Washington, DC: American Educational Research Association.

Harris Cooper

I

IDENTIFICATION WITH ACADEMICS

Identification with academics is related to the notion of domain identification introduced by William James (James, 1890/1981). James argued that every person has an almost infinite number of possible selves, but that individuals focus on a few core domains in defining the self. These core selves that a person identifies with can have a profound influence on everything from self-esteem and motivation to behavior. Other selves are regarded as unimportant. This process of placing more or less importance on certain aspects of the self is called "selective valuing." While there has been debate on whether these ideas can be empirically validated, many researchers accept them because of their intuitive appeal.

Identification with academics is a special case of domain identification and selective valuing. It refers to the extent to which an individual defines the self through a role or performance in a particular domain, in this case schooling and academics. The concept of domain identification is rooted in the Symbolic Interactionist perspective on self-esteem, which is presented graphically in Figure 1. In general, this model states that 1) individuals get lots of feedback in many different ways almost constantly and 2) if this feedback is received and viewed as accurate/valid, it is incorporated into an individual's domain-specific self-concept. If this part of self-concept is important, the feedback will affect self-esteem.

According to this model, outcomes in a domain will only affect an individual's self-esteem to the extent that the individual is identified with that domain. Another characteristic of this perspective is that there are not only individual differences in identification with a specific domain, but also changes within an individual over time in domain identification (e.g., Tesser, 1988). In other words, one person may view proficiency at tennis as a huge aspect of the self, while another could not care less about how well he or she plays tennis. Over time, as circumstances change, one's view of how important tennis is to the self might become less or more important.

IMPORTANCE OF IDENTIFICATION WITH ACADEMICS

If having a positive self-view feels good and a negative self-view feels bad (psychologists differ on this point), it follows that healthy individuals are motivated to maintain a positive self view. They are strategic and will value those domains that are most likely to produce positive feedback for the self, and will alter their domain valuing as conditions change, all with the goal of maximizing how positive the self-view is (Steele, 1988; Tesser, 1988).

From a simple reinforcement/punishment perspective, stronger identification should be related to more positive outcomes in that domain. Individuals should be motivated to behave in ways that maximize the probability of positive outcomes (and minimize the negative outcomes) in domains they strongly identify with. For students strongly identified with academics, good academic performance should be rewarding (leading to a more positive self-view, which feels good) whereas poor academic performance should be punishing (leading to a more negative self-view, which feels bad). Similarly, students not identified with academics should have little motivation to succeed in academics because there is no link between academic outcomes and

Representing identification with academics

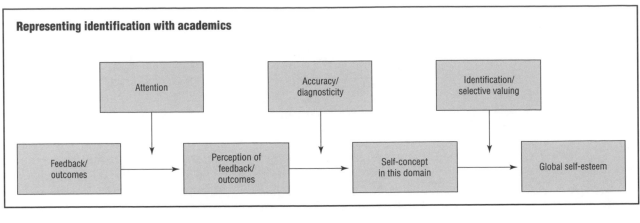

Figure 1 ILLUSTRATION BY GGS INFORMATION SERVICES. CENGAGE LEARNING, GALE.

self-esteem—good performance is not intrinsically reward-ing, and poor performance is not intrinsically punishing. For these students, motivation comes from other domains outside academics.

MOTIVATION AND/OR ACADEMIC OUTCOMES

Research supports the notion that identification with aca-demics increases the odds of success in academics (Osborne, Kellow, & Jones, 2007). Figure 2 shows the theoretical relationships between identification with academics and motivation to succeed as well as outcomes in that domain. (Other literatures, such as management and parenting literatures, have noted similar effects.)

Identification with academics predicts academic achieve-ment (Osborne, 1997a; Osborne & Rausch, 2001; Voelkl, 1997), receiving academic honors or being put on academic probation (Osborne, 1997a), engagement in learning/class-room activities (Osborne & Rausch, 2001; Voelkl, 1997; Walker, Greene, & Mansell, 2006), stronger academic self-efficacy (Walker et al., 2006), and even academic dishonesty (K. V. Finn & Frone, 2004). These studies show that stron-ger identification with academics increases motivation to succeed and the amount of effort students put into learning. Given this, it should not be surprising that these students are also more likely to achieve better outcomes in academics. Importantly, identification with academics has been linked to decreased likelihood of undesirable behaviors, such as cutting class, absenteeism, and dropping out (Osborne et al., 2007).

MEASURING IDENTIFICATION WITH ACADEMICS

There is no consensus on how to measure identification with academics. Valuing, belonging, positive predisposi-tions toward school, and behaviors that signal engagement in learning/schooling are theoretically linked to identifica-tion with academics, but do not capture the essence of it. Some researchers (Spencer, Steele, & Quinn, 1999) have argued that students who enroll in challenging academic courses and who possess well above average standardized scores are de facto classified as identified, but there are also gifted students who do exceedingly well and then drop out as soon as they can. Additionally, this perspective ignores extrinsic motivations for doing well in school. True identi-fication with academics is a purely intrinsic process (although it can be influenced by external forces). Others (e.g., Aronson et al., 1999) have supplemented these indicators with items that assess the relevance of the domain ("Mathematics is important to me") to students. Other researchers (Morgan & Mehta, 2004; Osborne, 1995, 1997b; Verkuyten & Thijs, 2004) have operationalized this as the relationship between measures of self-concept and academic outcomes. Referring to Figure 1, it is obvious that among students with strong identification, there should be a strong relationship between self-concept and academic outcomes. Yet this approach is severely limited in that it can only speak to large groups, although it may be important for initially establish-ing the validity of the general concept.

Researchers have published scales intended to measure identification with academics from the perspective presented above (Osborne, 1997a; Osborne & Walker, 2006, Voelkl, 1996, 1997, Finn,1989). These scales are designed to assess student feelings of belonging (i.e., acceptance of and respect for the self by others in the school, feelings of inclusion) and valuing (i.e., the extent to which the student views schooling as an important institution in society, and the material being learned as important and useful).

INDIVIDUAL AND GROUP DIFFERENCES

As James and many later theorists have argued, individ-uals differ not only in what domains they identify with,

476

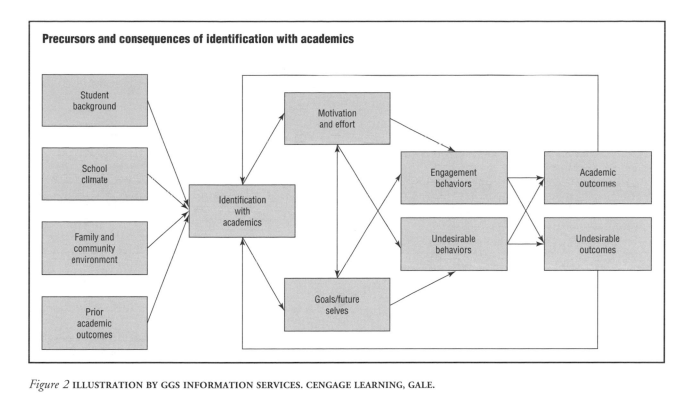

Precursors and consequences of identification with academics

Figure 2 ILLUSTRATION BY GGS INFORMATION SERVICES. CENGAGE LEARNING, GALE.

but also how complex the self is (i.e., how many domains they identify with. (For a review of self-complexity, see (Rafaeli-Mor & Steinberg, 2002.) Research strongly suggests that identification with academics is changeable, and as Finn (1989) and others argue, changes long before bad things happen academically (e.g., withdrawal from school). Therefore, there is significant hope that should students begin to disidentify, and if this change is diagnosed early enough, intervention can prevent serious consequences.

Identification with academics is also implicated in important social trends, such as the long-standing achievement gap between Caucasian students and students from disadvantaged/stigmatized groups (e.g., African American, Native American, Latino). Claude Steele's Stereotype Threat hypothesis (Steele, 1992, 1997, 1999; Steele & Aronson, 1995), for example, argues that members of academically stigmatized groups should show higher anxiety in school, and ultimately defensively disidentify with academics (see also Major & Schmader, 1998; Major, Spencer, Schmader, Wolfe, & Crocker, 1998). Research from several cultures and across many years has shown this disidentification effect predicted by Steele at the group level when comparing stigmatized and non-stigmatized groups (Cokley, 2002; Demo & Parker, 1987; Hansford & Hattie, 1982; Morgan & Mehta, 2004; Osborne, 1995, 1997b; Osborne, Major, & Crocker, 1992; Rosenberg & Simmons, 1972; Verkuyten

& Thijs, 2004). Interestingly, when stigmatized individuals (such as African American students) answer questionnaires about identification (valuing of) academics, there is often either no difference between the two groups or the African American students score higher than Caucasian Americans (e.g., Major & Schmader, 1998). On an individual level, parents, teachers, and others in power can reduce stereotype threat and/or enhance identification with academics. The literature gives many options, including (a) increasing positive outcomes, (b) promoting the importance of academic domains, (c) fostering a sense of belonging, and (d) lifting the situational threat. Those interested in this process should consult Osborne et al. (2007) for more on these strategies or Steele (1997) for other ideas specific to stereotype threat.

SEE ALSO *Expectancy Value Motivational Theory; Identity Development; Relevance of Self-Evaluations to Classroom Learning; School Belonging; Self-Esteem; Stereotype Threat.*

BIBLIOGRAPHY

Aronson, J., Lustina, M. J., Good, C., Keough, K., Steele, C. M., & Brown, J. (1999). When White men can't do math: Necessary and sufficient factors in stereotype threat. *Journal of Experimental Social Psychology, 35*(1), 29–46.

Cokley, K. O. (2002). Ethnicity, gender and academic self-concept: A preliminary examination of academic disidentification and implications for psychologists. *Cultural Diversity & Ethnic Minority Psychology, 8*(4), 378–388.

Demo, D. H., & Parker, K. D. (1987). Academic achievement and self-esteem among African-American and White college students. *Journal of Social Psychology, 127*(4), 345–355.

Finn, J. D. (1989). Withdrawing from school. *Review of Educational Research, 59*(2), 117–142.

Finn, K. V., & Frone, M. R. (2004). Academic Performance and Cheating: Moderating Role of School Identification and Self-Efficacy. *Journal of Educational Research, 97*(3), 115–122.

Hansford, B., & Hattie, J. (1982). The relationship between self and achievement performance measures. *Review of Educational Research, 52,* 123–142.

James, W. (1890/1981). *The principles of psychology.* Cambridge, MA: Harvard University Press.

Major, B., & Schmader, T. (1998). Coping with stigma through psychological disengagement. In J. K. Swim & C. Stangor (Eds.), *Prejudice: The target's perspective.* New York: Academic Press.

Major, B., Spencer, S. J., Schmader, T., Wolfe, C., & Crocker, J. (1998). Coping with negative stereotypes about intellectual performance: The role of psychological disengagement. *Personality and Social Psychology Bulletin, 24*(1), 34–50.

Morgan, S. L., & Mehta, J. D. (2004). Beyond the Laboratory: Evaluating the Survey Evidence for the Disidentification Explanation of Black-White Differences in Achievement. *Sociology of Education, 77*(1), 82–101.

Osborne, J. W. (1995). Academics, self-esteem, and race: A look at the assumptions underlying the Disidentification hypothesis. *Personality and Social Psychology Bulletin, 21*(5), 449–455.

Osborne, J. W. (1997a). Identification with Academics and Academic Success Among Community College Students. *Community College Review, 25*(1), 59–67.

Osborne, J. W. (1997b). Race and academic disidentification. *Journal of Educational Psychology, 89*(4), 728–735.

Osborne, J. W., Kellow, J. T., & Jones, B. (2007). Identification with academics, stereotype threat, and motivation to achieve in school. In D. M. McInerney, S. V. Etten & M. Dowson (Eds.), *Standards in education: A volume in research on sociocultural influences on motivation and learning.* Information Age Publishing.

Osborne, J. W., Major, B., & Crocker, J. (1992). *Social stigma and reactions to academic feedback.* Paper presented at the Eastern Psychological Association, Boston.

Osborne, J. W., & Rausch, J. L. (2001). *Identification with Academics and Academic Outcomes in Secondary Students.* Paper presented at the American Education Research Association, Seattle, WA.

Osborne, J. W., & Walker, C. (2006). Stereotype threat, identification with academics, and withdrawal from school: Why the most successful students of colour might be most likely to withdraw. *Educational Psychology, 26*(4), 563–577.

Rafaeli-Mor, E., & Steinberg, J. (2002). Self-complexity and well-being: A review and research synthesis. *Personality and Social Psychology Review, 6*(1), 31–58.

Rosenberg, M., & Simmons, R. (1972). *African-American and White self-esteem: The urban school child.* Washington DC: American Sociological Association.

Spencer, S. J., Steele, C. M., & Quinn, D. M. (1999). Stereotype threat and women's math performance. *Journal of Experimental Social Psychology, 35*(1), 4–28.

Steele, C. M. (1988). The psychology of self-affirmation: Sustaining the integrity of the self. In L. Berkowitz (Ed.), *Advances in experimental social psychology* (Vol. 21, pp. 261–302). San Diego, CA: Academic Press.

Steele, C. M. (1992, April). Race and the schooling of Black Americans. *The Atlantic Monthly,* 68–78.

Steele, C. M. (1997). A threat in the air: How stereotypes shape intellectual identity and performance. *American Psychologist, 52*(6), 613–629.

Steele, C. M. (1999). The psychology of self-affirmation: Sustaining the integrity of the self. In Baumeister, Roy F. (Ed.). (1999). *The self in social psychology: Key readings in social psychology* (pp. 372–390). Philadelphia: Psychology Press/Taylor & Francis.

Steele, C. M., & Aronson, J. (1995). Stereotype threat and the intellectual test performance of African Americans. *Journal of Personality and Social Psychology, 69*(5), 797–811.

Tesser, A. (1988). Toward a self-evaluation maintenance model of social behavior. In L. L. Berkowitz (Ed.), *Advances in experimental social psychology* (Vol. 21, pp. 181–228). San Diego, CA: Academic Press.

Verkuyten, M., & Thijs, J. (2004). Psychological disidentification with the academic domain among ethnic minority adolescents in The Netherlands. *British Journal of Educational Psychology, 74*(1), 109–125.

Voelkl, K. E. (1996). Measuring students' identification with school. *Educational and Psychological Measurement, 56,* 760–770.

Voelkl, K. E. (1997). Identification with school. *American Journal of Education, 105,* 294–318.

Walker, C. O., Greene, B. A., & Mansell, R. A. (2006). Identification with academics, intrinsic/extrinsic motivation, and self-efficacy as predictors of cognitive engagement. *Learning and individual differences, 16*(1), 1–12.

Jason W. Osborne

IDENTITY DEVELOPMENT

Identity is an individual's self definition that focuses on enduring characteristics of the self. In an established identity, the individual is able to explain the origins of these self-defined characteristics and the influences behind those origins. Complete identity includes a clarification of one's morals, ethics, and standards, as well as a commitment to a future occupation. Many development theorists see identity development as a means for an individual to explain the present as a bridge from the past to the future.

MAJOR PROCESSES IN IDENTITY DEVELOPMENT

The major processes that comprise identity development are addressed by Erik Erikson (1902–1994) in his theory of psychosocial development. Most psychologists appreciate Erikson's theory because of its "utility in many professional arenas [such as] clinical, theoretical and empirical" (McKinney, 2001).

Erikson was interested in explaining the development of the healthy personality, based on an enduring ego identity. The healthy ego identity evolves through a process of discovering the self within the various influences of a personal history, societal history, and social contexts. For Erikson this evolving of the ego identity takes place through stages of psychosocial development. In each stage, the psychological make-up of the individual interacts with the demands of the social context in a challenge that either brings about a healthy resolution or an unhealthy alternative. This age-related challenge is referred to as a crisis. Each of these crises represents a "direct reflection of the person's social maturity and societal expectations" (McKinney, 2001). All of the psychosocial stages are interdependent; the success of each earlier crisis is the foundation for the success of each later challenge.

Although identity is established in adolescence, the successful resolution of each previous psychosocial challenge contributes something to the make-up of the healthy ego identity. Infants learning trust are forming in their minds an enduring representation of the mother. This representation should guide growing children into understanding when to trust others and when not to trust them. Other childhood psychosocial challenges establish autonomy, initiative, and industry. Achieving these previous psychosocial functions facilitates establishing identity in adolescence.

NORMATIVE DEVELOPMENTAL CHANGES

Many theorists would agree that identity development begins with children establishing autonomy, recognizing that they are individuals separate from their mother. Autonomy and self awareness begins in the second year. It can be observed when children talk about themselves, using the concept of the self, when they resist control by parents, and recognize themselves in a mirror. Self concept starts to develop shortly after self awareness is established. Self concept is the rudimentary definition of self based on a collection of disconnected traits. The self concept relies on role models to suggest standards and preferences.

From 3 through 6 years of age, children nurture their self concept by making choices and following through on those choices. They experiment in this stage with doing things on their own. They are often told during this time period that what they have chosen to do is wrong. The shame that they feel in these situations leads to the beginnings of the self-evaluation that is so important in the next stage.

Across many cultures, middle childhood, from age 7 until the onset of puberty, is a time of increased responsibility and privilege. Children begin to learn what their culture deems important. More than in earlier years, they are involved in peer groups, putting them in a position to constantly compare themselves to others. When that comparison is favorable, they are inspired to work and accomplish more. When that comparison is not favorable, they may feel inferior to classmates. During this period self efficacy develops and becomes significant. Self efficacy is the attempt to assess one's worth through comparison with others.

According to Erikson, the most important process of identity development takes place during adolescence. During this time, individuals must establish their identity in order to make the transition from childhood to adulthood. Adolescents enter a psychosocial moratorium, which is a period of relative freedom from societal expectations. During this time, they feel free to experiment with different personalities and roles. From Erikson's perspective, everything that was established about self in childhood is re-evaluated in adolescence. Some of the components of the self concept, self worth, and childhood personality may be retained or rejected in the adolescent's search for identity. Adolescents have to internalize a comprehensive and consistent set of affirmations regarding their own strengths, weaknesses, values, and career choice. The positive influence of family and friends is important in this process, but the commitment must be made by adolescents as individuals. This process requires much experimentation and exploration, particularly in personality and vocational roles (Santrock, 2007).

The identity established during adolescence represents a major accomplishment. By young adulthood, individuals who have achieved their identity are prepared to adapt and contribute to society. That identity is expected to endure. However, many theorists who study identity achievement recognize that there is still much refinement, re-evaluation, and recommitment of identity in later life.

THE KEY THEORIES OF IDENTITY DEVELOPMENT

Although Erikson's theory of identity development is widely cited, other theories provide important knowledge about identity and its development. The attachment theories emphasize the value of the trust and security that a child learns from his/her mother in infancy. Social learning theories expand the constructs of self concept and self worth as the basis of self description in late childhood. Cognitive development theory describes the age-related processes leading to a child's limitation before adolescence and competence during adolescence for establishing identity. Researchers investigating Erikson's theory of identity development have provided important modifications to the theory.

Attachment Theory. Theorists such as Mary Ainsworth, who studied attachment in infancy, observed and explained concepts similar to those of Erikson. The description of attachment compares to Erikson's description of trust. In his theory, infants who have learned trust grow into children who accept that life has order and purpose. These growing children have a trusting and accepting relationship with their mother. Infants who have learned attachment grow into children who look to the mother for guidance and rely on her as a safe base for exploration. In both cases, these children's personality can be expected to have a basic confidence. Failure in attachment and in trust results in a confused child who is not sure about trusting parents and/ or may have little discretion in trusting others.

One difference in the two theories is that Erikson expected trust to be established in the first year. Ainsworth has shown that secure attachment can take as long as 18 months. Another difference is the strength of the influence on later development attributed to the mother-child bond. Ainsworth sees attachment as the most important influence on development. For Erikson, that influence is modified by the resolution of later psychosocial crises.

Social Learning Theory. As noted above, once self awareness is established, the self concept starts to develop. The self concept is the basic representation in children's minds of who they are and what they are like. Social learning theorists emphasize that the self concept is built upon the identification with role models, an assessment of self worth, and a preferred pattern in relating to the external world (Carver & Scheier, 1992).

Children learn to relate to the world through modeling and imitation of others, particularly role models. The same-sex parent is an influential role model for each child. Other role models in early childhood can be anyone the child admires. Children will identify with a role model and shape their behavior and tastes in imitation of that role model. The influences of a role model can affect individuals' personality, ambitions, interest, and tastes well into adulthood (Carver & Scheier, 1992).

Self worth is based on children's assessment of their capabilities in comparison to others. Children may feel that they are superior or inferior to others or may feel that they are capable but that others do not notice. Often the assessment is classified according to different areas of life such as sports, academics, or friendships. However, too many negative self assessments in the different areas may result in an overall feeling of helplessness.

The preferred pattern of relationships, influenced by the self concept, is different for individual children. Children seek social interaction in different ways. Although one pattern may be clearly seen as being more effective, some individuals are more likely to choose a pattern that is person-ally meaningful. For example, shy children may admire those children with more outgoing personalities but may continue to relate to others in a quiet manner.

The self concept can be a stronger motivator for behavior than an external reward. If children receive punishment in class for misbehaving, the punishment may not discourage them from repeating the behavior. If the children's see themselves as rebels, such a self concept would be encouraged by receiving punishment (Carver & Scheier, 1992).

Cognitive Development. The patterns of development that Erikson describes are related to what Jean Piaget (1896–1980) and the cognitive psychologists recognize about age-related strategies of children in reasoning. There are limits in children's reasoning until adolescence. Before adolescence, individuals are not capable of the cognitive reasoning necessary in establishing identity.

Evidence of cognition in infancy shows in babies' recognizing their mother's voice and smell even from birth. This perinatal cognitive ability facilitates the familiarity that leads to trust. Babies are comforted by their mother's voice and feel secure in her presence.

In early childhood, the self concept is constantly changing because of cognitive limitations. Piaget calls the period between 2 and 6 years of age the preoperational stage. Children at this age cannot use logical strategies. Therefore, they tend to focus on only one feature of an object. Also, children at this age do not understand the identity principle that some things do not change essentially even though they change one of their features. Even in describing themselves, children will focus on only one aspect of who they are without qualifying that aspect or relating it to another aspect of self. When preoperational children try to describe themselves, they cannot be sure they will not change.

During middle childhood, children develop the capacity for logical reasoning, but only in situations with concrete examples, which marks this as the cognitive stage of concrete operations. Children are increasingly capable of classifying and cross-classifying objects and characteristics. As they describe themselves in the stage of concrete operations, more qualifying occurs on the different attributes of self. Also, these individuals express an expectation of stability in their characteristics. Establishment of the psychosocial function of industry relies on the use of these newly learned cognitive capabilities. Through classification, children can identify their own strengths and weaknesses while being able to rank peers on their related abilities. Also, children can recognize that being inferior in one area does not make one inferior in another.

During adolescence individuals can reason beyond the concrete. Adolescents have increased capabilities for abstract reasoning. With this ability comes awareness that they have a future for which they need to prepare. This unexpected realization is the beginning of the identity crisis.

Other Identity Theories. Many theorists investigating identity achievement have expanded or modified Erikson's ideas. James Marcia investigated the major influences on identity achievement and identified four possible outcomes or statuses of the identity crisis based on whether the crisis has been met and a commitment has been made.

As with Erikson, Marcia sees the identity crisis as beginning when adolescents recognize the need to establish an identity that can prepare them to meet the challenges of adulthood. Marcia agrees with Erikson that adolescents need to explore the many possibilities in personality roles and career choices as well as lifestyles. Identity achievement is recognized as individuals gain a clear understanding of their own strengths and weaknesses and a clear set of personal standards.

For Marcia, true identity achievement is based on meeting the challenge and making the commitment. Some adolescents try to avoid the crisis; some try to avoid the commitment; some try to avoid both. If either the challenge or commitment is avoided, role confusion takes one of three forms. These three forms of role confusion in addition to identity achievement constitute the four identity statuses proposed by Marcia. Identity achievement is the first status. The second status is foreclosure, when the adolescent avoids the challenge by making a commitment without any exploration. This happens often when individuals surrender to the plans that their parents have made for their life. The third status is moratorium, when the youth perpetuates the exploration and challenge without making a commitment. Moratorium is not necessarily an unhealthy status. Because adolescence continues as long as society allows, the search for identity characterized by the moratorium status may continue into young adulthood. The fourth status is diffusion, when adolescents avoid the challenge and refuse to make a commitment. The danger of this status is that diffused adolescents are weak in resisting negative influences.

According to Santrock (2004), some experts investigating identity development challenge Erikson on several points. First, these experts have found substantial evidence that identity formation does not begin or end in adolescence. They also have found that it takes more time and is less dramatic than Erikson expected.

Later research found that moratorium may last into the college years. However, this finding does not contradict Erikson because Erikson, in his day, felt that more adolescents should attend college as a time of psychosocial moratorium. In contrast to the late 2000s, fewer adolescents attended college in the 1950s when Erikson was forming his theory. The age range he used to illustrate the identity challenge was appropriate for his time.

IDENTITY DEVELOPMENT AND SCHOOL ADJUSTMENT

During grade school years, children are still building their self concept. Choosing the right role models is very important during this time. Also important is developing a sense of industry, knowing what one's capabilities are. The social interaction with peers plays a role in supporting the self concept. School adjustment interacts with the positive development of the self concept.

Children's self concept leads them to associate with peers and influences the way they relate to those peers. In trying to understand their competence, these children compare themselves with others. If that comparison leads to a sense of self competence, the children will want to associate and cooperate with other children more than if that comparison leads to a sense of incompetence. If children define themselves as good students, they will want to live up to that self concept. Children who see themselves as loners will be more content to stay away from other children. A teacher can encourage children to develop a positive self concept.

A major threat to the self concept and self esteem of a school-age child is grade retention. One common reason for holding children back one year in the early grades is that these individuals are too immature for age-appropriate grade placement. However, retention has not been shown to have any long-term benefits and it may actually harm the child emotionally. "Children rate retention as the third most horrible thing they can imagine" (Lawson, 2007, p. 89).

VARIABLES REGARDING IDENTITY DEVELOPMENT PROCESS, GENDER, AND ETHNICITY

The development of gender identity leads to conceptual frameworks of perceived appropriate behavior and interests associated with gender. These concepts are influenced greatly by the same-sex parent who becomes a role model for establishing the appropriate gender role. The gender concepts developed in childhood will influence how identity is composed in adolescence. For adolescents from a minority ethnicity, the development of ethnic identity is an important part of identity achievement. In many cases, the preparation for adulthood is the first time that these adolescents have to confront their feelings about their background. While being exposed to alternative sources of group identity from the dominant culture, adolescents have to maintain connectedness with their own ethnicity. Researchers have found that those who establish and maintain an ethnic identity tend to have higher self esteem (Santrock, 2004).

Erikson found gender differences in vocational exploration with men more concerned with establishing a career and women more concerned about establishing a family. These claims were supported by research in the 1960s and the 1970s, but subsequent research has not found any support for gender differences. Women in the 2000s are just as likely to be career-oriented as men are (Santrock, 2007).

RISK AND PROTECTIVE FACTORS FOR SUCCESSFUL IDENTIFY DEVELOPMENT

Successful identity achievement is developed through accepting traditional values and expressing them in a contemporary manner. Therefore, adolescents need the influence of parents for traditional values and the influence of friends for contemporary expression. However, too much influence from either parents or friends may interfere with the adolescents' personal commitment.

Parenting styles influence the achievement of identity in adolescence. A parenting style emphasizing high standards and high communication encourages adolescents' exploration in a supportive environment. A parenting style that emphasizes high standards but low communication may interfere with the healthy exploration of identity potential. Permissive parents who do not establish standards for adolescents are encouraging a diffused identity with no clear commitments (Santrock, 2004).

SUGGESTIONS FOR TEACHERS AT VARIOUS GRADE LEVELS

Teachers can enhance children's identity development at all grade levels by taking an interest in the individual students and asking them to describe their impressions of self. This can be done as part of an age-appropriate class assignment. In preschool, during group conversation, the teacher can ask the children to describe their favorite memory. Although their memories will not go back too far, what the children describe will convey the influences of their developing self concepts. In grade school, a writing assignment might relate to the individual children's likes and dislikes, their favorite heroes, or their capabilities. In high school, students can be given a research assignment to explore specific vocations or the world of work in general.

Teachers should watch for signs of learned helplessness in grade school. If children describe themselves as individuals who cannot succeed, they will shirk the challenges of the classroom. A teacher can intervene by encouraging such students one-on-one or by establishing classroom support groups (Woolfolk, 2007).

It is important that children are constantly given the opportunity to succeed at increasingly challenging tasks. Teachers should avoid inappropriate comparison or competition with others. Students should be encouraged to compete against themselves to improve upon their previous accomplishments. The teacher should take the student's failing as an opportunity to point out how many times the child has succeeded (Woolfolk, 2006).

The high school teacher should be careful not to give into stereotyped perceptions of adolescence. Most adolescents, even those who appear to be antisocial, are involved in healthy exploration. The high school teacher should take the attitude that these students are young adults with the expectation that they will behave as adults. Most adolescents will feel free to approach such a teacher with their problems and concerns. Also, treating the young people as adults will lead to their seeing disciplinary actions as a natural consequence for misbehaviors.

SEE ALSO *Erikson, Erik.*

BIBLIOGRAPHY

Carver, C. S., & Scheier, M. F. (1992). *Perspectives on personality* (2nd ed.). Boston: Allyn & Bacon.

Erikson, E. H. (1963). *Childhood and society* (2nd ed.). New York: Norton.

Lawson, T. J. (2007). *Scientific perspective on pseudoscience and the paranormal: Readings for general psychology.* Upper Saddle River, NJ: Pearson Prentice Hall.

McKinney, K. G. (2001). Identity formation. In W. E. Craighead & C. B. Nemeroff (Eds.), *The Corsini encyclopedia of psychology and behavioral science* (3rd ed., pp. 723–724). New York: Wiley,

Santrock J. W. (2007). *Child development* (11th ed.). New York: McGraw-Hill.

Woolfolk, A. (2007). *Educational psychology* (10th ed.). Boston: Allyn & Bacon.

Ray Brogan

IEP

SEE *Individualized Education Program (IEP).*

IMPRESSION MANAGEMENT

Impression management refers to the process in which individuals attempt to influence the opinions or perceptions others hold of them. Impression management, also referred to as self-presentation, is a goal-directed activity that helps to establish the boundaries of what is considered acceptable behavior; conversely, it also aids in defining what behavior will be met with disapproval. In the classroom, impression management behaviors allow students to make sense of the complex social stratum and help to inform their social identities.

MODELS OF IMPRESSION MANAGEMENT

Writings on impression management were introduced by Goffman (1959). In his seminal book, *The Presentation of Self in Everyday Life*, Goffman shows that the individual is influenced by his or her environment and the perceived audience. Furthermore Goffman posits that the objective of individuals is to convey an image that is consistent with their desired goal (spoken or unspoken). While Goffman's theory is constructive (impressions can influence how individuals perceive themselves), Jones and his colleagues (Jones & Pittman, 1982; Jones & Wortman, 1972) championed strategic self-presentation. Strategic impression management emphasizes the power dynamics and goals that characterize most social interactions. Jones (1990) suggested that the goals or motives in strategic impression management are aimed at negotiating the power dynamics in social relationships such that the individual's power is never diminished.

Leary and Kowalski (1990) elaborated on the work of Goffman (1959) and Jones and his colleagues. Leary and Kowalski's (1990) model is distinctive, in that it elucidates reasons why people are concerned with others' impressions and why they choose to engage in specific impression management behaviors. Though other conceptualizations of impression management did not draw such a distinction, Leary and Kowalski's model posits that impression management is comprised of two distinct processes: *impression motivation* and *impression construction*. Impression motivation, they argue, is a function of several factors (goal-relevance, value of desired outcomes, discrepancy between desired image and current image) that determine whether or not an individual will engage in impression-related attempts. Goal relevance refers to whether or not one's actions are salient to obtaining prescribed goals. Value of desired goals refers to the importance placed on obtaining a particular goal; the value increases as the number of available desired objects decreases. The discrepancy between the desired image and the current image refers to the individual's perception of the closeness between the image others hold and the image he or she wants others to hold.

The second process, impression construction, is influenced by two intrapersonal and three interpersonal factors. Self-concept and desired image constitute the intrapersonal variables; role constraints, target values, and current or potential social image represent the interpersonal variables. Leary and Kowalski asserted that the self-concept variable is the chief impetus of a learner's impressions. Accordingly, students will display what they believe is their greatest asset. Thus, if academics do not constitute the best part of their self-concept, impression management for academic diligence will be low. Furthermore, the motivation to impression manage will be influenced by not only what the students think they are, but what they would like to be and not be; this refers to the second intrapersonal variable, desired and undesired identity image. It appears that attempts to impression manage are, in part, a function of the interaction between these two components. As mentioned above, three interpersonal variables also contribute to impression construction. The *role constraint* variable suggests that individuals who act in a manner that is inconsistent with social expectations risk losing the power associated with that position. The second interpersonal variable, *target values*, indicates that an individual will often modify or change his or her image so that it corresponds to an assumed value of a model. Lastly, *current or potential image*, states that impressions are further shaped by learners' perception of how they are presently perceived and how they believe others will see them in the future.

HOW IMPRESSION MANAGEMENT INFLUENCES CLASSROOM BEHAVIOR

Impression management theory provides a useful framework for understanding students' behavior in classroom situations. Studies on impression management generally indicate that academic diligence or effort is likely when individuals perceives their image as consistent with expectations of being academically competent and that the rewards of projecting such an image are greater than its possible repercussions. Research has demonstrated that if the potential repercussions of projecting an academically diligent image are sufficiently threatening, the student is less likely to project that image. The presence of multiple (and often competing) audiences necessitates an individual student's need to consider what image he or she is willing to project. It has become increasingly evident that classrooms are more than just academic environments; they are also social settings in which students must negotiate the demands/expectations of multiple audiences: the teacher and other students. While research has consistently demonstrated that teachers value and reward students who exhibit academic effort, peer groups, especially the "popular crowds," tend to ostracize those students whose identity or image is based largely on academic effort. Thus, while teachers possess legitimate power over the student, popular peers possess referent power, both of which are instrumental in determining the impression a student projects.

DEVELOPMENTAL AND INDIVIDUAL DIFFERENCES

Studies on impression management have also indicated that development affects impression management. One key assumption of the Leary and Kowalski (1990) model (as well as other explanations of impression management) is that the student must possess the ability to analyze potential interactions (including understanding what others value) and the ability to take another's perspective. Selman (1980) labeled these abilities as Level 3 perspective taking and argued that these abilities do not generally manifest until middle and junior high school years. However, a number of researchers have demonstrated that these abilities develop earlier than Selman (1980) argued. In their study of fourth, sixth and eighth grade students, Juvonen and Murdock (1995) found that younger students were able to demonstrate an understanding of the expectations of others. Another significant developmental difference identified by the authors was that older students, and not younger ones, modified their explanations of effort based on intended audience. What this finding seems to suggest is that while younger students are aware of what others expect, their perception that other students' and teachers' values are congruent represents a lack of understanding of the complexity of multiple audiences. Thus, it appears that the impression strategy a student employs is significantly influenced by cognitive development.

Though Juvonen and Murdock (1995) did not observe significant differences between males and females, gender differences in impression management related to academic diligence have consistently indicated that females are more likely than males to present an image that conveys a desire to be seen as conscientious of academic activities (Grabill, Lasane, Povitsky, Saxe, Munro, Phelps, & Straub, 2005). That this finding has been consistently reported is not surprising. Although academic achievement is seen as a masculine trait, this seems to apply only to one's natural abilities; effort (diligence) is largely viewed as a feminine characteristic. Impression management theory posits that since achievement with effort (compared to "natural" achievement) is by and large a feminine quality, most males would prefer to project images that would not call into question their masculinity for fear of disapproval.

Though few studies have explicitly investigated ethnic differences in impression management, it has been argued that many minority students (particularly African Americans) view academic diligence differently from Caucasian students. Several researchers (e.g., Czopp, Lasane, Swigard, Bradshaw & Hammer, 1998; Fordham & Ogbu, 1986) have reported that African American students attempt to conceal their academic selves for fear of social disapproval; instead, many of these students project an impression consistent with "Joe Cool," an image that is less concerned with academic effort. Furthermore, studies have suggested that the impression that some minority students adopt is based on the belief that academic diligence is a mostly "White" phenomenon; thus, to project an academic-conscious image would be perceived as denying one's culture. Though this theory has received considerable attention, additional research is warranted.

IMPLICATIONS FOR EDUCATORS

The ability of educators to recognize and acknowledge the effects of impression management on academic performance has important, yet feasible, implications for their ability to work effectively with diverse student populations. Foremost, educators need to actively and aggressively diversify the teacher pool. Administrators communicate to students their attitudes regarding academic achievement through those persons whom they hire to educate. Thus, there needs to be fair representation of men and women in academically rigorous courses as well as less academically rigorous ones. To that end, all physical education classes cannot be taught by Mr. Jones and not all of the language arts classes should be taught by Mrs. Smith.

Second, teachers are encouraged to reflect on their own attitudes towards students who tend to display academically disidentified behaviors. As research suggests, students' struggles with the problem of multiple audiences, for example, may manifest as academically disidentified (Osborne, 1995) or unconcerned behavior; this manifestation may, in turn, prejudice teacher-student interactions, particularly evaluations. It is possible (and likely) that unexamined attitudes could lead to interactions that result in negative evaluations, thus reinforcing an adversarial relationship with academically minded individuals and fostering a negative association with academic-related activities.

Lastly, teachers need to realize that students do contemplate the challenges of negotiating beliefs and stereotypes related to academic diligence. Teachers might consider purposefully addressing this issue with students in an effort to monitor and correct any detrimental views students may harbor. Also, an added benefit to this practice is that students may become more engaged in the learning process and, as research has indicated, students who are engaged in the learning process tend to evidence more positive long-term consequences.

BIBLIOGRAPHY

Baumeister, R. F. (1982). A self-presentational view of social phenomenon. *Psychological Bulletin, 91*, 3–26.

Czopp, A. M., Lasane, T. P., Sweigard, P. N., Bradshaw, S. D., & Hammer, E. D. (1998). Masculine styles of self-presentation in the classroom: Perceptions of Joe Cool. *Journal of Social Behavior and Personality, 13*, 281–294.

Fordham, S., & Ogbu, J. (1986). Black students' school success: Coping with the "burden of acting White." *Urban Review, 18,* 176–206.

Goffman, E. (1959). *The presentation of self in everyday life.* Garden City, NY: Doubleday Anchor.

Grabill, K., Lasane, T. P., Povitsky, W. T., Saxe, P., Mungro, G. B., Phelps, L. M., & Straub, J. (2005). Gender and study behavior: How social perception, social norm adherence, and structured academic behavior are predicted by gender. *North American Journal of Psychology, 7,* 7–24.

Jones, E. E. (1990). *Interpersonal perception.* New York: Freeman.

Jones, E. E., & Pittman, T. S. (1982). Toward a general theory of strategic self-presentation. In J. Suls (Ed.), *Psychological Perspectives on the self* (Vol. 1, pp. 231–262). Hillsdale, NJ: Erlbaum.

Jones, E. E., & Wortman, C. (1972). *Ingratiation: An attributional approach.* Morristown, NJ: General Learning Press.

Juvonen, J., & Murdock, T. B. (1995). Grade-level differences in the social value of effort: Implications for self-presentation tactics of early adolescents. *Child Development, 66,* 1694–1705.

Leary, M. R., & Kowalski, R. M. (1990). Impression management: A literature review and two-component model. *Psychological Bulletin 107,* 34–47.

Osborne, J. W. (1995). Academics, self-esteem, and race: A look at the assumptions underlying the disidentification hypothesis. *Personality and Social Psychology Bulletin, 21,* 449–455.

Schlenker, B. R. (1980). *Impression management: The self-concept, social identity, and interpersonal relations.* Monterey, CA: Brooks/Cole.

Selman, R. L. (1980). *The growth of interpersonal understanding.* San Diego, CA: Academic Press.

Chammie C. Austin

IMPULSIVE DECISION-MAKING

Decision-making can range from a highly rational style involving careful consideration of cognitive cues to a very impulsive act-without-thinking process that relies primarily on affective and physiological cues. Impulsive decision-makers are those who operate on the far end of this decision-making continuum. Whereas rational decision-makers carefully consider beliefs about the consequences of their actions when making decisions, impulsive decision-makers often fail to even consider such consequences, relying instead on cues that are often salient in the immediate present. As a result, individuals with an impulsive decision-making style often make decisions without a great deal of thought, fail to plan ahead for a variety of situations, and are more likely to act on impulse as compared to their rational decision-making counterparts (Donohew et al., 2000, 2004).

Impulsive decision-making is not, in and of itself, believed to be a personality trait. It is, however, thought to be a tendency that flows from the trait of impulsivity.

Impulsivity itself is conceptualized in different ways by different researchers in the field. For instance, some researchers treat impulsivity as a unidimensional trait (Grano et al., 2004), whereas others have provided evidence for multiple dimensions of impulsivity, identifying two (Dawe & Loxton, 2004) or as many as four dimensions (Whiteside & Lynam, 2001). The four-dimensional conceptualization of impulsivity includes: 1) urgency, 2) lack of premeditation, 3) lack of perseverance, and 4) sensation-seeking. Additionally, whereas other researchers view impulsivity and sensation-seeking (or thrill-seeking) as a single "supertrait" (Zuckerman & Kuhlman, 2000), some view impulsivity and sensation-seeking as different, albeit related dimensions (Donohew et al., 2000, 2004).

RELATION OF IMPULSIVE DECISION-MAKING TO PERSONALITY

While impulsivity is included at some level in many theories of personality, precisely how it fits into such theories, as well as how much emphasis it receives, tends to vary (Whiteside & Lynam, 2001). For instance, Eysenck and Eysenck's (1985) Three Factor Theory of personality focuses on the roles of neuroticism, extraversion, and psychoticism in an explication of personality processes. It considers impulsivity to consist of two components: venturesomeness and impulsiveness, which are thought to correspond to the extraversion and psychoticism factors, respectively.

McCrae and Costa's (1990) Five Factor Model of personality is focused on neuroticism, extraversion, openness to experience, agreeableness, and conscientiousness, each of which is composed of six facets. In this model, impulsivity is represented by a number of facets across the factors. For instance, the neuroticism factor contains an impulsiveness facet and the conscientiousness factor contains both self-control and deliberation facets. Facets on other dimensions, such as extraversion's excitement-seeking facet, also overlap with conceptualizations of impulsivity (Whiteside & Lynam, 2001).

Finally, Zuckerman and colleagues' (1993) Alternative Five Factor Model gives impulsivity perhaps its most prominent role compared to these other theories, combining it with sensation-seeking in a single "supertrait" termed "impulsive sensation-seeking." This model considers impulsive sensation-seeking to be one of five major traits that drive personality. The others are neuroticism-anxiety, aggression-hostility, activity, and sociability. Although early work with this model focused solely on the role of sensation-seeking as a predictor of a variety of behaviors, later work combined sensation-seeking with impulsivity to form this single trait (Zuckerman & Kuhlman, 2000).

IMPULSIVE DECISION-MAKING AND ACADEMIC OUTCOMES

One question concerns how impulsivity and impulsive decision-making affect behaviors. A number of studies exist on this topic across a variety of areas, with the overall theme being one of association with maladaptive and problem behaviors. For instance, impulsivity has been found to be related to a variety of antisocial behaviors, delinquency, and a lack of social adjustment (Cooper et al., 2003; Schwartz et al., 1999) and, thus, is a focal point among many theories of crime (Lynam & Miller, 2004). Impulsivity is a key diagnostic criterion for numerous disorders in the Diagnostic and Statistical Manual for Mental Disorders, or DSM-IV (American Psychiatric Association, 2000; Whiteside et al., 2005). Further, impulsive decision-making (and more generally, impulsivity) has been widely studied in the area of health risk behaviors among youth, exhibiting positive associations with alcohol use, drug use, risky sexual behavior, eating disorders, and even body piercing (Cooper et al., 2000, 2003; Dawe & Loxton, 2004; Donohew et al., 2000, 2004; Greif et al., 1999; Hoyle et al., 2000; Zuckerman & Kuhlman, 2000).

In the specific realm of education, impulsivity has been found to relate to, and may adversely affect, a number of key academic outcomes. Indeed, the educational process is a long-term, goal-oriented task. Given this fact, theoretically it might be expected that such an undertaking would be adversely affected by impulsivity, given that impulsive individuals exhibit a tendency to act on immediate demands instead of making decisions based on long-term goals (Spinella & Miley, 2003).

The research as of 2008 in the area of impulsivity and academic outcomes does, in fact, bear out this correlation. Impulsivity has been shown to be related to educational underachievement in a number of studies (Cooper et al., 2003; Lynam & Miller, 2004; Spinella & Miley, 2004; Weithorn, Kagen, & Marcus, 1984). In fact, those who are impulsive are more likely to fall behind their peers and achieve lower grades compared to those who exhibit a more rationale style. For instance, Meade (1981) found that first grade students with a low socio-economic status who exhibited impulsive behavior had lower grades and lower achievement scores than their peers, even when IQ was held constant. Among older students, another study found impulsivity and college students' grades to be inversely related, with higher impulsivity relating to lower grades (Spinella & Miley, 2003). Some researchers have even gone as far as to suggest that there is a positive association between impulsivity and academic failure (Vigil-Colet & Morales-Vives, 2005).

In addition, although limited research has been conducted on the association between impulsivity and academic cheating, some studies have examined the link between the two (Anderman & Cupp, 2006; Kelly & Worell, 1978; Miller et al, 2007). For instance, in one study, college students were given the opportunity to falsify scores in order to obtain course credit. Among the female participants, the students who cheated were significantly more impulsive than were the non-cheaters. Another study demonstrated a positive association between impulsivity and academic cheating among a large sample of high school students (Anderman & Cupp, 2006). These researchers have suggested that impulsive students experience difficulty with self-regulation, which leads to decreased self-control, and, in turn, increased cheating.

Finally, there is a large literature in the specific area of Attention Deficit Hyperactivity Disorder (ADHD). ADHD is itself characterized by impulsivity, inattention, and hyperactivity (American Psychiatric Association, 2000; Hoza, Owens, & Pelham, 1999). In the context of ADHD, impulsivity can manifest itself in a number of ways, including interrupting others, blurting out answers, not listening to instructions before beginning a task, and not waiting for a turn. A criterion of ADHD is that such difficulties impair functioning in academic, occupational, or social settings (American Psychiatric Association, 2000). Academic underachievement has also been identified as a primary long-term outcome associated with ADHD (Manuzza et al., 1993), with up to 80% of students with ADHD exhibiting problems in academic performance (Cantwell & Baker, 1991). Though impulsivity is a part of ADHD, impulsivity and impulsive decision-making can occur exclusive of ADHD (Furman, 2005). Thus, both impulsive ADHD and impulsive non-ADHD students may be at risk of similar poor academic outcomes (Merrell, & Tymms, 2001).

SUGGESTIONS FOR PRACTITIONERS

One challenge is identifying strategies to be used by those who work with impulsive youth. A primary obstacle which impulsive students struggle with is their lack of metacognition, that is, their ability to be reflective and think about thinking. Therefore, it is important to help impulsive students learn to think about making decisions instead of acting before thinking. Another general consideration is the fact that impulsive students do not consider alternatives effectively; therefore, it is important for those working with such students to emphasize the consideration of alternative options and alternative ways of thinking in decision-making (Margolis et al., 1977).

Moreover, many strategies for reducing students' impulsive behaviors have been reported in the literature. Cognitive and/or behavioral strategies are popular approaches given that students' problems with impulsivity are in regards to their thinking and behaviors (Baer & Nietzel, 1991). Self-instruction training, in which students learn to guide themselves through tasks by asking and then answering a series of questions, is a commonly used treatment (Baer & Nietzel, 1991). For example, in one self-instruction procedure, the impulsive student learns to size up the demands of a task, cognitively rehearse the task, guide their performance through self-instruction, and where appropriate, give self-reinforcements (Meichenbaum & Goodman, 1971).

Finally, the need for effective in-classroom interventions for impulsive students has also been identified. Given that there is a connection between impulsivity and a lack of metacognition, in-classroom interventions may help in this area (Bornas & Servera, 1992). In-class training, as opposed to out-of-class training, may be important in helping students to generalize learned skills to the classroom environment. Having students use strategies that are taught in real learning contexts may be important (Bornas & Servera, 1992), as is having peers model appropriate behaviors (Margolis et al., 1977). In addition, impulsive students may benefit from a classroom atmosphere that is mastery-oriented (Anderman & Cupp, 2006).

SEE ALSO *Sensation-Seeking.*

BIBLIOGRAPHY

American Psychiatric Association. (2000). *Diagnostic and statistical manual of mental disorders* (4th ed.). Washington DC: Author.

Anderman, E. M., & Cupp, P. K. (2006, August). Impulsivity and academic cheating. Paper presented at the annual meeting of the American Psychological Association, New Orleans, LA.

Baer, R., & Nietzel, M. (1991). Cognitive and behavioral treatment of impulsivity in children: A meta-analytic review of the outcome literature. *Journal of Clinical Child Psychology, 20,* 400–412.

Bornas, X., & Servera, M. (1992). Cognitive training programs to reduce impulsivity-related achievement problems: The need of in-classroom interventions. *Learning and Instruction, 2,* 89–100.

Cantwell, D. P., & Baker, L. (1991). Association between attention-deficit hyperactivity disorder and learning disorders. *Journal of Learning Disabilities, 24,* 88–95.

Cooper, M. L., Agocha, V. B., & Sheldon, M. S. (2000). A motivational perspective on risky behaviors: The role of personality and affect regulatory processes. *Journal of Personality, 68*(6), 1059–1087.

Cooper, M. L., Wood, P. K., Orcutt, H. K., & Albino, A. (2003). Personality and the predisposition to engage in risky or problem behaviors during adolescence. *Journal of Personality and Social Psychology, 84*(2), 390–410.

Costa, P. T., & McCrae, R. R. (1990). Personality disorders and the five factor model of personality. *Journal of Personality Disorders, 4,* 362-371.

Dawe, S., & Loxton, N. J. (2004). The role of impulsivity in the development of substance abuse and eating disorders. *Neuroscience and Biobehavioral Reviews, 28,* 343–351.

Donohew, L., Bardo, M. T., & Zimmerman, R. S. (2004). Personality and risky behavior: Communication and prevention. In R. M. Stelmack (Ed.), *On the psychobiology of personality: Essays in honor of Marvin Zuckerman* (pp. 223–245). Amsterdam: Elsevier.

Donohew, L., Zimmerman, R. S., Cupp, P. S., Novak, S., Colon, S., & Abell, R. (2000). Sensation seeking, impulsive decision-making, and risky sex: Implications for risk-taking and design of interventions. *Personality and Individual Differences, 28,* 1079–1091.

Furman, L. (2005). What is attention-deficit hyperactivity disorder (ADHD)? *Journal of Child Neurology, 20*(12), 994–1002.

Grano, N., Virtanen, M., Vahtera, J., Elovainio, M., & Kivimaki, M. (2004). Impulsivity as a predictor of smoking and alcohol consumption. *Personality and Individual Differences, 37,* 1693–1700.

Greif, J., Hewitt, W., Armstrong, M. L. (1999). Tattooing and body piercing: Body art practices among college students. *Clinical Nursing Research, 8,* 368–385.

Hoyle, R. H., Fejfar, M. C., & Miller, J. D. (2000). Personality and sexual risk taking: A quantitative review. *Journal of Personality, 68,* 1203–1231.

Hoza, B., Owens, J., & Pelham, W. (1999). *Attention-deficit/hyperactivity disorder.* Needham Heights, MA: Allyn & Bacon.

Kelly, J. A., & Worell, L. (1978). Personality characteristics, parent behaviors, and sex of subject in relation to cheating. *Journal of Research in Personality, 12,* 179–188.

Lynam, D. R., & Miller, J. D. (2004). Personality pathways to impulsive behavior and their relations to deviance: Results from three samples. *Journal of Quantitative Criminology, 20,* 319–341.

Manuzza, S., Gittelman-Klein, R., Bessler, A., Malloy, P., & LaPadula, M. (1993). Adult outcome of hyperactive boys: Educational achievement, occupational rank, and psychiatric status. *Archive of General Psychiatry, 50,* 565–576.

Margolis, H., Brannigan, G. G., & Poston, M. A. (1977). Modification of impulsivity. *Elementary School Journal, 77*(3), 231–237.

Meade, E. R. (1981). Impulse control and cognitive functioning in lower- and middle-SES children: A developmental study. *Merrill-Palmer Quarterly, 27*(3), 271–285.

Meichenbaum, D. H., & Goodman, J. (1971). Training impulsive children to talk to themselves: A means of developing self-control. *Journal of Abnormal Psychology, 77*(2), 115–126.

Merrell, C., & Tymms, P. B. (2001). Inattention, hyperactivity and impulsiveness: Their impact on academic achievement and progress. *British Journal of Educational Psychology, 77*(1), 43–56.

Miller, A. D., Murdock, T. B., Anderman, E. M., & Poindexter, A. L. (2007). Who are all these cheaters? Characteristics of academically dishonest students. In E. M. Anderman & T. B. Murdock (Eds.), *Psychology of Academic Cheating* (pp. 9 32). London: Elsevier.

Miller, J., Flory, K., Lynam, D., & Leukefeld, C. (2003). A test of the four-factor model of impulsivity-related traits. *Personality and Individual Differences, 34,* 1403–1418.

Reynolds, B., Ortengren, A., Richards, J. B., & de Wit, H. (2006). Dimensions of impulsive behavior: Personality and behavioral measures. *Personality and Individual Differences, 40,* 305–315.

Schwartz, D., McFayden-Ketchum, S., Dodge, K. E., Pettit, G. S., & Bates, J. E. (1999). Early behavior problems as a predictor of later peer group victimization: moderators and mediators in the pathways of social risk. Journal of *Abnormal Clinical Psychology, 27,* 191–201.

Spinella, M., & Miley, W. (2003). Impulsivity and Academic Achievement in College Students. *College Student Journal, 37*(4), 545–549.

Spinella, M., & Miley, W. (2004). Orbitofrontal function and educational attainment. *College Student Journal, 38*(3), 333–338.

Vigil-Colet, A., & Morales-Vives, F. (2005). How impulsivity is related to intelligence and academic achievement. *Spanish Journal of Psychology, 8*(2), 199–204.

Weithorn, C., Kagen, E., & Marcus, M. (1984). The relationship of activity level ratings and cognitive impulsivity to task performance and academic achievement. *Journal of Child Psychology and Psychiatry, 25*(4), 587–606.

Whiteside, S. P., & Lynam, D. R. (2001). The five factor model and impulsivity: Using a structural model of personality to understand impulsivity. *Personality and Individual Differences, 30,* 669–689.

Whiteside, S. P., Lynam, D. R., Miller, J. D., & Reynolds, S. K. (2005). Validation of the UPPS impulsive behaviour scale: A four-factor model of impulsivity. *European Journal of Personality, 19,* 559–574.

Zuckerman, M., & Kuhlman, D. M. (2000). Personality and risk taking: Common biosocial factors. *Journal of Personality, 68*(6), 999–1029.

Zuckerman, M., Kuhlman, D. M., Joireman, J., Teta, P., & Kraft, M. A. (1993). Comparison of three structural models for personality: The big three, the big five, and the alternative five. *Journal of Personality and Social Psychology, 65*(4), 757–768.

Seth M. Noar
Larson Pierce

INDIVIDUAL *VS.* GROUP ADMINISTERED TESTS

Psychological and educational assessment of students has been prominent since the early 1900s. The results garnered from these assessments have been used for a myriad of purposes, such as identifying children who (a) are suspected of having learning difficulties, (b) qualify for gifted programs or programs requiring specific talents (e.g., enrollment in a music or arts program), or (c) may be suffering from emotional distress (e.g., depression, anxiety). Further, group-based data focusing on a chosen index (e.g., standardized achievement scores, school drop-out rates) have also been compared across school districts and/or across states to examine learning outcomes. In common among all assessment processes is the gathering of data to make informed educational and mental health decisions (Neukrug & Fawcett, 2006).

The term *assessment* includes a broad array of methods. Sattler (2001) outlined four main types, or pillars, of assessment, each of which is complementary and adds unique information not found in the other methods. These pillars include (a) interviews with parents, teachers, and children, (b) observations of the child's behavior, and (c) informal assessment procedures such as reviewing class work, school records, or personal documents, for example, diaries, drawings, and self-report logs. The fourth and most frequently used method is the administration of norm-referenced tests (most notably intelligence and achievement measures) for diagnostic purposes. Such tests compare a child's results, in standardized form, against an established norm group. Considering the emphasis that teachers, parents, and schools often place on the results of norm-referenced tests, this entry focuses on this particular assessment method.

The results derived from norm-referenced tests often have been used to establish or support many legislative and educational policies (see Cohen & Swerdlik, 2002). The ramifications of these policies to schools, students, and the larger community underscore the need for tests to demonstrate sound psychometric properties (i.e., evidence of reliability and validity) and appropriateness for their intended use (Anastasi, 1988; Moreland, Fowler, & Honaker, 1997). A key factor in this regard is the manner in which tests are administered. Indeed, from the beginning of psychological testing much attention has been devoted to ensuring that test scores are invariant regardless of whether they are administered individually or in a group setting (Geisinger, 2000; Kline, 2005). Although strident measures have been taken to control method variance, each format contains inherent advantages and disadvantages. This entry reviews the most salient aspects of each format.

A BRIEF HISTORY OF TESTING

The history of psychological testing is one marked by necessity followed by innovation (Geisinger, 2000). Although the lineage of psychological measurement dates back at least 4,000 years (Thorndike & Lohman, 1990), the first modern test of intelligence was created at the turn of the 20th century, in response to problems reported by French public schools experiencing a sharp increase in student enrollment. The overcrowded conditions prompted a decision to remove children from the regular education classroom who were not learning at a satisfactory level. The 1905 work of Alfred Binet (1857–1911) and Theophile Simon led to the construction of a test containing a series of brief mental tasks, which could be individually administered to children ages 3 to 11. Revisions to this original test included expanding the age range to adulthood, increasing the number of items comprising each test, providing standard directions for administration, and introducing the concept of mental age, which was the chronological age of a group of typically developed children who performed at the same level as the examiner (Aiken, 2006).

A short time later, American psychologists made significant revisions to the original Binet-Simon scale. These changes included arranging the items in order of difficulty and assigning points for the level of correctness of an examinee's response. The most durable of these changes was provided by Lewis Terman and colleagues, who gathered extensive normative data on the Binet-Simon scale from hundreds of children in the Stanford, California, area. From this data, numerous revisions were made, most notably the inclusion of an intelligence quotient or IQ—a quantitative score that was defined as the ratio of the child's chronological age and mental age (Neukrug & Fawcett, 2006). Later known as the Stanford-Binet Intelligence Test, Terman's revised test served as the standard of testing for the first two decades of the 20th century (Aiken, 1996) and ushered in both the intelligence testing movement and the clinical testing movement (Boake, 2002; Cohen, Swerdlik, & Smith, 1992). The original Binet-Simon scales and their subsequent modifications also served as the prototype for most modern intelligence tests.

Group testing also was developed to address a pressing concern. The involvement of the United States in World War I prompted the need for a group-based cognitive test that could quickly determine if recruits were fit for military service and to identify those who could be trained as officers. Although considered crude by 21st century standards, two multiple-choice "intelligence" tests were created and administered to almost 2 million recruits. The Army Alpha was designed and administered to recruits who were literate and proficient in English, while the Army Beta was administered to foreign-born recruits or those who could not read with proficiency. Although both versions underwent significant revisions, their basis served as the foundation for most group-based intelligence tests used today. Further, these early tests served as the prototype for group tests examining other constructs (e.g., achievement, specific aptitude, psychopathology) across various environments (e.g., schools, mental health clinics)(Neukrug & Fawcett, 2006).

ADVANTAGES
AND DISADVANTAGES
OF INDIVIDUAL TESTING

Individually administered norm-referenced cognitive and achievement tests have been used for a wide variety of purposes. In conjunction with other norm-referenced tests and assessment methods, cognitive and achievement tests have typically been used to provide in-depth information on student's (a) intellectual functioning or academic standing in comparison to same-age peers, (b) ability to process certain mental or academic tasks, which can facilitate diagnostic impressions such as learning disabilities, giftedness, or mental retardation, and (c) initial or continuing eligibility for special education services. In most cases, cognitive and achievement tests provide a wide array of specific tasks that the student is asked to perform either within a given time frame or according to specific scoring guidelines. Each test is concluded when the allotted time is reached (i.e., a timed test) or the student gives a continuous number of failed responses (i.e., a power test). Most tests aggregate the task scores to yield a general or overall score, which is assumed to indicate a student's global level of cognitive or achievement functioning. Nevertheless, as the general score can be influenced by extremely high (or low) performance on one or more specific tasks, composite scores also are computed to assess functioning within a specific domain. For example, cognitive tasks that measure a student's verbal reasoning abilities and general knowledge would be combined to form a verbal composite. Likewise, achievement tasks that assess a student's aptitude for solving math problems or for identifying numbers would be combined to form a math composite.

There are numerous advantages for using individually administered cognitive and achievement tests. First, direct one-to-one attention allows the student and examiner to establish solid rapport, which is essential for obtaining valid results (Sattler, 2001). Also, the examiner has direct control of the testing environment, which includes ensuring that the environment itself is conducive to optimal student performance (e.g., making sure the temperature of the room is not too hot or cold, eliminating non-relevant stimuli that would distract the student). Second, the one-to-one attention allows the examiner to observe student behaviors that may be interfering with task performance but not reflected in the score (e.g., fatigue) or assist in diagnosis (e.g., difficulty remaining in seat). Third, because most task items are orally administered by the examiner, little reading is required by the student, which makes it possible to test very young students or those with limited reading skills (Thorndike, 2005). Finally, scores from individual tests can be interpreted across a variety of levels. For example, in addition to determining the general cognitive or achievement level of the student, composite and even subtest scores can be examined to determine specific processing deficits. Thus, individually administered tests yield detailed information on a student's cognitive or achievement functioning that is not typically obtained from group administered tests.

Nevertheless, there are some disadvantages to using individually administered tests. Perhaps the biggest limitation is the cost of the tests themselves, both monetarily and with respect to time. With the cost of most major tests close to or exceeding $1,000 (U.S.), purchasing these tests places a financial burden on school districts, especially those with limited economic resources. Further, learning to administer and interpret the results from the tests (particularly the cognitive tests) requires extensive training, and administration time ranges from one to four hours. Finally, the tests purposely include a wide array of tasks so that an adequate sampling of important cognitive or achievement domains are covered (Anastasi, 1988). Nevertheless, one of the most persistent criticisms (particularly with regard to cognitive tests) is that the underlying conceptual framework of most tests (and thus the tasks included) is largely atheoretical or based on different theories of intelligence (Flanagan & Ortiz, 2006). For example, the commonly used scales in the Wechsler series were originally based on clinical practice rather than a specific theory, while the original Stanford-Binet scales were based on the theory of general intelligence, or *g*, which proposed that all mental abilities can be explained by a single global intellectual functioning (Thorndike, 2005). More contemporary cognitive tests are based on neurophysiological modeling of the brain, while others are based on theories that emphasize broad fluid (i.e., innate) and crystallized (i.e., learned) abilities (Harrison & Flanagan, 2005). Thus, the use of one test may not adequately address domains covered by another test. In the early 2000s, attempts were made to create a cross-battery approach, whereby examiners are not relegated to using one test but instead use portions of multiple tests to ensure that specific domains are covered (e.g., McGrew & Flanagan, 1998). However, more research is needed to verify its clinical utility.

ADVANTAGES AND DISADVANTAGES OF GROUP TESTING

Most students will be administered a group administered cognitive or achievement test during their studies. Indeed, of the millions of cognitive tests that are administered to students annually, only a small fraction of these are individually administered (Cohen & Swerdlik, 2002). Considering their practicality, group tests are used across a variety of environments, including military, industrial/organizational, and educational. Thus, group administered tests have a broader application than individual tests (Aiken, 2006). Like their individually administered counterparts, most group administered tests consist of subtests that assess a variety of cognitive or academic domains and are either timed or power tests. However, the scoring format for most group administered tests is multiple-choice, which is less flexible and yields much less diagnostic information. For this reason, school-based group administered tests are used as screeners to determine whether further evaluation (often using an individually administered test) is warranted.

From their inception, it was clear that group administered tests could address some of the limitations inherent in individually administered tests. For example, by using only printed materials and following a standardized administration procedure, the financial and personnel resources are much less than the costs associated with individually administered tests. Further, most group administered tests have standardized and computerized scoring systems, which reduces the time necessary to score the protocols and thus minimizes scoring error. Moreover, given the nature of the format, group administered tests can be given to as many students who can comfortably fit into a room, which reduces test administration time and increases testing efficiency. Finally, considering the potentially unlimited number of students who would be administered a group administered test, the norms created are often based on a sample that is much larger than individually administered tests. This advantage allows for a direct comparison of scores across select demographic variables (e.g., race, disability status) that may not be possible when using individually administered tests.

Nevertheless, there are important disadvantages when considering group administered tests. For example, the format does not allow for in-depth observations of individual students as they complete the test. Thus, behaviors such as fatigue, low motivation, anxiety, hunger, and other states that may interfere with performance are not observed. Further, because the examiner may be less trained in the nuances of the test (in comparison to those who administer individual tests), the examiner may break standardization and inadvertently (and inappropriately) answer students' queries or not be able to monitor the testing environment with the same fidelity as can be given to the individual testing environment. Another limitation is the restriction of responses to multiple choice, whereas items on many individually administered tests have different levels of scoring depending on the complexity of the response. In this regard, group administered items may unduly penalize creative or original thinkers. Further, although the sample size of a group administered test may be large, it may also not be representative of children of a particular demographic. For example, many group administered cognitive and achievement tests are normed by students who take the test in the fall and in the spring. However, many students may choose not to take the test (when given a choice) or not be motivated to perform their best on the test (Aiken, 2006). Finally, the results of group administered tests can be used inappropriately. For example, the data obtained from such tests can be used to diagnose and place students into special programs, which should only occur from individually administered tests (Cohen & Swerdlik, 2002).

SEE ALSO *Criterion-Referenced Tests.*

BIBLIOGRAPHY

Anastasi, A. (1988). *Psychological testing* (6th ed.). New York: Macmillan.

Boake, C. (2002). From the Binet-Simon to the Wechsler-Bellevue: Tracing the history of intelligence testing. *Journal of Clinical and Experimental Neuropsychology, 24,* 383–405.

Cohen, R. J., & Swerdlik, M. E. (2002). *Psychological testing and measurement: An introduction to tests and measurement* (5th ed.). New York: McGraw-Hill.

Cohen, R. J., Swerdlik, M. E., & Smith, D. K. (1992). *Psychological testing and measurement: An introduction to tests and measurement* (2nd ed.). Mountain View, CA: Mayfield.

Flanagan, D. P., & Ortiz, S. O. (2006). Best practices in intellectual assessment: Future directions. In J. Grimes & A. Thomas, Alex (Eds.), *Best practices in school psychology IV* (pp. 1351–1372). Washington, DC: National Association of School Psychologists.

Geisinger, K. F. (2000). Psychological testing at the end of the millennium: A brief historical review. *Professional Psychology: Research and Practice, 31,* 117–118.

Harrison, P. L., & Flanagan, D. P. (2005). *Contemporary intellectual assessment: Theories, tests, and issues* (2nd ed.). New York: Guilford.

Kline, T. J. B. (2005). *Psychological testing: A practical approach to design and evaluation.* Thousand Oaks, CA: Sage.

McGrew, K. S., & Flanagan, D. P. (1998). *The intelligence test desk reference (ITDR): Gf-Gc cross-battery assessment.* Needham Heights, MA: Allyn & Bacon.

Moreland, K., Fowler, R. D., & Honaker, L. M. (1997). Future directions in the use of psychological assessment for treatment planning and outcome assessment: Predictions and recommendations. In M. E. Maruish (Ed.), *The use of psychological testing for treatment planning and outcomes assessment* (2nd ed.) (pp. 1415–1436). Mahwah, NJ: Erlbaum.

Neukrug, E. S., & Fawcett, R. C. (2006). *Essentials of testing and achievement: A practical guide for counselors, social workers, and psychologists.* Belmont, CA: Thompson Brooks/Cole.

Roid, G. H. (2003). *The Stanford-Binet Intelligence Scales* (5th ed.). Itasca, IL: Riverside.

Sattler, J. M. (2001). *Assessment of children: Cognitive applications* (4th ed.). San Diego, CA: Author.

Thorndike, R. M. (2005). *Measurement and evaluation in psychology and education* (7th ed.). Upper Saddle River, NJ: Pearson Education.

Thorndike, R. M., & Lohman, D. F. (1990). *A century of ability testing.* Chicago: Riverside.

Richard Gilman

INDIVIDUALIZED EDUCATION PROGRAM (IEP)

Individualized Education Programs, or IEPs as they are commonly called, are an integral part of the U.S. education system. They are the written documents that direct the provision of special education services to students with disabilities who need them. Increasing numbers of students in U.S. public schools have been deemed to need special education services, in a wider variety of categories, including learning disabilities, speech-language impairments, other health impairments, mental retardation, emotional disturbance, autism, visual impairments, hearing impairments, and others, totaling 13 separate categories in 2004. IEPs are considered a centerpiece of the special education process and, thus, necessary to understand for obtaining a perspective on special education as a whole.

DEFINITION OF THE INDIVIDUALIZED EDUCATION PROGRAM

The Individualized Education Program (IEP) is a written document required for each child who is eligible to receive special education services. It is provided to a student who has been determined first to have a disability and, second, to need special education services because of that disability. The IEP, the team that develops it, and what it must contain are governed by Part B of the Individuals with Disabilities Education Act (IDEA) and amendments to it. The IEP provides information on children's current levels of performance and directs the special services and supports that are provided to students who have IEPs. It includes provisions for defining annual goals, evaluating progress, and formalizing what is to be a free and appropriate public education (FAPE) for the student with the disability.

IEPs have several required components. Among the information that is to be included in IEPs are the following: (1) present levels of academic achievement and functional performance, (2) measurable annual goals, (3) special education, related services, and supplementary aids and services, (4) amount of time students will not participate in general education classes, (5) participation in state or district-wide academic assessments (including accommodations to be provided and reasons for using an alternate assessment if the child will not participate in the regular assessment), (6) initiation date and projected duration of IEP, (7) transition services, and (8) how student progress toward annual goals will be measured and when periodic reports will be provided to parents. Access to and participation in the general curriculum and use of research-based procedures are emphasized in the preparation of IEPs (Yell, Shriner, & Katsiyannis, 2006). States or districts may add to the basic components as they see appropriate, but failure to include all required components has been a source of litigation (Yell, 2006).

LEGISLATIVE HISTORY

The passage of the 1975 Education of the All Handicapped Children's Act (EHA), also commonly known as Public Law 94–142, contained the first requirement for the development of the Individualized Education Program (IEP) for a child with a disability requiring the provision of special education services. Subsequent to the 1975 EHA, reauthorizations of the law refined and adjusted the IEP requirements. Public Law 99–457 (EHA Amendments of 1986) added requirements for early intervention services for infants and toddlers. Public Law 101–476 (EHA Amendments of 1990) renamed the law as the Individuals with Disabilities Education Act (IDEA). Public Law 105–017 (IDEA Amendments of 1997) initiated alignment of IDEA with the Elementary and Secondary Education Act and required participation of students with disabilities in state and district-wide assessments. Public Law 108–446 (IDEA Amendments of 2004) adjusted the name of the law to the Individuals with Disabilities Education Improvement Act and further aligned its requirements to those of the Elementary and Secondary Education Act, particularly its accountability requirements.

With each reauthorization, IEP requirements were adjusted to address the new focus and challenges or needs that were identified during the time since the previous reauthorization. The IDEA amendments in 2004 introduced several adjustments to the IEP, with the intention of addressing the need for increased accountability in line with the requirements of the Elementary and Secondary Education Act, known as No Child Left Behind. The 2004 reauthorization also introduced an easier IEP process, including less paperwork and the need for fewer meetings (President's Commission on Excellence in Special Education, 2002; Yell, 2006).

Among the 2004 provisions were the ability to excuse from required IEP team membership anyone deemed to be unnecessary if agreed to by both school personnel and the child's parents, dropping the requirements to have short-term objectives (except for those students participating in the state alternate assessment) and allowing IEPs to be changed without reconvening the IEP team between annual meetings, as long as the IEP team and the parents agreed. In an attempt to study the idea of having IEP teams meet only every three years rather than the required annual meetings, a pilot program for up to 15 states was initiated in 2004 to test the implementation and consequences of three-year IEPs.

LEGAL REQUIREMENTS

The legal requirements for the Individualized Education Program (including the IEP team and the document itself) encompass not only what must be included in the IEP (see Definition) but also specifics of the process. The IEP team must meet to write the IEP within 30 calendar days of the date that the child was determined to be eligible for special education services. The team must include the child's parents (or guardians), a special education teacher, a general education teacher, a school or local education agency administrator, a person who is able to interpret evaluation

results, and, if appropriate, the child. An individual may fill more than one role. The child's participation is required when the IEP includes a focus on transition services, which must start by age 16. Other individuals may be members of the team, as desired by the parents or school.

Each year, at a minimum, the IEP must be reviewed and revised as needed (unless there is participation in the three-year IEP pilot program; see Legislative History). Attention is paid especially to the IEP goals, progress toward them, and whether they need to be revised, and the placement of the child (where and for how long the child is in specific settings within the school, such as the general education classroom, special education room, or other placements). Every three years, the IEP team must meet to examine reevaluation results, used to determine whether the child continues to meet criteria to be designated as having a disability that requires special education services.

DESIGNING AND IMPLEMENTING IEPS

The actual processes and procedures used in schools and districts to ensure that IEP teams carry out the letter and intent of the law vary and have been the subject of relatively little research. Concerns about the legal requirements have arisen because of perceptions that they have compromised the quality of IEPs (Beattie, Jordan, & Algozzine, 2006). At the same time, the 2004 reauthorization of the law focused on ways to make the process of developing and revising the IEP more efficient and on ways to reduce paperwork in developing IEPs. In practice, states or local education agencies often require or recommend a form to use in developing the IEP so that it meets federal and state requirements. Computer-based IEP development software gained popularity with the perception of increasingly complex IEP requirements. With improvements over time in technology and programming, computer-based IEPs came to be viewed as having the potential to aid in the production of well-thought through IEPs (Wilson, Michaels, & Margolis, 2005).

IEPs are implemented by carrying out the directives of the IEP. Ideally, everyone responsible for implementing the IEP for an individual child has access to a copy of the IEP, and each person knows which responsibilities to implement (Beattie et al., 2006). Along with providing the designated services, supports, and accommodations that are described in the IEP, the IEP defines how the child's progress toward meeting the goals stated in the IEP will be measured. Progress reports designed to indicate the extent to which the child is making sufficient progress to reach goals by the end of the year are given to parents. These progress reports on IEP goals are to be made as often as the parents of children without disabilities are informed of their children's progress.

Despite their importance to the special education process, IEPs often have been inaccessible to those who should use them. Some educators and administrators have treated them as though they define the curriculum for the child with disabilities who requires special education services, rather than as the delineation of the services, supports, and framework for access to the general curriculum provided in the least restrictive environment for each child. In the early 2000s the IEP continued to be the subject of revisions each time IDEA is reauthorized, all the while retaining its central position in the special education process.

SEE ALSO *Special Education.*

BIBLIOGRAPHY

Beattie, J., Jordan, L., & Algozzine, B. (2006). *Making inclusion work: Effective practices for all teachers.* Thousand Oaks, CA: Corwin Press.

President's Commission on Excellence in Special Education. (2002). *A new era: Revitalizing special education for children and their families.* Washington, DC: U.S. Department of Education, Office of Special Education and Rehabilitative Services.

Wilson, G. L., Michaels, G. A., & Margolis, H. (2005). Form versus function: Using technology to develop Individualized Education Programs for students with disabilities. *Journal of Special Education Technology, 20*(2), 37–48.

Yell, M. L. (2006). *The law and special education* (2nd ed.). Upper Saddle River, NJ: Pearson.

Yell, M. L., Shriner, J. G., & Katsiyannis, A. (2006). Individuals with Disabilities Education Improvement Act of 2004 and IDEA regulations of 2006: Implications for educators, administrators, and teacher trainers. *Focus on Exceptional Children, 39*(1), 1–24.

Martha L. Thurlow

INFORMATION PROCESSING THEORY

Humans process information with amazing efficiency and often perform better than highly sophisticated machines at tasks such as problem solving and critical thinking (Halpern, 2003; Kuhn, 1999). Yet despite the remarkable capabilities of the human mind, it was not until the 20th century that researchers developed systematic models of memory, cognition, and thinking. The best articulated and most heavily researched model is the information processing model (IPM) developed in the early 1950s. The IPM consists of three main components, sensory memory, working memory, and long-term memory (see Figure 1). Sensory and working memory enable people to manage limited amounts of incoming information during initial processing, whereas long-term memory serves as a permanent repository for knowledge. In this entry, the information processing model will be used as a metaphor for successful learning because it is well supported by research and provides a well-articulated means for describing the main cognitive structures (i.e., memory systems) and processes (i.e., strategies) in the learning cycle.

SENSORY MEMORY

Sensory memory processes incoming sensory information for very brief periods of time, usually on the order of 1/2 to 3 seconds. The amount of information held at any given moment in sensory memory is limited to five to seven discrete elements such as letters of the alphabet or pictures of human faces. Thus, if a person viewed 10 letters simultaneously for 1 second, it is unlikely that more than five to seven of those letters would be remembered.

The main purpose of sensory memory is to screen incoming stimuli and process only those stimuli that are most relevant at the present time. For example, drivers on a busy freeway in heavy traffic are constantly bombarded with visual and auditory stimuli. To maximize efficiency and safety, they process only information that is relevant to safe driving. Thus, they would attend to road conditions but not buildings they pass as they drive. Similarly, they would attend to sounds of other cars, but not to music from the radio or one passenger's casual conversation with another.

Researchers agree that information processing in sensory memory usually occurs too quickly for people to consciously control what they attend to. Rather, attention allocation and sensory processing are fast and unconscious. Information that is relevant to the task at hand, and information that is familiar and therefore subject to automatic processing, are the most likely types of information to be processed in sensory memory and forwarded to the working memory buffer. Information that is highly relevant may receive some degree of controlled, conscious processing if it is crucial to a task (e.g., attending to salient information such as animals along the road while driving at high speed). However, controlled processing in sensory memory would be likely further to reduce the limited amount of information that can be processed at any given moment.

WORKING MEMORY

After stimuli enter sensory memory, they are either forwarded to working memory or deleted from the system. Working memory is a term that is used to refer to a multi-component temporary memory system in which information is assigned meaning, linked to other information, and essential mental operations such as inferences are performed. A number of different models of working memory have been proposed (Shah & Miyake, 1999). However, the three-component model developed by Baddeley (1998, 2001) is the most common, and will be discussed shortly.

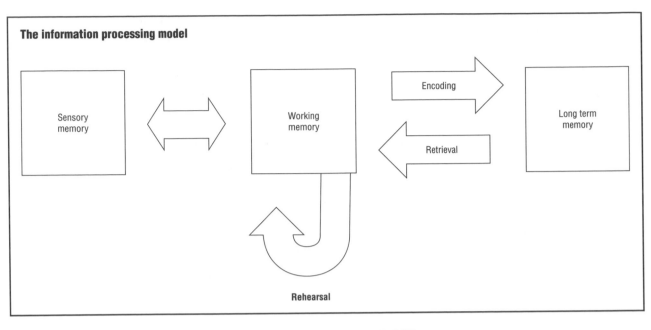

The information processing model

Sensory memory

Working memory

Encoding

Long term memory

Retrieval

Rehearsal

Figure 1 ILLUSTRATION BY GGS INFORMATION SERVICES. CENGAGE LEARNING, GALE.

Several useful terms have been developed to describe efficient cognitive processing in working memory. One term is *limited attentional resources*, which refers to the highly limited nature of information processing (Anderson, 2000; Neath, 1998). All individuals experience severe limitations in how much mental activity they can engage in due to limited cognitive resources (Kane & Engle, 2002). Although humans differ with respect to available cognitive resources, all learners experience severe limitations regardless of their skill and ability level. Often, differences between one learner and another are not due to the amount of resources, but how efficiently those resources are used.

Another key term is *automaticity*, which refers to being able to perform a task very quickly and efficiently due to repeated practice (Stanovich, 2003). Automated activities usually require few cognitive resources; thus, even a complex skill such as driving a car at 75 miles per hour can seem effortless. Effective information processing in sensory memory requires a high degree of automaticity with regard to recognition of familiar stimuli such as spoken or printed words, faces, and sounds.

A third key term is *selective processing*, which refers to the act of intentionally focusing one's limited cognitive resources on stimuli that are most relevant to the task at hand. For example, when driving in snow, one might allocate more of one's limited cognitive resources to watching the center line in the highway than one would allocate on a clear summer day. In contrast, on an extremely windy day, one would pay little attention to the whereabouts of the center line but pay special attention to any flying debris

that could cause an accident. In essence, selective processing enables learners to be optimally efficient by putting all of their cognitive eggs in one basket. It is no coincidence that highly effective learners succeed because they identify what is most important to learn and allocate limited attention to relevant information.

Baddeley's 2001 model of working memory consists of three components, the *executive control system, articulatory loop,* and *visual-spatial sketch pad.* The role of the executive control system is to select incoming information, determine how to best process that information, construct meaning through organization and inferences, and subsequently transfer the processed information to long-term memory or choose to delete that information from the memory system altogether (e.g., a telephone number that is no longer needed). Most models of working memory assume that the central executive is the place where humans "make conscious meaning" of the information they process (Shah & Miyake, 1999). The role of the articulatory loop is to maintain and further process verbal information. The role of the visual-spatial sketch pad is analogous to the articulatory loop in that it maintains and further processes non-verbal and visual information. Information is lost quickly from working memory (i.e., 5 to 15 seconds) unless some type of mental rehearsal occurs. Barring rehearsal (e.g., repeating a telephone number), information is either forwarded to long-term memory or is deleted from the system.

Baddeley's model makes several critical assumptions about the processing of information in working memory. One is that each of the three subsystems possesses its own

A comparison of sensory, working, and long term memory

Type of memory	Purpose	Capacity	Duration of retention
Sensory memory	Provides initial screening and processing of incoming stimuli.	3 to 7 discrete units	0.5 to 3 seconds
Working memory	Assigns meaning to stimuli and links individual pieces of information into larger units. Enables learner to construct meaning and perform visual-spatial mental operations.	7 to 9 units of information	5 to 15 seconds without rehearsal
Long term memory	Provides a permanent repository for different types knowledge	Infinite	Permanent

Table 1 ILLUSTRATION BY GGS INFORMATION SERVICES. CENGAGE LEARNING, GALE.

pool of limited cognitive resources. This means that, under normal information processing circumstances, each subsystem performs work without taxing the other subsystems. A second assumption is that the executive control system regulates the articulatory loop and visual-spatial sketch pad.

LONG-TERM MEMORY

Unlike sensory and working memory, long-term memory is not constrained by capacity or duration of attention limitations. The role of long-term memory is to provide a seemingly unlimited repository for all the facts and knowledge in memory. Most researchers believe that long-term memory is capable of holding millions of pieces of information for very long periods of time (Anderson, 2000). A great deal of research has gone into identifying two key aspects of long-term memory: (a) what types of information are represented, and (b) how information is organized. These two questions are addressed in the next section of this entry. For present purposes, there is universal agreement that qualitatively different types of information exist in long-term memory and that information must be organized, and therefore quickly accessible, to be of practical use to learners.

Figure 1 shows that working memory and long-term memory are connected by *encoding* and *retrieval* processes. Encoding refers to a large number of strategies that move information from temporary store in working memory into long-term memory. Examples include organization, inference, and elaboration strategies, which will be discussed later. Retrieval refers to processes that enable individuals to search memory and access information for active processing in working memory. Both encoding and retrieval greatly facilitate learning when information in long-term memory is organized for easy access.

A comparison of the three components of the IPM indicates that both sensory and working memory are relatively short term in nature (see Table 1). Their main roles are to screen incoming information, assign meaning, and relate individual units of information to other units. In contrast, the main role of long-term memory is to serve as a highly organized permanent storage system. Sensory and working memory process few pieces of information within a short time frame. Automaticity of processing and selective allocation of limited cognitive resources greatly increases the efficiency of information processing. Long-term memory is assumed to be more or less permanent and unlimited in terms of capacity. The main processing constraint on long-term memory is the individual's ability to quickly encode and retrieve information using an efficient organizational system.

The information processing model provides a conceptual model which explains the different functions and constraints on human memory. The IPM also has had a major impact on instructional theory and practice. Sweller and Chandler's 1994 work developed *cognitive load theory* to explain how different instructional and learner constraints affect optimal information processing. The crux of their argument is that each task imposes some degree of cognitive load, which must be met either by available cognitive resources or learner-based strategies such as selective attention and automaticity. Reducing cognitive load enables individuals to learn with less overall mental effort. Cognitive load theory has been especially helpful in terms of planning instruction and developing learning materials. Others researchers such as Mayer and Moreno (2003) have developed frameworks to increase learning by systematically reducing cognitive load through better design of learning materials and more strategic use of limited resources by students.

In summary, the information processing model postulates a three-component model of information processing. The IPM is consistent with empirical findings and provides an excellent framework for understanding principles of effective learning, which are considered later in this entry. Sensory and working memory are limited with respect to capacity and duration, whereas long-term memory is more or less unlimited. Information processing efficiency is increased due to automaticity and selectivity. Encoding and retrieval of information in long-term memory is increased due to efficient organizational strategies.

IMPLICATIONS FOR INSTRUCTION

The information processing model provides four important implications for improving learning and instruction. The first is that memory stores are extremely limited in both sensory and working memory. The two main strategies that effective learners use to cope with limited capacity are selectively focusing their attention on important information and engaging in as much automated processing as possible. From an educational perspective, it is essential for students to become automated at basic skills such as letter and word decoding, number recognition, and simple procedural skills such as handwriting, multiplication, and spelling. Automaticity makes available limited processing resources that can be used to engage in labor intensive self-regulation (Butler & Winne, 1995; Zeidner, Boekaerts, & Pintrich, 2000; Zimmerman, 2000) and comprehension monitoring (Schraw, 2001; Sternberg, 2001).

A second implication is that relevant prior knowledge facilitates encoding and retrieval processes. Highly effective learners possess a great deal of organized knowledge within a particular domain such as reading, mathematics, or science. They also possess general problem-solving and critical-thinking scripts that enable them to perform well across different domains. This knowledge guides information processing in sensory and working memory by providing easy-to-access retrieval structures in memory. It also serves as the basis for the development of expertise (Alexander, 2003; Ericsson, 2003). Thus, helping students use their prior knowledge when learning new information promotes learning.

A third implication is that automated information processing increases cognitive efficiency by reducing information processing demands. As discussed earlier, automaticity is an important aspect of effective learning for two reasons. One is that being automated makes it easier selectively to allocate limited resources to information that is most relevant to the task at hand. Unfortunately, there is no easy road to automaticity other than sustained, regular practice. In addition, automaticity frees limited resources that can be used for other activities such as drawing inferences and connecting new information to existing information in memory.

A fourth implication is that learning strategies improve information processing because learners are more efficient and process information at a deeper level (Pressley & Harris, 2006; Pressley & McDonald-Wharton, 1997). All effective learners draw from a repertoire of learning strategies in a flexible manner. Some of these strategies are used

automatically, while some require controlled processing and metacognitive control that place high demands on limited cognitive resources. Good learners use a wide variety of strategies and use them in a highly automatic fashion. However, there are three general strategies that all effective learners use in most situations. These include *organization, inferences,* and *elaboration* (Mayer & Moreno, 2003). Organization refers to how information is sorted and arranged in long-term memory. Information that is related to what one already knows is easier to encode and retrieve than isolated information. In some cases, individuals already possess well organized knowledge with empty slots that can be filled easily with new information. Activating existing knowledge prior to instruction, or providing a visual diagram of how information is organized, is one of the best ways to facilitate learning new information. Constructing inferences involves making connections between separate concepts. Elaboration refers to increasing the meaningfulness of information by connecting new information to ideas already known.

SEE ALSO *Cognitive Development: Information Processing Theories of Development; Cognitive Strategies; Memory; Metacognition.*

BIBLIOGRAPHY

Alexander, P. A. (2003). The development of expertise: The journey from acclimation to proficiency. *Educational Researcher, 32,* 10–14.

Anderson, J. R. (2000). *Cognitive psychology and its implication* (5th ed.). New York: Worth.

Baddeley, A. D. (1998). *Human memory: Theory and practice.* Boston: Allyn and Bacon.

Baddeley, A. D. (2001). Is working memory still working? *American Psychologist, 56,* 851–864.

Butler, D. L., and Winne, P. H. (1995) Feedback and self-regulated learning: A theoretical synthesis. *Review of Educational Research, 65,* 245–281.

Ericsson, K. A. (2003). The acquisition of expert performance as problem solving: Construction and modification of mediating mechanisms through deliberate practice. In J. E. Davidson and R. J. Sternberg (Eds.), *The psychology of problem solving* (pp. 31–83). Cambridge, England: Cambridge University Press.

Halpern, D. F. (2003). *Thought and knowledge: An introduction to critical thinking* (4th ed.). Mahwah, NJ: Erlbaum.

Kane, M. J., & Engle, R. W. (2002). The role of prefrontal cortex in working memory capacity, executive attention, and general fluid intelligence: An individual differences perspective. *Psychonomic Bulletin & Review, 9,* 637–671.

Kuhn, D. (1999). A developmental model of critical thinking. *Educational Researcher, 28,* 16–25.

Mayer, R. E. & Moreno, R. (2003). Nine ways to reduce cognitive load in multimedia learning. *Educational Psychologist, 38,* 43–53.

Neath, I. (1998). *Human memory: An introduction to research, data, and theory.* Pacific Grove, CA: Brooks/Cole.

Pressley, M., & Harris, K. R. (2006). Cognitive strategy instruction: From basic research to classroom instructions. In P. A. Alexander & P. H. Winne (Eds.), *Handbook of educational psychology* (2nd ed., pp. 265–287). Mahwah, NJ: Erlbaum.

Pressley, M., & Wharton-McDonald, R. (1997). Skilled comprehension and its development through instruction. *School Psychology Review, 26,* 448–466.

Schraw, G. (2001). Promoting general metacognitive awareness. In H. J. Hartman (Ed.), *Metacognition in learning and instruction: Theory, research and practice* (pp. 3–16). London: Kluwer.

Schraw, G. (2006). Knowledge: Structures and processes. In P. A. Alexander & P. II. Winne (Eds.), *Handbook of educational psychology* (2nd ed., pp. 245–264). Mahwah, NJ: Erlbaum.

Schunk, D. H., & Zimmerman, B. J. (2006). Competence and control beliefs: Distinguishing means and ends. In P. A. Alexander & P. H. Winne (Eds.), *Handbook of educational psychology* (2nd ed., pp. 349–368). Mahwah, NJ: Erlbaum.

Shah, P., & Miyake, A. (1999). Models of working memory. In A. Miyake & P. Shah (Eds.), *Models of working memory: Mechanisms of active maintenance and executive control* (pp. 1–25). Cambridge, England: Cambridge University Press.

Stanovich, K. E. (2003). The fundamental computational biases of human cognition: Heuristics that (sometimes) impair decision making and problem solving. In J. E. Davidson & R. J. Sternberg (Eds.), *The psychology of problem solving* (pp. 291–342). Cambridge, England: Cambridge University Press.

Sternberg, R. J. (2001). Metacognition, abilities, and developing expertise: What makes an expert student? In H. J. Hartman (Ed.), *Metacognition in learning and instruction: Theory, research, and practice* (pp. 247–260). Dordrecht, The Netherlands: Kluwer.

Sweller, J. & Chandler, P. (1994). Why some material is difficult to learn. *Cognition and Instruction, 12,* 185–253.

Zeidner, M., Boekaerts, M., & Pintrich, P. R. (2000). Self-regulation: Directions and challenges for future research. In M. Bockaerts, P. R. Pintrich, & M. Zeidner (Eds.), *Handbook of self-regulation* (pp. 13–39). San Diego, CA: Academic Press.

Zimmerman, B. J. (2000). Attaining self-regulation: A social cognitive perspective. In M. Boekaerts, P. R. Pintrich, & M. Zeidner (Eds.), *Handbook of self-regulation* (pp. 13–39). San Diego, CA: Academic Press.

Gregory Schraw
Matthew T. McCrudden

INQUIRY-BASED LEARNING

SEE *Constructivism: Inquiry-Based Learning.*.

INTELLIGENCE: AN OVERVIEW

This entry covers intelligence and intelligence testing. Intelligence is a difficult and often misused concept that has had an important impact on education. The entry will first review the definition and history of the concept of intelligence. Descriptions of the critical issues of measurement and application of the concept are then addressed. Intelligence tests commonly used in the schools are also described. Ways that tests are used in academic settings are covered with a short description of the qualifications for those who use the tests. Finally research trends and the emerging changes in the development of the concept of intelligence are addressed.

THE DEFINITIONS OF INTELLIGENCE

The specific meaning of intelligence in terms of how the concept is applied in education and schooling is difficult to convey. Everyone thinks they know intelligent performance when they see it, but when they try to define it, the elusiveness of the trait becomes apparent (Sternberg, Grigorenko, & Kidd, 2005). As Wagner (2000) has pointed out, definitions of intelligence have been notoriously inconsistent over the last century. Early definitions have tended to focus on specific or general abilities. For example, the work of Charles Spearman (1863–1945) over a century ago emphasized general ability (sometimes referred to as *g*) that involved recognition of relationships (e.g., Spearman, 1904), and intelligent activity involved combining this *g* with specific abilities. Alfred Binet (1857–1911) and Théodore Simon (1872–1961), working at around the same time, defined intelligence as "judgment, otherwise called good sense, practical sense, initiative, the faculty of adapting one's self to circumstances. To judge well, to comprehend well, to reason well, these are the essential activities of intelligence" (Binet & Simon, 1905, p. 43). Lewis Terman (1877–1956), largely credited for bringing intelligence testing into U.S. schools and developing the first versions of the Stanford-Binet Intelligence Test, emphasized knowledge and abstract thinking in defining intelligence (Aiken, 2003, Hegarty, 2007, Terman, 1918). The definition provided by David Wechsler (1896–1981) was "The aggregate or global capacity of the individual to act purposefully, to think rationally and to deal effectively with his environment" (Wechsler, 1958, p. 7).

Most of these definitions seemed to have an orientation to academic learning and performance. More recent definitions have been moving toward practical definitions with a view toward how the person functions in the real world as well as in traditional academic settings (Wagner, 2000). For example, in their 1998 book, Eleanor Amour-Thomas and Sharon-Ann Gopaul-McNichol have suggested the importance of a relativistic definition that recognized the significance of the interaction between the biological nature of the individual and the cultural and environmental context surrounding the person. Howard Gardner conceived intelligence as "a biopsychological potential to process information in certain ways, in order to solve problems or fashion products that are valued in a culture or community" (cited in Shearer, 2004, p. 3). Gardner saw intelligent behavior as related to specific kinds of functioning in the real world. Another of the more contemporary theorists, Robert Sternberg, defined intelligence from the perspective of research in cognitive information processing. His approach to intelligence implies successful performance in the real world and depends on an understanding of research in the ways in which the brain might work to produce intelligent behavior such as problem solving, adapting and learning. His theory is organized into three subtheories that address analytical, practical, and creative aspects of intelligent performance (Sternberg, 1994: Sternberg, Castejón, Prieto, Hautamäki, & Grigorenko, 2001). While many more definitions and approaches can be cited, they generally suggest that definitions of intelligence involve ability to learn, problem solve, and adapt. Further, later definitions move away from the notion of a unitary concept such as *g* to one that involves creativity, personal characteristics and traits, attention to the nature of the task or problem being addressed, the research on the brain and function, and environmental adaptation (Sternberg, Griegorenko, & Kidd, 2005; Sattler, 2001; Shearer, 2004).

Although many claim that intelligence is defined by what intelligence tests measure, many other theorists and researchers argue that this definition is too circular and narrow. Scores on intelligence tests are designed to reflect the definitions of intelligence rather than serve as the definition of intelligence (Gardner, Kornhaber, & Wake,1996), or an exact and unqualified representation of intellectual ability.

BRIEF HISTORY OF INTELLIGENCE TESTING

Interest in intelligence in some form has a long history. The Greek philosopher Aristotle (384–322 BCE) studied memory, logical thought, and what knowing means well before the mid- to late 19th-century investigations of the heritability of intelligence by Francis Galton (1822–1911) took place in England. Galton, considered one of the first scientific investigators of human intelligence, devised an array of simple tests covering an assortment of mental processes involving memory, senses, and motor behavior which he administered to a large sample of people. Performance was analyzed using statistical methods. These efforts are widely considered the beginning of the mental testing movement (Brennan, 2003). Binet, who was working in France at about the same time as Galton was doing his research, was more focused on mental processes such as the ability to adapt, comprehend, and reason. The idea of public education for the masses had just taken hold and schools were compelled to deal with much more widely divergent

abilities and behavior in children than was the case with the more privileged group that had previously attended school. Binet was asked by the French Ministry of Public Instruction to help identify the children who would be successful in school and those who would not (Gardner, Kornhaber, & Wake, 1996). Binet responded with a test for this purpose (Binet & Simon, 1905).

The concept of individual differences was gaining popularity around the world at the same time as Binet's work, spurred by the movement towards universal compulsory education in many countries. At the time, many psychologists were addressing the problem of how to identify children who would have success in education (Thorndike, 1990). In the United States, a number of psychologists, including Edward L. Thorndike (1874–1949) were addressing the problem. Thorndike, working at Teachers College of Columbia University, was central to the development of American and behavioral psychology and was very influential on American education practice (Brennan, 2003). Thorndike emphasized a neural basis of intelligence and felt that education should take advantage of natural intelligence and promote its development (Thorndike, 1990). Henry Goddard (1866–1957) translated the Binet scales and began experimenting with them. Terman standardized and normed the Binet test on California schoolchildren. He also added a concept developed by another psychologist, William Stern (1871–1938), which became the well-known Intelligence Quotient (IQ score). Originally the Binet tests yielded only a mental age, but Stern proposed dividing the mental age by the child's chronological age and multiplying by 100. Thus a child with a mental age score of 10 years, 6 months who is 9 years, 6 months old would have an IQ of 111 (i.e., MA/CA X 100 = (127 months)/(114 months) X 100 = 111) (Thorndike, 1990). A child with a score of 111 would be said to be performing above other children of the same age. A child whose mental age and chronological ages were the same would have an IQ of 100 and would be considered of average intelligence for the child's age.

Modern IQ tests use a scaling method based on the normal curve to compute the IQ score. This scaling method, known as *deviation IQ*, permits the test user to interpret a person's IQ score in terms of the proportion of people in the normative sample that had scores above and below the person's obtained score. This innovation was developed by Wechsler (1939) principally because the concept of mental age seemed inappropriate to use with adults. That is, intelligence tests of the time were designed with the assumption that a person's intelligence developed until the around the age of 20, at which time mature adult intelligence had been attained. Therefore the highest mental age that could be attained on a test was 20. However, Wechsler took the view that chronological age should be a predictor of mental age. This would not be the case if chronological age was increasing while mental age was not (Thorndike, 1990).

MODERN THEORIES OF INTELLIGENCE

Early intelligence theory emerged from an emphasis on a unitary concept of general ability, as can be seen in the definitions of Binet and Spearman. Spearman created a statistical technique called factor analysis to explore his approach. From his studies with this technique, he was able to report that about half of the variance in tests of mental ability was due to the general (*g*) factor (Kaplan & Sacuzzo, 2001). The remainder was due to the special ability (e.g., numerical reasoning, vocabulary, mechanical skill) that was required of a person to enable performance of the specific tasks on the test. Later approaches tended to emphasize expanded abilities. For example, Cattell divided *g* into fluid (*gf*) and crystallized (*gc*) intelligence (Horn & Cattell, 1966; Horn & Noll, 1997). *Fluid intelligence* encompasses abilities involved in thinking, reasoning, and in learning, while *crystallized intelligence* represents the knowledge and broader understanding that has developed through learning in the environmental setting.

Other theories further recognized the diversity of intelligent performance. In his 1967 book Joy Paul Guilford (1897–1987), using factor analysis, devised a model of intelligence he termed the *Structure of Intellect* in which he proposed three aspects of intelligence: operations, products, and contents. Each of these is broken down further into specific kinds of intellectual activity which Guilford considered interrelated to produce intelligent functioning of specific tasks.

Gardner (1993) proposed a theory of multiple intelligences based on the differential cognitive processing required for demonstration of intelligent or creative performance in different areas. Gardner's theory references eight intelligences. Linguistic and logico-mathematical intelligences are most often associated with academic performance, although others could be relevant depending on the task (Shearer, 2004). Other intelligences identified by Gardner were musical, kinesthetic, spatial, naturalistic, and personal (intrapersonal and interpersonal).

Robert Sternberg also proposed a theory informed by research from cognitive psychology. Sternberg's model is named the *triarchic theory* of intelligence because it is composed of three kinds of components: memory-analytic, creative-synthetic, and practical-contextual. The first component is related to the academic view of intelligence and is most similar to what most intelligence tests measure. The second component is necessary for creative endeavors, including traditionally academic areas such as science and mathematics. Finally, the practical-contextual is necessary for success in an everyday environment like school or business (Sternberg, 1994). Daniel Golman (1995) has proposed an emotional intelligence

that bears some similarity to the personal intelligences of Gardner and the practical intelligence of Sternberg, but goes further in tying emotion and personality to the capacity for intelligent behavior. For example, fear, excitement, or anger may contribute to how one behaves regardless of one's knowledge or capacity to reason.

In the first half of the 20th century, research in intelligence was heavily influenced by factor analysis (first used by Spearman). Factor analysis is a statistical procedure that enables the systematic study of the relationships within a set of variables in order to find the common aspects. Research and theory emerging in the second half of the 20th into the 21st century has begun to have an impact on the methods of assessment of intelligence (Gardner, et al., 1996). For example, research in cognitive psychology, neuro-psychology, cognitive science (Kolak, Hirstein, Mandik, & Waskan 2006), biopsychology and evolutionary processes (Geary, 2005), and cultural psychology (Armour-Thomas and Gopaul-McNicol, 1998) has begun to affect theory and research in intelligence, its measurement and applications.

MEASUREMENT OF INTELLIGENCE IN EDUCATIONAL SETTINGS

Two kinds of intelligence tests will be presented here. The first, group tests, are used to identify the range of IQ scores in a group, usually for research or administrative purposes. Group tests tend to have more specific content and question formats, and are designed for more specific purposes than individually administered tests, which aim for a relatively more comprehensive clinical picture of the individual's cognitive functioning. The individual tests are designed to provide much more information about the individual. They are only used by professionals who are trained and licensed to administer and interpret these assessment instruments as part of a comprehensive clinical assessment that contributes information useful for planning educational or therapeutic interventions. These tests provide a variety of scores and clinical information that licensed professional psychologists may use to plan interventions in schools, family, or other settings. In other words, the usefulness of individual intelligence tests goes well beyond the scores on the test. For this reason, group tests are not suitable substitutes for individual assessments when planning clinical or educational interventions.

Group Tests of Intelligence. Two examples of group intelligence test are discussed here. The Cognitive Abilities Test (Multilevel Edition, Form 6 [CogAT-6]) (Lohman 2001), and the Multidimensional Aptitude Battery, Second Edition (MAB-II) (Jackson, 1998) were chosen because they may be used in school or educational settings.

The Multidimensional Aptitude Battery-II (MAB-II) is a multiple-choice assessment of aptitude and intelligence that can be administered to groups or individuals above the age of 16. The instrument was designed to obtain scores similar to that of the individually administered Wechsler Adult Intelligence Scale-Revised (WAIS-R) in a group, as opposed to individual administration. The MAB-II produces composite scores: Verbal Scale (Information, Comprehension, Arithmetic, Similarities, Vocabulary), Performance Scale (Digit Symbol, Picture Completion, Spatial, Picture Arrangement, and Object Assembly) and Full Scale. The test can be pencil and paper or computer-administered.

The MAB-II is considered to be a useful tool for assessing cognitive abilities when large numbers of students must be screened. It is a well-developed and empirically sound instrument that provides correlations between subtest scores and occupational strengths (Thompson, 2003). The test can be administered by a proctor, rather than by a post-master's-level professional. As a result, the MAB-II should not be used for making clinical diagnoses about intelligence (Widaman, 2003). Additionally, MAB-II should not be administered to students with a learning disability related to reading comprehension or whose reading level is below ninth grade because the test relies on the test-takers' reading ability (Thompson, 2003).

The Cognitive Abilities Test—Multilevel Edition, Form 6 (CogAT-6) is one of the more widely used group ability tests for students in kindergarten through 12th grades. The test is intended to guide instruction to match the cognitive abilities and needs of each student, to provide an "alternative" measure of cognitive development, and to identify achievement-ability discrepancies. The test has a multitheoretical foundation as it is based on Vernon's model of hierarchical abilities, Cattell's model of crystallized and fluid abilities, and Carroll's work specifically on general abstract reasoning. The CogAT-6 is composed of two editions: the Primary and Multilevel Editions, both of which are intended to assess reasoning and problem-solving abilities and can be broken down into Verbal, Nonverbal, and Quantitative Batteries. The Primary Edition is designed for students in K–2nd grade and consists of six subtests. The Multilevel Edition is a nine-subtest instrument that is based on the Lorge-Thorndike Intelligence Tests (Lorge & Thorndike, 1954) and is appropriate for students in 3rd to12th grade. The CogAT-6 has a mean of 100 and standard deviation of 16.

DiPerna's 2005 review of the CogAT-6 suggested that the strengths of the test include a large, representative standardization sample, co-norming with the Iowa Tests, and a theoretical basis. In spite of these positive attributes, significant weaknesses were cited relative to the CogAT's purposes as described earlier. Criticisms included insuffi-

cient empirical evidence to support basing instructional recommendations on test results, a lack of reliability and predictive validity to measure cognitive ability and to predict cognitive ability-achievement discrepancies.

Individual Intelligence Tests. The following individual intelligence tests will be reviewed:

- Wechsler Intelligence Scale for Children-IV (WISC-IV)
- Woodcock-Johnson Tests of Cognitive Abilities-III (WJ COG III)
- Stanford-Binet Intelligence Scales, Fifth Edition (SB5)
- Das-Naglieri Cognitive Assessment System (CAS)
- Kaufman Assessment Battery for Children (K-ABC)

The Wechsler scales continue to be the most widely utilized individually administered tests of intelligence (Flanagan & Kaufman, 2004). As previously discussed, the Wechsler tests are based on the *g* factor or the "overall capacity of the individual to act purposefully, to think rationally, and to deal effectively with the environment" (Sternberg, 2000, p. 481) The Wechsler Intelligence Scale for Children, Fourth Edition (WISC-IV) is the current revision of the Wechsler scales for children 6.0 to 16.11 years of age. The WISC-IV comprises 15 subtests (5 of which are supplemental). Scores on these tasks contribute to the four composite indices (Verbal Comprehension, Perceptual Reasoning, Working Memory, and Processing Speed) in addition to a Full Scale IQ (FSIQ) score that can range from 40 (very low) to160 (very high), with a mean of 100 representing the average score, and a standard deviation of 15. A profile of the test taker's learning strengths and weaknesses are derived from the test performance. The FSIQ is derived from a combination of all subtest scores and is considered the most representative estimate of global intellectual functioning. However, when large discrepancies between Index scores exist, the FSIQ can be invalid and misleading. In this case, it is most helpful to describe the strengths and weaknesses in the profile and de-emphasize the FSIQ.

The WISC-IV continues to be a reliable and valid instrument. WISC-IV scores can be interpreted in combination with Wechsler Individual Achievement Test, Second Edition (WIAT-II) scores for comparisons between ability and achievement. Flanagan and Kaufman (2004) provide an extensive description of the strengths and limitations of this assessment tool. They cite the WISC-IV's most significant strengths as being "a robust four-factor structure across the age range of the test, increased developmental appropriateness, de-emphasis on time, improved psychometric properties, and an exemplary standardization sample (p. 171)." Flanagan & Kaufman (2004) indicate that none of the

WISC-IV's limitations are very serious, although they suggest ways in which its validity could be improved.

Other Weschler scales have been developed to assess IQ for young children and adults. The Wechsler Preschool and Primary Scale of Intelligence, Third Edition (WPPSI-III) (Harcourt Assessment, 2002) can be administered to children 2.6–7.3 years old and the Wechsler and the Wechsler Adult Intelligence Scale, Third Edition (WAIS-III) (Harcourt Assessment, 1997) is given to adults between 16 and 89 years of age.

The Woodcock-Johnson Tests of Cognitive Abilities-III (WJ COG III) is also widely used instrument in school settings. The WJ COG III is often administered as the examiner's second choice, if the age-appropriate Wechsler scale has been administered less than three years from the current assessment date. The WJ COG III is based on Catell, Horn, and Carroll's (CHC) concept of intelligence (Reynolds, Keith, Fine, Fisher & Low 2007). The WJ COG III has been normed on individuals age 2 through 90+. The standard battery includes 10 tests, while the extended battery consists of 20. Based on these scores, the examinee earns three Cluster Scores (Verbal Ability, Thinking Ability, and Cognitive Efficiency) and a General Intellectual Ability (GIA) score. Test scores in the standard and extended batteries are not weighted equally when the GIA score is computed.

The WJ COG III has high technical quality and is based on a well-respected theory of cognitive abilities (Schrank, Flanagan, Woodcock, & Mascolo, 2002). It assesses cognitive abilities for a wide age range and uses sophisticated scoring procedures to calculate scores and discrepancies (Sattler, 2001). Additionally, ability and achievement discrepancy norms are provided as the WJ COG III was co-normed with the Woodcock Johnson Tests of Achievement, Third Edition (WJ ACH III). Greater evidence is necessary to understand the utility of the clinical clusters (Schrank, Flanagan, Woodcock, & Mascolo, 2002). The WJ COG III may also overestimate abilities if interpreted incorrectly. For example, the Written Language test score emphasizes one's ability to write brief sentences rather than to develop and organize paragraphs.

The Stanford-Binet Intelligence Scales, Fifth Edition (SB5), a direct descendent of Terman's adaptation of the Binet test developed more than 100 years ago, is used occasionally in the educational setting. The SB5 is based on the CHC theory of intelligence. It is designed for assessing intelligence and cognitive abilities among individuals between the ages of 2 and 85+. The SB5 consists of ten subtests and these scores are used to calculate four composite scores: factor, domain, abbreviated, and full scale (score range 40–160, mean = 100, SD = 15). The five factors measured include Fluid Reasoning, Knowledge, Quantitative Reasoning, Visual-Spatial Reasoning, and Working Memory, each with verbal and nonverbal components. The SB5 contains two domain scales: Nonverbal IQ (NVIQ) and Verbal IQ (VIQ). An Abbreviated Battery IQ (ABIQ) can be determined with two routing subtest scores and the Full Scale IQ (FSIQ) is calculated using all 10 subtests.

The SB5 is advantageous as it is emphasizes both verbal and nonverbal abilities. The instrument is technically sound, according to Johnson and D'Amato (2005), although Kush's 2005 study cites technical limitations (e.g., lower stability for young children and individuals with low cognitive abilities, problematically high correlations with achievement, uncertain factor structure). In spite of these weaknesses, the SB5 is referred to as an outstanding measurement instrument for the assessment of cognitive abilities of children, adolescents, and adults (Johnson & D'Amato, 2005; Kush, 2005).

The Das-Naglieri Cognitive Abilities System (CAS) is a tool based on Luria's cognitive processing model that is intermittently used to evaluate cognitive abilities in schools. The CAS is useful for assessing Planning, Attention, Simultaneous, and Successive (PASS) abilities among students between the ages of 5.0 and 17.11. The instrument's basic battery comprises 8 subtests and the standard battery consists of 12 subtests.

The CAS is an innovative instrument and its development meets high standards of technical adequacy (Meikamp, 2003). When compared to other individually administered general ability tests, it takes less time to administer (Thompson, 2003). Additional empirical research must be completed to support the PASS construct. Factor analyses of subtests support both a 4-factor PASS model as well as a 3-factor model, which suggests that Planning and Attention may or may not be separate factors. (Thompson, 2003).

The Kaufman Assessment Battery for Children, Second Edition (KABC-II) is occasionally utilized in schools as a culture-fair assessment of cognitive abilities for students between the ages of 3 and 18. The KABC-II is based on a dual theoretical framework, Luria's neuropsychological model (Naglieri, 1998) and the CHC approach. The authors suggest that its multitheoretical base allows the examiner to select which model is most appropriate for interpretation of results depending on the culture and/or verbal skills of the examinee. This assessment instrument contains 20 subtests that contribute to 4 scale scores (Sequential Processing, Simultaneous Processing, Planning, Learning, and Knowledge). The KABC-II has a mean of 100 and standard deviation of 15.

The KABC-II is an acceptable option for measuring cognitive abilities as it provides a reasonable, well-normed, clinically appealing, and technically sound approach to measuring cognitive abilities and generating diagnoses (Braden, 2005). Other strengths of the KABC-II include smaller score discrepancies between ethnic groups and the ability to compare ability and achievement differences with the Kaufman Test of Educational Achievement, Second Edition, Comprehensive Form. However, it has been criticized for the suggestion that examiners can select the model (Luria or CHC) by which to interpret results. Braden (2005) and Thorndike (2005) suggest that the interchangeability of theoretical models is inappropriate and illogical.

Intelligence testing should not be conducted in a vacuum. In addition to using previously mentioned norm-referenced tests, an assessment should include a variety of other data from a multitude of informants. Sattler (2001) suggests that norm-referenced testing should be accompanied by interviews with a parent, teacher, and student; observations of the student during both the formal testing and natural environment (e.g., classroom, lunchroom, playground); and informal assessment procedures (e.g., district-wide criterion-referenced tests, school records). Such an assessment will provide the most accurate information by which educators can most effectively serve the student.

Group versus Individual Intelligence Tests. Whereas group-administered IQ tests can be very well constructed (Aiken 2003) and can provide valid and reliable information suitable for certain non-clinical applications, they do not provide the same kind of information as individual tests and should not be used for the same purposes. One reason is that group tests primarily emphasize multiple-choice question format, whereas individually administered tests provide a variety of response formats across the test. This allows clinicians to gather considerable clinically useful information about the person being tested, such as the approaches used in problem solving, quality of verbal expression, and other observational data (Domino 2000; Sattler 2001). Group tests were not designed to be used for clinical purposes and therefore should not be utilized in clinical settings or to substitute for individually administered intelligence tests for designing clinical interventions or individual educational programs (IEPs) in school settings.

Individual intelligence tests are designed to be administered by highly trained professionals who interpret data through the lens of learning, cognition, emotion, language, culture, health, and development. The one-on-one setting provides advantages to the test-taker and the examiner. First, it allows the examiner to develop rapport with the test-taker, which can benefit the shy or anxious test-taker. Second, the examiner has the opportunity to observe important test-taking behavior such as impulsiveness, compulsiveness, confidence, anxiety, and wandering attention. which may vary according to the task and contribute to the interpretation of the performance on the test. Third, the examiner can observe specific

problem-solving approaches, which may also vary with the task. The integration of these observations with test scores allows the examiner to take a holistic approach in interpreting scores and developing interventions.

APPLICATIONS IN CLASSROOMS AND SCHOOLS

Individual intelligence tests are used in schools and other educational settings to provide information about children's and adolescents' ability to express themselves, reason and problem solve, and perform on a variety of tasks. This information can be used to design programs for children with special needs or gifts in academic areas. Despite their shortcomings, intelligence tests are considered useful for identifying children for advanced programs for gifted learners (Pyryt, 1996). These tests also play an especially important role in special education. They can be useful for identifying an expected level of academic performance and also in helping school professionals design individual educational programs (IEP) for students with special needs (Sattler, 2001). However, Kim (2005) found in a meta-analysis of 21 studies that IQ tests are not effective for use in identifying students with special talents.

RESEARCH TRENDS

Research in intelligence is active and robust, and this section surveys the spectrum of investigations of intelligence related to school learning and performance. One active area of research is on the tests of intelligence themselves. Specifically, confirmatory factor analysis, a procedure for statistically examining the fit of data from a test to a hypothesized model, is being increasingly utilized to determine whether the theories and models of intelligence underlying tests is verifiable from performance on the test. For example, confirmatory factor analysis was used to verify the structure of the Kaufman Assessment Battery for Children, Second Edition, and the fit of the performance data to the Cattell-Horn-Carroll model of intelligence (Reynolds, Keith, Fine, Fisher, & Low, 2007). The technique was also used successfully to verify the factor structure of Sternberg's Triarchic Abilities Test Level-H (STAT) (Sternberg, Castejón, Prieto, Hautamäki, & Grigorenk, 2001). A related collection of research is directed at investigating the underlying theories and models of intelligence that have been proposed. Most of this research bases hypotheses and research questions on recent research in fields such as cognitive science, neuroscience, emotion, cultural psychology. An example of this kind of research is provided by Visser and her colleagues. Their research compared performance on tests of the components of Gardner's multiple intelligence theory with people's estimates of their own ability and found only modest significant relationships between estimated and measured abilities, and that people tended to overestimate their abilities (Visser, Ashton, & Vernon, 2008).

Research has shown that IQ scores seem to be trending upward (Flynn, 1984). The research has moved from documentation of the phenomenon across countries and cultures (Flynn, 1987; Daley, Whaley, Sigman, Espinosa, & Neumann, 2003), into investigations of whether people are truly becoming more intelligent or whether other explanations seem more plausible in explaining the phenomenon (Rodgers & Wänström, 2007). Some evidence has been provided that increase in measured IQ seems more related to areas considered more reflective of fluid rather than crystallized intelligence performance, such as mathematics test performance (Dickens & Flynn, 2001; Rodgers & Wänström, 2007).

The importance of cultural context in relation to intelligence cannot be minimized (Benson, 2003; Sternberg, 2004). The early definitions of intelligence were tied directly to school performance but have become more encompassing to include culture, language, social class, and related issues. For example, Sternberg's definition emphasizes success in life (Sternberg, 2004). However, a difficulty emerges in determining the standard criteria to use for this kind of intelligence (Benson, 2003). In primitive society, success might be simply be survival. Traditional IQ tests have long been considered culturally unfair because diverse groups such as those of Hispanic origin, African Americans, and Native Americans have not scored as well on them as White groups (Dickens & Flynn, 2006; Rushton & Jensen, 2006; Sternberg, Grigorenko, & Kidd, 2005). The discrepancy between Black and White Americans' test performance has been used to suggest a genetic determinant of IQ, a view has been attacked as unscientific and simplistic (Cooper, 2005; Cronshaw, Hamilton, Onyura & Wilson, 2006; Sternberg, Grigorenko, & Kidd, 2005). Recent research has shown the gap between Whites and Blacks narrowing (Dickens & Flynn, 2006).

The relationship between intelligence test performance and academic performance is well documented (Brody, 1997; Haywood, 2004; Sattler, 2001). Gagne and St. Pére (2002) found no significant relationship between motivation and IQ scores, and that IQ scores seemed to be even more related to achievement than motivation scores. Other studies have revealed strong relationship between IQ and academic performance. For example, in their 2007 study, Lynn and Mikk found significant relationships between IQ and academic performance in math and science among 10-year-olds in 25 countries and 14-year-olds in 46 countries. Barber (2005) reported significant relationships between literacy and having completed secondary education (among other variables) in 81 countries. Considerable research

suggests that one of the factors underlying the relationship between IQ and performance in academic subjects is mental processing speed (Luo, Thompson & Detterman, 2003). Sheppard's 2008 review of 172 studies of intelligence and the speed of information processing concluded that measures of intelligence and speed of mental processing are highly correlated, and males and females are faster on different types of speeded tasks.

This brief summary of the research relevant to theory and practice in intelligence shows that the field is active and dynamic. Also, it should be evident that intelligence researchers of the 21st century are addressing a broader, more complete concept of intelligence than was evident in the previous century. As related research in biology of the mind, emotion, neuropsychology, family dynamics, and cognitive processing progresses to new findings, these results will be incorporated into increasingly useful models and theories of the workings of intelligence and how to assess them.

Intelligence has been a useful concept for planning education for over a century. It is a difficult concept to define. Aspects of the definition that seem to have wide appeal include learning speed, adaptability, and ability to perform successfully. Group intelligence tests can be useful in research, or for assessing groups of students. They are not useful as a replacement for individual intelligence tests administered by qualified examiners in assessing for individual clinical or educational intervention. The Wechsler tests are among the most widely used instruments for assessing intelligence. Further, IQ score is a necessarily incomplete reflection of intelligence. It is far from perfect as an index of a person's total intellectual ability and is not useful in identifying specific talents. Cognitive and brain research has begun to impact theories of intelligence in important ways. Other areas that have impacted the field of intelligence are language, culture, biology, and the neurosciences. Recent theories of intelligence are emphasizing more than one unitary ability.

SEE ALSO *Intelligence Testing.*

BIBLIOGRAPHY

Aiken, L. R. (2003). *Psychological testing and assessment.* Boston: Allyn and Bacon.

Armour-Thomas, E., & Gopaul McNichol, S. (1998). *Assessing intelligence.* Thousand Oaks, CA: Sage.

Binet, A., & Simon, T. (1905). Methodes Nouvelles pour le Diagnostic du Niveau Intellectuel des Abnormaux. [New Methods for the Diagnosis of the Intellectual Level of Subnormals.] *L'Année Psychologique, 11,* 191–244. In A. Binet & T. Simon (E. S. Kite, Trans.). *The development of intelligence in children (The Binet-Simon Scale)* (pp. 37–90). Baltimore: Williams & Wilkins (1916).

Braden, J. P. (2005). Review of Kaufman Assessment Battery for Children, Second Edition. In R. A. Spies & B. S. Plake (Eds.),

The Sixteenth Mental Measurements Yearbook (pp. 517–520). Lincoln: University of Nebraska.

Brennan, J. F. (2003). *History and systems of psychology* (6th ed.). Upper Saddle River, NJ: Prentice-Hall.

Brody, N. (1997). Intelligence, schooling and society. *American Psychologist, 52*, 1046–1050.

Cooper, R. S. (2005). Race and IQ: Molecular Genetics as Deus ex Machina. *American Psychologist, 60*, 71–76.

Cronshaw, S. F., Hamilton, L. K., Onyura, B. R., & Winston, A. S. (2006). Case for non-biased intelligence testing against Black Africans has not been made. *International Journal of Selection and Assessment, 14*, 278–287.

Daley, T. C., Whaley, S. E., Sigman, M. D., Espinosa, M. P., & Neumann, D. (2003). IQ on the rise: The Flynn Effect in rural Kenyan children. *Psychological Science, 14, 215–219*.

Dickens, W. T., & Flynn, J. R. (2001). Heritability estimates versus large environmental effects: The IQ paradox resolved. *Psychological Review, 108*, 346–369.

Dickens, W. T., & Flynn, J. R. (2006). Black Americans reduce the racial IQ gap: Evidence from the standardization samples. *Psychological Science, 17*, 913–920.

DiPerna, J. C. (2005). Review of the Cognitive Abilities Test, Multilevel Edition, Form 6. In R. A. Spies & B. S. Plake (Eds.), *The sixteenth mental measurements yearbook* (pp. 228–234). Lincoln: University of Nebraska.

Domino, G. (2000). *Psychological testing: An introduction*. Upper Saddle River, NJ: Prentice-Hall.

Flanagan, D. P. & Kaufman, A. S. (2004) *Essentials of WISC-IV assessment*. New York: Wiley.

Flynn, J. R. (1984). The mean IQ of Americans: Massive gains 1932 to 1978. *Psychological Bulletin, 95*, 29–51.

Flynn, J. R. (1987). Massive IQ gains in 14 nations: What IQ tests really measure. *Psychological Bulletin, 101*, 171–191.

Gagne, F., & St. Pére, F. (January 1). When IQ is controlled, does motivation still predict achievement? *Intelligence, 30*(1), 71–100.

Gardner, H. (1993). *Frames of mind: The theory of multiple intelligences*. New York: Basic.

Gardner, H. (2000). The giftedness matrix: A developmental perspective. In R. C. Friedman & B. M. Shore (Eds.), *Talents unfolding: Cognition and development* (pp. 77–88). Washington, DC: American Psychological Association.

Gardner, H., Kornhaber, M. L., & Wake, W. K. (1996). *Intelligence: Multiple perspectives*. Belmont, CA: Wordsworth.

Geary, D. C. (2005). *The origin of mind: Evolution of brain, cognition, and general intelligence*. Washington, DC: American Psychological Association.

Golman, D. (1995). *Emotional intelligence: Why it can matter more than IQ*. New York: Bantam.

Guilford, J. P. (1967). *The nature of human intelligence*. New York: McGraw-Hill.

Haywood, H. (2004). Thinking in, around, and about the curriculum: The role of cognitive education. *International Journal of Disability Development and Education, 51*(3), 231.

Hegarty, P. (2007). From genius inverts to gendered intelligence: Lewis Terman and the power of the norm. *History of Psychology, 10*(2), 132–155.

Horn, J. L., & Cattell, R. B. (1996). Refinement and test of the theory of fluid and crystallized intelligence. *Journal of Educational Psychology, 57*, 253–276.

Horn, J. L., & Noll, J. (1997). Human cognitive capabilities: *Gf-Gc* theory. In D. P. Flanagan, J. L. Genshaft, & P. L. Harrison (Eds.), *Contemporary intellectual assessment: Theories, tests, and issues* (pp. 53–91). New York: Guilford.

Jackson, D. N. (1998). *Multidimensional Aptitude Battery II*. Port Huron, MI: Sigma Assessment Systems.

Johnson, J. A., & D'Amato, R. C. (2005). Review of the Stanford-Binet Intelligence Scales: Fifth Edition. In R. A. Spies & B. S. Plake (Eds.), *The sixteenth mental measurements yearbook* (pp. 975–979). Lincoln: University of Nebraska.

Kim, K. H. (2005). Can only intelligent people be creative? *The Journal of Secondary Gifted Education, 16*,(2/3), 57–66.

Kolak, D., Hirstein, W., Mandik, P., & Waskan, J. (2006). *Cognitive science: An introduction to mind and brain*. New York: Routledge.

Kaplan, R. M., & Saccuzzo, D. P. (2001). Psychological testing: Principles, applications and issues (5th Ed.). Belmont, CA: Wadsworth/Thomson.

Kush, J. C. (2005). Review of the Stanford-Binet Intelligence Scales: Fifth Edition. In R. A. Spies & B. S. Plake (Eds.), *The sixteenth mental measurements yearbook* (pp. 979–984). Lincoln: University of Nebraska.

Lorge, I., & Thorndike, R. M. (1954). *Lorge-Thorndike intelligence tests*. Boston: Houghton Mifflin.

Lohman, D. F., & Hagen, E. P. (2001). *Cognitive Abilities Test (Form 6)*. Itasca, IL: Riverside.

Luo, D., Thompson, L. A., & Detterman, D. K. (2003). The causal factor underlying the correlation between psychometric *g* and scholastic performance. *Intelligence, 31*, 67–83.

Meikamp, J. (2003). Review of Cognitive Abilities Scales, Revised. In B. Plake, J. Impara, & R. Spies (Eds.) *The fifteenth mental measurements yearbook* (pp. 201–203)). Lincoln: University of Nebraska.

Naglieri, J. A. (1998). A closer look at new kinds of intelligence tests. *American Psychologist, 53*, 1158–1159.

Pyryt, M. (1996). IQ: easy to bash, hard to replace. *Roeper Review, 18*(4), 255–258.

Reynolds, M. R., Keith, T. K., Fine, J. G., Fisher, M. E., & Low, J. A. (2007). Confirmatory factor structure of the Kaufman Assessment Battery for Children, Second Edition: Consistency with Cattell-Horn-Carroll theory. *School Psychology Quarterly 22*, 511–539.

Rodgers, J. L., & Wänström L. (2007). Identification of a Flynn Effect in the NLSY: Moving from the center to the boundaries. *Intelligence, 35* 187–196.

Rushton, J., & Jensen, A. (2005). Thirty years of research on race differences in cognitive ability. *Psychology, Public Policy, and Law, 11*(2), 235–294.

Rushton, J. P., & Jensen A. R. (2006). The totality of available evidence shows the race IQ gap still remains. *Psychological Science, 17*, 921–922.

Sattler, J. M. (2001). *Assessment of Children Cognitive Applications, Fourth Edition*. San Antonio: Sattler.

Schrank, F. A., Flanagan, D. P., Woodcock, R. W., & Mascolo, J. T. (2002). *Essentials of WJ-III Cognitive Abilities assessment*. New York: Wiley.

Shearer, B. (2004). Multiple intelligence theory after 20 years. *Teachers College Record, 106*(1), 2–16.

Spearman, C. (1904). General intelligence, objectively determined and measured. *American Journal of Psychology, 15*, 201–293.

Sternberg, R. J. (2000). *Handbook of Intelligence*. New York: Cambridge University Press.

Sternberg, R. J. (1994). A triarchic model for teaching and assessing students in general psychology. *General Psychologist, 30*(2), 42–48.

Sternberg, R. J., Castejón, J.L., Prieto, M.D., Hautamäki, J., & Grigorenko, E. L. (2001). Confirmatory factor analysis of the Sternberg Triarchic Abilities Test in three international samples: An empirical test of the triarchic theory of intelligence. *European Journal of Psychological Assessment, 17* (1), 1–16.

Sternberg, R., Grigorenko, E. L., & Kidd, K. K. (2005.) Intelligence, Race, and Genetics. *American Psychologist, 60,* 46–59.

Sternberg, R. J., & Grigorenko, E. L. (2005). Cultural explorations of the nature of intelligence. In Alice F. Healy (Ed.), *Experimental cognitive psychology and its applications* (pp. 225–235). Washington, DC: American Psychological Association.

Terman, L. M. (1918). *Tests of general intelligence. Psychological Bulletin, 15*(5) 160–167.

Thompson, D. L. (2003). Review of the Multidimensional Aptitude Battery, Second Edition. In B. Plake, J. Impara, & R. Spies (Eds.), *The fifteenth mental measurements yearbook* (pp. 603–607). Lincoln: University of Nebraska.

Thorndike, R. M. (with Lohman, D. F.) (1990). *A century of ability testing.* Chicago: Riverside.

Thorndike, R. M. (2005). Review of Kaufman Assessment Battery for Children, Second Edition. In R. A. Spies & B. S. Plake (Eds.), *The sixteenth mental measurements yearbook* (pp. 520–522). Lincoln: University of Nebraska.

Wagner, R. K. (2000). Practical Intelligence. In A. E. Kazdin (Ed). *Encyclopedia of psychology: Vol. 6* (pp. 266–270). Washington, DC: American Psychological Association; Oxford University Press.

Wechsler, D. (1939). *The measurement of adult intelligence.* Baltimore: Williams & Wilkins.

Wechsler, D. (1958). *The measurement and appraisal of adult intelligence* (4th ed.). Baltimore: Williams & Wilkins.

Wechsler, D. (1997). *Wechsler Adult Intelligence Scale, Third Edition.* San Antonio: Harcourt Assessment.

Wechsler, D. (1997). *Wechsler Preschool and Primary Scale of Intelligence, Third Edition.* San Antonio: Harcourt Assessment.

Widaman, K. F. (2003). Review of the Multidimensional Aptitude Battery, Second Edition. In B. Plake, J. Impara, & R. Spies (Eds.) *The fifteenth mental measurements Yearbook* (pp. 605–607). Lincoln: University of Nebraska.

Emanuel J. Mason
Kaila Wilcox

INTELLIGENCE TESTING

Intelligence and intelligence testing are two of the most controversial and highly polemic of all topics in the field of psychology. It seems that psychologists, educators, and indeed, the lay public alike, all have a love-hate relationship with the concept of intelligence and even more so with intelligence testing. Some form of intelligence test-ing is one of the most widely used of all forms of psychological tests. While tests for special aptitudes are available, and these are widely used for specialized diagnostic purposes as well as specialized aspects of personnel selection, these tests all measure some aspect of intellectual function. This entry describes more generally intelligence testing, provides a brief history of intelligence tests, presents their fundamental assumptions, applications, and an introduction to their interpretation.

INTELLIGENCE AND ACHIEVEMENT

Achievement tests as those designed to assess students' knowledge or skills in a content domain in which they have received instruction. In contrast, intelligence tests are broader in scope than achievement tests and are designed to measure the cognitive skills, abilities, and knowledge that individuals have accumulated as the result of their overall life experiences coupled with skills in application of these attributes to problem-solving. In other words, while achievement tests are tied to a specific program of instruction, intelligence tests reflect the cumulative impact of life experiences as a whole in concert with an individual's underlying or latent ability to use information. The general intelligence factor, *g*, is the most reliable component present in any multifactorial view of intelligence (Jensen, 1998). In the Cattell-Horn model (Horn & Cattell, 1966; Kamphaus, 2001) of intelligence, *g* is the dominant factor in the hierarchy of multiple abilities, with the next two dominant facets being crystallized and fluid intelligence.

Crystallized intelligence tends to be related more closely to verbal domains as a practical matter and is defined as the application of knowledge to problem solving. Fluid intelligence tends to be related more closely to non-verbal domains as a practical matter and is defined more strictly as reasoning and problem solving in the absence of any requirement for prior knowledge. It turns out that people do not really know how to assess reasoning and problem solving in the total absence of knowledge and so most tests of fluid intelligence attempt to approximate this perfect state to the extent possible by using principally nonverbal tasks that do not require knowledge of language or language concepts (Reynolds & Kamphaus, 2003).

The inclusion of crystallized intelligence measures as a component of most intelligence tests has led many people to believe, erroneously, that intelligence tests are simply measures of what people have learned. While intelligence and knowledge are certainly correlated, intelligence as measured on modern individually administered tests of intelligence and even many group measures is more directed at the assessment of problem solving and reasoning skill as opposed to static knowledge or learned content. The latter is the domain of achievement testing (Reynolds, Livingston, & Willson, 2006).

This introduction might suggest that there is a clear and universally accepted distinction between achievement and intelligence tests. However, in actual practice such is not the case and the distinction is actually a matter of degree. Many, if not most, testing experts conceptualize both achievement and intelligence tests as tests of developed cognitive abilities that can be ordered along a continuum in terms of how closely linked the assessed abilities are to specific learning experiences. The abilities measured by achievement tests are specifically linked to academic instruction or training. In contrast, the knowledge and abilities measured by intelligence tests are acquired through a broad-range of life experiences, including those at school, home, work, and all other settings.

General intelligence tests historically have been the most popular and widely used aptitude tests in school settings. While many people are familiar with the concept of intelligence and use the term in everyday conversations, it is not easy to develop a definition of intelligence on which everyone agrees. While many people, lay or professional, will have their own separate definition of intelligence, most of these definitions will incorporate abilities such as problem solving, abstract reasoning, and the ability to acquire knowledge. Developing a consensus beyond this point has proved quite difficult.

THE ORIGIN OF INTELLIGENCE TESTS

Intelligence tests had their beginning in the schools, in the early 1900s in France when a compulsory education program was initiated. Alfred Binet (1857–1911) and his colleague Theodore Simon (1873–1961) had been attempting to develop a measure of intelligence for some years and were commissioned by the French government to develop a test that could predict academic performance accurately. The result of their efforts was the first Binet-Simon Scale released in 1905. This test contained problems arranged in the order of their difficulty and assessing a wide range of abilities. The test contained some sensory-perceptual tests, but the emphasis was on verbal items assessing comprehension, reasoning, and judgment. Subsequent revisions of the Binet-Simon Scale were released in 1908 and 1911. These scales gained wide acceptance in France and were soon translated and standardized in the United States by Louis Terman (d. 1959) at Stanford University. Terman's work resulted in the Stanford-Binet Intelligence Test (1916), which has been revised numerous times and continues to be a prominent intelligence test used in the early 2000s.

The introduction of the Stanford Binet intelligence scales in the United States by Terman occurred in close proximity to World War I. Seeing the success of this approach to measuring mental ability, the U.S. Army set about to devise a means of evaluating recruits. A group of psychologists headed by Robert Yerkes (1876–1956) subsequently developed the Army Alpha and Army Beta examinations, which quickly became the most widely used group intelligence tests in the world. This widespread use also had the effect of familiarizing literally millions of individuals with the concept of intelligence testing and made it an acceptable enterprise. Not long afterward, the College Entrance Examination Board began development and employment of what became the SAT, a conglomerated measure of achievement and intelligence.

The development and success of the Binet-Simon Scale, and subsequently the Stanford-Binet Intelligence Test and the U.S. Army testing programs, ushered in the era of widespread intelligence testing in the United States. Following the model of the Stanford-Binet Intelligence Test, other assessment experts developed and released their own intelligence tests. Some of the tests were designed for individual administration (such as the Stanford-Binet Intelligence Test) while others were designed for group administration. Some of these tests placed more emphasis on verbal and quantitative abilities while others placed more emphasis on visual-spatial and/or abstract problem-solving abilities. As a general rule, research has shown with considerable consistency that contemporary intelligence tests are good predictors of academic success. This correlation is to be expected considering this was the precise purpose for which they were initially developed over 100 years earlier. In addition to being good predictors of school performance, research showed that IQs are fairly stable over time. Nevertheless, these tests became controversial as a result of the often-emotional debate over the meaning of intelligence. To try and avoid this association and possible misinterpretations, many test publishers adopted more neutral names such as "academic potential," "scholastic ability," "school ability," "mental ability," or simply "ability" to designate essentially the same construct to which the term intelligence referred.

THE USE OF APTITUDE AND INTELLIGENCE TESTS IN SCHOOLS

Clearly, aptitude and intelligence tests have a long history of use in the schools. Their widespread use continues in the early 2000s, with major applications including the following (Reynolds et al., 2006; Reynolds & Kamphaus, 2003):

> Providing alternative measures of cognitive abilities that reflect information not captured by standard achievement tests or school grades,

Providing objective evaluations of ability that do not reflect the subjective judgment of observers or others who may be influenced by irrelevant factors,

Helping teachers tailor instruction to meet a student's unique pattern of cognitive strengths and weaknesses,

Assessing how well students are prepared to profit from school experiences,

Identifying students who are underachieving and may need further assessment to rule-out learning disabilities or other cognitive disorders, including mental retardation or intellectual disability,

Identifying students for gifted and talented programs,

Helping guide parents and students with educational and vocational planning.

While this list identifies the most common uses of aptitude/intelligence tests in the schools, the list is not exhaustive. Classroom teachers and school administrators are involved to varying degrees with these applications. For example, teachers are frequently called on to administer and interpret many of the group aptitude tests for their own students. School psychologists or others professionals with specific training in administering and interpreting clinical and diagnostic tests typically administer and interpret the individual intelligence and aptitude tests.

COMMON INDIVIDUALLY ADMINISTERED TESTS OF INTELLIGENCE

As with achievement tests, group and individual intelligence tests are commonly used in schools. Whereas teachers are often asked to help administer and interpret the group aptitude tests, school psychologists and other professionals with special training in administering and interpreting clinical and diagnostic tests usually administer and interpret the individual tests. The most frequently employed individually administered intelligence tests are reviewed briefly below.

Wechsler Intelligence Scale for Children, Fourth Edition (WISC-IV). The WISC-IV is as of 2007 the most popular individual test of intellectual ability for children. Empirical surveys of school psychologists and other assessment personnel have consistently shown that the Wechsler scales are the most popular individual intelligence test used in clinical and school settings with children. The WISC-IV, as is true of virtually all individually administered intelligence tests, must be administered by professionals with extensive training in psychological assessment. The WISC-IV is one of the

longest of such intellectual assessments and takes approximately 2 to 3 hours to administer and score. Below are brief descriptions of the subtests (Wechsler, 2003):

Arithmetic—the student is presented a set of arithmetic problems that they solve mentally (i.e., no pencil and paper) and answer orally. This subtest involves numerical reasoning ability, mental manipulation, concentration, and auditory memory.

Block Design—the student reproduces a series of geometric patterns using red-and-white blocks. This subtest measures the ability to analyze and synthesize abstract visual stimuli, nonverbal concept formation, and perceptual organization.

Cancellation—the student scans sequences of visual stimuli and marks target forms. This subtest involves processing speed, visual attention, and vigilance.

Coding—the student matches and copies symbols that are associated with either objects (i.e., Coding A) or numbers (Coding B). This subtest is a measure of processing speed, short-term visual memory, mental flexibility, attention, and motivation.

Comprehension—the student responds to questions that are presented orally involving everyday problems or social situations. This subtest is a measure of verbal comprehension and reasoning as well as the ability to apply practical information.

Digit Span—the student is presented orally sequences of numbers that they repeat verbatim (i.e., Digits Forward) or in reverse order (i.e., Digits Backwards). This subtest involves short-term auditory memory, attention, and on Digits Backwards, mental manipulation.

Information—the student responds to questions that are presented orally involving a broad range of knowledge (e.g., science, history, and geography). This subtest measures the student's general fund of knowledge.

Letter-Number Sequencing   the student reads a list of letters and numbers and then recalls the letters in alphabetical order and the numbers in numerical order. This subtest involves short-term memory, sequencing, mental manipulation, and attention.

Matrix Reasoning—the student examines an incomplete matrix and then selects the item that correctly completes the matrix. This subtest is a measure of fluid intelligence and is considered a largely language-free and culture-fair measure of intelligence.

Picture Completion—the student is presented a set of pictures and must identify what important part is missing. This subtest measures visual scanning and organization as well as attention to essential details.

Picture Concepts—the student examines rows of objects and then selects objects that go together based on an underlying concept. This subtest involves nonverbal abstract reasoning and categorization.

Similarities—two words are presented orally to the student and the student must identify how they are similar. This subtest measures verbal comprehension, reasoning, and concept formation.

Symbol Search—the student scans groups of symbols and indicates if a target symbol is present. This subtest is a measure of processing speed, visual scanning, and concentration.

Vocabulary—the student is presented orally a series of words that the student must define. This subtest is primarily a measure of word knowledge and verbal conceptualization.

Word Reasoning—the student must identify the underlying or common concept that is implied by a series of clues. This subtest involves verbal comprehension, abstraction, and reasoning.

Information, Word Reasoning, Picture Completion, Arithmetic, and Cancellation are supplemental subtests while the other subtests are core subtests. The administration of supplemental subtests is not mandatory, but they may be used to substitute for a core subtest if the core subtest is seen as being inappropriate for a particular student (e.g., due to physical limitation). A supplemental subtest may also be used if a core subtest is invalidated for some reason (e.g., its administration is interrupted).

The WISC-IV produces four Index Scores. Below are brief descriptions of the Index Scores (Wechsler, 2003):

Verbal Comprehension Index (VCI) is a composite of Similarities, Vocabulary, and Comprehension. Information and Word Reasoning are supplemental VCI subtests. The VCI reflects verbal reasoning, verbal conceptualization, and knowledge of facts.

Perceptual Reasoning Index (PRI) is a composite of Block Design, Picture Concepts, and Matrix Reasoning. Picture Completion is a supplemental PRI subtest. The PRI reflects perceptual and nonverbal reasoning, spatial processing abilities, and visual-spatial-motor integration.

Working Memory Index (WMI) is a composite of Digit Span and Letter-Number Sequencing. Arithmetic is a supplemental WMI subtest. The WMI reflects the student's working memory capacity that includes attention, concentration, and mental control.

Processing Speed (PSI) is a composite of Coding and Symbol Search. Cancellation is a supplemental PSI subtest. The PSI reflects the student's ability to quickly process nonverbal material as well as attention and visual-motor coordination.

The WISC-IV and its predecessors are designed for use with children between the ages of 6 and 16 years of age. For early childhood assessment the Wechsler Preschool and Primary Scale of Intelligence, Third Edition (WPPSI-III) is available and is appropriate for children between 2 years 6 months to 7 years 3 months. The Wechsler Adult Intelligence Scale, Third Edition (WAIS-III) is appropriate for individuals between the ages of 16 and 89 years of age.

Stanford-Binet Intelligence Scales, Fifth Edition (SB5). The Stanford-Binet Intelligence Test was the first intelligence test to gain widespread acceptance in the United States. While the Wechsler scales have become the most popular and widely used intelligence tests in schools, the Stanford-Binet scales have continued to have a strong following. As of 2007. the most recent edition of these scales is the SB5 that was released in 2003. The SB5 is designed for use with individuals from 2 to 85 years of age. It contains 10 subtests which are combined to produce five factor indices (i.e., Fluid Reasoning, Knowledge, Quantitative Reasoning, Visual-Spatial Processing, and Working memory), two domain scores (i.e., Verbal IQ

Example of a common set of qualitative descriptions of performance levels expressed as IQs

Score level	Qualitative description	Approximate percent of population included
69≤	Significantly below average	2.34
70–79	Moderately Below average	6.87
80–89	Below average	16.12
90–109	Average	49.61
110–119	Above average	16.12
120–129	Moderately above average	6.87
≥130	Significantly above average	2.34

Table 1 ILLUSTRATION BY GGS INFORMATION SERVICES. CENGAGE LEARNING, GALE.

and Nonverbal IQ), and a Full Scale IQ reflecting overall intellectual ability. A potentially appealing aspect of the SB5 is the availability of an Extended IQ scale that allows the calculation of FSIQs higher than 160, which can be useful in the assessment of extremely gifted individuals.

Woodcock-Johnson III (WJ III) Tests of Cognitive Ability. The WJ III Tests of Cognitive Ability has gained a loyal following and has some unique qualities that warrant mentioning. The battery is designed for use with individuals 2 to 90 years of age. The WJ III Tests of Cognitive Ability is based on the Cattell-Horn-Carroll (CHC) theory of cognitive abilities, which incorporates Cattell's and Horn's Gf-Gc theory and Carroll's three-stratum theory. The CHC model provides a comprehensive model for assessing a broad range of cognitive abilities, and many clinicians like this battery because it measures such a broad range of abilities.

Reynolds Intellectual Assessment Scales (RIAS). The RIAS is a newcomer to the clinician's collection of intelligence tests. It is designed for use with individuals between 3 and 94 years of age and incorporates a co-normed supplemental memory test. One particularly desirable aspect of the RIAS is the ability to obtain a reliable and valid measure of intellectual ability that incorporates both verbal and non-verbal abilities (crystallized and fluid intelligence) in a relatively brief period (i.e., 20–25 minutes). Most other tests that assess verbal and nonverbal cognitive abilities require considerably more time. The supplemental memory tests require about 10 minutes for administration, so a clinician can assess both memory and intelligence in approximately 30 minutes.

INTELLIGENCE TEST SCORES

In the early decades of intelligence testing, intelligence test scores were expressed as a true quotient, hence the term IQ or intelligence quotient. An IQ was defined as a ratio of the examinees mental age to the examinees chronological age which was then multiplied by 100 to eliminate dealing with fractional scores [(MA/CA)X100]. This form calculation of an IQ has serious psychometric and related measurement problems and has been abandoned for decades although its presentation continues to be common in many introductory psychology and education textbooks. In the early 2000s, IQs are calculated in the form of age corrected deviation scaled scores. These are formal transformations of raw scores (i.e., number of points obtained or items answered correctly) into a standard score format that incorporates the use of the mean and the standard deviation of the raw scores at predetermined age intervals so that the IQ given by the test has the same percentile ranking at each age level, which is not true of the old ratio style IQ. Table 1 presents a common system for ascribing a qualitative descriptor to various score ranges found on most common

intelligence tests, nearly all of which (including all of those reviewed above) report IQs using a metric where the mean IQ is equal to 100 and the standard deviation is 15. When accompanied by significant deficits and adaptive behavior and occurring during the developmental period, scores below 70 are commonly associated with varying degrees of mental retardation or intellectual disability, while scores above 130 are often used to designate individuals as being intellectually talented or cognitively gifted.

The scores from intelligence tests are derived from large samples of individuals drawn using what is known as population proportion of stratified random sampling. Because all individuals in the United States cannot be tested, a sample is drawn to represent the entire population. This sample is typically chosen to be representative of the general population of the United States at large on the basis of gender, ethnicity, social economic status or educational level, region of residence within the United States, and community size, including urban and rural areas.

Scores from intelligence tests are interpreted properly only when the standardized instructions for administering and scoring the test have been followed rigidly. Deviations from standardized administration and scoring cause the scores to move up or down for an individual examinee inappropriately and in ways that are unpredictable, rendering the scores uninterpretable (Lee, Reynolds, & Willson, 2003). Intelligence test scores are viewed by some as reflecting innate potential but clearly that is not the case. While innate ability contributes to intelligence test performance, many other variables contribute to performance on ability measures as well.

Intelligence as measured on such tests as described here is a summative construct at any given point that is a reflection not only of a person's innate potential but the interaction of this potential with the entire life experiences of the individual as well as factors such as early stimulation, nutrition, prenatal care, and numerous other variables too extensive to list and discuss here. Proper interpretation of intelligence tests requires knowledge of the examinee's history, background, educational exposure, and generally the context of the examinee's life, especially when clinical diagnoses are being considered. Intelligence tests in the schools are very good predictors of academic achievement, but even this prediction is predicated upon averages among the various examinees. This qualification means that intelligence tests' predictions of future attainment are based on various assumptions about individuals taking such tests. Such assumptions, for example, would include the assumption that a particular examinee is no more motivated to achieve than the average person taking the test, that such an examinee would spend no more and no less time studying in any particular academic area, and would have no more or no less opportunity to acquire information in a particular academic domain. To the extent such assumptions are violated, the predictive schema of the intelligence test score interpretation would not hold.

SEE ALSO *Intelligence: An Overview.*

BIBLIOGRAPHY

Horn, J. L., & Cattell, R. B. (1966) Refinement and test of the theory of fluid and crystallized general intelligence. *Journal of Educational Psychology, 57,* 253–270.

Jensen, A. (1998). These suppressed relationship between IQ and the reaction time slope parameter of the Hick function. *Intelligence, 26,* 43–52.

Kamphaus, R. W. (2001) *Clinical assessment of child and adolescent intelligence,* 2nd ed. Boston: Allyn & Bacon.

Lee, D., Reynolds, C. R., Willson, V. L. (2003). Standardized test administration: why bother? *Journal of Forensic Neuropsychology, 3,* 55–81.

Reynolds, C. R., & Kamphaus, R. W. (2003). *Reynolds intellectual assessment scales* and *Reynolds intellectual screening test: Professional manual.* Lutz, FL: Psychological Assessment Resources Inc.

Reynolds, C. R., Livingston, R. A., & Willson, V. L. (2006). *Measurement and assessment in the classroom.* Boston: Allyn and Bacon.

Wechsler, D. (2003). *Wechsler intelligence scale for children,* 4th ed. San Antonio, TX: The Psychological Corporation.

Cecil R. Reynolds

INTEREST

Researchers have identified two types of interest. Situational interest is spontaneous, transitory, and environmentally activated, whereas personal interest, also referred to as individual interest, is less spontaneous, of enduring personal value, and activated internally. Situational interest often precedes and facilitates the development of personal interest. Situational interest appears to be especially important in catching students' attention, whereas personal interest may be more important in holding it (Durik & Harackewicz, 2007; Mitchell, 1993). Personal interest appears to be especially important for sustaining engagement and long-term learning (Hidi & Renninger, 2006).

Situational interest increases learning when the task or to-be-learned information is novel or when information is relevant to a task or learning goal. Text variables such as coherence, identification with characters, suspense, and the concreteness and image-ability of salient text segments also increase situational interest. Collectively, these variables can explain over 50 percent of sample variance in students' learning from text (Schraw, 1997).

Personal interest increases learning due to increased engagement, the acquisition of expert knowledge, and making mundane tasks more challenging. Personal interest

is also important because it appears to mediate the relationship between short-term situational interest and long-term mastery and learning within a domain (Hidi & Renninger, 2006). In addition, several studies suggest that personal interest increases the amount and quality of information processing. For example, Schiefele (1999) found that readers with personal interest in a topic were more likely to engage in deeper text processing, characterized by the construction of situational models (i.e., a mental representation of the people, setting, and events implied by the text).

CATCHING AND HOLDING INTEREST

Mitchell (1993) suggested that personal interest develops over time because some topic or event catches an individual's interest in a situational manner that is supported by learning events that help the person to hold that interest. Sustained interest increases engagement and motivation to learn, as well as facilitates strategy use and deeper processing. Thus, the development of sustained personal interest is an important component of learning.

Several researchers have investigated the development of interest in more detail. Ainley, Hidi, and Berndorff (2002) reported that situational factors lead to the development of sustained personal interest and that personal interest was related to positive affect, persistence, and learning. Durik and Harackiewicz (2007) described similar findings with one important exception. Experimental manipulations designed to catch learners' attention were effective if the learner has initial interest but undermined learning if the learner had little initial interest. Chen and Darst (2002) reported that background level of expertise had a mediating effect on situational and personal interest. These results suggested that both situational and personal interest are important but that manipulations designed to increase situational interest may not lead to sustained personal interest or learning. These findings also mirrored research on seductive details (i.e., text segments that are interesting but unimportant to a text's main themes), which found that seductive information may reduce learning (Harp & Mayer, 1998; Lehman, Schraw, McCrudden, & Hartley, 2007).

DEVELOPING SUSTAINED INTEREST

Mitchell (1993) originally proposed a simple three-stage model in which situational interest leads to personal interest, which leads to higher learning. Hidi and Renninger (2006) proposed a more sophisticated model in which interest develops through four continuous stages, including triggered situational interest, maintained situational interest, emerging personal interest, and well-developed individual interest. Triggered situational interest refers to a change in interest that is related directly to a temporary change in the stimuli, environment, or to-be-learned information. These changes may be evoked by a wide variety of factors, including highly relevant information, surprising or unexpected information, information that is incongruous with the task, a change in environment, or the enthusiasm of a teacher or mentor. Maintained situational interest refers to a state of focused attention and greater personal investment with the to-be-learned information. These changes usually are supported externally by a stimulating text, task, or teacher. In addition, maintained interest is sustained through meaningful tasks and personal involvement. Emerging individual interest refers to a state in which interest does not need to be sustained externally and one in which the interest becomes an enduring disposition. These changes are supported by increased curiosity, greater domain knowledge, and a perceived sense of pleasure and usefulness in the activity. Well-developed individual interest refers to an enduring change in disposition for the information or activity. These changes are characterized by positive affect, greater intrinsic motivation, extensive knowledge about the domain, a high level of procedural expertise, and an ability to monitor and self-regulate one's future development in the domain.

The four phase model of interest development provides a concise explanation of how interest develops, is sustained, and how it impacts engagement and learning. A number of studies provide empirical support for the model (Ainley et al., 2002; Durik & Harackiewicz, 2007). Nevertheless, a number of important issues remain as of 2008 for future research. One is whether the model is equally applicable across the lifespan. It may be the case that interest develops in a somewhat different way, or on a different developmental trajectory, for children compared to older students or adults. A second issue is whether interest is a necessary precursor of expertise or independent of expertise. For example, someone may develop considerable knowledge of investment strategies out of financial necessity rather than personal interest. A third is whether interest development is subject to reversals and, if so, how interest erodes and is replaced by new interests. A fourth issue pertains to how environmental factors affect the transition of early interest to sustained personal affect. As some research indicates, well meaning attempts to increase interest may actually have a negative effect on affect and learning (Lehman et al., 2007; Schraw & Lehman, 2001).

EFFECTS ON STUDENT LEARNING

Definitive evidence indicates that situational and personal interests are related to learning in three important ways. One way is that interest increases motivation, engagement, and persistence. Situational interest has a positive effect on extrinsic motivation, whereas personal interest has a positive long-term effect on intrinsic motivation. Presumably, external factors such as teachers and interesting textbooks provide external motivation to learn more about a domain. Once situational interest develops into well-developed individual interest, external factors likely play a smaller role in motivation, whereas intrinsic motivation and enjoyment play larger roles.

Extrinsic and intrinsic motivation are essential precursors to engagement. Students who are interested in a topic or activity are more likely to engage and persist, which in turn leads to the acquisition of new skills and knowledge. Motivation helps individuals to develop the confidence to undertake a new learning activity or to venture into an unfamiliar intellectual domain such as mathematics and science. For example, Renninger (2000) reported a compensatory effect in which high interest compensated for lower achievement and lower ability. Engagement enables learners to develop conceptual knowledge and essential procedural skills within a domain. In turn, motivation and engagement facilitate persistence within a domain that is necessary to develop true expertise. Persistence produces greater competence, which increases confidence and self-efficacy, and makes it easier and more enjoyable to learn.

A second way that interest is related to learning is through strategy use (Alexander & Jetton, 1996; Schraw & Lehman, 2001). Students who are interested in a topic report using more strategies are more likely to monitor their performance and shift strategies when necessary and are better able to self-regulate their learning. Increased strategy use, metacognitive monitoring, and self-regulation improve the efficiency of skill and knowledge acquisition as well as the amount of information learned.

A third way that interest affects learning is through deeper information processing. Schiefele (1999) found that high-interest learners were more likely to construct deeper mental representations of a text. This correlation may be due in part to the fact that high-interest learners are more likely to possess topic-specific knowledge and learning strategies. Yet regardless of knowledge and strategies, students with high levels of interest are more likely to engage in an activity, persist, report positive affect, and focus more of their effort on constructing a deeper understanding of the skill or domain that they are studying.

SUGGESTIONS FOR INCREASING INTEREST

Research suggests that interest is an important precursor to learning and is changeable. A number of suggestions are included below that are based on previous articles (Schraw, Flowerday & Lehman, 2001; Hidi & Renninger, 2006). Each of these strategies may have a unique facilitative effect;

thus, it is reasonable to use as many strategies as are feasible in the classroom.

1. Model interest and engagement in the classroom. Some teachers are enthusiastic about what they teach and demonstrate that enthusiasm on a day-to-day basis. Teacher enthusiasm develops initial interest due to events, topics, and observation. One way to promote and sustain interest is for teachers, tutors, or peers to model it.

2. Offer meaningful choices to students. Choice is hypothesized to promote a greater sense of self-determination because it satisfies students' need for autonomy. Empirical studies of choice support this view. Teachers also suggest that choice increases students' interest in a text.

Teachers interviewed by Flowerday and Schraw (2000) recommended offering a wide variety of choices to all students on a regular basis. In terms of when to use choice, teachers suggested offering meaningful choices to students of all ages, especially those who demonstrate low interest otherwise. Regarding where to offer choice, teachers do so in a variety of settings, including tasks such as homework and student assessment, as well as academic and social activities. Regarding how to use choice, teachers offered the following suggestions: offer simple choices at first, help students practice making good choices, provide feedback about the choices students make, use team choices for younger or less-experienced students, and provide information that clarifies the choice. For example, one teacher stated that she lets her students choose from a menu of five or six stories that she knows are interesting and suitable to her students.

Use engaging real-life problems. Students are engaged by interesting topics, but also by challenging and interesting activities. Several studies suggest that real-life problems are of interest to students and that even boring activities can be made more interesting if students challenge themselves. Hidi and Renninger (2006) recommended activities that require multiple students, including cooperative learning groups, team projects, one-on-one tutors, and interactive problem solving with or without teachers.

Use well organized texts and learning materials. Well organized texts are those that are coherent and informationally complete. These two variables are strongly related to interest and learning in text (Schraw, 1997). As texts become less user friendly or as students become less knowledgeable about text content, it is recommended that teachers make a greater effort to provide useful background knowledge about the text, given that knowledge and coherence appear to make separate contributions.

Select texts and learning materials that are vivid. Texts are vivid because they contain rich imagery, suspense, provocative information that surprises the reader, and engaging themes. Research suggests that text vividness has a positive impact on interest and learning provided the vivid information is germane to the learning task. Texts that include irrelevant or highly seductive information may actually interfere with learning by diverting readers' attention from important text segments (Harp & Mayer, 1998; Lehman et al., 2007).

Use texts that students know about. Prior knowledge is related positively to interest and deeper learning. Teachers should follow one of two strategies to promote interest. One is to use texts whose content is familiar, though not highly familiar, to the majority of students. Familiarity with text helps students generate thematic inferences within the text as well as between the text and prior knowledge. A second strategy is to provide pre-reading background information to help students better comprehend what they are asked to learn. This can be done directly by the teacher or via small group discussions among students.

Encourage students to be active learners. Students who actively make meaning learn more information at a deeper level. A number of researchers have suggested that interest increases active learning as well as the reverse (Mitchell, 1993; Hidi & Renninger, 2006). One way that students become more active is by using specific learning strategies such as predicting and summarizing. Another way is by using general study strategies in which students identify what they already know, want to know, and have learned.

Provide relevance cues for students. Relevance refers to whether information is salient to a task (McCrudden & Schraw, 2007). Almost any kind of information can become relevant to a learning situation. Understanding what is relevant to the learning task beforehand increases interest and learning. Teachers should highlight relevant themes and information for students before they begin to read or study. This is especially important for low-interest students. Several strategies may be used for highlighting the relevance of information: (a) encouraging students to set personal reading goals before reading, (b) helping students understand what is most important or salient to the reading task, c) asking students to focus on cause and effect relationships, and (d) asking students to explain the text to other students.

Highlighting the relevance of information or goals for learning may increase the perceived value of information. Previous research suggests that individuals are more motivated to process information they value. Although valuing may be due in part to personal interest, it also appears to be affected by the culture of the school as well as teacher values. Teachers who highlight the relevance and value of information and skills for students may also increase interest.

Do not use seductive information gratuitously. Research suggests that information that is irrelevant, out of place, or increases the relative cognitive load of information processing may actually interfere with learning. For example, Harp and Mayer (1998) found that highly interesting segments that were added to a text passage, but were not important or relevant, decreased learning of main idea, even though memory for the seductive information was quite high. One recommended rule is to incorporate a limited amount of highly interesting information, but make sure it is relevant to the learning task and does not seem incongruous with other to-be-learned information (Lehman et al., 2007).

SEE ALSO *Expectancy Value Motivational Theory; Intrinsic and Extrinsic Motivation.*

BIBLIOGRAPHY

Ainley, M., Hidi, S., & Berndorff, D. (2002). Interest, learning, and the psychological processes that mediate their relationship. *Journal of Educational Psychology, 94*, 545–561.

Alexander, P. A., & Jetton, T. L. (1996). The role of importance and interest in the processing of text. *Educational Psychology Review, 8*, 89–121.

Chen, E., & Darst, P. W. (2002). Individual and situational interest: The role of gender and skill. *Contemporary Educational Psychology, 27*, 250–269.

Durik, A. M., & Harackiewicz, J. (2007). Different strokes for different folks: How individual interest moderates the effects of situational factors on task interest. *Journal of Educational Psychology, 99*, 597–610.

Flowerday, T., & Schraw, G. (2000). Teacher beliefs about instructional choice. *Journal of Educational Psychology, 92*, 634–645.

Harp, S., F. & Mayer, R. E. (1998). How seductive details do their damage: A theory of cognitive interest in science learning. *Journal of Educational Psychology, 90*, 414–434.

Hidi, S., & Renninger, K. A. (2006). The four-phase model of interest development. *Educational Psychologist, 41*, 111–127.

Lehman, S., Schraw, G., McCrudden, M., & Hartley, K. (2007). The effects of seductive details on reading processes. *Contemporary Educational Psychology, 32*, 569–587.

McCrudden, M. T., & Schraw, G. (2007). Relevance and goal-focusing in text processing. *Educational Psychology Review, 19*, 113–139.

Mitchell, M. (1993). Situational Interest: Its multifaceted structure in the secondary school mathematics classroom. *Journal of Educational Psychology, 85*, 424–436.

Renninger, K. A. (2000). Individual interest and its implications for understanding intrinsic motivation. In C. Sansone & J. M. Harackiewicz (Eds.), *Intrinsic and extrinsic motivation: The search for optimal motivation and performance* (pp. 375–407). New York: Academic Press.

Schiefele, U. (1999). Interest and learning from text. *Scientific Studies of Reading, 3*, 257–280.

Schraw, G. (1997). Situational interest in literary text. *Contemporary Educational Psychology, 22*, 436–456.

Schraw, G., Flowerday, T., & Lehman, S. (2001). Promoting situational interest in the classroom. *Educational Psychology Review, 13*, 211–224.

Schraw, G., & Lehman, S. (2001). Situational interest: A review of the literature and directions for future research. *Educational Psychology Review, 13*, 23–52.

Gregory Schraw
Stephen Lehman

INTRINSIC AND EXTRINSIC MOTIVATION

Teachers can often readily identify students who demonstrate high or low motivation in a certain task. Motivated students engage in the task with intensity and feeling, whereas unmotivated students procrastinate and indicate in other ways that they would rather do something else. These differences exemplify the *quantitative* dimension of motivation, ranging from high to low. Teachers can often also identify highly motivated students who engage in tasks in different ways. Some may attempt to finish the task quickly, while others may seek more information. Some may persist, while others may begin enthusiastically but give-up when they encounter difficulty. These differences reflect the *qualitative* dimension of motivation. The distinction between intrinsic and extrinsic motivation has been one of the important theoretical conceptualizations of qualitative differences in engagement.

Intrinsic motivation refers to engagement in an activity with no reason other than the enjoyment and satisfaction of engagement itself. By comparison, extrinsic motivation refers to engagement that provides means to ends that go beyond the engagement itself. The goals of extrinsically motivated engagement might be the attainment of tangible rewards such as money, prizes, or other benefits; intangible rewards such as social approval, a sense of worthiness, or even a sense of conscientiousness; or the avoidance of tangible and intangible punishments such as time-out, scolding, rejection or sense of low self-worth.

THE ORGANISMIC SOURCES OF EXTRINSIC AND INTRINSIC MOTIVATION

Motivational theorists of the early 20th century searched for general principles of behavior. Theories of the period focused primarily on the motivations triggered by organismic physiological drives or needs such as food, sleep, procreation, and security (e.g., Hull, 1943). Organisms were perceived to be motivated to behave in ways that replenish biological deficits and secure survival. Because behavior that aims to satisfy a physiological deficit is done in order to achieve a goal and not for its own sake, it represents a type of extrinsic motivation.

Taking a different approach to motivation, behaviorist psychologists (e.g., Skinner, 1953) argued that behavior can be explained by the organisms' motivation to approach pleasant and desirable outcomes and to avoid unpleasant and undesirable outcomes. Pleasant outcomes constitute a reward, and enhance the chance that a behavior will recur, whereas unpleasant outcomes constitute a punishment and reduce the chance that a behavior will recur. Behaviorist psychologists argued that human (and animal) behavior can be explained by the various rewards and punishments in the environment. Thus, from a behaviorist perspective, all motivation is extrinsic.

However, during the middle of the 20th century, several theorists challenged the mechanistic models of the drive and behaviorist perspectives. These theorists relied on observations indicating that sometimes people (and animals) engage in behavior without an apparent reward. This engagement was seen to manifest universally early in life in children's exploration and play (Berlyne, 1960; White, 1959). But it also appears among older people who engage in games and hobbies. These observations seemed to suggest that such engagement is inherently enjoyable and satisfying. This type of motivation was contrasted with behavior propelled by "extrinsic" forces, and was labeled "intrinsic" motivation (Hunt, 1965).

Researchers of the period proposed a variety of theoretical explanations for intrinsic motivation, including characteristics of activities such as novelty and fantasy and biological mechanisms such as play instincts, curiosity, and need for stimulation. In a seminal paper, White (1959) reviewed several of these theoretical explanations and argued for their integration in a motive that developed along evolution, which he termed "effectance" motivation, or need for competence. White argued that this motive propels children to explore their surroundings, manipulate objects, and interact with others in ways that promote mastery of the environment. Unlike physiological needs, which operate on a homeostatic principle—that is, they are aroused when the organism is deficient in a resource, and operate to guide action towards reducing the deficiency—effectance motivation is aroused particularly when no deficiency exists. Engagement out of effectance motivation does not have a clear end-goal; rather, it is the engagement in the activity itself that elicits positive feelings of efficacy, which constitute an "intrinsic" reward.

Taking a different ideological approach, humanistic psychologists of the mid 20th century such as Maslow (1954) and Rogers (1963) challenged the drive and behaviorist perspectives by suggesting the existence of human needs that give rise to intrinsic motivation. Maslow, for example, argued that the physiological and safety needs, which he labeled "deficiency needs," are distinct from self-actualization needs, such as the need to develop talents, achieve comprehension, and fulfill potential, which he labeled "growth" needs. While the former provide the basis for extrinsic types of motivation, the latter provide the basis for intrinsic types of motivation.

At the beginning of the 21st century, many theorists still hold that intrinsic and extrinsic motivations are based in organismic needs. One such comprehensive theoretical framework—self-determination theory (SDT) (Deci & Ryan, 1985; Ryan & Deci, 2000)—explicitly asserts that humans are motivated by three basic psychological needs: for competence, relatedness, and autonomy. The need for competence in SDT is what White (1959) called effectance motivation. The need for relatedness refers to people's need to belong and to feel accepted by others. The need for autonomy refers to people's need to feel self-determined—to be the source of their own action (deCharms, 1968). Like physiological needs, these psychological needs are thought to represent necessary nourishment for psychological development and growth. When an individual's three needs are fully satisfied, engagement in action is intrinsically motivated and promotes adaptive development and well-being. When one of the needs is unsatisfied, engagement is likely to be extrinsically motivated and development may be hindered.

MODELS OF INTRINSIC AND EXTRINSIC MOTIVATION

Whereas organismic needs energize intrinsic and extrinsic motivations, the concept of need in itself is too general to explain engagement in specific behaviors and too vague to be a guide for empirical research (Harter, 1981; Pintrich & Schunk, 2002). Therefore, during the second half of the 20th century, researchers developed models that described how motivation triggered by needs manifests in intrinsic and extrinsic motivation in specific domains and activities. These models also explained how factors in the environment may shape and affect the type of motivation that people manifest in different domains.

In one important model of intrinsic motivation, Czikzentmihalyi (1990) focused on a phenomenological state of full absorption in an activity, which he labeled "flow." In this pure form of intrinsic motivation, "Concentration is so intense that there is no attention left over to think about anything irrelevant, or to worry about problems. Self-consciousness disappears, and the sense of time becomes distorted" (p. 71). Czikzentmihalyi interviewed professional artists, athletes, rock climbers, and chess players about their flow experiences and concluded that flow is most likely to be experienced when there are clear goals to be achieved and there is an optimal balance between the challenge posed by the activity and the person's level of skill. In addition, flow is experienced when there is immediate feedback on one's action and when the person feels a sense of control over the environment. According to Czikzentmihalyi, flow experiences promote further intrinsic motivation as well as skills in a domain. Since experiences of flow are rewarding, people are motivated to replicate the experience. Through engagement in challenging activities, skills develop and the person is motivated to seek more difficult challenges in the domain. Thus, growth of competencies and intrinsic motivation in the domain facilitate each other.

In a different program of research, Harter (1981, 1992) developed a model detailing how intrinsic motivation in different domains is shaped by experiences of success and failure as well as reinforcement from significant others. According to Harter, effectance motivation leads children to seek challenges, learn out of curiosity and for the experience of pleasure, and rely on themselves for a sense of success. When curiosity, independence, and exploration result with experiences of mastery and meet the approval and encouragement of parents or teachers, children experience pleasure, feel competent and in control of their environment, and have stronger intrinsic motivation for the domain or activity. However, when such engagement results with experiences of failure and meet disapproval by others, children feel anxious, perceive themselves to have low competence and control, and have lower intrinsic motivation. According to Harter, when parents and teachers demand compliance and employ extrinsic rewards and punishments, children develop extrinsic motivation for activities and domains.

In yet another elaborate model, self-determination theorists (Deci & Ryan, 1985; Ryan & Deci, 2000) suggested that intrinsic and extrinsic motivation can be arranged on an internal-external continuum according to the individual's perception of relative autonomy. Motivations that involve a higher perception of autonomy are more internal and represent a higher quality of engagement. Intrinsic motivation is positioned on the internal end of the continuum, and represents a perception of full autonomy in engagement. "External regulation" lies on the external end of the continuum and describes the sense of coercion and external control that individuals experience when they engage in an undesirable task in order to avoid punishment or achieve rewards. Between these poles are three other types of extrinsic motivation that vary in level of perceived relative autonomy. Whereas most activities may not be intrinsically motivating, SDT proposes that people have an organismic tendency to internalize motivation for uninteresting and enjoyable activities. However, internalization is likely to occur only if the

three psychological needs for competence, relatedness, and autonomy are satisfied.

ASSESSING INTRINSIC AND EXTRINSIC MOTIVATION

Researchers have used multiple methods to assess intrinsic and extrinsic motivation, either as a motivational "state"—the motivation a person has in a particular task—or as a motivational "trait"—the type of motivation a person has a tendency to display across domains and activities (Harter & Jackson, 1992). One common indicator of "state" intrinsic motivation is "free choice"—the amount of time spent on a task when alternative activities are available and no reward is offered (e.g., Deci, 1971; Lepper, Greene, & Nisbett, 1973). While an important measure in the literature, "free choice" is also somewhat problematic because there may be reasons other than intrinsic motivation for choosing a certain activity over others (e.g., wanting to prove worthiness) (Ryan, Koestner & Deci, 1991).

Perhaps the most frequently used method of assessing intrinsic and extrinsic motivation has been through participants' self-report. Early in her research, Harter (Harter & Zigler, 1974) assessed "trait" intrinsic motivation with an instrument comprised of four tasks, each targeting a different component of effectance motivation: seeking variation, preference for novelty, engagement for mastery, and preference for challenge. In each task, the child had a choice between two options indicating high or low level of effectance motivation. A few years later, Harter (1981) developed a different self-report instrument that was comprised of five scales of items, each assessing a different motivational component. Each item in the instrument *contrasted* intrinsic and extrinsic motivation (e.g., preference for challenging versus easy work). But several researchers, including Harter (1992) herself, recognized the possibility of adopting intrinsic and extrinsic motivation simultaneously—a possibility masked by instruments asking participants to choose *either* intrinsic *or* extrinsic motivation. Therefore, researchers divided Harter's instrument into separate intrinsic and extrinsic scales (Harter & Jackson, 1992; Lepper et al., 2005). Similar self-report scales have also been constructed by other motivational researchers (e.g., Pintrich et al., 1993; Ryan & Connell, 1989).

INTRINSIC MOTIVATION, EXTRINSIC REWARDS, AND OUTCOMES

The research literature is quite unanimous with regard to the benefits of intrinsic motivation to learning and development (Stipek, 1996). Engagement out of intrinsic motivation requires no external incentives and enhances motivation to engage again in the future. Studies also suggest that engagement out of intrinsic motivation is associated with enhanced comprehension, creativity, cognitive flexibility, achievement, and long-term well-being. By comparison, engagement out of extrinsic motivation may cease once the external motivator is removed. Moreover, extrinsic motivation is often associated with negative indicators of achievement and well-being. It is clear, however, that extrinsic motivation is preferable to having no motivation at all. Some perspectives also emphasize the possible motivational benefits of having both intrinsic and extrinsic motivation for an activity (Lepper & Henderlong, 2000). Unfortunately, research findings point quite consistently to a gradual decline in students' academic intrinsic motivation, and sometimes also extrinsic motivation, over years of schooling (Harter, 1981; Sansone & Morgan, 1992; Lepper et al., 2005). These trends have been attributed to the prevalence of extrinsic forces in schools such as tests and token economies, to the irrelevance of school tasks to students' lives and, more generally, to the growing mismatch between characteristics of school environments and the needs of adolescence for autonomy, self-expression, and meaningful social interaction (Eccles et al., 1993; Lepper & Henderlong, 2000).

The use of extrinsic rewards as a motivational strategy has spurred a persistent and heated debate in the literature (Sansone & Harackiewicz, 2000). Generally, humanistic motivation researchers argue that offering extrinsic rewards has detrimental effects on existing intrinsic motivation and is morally problematic (Kohn, 1993). Behaviorist researchers argue that offering extrinsic rewards has either negligible effects on intrinsic motivation or that it actually contributes to intrinsic motivation (Eisenberger & Cameron, 1996). What emerges from the research is that extrinsic rewards have no universal effect. Rather, the effect depends on the meaning of the reward to the child. Research also points to varying effects of different types of rewards and of different standards for their administration. For example, rewards that are expected, contingent on engagement or on task completion, and tangible are more likely to be detrimental to intrinsic motivation than rewards that are unexpected, not contingent, and intangible (e.g., verbal, social approval) (Lepper & Henderlong, 2000). More specifically, when positive rewards are perceived to provide valid information on student's competence—for example, performance-contingent rewards or feedback—they are likely to enhance intrinsic motivation. In contrast, when rewards are perceived as controlling and as suppressing the student's autonomy, they are likely to interfere with intrinsic motivation.

IMPLICATIONS FOR EDUCATORS

While some important variation exists (e.g., Nisan, 1992), there seems to be a wide-spread consensus among researchers and educators that enhancing intrinsic motivation among students is beneficial. Students' intrinsic motivation is enhanced when practices promote their sense of personal autonomy, when schoolwork is challenging and relevant to students, when social relationships are supportive, and when environments are physically and psychologically safe. Practices that promote these environmental characteristics include providing students with choices among activities and between ways of completing tasks, encouraging students to explore and pursue their interests, building on their backgrounds and prior experiences in constructing tasks, encouraging them to collaborate, incorporating fantasy in activities, providing feedback that is informative and frequent, and reducing rewards that are controlling (Lepper & Henderlong, 2000; Pintrich & Schunk, 2002).

Nevertheless, sometimes students are required to engage in tasks that they are not motivated to do. Thus, extrinsic motivation cannot be, and should not be, abandoned (Hidi & Harackiewicz, 2000). However, educators should pursue the internalization of students' extrinsic motivation for these tasks. Such internalization can be promoted by employing as many of the recommendations specified above as possible and, in addition, educators should make the value of the activity explicit and clear. This can be done most effectively through modeling and through providing a clear and age-appropriate rationale for the requirement (Assor et al., 2002).

BIBLIOGRAPHY

Assor, A., Kaplan, H., & Roth, G. (2002). Choice is good, but relevance is excellent: Autonomy-enhancing and suppressing teacher behaviours predicting students' engagement in schoolwork. *British Journal of Educational Psychology, 72,* 261–278.

Berlyne, D. E. (1960). *Conflict, arousal, and curiosity.* New York: McGraw-Hill.

Csikszentmihalyi, M. (1990). *Flow: The psychology of optimal experience.* New York: Harper Perennial.

Deci, E. L. (1971). Effects of externally mediated rewards on intrinsic motivation. *Journal of Personality and Social Psychology, 18,* 105–115.

Deci, E. L., & Ryan, R. M. (1985). *Intrinsic motivation and self-determination in human behavior.* New York: Plenum.

deCharms, R. (1968). *Personal causation: The internal affective determinants of behavior.* New York: Academic Press.

Eccles, J., Midgley, C., Wigfield, A., Buchanan, C., Reuman, D., Flanagan, C., & Mac Iver, D. (1993). Development during adolescence: The impact of stage-environment fit on young adolescents' experiences in schools and families. *American Psychologist, 48,* 90–101.

Eisenberger, R., & Cameron, J. (1996). Detrimental effects of reward: Reality or myth? *American Psychologist, 51,* 1153–1166.

Harter, S. (1981). A new self-report scale of intrinsic versus extrinsic orientation in the classroom: Motivational and informational components. *Developmental Psychology, 17,* 300–312.

Harter, S. (1992). The relationship between perceived competence, affect, and motivational orientation within the classroom: Processes and patterns of change. In A. K. Boggiano &

T. S. Pittman (Eds.) *Achievement and motivation: A social-developmental perspective.* Cambridge University Press.

Harter, S., & Jackson, B. K. (1992). Trait vs. nontrait conceptualizations of intrinsic/extrinsic motivational orientation. *Motivation and Emotion, 16,* 209–230.

Harter, S., & Zigler, E. (1974). The assessment of effectance motivation in normal and retarded children. *Developmental Psychology, 10,* 169–180.

Hull, C. L. (1943). *Principles of behavior.* New York: Appleton-Century-Crofts.

Hidi, S., & Harackiewicz, J. (2000). Motivating the academically unmotivated: A critical issue for the 21st century. *Review of Educational Research, 70,* 151–179.

Hunt, J. M. V. (1965). Intrinsic motivation and its role in psychological development. In D. Levine (Ed.), *Nebraska symposium on motivation* (Vol. 13, pp. 189–282). Lincoln, NE: University of Nebraska Press.

Kohn, A. (1993). *Punished by rewards: The trouble with gold stars, incentive plans, A's, praise, and other bribes.* New York: Houghton Mifflin.

Lepper, M. R., Greene, D., & Nisbett, R. E. (1973). Undermining children's intrinsic interest with extrinsic rewards: A test of the "overjustification" hypothesis. *Journal of Personality and Social Psychology, 28,* 129–137.

Lepper, M. R., & Henderlong, J. (2000). Turning "play" into "work" and "work" into "play": 25 years of research on intrinsic versus extrinsic motivation. In C. Sansone & J. M. Harackiewicz (Eds.), *Intrinsic and extrinsic motivation: The search for optimal motivation and performance* (pp. 257–307). San Diego, CA: Academic Press.

Lepper, M. R., Henderlong Corpus, J., & Iyengar, S. S. (2005). Intrinsic and extrinsic motivational orientations in the classroom: Age differences and academic correlates. *Journal of Educational Psychology, 97,* 184–196.

Maslow, A. (1954). *Motivation and personality.* New York: Harper.

Nisan, M. (1992). Beyond intrinsic motivation: Cultivating a sense of the desirable. In K. Oser, A. Dick, & J. L. Patry (Eds.), *Effective and responsible teaching: The new synthesis* (pp. 126–138). San Francisco: Jossey-Bass.

Pintrich, P. R., Smith, D. A. F., Garcia, T., & McKeachie, W. J. (1993). Reliability and predictive validity of the Motivated Strategies for Learning Questionnaire (MSLQ). *Educational and Psychological Measurement, 53,* 801–813.

Pintrich, P. R., & Schunk, D. (2002). *Motivation in education: Theory, research and applications* (2nd ed.). Upper Saddle River, NJ: Prentice-Hall.

Rogers, C. (1963). The actualizing tendency in relation to "motives" and to consciousness. In M. R. Jones (Ed.), *Nebraska symposium on motivation* (Vol. 11, pp. 1–24). Lincoln, NE: University of Nebraska Press.

Ryan, R. M., & Connell, J. P. (1989). Perceived locus of causality and internalization: Examining reasons for acting in two domains. *Journal of Personality and Social Psychology, 57,* 749–761.

Ryan, R. M., & Deci, E. L. (2000). Self-determination theory and the facilitation of intrinsic motivation, social development, and well-being. *American Psychologist, 55,* 68–78.

Ryan, R. M., Koestner, R., & Deci, E. L. (1991). Ego-involved persistence: When free choice behavior is not intrinsically motivated. *Motivation and Emotion, 15,* 185–205.

Sansone, C. & Harackiewicz, J. M. (Eds.) (2000). *Intrinsic and extrinsic motivation: The search for optimal motivation and performance.* San Diego, CA: Academic Press.

Sansone, C., & Morgan, C. (1992). Intrinsic motivation and education: Competence in context. *Motivation and Emotion, 16,* 249–270.

Skinner, B. F. (1953). *Science and human behavior.* New York: Macmillan.

Stipek, D. J. (1996). Motivation and instruction. In D. C. Berliner & R. C. Calfee (Eds.), *Handbook of educational psychology* (pp. 85–113). New York: Macmillan.

White, R. W. (1959). Motivation reconsidered: The concept of competence. *Psychological Review, 66,* 297–333.

Avi Kaplan

IQ

SEE *Misdiagnoses of Disabilities.*

ITEM ANALYSIS

Item analysis is a general term that refers to the specific methods used in education to evaluate test items, typically for the purpose of test construction and revision. Regarded as one of the most important aspects of test construction and increasingly receiving attention, it is an approach incorporated into item response theory (IRT), which serves as an alternative to classical measurement theory (CMT) or classical test theory (CTT). Classical measurement theory considers a score to be the direct result of a person's true score plus error. It is this error that is of interest as previous measurement theories have been unable to specify its source. However, item response theory uses item analysis to differentiate between types of error in order to gain a clearer understanding of any existing deficiencies. Particular attention is given to individual test items, item characteristics, probability of answering items correctly, overall ability of the test taker, and degrees or levels of knowledge being assessed.

THE PURPOSE OF ITEM ANALYSIS

There must be a match between what is taught and what is assessed. However, there must also be an effort to test for more complex levels of understanding, with care taken to avoid over-sampling items that assess only basic levels of knowledge. Tests that are too difficult (and have an insufficient floor) tend to lead to frustration and lead to deflated scores, whereas tests that are too easy (and have an insufficient ceiling) facilitate a decline in motivation and lead to inflated scores. Tests can be improved by maintaining and developing a pool of valid items from which future tests can be drawn and that cover a reasonable span of difficulty levels.

Item analysis helps improve test items and identify unfair or biased items. Results should be used to refine test item wording. In addition, closer examination of items will also reveal which questions were most difficult, perhaps indicating a concept that needs to be taught more thoroughly. If a particular distracter (that is, an incorrect answer choice) is the most often chosen answer, and especially if that distracter positively correlates with a high total score, the item must be examined more closely for correctness. This situation also provides an opportunity to identify and examine common misconceptions among students about a particular concept.

In general, once test items have been created, the value of these items can be systematically assessed using several methods representative of item analysis: a) a test item's level of difficulty, b) an item's capacity to discriminate, and c) the item characteristic curve. Difficulty is assessed by examining the number of persons correctly endorsing the answer. Discrimination can be examined by comparing the number of persons getting a particular item correct with the total test score. Finally, the item characteristic curve can be used to plot the likelihood of answering correctly with the level of success on the test.

ITEM DIFFICULTY

In test construction, item difficulty is determined by the number of people who answer a particular test item correctly. For example, if the first question on a test was answered correctly by 76% of the class, then the difficulty level (p or percentage passing) for that question is $p = .76$. If the second question on a test was answered correctly by only 48% of the class, then the difficulty level for that question is $p = .48$. The higher the percentage of people who answer correctly, the easier the item, so that a difficulty level of .48 indicates that question two was more difficult than question one, which had a difficulty level of .76.

Many educators find themselves wondering how difficult a good test item should be. Several things must be taken into consideration in order to determine appro-

priate difficulty level. The first task of any test maker should be to determine the probability of answering an item correctly by chance alone, also referred to as guessing or luck. For example, a true-false item, because it has only two choices, could be answered correctly by chance half of the time. Therefore, a true-false item with a demonstrated difficulty level of only $p = .50$ would not be a good test item because that level of success could be achieved through guessing alone and would not be an actual indication of knowledge or ability level. Similarly, a multiple-choice item with five alternatives could be answered correctly by chance 20% of the time. Therefore, an item difficulty greater than .20 would be necessary in order to discriminate between respondents' ability to guess correctly and respondents' level of knowledge. Desirable difficulty levels usually can be estimated as halfway between 100 percent and the percentage of success expected by guessing. So, the desirable difficulty level for a true-false item, for example, should be around $p = .75$, which is halfway between 100% and 50% correct.

In most instances, it is desirable for a test to contain items of various difficulty levels in order to distinguish between students who are not prepared at all, students who are fairly prepared, and students who are well prepared. In other words, educators do not want the same level of success for those students who did not study as for those who studied a fair amount, or for those who studied a fair amount and those who studied exceptionally hard. Therefore, it is necessary for a test to be composed of items of varying levels of difficulty. As a general rule for norm-referenced tests, items in the difficulty range of .30 to .70 yield important differences between individuals' level of knowledge, ability, and preparedness. There are a few exceptions to this, however, with regard to the purpose of the test and the characteristics of the test takers. For instance, if the test is to help determine entrance into graduate school, the items should be more difficult to be able to make finer distinctions between test takers. For a criterion-referenced test, most of the item difficulties should be clustered around the criterion cut-off score or higher. For example, if a passing score is 70%, the vast majority of items should have percentage passing values of

Extreme group method			
Item number	Correct response proportion in the top percentile	Correct response proportion in the bottom percentile	Discriminability index
1	.92	.40	.52
2	.97	.93	.04
3	.61	.74	−.13

Figure 1 ILLUSTRATION BY GGS INFORMATION SERVICES. CENGAGE LEARNING, GALE.

p = .60 or higher, with a number of items in the $p > .90$ range to enhance motivation and test for mastery of certain essential concepts.

DISCRIMINATION INDEX

According to Wilson (2005), item difficulty is the most essential component of item analysis. However, it is not the only way to evaluate test items. Discrimination goes beyond determining the proportion of people who answer correctly and looks more specifically at who answers correctly. In other words, item discrimination determines whether those who did well on the entire test did well on a particular item. An item should in fact be able to discriminate between upper and lower scoring groups. Membership in these groups is usually determined based on their total test score, and it is expected that those scoring higher on the overall test will also be more likely to endorse the correct response on a particular item. Sometimes an item will discriminate negatively, that is, a larger proportion of the lower group select the correct response, as compared to those in the higher scoring group. Such an item should be revised or discarded.

One way to determine an item's power to discriminate is to compare those who have done very well with those who have done very poorly, known as the extreme group method. First, identify the students who scored in the top one-third as well as those in the bottom one-third of the class. Next, calculate the proportion of each group that answered a particular test item correctly (i.e., percentage passing for the high and low groups on each item). Finally, subtract the p of the bottom performing group from the p for the top performing group to yield an item discrimination index (D). Item discriminations of D = .50 or higher are considered excellent. D = 0 means the item has no discrimination ability, while D = 1.00 means the item has perfect discrimination ability.

In Figure 1, it can be seen that Item 1 discriminates well with those in the top performing group obtaining the correct response far more often (p = .92) than those in the

low performing group (p = .40), thus resulting in an index of .52 (i.e., .92 - .40 = .52). Next, Item 2 is not difficult enough with a discriminability index of only .04, meaning this particular item was not useful in discriminating between the high and low scoring individuals. Finally, Item 3 is in need of revision or discarding as it discriminates negatively, meaning low performing group members actually obtained the correct keyed answer more often than high performing group members.

Another way to determine the discriminability of an item is to determine the correlation coefficient between performance on an item and performance on a test, or the tendency of students selecting the correct answer to have high overall scores. This coefficient is reported as the item discrimination coefficient, or the point-biserial correlation between item score (usually scored right or wrong) and total test score. This coefficient should be positive, indicating that students answering correctly tend to have higher overall scores or that students answering incorrectly tend to have lower overall scores. Also, the higher the magnitude, the better the item discriminates. The point-biserial correlation can be computed with procedures outlined in Figure 2.

In Figure 2, the point-biserial correlation between item score and total score is evaluated similarly to the extreme group discrimination index. If the resulting value is negative or low, the item should be revised or discarded. The closer the value is to 1.0, the stronger the item's discrimination power; the closer the value is to 0,

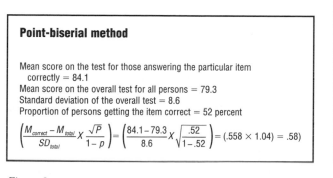

Point-biserial method

Mean score on the test for those answering the particular item correctly = 84.1
Mean score on the overall test for all persons = 79.3
Standard deviation of the overall test = 8.6
Proportion of persons getting the item correct = 52 percent

$$\left(\frac{M_{correct} - M_{total}}{SD_{total}} \times \frac{\sqrt{P}}{1-p}\right) = \left(\frac{84.1 - 79.3}{8.6} \times \sqrt{\frac{.52}{1-.52}}\right) = (.558 \times 1.04) = .58)$$

Figure 2 ILLUSTRATION BY GGS INFORMATION SERVICES. CENGAGE LEARNING, GALE.

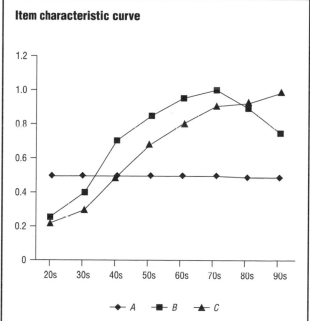

Figure 3 ILLUSTRATION BY GGS INFORMATION SERVICES. CENGAGE LEARNING, GALE.

the weaker the power. Items that are very easy and answered correctly by the majority of respondents will have poor point-biserial correlations.

CHARACTERISTIC CURVE

A third parameter used to conduct item analysis is known as the item characteristic curve (ICC). This is a graphical or pictorial depiction of the characteristics of a particular item, or taken collectively, can be representative of the entire test. In the item characteristic curve the total test score is represented on the horizontal axis and the proportion of test takers passing the item within that range of test scores is scaled along the vertical axis.

For Figure 3, three separate item characteristic curves are shown. Line A is considered a flat curve and indicates that test takers at all score levels were equally likely to get the item correct. This item was therefore not a useful discriminating item. Line B demonstrates a troublesome item as it gradually rises and then drops for those scoring highest on the overall test. Though this is unusual, it can sometimes result from those who studied most having ruled out the answer that was keyed as correct. Finally, Line C shows the item characteristic curve for a good test item. The gradual and consistent positive slope shows that the proportion of people passing the item gradually increases as test scores increase. Though it is not depicted here, if an ICC was seen in the shape of a backward *S*, negative item discrimination would be evident, meaning that those who scored lowest were most likely to endorse a correct response on the item.

SEE ALSO *Item Response Theory.*

BIBLIOGRAPHY

Anastasi, A., & Urbina, S. (1997). *Psychological testing* (7th ed.). Upper Saddle River, NJ: Prentice Hall.

Brown, F. (1983). *Principles of education and psychological testing* (3rd ed.). New York: Holt, Rinehart, & Winston.

DeVellis, R. (2003). *Scale development: Theory and applications* (2nd ed.). Thousand Oaks, CA: Sage.

Grunlund, N. (1993). *How to make achievement tests and assessments* (5th ed.). Boston: Allyn and Bacon.

Kaplan, R., & Saccuzzo, D. (2004). *Psychological testing: Principles, applications, and issues* (6th ed.) Pacific Grove, CA: Brooks/Cole.

Kehoe, J. (1995). Basic item analysis for multiple-choice tests. *Practical Assessment, Research & Evaluation, 4*(10), retrieved April 1, 2008, from http://pareonline.net/getvn.asp?v=4&n=10.

Patten, M. (2001). *Questionnaire research: A practical guide* (2nd ed.). Los Angeles: Pyrczak.

Wilson, M. (2005). *Constructing measures: An item response modeling approach.* Mahwah, NJ: Lawrence Erlbaum.

Susan H. Eaves
Bradley T. Erford

ITEM RESPONSE THEORY

Item response theory (IRT) is an approach to modern educational and psychological measurement that posits a particular notion about cognition and sets forth sophisticated statistics to appraise cognitive processes. Its objective is to reliably calibrate individuals and test stimuli (i.e., items and exercises) on a common scale that is interpreted to show the individuals' ability or proficiency and specified characteristics of the test stimuli.

IRT is attractive for a number of reasons but principally because it is presumed that IRT-based estimates of examinees' ability are more precise than can be garnered through traditional means, such as summing the number of correct responses to a set of test items or exercises. Also, IRT is applicable to many practical testing problems, such as generalizability of test results, various item analyses, examining test bias and differential item functioning, equating test forms, estimating construct parameters, domain scoring, and adaptive testing.

In the IRT theory, cognitive processes are hypothesized as abilities or proficiencies. Some examples are reading, computing, and reasoning problems through to credible solutions, as well as beliefs, attitudes, opinions, and likely desires and aspirations, too. In short, almost anything that is a cognitive process. Some skills or talents, like playing a musical instrument, giving a theatrical performance and some physical acts such as running or successfully hitting a baseball, can be accommodated in the theory as well. Each ability or proficiency is conceived as lying along a continuum that ranges from none at all to complete mastery. In statistical terms, the range is infinite ($\pm\infty$). Figure 1 depicts this notion graphically.

Graphical depiction of ability or proficiency continuum

Figure 1 ILLUSTRATION BY GGS INFORMATION SERVICES. CENGAGE LEARNING, GALE.

As cognitive processes, abilities and proficiencies are deeply seated in the brain and cannot be directly observed. For this reason, they are described as latent, and often as latent traits. Some persons working with IRT believe that describing aspects of cognition as traits is too limiting: It does not capture the fact of their malleability or the notion that they may be influenced by environmental and social factors; hence, more generic terms such as abilities and proficiencies are sometimes used. In this essay, the term ability is used.

The notion of mental abilities ranging along a continuum contrasts with classical testing theory (CTT) in which knowledge is conceived as being circumscribed within a domain (e.g., a reading domain), and a true score for any particular examinee can be estimated for that knowledge domain. In CTT, the more precisely the true score is estimated, the less error in measurement, and hence the greater reliability

A principal objective of IRT is to determine the point along the ability continuum that best calibrates a particular individual to the scale. This point—the test score expressed in IRT terms—is interpreted to reflect the individual's ability on whatever is the object of measurement (e.g., reading). Figure 2 illustrates this foundational IRT notion. For mathematical reason, ability is expressed as theta (θ) and when referring to individuals, the continuum is called the θ scale.

Graphical depiction of individuals along ability or proficiency continuum

Figure 2 ILLUSTRATION BY GGS INFORMATION SERVICES. CENGAGE LEARNING, GALE.

As seen in Figure 2, a given person may be low in the ability (shown as toward the left side of the θ scale), whereas another may be in the middle, while a third person may be high (shown as toward the right side of the θ scale). There is no assumption about the spread of individuals as in a bell-shaped (normal) distribution: all persons in a population could be high in the ability or all could be in the middle or have any other dispersion.

Of course, determining where a given individual's θ is situated along the scale (i.e., his or her ability) requires that some questions (test stimuli: items or exercises) be administered to the individual so that the θ estimate may be calculated. For the calculation, it is necessary to know characteristics of these test stimuli, a feature of IRT called *item characteristics*. Three commonly-used item characteristics are 1) its level of difficulty along the continuum, 2) its discrimination in detecting differences in ability between examinees (an item that everyone responds to correctly yields no discrimination), and 3) the likelihood of low ability examinees guessing a correct answer. Figure 3 depicts the notion of test characteristics being placed along the continuum.

Graphical depiction of many individuals dispersed along ability continuum

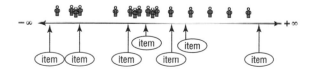

Figure 3 ILLUSTRATION BY GGS INFORMATION SERVICES. CENGAGE LEARNING, GALE.

Just as examinees may be located at any particular point along the continuum, so too may characteristics of items be situated at any point for their characteristic. In other words, any given items may be low in difficulty or have low discriminating power or be relatively simple to guess whereas another item may be middle or high in characteristics. Many items are typically situated all along the scale, reflecting wide dispersion.

To repeat, the three ingredients of IRT are: the scale, the examinees, and the items. As earlier stated, the scale's range is infinite, ($\pm\infty$). What remains is to determine the θ value for each examinee in the tested sample and the characteristics of the employed test items. Characteristics for the items can be discussed next.

In IRT (as well as in some other statistical contexts), item characteristics are plotted on a curve, called an ICC (item characteristics curve). While any number of characteristics may be plotted, it is common to display three of them: the discrimination, the difficulty, and the guessing. By convention, these are labeled as a, b, and c. In a statistical sense, the known characteristics of any given item are representative of a population of like items and hence are labeled *parameters*. The a, b, and c characteristics are thus labeled as a parameter or b parameter or c parameter. When all three characteristics are estimated, the IRT model is called the three-parameter model (3PL).

In IRT, there are many variations of ICCs. For instance, a common circumstance in IRT work is to estimate only a single item parameter, its difficulty (b parameter). This is the 1PL, and usually falls into an IRT category of estimation called the Rasch model, an eponym for the Danish mathematician Georg Rasch. The 3PL accounts for the most common IRT applications. Item characteristics for the 3PL are plotted in Figure 4.

ICC of one item, displaying three characteristics

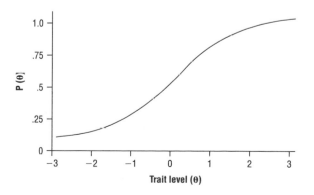

Figure 4 ILLUSTRATION BY GGS INFORMATION SERVICES. CENGAGE LEARNING, GALE.

In Figure 4, there are two scales, represented on the vertical X (abscissa) and horizontal Y (ordinate) axis. The X axis is the probability of θ, labeled P(θ) meaning the probability of a given θ value. It ranges from 0 to 1.0 and is considered the likelihood of getting the item correct (for dichotomous items). The Y axis is the IRT θ scale which (theoretically at least) ranges (±∞). For interpretability, however, the X scale is expressed in standardized units with a mean of 0 and standard deviation 1; since nearly all of the population is contained within the ±3 standard deviations, this is all of the range of the scale that is typically shown.

Regarding the ICC itself, the reader can see that the curve is shaped like a lazy S for an item with meritorious characteristics (but obviously it can assume almost any shape). Technically, the curve is an ogive, but many authors simply refer to it as the ICC. It begins at the lower left, which indicates the c parameter (guessing by low ability examinees: here almost -3 standard deviations from the mean 0). In the figure, this starting point is about .10, meaning that persons of very low ability still have about a ten percent probability of getting the item correct, even by mere guessing. As the curve progresses to the right, reflecting more and more ability, the curve slopes upward, indicating that as ability increases so does the probability of a correct response. The slope of the ICC represents the a parameter, the item's discriminating power. Next, the reader can observe that the overall location of the curve along the θ scale and imagine a vertical line drawn from its mid-point down to the Y axis. In this example, that line would intersect the Y axis at about .5, meaning that this item is best suited to examinees who are slightly more able that are average examinees (about a half standard deviation above the mean ability). It is important to realize from this example that an ICC can be situated anywhere along the θ scale, and its mid-point reflects its difficulty, the b parameter. In Figure 4, then, all three item characteristics can be seen: (a) the discrimination, (b) the difficulty, and (c) the guessing parameters.

When a person is learning IRT it is important to appreciate the fact that persons and items are calibrated on the same scale. This allows observers to learn features of each ingredient in IRT (persons and items) from the other. In other words, when test makers know the characteristics of items, they can observe (through the test) which ones a particular examinee gets right and wrong and thereby determine his or her ability. Conversely, when test makers know the θ values for a relatively large number of examinees, they can calibrate items to the scale. This reciprocal finding is something akin to saying that if a teacher knows a student's grade point average the teacher can ipso facto identify something about the stu-

dent's study habits and vice versa (not a perfect indicator but in the main a reliable one).

To persons new to IRT or not experienced in statistics, it may seem perplexing to state that items are calibrated to the scale from what test makers know about examinees' abilities and examinees are fitted to the scale from what test makers know about items. It seems a bit like the question: "Which came first, the chicken or the egg?" This is a relevant observation in IRT. Mathematically, this issue is addressed through the maximum likelihood function, a specialized statistical approach that determines the likelihood of observing a set of data in a hypothesized model. To explain how this works in IRT, one can suppose an item is well crafted and appropriate in its characteristics to a given examinee. The test maker presumes the examinee has a .5 chance of giving a correct response. This is expressed as syntactically as in Equation 1.

$$X = .5 \tag{1}$$

Next, the test maker can generalize this notion to a response (either correct or incorrect) to any item. Since the probability rests on ability, the generalization is written as follows.

$$P(U_i \mid \theta) \tag{2}$$

Equation 2 is read as the probability (P) of a response (U) on any given appropriate item (i) is a function of ability (θ). Thus, for the hypothetical examinee in the description of Equation 1 taking the item presumed that $P(U_i \mid \theta) = .5$. Examinees of another ability level would have a different probability.

Tests are composed of more than one item, of course, so the probability function is extended to include a test of any length (n items). Now, the probability of a correct response is conditioned upon several items and is accordingly a joint probability, meaning the probability of a response on all the items. A joint probability is calculated as the probability of a response on the first item times the probability of a response on the second item, and so forth to n items. This is written in Equation 3.

$$P(U_1, U_2 \ldots U_n \mid \theta = P(U_1 \mid \theta) P(U_2 \mid \theta) \ldots P(U_n \mid \theta) \tag{3}$$

To see Equation 3 in action, the reader may imagine that a particular examinee has 3 items presented to him on a test: a perfectly suited item (one in which the probability is .5 for his ability), another that is very easy for his ability (with, say, probability of .8), and a third item that is difficult relative to his ability, say, probability is .4). The joint probability of responding correctly to all the items on this short test is .16 (.5 x .8 x .4), or about 16 percent. Determining item characteristics is similarly done with a likelihood function, but this time using the examinee's presumed ability to inform an item's characteristics.

The mathematics of solving likelihood equations involves calculus and is not easily done when there are many items on a test. However, if the metric is in log units, the calculations are much simpler. Adding a small constant to the log-produced results yields answers that are nearly identical to what would be acquired in normal metric. Hence, most IRT calculations are done in log metric, and the θ scale is expressed in log units, called *logits*.

The mathematical expression for the 3PL, in logistic units, is as follows.

$$P_i(\theta) = c_i + (1 - c_i)\,\frac{e^{Da_i(\theta - b_i)}}{1 + e^{Da_i(\theta - b_i)}} \qquad i = 1, 2, \ldots, n \qquad (4)$$

While Equation 4 appears formidable, it is straightforward. In the equation, most terms are already known, including the probability (P), as well as the a, b, and c parameters. The *e* merely denotes that the expression is in log units of base e, and the *D* is a scaling constant to allow the results of log units to closely approximate a normal metric.

From this point on, IRT is mostly a search process wherein examinee responses to items give search to item characteristics and estimated item characteristics search for the best fitting examinee ability. When the process is complete, the test makerknows both IRT ingredients: examinee ability and item characteristics.

IRT is a powerful route to estimating an examinee's ability on the tested construct as well as learning about characteristics of test items. For these reasons, it is commonly used in many national testing programs such as the NAEP (National Assessment of Educational Progress), the SAT (Scholastic Achievement Test), GRE (Graduate Records Examination), LSAT (Law School Admission Test), MCAT (Medical College Admission Test), and many other assessment programs.

SEE ALSO *Classical Test Theory.*

BIBLIOGRAPHY

Baker, Frank (2001). *The Basics of Item Response Theory.* ERIC Clearinghouse on Assessment and Evaluation, University of Maryland, College Park, MD.

Embertson, S. E., Reise, S. P. (2000). *Item Response Theory for Psychologists.* Mahwah, NJ: Lawrence Erlbaum Associates.

Hambleton, R. K., Swaminathan, H., & Rogers, H. J. (1991). *Fundamentals of item response theory.* Newbury Park, CA: Sage Publications.

Lord, F. M. (1980). *Application of item response theory to practical testing problems.* Princeton, NJ: Educational Testing Service.

Thissen, D., & Wainer, H. (2001). *Test scoring.* Mahwah, NJ: Erlbaum.

Steven J. Osterlind

J

JAMES, WILLIAM
1842–1910

William James, often referred to as the Father of American Psychology, was born in New York City on January 11, 1842. As a youth, he was educated in private schools and had a succession of tutors in Europe and the United States. In 1864 he entered the Harvard Medical School, where five years later he received his medical degree, the only degree James ever received.

In 1873 James was offered a post at Harvard teaching physiology. His acceptance signaled the start of a prestigious career, for James was to become a gifted teacher, skilled orator, and prodigious thinker and writer. In 1875 he established the first laboratory of experimental psychology in the United States, and a year later he became the country's first professor of psychology. "The first lecture in psychology that I ever heard," he later wrote, "was the first I ever gave." In 1878 he married Alice Howe Gibbens. They had five children. His brother Henry became a famous novelist.

The Principles of Psychology, a two-volume work that had taken James 12 years to complete, was published in 1890. At the urging of his publisher to create a book with greater classroom appeal, James later condensed the two volumes into one, *Psychology: The Briefer Course* (1892). The complete work came to be known as *The James*, and the abridged tome as *The Jimmy*. For years, the two served as the standard psychology texts for generations of American university students.

The dawn of the 20th century found James at the height of his eminence both in philosophy and psychology. *The Will to Believe* (1897) and *Varieties of Religious Experience* (1902) reflected his growing spiritual and philosophical concerns. In 1907 he published *Pragmatism*, a concept that identified one of the prevailing philosophical movements of the 20th century. A method for resolving philosophical disputes, pragmatism aimed to discover the truth of an idea and to consider its value in terms of its practical, ethical/moral, and intellectual consequences.

James was the first American psychologist to directly address educational concerns. In July of 1892, he delivered the first of 12 lectures on psychology to teachers in Cambridge under the title of "Talks on Psychology of Interest to Teachers." Published in 1899 as *Talks to Teachers on Psychology*, the book became popular with educators, who subsequently used it prominently in teacher training programs throughout the world.

In *Talks*, James urged educators to familiarize themselves with the needs and interests of their students so that teaching practices could be geared to helping students develop the habits and make the associations and connections necessary to ensure effective learning. Progressive for its day, James's approach offered a view of teaching and learning in which freedom and compulsion each play an appropriate role. His educational psychology abounds with references to rigor, effort, ambition, competition, pugnacity, and pride.

The impact of James's ideas on modern educational psychology has been profound. In 1903 John Dewey referred to James as the "spiritual progenitor" of the progressive education movement launched at the University of Chicago. His emphasis on the importance of habit

William James THE LIBRARY OF CONGRESS.

and associations on human functioning influenced the behaviorist movement in psychology, but when humanistic psychologists searched for an antidote to behaviorism, they too stumbled on to James and his plea for a psychology centered on the individual and receptive to the importance of self-processes and introspection. Albert Bandura's social cognitive view of reciprocal determinism is also indebted to the Jamesian view of human functioning in which individuals and environments influence each other reciprocally.

Emphasis in the early 2000s on the importance of self-processes such as self-concept and self-efficacy in education is rooted in the critical aspects of self-awareness and personal cognition that James believed vital to the study of psychology. Moreover, 21st-century interest in conceptual change can be traced to James's vivid description of this process. Interest and research on habit (subsequently referred to as automaticity) also continues to

thrive. Additionally, motivation researchers are active in their study of Jamesian concepts such as interest, attention, memory processes, modeling and imitation, and transfer. Modern theories of constructivism can also be traced to James's theory of knowledge.

After his retirement from Harvard in 1907, James was in constant demand for lectures. In 1909 he published *A Pluralistic Universe* and *The Meaning of Truth.* Soon, however, his health began to deteriorate. On August 26, 1910, cradled in the arms of his wife Alice, William James died of an enlarged heart. He was 68. Two years after his death, a number of his articles were published as *Essays in Radical Empiricism.*

BIBLIOGRAPHY

WORKS BY

James, W. ([1890] 1981). *Principles of psychology.* 2 vols. Cambridge, MA: Harvard University Press.

James, W. ([1892] 2001) *Psychology: The briefer course.* New York: Dover.

James, W. ([1899-1900] 2001). *Talks to teachers on psychology and to students on some of life's ideals.* New York: Dover.

James, W. ([1902] 1990). *Varieties of religious experiences.* New York: Vintage Books.

James, W. ([1907] 1978). *Pragmatism: A new name for old ways of thinking.* Cambridge, MA: Harvard University Press.

James, W. ([1909] 1978). *The meaning of truth.* Cambridge, MA: Harvard University Press.

James, W. ([1912] 1996). *Esssays of Radical Empiricism.* Lincoln: University of Nebraska Press.

WORKS ABOUT

Dewey, J. Excerpt from a letter to William James, March 1903. In R. B. Perry, *The thought and character of William James as revealed in unpublished correspondence and notes, together with his published writings* (pp. 520–521). Boston: Little, Brown.

Gale, R. M. (2005). *The Philosophy of William James: an introduction.* New York: Cambridge University Press.

Garrison, J., Podeschi, R., & Bredo, E. (2002). *William James and education.* New York: Teachers College Press.

Pawelski, J. O. (2007). *The dynamic individualism of William James.* Albany: State University of New York Press.

Richardson, R. D. (2006). *William James: in the maelstrom of American modernism: a biography.* Boston: Houghton Mifflin.

Viegas, J. (2006). *William James: American philosopher, psychologist, and theologian.* New York: Rosen.

Frank Pajares